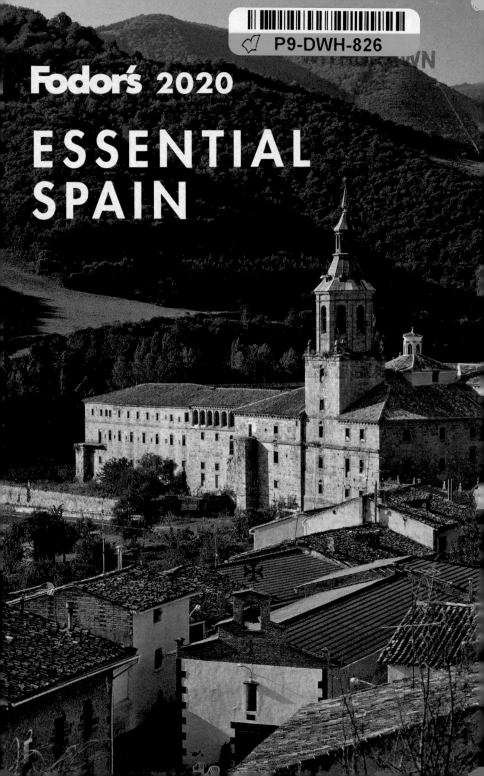

Fodor's 2020

ESSENTIAL SPAIN

Welcome to Spain

Spain conjures images of flamenco dancers, café-lined plazas, white hillside villages, and soaring cathedrals. Beyond these traditional associations, this modern country offers top-notch art museums, inventive cuisine, and exciting nightlife. From the Pyrenees to the coast, its landscapes and varied cultures are worth exploring. Especially enticing is the national insistence on enjoying everyday pleasures. The Spanish live life to its fullest whether they are strolling in the park, pausing for a siesta, lingering over lunch, or dancing until dawn.

TOP REASONS TO GO

★ **Cool Cities:** Barcelona, Madrid, Seville, Granada, Valencia, Bilbao, San Sebastián, and Salamanca.

★ **Amazing Architecture:** From the Moorish Alhambra to Gaudí's eclectic Sagrada Família.

★ **History:** From Segovia's Roman aqueduct to Córdoba's Mezquita, history comes alive.

★ **Superlative Art:** Masterpieces by Goya, El Greco, Picasso, Dalí, and Miró thrill.

★ **Tapas and Wine:** Spain's justly famed small bites pair perfectly with its Riojas.

★ **Beautiful Beaches:** From Barcelona's city beaches to Ibiza's celebrated strands.

Contents

Fodor's Features

Contents

Contents

Chapter 1

EXPERIENCE SPAIN

25 ULTIMATE EXPERIENCES

Spain offers terrific experiences that should be on every traveler's list. Here are Fodor's top picks for a memorable trip.

1 Park Güell

A sweeping view of Barcelona awaits you at this architectural park, Gaudí's pièce de résistance in urban planning. Peer out from the mosaic benches over gingerbread-like houses and fountains guarded by giant tiled lizards. *(Ch. 8)*

2 Picos de Europa

A national park where you can hike between lakes, meadows, and snowy peaks, this mountain range on Spain's northern coast is a top outdoor adventure. *(Ch. 5)*

3 Gorgeous cathedrals

Towering temples in cities including León and Burgos have been presided over by bishops for centuries and are some of the greatest marvels in Spain. *(Ch. 4)*

4 Food tours

Take a delicious dive into Spanish culture by trying dishes like tortilla española (Spanish potato omelet) and paella with a local guide who knows the best haunts. *(Ch. 2)*

5 Guggenheim Bilbao

Thought-provoking works by artists like Mark Rothko and Andy Warhol will entrance you at Bilbao's riverfront museum, a titanium work of art itself. *(Ch. 6)*

6 Beaches

You can't go wrong on the Iberian Peninsula, where you can choose between the sun-drenched beaches of the Mediterranean and the wild, brisk shores of the Atlantic. *(Ch. 9, 10, 12, 13)*

7 Flamenco

A foot-stomping whirlwind of click-clacking castanets, guitar solos, and gut-wrenching vocals will have you shouting "¡Olé!" at the tablaos (flamenco venues) of Sevilla. *(Ch. 11)*

8 El Escorial

A leisurely day trip from the hustle and bustle of Madrid, this medieval town's main attraction is a gargantuan royal residence set high on a hill. *(Ch. 4)*

9 Córdoba Mosque

The ancient Mezquita's engraved columns and candy cane–striped double arches are an enchanting reminder of Andalusia's 10th-century Islamic grandeur. *(Ch. 11)*

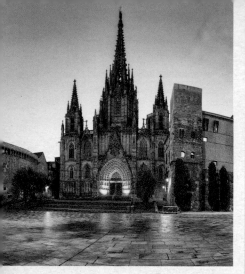

10 Barri Gòtic

Barcelona's most ancient quarter is a maze of cobblestone streets and stone arcades that empty into medieval plaças. It also boasts some of the city's chicest boutiques. *(Ch. 8)*

11 Rioja wine caves

Don't miss the bodegas in Haro, in the heart of Rioja Alta, for their centuries of history and mysterious cellars, draped with penicillin mold and cobwebs, or calados. *(Ch. 6)*

12 Mérida

Tour the remnants of an ancient Roman city, home to one of the best-preserved stone amphitheaters in Europe. The UNESCO site is the largest of its kind in Spain. *(Ch. 4)*

13 Canary Islands volcanoes

The tallest mountain in Spain is also an active volcano—and you can climb it. Make it to the peak of 12,000-foot El Teide, and you'll be rewarded with bird's-eye views. *(Ch. 13)*

14 Alhambra

Nothing epitomizes the Moors' power and ingenuity like this centuries-old fortress. Set aside a few hours to take in arched courtyards and intricate Arabesques. *(Ch. 11)*

15 Sagrada Família

Gaudí's iconic church is a soaring fantasy world of vivid stained glass and zoomorphic motifs. It is slated for completion in 2026 after 150 years of construction. *(Ch. 8)*

16 Toledo

When Toledo was the ancient capital of Spain, Muslims, Jews, and Christians cohabitated in harmony—hence the city's nickname, "City of Three Cultures." *(Ch. 4)*

17 Skiing

Some of the best slopes in western Europe (and with reasonable ticket prices) can be found in the Pyrenees, the mountain range Spain shares with France and Andorra. *(Ch. 7)*

18 Retiro Park

The tree-shaded trails, cafés, and French gardens here are an oasis right in Madrid's city center. Find the Palacio de Cristal, an impressive iron-and-glass greenhouse. *(Ch. 3)*

19 Feria!

Vibrant ferias, or fairs, are some of the country's wildest parties, with traditional dance performances, carnival rides, street food, and makeshift discotecas. *(Ch. 11)*

20 Paradores

Want to hole up in a property with personality and a true sense of place? Look to Paradores, a state-run network of accommodations housed in historic buildings. *(Ch. 5)*

21 Cuenca's hanging houses

It doesn't get much more picturesque than these buildings perched on a cliffside overlooking the Huécar River. They seem to defy gravity as they jut over the ravine. *(Ch. 4)*

22 Museums in Madrid

Madrid's Golden Triangle is home to three world-class museums within blocks of each other. Don't miss Guernica at Museo Reina Sofía. *(Ch. 3)*

23 Segovia aqueduct

This work of Roman engineering has stood for more than 2,000 years—mind-boggling, considering that mortar is entirely absent from construction. *(Ch. 4)*

24 Pueblos blancos

Road trip through these stark white villages on Andalusian hilltops, one of southern Spain's most postcard-perfect attractions. *(Ch. 11)*

25 Santiago de Compostela

The best way to reach the Galician capital is the Walk of St. James, a 1,000-year-old Christian pilgrimage—but you don't have to be religious to appreciate the hike. *(Ch. 5)*

WHAT'S WHERE

1 Madrid. Its boundless energy creates sights and sounds larger than life. The Prado, Reina Sofía, and Thyssen-Bornemisza museums make one of the greatest repositories of Western art in the world.

2 Central Spain. From Madrid there are several important excursions, notably Toledo, as well as Segovia and Salamanca. Other cities in Castile–La Mancha and Castile-León worth visiting include León, Burgos, Soria, Sigüenza, Ávila, and Cuenca. Extremadura, Spain's remote borderland with Portugal, is often overlooked, but has some intriguing places to discover.

3 Galicia and Asturias. On the way to Galicia to pay homage to St. James, pilgrims once crossed Europe to this corner of Spain so remote it was called *finis terrae* ("world's end"), and today Santiago de Compostela still resonates with mystic importance. In nearby Asturias, villages nestle in green highlands, backed by the snowcapped Picos de Europa mountains, while sandy beaches stretch out along the Atlantic. Farther east,

in Cantabria, is the Belle Époque beach resort of Santander.

4 The Basque Country, Navarra, and La Rioja. The Basque region is a country within a country, proud of its own language and culture as well as the wild, dramatic coast of the Bay of Biscay. Nearby Navarra and La Rioja are famous for the running of the bulls in Pamplona and for excellent wines, respectively.

5 The Pyrenees. Cut by some 23 steep north–south valleys on the Spanish side alone, with four independent geographical entities— the valleys of Camprodón, Cerdanya, Aran, and Baztán—the Pyrenees have a wealth of areas to explore, with different cultures and languages, as well as world-class ski resorts.

6 Barcelona. La Rambla, in the heart of the Ciutat Vella, is packed day and night with strollers, artists, street entertainers, vendors, and vamps, all preparing you for Barcelona's startling architectural landmarks. But treasures lie beyond the tourist path, including Antoni Gaudí's sinuous Casa Milà and unique Sagrada Família church, masterpieces of the Moderniste oeuvre.

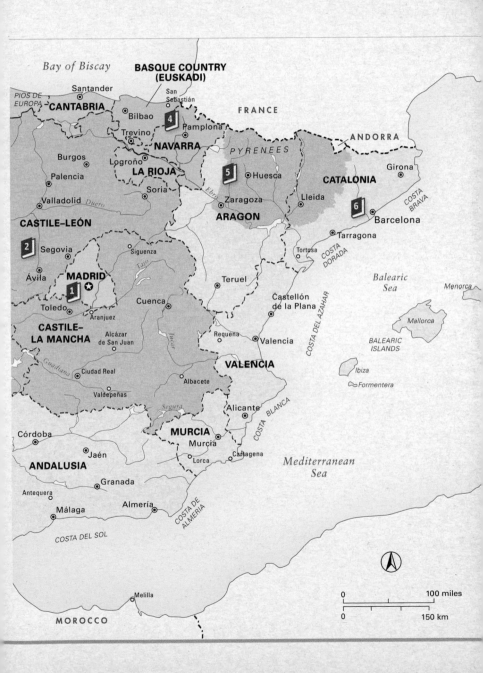

Bay of Biscay

**BASQUE COUNTRY
(EUSKADI)**

Santander

*PIOS DE
EUROPA*

San
Sebastián

FRANCE

CANTABRIA

Bilbao

4

Pamplona

ANDORRA

Trevino

Burgos

Logroño

NAVARRA

P Y R E N E E S

Girona

LA RIOJA

5

Huesca

CATALONIA

*COSTA
BRAVA*

Palencia

Soria

Valladolid

Duero

Zaragoza

Lleida

6

Barcelona

CASTILE–LEÓN

ARAGON

Tarragona

2

Segovia

Siguenza

Tortosa

*COSTA
DORADA*

Tajo

Ávila

MADRID ✪

Teruel

*Balearic
Sea*

Menorca

Toledo

Cuenca

Aranjuez

Castellón
de la Plana

Mallorca

**CASTILE–
LA MANCHA**

Alcázar
de San Juan

Jucar

Requena

Valencia

COSTA DEL AZAHAR

*BALEARIC
ISLANDS*

Guadiana

Ciudad Real

Albacete

VALENCIA

Ibiza

Valdepeñas

Segura

Alicante

Formentera

COSTA BLANCA

Córdoba

MURCIA

Jaén

Murcia

*Mediterranean
Sea*

ANDALUSIA

Lorca

Cartagena

Granada

Antequera

Málaga

Almería

*COSTA DE
ALMERÍA*

COSTA DEL SOL

Melilla

MOROCCO

0   100 miles

0   150 km

WHAT'S WHERE

7 Catalonia, Valencia, and the Costa Blanca. The mountain-backed plain of the Levante is dotted with Christian and Moorish landmarks and Roman ruins. Valencia's signature paella fortifies visitors touring the city's medieval masterpieces and modern architecture. The Costa Blanca has party-till-dawn resort towns. The rice paddies and orange groves of the Costa Blanca lead to the palm-fringed port city of Alicante.

8 Ibiza and the Balearic Islands. Ibiza still generates buzz as a summer playground for clubbers from all over, but even this isle has its quiet coves. Mallorca has some heavily touristed pockets, along with pristine mountain vistas in the island's interior. On serene Menorca, the two cities of Ciutadella and Mahón have different histories, cultures, and points of view.

9 Andalusia. Eight provinces—five of which are coastal (Huelva, Cádiz, Málaga, Granada, and Almería) and three of which are landlocked (Seville, Córdoba, and Jaén)— make up this southern autonomous community known for its Moorish influences. Highlights include the haunting Mezquita of Córdoba, Granada's romantic Alhambra, and seductive Seville.

10 Costa del Sol and Costa de Almería. A popular "sun-holiday" destination, the Costas have vast holiday resorts occupying much of the Mediterranean coast. Respites include Málaga, a vibrant city with world-class art museums; Marbella, a pristine Andalusian old quarter; and villages such as Casares seem immune to the goings-on along the water.

11 Canary Islands. Fuerteventura, the least visited and developed of the four largest volcanic islands, boasts endless white beaches. Gran Canaria is an isle of contrasts from the desert dunes in the south to the verdant central peaks. Lanzarote's ocher-and-gold landscape is dotted with long beaches and white villages. Tenerife has the most attractions plus Spain's highest peak, the Pico de Teide.

Bay of Biscay

BASQUE COUNTRY (EUSKADI)

Santander

CANTABRIA

San Sebastián

Bilbao

FRANCE

Trevino

NAVARRA

PYRENEES

ANDORRA

Burgos

Logroño

LA RIOJA

Huesca

CATALONIA

Girona

Palencia

Soria

Zaragoza

Lleida

COSTA BRAVA

Valladolid Duero

ARAGON

Tarragona

Barcelona

CASTILE–LEÓN

Tortosa

COSTA DORADA

Segovia

Tajo

Teruel

Balearic Sea

Menorca

Ciutadella

Ávila

MADRID

Castellón de la Plana

Mahon

Toledo

Cuenca

Mallorca

Aranjuez

Alcázar de San Juan

Requena

BALEARIC ISLANDS

CASTILE-LA MANCHA

Jucar

Valencia

COSTA DEL AZAHAR

Guadiana

VALENCIA

Ibiza

8

Ciudad Real

Albacete

Formentera

Valdepeñas

Benidorm

Segura

Alicante

COSTA BLANCA

Córdoba

Jaén

MURCIA

9

Murcia

Mediterranean Sea

ANDALUSIA

Lorca

Cartagena

Antequera

Granada

Almería

COSTA DE ALMERIA

10

Málaga

Marbella   COSTA DEL SOL

Melilla

0   100 miles

0   150 km

MOROCCO

7

Spain Today

POLITICS

Since the advent of democracy in 1978 and until 2014, Spanish politics was dominated by the two largest parties: the socialist Partido Socialista Obrero Español (PSOE) and the right-wing Partido Popular (PP). In 2014, however, as Spain continued to battle an economic crisis and as some high-profile corruption scandals came to light, the political scenario changed. "Renovation" became the watchword, and Spaniards clamored for more ethical behavior from public figures. On the back of this, two new parties entered the political arena: Unidas Podemos (Together We Can), a left-wing grassroots party; and Ciudadanos (Citizens), a pro-business, center-right party that strongly opposes Catalan nationalism. General elections in June 2016 resulted in a deadlock, with no party reaching the required 176-seat majority. The PP under Prime Minister Mariano Rajoy, however, formed a minority government with support from Ciudadanos.

A push for Catalan independence, led by separatist parties holding a slim majority in the Catalan regional legislature, then created a major constitutional crisis. On October 1, 2017, separatist politicians presided over an independence referendum (similar to the one celebrated in Scotland in 2014), which had been outlawed by Spanish courts. The ruling PP government in Madrid took a hardline stance against the independence movement, sending national police and civil guards into Catalonia to halt voting. Newspapers worldwide were splashed with images of police beating unarmed voters at polling stations. To punish its renegade region, Madrid imposed emergency rule on Catalonia, suspending its autonomy and jailing top regional politicians. Catalonia repeated regional elections in December 2017, with the same result: a slim majority for separatists, and a stalemate with Madrid.

A criminal trial of leading figures in the independence movement is likely to run for some time, but tensions in Barcelona have eased. Tourists are safe and there has been no appreciable violence even at large demonstrations, but it is advisable to avoid them when possible.

In 2018, Spain's national court found that the ruling PP had been profiting from illegal kickbacks in return for contracts since 1989 and confirmed that the party had been running an illegal, off-the-books accounting structure. The Socialist party under Pedro Sanchez won a parliamentary no-confidence motion and brought down Rajoy's government. Sanchez—who seeks a negotiated solution to the Catalan issue—became prime minister, supported in a coalition by Podemos and regional separatist parties.

THE ECONOMY

After Spain went into recession in 2008, stringent financial measures were imposed by the European Union and the IMF. Unemployment soared to 26%, and youth unemployment reached double that. Since 2014, the economy has bounced back: GDP growth for 2017 was 3.1%, one of the highest rates in Europe. Forecasts for 2019 expect Spain's economy to expand 2.2%, higher than for Germany, France, or Italy and nearly double the rate of the eurozone. While tourism to Catalonia briefly slumped in the fall of 2017, it has surged in the rest of the country. In 2017, Spain surpassed the United States to become the world's second-most-visited country after France.

RELIGION

The state-funded Catholic Church, closely tied to the right-wing PP and with the national Cadena Cope radio station as its voice, continues to hold considerable social and political influence in Spain, with members of secretive groups such as Opus Dei and the Legionarios de Cristo holding key government and industry positions.

Despite the church's influence, at street level Spain has become a secular country, as demonstrated by the fact that 70% of Spaniards supported the decidedly un-Catholic law allowing gay marriage. And although more than 75% of the population claims to be Catholic, less than 20% go to church on a regular basis.

More than 1 million Muslims reside in Spain, making Islam the country's second-largest religion.

THE ARTS

Spain's devotion to the arts is clearly shown by the attention, both national and international, paid to its annual Princesa de Asturias prize, where Princess Leonor hands out accolades to international high achievers such as Frank Gehry, Francis Ford Coppola, and Bob Dylan and to homegrown talent such as the writer Antonio Muñoz Molina, who has taught at the City University of New York.

Film is at the forefront of the Spanish arts scene. Spain's most acclaimed director, Pedro Almodóvar, is still at it, most recently with a 2019 film, *Pain and Glory*, starring fellow Spaniards Penélope Cruz and Antonio Banderas. *The Bookshop*, an English-language film directed and produced by Spaniards, won Best Film and Best Director awards at the 2018 Goya Awards, Spain's version of the Oscars.

While authors such as Miguel Delibes, Rosa Montero, and Maruja Torres flourish in Spain, few break onto the international scene, with the exception of Arturo Pérez Reverte, whose books include *Captain Alatriste* and *The Fencing Master*, and Carlos Ruiz Zafón, author of the acclaimed *Shadow of the Wind, The Angel's Game*, and *Prisoner of Heaven*. Spain's contribution to the fine arts is still dominated by three names: the Mallorca-born artist Miquel Barceló; the Basque sculptor Eduardo Chillida, who died in 2002; and the Catalan abstract painter Antoni Tàpies, who died in 2012.

SPORTS

With Real Madrid and FC Barcelona firmly established as international brands, and with La Liga recognized as one of the world's most exciting leagues, soccer remains the nation's favorite sport. The national soccer team, known as La Roja (The Red One), won the World Cup in 2010 and has won the European Cup three times—a record tied only by Germany. In other sports, national heroes include Rafael Nadal, the first tennis player to hold Grand Slam titles on clay, grass, and hard court; Garbiñe Muguruza, the 2017 Wimbledon champion; six-time NBA All-Star Pau Gasol and his two-time All-Star brother Marc; and WNBA star Anna Cruz, who plays for the Minnesota Lynx. Motorsports are hugely popular in Spain; Formula 1 champion Fernando Alonso has recently retired but all-time-great Marc Marquez continues to dominate in Grand Prix motorcycle road racing.

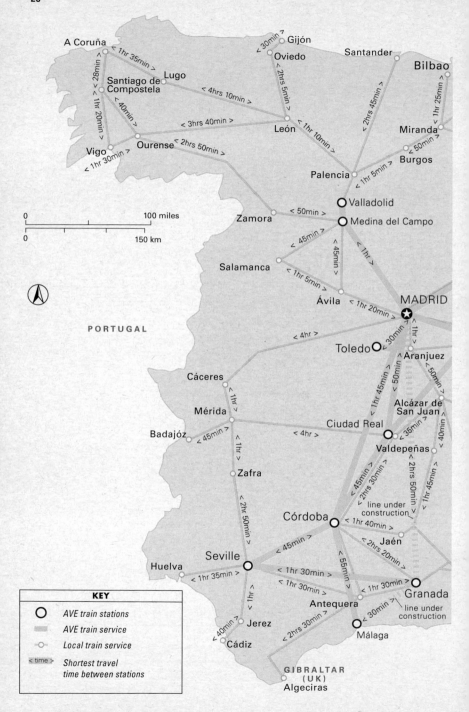

A Coruña
< 1hr 35min >
< 28min >
< 1hr 20min >
Santiago de
Compostela
Lugo
< 40min >
< 4hrs 10min >
< 3hrs 40min >
Vigo
< 1hr 30min >
Ourense < 2hrs 50min >

Gijón
< 30min >
Oviedo
< 2hrs 5min >
Santander
Bilbao
< 2hrs 45min >
< 1hr 25min >
Miranda
< 50min >
Burgos
León
< 1hr 10min >
< 1hr 5min >
Palencia

100 miles
0
0
150 km

Zamora
< 50min >
Valladolid
Medina del Campo
< 45min >
< 45min >
< 1hr >
Salamanca
< 1hr 5min >
Ávila < 1hr 20min >

MADRID

PORTUGAL

Toledo
< 4hr >
< 30min >
< 1hr >
Aranjuez
< 1hr 45min >
< 50min >
< 50min >
Cáceres
< 1hr >
Mérida
Badajóz
< 45min >
< 1hr >
Ciudad Real
< 4hr >
Alcázar de
San Juan
< 35min >
< 40min >
Valdepeñas
< 2hrs 50min >
< 1hr 45min >
Zafra
< 2hr 50min >
< 45min >
< 2hrs 30min >
line under
construction

Córdoba
< 1hr 40min >
< 45min >
Jaén
< 2hrs 20min >
Seville
< 1hr 30min >
< 55min >
Huelva
< 1hr 35min >
< 1hr 30min >
< 1hr 30min >
1hr 30min >
Granada
line under
construction
Antequera
< 30min >
< 1hr >
Jerez
< 40min >
< 2hrs 30min >
Málaga
Cádiz

GIBRALTAR
(UK)
Algeciras

KEY

○ AVE train stations

▬ AVE train service

–○– Local train service

< time > Shortest travel
time between stations

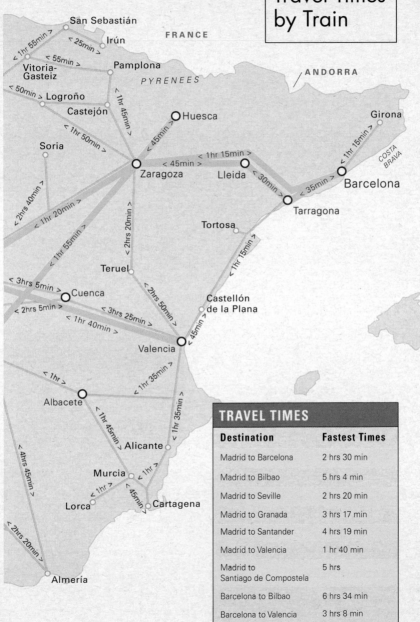

Travel Times by Train

1

San Sebastián
Irún
FRANCE
< 1hr 55min >
< 25min >
< 55min >
Vitoria-Gasteiz
Pamplona
PYRENEES
ANDORRA
< 50min >
Logroño
Castejón
< 1hr 45min >
Huesca
Girona
< 1hr 50min >
< 45min >
Soria
< 1hr 15min >
< 1hr 15min >
COSTA BRAVA
< 2hrs 40min >
< 1hr 20min >
< 45min >
Zaragoza
Lleida
< 30min >
< 35min >
Barcelona
< 1hr 55min >
< 2hrs 20min >
Tarragona
Teruel
Tortosa
< 1hr 15min >
< 3hrs 5min >
Cuenca
< 2hrs 50min >
Castellón de la Plana
< 2hrs 5min >
< 3hrs 25min >
< 1hr 40min >
< 45min >
Valencia
< 1hr >
< 1hr 36min >
Albacete
< 1hr 35min >
< 1hr 45min >
Alicante
< 4hrs 45min >
Murcia
< 1hr >
< 1hr >
< 1hr >
Lorca
< 45min >
Cartagena
< 2hrs 20min >
Almería

Spain's Best Museums

CIUDAD DE LAS ARTES Y LAS CIENCIAS (THE CITY OF ARTS AND SCIENCES)

This incredible collection of buildings located in Valencia houses some of the world's most cutting edge science and art exhibits in an enormous piece of modern sculpture.

DALÍ THEATRE-MUSEUM

Dalí himself supervised the renovation works on this former municipal building, which is recognizable for its red and gold paint job and the iconic white eggs that crown it. The museum pays homage to the artist's creativity and imagination and houses many memorable works. You won't find his greatest paintings here but you will find his crypt!

MUSEU NACIONAL D'ART DE CATALUNYA (MNAC)

Catalonia's national art museum isn't just a literal palace, it's also a shrine to history, culture, and the spirit of the Catalonian people. MNAC has the finest collection of Romanesque frescoes and devotional sculpture in the world, most rescued from abandoned chapels in the Pyrenees in an astonishing feat of restoration.

MUSEO NACIONAL DE ESCULTURA

Valladolid's National Museum of Sculpture houses both religious and nonreligious pieces and is divided into essentially two categories: original pieces made from polychrome wood, which date anywhere from the 13th through the 18th century, and reproductions made from plaster casts, which were produced in the 19th and 20th centuries.

THE GUGGENHEIM MUSEUM BILBAO

Frank Gehry's groundbreaking Guggenheim Museum Bilbao is a complex and swirling work of art in its own right and the first great building of the 21st century. It is also one of the world's best contemporary art museums. Highlights include works by Andy Warhol, Anish Kapoor, Jeff Koons, Louise Bourgeois, and Eduardo Chillida.

MUSEO THYSSEN-BORNEMISZA

Set in a palace on the Paseo del Prado the Thyssen offers the opportunity to check a lot of important art off your bucket list as you explore European painting from the Middle Ages through to the late 20th century.

MUSEO DEL PRADO

The Prado is one of Spain's largest and most visited museums and a highlight of a visit to Madrid. Wander through rooms filled with dazzling display of works by the great European masters, all housed in a magnificent neoclassical building that opened 200 years ago.

MUSEO NACIONAL CENTRO DE ARTE REINA SOFÍA

Unlike the Prado and the Thyssen, the Reina Sofía is specifically dedicated to Spanish modern and contemporary art with works by practically all the major Spanish artists of the 20th century—Picasso, Dalí, Miró, Julio González, Tàpies, Alfonso Ponce de León, and Antonio Saura. Picasso's Guernica is the top attraction but the museum also serves as a popular venue for concerts and events.

MUSEU PICASSO

Five elegant medieval and early Renaissance palaces in Barcelona's La Ribera house a collection of more than 4,000 works by Pablo Picasso, who studied at La Llotja art school. The collection focuses on these formative years and includes pre-adolescent portraits and sketchy landscapes—a treat for art lovers.

MUSEO ARQUEOLÓGICO NACIONAL (NATIONAL ARCHEOLOGICAL MUSEUM)

A modern showcase of ancient treasures, MAN went from hidden gem to one of Madrid's top museums and home to one of the most outstanding archaeological collections in Europe.

Spain's Best Beaches

CALA MACARELLA AND CALA MACARELLETA, MENORCA

These picture-perfect coves, situated alongside each other on the southwest coast of the island, offer impeccably clear waters, white beaches, and shallow, glimmering rock pools.

PLAYA LOS LANCES, TARIFA

Located where the Mediterranean and the Atlantic meet, Tarifa is ideal for kitesurfing and for spotting dolphins and whales. The main attraction is the 6-mile-long white powder sand paradise and the protected nature reserve.

PLAYA DE CORRALEJO, FUERTEVENTURA, CANARY ISLANDS

Incredibly popular with kite surfers, all the Grandes Playas (or big beaches) of the Corralejo Natural Park offer pristine white powder sand and crystal-clear turquoise water.

BOGATELL, BARCELONA

Even though Barceloneta is the best known of Barcelona's city beaches, Bogatell is the beach of choice among locals in the know. Why? Not only is it less crowded than tourist-heavy Barceloneta, it is also cleaner and less popular with local pickpockets. The downside, meanwhile, is that it requires a slightly longer trek from the city center. It's also home to one of Catalonia's best-loved seafood restaurants, Xiringuito Escribà.

PLAYA LAS ARENAS, VALENCIA

Given that Las Arenas literally translates as "the sands," it goes without saying that Valencia's most famous beach has been blessed with some pristine golden powder. The water is calm and shallow, making it suitable for swimmers of all ages and abilities, as well as windsurfers and sailors. Meanwhile, the wide, busy promenade that runs alongside the grand beach is packed with bars and restaurants.

LA KONTXA (OR LA CONCHA), SAN SEBASTIÁN

San Sebastián's emblematic seashell-shaped La Kontxa ranks as one of the most famous urban beaches in the world. Sheltered from the elements by Urgull hill on one side and Igueldo hill on the other, and facing Santa Clara island across a short stretch of water, La Kontxa's water is nearly always calm, making it an ideal spot for swimming, paddling, and sunbathing.

La Kontxa, San Sebastián

PLAYA DE LA RIBERA, SITGES

The dreamy seaside town of Sitges is located some 25 miles down the coast from Barcelona, and offers pristine, white powder sand and a lively scene. Sitges has gay-friendly and nudist beaches as well as family beaches.

EL PLAYAZO, COSTA DE ALMERIA

Few places in Europe remain as wild and unspoiled as Cabo de Gata, the UNESCO Biosphere Reserve in the southeastern corner of the Iberian Peninsula. Its wild, arid landscape is a mix of secluded rocky coves, jagged cliffs, and idyllic white, sandy beaches.

PLATJA DE SES ILLETES, FORMENTERA

While every corner of Formentera screams exclusivity, the chicest spot of all is Platja de Ses Illetes, part of the Ses Salines National Park. The residents are pretty, too.

ISLAS CIES, VIGO

One of the last unspoiled refuges of the Spanish coastline, these islands off the coast of Galicia in northernmost Spain are designated a nature conservation and wildlife site and home to seven beautiful beaches.

ES TRENC, MALLORCA

Popular with nudists and day-trippers, Es Trenc has excellent facilities and a variety of restaurants and beach bars and is an ideal spot to let it all hang out—if that's what you're into.

PLAYA DE LA VICTORIA, CÁDIZ

The most famous urban beach in the Andalusian city of Cádiz, Playa de la Victoria offers spacious, golden sand beach; a generous boardwalk with a seemingly infinite number of beach bars; and several popular beachfront hotels.

Most Beautiful Castle Hotels in Spain

CASTILLO DE MONDA

Midway between Málaga city and the beaches of Marbella, this Moorish citadel with roots in the 8th century lay in ruin for 400 years before reopening as a hotel in 2016. Moorish-themed rooms include arabesques, coffered ceilings, and colorful tiled bathrooms.

PARADOR DE HONDARRIBIA

Live like a feudal lord in this 10th-century bastion that hosted Spain's founding emperor, Carlos V. When you're not lounging on the outdoor terrace or the stone-walled lobby, retreat to simply outfitted rooms with dark wood floors and cushy beds.

CASTILLO DE ARTEAGA

This stunning French neo-Gothic castle erected by Napoleon III is now a Relais & Château–approved rural retreat. The castle's crenelated towers peek above the oak groves of the surrounding Urdaibai nature reserve.

TUGASA HOTEL CASTILLO DE CASTELLAR

If your Spain bucket list includes the pueblos blancos of southern Spain, stay in this budget 13th-century Moorish fortress in Los Alcornocales Natural Park, renowned for its cave paintings and groves of cork oak.

CASTILLO DE GRISEL

There are only eight rooms in this eclectic and affordable boutique hotel occupying a 12th-century Gothic castle, the best-preserved structure of its kind in the region. Between its sturdy ashlar walls you'll find palatial halls, an ancient cistern, and two sun-drenched patios strewn with plants. Grisel makes a good home base for travelers looking to explore the sandy canyons and steep cliffs of the Bardenas Reales, the otherworldly badlands of Navarra.

CASTILLO DEL BOSQUE LA ZOREDA

This stone mansion tucked among chestnut and oak trees in the backwoods of Asturias, 3 miles outside Oviedo, is far less ancient than meets the eye—it was commissioned in 1926 by a local business tycoon—but there's nothing newfangled about the pink-stone exterior, replete with arches and chimneys and crowned with ersatz battlements. Inside, things skew more modern with upscale amenities like room service and a sleek indoor pool.

Parador de Cardona

PARADOR DE CARDONA

Arguably the most important medieval fortress in Catalonia, the castillo (castle) was built in the 9th century by (the hilariously named) William the Hairy, a local count. The parador's barrel vaults and pointed arches make it a jewel of Romanesque and Gothic architecture, but even if you aren't an architecture buff, you'll be just as wowed by its period decor (think four-poster beds, beamed ceilings, antique wall art) and home-style Catalan restaurant.

CASTELL D'EMPORDÀ

Hidden in a fertile valley between the Pyrenees and the Costa Brava, this 14th-century castle is so heart-meltingly charming that Salvador Dalí is said to have offered to buy it in exchange for several of his works. The (evidently art-illiterate) owners declined. It was since sold and converted into a 38-room hotel complete with claw-foot tubs, two swimming pools, and a wraparound sundeck overlooking the golden farmscape.

HOTEL CASTILLO EL COLLADO

Built in 1900 by the Chimbo soap CEO, Víctor Tapia, this turreted castle in Álava province features the original stones from a disused 12th-century barracks. The sumptuous, delightfully old-fashioned rooms brim with antique furniture collected by Tapia, and the reception area—housed in the former chapel—sets the time-warpy mood with a gilded 17th-century altarpiece.

CASTILLO DEL BUEN AMOR

Towering above rolling farmland outside Salamanca, this 15th-century sandstone castle has vibrant gardens, coffered ceilings, and an arcaded dungeon (now occupied by an excellent restaurant), as well as modern amenities like a large outdoor pool, air-conditioning, and deep bathtubs.

Spain's Most Beautiful Villages

FORNELLS, MENORCA

For a guaranteed quiet escape, make a beeline to the northern fishing village of Fornells, whose whitewashed houses wrap around a picturesque marina. Dive by day then make your way to its seafood restaurants for the daily catch.

CADAQUÉS, GIRONA

Dalí, Lorca, Duchamp, Buñuel, Picasso—Spain's visionaries flocked to this whitewashed town on the Costa Brava for much the same reasons travelers continue to visit today: its laid-back, bohemian attitude; blindingly white houses; tiny harborside restaurants; and stupefyingly gorgeous sunsets.

CASARES, MÁLAGA

This quintessential Andalusian village—think whitewashed houses and terra-cotta roofs—produced one of the region's greatest thinkers and patriots, Blas Infante. Visit his childhood home museum, then head up the labyrinthine streets to the village's highest point, where you'll find the ruins of a Moorish castle.

SAN CRISTÓBAL DE LA LAGUNA

The UNESCO-protected center of San Cristóbal de La Laguna (simply "La Laguna" to locals) takes on a tropical feel with wide plazas, baroque churches, and pastel-painted houses with carved-wood balconies. What La Laguna may lack in beaches (it's 15 minutes from the coast) it makes up for with a student-driven nightlife scene, fascinating history (don't miss the Museo de Historia de Tenerife), and immaculately preserved colonial architecture.

ALQUÉZAR, HUESCA

One of the best-preserved villages of the region of Aragón, sandwiched between Catalonia and Navarra, Alquézar spirals out like a nautilus from its central castillo. Start there, and wind your way down to the base of the village through one-car-wide streets and arcaded plazas, pausing at the designated viewpoints to snap pics of the foothills of the Pyrenees.

COMBARRO, PONTEVEDRA

Combarro is a quintessentially Galician village with its old town of granite buildings, churches with stone crosses peeking above the skyline, and rows and rows of hórreos, medieval granaries built on stone stilts. The town is influenced by both land and sea, bordered to the south by rolling farmland and to the north by the temperamental Atlantic.

Cudillero

CUDILLERO, ASTURIAS
Gravity-defying cliff-top houses? Check. Sleepy port surrounded by cafés and seafood restaurants? Check. Centuries-old churches and palaces? Claro que sí.

ALMAGRO, CIUDAD REAL
Drama geeks and literature buffs fawn over Almagro, whose Corral de Comedias is the only preserved medieval theater in Europe, founded in 1628. This quaint Manchegan town is known for its berenjenas de Almagro (pickled baby eggplant) best sampled at the tapas bars that line the green-and-white Plaza Mayor, a relic of the 1500s; near the plaza are granite mansions bearing the heraldic shields of their former owners and a splendid parador housed in a 17th-century convent.

PEDRAZA, SEGOVIA
When it comes to day trips from Madrid, Segovia and Toledo are most travelers' go-tos. Avoid the crowds and visit Pedraza, a fairy-tale town 40 minutes northeast of Segovia whose architecture will transport you to the Middle Ages. After wandering the dim halls of the town's 15th-century castle, make your way down to the Plaza Mayor, a porticoed square built in the 16th century. Each July this small hilltop village hosts the Concierto de las Velas, during which the village is filled with live classical music and lit entirely by candles.

HONDARRIBIA, GIPUZKOA
Hondarribia is one of the Basque Country's most charming towns, thanks to its white, green, and red fishermen's homes and tree-shaded promenades. Wind your way down to the harbor on foot, and ferry over to the town of Hendaye. Then stay at the parador, housed in a medieval bastion.

What to Watch and Read Before You Go to Spain

HOMAGE TO CATALONIA BY GEORGE ORWELL

George Orwell's life was strongly influenced by his time in Spain fighting against the Nationalist army led by future Fascist dictator Francisco Franco. Orwell's journals directly document his time at war in Catalonia and his first-person narrative provides a view of war-torn Barcelona.

FOR WHOM THE BELL TOLLS BY ERNEST HEMINGWAY

All the typical Hemingway elements are present in this fictional account of the Spanish Civil War: romance, bravado, glory, death, and tragedy. It's an incredibly evocative slice of historical fiction that is almost impossible to put down once started.

DRIVING OVER LEMONS BY CHRIS STEWART

In this hilarious bestseller memoir by the ex-drummer for the rock band Genesis, Stewart tells the story of buying a peasant farm (complete with a resident previous owner) in Andalusia's Alpujarras mountains.

MONSIGNOR QUIXOTE BY GRAHAM GREENE

This novel provides a wonderful journey through Spain in the company of Monsignor Quixote, an aging village priest, and his friend Sancho Panza, the communist ex-mayor. It's a contemporary reimagining of Miguel Cervantes's classic Don Quixote but set in Spain in the 1980s rather than the 1600s.

THE NEW SPANIARDS BY JOHN HOOPER

How was the transition from dictatorship to democracy accomplished so smoothly? How did a country noted for sexual repression find itself in the European vanguard in legalizing gay marriage? What's the deal with the Spanish royal family? Read Hooper's fascinating study, considered one of the clearest insights into the sociology and culture of modern Spain.

THE SHADOW OF THE WIND BY CARLOS RUIZ ZAFÓN

Daniel Sempere is 10 years old when his father, a bookseller in post–civil war Barcelona, takes him to a mysterious labyrinth filled with treasured but forgotten tomes and tells him to pick one that he will then dedicate his life to preserving. What follows is a tale of a young man who discovers a mysterious person—or perhaps creature—is destroying all remaining works of Julián Carax, the author whose book he now protects. *The Shadow of the Wind*'s story of life, death, and history may be fictional, but its setting in a war-torn Spain is forceful, and the fact that it's sold more than 15 million copies hints at its compelling universe.

THE CITY OF MARVELS BY EDUARDO MENDOZA

The tale of a boy who rises from abject poverty to great wealth and power and a city—Barcelona—that expands from a small provincial capital to a metropolitan city. The action spans the years between Barcelona's two economically disastrous World's Fairs of 1888 and 1929.

HOMAGE TO BARCELONA BY COLM TÓIBÍN

Irish author Colm Tóibín moved to Barcelona in 1975 when he was twenty. In this book, written with deep affection and knowledge, Tóibín celebrates one of Europe's greatest cities and explores its history, moving from its foundations through to nationalism, civil war, and the transition from dictatorship to democracy. He looks at the lives of Barcelona's great artists—Gaudí, Miró, Picasso, Casals, and Dali. Tóibín is the perfect guide to Barcelona and this is a sensuous and beguiling portrait of a unique Mediterranean port and an adopted home.

THE TIME OF THE DOVES BY MERCÈ RODOREDA

Written by exiled Catalan writer Mercè Rodoreda, *The Time of the Doves* is a novel about a shopkeeper named Natalia who endures a controlling husband and an increasingly challenging life during the Spanish Civil War. This is widely considered a classic of Catalan literature and is required reading in Catalan secondary schools. It's a story about hope and endurance in the face of great adversity. After the Spanish Civil War, when the Catalan language was banned in public and the culture harshly supressed, Rodoreda went into exile. In 1962 she published La plaça del Diamant (translated as The Time of the Doves by David Rosenthal in 1981), widely regarded as her masterpiece and a masterpiece of Catalan literature. It is not your usual account of the civil war in that there is no fighting and no scenes from the front. We learn about the war from the perspective of a woman whose husband is fighting with the Republicans while she works hard to feed herself and her two children. Gabriel García Márquez learned Catalan just to read this book and declared it "the most beautiful novel that's been published in Spain after the Civil War." The author, who died in 1983, is also known for her first novel, *Aloma*.

¡AY CARMELA! DIRECTED BY CARLOS SAURA

This 1991 film portrays the ethical and personal dilemmas a group of nomadic comedians face during the Spanish Civil War. The film features a scene where Carmela, played by Carmen Maura, tries to teach a Polish prisoner, an International Brigadist, how to pronounce the /ñ/ sound in the word "España."

WOMEN ON THE VERGE OF A NERVOUS BREAKDOWN DIRECTED BY PEDRO ALMODÓVAR

This Academy Award–nominated black comedy was Pedro Almodóvar's international breakthrough and secured his place at the vanguard of modern Spanish cinema. Madrid-based Pepa resolves to kill herself with a batch of sleeping-pill-laced gazpacho after her lover leaves her. Fortunately, she is interrupted by a deliciously chaotic series of events.

TODO SOBRE MI MADRE (ALL ABOUT MY MOTHER) DIRECTED BY PEDRO ALMODÓVAR

After Manuela's 17-year-old son Esteban is killed before her eyes she decides to move to Barcelona in order to find his father, a transvestite named Lola who doesn't know that Esteban exists. It's a brilliantly directed tale which sensitively examines a variety of complex topics such as bereavement, addiction, gender identity, and the impacts of HIV. It also earned director Pedro Almodóvar the Best Director award at the 1999 Cannes Film Festival and the Academy Award for Best Foreign Language Film in 2000.

BELLE EPOQUE DIRECTED BY FERNANDO TRUEBA

It is 1931 in Spain and the country's monarchy is facing its final days. During this time of confusion and conflicting loyalties, Fernando, whose allegiance is to the republic, deserts from the army and goes on the run into the beautiful Spanish countryside. There, he meets Manolo, a painter with the same political beliefs and four young, beautiful daughters.

PAN'S LABYRINTH DIRECTED BY GUILLERMO DEL TORO

Set in the early years of Franco's dictatorship, this film follows an imaginative kid, Ofelia, who moves with her pregnant mother to her future stepfather's house. In her new home, she meets the faun, Pan, who tells her she might be the lost princess of an underground world. While she faces mythological creatures and terrifying beasts, a rebellion is taking place in her stepfather's military post.

FAMILY UNITED DIRECTED BY DANIEL SANCHEZ AREVALO

Combining two of Spain's greatest passions—football and family, this Spanish comedy takes place at a family wedding in a mountain-village near Madrid during the 2010 World Cup soccer final.

BIUTIFUL DIRECTED BY ALEJANDRO GONZÁLEZ IÑÁRRITU

Iñárritu's first feature since *Babel*, and his fourth moving film is the story of a single father of two (Javier Bardem) in Barcelona who finds out he has terminal cancer and tries to find someone to care for his children before his death. While melancholy, this is also a story of redemption as a father seeks a better life for his children.

History You Can See

ANCIENT SPAIN

The story of Spain, a romance-tinged tale of counts, caliphs, crusaders, and kings, begins long before written history. The Basques were among the first here, fiercely defending the green mountain valleys of the Pyrenees. Then came the Iberians, apparently crossing the Mediterranean from North Africa around 3000 BC. The Celts arrived from the north about a thousand years later. The seafaring Phoenicians founded Gàdir (now Cádiz) and several coastal cities in the south three millennia ago. The parade continued with the Greeks, who settled parts of the east coast, and then the Carthaginians, who founded Cartagena around 225 BC and dubbed the then-wild, forested, and game-rich country "Ispania," after their word for rabbit: *span*.

What to See: Near Barcelona, on the Costa Brava, rocket yourself back almost 3,000 years at **Ullastret,** a settlement occupied by an Iberian people known as the Indiketas. On a tour, actors guide groups through the homes and fortifications of some of the peninsula's earliest inhabitants, the defensive walls attesting to the constant threat of attack and the bits of pottery evidence of the settlement's early ceramic industry. Not far away in **Empúries** are ruins of the Greek colony established in the 6th century BC. At the **Museo de Cádiz** in Andalusia, you can view sarcophagi dating back to the 1100 BC founding of the city.

In Madrid, the outstanding, newly renovated **National Archaeological Museum** displays more than 1 million years of artifacts unearthed in what is now Spain: from Paleolithic tools found in Madrid's Manzanares River basin to 19th-century textiles and musical instruments.

THE ROMAN EPOCH

Modern civilization in Iberia began with the Romans, who expelled the Carthaginians and turned the peninsula into three imperial provinces. It took the Romans 200 years to subdue the fiercely resisting Iberians, but their influence is seen today in the fortifications, amphitheaters, aqueducts, and other ruins in cities across Spain, as well as in the country's legal system and in the Latin base of Spain's Romance languages and dialects.

What to See: Segovia's nearly 3,000-foot-long **Acueducto Romano** is a marvel of Roman engineering. Mérida's Roman ruins are some of Spain's finest, including its **bridge, theater,** and **outdoor amphitheater.** Tarragona was Rome's most important city in Catalonia, as the **walls, circus,** and **amphitheater** bear witness, while Zaragoza boasts a **Roman amphitheater** and a **Roman fluvial port** that dispatched flat-bottom riverboats loaded with wine and olive oil down the Ebro.

THE VISIGOTHS AND MOORS

In the early 5th century, invading tribes crossed the Pyrenees to attack the weakening Roman Empire. The Visigoths became the dominant force in central and northern Spain by AD 419, establishing their kingdom at Toledo and eventually adopting Christianity. But the Visigoths, too, were to fall before a wave of invaders. The Moors, an Arab-led Berber force, crossed the Strait of Gibraltar in AD 711 and swept through Spain in an astonishingly short time, launching almost eight centuries of Muslim rule. The Moorish architecture and Mudejar Moorish-inspired Gothic decorative details found throughout most of Spain tell much about the splendor of the Islamic culture that flourished here.

What to See: Moorish culture is most spectacularly evident in Andalusia, derived from the Arabic name for the Moorish reign on the Iberian Peninsula, al-Andalus, which meant "western lands." The fairy-tale **Alhambra** palace overlooking Granada captures the refinement of the Moorish aesthetic, while the earlier 9th-century **Mezquita** at Córdoba bears witness to the power of Islam in al-Andalus.

SPAIN'S GOLDEN AGE

By 1085, Alfonso VI of Castile had captured Toledo, giving the Christians a firm grip on the north. In the 13th century, Valencia, Seville, and finally Córdoba—the capital of the Muslim caliphate in Spain—fell to Christian forces, leaving only Granada in Moorish hands. Nearly 200 years later, the so-called Catholic Monarchs—Ferdinand of Aragón and Isabella of Castile—were joined in a marriage that would change the world. Finally, on January 2, 1492—244 years after the fall of Córdoba—Granada surrendered and the Moorish reign was over.

The year 1492 was the beginning of the nation's political golden age: Christian forces conquered Granada and unified all of present-day Spain as a single kingdom; in what was, at the time, viewed as a measure promoting national unity, Jews and Muslims who did not convert to Christianity were expelled from the country. The departure of educated Muslims and Jews was a blow to the nation's agriculture, science, and economy from which it would take nearly 500 years to recover. The Catholic Monarchs and their centralizing successors maintained Spain's unity, but they sacrificed the spirit of international free trade that was bringing prosperity to other parts of Europe. Carlos V weakened Spain with his penchant for waging war, and his son, Felipe II, followed in the same expensive path, defeating the Turks in 1571 but losing the "Invincible Spanish Armada" in the English Channel in 1588.

What to See: Celebrate Columbus's voyage to America with festivities in Seville, Huelva, Granada, Cádiz, and Barcelona, all of which display venues where "the Discoverer" was commissioned, was confirmed, set out from, returned to, or was buried. Wander through the somber **Escorial,** a monastery northwest of Madrid commissioned by Felipe II in 1557 and finished in 1584, the final resting place of most of the Habsburg and Bourbon kings of Spain ever since.

WAR OF THE SPANISH SUCCESSION

The War of the Spanish Succession (1700–14) ended with the fall of Barcelona, which sided with the Habsburg Archduke Carlos against the Bourbon Prince Felipe V. El Born market, completed in 1876, covered the buried remains of the Ribera neighborhood, where the decisive battle took place. Ribera citizens were required to tear down a thousand houses to clear space for the Ciutadella fortress, from which fields of fire were directed, quite naturally, toward the city the Spanish and French forces had taken a year to subdue. The leveled neighborhood, then about a third of Barcelona, was plowed under and forgotten by the victors, though never by barcelonins.

What to See: In Barcelona, the **Fossar de les Moreres cemetery,** next to the Santa María del Mar basilica, remains a powerful symbol for Catalan nationalists who gather there every September 11, Catalonia's National Day, to commemorate the fall of the city in 1714.

SPANISH CIVIL WAR

Spain's early-19th-century War of Independence required five years of bitter guerrilla fighting to rid the peninsula of Napoleonic troops. Later, the Carlist wars set the stage for the Spanish Civil War (1936–39), which claimed more than half a million lives. Intellectuals and leftists sympathized with the elected government; the International Brigades, with many American, British, and Canadian volunteers, took part in some of the worst fighting, including the storied defense of Madrid. But General Francisco Franco, backed by the Catholic Church, got far more help from Nazi Germany, whose Condor legions destroyed the Basque town of Gernika (in a horror made infamous by Picasso's monumental painting *Guernica*), and from Fascist Italy. For three years, European governments stood by as Franco's armies ground their way to victory. After the fall of Barcelona in January 1939, the Republican cause became hopeless. Franco's Nationalist forces entered Madrid on March 27, 1939, and thus began nearly 40 years of dictatorship under Franco. This dark period in recent Spanish history ended on November 20, 1975, when Franco died.

What to See: Snap a shot of **Madrid's Plaza Dos de Mayo,** in the Malasaña neighborhood, where officers Daoiz and Velarde held their ground against the superior French forces at the start of the popular uprising against Napoléon. The archway in the square is all that remains of the armory Daoiz and Velarde defended to the death. Trace the shrapnel marks on the wall of the **Sant Felip Neri church** in Barcelona, evidence of the 1938 bombing of the city by Italian warplanes under Franco's orders. East of Zaragoza, **Belchite** was the scene of bloody fighting during the decisive Battle of the Ebro. The town has been left exactly as it appeared on September 7, 1937, the day the battle ended.

RETURN TO DEMOCRACY

After Franco's death, Spain began the complex process of national reconciliation and a return to democracy. Despite opposition from radical right-wing factions and an attempted coup d'etat in February 1981, Spain celebrated the first general elections for 40 years in 1977 and approved a democratic constitution in 1978.

Chapter 2

TRAVEL SMART SPAIN

Updated by
Benjamin Kemper,
Isabelle Kliger

★ CAPITAL:
Madrid

POPULATION:
46.57 million

LANGUAGE:
Spanish

$ CURRENCY:
Euro

COUNTRY CODE:
34

⚠ EMERGENCIES:
112

DRIVING:
On the right

ELECTRICITY:
220v/50 cycles; electrical plugs have two round prongs

TIME:
Six hours ahead of New York

WEB RESOURCES:
www.spain.info
www.parador.es
www.spainisculture.com

What You Need to Know Before You Go

Should you tip? When can you eat? Do you need to plan ahead for the major attractions or can you just show up? We've got answers and a few tips to help you make the most of your visit to this beautiful country.

CATALAN CULTURE IS STRONG

Before the rise of modern-day Spain there was Aragon, a kingdom on the Iberian Peninsula whose territories included the regions we know as Catalonia and Aragon, as well as Roussillon, a part of southern France. The Catalan people and their culture are tenacious and Barcelona—the capital of Catalonia—remains strongly Catalan. This means that you'll see signage printed in both Spanish and Catalan and will also hear Catalan being spoken. The wealthy Catalan region has about 7.5 million people, with their own language, parliament, flag, and anthem. While you won't be expected to learn the language, it's a sign of respect to learn at least a few Catalan words. (Speaking of regional differences, in the Spanish south, the culture and architecture was strongly influenced by the Moors, the name given to Spain's Muslim population which came across the Straight of Gibraltar from northern Africa.)

AVOID TALKING POLITICS

The Catalan bid for independence is an ongoing and touchy topic in Spain, and it's probably best to avoid asking locals about it. When a majority of the members of the Catalan regional Parliament declared the region's independence from Spain in 2017, a referendum vote was held shortly after and saw most voters indicating that they too wanted to separate from Spain. As a result the central Spanish government cracked down on the separatists, igniting fierce debate and sometimes violent protests. You may notice flags with a single star––known as the Estelada––and oversize yellow ribbons displayed prominently as you explore Barcelona and beyond; these are signs of support for the Catalan secessionist movement.

DESPACITO

Spanish life has a slower rhythm than you may be accustomed to. Meals are later (lunch starts at around 2 and dinner at around 10 or 11) and are languorous experiences that last for hours. Sundays are especially slow, especially in smaller towns (and in the off season) where many stores and some restaurants are closed for the day. Stores and restaurants keep familiar hours in tourist-centric areas, and while it's unlikely that you'll be refused service if you want to eat lunch at noon, you'll definitely stand out as a tourist. As for the fabled afternoon siesta, while it does still exist in some more rural communities, in cities like Barcelona and Madrid, it really just takes the form of a long, leisurely lunch.

SPAIN IS GAY FRIENDLY

While it's true that Spain is Catholic-majority and generally takes religion quite seriously, this country also legalized gay marriage in 2005, a full decade before the United States. While Spain as a whole is generally tolerant, specific areas have also built international reputations for being welcoming to gay travelers and have gay-friendly beaches, restaurants, and nightclubs, and hold yearly Pride parades. Some particularly welcoming destinations are the capital city Madrid, which is said to be one of the most LGBT-friendly cities in all of Europe, the seaside resort town of Sitges, the island of Maspalomas in the Canary Islands, and parts of the bass-thumping club island Ibiza.

BOOK AHEAD

There are a few major attractions in Spain that rank highly on most traveler bucket lists and if you are hoping to check some of the world's top attractions off your list, too, you'll need to plan ahead. For big-ticket sights like the Alhambra, the Sagrada Família, Parc Güell, and the Picasso Museum, you will need to book tickets before you arrive. Otherwise, lines can be long and there is no guarantee that tickets will be available when you visit, especially at peak times. Booking in advance gives you an allocated time (there is zero flexibility with this at most attractions so be sure to arrive on time).

PACK FOR A VARIED CLIMATE AND TERRAIN
If you're planning to travel across Spain's different regions, keep in mind that the landscape and climate can change rather dramatically. While Catalonia and Aragon are rolling, arid, and quite dry, Basque Country has generally mild temperatures but significant rainfall, even during the drier months, and southern cities like Seville have a dry Mediterranean climate that can get quite hot during the day. Spain also has placid beaches, coastal plains, tropical islands, and the dramatic Pyrenees mountain range. You'll need to pack accordingly if you will be in more than one climate zone.

SKIP THE PLANE AND TAKE A TRAIN
Flights from one region of Spain to another are cheap and easy, but don't discount the country's high-speed rail network. It's fast, comfortable, and a great way to get from city to city.

You can get from Madrid to Seville in 2 hours and 20 minutes without any of the hassles or stresses of air travel. Also, did we mention that you can bring food and alcohol on board with you?

AVOID PRICING PSYCHOLOGY
Spain is the third largest producer of wine in the world, after France and Italy, and almost half the wine (in a normal vintage) production is sold at low prices—like 3- to 5 euros a bottle. It's key to a fun and frugal vacation to know that just because this wine is inexpensive, it doesn't mean it's cheap.

DON'T JUST EAT PAELLA
Delicious as it is, there's a lot more to Spanish cuisine than paella. As with any country, Spanish recipes are strongly influenced by culture, tradition, and environment. In northwestern Basque Country the name of the game is pintxos (pronounced pinchos), which is that region's version of tapas—numerous little bites, often on a toothpick, eaten alongside beer or wine. Vegetables are the main attraction in the Navarra region: look for Lodosa piquillo peppers, Tudela artichokes, and white asparagus. On the western border where Spain meets Portugal the greatest treasure is jamón ibérico, thinly sliced cured ham made from pigs fattened up on foraged acorns. In the Andalusian south—where they were invented—tapas reign supreme. Think about the region you're in before you order. If you're on the

coast, fish is the way to go. If you're inland, consider a dish made with meat.

BEACH YOURSELF
While most of Europe visits Spain for their beach holidays, the rest of the world is more interested in Spain's vibrant cities, culture, and history. But if you find yourself on one of Spain's gorgeous beaches surrounded by half- (or more likely, fully) naked beautiful people and you'll wonder why people don't visit just for the beaches alone. Spain has a great many seaside towns that offer a range of popular and less-traveled stretches of sand. Even major coastal cities like Barcelona have beaches. Sure, they can be crowded but they're still a major draw and certainly an added bonus if you're already in a city and looking to catch some sun. If you're looking for something truly special though, head to the Canary Islands, which are famous for their soft sands and clear, azure waters.

TIPPING ISN'T MANDATORY (MOST OF THE TIME)
Thanks to decent worker protections, Spanish servers earn a living wage and don't depend on tips to survive. That said, it is customary in a casual restaurant to round up your bill and leave the change, but it isn't expected or required. If you eat in a formal restaurant there is an expectation that you'll tip, but the maximum is still only 10%.

Getting Here and Around

✈ Air Travel

Flying time from New York to Madrid is about seven hours; from London, it's just over two hours.

Regular nonstop flights serve Spain from many major cities in the eastern United States; flying from other North American cities usually involves a stop. If you're coming from North America and want to land in a city other than Madrid or Barcelona, consider flying a European carrier.

A number of low-cost carriers operate from the United Kingdom to Spain such as Vueling (⊕ www.vueling.com), Jet2 (⊕ www.jet2.com), and flybe (⊕ www.flybe.com). They provide competition to the market's main players, easyJet (⊕ www.easyjet.com) and Ryanair (⊕ www.ryanair.com). All these carriers offer frequent flights, cover small cities as well as large ones, and have very competitive fares.

AIRPORTS

Most flights from North America land in, or pass through, Madrid's Barajas Airport (MAD). The other major gateway is Barcelona's Prat de Llobregat (BCN). From the United Kingdom and elsewhere in Europe, regular flights also touch down in Málaga (AGP), Alicante (ALC), Palma de Mallorca (PMI), and many other smaller cities.

FLIGHTS

From North America, Air Europa flies to Madrid; American Airlines, part of the Oneworld Alliance, and Iberia fly to Madrid and Barcelona; Delta flies direct to Barcelona, Madrid, and Málaga (June–September). Note that some of these airlines use shared facilities and do not operate their own flights. Within Spain, Iberia is the main domestic airline and also operates low-cost flights through its budget airlines Iberia Express and Vueling. Air Europa and Ryanair both offer inexpensive flights on most domestic routes. The earlier before your travel date you purchase the ticket, the more bargains you're likely to find. Air Europa, Iberia Express, Vueling, and Ryanair also have flights from Spain to other destinations in Europe.

⛴ Boat Travel

Regular car ferries connect the United Kingdom with northern Spain. Brittany Ferries sails from Plymouth to Santander, and from Portsmouth to Santander and Bilbao. Trasmediterránea and Baleària connect mainland Spain to the Balearic and Canary islands.

Direct ferries from Spain to Tangier leave daily from Tarifa and Algeciras on FRS, International Shipping, and Trasmediterránea. Otherwise, you can take your car either to Ceuta (via Algeciras, on Baleària) or Melilla (via Málaga, on Trasmediterránea)—two Spanish enclaves on the North African coast—and then move on to Morocco.

CONTACTS Baleària. ☎ 902/160180 ⊕ www.balearia.com. **Brittany Ferries.** ☎ 01752/648000 in U.K., 902/108147 in Spain ⊕ www.brittany-ferries.com. **FRS.** ☎ 956/681830 ⊕ www.frs.es. **Trasmediterránea.** ☎ 902/454645 ⊕ www.trasmediterranea.es.

🚌 Bus Travel

Within Spain, a number of private companies provides bus service, ranging from knee-crunchingly basic to luxurious. Fares are almost always lower than the corresponding train fares, and service covers more towns, though buses are less frequent on weekends. Smaller towns don't usually have a central bus depot, so ask the tourist office where to wait for the bus. Spain's major national long-haul bus line is ALSA.

ALSA has four luxury classes in addition to its regular seating. Premium, available on limited routes from Madrid, includes a number of services such as à la carte meals and a private waiting room, while Supra+ and Supra Economy include roomy leather seats and onboard meals. You also have the option of *asientos individuales,* individual seats (with no other seat on either side) that line one side of the bus. The last class is Eurobus, with a private waiting room, comfortable seats, and plenty of legroom. The Supra+ and Eurobus usually cost, respectively, up to one-third and one-fourth more than the regular seats.

🚗 Car Travel

Your own driver's license is valid in Spain, but U.S. citizens are highly encouraged to obtain an International Driving Permit (IDP). The IDP may facilitate car rental and help you avoid traffic fines—it translates your state-issued driver's license into 10 languages so officials can easily interpret the information on it. Permits are available from the American Automobile Association.

Driving is the best way to see Spain's rural areas. The main cities are connected by a network of excellent four-lane divided highways (*autovías* and *autopistas*), which are designated by the letter A and have speed limits—depending on the area—of 80 kph (50 mph)–120 kph (75 mph). If the artery is a toll highway (*peaje*), it is designated AP. The letter N indicates a *carretera nacional*: a national or intercity route, with local traffic, which may have four or two lanes. Smaller towns and villages are connected by a

network of secondary roads maintained by regional, provincial, and local governments, with an alphabet soup of different letter designations.

RENTAL CARS
Alamo, Avis, Budget, Europcar, Hertz, and Enterprise have branches at major Spanish airports and in large cities. Smaller, regional companies and wholesalers offer lower rates. The online outfit Pepe Car has been a big hit with travelers; in general, the earlier you book, the less you pay. Rates run as low as €15 per day, taxes included—but note that pickups at its center-city locations are considerably cheaper than at the airports. All agencies have a range of models, but virtually all cars in Spain have manual transmission. Rates in Madrid begin at the equivalents of $60 per day and $190 per week for an economy car with air-conditioning, manual transmission, and unlimited mileage, including 21% tax. A small car is cheaper and prudent for the tiny roads and parking spaces in many parts of Spain.

Anyone age 18 or older with a valid license can drive in Spain, but most rental agencies will not rent cars to drivers under 23.

RULES OF THE ROAD
Spaniards drive on the right and pass on the left, so stay in the right-hand lane when not passing. Children under 12 may not ride in the front seat, and seat belts are compulsory for both front- and backseat riders. Speed limits are 30 kph (19 mph) or 50 kph (31 mph) in cities, depending on the type of street, 100 kph (62 mph) on national highways, 120 kph (75 mph) on the autopista or autovía. The use of cell phones by drivers, even on the side of the road, is illegal, except with completely hands-free devices.

Severe fines are enforced throughout Spain for driving under the influence of

Getting Here and Around

alcohol. Spot Breathalyzer checks are often carried out, and you will be cited if the level of alcohol in your bloodstream is found to be 0.05% or above.

🚇 Train Travel

The chart here has information about popular train routes. Prices are for one-way fares (depending on seating and where purchased) and subject to change.

International trains run from Madrid to Lisbon (10 hours 30 minutes, overnight) and Barcelona to Paris (6 hours 20 minutes).

Spain's wonderful high-speed train, the 290-kph (180-mph) AVE, travels between Madrid and Seville (with a stop in Córdoba) in 2½ hours; prices start at about €50 each way. It also serves the Madrid–Barcelona route, cutting travel time to just under three hours. From Madrid you can also reach Lleida, Huesca (one AVE train daily), Valencia, Málaga, Toledo, and Valladolid.

The fast Talgo service is also efficient, but other elements of the state-run rail system (RENFE) are still a bit subpar by European standards, and some long-distance trips with multiple stops can be tediously slow. Although some overnight trains have comfortable sleeper cars, first-class fares that include a sleeping compartment are comparable to, or more expensive than, airfares.

DISCOUNTS

If you purchase a ticket on the REN-FE website for the AVE or any of the Grandes Líneas (the faster, long-distance trains, including the Talgo) you can get a discount of 20%–60%, depending on how far ahead you book and how you travel: discounts on one-way tickets tend to be higher than on round-trips.

Discount availabilities disappear fast: the earliest opportunity is 62 days in advance of travel. If you have a domestic or an international airline ticket and want to take the AVE within 48 hours of your arrival but haven't booked online, you can still get a 10% discount on the AVE one-way ticket and 25% for a round-trip ticket with a dated return. On regional trains, you get a 10% discount on round-trip tickets (15% on AVE medium-distance trains).

■ **TIP→** If there are more than two of you traveling on the AVE, look for the word "mesa" in the fare column, quoting the price per person for four people traveling together and sitting at the same table. If you select the price, it tells you how much the deal is for one, two, and three people. You have to buy all the tickets at the same time, but they're between 20% and 60% cheaper than regular tickets.

RAIL PASSES

Spain is one of 28 European countries in which you can use the Eurail Global Pass, which buys you unlimited rail travel in all participating countries for the duration of the pass. Choose from passes that allow a set number of days to travel during a one-, two-, or three-month period, or passes offering continuous travel within the chosen period. There are discounts for children (ages 4–11) and youths (ages 12–27).

If Spain is your only destination, a Eurail Spain Pass allows between three and eight days of unlimited train travel in Spain within a one-month period for $263–$432 (first class) and $198–$325 (second class). There are also combination passes for those visiting Spain and Portugal, Spain and France, and Spain and Italy.

Before You Go

 Immunizations

There are no immunization requirements for visitors traveling to Spain for tourism.

🌐 Passports and Visas

Visitors from the United States, Australia, Canada, New Zealand, and the United Kingdom need a valid passport to enter Spain.

VISAS

Visas are not necessary for those with U.S. passports valid for a minimum of six months and who plan to stay in Spain for tourist or business purposes for up to 90 days. Should you need a visa to stay longer than this, contact the Spanish consulate office nearest to you in the United States to apply for the appropriate documents.

🇺🇸 U.S. Embassy/Consulate

Embassies are located in Madrid while some countries also maintain consulates in Barcelona. The United States also maintains consular agencies in A Coruña, Fuengirola, Palma de Mallorca, Seville, and Valencia.

🧳 What to Pack

Pack light. Although baggage carts are free and plentiful in most Spanish airports, they're rare in smaller train stations and most bus stations. Madrid, north and northeastern Spain, and Granada and the Sierra Nevada can be bitterly cold from late fall through early spring, while the Mediterranean and southern regions are generally much milder, if not warm. It makes sense to wear casual, comfortable clothing and shoes for sightseeing, but you'll want to dress up a bit in large cities, especially for fine restaurants and nightclubs. On the beach, anything goes; it's common to see women of all ages wearing only bikini bottoms, and many of the more remote beaches allow nude sunbathing.

📅 When to Go

High season: June through mid-September is the most expensive and popular time to visit the coast and islands; July and August are especially crowded. Inland cities are quieter but hot, and many businesses close for August. Sunshine is guaranteed almost everywhere, except in the north where weather is changeable.

Low season: Winter offers the least appealing weather, though it's the best time for airfares and hotel deals. The Mediterranean coast can be balmy during the daytime, even in December—and there are no crowds—but nighttime temperatures drop.

Value season: May, June, and September are lovely with warm weather, saner airfares, and good hotel offers. You can hang with the locals without the tourist crowds. October still has great weather, though temperatures start to fall by November. Bring an umbrella in March and April.

Essentials

◉ Communications

PHONES

The country code for Spain is 34. The country code is 1 for the United States and Canada.

If you're going to be traveling in Spain for an extended period, buy a local SIM card (ensure your phone is unlocked), use Skype or FaceTime, or install a free messenger app on your smartphone, such as Viber or WhatsApp.

🍴 Dining

Although Spain has always had an extraordinary range of regional cuisines, in the past decade or so its restaurants have won it international recognition at the highest levels. A new generation of Spanish chefs—led by the revolutionary Ferran Adrià—has transformed classic dishes to suit contemporary tastes, drawing on some of the freshest ingredients in Europe and bringing an astonishing range of new technologies into the kitchen.

Smoking is banned in all eating and drinking establishments in Spain.

MEALS AND MEALTIMES

Outside major hotels, which serve morning buffets, breakfast (*desayuno*) is usually limited to coffee and toast or a roll. Lunch (*comida* or *almuerzo*) traditionally consists of an appetizer, a main course, and dessert, followed by coffee and perhaps a liqueur. Between lunch and dinner the best way to snack is to sample some tapas at a bar; normally you can choose from quite a variety. Dinner (*cena*) is somewhat lighter, with perhaps only one course. In addition to à la carte selections, most restaurants offer a *menú del día* (daily fixed-price menu) consisting of a starter, main plate, beverage, and dessert. The menú del día is traditionally offered only at lunch, but increasingly it's also offered at dinner in popular tourist destinations. If your waiter does not suggest it when you're seated, ask for it: "*¿Hay menú del día, por favor?*"

Mealtimes in Spain are later than elsewhere in Europe, and later still in Madrid and the southern region of Andalusia. Lunch starts around 2 or 2:30 (closer to 3 in Madrid) and dinner after 9 (as late as 11 or midnight in Madrid). Weekend eating times, especially dinner, can begin upward of an hour later. In areas with heavy tourist traffic, some restaurants open a bit earlier.

Most prices listed in menus are inclusive of 10% value-added tax (I.V.A.), but not all. If I.V.A. isn't included, it should read, "*10% I.V.A. no incluido en los precios*" at the bottom of the menu. Unless otherwise noted, the restaurants listed in this guide are open daily for lunch and dinner. *Prices in the reviews are the average cost of a main course or equivalent combination of smaller dishes at dinner or, if dinner is not served, at lunch.*

WINES, BEER, AND SPIRITS

Apart from its famous wines, Spain produces many brands of lager, the most popular of which are San Miguel, Cruzcampo, Aguila, Voll Damm, Mahou, and Estrella. There's also a thriving craft-beer industry and most large towns and cities have bars specializing in local brews. Jerez de la Frontera is Europe's largest producer of brandy and is a major source of sherry. Catalonia is a major producer of cava (sparkling wine). Spanish law prohibits the sale of alcohol to people age 18 or younger.

🛏 Lodging

By law, hotel prices in Spain must be posted at the reception desk and should indicate whether the value-added tax (I.V.A. 10%) is included. Note that high-season rates prevail not only in summer but also during Holy Week and local fiestas. In much of Spain, breakfast is normally *not* included.

HOTELS AND BED-AND-BREAKFASTS

The Spanish government classifies hotels with one to five stars, with an additional rating of five-star GL (Gran Lujo) indicating the highest quality. Although quality is a factor, the rating is technically only an indication of how many facilities the hotel offers. For example, a three-star hotel may be just as comfortable as a four-star hotel but lack a swimming pool.

All hotel entrances are marked with a blue plaque bearing the letter *H* and the number of stars. The letter *R* (for *residencia*) after the letter *H* indicates an establishment with no meal service, with the possible exception of breakfast. The designations *fonda* (*F*), *pensión* (*P*), *casa de huéspedes* (*CH*), and *hostal* (*Hs*) indicate budget accommodations: these are no longer official categories, but you'll still find them across the country. In most cases, especially in smaller villages, rooms in such buildings will be basic but clean; in large cities, these rooms can be downright dreary.

When inquiring in Spanish about whether a hotel has a private bath, ask if it's an *habitación con baño.* Although a single room (*habitación sencilla*) is usually available, singles are often on the small side. Solo travelers might prefer to pay a bit extra for single occupancy of a double room (*habitación doble uso individual*). Make sure you request a double bed (*cama de matrimonio*) if you want one—if you don't ask, you will usually end up with two singles.

The Spanish love small country hotels and agritourism. Rusticae (⊕ *www.rusticae.es*) is an association of more than 170 independently owned hotels in restored palaces, monasteries, mills, and estates, generally in rural Spain. Similar associations serve individual regions, and tourist offices also provide lists of establishments. In Galicia, *pazos* are beautiful, old, often stately homes converted into small luxury hotels; Pazos de Galicia (⊕ *www.pazosdegalicia.com*) is the main organization for them. In Cantabria, *casonas* are small-to-large country houses, but they may not have individual websites, so check the regional tourist office websites for booking and contact information.

A number of *casas rurales* (country houses similar to B&Bs) offer pastoral lodging either in guest rooms or in self-catering cottages. You may also come across the term *finca,* for country estate house. Many *agroturismo* accommodations are fincas converted to upscale B&Bs.

PARADORES

The Spanish government operates nearly 100 paradores—upscale hotels often in historic buildings or near significant sites. Rates are reasonable, considering that most paradores have four- or five-star amenities, and the premises are invariably immaculate and tastefully furnished, often with antiques or reproductions. Each parador has a restaurant serving regional specialties, and you can stop in for a meal without spending the night. Paradores are popular with foreigners and Spaniards alike, so make reservations well in advance.

Essentials

Tipping

Aside from tipping waiters and taxi drivers, Spaniards tend not to leave extra in addition to the bill. Restaurant checks do not list a service charge on the bill but consider the tip included. If you want to leave a small tip in addition to the bill, tip 5%–10% of the bill (and only if you think the service was worth it), and leave less if you eat tapas or sandwiches at a bar—just enough to round out the bill to the nearest €1.

Tours

SPECIAL-INTEREST TOURS
Madrid and Beyond

SPECIAL-INTEREST | An array of customized private luxury tours (no two are the same) are offered by this company, focusing on culinary, cultural, and sports-related themes. ☎ 91/758–0063 in Spain, 917/470–9460 in U.S. ⊕ www.madridandbeyond.com ✉ Prices available on application.

Toma Tours

SPECIAL-INTEREST | This company provides personalized and small-group tours with the focus on discovering Andalusia's culture, landscape, and gastronomy beyond the guidebook. ☎ 650/733116 ⊕ tomaandcoe.com ✉ From €1690.

ART
Atlas Travel Center/Escorted Spain Tours

SPECIAL-INTEREST | Based in the United States, this company offers a range of tours with accents on art, cultural history, and the outdoors. ☎ 888/942–3301 ⊕ www.escortedspaintours.com ✉ From €1030.

Heritage Tours

SPECIAL-INTEREST | Based in New York, this company helps arrange customized cultural tours based on your interests and budget. Guides are drawn from a network of curators, gallery owners, and art critics. ☎ 800/378–4555, 212/206–8400 ⊕ www.heritagetours.com ✉ Prices vary.

Olé Spain Tours

SPECIAL-INTEREST | This guide offers art and historical tours to Spain. ☎ 915/515294 ⊕ www.olespaintours.com ✉ From €310.

BIRD-WATCHING
Discovering Doñana

SPECIAL-INTEREST | In the Coto Doñana National Park in Andalusia, this company offers some of the best guided bird-watching tours and expeditions in Spain. ☎ 620/964369 ⊕ www.discoveringdonana.com ✉ From €35.

CULINARY AND WINE
Artisans of Leisure

SPECIAL-INTEREST | This company offers personalized food-and-wine and cultural tours to Spain. ☎ 800/214–8144, 212/243–3239 ⊕ www.artisansofleisure.com ✉ From €8560.

Cellar Tours

SPECIAL-INTEREST | Based in Madrid, Cellar Tours offers a wide array of wine and cooking tours to Spain's main wine regions. ☎ 911/436553 in Spain, 310/496–8061 in U.S. ⊕ www.cellartours.com ✉ From €2800.

HIKING
Spain Adventures

SPECIAL-INTEREST | This company offers hiking and biking around Spain, as well as unusual tours such as yoga and cooking. ☎ 772/564–0330 ⊕ www.spainadventures.com ✉ From €3090.

LANGUAGE PROGRAMS
Go Abroad

SPECIAL-INTEREST | This is one of the best resources for language schools in Spain. ☎ 720/570–1702 ⊕ www.goabroad.com.

Contacts

✈ Air Travel

CONTACTS Air Europa.
☎ *844/415–3955 in U.S.,
902/401501 in Spain*
⊕ *www.aireuropa.com.*
Iberia. ☎ *800/772–4642
in U.S., 901/111–500 in
Spain* ⊕ *www.iberia.com.*
**Transportation Security
Administration.** ⊕ *www.
tsa.gov.* **Visit Europe Pass.**
⊕ *www.oneworld.com.*

AIRLINES Air Europa.
☎ *844/415–3955 in U.S.,
902/401501 in Spain*
⊕ *www.aireuropa.com.*
Iberia. ☎ *901/111500,
800/772–4642 in U.S.
and Canada* ⊕ *www.
iberia.com.* **Iberia Express.**
☎ *901/111500* ⊕ *www.ibe-
riaexpress.com.* **Vueling.**
☎ *902/808022* ⊕ *www.
vueling.com.*

AIRPORTS AENA.
☎ *902/404704, 91/321–
1000 when calling from
outside Spain* ⊕ *www.
aena.es.*

🚌 Bus Travel

CONTACTS ALSA.
☎ *902/422242* ⊕ *www.
alsa.es.* **Eurolines
Spain.** ☎ *902/405040,
933/674400* ⊕ *www.
eurolines.es.*

🚗 Car Travel

**CAR RENTAL COMPANIES
Avis.** ☎ *800/633–3469,
902/180854 in Spain*
⊕ *www.avis.com.*
Budget. ☎ *800/214–6094,
902/112585 in Spain*
⊕ *www.budget.com.*
Enterprise. ☎ *902/111902
in Spain* ⊕ *www.
enterprise.es.* **Europcar.**
☎ *902/503010 in Spain*
⊕ *www.europcar.es.*
Hertz. ☎ *800/654–3001,
902/027659 in Spain*
⊕ *www.hertz.com.* **Pepe
Car.** ☎ *902/996666 in
Spain* ⊕ *www.pepecar.
com.*

**EMERGENCY SERVICE
RACE.** ☎ *900/100992 for
info, 900/112222 for assis-
tance* ⊕ *www.race.es.*

🚆 Train Travel

TRAIN CONTACTS Eurail.
⊕ *www.eurail.com.* **Rail
Europe.** ☎ *800/622–8600
in U.S. and Canada*
⊕ *www.raileurope.com.*
RENFE. ☎ *912/320320 for
tickets and info* ⊕ *www.
renfe.es.*

🇺🇸 Emergencies

**FOREIGN EMBASSIES
AND CONSULATES U.S.
Embassy.** ✉ *Calle Serrano
75, Madrid* ☎ *91/587–
2200 for U.S.-citizen emergencies* ⊕ *es.usembassy.
gov.*

**GENERAL EMERGENCY
CONTACTS Emergency tele-
phone number.** ☎ *112.* **Fire
department.** ☎ *080.* **Local
police.** ☎ *092.* **Medical
service.** ☎ *061.* **National
police.** ☎ *091.*

🛏 Lodging

**APARTMENT RENTALS
HolidayLettings.** ⊕ *www.
holidaylettings.co.uk.*
HomeAway. ⊕ *www.
homeaway.com.* **Interhome.**
☎ *800/882–6864* ⊕ *www.
interhomeusa.com.* **Villas
and Apartments Abroad.**
☎ *212/213–6435* ⊕ *www.
vaanyc.com.* **Villas International.** ☎ *415/499–9490,
800/221–2260* ⊕ *www.
villasintl.com.*

**PARADORES Paradores de
España.** ☎ *902/547979 in
Spain, 818/884–1984 in
U.S.* ⊕ *www.parador.es.*

Great Itineraries

Madrid, Castile, and Andalusia, 10-Day Itinerary

This trip takes in the best of vibrant Madrid and its world-class art museums and showcases some of Castile's historic gems before whisking you to the Moorish south where Córdoba's majestic mosque, Seville's fragrant orange blossoms, and Granada's "heaven on earth" await.

DAYS 1–3: MADRID

Start the day with a visit to either the **Prado,** the **Museo Thyssen-Bornemisza,** or the **Centro de Arte Reina Sofía.** Then head to the elegant **Plaza Mayor**—a perfect jumping-off point for a tour of the Spanish capital. To the west, see the **Plaza de la Villa, Palacio Real** (the Royal Palace), **Teatro Real** (Royal Theater), and the royal convents; to the south, wander around the maze of streets of **La Latina** and **El Rastro** and try some local tapas.

On Day 2, visit the sprawling **Barrio de las Letras,** centered on the Plaza de Santa Ana. This was the favorite neighborhood of writers during the Spanish golden literary age in the 17th century (Cervantes lies buried under a convent nearby), and it's still crammed with theaters, cafés, and good tapas bars. It borders the Paseo del Prado on the east, allowing you to comfortably walk to any of the art museums in the area. If the weather is pleasant, take an afternoon stroll in the **Parque del Buen Retiro.**

For your third day in the capital, wander in **Chueca** and **Malasaña,** the two funky hipster neighborhoods most favored by young madrileños. Fuencarral, a landmark pedestrianized street that serves as the border between the two, is one of the city's trendiest shopping enclaves. From there you can walk to the **Parque del Oeste** and the **Templo de Debod**—the best spot from which to see the city's sunset. Among the lesser-known museums, consider visiting the captivating **Museo Sorolla,** Goya's frescoes and tomb at the **Ermita de San Antonio de la Florida,** or the **Real Academia de Bellas Artes de San Fernando** for classic painting. People-watch at any of the terrace bars in either Plaza de Chueca or Plaza 2 de Mayo in Malasaña.

Logistics: If you're traveling light, the subway (Metro Línea 8) or the bus (No. 203 during the day and N27 at night) will take you from the airport to the city for €5. The train costs €2.60 and a taxi is a fixed price of €30. Once in the center consider walking or taking the subway rather than cabbing it in gridlock traffic.

DAYS 4 AND 5: CASTILIAN CITIES

There are several excellent options for half- or full-day side trips from Madrid to occupy Days 4 and 5. **Toledo** and **Segovia** are two of the oldest Castilian cities—both have delightful old quarters dating back to the Romans. There's also **El Escorial,** which houses the massive monastery built by Felipe II. Two other nearby towns also worth visiting are **Aranjuez** and **Alcalá de Henares.**

Logistics: Toledo and Segovia are stops on the high-speed train line (AVE), so you can get to either of them in a half hour from Madrid. To reach the old quarters of both cities, take a bus or cab from the train station or take the bus from Madrid. Buses and trains both go to El Escorial. Reach Aranjuez and Alcalá de Henares via the intercity train system.

DAY 6: CÓRDOBA OR EXTREMADURA

Córdoba, the capital of both Roman and Moorish Spain, was the center of Western art and culture between the 8th and 11th centuries. The city's breathtaking **Mezquita** (mosque), which is now a cathedral, and the medieval **Jewish Quarter** bear witness to the city's brilliant past. From Madrid you could also rent a car and visit the lesser-known cities in the north of **Extremadura,** such as **Guadalupe** and **Trujillo,** and overnight in **Cáceres,** a UNESCO World Heritage Site, then return to Madrid the next day.

Logistics: The AVE will take you to Córdoba from Madrid in less than two hours. One alternative is to stay in Toledo, also on the route heading south, and then head to Córdoba the next day, although you need to return to Madrid by train first. Once in Córdoba, take a taxi for a visit out to the summer palace at Medina Azahara.

DAYS 7 AND 8: SEVILLE

Seville's **cathedral,** with its tower La Giralda, **Plaza de Toros Real Maestranza,** and **Barrio de Santa Cruz** are visual feasts. Forty minutes south by train, you can sip the world-famous sherries of **Jerez de la Frontera,** then munch jumbo shrimp on the beach at **Sanlúcar de Barrameda.**

Logistics: From Seville's AVE station, take a taxi to your hotel. After that, walking and hailing the occasional taxi are the best ways to explore the city. A rental car is the best option to reach towns beyond Seville, except for Jerez de la Frontera, where the train station is an architectural gem in its own right.

DAYS 9 AND 10: GRANADA

The hilltop **Alhambra** palace, Spain's most visited attraction, was conceived by the Moorish caliphs as heaven on earth. Try any of the city's famous tapas bars and tea shops, and make sure to roam the magical, steep streets of the **Albayzín,** the ancient Moorish quarter.

Logistics: The Seville–Granada leg of this trip is best accomplished by renting a car; Antequera makes a good quick stop on the way. However, the Seville–Granada trains (four daily, about 3½ hours, €30) are one alternative. Another idea is to head first from Madrid to Granada, and then from Granada to Seville via Córdoba.

Great Itineraries

The North Coast, and Galicia, 16-Day Itinerary

Dive into happening Barcelona, with its unique blend of Gothic and Gaudí architecture, colorful markets, and long city beaches. Then head to the verdant north for culinary sophistication in San Sebastián and to check out the Guggenheim in chic Bilbao. Next, wind your way along the wild, rugged coastline, taking in the mountains, fishing ports, bagpipes, and Europe's best seafood along the way.

DAYS 1–3: BARCELONA

To get a feel for Barcelona, begin with **La Rambla** and the **Bouqería** market. Then set off for the **Gothic Quarter** to see the **Catedral de la Seu, Plaça del Rei,** and the Catalan and Barcelona government palaces in **Plaça Sant Jaume.** Next, cross Via Laietana to the **Born-Ribera** (waterfront neighborhood) for the Gothic **Santa Maria del Mar** and nearby **Museu Picasso.**

Make Day 2 a Gaudí day: Visit the **Temple Expiatori de la Sagrada Família,** then **Park Güell.** In the afternoon see the **Casa Milà** and **Casa Batlló,** part of the Manzana de la Discòrdia on Passeig de Gràcia. **Palau Güell,** off the lower Rambla, is probably too much Gaudí for one day, but don't miss it.

On Day 3, climb **Montjuïc** for the **Museu Nacional d'Art de Catalunya,** in the hulking **Palau Nacional.** Investigate the **Fundació Miró, Estadi Olímpic,** the **Mies van der Rohe Pavilion,** and **CaixaForum** exhibition center. At lunchtime, take the cable car across the port for seafood in **Barceloneta** and then stroll along the beach.

Logistics: In Barcelona, walking or taking the subway is better than cabbing it.

DAY 4: SAN SEBASTIÁN

San Sebastián is one of Spain's most beautiful—and delicious—cities. Belle Époque buildings nearly encircle the tiny bay, and tapas bars flourish in the old quarter. Not far from San Sebastián is historic **Pasajes (Pasaia) de San Juan.**

Logistics: Take the train from Barcelona to San Sebastián (5 hours 30 minutes) first thing in the morning. You don't need a car in San Sebastián proper, but visits to cider houses in Astigarraga, Chillida Leku on the outskirts of town, and many of the finest restaurants around San Sebastián are possible only with your own transportation or a taxi (the latter with the advantage that you won't get lost). The freeway west to Bilbao is beautiful and fast, but the coastal road is recommended at least as far as Zumaia.

DAYS 5 AND 6: THE BASQUE COAST

The Basque coast between San Sebastián and Bilbao has a succession of fine beaches, rocky cliffs, and picture-perfect fishing ports. The wide beach at **Zarautz,** the fishermen's village of **Getaria,** the **Zuloaga Museum in Zumaia,** and **Bermeo's** port and fishing museum should all be near the top of your list.

DAYS 7 AND 8: BILBAO

Bilbao's **Guggenheim Museum** is worth a trip for the building itself, and the **Museo de Bellas Artes** has an impressive collection of Basque and Spanish paintings. Restaurants and tapas bars are famously good in Bilbao.

Logistics: In Bilbao, use the subway or the Euskotram, which runs up and down the Nervión estuary.

DAYS 9 AND 10: SANTANDER AND CANTABRIA

The elegant beach town of **Santander** has an excellent summer music festival every August. Nearby, **Santillana del Mar** is one of Spain's best Renaissance towns, and the museum of the **Altamira Caves** displays reproductions of the famous underground Neolithic rock paintings discovered here. Exploring the **Picos de Europa** will take you through some of the peninsula's wildest reaches, and the port towns along the coast provide some of Spain's most pristine beaches.

DAYS 11–13: OVIEDO AND ASTURIAS

The coast road through **Ribadesella** and the cider capital **Villaviciosa** to **Oviedo** is scenic and punctuated with tempting beaches. Oviedo, its **cathedral,** and the simplicity of its pre-Romanesque churches are worlds away from the richness of Córdoba's Mezquita and Granada's Alhambra.

Logistics: The A8 coastal freeway gets you quickly and comfortably to Gijón, then hop on the A66 to Oviedo. From there, head back to the A8 and go west through Avilés and into Galicia via the coastal N634—a slow but scenic route to Santiago.

DAYS 14–16: SANTIAGO DE COMPOSTELA AND GALICIA

Spain's northwest corner, with **Santiago de Compostela** at its spiritual and geographic center, is a green land of bagpipes and apple orchards. The Albariño wine country, along the Río Miño border with Portugal, and the *rías* (estuaries), full of delicious seafood, will keep you steeped in *enxebre*—Gallego for "local specialties and atmosphere."

Logistics: The four-lane freeways AP9 and A6 whisk you from Lugo and Castro to Santiago de Compostela and to the Rías Baixas. By car is the only way to tour Galicia. The AC862 route around the upper northwest corner and the Rías Altas turns into the AP9 coming back into Santiago.

Great Itineraries

Madrid and Barcelona, 6-Day Itinerary

Combining Spain's two largest and greatest cities on a six-day itinerary gives you the chance to take in the contrasts of imperial Madrid and Moderniste Barcelona. Both cities are vibrant, energetic cultural centers showcasing some of Europe's greatest art and architecture as well as Spanish gastronomy at its best. You can also get a taste for Spain's late-night fun, sample its colorful markets, and stay at some of the country's best lodgings. However, Madrid and Barcelona feel very different, and you'll find huge contrasts in their landscapes, culture, and ambience. By visiting them both you'll get a good idea of the many facets that make up Spain.

For what to do on your days in Madrid, see the "Madrid to the Alhambra" itinerary above. For Barcelona, see the "Barcelona, the North Coast, and Galicia" itinerary above.

Logistics: Take the high-speed train (AVE) from Madrid to Barcelona (2 hours 30 minutes). For the return journey, fly from Barcelona to Madrid Barajas Airport in time to catch your flight home.

Andalusia 7-Day Itinerary

Head south to a land of fiery flamenco passion, unique Moorish treasures, impossibly white villages, and delicious sherry and tapas. As you make your way from Córdoba to Granada via Seville, Jerez de la Frontera, and Málaga, prepare yourself to see some of Europe's finest monuments, prettiest villages, and loveliest—albeit most sweltering—landscapes.

DAY 1: CÓRDOBA
Córdoba's breathtaking **Mezquita** (mosque), now a cathedral, is an Andalusian highlight, and the medieval **Jewish Quarter** is lovely to explore. If you're here during May, visit the **Festival de los Patios** (Patio Festival).

DAYS 2–3: SEVILLE
The city that launched Christopher Columbus to the New World, **Seville** is a treasure trove of sights. Start with the **cathedral** and climb La Giralda for great views of the city. Move on to the richly decorated *alcázar* (fortress), still an official royal residence, with its many beautiful patios, and where, more recently, much of the *Game of Thrones* epic was filmed. The **Jewish Quarter** in Santa Cruz is a charming labyrinth of alleyways and squares. In the afternoon, cross to **Triana** over the Guadalquivir River and lose yourself in the quiet streets, which are the birthplace of many a flamenco artist.

Logistics: Take the high-speed train (AVE) to Seville from Córdoba (45 minutes). Seville is a compact city and easy to navigate so it's best to explore on foot—or pick up a municipal bicycle at one of the hundreds of Sevici bike stations spread out across the city

DAY 4: JEREZ DE LA FRONTERA AND RONDA VIA ARCOS DE LA FRONTERA
Jerez de la Frontera is the world's sherry headquarters and home to some of the greatest *bodegas* (wineries). Visit Domecq, Harvey, or Sandeman, and, if you have time, watch the world's finest dancing horses at the prestigious Royal Andalusian School of Equestrian Art. The lovely cliff-top village of **Arcos de la Frontera,** one of Andalusia's prettiest *pueblos blancos* (white villages), makes a great stop on the way to **Ronda.** One of the oldest towns in Spain, Ronda is famed for its spectacular position and views;

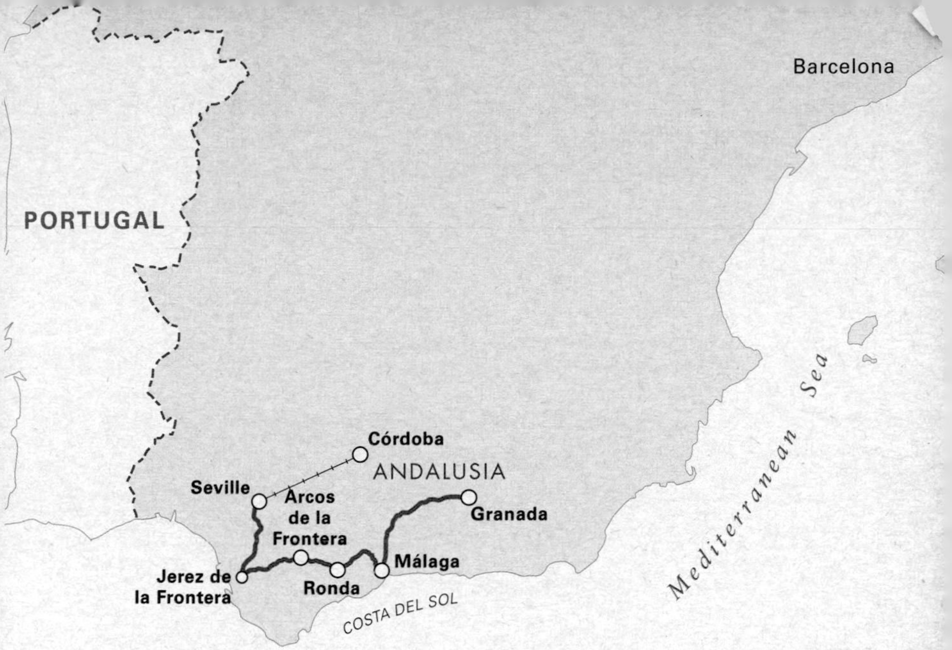

PORTUGAL

Córdoba

ANDALUSIA

Seville

Arcos
de la
Frontera

Granada

Málaga

Jerez de
la Frontera

Ronda

COSTA DEL SOL

Mediterranean Sea

get the best photo from the Juan Peña El Lebrijano Bridge.

Logistics: Rent a car in Seville and take the highway to Jerez de la Frontera before making your way to Ronda via Arcos de la Frontera. If you have time, stop off in the lovely village of Grazalema.

DAY 5: MÁLAGA

Start your exploration of the capital of the **Costa del Sol, Málaga,** with the **Roman theater,** Moorish alcazaba (citadel), and Gothic **cathedral.** Stroll down to the Muelle Uno on the port for views of the city skyline and **Gibralfaro** castle before returning to the center to visit the **Museo Picasso** and browse the shops in Larios and surrounding streets.

Logistics: Leave Ronda early and enjoy the scenic drive to Málaga via the A367 and A357. In Málaga, explore on foot, leaving your car in a central lot or at your hotel.

DAYS 6–7: GRANADA

Allow a good half day to visit the hilltop **Alhambra** palace and Generalife gardens. From there, walk down to the city center

Tip

Rent a car with a GPS navigation system to help you find your way from one Andalusian city to the next. Help with navigating is also useful in the cities themselves.

to the **cathedral** and **Capilla Real,** the shrine of Isabella of Castile and Ferdinand of Aragón. Finish your day with some tapas at one of the many famous tapas bars. On Day 7, walk up to the Albayzín, the ancient Moorish quarter, for a leisurely wander around the narrow streets. Take your time in the Plaza de San Nicolás and admire the magnificent views of the Alhambra and Sierra Nevada before you leave.

Logistics: The drive to Granada from Málaga takes about 1 hour 30 minutes. Granada is best explored on foot, so leave your car at the hotel.

Helpful Phrases in Spanish

BASICS

Hello	Hola	**oh**-lah
Yes/no	Sí/no	see/no
Please	Por favor	pore fah-**vore**
May I?	¿Me permite?	may pair-**mee**-tay
Thank you	Gracias	**Grah**-see-as
You're welcome	De nada	day **nah**-dah
I'm sorry	Lo siento	lo see-**en**-toh
Good morning!	¡Buenos días!	**bway**-nohs **dee**-ahs
Good evening!	¡Buenas tardes! (after 2pm)	**bway**-nahs-**tar**-dess
	¡Buenas noches! (after 8pm)	**bway**-nahs **no**-chess
Good-bye!	¡Adiós!/¡Hasta luego!	ah-dee-**ohss/ah**-stah **lwe**-go
Mr./Mrs.	Señor/Señora	sen-**yor**/sen-**yohr**-ah
Miss	Señorita	sen-yo-**ree**-tah
Pleased to meet you	Mucho gusto	**moo**-cho **goose**-toh
How are you?	¿Que tal?	keh-tal

NUMBERS

one	un, uno	oon, **oo**-no
two	dos	dos
three	tres	tress
four	cuatro	**kwah**-tro
five	cinco	**sink**-oh
six	seis	saice
seven	siete	see-**et**-eh
eight	ocho	**o**-cho
nine	nueve	new-**eh**-vey
ten	diez	dee-**es**
eleven	once	**ohn**-seh
twelve	doce	**doh**-seh
thirteen	trece	**treh**-seh
fourteen	catorce	ka-**tohr**-seh
fifteen	quince	**keen**-seh
sixteen	dieciséis	dee-es-ee-**saice**
seventeen	diecisiete	dee-es-ee-see-**et**-eh
eighteen	dieciocho	dee-**es**-ee-**o**-cho
nineteen	diecinueve	dee-**es**-ee-new-**ev**-eh
twenty	veinte	**vain**-teh
twenty-one	veintiuno	**vain**-te-**oo**-noh
thirty	treinta	**train**-tah
forty	cuarenta	kwah-**ren**-tah
fifty	cincuenta	seen-**kwen**-tah
sixty	sesenta	sess-**en**-tah
seventy	setenta	set-**en**-tah
eighty	ochenta	oh-**chen**-tah
ninety	noventa	no-**ven**-tah
one hundred	cien	see-**en**
one thousand	mil	meel
one million	un millón	oon meel-**yohn**

COLORS

black	negro	**neh**-groh
blue	azul	ah-**sool**
brown	marrón	mah-**ron**
green	verde	**ver**-deh
orange	naranja	na-**rahn**-hah
red	rojo	**roh**-hoh
white	blanco	**blahn**-koh
yellow	amarillo	ah-mah-**ree**-yoh

DAYS OF THE WEEK

Sunday	domingo	doe-**meen**-goh
Monday	lunes	**loo**-ness
Tuesday	martes	**mahr**-tess
Wednesday	miércoles	me-**air**-koh-less
Thursday	jueves	hoo-**ev**-ess
Friday	viernes	vee-**air**-ness
Saturday	sábado	**sah**-bah-doh

MONTHS

January	enero	eh-**neh**-roh
February	febrero	feh-**breh**-roh
March	marzo	**mahr**-soh
April	abril	ah-**breel**
May	mayo	**my**-oh
June	junio	**hoo**-nee-oh
July	julio	**hoo**-lee-yoh
August	agosto	ah-**ghost**-toh
September	septiembre	sep-tee-**em**-breh
October	octubre	oak-**too**-breh
November	noviembre	no-vee-**em**-breh
December	diciembre	dee-see-**em**-breh

USEFUL WORDS AND PHRASES

Do you speak English?	¿Habla usted inglés?	**ah**-blah oos-**ted** in-**glehs**
I don't speak Spanish.	No hablo español	no **ah**-bloh es-pahn-**yol**
I don't understand.	No entiendo	no en-tee-**en**-doh
I understand.	Entiendo	en-tee-**en**-doh
I don't know.	No sé	no **seh**
I'm American.	Soy americano (americana)	soy ah-meh-ree-**kah**-no (ah-meh-ree-**kah**-nah)
What's your name?	¿Cómo se llama ?	koh-mo seh **yah**-mah
My name is ...	Me llamo ...	may **yah**-moh
What time is it?	¿Qué hora es?	keh **o**-rah es
How?	¿Cómo?	**koh**-mo
When?	¿Cuándo?	**kwahn**-doh
Yesterday	Ayer	ah-**yehr**
Today	hoy	oy
Tomorrow	mañana	mahn-**yah**-nah

Tonight	Esta noche	es-tah no-cheh
What?	¿Qué?	keh
What is it?	¿Qué es esto?	keh es es-toh
Why?	¿Por qué?	pore keh
Who?	¿Quién?	kee-yen
Where is...	¿Dónde está...	dohn-deh es-tah
...the train station?	la estación del tren?	la es-tah-see-on del trehn
...the subway station?	estación de metro	la es-ta-see-on del meh-tro
...the bus stop?	la parada del autobus?	la pah-rah-dah del ow-toh-boos
...the terminal? (airport)	el aeropuerto	el air-oh-pwar-toh
...the post office?	la oficina de correos?	la oh-fee-see- nah deh koh-rreh-os
...the bank?	el banco?	el bahn-koh
...the hotel?	el hotel?	el oh-tel
...the museum?	el museo?	el moo-seh-oh
...the hospital?	el hospital?	el ohss-pee-tal
...the elevator?	el ascensor?	el ah-sen-sohr
Where are the restrooms?	el baño?	el bahn-yoh
Here/there	Aquí/allí	ah-key/ah-yee
Open/closed	Abierto/cerrado	ah-bee-er-toh/ser-ah-doh
Left/right	Izquierda/derecha	iss-key-eh-dah/dare-eh-chah
Is it near?	¿Está cerca?	es-tah sehr-kah
Is it far?	¿Está lejos?	es-tah leh-hoss
I'd like...	Quisiera...	kee-see-ehr-ah
...a room	un cuarto/una habitación	oon kwahr-toh/oo-nah ah-bee-tah-see-on
...the key	la llave	lah yah-veh
...a newspaper	un periódico	oon pehr-ee-oh-dee-koh
...a stamp	un sello de correo	oon seh-yo deh korr-eh-oh
I'd like to buy...	Quisiera comprar...	kee-see-ehr-ah kohm-prahr
...soap	jabón	hah-bohn
...suntan lotion	crema solar	kreh-mah soh-lar
...envelopes	sobres	so-brehs
...writing paper	papel	pah-pel
...a postcard	una tarjeta postal	oon-ah tar-het-ah post-ahl
...a ticket	un billete (travel)	oon bee-yee-teh
	una entrada (concert etc.)	oona en-trah-dah
How much is it?	¿Cuánto cuesta?	kwahn-toh kwes-tah
It's expensive/cheap	Es caro/barato	es kah-roh/bah-rah-toh
A little/a lot	Un poquito/mucho	oon poh-kee-toh/moo-choh
More/less	Más/menos	mahss/men-ohss
Enough/too (much)	Suficiente/	soo-fee-see-en-teh/

I am ill/sick	Estoy enfermo(a)	es-toy en-fehr-moh(mah)
Call a doctor	Llame a un medico	ya-meh ah oon med-ee-koh
Help!	Socorro	soh-koh-roh
Stop!	Pare	pah-reh

DINING OUT

I'd like to reserve a table...	Quisiera reservar una mesa...	kee-syeh-rah rreh-sehr-bahr oo-nah meh-sah...
...for two people.	para dos personas.	pah-rah dohs pehr-soh-nahs
...for this evening.	para esta noche.	pah-rah ehs-tah noh-cheh
...for 8 PM	para las ocho de la noche.	pah-rah lahs oh-choh deh lah noh-cheh
A bottle of...	Una botella de...	oo-nah bo-teh-yah deh
A cup of...	Una taza de...	oo-nah tah-sah deh
A glass of...	Un vaso (water, soda, etc.) de...	oon vah-so deh
	Una copa (wine, spirits, etc.) de...	oona coh-pah deh
Bill/check	La cuenta	lah kwen-tah
Bread	El pan	el pahn
Breakfast	El desayuno	el deh-sah-yoon-oh
Butter	La mantequilla	lah man-teh-kee-yah
Coffee	Café	kah-feh
Dinner	La cena	lah seh-nah
Fork	El tenedor	el ten-eh-dor
I don't eat meat	No como carne	noh koh-moh kahr-neh
I cannot eat...	No puedo comer...	noh pweh-doh koh-mehr
I'd like to order...	Quiero pedir...	kee-yehr-oh peh-deer
I'd like...	Me gustaría...	Meh goo-stah-ee-ah
I'm hungry/thirsty	Tengo hambre/sed	Tehn-goh hahm-breh/seth
Is service/the tip included?	¿Está incluida la propina?	es-tah in-cloo-ee-dah lah pro-pee-nah
Knife	El cuchillo	el koo-chee-yo
Lunch	La comida	lah koh-mee-dah
Menu	La carta, el menú	lah cart-ah, el meh-noo
Napkin	La servilleta	lah sehr-vee-yet-ah
Pepper	La pimienta	lah pee-mee-en-tah
Plate	plato	plato
Please give me...	Por favor déme...	pore fah-vor deh-meh
Salt	La sal	lah sahl
Spoon	Una cuchara	oo-nah koo-chah-rah
Sugar	El ázucar	el ah-su-kar

On the Calendar

January

La Tamborrada. Every January 19 and 20, more than 100 platoons of donostiarras (San Sebastián natives) dress up as chefs and Napoleonic soldiers and bang drums as they parade through the streets. The tradition was born out of a mockery of Napoleon's troops, who would march around the city in a similar fashion. Today it's San Sebastián's biggest street party. ⊠ *San Sebastián.*

Processo dels Tres Tocs (*Procession of the Three Knocks*). This festival, held in Ciutadella on January 17, celebrates the 1287 victory of King Alfonso III of Aragón over the Moors. ⊠ *Ciutadella.*

February

Carnival. In February and March, on this first major fiesta of the year after Three Kings' Day (January 6), cities, towns, and villages across the region erupt with festive fun, including parades, parties, and wild costumes.

Festes de Santa Eularia. Ibiza's boisterous winter carnival, held on February 12, includes folk dancing and music. ⊠ *Eivissa.*

March

Cherry Blossom Festival (*Fiesta del Cerezo en Flor*). For approximately two weeks between March and early May, depending on the year, Spain's prized cherry-growing region, the Jerte Valley, turns pink and white as more than a million cherry trees bloom in unison. Throughout the area, a series of live concerts, street markets, and gastronomic presentations accompany nature's show. ⊠ *Jaraíz de la Vera* ☎ *92/747–2558* ⊕ *www.turismovalledeljerte.com.*

April

Feria de Abril (*April Fair*). Held two weeks after Easter, this secular celebration focuses on horses, pageantry, and bullfights. ⊠ *Seville.*

May

Antxua Eguna (*Getaria Anchovy Festival*). Join Getaria locals in early May as they ring in anchovy season with gallons of Txakoli and mountains of grilled fresh fish. ⊠ *Getaria.*

Cruces de Mayo (*Festival of Crosses*). Celebrated throughout the Spanish-speaking world, this ancient festival is a highlight of Córdoba's calendar of events, with lots of flower-decked crosses and other floral displays, processions, and music in early May. ⊠ *Córdoba.*

Feria Nacional del Queso de Trujillo. Trujillo's cheese festival, in early May, brings together Spain's finest cheese makers with hundreds of varieties to taste and buy (don't pass up Pascualete, named the best cheese in Spain by the World Cheese Awards). The event is understandably popular with foodies. ⊠ *Trujillo* ☎ *92/732–1450* ⊕ *www.feriadelquesotrujillo.es.*

Festival de los Patios (*Patio Festival*). This celebration, awarded UNESCO World Heritage status in 2012, is held during the second week of May, a fun time to be in the city, when owners throw open their flower-decked patios to visitors (and to judges, who nominate the best), and the city celebrates with food, drink, and flamenco. ⊠ *Córdoba* ⊕ *patios.cordoba.es.*

WOMAD Cáceres. The World of Music, Arts and Dance draws crowds of around 75,000 in early May. Main stages are set up in the magical surroundings of this ancient city's plazas for free concerts, and other events include shows staged in the Gran Teatro, children's events, and a grand procession. ⊠ *Calle San Antón 0, Cáceres* ☎ *92/701–0884* ⊕ *www.womad. org.*

June

Festes de Sant Joan. At this event June 23–24, riders in costume parade through the streets of Ciutadella on horseback, urging the horses up to dance on their hind legs while spectators pass dangerously under their hooves. ⊠ *Ciutadella.*

July

Bilbao BBK Live. One of Spain's hottest pop and rock music festivals, BBK Live draws more than 100,000 fans each year with its lineup of big-name artists. In 2019, headliners included The Strokes, Rosalía, Weezer, and Liam Gallagher. Those with an aversion to mud and noisy campgrounds will appreciate the "glamping" accommodation option. ⊠ *Bilbao* ⊕ *www.bilbaobbklive.com.*

Festival de Teatro Clásico. In Mérida, the highlight of the cultural calendar is this annual festival held in the restored Roman amphitheater from early July through mid-August. It features opera as well as classical drama and celebrated its 65th year in 2019. ⊠ *Pl. Margarita Xirgu, Mérida* ☎ *92/400–9480* ⊕ *www.festivald-emerida.es.*

Heineken Jazzaldia. Drawing many of the world's top performers, this late-July festival in San Sebastián attracts an international crowd of jazz devotees. Headliners in 2019 included Diana Krall, Jamie Cullum, Neneh Cherry, and Joan Baez. ⊠ *San Sebastián* ⊕ *www.heineken-jazzaldia.com.*

Ortigueira Festival. This major Celtic music festival, which takes place in early or mid-July over four days in the coastal city of Ortigueira, attracts folk musicians from around the world. ⊠ *A Coruña* ☎ *981/422089 for tourist office* ⊕ *www.festivaldeortigueira.com.*

San Fermín. Pamplona's main event, immortalized by Ernest Hemingway in his 1926 novel *The Sun Also Rises,* is best known for its running of the bulls, a tradition that's dangerous for humans and ultimately lethal for the animals involved. Ethics aside, a huge part of the festival is consumed by nontaurine activities such as processions, live music acts, and fireworks. Held each year July 6–14, every day begins at 8 am with a herd of fighting bulls let loose to run through the narrow streets to the bullring alongside daredevils testing their speed and agility in the face of possible injury or death. The atmosphere is electric, and hotel rooms overlooking the course come at a price. ⚠ **Recent years have seen a disturbing increase in sex crimes; it's advisable for travelers, especially women, to take commonsense precautions, including being aware of your surroundings and not walking alone at night**. ⊠ *Pamplona* ⊕ *www.sanfermin.com.*

Virgen del Carmen. The patron saint of sailors (Our Lady of Mount Carmel) is honored July 15–16 in Formentera with a blessing of the boats in the harbor. The holiday is also celebrated on Ibiza. ⊠ *Sant Antoni.*

August

Aste Nagusia. The "Big Week," a nine-day event celebrating Basque culture, is held in Bilbao in mid-August with a fine

On the Calendar

series of street concerts, bullfights, and fireworks displays. ⊠ *Bilbao*.

Festa do Viño Albariño (*Albariño Wine Festival*). On the first Sunday of August, the town of Cambados, capital of Albariño country, draws thousands to witness its processions, concerts, cultural events, fireworks, and other revelry honoring local vineyards and wineries—including wine tastings from around 40 different Rías Baixas wineries. The festival has been held since the early 1950s. ⊠ *Cambados* ⊕ *www.fiestadelalbariño.com*.

Fiesta de la Virgen Blanca (*Festival of the White Virgin*). This weeklong festival (August 4–9) celebrates Vitoria's patron saint with bullfights and street parties. The festivities begin with the arrival of Celedón, a well-dressed dummy that "flies" over the main square holding an umbrella. ⊠ *Vitoria*.

Sant Ciriac. Capped with a spectacular fireworks display over the walls of Eivissa's old city, this festival (on August 8) celebrates the Reconquest of Ibiza from the Moors. ⊠ *Eivissa*.

Sant Lluís. Celebrations of this saint's day, which are held during the last weekend of August in the town of Sant Lluís, on Menorca, center on an equestrian cavalcade called La Qualcada. ⊠ *Sant Lluís*.

September

Fiestas de la Mare de Déu de Gràcia. Held September 6–9 in Mahón, this celebration is Menorca's final blowout of the season. ⊠ *Mahón*.

Fiesta de Otoño (*Autumn Festival*). In September, this festival in Jerez celebrates the grape harvest and includes a procession, the blessing of the harvest on the steps of the cathedral, and traditional-style grape treading. ⊠ *Jerez de la Frontera*.

San Sebastián Film Festival. Glitterati descend on the city for its international film fest in the second half of September. Exact dates vary, so check the website for details. ⊠ *San Sebastián* ⊕ *www.sansebastianfestival.com*.

October

Festa do Marisco (*Seafood Festival*). Galicia's famous culinary event, held in O Grove in October, draws crowds to feast on a stunning number of seafood delicacies. ⊠ *O Grove* ⊕ *www.turismogrove.es*.

Fiesta de la Rosa del Azafrán (*Consuegra Saffron Festival*). This festival, held in the last week of October since 1963, celebrates the annual saffron harvest, one of La Mancha's longest-standing traditions. Watch a saffron-plucking contest, savor locally made manchego cheeses, and marvel at folk dance spectacles—all with a backdrop of Don Quixote–style windmills. ☎ *92/547–5731 Consuegra tourist office* ⊕ *www.consuegra.es/fiestas/fiesta-de-la-rosa-del-azafrán*.

December

Encuentros Flamencos. Some of the country's best performers are featured in this early-December event in Granada. ⊠ *Granada*.

Los Escobazos. On December 7, the city is filled with bonfires celebrating the Virgen de la Concepción. Watch out for the locals play-fighting with torches made out of brooms—or if you're feeling daredevilish, join in. ⊠ *Jarandilla de la Vera* ☎ *92/756–0045 tourist office* ⊕ *www.jarandilladelavera.es*.

Chapter 3

MADRID

Updated by
Benjamin Kemper

👁 Sights   🍴 Restaurants   🛏 Hotels   🛍 Shopping   🍸 Nightlife
★★★★☆   ★★★★★   ★★★★☆   ★★★★★   ★★★★★

WELCOME TO MADRID

TOP REASONS TO GO

★ **Hit the Centro Histórico:** The Plaza Mayor, on any late night when it's almost empty, evokes the glory of Spain's Golden Age.

★ **Stroll down museum row:** Find a pleasant mix of art and architecture in the Prado, the Reina Sofía, and the Thyssen-Bornemisza, all of which display extensive and impressive collections.

★ **Nibble tapas into the night:** Indulge in a madrileño way of socializing. Learn about the art of tapas and sample local wines while wandering among the bars of Cava Baja, Calle Ponzano, and beyond.

★ **Relax in the Retiro gardens:** Unwind at a *chiringuito* (refreshment stand) and enjoy some primo people-watching.

★ **Burn the midnight oil:** As other Europeans tuck themselves in, madrileños swarm to the bars of the liveliest neighborhoods—Malasaña, Chueca, Lavapiés, Barrio de las Letras, and more—and stretch the party out until dawn.

Madrid comprises 21 districts, each broken down into several neighborhoods. The most central district is called just that: Centro. Here you'll find all of Madrid's oldest neighborhoods: Palacio, Sol, La Latina, Lavapiés, Barrio de las Letras, Malasaña, and Chueca. Other well-known districts, a term we'll use interchangeably with "neighborhoods" for the sake of convenience, are Salamanca, Retiro, Chamberí (north of Centro), Moncloa (east of Chamberí), and Chamartín.

1 Palacio. Tour Madrid's most noble corner encompassing the Royal Palace, Sabatini Gardens, and Royal Theater.

2 La Latina. Throw a few elbows at El Rastro flea market and sample ultra-traditional tapas.

3 Sol. Shop for clothes, souvenirs, electronics, and more in the commercial and touristic epicenter.

4 Moncloa. Visit a real Ancient Egyptian temple and wander a blissfully off-the-radar park.

5 Barrio de las Letras. Walk in the footsteps of Spain's great writers, and sample some trendy tapas while you're at it.

6 Lavapiés. Sneak into a graffitied art squat and gobble down budget-friendly Senegalese food in this rebellious, multicultural neighborhood.

7 El Rastro. Home to the most popular open air flea market in Madrid.

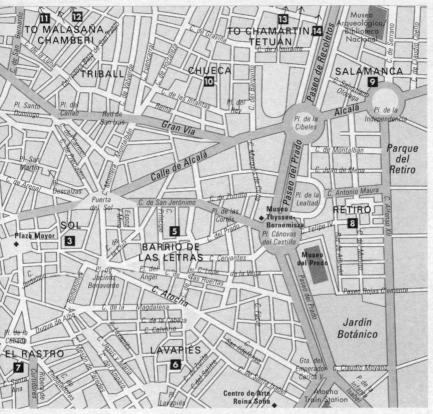

8 **Retiro.** After a leisurely stroll through the park, get lost among the nontouristy side streets to get a feel for residential Madrid.

9 **Salamanca.** Sip *gin-tónics* and shop for top-quality clothes and jewelry alongside high-society Madrileños.

10 **Chueca.** Discover Madrid's "gayborhood," as famous for its come-one-come-all nightclubs as it is for its independently owned boutiques.

11 **Malasaña.** Join the bearded-and-bunned Euro-hipsters at third-wave coffee shops and trendy cocktail bars.

12 **Chamberí.** Go on a taste tour of Madrid's new (and pleasantly unpretentious) culinary nerve center.

13 **Chamartín.** Cheer till you're hoarse at a Real Madrid soccer match.

14 **Tetuán.** Make the trek to this working-class neighborhood for solid international restaurants and old-timey tapas bars.

EATING AND DRINKING WELL IN MADRID

As Spain's most vibrant melting pot, Madrid is home to countless regional Spanish restaurants serving everything from Valencian paella to Basque pintxos, but the most classic fare closely resembles that of Castile.

With a climate sometimes described as *nueve meses de invierno y tres de infierno* (nine months of winter and three of hell), it's no surprise that the local cuisine is essentially comfort food. Garlic soup, stewed chickpeas, and roast suckling pig and lamb are standard components of Madrid feasts, as are baby goat and deeply flavored beef from Ávila and the Sierra de Guadarrama. *Cocido madrileño* (a meat-packed winter stew) and *callos a la madrileña* (stewed tripe) are favored local specialties, while *jamón ibérico de bellota* (acorn-fed Iberian ham)—a specialty from *las dehesas,* the rolling oak forests of Extremadura and Andalusia—is a staple on special occasions. Summer fare hinges on minimally manipulated fruits and vegetables, while contemporary restaurants frequently offer lighter dishes.

TAPAS

Itinerant grazing from tavern to tavern is especially popular in Madrid, beneficiary of tapas traditions from every corner of Spain. The areas around Plaza Santa Ana, Plaza Mayor, Calle Ponzano, and Cava Baja buzz with excitement as crowds drink beer and wine while devouring platefuls of *boquerones en vinagre* (vinegar-cured anchovies), *calamares a la romana* (fried squid), or *albóndigas* (meatballs).

SOUPS

Sopa de ajo (garlic soup), also known as *sopa castellana,* is a homey soup that starts with an unapologetically garlicky ham-bone stock. Stale bread is then torn in to thicken it up, followed by a cracked egg—a final enriching flourish. *Caldo* (hot chicken or beef broth), a Madrid favorite on wet winter days, is often offered free of charge in traditional bars and cafés with an order of anything else.

STEWS

Cocido madrileño is Madrid's ultimate comfort food, a boiled dinner of garbanzo beans, vegetables, potatoes, sausages, pork, and hen simmered for hours in earthenware crocks over coals and presented in multiple courses. It is usually served in an earthenware casserole to keep the stew piping hot. *Estofado de judiones de La Granja* (broad-bean stew) is another soul-satisfying favorite: pork, quail, ham, or whatever meat is available simmers with onions, tomatoes, carrots, and luxuriously creamy broad beans from the Segovian town of La Granja de San Ildefonso.

ROASTS

Asadores (restaurants specializing in roasts) are an institution in and around Madrid, where the *cochinillo asado,* or

roast suckling pig, is the crown jewel. Whether you taste this culinary specialty at Casa Botín in Madrid or Mesón de Cándido in Segovia or Adolfo Restaurant in Toledo, the preparation is largely the same: milk-fed piglets are roasted in oak-burning wood ovens and emerge shatteringly crisp yet tender enough to carve using the edge of a plate. *Lechazo,* or milk-fed lamb, is another asador stalwart that emerges from wood ovens accompanied by the aromas of oak and Castile's wide *meseta*: thistle, rosemary, and thyme.

WINES

The traditional Madrid house wine, a coarse Valdepeñas from La Mancha, south of the capital, has fallen out of favor as better-quality cuvées from Rioja and Ribera del Duero (for reds) and Rueda and Rías Baixas (for whites) have become more readily available. Deep-pink *rosados,* the best of which hail from Rioja, Catalonia, and Navarra, are increasingly popular in the summer. Natural wines—made largely without additives and pesticides in family-run *bodegas* (wineries)—are becoming trendier by the minute and can be enjoyed at a number of specialty bars and restaurants.

Madrid, the Spanish capital since 1561, is Europe's city that never sleeps. A vibrant and increasingly international metropolis, Madrid has an infectious appetite for art, music, and epicurean pleasures yet remains steadfast in its age-old traditions.

Madrid takes in plenty of "modern" barrios such as Salamanca, Chamberí, and Chamartín, but the part of Madrid that draws visitors the world over is its historic center, situated between the Palacio Real and the city's green lung, the Parque del Buen Retiro. A conglomeration of Belle Époque buildings with intricate facades, terra-cotta-roofed residences, and redbrick Mudejar Revival churches, Madrid is a stately stunner. Madrileños love being outdoors as much as possible: restaurant patios, flea markets, and parks and plazas are always abuzz, particularly if the sun's out.

Then there's the art—the legacy of one of the most important global empires ever assembled. King Carlos I (1500–58), who later became Emperor Carlos V (or Charles V), set out to collect the best specimens from all European schools of art, many of which found their way to Spain's palaces and, later, to the Prado Museum. Between the classical Prado, the contemporary Reina Sofía, the wide-ranging Thyssen-Bornemisza, and Madrid's smaller artistic repositories— the Real Academia de Bellas Artes de San Fernando, the Convento de las Descalzas Reales, the Sorolla Museum, and the Lázaro Galdiano Museum, to name a few—there are more paintings here than you could admire in a lifetime.

Not all of the city's most memorable attractions are centuries old. The CaixaForum arts center is an architectural triumph by Jacques Herzog and Pierre de Meuron. Futuristic towers by Norman Foster and César Pelli have changed the city's northern landscape. Other newly finished projects include Madrid Río, which has added nearly 20 miles of green space along the banks of the Manzanares River, and the Conde Duque cultural center, a multidisciplinary haven that hosts film screenings, dance nights, poetry readings, and more.

Planning

WHEN TO GO

Madrid is hot and dry in summer—with temperatures reaching 40°C (105°F) in July and August—and chilly and damp in winter, with minimum temperatures around 1°C (low 30s). Snow in the city is rare. The most pleasant time to visit is spring, especially May, when the city honors its patron saint with street fairs and celebrations. June and September–December are also fine times to visit.

Avoid Madrid in July and August—especially August as locals flee the punishing heat and head to the coast or to the mountains and many restaurants, bars, and shops are closed. Winter is a pleasant time to visit, if you don't mind bundling up a bit in the evenings.

PLANNING YOUR TIME

Madrid's most valuable art treasures are all on display within a few blocks of Paseo del Prado. This area is home to the Museo del Prado, whose collection amasses masterworks by Velázquez, Goya, El Greco, and others; the Centro de Arte Reina Sofía, whose eclectic contemporary art pieces include Picasso's *Guernica*; and the Museo Thyssen-Bornemisza, whose collection stretches from the Renaissance to the 21st century. Each can take hours to explore, so it's best to alternate museum visits with less intellectually rigorous attractions. If you're running short on time and want to pack everything in, recharge at any of the tapas bars or restaurants in the Barrio de las Letras (behind the Paseo del Prado, across from the Prado).

Any visit to Madrid should include a walk through the historic area between Puerta del Sol and the Palacio Real. Leave the map in your back pocket and wander through the Plaza Mayor, Plaza de la Villa, and Plaza de Oriente, pausing to marvel at some of the city's oldest churches and convents.

GETTING HERE AND AROUND
AIR TRAVEL

Madrid's Adolfo Suárez Madrid–Barajas Airport is Europe's fifth-busiest. Terminal 4 (T4) handles flights from 22 carriers, including American Airlines, British Airways, and Iberia. All other U.S. airlines use Terminal 1 (T1).

Airport terminals are connected by bus service and also to Línea 8 of the metro, which reaches the city center in 30–45 minutes for around €5 (€1.50–€2 plus a €3 airport supplement). For €5 there are also convenient buses (Nos. 203 and 203 Exprés) to the Atocha train station (with stops on Calle de O'Donnell and Plaza de Cibeles) and to Avenida de América (note that bus drivers don't take bills

greater than €20), where you can catch the metro or a taxi to your hotel. Taxis charge a flat fee of €30 from the airport to anywhere in the city center.

BIKE TRAVEL

BiciMAD (⊕ *www.bicimad.com*) is Madrid's public bike-share service with 208 docks scattered around the city center. The bikes are electric, meaning you hardly have to pedal, and are an excellent alternative to the metro and buses, provided the weather is good and you're comfortable riding in traffic (separate bike lanes are virtually nonexistent). Avid urban cyclists staying for a month or more may wish to purchase a €25 yearly membership, which drastically lowers the cost of individual rides to €0.60 for up to one hour, but occasional users can pay €2 per 30-minute ride, buying a ticket at each service station. The bikes can be borrowed from, and returned to, any station in the system.

BUS TRAVEL

Buses are generally less popular than trains, though they're sometimes faster and cheaper. Madrid has no central bus station: most destinations south and east of Madrid are serviced by the Estación del Sur, while Intercambiador de Moncloa and Estación de Avenida de América service northern destinations. All have eponymous metro stops (except for Estación del Sur, serviced by Méndez Álvaro).

Blue city buses (€1.50 one-way) run about 6 am–11:30 pm. Less frequent night buses run through the night on heavily trafficked routes.

BUS STATIONS Estación de Avenida de América ✉ *Av. de América 9, Salamanca* ☎ *90/242–2242 for ALSA Bus Company* ⊕ *www.crtm.es/tu-transporte-publico/ intercambiadores.aspx* Ⓜ *Av. de América.* **Estación del Sur** ✉ *Calle Méndez Álvaro s/n, Atocha* ☎ *91/468–4200* ⊕ *www.estaciondeautobuses.com* Ⓜ *Méndez Álvaro.* **Intercambiador de Moncloa** ✉ *Princesa 89,*

Moncloa ☎ *012 for Madrid city hotline* ⊕ *www.crtm.es* Ⓜ *Moncloa.*

CAR TRAVEL

November 2018 marked the beginning of **Madrid Central,** a sweeping, environmentally driven law that prohibits most vehicles—rentals included—from entering the city center. This zone is delineated by double red lines, large roadside signs, and nautilus-like "Madrid Central" logos painted clearly on the asphalt; entering without the proper permissions will result in fines. Be sure to ask your rental car agency about the specific restrictions on your vehicle as they relate to Madrid Central. Zero-emissions vehicles are not affected, so if you plan on driving in the city center, it may be worth spending the extra euros on an eco-friendly car.

Blablacar is Spain's leading rideshare app in intercity travel with more global users than Uber. Its free platform allows you to book ahead using a credit card, and message with the driver to set meeting and drop-off points. Blablacar is the most affordable way to travel to Madrid's outlying cities and beyond as drivers aren't allowed to make a profit (you essentially help the driver offset the price of gas and tolls).

SUBWAY TRAVEL

To ride the metro, you must buy a refillable Tarjeta de Transporte Público (Public Transportation Card), which costs an unrefundable €2.50 and can be obtained at ticketing machines inside any metro station. Each journey costs €1.50–€2, depending on how far you're traveling within the city; you can also buy a 10-ride Metrobus ticket (€12.20). There are no free transfers between the metro and bus systems. The **Abono Turístico** (Tourist Pass) allows unlimited use of public buses and the metro for one day (€8.40 for Zone A, €17 for Zone T) to seven days (€35.40 for Zone A, €70.80 for Zone T); buy it at tourist offices, metro stations, or select newsstands. The metro runs 6 am–1:30 am, though a few entrances close earlier. *(See the metro map in this chapter.)*

SUBWAY INFORMATION Metro Madrid ☎ *90/244–4403* ⊕ *www.metromadrid.es.*

TAXI TRAVEL

Taxis work under several tariff schemes. Tariff 1 is for the city center 7 am–9 pm; meters start at €2.40. There is a fixed taxi fare of €30 to or from the airport from the city center. Supplements include €3 to or from bus and train stations. Tariff 2 is for the city center 9 pm–7 am on weekdays (and 7 am–9 pm on weekends and holidays); the meter starts at €2.90 and charges more per kilometer. Besides reserving a taxi by phone, you can also do it through mobile app MyTaxi, which works with local official taxi drivers. As of mid-2019, Uber and Cabify are back in operation after a hiatus due to legal restrictions; in 2017, UberONE, Uber's premium service, added 50 Teslas to its Madrid fleet.

The rise of Uber and similar ride-hailing apps has led to a standoff between traditional taxis and vehicles for hire. Taxi strikes are increasingly frequent, so if you plan on using a taxi service, be sure to inquire locally to ensure they're running to cover your bases.

TAXI SERVICES Radio Taxi Gremial ☎ *91/447–3232, 91/447–5180* ⊕ *www. radiotaxigremial.com.* **Radioteléfono Taxi** ☎ *91/547–8200* ⊕ *www.radiotele-fono-taxi.com.* **Tele-Taxi** ☎ *91/371–2131* ⊕ *www.tele-taxi.es.*

TRAIN TRAVEL

Madrid is the geographical center of Spain, and all major train lines depart from one of its two main train stations (Chamartín and Atocha) or pass through Madrid. Though train travel is comfortable, for some destinations buses run more frequently and make fewer stops; this is true for Segovia and Toledo, unless you take the more expensive high-speed train.

Commuter trains to El Escorial, Aranjuez, and Alcalá de Henares run frequently. The best way to get a ticket for such trains is to use one of the automated reservation terminals at the station. You can reach Segovia and Toledo from Atocha station in a half hour on the high-speed Alvia and Avant lines; if you book ahead, the ticket may cost less than €25. Train stations in Toledo and Segovia are outside the city, meaning once there you'll have to take a bus or a taxi into the center.

The high-speed AVE can get you to Barcelona in less than three hours. If you buy the ticket ahead online (with discounts up to 60% off the official fare), you may pay less than €40 each way for (often nonrefundable) tickets. Otherwise expect to pay between €60 and €100 each way—the higher price is for non-stop service.

⇨ *For more information about buying train tickets, see the Travel Smart chapter.*

TRAIN INFORMATION Estación de Atocha
⊠ *Glorieta del Emperador Carlos V, Atocha* ☎ *91/232–0320* ⊕ *www.adif. es* Ⓜ *Atocha.* **Estación de Chamartín** ⊠ *Calle Agustín de Foxá s/n, Chamartín* ☎ *91/232–0320* ⊕ *www.adif.es* Ⓜ *Chamartín.* **Estación de Príncipe Pío (Norte)** ⊠ *Paseo de la Florida s/n, Moncloa* ☎ *90/210–9804* Ⓜ *Príncipe Pío.*

TOURS
Plaza Mayor Tourist Office
BUS TOURS | Madrid's main tourist office, open 365 days a year, is a treasure trove of maps and resources and will happily recommend popular bus, segway, cycling, and walking tours to meet your needs. ⊠ *Pl. Mayor 27, Sol* ☎ *91/531– 0074* ⊕ *www.esmadrid.com.*

BIKE TOURS
Biking in Madrid can be a white-knuckle experience for those unaccustomed to biking in traffic, but for leisurely sightseeing through parks and along the river, bike tours can be a pleasant activity.

BravoBike
BICYCLE TOURS | BravoBike offers guided bike tours in English (from €15 for two hours). It also offers multiday guided and self-guided bike tours near Madrid, in Toledo, Aranjuez, Chinchón, and Segovia, as well as tours along the pilgrimage route to Santiago de Compostela and Andalusia, among others. ⊠ *Calle Juan Álvarez Mendizábal 19, Calle Juan Álvarez Mendizábal 19, Moncloa* ☎ *91/758–2945, 60/744–8440 for WhatsApp* ⊕ *www. bravobike.com* 🖶 *From €15.*

BUS TOURS
Madrid City Tours
BUS TOURS | These ubiquitous red double-decker tourist buses make 1½-hour circuits of the city, allowing you to get on and off at various attractions (there is a Historic Madrid tour and a Modern Madrid tour, plus a Night Tour June 16– September 15) with recorded English commentary. There are one- and two-day passes. ☎ *90/202–4758* ⊕ *www.madrid. city-tour.com* 🖶 *From €20.*

WALKING TOURS
Asociación Nacional de Guías de Turismo (APIT)
This tour operator offers custom history and art walks by government-certified travel guides. ⊠ *Calle Jacometrezo 4, 9° 13, Sol* ☎ *91/542–1214* ⊕ *www.apit.es.*

Carpetania Madrid
WALKING TOURS | This company offers niche, brainy tours and literary walks on topics like "Women of Malasaña" and "Almodóvar's Madrid." (Spanish only.) ⊠ *Calle Jesús del Valle 11, Malasaña* ☎ *91/531–1418* ⊕ *www.carpetaniama-drid.com* 🖶 *From €10.*

★ Devour Madrid
SPECIAL-INTEREST | FAMILY | A hip, young tour company catering to foodie travelers of all interests and ages (custom and kids' tours are available), Devour Madrid hosts walks that run the gamut from an "Ultimate Spanish Cuisine" neighborhood crawl to a "Prado Museum Tour"

that culminates in a lunch at Botín, the world's oldest restaurant, according to Guinness World Records. ⊠ *Calle de la Torrecilla del Leal 10, Cortes* ☎ *94/458–1022* ⊕ *www.madridfoodtour.com* ✉ *From €49.*

RESTAURANTS

When it comes to dining, younger madrileños gravitate toward trendy neighborhoods like bearded-and-bunned Malasaña, gay-friendly Chueca, rootsy La Latina, and multicultural Lavapiés for their boisterous and affordable restaurants and bars. Dressier travelers, and those visiting with kids, will feel more at home in the quieter, more buttoned-up restaurants of Salamanca, Chamartín, and Retiro. Of course, these are broad-brush generalizations, and there are plenty of exceptions.

The house wine in old-timey Madrid restaurants is often a sturdy, uncomplicated Valdepeñas from La Mancha. A plummy Rioja or a gutsy Ribera del Duero—the latter from northern Castile—are the usual choices for reds by the glass in chicer establishments, while popular whites include fruity Verdejo varietals from Rueda and slatey albariños from Galicia After dinner, try the anise-flavored liqueur (*anís*), produced outside the nearby village of Chinchón, or a fruitier *patxaran*, a digestif made with sloe berries.

WHAT IT COSTS in Euros

$	$$	$$$	$$$$
RESTAURANTS			
under €16	€16–€22	€23–€29	over €29

HOTELS

Spain overtook the United States as the world's second-most-visited country in 2018, so it's no surprise that Madrid is in the throes of a hotel construction boom, the first since the economic crisis hit in 2008. The Old Guard of hotels is shaking in its boots as newcomers offer

modern-day amenities (Bluetooth speakers, international power outlets, bedside thermostats, etc.) at affordable prices: The Westin Palace is in the midst of a seemingly never-ending remodel, while the Ritz Madrid will remain closed for massive renovations until late 2020. The last couple of years have also ushered in several cutting-edge boutique and designer properties, the likes of which the city has never seen, such as Barceló Torre de Madrid, Tótem, and Only You Atocha. And Madrid can finally lay claim to a chic, immaculately clean hostel in The Hat. The next big game-changer? Four Seasons Hotel Madrid, set to usher in its first guests in late 2019.

WHAT IT COSTS in Euros

$	$$	$$$	$$$$
HOTELS			
under €125	€125–€174	€175–€225	over €225

NIGHTLIFE

Unlike in other European cities, where partying is a pastime geared only toward the young, there are plenty of bars and discotecas with mixed-age crowds, and it's not uncommon for children to play on the sidewalks past midnight while multi-generational families and friends convene over coffee or cocktails at an outdoor café. For those who don't plan on staying out until sunrise, the best options are the bars along the Cava Alta and Cava Baja, Calle Huertas near Plaza de Santa Ana, and Calle Moratín near Antón Martín. Those who want to stay out till the wee hours have more options: Calle Príncipe and Calle De la Cruz, lined with sardine-can bars lined with locals, and the scruffier streets that snake down toward Plaza de Lavapiés. But the neighborhood most synonymous with *la vida nocturna* is Malasaña, which has plenty of trendy hangouts along Calle San Vicente Ferrer, Calle La Palma, and all around Plaza de Dos de Mayo. Another major nightlife contender is is Chueca, where tattoo parlors and street-chic boutiques sit between LGBT+ (yet hetero-friendly) bars, dance clubs, and after-hours clubs.

In general, cafés in Madrid can be classified into two groups: those that have been around for many years (La Pecera del Círculo, Café de Oriente), where writers, singers, poets, and discussion groups still meet and where conversations are usually more important than the coffee itself, and Nordic-style third-wave venues (Hanso, Toma Café, Hola Coffee, Federal Café) tailored to hip and hurried urbanites that tend to have a wider product selection, modern interiors, and Wi-Fi.

SHOPPING

Madrid has three main shopping areas. The first stretches from Callao to Puerta del Sol (Calle Preciados, Gran Vía on both sides of Callao, and the streets around the Puerta del Sol) and includes the major department stores (El Corte Inglés and the French music, book, and electronics chain FNAC) and popular Spanish brands such as Zara.

The second area, far more elegant and expensive, is in the eastern Salamanca district, bounded roughly by Serrano, Juan Bravo, Jorge Juan (and its mews), and Velázquez; the shops on Goya extend as far as Alcalá. The streets just off the Plaza de Colón, particularly Calle Serrano and Calle Ortega y Gasset, have the widest selection of designer goods—think Prada, Loewe, Armani, and Louis Vuitton—as well as other mainstream and popular local designers (Purificación García, Pedro del Hierro, Adolfo Domínguez, Roberto Verino). Calle Jorge Juan, Calle Lagasca, and Calle Claudio Coello hold the widest selection of smart boutiques from renowned Spanish designers such as Sybilla, DelPozo, and Dolores Promesas.

Finally, for hipper clothes, Chueca, Malasaña, and the streets around the Conde Duque cultural center are your best bets. Calle Fuencarral, between Gran Vía and Tribunal, has the most shops in this area with outposts from Diesel, Adidas, and Footlocker, but also local brands such as El Ganso, Adolfo Domínguez U (selling the Galician designer's younger collection), and Custo as well as some cosmetics stores (Madame B and M.A.C). Less mainstream and sometimes more exciting is the selection you can find on nearby Calles Hortaleza, Almirante, and Piamonte and around the Conde Duque cultural center.

Palacio

Madrid's oldest neighborhood, Palacio is the home of the imposing Palacio Real. This is where Muhammad I established the city's first military post in the 9th century, essentially founding the city. The quarter, bounded by the Plaza Mayor to the east, is a maze of cobblestone streets lined with homey restaurants and old-school cafés and shops.

◉ Sights

Catedral de la Almudena

RELIGIOUS SITE | The first stone of the cathedral, which faces the Royal Palace, was laid in 1883 by King Alfonso XII, and the resulting edifice was consecrated by Pope John Paul II in 1993. Built on the site of the old church of Santa María de la Almudena (the city's main mosque during Arab rule), the cathedral has a wooden statue of Madrid's female patron saint, the Virgin of Almudena, reportedly discovered after the Christian Reconquest of Madrid. Legend has it that when the Arabs invaded Spain, the local Christian population hid the statue of the Virgin in a vault carved in the old Roman wall that encircled the city. When the Christians reconquered Madrid in 1083, they looked for it, and after nine days of intensive praying—others say it was after a

Madrid Metro

KEY

1 Metro Terminals
O Metro Stations
▣ Transfer Stations
╫ Railway Lines
• Train Stations

procession honoring the Virgin—the wall opened up to show the statue framed by two lighted candles. Its name is derived from the place where it was found: the wall of the old citadel (in Arabic, *al-mudayna*). ✉ *Calle Bailén 10, Palacio* ☎ *91/542–2200* ⊕ *www.catedraldelaalmudena.es* ✉ *Free, museum and cupola €6* Ⓜ *Ópera.*

Jardines de Sabatini (*Sabatini Gardens*)
GARDEN | The meticulously manicured gardens to the north of the Palacio Real, located where the royal stables once were, are a pleasant place to rest or watch the sun set. ✉ *Calle Bailén s/n, Palacio* Ⓜ *Ópera, Príncipe Pío, Plaza de España.*

Madrid Río
CITY PARK | FAMILY | Madrid Río, the city's most ambitious urban planning initiative in recent history, has added nearly 32 km (20 miles) of green space and bike-friendly paths along the Manzanares River, just downhill from the Palacio Real. But there's no need to break a sweat to make the most of the new esplanade: outdoor concerts (check out the Veranos de la Villa series; lineups are posted online) and riverside dining round out the park's offerings. Note to nature lovers: Madrid Río connects to Casa de Campo, Parque del Oeste, and Madrid's 64-km (40-mile) Anillo Verde ("Green Ring") bike path. ✉ *Palacio* ⊕ *www.veranosdelavilla. madrid.es* Ⓜ *Príncipe Pío, Pirámides, Legazpi.*

Monasterio de la Encarnación (*Monastery of the Incarnation*)
RELIGIOUS SITE | Once connected to the Palacio Real by an underground passageway, this Augustinian convent now houses fewer than a dozen nuns. Founded in 1611 by Queen Margarita de Austria, the wife of Felipe III, it has several artistic treasures, including a reliquary where a vial with the dried blood of St. Pantaleón is said to liquefy every July 27. The ornate church has superb acoustics for medieval and Renaissance choral concerts. ✉ *Pl.*

de la Encarnación 1, Palacio ☎ *91/454–8800 for tourist office* ✉ *From €6* ⊘ *Closed Mon.* Ⓜ *Ópera.*

Monasterio de las Descalzas Reales (*Monastery of the Royal Discalced, or Barefoot, Nuns*)
RELIGIOUS SITE | This 16th-century building was restricted for 200 years to women of royal blood. Its plain, brick-and-stone facade begets an opulent interior strewn with paintings by Francisco de Zurbarán, Titian, and Pieter Brueghel the Elder—all part of the dowry that novices had to provide when they joined the monastery—as well as a hall of sumptuous tapestries crafted from drawings by Peter Paul Rubens. The convent was founded in 1559 by Juana of Austria, one of Felipe II's sisters, who ruled Spain while he was in England and the Netherlands. It houses 33 different chapels—the age of Christ when he died and the maximum number of nuns allowed to live at the monastery—and more than 100 sculptures of Jesus as a baby. About 30 nuns (not necessarily of royal blood) still live here and grow vegetables in the convent's garden. ■TIP→ **You must take a (Spanish-only) tour in order to visit the convent.** ✉ *Pl. de las Descalzas Reales 3, Palacio* ☎ *91/454–8800* ✉ *From €6* ⊘ *Closed Mon.* Ⓜ *Sol.*

★ **Palacio Real**
CASTLE/PALACE | Emblematic of the oldest part of the city, the Royal Palace awes visitors with its sheer size and monumental presence. The palace was commissioned in the early 18th century by the first of Spain's Bourbon rulers, Felipe V. Outside, you can see the classical French architecture on the graceful Patio de Armas; inside, 2,800 rooms compete with each other for over-the-top opulence. A two-hour guided tour in English points out highlights including the Salón de Gasparini, King Carlos III's private apartments; the Salón del Trono, a grand throne room; and the banquet hall. Also worth visiting are the Museo de Música

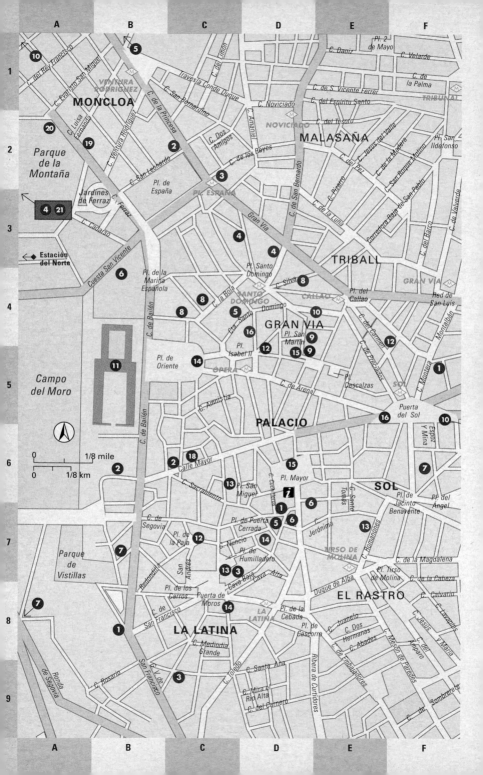

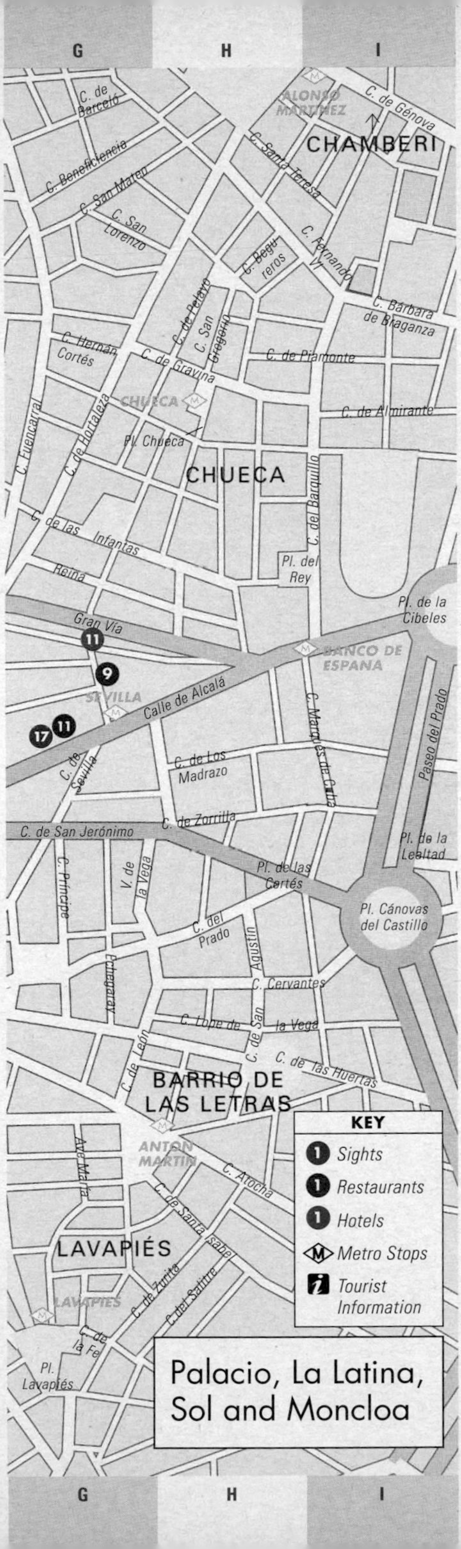

CHAMBERÍ

CHUECA

BANCO DE ESPAÑA

SEVILLA

BARRIO DE LAS LETRAS

LAVAPIÉS

KEY

- ❶ Sights
- ❶ Restaurants
- ❶ Hotels
- Ⓜ Metro Stops
- 🛈 Tourist Information

Palacio, La Latina, Sol and Moncloa

Sights ▼

1 Basílica de San Francisco el Grande B8
2 Catedral de la Almudena................ B6
3 Cava Baja.................C7
4 Ermita de San Antonio de la Florida A3
5 Faro de Moncloa........ B1
6 Jardines de Sabatini ... B4
7 Madrid Río............... A8
8 Monasterio de la Encarnación...............C4
9 Monasterio de las Descalzas Reales....... D5
10 Museo del Traje....... A1
11 Palacio Real............. B5
12 Plaza de la Paja.........C7
13 Plaza de la Villa C6
14 Plaza de Oriente C5
15 Plaza Mayor............. D6
16 Puerta del Sol E5
17 Real Academia de Bellas Artes de San Fernando........ G5
18 San Nicolás de los Servitas C6
19 Teleférico................. A2
20 Templo de Debod A2
21 Zoo-Aquarium........... A3

Restaurants ▼

1 Casa Botín............... D7
2 Casa Ciriaco...............C6
3 Casa Gerardo C9
4 Casa Lafu C3
5 Casa Paco D7
6 Casa Revuelta........... D7
7 El Landó.................. B7
8 La Bola C4
9 La Hojaldreria G4
10 La Pulpería de Victoria.................... F5
11 La Terraza del Casino de Madrid.............. G5
12 Lambuzo D5
13 Taberna Almendro 13 ...C7
14 Txirimiri C8

Hotels ▼

1 Ateneo Hotel F5
2 Barceló Torre de Madrid..........C2
3 Dear Hotel C2
4 Generator Madrid D3
5 Gran Meliá Palacio de los Duques.............C4
6 The Hat................... D6
7 Hostal Adriano F6
8 Hotel Indigo Madrid D4
9 Hotel Intur Palacio San Martín............... D4
10 Hotel Preciados......... D4
11 Iberostar Las Letras Gran Vía................. G4
12 Liabeny.................... F4
13 Mayerling Hotel..........E7
14 Posada del León de Oro D7
15 Room Mate Laura....... D5
16 Room Mate Mario D4

(Music Museum), the world's largest collection of five-stringed instruments by Antonio Stradivari; the Painting Gallery, with works by Spanish, Flemish, and Italian artists; the Armería Real (Royal Armory), with suits of armor and medieval torture implements; and the Real Oficina de Farmacía (Royal Pharmacy). The palace also takes in the Biblioteca Real (Royal Library), with a first edition of Miguel de Cervantes's *Don Quijote,* and the Real Cocina (Royal Kitchen; tickets sold separately), which occupies 800 square meters and has remained largely unchanged since the late 18th century. ⊠ *Calle Bailén s/n, Palacio* ☎ *91/454–8800* ☑ *From €11* Ⓜ *Ópera.*

Plaza de la Villa
GOVERNMENT BUILDING | Madrid's town council met in the medieval-looking complex here from the Middle Ages until 2009, when it moved to the new city hall headquarters in the Palacio de Cibeles. It now houses municipal offices. The oldest building on the plaza is the **Casa de los Lujanes**—it's the one with the Mudejar tower. Built as a private home in the late 15th century, the house carries the Lujanes crest over the main doorway. Also on the plaza's east end is the brick-and-stone **Casa de la Villa,** built in 1629, a classic example of Madrid design, with clean lines and spire-topped corner towers. Connected by an overhead walkway, the **Casa de Cisneros** was commissioned in 1537 by the nephew of Cardinal Cisneros. It's one of Madrid's rare examples of the flamboyant plateresque style, which has been likened to splashed water. Sadly, none of these landmarks are open to the public. ⊠ *Palacio* Ⓜ *Sol, Ópera.*

Plaza de Oriente
PLAZA | This stately plaza, in front of the Palacio Real, is flanked by massive statues of Spanish monarchs. They were meant to be mounted on the railing on top of the palace, but Queen Isabel of Farnesio, one of the first royals to live in the palace, had them removed because she was afraid their enormous weight would bring the roof down. (At least that's the *official* reason; according to local lore, the queen wanted the statues removed because her own likeness wouldn't have been placed front and center.) A Velázquez drawing of King Felipe IV is the inspiration for the statue in the plaza's center. It's the first equestrian bronze ever cast with a rearing horse. The sculptor, Italian artist Pietro de Tacca, enlisted Galileo Galilei's help in configuring the statue's weight so it wouldn't tip over. ⊠ *Palacio* Ⓜ *Ópera.*

San Nicolás de los Servitas (*Church of St. Nicholas of the Servites*)
RELIGIOUS SITE | There's some debate over whether the oldest church in Madrid once formed part of an Arab mosque. It was more likely built after the Christian Reconquest of Madrid in 1083, but the brickwork and horseshoe arches are evidence that it was crafted by either Mudejars (Moorish workers) or Spaniards well versed in the style. Inside, exhibits detail the Islamic history of early Madrid. ⊠ *Pl. de San Nicolás, Palacio* ☎ *91/559–4064* ☑ *Suggested donation* Ⓜ *Ópera.*

🍴 Restaurants

Casa Ciriaco
$$$ | **SPANISH** | Casa Ciriaco rang in its 90th anniversary in 2019, and its wine cellar is even older, dating to 1897. The Madrid institution is as famous for its callos a la madrileña as it is for *gallina en pepitoria* , an old-school Spanish stew of wine-braised chicken thickened with hard-boiled yolks that's become increasingly hard to find. **Known for:** abuela-approved local comfort food; a neighborhood institution; fame in Spanish literature. Ⓢ *Average main: €23* ⊠ *Calle Mayor 84, Palacio* ☎ *91/548–0620* ⊕ *www.casaciriaco.es.*

Casa Lafu

$$ | **CHINESE** | **FAMILY** | Madrid has a vibrant Chinese community, which means there are noodles to slurp and dumplings to dunk all around town. Casa Lafu stands out for its expertly prepared repertoire of dishes, a veritable taste tour of the enormous country, from Sichuan-style *má là* (spicy) plates to Shanghainese wine-cooked meats and Cantonese dim sum. **Known for:** hot pot; white-tablecloth Chinese cuisine at affordable prices; rare regional specialties. [$] *Average main: €17* ✉ *Calle Flor Baja 1, Palacio* ☎ *91/548–7096* 🌐 *www.casalafu.com* [M] *Santo Domingo.*

Chocolatería Valor

$ | **CAFÉ** | Despite what the ads say, Madrid is not always sunny. If you hit a rainy or chilly day, walk along the western side of the Monasterio de las Descalzas Reales until you reach Chocolatería Valor, an ideal spot to indulge in piping-hot churros dipped in thick hot chocolate. **Known for:** one of the best chocolaterías in town; churros in chocolate; outdoor seating. [$] *Average main: €6* ✉ *Calle Postigo de San Martín 7, Palacio* ☎ *91/899–4062* 🌐 *www.valor.es* [M] *Callao.*

La Bola

$$ | **SPANISH** | La Bola is renowned for its cocido madrileño, a soul-satisfying chickpea and meat stew, and for its decor, which has hardly changed a lick since 1868, when the restaurant was founded. Originally, La Bola served three types of cocido: a simple rendition at noon for blue-collar workers and employees, a chicken-only version at 1 for students, and a multimeat extravaganza at 2 for politicians and journalists. **Known for:** cocido madrileño; 19th-century decor; palace-side dining. [$] *Average main: €22* ✉ *Calle La Bola 5, Palacio* ☎ *91/547–6930* 🌐 *www.labola.es* 💳 *No credit cards* 🕒 *No dinner Sun.* [M] *Ópera.*

🛏 Hotels

Generator Madrid

$ | **HOTEL** | Forget the grotty, dilapidated "youth hostels" from your study-abroad days—Generator Madrid (opened in 2018) might be a budget hotel with shared (up to eight-person) rooms, but it's as much a "hotel" as any of the major brands. **Pros:** bubbly staff and fellow guests; PlayStation in the lobby; USB sockets in rooms. **Cons:** towels (€5 rental) not included in the rate; storing luggage in lockers is exorbitant at €2 per hour; no laundry facilities or kitchen. [$] *Rooms from: €44* ✉ *Calle de San Bernardo 2, Palacio* ☎ *91/047–9801* 🌐 *www.staygenerator.com* 🔑 *129 rooms* 🍴 *No meals* [M] *Callao.*

★ **Gran Meliá Palacio de Los Duques**

$$$$ | **HOTEL** | Spanish-art lovers will geek out at the new Gran Meliá Palacio de los Duques, a luxury hotel tucked behind Gran Vía where reproductions of famous Diego Velázquez paintings feature in every room. **Pros:** Dos Cielos, one of the city's best hotel restaurants; underfloor heating and deep-soak tubs; rooftop pool and bar. **Cons:** rooms are distinctly less attractive than public areas; rooftop often off-limits because of private events; no great views from rooms. [$] *Rooms from: €350* ✉ *Cuesta Santo Domingo 5, Palacio* ☎ *91/276–4747* 🌐 *www.melia.com* 🔑 *180 rooms* 🍴 *No meals* [M] *Santo Domingo.*

Hotel Índigo Madrid

$$ | **HOTEL** | A hip, vibrant hotel off the bustling Gran Vía thoroughfare, Hotel Índigo is best known for its stunning rooftop lounge and outdoor infinity pool, rare features in Madrid. **Pros:** sceney rooftop infinity pool; restaurant that punches above its weight; surprisingly well-equipped gym. **Cons:** interior rooms get little natural light; loses much of its vitality in cold-weather months; decor borders on gaudy. [$] *Rooms from: €170* ✉ *Calle de Silva 6, Palacio*

Did You Know?

In 1997 the Teatro Real returned to its intended use as a dedicated opera house—it was a major European opera venue when it first opened in 1850, but in the interim years it was also used as a parliamentary debate chamber, a dance hall, a temporary war barracks, and even a gunpowder storage facility.

☎ *91/200–8585* 🌐 *www.indigomadrid.com* 🛏 *85 rooms* 🍴 *No meals.*

Hotel Intur Palacio San Martín

$$ | HOTEL | In an unbeatable location across from one of Madrid's most celebrated landmarks (Monasterio de las Descalzas Reales), this newly renovated hotel—once the U.S. embassy and later a luxurious residential building crowded with noblemen—has the architectural bones of a turn-of-the-century mansion with its hand-carved ceilings, marble foyers, and intricate iron balconies. **Pros:** good variety at breakfast; spacious rooms; lobby with glass-domed atrium. **Cons:** bland interiors; bare-bones gym; head-splitting church bells in the morning. [$] *Rooms from: €160* ✉ *Pl. de San Martín 5, Palacio* ☎ *91/701–5000* 🌐 *www.intur.com* 🛏 *94 rooms, 8 suites* 🍴 *No meals* [M] *Ópera, Callao.*

Room Mate Laura

$$ | HOTEL | A quirky, clubby hotel located overlooking Plaza de San Martín near the Royal Theater and Palace, Room Mate Laura feels like a time warp to an IKEA catalog of the early aughts—so thank god the service and amenities are so outstanding. **Pros:** free portable Wi-Fi gadgets; kitchenettes; clean and comfortable. **Cons:** only the best rooms have views of the convent; no restaurant; some bathrooms need to be revamped. [$] *Rooms from: €161* ✉ *Travesía de Trujillos 3, Palacio* ☎ *91/701–1670* 🌐 *www.room-matehotels.com* 🛏 *36 rooms* 🍴 *No meals* [M] *Ópera.*

Room Mate Mario

$$ | HOTEL | In the city center, steps from the Royal Palace and Teatro Real, Mario is small with limited services but a welcome alternative to Madrid's traditional hotel options at a good price. **Pros:** centrally located; good breakfast served until noon; most affordable of the Room Mate cohort in Madrid. **Cons:** no restaurant; cramped entry-level rooms; unremarkable views compared to other Room Mate hotels. [$] *Rooms from: €170* ✉ *Calle Campomanes 4, Palacio* ☎ *91/548–8548* 🌐 *www.room-matehotels.com* 🛏 *57 rooms* 🍴 *Free Breakfast* [M] *Ópera.*

Nightlife

DANCE CLUBS

Cool

DANCE CLUBS | This gritty, Berlin-style underground club hosts techno-driven dance parties on weekend nights for a young, primarily LGBT+ clientele. ✉ *Calle Isabel la Católica 6, Palacio* ☎ *63/459–6212* [M] *Santo Domingo.*

Velvet

DANCE CLUBS | Magical and chameleon-like, thanks to the use of LED lighting and the undulating shapes of the columns and walls, this is the place to go if you want a late-night drink—it opens at 11 and closes at 5:30 am—without the thunder of a full-blown DJ. ✉ *Calle Jacometrezo 6, Palacio* ☎ *63/341–4887* 🌐 *www.velvetdisco.es* [M] *Callao.*

MUSIC CLUBS

★ Café Berlín

MUSIC CLUBS | For a space so small, Café Berlín packs quite the acoustic punch and draws an international, eclectic crowd. Before midnight, catch nightly live music acts in a panoply of styles (flamenco, swing, soul, and more); from around 1 am on, drop in for the disco-inflected DJ sets that ooze good vibes until 6 am. ✉ *Costanilla de los Ángeles 20, Palacio* ☎ *91/559–7429* 🌐 *www.berlincafe.es* [M] *Santo Domingo.*

★ Corral de la Morería

MUSIC CLUBS | A Michelin-starred dinner followed by a world-class flamenco performance in the same building sounds too good to be true, but at Corral de la Morería, the food (Basque with an Andalusian twist) is as invigorating as the twirling and stomping *bailaoras*. Opt for an elegant, market-driven prix-fixe menu to be enjoyed during the show, or splurge on a truly sublime tasting experience at the four-table Gastronómico restaurant that earned the venue its coveted star. Wine pairings, which hinge on rare back-vintage sherries and other *v inos generosos* (fortified wines), are well worth the extra euros. ⊠ *Calle de la Moreria 17, Palacio* ☎ *91/365–8446* Ⓜ *La Latina.*

El Amante

MUSIC CLUBS | Blocks from Plaza Mayor, this might be the closest thing you'll find in Madrid to a posh private New York club. Its creative and lush spaces, two winding floors filled with nooks, host the city's poshest crowds. There's a tough door policy, so be sure to dress to impress (no sneakers allowed, gents). Get here before 1:30 am or be ready to wait in line. ⊠ *Calle Santiago 3, Palacio* ☎ *91/755–4460* Ⓜ *Ópera.*

Marula

MUSIC CLUBS | Popular for its quiet summer terrace under the Puente de Segovia arches, its unbeatable electro-funk mixes, and for staying open into the wee hours, this is a cleverly designed narrow space with lots of illuminated wall art. There's a branch in Barcelona, too. Check the website for concert listings. Live music usually begins at 11 pm. ⊠ *Calle Caños Viejos 3, Palacio* ☎ *91/366–1596* ⊕ *www.marulacafe.com* Ⓜ *La Latina.*

🎭 Performing Arts

Teatro Real

CONCERTS | This resplendent theater is the venue for opera and dance performances. Built in 1850, this neoclassical theater was long a cultural center for madrileño high society. A major restoration project endowed it with golden balconies, plush seats, and state-of-the-art stage equipment. ⊠ *Pl. de Isabel II, Palacio* ☎ *91/516–0660* ⊕ *www.teatro-real.com* Ⓜ *Ópera.*

FLAMENCO

Café de Chinitas

DANCE | This touristy spot fills up fast. Make reservations, because shows often

sell out. The restaurant opens at 8 and there are performances Monday–Saturday at 8:15 and 10:30. ⊠ *Calle Torija 7, Palacio* ☎ *91/559–5135* ⊕ *www.chinitas. com* Ⓜ *Santo Domingo.*

🛍 Shopping

CERAMICS

★ Antigua Casa Talavera

CERAMICS/GLASSWARE | This is the best of Madrid's many ceramics shops. Despite the name, the finest wares sold here are from Manises, near Valencia, but the blue-and-yellow Talavera ceramics are also excellent. All pieces are hand-painted and bear traditional Spanish motifs that have been used for centuries. ⊠ *Calle de Isabel la Católica 2, Palacio* ☎ *91/547–3417* ⊕ *www.antiguacasatalavera.com* Ⓜ *Santo Domingo.*

SPECIALTY STORES

Alambique

SPECIALTY STORES | Amateur and professional cooks will love this terrific little shop (est. 1978) that sells everything from paella pans to earthenware cazuelas to olive-wood cheese boards. Cooking classes (in Spanish) are also available. ⊠ *Pl. de la Encarnación 2, Palacio* ☎ *91/547–4220* ⊕ *www.alambique.com.*

La Latina

Officially part of the Palacio neighborhood, this bustling area bordered by Calle de Segovia to the north; Calle Toledo to the east; Puerta de Toledo to the south; and Calle Bailén, with its imposing Basílica de San Francisco, to the west houses some of the city's oldest buildings, plenty of sloping streets, and an array of unmissable tapas spots—especially on Cava Baja and Cava Alta, and in the area around Plaza de la Paja.

◉ Sights

Basílica de San Francisco el Grande

RELIGIOUS SITE | In 1760 Carlos III built this basilica on the site of a Franciscan convent, allegedly founded by St. Francis of Assisi in 1217. The dome, 108 feet in diameter, is the largest in Spain, even larger than that of St. Paul's in London. The seven main doors, of American walnut, were carved by Casa Juan Guas. Three chapels adjoin the circular church, the most famous being that of **San Bernardino de Siena,** which contains a Goya masterpiece depicting a preaching San Bernardino. The figure standing on the right, not looking up, is a self-portrait of Goya. The 16th-century Gothic choir stalls came from La Cartuja del Paular, in rural Segovia Province. ⊠ *Pl. de San Francisco, La Latina* 🕾 *91/365–3800* 🕾 *€3 guided tour (in Spanish)* ⊗ *Closed Mon. and some Sat.* Ⓜ *Puerta de Toledo, La Latina.*

Cava Baja

NEIGHBORHOOD | Madrid's most popular tapas street is crowded with excellent (if overpriced) tapas bars and traditional *tabernas.* Its lively, and rather touristy, atmosphere spills over onto nearby streets and squares including Almendro, Cava Alta, Plaza del Humilladero, and Plaza de la Paja. Expect full houses and long wait times on weekend nights. ⊠ *La Latina* Ⓜ *La Latina.*

Plaza de la Paja

PLAZA | At the top of the hill, on Costanilla San Andrés, sits the most important square in medieval Madrid. It predates the Plaza Mayor by at least two centuries. The sloped plaza's jewel is the **Capilla del Obispo** (Bishop's Chapel), built between 1520 and 1530, where peasants deposited their tithes, called *diezmas*— one-tenth of their crop. Architecturally the chapel embodies the transition from the blocky Gothic period, which gave the structure its basic shape, to the Renaissance, the source of its decorations. It houses an intricately carved polychrome

altarpiece by Francisco Giralta with scenes from the life of Christ. To visit the chapel (*Tuesday 9:30–12:30, Thursday 4–5:30*) reserve in advance (*91/559–2874* or *reservascapilladelobispo@archimadrid. es*). The chapel is part of the complex of the domed church of San Andrés, one of Madrid's oldest. ⊠ *La Latina* Ⓜ *La Latina.*

🍴 Restaurants

Casa Botín

$$$ | SPANISH | According to *Guinness World Records*, Madrid is home to the world's oldest restaurant, Botín, established in 1725 and a favorite of Ernest Hemingway (the final scene of *The Sun Also Rises* is set in this very place). A menu must, by all accounts, is the cochinillo asado, which is stuffed with aromatics, doused with wine, and crisped in the original wood-burning oven. **Known for:** being the world's oldest restaurant; roast lamb and suckling pig; roving traditional musical groups. Ⓢ *Average main: €25* ⊠ *Calle Cuchilleros 17, La Latina* 🕾 *91/366–4217* ⊕ *www.botin.es* Ⓜ *Tirso de Molina.*

★ Casa Gerardo

$$ | TAPAS | Huge *tinajas*, clay vessels once filled to the brim with bulk wine (yet now defunct), sit behind the bar at this raucous, no-frills bodega specializing in Spanish cheese and charcuterie. Ask the waiters what they've been drinking and eating lately, and order precisely that. **Known for:** unforgettable old-world atmosphere; wide selection of wines and charcuterie; frazzled yet friendly staff. Ⓢ *Average main: €16* ⊠ *Calle Calatrava 21, La Latina* 🕾 *91/221–9660* Ⓜ *La Latina.*

Casa Paco

$$$ | STEAKHOUSE | Packed with madrileños downing Valdepeñas wine, this Castilian tavern, with its zinc-top bar and tiled walls, wouldn't have looked out of place a century ago; indeed, it opened in 1933. Warm up with the city's best rendition of sopa de ajo, garlic soup crowned

with a poached egg, and then feast on thick slabs of Spanish beef *chuletones* , served medium rare and sizzling. **Known for:** ornate wooden zinc-topped bar; rustic Valdepeñas wine; city's best garlic soup. $ *Average main: €23* ⊠ *Pl. Puerta Cerrada 11, La Latina* ☎ *91/366–3166* ⊕ *www. casapaco1933.es* ⟳ *Closed Mon. No dinner Sun.* Ⓜ *Tirso de Molina.*

★ Casa Revuelta

$ | SPANISH | There's a cod—yes, cod—war in Madrid between Casa Lavra and Casa Revulta: Both claim to make the city's best *pincho de bacalao*, or battered salt cod. As locals will tell you, Revuelta's rendition is far and away the superior choice—provided you're successful at elbowing your way to the 1930s-era bar. **Known for:** battered salt cod canapés; midmorning vermú (vermouth) rush; time-warp decor. $ *Average main: €5* ⊠ *Calle Latoneros 3, La Latina* ☎ *91/366–3332* ⟳ *Closed Mon. No dinner Sun.* ▭ *No credit cards.*

El Landó

$$$ | SPANISH | This *castizo* ("rootsy") restaurant, with dark wood-paneled walls lined with bottles of wine, serves classic Spanish food like *huevos estrellados* (fried eggs with potatoes and sausage), grilled meats, a good selection of fish (sea bass, haddock, grouper) with many different sauces, and steak tartare. Check out the pictures of famous celebrities who've eaten at this typically noisy landmark; they line the staircase that leads to the main dining area. **Known for:** castizo ambience; huevos estrellados; impeccably cooked seafood. $ *Average main: €26* ⊠ *Pl. Gabriel Miró 8, La Latina* ☎ *91/366–7681* ⟳ *No dinner Sun.* Ⓜ *La Latina.*

Taberna Almendro 13

$ | TAPAS | Getting a weekend seat in this rustic old favorite is a feat, but drop by any other time and you'll be served ample, stick-to-your-ribs *raciones* (shared plates) such as *roscas* (hot bread rounds filled with cured meats), *huevos rotos*

(fried eggs over homemade potato chips), and *revueltos* (scrambled eggs; opt for the habanero with fava beans and black pudding). **Known for:** roscas sandwiches; greasy-spoon tapas (in the best way); old-timey decor. $ *Average main: €13* ⊠ *Calle del Almendro 13, La Latina* ☎ *91/365–4252* ⊕ *www.almendro13.com* ▭ *No credit cards* Ⓜ *La Latina.*

Txirimiri

$$ | TAPAS | One of four branches in a beloved local chain, this perennially packed Basque tapas spot is famous for its Unai slider, fried in tempura and topped with a boletus sauce, and killer Spanish omelet. Arrive early and you may be lucky enough to snag one of the tables in the back. **Known for:** tortilla española; nueva cocina tapas; sardine-can digs. $ *Average main: €18* ⊠ *Calle Humilladero 6, La Latina* ☎ *91/364–1196* ⊕ *www.txirimiri.es* ▭ *No credit cards* Ⓜ *La Latina.*

Hotels

★ The Hat

$ | HOTEL | The Hat epitomizes the fast-growing category of "designer hostels," affordable properties geared toward the millennial set with sleek multiperson (and private) rooms, bumping weekend events, and generous breakfasts. **Pros:** rooftop bar; steps from the Plaza Mayor; bountiful breakfasts. **Cons:** hotel guests not prioritized on rooftop, which fills up fast; some rooms are dark; location means tourists are everywhere. $ *Rooms from: €45* ⊠ *Calle Imperial 9, La Latina* ☎ *91/772–8572* ⊕ *www. thehatmadrid.com* ⤸ *42 rooms* ⦿ *Free Breakfast* Ⓜ *Tirso de Molina.*

Posada del León de Oro

$$ | HOTEL | More like a village guesthouse than a metropolitan hotel, this refurbished late-19th-century property was built atop the remains of a stone wall that encircled the city in the 12th century, which you can see through glass

floor panels at the hotel entrance and in the restaurant. **Pros:** unbeatable location; restaurant with more than 300 Spanish wines; high ceilings with exposed wood beams. **Cons:** rooms facing the courtyard are quite small; late-night noise on weekends; cramped entry-level rooms. ⓢ *Rooms from: €160* ✉ *Calle Cava Baja 12, La Latina* ☎ *91/119–1494* ⊕ *www. posadadelleondeoro.com* ⬫ *27 rooms* ⑪ *No meals* Ⓜ *La Latina.*

Nightlife

BARS AND CAFÉS
Delic

CAFES—NIGHTLIFE | This warm, inviting café is an all-hours hangout for Madrid's trendy crowd. Homesick travelers will find comfort in Delic's carrot cake, brownies, and pumpkin pie (seasonal), while low-key revelers will appreciate the bar's coziness and late hours (open until 2:30 on weekends). ✉ *Pl. de la Paja, Costanilla de San Andrés 14, La Latina* ☎ *91/364–5450* ⊕ *www.delic.es* ⊘ *Closed Mon.* Ⓜ *La Latina.*

El Viajero

BARS/PUBS | You can find fine modern raciones here (the ultracreamy burrata stands out), but this place is better known among madrileños for its middle-floor bar, which fills up with a cocktail-drinking after-work crowd, and its rooftop terrace. Beware of the 10% surcharge that comes with outdoor dining. ✉ *Pl. de la Cebada 11, La Latina* ☎ *91/366–9064* ⊕ *www.elviajeromadrid. com* ⊘ *Closed Sun. night and Mon.* Ⓜ *La Latina.*

 Performing Arts

FLAMENCO
Las Carboneras

DANCE | A prime flamenco showcase, this venue rivals Corral de la Morería as the best option in terms of quality and price. Performers here include both the young, less commercial artists and more

Mercado de San Miguel

Adjacent to the Plaza Mayor, this "gastronomic market" is a feast for the senses. Its bustling interior—a mixture of tapas spots and immaculately arranged grocery stalls—sits beneath a fin-de-siècle glass dome reinforced by elaborate wrought iron. Enjoy a glass of wine and maybe a snack here, but save your appetite: the market, as gorgeous as it may be, has become an overpriced tourist trap in recent years, and most locals have stopped going altogether, but don't let that stop you! ⊕ *www.mercadodesanmiguel.es*

established stars on tour. The show is staged at 8:30 and 10:30 Monday–Thursday and at 8:30 and 11 Friday and Saturday. ✉ *Pl. del Conde de Miranda 1, La Latina* ☎ *91/542–8677* ⊕ *www. tablaolascarboneras.com* ⊘ *Closed Sun.* Ⓜ *La Latina, Ópera.*

🛍 Shopping

CRAFTS AND DESIGN
★ **Cocol**

CRAFTS | There's no better shop in Madrid for top-quality Spanish artisan wares. The shelves in this tiny independently owned boutique off Plaza de la Paja are lined with everything from exquisite Andalusian pottery to hand-sewn blankets, antique esparto baskets, and leather soccer balls. ✉ *Costanilla de San Andrés 18, La Latina* ☎ *91/919–6770* ⊕ *www. cocolmadrid.es* Ⓜ *La Latina.*

Sol

This neighborhood, built in the 16th century around the Puerta del Sol, used to mark the city's geographic center, which today sits a tad to its east. Sol encompasses, among other sites, the monumental Plaza Mayor and the popular pedestrian shopping area around Callao. It remains the nerve center of Madrid.

◉ Sights

★ Plaza Mayor

PLAZA | Austere, grand, and sometimes surprisingly quiet compared to other plazas in the city, this public square, finished in 1619 under Felipe III—whose equestrian statue stands in the center—is one of the largest in Europe, measuring 360 feet by 300 feet. It's seen it all: autos-da-fé (public burnings of heretics), the canonization of saints, criminal executions, royal marriages, bullfights (until 1847), and all manner of other events. The plot was once occupied by a city market, and many of the surrounding streets retain names of the trades and foods once headquartered there (e.g., Knife Makers' Street, Lettuce Street). The plaza's oldest building, Casa de la Panadería (Bakery House), has brightly painted murals and gray spires; it is now the tourist office. Opposite sits Casa de la Carnicería (Butcher Shop), now a police station. The plaza is closed to motorized traffic, making it a pleasant if touristy spot to enjoy a cup of coffee. ⊠ Sol Ⓜ Sol.

Puerta del Sol

PLAZA | Crowded with locals, tourists, hawkers, and street performers—and the site of many important protests in recent decades—the Puerta del Sol is the nerve center of Madrid. The city's main metro interchange, the largest in the world, is below. A brass plaque in the sidewalk on the south side of the plaza marks Kilometer 0, the point from which all distances in Spain are measured. The restored 1756

Gourmet Experience Callao 🍴

On the rooftop of El Corte Inglés, Spain's largest department store, there's a gourmet food court with some of the best views in the city. Grab a couple of tapas and a glass of wine here after perusing the shops around Callao. The space features outposts of well-known Spanish restaurants like La Máquina (seafood) and Asador Imanol (pinchos) as well as international options (hamburgers, Mexican, and Chinese, for example). Take the second entrance to El Corte Inglés as you're walking down Callao on Calle Carmen and across from Fnac.

French-neoclassical building near the marker now houses the offices of the regional government, but during Franco's reign, it was the headquarters of his secret police and is still known colloquially as the Casa de los Gritos (House of Screams). Across the square are a bronze statue of Madrid's official symbol, a bear with a madroño (strawberry tree), and a statue of King and Mayor Carlos III on horseback. ⊠ Sol Ⓜ Sol.

Real Academia de Bellas Artes de San Fernando (St. Ferdinand Royal Academy of Fine Arts)

MUSEUM | Designed by José Benito de Churriguera in the waning baroque years of the early 18th century, this museum showcases 500 years of Spanish painting, from José Ribera and Bartolomé Esteban Murillo to Joaquín Sorolla and Ignacio Zuloaga. The tapestries along the stairways are stunning. The gallery displays paintings up to the 18th century, including some by Goya. Worthwhile guided tours are available on Tuesday, Thursday, and Friday at 11, except during August. The same building houses the

The Puerta del Sol, Madrid's central transportation hub, is sure to be passed through by every visitor to the city.

Instituto de Calcografía (Prints Institute), which sells limited-edition prints from original plates engraved by Spanish artists. Check the website for classical concerts and literary events in the small upstairs hall. ⊠ *Calle de Alcalá 13, Sol* ☎ *91/524–0864* ⊕ *www.realacademia-bellasartessanfernando.com* ✉ *€8 (free Wed.)* ⊘ *Closed Mon.* Ⓜ *Sol.*

🍴 Restaurants

La Hojaldrería

$$ | CAFÉ | A veritable temple of all things flaky and buttery (*hojaldre* is Spanish for "puff pastry"), this new concept café by Javier Bonet (the brains behind the buzzy Sala de Despiece and Muta) is a sophisticated spot to enjoy a fancy pastry and a well-made cappuccino at breakfast or innovative bistro fare at lunch and dinner.
Known for: exquisite viennoiserie; throwback rococo decor; gourmet sandwiches. Ⓢ *Average main: €16* ⊠ *Calle Virgen de los Peligros 8, Sol* ☎ *91/059–5193* ⊕ *www.hojaldreria.com* ⊘ *No dinner Sun.* Ⓜ *Sevilla.*

La Pulpería de Victoria

$$ | SPANISH | FAMILY | A modern, urban interpretation of a traditional Galician *pulpería* (octopus restaurant), this casual restaurant specializes in *polbo à feira*, boiled octopus cut into coins, drizzled with olive oil, and dusted with smoked paprika. Pair with an icy glass of Albariño and a heap of blistered Padrón peppers.
Known for: perfectly executed Galician-style octopus; ocean-fresh shellfish; great variety of Galician wines. Ⓢ *Average main: €16* ⊠ *Calle de La Victoria 2, Sol* ☎ *91/080–4929* ⊕ *www.pulperiade-victoria.com* Ⓜ *Sol.*

La Terraza del Casino de Madrid

$$$$ | ECLECTIC | This award-winning restaurant by chef Paco Roncero is in an aerie above one of Madrid's oldest, most exclusive gentlemen's clubs but its recently revamped dining room is a vivid and colorful display of youthful levity. Awaken your palate with mousses, foams, and liquid jellies, or indulge in gustatory experiments in flavor, texture, and temperature such as the gazpacho

"sandwich," assembled tableside, or the uni enriched with beef tallow. **Known for:** "thousand-year-old" olive oil; two Michelin stars; foams, jellies, and tweezed garnishes. $ *Average main: €38* ⊠ *Calle Alcalá 15, Sol* ☎ *91/521–8700* ⊕ *www. casinodemadrid.es* ⊘ *Closed Sun. and Mon.* 🎩 *Jacket required* Ⓜ *Sol.*

Lambuzo

$$ | **SPANISH** | **FAMILY** | This laid-back Andalusian tavern, one of three locations in the city, embodies the soul and joyful spirit of that sunny region. Let cheerful waiters help guide you through the extensive menu, which includes fried seafood, unconventional *croquetas* (croquettes, here flecked with garlicky shrimp, for instance), and more filling dishes like cuttlefish meatballs and seared Barbate tuna loin. **Known for:** sunny Andalusian vibe; an ocean's worth of seafood dishes; chatty owners. $ *Average main: €16* ⊠ *Calle de las Conchas 9, Sol* ☎ *91/143–4862* ⊕ *www.barlambuzo.com* ⊘ *Closed Mon. No dinner Sun.* Ⓜ *Ópera.*

Hotels

Ateneo Hotel

$ | **HOTEL** | This clean and economical property is set in an 18th-century building that was once home to the Ateneo, a club founded in 1835 to promote freedom of thought. **Pros:** sizeable rooms; triple and quadruple rooms available; some rooms have skylights and balconies. **Cons:** safe yet slightly sketchy street; noisy area; dated decor. $ *Rooms from: €120* ⊠ *Calle de la Montera 22, Sol* ☎ *91/521–2012* ⊕ *www.hotel-ateneo. com* ⟿ *44 rooms* ⦿ *Free Breakfast* Ⓜ *Gran Vía, Sol.*

Hostal Adriano

$ | **HOTEL** | On a street with dozens of bland competitors a couple of blocks from Sol, this budget hotel stands out for its price and quality. **Pros:** friendly service; good value; charming touches. **Cons:** shares the building with other hostales;

reception desk not staffed 24 hours; street noise. $ *Rooms from: €75* ⊠ *Calle de la Cruz 26, 4th fl., Sol* ☎ *91/521–1339* ⊕ *www.hostaladriano.com* ⟿ *22 rooms* ⦿ *No meals* Ⓜ *Sol.*

Hotel Preciados

$$ | **HOTEL** | In a 19th-century building on the quieter edge of one of Madrid's main shopping districts, Preciados is a charming midrange hotel ideal for travelers who value space and comfort. **Pros:** conveniently located; complimentary minibar (you read that correctly!); valet parking a steal at €19.50 per day. **Cons:** expensive breakfast; chaotic street; dated decor. $ *Rooms from: €173* ⊠ *Calle Preciados 37, Sol* ☎ *91/454–4400* ⊕ *www.preciadoshotel.com* ⟿ *101 rooms* ⦿ *No meals* Ⓜ *Callao.*

★ Iberostar Las Letras Gran Vía

$$$ | **HOTEL** | A modern, clubby hotel on the stately avenue of Gran Vía, Iberostar Las Letras is a welcoming oasis from the area's constant hubbub of tourists and shoppers. **Pros:** state-of-the-art gym; many rooms have balconies; happening rooftop bar. **Cons:** finicky a/c; no spa; awkward bathroom design. $ *Rooms from: €220* ⊠ *Gran Vía 11, Sol* ☎ *91/523–7980* ⊕ *www.hoteldelasletras.com* ⟿ *110 rooms* ⦿ *No meals* Ⓜ *Banco de España.*

Liabeny

$$ | **HOTEL** | This classically decorated hotel situated between Gran Vía and Puerta del Sol has large, comfortable carpeted rooms with striped fabrics and big windows. **Pros:** spacious bathrooms; near Princesa shopping area; upscale Castilian restaurant. **Cons:** small rooms; crowded, noisy neighborhood; stairs to access public areas. $ *Rooms from: €140* ⊠ *Calle de la Salud 3, Sol* ☎ *91/531–9000* ⊕ *www. liabeny.es* ⟿ *220 rooms* Ⓜ *Sol.*

Mayerling Hotel

$ | **HOTEL** | Sleek minimalism at just the right value can be found on this former textile wholesaler's premises, now a 22-room boutique hotel a few blocks off

Did You Know?

The Gran Vía, one of modern Madrid's main arteries, was devised by urban planners in the mid-19th century; the grand buildings that line it are home to hotels, shops, and restaurants.

Plaza Mayor and Plaza Santa Ana. Serene (if slightly clinical) white rooms come in three sizes—standard, superior, and triple—and are decorated with colorful headboards, charcoal valances, and small open closets. **Pros:** some rooms accommodate up to three people; 24-hour "help yourself" bar with coffee, snacks, and juices; prime location. **Cons:** rooms are smallish by U.S. standards; white walls show smudges; no restaurant or gym. $ *Rooms from: €120* ⊠ *Calle del Conde de Romanones 6, Sol* ☎ *91/420–1580* ⊕ *www.mayerlinghotel.com* ⌁ *22 rooms* ❘○❘ *No meals* Ⓜ *Tirso de Molina.*

Nightlife

CAFÉS
Chocolatería San Ginés
CAFES—NIGHTLIFE | FAMILY | San Ginés is to Madrid what Café du Monde is to New Orleans. A national sensation, for generations this 19th-century café has been frying spirals of piping-hot churros and *porras* (a churro's larger cousin—try them) day and night. Dunk your breakfast in *café con leche* or Cola Cao (Spanish chocolate milk)—the melted dark chocolate, which tastes processed, isn't what it used to be. ⊠ *Pasadizo de San Ginés, Sol* ⌖ *Enter by Arenal 11* ☎ *91/365–6546* ⊕ *www.chocolateriasangines.com* Ⓜ *Sol.*

DANCE CLUBS
★ Cha Chá the Club
DANCE CLUBS | For trendy twentysomethings, there's no buzzier place to be on Friday nights than this converted multifloor movie theater that erupts into epic DJ-fueled parties. Expect a mixed, LGBTQ-friendly crowd. Buy tickets online ahead of time. ⊠ *Calle de Alcalá 20, Sol* ⊕ *www.xceed.me/tickets-club/madrid/cha-cha-the-club* Ⓜ *Sol.*

Cocó Madrid
DANCE CLUBS | This club, with its wild color palette, huge dance floor, and better-than-average cocktails, is best known for its Mondo Disko nights (Thursday and Saturday) that rage until dawn with house and electronic music often by international DJs. ⊠ *Calle Alcalá 20, Sol* ☎ *91/445–7938* ⊕ *www.web-mondo.com* ◔ *Closed Mon.–Wed.* Ⓜ *Sevilla.*

El Sol
DANCE CLUBS | Madrid's oldest discoteca continues to win over its patrons with all-night dancing to live music (around midnight Thursday–Saturday) and DJ sets. ⊠ *Calle Jardines 3, Sol* ☎ *91/532–6490* ⊕ *www.elsolmad.com* ◔ *Closed Mon.* Ⓜ *Gran Vía.*

Joy Eslava
DANCE CLUBS | A downtown club in a converted theater, this is a long-established standby that attracts a varied, somewhat bourgeois crowd of locals and tourists. ⊠ *Calle del Arenal 11, Sol* ☎ *91/366–3733* ⊕ *www.joy-eslava.com* Ⓜ *Sol.*

MUSIC CLUBS
Costello
MUSIC CLUBS | A multiuse space that combines a café and a lounge, this place caters to a relaxed, conversational crowd; the bottom floor is suited to partygoers, with the latest in live and club music. On weekdays, there are theater and stand-up comedy shows. Check the website for events and ticket prices. ⊠ *Calle Caballero de Gracia 10, Sol* ☎ *91/522–1815* ⊕ *www.costelloclub.com* Ⓜ *Gran Vía.*

🎭 Performing Arts

Círculo de Bellas Artes
CONCERTS | Concerts, theater, dance performances, art exhibitions, and events are all part of the calendar here. There is also an extremely popular (and wildly overpriced) café and a rooftop restaurant-bar with great views of the city. ⊠ *Calle del Marqués de Casa Riera 2, Sol* ☎ *90/242–2442* ⊕ *www.circulobellasartes.com* Ⓜ *Banco de España.*

Shopping

CLOTHING

Capas Seseña

CLOTHING | Seseña is the oldest cape tailor in the world. Since 1901, this family-run business, now in its fourth generation, has outfitted the likes of Picasso, Hemingway, and Michael Jackson in traditional merino wool and velvet capes, some lined with red satin. ✉ *Calle de la Cruz 23, Sol* ☎ *91/531–6840* ⊕ *www. sesena.com* ⊘ *Closed Sun.* Ⓜ *Puerta del Sol.*

CRAFTS AND DESIGN

El Arco Artesanía

CRAFTS | El Arco sells contemporary, whimsical handicrafts from all over Spain, including modern ceramics, handblown glassware, jewelry, and leather items. ✉ *Pl. Mayor 9, Sol* ☎ *91/365–2680* ⊕ *www.artesaniaelarco.com* Ⓜ *Sol.*

Taller Puntera

SHOES/LUGGAGE/LEATHER GOODS | You can watch the artisans at work at this inviting atelier-boutique hybrid situated steps from the Plaza Mayor. Regardless of what catches your eye—a leather card holder, handbag, or perhaps a handbound notebook—you'll be pleasantly surprised by the affordable prices. ✉ *Pl. del Conde de Barajas 4, Sol* ☎ *91/364–2926* ⊕ *www.puntera.com* ⊘ *Closed Sun.*

Moncloa

A large neighborhood extending to the northwest of Madrid, Moncloa includes high-class residential areas, such as Puerta de Hierro and Aravaca; more urban ones such as Argüelles, teeming with college students and budget bars; and wonderfully scenic parks including Casa de Campo, Parque del Oeste (with the Templo de Debod gardens), a section of Madrid Río, and Dehesa de la Villa.

Sights

Ermita de San Antonio de la Florida (*Goya's Tomb*)

MUSEUM | Built between 1792 and 1798 by the Italian architect Francisco Fontana, this neoclassical chapel was financed by King Carlos IV, who also commissioned Goya to paint the vaults and the main dome: it took him 120 days to fully depict events of the 13th century (St. Anthony of Padua resurrecting a dead man) as if they had happened five centuries later, with naturalistic images never used before to paint religious scenes. Opposite the image of the frightening dead man on the main dome, Goya painted himself as a man covered with a black cloak. Goya, who died in Bordeaux in 1828, is buried here (without his head, because it was stolen in France) under an unadorned gravestone. ✉ *Glorieta de San Antonio de la Florida 5, Moncloa* ☎ *91/542–0722* ⊕ *www.sanantoniodelaflorida.es* 🎫 *Free* ⊘ *Closed Mon.* Ⓜ *Príncipe Pío.*

Faro de Moncloa

BUILDING | This UFO-like tower is 360 feet tall and an excellent viewpoint from which to gaze at some of the city's most outstanding buildings including the Palacio Real, Palacio de Cibeles (city hall), the four skyscrapers to the north, and up to 50 landmarks for which you'll find descriptions in English and Spanish. ✉ *Av. Arco de la Victoria 2, Moncloa* ⊕ *www.esmadrid.com/en* 🎫 *€3* Ⓜ *Moncloa.*

Museo del Traje (*Costume Museum*)

MUSEUM | This museum traces the evolution of dress in Spain, from old royal burial garments (very few of which remain) to French fashion pieces of Felipe V's reign and the haute couture creations of Balenciaga and Pertegaz. Explanatory notes are in English, and the museum has a superb restaurant, Café de Oriente, overlooking the gardens that specializes in modern Spanish fare. ✉ *Av.*

Juan de Herrera 2, Moncloa ☎ *91/550–4700* 🌐 *museodeltraje.mcu.es* 🎫 *€3 (free Sat. after 2:30 and Sun.)* 🕒 *Closed Mon.* [M] *Ciudad Universitaria.*

Teleférico

TRANSPORTATION SITE (AIRPORT/BUS/FERRY/TRAIN) | FAMILY | Kids and adults alike appreciate the sweeping views from this retro cable car, which takes you 2.5 km (1.6 miles) from the Rosaleda gardens in the Parque del Oeste to the center of Casa de Campo in about 10 minutes. If you're feeling active, take the (very) long hike to the top and ride the car down, or you can find well-marked trails and primo picnic spots at the top. **■TIP→ This is not the best way to get to the zoo and theme park, located approximately 2 km (1 mile) from the drop-off point in Casa de Campo. You're better off riding the Teléferico out and back, then taking the bus to the zoo.** ✉ *Estación Terminal Teleférico, Paseo de Pintor Rosales, at C. Marqués de Urquijo, Moncloa* ☎ *91/541–1118* 🌐 *www.teleferi-comadrid.es* 🎫 *From €5* [M] *Arguelles.*

Templo de Debod

RELIGIOUS SITE | It's not every day that you can marvel at a fully reconstructed ancient Egyptian temple from the 4th century BC, but thanks to the Egyptian government, which bequeathed the edifice to the Spanish government in 1968 for its assistance with the construction of the Aswan Dam, it's free for the public to appreciate. Visit at sunset and watch as the day's last light radiates off the timeworn stones. The interior of the temple is closed until further notice. ✉ *Paseo del Pintor Rosales, Moncloa* ☎ *91/765–1008* 🎫 *Free* [M] *Pl. de España, Ventura Rodríguez.*

Zoo-Aquarium

ZOO | FAMILY | Madrid's zoo-aquarium houses one of Europe's largest variety of animals (including rarities such as an albino tiger) that are grouped according to their geographical origin. It also has a dolphinarium and a wild bird sanctuary that hold entertaining exhibitions twice a day on weekdays and more often on weekends—check times on arrival and show up early to get a good seat. **■TIP→ Although the nearest metro stop is Casa de Campo, it's best reached via the Príncipe Pío stop, then Bus No. 33.** ✉ *Casa de Campo s/n, Moncloa* ☎ *91/154–7479* 🌐 *www.zoomadrid.com* 🎫 *€24* [M] *Casa de Campo; Príncipe Pío, then Bus No. 33.*

Hotels

★ Barceló Torre de Madrid

$$$ | HOTEL | A jewel box of glowing lights, harlequin furniture, and gilded mirrors, the soaring Barceló Torre de Madrid is the trendiest hotel in town—and one of the newest, opened in February 2017. **Pros:** cutting-edge design by local artists; offers experiences with local influencers; excellent Somos restaurant. **Cons:** certain bathrooms offer questionable privacy; some minor technical foibles; still ironing out kinks in service. [$] *Rooms from: €210* ✉ *Pl. de España 18, Moncloa* ☎ *91/524–2339* 🌐 *www.barcelo.com* 🛏 *256 rooms* 🍴 *No meals* [M] *Plaza de España.*

Dear Hotel

$$ | HOTEL | On Gran Vía overlooking the tree-lined Plaza de España, Dear Hotel is a sleek urban property designed by Tarruella Trenchs Studio, the firm behind such lauded projects as H10 La Mimosa hotel in Barcelona and La Bien Aparecida restaurant in Madrid. **Pros:** all rooms face out; swanky rooftop bar; Scandy-chic decor. **Cons:** tiny pool; no gym or spa; cramped lobby. [$] *Rooms from: €160* ✉ *Gran Vía 80, Moncloa* ☎ *91/412–3200* 🌐 *www.dearhotelmadrid.com* 🛏 *162 rooms* 🍴 *No meals* [M] *Plaza de España.*

Barrio de las Letras

The Barrio de las Letras, long favored by tourists for its charming buildings and mix of historic and trendy bars and restaurants, is named for the many writers and playwrights from the Spanish

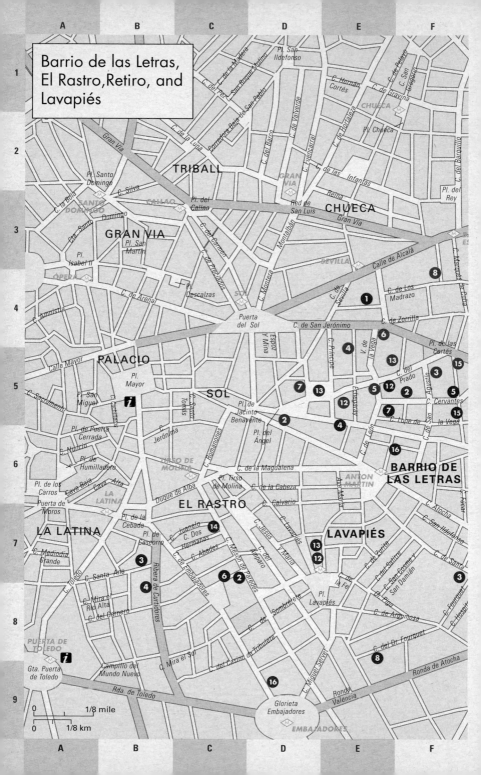

Barrio de las Letras,
El Rastro, Retiro, and
Lavapiés

Sights ▼

1 CaixaForum.............. G6
2 Casa Museo Lope de Vega F5
3 Centro de Arte Reina Sofía F7
4 El Rastro B8
5 Estación de Atocha..... H8
6 Museo del Prado G5
7 Museo Nacional de Artes Decorativas.....I4
8 Museo Naval............ H4
9 Museo Thyssen-Bornemisza... G5
10 Parque del Buen Retiro................I5
11 Plaza de Cibeles G3
12 Plaza de Lavapiés D7
13 Plaza de Santa Ana.... D5
14 Real Fábrica de Tapices.................I8
15 Real Jardín Botánico... H6
16 Tabacalera D9

Hotels ▼

1 AC Palacio del Retiro.....I4
2 Catalonia Puerta del Sol D5
3 DoubleTree by Hilton Madrid-Prado............ F5
4 Gran Hotel Inglés E5
5 Hotel Catalonia Las Cortes E5
6 Hotel Urban............... E4
7 ME by Meliá Madrid.... D5
8 NH Collection Madrid Suecia..................... F4
9 NH Collection Paseo del Prado G5
10 Only YOU Atocha I8
11 Radisson Blu G6
12 Room Mate Alicia........ E5
13 Suite Prado............... E5
14 Urban Sea Atocha 113............... G7
15 Westin Palace F5

Restaurants ▼

1 AskuaBarra............... E4
2 Baobab................... C7
3 Bar Santurce............ B7
4 Casa Alberto E6
5 Cervecería Cervantes... F5
6 El Rincón de Marco C7
7 Gofio...................... E5
8 Hola Coffee............... E9
9 Horcher I3
10 La Castela I4
11 La Catapa I4
12 La Huerta de Tudela..... E5
13 Melo's.................... D7
14 Taberna de Antonio Sanchez.................C7
15 Taberna de la Dolores... F5
16 TriCiclo.................... F6

Golden Age (16th and 17th centuries) who lived within a few blocks of Plaza de Santa Ana. Once a shelter to *los madrileños castizos*—the word *castizo* roughly translates to "authentic"—it is now the favored living area of Spanish and international yuppies. Calle de las Huertas (full of bars and clubs) is pedestrian-only, making the neighborhood even more attractive for walking around and hobnobbing with locals.

Sights

CaixaForum

MUSEUM | Swiss architects Jacques Herzog and Pierre de Meuron, who transformed a former London power station into that city's Tate Modern, performed a similar feat here. Their conversion of this early-20th-century power station has created a stunning arts complex fit to become the fourth point in Madrid's former triangle of great art institutions—the Prado, the Reina Sofía, and the Thyssen-Bornemisza museums. Belonging to one of the country's wealthiest foundations (La Caixa), the structure seems to float on the sloped public plaza, with a tall vertical garden designed by French botanist Patrick Blanc on its northern side contrasting with a geometric rust-color roof. Inside, the huge exhibition halls display ancient as well as contemporary art, including a sample of La Caixa's own collection. The restaurant on the fourth floor has good views. Visits are by online appointment only. ⊠ *Paseo del Prado 36, Barrio de las Letras* ☎ *91/330–7300* ⊕ *www.caixaforum.es* ⚏ *€3* Ⓜ *Atocha.*

Casa Museo Lope de Vega

HOUSE | A contemporary and adversary of Cervantes, Lope de Vega (1562–1635) wrote some 1,800 plays and enjoyed great success during his lifetime. His former home is now a museum with an intimate look into a bygone era: everything from the whale-oil lamps and candles to the well in the tiny garden and the pans used to warm the bedsheets brings you closer to the great dramatist. There is a 35-minute guided tour in English starting every half an hour (reservations are necessary, either by phone or email) that runs through the playwright's professional and personal life—including his lurid love life—and touches on 17th-century traditions. ⊠ *Calle Cervantes 11, Barrio de las Letras* ☎ *91/429–9216* ⊕ *www.casamuseolopedevega.org* ⚏ *Free* ⊘ *Closed Mon.* ☞ *Advance booking by phone or email required* Ⓜ *Antón Martin, Sevilla.*

★ Museo Thyssen-Bornemisza

MUSEUM | Opened in 1992, the Thyssen occupies the spacious salmon-painted galleries of the late-18th-century Villahermosa Palace. Its ambitious collection of almost 1,000 paintings traces the history of Western art with examples from every important movement, from the 13th-century Italian Gothic through 20th-century American pop art. The works were gathered from the 1920s to the 1980s by Swiss industrialist Baron Hans Heinrich Thyssen-Bornemisza and his father. The baron donated the entire collection to Spain in 1993, and a renovation in 2004 increased the number of paintings on display to include the baroness's personal collection (considered of lesser quality). Critics have described the museum's paintings as the minor works of major artists and the major works of minor artists, but the collection still traces the development of Western humanism as no other in the world. It includes works by Hans Holbein, Gilbert Stuart, many impressionists and postimpressionists, and a number of German expressionist paintings. ⊠ *Paseo del Prado 8, Barrio de las Letras* ☎ *91/369–0151* ⊕ *www.museothyssen.org* ⚏ *From €13* Ⓜ *Banco de España.*

Plaza de Santa Ana

PLAZA | This plaza was the heart of the theater district in the 17th century—the Golden Age of Spanish literature—and is now one of Madrid's many thumping

The vertical outdoor garden is a stunning element of the CaixaForum cultural center. The sculpture in front of the building is changed periodically.

nightlife centers. A statue of 17th-century playwright Pedro Calderón de la Barca faces the **Teatro Español,** where playwrights such as Lope de Vega, Tirso de Molina, Pedro Calderón de la Barca, and Ramón del Valle-Inclán released some of their plays. Opposite the theater, beside the ME by Meliá hotel, is the diminutive **Plaza del Ángel,** with one of Madrid's best jazz clubs, **Café Central. Cervecería Alemana,** a favorite haunt of Hemingway, is on Plaza Santa Ana and is worth a visit for its fried calamari (always fresh, never frozen) alone. ⊠ *Barrio de las Letras* Ⓜ *Sevilla.*

🍴 Restaurants

AskuaBarra

$$$ | **SPANISH** | This austere yet polished restaurant, with about 10 tables, has a meat-focused menu with highlights like roasted bone marrow with cilantro salad, grilled lamb sweetbreads, and an outstanding steak tartare. **Known for:** butter-smooth steak tartare; eclectic offal dishes; cozy digs. Ⓢ *Average main: €23*

⊠ *Calle Arlabán 7, Barrio de las Letras* ☎ *91/593–7507* ⊕ *www.askuabarra.com* ⊙ *Closed Sun.* Ⓜ *Sevilla.*

★ Casa Alberto

$$ | **SPANISH** | Enter through the firetruck-red facade of this 193-year-old bar and restaurant and be blown away by impeccably executed fried *bacalao* (cod), croquetas, meatballs, oxtail, and more. **Known for:** old-world decor; fantastic traditional tapas; surprisingly reasonable prices. Ⓢ *Average main: €18* ⊠ *Calle Huertas 18, Barrio de las Letras* ☎ *91/429–9356* ⊕ *www.casaalberto.es* ⊙ *Closed Mon.* Ⓜ *Anton Martin.*

Cervecería Cervantes

$ | **TAPAS** | Cervecería Cervantes is an improbably down-to-earth neighborhood bar—the type where you throw your olive pits and napkins right onto the floor—among the glut of underwhelming, tourist-oriented eateries in the area. Most patrons come for the ice-cold *cañas* (half pints), but if you're peckish, there's a fine menu of Spanish standbys including *pulpo a la gallega* (octopus with potatoes, olive oil, and paprika), *empanada* (tuna-stuffed pastry), stuffed piquillo peppers, and more. **Known for:** free tapa with beer; diamond in the touristy rough; generous portions of Galician-style octopus. $ *Average main: €13* ⊠ *Pl. de Jesús 7, Barrio de las Letras* ☎ *91/429–6093* ⊙ *No dinner Sun.* Ⓜ *Antón Martín.*

Gofio

$$$ | **SPANISH** | Savor a rare taste of Canary Islands cuisine—with quite a few twists—at this envelope-pushing restaurant helmed by Canarian chef Safe Cruz. Dinner might start with olives marinated in green *mojo,* a garlicky cilantro-and-parsley sauce ground in a mortar, and continue with crispy goat tacos or Gomero cheese (smoked tableside) before finishing with *gofio* ice cream, made with the Canarian corn flour from which the restaurant takes its name. **Known for:** Canarian "fusion" cuisine; smoky volcanic wines; gorgeous, uncontrived plating. $ *Average main: €23* ⊠ *Calle Lope de Vega 9, Barrio de las Letras* ☎ *91/599–4404* ⊕ *gofiobycicero. com* ⊙ *Closed Mon. and Tues.* Ⓜ *Anton Martin.*

La Huerta de Tudela

$$ | **SPANISH** | It can be hard to find a vegetable in Madrid, but in Navarra, the region this restaurant looks to for inspiration, there's never a shortage of tender asparagus, fresh artichokes, piquillo peppers, and other seasonal delicacies. Savor a vegetable-centric tasting menu that hinges on ingredients from the owners' family farm for €40, a steal in this increasingly overpriced neighborhood. **Known for:** vegetarian- and celiac-friendly cuisine; bottles of wine starting at €15; delectable crispy artichokes. $ *Average main: €22* ⊠ *Calle del Prado 15, Barrio de las Letras* ☎ *91/420–4418* ⊕ *www. lahuertadetudela.com* ⊙ *No dinner Sun. or Mon.* Ⓜ *Anton Martin.*

Taberna de la Dolores

$ | **TAPAS** | A lively corner bar with a colorful tiled facade, this is a solid spot for a cold beer and a quick bite after visiting the nearby museums. Try the *matrimonio* ("marriage") tapa, which weds a pickled and a cured anchovy on a crusty baguette. **Known for:** affordable, no-nonsense tapas; ice-cold cañas; mixed crowd of expats and locals. $ *Average main: €12* ⊠ *Pl. de Jesús 4, Barrio de las Letras* ☎ *91/429–2243* ▭ *No credit cards* Ⓜ *Antón Martín.*

TriCiclo

$$ | **TAPAS** | A Spanish-style bistro, TriCiclo serves inventive tapas—think surf-and-turf livers and *ibérico* (Iberian) pork tartare—in an environment where you don't have to throw elbows to place your order. This may be the only restaurant in town that serves raciones in one-third portions as well as half and full ones—ideal for creating your own tasting menu. **Known for:** traditional and modern tapas; tranquil ambience; excellent service. $ *Average main: €19* ⊠ *Calle Santa María 28, Barrio de las Letras* ☎ *91/024–4798* ⊕ *www. eltriciclo.es* ⊙ *Closed Sun.* Ⓜ *Antón Martín.*

Hotels

Catalonia Puerta del Sol

$$ | **HOTEL** | The regal cobblestone corridor leading to the reception desk, the atrium with walls made partly of original granite blocks, and the magnificent main wooden staircase (presided over by a lion statue) reveal this building's 18th-century origins. **Pros:** grand, quiet building; spacious rooms; room service. **Cons:** street looks a bit scruffy; rooms and common areas lack character; smoking permitted in the courtyard. $ *Rooms from: €140* ⊠ *Calle de Atocha 23, Barrio de las Letras* ☎ *91/369–7171* ⊕ *www.hoteles-catalonia.es* ⇲ *63 rooms* ⅩⅠ *No meals* Ⓜ *Tirso de Molina.*

DoubleTree by Hilton Madrid-Prado

$$$ | **HOTEL** | Opened in January 2017, this DoubleTree is a sparkling, immaculately designed hotel two blocks from the

Prado Museum. **Pros:** relaxing earth-tone accents; excellent in-room amenities; arguably the city's best Japanese restaurant. **Cons:** no valet parking; dull bar; no sense of place. [$] *Rooms from: €220* ✉ *Calle de San Agustín 3, Barrio de las Letras* ☎ *91/360–0820* 🌐 *www.doubletree3.hilton.com* 🛏 *61 rooms* 🍴 *No meals* [M] *Anton Martin.*

Gran Hotel Inglés

$$$$ | **HOTEL** | This grand hotel, opened in 1853, is the oldest in Madrid—and after a long, painstaking renovation, it reopened in 2018 to great fanfare. **Pros:** one of the city's most historic hotels; impeccable design; all rooms at least 280 square feet. **Cons:** pricey food and beverages; stairs to get to some rooms; occasional weekend street noise. [$] *Rooms from: €310* ✉ *Calle Echegaray 8, Barrio de las Letras* ☎ *91/360–0001* 🌐 *www.granhotelingles.com* 🛏 *48 rooms* 🍴 *No meals* [M] *Sevilla.*

Hotel Catalonia Las Cortes

$$ | **HOTEL** | A late-18th-century palace formerly owned by the Duke of Noblejas, this hotel, situated a few yards from Plaza Santa Ana, still bears traces of opulence and grandeur. **Pros:** tastefully decorated rooms; big walk-in showers; gorgeous architectural details. **Cons:** common areas are rather dull; no gym, pool, or spa; no bar. [$] *Rooms from: €150* ✉ *Calle del Prado 6, Barrio de las Letras* ☎ *91/389–6051* 🌐 *www.cataloniahotels.com/en/hotel/catalonia-las-corte* 🛏 *74 rooms* 🍴 *No meals* [M] *Sevilla, Antón Martín.*

★ Hotel Urban

$$$$ | **HOTEL** | A five-minute walk from Puerta del Sol, Hotel Urban conveys Madrid's cosmopolitan spirit with its stylish mix of Papua New Guinean artifacts and rare designer wares. **Pros:** eclectic, internationally sourced art; rooftop swimming pool; Michelin-starred restaurant. **Cons:** some rooms are small, and those near the elevator can be noisy; forgettable gym; no coffeemakers in entry-level rooms. [$] *Rooms from: €230* ✉ *Carrera de San Jerónimo 34, Barrio de las Letras* ☎ *91/787–7770* 🌐 *www.derbyhotels.com* 🛏 *103 rooms* 🍴 *No meals* [M] *Sevilla.*

ME by Meliá Madrid

$$$$ | **HOTEL** | In an unbeatable location, this ultramodern hotel bears a few reminders of the era when bullfighters would convene here before setting off to Las Ventas—a few bulls' heads hang in the lounge and some abstract pictures of bullfighting are scattered around, but the old flair has been superseded by cutting-edge amenities. **Pros:** cool, clubby vibe; popular restaurant; rooftop bar boasts great views of city. **Cons:** some rooms are cramped; plaza-facing rooms can be noisy; key cards demagnetize easily. [$] *Rooms from: €280* ✉ *Pl. Santa Ana 14, Barrio de las Letras* ☎ *91/531–4500* 🌐 *www.melia.com* 🛏 *191 rooms* 🍴 *No meals* [M] *Sol.*

NH Collection Madrid Suecia

$$$$ | **HOTEL** | The 1956 building the NH Collection Madrid Suecia occupies was once home to Ernest Hemingway and Che Guevara; today's guests are decidedly tamer, but the retro aesthetic lives on in the hotel's brown velvet couches, towering tropical plants, and suave concierges. **Pros:** renovated in 2016, well maintained since; rooftop bar with great views; stylish rooms. **Cons:** robes and slippers not provided in entry-level rooms; windowless gym; overpriced restaurant. [$] *Rooms from: €230* ✉ *Calle del Marqués de Casa Riera 4, Barrio de las Letras* ☎ *91/200–0570* 🌐 *www.nh-hotels.com* 🛏 *123 rooms* 🍴 *No meals.*

NH Collection Paseo del Prado

$$$ | **HOTEL** | In a turn-of-the-20th-century palace overlooking Plaza de Neptuno, this hotel preserves the building's erstwhile grandeur with canopy beds, gold-framed mirrors, and wing chairs. **Pros:** within the Golden Triangle of museums; gym with panoramic views; "lazy Sunday check-out" at 3 pm. **Cons:** need to upgrade to get good views; inconsistent food

Lodging Alternatives

If you want a home base that's roomy enough for a family and comes with cooking facilities, consider a furnished rental. Apartment rentals are increasingly popular in Madrid, and they can save you money, too. Prices run €50–€250 per person per night, and perfectly acceptable lodging for four can be found for around €150 per night. These are just a few of the apartment rental agencies that Fodorites are using these days: ⊕ www.airbnb.com; ⊕ www.niumba. com; ⊕ www.homeclub.com; ⊕ www. habitatapartments.com/madrid-apart-ments; ⊕ www.idealista.com; ⊕ www. apartinmadrid.com.

at Estado Puro; dated decor. $ Rooms from: €200 ⊠ Pl. Cánovas del Castillo 4, Barrio de las Letras ☎ 91/330–2400 ⊕ www.nh-hoteles.es ⮢ 115 rooms ⦿ No meals Ⓜ Banco de España.

★ Only YOU Atocha
$$ | HOTEL | Arguably the hottest hotel in town, the newly opened Only YOU Atocha is a stunner with its swanky lobby, rooftop restaurant, and well-appointed, industrial-chic accommodations. **Pros:** sceney rooftop brunch; interesting pop-ups in the lobby; cutting-edge design. **Cons:** exterior-facing rooms can be noisy; food quality could be better in both restaurants; ugly views of major intersection. $ Rooms from: €170 ⊠ Paseo de la Infanta Isabel 13, Barrio de las Letras ☎ 91/409–7876 ⊕ www. onlyyouhotels.com ⮢ 205 rooms ⦿ No meals Ⓜ Atocha.

Radisson Blu
$$$ | HOTEL | Surprisingly "boutique" for a Radisson Blu, this hotel has an intimate, urban feel that suits its middle-of-it-all location. **Pros:** pool and spa access; great location; breakfast from 6:30 am. **Cons:** some standard rooms are rather small; pricey breakfast; middling restaurant. $ Rooms from: €190 ⊠ Calle de Moratín 52, Barrio de las Letras ☎ 91/524–2626 ⊕ www.radissonblu.com ⮢ 54 rooms ⦿ No meals Ⓜ Atocha.

Room Mate Alicia
$$ | HOTEL | The all-white lobby, with curving walls, backlit ceiling panels, and gilded columns, may have looked trendy 10 years ago, when the hotel opened, but today it verges on tacky, so it's a good thing, then, that Room Mate Alicia's prime location and competitive rates continue to make it a worthwhile contender. **Pros:** good value; brightly colored rooms; laid-back atmosphere. **Cons:** standard rooms are small; zero-privacy bathroom spaces; no restaurant or gym. $ Rooms from: €165 ⊠ Calle Prado 2, Barrio de las Letras ☎ 91/389–6095 ⊕ www. room-matehoteles.com ⮢ 34 rooms ⦿ No meals Ⓜ Sevilla.

Suite Prado
$$ | HOTEL | Popular with Americans, this basic yet comfortable apartment hotel is situated a few steps from the Prado, the Thyssen-Bornemisza, and the Plaza Santa Ana tapas area. **Pros:** variety of room options; great for families and longer stays; complimentary room-service breakfasts. **Cons:** a bit noisy; dated decor; low ceilings on the top floor. $ Rooms from: €160 ⊠ Calle Manuel Fernández y González 10, Barrio de las Letras ☎ 91/420–2318 ⊕ www.suiteprado. com ⮢ 18 apartments ⦿ Free Breakfast Ⓜ Sevilla.

Urban Sea Atocha 113
$ | HOTEL | A metropolitan outpost of the Blue Sea resort chain, Urban Sea Atocha

113 is a no-frills 36-room hotel just north of the eponymous railway station. **Pros:** equidistant between Barrio de las Letras and Lavapiés; rooftop terrace with gorgeous views; single rooms ideal for solo travelers. **Cons:** bare-bones services; in-room sinks; exterior rooms facing Calle Atocha are pricey. [$] *Rooms from: €100* ✉ *Calle Atocha 113, Barrio de las Letras* ☎ *91/369–2895* 🌐 *www.blueseahotels.com* 🛏 *36 rooms* 🍴 *No meals* [M] *Atocha.*

Westin Palace

$$$$ | **HOTEL** | An iconic hotel situated inside the "Golden Triangle" (the district connecting the Prado, Reina Sofía, and Thyssen museums), the Westin Palace is known for its unbeatable location, stately facade, and classical decor. **Pros:** historic grand hotel; 24-hour gym with adjoining roof deck; spacious bathrooms. **Cons:** standard rooms face a backstreet; daily turndown provided only on request; redesigned areas clash with those that haven't been updated. [$] *Rooms from: €282* ✉ *Pl. de las Cortés 7, Barrio de las Letras* ☎ *91/360–8000* 🌐 *www.palace-madrid.com* 🛏 *467 rooms* 🍴 *No meals* [M] *Banco de España, Sevilla.*

🍸 Nightlife

BARS AND CAFÉS

★ Salmon Guru

BARS/PUBS | Regularly featured on best-of lists, Salmon Guru is Madrid's—and perhaps Spain's—most innovative *coctelería.* Come here to impress your boss or date or to geek out with mixology-loving friends over eye-popping concoctions like the Chipotle Chillón, made with mezcal, absinthe, and chipotle syrup. The nueva cocina tapas are almost as impressive as the drinks. No tables or barstools available? Wander around the corner to Viva Madrid, the newest project (opened in 2019) by Salmon Guru's celebrity mixologist, Diego Cabrera. ✉ *Calle de Echegaray 21, Barrio de las Letras* ☎ *91/000–6185* 🌐 *www.salmonguru.es* [M] *Anton Martin.*

Radio

CAFES—NIGHTLIFE | This bar in the ME Madrid Reina Victoria is split between a bottom-floor lounge, ideal for after-work martinis, and a more exclusive rooftop terrace with 360-degree views—a boon to chic summer revelers. ✉ *ME Madrid Reina Victoria, Pl. Santa Ana 14, Barrio de las Letras* ☎ *91/445–6886* 🌐 *www.melia.com* [M] *Antón Martín.*

DANCE CLUBS

Azúcar

DANCE CLUBS | Salsa has become a fixture of Madrid nightlife. Even if you don't have the guts to twirl and shake with the pros on the dance floor, you'll be almost as entertained sipping a mojito on the sidelines. Entry costs €11. ✉ *Calle de Atocha 107, Barrio de las Letras* ☎ *91/429–6208* 🕓 *Closed Sun.–Wed.* [M] *Atocha.*

★ Teatro Kapital

DANCE CLUBS | Easlly Madrid's most famous nightclub, Kapital has seven floors—each of which plays a different type of music (spun by the city's top DJs, of course)—plus a small movie theater and rooftop terrace. Dress to impress for this one: no sneakers, shorts, or tanks allowed. ✉ *Calle Atocha 125, Barrio de las Letras* ☎ *91/420–2906* 🌐 *www.grupo-kapital.com* [M] *Estacion del Arte.*

MUSIC CLUBS

★ Café Central

MUSIC CLUBS | Madrid's best-known jazz venue is chic, and the musicians are often internationally known. Performances are usually 9–11 nightly, and tickets can be bought at the door or online (the latter is advisable if traveling around holiday time). ✉ *Pl. de Ángel 10, Barrio de las Letras* ☎ *91/369–4143* 🌐 *www.cafecentralmadrid.com* [M] *Antón Martín.*

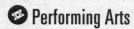 Performing Arts

FLAMENCO
Casa Patas
DANCE | Along with tapas, this well-known space offers good, authentic flamenco. Prices are more reasonable than elsewhere. Shows are at 10:30 pm Monday–Thursday, and at 9 pm and midnight on Friday and Saturday. ✉ *Calle Canizares 10, Barrio de las Letras* ☎ *91/369–0496* ⊕ *www.casapatas.com* Ⓜ *Antón Martín.*

Shopping

BOUTIQUES AND FASHION
Andrés Gallardo
JEWELRY/ACCESSORIES | Madrid's porcelain whisperer, Gallardo fashions second-hand shards and custom-made porcelain elements into runway-ready jewelry and accessories. ✉ *Calle Moratín 17, Barrio de las Letras* ☎ *91/053–5352* ⊕ *www.andresgallardo.com* ⊘ *Closed Sun.* Ⓜ *Anton Martin.*

The Concrete
CLOTHING | Fashion designer Fernando García de la Calera is redefining what it means to be a tailor by custom-making garments out of materials usually associated with streetwear such as denim and canvas. His creations are surprisingly affordable for being artisan made. ✉ *Calle de San Pedro 10, Barrio de las Letras* ☎ *91/242–1803* ⊕ *www.concretemadrid. com* ⊘ *Closed Sun. and Mon.* Ⓜ *Anton Martin.*

Eduardo Rivera
CLOTHING | A block off Plaza de Santa Ana, this is the flagship store of a young Spanish designer with clothes and accessories for both men and women. Other outposts can be found on Calle Sagasta 4 and Calle Clavel 4. ✉ *Pl. del Ángel 4, Barrio de las Letras* ☎ *91/843–5852* ⊕ *www. eduardorivera.es* Ⓜ *Puerta del Sol.*

Peseta
JEWELRY/ACCESSORIES | Shop made-in-Spain handbags, backpacks, clutches, totes, and more at this boutique by Asturian seamstress and fashion designer Laura Martínez. Expect splashy, wild patterns in every hue. ✉ *Calle San Vicente Ferrer 8* ☎ *91/052–5971* ⊕ *www. peseta.org* Ⓜ *Tribunal.*

Santacana
JEWELRY/ACCESSORIES | Keep your hands warm—and stylish—during Madrid's chilly winters with a pair of custom handmade gloves by Santacana, a family-run business that's been open since 1896. ✉ *Calle Huertas 1, Barrio de las Letras* ☎ *91/704–9670* ⊕ *www.santacana.es* Ⓜ *Anton Martin.*

FLEA MARKETS
★ El Rastro
OUTDOOR/FLEA/GREEN MARKETS | FAMILY | On Sunday morning, Calle de Ribera de Curtidores is closed to traffic and jammed with outdoor booths selling everything under the sun—this is its weekly transformation into the Rastro flea market. Find everything from antique furniture to rare vinyls of flamenco music and keychains emblazoned with "CNT," Spain's old anarchist trade union. Practice your Spanish by bargaining with vendors over paintings, heraldic iron gates, new and used clothes, and even hashish pipes. Plaza General Vara del Rey has some of El Rastro's best antiques, and the streets beyond—Calles Mira el Río Alta and Mira el Río Baja—boast all sorts of miscellany and bric-a-brac. The market shuts down shortly after 2 pm, in time for a street party to start in the area known as La Latina, centered on the bar El Viajero in Plaza Humilladero. ■TIP→ Off the Ribera are two galerías, courtyards with higher-quality, higher-price antiques shops. ✉ *Calle de Ribera de Curtidores, Barrio de las Letras* Ⓜ *Puerta de Toledo.*

FOOD AND WINE
★ Casa González
FOOD/CANDY | This food store (est. 1931) contains a cozy bar where you can sample most of its fare including canned asparagus, charcuterie, anchovies, and a good, well-priced selection of Spanish cheeses and wines. It also serves good, inexpensive breakfasts. ⊠ *Calle León 12, Barrio de las Letras* ☎ *91/429–5618* ⊕ *www.casagonzalez.es* Ⓜ *Antón Martín.*

Lavapiés

Lavapiés, which has overtaken Malasaña and La Latina as Madrid's trendiest neighborhood, has the city's highest concentration of immigrants—mostly Chinese, Indian, and North and West African—and as a result the area has plenty of international markets and inexpensive restaurants. The area also has the highest number of extant *corralas*—a type of building (now protected by the city after many years of abandonment) popular in Madrid in the 17th century. In the corralas, all the apartments are connected to a central patio, which serves as the community's social hub.

◉ Sights

★ Centro de Arte Reina Sofía (*Queen Sofía Art Center*)
MUSEUM | Madrid's premier museum of modern art, housed in a historic hospital building, features more than 1,000 works on four floors. Painting is the focus here, but photography and cinema are also represented. The new collection contextualizes the works of the great modern masters—Picasso, Miró, and Salvador Dalí—and of other famed artists, such as Juan Gris, Jorge Oteiza, Pablo Gargallo, Julio Gonzalez, Eduardo Chillida, and Antoni Tàpies, into broader narratives that attempt to better explain the evolution of modern art. This means, for instance, that the Dalís are not all displayed together in a single area, but scattered around the 38 rooms. The museum's showpiece is Picasso's *Guernica,* in Room No. 206 on the second floor. The huge black-and-white canvas depicts the horror of the Nazi Condor Legion's bombing of the ancient Basque town of Gernika in 1937 during the Spanish Civil War. Check out the rooftop area for scenic city views. ⊠ *Calle de Santa Isabel 52, Lavapiés* ☎ *91/467–5062* ⊕ *www.museoreinasofia.es* 🎫 *From €10 (free Mon. and Wed.–Sat. after 7 pm, Sun. 1:30–7)* ⊘ *Closed Tues.* Ⓜ *Atocha.*

Plaza de Lavapiés
PLAZA | The heart of what may have been Madrid's *judería* , or Jewish quarter, this plaza is Lavapiés's nerve center. To the east is Calle de la Fé (Street of Faith), called Calle Sinagoga until the expulsion of the Jews in 1492 for the synagogue once situated on it; the church of **San Lorenzo** sits in its place now. ⊠ *Lavapiés* Ⓜ *Lavapiés.*

Tabacalera (*Tabacalera Art Promotion*)
ARTS VENUE | This cultural center, which occupies an 18th-century cigarette factory, is divided in two parts: on the building's northwest corner, there's the city-funded exhibition and event space (called Espacio Promoción del Arte), a hub of contemporary art, while at its southwest corner is an entrance to the city's most famous art squat. Both venues are worth visiting, but the latter (with no official opening schedule) is truly unique with its thought-provoking graffiti and sculptural art. ⊠ *Calle de Embajadores 51, Lavapiés* ☎ *91/701–7045* ⊕ *www.latabacalera.net* 🎫 *Free* ⊘ *Closed Mon.*

🍴 Restaurants

Baobab
$ | **AFRICAN** | Get a taste of Lavapiés's vibrant Senegalese community at Baobab, an indoor-outdoor restaurant on Plaza de Nelson Mandela that serves up €7

thiéboudienne, a rich fish-and-vegetable braise ladled over *fonio* (a West African "supergrain"). The fountain beside the restaurant, called Fuente de Cabestreros, displays one of the city's only remaining references to "La República" that survived Franco's anti-Republican propaganda campaign following the Spanish Civil War. **Known for:** feast for under €10; real-deal thiéboudienne; primo people-watching. [$] *Average main: €8* ✉ *Calle de Cabestreros 1, Lavapiés* ☎ *63/211–5681* ⏲ *Closed Tues.* [M] *Lavapiés.*

★ Bar Santurce

$ | **TAPAS** | This *abuelo* bar near the top of the Rastro is famous for grilled sardines, blistered Padrón peppers, and fried calamari. **Known for:** delicious grilled sardines; inexpensive and unfussy; busy on Sunday. [$] *Average main: €10* ✉ *Pl. General Vara del Rey 14, Lavapiés* ☎ *64/623–8303* 🌐 *www.barsanturce.com* 💳 *No credit cards* [M] *La Latina.*

El Rincón de Marco

$ | **CUBAN** | Step straight into Havana at this hidden Cuban bar and restaurant where rumbas and *sones* flow from the speakers and regulars burst into impromptu dance parties. Whatever you end up eating—a €6 *ropa vieja* (cumin-scented beef stew), or perhaps the heftier €10 *picapollo* (fried chicken)—be sure to nab an order or two of fried plaintains for the table. **Known for:** home-cooked Cuban food; kitschy decor; music that makes you want to dance. [$] *Average main: €8* ✉ *Calle Cabestreros 8, Lavapiés* ☎ *91/210–7500* ⏲ *Closed Mon.* [M] *Lavapiés.*

★ Hola Coffee

$ | **CAFÉ** | Spaniards love their morning cafés con leche and afternoon *cortados* (espresso with steamed milk), but it's never been easy to find a great-quality cup of joe in Madrid—until now: Hola Coffee, a pocket coffee shop that pulls complex-tasting third-wave espressos and cappuccinos using beans they roast themselves. Larger groups should head to Mision Café, Hola's shiny new outpost in Malasaña that makes its own croissants by hand and just started serving phenomenal (and often vegan-friendly) €13 *menús del día* (prix-fixe lunches) on weekdays. **Known for:** third-wave coffees made with house-roasted beans; expat staff and clientele; great music and atmosphere. [$] *Average main: €5* ✉ *Calle del Dr. Fourquet 33, Lavapiés* ☎ *91/056–8263* 🌐 *www.hola.coffee* [M] *Lavapies.*

Melo's

$ | **SPANISH** | This old-timey Galician bar serves eight simple dishes, and they're infallible. Come for the ultracreamy croquetas, blistered Padrón peppers, and football-sized *zapatilla* sandwiches; stay for the dressed-down conviviality and the *cuncos* (ceramic bowls) overflowing with slatey Albariño. **Known for:** old-school Galician bar food; oversize ham croquetas; cheap, good Albariño. [$] *Average main: €8* ✉ *Calle del Ave María 44, Lavapiés* ☎ *91/527–5054* ⏲ *Closed Sun. and Mon.* 💳 *No credit cards* [M] *Lavapiés.*

★ Taberna de Antonio Sánchez

$$ | **SPANISH** | A Lavapiés landmark opened in 1786, this taberna's regulars have included realist painter Ignacio Zuloaga, countless champion bullfighters, and King Alfonso XIII. Sip on a sudsy caña, or half pint, in the creaky bar area, and nibble on house specialties like *cazón en adobo* (fried shark bites with cumin) and *torrijas* (custardy fried bread dusted with cinnamon). **Known for:** centuries-old decor; museum-grade bullfighting paraphernalia; cazón (fried shark). [$] *Average main: €16* ✉ *Calle del Mesón de Paredes, Lavapiés* ☎ *91/539–7826* ⏲ *No dinner Sun.* [M] *Lavapiés.*

🍸 Nightlife

BARS AND CAFÉS

★ Bendito Vinos y Vinilos

WINE BARS—NIGHTLIFE | This unassuming stall inside Mercado de San Fernando is a wine-industry hangout—one of the city's top spots for sampling hard-to-find natural and biodynamic wines from Spain and beyond. Pair whatever wine the owner, José, is drinking lately with Bendito's hand-selected cheeses and charcuterie sourced from independent producers. ✉ *Mercado de San Fernando, Calle de Embajadores 41, Lavapiés* ☎ *66/175–0061* Ⓜ *Lavapiés.*

La Fisna
WINE BARS—NIGHTLIFE | An ideal date spot, this understated yet elegant *vinoteca* pours over 50 wines by the glass and serves a delectable if overpriced menu of market-driven tapas. You won't find a more impressive roster of French wines anywhere in the city. ✉ *Calle Amparo 91, Lavapiés* ☎ *91/539–5615* ⊕ *www.lafisna. com.*

MUSIC AND DANCE CLUBS
Club 33
DANCE CLUBS | This intimate nightclub caters to a local, alternative crowd and has quickly become a stalwart on the lesbian party circuit, though partiers of all orientations are welcome. ✉ *Calle de la Cabeza 33, Lavapiés* ☎ *91/369–3302* ⊕ *www.club33madrid.es* Ⓜ *Lavapiés.*

Medias Puri
DANCE CLUBS | A decades-old, exclusive underground party made public in 2017, Medias Puri is the brainchild of Puri, an ageless Madrid socialite who rolled with Ava Gardner and Lola Flores back in the day. It's one of the hottest venues in town. ✉ *Pl. Tirso de Molina 1, Lavapiés* ☎ *91/521–6911* ⊕ *www.mediaspuri.com* Ⓜ *Tirso de Molina.*

★ Sala Juglar
MUSIC CLUBS | Sala Juglar is proof that nontouristy, affordable, and skillful flamenco still exists in Madrid (check the website for weekly performance times). Tropical-inflected dance parties, often held on the weekends, are another draw. ✉ *Calle de Lavapiés 37, Lavapiés* ☎ *91/528–4381* ⊕ *www.salajuglar.com* Ⓜ *Lavapiés.*

 Shopping

CRAFTS
★ Yolanda Andrés
CRAFTS | These are not your grandma's embroideries: In Yolanda Andrés's thought-provoking pieces, which she describes as "paintings with thread," she interprets the centuries-old technique through a modern-day lens—with stunning results. Beyond the framed artwork (don't miss the technicolor "Artichoke" line), there are embroidered pillow cases, totes, and more. ✉ *Calle Encomienda 15, Lavapiés* ☎ *91/026–0742* ⊕ *www. yolandaandres.com* ☯ *Closed Tues. and Sun.*

MUSIC
Percusión Campos
MUSIC STORES | This percussion shop and workshop—where Canarian Pedro Navarro crafts his own *cajones flamencos,* or flamenco box drums—is hard to find, but his pieces are greatly appreciated among professionals. Prices run €90–€220 and vary according to the quality of woods used. ✉ *Calle Olivar 36, Lavapiés* ☎ *91/539–2178* ⊕ *www.percusioncampos.com* Ⓜ *Lavapiés.*

El Rastro

The Rastro area in Embajadores traces back to the last third of the 16th century, when it marked the lower part of the old city's wall. The old slaughterhouses of this quarter (and all the other businesses related to that trade) are the origins of today's flea market, which spreads all over the neighborhood on Sunday. It gets quite busy on the weekends, especially on Sunday morning.

Sights

★ El Rastro

MARKET | Named for the *arrastre* (dragging) of animals in and out of the slaughterhouse that once stood here and, specifically, the *rastro* (blood trail) left behind, this site explodes into a rollicking flea market every Sunday 9–3 with dozens and dozens of street vendors with truly bizarre bric-a-brac ranging from costume earrings to mailed postcards and thrown-out love letters. There are also more formal shops, where it's easy to turn up treasures such as old iron grillwork, a marble tabletop, or a gilt picture frame. The shops (not the vendors) are open during the week, allowing for quieter and more serious bargaining. Even so, people-watching on Sunday is the best part. ⊠ *Calle de la Ribera de los Curtidores s/n, Embajadores* Ⓜ *La Latina, Puerta de Toledo.*

Retiro

The Retiro holds the city's best-known park, Parque del Buen Retiro, and best known museum, the Museo del Prado, and the neighborhood's borders extend to its east and west. The area between the western side of the park and the Paseo del Prado showcases some of the city's most exclusive and expensive real estate. The area on the opposite side of the park is livelier and more casual with plentiful tapas bars and mom-and-pop restaurants.

Sights

Estación de Atocha

TRANSPORTATION SITE (AIRPORT/BUS/FERRY/TRAIN) | A steel-and-glass hangar, Madrid's main train station was built in the late 19th century by Alberto Palacio Elissague, who became famous for his work with Ricardo Velázquez in the creation of the Palacio de Cristal (Glass Palace) in Madrid's Parque del Buen Retiro. Today, following renovations by architect Rafael Moneo, the station's main hall resembles a greenhouse; it's filled with tropical trees and contains a busy little turtle pool, a magnet for kids. ⊠ *Paseo de Atocha, Retiro* ☎ *91/243–2323* Ⓜ *Atocha.*

★ Museo del Prado (*Prado Museum*)

MUSEUM | When the Prado was commissioned by King/Mayor Carlos III, in 1785, it was as a natural-science museum. By the time the building was completed in 1819, its purpose had changed to exhibiting the art gathered by Spanish royalty since the time of Ferdinand and Isabella. The Prado's jewels are its works by the nation's three great masters: Goya, Velázquez, and El Greco. The museum also holds masterpieces by Flemish, Dutch, German, French, and Italian artists, collected when their lands were part of the Spanish Empire. The most famous canvas, Velázquez's *Las Meninas* (*The Maids of Honor*), combines a self-portrait of the artist with a mirror reflection of the king and queen. Among Goya's early masterpieces are portraits of the family of King Carlos IV; later works include his famous "black paintings." Other highlights include the *Garden of Earthly Delights* by Hieronymus Bosch, and two of El Greco's greatest paintings, *The Resurrection* and *The Adoration of the Shepherds.* ⊠ *Paseo del Prado s/n, Retiro* ☎ *91/330–2800* ⊕ *www.museodelprado.es* 🎟 *€15 (permanent collection free Mon.–Sat. 6–8 pm, Sun. 5–7 pm)* Ⓜ *Banco de España, Atocha.*

Museo Nacional de Artes Decorativas

MUSEUM | This newly renovated palatial building showcases 70,000 items including textiles, furniture, jewelry, ceramics, glass, crystal, and metalwork. The collection, displayed in chronological order, starts with medieval and Renaissance items on the first floor and ends with 18th- and 19th-century pieces on the top floor. The ground floor, currently devoted to works by the inmates of a

The bustling Rastro flea market takes place every Sunday 10–2; you never know what kind of treasures you might find.

local penitentiary, rotates temporary exhibitions and some avant-garde works. This museum can be seen as part of the Abono Cinco Palacios, a €12 pass that grants access to five mansion-museums. ✉ *Montalbán 12, Retiro* ☎ *91/532–6499* ⊕ *mnartesdecorativas.mcu.es* ✉ *€3 (free Thurs. after 5, Sun. all day)* ⏀ *Closed Mon.* Ⓜ *Retiro.*

Museo Naval

MUSEUM | Anyone interested in Patrick O'Brian's painstakingly detailed naval novels or in old vessels and warships shouldn't miss the 500 years of Spanish naval history displayed in this museum. The collection, which includes documents, maps, weaponry, paintings, and hundreds of ship models of different sizes, is best enjoyed by those who speak some Spanish. Beginning with Queen Isabella and King Ferdinand's reign and the expeditions led by Christopher Columbus and the conquistadores, exhibits also reveal how Spain built a naval empire that battled Turkish, Algerian, French, Portuguese, and English armies and commanded the oceans and the shipping routes for a century and a half. Moving to the present day, the museum covers Spain's more recent shipyard and naval construction accomplishments. ✉ *Paseo del Prado 5, Retiro* ☎ *91/523–8789* ⊕ *www.armada.mde.es/museonaval* ✉ *€3 suggested donation* ⏀ *Closed Mon.* Ⓜ *Banco de España.*

★ Parque del Buen Retiro (*El Retiro*)

NATIONAL/STATE PARK | **FAMILY** | Once the private playground of royalty, Madrid's crowning park is a vast expanse of green encompassing formal gardens, fountains, lakes, exhibition halls, children's play areas, outdoor cafés, and a puppet theater (shows on Saturday at 1 and on Sunday at 1, 6, and 7). The park, especially lively on weekends, also holds a book fair in May and occasional flamenco concerts in summer. From the entrance at the Puerta de Alcalá, head straight toward the center to find the Estanque (lake), presided over by a grandiose equestrian statue of King Alfonso XII. The 19th-century Palacio de Cristal (Glass Palace) was built

Continued on page 113

EL PRADO:
MADRID'S BRUSH
WITH GREATNESS

One of the world's top museums, the Prado is to Madrid what the Louvre is to Paris, or the Uffizi to Florence: a majestic city landmark and premiere art institution that merits the attention of every traveler who visits the city.

The Prado celebrated its 200th anniversary in 2019, and its unparalleled collection of Spanish paintings (from the Romanesque period to the 19th century—don't expect to find Picassos here) makes it one of the most visited museums in the world. Foreign artists are also well represented—the collection includes masterpieces of European painting such as Hieronymus Bosch's *Garden of Earthly Delights*, *The Annunciation by Fra Angelico*, *Christ Washing the Disciples' Feet* by Tintoretto, and *The Three Graces* by Rubens—but the Prado is best known as home to more paintings by Diego Velázquez and Francisco de Goya than anywhere else.

Originally meant by King Charles III to become a museum of natural history, the Prado nevertheless opened, in 1819, as a sculpture and painting museum under the patronage of his grandchild, King Philip VII. For the first bewildered *madrileños* who crossed the museum's entrance back then, there were only about 300 paintings

on display. Today there are more than 3 million visitors a year and 2,000-plus paintings are on display (the whole collection is estimated at about 8,000 canvases, plus 1,000 sculptures).

WHEN TO GO
The best time to visit the Prado is during lunch time, from 1-3, to beat the rush.

HUNGRY?
If your stomach rumbles during your visit, check out the café/restaurant in the foyer of the new building.

CONTACT INFORMATION
✉ Paseo del Prado s/n, 28014 Madrid
☎ (+34) 91 330 2800.
🌐 www.museodelprado.es
Ⓜ Banco de España, Estacíon del Arte

HOURS OF OPERATION
🕑 Mon.–Sat. 10 AM–8 PM, Sun. 10 AM–7 PM, Closed New Year's Day, Fiesta del Trabajo (May 1), and Christmas.

ADMISSION
💳 €15. Free Mon. to Sat. 6 PM–8 PM, Sun. 5 PM-7 PM. To avoid lines, buy tickets in advance online.

The Trinity by El Greco, 1577. Oil on canvas.

THREE GREAT MASTERS

FRANCISCO DE GOYA 1746–1828
Goya's work spans a staggering range of tone, from bucolic to horrific, his idyllic paintings of Spaniards at play and portraits of the family of King Carlos IV contrasting with his dark, disturbing "black paintings." Goya's attraction to the macabre assured him a place in posterity, an ironic statement at the end of a long career in which he served as the official court painter to a succession of Spanish kings, bringing the art of royal portraiture to unknown heights.

Francisco de Goya

Goya found fame in his day as a portraitist, but he is admired by modern audiences for his depictions of the bizarre and the morbid. Beginning as a painter of decorative Rococo figures, he evolved into an artist of great depth in the employ of King Charles IV. The push-pull between Goya's love for his country and his disdain for the enemies of Spain yielded such masterpieces as *Third of May 1808*, painted after the French occupation ended. In the early 19th century, Goya's scandalous *The Naked Maja* brought him before the Spanish Inquisition, whose judgment was to end his tenure as a court painter.

DIEGO VELÁZQUEZ 1599–1660
A native of Seville, Velázquez gained fame at age 24 as court painter to King Philip IV. He developed a lifelike approach to religious art in which both saints and sinners were specific people rather than generic types. The supple brushwork of his ambitious history paintings and portraits was unsurpassed. Several visits to Rome, and his friendship with Rubens, made him the quintessential baroque painter with an international purview.

Diego Velázquez

DOMENIKOS THEOTOKOPOULOS (AKA "EL GRECO") 1541–1614
El Greco's art was one of rapture and devotion, but beyond that his style is almost impossible to categorize. "The Greek" found his way from his native Crete to Spain through Venice; he spent most of his life in Toledo. His twisted, elongated figures imbue both his religious subjects and portraits with a sense of otherworldliness. While his palette and brushstrokes were inspired by Italian Mannerism, his approach to painting was uniquely his own. His inimitable style left few followers.

Domenikos Theotokopoulos

SIX PAINTINGS TO SEE

SATURN DEVOURING ONE OF HIS SONS (1819)
FRANCISCO DE GOYA Y LUCIENTES
In one of fourteen nightmarish "black paintings" executed by Goya to decorate the walls of his home in the later years of his life, the mythological God Kronos, or Saturn, cannibalizes one of his children in order to derail a prophecy that one of them would take over his throne. *Mural transferred to canvas.*

Saturn Devouring One of His Sons

THE GARDEN OF DELIGHTS OR LA PINTURA DEL MADROÑO (1500)
HIËRONYMUS BOSCH
Very little about the small-town environment of the Low Countries where the Roman Catholic Bosch lived in the late Middle Ages can explain his thought-provoking, and downright bizarre, paintings. His depictions of mankind's sins and virtues, and the heavenly rewards or demonic punishments that await us all, have fascinated many generations of viewers. The devout painter has been called a "heretic," and compared to Salvador Dalí for his disturbingly twisted renderings. In this three-panel painting, Adam and Eve are created, mankind celebrates its humanity, and hell awaits the wicked, all within a journey of 152 inches! *Wooden Triptych.*

The Garden of Delights

LAS MENINAS (THE MAIDS OF HONOR) (1656-57)
DIEGO VELÁZQUEZ DE SILVA
Velázquez's masterpiece of spatial perspective occupies pride-of-place in the center of the Spanish baroque galleries. In this complex visual game, *you* are the king and queen of Spain, reflected in a distant hazy mirror as the court painter (Velázquez) pauses in front of his easel to observe your features. The actual subject is the Princess Margarita, heir to the throne in 1656. *Oil on canvas.*

Las Meninas

STILL LIFE (17th Century; no date)
FRANCISCO DE ZURBARÁN
Best known as a painter of contemplative saints, Zurbarán, a native of Extremadura who found success working with Velázquez in Seville, was a peerless observer of beauty in the everyday. His rendering of the surfaces of these homely objects elevates them to the stature of holy relics, urging the viewer to touch them. But the overriding mood is one of serenity and order. *Oil on canvas.*

Still Life

DAVID VICTORIOUS OVER GOLIATH (1599)
MICHELANGELO MERISI (CARAVAGGIO)

Caravaggio used intense contrasts between his dark and light passages (called *chiaroscuro* in Italian) to create drama in his bold baroque paintings. Here, a surprisingly childlike David calmly ties up the severed head of the giant Philistine Goliath, gruesomely featured in the foreground plane of the picture. The astonishing realism of the Italian painter, who was as well known for his tempestuous personal life as for his deftness with a paint brush, had a profound influence on 17th century Spanish art. *Oil on canvas.*

David Victorious over Goliath

THE TRINITY (1577)
DOMENIKOS THEOTOKOPOULOS (EL GRECO)

Soon after arriving in Spain, Domenikos Theotokopoulos created this view of Christ ascending into heaven supported by angels, God the Father, and the Holy Spirit. It was commissioned for the altar of a convent in Toledo. The acid colors recall the Mannerist paintings of Venice, where El Greco was trained, and the distortions of the upward-floating bodies show more gracefulness than the anatomical contortions that characterize his later works. *Oil on canvas.*

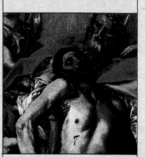

The Trinity

PICASSO AND THE PRADO

The Prado contains no modern art, but one of the greatest artists of the 20th century had an important history with the museum. **Pablo Picasso** (1891–1973) served as the director of the Prado during the Spanish civil war, from 1936 to 1939. The Prado was a "phantom museum" in that period, Picasso once noted, since it was closed for most of the war and its collections hidden elsewhere for safety.

Picasso with his wife
Jacqueline Roque

Later that century, the abstract artist's enormous *Guernica* hung briefly on the Prado's walls, returning to Spain from the Museum of Modern Art in 1981. Picasso had stipulated that MoMA give up his anti-war masterpiece after the death of fascist dictator Francisco Franco, and it was displayed at the Prado and the Casón del Buen Retiro until the nearby Reina Sofia was built to house it in 1992.

Picasso in his atelier

to house exotic plants—and, incredibly, actual tribesmen displayed as a "human zoo"—from the Philippines; the Rosaleda (Rose Garden) is bursting with color and heady with floral scents for most of the summer. Madrileños claim that a statue called the *Ángel Caído* (*Fallen Angel*) is the only one in the world depicting the Prince of Darkness before his fall from grace. ✉ *Puerta de Alcalá, Retiro* 🎫 *Free* Ⓜ *Retiro.*

Plaza de Cibeles

FOUNTAIN | The Plaza de Cibeles, where three of Madrid's most affluent neighborhoods (Centro, Retiro, and Salamanca) intersect, is both an epicenter of municipal grandeur and a crash course in Spanish architecture. Two palaces, Buenavista and Linares (baroque and baroque revival, respectively), sit on the northerly corners of the plaza and are dwarfed by the ornate Palacio de Cibeles. In the center of the plaza sits one of Madrid's most defining symbols, the Cybele Fountain, a depiction of the Roman goddess of the Earth driving a lion-drawn chariot. (During the civil war, patriotic madrileños risked life and limb to sandbag it as Nationalist aircraft bombed the city.) ✉ *Retiro* Ⓜ *Banco de España.*

Real Fábrica de Tapices

FACTORY | Tired of previous monarchs' dependency on Belgian and Flemish thread mills and craftsmen, King Felipe V decided to establish the Royal Tapestry Factory in Madrid in 1721. It was originally housed near Alonso Martínez and moved to its current location in 1889. Some of Europe's best artists collaborated on the factory's tapestry designs, the most famous of whom was Goya, who produced a number of works that can be seen at the Prado. The factory, the most renowned of its kind in Europe, is still in operation—you can tour the workshop floor and watch weavers at work. They apply traditional weaving techniques from the 18th and 19th centuries to modern and classic designs—including

An Uphill Jog

Explore Madrid on your morning run but be prepared for hills. The best running spots are the Parque del Buen Retiro—where the main path circles the park (approximately 2½ miles) and others weave under trees and through gardens— and the Parque del Oeste, which has more uneven terrain and fewer people. Casa de Campo is crisscrossed by hilly trails and ideal for distance runners (bring your phone so you don't get lost); same goes for the Madrid Río esplanade and much longer Anillo Verde ("Green Ring"), which you can access by crossing a bridge at the northwest corner of Parque del Oeste.

Goya's. ✉ *Calle de Fuenterrabía 2, Retiro* ☎ *91/434–0550* ⊕ *www.realfabricadetapices.com* 🎫 *€5* 🕐 *Closed weekends, and Aug.* Ⓜ *Atocha.*

Real Jardín Botánico (*Botanical Garden*)
GARDEN | You don't have to be a horticulturalist to appreciate the exotic plant collection here. Opened in 1781 and emblematic of the Age of Enlightenment, this lush Eden of bonsais, orchids, cacti, and more houses more than 5,000 species of living plants and trees in just 20 acres. Its dried specimens number over a million, and many were brought back from exploratory voyages to the New World. ✉ *Pl. de Murillo 2, Retiro* ☎ *91/420–3017* ⊕ *www.rjb.csic.es* 🎫 *€6* Ⓜ *Atocha.*

🍽 Restaurants

Horcher

$$$$ | **GERMAN** | A beacon of old-world Spanish hospitality, Horcher is a Madrid classic with German influences. Wild game—boar, venison, partridge, and

Performing Arts Tickets

As Madrid's reputation as a vibrant, contemporary arts center has grown, artists and performers have been arriving in droves. Consult the daily listings and Friday city-guide supplements in any of the leading newspapers—*El País*, *El Mundo*, or *ABC*—all of which are fairly easy to understand, even if you don't read much Spanish. Websites such as ⊕ *www.guiadelocio.com* and ⊕ *www.timeout.es* are also useful.

El Corte Inglés You can buy tickets for major concerts online. ☎ 90/240–0222 ⊕ *www.elcorteingles.es/entradas.*

Entradas.com This website sells tickets for musicals and big-name concerts. ☎ 90/222–1622 ⊕ *www.entradas.com.*

Ticketea ☎ 90/204–4226 ⊕ *www. ticketea.com.*

duck—is the centerpiece of the menu, which also includes comfort-food classics like ox Stroganoff with a Pommery mustard sauce and pork chops with sauerkraut. **Known for:** wild game dishes; German-inflected wine list; to-die-for baumkuchen (a German-style spit cake). ⓈAverage main: €37 ⊠ Calle de Alfonso XII 6, Retiro ☎ 91/522–0731 ⊕ www. restaurantehorcher.com ☉ Closed Sun. No lunch Sat. ⚏ Jacket and tie Ⓜ Retiro.

★ La Castela
$$ | TAPAS | Traditional taverns with tin-top bars, vermouth on tap, and no-nonsense waiters are a dying breed in Madrid, but this one, just a couple of blocks from the Parque del Buen Retiro, has stood the test of time. It's always busy with locals clamoring over plates of sautéed wild mushrooms, anchovies served with a *pipirrana* (cucumber and tomato salad), and clams in white wine. **Known for:** fresh seafood and fish; vintage bar; local crowd. ⓈAverage main: €18 ⊠ Calle Doctor Castelo 22, Retiro ☎ 91/574–0015 ⊕ www.lacastela.com ☉ No dinner Sun. Ⓜ Ibiza.

La Catapa
$$ | SPANISH | La Catapa's tapas are classic but never old hat, inventive but never pretentious. The burst-in-your-mouth croquetas and garlicky razor clams may lure the crowds, but the hidden gems are in the vegetable section: it's hard to decide between the artichoke confit "flowers" with crunchy salt, peeled tomatoes dressed with olive oil, and umami-packed seared mushrooms. **Known for:** elevated tapas; market-driven specials; eclectic wines. ⓈAverage main: €16 ⊠ Calle Menorca 14, Retiro ☎ 68/614–3823 ☉ Closed Sun. and Mon.

Hotels

★ AC Palacio del Retiro
$$$$ | HOTEL | A palatial early-20th-century building, once owned by a noble family with extravagant habits (the elevator carried their horses up and down from the rooftop exercise ring), this spectacular hotel shows that mixing classical and modern decor can work when done right. **Pros:** spacious, stylish rooms; within walking distance of the Prado; bathrooms stocked with all sorts of complimentary products. **Cons:** pricey breakfast; lower rooms facing the park can get noisy; cumbersome room keys. ⓈRooms from: €260 ⊠ Calle de Alfonso XII 14, Retiro ☎ 91/523–7460 ⊕ www.ac-hotels.com ⤶ 58 rooms ⓘⓄ No meals Ⓜ Retiro.

You can rent rowboats at the lake in the Parque del Buen Retiro; it's a great way to cool off in the summer.

Salamanca

The Salamanca neighborhood, one of the new areas included in the program of city expansions which started in the second half of the 19th century, was originally supposed to provide shelter for the working classes. However, it soon became a favorite location for the bourgeois, the upper class, and the aristocracy, a legacy that's still apparent in the neighborhood's myriad expensive restaurants and luxury shops.

Sights

Museo Arqueológico Nacional (*Museum of Archaeology*)

MUSEUM | This museum boasts three large floors filled with Spanish relics, artifacts, and treasures ranging from ancient history to the 19th century. Among the highlights are *La Dama de Elche* , the bust of a wealthy 5th-century-BC Iberian woman (notice that her headgear vaguely resembles the mantillas and hair combs still associated with traditional Spanish dress); the ancient Visigothic votive crowns discovered in 1859 near Toledo, believed to date back to the 7th century; and the medieval ivory crucifix of Ferdinand and Sancha. There is also a replica of the early cave paintings in Altamira (access to the real thing, in Cantabria Province, is highly restricted). ■**TIP**➜ **Consider getting the multimedia guide offering select itineraries to make your visit more manageable.** ✉ *Calle de Serrano 13, Salamanca* ☎ *91/577–7912* ⊕ *www.man.es* ✉ *€3 (free Sat. after 2 and Sun. before 2)* ⊗ *Closed Mon.* Ⓜ *Colón.*

Museo Lázaro Galdiano

MUSEUM | This stately mansion of writer and editor José Lázaro Galdiano (1862–1947), a 10-minute walk across the Castellana from the Museo Sorolla, has decorative items and paintings by Bosch, El Greco, Murillo, and Goya, among others. The remarkable collection comprises five centuries of Spanish, Flemish, English, and Italian art. Bosch's *St. John the*

KEY
- **1** Sights
- **1** Restaurants
- **1** Hotels
- **Ⓜ** Metro Stops
- **ⓘ** Tourist Information

Chueca, Malasaña, Salamanca, Chamberí, Chamartín, and Tetuán

Baptist and the many Goyas are the stars of the show, with El Greco's *San Francisco de Assisi* and Zurbarán's *San Diego de Alcalá* close behind. This museum can be seen as part of the Abono Cinco Palacios, a €12 pass that grants access to five mansion-museums. ✉ *Calle de Serrano 122, Salamanca* ☎ *91/561–6084* 🌐 *www.flg.es* 🎟 *€6 (free last hr)* 🕒 *Closed Mon.* [M] *Gregorio Marañón.*

Plaza Colón

PLAZA | Named for Christopher Columbus, this plaza has a statue of the explorer (identical to the one in Barcelona's port) looking west from a high tower in the middle of the square. Behind Plaza Colón is **Calle de Serrano,** the city's premier shopping street (think Gucci, Prada, and Loewe). Stroll in either direction on Serrano for some window-shopping. ✉ *Salamanca* [M] *Colón.*

🍴 Restaurants

Álbora

$$$ | **TAPAS** | The owners of this sleek award-winning restaurant also produce cured hams and top-notch canned foods, and these quality ingredients are included in a menu that manages to be both traditional and creative. There's an avant-garde tapas bar on the street level, ideal for cocktails and quick bites, and a more refined restaurant on the second floor, perfect for impressing a client or a date. **Known for:** top-quality charcutería; experimental Spanish cuisine; well-heeled clientele. [$] *Average main: €25* ✉ *Calle de Jorge Juan 33, Salamanca* ☎ *91/781–6197* 🌐 *www.restaurantealbora.com* 🕒 *No dinner Sun.* [M] *Velázquez.*

★ **Casa Dani**

$ | **SPANISH** | Hidden in a back corner of Mercado de la Paz, the neighborhood's famed traditional market, Casa Dani is a no-frills bar that happens to serve one of the best Spanish omelets in town; each hefty wedge is packed with caramelized onions and served hot and slightly runny (adventurous eaters should opt for the *con callos* version, topped with braised tripe). The €10 prix fixe, which hinges on market ingredients, is the best lunch deal in the area. **Known for:** top-notch tortilla española; €10 prix-fixe lunch; local crowd. [$] *Average main: €10* ✉ *Calle de Ayala 28, Salamanca* ☎ *91/575–5925* 🌐 *www.casadanimadrid.blogspot.com* 🕒 *Closed Sun. No dinner* [M] *Serrano.*

El Pescador

$$$ | **SEAFOOD** | Owned by the proprietors of the best fish market in town, this seafood restaurant with a warm modern interior welcomes guests with an impressive window display of fresh seafood—red and white prawns, Kumamoto oysters, goose barnacles, and the renowned Galician Carril clams are just some of what you might see. Fish (including turbot, sole, grouper, and sea bass) is cooked to each customer's liking in the oven, on the grill, in a pan with garlic, or battered and fried. **Known for:** extravagant seafood displays; dayboat fish; crisp Albariño. [$] *Average main: €25* ✉ *Calle de José Ortega y Gasset 75, Salamanca* ☎ *91/402–1290* 🌐 *www.marisqueriaelpescador.net* 🕒 *Closed Sun.* [M] *Lista, Núñez de Balboa.*

El Rincón de Jaén

$$ | **SPANISH** | **FAMILY** | An Andalusian-style taberna, El Rincón de Jaén evokes the raucous energy and down-home cuisine of that sunny region. Start with the *pescaíto frito,* a mix of seafood that's lightly fried and served with lemon halves, before moving on to more substantial dishes like the peeled tomato salad topped with oil-cured tuna belly (easily one of the best salads in town) and whole roasted fish and braised meats. **Known for:** Andalusian joie de vivre; tomato and tuna salad; complimentary tapas with drinks. [$] *Average main: €22* ✉ *Calle Don Ramón de la Cruz 88, Salamanca* ☎ *91/401–6334* 🌐 *www.elrincondejaen.es* [M] *Lista.*

Estay

$$ | SPANISH | A spacious, tranquil place presided over by white-jacketed waitstaff that makes fine breakfasts (choose from *pan con tomate,* toast with jam, or a griddled all-butter croissant plus coffee) for less than €3—this is the quintessential Salamanca restaurant. The interiors got a makeover in 2016, but the unassuming elegance of Estay was retained. **Known for:** runny tortilla española; weekday prix fixe; preppy Salamanca atmosphere. $ *Average main: €20* ⊠ *Calle de Hermosilla 46, Salamanca* ☎ *91/578–0470* ⊕ *www.estayrestaurante.com* ⊗ *Closed Sun.* Ⓜ *Velázquez.*

Goizeko Wellington

$$$ | SPANISH | Aware of the sophisticated palate of Spain's new generation of diners, the owners of Goizeko Kabi (a terrific restaurant in its own right) opened this more modern restaurant, which shares the virtues of its kin but none of its stuffiness. Think neutral tones, bright wood paneling, and personable service. **Known for:** elevated Basque cuisine; simply perfect seafood; elegant atmosphere. $ *Average main: €27* ⊠ *Hotel Wellington, Calle de Villanueva 34, Salamanca* ☎ *91/577–6026* ⊕ *www.goizekogaztelupe.com* ⊗ *Closed Sun.* Ⓜ *Retiro, Príncipe de Vergara.*

★ Punto MX

$$$$ | MEXICAN | The first Mexican restaurant in Europe to land a Michelin star, Punto MX, helmed by Roberto Ruiz, draws on Spanish ingredients and international techniques to redefine Mexican food with dishes like nopal "ceviche," ibérico pork tacos, and squab mole. If you can't snag a reservation in the dining room, book a more casual experience in the Mezcal Lab bar area. **Known for:** award-winning Mexican restaurant; real-deal Oaxacan moles; Spanish twists on Mexican classics. $ *Average main: €38* ⊠ *Calle de General Pardiñas 40, Salamanca* ☎ *91/402–2226* ⊕ *www.puntomx.es* ⊗ *Closed Sun. and Mon.* Ⓜ *Lista.*

★ Ten Con Ten

$$$ | SPANISH | This is one of the "gin bars" that started the Spanish gin-tónic craze of the late aughts, and though perhaps not as avant-garde as it once was, the quality of food and drinks at Ten Con Ten is consistently excellent. Grab a cocktail at one of the wooden high-tops in the bar area, or sit down for a soup-to-nuts dinner in the classy dining room at the back—just remember to book a table weeks, if not months, in advance. **Known for:** expertly made gin-tónics; memorable gastro-bar fare; hand-cut jamón ibérico. $ *Average main: €24* ⊠ *Calle de Ayala 6, Salamanca* ☎ *91/575–9254* ⊕ *www.restaurantetenconten.com* Ⓜ *Serrano.*

Zalacaín

$$$$ | BASQUE | This newly renovated restaurant, which in its heyday held three Michelin stars, introduced nouvelle Basque cuisine to Spain in the 1970s and has since become a Madrid classic. It's particularly known for using the best and freshest seasonal products available in signature dishes like steak tartare with *pommes soufflés* (puffed potatoes) prepared tableside. *¡Ojo!* Zalacaín is back with a vengeance and ready for its close-up. **Known for:** old-guard Spanish fine dining; revamped interiors and menus; unbeatable "materia prima". $ *Average main: €34* ⊠ *Calle Álvarez de Baena 4, Salamanca* ☎ *91/561–4840* ⊕ *www.restaurantezalacain.com* ⊗ *Closed Sun., Easter wk, and Aug. No lunch Sat.* 🍴 *Jacket and tie* Ⓜ *Gregorio Marañón.*

🛏 Hotels

Barceló Emperatriz

$$$ | HOTEL | Worthy of an empress, as its name implies, this swanky property on a tree-shaded block opened in 2016 and offers knowledgeable concierge services, healthy breakfast options, and an extensive pillow menu. **Pros:** private terraces; king-size beds and in-room hot tubs; portable Wi-Fi hot spot. **Cons:** cramped lobby; 10-minute taxi from center of

town; small pool and gym. [$] *Rooms from: €190* ✉ *Calle de López de Hoyos 4, Salamanca* ☎ *91/342–2490* 🌐 *www.barcelo.com* 🛏 *146 rooms* 🍴 *No meals* Ⓜ *Núñez de Balboa.*

Gran Meliá Fénix

$$$$ | **HOTEL** | A Madrid institution that has played host to the likes of the Beatles, Cary Grant, and Rita Hayworth, this hotel is a mere hop from the posh shops of Calle Serrano. **Pros:** close to shopping; great breakfast buffet; opulent, spacious rooms. **Cons:** small bathrooms; below-average restaurant; elitist VIP policy that excludes standard-room guests from certain areas. [$] *Rooms from: €230* ✉ *Calle de Hermosilla 2, Salamanca* ☎ *91/431–6700* 🌐 *www.melia.com* 🛏 *225 rooms* 🍴 *No meals* Ⓜ *Colón.*

★ Tótem Madrid

$$$ | **HOTEL** | A breath of fresh air on the Madrid hotel scene, particularly in this notoriously stuffy part of town, Tótem checks all the boxes: genial service, state-of-the-art design, sought-after location, terrific food and cocktails—you name it, they've got it. **Pros:** charming tree-lined block; excellent cocktail bar and restaurant; stylish and modern. **Cons:** main attractions not within walking distance; slightly stodgy neighborhood; interior rooms not as pleasant. [$] *Rooms from: €200* ✉ *Calle Hermosilla 23, Salamanca* ☎ *91/426–0035* 🌐 *www.totem-madrid.com* 🛏 *64 rooms* 🍴 *No meals* Ⓜ *Serrano.*

★ Villa Magna

$$$$ | **HOTEL** | If the Ritz caters to old-money Madrid, then Villa Magna, located on the shady Castellana mall, is its low-profile, new-money counterpart, frequented by celebrities, foreign financiers, and other high-society types. **Pros:** exceptional service; arguably the best breakfast in Madrid; sleek new spa unveiled in 2019. **Cons:** expensive room service; the exterior is a little dull; occasionally starchy staff. [$] *Rooms from: €415* ✉ *Paseo de la Castellana 22, Salamanca* ☎ *91/587–1234* 🌐 *www.mythahotels.com* 🛏 *150 rooms* 🍴 *No meals* Ⓜ *Rubén Darío.*

VP Jardín de Recoletos

$$ | **HOTEL** | **FAMILY** | This boutique apartment hotel offers great value on a quiet street just a couple of blocks from Retiro Park, the Prado, and Madrid's main shopping area. **Pros:** spacious rooms with kitchens; good restaurant; periodic deals on the hotel's website. **Cons:** the garden closes at midnight and, when crowded, can be noisy; design is a bit outmoded; breakfast not served in the garden. [$] *Rooms from: €160* ✉ *Calle Gil de Santivañes 6, Salamanca* ☎ *91/781–1640* 🌐 *www.recoletos-hotel.com* 🛏 *43 rooms* 🍴 *No meals* Ⓜ *Colón.*

Nightlife

DANCE CLUBS

Bling Bling

DANCE CLUBS | This glitzy nightclub (opened in 2018 by the owners of equally exclusive Opium Madrid) attracts a well-heeled local crowd. Dress to impress: this isn't an easy door. ✉ *Calle Génova 28, Salamanca* ☎ *91/064–4479* Ⓜ *Colón.*

Performing Arts

Auditorio Nacional de Música

CONCERTS | This is Madrid's main concert hall, with spaces for both symphonic and chamber music. ✉ *Calle del Príncipe de Vergara 146, Salamanca* ☎ *91/337–0140* 🌐 *www.auditorionacional.mcu.es* Ⓜ *Cruz del Rayo.*

Shopping

BOUTIQUES AND FASHION

Salamanca is Madrid's quintessential shopping district with a high concentration of large and small shops and boutiques on Calles Claudio Coello, Lagasca, and the first few blocks of Serrano.

Adolfo Domínguez

CLOTHING | This popular Galician designer creates simple, sober, and elegant lines for both men and women. Of the numerous locations around the city, the flagship at Calle Serrano 5 is the most varied. There's also a large store at Madrid–Barajas Airport. ⊠ *Calle de Serrano 5, Salamanca* ☎ *91/436–2600* ⊕ *www. adolfodominguez.com* Ⓜ *Serrano.*

Delpozo

CLOTHING | Jesús del Pozo, the prominent designer behind this renowned fashion house, died in 2011, and it's now Josep Font who extends its creative legacy with modern clothes for both sexes. It's an excellent, if pricey, place to try on some modern Spanish couture. ⊠ *Calle de Lagasca 19, Salamanca* ☎ *91/219–4038* ⊕ *www.delpozo.com* Ⓜ *Serrano.*

Intropia

CLOTHING | Intropia's fashion lines are consistently subtle, gossamer, and flowy. (Note that this brand used to be called Hoss.) ⊠ *Calle de Serrano 18, Salamanca* ☎ *91/781–0612* ⊕ *www.intropia.com* Ⓜ *Serrano.*

Loewe

CLOTHING | This sumptuous store carries high-quality designer purses, accessories, and clothing made of butter-soft leather in gorgeous jewel tones. The store at Serrano 26 displays the women's collection; men's items are a block away, at Serrano 34. The Gran Vía location opened a small fashion museum (free entry) in 2019 chronicling the history of the iconic Spanish brand with pieces dating back to the 19th century. ⊠ *Calle de Serrano 26 and 34, Salamanca* ☎ *91/577–6056* ⊕ *www.loewe.com* Ⓜ *Serrano.*

Pedro del Hierro

CLOTHING | This Madrileño designer has a solid reputation for his sophisticated but uncomplicated clothes for both sexes. ⊠ *Calle de Serrano 29 and 40, Salamanca* ☎ *91/575–6906* ⊕ *www.pedrodelhierro. com* Ⓜ *Serrano.*

FOOD AND WINE

★ Lavinia

WINE/SPIRITS | Welcome to one of the largest wine stores in Europe. Beyond the encyclopedic selection of bottles, find books, glasses, and bar accessories here as well as a restaurant, Enomatic tasting bar, and newly opened outdoor patio. ⊠ *Calle de José Ortega y Gasset 16, Salamanca* ☎ *91/426–0604* ⊕ *www. lavinia.es* Ⓜ *Núñez de Balboa.*

Mantequerías Bravo

FOOD/CANDY | In the heart of Salamanca's shopping area, this store sells Spanish wines, olive oils, cheeses, and hams. ⊠ *Calle de Ayala 24, Salamanca* ☎ *91/576–7641* ⊕ *www.mantequeriasbravo.com* Ⓜ *Serrano.*

TEXTILES

★ Ábbatte

TEXTILES/SEWING | Every blanket, tablecloth, throw, and rug sold at this contemporary textile shop is woven by hand using the finest natural fibers in the Cistercian abbey of Santa María de la Sierra in Segovia. ⊠ *Calle Villanueva 27, Salamanca* ☎ *91/622–5530* ⊕ *www. abbatte.com* ⊙ *Closed Sun.*

Chueca

Chueca is named after Plaza de Chueca, a central square in the neighborhood that is named for Federico Chueca, a Spanish composer and writer. It's small but lively and known for its nightlife and bar scene. Chueca is part of the larger neighborhood of Justicia and borders Malasaña to the west.

🍽 Restaurants

★ Casa Hortensia Restaurante y Sidrería

$$ | SPANISH | FAMILY | Approximate a vacation to the north of Spain by dining at this true-blue Asturian restaurant (or at the more casual *sidrería*, located in the bar area), where that region's unsung

comfort-food dishes—such as *fabada* (pork-and-bean stew), Cabrales cheese, and *cachopo* (cheese-stuffed beef cutlets)—take center stage. The obligatory tipple is *sidra,* bone-dry Asturian cider that's aerated using a battery-powered gadget designed for this task. **Known for:** authentic fabada; cider bottles with DIY aerators; locals-only crowd. [$] *Average main: €19* ✉ *Calle Farmacia 2, 2nd and 3rd fl., Chueca* ✣ *Situated in what appears to be an apartment building* ☎ *91/539–0090* 🌐 *www.casahortensia.com* 🕓 *Closed Mon. No dinner Sun.* [M] *Chueca.*

★ Casa Salvador

$$ | **SPANISH** | Whether you approve of bullfighting or not, the culinary excellence of Casa Salvador—a checkered-tablecloth, taurine-themed restaurant that opened in 1941—isn't up for debate. Sit down to generous servings of feather-light fried hake, hearty oxtail stew, and other stodgy (in the best way) Spanish classics, all served by hale old-school waiters clad in white jackets. **Known for:** time-warpy decor; walls packed with bullfighting paraphernalia; killer fried hake and stewed oxtail. [$] *Average main: €18* ✉ *Calle de Barbieri 12, Chueca* ☎ *91/521–4524* 🌐 *www.casasalvadormadrid.com* 🕓 *Closed Sun.* [M] *Chueca.*

Celso y Manolo

$ | **TAPAS** | **FAMILY** | Named after the brothers who founded the restaurant (though under new ownership), this place has around a dozen tables and an extensive, eclectic menu geared toward sharing that hinges on natural products—game meats, seafood, cheeses—from the mountainous northerly region of Cantabria. Natural and often organic wines sourced from around the country make for spot-on pairings. **Known for:** market-driven cuisine; Cantabrian specialties; extremely varied menu. [$] *Average main: €14* ✉ *Calle Libertad 1, Chueca* ☎ *91/531–8079* 🌐 *www.celsoymanolo.es* [M] *Chueca.*

La Tita Rivera

$ | **SPANISH** | This budget-friendly place—specializing in hot stuffed bread rolls (called *casis*) and flavored hard cider—has an industrial vibe, thanks to exposed pipes, high ceilings, and a semiopen kitchen. But the bar's most exceptional asset is its interior patio area, a well-kept secret among madrileños living in the area. **Known for:** stuffed bread rolls; hidden interior patio; flavored draft ciders. [$] *Average main: €11* ✉ *Calle Pérez Galdós 4, Chueca* ☎ *91/522–1890* 🌐 *www.latitarivera.com* [M] *Chueca.*

Mercado de la Reina

$$ | **TAPAS** | Perhaps the only worthwhile tapas restaurant on Gran Vía, Madrid's main commercial artery, Mercado de la Reina serves everything from croquetas to grilled vegetables to tossed salads. Enjoy them in the casual bar area, in the slightly more formal dining room, or on the outdoor patio. **Known for:** inexpensive eats; being the only decent spot on Gran Vía; lounge bar downstairs. [$] *Average main: €17* ✉ *Calle Gran Vía 12, Chueca* ☎ *91/521–3198* 🌐 *www.grupomercado-delareina.com* [M] *Banco de España.*

Trattoria Pulcinella

$ | **ITALIAN** | **FAMILY** | When Enrico Bosco arrived in Madrid from Italy in the early '90s, he couldn't find a decent Italian restaurant—so he decided to open one. Always bustling and frequented by families and young couples, this trattoria seems like a direct transplant from Naples with its superb fresh pastas, pizzas, and focaccias. (La Cantina di Pulcinella, located across the street, is under the same ownership and serves the same food.) **Known for:** affordable down-home Italian fare; family-friendly vibe; excellent fresh pastas. [$] *Average main: €14* ✉ *Calle de Regueros 7, Chueca* ☎ *91/319–7363* 🌐 *www.gruppopulcinella.com* [M] *Chueca.*

Hotels

★ Only YOU Boutique Hotel

$$$$ | HOTEL | The Ibizan owners of this hotel bring that island's mix of glamour, energy, and cutting-edge music and design to one of Madrid's most happening neighborhoods. **Pros:** location among trendy cafés and shops; double-paned glass blocks out street noise; late checkout. **Cons:** sleeping area is a bit cramped; rooms with views of Calle Barquillo are pricey; scant storage space for suitcases. $ *Rooms from: €260* ✉ *Calle Barquillo 21, Chueca* ☎ *91/005–2222* ⊕ *www. onlyyouhotels.com/en* ⤴ *70 rooms* ⦾ *No meals* Ⓜ *Chueca.*

The Principal Madrid

$$$$ | HOTEL | Dozens of hotels flank Gran Vía, Madrid's main artery, but only the Principal can claim five stars. **Pros:** hotel rooftop with best views in Madrid; Ramón Freixa–helmed restaurant; luxury feel with personal touches. **Cons:** rooms not properly soundproofed; rooftop pool is tiny; gym doesn't open until 10 am. $ *Rooms from: €280* ✉ *Calle Marqués de Valdeiglesias 1, Chueca* ☎ *91/521– 8743* ⊕ *www.theprincipalmadridhotel. com* ⤴ *76 rooms* ⦾ *No meals* Ⓜ *Chueca.*

★ Room Mate Óscar

$$$ | HOTEL | Boasting one of the swankiest rooftop pools in the heart of Chueca, Madrid's "gayborhood," Room Mate Óscar caters to an artsy crowd. **Pros:** playful design accents; see-and-be-seen clientele; rooftop pool and lounge. **Cons:** noisy street and rooftop; might be too happening for some; pool only open in summer. $ *Rooms from: €175* ✉ *Pl. Vázquez de Mella 12, Chueca* ☎ *91/701–1173* ⊕ *www.room-matehotels.com* ⤴ *69 rooms* ⦾ *Free Breakfast* Ⓜ *Chueca.*

★ URSO Hotel and Spa

$$$ | HOTEL | Housed in a regal turn-of-the-20th-century municipal building, this luxury hotel and spa boasts old-world luxury and avant-garde design to satisfy alternative types and jet-setters alike. **Pros:** stunning facade; Natura Bissé spa with 7-meter hydromassage pool; sanctuary-like rooms. **Cons:** bar closes at midnight; construction next door; smallish gym. $ *Rooms from: €210* ✉ *Calle de Mejía Lequerica 8, Chueca* ☎ *91/444– 4458* ⊕ *www.hotelurso.com* ⤴ *78 rooms* ⦾ *No meals* Ⓜ *Alonso Martinez.*

Shopping

BOUTIQUES AND FASHION

Oteyza

CLOTHING | Every garment sold at master tailor Oteyza takes at least two months to make, and the classic craftsmanship shows in the immaculate suits, jackets, and shirts. Get fitted while you're in Madrid and pony up the euros for shipping—you won't regret it. ✉ *Calle Conde de Xiquena 11, Chueca* ☎ *91/448–8623* ⊕ *www.deoteyza.com* ⦿ *Closed Sun.* Ⓜ *Chueca.*

Pez

CLOTHING | A favorite among fashion-magazine editors, this store has two branches—one dedicated to high-end women's wear and another to furniture and decor—on the same street. ✉ *Calle de Regueros 2 and 15, Chueca* ☎ *91/308– 6677* ⊕ *www.pez-pez.es* Ⓜ *Chueca.*

Próxima Parada

CLOTHING | The bubbly owner of this womenswear store culls daring, colorful garments from Spanish designers for her devoted (mostly 40-and-above) clientele. ✉ *Calle Conde de Xiquena 9, Chueca* ☎ *91/523–1929* ⦿ *Closed Sun.* Ⓜ *Chueca.*

CERAMICS

Guille García-Hoz

CERAMICS/GLASSWARE | Take home one of this iconic ceramicist's painted plates or gleaming white urns decorated with animal motifs. ✉ *Calle Pelayo 43, Chueca* ☎ *91/022–4745* ⊕ *www.guillegarciahoz. com* ⦿ *Closed Sun.* Ⓜ *Chueca.*

FOOD AND WINE

Poncelet Cheese Bar

FOOD/CANDY | At this gourmet cheese bar and shop, you can find more than 120 different cheeses from all over Spain as well as some 300 others from France, Portugal, Italy, and the Netherlands. Marmalades, wines, and other assorted cheese accompaniments are available. ✉ *Calle José Abascal 61, Chamberí* ☎ *91/399–2550* 🌐 *www.ponceletcheese-bar.es* [M] *Gregorio Marañón.*

Malasaña

Malasaña is in the center of Madrid, just north of the Gran Vía and south of the traditional Madrid neighborhood of Chamberi. It's known primarily for its party scene and nightlife but also as one of Madrid's coolest neighborhoods.

🍴 Restaurants

★ Bodega de la Ardosa

$ | **SPANISH** | A 19th-century bodega, with barrel tables and dusty gewgaws hanging from the walls, Bodega de la Ardosa is an anachronism in Malasaña, an unapologetically gentrified neighborhood. La Ardosa pours refreshing vermouth and draft beers, but the bar's claim to fame—and the dish madrileños make special trips for—is its award-winning *tortilla española,* or Spanish omelet, always served warm with a gooey center. **Known for:** 100-plus years of history; award-winning tortilla española; draft vermú and unfiltered fino sherry. [$] *Average main: €13* ✉ *Calle Colón 13, Malasaña* ☎ *91/521–4979* 🌐 *www.laardosa.es* 💳 *No credit cards* [M] *Tribunal.*

Café Comercial

$$ | **SPANISH** | When this centenary café—one of the oldest in Madrid—shuttered in 2015, ostensibly for good, the public outcry was so great that it inspired Grupo El Escondite (of Lady Madonna, Barbara Ann, and El Escondite) to buy the property and give it a much-needed revamp in 2017. In a dining room that combines original design elements (huge mirrors, carved wooden columns) with new cutting-edge fixtures, feast on a menu that's a dance between Café Comercial *clásicos* and novel creations by chef Pepe Roch. **Known for:** history as one of Madrid's first literary cafés; modern menus by Pepe Roch; outstanding seafood rice. [$] *Average main: €18* ✉ *Glorieta de Bilbao 7, Malasaña* ☎ *91/088–2525* 🌐 *www.cafecomercialmadrid.com.*

🍸 Nightlife

BARS AND CAFÉS

Cazador

BARS/PUBS | You may as well be in Williamsburg or Kreuzberg at this popular and unflamboyant (mostly) gay bar where a bearded-and-bunned clientele sips cañas and cocktails before heading out to the discoteca. ✉ *Calle Pozas 7, Malasaña* ☎ *63/997–0916* [M] *Noviciado.*

De Vinos

WINE BARS—NIGHTLIFE | A snug, casual wine bar situated in the artsy Conde Duque area of Malasaña, De Vinos pours hard-to-find wines from regions like Bierzo, Somontano, and—*claro que sí*—Madrid. Cured sausages and Spanish cheeses make fine accompaniments. ✉ *Calle de la Palma 76, Malasaña* ☎ *91/182–3499* [M] *Noviciado.*

1862 Dry Bar

BARS/PUBS | One of Madrid's swankiest and most skilled coctelerías, 1862 Dry Bar shakes and stirs meticulously prepared cocktails that incorporate sherries and unconventional aromatics. The only snag? On busy nights, drinks take forever to arrive. ✉ *Calle Pez 27, Malasaña* ☎ *60/953–1151* 🌐 *www.1862drybar.com* [M] *Plaza de España.*

Fábrica Maravillas

BREWPUBS/BEER GARDENS | This is Madrid's only city-center brewpub; taste fun and funky beers that were fermented in the

"beer lab" a few feet from your barstool. ⊠ *Calle de Valverde 29, Malasaña* ☎ *91/521–8753* ⊕ *www.fmaravillas.com* Ⓜ *Gran Via*.

★ Toma Café

CAFES—NIGHTLIFE | The originator of Madrid's third-wave coffee revolution, Toma is a Malasaña institution and a favorite among expats and coffee-geek locals. After satisfying your cold brew, flat white, or pour-over cravings, indulge in any of the delicious open-face *tostas*. Toma opened a second outpost in 2017 off Plaza de Olavide at Calle Santa Feliciana 5; it's less packed and more conducive to leisurely laptopping. ⊠ *Calle de la Palma 49, Malasaña* ☎ *91/704–9344* ⊕ *www.tomacafe.es* Ⓜ *Plaza de España*.

Santamaría

BARS/PUBS | This cocktail bar mixes vintage design with artsy touches and caters to a laid-back, bohemian crowd. Choose from a variety of not-too-fussy cocktails including one bearing the club's name, made with mixed-berry juice and vodka or gin. ⊠ *Calle de la Ballesta 6, Malasaña* ☎ *91/166–0511* Ⓜ *Gran Via*.

DANCE CLUBS
★ BarCo

DANCE CLUBS | One of Malasaña's most popular nightclubs, for both its live shows (funk, jazz, and more) and late-night DJ sets, BarCo is a guaranteed good time. Acoustics here are top-notch. ⊠ *Calle del Barco 34, Malasaña* ☎ *91/531–7754* ⊕ *www.barcobar.com* Ⓜ *Plaza de España*.

Ocho y Medio

DANCE CLUBS | If you like booze-fueled pop and techno parties frequented by college kids that peak at 3 am, then Ocho y Medio is for you. Arrive before 1 am to avoid slow, snaking lines. ⊠ *Calle Barceló 11, Malasaña* ☎ *91/541–3500* ⊕ *www. ochoymedioclub.com* ☉ *Closed Mon.– Wed.* Ⓜ *Tribunal*.

MUSIC CLUBS
Café la Palma

MUSIC CLUBS | There are four different spaces in this divey local favorite: a bar in front, a music venue for intimate concerts (pop, rock, electronic, hip-hop), a chill-out room in the back, and a café in the center room. ⊠ *Calle de La Palma 62, Malasaña* ☎ *91/522–5031* ⊕ *www. cafelapalma.com* Ⓜ *Noviciado*.

🆕 Performing Arts

Centro Cultural de Conde Duque

CONCERTS | This massive venue is best known for its summer live music concerts (flamenco, jazz, pop) and also has free and often interesting exhibitions, lectures, and theater performances. The pleasant, quiet library is a good place for studying or working. ⊠ *Calle Conde Duque 11, Malasaña* ☎ *91/588–5834* ⊕ *www.condeduquemadrid.es* Ⓜ *Ventura Rodríguez*.

FLAMENCO
★ Teatro Flamenco

CONCERTS | FAMILY | Less traditional *tablao* and more modern performance venue, Teatro Flamenco hosts a variety of classical and modern interpretations of flamenco dance and song. Check the website for upcoming acts. ⊠ *Calle del Pez 10, Malasaña* ☎ *91/159–2005* ⊕ *www.teatroflamencomadrid.com* Ⓜ *Noviciado*.

💼 Shopping

ART AND DESIGN
La Fiambrera

ART GALLERIES | The polar opposite of your standard stuffy gallery, La Fiambrera sells colorful pop art at affordable prices. There's a small bookshop and café, should your feet need a rest. ⊠ *Calle del Pez 7, Malasaña* ☎ *91/704–6030* ⊕ *www. lafiambrera.net* Ⓜ *Plaza de España*.

BOUTIQUES AND FASHION
Magpie Vintage

CLOTHING | A fashion temple that screams "Movida Madrileña," the '80s counter-cultural movement that ushered Madrid into the modern era, this vintage store is decked out with wildly patterned skirts and dresses and fluorescent track jackets. ⊠ *Calle Velarde 3, Malasaña* ☎ *91/448–3104* ⊕ *www.magpie.es* Ⓜ *Bilbao.*

Muroexe

SHOES/LUGGAGE/LEATHER GOODS | Try on Muroexe's ultracomfy, streamlined lace-ups that toe the line between sneakers and dress shoes, and you'll likely walk out the door wearing them. The independently owned boutique also sells durable backpacks, slippers, and raincoats. ⊠ *Calle de Fuencarral 67, Malasaña* ☎ *91/046–8383* ⊕ *www.muroexe.com* Ⓜ *Muroexe.*

★ Natalia Lumbreras

JEWELRY/ACCESSORIES | Splurge on eye-popping hand-painted (and printed) silk scarves at this appointment-only boutique. Lumbreras's handiwork has been sold as far afield as Paris, Tokyo, and New York. ⊠ *Calle San Lorenzo 11, Malasaña* ☎ *63/087–5700* ⊕ *www.natalialumbreras.com* Ⓜ *Alonzo Martinez.*

★ Sportivo

CLOTHING | Feast your eyes on the best menswear boutique in the city with two floors of hand-picked garments by the buzziest designers out of Spain, France, Japan, and beyond. ⊠ *Calle Conde Duque 20, Malasaña* ☎ *91/542–5661* ⊕ *www.sportivostore.com.*

FOOD
★ Quesería Cultivo

FOOD/CANDY | This sleek *quesería,* which opened in 2014, might be the city's best cheese shop. Seek out rare treasures like Torrejón, a raw ashed-rind sheep's cheese from Castile. ⊠ *Calle Conde Duque 15, Malasaña* ☎ *91/127–3126* ⊕ *www.queseriacultivo.com* Ⓜ *San Bernardo.*

Chamberí

Chamberí is a large area to the north of Malasaña, Chueca, and Barrio de las Letras. It's mostly residential but has a few lively spots, especially the streets around Plaza de Olavide and Calle Ponzano, a favorite high-end tapas drag.

Sights

★ Museo Sorolla

MUSEUM | See the world through the exceptional eye of Spain's most famous impressionist painter, Joaquín Sorolla (1863–1923), who lived and worked most of his life at the home and garden he designed. Every corner is filled with exquisite artwork—including plenty of original Sorollas—and impeccably selected furnishings, which pop against brightly colored walls that evoke the Mediterranean coast, where the painter was born. This museum can be seen as part of the Abono Cinco Palacios, a €12 pass that grants access to five mansion-museums. ⊠ *Paseo del General Martinez Campos 37, Chamberí* ☎ *91/310–1584* ⊕ *museosorolla.mcu.es* ⊡ *€3 (free Sat. after 2 and all day Sun.)* ⊙ *Closed Mon.* Ⓜ *Rubén Darío, Gregorio Marañón.*

 Restaurants

Lakasa

$$$ | SPANISH | Basque chef César Martín has a devoted local following for his hyperseasonal menus that show a sincere dedication to food sustainability. Lakasa may have moved into a bigger, more modern space, but Martín's specialties haven't wavered: be sure to indulge in the Idiazabal fritters, crisp orbs redolent of smoky sheep's cheese. **Known for:** experimental Basque cuisine; Idiazabal fritters; pristine seafood. Ⓢ *Average main: €24* ⊠ *Calle Santa Engracia 120, Chamberí* ☎ *91/533–8715* ⊕ *www.lakasa.es* ⊙ *Closed Sun. and Mon.* Ⓜ *Cuatro Caminos.*

A typical evening scene: beer and tapas on the terrace of one of Madrid's many tapas bars

Las Tortillas de Gabino

$$ | **TAPAS** | At this lively restaurant you'll find crowds of Spaniards gobbling up one of the city's finest, most upmarket renditions of the tortilla española with unconventional add-ins like octopus, potato chips, and truffles. Travelers with tortilla fatigue can rest easy knowing that the menu includes plenty of equally succulent non-egg choices (the rice dishes in particular stand out). **Known for:** fancy tortillas; date-night ambience; carefully selected wines. $ *Average main: €16* ⊠ *Calle Rafael Calvo 20, Chamberí* ☎ *91/319–7505* ⊕ *www.lastortillasdegabino.com* ⊘ *Closed Sun.* Ⓜ *Rubén Darío.*

Nakeima Dumpling Bar

$$ | **ASIAN FUSION** | Good thing the *bao*s, dumplings, and *nigiri*s are out-of-this-world spectacular at Nakeima—if not, no one would wait the hour (on average) it takes to get in. Dishes here are "Asian freestyle" (their term) and bridge the gap between East and West with dishes like Thai-spiced tripe and a squab "Kit Kat." **Known for:** Spanish-Asian fusion cuisine;

eclectic dumplings and baos; lines out the door. $ *Average main: €22* ⊠ *Calle de Meléndez Valdés 54, Chamberí* ☎ *62/070–9399* ⊘ *Closed Sun. and Mon.*

Sala de Despiece

$$ | **SPANISH** | The opening of this ultratrendy butcher-shop-themed restaurant spurred the revival of Calle Ponzano as Madrid's most exciting tapas street. Feast on eye-catching, impeccably prepared dishes like carpaccio-truffle roll-ups and grilled octopus slathered in chimichurri. **Known for:** local celebrity chef; playful industrial decor; see-and-be-seen crowd. $ *Average main: €19* ⊠ *Calle de Ponzano 11, Chamberí* ☎ *91/752–6106* ⊕ *www.saladedespiece.com.*

Santceloni

$$$$ | **MEDITERRANEAN** | Chef Óscar Velasco delivers exquisite combinations of Mediterranean ingredients accompanied by a comprehensive and unusual wine list. Go with an appetite and lots of time (a minimum of three hours), because a meal here is ceremonious. **Known for:**

wide cocktail and wine menu; highly orchestrated tasting menus; standout cheese course. $ *Average main: €50* ✉ *Hotel Hesperia, Paseo de la Castellana 57, Chamberí* ☎ *91/210–8840* ⊕ *www.restaurantesantceloni.com* ⊘ *Closed Sun. No lunch Sat.* Ⓜ *Gregorio Marañón.*

★ Tripea
$$$$ | FUSION | Young-gun chef Roberto Martínez Foronda is turning food critics' heads with his newcomer Spanish-fusion restaurant hidden inside the Mercado de Vallehermoso, Chamberí's traditional market. It earned a coveted Bib Gourmand in 2019. **Known for:** experimental tasting menus; Spanish-fusion cuisine; foodie buzz. $ *Average main: €35* ✉ *Calle de Vallehermoso 36, Chamberí* ☎ *91/828–6947* ⊕ *www.tripea.es* ⊘ *Closed Sun. and Mon.* Ⓜ *Quevedo.*

Hotels

★ AC Santo Mauro, Autograph Collection
$$$$ | HOTEL | This fin-de-siècle palace in the Chamberí district, first a duke's residence and later the Canadian embassy, is now an intimate luxury hotel (managed by Marriott), an oasis of calm removed from the city center. **Pros:** a world away from the city's hustle and bustle; cloudlike beds; fine restaurant. **Cons:** pricey breakfast; not in the historic center; some rooms on the smaller side. $ *Rooms from: €320* ✉ *Calle Zurbano 36, Chamberí* ☎ *91/319–6900* ⊕ *www. ac-hotels.com* ⤴ *51 rooms* ⓞ *No meals* Ⓜ *Alonso Martínez, Rubén Darío.*

Hotel Sardinero
$$ | HOTEL | Steps from the trendy Malasaña and gay-friendly Chueca districts, and slightly off the tourist track, Hotel Sardinero opened in May 2017 in a turn-of-the-century palace previously occupied by Innside Génova. **Pros:** mellow earth-tone interiors; two rooftop terraces; gorgeous neoclassical facade. **Cons:** gym could be bigger; no restaurant; kettles and coffeemakers only available upon request. $ *Rooms from: €130* ✉ *Pl. Alonso Martínez 3, Chamberí* ☎ *91/206–2160* ⊕ *www.hotelsardineromadrid.com* ⤴ *63 rooms* ⓞ *No meals* Ⓜ *Bilbao.*

Intercontinental Madrid
$$$$ | HOTEL | Chauffeur-driven town cars snake around the block day and night at the Intercontinental Madrid, a classically decorated hotel frequented by dignitaries, diplomats, and other international bigwigs. **Pros:** starchy, dependable elegance; newly refurbished 24-hour gym; excellent business facilities. **Cons:** cookie-cutter business hotel decor; removed from the center; street-facing rooms can be noisy. $ *Rooms from: €230* ✉ *Paseo de la Castellana 49, Chamberí* ☎ *91/700–7300* ⊕ *www.ihg.com* ⤴ *302 rooms* ⓞ *No meals* Ⓜ *Gregorio Marañón.*

Orfila
$$$$ | HOTEL | On a leafy residential street not far from Plaza Colón and the gallery-lined Chueca district, this elegant 1886 town house boasts every comfort of larger five-star Madrid hotels—sans the stuffy corporate vibes. **Pros:** quiet street; refined, classic interiors; attentive service. **Cons:** decidedly unhip decor; no gym; low-key neighborhood without much nightlife. $ *Rooms from: €345* ✉ *Calle Orfila 6, Chamberí* ☎ *91/702–7770* ⊕ *www.hotelorfila.com* ⤴ *32 rooms* ⓞ *No meals* Ⓜ *Alonso Martínez.*

Nightlife

MUSIC CLUBS
Clamores
DANCE CLUBS | Hear good jazz concerts and world music until 5:30 am on weekdays and 6 am on weekends. Check the website for performance listings and to buy tickets. ✉ *Albuquerque 14, Chamberí* ☎ *91/445–5480* ⊕ *www.salaclamores.es* ⊘ *Closes at 11 pm Sun.* Ⓜ *Bilbao.*

GOOOOOALL!

Fútbol (or soccer) is Spain's number-one sport, and Madrid has four teams: Real Madrid, Atlético Madrid, Rayo Vallecano, and Getafe. The two major teams are Real Madrid and Atlético Madrid. For tickets, book online or call a week in advance to reserve and pick them up at the stadium—or, if the match isn't sold out, stand in line at the stadium of your choice. Ticket prices vary according to several factors: the importance of the rival, the seat location, the day of the week the match takes place, whether the match is aired on free TV or not, and the competition (Liga, Copa del Rey, Champions League or Europa League). Final dates and match times are often confirmed only a few days before so it can be hard to reserve in advance. That said, Real Madrid CF and Atlético Madrid never play at home the same week so there is a football match every single week in the city. So if you don't care which club you see, you always have a chance to get tickets.

Stadiums

Santiago Bernabéu Stadium Home to Real Madrid, this stadium seats 85,400 and offers daytime tours of the facilities. A controversial $590 million renovation was approved by the city council in May 2019 and will take approximately 3½ years to complete; tour and game schedules may be affected, so check the website for updates. ⊠ *Paseo de la Castellana 140, Chamartín* ☎ *91/398–4300* ⊕ *www.realmadrid.es* Ⓜ *Santiago Bernabeu.*

Wanda Metropolitano Since 2017, Atlético Madrid has called this stadium in the San Blas–Canillejas district home. ⊠ *Av. de Luis Aragones 4* ☎ *90/226–0403* ⊕ *www.atleticomadrid.com* Ⓜ *Estadio Metropolitano.*

■**TIP→ On the ticket, "Puerta" is the door number that you enter, "Fila" is the row, and "Número" is the seat number.**

🛍 Shopping

Nac

CLOTHING | You'll find a good selection of European designer brands (like Berga-mot, Forte Forte, Pomandere, Babo) at Nac. The store on Calle Génova is the biggest of the six in Madrid. ⊠ *Calle de Génova 18, Chamberí* ☎ *91/310–6050* ⊕ *www.nac.es* Ⓜ *Colón, Alonso Martínez.*

Chamartín

This sprawling neighborhood, which extends to the north of the city from Avenida de América, wasn't annexed to Madrid until 1948. During the following decades, and due to the construction of new sites such as the Chamartín Train Station and the National Auditorium of Music, it has been gaining popularity among madrileños as a good and lively place to live. The famous leaning "Gate of Europe" towers are situated here, as are many office buildings, convention centers, and business hotels.

🍴 Restaurants

★ Casa Benigna

$$$ | SPANISH | Owner Don Norberto, a quirky, jolly gent, offers a health-con-scious menu with painstakingly selected wines to match at this snug, book-lined restaurant. Rice dishes are the house specialty, and they're cooked in extra-flat paella pans specially manufactured for the restaurant. **Known for:** city's best paella; larger-than-life owner; homey atmosphere. $ *Average main: €26* ⊠ *Calle de Benigno Soto 9, Chamartín* 🕾 *91/416–9357* ⊙ *No dinner Sun. and Mon.* Ⓜ *Concha Espina, Prosperidad.*

★ DiverXO

$$$$ | ECLECTIC | When you ask a madrileño about a remarkable food experience—something that stirs the senses beyond feeding one's appetite—David Muñoz's bombastic venue is often the first name you'll hear. Nothing is offered à la carte; the restaurant serves tasting menus (called "canvases") only, running €195–€250. **Known for:** punk-rock fine dining; courses that use the whole table as a canvas; Madrid's only Michelin three-star. $ *Average main: €200* ⊠ *NH Hotel Eurobuilding, Calle Padre Damían 23, Chamartín* 🕾 *91/570–0766* ⊕ *www.diverxo.com* ⊙ *Closed Sun. and Mon.* Ⓜ *Cuzco.*

Sacha

$$$ | SPANISH | Settle into a unhurried feast at Sacha, a cozy bistro with soul-satisfying food and hand-selected wines, and you might never want to leave—especially if you strike up a conversation with Sacha himself, who's quite the character. The cuisine is regional Spanish—think *butifarra* sausages with sautéed mushrooms or razor clams with black garlic emulsion—with just enough imagination to make you wonder why the restaurant isn't better known. **Known for:** Spanish bistro fare; impeccable steak tartare; hard-to-find wines. $ *Average main: €24* ⊠ *Calle Juan Hurtado de Mendoza 11, Chamartín* 🕾 *91/345–5952* ⊙ *Closed Sun.* Ⓜ *Cuzco.*

Hotels

Hesperia Madrid

$$$ | HOTEL | A five-star hotel geared toward the business traveler, Hesperia Madrid is located in the city's financial district, miles away from the tourist hubbub and within walking distance of Bernabéu Stadium and the National Museum of Natural Sciences. **Pros:** open-air gym; award-winning restaurant; 24-hour room service. **Cons:** interior rooms can be dark; stuffy, corporate feel; miles from the center. $ *Rooms from: €179* ⊠ *Paseo de la Castellana 57, Chamartín* 🕾 *91/210–8800* ⊕ *www.hesperia-madrid.com* 🛏 *170 rooms* ⊙ *No meals* Ⓜ *Gregorio Marañón.*

★ Hotel NH Collection Madrid Eurobuilding

$$ | HOTEL | The towering NH Collection Madrid Eurobuilding, located blocks from Real Madrid's home stadium, is a state-of-the-art luxury property with large, airy rooms, and an enormous pool and gym complex. **Pros:** 180-degree views from some rooms; excellent gym and spa; one of Madrid's top restaurants. **Cons:** inconsistent service; hotel can't secure bookings at DiverXO; area dies at night. $ *Rooms from: €145* ⊠ *Calle de Padre Damián 23, Chamartín* 🕾 *91/353–7300* ⊕ *www.nh-hotels.com* 🛏 *440 rooms* ⊙ *No meals* Ⓜ *Cuzco.*

Hotel Puerta de América

$$ | HOTEL | Inspired by Paul Eluard's *La Liberté*, whose verses are written across the facade, the owners of this hotel granted an unlimited budget to 19 of the world's top architects and designers. **Pros:** an architect's dreamland; top-notch restaurant and bars; candlelit pool and steam room area. **Cons:** miles from the center; interiors doesn't always get the required maintenance; design impractical in places. $ *Rooms from: €130* ⊠ *Av. de América 41, Chamartín* 🕾 *91/744–5400* ⊕ *www.hotelpuertamerica.com* 🛏 *315 rooms* ⊙ *No meals* Ⓜ *Av. de América.*

Nightlife

CAFÉS
Domo Lounge and Terrace
BARS/PUBS | The NH hotel chain is building a top-notch food-and-drink stronghold north of the city around its Eurobuilding property. Besides DiverXO and Domo restaurants there's now a cocktail bar with an enclosed terrace, run by Diego Cabrera, the city's top mixologist. Choose from all-time classic cocktails and original creations. ⊠ *Calle de Padre Damián 23, Chamartín* ☎ *91/353–7300* ⊕ *www.nh-hotels.com* Ⓜ *Cuzco.*

Tetuán

As Madrid grew dramatically in the second half of the 19th century, rough-and-tumble barrios like Tetuán got a face-lift. Today, it's main artery, Bravo Murillo, divides the more developed, business-oriented eastern section from the more residential and multicultural western area of the neighborhood.

 Restaurants

Al-Aga
$ | **MIDDLE EASTERN** | **FAMILY** | Madrileños love kebabs, and the smoky, juicy version served at Al-Aga is far and away the city's best. Opened by a family of refugees fleeing Syria's civil war, Al-Aga draws on recipes handed down to the chef and owner, Labib, who cooks with care and attention to detail: meat is ground by hand for each order, and all the sauces are homemade. **Known for:** flame-grilled kebabs; grab-and-go style; Syrian specialties. Ⓢ *Average main: €9* ⊠ *Calle Villaamil 52, Tetuán* ☎ *91/070–3115* Ⓜ *Tetuán.*

Nightlife

DANCE CLUBS
New Garamond
DANCE CLUBS | At this hopping venue, popular among Latino locals, you'll find plenty of space to dance (under the gaze of go-go girls), and also quieter nooks where you can chat and sip a drink. It's open nights Tuesday–Saturday. ⊠ *Calle Rosario Pino 14, Tetuán* ☎ *62/053–2656* ⊕ *www.newgaramondmadrid.es* ⊘ *Closed Sun.–Wed.* Ⓜ *Cuzco.*

Chapter 4

CENTRAL SPAIN

Updated by
Benjamin Kemper

4

WELCOME TO CENTRAL SPAIN

TOP REASONS TO GO

★ **See El Greco's Toledo:** Tour the Renaissance painter's home and studio on an El Greco–themed tourist trail in the stunning city that the Greek-born painter called home.

★ **Be mesmerized by Cuenca's Hanging Houses:** The Casas Colgadas seem to defy gravity, clinging to a cliffside with views over Castile–La Mancha's parched plains.

★ **See Salamanca's old and new cathedrals:** Compare the intricate late Gothic detail of the new with the Romanesque simplicity of the old.

★ **Visit Segovia's aqueduct:** Against all odds, this soaring 2,000-year-old Roman aqueduct, constructed without mortar, still functions today.

★ **Time-travel to the Middle Ages:** The walled city of Cáceres is especially evocative at dusk with its skyline of ancient spires, towers, and cupolas, many of which play host to swooping storks.

1 Toledo. Discover a treasure trove of medieval art and restored synagogues, mosques, and churches in the ancient capital of Castile.

2 Almagro. Small-town charm and evening *tapeo* (tapas scene) on the plaza.

3 Cuenca. See the Hanging Houses, then explore the Ciudad Encantada ("Enchanted City") with its alien rock formations.

4 Sigüenza. Home to one of Spain's most stunning Gothic cathedrals.

5 Segovia. The watchtower of the Alcázar is said to have inspired the Disney castle.

6 Sepúlveda. A medieval dungeon and an 11th-century church in a town some call the most beautiful in Spain.

7 San Lorenzo de El Escorial. Less than an hour from Madrid, El Escorial is one of the region's top attractions.

8 Ávila. Some of the best-preserved city walls in Europe and ancient convents with sweet treats baked by nuns.

9 Salamanca. The frog on the plateresque facade of Spain's oldest university is said to bring good luck.

10 Burgos. Blood sausage and a Gothic cathedral that's well worth the pilgrimage.

11 León. The vivid stained-glass panels in the cathedral are second only to Sainte-Chapelle's in Paris.

12 Astorga. Uncover one of Gaudí's least-known masterpieces, the Episcopal Palace.

13 Villafranca del Bierzo. Vineyard-hop through the surrounding Bierzo wine region.

14 Jerte and El Valle del Jerte. One of Spain's most breathtaking natural displays.

15 La Vera and Monasterio de Yuste. Natural springs, locally made *pimentón* (paprika), and the retirement estate of King Carlos V.

16 Cáceres. This UNESCO-protected old town was a filming site for *Game of Thrones*.

17 Trujillo. Learn about Spain's colonial past in the cradle of the conquistadores.

18 Guadalupe. A bucket-list jewel in the foothills of the Sierra de las Villuercas.

19 Mérida. One of the most immaculately restored Roman amphitheaters in Europe.

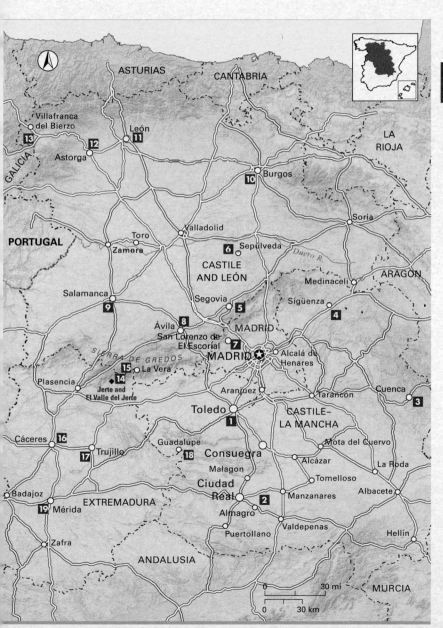

ASTURIAS

CANTABRIA

Villafranca
del Bierzo

13

León

11

GALICIA

12

Astorga

LA
RIOJA

Burgos

10

Soria

PORTUGAL

Toro

Valladolid

Zamora

Sepúlveda

6

Duero R.

CASTILE
AND LEÓN

Medinaceli

ARAGON

Salamanca

Segovia

Sigüenza

9

5

4

Ávila

8

San Lorenzo de
El Escorial

MADRID

7

MADRID

Alcalá de
Henares

SIERRA DE GREDOS

La Vera

15

Plasencia

14

Jerte and
El Valle del Jerte

Aranjuez

Tarancón

Cuenca

3

Toledo

1

CASTILE–
LA MANCHA

Cáceres

16

Guadalupe

Mota del Cuervo

17

Trujillo

18

Consuegra

Alcázar

La Roda

Malagón

Tomelloso

Ciudad
Real

Manzanares

Albacete

Badajoz

2

EXTREMADURA

19

Mérida

Almagro

Puertollano

Valdepeñas

Hellín

Zafra

ANDALUSIA

MURCIA

0   30 mi

0   30 km

EATING AND DRINKING WELL IN CASTILE AND EXTREMADURA

In Spain's central *meseta*, an arid, high plateau, peasant cooking provides comfort and energy. Roast lamb, pork, and goat are staples, as are soups, stews, and dishes made from scraps, such as the classic *migas*, bread crumbs fried with sundry meats and sausages.

Classic Castilian dishes include *cordero* (lamb) and *cochinillo* (suckling pig) roasted in wood ovens, and other prized entrées include *perdiz en escabeche* (marinated partridge) and *perdices a la toledana* (stewed partridge, Toledo style). Broad-bean dishes are specialties in the areas around Ávila and La Granja (Segovia), while *trucha* (trout) and *cangrejos de río* (river crayfish) are Guadalajara specialties. Some of Castile's most surprising cuisine is found in Cuenca, where a Moorish influence appears in such dishes as *gazpacho pastor,* a stew made with several meats and a matzo-like flatbread. Wild mushrooms enhance aromas in meat dishes and stews or are served on their own in earthenware dishes.

DON QUIXOTE FOOD

"Somewhere in La Mancha, in a place whose name I do not care to remember..." begins the epic tale of *Don Quixote*, and yet the wines and hearty dishes here are quite unforgettable. Cervantine menus are favorites at taverns and inns throughout Quixote country southeast of Madrid. They usually feature *gachas manchegas* (a thick peasant porridge based on fried grass-pea flour and pork) and *duelos y quebrantos* (scrambled eggs and bacon), dishes mentioned in the novel.

LAMB

Roast lamb, *cordero asado,* is a favorite throughout Castile. *Lechazo,* or milk-fed lamb, is handled with great care and roasted slowly to render a mild, ultra-tender meat that's a true delicacy.

PARTRIDGE

Perdiz a la toledana is one of Castile–La Mancha's most sought-after dishes. Toldeo partridges are neither *estofada* (stewed) nor *escabechada* (marinated) but, rather, cooked on low heat in wine with vinegar, olive oil, onions, garlic, and bay leaves until the sauce is thick and rich. October to February is the hunting season for partridge and the best time to try it.

VEGETABLE STEW

La Mancha has moist vegetable-growing pockets along the Tajo River. *Pisto manchego,* a ratatouille-like vegetable stew with peppers, onions, tomatoes, and zucchini, is a classic. Served in an earthenware vessel with a fried egg on top, it makes a wonderful light lunch.

MIGAS

Translated as "shepherd's bread crumbs," this ancient dish is made with stale bread that's been softened with water and fried in olive oil with lots of garlic and (sometimes) eggs, as well as finely chopped bacon, chorizo, peppers, and potato. Fresh grapes are a tradition-al accompaniment.

GAZPACHO PASTOR (SHEPHERD'S STEW)

Andalusian gazpacho is a cold soup, but in La Mancha, especially around Cuenca, gazpacho is a thick, hot braise made with virtually everything in the barnyard. Partridge, hare, rabbit, hen, peppers, paprika, and *tortas de cenceña* (flatbread made especially for this dish) complete the stew.

CASTILIAN WINES

In Toledo, Carlos Falcó (aka El Marqués de Griñón) has developed excellent Dominio de Valdepusa wines using petit verdot and syrah grapes. In Ribera del Duero, winemakers from Pingus and Protos to Pago de Carraovejas offer full-bodied wines using tempranillo, while Bierzo, northwest of León, is a region to watch for its herbaceous, multilayered wines made from the local mencía grape.

Madrid, in the center of Spain, is an excellent jumping-off point for exploring, and the high-speed train puts many destinations within easy reach. The Castiles, which bracket Madrid to the north and south, and Extremadura, bordering Portugal, are filled with compelling destinations steeped in tradition.

There's something of an underlying unity in Castile, the high, wide steppe of central Spain planted with olive trees and grapevines and punctuated with tiny medieval towns and the occasional scrubby sierra.

Over the centuries, poets and others have characterized Castile as austere and melancholy. Gaunt mountain ranges frame the horizons; gorges and rocky outcrops break up flat expanses; and the fields around Ávila and Segovia are littered with giant boulders. Castilian villages are built predominantly of granite, and their severe, formidable look contrasts markedly with the whitewashed walls of most of southern Spain.

The very name Extremadura, literally "the far end of the Duero" (as in the Douro River), expresses the wild, isolated, and end-of-the-line character of the region bordering Portugal. With its poor soil and minimal industry, Extremadura hardly experienced the economic booms felt in other parts of Spain, and it's still the country's poorest province—but for the tourist, this otherworldly, lost-in-time feel is unforgettable. No other place in Spain has as many Roman monuments as Mérida, capital of the vast Roman province of Lusitania, which included most of the western half of the Iberian Peninsula. Mérida guarded the Vía de la Plata, the major Roman highway that crossed Extremadura from north to south, connecting Gijón with Seville. The economy and the arts declined after the Romans left, but the region revived in the 16th century when explorers and conquerors of the New World—from Francisco Pizarro and Hernán Cortés to Francisco de Orellana, first navigator of the Amazon—returned to their birthplace. These men built the magnificent palaces that now glorify towns such as Cáceres and Trujillo, and they turned the remote monastery of Guadalupe into one of the great artistic repositories of Spain.

MAJOR REGIONS

Castile–La Mancha is the land of Don Quixote, Miguel de Cervantes's chivalrous hero. Some of Spain's oldest and noblest cities are found here, steeped in culture and legend, though many have fallen into neglect. In 2016, these mostly untouristed cities marked the 400th anniversary of the death of Cervantes, who died within days of his contemporary, William Shakespeare. **Toledo,** the pre-Madrid capital of Spain, is the main destination, though travelers willing to venture farther afield can explore **Cuenca** with its Hanging Houses, **Almagro** with its green-and-white plaza and splendid parador, or Consuegra or Campo de Criptana, both of which sit under the gaze of Don Quixote–esque windmills.

Castile and León. This is Spain's wind-swept interior, stretching from the dry plains of Castile–La Mancha to the hilly vineyards of Ribera del Duero, and up to the foot of several mountain ranges: the Sierra de Gredos, Sierra de Francia, and northward toward the towering Picos de Europa. The area combines two of Spain's old kingdoms, Léon and Old Castile, each with their many treasures of palaces, castles, and cathedrals. The region's crown jewel is **Segovia** with its Roman aqueduct and 12th-century alcázar, though medieval **Ávila** is a close second. Farther north lie **Salamanca,** dominated by luminescent sandstone buildings, and the ancient capitals of **Burgos** and **León.** Burgos, an early outpost of Christianity, is said to have the most beautiful Gothic cathedral in Spain. León is a vibrant college town with a budget-friendly tapas scene and nationally famous modern art museum.

Rugged **Extremadura** is a nature lover's paradise, so bring your mountain bike (or plan on renting one), hiking boots, and binoculars. The lush **Jerte Valley** and the craggy peaks of the Sierra de Gredos mark Upper Extremadura's fertile landscape. South of the Jerte Valley is the 15th-century Yuste Monastery in the village of Cuacos de Yuste. Don't miss medieval **Cáceres**—boasting one of the best-preserved old towns in Europe—and **Mérida,** with its immaculately preserved Roman amphitheater. Extremadura's other main towns—Badajoz, **Trujillo,** Olivenza, and Zafra—are charming (if a tad sleepy) and virtually tourist free.

Planning

When to Go

July and August can be brutally hot, and November through February can get bitterly cold, especially in the mountains. May and October, when the weather is sunny but relatively cool, are the two best months to visit

Spring is the ideal season in Extremadura, especially in the countryside, when the valleys and hills bloom with wildflowers. The stunning spectacle of cherry blossom season in the Jerte Valley and La Vera takes place around mid-March. Fall is also a good time for Extremadura, though there may be rain starting in late October.

Planning Your Time

Madrid is an excellent hub for venturing farther into Spain, but with so many choices, we've divided them into must-see stand-alone destinations and worthy stops en route to other parts of the country. Some are day trips; others are best overnight.

Must-see, short-trip destinations from Madrid are **Toledo, Segovia** (add **Sepúlveda** if time allows), **Sigüenza,** and **Salamanca.** Salamanca should be an overnight trip as it's farther and has buzzy nightlife.

If you're traveling to other areas in Spain, we suggest the following stopover destinations:

If you're on your way to Salamanca, stop in **Ávila** (buses go direct to Salamanca without stopping, but most trains stop in Ávila).

If you're on your way to Santander, San Sebastián, or Bilbao, stop in **Burgos.**

If you're on your way to Asturias, stop in **León.**

If you're on your way to Lugo and A Coruña, in Galicia, stop in **Villafranca del Bierzo** or **Astorga.**

If you're on your way to Córdoba or Granada, stop in **Almagro.**

If you're on your way to Valencia, detour to **Cuenca.** Most trains, including the high-speed AVE to Valencia, stop in Cuenca.

Extremadura is a neglected destination, even for Spanish tourists, but it's a beautiful part of the country with fascinating cities like Cáceres (a UNESCO World Heritage Site) and Trujillo, both of which have been used as filming locations for *Game of Thrones.* You can get a lightning impression of Extremadura in a day's drive from Madrid (or on a pit stop on the way to Lisbon), though overnighting is preferable. It's about 2½ hours from Madrid to **Jerte**; from there, take the A66 south to **Cáceres** before heading east to **Trujillo** on the N521. Split your time evenly between Cáceres and Trujillo. If you have more time, spend a day exploring the Roman monuments in **Mérida** and do some world-famous bird-watching in the **Parque Natural de Monfragüe**, near **Plasencia.** If you can, visit the **Monasterio de Yuste,** where Spain's founding emperor, Carlos V, died in 1558.

Getting Here and Around

AIR TRAVEL

The only international airport near Castile is Madrid's Barajas; Salamanca, León, and Valladolid have domestic airports, but the economic crisis has led to a reduction in traffic and they receive very few flights these days. Extremadura's only airport is Badajoz, which receives domestic flights from Madrid, Barcelona, and Tenerife.

AIRPORT CONTACTS Madrid–Barajas Adolfo Suárez Airport ⊠ *Barajas* ☎ *91/321–1000* ⊕ *www.aena.es.*

BUS TRAVEL

Bus connections between Madrid and Castile are frequent and cheap; there are several stations and stops in Madrid. Buses to Toledo (1 hour) leave every half hour from the southerly Plaza Elíptica, and buses to Segovia (1¼ hours) leave every hour from La Sepulvedana's headquarters, near Príncipe Pío. Jiménez Dorado sends buses to Ávila (1¾ hours) from the Estación del Sur. ALSA has service to León (4½ hours), Valladolid (2¼ hours), and Soria (3 hours). Avanza serves Cuenca (2¾ hours), Salamanca (3 hours), and Burgos (2½ hours).

From Burgos, buses head north to the Basque Country; from León, you can press on to Asturias. Service between towns is not as frequent as it is to and from Madrid, so you may find it quicker to return to Madrid and make your way from there. Online reservations are rarely necessary but might save you a few bucks and the minutes you'd otherwise spend waiting in line.

Buses to Extremadura's main cities from Madrid are reliable. The first bus of the day on lesser routes often sets off early in the morning, so plan carefully to avoid getting stranded. Some examples of destinations from Madrid are: Cáceres (7 daily), Guadalupe (2 daily), Trujillo (12 daily), and Mérida (7 daily). For schedules and prices, check the tourist offices or consult the individual bus lines. Note that it's best to avoid rush hour as journeys can be delayed.

■ **TIP→ The easiest way to plan bus travel is on www.goeuro.com, a scheduling and purchasing site that allows you to view different prices and bus companies on one platform.**

BUS CONTACTS ALSA ☎ *90/242–2242* ⊕ *www.alsa.es.* **Avanza** (*Auto-Res*) ☎ *91/272–2832* ⊕ *www.avanzabus.com.* **La Sepulvedana** ☎ *90/211–9699* ⊕ *www.lasepulvedana.es.* **Larrea** (*Avanza*) ☎ *91/851–5592* ⊕ *www.autobuseslarrea.*

com. **Movelia** ☎ *90/264–6428* ⊕ *www.*
movelia.es.

CAR TRAVEL

Major highways—the A1 through A6—
spoke out from Madrid, making Spain's
farthest corners no more than five- to six-
hour drives. If possible, avoid returning to
Madrid on major highways at the end of a
weekend or a holiday. The beginning and
end of August are notorious for traffic
jams, as is Semana Santa (Holy Week),
which starts on Palm Sunday and ends
on Easter Sunday. National (toll-free)
highways and back roads are slower but
provide one of the great pleasures of
driving around the Castilian countryside:
surprise encounters with historical monuments and spectacular vistas.

If you're driving from Madrid to Extremadura, the six-lane A5 moves quickly. The
A66, or Vía de la Plata, which crosses
Extremadura from north to south, is also
effective. The fastest way from Portugal
is the (Portuguese) A6 from Lisbon to
Badajoz (not to be confused with the
Spanish A6, which runs northwest from
Madrid to Galicia). Side roads—particularly those that cross the wilder mountainous districts, such as the Sierra de
Guadalupe—differ in terms of upkeep but
are wonderfully scenic.

Mileage from Madrid:

Madrid to Burgos is 243 km (151 miles).

Madrid to Cáceres is 299 km (186 miles).

Madrid to Cuenca is 168 km (104 miles).

Madrid to Granada is 428 km (266 miles).

Madrid to Léon is 334 km (208 miles).

Madrid to Salamanca is 212 km (132
miles).

Madrid to Segovia is 91 km (57 miles).

Madrid to Toledo is 88 km (55 miles).

Madrid to Ávila is 114 km (71 miles).

⇨ *The Travel Smart chapter has contact
information for major car rental agencies.*

RIDESHARE TRAVEL

As right-lane-cruising buses and low-
speed trains make intercity travel in
Castile a nuisance, travelers of all ages
are increasingly taking rideshares, the
most popular of which is Blablacar, an
app with more global users than Uber. Its
free platform allows you to book ahead
via debit or credit card and message with
the driver to set up pickup and drop-off
points. It's not only the quickest way
from A to B without a rental car but also
often the cheapest, since drivers aren't
allowed to make a profit on trips (the
amount you pay only offsets costs for
tolls and gas). Check ⊕ *www.blablacar.
com* for details.

TRAIN TRAVEL

The main towns in Castile and León and
Castile–La Mancha are accessible by
multiple daily trains from Madrid, with
tickets running about €10–€30, depending on train speed (the high-speed
AVE service costs more), the time of
day, and the day of the week. Several
towns make feasible day trips: there are
commuter trains from Madrid to Segovia
(30 minutes), Guadalajara (30 minutes),
and Toledo (30 minutes). Trains to Toledo
depart from Madrid's Atocha station;
trains to Salamanca, Burgos, and León
depart from Chamartín; and both stations
serve Ávila, Segovia, and Sigüenza,
though Chamartín has more frequent
service. Trains from Segovia go only to
Madrid, but you can change at Villalba for
Ávila and Salamanca.

For Extremadura, (notoriously rickety
and sluggish) trains from Madrid stop at
Monfragüe, Plasencia, Cáceres, Mérida,
Zafra, and Badajoz and run as often as
six times daily. The journey from Madrid
to Cáceres takes about four hours.
Within the province there are services
from Badajoz to Cáceres (three daily, 1
hour 55 minutes), to Mérida (five daily,
40 minutes), and to Plasencia (two daily,
2 hours 40 minutes); from Cáceres to
Badajoz (three daily, 1 hour 55 minutes),
to Mérida (five daily, 1 hour), to Plasencia

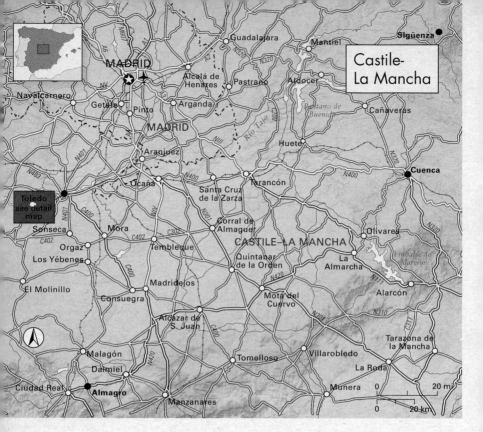

(four daily, 1 hour 10 minutes), and to Zafra (two daily, 2 hours 10 minutes); from Plasencia to Badajoz (two daily, 3 hours), to Cáceres (four daily, 1 hour 10 minutes), and to Mérida (four daily, 2 hours 10 minutes). Several cities have separate train stations for normal versus AVE high-speed rail service; the newer AVE stations are often farther from town centers. ⚠ **Through 2020, expect delays and schedule changes as the government continues to roll out a €20 million project to update the Extremaduran train network.**

TRAIN CONTACTS RENFE ☎ *90/232–0320* 🌐 *www.renfe.com.*

Restaurants

This is Spain's rugged heartland, bereft of touristy hamburger joints and filled instead with the country's most traditional *tavernas,* which attract Spanish foodies from across the country. Some of the most renowned restaurants in this region are small and family run, while a few new avant-garde spots in urban areas serve up modern architecture as well as experimental fusion dishes.

Hotels

Small, independently owned hotels abound in Castile and León, and many of the country's best-reviewed paradores (🌐 *www.paradores.es*) can be found here as well in quiet towns such as Almagro, Ávila, Cuenca, and Sigüenza. Those in Toledo, Segovia, and Salamanca are modern buildings with magnificent views and, in the case of Segovia, have wonderful indoor and outdoor swimming pools. Reacting to a spate of bad press and unsatisfactory customer reviews, the Parador brand invested €21 million in its Castile and León properties in 2019. There are plenty of pleasant alternatives to paradores, too, such as Segovia's Hotel Infanta Isabel, Salamanca's Hotel Rector, and Cuenca's Posada de San José, housed in a 16th-century convent.

In Extremadura the paradores occupy buildings of great historic or architectural interest; the Extremaduran government also runs a few *hospederías,* regional offshoots of the Parador chain. Most "high-end" hotels, with a few exceptions, are modern boxes with little character. You're almost always better off staying in a charming, underrated *hotel rural* (bed-and-breakfast inn) or *casa rural* (guesthouse).

⇨ *Hotel reviews have been shortened. For full information, visit Fodors.com.*

What It Costs in Euros			
$	$$	$$$	$$$$
RESTAURANTS			
under €12	€12–€17	€18–€22	over €22
HOTELS			
under €90	€90–€125	€126–€180	over €180

Tours

In summer the tourist offices of Segovia, Toledo, and Sigüenza organize Trenes Turísticos (miniature tourist trains) that glide past all the major sights; contact local tourist offices for schedules.

A great way to really get to know Extremadura is by bike (in any season but scorching summer), and you can essentially forego all maps by following the ancient Roman road, the Vía de la Plata. It runs through Extremadura from north to south along the A66 and passes by Plasencia, Cáceres, Mérida, and Zafra. Note that the region north of the province of Cáceres, including the Jerte

Valley, La Vera, and the area surrounding Guadalupe, is mountainous and uneven: be prepared for a bumpy and exhausting ride. The regional government has also opened four Vías Verdes, or "green way" paths geared toward hiking and biking, along disused railroads; a notable (if rugged) one goes from Logrosán (a couple of miles southwest of Guadalupe) to Villanueva de la Serena (east of Mérida and near Don Benito). Check ⊕ *www. viasverdes.com* for maps of this and other trails.

Equiberia
GUIDED TOURS | FAMILY | Horseback tours, ranging 1–10 days, offer a unique way to experience the gorges, fields, and forests of the Sierra de Guadarrama, Segovia, Ávila, and beyond. ✉ *Navarredonda de Gredos, Ávila* ☎ 68/934–3974 ⊕ *www. equiberia.com* ✉ *From €150.*

Valle Aventura
GUIDED TOURS | FAMILY | Hiking, horseback riding, cycling, and kayaking trips in the Jerte Valley can be organized with this company. Prices may not include meals. ☎ 63/663–1182 ⊕ *www.valleaventura. oom* ✉ *From €180.*

Toledo

88 km (55 miles) southwest of Madrid.

The spiritual capital of Castile, Toledo sits atop a rocky mount surrounded on three sides by the Río Tajo (Tagus River). When the Romans arrived here in 192 BC, they built their fortress (the Alcázar) on the highest point of the rock. Later, the Visigoths remodeled the stronghold.

In the 8th century, the Moors arrived and strengthened Toledo's reputation as a center of religion and learning. Today, the Moorish legacy is evident in Toledo's strong crafts tradition, the mazelike streets, and the predominance of brick construction (rather than the stone of many of Spain's historical cities). For the Moors, beauty was to be savored from within rather than displayed on the surface. Even Toledo's cathedral—one of the most richly endowed in Spain—is hard to see from the outside, largely obscured by the warren of houses around it.

Under Toledo's long line of cardinals—most notably Mendoza, Tavera, and Cisneros—Renaissance Toledo was a center of the humanities. Economically and politically, however, Toledo began to decline at the end of the 15th century. The expulsion of the Jews from Spain in 1492, as part of the Spanish Inquisition, eroded Toledo's economic and intellectual prowess. When Madrid became the permanent center of the Spanish court in 1561, Toledo lost its political importance, and the expulsion from Spain of the converted Arabs (Moriscos) in 1601 meant the departure of most of the city's artisans. The years the painter El Greco spent in Toledo—from 1572 to his death in 1614—were those of the city's decline, which is greatly reflected in his works. In the late 19th century, after hundreds of years of neglect, the works of El Greco came to be widely appreciated, and Toledo was transformed into a major tourist destination. Today, Toledo is conservative, prosperous, and proud—and a bit provincial (don't expect cosmopolitan luxury here). Its winding streets and steep hills can be exasperating, especially when you're searching for a specific sight, so take a full day (or three) to absorb the town's medieval trappings—and expect to get a little lost.

GETTING HERE AND AROUND

The best way to get to Toledo from Madrid is the high-speed AVE train, which leaves from Madrid at least nine times daily from Atocha station and gets you there in 30 minutes.

ALSA buses leave every half hour from Plaza Elíptica and take 1¼ hours.

TOURS

Cuéntame Toledo

GUIDED TOURS | The name means "Tell me about Toledo," and that's what they do.

The company offers free tours (in English and Spanish; donation encouraged) of Toledo's historic center at 5 pm daily, plus a range of other paid tours of the city's monuments, best-kept secrets, underground passageways, and urban legends. There are also El Greco–themed tours, nighttime ghost tours, and other routes that include visits to ancient Arab baths. ⊠ *Corral de Don Diego 5* ☎ *92/521–0767, 60/893–5856* ⊕ *www.cuentametoledo. com* ⊠ *Historic center tour free, other tours from €12.*

★ Toledo de la Mano

GUIDED TOURS | Toledophile Adolfo Ferrero, author of a 200-page guidebook on the town, delves far deeper on his private tours than those run by competitors, touching on the city's history of multiculturalism and its significance in medieval Europe. Groups of up to 55 people can be accommodated. ⊠ *Calle Nuncio Viejo 10* ☎ *62/917–7810* ⊕ *www.toledodelamano.com* ⊠ *From €140.*

★ Toledo Tours

GUIDED TOURS | Self-guided tours cater to those interested in the city's gastronomy, art, history, and other aspects, with various mix-and-match "Toledopass" packages including admission to various museums and landmarks. Pick the itinerary that best suits your interests and cut the lines. ⊠ *Toledo* ☎ *92/582–6616* ⊕ *www.toledoturismo.org* ⊠ *From €19.*

Toledo Train Vision

TRAIN TOURS | FAMILY | This unabashedly touristy "train" chugs past many of Toledo's main sights, departing from the Plaza de Zocodover every hour on the hour during the week, and every 30 minutes on weekends. The tour takes 45–50 minutes and has recorded information in 13 languages (including English, Spanish, and French) plus children's versions in those three languages, too. Buy tickets at the kiosk in Plaza de Zocodover. ⊠ *Pl. de Zocodover* ☎ *62/530–1890* ⊠ *€6.*

ESSENTIALS
VISITOR INFORMATION Toledo Tourist Office ⊠ *Pl. de Zocodover 8* ☎ *92/526–7666, 68/785–4965, 92/523–9121* ⊕ *www.turismo.toledo.es.*

Sights

Alcázar
CASTLE/PALACE | Originally a Moorish citadel (*al-qasr* is Arabic for "fortress") and occupied from the 10th century until the Reconquest, Toledo's alcázar is on a hill just outside the walled city, dominating the horizon. The south facade—the building's most severe—is the work of Juan de Herrera, of Escorial fame, while the east facade incorporates a large section of battlements. The finest facade is the northern, one of many Toledan works by Miguel Covarrubias, who did more than any other architect to introduce the Renaissance style here. The building's architectural highlight is his Italianate courtyard, which, like most other parts of the building, was largely rebuilt after the Spanish Civil War, when the alcázar was besieged by the Republicans. Though the Nationalists' ranks were depleted, they held on to the building. General Francisco Franco later turned the alcázar into a monument to Nationalist bravery. The alcázar now houses the **Museo del Ejército** (Military Museum), which was formerly in Madrid. ■**TIP→ Be sure to keep your ticket—it's needed when you exit the museum.** ⊠ *Cuesta de los Capuchinos* ☎ *92/523–8800* ⊕ *www.museo.ejercito. es* ⊠ *From €5 (free Sun. 10–3).*

Calle del Comercio
NEIGHBORHOOD | Near Plaza de Zocodover, this is the town's narrow and busy pedestrian thoroughfare. It's lined with bars and shops and shaded in summer by awnings. ⊠ *Toledo.*

★ Cathedral
RELIGIOUS SITE | One of the most impressive structures in all of Spain, this is a must-see on any visit to the city. The elaborate structure owes its impressive

Mozarabic chapel, with an elongated dome crowning the west facade, to Jorge Manuel Theotokópoulos. The rest of the facade is mainly early 15th century. Immediately to your right is a beautifully carved plateresque doorway by Covarrubias, marking the entrance to the Treasury, which houses a small Crucifixion by the Italian painter Cimabue and an extraordinarily intricate late-15th-century monstrance by Juan del Arfe. The ceiling is an excellent example of Mudejar (11th- to 16th-century Moorish-influenced) workmanship. From here, walk around to the ambulatory. In addition to Italianate frescoes by Juan de Borgoña and an exemplary baroque illusionism by Narciso Tomé known as the Transparente, you'll find several El Grecos, including one version of El Espolio (Christ Being Stripped of His Raiment), the first recorded instance of the painter in Spain. ⊠ *Calle Cardenal Cisneros 1* ☎ *92/522–2241* ⊕ *www.catedralprimada.es* ⊠ *From €10.*

★ Convento de San Clemente
RELIGIOUS SITE | Founded in 1131, this is Toledo's oldest convent—and it's still in use. The 20 nuns who live here produce their own sweet wine and marzipan. The impressive complex, a bit outside the city center, includes ruins of a mosque on which a chapel was built in the Middle Ages, those of an Islamic house and courtyard (with an ancient well and Arab baths), and those of a Jewish house from the same period. Free tours, offered twice daily (though not dependably—be forewarned), might include a visit to the kitchen where the Mother Superior will let you sample some sweets if she's in a good mood. Skip the touristy marzipan shops and buy the real stuff here. There's also an adjacent cultural center with rotating history exhibits. ⊠ *Calle San Clemente* ☎ *92/525–3080* ⊠ *Free* ☽ *Closed sporadically (call before visiting).*

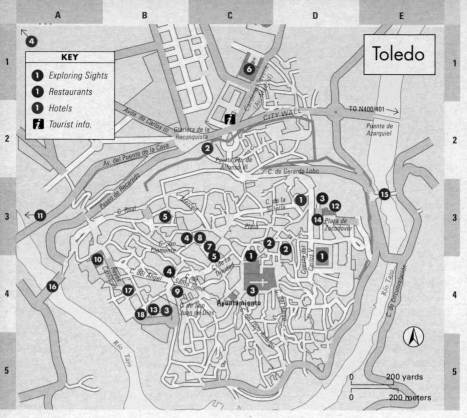

Toledo

KEY

1 Exploring Sights
1 Restaurants
1 Hotels
i Tourist info.

Sights ▼

1 Alcázar.................. **D4**
2 Calle del Comercio **C3**
3 Cathedral **C4**
4 Convento de
San Clemente **C3**
5 Convento de Santo
Domingo el Antiguo **B3**
6 Hospital de Tavera....... **C1**
7 Iglesia de
San Ildefonso **C3**
8 Iglesia de San Román ... **C3**
9 Iglesia de Santo Tomé.. **B4**

10 Monasterio de San Juan
de los Reyes............. **B4**
11 Museo Cerámica
Ruiz de Luna............. **A3**
12 Museo de Santa Cruz .. **D3**
13 Museo del Greco **B4**
14 Plaza de Zocodover **D3**
15 Puente de Alcántara **E3**
16 Puente de San Martín.. **A4**
17 Sinagoga de Santa María
La Blanca................ **B4**
18 Sinagoga del Tránsito .. **B4**

Restaurants ▼

1 Adolfo Restaurant **C3**
2 Bar Ludeña **D3**
3 Cervecería El Trébol.... **D3**
4 Churrería
Santo Tomé............. **B4**
5 La Flor de la Esquina **C4**

Hotels ▼

1 Antídoto Rooms......... **D3**
2 Hacienda del
Cardenal.................. **C2**
3 Hotel Pintor El Greco
Sercotel................. **B4**
4 Miluna................... **A1**

Convento de Santo Domingo el Antiguo
(*Convento de Santo Domingo de Silos; Santo Domingo Convent*)
RELIGIOUS SITE | This 16th-century Cistercian convent houses the earliest of El Greco's Toledo paintings as well as the crypt where the artist is believed to be buried. The friendly nuns at the convent will show you around its odd little museum, which includes decaying bone relics of little-known saints and a life-size model of John the Baptist's decapitated head. ⊠ *Pl. Santo Domingo el Antiguo* ☎ *92/522–2930* ✉ *€3.*

Hospital de Tavera (*Hospital de San Juan Bautista*)
HOSPITAL—SIGHT | Architect Alonso de Covarrubias's last work, this hospital lies outside the city walls, beyond Toledo's main northern gate. A fine example of Spanish Renaissance architecture, the building also houses the **Museo de Duque de Lema** in its southern wing. The most important work in the museum's miscellaneous collection is a painting by the 17th-century artist José Ribera. The hospital's monumental chapel holds El Greco's *Baptism of Christ* and the exquisitely carved marble tomb of Cardinal Tavera, the last work of Alonso de Berruguete. Descend into the crypt to experience some bizarre acoustical effects. A full ticket includes the hospital, museum, old pharmacy, and Renaissance patios; a partial ticket includes everything except the museum. Guided tours are available at 45-minute intervals. ⊠ *Calle Duque de Lerma 2 (aka Calle Cardenal Tavera)* ☎ *92/522–0451* ✉ *From €4.*

★ **Iglesia de San Ildefonso** (*San Ildefonso Church, The Jesuits*)
RELIGIOUS SITE | Sometimes simply called "Jesuitas," for the religious order that founded it, the Iglesia de San Ildefonso is named for Toledo's patron saint, a local bishop in the 7th century. It was finally consecrated in 1718, after taking 150 years to build the baroque stone facade with twin Corinthian columns. Its semispherical dome is one of the icons of Toledo's skyline. This impressive building deserves a visit, and a climb up its tower (€3) affords some of the best views over Toledo. ⊠ *Pl. Juan de Mariana 1* ☎ *92/525–1507* ✉ *€3.*

Iglesia de San Román
MUSEUM | Hidden in a virtually unspoiled part of Toledo, this early-13th-century Mudejar church (built on the site of an earlier Visigoth one) is now the **Museo de los Concilios y de la Cultura Visigoda** (Visigoth Museum) with exhibits of statuary, manuscript illustrations, jewelry, and an extensive collection of frescoes. The church tower is adjacent to the ruins of Roman baths. ⊠ *Calle San Román* ☎ *92/522–7872* ✉ *€6 (free Fri. and Sat. 4:30–6:30 and Sun. 10–2:30).*

★ **Iglesia de Santo Tomé** (*Santo Tomé Church*)
RELIGIOUS SITE | Not to be confused with the marzipan shop bearing the same name, this chapel topped with a Mudejar tower was built specially to house El Greco's most masterful painting, *The Burial of Count Orgaz.* Using vivid colors and splashes of light, he portrays the benefactor of the church being buried with the posthumous assistance of St. Augustine and St. Stephen, who have appeared at the funeral to thank the count for his donations to religious institutions named after the two saints. Though the count's burial took place in the 14th century, El Greco painted the onlookers in contemporary 16th-century costumes and included people he knew; the boy in the foreground is one of El Greco's sons, and the sixth figure on the left is said to be the artist himself. Santo Tomé is Toledo's most visited church besides the cathedral, so to avoid crowds, plan to visit as soon as the building opens. ⊠ *Pl. del Conde 4, Calle Santo Tomé* ☎ *92/525–6098* ⊕ *www.santotome.org* ✉ *€3.*

★ **Monasterio de San Juan de los Reyes**
RELIGIOUS SITE | This convent church in western Toledo was erected by Ferdinand and Isabella to commemorate their

victory at the Battle of Toro in 1476. (It was also intended to be their burial place, but their wish changed after Granada was recaptured from the Moors in 1492, and their actual tomb is in that city's Capilla Real.) The breathtakingly intricate building is largely the work of architect Juan Guas, who considered it his masterpiece and asked to be buried there himself. In true plateresque fashion, the white interior is covered with inscriptions and heraldic motifs. ✉ *Calle San Juan de los Reyes 2* ☎ *92/522–3802* ⊕ *www. sanjuandelosreyes.org* 🎫 *€3*.

Museo Cerámica Ruiz de Luna Most of the region's pottery is made in Talavera de la Reina, 76 km (47 miles) west of Toledo. At this museum you can watch artisans throw local clay, then trace the development of Talavera's world-famous ceramics, chronicled through some 1,500 tiles, bowls, vases, and plates dating back to the 15th century. ✉ *Place de San Augustín, Calle San Agustín el Viejo 13, Talavera de la Reina* ☎ *92/580–0149* 🎫 *€3* 🌣 *Closed Mon.*

Museo de Santa Cruz
HOSPITAL—SIGHT | In a 16th-century Renaissance hospital with a stunning classical-plateresque facade, this museum is open all day without a break (unlike many of Toledo's other sights). Works of art have replaced the hospital beds, and among the displays is El Greco's *Assumption* of 1613, the artist's last known work. A small **Museo de Arqueología** (Museum of Archaeology) is in and around the hospital's delightful cloister. ✉ *Calle Cervantes 3* ☎ *92/522–1036* 🎫 *Free, art exhibit €4* 🌣 *Closed Sun. after 2:30.*

Museo del Greco (*El Greco Museum*)
HOUSE | This house that once belonged to Peter the Cruel's treasurer, Samuel Levi, is said to have later been El Greco's home, though historians now believe he actually lived across the street. Nevertheless, the interior of the El Greco Museum is decorated to resemble a typical house

of the artist's time. The house is now incorporated into a revamped El Greco museum with several of the artist's paintings, including a panorama of Toledo with the Hospital of Tavera in the foreground, and works by several of El Greco's students (including his son) and other 16th- and 17th-century artists. Medieval caves have been excavated at the site, and there's a beautiful garden in which to take refuge from Toledo's often-scorching summer heat. The impressive museum complex has been the centerpiece for Toledo tourism since the "El Greco 2014" festival, marking the 400th anniversary of the artist's death. ✉ *Paseo del Tránsito s/n* ☎ *92/522–3665* 🎫 *€3 (free Sat. after 2).*

Plaza de Zocodover
PLAZA | Toledo's main square was built in the early 17th century as part of an unsuccessful attempt to impose a rigid geometry on the chaotic Moorish streets. Over the centuries, this tiny plaza has hosted bullfights, executions (autos-da-fé) of heretics during the Spanish Inquisition, and countless street fairs. Today it's home to the largest and oldest marzipan store in town, Santo Tomé. You can catch intracity buses here, and the tourist office is on the south side of the plaza. ✉ *Toledo.*

Puente de Alcántara
BRIDGE/TUNNEL | Roman in origin, this is the city's oldest bridge. Next to it is a heavily restored castle built after the Christian capture of 1085 and, above this, a vast and severe military academy, an eyesore of Franquist architecture. From the other side of the Río Tajo, the bridge offers fine views of Toledo's historic center and the alcázar. ✉ *Calle Gerardo Lobo.*

Puente de San Martín
BRIDGE/TUNNEL | This pedestrian bridge on the western edge of Toledo dates to 1203 and has splendid horseshoe arches. ✉ *Toledo.*

Did You Know?

The alcázar of Toledo has dominated the city since at least the 3rd century. It is the setting for an important scene of Franquist lore: During the Spanish Civil War, the Nationalist colonel Moscardó was defending the building against overwhelming Republican forces. The Republicans held his son hostage, demanding the alcázar be surrendered. To his son's entreaties to "surrender or they will shoot me," the father replied, "Then commend your soul to God and die like a hero."

★ Sinagoga de Santa María La Blanca

RELIGIOUS SITE | Founded in 1203, Toledo's second synagogue—situated in the heart of the Jewish Quarter—is nearly two centuries older than the more elaborate Tránsito, just down the street. Santa María's white interior has a forest of columns supporting capitals with fine filigree work. ✉ *Calle de los Reyes Católicos 4* ☎ *92/522–7257* 🎫 *€3.*

★ Sinagoga del Tránsito (*Museo Sefardí, Sephardic Museum*)

MUSEUM | This 14th-century synagogue's plain exterior belies sumptuous interior walls embellished with colorful Mudejar decoration. There are inscriptions in Hebrew and Arabic glorifying God, Peter the Cruel, and Samuel Levi (the original patron). It's a rare example of architecture reflecting Arabic as the lingua franca of medieval Spanish Jews. It's said that Levi imported cedars from Lebanon for the building's construction, echoing Solomon when he built the First Temple in Jerusalem. This is one of only three synagogues still fully standing in Spain (two in Toledo, one in Córdoba), from an era when there were hundreds—though more are in the process of being excavated. Adjoining the main hall is the **Museo Sefardí,** a small but informative museum of Jewish culture in Spain. ✉ *Calle Samuel Levi 2* ☎ *92/522–3665* 🌐 *www.mecd.gob.es/msefardi/home.html* 🎫 *€3 (free Sat. afternoon and Sun.).*

🍴 Restaurants

★ Adolfo Restaurant

$$$$ | **SPANISH** | Visit this white-tablecloth restaurant, situated steps from the cathedral, for traditional Toledan recipes with fine-dining twists, complemented by a 2,800-bottle-deep wine list. Don't pass up the hearty partridge stew, deemed the best in Spain by the former Spanish king Juan Carlos I; it sings alongside a glass of Adolfo's proprietary red wine. **Known for:** chef's menu; historic building; game dishes. [$] *Average main: €50* ✉ *Calle del Hombre de Palo 7* ☎ *92/522–7321* 🌐 *www.grupoadolfo.com* 🕒 *No dinner Sun.*

Bar Ludeña

$$ | **SPANISH** | Locals and visitors come together at this old-timey tapas bar for steaming cauldrons of *carcamusa*, a traditional Toledan meat stew studded with peas and chorizo. (The rest of the menu is nothing special.) **Known for:** hearty carcamusa stew; free tapa with every drink; rustic ambience. [$] *Average main: €12* ✉ *Pl. de la Magdalena 10* ☎ *92/522–3384* 🕒 *Closed Wed.*

★ Cervecería El Trébol

$$ | **SPANISH** | You can't leave Toledo without indulging in one of El Trébol's famous *bombas*, fried fist-sized spheres of mashed potato stuffed with spiced meat and anointed with aioli. They're best enjoyed on the twinkly outdoor patio with a locally brewed beer in hand. **Known for:** to-die-for bombas; most pleasant patio in town; local craft beers. [$] *Average main: €15* ✉ *Calle de Santa Fe 1* ☎ *92/528–1297* 🌐 *www.cerveceriatrebol.com.*

★ Churrería Santo Tomé

$ | **SPANISH** | **FAMILY** | Recharge at this adorable four-table *churrería*, established over a century ago, with hot homemade churros dipped in ultrathick melted chocolate. This churrería opens at 6am so look like a local and come have light-but-crispy churros for breakfast. **Known for:** churros made on site; churros for breakfast; local institution. [$] *Average main: €5* ✉ *Calle Santo Tomé 27* ☎ *92/521–6324* 💳 *No credit cards.*

La Flor de la Esquina

$$$ | **SPANISH** | The most coveted seats at this charming restaurant are the patio tables on the Plaza del Padre, which boast views of Toledo's cathedral spires. Three-course lunch menus are a great value at €10 (don't expect anything too fancy), and there are tapas menus and charcuterie boards for those looking to sample a bit of everything. **Known for:** steal prix-fixe menu; cathedral views;

Toledo's Santa María la Blanca synagogue is a fascinating symbol of cultural cooperation: built by Islamic architects, in a Christian land, for Jewish use.

top-quality cured meats. $ *Average main: €20* ✉ *Pl. del Padre Juan de Mariana 2* ☎ *62/794–5020.*

Hotels

★ Antídoto Rooms

$$ | HOTEL | Antídoto is a breath of fresh air in Toledo's mostly staid hotel scene: expect turquoise beamed ceilings, poured-concrete floors, and designer light fixtures. **Pros:** highly Instagrammable rooms; in the heart of the old town; friendly staff. **Cons:** awkward room layout; in-room bathrooms with no curtains and transparent doors; sheets feel rough on the skin. $ *Rooms from: €120* ✉ *Calle Recoletos 2* ☎ *92/522–8851* ⊕ *www.antidotorooms.com* ⇨ *10 rooms* ⦿ *No meals.*

Hacienda del Cardenal

$$ | HOTEL | Once a summer palace for Cardinal Lorenzana, who lived in the 1700s, this serene three-star hotel on the outskirts of the old town hits the sweet spot between rustic and refined. **Pros:** lovely courtyard; convenient dining; spacious rooms. **Cons:** restaurant often full; parking is pricey; stairs inconvenient for those with heavy luggage. $ *Rooms from: €100* ✉ *Paseo de Recaredo 24* ☎ *92/522–4900* ⊕ *www.elhostaldelcardenal.com* ⇨ *27 rooms* ⦿ *No meals.*

Hotel Pintor El Greco Sercotel

$$$ | HOTEL | Next door to the painter's house, this former 17th-century bakery is now a chic, contemporary hotel managed by the Sercotel chain. **Pros:** parking garage adjacent; cozy decor; complimentary wine and olives. **Cons:** street noise in most rooms; elevator goes to the second floor only; bar area sometimes closed for private events. $ *Rooms from: €130* ✉ *Alamillos del Tránsito 13* ☎ *92/528–5191* ⊕ *www.hotelpintorelgreco.com* ⇨ *60 rooms* ⦿ *No meals.*

★ Miluna

$$$$ | HOTEL | Taking a page from Aire de Bardenas, Navarra's avant-garde bubble hotel, Miluna opened in September 2018 on the outskirts of Toledo. **Pros:** a bubble hotel that won't break the budget; telescopes in every room; the ideal place

to unplug. **Cons:** so popular it's difficult to get a reservation; outdoor temperatures can be extreme in winter and summer; no alternate dining options in vicinity. [$] *Rooms from: €189* ✉ *C. Valdecarretas, Parcela 364* ☎ *92/567–9229* 🌐 *www.miluna.es* 🛏 *4 rooms* 🍴 *Free Breakfast.*

Shopping

The Moors established silverwork, damascene (metalwork inlaid with gold or silver), pottery, embroidery, and marzipan traditions here. A turn-of-the-20th-century art school next to the Monasterio de San Juan de los Reyes keeps some of these crafts alive. For inexpensive pottery, stop at the large stores on the outskirts of town, on the main road to Madrid. Many shops are closed on Sunday.

La Encina de Ortega

FOOD/CANDY | This is a one-stop-shop for local wines, olive oil, manchego cheese, and—most notably—*ibérico* pork products (ham, chorizo, dry-cured sausages) made from pigs raised on the family farm. ✉ *Calle La Plata 22* ☎ *92/510–2072* 🌐 *www.laencinadeortega.com.*

Santo Tomé Marzipan

FOOD/CANDY | Since 1856, Santo Tomé has been Spain's most famous maker of marzipan, a Spanish confection made from sugar, honey, and almond paste. Visit the main shop on the Plaza de Zocodover, or take a tour of the old convent-turned-factory where it's actually made at Calle Santo Tomé 3 (advance booking required). ✉ *Pl. de Zocodover 7* ☎ *92/522–1168, 92/522–3763* 🌐 *www.mazapan.com.*

Tea Break

Teteria Dar Al-Chai Rest your legs at this Arabian tea house–bar, appointed with plush couches, low tables, and colorful tapestries. Sample specially blended teas incorporating flowers, dried fruit, and spices. **Known for:** specially blended teas; delicious crepes and cakes; peaceful spot. ✉ *Pl. Barrio Nuevo 5* ☎ *92/522–5625.*

Almagro

215 km (134 miles) south of Madrid.

The center of this noble town contains the only preserved medieval theater in Europe. It stands beside the ancient Plaza Mayor, where 85 Roman columns form two colonnades supporting green-frame 16th-century buildings. Enjoy casual tapas (such as pickled baby eggplant, an Almagro specialty known the country over) and rustic local wines in the unfussy bars lining the square. Near the plaza are granite mansions emblazoned with the heraldic shields of their former owners and a splendid parador in a restored 17th-century convent.

GETTING HERE AND AROUND

Almagro can be reached by train from Madrid, with one scheduled departure per day departing from Atocha or Chamartín stations for the 2½-hour journey, but it's probably best to rent a car or book a Blablacar rideshare. The drive south from the capital takes you across the plains of La Mancha, where Don Quixote's adventures unfolded.

ESSENTIALS

VISITOR INFORMATION Almagro ✉ *Pl. Mayor 1* ☎ *92/686–0717* 🌐 *www.ciudad-almagro.com.*

Sights

★ Corral de Comedias

ARTS VENUE | Appearing almost as it did in 1628 when it was built, this theater has wooden balconies on four sides and the stage at one end of the open patio. During the golden age of Spanish theater—the time of playwrights Pedro Calderón de la Barca, Cervantes, and Lope de

Vega—touring actors came to Almagro, once a burgeoning urban center for its mercury mines and lace industry. Forego the tourist-oriented spectacles unless you're a Spanish theater buff: poor acoustics and archaic Spanish scripts make it difficult to understand what's going on. ✉ *Pl. Mayor 18* ☎ *92/686–1539* 🌐 *www.corraldecomedias.com* 🎟 *From €4.*

★ Museo Etnográfico Campo de Calatrava
MUSEUM | For a window into what agrarian life was like in this area in centuries past, pop into this tiny museum presided over by the passionate historian who amassed the (mostly obsolete) curiosities on display. A guided tour, in Spanish, takes a little less than an hour and is well worth it. ✉ *Calle Chile 6* ☎ *65/701–0077* 🌐 *www.museodealmagro.com* 🎟 *€5.*

Museo Nacional del Teatro
MUSEUM | This museum displays models of the Roman amphitheaters in Mérida (Extremadura) and Sagunto (near Valencia), both still in use, as well as costumes, pictures, and documents relating to the history of Spanish theater. ✉ *Calle del Gran Maestre 2* ☎ *92/626–1014, 92/626–1018* 🌐 *museoteatro.mcu.es* 🎟 *€3 (free Sat. afternoon and Sun. morning)* 🕒 *Closed Mon.*

🛏 Hotels

★ Parador de Almagro
$$$ | **HOTEL** | Five minutes from the Plaza Mayor of Almagro, this parador is a finely restored 16th-century Franciscan convent with cells, cloisters, and patios. **Pros:** pretty indoor courtyards; outdoor pool; ample parking. **Cons:** untidy public areas; double-bed rooms smaller than normal rooms; inconsistent restaurant. [$] *Rooms from: €135* ✉ *Ronda de San Francisco 31* ☎ *92/686–0100* 🌐 *www.parador.es* 🛏 *54 rooms* 🍴 *Free Breakfast.*

Cuenca

168 km (105 miles) southeast of Madrid, 150 km (93 miles) northwest of Valencia.

The delightful old town of Cuenca is one of the most surreal looking in Spain, built on a sloping rock with precipitous sides that plunge to the gorges of the Huécar and Júcar rivers. Because the town ran out of room to expand, some medieval houses dangle right over the abyss and are now a unique architectural attraction, the Casas Colgadas (Hanging Houses). The old town's dramatic setting grants spectacular views of the surrounding countryside, and its cobblestone streets, cathedral, churches, and taverns contrast starkly with the modern town, which sprawls beyond the river gorges. Though somewhat isolated, Cuenca makes a good overnight stop if you're traveling between Madrid and Valencia, or even a worthwhile detour between Madrid and Barcelona.

GETTING HERE AND AROUND

From Madrid, buses leave for Cuenca about every two hours from Conde de Casal. From Valencia, four buses leave every four to six hours, starting at 8:30 am. A high-speed AVE train leaves Madrid approximately every hour and stops in Cuenca (after about 55 minutes) on its way to Valencia. Slower, cheaper trains also run several times daily between Cuenca and Valencia, Madrid, Albacete, and Alicante, on the coast. Rideshares (via Blablacar) to and from the city are plentiful.

ESSENTIALS

VISITOR INFORMATION Cuenca ✉ *Av. Cruz Roja 1* ☎ *96/924–1050.*

👁 Sights

Cuenca has more than a dozen churches and two cathedrals, but visitors are allowed inside only about half of them. The best views of the city are from the square in front of a small palace at the very top of Cuenca, where the town tapers out to the narrowest of ledges. Here, gorges flank the precipice, and old houses sweep down toward a distant plateau. The lower half of the old town is a maze of tiny streets, any of which will take you up to the Plaza del Carmen. From here the town narrows and a single street, Calle Alfonso VIII, continues the ascent to the Plaza Mayor, which passes under the arch of the town hall.

★ **Casas Colgadas** (*Hanging Houses*)
BUILDING | As if Cuenca's famous Casas Colgadas, suspended impossibly over the cliffs below, were not eye-popping enough, they also house one of Spain's finest and most curious museums, the **Museo de Arte Abstracto Español** (Museum of Spanish Abstract Art)—not to be confused with the adjacent Museo Municipal de Arte Moderno. Projecting over the town's eastern precipice, these houses originally formed a 15th-century palace, which later served as a town hall before falling into disrepair in the 19th century. In 1927 the cantilevered balconies that had once hung over the gorge were rebuilt, and in 1966 the painter Fernando Zóbel decided to create (inside the houses) the world's first museum devoted exclusively to abstract art. The works he gathered—by such renowned names as Carlos Saura, Eduardo Chillida, Lucio Muñoz, and Antoni Tàpies—are primarily by exiled Spanish artists who grew up under Franco's regime. The museum has free smartphone audio guides that can be downloaded from the website. A plan to build a fine-dining restaurant within one of the historic houses was approved in spring 2019, though an opening date has yet to be confirmed. ⊠ *Calle de los Canónigos* ☎ *96/921–2983* ⊕ *www. march.es/arte/cuenca* ⊠ *Free.*

Catedral de Cuenca
RELIGIOUS SITE | This cathedral looms large and casts an enormous shadow in the evening throughout the adjacent Plaza Mayor. Built during the Gothic era in the 12th century atop ruins of a conquered

mosque, the cathedral's massive triptych facade lost its Gothic character in the Renaissance. Inside are the tombs of the cathedral's founding bishops, an impressive portico of the Apostles, and a Byzantine reliquary. ⊠ *Pl. Mayor* ☎ *96/922–4626* ⊕ *www.catedralcuenca. es* ⊠ *From €5 (free 1st Mon. of month).*

★ Puente de San Pablo
BRIDGE/TUNNEL | The 16th-century stone footbridge over the Huécar gorge was fortified with iron in 1903 for the convenience of the Dominican monks of San Pablo, who lived on the other side. If you don't have a fear of heights, cross the narrow bridge to take in the vertiginous view of the river and equally thrilling panorama of the Casas Colgadas. It's by far the best view of the city. If you've read the popular English novel *Winter in Madrid,* you'll recognize this bridge from the book's final scene. ⊠ *Cuenca.*

Cuenca's precarious Casas Colgadas (Hanging Houses) are also home to the well-regarded Museum of Abstract Art.

🍴 Restaurants

Much of Cuenca's cuisine is based on wild game, and partridge, lamb, rabbit, and hen are ubiquitous on menus. Trucha from the adjacent river is the fish of choice, and it turns up in entrées and soups. In almost every town restaurant, you can find *morteruelo*—Cuenca's pâté of *jabalí* (wild boar), rabbit, partridge, hen, liver, pork loin, and spices—as well as *gazpacho manchego* (aka *galiano*), a meat stew thickened with dry flatbread. For dessert, try the almond-based confection called *alajú,* which is enriched with honey, nuts, and lemon, and *torrija,* bread dipped in milk, fried until custardy, and sprinkled with powdered sugar.

Figón del Huécar

$$$$ | **SPANISH** | This family-run tavern serves updated Castilian classics in an airy dining room set within a medieval stone house with sweeping views of the city (ask for an outdoor table when booking). Specialty dishes include Manchegan migas and "old wine," veal with potatoes *al montón* (fried with garlic). **Known for:** breathtaking views; scrumptious desserts; elegant dining room. [$] *Average main: €35* ✉ *Ronda de Julián Romero 6* ☎ *96/924–0062, 62/906–3366* 🌐 *www.figondelhuecar.es* 🕒 *Closed Mon. No dinner Sun.*

★ La Ponderosa

$$ | **TAPAS** | La Ponderosa is a quintessential yet elevated Castilian bar where locals mingle at high volume while tossing back local wine and munching on well-priced seasonal delicacies like griddled wild asparagus, suckling lamb chops, and seared wild mushrooms. It's a standing-room-only joint, so if you want to sit, you'll have to come early and find a place on the terrace. **Known for:** hidden-gem local wines; simple and delicious vegetable dishes; buzzy atmosphere. [$] *Average main: €15* ✉ *Calle de San Francisco 20* ☎ *96/921–3214* 🕒 *Closed Sun., and July.*

Trivio

$$$$ | **SPANISH** | The punchy, artfully presented dishes at Trivio—think wild game tartare and house-pickled vegetables—are an anomaly in a region known

154

for its stodgy country fare. Choose from three well-priced tasting menus in the dining room, or opt for a more casual experience in the Bistró-Bar. **Known for:** bold tasting menus; award-winning croquettes; pretty plating. $ *Average main: €30* ✉ *Calle Colón 25* ☎ *96/903–0593* ⊕ *www.restaurantetrivio.com* ⊘ *Closed Mon. No dinner Sun.*

Hotels

Cueva del Fraile
$ | HOTEL | FAMILY | Surrounded by dramatic landscapes, this family-friendly three-star lodging occupies a 16th-century building on the outskirts of town. **Pros:** beautiful interior garden terrace; outdoor swimming pool and tennis courts; good value. **Cons:** location 7 km (4½ miles) from town; no a/c in some rooms; some rooms have leaky showers. $ *Rooms from: €50* ✉ *Ctra. Cuenca–Buenache, Km 7* ☎ *96/921–1571* ⊕ *www.hotelcuevadelfraile.com* ⊘ *Closed Jan.* ⟿ *75 rooms* �◎ *No meals.*

Hostal Cánovas
$ | B&B/INN | Near Plaza de España, in the heart of the new town, this quirky inn is one of Cuenca's best bargains, and though the lobby's not impressive, the inviting rooms more than compensate. **Pros:** low prices even during high season; spacious digs; clean rooms. **Cons:** uphill trek to the old quarter; thin walls; slightly sunken beds. $ *Rooms from: €55* ✉ *Calle Fray Luis de León 38* ☎ *96/921–3973* ⊕ *www.hostalcanovas.com* ⟿ *17 rooms* ◎ *No meals.*

★ Parador de Cuenca
$$$ | HOTEL | The rooms are luxurious and serene at the exquisitely restored 16th-century convent of San Pablo, pitched on a precipice across a dramatic gorge from Cuenca's city center. **Pros:** great views of the hanging houses and gorge; spacious rooms; consistently good restaurant. **Cons:** expensive breakfast not always included in room rate; secure garage parking not always

available; calls to reception sometimes go unanswered. $ *Rooms from: €180* ✉ *Subida a San Pablo* ☎ *96/923–2320* ⊕ *www.parador.es* ⟿ *63 rooms* ◎ *No meals.*

★ Posada de San José
$ | B&B/INN | FAMILY | This family-friendly inn, housed in a centuries-old convent, clings to the top of the Huécar gorge in Cuenca's old town. **Pros:** cozy historical rooms; stunning views of the gorge; well-prepared local food. **Cons:** built to 17th-century proportions, some doorways are low; certain rooms are cramped; sloping floors can be vertiginous when lying in bed. $ *Rooms from: €50* ✉ *Calle Julián Romero 4* ☎ *96/921–1300, 63/981–6825* ⊕ *www.posadasanjose.com* ⟿ *31 rooms* ◎ *Free Breakfast.*

Sigüenza

132 km (82 miles) northeast of Madrid.

The ancient university town of Sigüenza dates back to Roman, Visigothic, and Moorish times and still has splendid architecture and one of the most impressive gothic cathedrals in Castile. It's one of the rare Spanish towns that has not surrendered to modern development and sprawl. If you're coming from Madrid via the A2, the approach, through craggy hills and ravines, is dramatic. Sigüenza is an ideal base for exploring the countryside on foot or by bike, thanks to the Ruta de Don Quixote, a network of paths named for Cervantes's literary hero that passes through Sigüenza and nearby villages.

GETTING HERE AND AROUND
There are five train departures daily to Sigüenza from Madrid's Chamartín station, and the journey takes about 1½ hours. Sigüenza's train station is an easy walk from the historic walled center. Buses depart from Madrid's Avenida de América station once a day and take two hours. If you arrive by car, park near

the train station to avoid the narrow cobblestone streets of the city center. Rideshares, such as Blablacar, are another option, provided there are trips that align with your schedule.

ESSENTIALS
BICYCLE RENTAL
Bicicletas del Olmo
This company rents mountain bikes for €10 per day or €17 for two. Call ahead to reserve on busy holiday weekends. Note to parents: they don't have trailers or child seats. ⊠ *Ctra. de Moratilla, Nave 1* ☎ *94/939–0754, 60/578–7650.*

VISITOR INFORMATION
Sigüenza Tourist Office
Guided tours depart daily except Sunday from the tourist office in front of the cathedral at noon and 4:30, and at 5:15 May through September. A minimum of 10 people is required. ⊠ *Calle Serrano Sanz 9* ☎ *94/934–7007* ⊕ *www.siguenza. es* ☎ *Tours €7.*

Sights

Castillo de Sigüenza
CASTLE/PALACE | FAMILY | This enchanting castle overlooking wild, hilly countryside from above Sigüenza is now a parador. Nonguests can visit the dining room and common areas. The structure was founded by the Romans and rebuilt at various later periods. Most of the current structure was erected in the 14th century, when it became a residence for the queen of Castile, Doña Blanca de Borbón, who was banished here by her husband, Pedro the Cruel. During the Spanish Civil War (1936–39), the castle was the scene of fierce battles, and much of the structure was destroyed. The parador's lobby has an exhibit on the subsequent restoration with photographs of the bomb damage. If you've got half an hour to spare, there's a lovely walking path around the hilltop castle with a 360-degree view of the city and countryside below. ⊠ *Pl. de Castillo* ☎ *949/390100.*

Catedral de Sigüenza
RELIGIOUS SITE | Begun around 1150 and completed in the 16th century, Sigüenza's cathedral combines architecture from the Romanesque period to the Renaissance. Ask the sacristan (the officer in charge of the care of the sacristy, which holds sacred vestments) for a peek at the cathedral's wealth of ornamental and artistic masterpieces. From there, take a guided tour from the late-Gothic cloister to a room lined with 17th-century Flemish tapestries and onto the north transept, where the 15th-century plateresque sepulchre of Dom Fadrique of Portugal is housed. The Chapel of the Doncel (to the right of the sanctuary) contains Don Martín Vázquez de Arca's tomb, commissioned by Queen Isabella, to whom Don Martín served as *doncel* (page) before dying young (at 25) at the gates of Granada in 1486. Tours of the catacombs, on weekends only, are run by the Museo Diocesano de Sigüenza. ⊠ *Calle Serrano Sanz 2* ☎ *61/936–2715* ⊕ *www.lacatedraldesiguenza.com* ☎ *Free, €4 for tour of chapel, cloister, and tower.*

Museo Diocesano de Sigüenza (*Diocesan Museum of Sacred Art*)
MUSEUM | FAMILY | In a refurbished early-19th-century house next to the cathedral's west facade, the small Diocesan Museum has a prehistoric section and mostly religious art from the 12th to 18th century. It also runs the tours of the burial chambers (catacombs) under the cathedral—a spooky favorite for kids. ⊠ *Pl. Obispo Don Bernardo* ☎ *94/939–1023* ⊕ *www.lacatedraldesiguenza.com* ☎ *From €1 (free on 3rd Wed. of month).*

Plaza Mayor
PLAZA | The south side of the cathedral overlooks this harmonious, arcaded Renaissance square, which hosts a medieval market on weekends. Legend has it, a group of American tycoons found the plaza so charming that they offered to buy it, in order to reconstruct it, piece by piece, stateside. ⊠ *Sigüenza.*

Tren Medieval

SCENIC DRIVE | **FAMILY** | Leaving from Madrid's Chamartín station, this delightful medieval-themed train service runs to Sigüenza mid-April through mid-November. The (otherwise thoroughly modern) train comes populated with minstrels, jugglers, and other entertainers, and it's a great activity for Spanish-speaking children. The ticket price includes round-trip fare, a guided visit to Sigüenza, entry to the main monuments and museums, and discounts at area restaurants. ✉ *Sigüenza* ☎ *90/232–0320* 🌐 *www.renfe.com/trenesturisticos/otros-trenes-renfe.html* 🎫 *€35* 🕒 *Closed mid-Nov.–mid-Apr.*

🍴 Restaurants

★ Bar Alameda

$$ | **TAPAS** | **FAMILY** | This family-run bar and restaurant punches above its weight with market-driven tapas that reflect a sense of place. Spring for the stuffed foraged mushrooms or seared Sigüenza-style blood sausage. **Known for:** thoughtfully prepared tapas; local wines by the glass; family-friendly atmosphere. [$] *Average main: €15* ✉ *Calle de la Alameda 2* ☎ *94/939–0553* 💳 *No credit cards* 🕒 *Closed Thurs.*

🛏 Hotels

★ Parador de Sigüenza

$$$$ | **HOTEL** | **FAMILY** | This fairy-tale 12th-century castle has hosted royalty for centuries, from Ferdinand and Isabella right up to Spain's present king, Felipe VI. **Pros:** excellent food; sense of history and place; plenty of parking. **Cons:** much of castle is a neo-medieval replica; bland, modern furniture that doesn't jibe with the space; occasionally surly service. [$] *Rooms from: €185* ✉ *Pl. del Castillo* ☎ *94/939–0100* 🌐 *www.parador.es* 🛏 *81 rooms* 🍽 *Free Breakfast.*

Segovia

91 km (57 miles) north of Madrid.

Medieval Segovia rises on a steep ridge that juts above a stark, undulating plain. It's defined by its ancient monuments, excellent cuisine, embroideries and textiles, and small-town charm. An important military town in Roman times, Segovia was later established by the Moors as a major textile center. Captured by the Christians in 1085, it was enriched by a royal residence, and in 1474 the half sister of Henry IV, Isabella the Catholic (married to Ferdinand of Aragón), was crowned queen of Castile here. By that time Segovia was a bustling city of about 60,000 (its population is about 80,000 today), but its importance soon diminished as a result of its taking the losing side of the Comuneros in the popular revolt against Emperor Carlos V. Though the construction of a royal palace in nearby La Granja in the 18th century somewhat revived Segovia's fortunes, it never recovered its former vitality. Early in the 20th century, Segovia's sleepy charm came to be appreciated by artists and writers, among them painter Ignacio Zuloaga and poet Antonio Machado. Today the streets swarm with day-trippers from Madrid—if you can, visit sometime other than in summer, and spend the night.

Tourists on a day trip from Madrid generally hit the triumvirate of basic sights: the aqueduct, the alcázar, and the cathedral. If you have time, an overnight visit will allow you to sample Segovia's renowned food and nightlife in the Plaza Mayor, where you'll see segovianos of all ages out until the early hours.

GETTING HERE AND AROUND

High-speed AVE trains from Madrid's Chamartín station—the fastest and costliest option—take 30 minutes and drop you at the Guiomar station, about 7 km (4 miles) outside Segovia's center. Buses 11 and 12 are timed to coincide

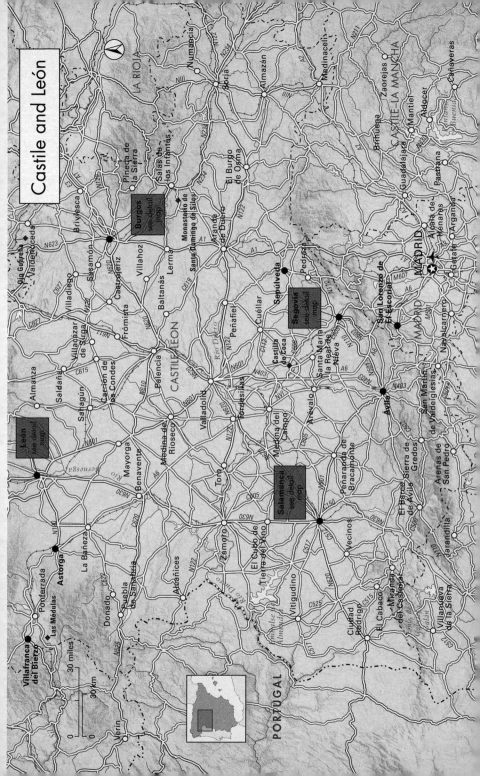

Castile and León

with arriving trains. Bus 11 will take you to the foot of the aqueduct after about a 15-minute ride, and Bus 12 drops you near the bus station.

La Sepulvedana buses depart Madrid (Moncloa station) for Segovia some 28 times a day. Direct routes take 55 minutes and cost €8 each way. There are also plentiful Blablacar options. (Check ⊕ *www.blablacar.com* or the app for details.)

Urbanos de Segovia operates the 13 inner-city bus lines and one tourist line, which are better options for getting around than struggling through the narrow streets (and problematic parking) with a car. Segovia's central bus station is a five-minute walk from the aqueduct along the car-free Paseo de Ezequiel González.

ESSENTIALS

BUS CONTACTS Bus Station ⊠ *Paseo de Ezequiel González* ☎ *92/142–7705.* **La Sepulvedana** ⊠ *Pl. la Estación de Autobuses* ☎ *90/211–9699* ⊕ *www.lasepulvedana.es.* **Urbanos de Segovia** ☎ *90/233–0080* ⊕ *segovia.avanzagrupo.com.*

VISITOR INFORMATION Segovia Tourist Office ⊠ *Azoguejo 1* ☎ *92/146–6720, 92/146–6721* ⊕ *www.turismodesegovia.com.*

 # Sights

★ Acueducto Romano

ARCHAEOLOGICAL SITE | Segovia's Roman aqueduct is one of the greatest surviving examples of Roman engineering and the city's main sight. Stretching from the walls of the old town to the lower slopes of the Sierra de Guadarrama, it's about 2,952 feet long and rises in two tiers to a height of 115 feet. The raised section of stonework in the center originally carried an inscription, of which only the holes for the bronze letters remain. Neither mortar nor clamps hold the massive granite blocks together, but miraculously, the

aqueduct has stood since the end of the 1st century AD. ⊠ *Pl. del Azoguejo.*

★ Alcázar

CASTLE/PALACE | **FAMILY** | It's widely believed that the Walt Disney logo is modeled after the silhouette of this castle, whose crenellated towers appear to have been carved out of icing. Possibly dating to Roman times, this castle was considerably expanded in the 14th century, remodeled in the 15th, altered again toward the end of the 16th, and completely reconstructed after being gutted by a fire in 1862, when it was used as an artillery school. The exterior, especially when seen below from the Ruta Panorámica, is awe-inspiring, as are the superb views from the ramparts. Inside, you can enter the throne room, chapel, and bedroom used by Ferdinand and Isabella as well as a claustrophobia-inducing winding tower. The intricate woodwork on the ceiling is marvelous, and the first room you enter, lined with knights in shining armor, is a crowd pleaser, particularly for kids. There's also a small armory museum, included in the ticket price. ⊠ *Pl. de la Reina Victoria* ☎ *92/146–0759, 92/146–0452* ⊕ *www.alcazardesegovia.com* 💶 *From €3.*

★ Catedral de Segovia

RELIGIOUS SITE | Segovia's 16th-century cathedral was built to replace an earlier one destroyed during the revolt of the Comuneros against Carlos V. It's one of the country's last great examples of the Gothic style. The designs were drawn up by the leading late-Gothicist Juan Gil de Hontañón and executed by his son Rodrigo, in whose work you can see a transition from the Gothic to the Renaissance style. The interior, illuminated by 16th-century Flemish windows, is light and uncluttered (save the wooden neoclassical choir). Across from the entrance, on the southern transept, is a door opening into the late-Gothic cloister, the work of architect Juan Guas. Off the cloister, a small museum of religious art, installed partly in the first-floor chapter

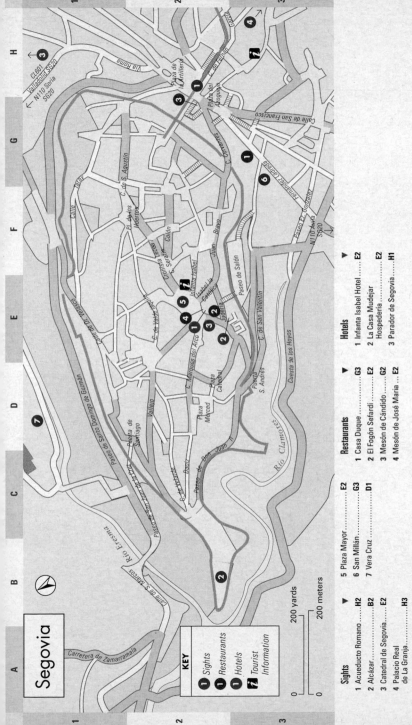

Segovia

4

Central Spain SEGOVIA

Hotels ▶
1 Infanta Isabel Hotel **E2**
2 La Casa Mudejar
  Hospedería..................**E2**
3 Parador de Segovia...**H1**

Restaurants ▶
1 Casa Duque.................**G3**
2 El Fogón Sefardí...........**E2**
3 Mesón de Cándido.......**G2**
4 Mesón de José María ...**E2**

Sights ▶
1 Acueducto Romano......**H2**
2 Alcázar.........................**B2**
3 Catedral de Segovia......**E2**
4 Palacio Real
  de La Granja............**H3**
5 Plaza Mayor................**E2**
6 San Millán..................**G3**
7 Vera Cruz...................**D1**

KEY
1 Sights
1 Restaurants
1 Hotels
🛈 Tourist
  Information

0 ———— 200 yards
0 ———— 200 meters

Carretera de Zamarramala

Off the Beaten Path

Palacio Real de La Granja (Royal Palace of La Granja) If you have a car, don't miss the Palacio Real de La Granja (Royal Palace of La Granja) in the town of La Granja de San Ildefonso, on the northern slopes of the Sierra de Guadarrama. The palace site was once occupied by a hunting lodge and a shrine to San Ildefonso, administered by Hieronymite monks from the Segovian monastery of El Parral. Commissioned by the Bourbon king Felipe V in 1719, the palace has been described as the first great building of the Spanish Bourbon dynasty. The Italian architects Juvarra and Sachetti, who finished it in 1739, were responsible for the imposing garden facade, a late-baroque masterpiece anchored throughout its length by a giant order of columns. The interior has been badly gutted by fire, but the collection of 15th- to 18th-century tapestries warrants a visit. Even if you don't go into the palace, walk through the magnificent gardens: terraces, ornamental ponds, lakes, classical statuary, woods, and baroque fountains dot the mountainside. On Wednesday, Saturday, and Sunday evenings in the summer (April–August, 5:30–7 pm), the illuminated fountains are turned on, one by one, creating an effect to rival that of Versailles. The starting time has been known to change on a whim, so call ahead. ⊠ *Pl. de España 15, San Ildefonso* ✛ *About 11 km (7 miles) southeast of Segovia on N601* ☎ *92/147–0019, 92/147–0020* ⊕ *www.patrimonionacional.es* ☜ *From €4.*

house, has a white-and-gold 17th-century ceiling, a late example of Mudejar *artesonado* (a type of intricately joined wooden ceiling) work. ⊠ *Pl. Mayor* ☎ *92/146–2205* ⊕ *www.catedralsegovia.es* ☜ *From €3 (free cathedral entrance for Sun. Mass only).*

Plaza Mayor
PLAZA | In front of the cathedral, this lovely historic square comes alive every night and especially on weekends, when visiting madrileños and locals gather at casual cafés that line the square's perimeter. There's a charming gazebo in the middle that occasionally hosts live music. (Otherwise it's occupied by children playing while their parents dine nearby.) ⊠ *Segovia.*

San Millán
RELIGIOUS SITE | Built in the 12th century and a perfect example of the Segovian Romanesque style, this church, a five-minute walk outside the town walls, may be the finest in town, aside from the cathedral. The exterior is notable for its arcaded porch, where church meetings were once held. The virtually untouched interior is dominated by massive columns, whose capitals carry such carved scenes as the Flight into Egypt and the Adoration of the Magi. The vaulting on the crossing shows the Moorish influence on Spanish medieval architecture. It's open for Mass only. ⊠ *Av. Fernández Ladreda 26* ⊕ *www.parroquiasanmillansegovia.com.*

Vera Cruz
RELIGIOUS SITE | This isolated Romanesque church on the outskirts of town was built in 1208 for the Knights Templar. Like other buildings associated with this order, it has 12 sides, inspired by the Church of the Holy Sepulchre in Jerusalem. It's about a 45-minute walk outside town (you can see this church on a cliff side from the castle windows), but the trek pays off in full when you climb the bell tower and see all of Segovia silhouetted

Segovia's Roman aqueduct, built more than 2,000 years ago, is remarkably well preserved.

against the Sierra de Guadarrama. ⊠ *Ctra. de Zamarramia* ☎ *92/143–1475* ⊕ *www. ordendemalta.es* ✉ *€2 (free Tues. 4–6 pm).*

🍽 Restaurants

Casa Duque

$$$$ | SPANISH | Segovia's oldest restaurant, founded in 1895 and still run by the same family, has a rustic interior with wood beams and bric-a-brac hanging on the walls. The decor suits the unfussy (if overpriced) cuisine, which features roast meats and stewed broad beans. **Known for:** ultratender cochinillo asado (roast suckling pig); tourist-friendly menus and service; historic setting. $ *Average main: €30* ⊠ *Calle Cervantes 12* ☎ *92/146–2487, 92/146–2486* ⊕ *www.restaurant-eduque.es.*

★ El Fogón Sefardí

$$$ | SPANISH | This tavern in Segovia's historic Jewish quarter is owned by La Casa Mudejar Hospedería hotel and wins awards year after year for the region's best tapas. The menu is exquisite,

featuring Segovian specialties like cochinillo as well as traditional Sephardic Jewish cuisine (though it's not a kosher kitchen), plus a variety of well-executed *raciones* (tapas). **Known for:** traditional Sephardic Jewish cuisine; cochinillo; generous salads. $ *Average main: €20* ⊠ *Calle Judería Vieja 17* ☎ *92/146–6250* ⊕ *www.lacasamudejar.com* ▭ *No credit cards.*

Mesón de Cándido

$$$$ | SPANISH | Amid the dark-wood beams and Castilian knickknacks of this restaurant beneath the aqueduct hang photos of celebrities who have dined here, among them Ernest Hemingway and Princess Grace. The suckling pig (cochinillo) is the star; partridge stew and roast lamb are also memorable, especially on cold afternoons. **Known for:** wood-fire-oven-roasted cochinillo; historic building; famous former patrons like Ernest Hemingway. $ *Average main: €30* ⊠ *Pl. de Azoguejo 5* ☎ *92/142–5911* ⊕ *www.mesondecandido.es.*

★ Mesón de José María
$$$$ | **SPANISH** | According to foodies, this old-timey *mesón* (traditional tavern-restaurant) serves the most delectable cochinillo asado in town, but there are plenty of lighter, fresher dishes to choose from as well. Expect a boisterous mix of locals and tourists. **Known for:** best cochinillo in town; beamed dining room; local crowd (a rarity in this touristy town). [$] *Average main: €35* ✉ *Calle Cronista Lecea 11, off Pl. Mayor* ☎ *92/146–1111, 92/146–6017* 🌐 *www.restaurantejosemaria.com.*

Hotels

Infanta Isabel Hotel
$$ | **HOTEL** | On the corner of the Plaza Mayor, this classically appointed hotel boasts cathedral views in a bustling shopping area. **Pros:** lived-in, cozy ambience; central location; some rooms have balconies overlooking the plaza. **Cons:** some rooms are cramped and oddly shaped; rooms facing the plaza can be noisy on weekends; decidedly unhip decor. [$] *Rooms from: €120* ✉ *Pl. Mayor 12* ☎ *92/146–1300* 🌐 *www.hotelinfantaisabel.com* 🛏 *37 rooms* 🍴 *No meals.*

La Casa Mudejar Hospedería
$$ | **HOTEL** | Built in the 15th century as a Mudejar palace, this historical property has spacious rooms and a well-priced spa (€30 per person) that's extremely popular, even with nonguests. **Pros:** terrific restaurant serving rare Sephardic dishes; historic building with Roman ruins; affordable spa. **Cons:** forgettable interiors; no nearby parking; beds nothing special. [$] *Rooms from: €100* ✉ *Calle Isabel la Católica 8* ☎ *92/146–6250* 🌐 *www.lacasamudejar.com* 🛏 *40 rooms* 🍴 *No meals.*

Parador de Segovia
$$ | **HOTEL** | From the large windows of this modern-style parador, 3 km (2 miles) from the old town, you can take in spectacular views of the cathedral and aqueduct. **Pros:** beautiful views of the city; sunny, picturesque pool area; spacious rooms. **Cons:** need a car to get here; uncozy, passé decor; lacks antique touches of more historic paradores. [$] *Rooms from: €120* ✉ *Ctra. de Valladolid* ☎ *92/144–3737* 🌐 *www.parador.es* 🛏 *113 rooms* 🍴 *No meals.*

Shopping

After Toledo, the province of Segovia is Castile's most important area for traditional artisanry. Glass and crystal are specialties of La Granja, and ironwork, lace, basketry, and embroidery are famous in Segovia. You can buy good lace from the Romani vendors in Segovia's Plaza del Alcázar, but be prepared for some strenuous bargaining, and never offer more than half the opening price. The area around Plaza San Martín is a good place to buy crafts.

Calle Daoíz
CERAMICS/GLASSWARE | Leading to the Alcázar, this street overflows with locally made (if tourist-oriented) ceramics, textiles, and gift shops. ✉ *Segovia.*

Plaza San Martín
ANTIQUES/COLLECTIBLES | Several antiques shops line this small plaza. ✉ *Segovia.*

Salchichería Briz
FOOD/CANDY | The city's best artisanal sausages—from chorizo to *morcilla* (blood sausage) and *lomo* (cured pork loin)—can be found at this 40-year-old butcher shop. The cured meats travel well and can be kept for months at a cool room temperature. ✉ *Calle Fernández Ladreda 20* ☎ *92/146–1755* 🌐 *www.salchicheriabriz.es.*

Sepúlveda

58 km (36 miles) northeast of Segovia.

A walled village with a commanding position, Sepúlveda has a charming main square, but the main reasons to visit are its 11th-century Romanesque church and striking gorge with a scenic hiking trail.

GETTING HERE AND AROUND

Sepúlveda is about an hour north of Madrid on the A1. There are also several buses (and Blablacar rideshares) a day from both Segovia and Madrid. The city is perched atop a hill overlooking a ravine, so you'll likely want transportation to the top. Don't park or get off the bus too soon.

ESSENTIALS

VISITOR INFORMATION Sepúlveda Tourist Office ⊠ *Pl. del Trigo 6* ☎ *92/154–0237* ⊕ *www.sepulveda.es.*

Sights

Iglesia de San Salvador

RELIGIOUS SITE | This 11th-century church is the oldest Romanesque church in Segovia Province. The carvings on its capitals, probably by a Moorish convert, are quite outlandish. ⊠ *Calle Subida a El Salvador 10.*

★ Ermita de San Frutos

RELIGIOUS SITE | This 11th-century hermitage is in ruins, but its location, on a peninsula jutting out into a bend 100 meters above the Duratón River, is extraordinary. You'll need a car to get there, about 15 minutes' drive west of Sepúlveda. Stay on the marked paths—the surrounding area is a natural park and a protected nesting ground for rare vultures—and try to go at sunset, when the light enhances spectacular views of the sandstone monastery and river below. Inside the monastery, there's a small chapel and plaque describing the life of San Frutos, the patron saint of Segovia. An ancient pilgrimage route stretches 77 km (48 miles) from the monastery to Segovia's cathedral, and pilgrims still walk it each year. As an add-on to the trip, you can rent kayaks from **NaturalTur** (☎ *92/152–1727* ⊕ *www.naturaltur.com*) to paddle the river. ⊠ *Carrascal del Rio, Burgomillodo* ⊕ *www.caminodesanfrutos.org* ✉ *Free.*

San Lorenzo de El Escorial

50 km (31 miles) northwest of Madrid

An hour from Madrid, San Lorenzo del Escorial makes for a leisurely day trip away from the hustle and bustle of the Spanish capital. The medieval town's main attraction is the Real Sitio de San Lorenzo de El Escoriala, the Royal Site of San Lorenzo of El Escorial. The easiest way to visit is on a guided tour. There are also a number of trains that leave every day from the Madrid Sol train station that will take you to El Escorial. You can take the C3 regional line from Atocha, Chamartin, Nuevos Ministerios, or Recoletos. The journey takes about an hour and the entrance to El Escorial is about a ten minute walk from the train station.

Sights

★ El Escorial

CASTLE/PALACE | A UNESCO World Heritage Site and one of Spain's most visited landmarks, the imposing Monastery and Real Sitio de San Lorenzo de El Escorial (or just El Escorial) was commissioned by Felipe II after the death of his father in the 1500s and remains the most complete and impressive monument of the later Renaissance in Spain. The monastery was built as an eternal memorial for his relatives and the crypt here is the resting place of the majority of Spain's kings, from Charles V to Alfonso XIII. A veritable labyrinth of gilded halls, hand-painted chambers, and manicured French gardens, this gargantuan royal residence houses an important collection of paintings by Renaissance and baroque artists donated by the crown, among its many artistic treasures. It's worth paying the €12 entry fee to see the library alone, whose vibrant frescoes and leather-bound tomes spur the imagination. ■**TIP→ Combine your El Escorial visit with a trip to the El Valle de los Caidos, or the**

Castillo de Coca

Perhaps the most famous medieval sight near Segovia—worth the 52 km (32-mile) detour northwest of the city en route to Ávila or Valladolid—is the Castillo de Coca. Built in the 15th century for Archbishop Alonso de Fonseca I, the castle is a turreted Mudejar structure of plaster and red brick surrounded by a deep moat. Highly Instagrammable, it looks like a stage set for a fairy tale, and, indeed, it was intended not as a fortress but as a place for the notoriously pleasure-loving archbishop to hold riotous parties. The interior, now occupied by a forestry school, has been modernized, with only fragments of the original decoration preserved. ⊕ *www.castillodecoca.com*

Valley of the Fallen. Here, you'll find final resting place of General Franco. ⊠ *Plaza de España, 1, San Lorenzo de El Escorial* ☎ *91/890–5903* ⊕ *el-escorial.com* ⊠ *€12* ⊗ *Closed Mon.* Ⓜ *El Escorial.*

Ávila

114 km (71 miles) northwest of Madrid.

On a windy plateau littered with giant boulders, with the Sierra de Gredos in the background, Ávila is a walled fairy-tale town that wouldn't look out of place in *Game of Thrones*. Shortly after the town was reclaimed from the Moors in 1090, crenelated walls were erected in just nine years—thanks to the employment of an estimated 1,900 builders. The walls have nine gates and 88 cylindrical towers bunched together, making them unique to Spain in form—they're quite unlike the Moorish defense architecture that the Christians adapted elsewhere. They're most striking when seen from afar; for the best views (and photos), cross the Adaja River, turn right on the Carretera de Salamanca, and walk uphill about 250 yards to a monument of pilasters surrounding a cross known as the "Four Posts."

Ávila's fame is largely due to St. Teresa. Born here in 1515 to a noble family of Jewish origin, Teresa spent much of her life in Ávila, leaving a legacy of convents and the ubiquitous *yemas* (candied egg yolks), originally distributed free to the poor and now sold for high prices to tourists. The town comes to life during the Fiestas de la Santa Teresa in October, a weeklong celebration that includes lighted decorations, parades, singing in the streets, and religious observances.

GETTING HERE AND AROUND

Jiménez Dorado (⊕ *www.jimenezdorado.com*) and Avilabus (⊕ *www.avilabus.com*) serve Ávila and its surrounding villages. Twenty-three trains depart for Ávila each day from Chamartín station, and there are usually plentiful Blablacar rideshares available. The city itself is easily managed on foot.

ESSENTIALS

VISITOR INFORMATION **Ávila Tourist Office** ⊠ *Pl. de la Catedral, Av. de Madrid 39* ☎ *92/021–1387* ⊕ *www.avilaturismo.com.*

Sights

Basílica de San Vicente (*Basilica of St. Vincent*)
RELIGIOUS SITE | On this site, now a Romanesque basilica, it's said that St. Vincent was martyred in AD 303 with his sisters, Sts. Sabina and Cristeta. Construction began in 1130 and continued through the 12th century, and the massive church complex was restored in the late 19th and early 20th centuries.

Ávila's city walls, which still encircle the old city, have a perimeter of about 2.5 km (1½ miles).

The west front, shielded by a vestibule, displays damaged but expressive Romanesque carvings depicting the death of Lazarus and the parable of the rich man's table. The sarcophagus of St. Vincent forms the centerpiece of the basilica's Romanesque interior. The extraordinary, Eastern-influenced canopy above the sarcophagus is a 15th-century addition. ⊠ *Pl. de San Vicente 1* ☏ *92/022–5969* ⊕ *www.basilicasanvicente.es* ⊠ *€3 (free Sun.).*

Casa de los Deanes (*Deans' Mansion*) **MUSEUM** | This 15th-century building houses the cheerful **Museo Provincial de Ávila,** full of local archaeology and folklore. Part of the museum's collection is housed in the adjacent Romanesque temple of San Tomé el Viejo, a few minutes' walk east of the cathedral apse. ⊠ *Pl. de Nalvillos 3* ☏ *92/021–1003* ⊠ *€2 (free on weekends)* ☉ *Closed Mon.*

★ Catedral de Ávila

RELIGIOUS SITE | The battlement apse of Ávila's cathedral forms the most impressive part of the city's walls. Entering the town gate to the right of the apse, you can reach the sculpted north portal by turning left and walking a few steps. The west portal, flanked by 18th-century towers, is notable for the crude carvings of hairy male figures on each side. Known as "wild men," these figures appear in many Castilian palaces of this period. The Transitional Gothic structure, with its granite nave, is considered to be the first Gothic cathedral in Spain. Look for the early-16th-century marble sepulchre of Bishop Alonso de Madrigal. Known as El Tostado (the Toasted One) for his swarthy complexion, the bishop was a tiny man of enormous intellect. When on one occasion Pope Eugenius IV ordered him to stand—mistakenly thinking him to still be on his knees—the bishop pointed to the space between his eyebrows and hairline, and retorted, "A man's stature is to be measured from here to here!" ⊠ *Pl. de la Catedral s/n* ☏ *92/021–1641* ⊕ *catedralavila.es* ⊠ *€6.*

Convento de Santa Teresa

RELIGIOUS SITE | This Carmelite convent was founded in the 17th century on the site of the St. Teresa's birthplace. Teresa's account of an ecstatic vision, in which an angel pierced her heart, inspired many baroque artists, most famously the Italian sculptor Giovanni Bernini. The convent has a small museum with creepy relics including one of Teresa's fingers. You also can see the small and rather gloomy garden where she played as a child. ⊠ *Pl. de la Santa 2* ☎ *92/021–1030* ⊕ *www. santateresadejesus.com* ✍ *Church and reliquary free, museum €2.*

Mysticism Interpretation Center

MUSEUM | The only such museum of its kind in Europe, this small modern museum is devoted to mysticism, the idea made famous by Ávila's native daughter, St. Teresa—one of Christianity's first female mystics. Exhibits explain the role of mysticism in Judaism, Christianity, and a number of Eastern religions. While the exterior of the building, a medieval house, is original, architects installed a giant prism ceiling that reflects light throughout the interior. ⊠ *Paseo del Rastro s/n* ☎ *92/021–2154* ⊕ *www.avilamistica.es* ✍ *€3* ☞ *Closed Mon.*

Real Monasterio de Santo Tomás

RELIGIOUS SITE | In a most unlikely location—among apartment blocks a good 10-minute walk from the walls—is one of the most important religious institutions in Castile. The monastery was founded by Ferdinand and Isabella with the backing of the Inquisitor-General Tomás de Torquemada, largely responsible for the explusion of the Jews per the Alhambra Decree, who is buried in the sacristy. Further funds were provided by the confiscated property of converted Jews who were dispossessed during the Inquisition. Three decorated cloisters lead to the church; inside, a masterful high altar (circa 1506) by Pedro Berruguete overlooks a serene marble tomb by the Italian artist Domenico Fancelli. One of the earliest examples of the Italian Renaissance style in Spain, this work was built for Prince Juan, the only son of Ferdinand and Isabella, who died at 19.

After Juan's burial here, his heartbroken parents found themselves unable to return. There are free guided tours at 6 pm on weekends and holidays. ⊠ *Pl. de Granada 1* ☎ *92/022–0400* ⊕ *www. monasteriosantotomas.com* ✍ *€4.*

 Restaurants

Las Cancelas

$$$ | SPANISH | Locals flock to this little tavern for the tapas and fat, juicy steaks served in the boisterous barroom or white-tablecloth dining area, set in a covered arcaded courtyard. There are 14 hotel rooms available, too—simple, slightly ramshackle arrangements at moderate prices. **Known for:** chuletón de Ávila (gargantuan local steaks); quaint, romantic dining room; good value. Ⓢ *Average main: €20* ⊠ *Calle de la Cruz Vieja 6* ☎ *92/021–2249* ⊕ *www.lascancelas. com* ⊘ *Closed early Jan.–early Feb. No dinner Sun.*

Restaurante El Molino de la Losa

$$$$ | SPANISH | FAMILY | Sitting at the edge of the serene Adaja River, El Molino, housed in a 15th-century mill, enjoys one of the best views of the town walls. Lamb, the restaurant's specialty, is roasted in a medieval wood oven, and the beans from nearby El Barco de Ávila (*judías de El Barco*) are famous. **Known for:** succulent roast lamb; views of the river and city walls; refined cuisine. Ⓢ *Average main: €30* ⊠ *Calle Bajada de la Losa 12* ☎ *92/021–1101, 92/021–1102* ⊕ *www.elmolinodelalosa.com* ⊘ *No dinner Sun.*

Hotels

★ Palacio de los Velada

$$$ | HOTEL | Ávila's top four-star hotel occupies a beautifully restored 16th-century palace in the heart of the city next to the cathedral, an ideal spot if you like to relax between sightseeing. **Pros:** gorgeous glass-covered patio; amiable service; bountiful breakfast buffet. **Cons:**

some rooms don't have views because the windows are so high; expensive off-site parking; lack of power outlets. $ *Rooms from: €150* ✉ *Pl. de la Catedral 10* ☎ *92/025–5100* ⊕ *www.veladahoteles.com* ➘ *145 rooms* ⦿ *No meals.*

Parador de Ávila

$$$ | HOTEL | FAMILY | This largely rebuilt 16th-century medieval castle is attached to the massive town walls, and a standout feature is its lush garden containing archaeological ruins. **Pros:** gorgeous garden and views; good restaurant; family-friendly rooms and services. **Cons:** long walk into town; interiors need a refresh; underwhelming breakfast. $ *Rooms from: €130* ✉ *Marqués de Canales de Chozas 2* ☎ *92/021–1340* ⊕ *www.parador.es* ➘ *61 rooms* ⦿ *No meals.*

Salamanca

212 km (132 miles) northwest of Madrid.

Salamanca's radiant sandstone buildings, postcard-perfect Plaza Mayor, and meandering river make it one of the most majestic and beloved cities in Spain. Today, as it did centuries ago, the university imbues the city with an intellectual verve, a stimulating arts scene, and raging nightlife to match. You'll see more foreign students here per capita than anywhere else in Spain.

If you approach from Madrid or Ávila, your first glimpse of Salamanca will be of the city rising on the northern banks of the wide and winding Tormes River. In the foreground is its sturdy, 15-arch Roman bridge; soaring above it is the combined bulk of the old and new cathedrals. Piercing the skyline to the right is the Renaissance monastery and church of San Esteban. Behind San Esteban and the cathedrals, and largely out of sight from the river, extends a stunning series of palaces, convents, and university buildings that culminates in the Plaza Mayor. Despite enduring considerable

damage over the centuries, Salamanca remains one of Spain's greatest cities architecturally, a showpiece of the Spanish Renaissance.

GETTING HERE AND AROUND

You'll probably feel rushed if you try to visit Salamanca from Toledo in an out-and-back day trip: to take in its splendor, plan on an overnight. Approximately 13 trains depart Madrid for Salamanca daily, several of which are high-speed ALVIA itineraries that take just over an hour and a half. Avanza buses leave from the Estación Sur de Autobuses; Blablacar rideshares (about 2 hours and 15 minutes) are faster and more affordable.

Once in town, Salamanca de Transportes runs 64 municipal buses equipped with lifts for passengers with disabilities on routes throughout the city of Salamanca. You may opt to take a bus in order to reach the train and bus stations on the outskirts of the city.

INTRACITY BUS CONTACT Salamanca de Transportes ☎ *92/319–0545* ⊕ *www.salamancadetransportes.com.*

ESSENTIALS

VISITOR INFORMATION Salamanca Municipal Tourist Office ✉ *Pl. Mayor 32* ☎ *92/321–8342* ⊕ *www.salamanca.es.* **Salamanca Regional Tourist Office** ✉ *Rúa Mayor s/n* ☎ *92/326–8571, 90/220–3030* ⊕ *www.salamanca.es.*

 Sights

★ **Casa de Las Conchas** (*House of Shells*) HOUSE | This house, whose facade is covered in scallop shell carvings, was built around 1500 for Dr. Rodrigo Maldonado de Talavera, a chancellor of the Order of St. James, whose symbol is the shell. Among the playful plateresque details are the lions over the main entrance, engaged in a fearful tug-of-war with the Talavera crest. The interior has been converted into a public library. Duck into the charming courtyard, which has an intricately carved upper balustrade that imitates basketwork. ⌧ *Calle Compañia 2* ☎ *92/326–9317* ⌧ *Free.*

★ Catedrals Vieja and Nueva

RELIGIOUS SITE | Nearest the river stands the **Catedral Vieja** (Old Cathedral), built in the late 12th century and one of the most riveting examples of the Spanish Romanesque. Because the dome of the crossing tower has strange, plumelike ribbing, it's known as the Torre del Gallo (Rooster's Tower). The much larger **Catedral Nueva** (New Cathedral) was built between 1513 and 1526 under the late-Gothic architect Juan Gil de Hontañón. The two cathedrals are part of the same complex, though they have different visiting hours, and you need to enter the new one to get to the Old Cathedral. Take a moment to marvel at the west facade, dazzling in its sculptural complexity. ⌧ *Pl. de Anaya and Calle Cardenal Pla y Deniel* ☎ *92/321–7476, 92/328–1123* ⊕ *www.catedralsalamanca. org* ⌧ *Catedral Nueva free, Catedral Vieja €5 (free Tues. 10–noon).*

★ Convento de Las Dueñas (*Convent of the Dames*)

RELIGIOUS SITE | Founded in 1419, this convent hides a 16th-century cloister that is the most fantastically decorated in Salamanca, if not in all of Spain. The capitals of its two superimposed Salmantine arcades are crowded with a baffling profusion of grotesques that can absorb you for hours. Don't forget to look down: the interlocking diamond pattern on the ground floor of the cloister is decorated with the knobby vertebrae of goats and sheep. It's an eerie yet perfect accompaniment to all the grinning, disfigured heads sprouting from the capitals looming above you. The museum has a fascinating exhibit on Spain's little-known slavery industry. And don't leave without buying some sweets—the nuns are excellent bakers. ⌧ *Pl. del Concilio de Trento s/n* ☎ *92/321–5442* ⌧ *€2.*

Fonseca's Mark

Nearly all of Salamanca's outstanding Renaissance buildings bear the five-star crest of the all-powerful and ostentatious Fonseca family. The most famous of them, Alonso de Fonseca I, was the archbishop of Santiago and then of Seville; he was also a notorious womanizer and a patron of the Spanish Renaissance.

Convento de Las Úrsulas (*Convento de la Anunciación*)

RELIGIOUS SITE | Archbishop Alonso de Fonseca I lies here, in this splendid Gothic-style marble tomb created by Diego de Siloe during the early 1500s on the outskirts of the historic center. Magnificent churrigueresque altarpieces depicting scenes in the life of Jesus were restored in 2014. The cloister is closed to the public as the convent is still active. ⌧ *Calle de las Úrsulas 2* ☎ *92/321–9877* ⌧ *€3.*

★ Convento de San Estéban (*Convent of St. Stephen*)

RELIGIOUS SITE | The convent's monks, among the most enlightened teachers at the university in medieval times, introduced Christopher Columbus to Isabella (hence his statue in the nearby Plaza de Colón, back toward Calle de San Pablo). The complex was designed by one of the monks who lived here, Juan de Álava. The massive west facade, a thrilling plateresque work in which sculpted figures and ornamentation are piled up to a height of more than 98 feet, is a gathering spot for tired tourists and picnicking locals, but the crown jewel of the structure is a glowing golden sandstone cloister with Gothic arcading punctuated by tall, spindly columns adorned with classical motifs. The church, unified and uncluttered but also dark and severe, allows the one note of color provided by the ornate and gilded high altar of 1692.

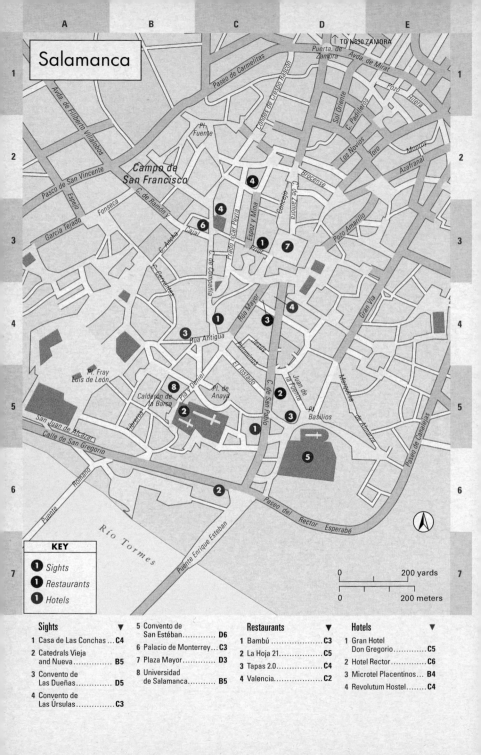

Salamanca

KEY

- ● Sights
- ● Restaurants
- ● Hotels

| 0 | | 200 yards |
| 0 | | 200 meters |

Sights ▼

1 Casa de Las Conchas ... **C4**
2 Catedrals Vieja
   and Nueva **B5**
3 Convento de
   Las Dueñas **D5**
4 Convento de
   Las Úrsulas **C3**
5 Convento de
   San Estéban **D6**
6 Palacio de Monterrey ... **C3**
7 Plaza Mayor **D3**
8 Universidad
   de Salamanca **B5**

Restaurants ▼

1 Bambú **C3**
2 La Hoja 21 .... **C5**
3 Tapas 2.0 .... **C4**
4 Valencia **C2**

Hotels ▼

1 Gran Hotel
   Don Gregorio **C5**
2 Hotel Rector **C6**
3 Microtel Placentinos ... **B4**
4 Revolutum Hostel **C4**

An awe-inspiring baroque masterpiece by José Churriguera, it deserves five minutes of just sitting and staring. You can book free guided tours on the website. ✉ *Pl. Concilio de Trento 1* ☎ *92/321–5000* 🌐 *www.conventosanesteban.es* 🎟 *€4* 🕒 *Museum closed Mon.*

Palacio de Monterrey

CASTLE/PALACE | Built in the mid-16th century by Rodrigo Gil de Hontañón and one of the most stunning Renaissance palaces in Spain, this lavish edifice was meant for an illegitimate son of Alonso de Fonseca I. The building is flanked by towers and has an open arcaded gallery running the length of the upper level. Such galleries—often seen on the ground floor of palaces in Italy—were intended to provide privacy for the women of the house and to cool the floor below during the summer. Following years of renovations and much anticipation, the palace finally opened to the public in 2018; tours, which cost €5 per person, are by appointment only (reservations must be made in person at the Plaza Mayor tourist office). Feast your eyes on seldom-before-seen Titians, Coellos, and other masterpieces presided over by the Alba family. ✉ *Pl. de las Agustinas* 🌐 *www.fundacioncasadealba.com* 🎟 *€5 tour.*

★ Plaza Mayor

PLAZA | Built in the 1730s by Alberto and Nicolás Churriguera, Salamanca's Plaza Mayor is one of the largest and most beautiful squares in Spain. The lavishly elegant, pinkish **ayuntamiento** dominates its northern side. The square and its arcades are popular gathering spots for salmantinos of all ages, and its *terrazas* are the perfect spot for a coffee break. At night, the plaza swarms with students meeting "under the clock" on the plaza's north side. *Tunas* (strolling musicians in traditional garb) often meander among the cafés and crowds, playing for smiles and applause rather than tips. The plaza was in the news in 2017, when, after decades of controversy, the infamous medallion portraying Franco was removed from one of its capitals. ✉ *Salamanca.*

Universidad de Salamanca

COLLEGE | Parts of the university's walls, like those of the cathedral and other structures in Salamanca, are covered with large ocher lettering recording the names of famous university graduates. The earliest names are said to have been written in the blood of the bulls killed to celebrate the successful completion of a doctorate (call it medieval graffiti). The elaborate facade of the **Escuelas Mayores** (Upper Schools) dates to the early 16th century; see if you can spy the "lucky" frog that's become the symbol of the city—legend has it that students who spot the frog on their first try will pass all their exams. ✉ *Calle Libreros* ☎ *92/329–4400, 95/222–2998* 🌐 *www.usal.es* 🎟 *Free to view facade, €10 to enter (free Mon. morning).*

🍴 Restaurants

Bambú

$$ | **TAPAS** | Bambú is two restaurants in one: there's a jovial basement tapas bar serving gargantuan tapas and beers to hungry locals, and then there's the far more sedate white-tablecloth dining room, whose *nueva cocina* (new cuisine) menu is subtler, fussier, and more expensive. Both are worthwhile options; go with the vibe that suits you best. **Known for:** free tapas with every drink at the bar; sedate nueva cocina dining room; friendly collegiate ambience. [$] *Average main: €12* ✉ *Calle Prior 4* ☎ *92/326–0092.*

★ La Hoja 21

$$$$ | **SPANISH** | Just off the Plaza Mayor, this upscale restaurant has a glass facade, high ceilings, butter-yellow walls, and minimalist art—a welcome relief from the dime-a-dozen Castilian mesones. Savor traditional fare with a twist, such as ibérico pork ravioli and langoustine-stuffed trotters at dinner, or spring for the €16 lunch prix fixe, an

Salamanca's Plaza Mayor once hosted bullfights.

absolute steal served Tuesday through Thursday. **Known for:** nuanced yet unpretentious modern fare; phenomenally affordable menú del día (prix fixe); romantic, low-key atmosphere. *Average main: €30* ⊠ *Calle San Pablo 21* ☎ *92/326–4028* ⊕ *www.lahoja21.com* ⊗ *Closed Mon. No dinner Sun.*

★ Tapas 2.0

$$ | TAPAS | Decidedly modern, dependably delicious, and shockingly cheap, Tapas 2.0 might pull you back for a second meal. The cool *ensaladilla rusa* (potato salad mixed with tuna), a specialty, is one of the best in Spain; then there are more substantial dishes, like "Momofuku-style" fried chicken and saucy lamb meatballs, all complemented by a wine list featuring unexpected wines like German Riesling. **Known for:** ensaladilla rusa; uncommon wines; the best tapas in town. $ *Average main: €14* ⊠ *Calle Felipe Espino 10* ☎ *92/321–6448* ⊕ *www.tapastrespuntocero.es.*

★ Valencia

$$$ | SPANISH | Despite its Mediterranean name, this traditional, family-run restaurant serves up Castilian specialties like garlic soup, partridge salad, local river trout, white asparagus, and suckling lamb. The tiny front bar is decorated with black-and-white photos of local bullfighters, and is usually packed with locals (as is the back room). **Known for:** hidden-gem local hangout; soul-warming Castilian fare; outdoor seating. $ *Average main: €20* ⊠ *Calle Concejo 15* ☎ *92/321–7868* ⊕ *www.restaurantevalencia.com* ⊗ *Closed Mon. Nov., Tues. Sept.–May, and Sun. June–Aug.*

🛏 Hotels

Grand Hotel Don Gregorio

$$$$ | HOTEL | This upscale boutique hotel has spacious, contemporary rooms in a building with roots in the 15th century. **Pros:** chic, contemporary facilities; complimentary cava upon arrival; spa and in-room massages. **Cons:** restaurant is expensive—the more casual cafeteria

is a better bet; no outdoor space for lounging; some receptionists speak poor English. $ Rooms from: €220 ⊠ Calle San Pablo 80–82 ☎ 92/321–7015 ⊕ www.hoteldongregorio.com ⇆ 17 rooms ⦿❙ Free Breakfast.

★ Hotel Rector

$$$ | HOTEL | From the stately entrance to the high-ceiling guest rooms, this lovely hotel offers a fairy-tale European experience. **Pros:** terrific value for a luxury hotel; personal service; good location. **Cons:** parking costs extra; no balconies; breakfast could be more ample. $ Rooms from: €160 ⊠ Paseo Rector Esperabé 10 ☎ 92/321–8482 ⊕ www.hotelrector.com ⇆ 13 rooms ⦿❙ No meals.

★ Microtel Placentinos

$$ | B&B/INN | This is a lovely B&B tucked down a quiet pedestrian street in Salamanca's historic center, near the Palacio de Congresos convention center and a short walk from the Plaza Mayor. **Pros:** some rooms have whirlpool baths; quirky decor; short walk to bus station. **Cons:** rooms by interior staircase can be noisy; some accommodations are cramped; boring breakfast buffet. $ Rooms from: €90 ⊠ Calle Placentinos 9 ☎ 92/328–1531 ⊕ www.microtelplacentinos.com ⇆ 9 rooms ⦿❙ Free Breakfast.

Revolutum Hostel

$ | HOTEL | Embodying the swiftly growing hotel category of "designer hostel," this is the best budget option in Salamanca. **Pros:** breakfast included; all rooms have private bathrooms; special rates for families and longer stays. **Cons:** deposit required for towels; you have to make your own bed in some rooms; small bathrooms in some rooms. $ Rooms from: €49 ⊠ Calle Sánchez Barbero 7 ☎ 92/321–7656 ⊕ www.revolutumhostel.com ⇆ 20 rooms ⦿❙ Free Breakfast.

Nightlife

Particularly in summer, Salamanca sees the greatest influx of foreign students of any city in Spain: by day they study Spanish, and by night they fill Salamanca's bars and clubs.

BARS AND CAFÉS

Café Corrillo

CAFES—NIGHTLIFE | This lively (if unstylish) restaurant-bar-café is the main hangout for fans of live music, especially jazz, and solid tapas seal the deal. Call ahead for the concert list and special events like craft beer nights. ⊠ Calle Meléndez 18 ☎ 92/327–1917.

★ The Doctor Cocktail Bar

BARS/PUBS | This petite, unpretentious coctelería off the Plaza Mayor serves an enormous breadth of drinks, from colorful tiki numbers (some with pyrotechnics) to Prohibition-era classics until 1:30 am daily. ⊠ Calle Doctor Pinuela 5 ☎ 92/326–3151.

Gran Café Moderno

BARS/PUBS | After-hours types end the night here, snacking on churros with chocolate at daybreak. ⊠ Gran Vía 75–77 ☎ 63/753–8165, 92/326–0147.

Performing Arts

Teatro Liceo

ARTS VENUE | This 732-seat theater, 40 yards from Plaza Mayor, got a face-lift in 2002, but traces of the old 19th-century theater, built over an 18th-century convent, remain. It hosts classic and modern performances of opera, dance, and flamenco as well as film festivals. ⊠ Calle del Toro 23 ☎ 92/328–0619 ⊕ www.ciudaddecultura.org.

🛍 Shopping

El Rastro

OUTDOOR/FLEA/GREEN MARKETS | On Sunday, this flea market—named after the larger one in Madrid—is held just outside

Salamanca's historic center. It has some 400 stalls. Buses leave from Plaza de España. ⊠ *Av. de Aldehuela.*

Isisa Duende

CRAFTS | If you have a car, skip the souvenir shops in Salamanca's center and instead head 35 km (22 miles) through the countryside along the rural SA300 road to Isisa Duende, a wooden crafts workshop run by a charming husband-and-wife team. Their music boxes, photo frames, and other items are carved with local themes, from the *bailes charros,* Salamanca's regional dance, to the floral designs embroidered on the hems of provincial dresses. Because the store has limited hours (primarily weekends only), it's best to call ahead to schedule a free, personal tour; if you're pressed for time, you can buy some of their wares in the tourist office on the Plaza Mayor. ⊠ *Calle San Miguel 1, Ledesma* ☏ *62/651–0527, 62/533–6703* ⊕ *www.isisa-duende.es.*

Mercado Central

FOOD/CANDY | **FAMILY** | At Salamanca's most historic market you can stock up on local gourmet specialties—such as *farinato* sausages, *jamón ibérico* (Iberian ham), and sheep's cheeses—and round out your shopping spree with a glass of wine at any of the market's traditional tapas counters. The 53 stalls are sure to keep any foodie occupied. ⊠ *Pl. del Mercado* ☏ *92/321–3000* ⊕ *www.mercadocentral-salamanca.com.*

Burgos

243 km (151 miles) north of Madrid on A1.

On the banks of the Arlanzón River, this small city boasts some of Spain's most outstanding Gothic architecture. If you approach on the A1 from Madrid, the spiky twin spires of Burgos's cathedral, rising above the main bridge, welcome you to the city. Burgos's second pride is its heritage as the city of El Cid, the part-historical, part-mythical hero of the Christian Reconquest of Spain. The city has been known for centuries as a center of both militarism and religion, and even today more nuns fill the streets than almost anywhere else in Spain. Burgos was born as a military camp—a fortress built in 884 on the orders of the Christian king Alfonso III, who was struggling to defend the upper reaches of Old Castile from the constant forays of the Arabs. It quickly became vital in the defense of Christian Spain, and its reputation as an early outpost of Christianity was cemented with the founding of the Royal Convent of Las Huelgas, in 1187. Burgos also became a place of rest and sustenance for Christian pilgrims on the Camino de Santiago. These days, it's also a food town, known for its namesake *queso fresco* and morcilla.

GETTING HERE AND AROUND

Burgos can be reached by train from Madrid, with 13 departures daily from Chamartín (2½ hours on the fast ALVIA train and 4½ on the regional line) and by bus, with hourly service from various Madrid stations. There are usually several Blablacar rideshares available as well. Once there, municipal buses cover 45 routes throughout the city, many of them originating in Plaza de España.

ESSENTIALS

VISITOR INFORMATION Burgos Tourist Office ⊠ *Calle Nuño Rasura 7* ☏ *94/728–8874* ⊕ *www.turismoburgos.org.*

◉ Sights

Cartuja de Miraflores (*Miraflores Charterhouse*)

RELIGIOUS SITE | The plain facade of this 15th-century Carthusian monastery, some 3 km (2 miles) outside the historic center, belies a richly decorated interior. There's an altarpiece by Gil de Siloe that is said to be gilded with the first gold brought back from the Americas. ⊠ *Ctra. Fuentes Blancas* ☏ *94/725–2586* ⊕ *www.cartuja.org* *Free.*

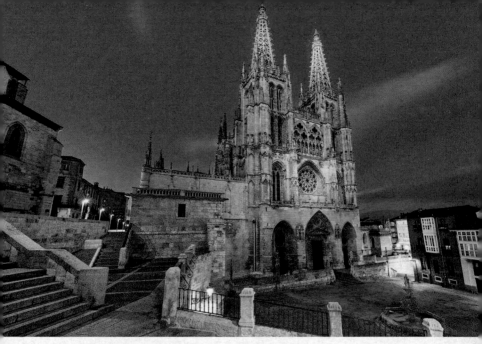

The small city of Burgos is famous for its magnificent Gothic cathedral.

★ Catedral de Burgos

RELIGIOUS SITE | Start your tour of the city with the cathedral, which contains such a wealth of art and other treasures that the local burghers lynched their civil governor in 1869 for trying to take an inventory of it: the proud citizens feared that the man was plotting to steal their riches. Just as opulent as what's inside is the sculpted flamboyant Gothic facade. The cornerstone was laid in 1221, and the two 275-foot towers were completed by the middle of the 14th century, though the final chapel was not finished until 1731. There are 13 chapels, the most elaborate of which is the hexagonal Condestable Chapel. You'll find the **tomb of El Cid** (1026–99) and his wife, Ximena, under the transept. El Cid (whose real name was Rodrigo Díaz de Vivar) was a feudal warlord revered for his victories over the Moors; the medieval *Song of My Cid* transformed him into a Spanish national hero.

At the other end of the cathedral, high above the West Door, is the **Reloj de Papamoscas** (Flycatcher Clock), so named for the sculptured bird that opens its mouth as the hands mark each hour. The grilles around the choir have some of the finest wrought-iron work in central Spain, and the choir itself has 103 delicately carved walnut stalls, no two alike. The 13th-century stained-glass windows that once shed a beautiful, filtered light were destroyed in 1813, one of many cultural casualties of Napoléon's retreating troops. ⊠ *Pl. de Santa María* ☎ *94/720–4712* ⊕ *www.catedraldeburgos.es* ⊠ *€7.*

Espolón

PROMENADE | The Arco de Santa María frames the city's loveliest promenade, the Espolón. Shaded with black poplars, it follows the riverbank. ⊠ *Burgos.*

Monasterio de Santa María la Real de las Huelgas (*Monasterio de las Huelgas*)

MUSEUM | This convent on the outskirts of town, founded in 1187 by King Alfonso VIII, is still run by nuns. There's a small on-site textile museum, but the building's main attraction is its stained-glass panels, some of the oldest in Spain. Admission includes a guided tour (Spanish only)

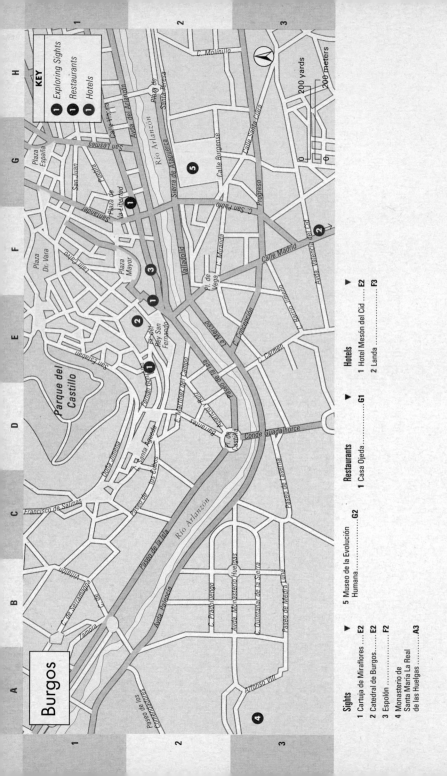

Burgos

KEY

- ● Exploring Sights
- ● Restaurants
- ● Hotels

Parque del Castillo

Río Arlanzón

C. Molinillo

200 yards

200 meters

Sights ►

1 Cartuja de Miraflores	.....**E2**
2 Catedral de Burgos	.......**E2**
3 Espolón	.........**F2**
4 Monasterio de Santa María La Real de las Huelgas	..........**A3**
5 Museo de la Evolución Humana	.............**G2**

Restaurants ►

1 Casa Ojeda	..............**G1**

Hotels ►

1 Hotel Mesón del Cid	.....**E2**
2 Landa	..................**F3**

of the monastery which is the only way to view the monastery. The monastery is closed to the public between 1.30 and 4. ✉ *Calle de Los Compases s/n* ☎ *94/720–1630* 🌐 *www.patrimonionacional.es* 🎫 *€6.*

★ Museo de la Evolución Humana
MUSEUM | **FAMILY** | This airy, modern complex is one of the best natural history museums in the world and traces human evolution from primate to the present day. There are life-size replicas of our ancient ancestors, plus hands-on exhibits and in-depth scientific explanations (in English) that will fascinate visitors of all ages. Pair with a museum-led visit to the Atapuerca archaeological site (inquire at reception or online to arrange). ✉ *Paseo Sierra de Atapuerca* ☎ *94/725–7103* 🌐 *www.museoevolucionhumana.com* 🎫 *€6* 🕒 *Closed Mon.*

🍴 Restaurants

Casa Ojeda
$$$$ | **SPANISH** | This centennial restaurant—a Castilian classic—is known for refined Burgos standbys, especially cochinillo and lamb straight from the 200-year-old wood oven. Wines by the glass are local and reasonable. **Known for:** fall-off-the-bone lamb; old-school waitstaff; tried-and-true Castilian cuisine. [$] *Average main: €32* ✉ *Calle Vitoria 5* ☎ *94/720–9052* 🌐 *www.restauranteojeda.com* 🕒 *No dinner Sun.*

🛏 Hotels

Hotel Mesón del Cid
$ | **HOTEL** | Once home to a 15th-century printing press, this independently owned hotel and restaurant has been hosting travelers for generations in light, airy guest rooms (ask for one facing the cathedral). **Pros:** cathedral views from upgraded rooms; comfy, clean digs; central location. **Cons:** parking is a tight squeeze; could use a face-lift; some rooms noisy. [$] *Rooms from: €80* ✉ *Pl. Santa María 8* ☎ *94/720–8715* 🌐 *www.mesondelcid.es* 🔑 *55 rooms* 🍽 *No meals.*

Landa
$$$ | **HOTEL** | **FAMILY** | If you've ever dreamed of holing up in a luxurious castle, consider booking a room at Landa, a converted 14th-century palace some 5 km (3 miles) from the city center surrounded by lush gardens. **Pros:** stunning indoor-outdoor swimming pool; surprisingly affordable for level of luxury; beautiful lobby. **Cons:** roads to and from town are busy; you'll need your own transportation to get here; inconsistent food quality. [$] *Rooms from: €140* ✉ *Ctra. de Madrid–Irún, Km 235* ☎ *94/725–7777* 🌐 *www.landa.as* 🔑 *37 rooms* 🍽 *No meals.*

🍸 Nightlife

Due to its student population, Burgos has a lively *vida nocturna* (nightlife) in **Las Llanas,** near the cathedral. House wines and *cañas* (small glasses of beer) flow freely through the crowded tapas bars along Calles Laín Calvo and San Juan, near the Plaza Mayor. Calle Puebla, a small, dark street off Calle San Juan, also gets constant revelers. When you order a drink at any Burgos bar, the bartender plunks down a free *pinchito* (small tapa)—a long-standing tradition.

El Camino 👁

West of Burgos, the N120 to León crosses the ancient Camino de Santiago, or Way of St. James, revealing lovely old churches, tiny hermitages, ruined monasteries, and medieval villages across rolling fields. West of León, you can follow the well-worn Camino pilgrimage route as it approaches the giant cathedral in Santiago de Compostela.

Side Trips from Burgos

Monastery of Santo Domingo de Silos

For a sojourn with masters of the Gregorian chant, head to the monastery where 1994's triple-platinum album *Chant* was recorded in the 1970s and '80s. Located 58 km (36 miles) southeast of Burgos, the monastery has an impressive two-story cloister that's lined with intricate Romanesque carvings. Try to drop in for an evening vespers service. It's a unique experience that's well off the tourist path. Single men can stay here for up to eight days (€42 per night with full board). Guests are expected to be present for breakfast, lunch, and dinner but are otherwise left to their own devices. ⊕ *www.abadiadesilos.es*

Ojo Guareña

If you have a day to spare or are traveling on to Cantabria, stop at this breathtaking hermitage hewn into a karst cliffside surrounded by leafy woodlands and less than a mile south of Cueva. Declared a national monument, the cave complex housing the religious structure stretches some 90 km (56 miles), and there's rock art throughout the many chambers that depicts the cave as a dwelling for early humans. Archeologists date the site from from the Middle Palaeolithic time period to the Middle Ages. A worthwhile guided tour of the hermitage lasts 45 minutes; far more scintillating is the tour of nearby Palomera Cave (by appointment only). ⊕ *www.merindaddesotoscueva.es*

Bardeblás

CAFES—NIGHTLIFE | This intimate bar stays open until 4:30 on the weekends, inviting you to stay awhile—and you just might, thanks to its strong and affordable drinks and catchy throwback jams. ⊠ *Calle de la Puebla 29* ☎ *94/720–1162.*

🛍 Shopping

Ribera del Duero reds, bottled south of the city along the eponymous river, might not be as well known as those from Rioja, but they can be equally (if not more) sublime. You also can stock up on Burgos-style morcilla and local cheese. Beyond culinary finds, keep your eye out for small artisan shops specializing in ceramics and textiles.

★ Delicatessen Ojeda

FOOD/CANDY | A food lover's paradise, this pristine, well-lit store carries all the Castilian delicacies you can imagine, from Burgos-style morcilla and cheese to roasted oil-packed peppers and top-quality dried beans and pulses. ⊠ *Calle de Vitoria 5* ☎ *94/720–4832* ⊕ *www.delicatessenojeda.com.*

León

334 km (208 miles) northwest of Madrid, 184 km (114 miles) west of Burgos.

León, the ancient capital of Castile and León, sits on the banks of the Bernesga River in the high plains of Old Castile; today it's a wealthy and conservative provincial capital and prestigious university town. The wide avenues of western León are lined with boutiques, and the twisting alleys of the half-timber old town hide the bars, bookstores, and *chocolaterías* most popular with students.

Historians say that the city was not named for the proud lion that has been its emblem for centuries; rather, they assert that the name is a corruption of the Roman word *legio* (legion), from the fact that the city was founded as a permanent camp for the Roman legions in AD 70. The capital of Christian Spain was moved here from Oviedo in 914 as the Reconquest spread south, ushering in the city's richest era.

As you wander the old town, you can still see fragments of the 6-foot-thick ramparts that were once part of the Roman walls. Look down and you might notice small brass scallop shells set into the street. The scallop is the symbol of St. James; the town government installed them to mark the path for modern-day pilgrims heading north to Santiago de Compostela.

León was chosen as Spain's "Capital of Gastronomy" in 2018, which lured hordes of foodie tourists, inspired restaurants to up their game, and confirmed what those who've been to León already knew—that the city is a fantastic food town.

GETTING HERE AND AROUND
León can be reached by train from Madrid with 13 departures daily from Chamartín station; the journey takes two hours 15 minutes on the high-speed lines (ALVIA and AVE) and between three and four on trains making local stops. ALSA has several bus departures daily, and there are generally plentiful Blablacar rideshares available.

ESSENTIALS
VISITOR INFORMATION León Tourist Office ✉ *Pl. de San Marcelo 1* ☎ *98/787–8327* ⊕ *www.turismoleon.org.*

◉ Sights

Antiguo Convento de San Marcos
BUILDING | Originally a home for knights of the Order of St. James, who patrolled the Camino de Santiago, this monastery was begun in 1513 by the head of the order, King Ferdinand. It is now a parador. The plateresque facade is a majestic swath of small, intricate sculptures (many depicting knights and lords) and

ornamentation—one of the most impressive Renaissance works in Spain. Inside, a cloister full of medieval statues leads you to the bar, which still has the original defensive arrow slits as windows. As the Anexo Monumental del Museo de León, the convent also displays historic paintings and artifacts. ✉ *Pl. de San Marcos 7* ☎ *98/724–5061, 98/723–7300* ⊕ *www. parador.es* 🎟 *Museum €1* ⊗ *Closed Mon.*

Casa Botines
BUILDING | This Gaudí masterpiece, which previously housed a bank, was converted into an excellent museum dedicated to the Moderniste architect in April 2017. Under its conical spires and behind its fish-scale-patterned facade are more than 5,000 works of art spanning eight centuries by such renowned masters as Sorolla, Madrazo, Gutiérrez, and Solana. Given that this is the largest of Gaudí's buildings to be opened as a museum, it's worth ponying up the extra few euros for a guided tour. ✉ *Calle Legión VII 3* ⊕ *www.casabotines.es* 🎟 *From €5* ⊗ *Closed Wed. morning and Sun. afternoon.*

★ Catedral de León
MUSEUM | The pride of León is its soaring cathedral, begun in 1205. It is an outstanding example of Gothic architecture complete with gargoyles, flying buttresses, and pointed arches. Its 2,000 square yards of vivid stained-glass panels—second only, perhaps, to those in Chartres, France—depict biblical stories and Castilian landscapes. A glass door to the choir gives an unobstructed view of nave windows and the painted altarpiece, framed with gold leaf. The cathedral also contains the sculpted tomb of King Ordoño II, who moved the capital of Christian Spain to León. The museum's collection boasts giant medieval hymnals, textiles, sculptures, wood carvings, and paintings. Look for the carved-wood Mudejar archive, with a letter of the alphabet above each door—it's one of the world's oldest file cabinets. ✉ *Pl.*

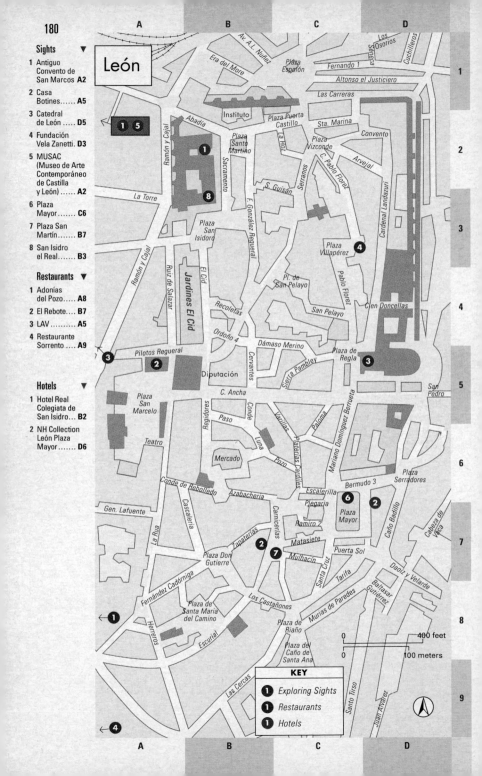

León

Sights ▼

1 Antiguo Convento de San Marcos **A2**
2 Casa Botines...... **A5**
3 Catedral de León **D5**
4 Fundación Vela Zanetti. **D3**
5 MUSAC (Museo de Arte Contemporáneo de Castilla y León) **A2**
6 Plaza Mayor....... **C6**
7 Plaza San Martín....... **B7**
8 San Isidro el Real....... **B3**

Restaurants ▼

1 Adonías del Pozo..... **A8**
2 El Rebote.... **B7**
3 LAV **A5**
4 Restaurante Sorrento **A9**

Hotels ▼

1 Hotel Real Colegiata de San Isidro... **B2**
2 NH Collection León Plaza Mayor **D6**

KEY

- 1 *Exploring Sights*
- 1 *Restaurants*
- 1 *Hotels*

400 feet
100 meters

de Regla s/n ☎ *98/787–5770* 🌐 *www.catedraldeleon.org* 🎫 *From €6.*

Fundación Vela Zanetti

MUSEUM | This contemporary art museum, constructed using minimalist wood beams and glass panels inside a 15th-century mansion, pays homage to Zanetti, a 20th-century Castilian artist known for his thought-provoking murals portraying agrarian life. Some of his portraits recall works by El Greco for their shimmering luminosity. It's worth the stop, and you can view it in under an hour. ✉ *Casona de Villapérez, Calle Pablo Flórez s/n* ☎ *98/724–4121* 🎫 *Free* 🕒 *Closed Sun. and Mon.*

MUSAC (Museo de Arte Contemporáneo de Castilla y León) *(Museum of Modern Art of Castilla y León)*

MUSEUM | It's worth a visit to this museum for its facade alone, a modern technicolor masterpiece by famed Spanish architects Mansilla + Tuñón. The endless rainbow of rectangles that encloses the building is an homage to the colorful stained glass of the cathedral. Inside, wander through rooms bearing the latest art and multimedia projects by locally and nationally acclaimed artists. Films and concerts are also shown throughout the year. ✉ *Av. de los Reyes Leoneses 24* ☎ *98/709–0000* 🌐 *www.musac.es* 🎫 *€3 (free Sun. 5–9)* 🕒 *Closed Mon.*

Plaza Mayor

MARKET | This is the heart of the old town, and on Wednesday and Saturday mornings the arcaded plaza bustles with farmers selling produce and cheeses. ✉ *León.*

Plaza San Martín

PLAZA | Most of León's tapas bars are in this 12th-century square. The surrounding area is called the Barrio Húmedo, or "Wet Neighborhood," allegedly because of the large amount of wine spilled here late at night. ✉ *León.*

San Isidoro el Real

MUSEUM | This sandstone basilica was built into the side of the city wall in 1063 and rebuilt in the 12th century on the site of an ancient Roman temple. Adjoining the basilica, the **Panteón de los Reyes** (Royal Pantheon), which has been called "the Sistine Chapel of Romanesque art," has vibrant 12th-century frescoes on its pillars and ceiling. Look for the agricultural calendar painted on one archway, showing which farming task should be performed each month. Twenty-three kings and queens were buried here, but their tombs were destroyed by French troops during the Napoleonic Wars. Treasures in the adjacent **Museo de San Isidoro** include a jewel-encrusted agate chalice, a richly illustrated handwritten Bible, and polychrome wood statues of the Virgin Mary. Admission includes a guided tour of the Royal Pantheon and museum. ✉ *Pl. de San Isidoro 4* ☎ *98/787–6161* 🌐 *www.museosanisidorodeleon.com* 🎫 *€5 (free after 4 on last Thurs. of month).*

🍴 Restaurants

Adonías del Pozo

$$$$ | **SPANISH** | In this softly lit dining room furnished with rustic tables and colorful ceramics, feast on top-of-the-line cured ham, roasted peppers, and chorizo. Grilled sea bream is a treat for seafood lovers; banana pudding with chocolate sauce is a treat for just about everyone. **Known for:** well-priced menú del día; excellent sausages and roast meats; homey dining room. [$] *Average main: €30* ✉ *Calle Santa Nonia 16* ☎ *98/720–6768, 98/725–2665* 🕒 *Closed Sun.*

El Rebote

$ | **TAPAS** | Though every drink comes with a complimentary croqueta at this pocket-size bar frequented by locals, the crisp, gooey orbs are so succulent that you'll want to order a few extra. Be sure to sample the smoky *cecina* rendition incorporating the Leonese air-cured beef delicacy. **Known for:** to-die-for croquetas;

The colorful panels on León's MUSAC, the Museum of Modern Art, were inspired by the rose window of the city's Gothic cathedral.

quirky local wines by the glass; sardine-can digs. [$] *Average main: €8* ✉ *Pl. San Martín 9* ☎ *98/721–3510* ⏲ *Closed Mon.*

LAV

$$$$ | **SPANISH** | The most exciting nueva cocina restaurant on the León dining scene, LAV appeals to all the senses with unexpected flavor combinations, playful plating, and personable service. Tasting menus—a steal at €39—begin with "surprise sandwiches" at the bar and progress into the kitchen for a brief "show cooking" demo before winding up in the dining room. **Known for:** fine dining that doesn't take itself too seriously; terrific-value tasting menu; local ingredients used in ways you've never seen before. [$] *Average main: €39* ✉ *Av. del Padre Isla 1* ☎ *98/779–8190* 🌐 *www.restaurantelav.com* ⏲ *Closed Sun.*

★ Restaurante Sorrento

$$$ | **SPANISH** | **FAMILY** | León is a cold, windy town for much of the year, so it's no surprise that the local version of *cocido* (boiled dinner) is heartier than usual with mounds of green cabbage, spoonable blood sausage, and some 10 types of meat (chorizo, beef shanks, pork belly, and chicken, to name a few). Sample the city's best rendition at this spartan yet inviting restaurant outside the historic center—and be sure to bring an appetite. **Known for:** soul-satisfying cocido leonés; warm service; local crowd. [$] *Average main: €18* ✉ *Calle Bernardo del Carpio 1* ☎ *98/707–3270* ⏲ *Closed Mon.*

Hotels

Hotel Real Colegiata de San Isidoro

$$$ | **HOTEL** | Other hotels around town bill themselves as being steps from the main tourist attractions, but the Hotel Real Colegiata, which houses a Romanesque collegiate library and museum, is located within one. **Pros:** gorgeous historic building; modern Spanish restaurant; free tour of the grounds. **Cons:** no gym, pool, or spa; furnishings lack style; cleanliness can be inconsistent. [$] *Rooms from: €140* ✉ *Pl. Santo Martino*

5 ⌂ *98/787–5088* ⊕ *www.hotelrealcole-giata.com* ↪ *32 rooms* ⏍ *Free Breakfast.*

★ NH Collection León Plaza Mayor

$$$ | **HOTEL** | This handsome hotel, housed in a palace overlooking the 17th-century Plaza Mayor, is awash with whites, dark woods, and neutral tones. **Pros:** subdued, elegant interiors; parking below building; varied breakfasts. **Cons:** some furniture could use replacing; maintenance a little inconsistent; parking is a tight squeeze. **$** *Rooms from: €170* ✉ *Pl. Mayor 15–17* ⌂ *98/734–4357* ⊕ *www.nh-collection. com* ↪ *51 rooms* ⏍ *No meals.*

Nightlife

León's most popular hangouts are clustered around the Plaza Mayor, frequented mainly by couples and families, and Plaza San Martín, where the college kids go. The surrounding streets (Calles Escalerilla, Plegaria, Ramiro 2, Matasiete, and Mulhacén) are packed with tapas bars. In the Plaza Mayor, you might want to start at **La Pañería, The Harley,** or **Mishiara.** In the Plaza San Martín, begin your evening with tapas and *cortitos* (local slang for two-gulp glasses of beer) at **Taberna Los Cazurros, El Rebote,** or **Mesón Jabugo.** Then, go clubbing at **Studio 54,** a *discoteca* housed in an old theater whose crowd gets progressively younger (and LGBT friendly) as the night goes on.

⊖ Shopping

Tasty regional treats include roasted red peppers, potent brandy-soaked cherries, and candied chestnuts—but León's most prized and artisinal product is cecina, air-dried beef that packs an umami punch similar to that of a dry-aged steak. You can buy all of these items in food shops around the city. Please note that many stores in León are closed on Sunday.

Prada a Tope

FOOD/CANDY | This restaurant, winery, and gourmet store has a huge estate in the countryside just outside León

and operates a small café and shop in the city. Delicacies include chestnuts in syrup, bittersweet figs and pears in wine, jams, and liqueurs. Not enough room in your suitcase? You can also order by mail from its website. ✉ *Calle Alfonso IX 9* ⌂ *98/725–7221, 98/756–3366* ⊕ *www. pradaatope.es.*

Astorga

46 km (29 miles) southwest of León.

Astorga, where the pilgrimage roads from France and Portugal merge, once had 22 hospitals to lodge and care for ailing travelers. Though the city is no longer the crossroads that it once was, plenty of travelers visit this charming town for its eye-popping Gaudí masterpiece, El Palacio Episcopal, and its famed *cocido maragato*, a stick-to-your-ribs stew. Astorga is in an area once known as La Maragatería, home to a community that once stood apart from its neighbors for its special dialect, elaborate dress, and distinctive folk music.

GETTING HERE AND AROUND

Sixteen buses depart daily from León; the trip takes about 45 minutes. If you're driving yourself, there's ample parking, and the city is navigable on foot.

ESSENTIALS

VISITOR INFORMATION Astorga Tourist Office ✉ *Pl. Eduardo de Castro 5* ⌂ *98/761–8222* ⊕ *www.aytoastorga.es.*

Sights

Museo Catedralicio

MUSEUM | This museum within the cathedral displays 10th- and 12th-century chests, religious silverware, and paintings and sculptures by Astorgans through the ages. ✉ *Pl. de la Catedral* ⌂ *98/761–5820* ✉ *€5.*

★ Museo Romano *(Roman Museum)*

ARCHAEOLOGICAL SITE | **FAMILY** | This hidden-gem museum uses the archaeological record to show what life was like in Astorga during Roman times, when the city was called Asturica Augusta. The most memorable part of the experience is the **Ruta Romana,** a walking tour of Roman archaeological remains in Astorga (combined tickets can be bought at the museum). ✉ *Pl. San Bartolomé 2* ☎ *98/761–6937* 🌐 *www.asturica.com* 🎫 *From €3* 🕒 *Closed Mon.*

Palacio de Gaudí (*Palacio Episcopal*)
BUILDING | Just opposite Astorga's cathedral is this fairy-tale neo-Gothic palace, designed for a Catalan cleric by Antoni Gaudí in 1889. Though the interiors pale in comparison to the eye-popping exteriors, those interested in local ecclesiastical history shouldn't miss visiting the **Museo de Los Caminos** (Museum of the Way). ✉ *Pl. de la Catedral , Glorieta Eduardo de Castro s/n* ☎ *98/761–6882* 🌐 *www.palaciodegaudi.es* 🎫 *€5* 🕒 *Closed Mon.*

🍴 Restaurants

Restaurante Serrano
$$$$ | **SPANISH** | This local hangout serves Astorgan dishes that incorporate wild game, foraged mushrooms, and regional meats. For a break from carniverous Castilian cuisine, tuck into handmade pasta dishes or chickpeas stewed with fresh octopus, a house specialty. **Known for:** dishes using local "pico pardal" garbanzos; attentive old-school service; wild game. [$] *Average main: €35* ✉ *Calle Portería 2* ☎ *98/761–7866, 64/607–1736* 🌐 *www.restauranteserrano.es* 🕒 *Closed Mon.*

🛏 Hotels

★ Hotel Vía de la Plata
$$ | **HOTEL** | **FAMILY** | A giant slate terrace with views of the countryside is the main draw of this airy, modern hotel. **Pros:** great views and service; gorgeous terrace; free parking. **Cons:** wedding parties can be noisy; small breakfast area; spa not included in rate. [$] *Rooms from: €90* ✉ *Calle Padres Redentoristas 5* ☎ *98/761–9000 for hotel, 98/760–4165 for spa* 🌐 *www.hotelviadelaplata.com* 🔑 *38 rooms* 🍽 *No meals.*

Villafranca del Bierzo

135 km (84 miles) west of León.

After crossing León's grape-growing region, where the funky, floral Bierzo wines are produced, you'll arrive in this medieval village, dominated by a massive (and still-inhabited) feudal fortress. Visit the Romanesque church of Santiago to see the Puerta del Perdón (Door of Pardon), a sort of spiritual consolation prize for exhausted Camino pilgrims who couldn't make it over the mountains. Stroll the streets and seek out the onetime home of the infamous Grand Inquisitor Tomás de Torquemada. If you've made it all the way here, don't leave Bierzo without visiting the area's most famous archaeological site, Las Médulas, whose bizarre stone formations are the remnants of Roman gold mines.

GETTING HERE AND AROUND

Charter bus trips from León—or better yet, a rental car—remain the best ways to get to this rural region. You'll likely want your own transportation once you get here, to visit Las Medulas, which is several kilometers away. It's also possible to hike or get there by bicycle.

ESSENTIALS

VISITOR INFORMATION Villafranca del Bierzo Tourist Office ✉ *Av. Díaz Ovelar 10* ☎ *98/754–0028* 🌐 *www.villafrancadelbierzo.org.*

👁 Sights

★ Las Médulas
ARCHAEOLOGICAL SITE | **FAMILY** | One of northern Spain's most impressive archaeological sites, this mountainous area of former Roman gold mines—located 24

km (15 miles) south of town—is now a UNESCO World Heritage Site. The landscape is the result of an ancient mining technique in which myriad water tunnels were burrowed into a mountain, causing it to collapse. Miners would then sift through the rubble for gold. What's left at Las Médulas are half-collapsed mountains of golden clay, with exposed tunnels, peeking through lush green forest. Take in the best panorama from the Orellán viewpoint. There are hiking paths, a small archaeology exhibit (open only on weekends), and a visitor center. You can pay to enter some of the tunnels or browse the larger area for free. The visitor center also organizes 3-km (2-mile) walking tours—call ahead to book. ⊠ *Carucedo* ☎ *98/742–2848* ⊕ *www. espaciolasmedulas.es* ⊠ *Free, archaeology center €2, Orellán tunnel €2, guided walking tour €3.*

 Hotels

★ Casa do Louteiro

$ | B&B/INN | FAMILY | This charming, rustic inn, in a tiny village near the archaeological site of Las Médulas, was lovingly converted from a series of medieval ruins. **Pros:** rustic details; friendly staff; fire pit on winter evenings. **Cons:** plenty of hiking and biking nearby, but you'll need a car to get here; disorganized front-desk management; no housekeeping service. Ⓢ *Rooms from: €70* ⊠ *Calle Louteiro 6, Orellán* ☎ *65/293–3419, 65/293–3971* ⊅ *3 cottages* ⦿ *No meals.*

Parador de Villafranca del Bierzo

$$ | HOTEL | FAMILY | This modern two-story hotel built with local stone looks out over the Bierzo valley. **Pros:** indoor and outdoor swimming pools; quiet surroundings; comfortable beds. **Cons:** lacks history of other paradores; some rooms overlook parking lot; noisy a/c in some rooms. Ⓢ *Rooms from: €100* ⊠ *Av. de Calvo Sotelo 28* ☎ *98/754–0175* ⊕ *www.parador.es* ⊅ *51 rooms* ⦿ *No meals.*

Jerte and El Valle del Jerte (Jerte Valley)

220 km (137 miles) west of Madrid.

Every spring, the Jerte Valley in northern Extremadura becomes one of Spain's top attractions for its riot of cherry blossoms. Unsurprisingly, this is where Spain's biggest cherry harvest originates, backed by the snowcapped Gredos mountains. Book ahead for March and April—peak cherry blossom season.

GETTING HERE AND AROUND

You will need a car to get here and explore the valley. For a scenic route, follow N110 southwest from Ávila to Plasencia.

ESSENTIALS

VISITOR INFORMATION Valle del Jerte Tourist Office ⊠ *Paraje Virgen de Peñas Albas (N110) s/n, Cabezuela del Valle* ☎ *92/747–2558* ⊕ *www.turismovalledeljerte.com.*

 Sights

Cabezuela del Valle

TOWN | Full of half-timber stone houses, this is one of the valley's best-preserved villages. Follow N110 to Plasencia, or, if you enjoy mountain scenery, detour from the village of Jerte to Hervás, traveling a narrow road that winds 35 km (22 miles) through forests of low-growing oak trees and over the Honduras Pass. ⊠ *Cabezuela del Valle.*

Puerto de Tornavacas (*Tornavacas Pass*)

VIEWPOINT | There's no more striking introduction to Extremadura than the Puerto de Tornavacas—literally, the "point where the cows turn back." Part of the N110 road northeast of Plasencia, the pass marks the border between Extremadura and the stark plateau of Castile. At 4,183 feet above sea level, it boasts a breathtaking view of the valley formed by the fast-flowing Jerte River. The valley's

Cherry trees blossom in the Jerte Valley.

lower slopes are covered with a dense mantle of ash, chestnut, and cherry trees, whose richness contrasts with the granite cliffs of Castile's Sierra de Gredos. Cherries are the principal crop. To catch their brilliant blossoms, visit in spring. Camping is popular in this region, and even the most experienced hikers can find some challenging trails. ✉ *Plasencia.*

🍴 Restaurants

★ La Cabaña

$$ | SPANISH | This homey, sun-drenched restaurant serves honest Extremaduran fare at an excellent price. Unlike other dining options in the area, cooks here pay special attention to presentation and ingredient quality—attributes on display in the not-too-greasy migas, ultrajuicy Iberian pork dishes, and refreshing tomato salads. **Known for:** home-cooked food; Iberian pork dishes; bright, casual dining room. [$] *Average main: €15* ✉ *Av. Ramón y Cajal 17, Jerte* ☎ *64/523–3953* 🌐 *www.restaurantelacabañajerte.es.*

🛏 Hotels

Finca El Carpintero

$ | B&B/INN | FAMILY | This restored 150-year-old stone mill and farmhouse makes an ideal base for enjoying the area's great outdoors. **Pros:** cozy atmosphere; picturesque grounds with swimming pool; ideal country escape, especially in spring and fall. **Cons:** disparity in quality between rooms and suites; need a car to get here; spent towels and small TVs. [$] *Rooms from: €76* ✉ *N110, Km 360.5, Tornavacas* ✣ *9 km (5½ miles) northeast of Jerte* ☎ *92/717–7089, 65/932–8110* 🌐 *www.fincaelcarpintero.com* 🛏 *8 rooms* 🍴 *Free Breakfast.*

La Casería

$ | B&B/INN | FAMILY | One of Extremadura's first rural guesthouses, this rambling home 10 km (6 miles) southeast of Jerte is on a spectacular 120-acre working farm, once a 16th-century Franciscan convent. **Pros:** privacy in the cottages; outdoor activities; views of Jerte Valley. **Cons:** main lodge often rented out to groups; need a car to get here; far from all main sights and national parks. [$] *Rooms from: €80* ✉ *N110, Km 378.5, Navaconcejo* ☎ *92/717–3141* 🌐 *www.lac-aseria.es* 🛏 *9 rooms* 🍴 *Free Breakfast.*

La Vera and Monasterio de Yuste

45 km (28 miles) east of Plasencia.

In northern Extremadura, the fertile La Vera region sits at the foot of the Gredos mountains, which are usually snow-capped through June. With its wildflowers, mountain vistas, and world-famous Yuste Monastery, the area welcomes hordes of tourists, especially in spring, its most beautiful season. One of the favorite souvenirs to take home is La Vera's famous smoky paprika—pimentón, available in three types: *dulce* (mild), *agridulce* (medium), and *picante* (hot). You're likely to see strings of red peppers hanging out to dry on the windowsills of area homes.

GETTING HERE AND AROUND

You'll need a car to get here. Turn left off the C501 at Cuacos and follow signs for the monastery (1 km [½ mile]).

ESSENTIALS

VISITOR INFORMATION Jaraíz de la Vera Tourist Office ✉ *Calle Mérida 17, Jaraíz de la Vera* ☎ *92/717–0587.*

👁 Sights

★ **Monasterio de Yuste** (*Yuste Monastery*)
RELIGIOUS SITE | In the heart of La Vera—a region of steep ravines (*gargantas*), rushing rivers, and sleepy villages—lies the Monasterio de San Jerónimo de Yuste, founded by Hieronymite monks in the early 15th century. Badly damaged in the Peninsular War, it was left to decay after the suppression of Spain's monasteries in 1835, but it has since been restored by the Hieronymites. Today it's one of the most impressive monasteries in all of Spain. Carlos V (1500–58), founder of Spain's vast 16th-century empire, spent his last two years in the Royal Chambers, enabling the emperor to attend mass within a short stumble of his bed. The guided tour also covers the church, the crypt where Carlos V was buried before being moved to El Escorial (near Madrid), and a glimpse of the monastery's cloisters. ✉ *Carretera de Yuste s/n, Cuacos* ☎ *92/717–2197* 🌐 *www.patrimonionacional.es* 🎫 *From €7 (free Apr.–Sept., Wed. and Thurs. 5–8; Oct.–Mar., Wed. and Thurs. 3–6).*

Museo del Pimentón (*Paprika Museum*)
MUSEUM | Tucked away in a 17th-century row house, this quirky museum tells the history of the locally made paprika, dubbed "red gold," for which Jaraíz de la Vera is probably best known nationally. The three floors feature audiovisual presentations and examples of grinding tools and recipes. The museum is the centerpiece of the village's annual pepper festival, held In August. ✉ *Pl. Mayor 7, Jaraíz de la Vera* ☎ *92/746–0810* 🌐 *museodelpimenton.business.site* 🎫 *Free* 🕒 *Closed Sun. afternoon and Mon.*

🛏 Hotels

La Casona
$ | B&B/INN | FAMILY | This rustic estate with spectacular views of the Gredos mountains has six cozy rooms in the main house and six log-cabin bungalows. **Pros:** great service; very family-friendly; bevy of outdoor activities. **Cons:** need your own transportation; has gone downhill in recent years; hard to find because there's hardly any signage. [$] *Rooms from: €60* ✉ *Ctra. Navalmoral (EX392), Km 15, Jaraíz de la Vera* ☎ *92/719–4145, 62/964–5930* 🛏 *12 rooms* 🍴 *No meals.*

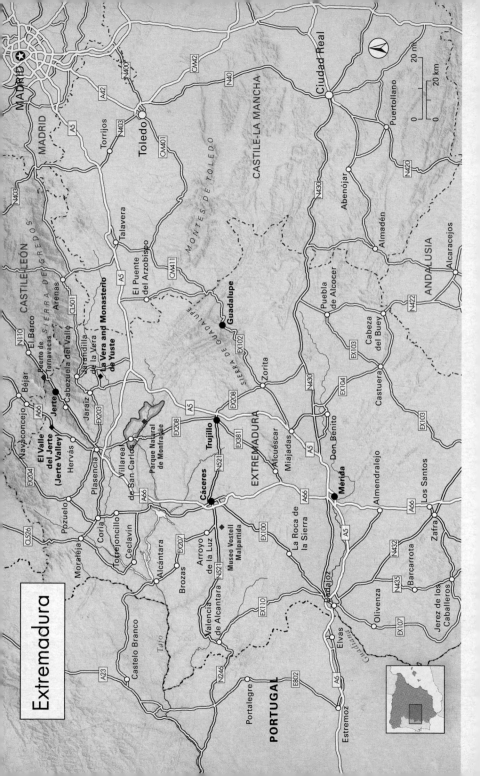

Parque Natural de Monfragüe

At the junction of the Tiétar and Tajo Rivers, 20 km (12 miles) south of Plasencia on the EX208 and 60 km (37 miles) southwest of La Vera via the EX203, lies Extremadura's only national park. This rocky, mountainous wilderness is known for its diverse plant and animal life including lynxes, boars, deer, foxes, black storks, imperial eagles, and the world's largest colony of black vultures, attracting bird-watchers from around the world. Bring binoculars and head for the lookout point called Salto del Gitano (Gypsy's Leap), on the C524 just south of the Tajo River—vultures can often be spotted wheeling in the dozens at close range. The park's visitor center and main entrance is in the hamlet of Villareal de San Carlos. ⊕ *www.parquedemonfrague.com*

Cáceres

299 km (186 miles) west of Madrid, 125 km (78 miles) southwest of Monasterio de Yuste.

The provincial capital and one of Spain's oldest cities, Cáceres is known for its UNESCO-protected old town and lively tapeo. The Roman colony called Norba Caesarina was founded in 35 BC, but when the Moors took over in the 8th century, they named the city Quazris, which eventually morphed into the Spanish Cáceres. Amazingly, some 22 Moorish towers survive in the historic center today. Ever since noble families helped Alfonso IX expel the Moors in 1229, the city has prospered; the pristine condition of the medieval and Renaissance quarter is the result of the families' continued occupancy of the palaces erected in the 15th century.

GETTING HERE AND AROUND

Trains from Madrid take about 2½ hours and are the cheapest and easiest way to get to Cáceres. Catch a city bus outside the train station, which takes you to Plaza Mayor in the historic quarter, or walk 15 minutes into town. From Madrid, Blablacar rideshares are an excellent option as well. The city center is navigable on foot. If you drive, park on the outskirts as the winding, narrow medieval streets are difficult for parking.

TRAIN STATION Cáceres ⊠ *Av. Juan Pablo II 6* ☎ *92/723–5061, 90/224–0202* ⊕ *www.renfe.com.*

TOURS

★ **Cuenta Trovas de Cordel**

One of the best ways to see Cáceres is by night. The energetic local guides Vicente and Patxi weave lots of knowledge about Cáceres folklore, legends, and ghost stories into their multilingual weekend tours of Cáceres's old quarter, which they present in medieval costume. Call ahead to reserve, or book online. ⊠ *Pl. Mayor* ☎ *66/728–3187, 66/777–6205* ⊕ *www.cuentatrovas.com* ☞ *From €10.*

ESSENTIALS

VISITOR INFORMATION Cáceres ⊠ *Pl. Mayor* ☎ *92/701–0834, 92/721–7237 tours* ⊕ *turismo.ayto-caceres.es.*

Sights

Ciudad Vieja de Cáceres (Old Cáceres), which begins just east of Plaza San Juan, is where all the action is.

★ **Ciudad Monumental**

NEIGHBORHOOD | Travel back a few centuries in Cáceres's Ciudad Monumental (aka *casco antiguo* or *ciudad vieja*), one of the best-preserved medieval quarters in Europe. It's so convincingly ancient that *Game of Thrones* used it as a filming location in 2017. There isn't a single modern building to detract from its aura. It's virtually deserted in winter and occasionally dusted with a light coating of snow—a fairy-tale sight. Most of the city's main monuments are located here, but of Cáceres's approximately 100,000 residents, only 380 reside within this tiny enclave. ⊠ *Cáceres.*

Concatedral de Santa María

RELIGIOUS SITE | This Gothic church, built mainly in the 16th century, is now the cathedral and the city's most important religious site. The elegantly carved wooden reredos (dating to 1551), left unpainted according to Extremaduran custom, is barely visible in the gloom. Follow the lines of pilgrims to the statue of San Pedro de Alcántara in the corner; legend says that touching the stone figure's shoes brings luck. A small museum in the back displays religious artifacts. ⊠ *Pl. de Santa María s/n* ☎ *92/721–5313* ⊕ *www.concatedralcaceres.com* ⊠ *€4.*

Fundación Helga de Alvear (*Visual Arts Center Foundation Helga de Alvear*)

MUSEUM | After a day spent meandering through medieval passageways and marveling at ancient churches, this small contemporary art museum, presided over by one of Europe's great modern art collectors, is a breath of fresh air. Highlights include sculptures by Ai Weiwei and Dan Graham and paintings by Josef Albers and John Baldessari. A much-anticipated renovation by Tuñón Arquitectos (of Atrio fame), which will add additional rooms and multimedia spaces, is under way and set to be completed by the end of 2019. ⊠ *Calle Pizarro 8* ☎ *92/762–6414* ⊕ *www. fundacionhelgadealvear.es* ⊠ *Free* ⊘ *Closed Mon.*

Museo Apple e Historia de la Computación

MUSEUM | Medieval Cáceres is about the last place you'd expect to find an eclectic collection of more than 150 Apple computers through the ages, but in this pocket-sized space you can see (and sometimes play around with) museum curator Carlos's prehistoric-looking machines from the '80s, '90s, and early 2000s. Tours take about an hour and are well worth the nominal fee. ⊠ *Pl. de San Juan 13* ☎ *92/731–6501* ⊕ *www.museo-apple.com* ⊠ *€5* ⊘ *Closed Mon.*

★ Museo de Cáceres

MUSEUM | The Casa de las Veletas (House of the Weather Vanes) is a 12th-century Moorish mansion that is now used as the city's museum. Filled with archaeological finds from the Paleolithic through Visigothic periods, the museum also includes an art section with works by El Greco, Picasso, and Miró. The highlight is the superbly preserved Moorish cistern—the *aljibe*—with horseshoe arches supported by mildewy stone pillars. ⊠ *Pl. de las Veletas 1* ☎ *92/701–0877* ⊕ *museode-caceres.juntaex.es* ⊠ *€2 (free for EU residents)* ⊘ *Closed Mon.*

★ Museo Vostell Malpartida

NATURE SITE | The first thing that grabs your attention at this museum—located 14 km (9 miles) outside town—is the landscape that surrounds it: the Los Barruecos nature reserve. Spanning 800 acres, the park's otherworldly landscape comprises rolling grasslands, lakes, and enormous, peculiarly shaped boulders, which you can explore on foot. These curious natural forms inspired Wolf Vostell, a German artist of the Fluxus and Happening movements (whose wife was extremeña), to turn a defunct yarn factory located within the park into a museum. Today you can still take in his bizarre, thought-provoking work—including a Cadillac surrounded by dinner plates and a wall of rusty Guardia Civil motorcycles—much as it was when he was alive. ⊠ *Calle Los Barruecos s/n* ☎ *92/701–0812* ⊕ *museovostell.gobex.es* ⊠ *€3* ⊘ *Closed Mon.*

Palacio de Carvajal

CASTLE/PALACE | This palace has an imposing granite facade, arched doorway, and

The San Mateo church, with the Torre de las Cigüeñas (Tower of the Storks) in the background

tower, and the interior has been restored with period furnishings and art to look as it did when the Carvajal family lived here in the 16th century. Legend has it that King Ferdinand IV ordered the execution of two brothers from the Carvajal family, whom he accused of killing one of his knights. Thirty days later, the king was sued in the Court of God. Judgment was postponed until after the king's death, when the Carvajal brothers were declared innocent. ⊠ *Calle Amargura 1, at Pl. Santa María* ☎ *92/725–5597* ✉ *Free.*

Palacio de los Golfines de Abajo

CASTLE/PALACE | The stony severity of this palace on the Plaza Mayor seems appropriate when you consider it was once the headquarters of General Franco. The exterior is somewhat relieved by elaborate Mudejar and Renaissance decorative motifs. Some 400 years before Franco, the so-called Reyes Católicos purportedly slept here. Guided tours by appointment only. ⊠ *Pl. de los Golfines* ⊕ *www.palaciogolfinesdeabajo.com* ✉ *€3* ⊗ *Closed Mon.*

Palacio de los Golfines de Arriba

CASTLE/PALACE | After you pass through the gate leading to the old quarter, you'll see this palace, dominated by a soaring tower dating to 1515. Only three of the four corner towers remain, adorned with various coats of arms of the families who once lived here. Inside, there are classical colonnaded courtyards with Renaissance details, but they're no longer open to the public. Still, the impressive building is worth a stop. ⊠ *C. de los Olmos 2.*

Palacio del Capitán Diego de Cáceres

CASTLE/PALACE | The battlement tower of this palace is also known as the Torre de las Cigüeñas (Tower of the Storks) for obvious reasons. It's now a military residence, but some rooms are occasionally opened for exhibitions. ⊠ *Pl. San Mateo.*

Plaza Mayor

PLAZA | This long, inclined, arcaded plaza contains several cafés, the tourist office, and—on breezy summer nights—nearly everyone in town. In the middle of the arcade opposite the old quarter is the entrance to the lively Calle General

Ezponda, lined with tapas bars, student hangouts, and discotecas that keep the neighborhood awake and moving until dawn. ✉ *Cáceres.*

San Mateo

RELIGIOUS SITE | Construction on this church began in the 14th century, purportedly over the ruins of a mosque, and took nearly 300 years to finish. The interior is austere, with a 16th-century choir and walls lined with the tombs of prominent Cáceres citizens. The church opens at 10 most mornings, but check with the tourist office in case of changes. ✉ *Pl. de San Mateo* ☎ *92/724–6329* 🎫 *Free.*

Santuario de la Virgen de la Montaña

(*Sanctuary of the Virgin of the Mountain*) **RELIGIOUS SITE** | Overlooking Cáceres's Ciudad Monumental is this 18th-century shrine dedicated to the city's patron saint. It's built on a mountain with highly Instagrammable views of the old town, especially at sunset. The panorama is worth the 15-minute drive—or even the grueling two-hour walk past chalets and farms—despite the rather mundane interior of the church (the golden baroque altar being the only exception). ✉ *Ctra. Santuario Virgin de la Montaña s/n* 🎫 *Free.*

🍴 Restaurants

★ Atrio

$$$$ | **SPANISH** | This elegant, award-winning restaurant (in a drool-worthy boutique hotel with a rooftop pool), housed in a medieval building redesigned by star architect firm Mansilla + Tuñón, is easily the best in Extremadura. It specializes in refined contemporary cooking, and the menu changes according to what's in season in chef Toño Pérez's private garden. **Known for:** affordability for a two-Michelin-star restaurant; stunning interiors with bespoke furniture and Warhols; tasting menu only. [$] *Average main: €75* ✉ *Pl. de San Mateo 1* ☎ *92/724–2928* 🌐 *www.restauranteatrio.com.*

El Figón de Eustaquio

$$$$ | **SPANISH** | A fixture on the quiet and pleasant Plaza San Juan, this restaurant has been run by the same family for 70 years and counting. In its jumble of old-fashioned dining rooms with wood-beam ceilings, feast on regional delicacies including *venado de montería* (wild venison) or *perdiz estofada* (partridge stew) complemented by bold local wines. **Known for:** old-school Extremaduran cooking; good selection of local wines; pleasant outdoor patio. [$] *Average main: €30* ✉ *Pl. San Juan 12–14* ☎ *92/724–4362, 92/724–8194* 🌐 *www.elfigondeeustaquio.com.*

★ La Tapería

$$ | **TAPAS** | This tiny taverna, which serves some of the best tapas in town, is always packed with locals. Order a few *tostas* (a piece of sliced crunchy bread with ingredients on top) and raciones, and pair them with wines from local vineyards. **Known for:** fresh, filling tostas; local hangout; free tapa with every drink. [$] *Average main: €12* ✉ *Calle Sánchez Garrido 1, bajo* ☎ *92/722–5147* 💳 *No credit cards* 🕒 *Closed Mon.*

🛏 Hotels

Hotel Iberia Plaza Mayor

$ | **HOTEL** | **FAMILY** | Confusingly, this budget-friendly hotel isn't on the Plaza Mayor but rather 100 yards down a quiet side street. **Pros:** great value; generous breakfast buffet; great location. **Cons:** dated furniture; no on-site parking; soundproofing could be better. [$] *Rooms from: €50* ✉ *Calle Pintores 2* ☎ *92/724–7634* 🌐 *www.iberiahotel.com* 🛏 *38 rooms* 🍽 *Free Breakfast.*

★ NH Collection Cáceres Palacio de Oquendo

$$$ | **HOTEL** | This 16th-century palace, which spans the length of Plaza San Juan on the edge of the old quarter, is now an impressive NH Collection hotel that rivals the town's parador—at much lower rates. **Pros:** excellent value; new design;

quiet area close to Plaza Mayor. **Cons:** no parking; pricey breakfast and mediocre restaurant; some rooms have only skylights (no windows). [$] *Rooms from: €135* ✉ *Pl. San Juan 11* ☎ *92/721–5800* 🌐 *www.nh-hotels.com* 🛏 *86 rooms* 🍴 *No meals.*

Parador de Cáceres
$$$$ | **HOTEL** | This 14th-century palace in the old town boasts elegant public spaces filled with antiques. **Pros:** gorgeous old building; inviting outdoor dining area; spacious rooms. **Cons:** spartan decor; unattractive indoor dining room; some bathrooms need work. [$] *Rooms from: €205* ✉ *Calle Ancha 6* ☎ *92/721–1759* 🌐 *www.parador.es* 🛏 *39 rooms* 🍴 *Free Breakfast.*

🛍 Shopping

Some of the best shopping in Cáceres is culinary: the city and surrounding countryside are renowned for producing unparalleled Iberian ham and chorizo, complex cheeses, grippy wines, and mouthwatering pastries. But there are also distinctive artisan crafts worth seeking out.

Centro de Artesanía Casa Palacio de los Moraga
CRAFTS | Eschew the usual souvenir shops and instead drop by this art collective that sells wallets, purses, pins, toys, clothes, and other decorative elements in leather and ceramics made by local artisans. ✉ *Calle Cuesta de Aldana 1* ☎ *92/722–7453* 🌐 *www.extremadurartesana.com.*

Pastelería Isa
FOOD/CANDY | The city's premier pastry shop since opening in 1952, "La Isa" is best known for its *mojicón*, an oversized orange-scented muffin native to Extremadura that's the perfect *café con leche* sidekick. ✉ *Pl. Mayor 25* ☎ *92/724–8185.*

★ Sierra de Montánchez
FOOD/CANDY | Satisfy your jamón cravings at this gourmet shop specializing in acorn-fed pork products. There are usually baskets of terrific-quality La Dalia pimentón on sale as well; grab one or two tins here as they're hard to find outside Extremadura. ✉ *Pl. de la Concepción 5* ☎ *62/547–1315* 🌐 *www.sierrademontanchez.es.*

Trujillo

45 km (28 miles) east of Cáceres, 256 km (159 miles) southwest of Madrid.

Trujillo rises up from the boulder-strewn fields like a great granite schooner under full sail. From above, the rooftops and towers are worn and medieval looking. At street level, Renaissance architecture flourishes in squares such as the Plaza Mayor, with its elegant San Martín church. As in Cáceres, storks' nests top many towers—the birds have become a symbol of Trujillo. With roots in Roman times, the city was captured from the Moors in 1232 and colonized by a number of leading military families.

GETTING HERE AND AROUND

There is no train service to Trujillo, but Avanza bus (🌐 *www.avanzabus.com*) offers five departures daily from Madrid's Estacion de Sur (3½ hours). There are usually several Blablacar rideshares available each day as well. Take in Trujillo on foot, as the streets are mostly cobbled or crudely paved with stone (suitable footwear needed; prepare for hills, too). The two main roads into Trujillo leave you at the unattractive bottom end of town. Things get progressively older the farther you climb, but even on the lower slopes—where most of the shops are concentrated—you need walk only a few yards to step into what seems like the Middle Ages.

BUS CONTACTS Avanza Bus ☎ *91/272–2832* 🌐 *www.avanzabus.com.*

ESSENTIALS
VISITOR INFORMATION Trujillo Tourist Office ✉ *Pl. Mayor* ☎ *92/732–2677* ⊕ *www.trujillo.es.*

Sights

Casa Museo de Pizarro
MUSEUM | The Pizarro family residence is now a modest museum dedicated to the connection between Spain and Latin America. The first floor emulates a typical home from 15th-century Trujillo, and the second floor is divided into exhibits on Peru and Pizarro's life there. The museum explains the "Curse of the Pizarro," recounting how the conquistador and his brothers were killed in brutal battles with rivals; those who survived never again enjoyed the wealth they had achieved in Peru. ✉ *Pl. de Santa María and Calle Merced s/n* ☞ *€2.*

Castillo
CASTLE/PALACE | For spectacular views, climb this large fortress, built by the Moors in the 9th century over old Roman foundations. To the south are silos, warehouses, and residential neighborhoods. To the north are green fields and brilliant flowers, partitioned by a maze of nearly leveled Roman stone walls, and an ancient cistern. The castle's size underscores the historic importance of now-tiny Trujillo. ✉ *Cerro Cabeza de Zorro* ☞ *€2.*

Iglesia de Santa María La Mayor
RELIGIOUS SITE | Attached to a Romanesque bell tower, this Gothic church is the most beautiful in Trujillo. It's only occasionally used for Mass, and its interior has been virtually untouched since the 16th century. The upper choir has an exquisitely carved balustrade, and the coats of arms at each end indicate the seats Ferdinand and Isabella occupied when they came here to worship. Note the high altar, circa 1480, adorned with great 15th-century Spanish paintings. To see it properly illuminated, place a coin in the box next to the church entrance.

Climb the tower for stunning views of the town and vast plains stretching toward Cáceres and the Sierra de Gredos. ✉ *Pl. de Santa María* ☞ *From €1.*

★ La Villa
HISTORIC SITE | This is Trujillo's oldest area, enclosed by restored stone walls. Follow them along Calle Almenas, which runs west from the Palacio de Orellana-Pizarro, beneath the **Alcázar de Los Chaves,** a castle-fortress that was converted into a guest lodge in the 15th century and hosted visiting dignitaries including Ferdinand and Isabella. Now a college, the building has seen better days. Passing the alcázar, continue west along the wall to the **Puerta de San Andrés,** one of La Villa's four surviving gates (there were originally seven). Views from the hilltop are particularly memorable at sunset, when spotlights illuminate the old quarter. ✉ *Trujillo.*

Museo de la Coria (*Fundación Xavier de Salas*)
MUSEUM | Near the Puerta de la Coria and occupying a former Franciscan convent built in the 15th century, this museum's exhibits on the relationship between Spain and Latin America are similar to those in the Casa Museo de Pizarro but with an emphasis on the troops as well as other conquistadores who led missions across the water. The museum is worth visiting if only for a look inside the old convent's two-tier central cloister. ✉ *Pl. de Santa María* ☎ *92/765–9032, 92/732–1898* ⊕ *www.fundacionxavierdesalas.com* ☞ *Free* ⊘ *Closed weekdays.*

Palacio de Orellana-Pizarro
CASTLE/PALACE | The Palacio de Orellana-Pizarro, renovated by Juan Pizarro himself in the 16th century, now serves as a school and has one of the most elegant Renaissance courtyards in town. The ground floor, open to visitors, has a deep, arched front doorway; on the second story is an elaborate Renaissance balcony bearing the crest of the Pizarro family. Miguel de Cervantes, on his way

to thank the Virgin of Guadalupe for his release from prison, spent time writing in the palace. ✉ *Trujillo* ✥ *Behind Pl. Mayor* 🎟 *Free.*

★ Plaza Mayor

PLAZA | One of the finest plazas in Spain, this superb Renaissance creation is dominated by a bronze equestrian statue of Francisco Pizarro—the work of an American sculptor, Charles Rumsey. Notice the Palacio del Marqués de la Conquista, the most dramatic building on the square with plateresque ornamentation and imaginative busts of the Pizarro family flanking its corner balcony. It was built by Francisco Pizarro's half-brother Hernando. ✉ *Trujillo.*

🍴 Restaurants

★ El 7 de Sillerías

$$$ | **SPANISH** | Ask Trujillo locals for the best food in town, and many will point you here for fresh, reasonably priced tapas and mains including croquetas (try the wild mushroom rendition) and *secreto ibérico* (seared Iberian pork shoulder steak). For just €14, the weekday lunch menú del día—including three courses and wine—is a steal. **Known for:** pleasant patio out back; secreto ibérico, a specialty pork dish; prix-fixe weekday lunch deal. [$] *Average main: €20* ✉ *Calle Sillerías 7* ☎ *92/732–1856* 🌐 *www.el7desillerias.com.*

Restaurante Bizcocho Plaza

$$$ | **SPANISH** | A Trujillo institution conveniently located on the Plaza Mayor, Bizcocho specializes in (slightly overpriced) Extramaduran cuisine—think local jamón, cheese, and migas—and the stone-and-tile dining room is cozy and cool even in the summer. Reservations are essential on holiday weekends. **Known for:** central location; excellent Iberian pork dishes; well-presented plates. [$] *Average main: €20* ✉ *Pl. Mayor 11* ☎ *92/732–2017* 🌐 *www.restaurantebizcochoplaza.com* 💳 *No credit cards.*

🛏 Hotels

Izán Trujillo

$$ | **HOTEL** | **FAMILY** | Once a 16th-century convent, this splendid four-star hotel is a short walk from the historic center. **Pros:** air of calm throughout the property; friendly and efficient staff; central location. **Cons:** small swimming pool; rooms vary in size; unpredictable food quality in restaurant. [$] *Rooms from: €90* ✉ *Pl. del Campillo 1* ☎ *92/745–8900* 🌐 *www.izanhoteles.es* 🛏 *78 rooms* 🍴 *No meals.*

★ Parador de Trujillo

$$$ | **HOTEL** | **FAMILY** | In another of the region's 16th-century convents, this parador is the essence of peace and tranquility, with rooms that are cozy and serene. **Pros:** peace and quiet in the heart of town; swimming pool; homey decor. **Cons:** somewhat overpriced; rooms are a bit like monastery quarters—on the small side; poor-quality bath products. [$] *Rooms from: €175* ✉ *Calle Santa Beatriz de Silva 1* ☎ *92/732–1350* 🌐 *www.parador.es* 🛏 *50 rooms* 🍴 *Free Breakfast.*

★ Posada Dos Orillas

$ | **HOTEL** | This hotel occupies a 16th-century stagecoach inn on a quiet pedestrian street uphill from the Plaza Mayor. **Pros:** pleasant interiors; beautiful terrace; good weekend rates. **Cons:** no reserved parking; beds a little basic; small TVs. [$] *Rooms from: €75* ✉ *Calle de los Cambrones 6* ☎ *92/765–9079* 🌐 *www.dosorillas.com* 🛏 *13 rooms* 🍴 *Free Breakfast.*

🛍 Shopping

Trujillo is a good place to shop for folk art. Look for multicolor rugs, blankets, and embroidery.

Eduardo Pablos Mateos

CRAFTS | This workshop specializes in wood carvings, basketwork, and furniture. Call ahead to schedule a personal tour. ✉ *Calle de San Judas 3* ☎ *92/732–1066, 60/617–4382 mobile.*

★ La Despensa

FOOD/CANDY | This gourmet shop on the corner of Plaza Mayor used to be the wine cellar of a 16th-century palace. Now it sells local products including jamón, cheese, wine, and locally made beer at excellent prices. ✉ *Cuesta de la Sangre s/n* ☎ *65/450–3419.*

Guadalupe

200 km (125 miles) southwest of Madrid, 96 km (60 miles) east of Trujillo.

Guadalupe's monastery is one of the most inspiring sights in Extremadura, and its story begins around 1300, when a local shepherd uncovered a statue of the Virgin, supposedly carved by St. Luke. King Alfonso XI, who often hunted here, had a church built to house the statue and vowed to found a monastery should he defeat the Moors at the battle of Salado in 1340. After his victory, he kept his promise. The greatest period in the monastery's history was between the 15th and 18th centuries, when, under the rule of the Hieronymites, it was turned into a pilgrimage center rivaling Santiago de Compostela in importance. Pilgrims have been coming here since the 14th century and have been joined by a growing number of tourists. Yet the monastery's isolation—a good two-hour drive from the nearest town—has protected it from commercial excess. The monastery's decline coincided with Spain's loss of overseas territories in the 19th century. Guadalupe is also known for its copper-ware, crafted here since the 16th century.

GETTING HERE AND AROUND

There's no train to Guadalupe, and bus service is sporadic. It's easiest if you have your own car and park on the outskirts of town. It's small enough to explore on foot but hilly with cobblestone streets, so wear comfortable shoes.

ESSENTIALS

VISITOR INFORMATION Guadalupe Tourist Office ✉ *Pl. Santa María de Guadalupe* ☎ *92/715–4128* *www.turismoextremadura.com/ viajar/turismo/en/organiza-tu-viaje/ Oficina-de-Turismo-de-Guadalupe.*

◉ Sights

★ Real Monasterio de Santa María de Guadalupe (*Royal Monastery of Our Lady of Guadalupe*)

RELIGIOUS SITE | Looming in the background of the Plaza Mayor is the late-Gothic facade of Guadalupe's colossal **monastery church,** flanked by battlement towers. The (required) guided tour begins in the Mudejar cloister and continues on to the **chapter house,** with hymnals, vestments, and paintings including a series of small panels by Zurbarán. The ornate 17th-century **sacristy** has a series of eight Zurbarán paintings, from 1638 to 1647. These austere representations of monks of the Hieronymite order and scenes from the life of St. Jerome are the artist's only significant paintings housed in the setting for which they were intended. The tour concludes in the garish, late-baroque **Camarín,** the chapel where the famous *Virgen Morena* (*Black Virgin*) is housed. Each September 8, the virgin is brought down from the altarpiece and walked around the cloister in a procession with pilgrims following on their knees. Outside, the monastery's gardens have been restored to their original, geometric Moorish style. ✉ *Guadalupe* ✛ *Entrance on Pl. Mayor* ☎ *92/736–7000* *www.monasterioguadalupe.com* 🎟 *€5.*

🛏 Hotels

Casa Rural Abacería de Guadalupe

$ | **B&B/INN** | **FAMILY** | For a simple, inexpensive overnight stay, try this small, tidy guesthouse on a quiet side street near the center of the village, around the corner from the parador. **Pros:** private

Did You Know?

The city of Guadalupe has been a tourist attraction—or pilgrimage destination—since the early 1300s, when a local man found a half-buried statue of the Virgin Mary, rumored to have been carved by St. Luke.

location; good for families; plenty of peace and quiet. **Cons:** individual rooms are a bit small; cold hallways in the winter; no Wi-Fi. $ *Rooms from: €50* ✉ *Calle Marqués de la Romana* ☎ *92/715–4282, 65/020–8405* ⊕ *www.guadaluperural. com* ▤ *No credit cards* ⤳ *3 rooms* ❍❘ *Free Breakfast.*

★ **Hospedería del Real Monasterio**

$ | **HOTEL** | An excellent and considerably cheaper alternative to the town parador, this inn was built around the 16th-century Gothic cloister of the monastery itself. **Pros:** guests get free monastery admission; excellent restaurant; helpful staff. **Cons:** the monastery's church bells chime around the clock; a bit pricey; uncomfortable beds. $ *Rooms from: €75* ✉ *Pl. Juan Carlos I* ☎ *92/736–7000* ⊕ *www. hotelhospederiamonasterioguadalupe. com* ⊘ *Closed mid-Jan.–mid-Feb.* ⤳ *47 rooms* ❍❘ *No meals.*

Parador de Guadalupe

$$$ | **HOTEL** | This exquisite estate, once the 15th-century palace of the Marquis de la Romana, now houses one of Spain's finest paradores. **Pros:** stunning architecture; authentic extremeño cooking; idyllic balconies. **Cons:** tight parking; long hike from reception to the farthest rooms; old-world property with old-world amenities. $ *Rooms from: €150* ✉ *Calle Marqués de la Romana 12* ☎ *92/736–7075* ⊕ *www.parador.es* ⤳ *41 rooms* ❍❘ *Free Breakfast.*

Mérida

76 km (47 miles) south of Cáceres, 191 km (119 miles) north of Seville, 347 km (216 miles) southwest of Madrid.

Mérida has some of the most impressive Roman ruins in Iberia. Founded by the Romans in 25 BC on the banks of the Río Guadiana, the city is strategically located at the junction of major Roman roads from León to Seville and Toledo to Lisbon.

The glass-and-steel bus station, on the other side of the river from the town center, commands a good view of the exceptionally long **Roman bridge.** On the bank opposite the ruins is the *alcazaba* (fortress).

Other Roman sites nearby require a drive. Across the train tracks in a modern neighborhood is the *circo* (circus), where chariot races were held. Little remains of the grandstands, which seated 30,000, but the outline of the circus is clearly visible and impressive for its size. Of the existing aqueduct remains, the most impressive is the **Acueducto de los Milagros** (Aqueduct of Miracles), north of the train station.

GETTING HERE AND AROUND

There are several buses daily to Mérida from Badajoz (1 hour), Sevilla (2½ hours), Cáceres (45 minutes), Trujillo (1½ hours), and Madrid (4½ hours). There are also several daily trains, which take about the same travel time but cost more. Check the RENFE website (⊕ *www.renfe.com*) or tourist office for schedules. Alternatively, there are usually several Blablacar rideshare departures from Madrid and Mérida's neighboring cities each day. Once in Mérida, the city center is navigable on foot or by tourist train.

ESSENTIALS

VISITOR INFORMATION Mérida Tourist Office ✉ *Paseo José Álvarez Sáenz de Buruaga* ☎ *92/433–0722* ⊕ *www.turismo-merida.org.*

TOURS

Tren Turístico

TRAIN TOURS | Mérida is walkable, but this tourist train follows a 35-minute circular route past all the sites, starting at the tourist office in front of the Roman theater. Call ahead to book, because service is sometimes canceled if there isn't a minimum number of passengers. ✉ *Paseo José Álvarez Sáenz de Buruaga* ☎ *66/747–1907* ▤ *€5.*

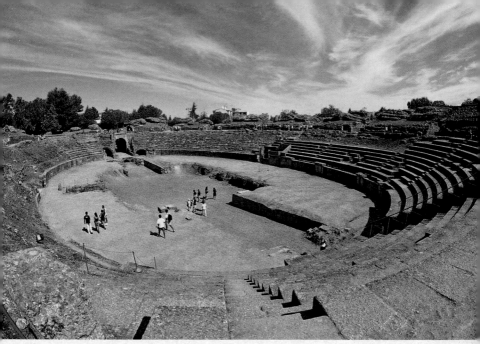

Mérida's excellently preserved Roman amphitheater is the site of a drama festival every July.

⊙ Sights

Alcazaba Árabe (*Fortress*)
ARCHAEOLOGICAL SITE | To get to this sturdy square fortress, built by the Romans and strengthened by the Visigoths and Moors, continue west from the Museo Nacional de Arte Romano, down Suarez Somontes toward the river and the city center. Turn right at Calle Baños and you can see the towering columns of the **Templo de Diana,** the oldest of Mérida's Roman buildings. To enter the alcazaba, follow the fortress walls around to the side farthest from the river. Climb up to the battlements for sweeping river views, or go underground to see the aljibe, or cistern. ⊠ *Calle de Graciano* 🖭 *€6.*

★ Museo Nacional de Arte Romano
(*National Museum of Roman Art*)
MUSEUM | Across the street from the entrance to the Roman sites and connected by an underground passageway is Mérida's superb Roman art museum, in a monumental building designed by the renowned Spanish architect Rafael Moneo. Walk through a series of passageways to the luminous, cathedral-like main exhibition hall, which is supported by arches the same proportion and size (50 feet) as the Roman arch in the center of Mérida, the Arco de Trajano (Trajan's Arch). The exhibits include mosaics, frescoes, jewelry, statues, pottery, household utensils, and other Roman works. Be sure to visit the **crypt** beneath the museum—it contains the remains of several homes and a necropolis that were uncovered while the museum was being built in 1981. ⊠ *Calle José Ramón Mélida s/n* 🕾 *92/431–1690, 92/431–1912* ⊕ *www.mecd.gob.es/mnromano/home. html* 🖭 *€3* ⊙ *Closed Mon.*

★ Plaza de España
PLAZA | Mérida's main square adjoins the northwestern corner of the alcazaba and is lively both day and night. The plaza's oldest building is a 16th-century palace, now the Mérida Palace hotel. Behind the palace stretches Mérida's most charming area with Andalusian-style white houses shaded by palms, in the midst of which stands the **Arco de Trajano,** part of a

Roman city gate. This is a great place to people-watch over tapas at sunset. ✉ *Mérida.*

★ Roman Monuments

ARCHAEOLOGICAL SITE | FAMILY | Mérida's Roman **teatro** (theater) and **anfiteatro** (amphitheater) are set in a verdant park, and the theater—the best preserved in Spain—seats 6,000 and is used for a classical drama festival each July. The amphitheater, which holds 15,000 spectators, opened in 8 BC for gladiatorial contests. Next to the entrance to the ruins is the **main tourist office,** where you can pick up maps and brochures. You can buy a ticket to see only the Roman ruins or, for a slightly higher fee, an *entrada conjunta* (joint admission), which also grants access to the Basílica de Santa Eulalia and the alcazaba. To reach the monuments by car, follow signs to the "Museo de Arte Romano." Parking is usually easy to find. ✉ *Av. de los Estudiantes* ☎ *92/431–2530* 🎟 *From €12.*

🍴 Restaurants

Vía de la Tapa

$ | TAPAS | FAMILY | One of the specialties at this local hangout, known for its cheap, thoughtfully prepared tapas, is morcilla de Guadalupe, blood sausage made in the nearby town of the same name. Note to diners with time constraints: the service is notoriously slow (and churlish) when the restaurant is packed. **Known for:** €10 menú del día; fall-off-the-bone stewed meats; worth-the-wait outdoor seating. [$] *Average main: €11* ✉ *Calle José Ramón Mélida 48* ☎ *92/431–5859* 🌐 *www.viadelatapa.es* 💳 *No credit cards.*

🛏 Hotels

★ Ilunion Mérida Palace

$$ | HOTEL | FAMILY | Dominating the Plaza de España, this five-star luxury hotel has a rooftop pool deck, Moorish-themed design elements, and a twinkly central courtyard. **Pros:** outdoor pool, terrace, and solarium; gym facilities; excellent restaurant. **Cons:** some front rooms facing the Plaza de España can be noisy in summer; valet parking is expensive and alternatives are scarce; a bit far from the Roman ruins. [$] *Rooms from: €120* ✉ *Pl. de España 19* ☎ *92/438–3800* 🌐 *www.ilunionmeridapalace.com* 🔑 *76 rooms* 🍽 *No meals.*

Parador de Mérida (*Parador Vía de la Plata*)

$$$ | HOTEL | FAMILY | This spacious hotel exudes Andalusian cheerfulness with hints at its Roman and Moorish past—it was built over the remains of a Roman temple, later became a baroque convent, and then served as a prison. **Pros:** central location; stunning interior courtyard; dazzling-white interior. **Cons:** expensive parking; erratic Wi-Fi; could use a revamp. [$] *Rooms from: €165* ✉ *Pl. de la Constitución and Calle Almendralejo 56* ☎ *92/431–3800* 🌐 *www.parador.es* 🔑 *81 rooms* 🍽 *No meals.*

GALICIA AND ASTURIAS

Updated by
Elizabeth Prosser

👁 **Sights**
★★★★☆

🍽 **Restaurants**
★★★★☆

🛏 **Hotels**
★★★☆☆

🛍 **Shopping**
★★★☆☆

🍸 **Nightlife**
★★★☆☆

WELCOME TO GALICIA AND ASTURIAS

TOP REASONS TO GO

★ **Experience gourmet heaven:** Beautiful Santiago de Compostela is said to contain more restaurants and bars per square mile than any other city in Spain.

★ **Go on rugged hikes:** Spend days in the spectacular Picos de Europa range getting lost in forgotten mountain villages.

★ **Get in on the grapevine:** The Ribeiro region yields Spain's finest white wines.

★ **Enjoy the waterfront activity:** Watch the oyster hawkers at work while dining on a fresh catch on Vigo's Rúa Pescadería.

★ **Discover Santander:** With its intoxicating schedule of live music, opera, and theater performances on the beach and in gardens and monasteries, the city's August festival of music and dance is the perfect backdrop for exploring this vibrant city.

The bewitching provinces of Galicia and Asturias lie in Spain's northwest; these rugged Atlantic regions hide a corner of Spain so remote it was once called finis terrae (the end of the earth).

1 Santiago de Compostela. For centuries a destination for Christian pilgrims seeking to pay homage to St. James.

2 Ourense and La Ribeira Sacra. An attractive medieval quarter and bubbling thermal springs.

3 Lugo. Beautifully preserved Roman ramparts.

4 Muxia. A small fishing village in stunning surrounds.

5 Fisterra. Once considered the end of the earth, now the unofficial added-on end of the pilgrimage for many.

6 Muros. Famous for its 6 pm fish auction.

7 Cambados. Charming seaside town and home to Albariño white wine.

8 Pontevedra. Base for exploring the Rías Baixas.

9 Vigo. A formidable port, red-roofed fisherman's houses, and appealing old town.

10 Baiona. Home to one of Spain's most popular paradores.

11 Tui. An important border town.

12 A Coruña. Lots of interesting sights and a buzzing nightlife scene.

13 Betanzos. A charming medieval town.

14 Viveiro. Great beaches make this a popular summer resort.

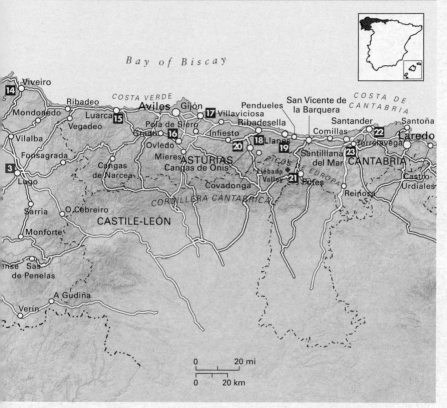

15 Luarca. Cobblestone streets, stone stairways, and whitewashed houses.

16 Oviedo. A city of ancient charm and youthful energy.

17 Gijón. An ancient Roman port with lively bars.

18 Ribadesella. Famous for its seafood, its cave, and the canoe races.

19 Llanes. Beach town with colorful houses with glass galleries against a backdrop of the Picos de Europa.

20 Cangas de Onís. The unofficial capital of the Picos de Europa National Park.

21 Potes. Known for its fine cheeses and 9th century monasteries.

22 Santander. Busy port with great beaches.

23 Santillana del Mar. Home to some of Spain's most stunning 15th- to 17th-century stone houses.

EATING AND DRINKING WELL IN GALICIA AND ASTURIAS

Galicia, Asturias, and Cantabria are famous for seafood and fish so fresh that chefs frown on drowning the inherent flavors in sauces and seasonings. Inland, the Picos de Europa and the mountain meadows are rich in game, lamb, and beef.

The northern coast of Spain is justly famous for fish and seafood, and specialties include *merluza a la gallega* (steamed hake with paprika sauce) in Galicia and *merluza a la sidra* (hake in a cider sauce) in Asturias. Look also for Galician seafood treasures such as *vieiras* (scallops) and *pulpo a la gallega* (boiled octopus that's drizzled with olive oil and dusted with salt and paprika). The rainy weather means that bracing stews are a favorite form of sustenance, especially *fabada asturiana* (Asturian bean-and-sausage stew) and Galicia's *caldo gallego* (a thick soup of white beans, turnip greens, ham, and potatoes). Cantabria's cooking is part mountain fare, such as roast kid and lamb or *cocidos* (pork-and-bean stews) in the highlands, and part seafood dishes, such as *sorropotún* (a bonito, potato, and vegetable stew) along the coast.

CABRALES CHEESE

Asturias is known for having Spain's bluest and most pungent cheese, Cabrales, made of raw cow's milk (with goat curd added for a softer consistency). Produced in the Picos de Europa mountains of eastern Asturias, the cheese gets such praise because of the quality of the milk and the dry highland air used to cure it. Cabrales is ideal melted over meat or for dessert with a sweet sherry.

BEANS AND LEGUMES

Fabada asturiana is as well known in Spain as Valencia's paella or Andalusia's gazpacho. A meal in itself, fabada is usually consumed in copious quantities. The secret to great fabada lies in slow simmering while adding small quantities of cold water, and crushing some of the beans so that the creamy paste becomes part of the sauce. Fatback, *morcilla* (blood sausage), chorizo, and pork chops are added to this powerful dose of protein and vitamin B, and it's cooked on low heat for at least 2½ hours.

VEGETABLES

Turnip greens (*grelos* in Gallego) are a favorite vegetable in Galicia, celebrated in La Festa do Grelo during Carnavales in February and March. *Lacón con grelos* is a classic Galician specialty combining cured pork shoulder, turnip stalks and greens, potatoes, and chorizo, all boiled for about four hours. The grelos' acidity and the pork shoulder's heavy fat content make the marriage of these two products an ideal union. Similarly, caldo gallego is a powerful mountain or seafarer's stew, the whole garden in a pot—including grelos stalks and greens, *alubias* (white beans), and potatoes—with pork for ballast and taste. Traditionally served in earthenware cups called *cuncas,* the diverse ingredients and the fat from the pork make this a fortifying antidote to the bitter Atlantic climate of Spain's northwest corner.

PULPO A LA GALLEGA

This typical Galician specialty, also known as *polbo á feira*, consists of octopus that's been boiled (traditionally in a copper cauldron), cut into slices, drizzled with olive oil, sprinkled with salt and bittersweet paprika, and served on a wooden plate. A variation is served atop slices of boiled potato; the texture of the potato slices balances the consistency of the octopus.

TO DRINK

The best Galician wine is the fresh, full-bodied, white Albariño from Rías Baixas, perfect with seafood. Ribeiro, traditionally sipped from shallow white ceramic cups, or *tazas,* in order to allow aromas to expand, is lighter and fresher. Asturias is known for its *sidra* (hard cider), poured from overhead and quaffed in a single gulp for full enjoyment. Brandy buffs should try Galicia's *queimada* (which some locals claim is a witches' brew), made of potent, grappa-like *orujo* mixed with lemon peel, coffee beans, and sugar in an earthenware bowl and then set aflame and stirred until the desired amount of alcohol is burned off.

EL CAMINO DE SANTIAGO

Traversing meadows, mountains, and villages across Spain, about 100,000 travelers embark each year on a pilgrimage to Galicia's Santiago de Compostela, the sacred city of St. James— they're not all deeply religious these days, though a spiritual quest is generally the motivation.

HISTORY OF THE CAMINO

The surge of spiritual seekers heading to Spain's northwest coast began as early as the 9th century, when news spread that the apostle James's remains were there. By the middle of the 12th century, about 1 million pilgrims were arriving in Santiago de Compostela each year. An entire industry of food hawkers, hoteliers, and trinket sellers awaited their arrival. They even had the world's first travel guide, the Codex Calixtinus (published in the 1130s), to help them on their way. Some made the journey in response to their conscience, to do penance for their sins against God, while others were sentenced by law to make the long walk as payment for crimes against the state. Legend claims that St. James's body was transported secretly to the area by boat after his martyrdom in Jerusalem in AD 44. The idea picked up steam in 814, when a hermit claimed to see miraculous lights in the sky, accompanied by the sound of angels singing, on a wooded hillside near Padrón. Human bones were quickly discovered at the site, and immediately—and perhaps somewhat conveniently—declared to be those of the apostle (the bones may actually have belonged to Priscillian, the leader of a 4th-century Christian sect). Word of this important find quickly spread across a relic-hungry Europe. Within a couple of centuries, the road to Santiago had become as popular as the other two major medieval pilgrimages, to Rome and to Jerusalem. After the 12th century, pilgrim numbers began to gradually decline, due to the dangers of robbery along the route, a growing skepticism about the genuineness of St. James's remains, and the popular rise of science in place of religion.

THE PILGRIMAGE TODAY

The pilgrims follow one of seven main routes, walking about 19 miles per day in a nearly 500-mile journey. Along the way, they encounter incredible local hospitality and trade stories with fellow adventurers. By the late 1980s, there were only about 3,000 pilgrims a year, but in 1993 the Galician govern-ment launched an initiative called the Xacobeo (i.e., Jacobean; the name James comes from the Hebrew word "Jacob") to increase the number of visitors to the region, and the popularity of the pilgrimage soared. Numbers increased exponentially, and there have been more than 100,000 annually since 2006. In holy years, when St. James's Day (July 25) falls on a Sunday, the number of pilgrims usually doubles.

WHO WAS ST. JAMES?

St. James the Great, brother of St. John the Evangelist (author of the Gospel of

John and the Book of Revelation), was one of Jesus's first apostles. Sent by Jesus to preach that the kingdom of heaven had come, he crossed Europe and ended up in Spain. Along the way, he saved a knight from drowning in the sea. As legend goes, the knight resurfaced, covered in scallop shells: this is why Camino pilgrims carry this seashell on their journey. Legend has it that St. James was beheaded by King Herod Agrippa on his return to Judea in AD 44 but that he was rescued by angels and transported in a rudderless stone boat back to Spain, where his lifeless body was encased in a rock. James is said to have resurfaced to aid the Christians in the Reconquest Battle of Clavijo, gaining him the title of Matamoros, or Moor Killer. When the body of St. James was found, people came in droves to see his remains—the Spanish and Portuguese name for St. James is Santiago. The belief arose that sins would be cleansed through the penance of this long walk, an idea no doubt encouraged by the Church at the time.

THE PILGRIMAGE EXPERIENCE

Not everyone does the route in one trip. Some split it into manageable chunks and take years to complete the whole course. Most, however, walk an average of 30 km (19 miles)

per day to arrive in Santiago after a monthlong trek. The Camino, which sometimes follows a mountain trail and other times passes through a village or across a field, is generally so well marked that most travelers claim not to need a map (bringing one is highly recommended, however). Travelers simply follow the route markers—gold scallop-shell designs on blue backgrounds posted on buildings or painted on rocks and trail posts. Walking is not the only option: bicycles are common and will cut the time needed to complete the pilgrimage in half; horseback riding, or walking with a donkey in tow, carrying the bags, are also options. Every town along the route has an official Camino *albergue,* or hostel, often in an ancient monastery or original pilgrim's hospice. They generally accommodate 40–150 people. You can bunk for free—though a donation is expected—in the company of fellow walkers but may only stay one night, unless severe Camino injuries prevent you from moving on. Be aware that these places can fill up fast. Walkers get first priority, followed by cyclists and those on horseback, with organized walking groups at the bottom

of the pecking order. If there is no room at the official albergues, there are plenty of paid hostels along the route. Wherever you stay, get your Pilgrims' Passport, or *credencial,* stamped, as proof of how far you've walked.

A TYPICAL DAY

A typical day on the Camino involves walking hard through the morning to the next village in time to get a free bed. The afternoon is for catching up with fellow pilgrims, having a look around town, and doing a bit of washing. The Spanish people you meet along the way and the camaraderie with fellow pilgrims is a highlight of the trip for many. Some albergues serve a communal evening meal, but there is always a bar in town that offers a lively atmosphere and a cheap (€8–€10) pilgrim's set menu (quality and fare varies; it consists of three courses plus bread and beverage). Sore feet are compared, local wine is consumed, and new walking partners are found for the following day's stage. Just make sure you get back to the albergue before curfew, around 10 or 11, or you may find a locked door.

THE FINISH LINE

Arriving at the end of the Camino de Santiago is an emotional experience. It is common to see small groups of pilgrims, hands clasped tightly together, tearfully approaching the moss- and lichen-covered cathedral in Santiago's Plaza del Obradoiro. After entering the building through the Pilgrim's Door and hugging the statue of St. James, a special mass awaits them at midday, the highlight of which is seeing the *botafumeiro*, a giant incense-filled censer, swinging from the ceiling. Those that have covered more than 100 km (62 miles) on foot, or twice that distance on a bicycle—as shown by the stamped passport—can then collect their Compostela certificate from the pilgrim's office (near the cathedral, at Rúa do Vilar 1).

USEFUL WEBSITES

The modern pilgrim has technology at his or her fingertips. The official Xacobeo website (⊕ *www.xacobeo. es/en*) not only can help you plan your trip, with detailed route maps and hostel locations, it also has a Xacoblog where you can share videos, photos, and comments, as well as a forum for asking questions and getting feedback. A cell phone application helps you check routes, hostels, and sites to see while you're walking. Other websites include: ⊕ *www.caminodesantiago.me*, ⊕ *www.csj.org.uk*, ⊕ *www.caminoadventures.com*, and ⊕ *www.caminosantiagodecompostela.com*.

CAMINO TIPS

The most popular of the seven main routes of the Camino de Santiago is the 791-km (480-mile) **Camino Francés** (French Way), which starts in France (in Saint-Jean-Pied-de-Port) and crosses the high *meseta* plains into Galicia. The **Camino Norte** (Northern Way), which runs through the woodlands of Spain's rugged north coast, is also gaining in popularity.

The busiest time on the Camino is in the summer months, June–September. That means crowded paths and problems finding a room at night, particularly if you start the Camino on the first few days of any month, plus hot temperatures. Consider starting in April, May, or September instead. Making the journey in winter is not advised.

To get your credencial, contact one of the Camino confraternity groups. These are not-for-profit associations formed by previous pilgrims to help those who are thinking about doing the Camino (⊕ *www.csj.org.uk*). You can also pick up a passport at many of the common starting points, local churches, and Amigos del Camino de Santiago in villages throughout Spain. Many albergues throughout Spain also can provide you with a valid credencial for a small fee.

PACKING TIPS:

A lightweight but sturdy 30–50 liter hiking pack is a good investment for this hike. You won't need the full ankle support of hiking boots for the Camino's terrain; a pair of hiking shoes with a good grip will do. Good socks are crucial to prevent blisters. Otherwise, pack light, quick-drying fabrics.

Spain's westernmost region is en route to nowhere, an end in itself. This magical, remote area is sure to pull at your heartstrings, so be prepared to fall in love. In Gallego they call the feeling *morriña*, a powerful longing for a person or place you've left behind.

Stretching northwest from the lonesome Castilian plains to the rocky seacoast, Asturias and Galicia incorporate lush hills and vineyards, gorgeous *rías* (estuaries), and the country's wildest mountains, the Picos de Europa. Santander and the entire Cantabrian region are cool summer refuges with sandy beaches, high sierras (including part of the Picos de Europa), and tiny highland towns. Santander, once the main seaport for Old Castile on the Bay of Biscay, is in a mountainous zone wedged between the Basque Country and Asturias.

Northwestern Spain is a series of rainy landscapes, stretching from your feet to the horizon. Ancient granite buildings wear a blanket of moss, and even the stone *hórreos* (granaries) are built on stilts above the damp ground. Swirling fog and heavy mist help keep local folktales of the supernatural alive. Rather than a guitar, you'll hear the *gaita* (bagpipe), a legacy of the Celts' settlements here in the 5th and 6th centuries BC. Spanish families flock to these cool northern beaches and mountains each summer. Santiago de Compostela, where the cathedral holds the remains of the apostle James, has drawn pilgrims for 900 years, leaving churches, shrines, and former hospitals in their path. Asturias, north of the main pilgrim trail, has always maintained a separate identity, isolated by the rocky Picos de Europa. This and the Basque Country are the only parts of Spain never conquered by the Moors, so Asturian architecture shows little Moorish influence. It was from a mountain base at Covadonga that the Christians won their first decisive battle against the Moors and launched the Reconquest of Spain. Despite being very much its own region, Cantabria is in spirit much closer to Asturias—with which it shares the Picos de Europa, Castilian Spanish, and similar architecture—than its passionately independent neighbor, the Basque Country.

MAJOR REGIONS

Santiago de Compostela and Eastern Galicia. Books and movies have been written about it and millions have walked it, but you don't have to be a pilgrim to enjoy the **Camino de Santiago.** At the end of the path is Santiago itself, a vibrant university town embedded in hills around the soaring spires of one of Spain's most emblematic cathedrals.

The Costa da Morte and Rías Baixas. From the small fishing village of Malpica to **Muros,** from **Fisterra** (World's End) down to **Vigo** and the Portuguese border, this area takes in the peaceful seaside towns of **Cambados** and Baiona, the exquisite beaches of Las Islas Cíes, and the beautifully preserved medieval streets of **Pontevedra.**

A Coruña and Rías Altas. Galicia has more coastline and unspoiled, nontouristy beaches than anywhere else in Spain. Opt for vast expanses of sand facing the Atlantic Ocean or tiny, tucked-away coves, but take note: the water is colder than the Mediterranean, and the weather is more unreliable.

Asturias. Also known as the Senda Costera (Coastal Way), this partly paved nature route between Pendueles and **Llanes** takes in some of Asturias's most spectacular coastal scenery, including noisy *bufones* (large waterspouts created naturally by erosion) and the Playa de Ballota. Asturias is bordered to the southeast by the imposing Picos de Europa, which are best accessed via the scenic coastal towns of **Llanes** or **Ribadesella.**

The Picos de Europa. One of Spain's best-kept secrets, the "Peaks of Europe" lie across Asturias, Cantabria, and León. In addition to 8,910-foot peaks, the area has deep caves, excellent mountain refuges, and interesting wildlife. This region is also known for its fine cheeses.

Cantabria. Santander's wide beaches and summer music-and-dance festival are highlights of this mountain and maritime community. The Liébana Valley, the Renaissance town at **Santillana del Mar,** and ports and beaches like **San Vicente de la Barquera** all rank among northern Spain's finest treasures. The most scenic route from Madrid via Burgos to Santander is the slow but spectacular N62, past the Ebro reservoir. Faster and safer is the N627 from Burgos to Aguilar de Campóo connecting to the A67 freeway down to Santander.

Planning

When to Go

Galicia can get very hot (more than 90°F [30°C]) June–September, although summer is the best time for swimming and water sports and for Celtic music festivals. Asturias, in the mountains, is cooler. Galicia can be rainy to the point of saturation—not for nothing is this region called Green Spain—so avoid the area in winter: the rain, wind, and freezing temperatures make driving an arduous experience. Spring and fall are ideal, as the weather is reasonable and crowds are few. At any time of year in Galicia, it is not unusual to experience all seasons in one day.

Planning Your Time

You can fly into Santiago de Compostela, and a week should be long enough to cover the Santiago area and Galicia's south. From Santiago, you can drive down the PO550 to Cambados, stopping on the way at fishing villages along the Ría de Arousa. If you take the coastal road to Pontevedra, you can spend time there exploring the medieval streets and tapas bars and then drive down to Vigo for a lunch of oysters on Rúa Pescadería. Continue south and arrive before dark at the Baiona parador. Alternatively, travel to A Coruña, and from there head north to some of Spain's loveliest beaches and Viveiro. From here cross into Asturias and spend time in Luarca or Gijón. Another attractive option is getting lost in a small village in the Picos de Europa.

Heading farther east, Santillana del Mar's Renaissance architecture, the Altamira Caves, and the Sardinero Beach at Santander are top spots, while the fishing villages and beaches around Llanes in eastern Asturias, and San Vicente de la Barquera in Cantabria have charming ports and inlets. If you want to delve more deeply into the Picos de Europa and the region's pretty coastline, Asturias and Cantabria merit more than a week's exploration.

Getting Here and Around

AIR TRAVEL

The region's domestic airports are in Santander, A Coruña, Vigo, and near San Estéban de Pravia, 47 km (29 miles) north of Oviedo. Santiago de Compostela is a hub for both domestic and international flights. Airport shuttles usually take the form of ALSA buses from the city bus station. Iberia sometimes runs a private shuttle from its office to the airport; inquire when you book your ticket.

BIKE TRAVEL

Cycling the Camino de Santiago de Compostela is becoming increasingly popular every year, particularly with international visitors. The official *French Way by Bicycle* booklet, available from **Xacobeo** or from the Santiago tourist office, warns that the approximately 800-km (500-mile) route from the French border to Santiago is a very tough bike trip—bridle paths, dirt tracks, rough stones, and mountain passes. The best time of year to tackle it is late spring or early autumn. The Asturias tourist office's booklet, *Sus Rutas de Montaña y Costa,* available online (⊕ *www.asturias.es*), outlines additional routes. For something a little less arduous, try the final leg of the Camino Francés, from Sarria to Santiago.

BIKE ROUTES

CaminoWays.com
This tour operator can help you bike the Camino with tailor-made packages for individuals and families, child-friendly accommodations if necessary, meals, luggage transfer, and bike rental. ⊠ *Calle Gomez Ulla 6, Santiago de Compostela* ☎ *923/990672* ⊕ *www.caminoways.com.*

Xacobeo
This is the definitive website for pilgrims embarking upon the Camino de Santiago, maintained by the Galicia's tourism department. ⊕ *www.xacobeo.es.*

BUS TRAVEL

ALSA runs daily buses from Madrid to Galicia and Asturias. Once here, there is good bus service between the larger destinations in the area, like Santiago, Vigo, Pontevedra, Lugo, A Coruña, Gijón, Oviedo, and Santander, though train travel is generally smoother, faster, and easier. Getting to the smaller towns by bus is more difficult. Galicia-based Monbus offers quick, inexpensive transportation between major cities like Santiago, A Coruña, Vigo, and Pontevedra, as well as smaller towns that may not be easily accessible by train.

CONTACTS ALSA ☎ *902/422242* ⊕ *www.alsa.com.* **Monbus** ☎ *982/292900* ⊕ *www.monbus.es.*

CAR TRAVEL

Driving is the best way to get around. The four-lane A6 expressway links the area with central Spain; it takes about 6½ hours to cover the 650 km (403 miles) from Madrid to Santiago, and from Madrid, it's 240 km (149 miles) on the N1 or the A1 toll road to Burgos, after which you can take the N623 to complete the 162 km (100 miles) to Santander.

The expressway north from León to Oviedo and Gijón is the fastest way to cross the Cantabrian Mountains. The AP9 north–south Galician ("Atlantic") expressway links A Coruña, Santiago, Pontevedra, and Vigo, and the A8 in Asturias links Santander to Luarca and beyond. Local roads along the coast or through the hills are more scenic but slower.

TRAIN TRAVEL

RENFE (⊕ *www.renfe.es*) runs several trains a day from Madrid to Santander (4½ hours), Oviedo (7 hours), and Gijón (8 hours), and a separate line serves Santiago (11 hours). Local RENFE trains connect the region's major cities with most of the surrounding small towns, but there may be dozens of stops on the way. Narrow-gauge FEVE trains clatter slowly across northern Spain, connecting Galicia and Asturias with Santander, Bilbao, and Irún, on the French border.

FEVE's Transcantábrico narrow-gauge train tour (⊕ www.eltranscantabricogranlujo.com) is an eight-day, 1,000-km (600-mile) journey through the Basque Country, Cantabria, Asturias, and Galicia. English-speaking guides narrate, and a private bus takes the group from train stations to natural attractions. Passengers sleep on the train in suites and dine on local specialties. Trains run April–October; the all-inclusive cost is €5,150 for seven nights per person in a deluxe suite.

Hotels

Expect to feel at home in the region's classic inns: they're usually small, centuries-old, family-owned properties, with plenty that's pleasing, such as gardens, exposed stone walls, and genuinely friendly service. City hotels may not have the same country charm, but they make up for it with professional service, sparkling facilities, and spacious, comfortable rooms. Many big chain hotels may resemble their American counterparts, but you may not be able to assume that they also come with ample parking, big breakfasts, fitness rooms, or other amenities that are more-or-less standard back home. It's a very good idea to book ahead of time May–September, particularly if your stay includes a weekend.

Hotel reviews have been shortened. For full information, visit Fodors.com.

What It Costs in Euros			
$	$$	$$$	$$$$
RESTAURANTS			
under €12	€12–€17	€18–€22	over €22
HOTELS			
under €90	€90–€125	€126–€180	over €180

Santiago de Compostela

650 km (403 miles) northwest of Madrid.

You don't need to be a pilgrim to enjoy this medieval city, which is one of the most popular and beautiful in all of Galicia. Wander down the cobblestone streets of the picturesque old town, and admire the unique mix of Romanesque, Gothic, and baroque buildings. Or pop into an art gallery or one of the city's many chic literary cafés to catch some poetry or local music. A large, lively university makes Santiago one of the most exciting cities in Spain, and its cathedral makes it one of the most impressive. The building is opulent and awesome, yet its towers create a sense of harmony as a benign St. James, dressed in pilgrim's costume, looks down from his perch. Santiago de Compostela welcomes more than 4½ million visitors a year, with an extra million during Holy Years (the next will be in 2021), when St. James's Day (July 25) next falls on a Sunday.

GETTING HERE AND AROUND

Santiago is connected to Pontevedra (61 km [38 miles]) and A Coruña (57 km [35 miles]) via the AP9 tollway. The N550 is free but slower. Parking anywhere in the city center can be difficult unless you use one of the numerous car parks around the outside edge of the historical quarter.

Bus service out of Santiago's station is plentiful, with eight daily buses to Madrid (7–9 hours) and hourly buses to A Coruña and to the Santiago Airport.

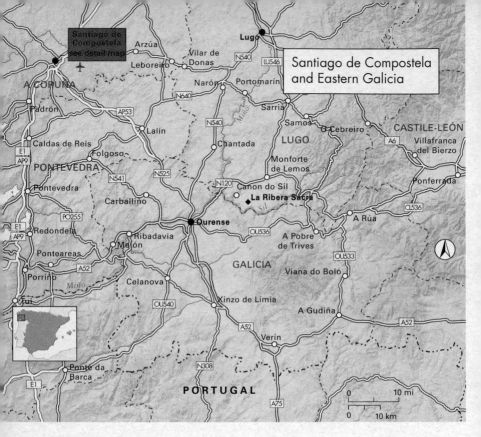

Santiago de Compostela
and Eastern Galicia

High-speed Talgo trains to Madrid take just over six hours; there is daily service to Irún, on the French border, via León and Santander. Trains depart every hour for Galicia's other major towns.

Santiago's center is very pedestrian friendly, and the distances between attractions are relatively short, so walking is the best and often the only way around town.

BUS STATION Santiago de Compostela Bus Station ✉ *Praza de Camilo Díaz Baliño s/n* ☎ *981/542416.*

TRAIN STATION Santiago de Compostela Train Station ✉ *Rúa do Hórreo 75A* ☎ *912/320320 RENFE.*

VISITOR INFORMATION
CONTACTS Santiago de Compostela Turismo ✉ *Rúa do Vilar 63* ☎ *981/555129* ⊕ *www. santiagoturismo.com.*

TOURS
La Asociación Profesional de Guías Turísticos de Galicia

WALKING TOURS | Santiago's association of well-informed guides, which is part of the tourist office, can arrange walking tours of the city or tours to any place in Galicia. Tours in English each Saturday begin at 3:30 year round (and also Thursday–Sunday June–September) and are priced from €12. Look out for the yellow umbrella at the meeting point on Plaza de Praterías. ✉ *Dársena de Xoan XXIII, Av. Xoan XXIII* ☎ *981/576698* ⊕ *www. guiasdegalicia.org* ⊠ *From €12.*

Sights

★ Casco Antiguo *(Old Town)*
NEIGHBORHOOD | The best way to spend your time in Santiago de Compostela is simply to walk around the *casco antiguo*

(old town), losing yourself in its maze of stone-paved narrow streets and little plazas. The streets hold many old *pazos* (manor houses), convents, and churches. The most beautiful pedestrian thoroughfares are Rúa do Vilar, Rúa do Franco, and Rúa Nova—portions of which are covered by arcaded walkways called *soportales,* designed to keep walkers out of the rain. Don't miss the Praza da Quintana, a small enclosed square surrounded by the majestic walls of the cathedral and the 9th-century Monastery of San Paio de Antealtares, founded by Alfonso II—it's the haunt of young travelers and folk musicians in summer. ✉ *Santiago de Compostela.*

★ **Catedral de Santiago de Compostela**
(*Cathedral of Santiago de Compostela*)
RELIGIOUS SITE | Although the facade is baroque, the interior holds one of the finest Romanesque sculptures in the world, the **Pórtico de la Gloria.** Completed in 1188 by Maestro Mateo, this is the cathedral's original entrance, its three arches carved with figures from the Apocalypse, the Last Judgment, and purgatory. Below Jesus is a serene St. James, poised on a carved column. Look carefully and you can see five smooth grooves, formed by the millions of pilgrims who have placed their hands here over the centuries. On the back of the pillar, people lean forward to touch foreheads in the hope that his genius can be shared.

In his bejeweled cloak, St. James presides over the **high altar.** The stairs behind it are the cathedral's focal point, surrounded by dazzling baroque decoration, sculpture, and drapery. Here, as the grand finale of their spiritual journey, pilgrims embrace St. James and kiss his cloak. In the crypt beneath the altar lie the remains of James and his disciples St. Theodore and St. Athenasius. A pilgrims' Mass is celebrated every day at noon.

✉ *Praza do Obradoiro* ☎ *902/044077 museum – information and bookings*

⊕ *www.catedraldesantiago.es/en* ✉ *Cathedral free, museum €6.*

Centro Galego de Arte Contemporánea
(*Galician Center for Contemporary Art*)
MUSEUM | On the north side of town, off the Porta do Camino, the CGAC is a stark but elegant modern building that contrasts with the ancient feel of most other places in Santiago. The Portuguese designer Álvaro Siza built the museum of smooth, angled granite, which mirrors the medieval convent of San Domingos de Bonaval next door. Inside, a gleaming lobby of white Italian marble gives way to white-walled, high-ceilinged exhibition halls flooded with light from massive windows and skylights. The museum has a good permanent collection and even better changing exhibits. ✉ *Rúa Valle Inclán 2* ☎ *981/546619* ⊕ *www.cgac.org* ✉ *Free* ⊙ *Closed Mon.*

Hostal de los Reyes Católicos (*Hostel of the Catholic Monarchs*)
HOTEL—SIGHT | Facing the cathedral from the left, the hostal was built in 1499 by Ferdinand and Isabella to house the pilgrims who slept on Santiago's streets every night. Having lodged and revived travelers for more than 500 years, it's the oldest refuge in the world; it was converted from a hospital to a parador in 1954. The facade bears two Castilian coats of arms along with Adam, Eve, and various saints; inside, the four arcaded patios have gargoyle rainspouts said to be caricatures of 16th-century townsfolk. Behind the lobby is the building's focal point, a Renaissance chapel in the shape of a cross. Thanks to the Parador Museo initiative, visitors (as opposed to just guests staying at the parador) can behold these architectural treasures on a guided tour. ✉ *Praza do Obradoiro 1* ☎ *981/114873 tours* ⊕ *www.freetoursantiagodecompostela.com/en/tours/tour-hostal-de-los-reyes-catolicos* ✉ *€12.*

★ Mercado de Abastos de Santiago (*Santiago City Market*)
MARKET | Built in 1941 and designed by architect Joaquín Vaquero Palacios, this charming stone building houses a lively and bustling market. Open from 7 am until about 3 pm, the market gets particularly busy around 11, when locals come to buy food in preparation for the traditional midday meal. Whether you want to buy local cheeses and tinned fish to take home or merely ogle Galicia's bounty of shellfish and colorful fruits and vegetables, it's a destination not to be missed. ✉ *Rúa Ameás s/n* 🌐 *www.mercadodeabastosdesantiago.com* 🕒 *Closed Sun.*

Museo das Peregrinacións (*Pilgrimage Museum*)
MUSEUM | North of Acibechería (follow Ruela de Xerusalén) is the Museo das Peregrinacións, with Camino de Santiago iconography from sculptures and carvings to *azabache* (compact black coal, or jet) items. For an overview of the history of St. James, the cathedral, and the pilgrimage, as well as the Camino's role in the development of the city itself, this is a key visit. ✉ *Praza das Praterías 2* ☎ *981/566110* 🌐 *museoperegrinacions.xunta.gal* 🎫 *€3 (free Sat. afternoon and Sun.)* 🕒 *Closed Mon. and some public holidays.*

Museo do Pobo Galego (*Galician Folk Museum*)
MUSEUM | Next door to the Centro Galego de Arte Contemporánea stands the medieval convent of San Domingos de Bonaval. The museum within includes photos, farm implements, traditional costumes, and other items illustrating aspects of traditional Galician life. The star attraction is the 13th-century self-supporting spiral granite staircase that still connects three floors. ✉ *San Domingos de Bonaval s/n* ☎ *981/583620* 🌐 *www.museodopobo.gal* 🎫 *€3 (free Sun.)* 🕒 *Closed Mon.*

Pazo de Xelmírez (*Palace of Archbishop Xelmírez*)
CASTLE/PALACE | Step into this rich 12th-century building to view an unusual example of Romanesque civic architecture, with a cool, clean, vaulted dining hall. The little figures carved on the corbels in this graceful, 100-foot-long space are drinking, eating, and listening to music with great medieval gusto. Each is different, so stroll around for a tableau of mealtime merriment. ■ **TIP→ The palace is attached to the cathedral. However, the entrance varies—it's best to ask at the cathedral museum where to enter the Pazo de Xelmírez.** ✉ *Praza do Obradoiro* ☎ *981/552985* 🌐 *www.catedraldesantiago.es* 🎫 *€6, includes cathedral museum.*

Praza do Obradoiro
PLAZA | This vast square is presided over by the intricate baroque facade of the cathedral. Look out for the stone slab in the center, which indicates "kilometer zero" on the pilgrimage trail. It is also the setting for the spectacular fireworks display on July 24 (the eve of St. James's Day). Traffic free, and flanked on all sides by historical buildings—including the 16th-century Hostal de los Reyes Católicos—it is a unique place to soak up the city's atmosphere. ✉ *Santiago de Compostela.*

🍴 Restaurants

★ Abastos 2.0
$$$$ | **TAPAS** | "From the market to the plate" is the philosophy here, where the chefs start and finish the day with an empty larder and a blank menu. Ingredients are handpicked at market each morning and crafted into impeccable dishes bursting with fresh flavors and new ideas. **Known for:** inventive tapas; market-fresh ingredients; contemporary design. [$] *Average main: €25* ✉ *Casetas 13–18, Pl. de Abastos s/n* ☎ *654/015937* 🌐 *www.abastosdouspuntocero.es* 💳 *No credit cards* 🕒 *Closed Sun.*

Santiago de Compostela's Praza do Obradoiro

Bierzo Enxebre

$$ | SPANISH | Tucked behind the cathedral, this tapas bar specializes in products from El Bierzo, a *comarca* (subdivision) in Castile-León, either in the animated bar or in one of the stone-walled dining rooms. Visitors stopping in for a drink at the bar can expect a generous portion of free tapas, while the menu has a selection of grilled meats, *revueltos* (scrambled eggs with a variety of toppings), cold meats, and cheeses. **Known for:** food and wine from El Bierzo; good-value prix-fixe lunch menu; grilled meat. $ *Average main: €15* ⊠ *Rúa La Troia 10* ☎ *981/581909* ⊕ *www.bierzoenxebre.es* ▭ *No credit cards* ⊙ *No dinner Sun.*

Carretas

$$$$ | SEAFOOD | This casual spot for fresh Galician seafood is around the corner from the Hostal de los Reyes Católicos, and the specialty here is shellfish. Start with a plate of melt-in-your-mouth battered mini-scallops, then, for the full experience, order the *variado de mariscos*, a comprehensive platter of langostinos, king prawns, crab, and goose barnacles, a white or gray crustacean found in deep waters. **Known for:** fresh seafood; lively atmosphere; variado de mariscos platter. $ *Average main: €25* ⊠ *Rúa das Carretas 21* ☎ *981/563111* ⊕ *www.restaurantecarretas.com* ⊙ *No dinner Sun. Closed Mon.*

Casa Marcelo

$$$$ | FUSION | Fusing traditional Galician cooking with varying international influences including Japan, Mexico, and Peru, each dish is prepared in an open-plan kitchen while the jovial dining area—always full and always loud—is made up of long communal tables. As all creations are intended to be shared, the fact that diners sit at communal tables only adds to the immersive experience. **Known for:** fusion tapas; no bookings; extremely popular. $ *Average main: €30* ⊠ *Rúa Hortes 1* ☎ *981/558580* ⊕ *www.casa-marcelo.net* ⊙ *Closed Sun. and Mon.*

La Bodeguilla de San Roque

$$ | TAPAS | This is one of Santiago's favorite spots for *tapeo* (tapas grazing)

Santiago de Compostela

KEY

- **1** Sights
- **1** Restaurants
- **1** Hotels
- **i** Tourist Information

and *chiquiteo* (wine sampling); it's just a five-minute walk from the cathedral. The traditional bar area takes center stage, playing host to locals, pilgrims, and tourists alike, all gathering for wine, Iberian cured meats, cheeses, and seasonal dishes. **Known for:** tapas; wine; lively crowd. $ *Average main: €15* ✉ *C. San Roque 13* ☎ *981/564379* ⊕ *www. labodeguilladesanroque.com* ▤ *No credit cards.*

O Curro da Parra

$$ | SPANISH | Located directly across from the market, this lively, two-floor restaurant has exposed brick walls, wooden tables, and gastronomic delicacies such as *menestra crujiente de verduras y algas, pesto de cacahuete y mayonesa de wasabi* (crunchy vegetable–and-seaweed warm salad with peanut pesto sauce and wasabi mayo), *langostinos, pil-pil, jugo de sus cabezas, sal de ajo, jalapeños y cebollino* (king prawns, garlic salt, chili peppers, and spring onion), and *croquetas de jamón ibérico* (croquettes made with Iberian ham). **Known for:** king prawns; pork belly; wine list. $ *Average main: €17* ✉ *Rúa Travesa 20* ☎ *981/556059* ⊕ *www.ocurrodaparra. com* ⊙ *Closed Mon.*

Restaurante A Tafona

$$$ | SPANISH | Located a block away from the Mercado de Abastos, Santiago's premier food market, this excellent restaurant serves tapas and more substantial dishes made exclusively from seasonal, locally sourced ingredients. The chefs are relentlessly inventive, serving up traditional Galician specialties with an avant-garde touch in the modern, minimalist dining room with exposed stone walls. **Known for:** creative menu; traditional Galician specialties; garden tomatoes with tuna and figs. $ *Average main: €18* ✉ *Virxe da Cerca 7* ☎ *981/562314* ⊕ *www.restauranteatafona.com* ⊙ *Closed Mon. No dinner Sun.*

★ Restaurante Filigrana

$$$$ | SPANISH | Although the cheery yellow walls, crystal chandeliers, and carefully chosen antique furniture may evoke a traditional French bistro, the food prepared by this restaurant attached to the Hotel Spa Relais & Châteaux A Quinta da Auga is undeniably Galician. Try delicacies such as Galician chestnut cream soup, fresh-caught *merluza* (hake), or bay scallops roasted in their shells with garlic parsley oil. **Known for:** reputation as one of the best restaurants in Galicia; good-value lunch menu; exquisitely presented seafood. $ *Average main: €25* ✉ *Hotel Spa Relais & Châteaux A Quinta da Auga, Paseo da Amaia 23B* ☎ *981/534636* ⊕ *www.aquintadaauga. com.*

Hotels

Hotel Costa Vella

$ | B&B/INN | At this classically Galician inn, there's a perfect little garden and views of red-tile rooftops, the baroque convent of San Francisco, and the green hills beyond (ask for a garden view). **Pros:** charming views; ideal location; warm, accommodating staff. **Cons:** creaky floors; thin walls and noise from other rooms carries; no elevator. $ *Rooms from: €85* ✉ *Rúa Porta da Pena 17* ☎ *981/569530* ⊕ *www.costavella.com* ⤳ *14 rooms* ⊙ *No meals.*

Hotel Monumento San Francisco

$$$ | HOTEL | Contemporary stained-glass windows add a touch of pizzazz to the solemn interior of this converted 13th-century convent, adjoining the church of the same name. **Pros:** indoor swimming pool and Jacuzzi; easily accessible by car; very tidy. **Cons:** a bit too quiet at times; decor a bit dated; can get a bit chilly. $ *Rooms from: €150* ✉ *Campillo San Francisco 3* ☎ *981/581634* ⊕ *www.sanfranciscohm.com* ⤳ *81 rooms* ⊙ *No meals.*

★ Hotel Spa Relais & Châteaux A Quinta da Auga

$$$$ | **HOTEL** | Tastefully converted from a 14th-century printing factory, this elegantly restored building is surrounded by manicured gardens, with a view of the burbling Río Sar. Adorned with French crystal chandeliers and carefully restored antique furniture—handpicked by the owner for each room—and managed with exquisite attention to detail, this illustrious hotel feels both classic and fresh at once. **Pros:** excellent restaurant; warm, professional, and attentive staff; designer spa. **Cons:** a 10-minute car ride from the center of Santiago de Compostela; Wi-Fi spotty in some rooms; additional charge for the spa. [$] *Rooms from: €186* ✉ *Paseo da Amaia 23B* ☎ *981/534636* 🌐 *www.aquintadaauga.com* 🛏 *61 rooms* 🍴 *Free Breakfast.*

★ Parador de Santiago de Compostela: Hostal dos Reis Católicos

$$$$ | **HOTEL** | One of the parador chain's most highly regarded hotels, this 15th-century masterpiece, once a royal hostel and hospital for sick pilgrims, has a mammoth baroque doorway that gives way to austere courtyards of box hedge and simple fountains, and to rooms furnished with antiques, some with canopy beds. **Pros:** views of Praza do Obradoiro; excellent cuisine; fascinating collection of antiques and paintings. **Cons:** confusing corridors; often filled with people on guided tours; pricey. [$] *Rooms from: €284* ✉ *Praza do Obradoiro 1* ☎ *981/582200* 🌐 *www.parador.es* 🛏 *137 rooms* 🍴 *Free Breakfast.*

Pazo Cibrán

$ | **B&B/INN** | This comfortable 18th-century Galician manor house, 7 km (4 miles) from Santiago de Compostela, has an antiques-packed living room that overlooks gardens with camellias, magnolias, palms, vines, and a bamboo walk. **Pros:** personal hospitality; authentic and stately country house; delightful gardens. **Cons:** inaccessible without a car; poor local dining options; only open for groups November–March. [$] *Rooms from: €70* ✉ *San Xulián de Sales s/n, Vedra* ✥ *Take N525 toward Ourense from Santiago and turn right at Km 11, after gas station* ☎ *981/511515* 🌐 *www.pazocibran.com* 🛏 *11 rooms* 🍴 *No meals.*

Local Lingo

In the Gallego language, the Castilian Spanish *plaza* (town square) is *praza* and the Castilian *playa* (beach) is *praia*. Closer to Portuguese than to Castilian Spanish, Gallego is the language of nearly all road signs in Galicia.

Nightlife

Santiago's nightlife peaks on Thursday night, because many students spend weekends at home with their families. For up-to-date info on concerts, films, and clubs, pick up the monthly *Compostela Capital Cultural,* available at the main tourist office on Rúa do Vilar, or visit the official tourism website (🌐 *www.santiagoturismo.com*). Bars and seafood-themed tapas joints line the old streets south of the cathedral, particularly **Rúa do Franco, Rúa da Raiña,** and **Rúa do Vilar.** A great first stop, especially if you haven't eaten dinner, is **Rúa de San Clemente,** off the Praza do Obradoiro, where several bars offer two or three plates of tapas free with each drink.

BARS

Casa das Crechas

BARS/PUBS | Drink to Galicia's Celtic roots here, with live music and Celtic wood carvings hanging from thick stone walls, while dolls of playful Galician witches ride their brooms above the bar. ✉ *Vía Sacra 3* ☎ *981/560751.*

Modus Vivendi

BARS/PUBS | Galicia's oldest pub is also one of its most unusual: Modus Vivendi is in a former stable. The old stone feeding trough is now a low table, and instead of stairs you walk on ridged stone inclines designed for the former occupants—horses and cattle. On weekends the bar hosts live music (jazz, Spanish, Celtic) and sometimes storytelling. ⊠ *Praza Feixóo 1* ☎ *607/804140.*

O Filandón

TAPAS BARS | Venture forth through the narrow cheese shop and you'll discover a cozy bar in the back, where an inviting log fire burns on chilly evenings, and pilgrims gather and swap stories and pin handwritten notes to the walls (there are literally thousands). The free *pinchos* (snacks) are more than generous with hunks of freshly baked bread, cold meats, and cheese standard with every drink. ⊠ *Rua Acibecheria 6.*

CAFÉS

Santiago is a great city for coffee drinking and people-watching. Most of the cafés are clustered around the cathedral, in the casco antiguo, especially on Rúa Caldería and Rúa do Vilar.

Café Casino

CAFES—NIGHTLIFE | Upholstered armchairs, mirrors, and wood paneling make this atmospheric Art Nouveau café feel like an elegant and comfortable library. ⊠ *Rúa do Vilar 35* ☎ *981/577503* ⊕ *www.cafecasino.gal.*

Cafe Literarios

CAFES—NIGHTLIFE | Tranquil by day and lively at night, Cafe Literarios comes with colorful paintings, large windows, and a good supply of outdoor tables. It overlooks the plaza. ⊠ *Praza da Quintana 1* ☎ *981/565630.*

Iacobus

CAFES—NIGHTLIFE | Cozy Iacobus blends stone walls with contemporary wood trim and light fixtures; there's a glass cache of coffee beans in the floor.

Another branch is located at Rúa Caldería 42. ⊠ *Rúa da Senra 24* ☎ *981/585967.*

Shopping

Bolillos

TEXTILES/SEWING | In the fishing town of Camariñas, women fashion exquisite lace collars, scarves, and table linens. This is the best place to buy their work and watch some of it being crafted. ⊠ *Rúa Nova 40* ☎ *981/589776.*

Catrineta

FOOD/CANDY | This is a great place to buy locally produced gourmet preserves typical of the region, such as *bacalao a gallega "Los Peperetes"* (Galician cod), *bonito en aceite de oliva "La Pureza"* (bonito tuna fish in olive oil), *mejillones en escaveche* (mussels marinated in a vinegary pimiento sauce often used to preserve fish), and *calamares en su tinta* (squid in its ink). ⊠ *Ruela Altamira 2-baixo* ☎ *981/577544* ⊕ *www.catrineta.com.*

Sargadelos

CERAMICS/GLASSWARE | Galicia is known throughout Spain for its distinctive blue-and-white ceramics with bold modern designs, made in Cervo and O Castro. There is a wide selection at Sargadelos. It's often possible to watch artisans work at their workshops in Cervo and O Castro (weekdays 8:30–2), but call ahead to confirm. ⊠ *Rúa Nova 16* ☎ *981/581905* ⊕ *www.sargadelos.com* ⊙ *Closed Sun.*

Vide, Vide!

WINE/SPIRITS | The definitive place to buy, taste, and learn about Galician wines, this shop is well stocked with a wide range of wine of various types and vintages from local *bodegas* (wineries) across the region. ⊠ *Rúa Fonte de Sano Antonio 10-baixo* ☎ *981/582911* ⊕ *www.videvide.net.*

Ourense and La Ribeira Sacra

105 km (65 miles) southeast of Santiago de Compostela, 95 km (59 miles) east of Vigo.

Despite the uninspiring backdrop of Ourense's new town, Galicia's third-largest city has bubbling thermal springs and an attractive medieval quarter whose animated streets, tapas bars, and plazas come alive on weekends. A smattering of notable historical monuments includes the colossal arches of the Ponte Vella spanning the Río Miño and the 13th-century Cathedral of San Martino. Ourense is a good starting point for exploring the surrounding dramatic landscapes of the Ribeira Sacra (Sacred Riverbank) and Cañon do Sil (Sil River Canyon). This less explored region of interior Galicia is dotted with vineyards, Romanesque churches, and monasteries. Well worth a visit or a short stay is the Parador de Santo Estevo, converted from the Benedictine 10th-century Monasterio de Santo Estevo and perched high above the spectacular scenery of the Cañon do Sil.

GETTING HERE AND AROUND
RENFE and Monbus offer frequent services to Ourense from Santiago and Vigo in less than two hours. The A52 links Ourense to Vigo and Pontevedra, and the AG53 with Santiago.

CONTACTS Ourense Turismo ✉ *Isabel la Católica 2* ☎ *988/366064* ⊕ *www.turismodeourense.gal.*

Sights

Thermal Baths
HOT SPRINGS | Several hot springs along the Minho River at varying temperatures draw visitors from far and wide and are ideal for soaking weary muscles on the pilgrim trail. Some are free and others charge a small entrance fee. There is a tourist train that stops at the main baths, such as A Chavasqueira and Outariz. ✉ *A Chavasqueira Thermal Baths, Campo da Feira s/n* ⊕ *www.turismodeourense.gal.*

Hotels

Hotel Carrís Cardenal Quevedo
$$ | HOTEL | Offering stylish city-chic accommodations, this hotel is in a handy location for Ourense's shopping district, restaurants, and lively tapas scene and is only a five-minute stroll from the historical quarter. **Pros:** well positioned for both shopping district and historical quarter; restaurant serves regional cuisine; modern and spotless. **Cons:** expensive breakfast; tight parking space; uninspiring views. $ *Rooms from: €105* ✉ *Rúa Cardenal Quevedo 28–30* ☎ *988/375523* ⊕ *www.carrishoteles.com* ▤ *No credit cards* ⇌ *39 rooms* ⦿ *No meals.*

★ Parador de Santo Estevo
$$$ | HOTEL | Clinging to the edge of the Cañon do Sil, this parador, carefully built into the colossal 12th-century Benedictine Monasterio de Santo Estevo, stands out for its atmospheric setting and spectacular vistas. **Pros:** magnificent setting with views; historical sanctuary surrounded by nature; spa on-site. **Cons:** mediocre food; can get booked up by wedding parties; remote. $ *Rooms from: €150* ✉ *Monasterio de Santo Estevo* ✛ *Off CV323 beyond Luintra, 26 km (16 miles) northeast of Ourense* ☎ *988/010110* ⊕ *www.parador.es* ▤ *No credit cards* ⊙ *Closed Dec.–Feb.* ⇌ *77 rooms* ⦿ *No meals.*

Lugo

102 km (63 miles) east of Santiago de Compostela.

Just off the A6 freeway, Galicia's oldest provincial capital is most notable for its 2-km (1½-mile) **Roman wall.** These beautifully preserved ramparts completely surround the streets of the old town. The walkway on top has good views. The baroque *ayuntamiento* (town hall) has a magnificent rococo facade overlooking the tree-lined **Praza Maior** (Plaza Mayor). There's a good view of the Río Miño valley from the **Parque Rosalía de Castro,** outside the Roman walls near the cathedral, which is a mixture of Romanesque, Gothic, baroque, and neoclassical styles.

GETTING HERE AND AROUND

RENFE runs eight trains per day to and from A Coruña, a journey of 1½–2 hours. Several daily ALSA buses connect Lugo to Santiago de Compostela, Oviedo, and Gijón.

CONTACTS Estación de Autobuses Lugo ✉ *Prazo da Constitución s/n.* **Estación de Tren Lugo** ✉ *Pl. Conde de Fontao s/n* ☎ *912/320320 RENFE* 🌐 *www.renfe.com.*

VISITOR INFORMATION

CONTACTS Ourense Turismo ✉ *Isabel la Católica 2, Ourense* ☎ *988/366064* 🌐 *www.turismodeourense.gal.*

👁 Sights

City Walls

PROMENADE | Declared a UNESCO World Heritage Site, the Roman walls encircling Lugo, built in the 3rd century, provide a picturesque 2-km (1-mile) walk and the best bird's-eye views of the town. Comprised of 85 towers and 10 gates, the walls have four staircases and two ramps providing access to the top. ✉ *Lugo.*

🍴 Restaurants

Mesón de Alberto

$$$ | **SPANISH** | A hundred meters from the cathedral, this cozy venue has excellent Galician fare and professional service. The bar and adjoining bodega serve plenty of cheap *raciones* (appetizers). **Known for:** small size, so reservations recommended; authentic Galician food; local cheeses with quince jelly. [$] *Average main: €20* ✉ *C. de la Cruz 4* ☎ *982/228310* 🕒 *No dinner Sun. and Mon. Closed Tues.*

🛏 Hotels

Casa Grande da Fervenza

$ | **B&B/INN** | This graceful 17th- to 19th-century manor house, set in a forested area on the banks of the Río Miño 14 km (8 miles) south of Lugo, has rustic but comfortable rooms. **Pros:** intimate feel; excellent restaurant; great base for hiking. **Cons:** a bit out of town; rooms are dark and could stand to be refurbished; creaky floor boards and noise from other rooms carries. [$] *Rooms from: €76* ✉ *Ctra. Lugo–Paramo, Km 11, O Corgo* ☎ *982/151610* 🌐 *www.fervenza.com* 🛏 *9 rooms* 🍽 *No meals.*

Muxia

75 km (47 miles) northwest of Santiago de Compostela, 30 km (18 miles) north of Fisterra.

A small fishing village far off the beaten path, surrounded by the stunning rocky cliffs and virgin beaches of the Costa da Morte, close to great hiking trails and lush green forests, Muxia is the perfect destination for a rural getaway.

👁 Sights

O Camiño dos Faros (*Way of the Lighthouses*)

LOCAL INTEREST | For a pleasant excursion, the Faro de Cabo Turiñan, Faro Punto de Barca, and Faro de Cabo Vilán, three lighthouses in the region of Muxia, can all be visited by car within an hour and a half and offer extraordinary views of the rocky cliffs and churning waters below that have earned this part of Galicia its nickname, the Costa da Morte. The lighthouses are part of a 200-km (124-mile) hiking route, the Way of the Lighthouses, that begins in Malpica and ends in

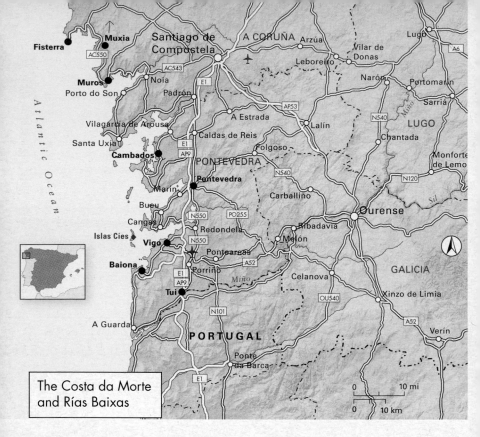

The Costa da Morte
and Rías Baixas

Finiesterre. Start with the Faro de Cabo Turiñan, which guards a narrow peninsula that marks the westernmost point of continental Europe. Just a 20-minute drive away is the Faro Punto de Barca, a stone lighthouse built in 1926 alongside the 16th-century Sanctuario de Virxe da Barca (Sanctuary of the Virgin of the Boat). Finish with Faro de Cabo Vilán, a lighthouse with unique architecture that emerges seamlessly from the surrounding red rock; it was the first in Spain to run by electricity. ⊠ *Muxia* ⊕ *www. caminodosfaros.com/en.*

Beaches

Playa Nemiña
BEACH—SIGHT | A favorite with surfers and sport fisherman, this virgin beach is buffered from the wind by the green forested hills on either side. Still relatively undiscovered by tourists, this semiprivate beach is an excellent place for a romantic stroll at sunset, or a midday picnic on the fine white sand. **Amenities:** showers. **Best for:** sunset; surfing; walking. ⊠ *Muxia.*

🛏 Hotels

Hotel Rústico Fontequeiroso
$ | **B&B/INN** | Surrounded by green hills and pine forests, just a five-minute drive from the stunning, pristine beaches of the Costa da Morte, this small bed-and-breakfast is the ideal base from which to explore Galicia's natural bounty. **Pros:** beautiful surroundings; excellent local fare; bicycles available for guests. **Cons:** remote; lunch and dinner must

be prebooked; no amenities nearby. [$] *Rooms from: €80* ✉ *Lugar de Queiroso, Nemiña* ☎ *981/748946* 🌐 *www.casafontequeiroso.com* 🛏 *6 rooms* 🍴 *Free Breakfast* 💳 *No credit cards.*

Fisterra

50 km (31 miles) west of Santiago de Compostela, 75 km (48 miles) southwest of A Coruña.

There was a time when this lonely, windswept outcrop over raging waters was thought to be the end of the earth—the *finis terrae.* In fact, the official westernmost point of Europe is in Portugal. Despite this, many Camino pilgrims choose to continue the tradition of continuing on to the "end of the earth" from Santiago de Compostela to triumphantly finish at Fisterra's windswept lighthouse, beyond which there is nothing but the boundless expanse of the Atlantic Ocean. Fisterra all but shuts down in winter, but in summer it's a pleasant seaside resort with an attractive harbor.

VISITOR INFORMATION

CONTACTS Fisterra Turismo ✉ *Calle Real 2* ☎ *981/740781.*

Sights

Santa María das Areas

RELIGIOUS SITE | Aside from legends, another draw in this tiny seaside town is its main plaza and the 12th-century church of Santa María das Areas. Romanesque, Gothic, and baroque elements combine in an impressive (but gloomy) facade. ✉ *Manuel Lago País s/n.*

Hotels

Hotel Naturaleza y Playa Mar da Ardora

$$ | **HOTEL** | Just a two-minute walk from Fisterra's Mar de Fora Beach, this small boutique hotel is surrounded by gardens, with stunning views of the beach. **Pros:** exquisite views of the sea; spa and wellness center; dinner on the terrace. **Cons:** expensive compared to other regional options; noise carries between the rooms; outside the town center. [$] *Rooms from: €110* ✉ *Playa de la Potiña 15* ☎ *667/641304* 🌐 *www.hotelmardaardora.com* 🛏 *6 rooms* 🍴 *No meals.*

Muros

65 km (40 miles) southwest of Santiago de Compostela, 55 km (34 miles) southeast of Fisterra.

Muros is a popular summer resort with lovely, arcaded streets framed by Gothic arches. The quiet back alleys of the old town reveal some well-preserved Galician granite houses, but the real action takes place when fishing boats return to dock from the mussel-breeding platforms that dot the bay. At around 6 pm, a siren signals the start of the *lonja* (fish auction), to which anyone is welcome, although you need a special license to buy. Trays spilling over with slimy octopus or cod line the floor, covered in a sheen of salt water, squid ink, and fish blood; the favored footwear is knee-high rubber boots. Good beaches nearby include Praia de San Francisco and Praia de Area.

GETTING HERE AND AROUND

Monbus runs frequent buses between Muros and Santiago de Compostela and A Coruña. By car, take the AP9 north from Vigo and Pontevedra (just under 2 hours away) or the AC550 west from Santiago de Compostela and A Coruña (1½ hours).

VISITOR INFORMATION

CONTACTS Muros Turismo ✉ *C. Curro da Praza 1* ☎ *981/826050.*

Wine Tasting in Rías Baixas

Albariño Wine

The Rías Baixas region, in the southern part of Galicia, is the most important Denomination of Origin (D.O.) in the province and is the largest global producer of Albariño, a crisp, young, aromatic white wine that has earned international prestige. Albariño has been compared to Riesling for its pungent acidity, to Petit Manseng and Viognier for fruity qualities suggesting peach and apricot, and to Pinot Gris for its distinctive floral bouquet. Classically paired with Galician seafood dishes, Albariño's ripe fruit flavor and relatively low alcohol content also make it an excellent complement to more exotic fare, such as Indian and Thai food.

The Rías Baixas vineyards and bodegas are spread throughout the Pontevedra region, with a particularly high density in Cambados, the capital of the Albariño-producing region. With more than 6,500 growers and 20,000 individual vineyard plots in Rías Baixas, planning a wine trip to the region can feel overwhelming. **Ruta do Viño Rías Baixas** (⊕ www. rutadelvinoriasbaixas.com/en) and **Rías Baixas Wines** (⊕ www.

riasbaixaswines.com/index.php) have information about wine tasting in the Rías Baixas region, including a detailed explanation of Albariño, a list of wineries, and places to stay. Guiados Pontevedra and North West Iberia Wine Tours can arrange a tour, but you don't need to hire a guide to enjoy wine tasting in the region. Head to these bodegas in Pontevedra: Adega Eidos and Pazo Baión; or these in Cambados: Don Oligario and Palacio de Fefiñánes, for a do-it-yourself tour.

Wine Tours

Guiados Pontevedra You can arrange custom tours of two to three bodegas in the region, including an English-speaking guide, for €90 for four hours (minimum two people). ☎ 654/222081 ⊕ www.guiadospontevedra.com ✉ From €90.

North West Iberia Wine Tours One- or three-day wine tours include transport, admissions, gourmet lunch, and wine tasting at two different locations, as well as a visit to a local pazo and camellia garden. ✉ C. Enrique Marinas Romero 30–5H, A Coruña ☎ 881/879910 ⊕ www.northwestiberi-awinetours.com ✉ From €180.

Cambados

34 km (21 miles) north of Pontevedra, 61 km (37 miles) southwest of Santiago de Compostela.

This breezy seaside town has a charming, almost entirely residential old quarter and is the center for the full-bodied and fruity Albariño, one of Spain's best white wines. The impressive main square, **Praza de Fefiñanes,** is bordered by an imposing bodega.

GETTING HERE AND AROUND

Cambados is less than an hour from Santiago de Compostela, to the north, and Vigo and Pontevedra, to the south, via the AP9.

Sights

Bodegas del Palacio de Fefiñanes

WINERY/DISTILLERY | Set in a 16th-century stone palace, this illustrious winery has been involved in wine making since the 17th century and crafts classic Albariños, such as the full-bodied and powerful 1583 Albariño de Fefiñanes, a ripe, fruity wine aged one to five years in Bordeaux barrels. A 30-minute guided tour without a tasting costs €3; a 45-minute guided tour with a tasting of Albariño de Fefiñanes costs €6; and an hour-long tour with two wine tastings costs €10. Reservations advised. ⊠ *Pl. de Fefiñanes* ☎ *986/542204* ⊕ *www.fefinanes.com* ✉ *From €3.*

Don Olegario

WINERY/DISTILLERY | This award-winning family-run winery offers an intimate guided visit of the winery, followed by a tasting on their terrace, with a view of the vineyards. A 45-minute guided tour costs €6 including two wine tastings (€10 with tapas). ⊠ *Refoxos, Corbillón* ☎ *986/520886* ⊕ *www.donolegario.com* ✉ *From €6.*

Pazo de Rubianes

BUILDING | The jewel of this property is the camellia garden, one of the largest and most impressive collections of flowers in the world. The camellias bloom November–May, with peak viewing season February–April. The 15th-century manor house is decadently furnished and also worth a visit, as is the attached bodega and chapel. Gourmet picnic baskets with local products can be arranged for those who want to enjoy a leisurely lunch amid the grapevines and flowers. There are also guided tours available, which last about two hours and include the gardens, winery, pazo, chapel, and a wine tasting. ⊠ *Rúa do Pazo 7* ☎ *986/510534* ⊕ *www. pazoderubianes.com* ✉ *Self-guided tour (by appointment) free, guided tour €16.*

🍴 Restaurants

★ Yayo Daporta

$$$$ | SPANISH | The chef, Yayo Daporta, for whom the restaurant is named, is something of a local celebrity and a true food artist who produces gastronomic masterpieces, such as a cocktail glass filled with cauliflower mousse and fresh-caught local clams with a drizzle of basil-infused olive oil and coffee vinaigrette. Inventive dishes include scallop carpaccio and tempura clam on an algae crisp with clam foam and greens. **Known for:** locally admired chef; inventive dishes; fresh clams. 🛉 *Average main: €48* ⊠ *Rúa Hospital 7* ☎ *986/526062* ⊕ *www.yayodaporta.com* ⊘ *Closed Mon. and Nov. 14–28. No dinner Sun.*

Hotels

Parador de Cambados (El Albariño)

$$$ | HOTEL | This airy mansion's rooms are warmly furnished with wrought-iron lamps, area rugs, and full-length wood shutters over small-pane windows. **Pros:** easily accessible; comfortable rooms; excellent dining. **Cons:** Wi-Fi is patchy in some rooms; old-fashioned room decor; limited parking. 🛉 *Rooms from: €180* ⊠ *Paseo Calzada s/n* ☎ *986/542250* ⊕ *www.parador.es* ⊘ *Closed Jan.* ✍ *58 rooms* 🍽 *Free Breakfast.*

★ Quinta de San Amaro

$$$ | HOTEL | This stylish rural hotel is a great base for exploring the surrounding wine region—a stay here includes gorgeous vineyard views as well as a local winery visit and wine tasting. **Pros:** excellent service and great restaurant; good base for exploring local wineries; beautiful views. **Cons:** need a car to get here; somewhat remote at a 15-minute drive from Cambados; small swimming pool. 🛉 *Rooms from: €130* ⊠ *Rúa San Amaro 6* ☎ *630/877590* ⊕ *www.quintadesanamaro.com* ✍ *14 rooms* 🍽 *Free Breakfast.*

Nightlife

Bar Laya

BARS/PUBS | This wine bar is easy to spot day or night, because it's always filled with a youngish crowd. Its stone walls and close quarters feel very inviting, and one of its corners is used for a wineshop. ⊠ *Rúa Real 13* ☎ *986/542436.*

Shopping

Cucadas

CRAFTS | Head to this crafts shop for its large selection of baskets, copper items, and lace. ✉ *Praza de Fefiñáns 8* ☎ *986/542511.*

Pontevedra

135 km (84 miles) southeast of Fisterra, 59 km (37 miles) south of Santiago de Compostela.

At the head of its ría, right where it joins the sea, Pontevedra is a delightful starting point for exploring the Rías Baixas. Its well-preserved old quarter is a dense network of pedestrian-only streets and handsome plazas flanked with elegant stone buildings, many of which are dressed in cascading flowers in spring and summer. The city got its start as a Roman settlement (its name comes from an old Roman bridge over the Río Lérez). As a powerful base for fishing and international trade, Pontevedra was a major presence in the Atlantic in the 16th century. Nowadays, its streets and plazas are awash with bars and restaurants, and it can get very busy on weekends. It also has the only operating *plaza de toros* (bullring) in Galicia.

GETTING HERE AND AROUND

RENFE and Monbus offer quick, frequent service between Vigo and Pontevedra, a half-hour journey; the same bus and train routes also link Pontevedra to Santiago de Compostela and A Coruña to the north along the AP9.

CONTACTS Estación de Autobuses Pontevedra ✉ *Calle de la Estación s/n* ☎ *986/852408* ⊕ *www.autobusesponte-vedra.com.*

VISITOR INFORMATION

CONTACTS Turismo Pontevedra ✉ *Casa da Luz, Praza da Verdura s/n* ☎ *986/090890.*

Sights

Adega Eidos

WINERY/DISTILLERY | This sleek winery overlooks the beautiful Sanxenxo harbor, and produces modern takes on traditional Albariño harvested from 50-year-old ungrafted vines grown on granite slopes on the westernmost edge of Rías Baixas and fermented with natural yeasts. A one-hour tour of the bodega with three wine and liquor tastings, plus a snack, costs €3.50, with gourmet preserves €7.50; €8 includes a bottle of wine. ✉ *Padriñán 65, Sanxenxo* ☎ *986/690009* ⊕ *www.adegaeidos.com* 🍷 *From €4.*

Pazo Baión

WINERY/DISTILLERY | Surrounded by lush Albariño vineyards, this classic 15th-century stone Galician manor house stands in pleasant contrast to its 100-year-old boutique wine cellar, built in an art deco style. Winemaker José Hidalgo produces a silky Albariño with notes of citrus and floral aromas. The 60-minute tour costs €10 and includes one wine tasting; a tasting of three wines costs €15. Reservations are required. ✉ *Abelleira 6, Vilanova de Arousa* ☎ *986/543535* ⊕ *www.pazobaion.com* 🍷 *From €10.*

Real Basilica de Santa María la Mayor

RELIGIOUS SITE | The 16th-century seafarers' basilica has lovely, sinuous vaulting and, at the back of the nave, a Romanesque portal. There's also an 18th-century Christ by the Galician sculptor Ferreiro. ✉ *Av. de Santa María 24* 🍷 *Free.*

🍴 Restaurants

Casa Solla

$$$$ | **SPANISH** | Pepe Solla brings Galicia's bounty to his terrace garden restaurant, 2 km (1 mile) outside of town toward O Grove. Try the *menú de degustación* (tasting menu) to sample a selection of regional favorites, such as *lomo de caballa* (grilled mackerel), *caldo gallego de chorizo* (Galician chorizo sausage

soup), *merluza con acelga* (cod with chard), or *jarrete de cordero* (sliced lamb shank). **Known for:** award-winning menu; presentation; tasting menu. [$] *Average main: €80* ✉ *Av. Sineiro 7, San Salvador de Poio* ☎ *986/872884* 🕒 *Closed Mon. No dinner Thurs. and Sun.*

Hotels

Parador de Pontevedra (Casa del Barón)
$$$ | **HOTEL** | A 16th-century manor house in the heart of the old quarter, this rather dark parador has guest rooms with recessed windows embellished with lace curtains and large wooden shutters; some face a small rose garden. **Pros:** interesting collection of bric-a-brac; tranquil yet central location; free parking. **Cons:** confusing corridors; limited parking; gloomy rooms—a bit haunted house–ish. [$] *Rooms from: €140* ✉ *Rúa Barón 19* ☎ *986/855800* 🌐 *www.parador.es* 🛏 *47 rooms* 🍴 *No meals.*

Activities

GOLF

Campo de Golf Meis
GOLF | Set on top of the hilly plateau of Monte Castrove more than 1,640 feet above sea level, Campo de Golf de Meis is a public 18-hole course surrounded by a light pine forest, with a magnificent view of the white sandy beaches and glittering waters of Ría de Arousa below. The wide fairway is framed by stony pines and has six lakes that make for a more challenging game. It's also an excellent value. ✉ *Silván de Armenteira* ☎ *986/680400* 🌐 *www.campodegolf-meis.com* 🎫 *€28 weekdays, €40 weekends and public holidays* ⛳ *18 holes, 6849 yards, par 72.*

Ría de Vigo Golf Club
GOLF | The 18-hole Ría de Vigo Golf Club comes with breathtaking views overlooking the estuary and city. ✉ *San Lorenzo Domaio, Moaña* ☎ *986/327051* 🌐 *www.riadevigogolf.com* 🎫 *€70* ⛳ *18 holes, 6683 yards, par 72.*

Vigo

31 km (19 miles) south of Pontevedra, 90 km (56 miles) south of Santiago de Compostela.

Fishing is central to the livelihood of thousands who live and work in Vigo, and its fish market handles some of the largest quantities of fresh fish in Europe, which is consumed across the continent. From 10 to 3:30 daily, on **Rúa Pescadería** in the barrio called **La Piedra,** Vigo's famed *ostreras*—a group of rubber-gloved fisherwomen who have been peddling fresh oysters to passersby for more than 50 years—shuck the bushels of oysters hauled into port that morning. Competition has made them expert hawkers who cheerfully badger all who walk by their pavement stalls. When you buy half a dozen (for about €8), the women plate them and plunk a lemon on top; you can then take your catch into any nearby restaurant and turn it into a meal. A short stroll southwest of the old town brings you to the fishermen's barrio of **El Berbés. Ribera del Berbés,** facing the port, has several seafood restaurants, most with outdoor tables in summer.

GETTING HERE AND AROUND

A small airport connects Vigo to a handful of destinations, like Madrid and Barcelona, but trains and buses are your best bet for transportation within Galicia. Northbound RENFE trains leave on the hour for Pontevedra, Santiago de Compostela, and A Coruña, making stops at the smaller towns in between. Monbus and ALSA also connect Vigo to the same destinations via the AP9, while AUTNA runs a daily shuttle south to Porto and its international airport, a 2½-hour trip.

CONTACTS **Vigo Bus Station** ✉ *Av. de Madrid 57* ☎ *986/373411.* **Vigo Train**

The coastline of Baiona is one of the first things the crew of Columbus's ship the *Pinta* saw when they returned from their discovery of America.

Station ✉ *C. Areal s/n* ☎ *912/320320 REN-FE* ⊕ *www.renfe.com.*

VISITOR INFORMATION

CONTACTS Vigo ✉ *Estación Marítima de Ría, C. Cánovas del Castillo 3, Oficina 4* ☎ *986/224757.*

Sights

★ Islas Cíes

NATURE PRESERVE | The Cíes Islands, 35 km (21 miles) west of Vigo, are among Spain's best-kept secrets. They form a pristine nature preserve that's one of the last unspoiled refuges on the Spanish coast. Starting on weekends in May and then daily June–late September, **Naviera Mar de Ons** (*986/225272; www. mardeons.com*) runs about eight boats from Vigo's harbor (subject to weather conditions), returning later in the day, for the €18.50 round-trip fare (tickets must be booked in advance on the website). The 45-minute ride brings you to white-sand beaches surrounded by turquoise waters brimming with marine life; there's

also great birding. The only way to get around is your own two feet: it takes about an hour to cross the main island. If you want to stay overnight, there's a designated camping area. The tourist office has up-to-date information on timetables and crossings. ■**TIP**➜ **It is mandatory for travelers to the Cíes Islands to first obtain authorization from the Xunta de Galicia.** ✉ *Estación Marítima* ⊕ *www.campingis-lascies.com.*

MARCO (*Museum of Contemporary Art*) **MUSEUM** | Housed in a refurbished prison on Vigo's main shopping drag, this gallery hosts intriguing temporary exhibitions along with solo shows of featured artists. ✉ *C. del Príncipe 54* ☎ *986/113900* ⊕ *www.marcovigo.com* ✉ *Free* ⊗ *Closed Mon.*

Parque del Castro

CITY PARK | South of Vigo's old town, this is a quiet, stately park with sandy paths, palm trees, mossy embankments, and stone benches. Atop a series of steps are the remains of an old fort and a *mirador* (lookout) with fetching views of

Vigo's coastline and the Islas Cíes. Along its shady western side lies the Castro de Vigo, the remains of Vigo's first Celtic settlement, which dates back to the 3rd century BC. ✉ *Av. Marqués de Alcedo, between Praza de España and Praza do Rei* 🎫 *Free* 🕒 *Castro de Vigo closed Sun. and Mon.* ☞ *Reservations required for Castro de Vigo.*

🍴 Restaurants

Bar Cocedero La Piedra

$ | **SPANISH** | Elegant it may not be, but this jovial tapas bar is a perfect place to devour the freshest catch from the Rúa Pescadería fisherwomen, and it does a roaring lunch trade with Vigo locals. The chefs serve heaping plates of *mariscos* (shellfish) and scallops with roe at market prices; fresh and fruity Albariño is the beverage of choice. **Known for:** fresh seafood; front-row seats for oyster hawkers; simple, down-to-earth atmosphere. [$] *Average main: €10* ✉ *Rúa Pescadería 3* ☎ *986/431204.*

El Mosquito

$$$$ | **SPANISH** | Signed photos from the likes of KIng Juan Carlos and Julio Iglesias cover the walls of this elegant rose- and stone-wall restaurant, open since 1928. Specialties include *lenguado a la plancha* (grilled sole) and *navajas* (razor clams). **Known for:** seafood; caramel flan; extensive wine cellar. [$] *Average main: €25* ✉ *Praza da Pedra 4* ☎ *616/504544* 🌐 *elmosquitorestaurante.com* 🕒 *No dinner Sun.*

Tapas Areal

$$$ | **TAPAS** | This ample and lively bar flanked by ancient stone and exposed redbrick walls is a good spot for tapas and beer, as well as Albariños and Ribeiros. **Known for:** buzzing atmosphere; Albariños; tapas. [$] *Average main: €18* ✉ *C. México 36* ☎ *986/418643* 🕒 *Closed Sun.*

🛏 Hotels

Gran Hotel Nagari Boutique and Spa

$$$$ | **HOTEL** | A short walk from Vigo's pretty harbor, a major fishing port on Spain's northwest coast, this boutique hotel offers a welcoming, stylish lobby with polished surfaces and sleek lines, softened by thick gold brocade curtains and soft leather seating. **Pros:** a short stroll from the old town; rooftop pool with city and Atlantic views; excellent spa. **Cons:** parking additional cost; spa and pool additional cost; confusing panel controls in rooms. [$] *Rooms from: €220* ✉ *Pl. de Compostela 21* ☎ *986/211111* 🌐 *www.granhotelnagari.com* 🛏 *63 rooms.*

🏃 Activities

There are several horse-riding clubs in the hills around Vigo. The Galician Equestrian Federation is an excellent source of information. And golfers can work on their game at the nearby Ría de Vigo Golf Club.

HORSEBACK RIDING

Granja O Castelo

HORSEBACK RIDING | The Granja O Castelo conducts horseback rides along the pilgrimage routes to Santiago from O Cebreiro and Braga (Portugal). ✉ *Castelo 41, Ponte Caldelas* ☎ *986/425937, 608/381334* 🌐 *www.caminoacaballo.com.*

Baiona

12 km (8 miles) southwest of Vigo.

At the southern end of the AP9 freeway and the Ría de Vigo, Baiona (Bayona in Castilian) is a summer haunt of affluent gallegos. When Columbus's *Pinta* landed here in 1492, Baiona became the first town to receive the news of the discovery of the New World. Once a castle, **Monte Real** is one of Spain's most popular paradores; walk around the battlements for superb views. Inland from Baiona's waterfront is the jumble of streets that make up Paseo Marítima: head here for seafood restaurants and lively cafés and bars. Calle Ventura Misa is one of the main drags. On your way into or out of town, check out Baiona's **Roman bridge.** The best nearby beach is Praia de América, north of town toward Vigo.

GETTING HERE AND AROUND
ATSA buses leave every half hour from Vigo, bound for Baiona and Nigrán. By car, take the AG57 from Vigo to the north or the PO340 from Tui to the southeast.

 ## Hotels

★ Parador de Baiona
$$$$ | HOTEL | This baronial parador, positioned on a hill within the perimeter walls of a medieval castle, has plush rooms, some with balconies and ocean views toward the Islas Cíes. **Pros:** stupendous medieval architecture; views of the ría; luxurious bathrooms. **Cons:** especially pricey for rooms with sea views; occasional plumbing problems; dark rooms. $ *Rooms from: €290 ⊠ Av. Arquitecto Jesús Valverde ☎ 986/355000 ⊕ www.parador.es ⤳ 122 rooms ⦿ Free Breakfast.*

Pazo de Touza
$$ | HOTEL | This 16th-century stone manor house is surrounded by manicured gardens, with a terrace that looks out onto a hedge labyrinth. **Pros:** historical manor house; beautiful gardens; tranquil setting. **Cons:** 15-minute drive from Baiona; some traffic noise from a nearby road; can be booked out for weddings. $ *Rooms from: €110 ⊠ Rúa dos Pazos ☎ 986/383047 ⊕ www.pazodatouza.info ⤳ 8 rooms ⦿ No meals.*

Tui

14 km (9 miles) southeast of Baiona, 26 km (16 miles) south of Vigo.

The steep, narrow streets of Tui, rich with emblazoned mansions, suggest the town's past as one of the seven capitals of the Galician kingdom. Today it's an important border town; the mountains of Portugal are visible from the cathedral. Across the river in Portugal, the old fortress town of Valença contains reasonably priced shops, bars, restaurants, and a hotel with splendid views of Tui.

GETTING HERE AND AROUND
From Vigo, take the scenic coastal route PO552, which goes up the banks of the Río Miño along the Portuguese border or, if time is short, jump on the inland A55; both routes lead to Tui.

 ## Sights

Cathedral de Santa María de Tuí
RELIGIOUS SITE | A crucial building during the medieval wars between Castile and Portugal, Tuí's 13th-century cathedral looks like a fortress. The cathedral's majestic cloisters surround a lush formal garden. ⊠ *Pl. de San Fernando ☎ 986/600511 ⊕ www.catedraldetui.com.*

 ## Hotels

Parador de Tui
$$$ | HOTEL | This stately granite-and-chestnut hotel on the bluffs overlooking the Miño is filled with local art, and the rooms are furnished with antiques. **Pros:** enticing gardens; fine fish cuisine; swimming pool (seasonal). **Cons:** a bit of a walk from Tui proper; somewhat pricey; dark rooms. $ *Rooms from: €150 ⊠ Av. Portugal s/n ☎ 986/600300 ⊕ www. parador.es ⊗ Closed Jan.–mid-Feb. ⤳ 32 rooms ⦿ No meals.*

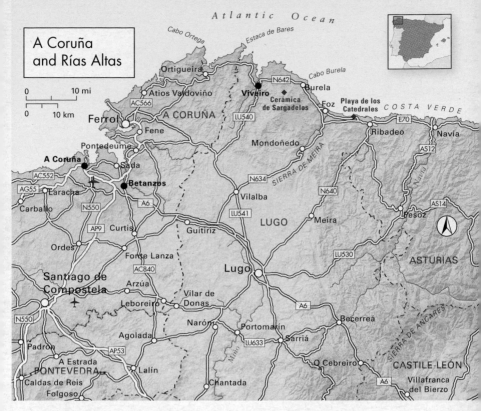

A Coruña and Rías Altas

Atlantic Ocean

Cabo Ortega

Estaca de Bares

Ortigueira

Cabo Burela

0   10 mi
0   10 km

Atios Valdoviño   Viveiro   Burela
AC566   Cerámica   Foz   Playa de los   COSTA VERDE
de Sargadelos   Catedrales

Ferrol

Fene   A CORUÑA   LU540   E70

Pontedeume   Mondoñedo   Ribadeo   Navía

A Coruña   Sada   AS12

AC552   N634   SIERRA DE MEIRA

AG55   Laracha   Betanzos   Meira   Pesoz

Carballo   N550   A6   Vilalba   N640   AS14

AP9   Curtis   LU541   LUGO

Ordes   Guitiríz   LU530   ASTURIAS

Fonte Lanza   AC840   Lugo

Santiago de   Arzúa

Compostela   Vilar de   A6   Becerreá

N550   Leboreiro   Donas   SIERRA DE ANCARES

Narón   Portomarín

Padrón   Agolada   LU633   Sarriá

A Estrada   AP53   Lalín   O Cebreiro   CASTILE-LEÓN

Caldas de Reis   PONTEVEDRA   Chantada   A6   Villafranca
del Bierzo

Folgoso

A Coruña

57 km (35 miles) north of Santiago de Compostela.

One of Spain's busiest ports, A Coruña is often (mistakenly) overlooked by travelers. While the weather can be fierce, wet, and windy, it does give way to bouts of sunshine (it's not uncommon to experience all in one day). This unpredictable weather, along with a thriving commercial center and intriguing historic quarter, gives the city and its people its unique, endearing personality. A Coruña takes pride in its gastronomy and there is a buzzing nightlife scene, as well as a host of interesting sights, including the world's oldest still-functioning lighthouse. Its shining jewel is the city's emblematic row of glass-enclosed, white-paned galleries on the houses that line the harbor—a remarkable sight when the light catches them on a sunny day.

GETTING HERE AND AROUND

The A9 motorway provides excellent access to and from Santiago de Compostela, Pontevedra, Vigo, and Portugal, while Spain's north coast and France are accessible along the N634.

Buses run every hour from A Coruña to Santiago. Trains also operate on an hourly basis to Santiago and Pontevedra from the city's San Cristóbal train station; Madrid can be reached in eight hours on high-speed Talgo trains.

Outside the old town, the city's local buses shuttle back and forth between the Dársena de la Marina seafront and more far-flung attractions, such as the Torre de Hércules lighthouse.

A Coruña is a major port town, but fashionistas might know it as where the first Zara clothing shop opened, back in 1975.

CONTACTS A Coruña Bus Station
✉ *Rúa Caballeros 21* ☎ *981/184335.* **A Coruña Train Station** ✉ *Av. Ferrocaril s/n* ☎ *912/320320* ⊕ *www.renfe.com.*

VISITOR INFORMATION

CONTACTS A Coruña ✉ *Oficina de Turismo, Pl. de María Pita 6* ☎ *981/923093* ⊕ *www.turismocoruna.com.*

 Sights

Castillo de San Antón

MUSEUM | At the northeastern tip of the old town is St. Anthony's Castle, a 16th-century fort that houses A Coruña's **Museum of Archaeology.** The collection includes remnants of the prehistoric Celtic culture that once thrived in these parts, including silver artifacts as well as pieces of the stone forts called *castros.* ✉ *Paseo Alcalde Francisco Vázquez 2* ☎ *981/189850* 🎟 *€2* ⏱ *Closed Mon.*

Iglesia de Santiago

RELIGIOUS SITE | This 12th-century church, the oldest church in A Coruña, was the first stop on the Camino Inglés (English route) toward Santiago de Compostela. Originally Romanesque, it's now a hodge-podge that includes Gothic arches, a baroque altarpiece, and two 18th-century rose windows. ✉ *Rúa do Parrote, 1.*

Paseo Marítimo

PROMENADE | To see why sailors once nicknamed A Coruña *la ciudad de cristal* (the glass city), stroll the Paseo Marítimo, said to be the longest seaside promenade in Europe. Although the congregation of boats is charming, the real sight is across the street: a long, gracefully curved row of houses. Built by fishermen in the 18th century, they face *away* from the sea—at the end of a long day, these men were tired of looking at the water. Nets were hung from the porches to dry, and fish was sold on the street below. When Galicia's first glass factory opened nearby, someone thought to enclose these porches in glass, like the latticed stern galleries of oceangoing galleons, to keep wind and rain at bay. The resulting emblematic **glass galleries** spread across the harbor and eventually throughout Galicia. ✉ *Paseo Marítimo.*

Plaza de María Pita

PLAZA | The focal point of the *ciudad vieja* (old town), this stirring plaza has a north side that's given over to the neoclassical **Palacio Municipal,** or city hall, built 1908–12 with three Italianate domes. The **monument** in the center, built in 1998, depicts the heroine Maior (María) Pita. When England's Sir Francis Drake arrived to sack A Coruña in 1589, the locals were only half finished building the defensive Castillo de San Antón, and a 13-day battle ensued. When María Pita's husband died, she took up his lance, slew the Briton who tried to plant the Union Jack here, and revived the exhausted coruñeses, inspiring other women to join the battle. The surrounding streets of the old town are a hive of activity, lined with tapas bars and shops. ✉ *A Coruña.*

Torre de Hércules

LIGHTHOUSE | Much of A Coruña sits on a peninsula, on the tip of which sits this city landmark and UNESCO World Heritage Site—the oldest still-functioning lighthouse in the world. First installed during the reign of Trajan, the Roman emperor born in Spain in AD 98, the lighthouse was rebuilt in the 18th century and looks strikingly modern; all that remains from Roman times are inscribed foundation stones. Scale the 245 steps for superb views of the city and coastline—if you're here on a summer weekend, the tower opens for views of city lights along the Atlantic. Lining the approach to the lighthouse are sculptures depicting figures from Galician and Celtic legends. ✉ *Av. de Navarra s/n* ☎ *981/223730* 🌐 *www.torredeherculesacoruna.es* 🎟 *€3 (free Mon.).*

Beaches

Playas Orzán and Riazor

BEACH—SIGHT | A Coruña's sweeping Paseo Marítimo overlooks two excellent, well-maintained beaches, Playa del Orzán and Playa de Riazor. These long curves of fine golden sand tend to be busy in summer with chattering groups of local families and friends enjoying the milder climate. The area of Playa del Orzán in front of Hotel Melía Pita is popular with surfers. Cross the Paseo Marítimo for a choice of cafés and restaurants with animated terraces, while on the seafront, kiosks sell ice cream and snacks. Keep in mind that this is the Atlantic, so test the temperature before taking the plunge. There is no natural shade, but you can rent sun loungers and parasols in summer. **Amenities:** food and drink; lifeguards; showers; toilets. **Best for:** surfing; swimming; walking. ✉ *Paseo Marítimo.*

Restaurants

Adega O Bebedeiro

$$ | **SPANISH** | This tiny restaurant is beloved by locals for its authentic food. It feels like an old farmhouse, with stone walls and floors, a fireplace, pine tables and stools, and dusty wine bottles (*adega* is Gallego for bodega, or wine cellar). **Known for:** octopus with clams in garlic sauce; baked scallops; wine cellar. [$] *Average main: €17* ✉ *C. Ángel Rebollo 34* ☎ *981/210609* ⏲ *Closed Mon., and 1st wk in Jan. No dinner Sun.*

El De Alberto

$$$ | **SPANISH** | Steps from the ultramodern Domus, El De Alberto marries the traditional flavors of Galicia with impeccable modern presentation. Alberto, the passionate and friendly owner (and chef), devises repeatedly exciting flavor combinations, such as *pulpo a la brasa con puró de calabaza, salsa kimchi y crujientes de patata* (grilled octopus with pumpkin puree, kimchi sauce, and crispy potatoes), or *zamburiñas en salsa de trufa* (baked scallops with truffle sauce). **Known for:** presentation; grilled octopus; baked scallops. [$] *Average main: €18* ✉ *Rúa Ángel Rebollo 18* ☎ *981/907411* ⏲ *Closed Mon. No dinner Sun.*

La Penela

$$$ | SEAFOOD | This contemporary, bottle-green dining room is the perfect place to feast on fresh fish while sipping Albariño—try at least a few crabs or mussels with béchamel, a dish that La Penela is locally famous for. If shellfish isn't your speed, the roast veal is also popular. **Known for:** views of the harbor and Plaza de María Pita; terrace dining; mussels with béchamel. $ *Average main: €18* ✉ *Plaza de María Pita 12* ☎ *981/209200* ⊕ *www.lapenela.com* ◐ *Closed last 2 wks of Jan. No dinner Sun.*

Hotels

Hotel Lois

$$ | B&B/INN | Positioned in a quiet part of the street, a few steps from the tapas bars of Calle Estrella, Hotel Lois is an excellent choice for location alone, as well as its clean, contemporary style and excellent value for money. **Pros:** central location; surrounded by restaurants; discount at nearby car park. **Cons:** patchy Wi-Fi in some rooms; no parking on-site; no access to street with car. $ *Rooms from: €90* ✉ *Estrella 40* ☎ *981/212269* ⊕ *www.loisestrella.com* 🛏 *10 rooms* ⭐ *No meals.*

NH Collection A Coruña Finisterre

$$$$ | HOTEL | A favorite with businesspeople and families, the oldest and busiest of A Coruña's top hotels is only a few minutes' walk from the port, and is bursting with on-site amenities. **Pros:** port and city views; heated pool; spa. **Cons:** inconvenient outdoor parking; unimpressive breakfast; additional charge for parking. $ *Rooms from: €186* ✉ *Paseo del Parrote 2–4* ☎ *855/215-4084* ⊕ *www.nh-hotels. com/hotel/nh-collection-a-coruna-finisterre* 🛏 *92 rooms* ⭐ *No meals.*

Nightlife

Begin your evening in the **Plaza de María Pita**: cafés and tapas bars proliferate off its western corners and inland. **Calles**

Estrella, Franja, Riego de Agua, Barrera, and Galera and the **Plaza del Humor** have many tapas bars that get progressively busier as the night develops, some of which serve Ribeiro wine in bowls and free tapas with every drink. Start at the top of Calle Estrella (at the farthest end from Plaza de María Pita) beginning with A Taberna de Cunqueiro (Rúa Estrella 22) and work your way back. Night owls head for the posh and pricey clubs around **Playa del Orzán** (Orzán Beach), particularly along Calle Juan Canalejo. For lower-key entertainment, the old town has cozy taverns and plenty of bars that stay open into the early hours.

A Lagareta

TAPAS BARS | Tucked behind a thick (yet easy-to-miss) wooden door, this vivacious, cozy stone-walled tavern is popular with locals. The bar serves cheese and cold cuts on slate, freshly made tortillas, and modern spins on Galician tapas, accompanied by a good choice of local wines by the glass. ✉ *Rúa Franja 24* ☎ *881/897813.*

Taberna da Galera

TAPAS BARS | This popular and stylish tapas bar, in the heart of the old town, serves Galician raciones to a lively crowd. Prop up at the bar or squeeze into a small wooden table and feast on *tigres* (stuffed mussels) or *pulpo* (octopus) in tempura, and accompany it all with a glass of fresh Ribeiro wine. ✉ *Rúa Galera 32* ☎ *881/923996* ⊕ *www.tabernadagalera. com.*

Shopping

Calle Real and **Plaza de Lugo** have boutiques with contemporary fashions. A stroll down **Calle San Andrés,** two blocks inland from Calle Real, or **Avenida Juan Flórez,** leading into the newer town, can yield some sartorial treasures. El Mercado Municipal de San Agustín close to Plaza de María Pita is the place to go for local produce.

Alfarería Aparicio

CRAFTS | The glazed terra-cotta ceramics from Buño, a town 40 km (25 miles) west of A Coruña on the C552, are prized by aficionados. To see where they're made, drive out to Buño itself, where potters work in private studios all over town; then stop in to this store to see the results. ⊠ *Rúa Nova 4* 🕾 *981/711136* ⊕ *www.alfareriaaparicio.es.*

Mundo Galego

FOOD/CANDY | Stop here for local cheese, wine, liqueur, and other Galician specialties. The shop also organizes tastings. ⊠ *Rúa Galera 40* 🕾 *981/912038.*

Betanzos

25 km (15 miles) east of A Coruña, 65 km (40 miles) northeast of Santiago de Compostela.

The charming, slightly ramshackle medieval town of Betanzos is still surrounded by parts of its old city wall. An important Galician port in the 13th century, the old town straddles the confluence of the Mendo River and the Mandeo River and is known today for its white galleried houses, stately Gothic monuments, and lively taverns.

GETTING HERE AND AROUND

From Vigo and other destinations to the south, head north up the AP9; from A Coruña, head east for half an hour along the same motorway. The medieval center, with its narrow lanes rising up from the Pont Nova, is best explored on foot.

VISITOR INFORMATION

CONTACTS **Betanzos** ⊠ *Praza de Galicia 1* 🕾 *981/776666* ⊕ *www.betanzos.es.*

 Sights

Iglesia de San Francisco

RELIGIOUS SITE | The 1292 monastery of San Francisco was converted into a church in 1387 by the nobleman Fernán Pérez de Andrade. His magnificent tomb, to the left of the west door, has him lying on the backs of a stone bear and boar, with hunting dogs at his feet and an angel receiving his soul by his head. ⊠ *Pl. de Fernán Pérez Andrade.*

Iglesia de Santa María de Azogue

RELIGIOUS SITE | This 15th-century church, a few steps uphill from the church of San Francisco, is a national monument. It has Renaissance statues that were stolen in 1981 but subsequently recovered. ⊠ *Pl. de Fernán Pérez Andrade.*

Iglesia de Santiago

RELIGIOUS SITE | The tailors' guild put up the Gothic-style church of Santiago, which includes a Pórtico de la Gloria inspired by the one in Santiago's cathedral. Above the door is a carving of St. James as the Slayer of the Moors. ⊠ *Pl. de Lanzós.*

Viveiro

121 km (75 miles) northeast of Betanzos.

The once-turreted city walls of this popular summer resort are still partially intact. The **Semana Santa** processions, when penitents follow religious processions on their knees, are particularly noteworthy here. The beaches in Viveiro Bay are some of the north's finest.

GETTING HERE AND AROUND

Narrow-gauge FEVE trains connect Viveiro to Oviedo, Gijón, and other points eastward. By car, head east on the AP9 from A Coruña and then take the LU540 to Viveiro.

VISITOR INFORMATION

CONTACTS **Viveiro** ⊠ *Av. Ramón Canosa 3* 🕾 *982/560879* ⊕ *www.viveiroturismo.com.*

Hotels

Hotel Ego

$$$ | **HOTEL** | The view of the ría from this hilltop hotel outside Viveiro is unbeatable, and every room has one. **Pros:** hilltop views; relaxing public areas; excellent restaurant. **Cons:** a little generic; the facade resembles an airport terminal; small spa. [$] *Rooms from: €143* ✉ *Playa de Area 1, off N642, Faro (San Xiao)* ☎ *982/560987* 🌐 *www.hotelego.es* 🛏 *45 rooms* 🍴 *No meals.*

Luarca

92 km (57 miles) northeast of Oviedo.

The village of Luarca is tucked into a cove at the end of a final twist of the Río Negro, with a fishing port and, to the west, a sparkling bay. The town is a maze of cobblestone streets, stone stairways, and whitewashed houses, with a harborside decorated with painted flowerpots.

GETTING HERE AND AROUND

To get to Oviedo, Gijón, and other destinations to the east, you can take a FEVE train or an ALSA bus; it's about a two-hour trip. By car, take the A8 west along the coast from Oviedo and Gijón or east from A Coruña.

VISITOR INFORMATION

CONTACTS Luarca ✉ *Pl. de Alfonso X El Sabio s/n* ☎ *985/640083* 🌐 *www.turismoluarca.com.*

Restaurants

El Barómetro

$$$ | **SEAFOOD** | Decorated with an ornate barometer to gauge the famously unpredictable local weather, this small, family-run seafood eatery is in a 19th-century building in the middle of the harborfront. In addition to an inexpensive *menú del día* (prix fixe), there's also a good choice of local fresh fish, including *calamares* (squid) and *espárragos rellenos de erizo de mar* (asparagus stuffed with sea urchins). **Known for:** excellent-value prix-fixe lunch; seafood fideo (noodles); popularity with locals. [$] *Average main: €18* ✉ *Paseo del Muelle 5* ☎ *985/470662.*

Restaurante Sport

$$$ | **SPANISH** | This friendly, family-run restaurant has been going since the 1950s. Here you will find large windows overlooking river views, walls adorned with artwork, and a kitchen adept at *fabada asturiana* (fava-bean-and-sausage stew) and seafood. **Known for:** riverside setting; seafood; rollo de bonito (tuna meatballs in tomato sauce). [$] *Average main: €22* ✉ *Calle Rivero 9* ☎ *985/641078* 🕒 *No dinner Wed. Closed Sun.*

Hotels

★ Hotel Rural 3 Cabos

$$ | **B&B/INN** | **FAMILY** | Built on a grassy hill with spectacular views of the ocean and Luarca's three famous bays in the distance, this luxurious B&B makes for a charming stay. **Pros:** excellent food; stunning views of green rolling hills and the ocean in the distance; fast Wi-Fi, use of bicycles, and an on-site playground. **Cons:** somewhat out of the way (15-minute drive to Luarca); car needed; restaurant only open to guests. [$] *Rooms from: €105* ✉ *Ctra. de El Vallín, Km 4* ☎ *985/924252* 🌐 *www.hotelrural3cabos.com* 🕒 *Closed Jan. (can vary)* 🛏 *6 rooms* 🍴 *Free Breakfast.*

Villa La Argentina

$$ | **B&B/INN** | Built in 1899 by a wealthy *indiano* (a Spaniard who made his fortune in South America), this charming Asturian mansion, on the hill above Luarca, offers modern apartments in the garden or Belle Époque suites in the main building. **Pros:** swimming pool; lovely gardens; peace and quiet. **Cons:** a short uphill walk from town; not central; simple breakfast. [$] *Rooms from: €118* ✉ *Villar s/n* ☎ *985/640102* 🌐 *www.villalaargentina.com* 🕒 *Closed Jan. and Feb.* 🛏 *12 rooms* 🍴 *No meals.*

Two Great Detours

A Beach Detour

Playa de las Catedrales *(Las Catedrais Beach)* One of Spain's best-kept secrets, this spectacular stretch of sand, also known as Praia de Augas Santas (Beach of the Holy Waters) features vast rock formations, domes, arches, and caves that have been naturally formed over time by the wind and the sea. In high season it is mandatory to reserve a ticket to access the actual beach (July–September). **Amenities:** parking. **Best for:** spectacular natural scenery; beach walks; rock formations. ✉ *A8, 516 exit, Ribadeo.*

Shopping Side Trip

Cerámica de Sargadelos Distinctive blue-and-white-glazed contemporary ceramics are made at Cerámica de Sargadelos, 21 km (13 miles) east of Viveiro. It's usually possible to watch artisans work (weekdays 9–1:15), but call ahead and check. ✉ *Ctra. Paraño s/n, Cervo* ☏ *982/557841* ⊕ *www. sargadelos.com.*

Oviedo

92 km (57 miles) southeast of Luarca, 50 km (31 miles) southeast of Cudillero, 30 km (19 miles) south of Gijón.

Inland, the Asturian countryside starts to look picture-perfect. Gently rolling green hills, and wooden, tile-roof hórreos strung with golden bundles of drying corn replace the stark granite sheds of Galicia. A drive through the hills and valleys brings you to the capital city, Oviedo. Although its surrounds are primarily industrial, Oviedo has three of the most famous pre-Romanesque churches in Spain and a large university, giving it both ancient charm and youthful zest. Start your explorations with the two exquisite 9th-century chapels outside the city, on the slopes of Monte Naranco.

GETTING HERE AND AROUND

Oviedo is served by the A66 tollway, which links to Gijón and Avilés, where you can get on the A8 west to A Coruña or east toward Santander. Madrid is reached on the N630 south.

There are several buses per day to Gijón (30 minutes) and to Santiago and A Coruña (5 hours). Madrid is 5½ hours away by rail from Oviedo's RENFE station, situated on Calle Uría. The FEVE service operates across the north coast, with Gijón easily reached in half an hour and Bilbao just under eight hours away.

CONTACTS Oviedo Bus Station ✉ *Calle Pepe Cosmen* ⊕ *www.estaciondeauto-busesdeoviedo.com.* **Oviedo Train Station** ✉ *Calle Uria s/n* ☏ *912/320320 RENFE.*

VISITOR INFORMATION

CONTACTS Oviedo ✉ *Pl. de la Constitución 4* ☏ *984/493563.*

Sights

Cathedral

RELIGIOUS SITE | Oviedo's Gothic cathedral was built between the 14th and 16th centuries around the city's most cherished monument, the **Cámara Santa** (Holy Chamber). King Ramiro's predecessor, Alfonso the Chaste (792–842), built it to hide the treasures of Christian Spain during the struggle with the Moors. Damaged during the Spanish Civil War, it has since been rebuilt. Inside is the gold-leaf **Cross of the Angels,** commissioned by Alfonso in 808 and encrusted with pearls and jewels. On the left is the more elegant **Victory Cross,** actually a jeweled sheath crafted in 908 to cover the oak cross used by Pelayo in the battle

of Covadonga. ✉ *Pl. Alfonso II El Casto* ☎ *985/219642* ⊕ *www.catedraldeoviedo. es* ✉ *€7 (incudes audio guide).*

San Julián de los Prados (*Santullano*)
RELIGIOUS SITE | Older than its more famous pre-Romanesque counterparts on Monte Naranco, the 9th-century church of Santullano has surprisingly well-preserved frescoes inside. Geometric patterns, rather than representations of humans or animals, cover almost every surface, along with a cross containing Greek letters. ✉ *C. Selgas 1* ☎ *687/052826* ✉ *€2 (free 1st Mon. of each month)* ⊘ *Closed Sun.*

Santa María del Naranco and San Miguel de Lillo
RELIGIOUS SITE | These two churches—the first with superb views and its plainer sister 300 yards uphill—are the jewels of an early architectural style called Asturian pre-Romanesque, a more primitive, hulking, defensive line that preceded Romanesque architecture by nearly three centuries. Commissioned as part of a summer palace by King Ramiro I when Oviedo was the capital of Christian Spain, these masterpieces have survived for more than 1,000 years. Tickets for both sites are available in the church of Santa María del Naranco. ✉ *Monte Naranco ⊹ 2 km (1 mile) north of Oviedo* ☎ *638/260163* ⊕ *www.santamariadel-naranco.es* ✉ *€3, includes guided tour (free Mon., without guide).*

🍴 Restaurants

Casa Chema
$$$ | **SPANISH** | With a sun-dappled terrace overlooking rolling green hills and a sparkling river, this restaurant, 11 km (7 miles) outside Oviedo, is an inviting—and

peaceful—spot to savor some of Asturias's best traditional cooking. The fabada, with its buttery soft beans and slow-simmered rich broth, served in earthenware pots, has won the restaurant awards. **Known for:** award-winning fabada; terrace with views; laid-back lunch. [$] *Average main: €20* ✉ *La Arquera 184 (Puerto)* ☎ *985/798200* 🌐 *www.casachema.com* 🕒 *No dinner Sun.–Fri.*

Casa Fermín

$$$$ | **SPANISH** | Skylights, plants, and an air of modernity belie the age of this sophisticated restaurant, which opened in 1924 and is now in its fourth generation. The creative menu changes seasonally and there is also a tasting menu (€70). **Known for:** langoustines with cream of leek; roasted sea bass; elegant setting. [$] *Average main: €26* ✉ *C. San Francisco 8* ☎ *985/216452* 🌐 *www.casafermin.com* 🕒 *Closed Sun.*

La Corte de Pelayo

$$$ | **SPANISH** | Head to this renowned restaurant and meeting spot on one of Oviedo's main thoroughfares for a famous Asturian dish called *cachopo* (a heart-stopping combination of veal, ham, and Asturian cheese wrapped in bread crumbs and deep-fried). If you prefer something a bit lighter, the menu also includes salads, fresh fish, and meat dishes. **Known for:** cachopo; lively atmosphere; central location. [$] *Average main: €20* ✉ *Calle San Francisco 21* ☎ *985/213145* 🌐 *www.lacortedepelayo.com* 🕒 *No dinner Sun. Closed Mon.*

Tierra Astur

$$ | **SPANISH** | This bustling *sidrería* (cider bar) is a popular and classic destination for locals and tourists alike, who come to enjoy the lively atmosphere, a cup of cider poured from a great height, and the traditional, family-style Asturian fare. Try the fabada, or sample from an array of traditional *tablas* (boards) with choice selections from more than 40 artisanal cheeses and local cold cuts, preserved seafood, and fresh fish and meat dishes. **Known for:** cider; cheese platters; succulent chuleton (rib-eye steak). [$] *Average main: €15* ✉ *Calle Gascona 1* ☎ *985/202502* 🌐 *www.tierra-astur.com.*

Cudillero 👁

The coastal road leads 35 km (22 miles) east of Luarca to this little fishing village, clustered around its tiny port. The emerald green of the surrounding hills, the bright blue of the water, and the pops of color among the white houses make this village one of the prettiest and most touristic in Asturias. Seafood and cider restaurants line the central street, which turns into a boat ramp at the bottom of town.

🛏 Hotels

Barceló Oviedo Cervantes

$$ | **HOTEL** | A playful revamp of this town house in the city center added a neo-Moorish portico to the original latticed facade and indulgent amenities like entertainment systems in some of the bathrooms. **Pros:** fun '70s design; central location close to train station; on-site bar and restaurant. **Cons:** uninteresting views; erratic service; below par lighting in rooms. [$] *Rooms from: €104* ✉ *C. Cervantes 13* ☎ *985/255000* 🌐 *www.barcelo.com* 🔑 *72 rooms* 🍴 *No meals.*

★ Eurostars Hotel de la Reconquista

$$$ | **HOTEL** | Occupying an 18th-century hospice emblazoned with a huge stone coat of arms, the luxurious Reconquista is by far the most distinguished hotel in Oviedo. **Pros:** great location; spacious rooms; good breakfast buffet. **Cons:** some rooms have uninteresting views; poorly lighted rooms; tired room decor. [$] *Rooms from: €180* ✉ *C. Gil de Jaz 16* ☎ *913/342196* 🌐 *www.hoteldelareconquista.com* 🔑 *142 rooms* 🍴 *Free Breakfast.*

Shopping

Shops throughout the city carry **azabache jewelry** made of jet.

Joyería Santirso

JEWELRY/ACCESSORIES | This family-run shop has been selling silver jewelry, including Asturias' world-famous azabache, for five generations. ⊠ *Calle de la Rúa 7* ☎ *985/225304.*

Mercado El Fontan

LOCAL SPECIALTIES | Shop for fish, vegetables, and local products at Mercado El Fontan, a market that has been in this spot since the 13th century (although the current property was built in the 19th century). The narrow streets surrounding the market are lined with colorful flower stalls and small shops selling Asturian goods, such as vacuum-packed fava beans and cheeses. ⊠ *Pl. 19 de Octubre* ☎ *985/204394* ⊕ *mercadofontan.es.*

Activities

SKIING

Fuentes de Invierno

SKIING/SNOWBOARDING | An hour's drive from Oviedo in the heart of the Cantabrian Mountains, Fuentes de Invierno has five chairlifts and 15 trails of varying difficulty. ⊠ *Ctra. del Puerto de San Isidro* ☎ *985/959106* ⊕ *www.fuentesdeinvierno.com* ☜ *€26.*

Valgrande Pajares

SKIING/SNOWBOARDING | This resort has two chairlifts, eight slopes, and cross-country trails. ⊠ *Estación Invernal y de Montaña Valgrande-Pajares, Brañillín, Pajares* ✛ *60 km (37 miles) south of Oviedo* ☎ *985/957097* ⊕ *www.valgrande-pajares.com.*

Gijón

30 km (19 miles) north of Oviedo.

The Campo Valdés baths, dating back to the 1st century AD, and other reminders of Gijón's time as an ancient Roman port remain visible downtown. Gijón was almost destroyed in a 14th-century struggle over the Castilian throne, but by the 19th century it was a thriving port and industrial city. The lively modern-day city is part fishing port, part summer resort, and part university town, packed with cafés, restaurants, and sidrerías.

GETTING HERE AND AROUND

Oviedo is only 30 minutes away by ALSA bus or FEVE train, both of which run every half hour throughout the day. The A8 coastal highway runs east from Gijón to Santander, and west to Luarca, and eventually A Coruña.

CONTACTS Gijón Bus Station ⊠ *C. Magnus Blikstad 1.* **Gijón Train Station** ⊠ *C. Sanz Crespo s/n* ☎ *912/320320* ⊕ *www.renfe.com.*

VISITOR INFORMATION

CONTACTS Gijón ⊠ *Espigón Central de Fomento, C. Rodriguez San Pedro* ☎ *985/341771* ⊕ *www.gijon.info.*

Sights

Cimadevilla

NEIGHBORHOOD | This steep peninsula, the old fishermen's quarter, is now the hub of Gijón's nightlife. At sunset, the sidewalk in front of bar El Planeta (Tránsito de las Ballenas 4), overlooking the harbor, is a prime spot to join in with the locals and drink Asturian cider. From the park at the highest point on the headland, beside Basque artist Eduardo Chillida's massive sculpture *Elogio del Horizonte* (*In Praise of the Horizon*), there's a panoramic view of the coast and city. ⊠ *Gijón.*

Muséu del Pueblu d'Asturies (*Museum of the People of Asturias*)
MUSEUM | Across the river on the eastern edge of town, past Parque Isabel la Católica, this rustic museum contains traditional Asturian houses, cider presses, a mill, and an exquisitely painted granary. Also here is the **Museo de la Gaita** (Bagpipe Museum). This collection of wind instruments explains their evolution both around the world and within Asturias. ✉ *Paseo del Doctor Fleming 877, La Güelga s/n* ☎ *985/182960* 🎟 *€3 (free Sun.)* 🕒 *Closed Mon.*

Termas Romanas de Campo Valdés (*Roman Baths*)
HOT SPRINGS | Dating back to the time of Augustus, Gijón's baths are under the plaza at the end of the beach. ✉ *Campo Valdés s/n* ☎ *985/185151* 🎟 *€3 (free Sun.)* 🕒 *Closed Mon.*

Beaches

The capital of the Costa Verde, Gijón, overlooks two attractive sandy beaches that are large enough to avoid overcrowding in summer.

Playa de Poniente (*Sunset Beach*)
BEACH—SIGHT | Tucked into the city's harbor, this horseshoe-shape curve of fine artificial sand and calm waters is wonderful for a stroll as the evening draws in. **Amenities:** lifeguards; showers; toilets. **Best for:** sunset; swimming; walking. ✉ *C. Rodriguez San Pedro.*

Playa de San Lorenzo
BEACH—SIGHT | Gijón's second popular beach, on the other side of the headland from Playa de Poniente, is a large stretch of golden sand backed by a promenade that extends from one end of town to the other. Across the narrow peninsula and the Plaza Mayor is the harbor, where the fishing fleet comes in with the day's catch. As long as the tide is out, you can sunbathe. The waves are generally moderate, although the weather and sea currents can be unpredictable along the northern coast. **Amenities:** food and drink; lifeguards; showers; toilets; water sports. **Best for:** sunset; swimming; walking. ✉ *Av. Rufo García Rendueles.*

Restaurants

La Galana
$$$ | **SPANISH** | La Galana has all the ingredients of a typical Asturian sidrería, with colossal barrels lining the walls, thick wooden tables, and plenty of standing room at the bar, where locals munch on Cabrales cheese. The kitchen serves classic cider-house fare, but the portions are smaller and the presentation more refined. **Known for:** cider; seafood; refined, creative dishes. [$] *Average main: €20* ✉ *Pl. Mayor 10* ☎ *985/172429* 🌐 *www.restauranteasturianolagalana.es.*

Restaurante Auga
$$$$ | **SPANISH** | This glass-enclosed dining room, housed in what was once Gijón's fish market, overlooks the harbor and serves fine, imaginative seafood and meat dishes. The renowned restaurant's emphasis is on its Cantabrian catch, with specialties like *langostinos frescos en su jugo y tocino ibérico* (fresh prawns in their juice with Iberian bacon) and *merluza de pino "Puerto de Celeiro" con sopa de patata, citricos y cardamomo* (Port of Celeiro line-caught hake, served with potato soup seasoned with citrus and cardamom). **Known for:** harbor and sea views; contemporary seafood dishes; alfresco dining. [$] *Average main: €26* ✉ *C. Claudio Alvargonzález s/n* ☎ *985/168186* 🌐 *www.restauranteauga.com* 🕒 *Closed Mon. No dinner Sun.*

Hotels

Hostel Gijón Centro
$ | **B&B/INN** | Brilliantly located a few steps from the harbor and Plaza Mayor, this tiny guesthouse offers rooms with large windows affording plenty of natural light, plus simple, modern decor and comfortable beds. **Pros:** excellent value; central

location; quiet. **Cons:** tiny bathrooms; no on-site facilities; simple lodging. [$] *Rooms from: €70* ✉ *Calle San Antonio 12, Flat 1* ☎ *657/029242* 🌐 *www.hostelgijoncentro.es* 🛏 *6 rooms* 🍴 *No meals.*

Hotel El Mirador de Ordiales

$ | **B&B/INN** | Built on the top of a hill, this cozy B&B offers an exquisite view of the valley below and the snowcapped Picos de Europa in the distance. **Pros:** stunning views; good base for hiking; spacious rooms. **Cons:** remote—need a car; 25-minute drive from Gijón city center; breakfast is extra. [$] *Rooms from: €85* ✉ *Ordiales 11B, Siero* ☎ *653/938156, 985/721020* 🌐 *www.elmiradordeordiales.com* 🛏 *3 rooms* 🍴 *No meals.*

Parador de Gijón

$$$$ | **HOTEL** | This is one of the simplest and friendliest paradores in Spain, and most of the rooms in the new wing have wonderful views over the lake or the park. **Pros:** park views; welcoming, down-to-earth staff; great food. **Cons:** austere guest rooms; fairly expensive; some distance from the old town. [$] *Rooms from: €185* ✉ *Av. Torcuato Fernández Miranda 15* ☎ *985/370511* 🌐 *www.parador.es* 🛏 *40 rooms* 🍴 *Free Breakfast.*

Ribadesella

67 km (40 miles) east of Gijón, 84 km (50 miles) northeast of Oviedo.

The N632 twists around green hills dappled with eucalyptus groves, allowing glimpses of the sea and sandy beaches below and the snowcapped Picos de Europa looming inland. This fishing village and beach resort is famous for its seafood, its cave, and the canoe races held on the Río Sella the first Saturday in August.

GETTING HERE AND AROUND

FEVE and ALSA connect Ribadesella to Gijón and Oviedo by train and bus, a journey of 1½–2 hours. By car, you can take the A8 from Gijón and Oviedo past Villaviciosa to Ribadesella.

VISITOR INFORMATION

CONTACTS Ribadesella ✉ *Paseo Princesa Letizia s/n* ☎ *985/860038* 🌐 *www.ribadesella.es.*

Sights

Centro de Arte Rupestre Tito Bustillo

CAVE | Discovered in 1968, the cave here has 20,000-year-old paintings on a par with those in Lascaux, France, and Altamira. Giant horses and deer prance about the walls. To protect the paintings, no more than 375 visitors are allowed inside each day, so reservations are essential. The guided tour is in Spanish. Audio guides are available in English. There's also a **museum** of Asturian cave finds, open year-round. ✉ *Av. de Tito Bustillo s/n* ☎ *902/306600* 🌐 *www.centrotitobustillo.com* 🎟 *From €6* 🕒 *Closed Mon. and Tues., and Jan.*

Beaches

Playa Santa Marina

BEACH—SIGHT | To the west of the Río Sella estuary, which divides the town, this gentle curve of golden sand is one of the prettiest beaches in Asturias, tucked neatly beneath the town's seafront promenade, which is lined with elegant 20th-century mansions. Moderate waves provide safe swimming conditions, although, as with all of Spain's Atlantic-facing beaches, currents and weather can be unpredictable. In high season (particularly in August) the beach can get very busy. This part of the coast is not called the "dinosaur coast" for nothing; over by the Punta'l Pozu Viewpoint, you can see footprints embedded in the rocks and cliff faces where they left their mark millions of years ago. Amenities listed are only available June–September. **Amenities:** food and drink; lifeguards; showers; toilets. **Best for:** surfing; swimming. ✉ *Paseo Agustin de Argüelles Marina.*

Hiking in the Picos de Europa

🍴 Restaurants

Arbidel

$$$$ | **SPANISH** | This one-Michelin-starred restaurant, tucked into the narrow streets of Ribadesella's old town, is adorned with rustic stone walls and a hand-painted mural. It serves traditional Asturian fare with a modern twist, as well as gourmet tapas and a tasting menu (€55–€88). **Known for:** Michelin star; good-value tasting menu; apple gazpacho with sardine. [$] *Average main: €28* ✉ *Calle Oscuro 1* ☎ *985/861440* 🌐 *www.arbidel.com* 🕒 *No dinner Sun. Closed Mon.–Thurs. in Jan. No dinner weekends in Jan.*

Llanes

40 km (25 miles) east of Ribadesella.

This beach town is on a pristine stretch of the Costa Verde. The shores in both directions outside town have vistas of cliffs looming over white-sand beaches and isolated caves. A long canal connected to a small harbor cuts through the heart of Llanes, and along its banks rise colorful houses with glass galleries against a backdrop of the Picos de Europa. At the daily port-side fish market, usually held around 1 pm, vendors display heaping mounds of freshly caught seafood.

GETTING HERE AND AROUND

The scenic A8 coastal route from Gijón continues past Villaviciosa and Ribadesella and then winds through Llanes before heading east toward Santander. FEVE trains and ALSA buses make the trip in 2–3½ hours.

VISITOR INFORMATION

CONTACTS Llanes ✉ *Antigua Lonja de Pescado, Calle Marqués de Canillejas 1* ☎ *985/400164* 🌐 *www.llanes.es.*

👁 Sights

Basílica de Santa María del Conceyu

RELIGIOUS SITE | This 13th-century church, which rises over the main square here, is an excellent example of Romantic Gothic architecture. ✉ *Pl. Christo Rey.*

Mirador Panorámico La Boriza

VIEWPOINT | Dotting the Asturian coast east and west of Llanes are bufones , cavelike cavities that expel water when waves are sucked in. Active blowholes shoot streams of water as high as 100 feet into the air, although it's hard to predict when this will happen, as it depends on the tide and the size of the surf. They are clearly marked so you can find them, and there are barriers to protect you when they expel water. There's a blowhole east of Playa Ballota; try to watch it in action from this mirador east of Llanes, between the villages of Cué and Andrin, near the entrance to Campo de Golf Municipal de Llanes. If you miss it, the view is still worth a stop—on a clear day you can see the coastline all the way east to Santander. ✉ *Llanes.*

Plaza Cristo Rey

PLAZA | Peaceful and well conserved, this plaza marks the center of the old town, which is partially surrounded by the remains of its medieval walls. ✉ *Llanes.*

Beaches

Playa Ballota

BEACH—SIGHT | Just 1 km (½ mile) east of Llanes is one of the area's most secluded beaches, the pristine Playa Ballota, with private coves and one of the few stretches of nudist sand in Asturias. **Amenities:** food and drink (seasonal). **Best for:** nudists; swimming; walking. ✉ *C. Ballota.*

Playa de Torimbia

BEACH—SIGHT | Farther west of Llanes is the partially nudist Playa de Torimbia, a wild, virgin beach as yet untouched by development. It can be reached only via a footpath—roughly a 15-minute walk. This secluded crescent of fine, white sand and crystal-clear waters is backed by Asturias's green hills, making it one of the region's most picturesque beaches. Winds can be strong, and there is no real infrastructure. **Amenities:** none. **Best for:** nudists; solitude; swimming; walking. ✉ *Llanes* ✣ *Off C. Niembru, 8 km (5 miles) west of Llanes.*

Playa de Toró

BEACH—SIGHT | On the eastern edge of town is the Playa de Toró, where fine white sands are peppered with unique rock formations. This pristine beach is ideal for sunbathing and families. **Amenities:** lifeguards; showers; toilets. **Best for:** swimming. ✉ *Av. de Toró.*

Playa del Sablón

BEACH—SIGHT | Steps from the old town is the protected Playa del Sablón (whose name derives from the Asturian word for "sand"), a little swath of beach that gets crowded on weekends. **Amenities:** food and drink; lifeguards; showers; toilets. **Best for:** swimming. ✉ *C. Sablón.*

🍴 Restaurants

La Casa del Mar

$ | **SEAFOOD** | Llanes has prettier, cleaner, and less noisy places to enjoy seafood, but if you feel like rubbing shoulders with Asturian fishermen and eating their catch cooked just the way they like it, then this spot by the port, guarded by a parrot named Paco, is for you. The glassed-in terrace has a view of the small harbor bobbing with boats, and the menu offers such local classics as baby squid in ink, spider crab, seafood meatballs, and razor clams, all with a minimum of fuss but maximum value. **Known for:** seafood; good value; popular with locals. [$] *Average main: €10* ✉ *Calle Muelle 4, C. Marinero* ☎ *985/401215* 💳 *No credit cards.*

🛏 Hotels

Hotel CAEaCLAVELES

$$ | **HOTEL** | This sleek, modern-design hotel is architecturally captivating, with organic curves, full-length windows, polished cement ceilings, and a

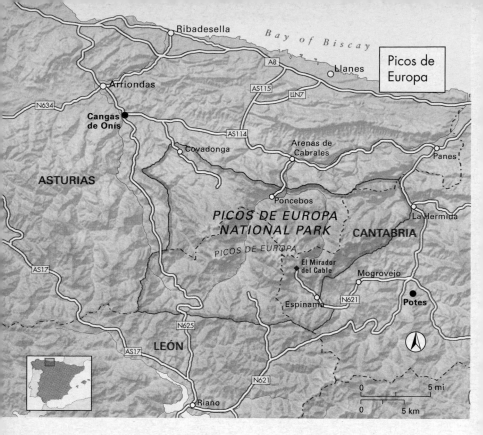

grass-covered roof that gently slopes down to the ground on either side of the building, allowing guests to walk up and enjoy the views. **Pros:** award-winning architecture; plenty of natural light; quiet and scenic. **Cons:** bathrooms lack privacy; somewhat remote, car needed; no children under nine. $ *Rooms from: €115* ✉ *La Pereda* ☎ *985/925981* ⊕ *www. caeaclaveles.com* ☉ *Closed mid-Dec.–mid-Jan.* ➴ *5 rooms* ❍⃨ *No meals.*

La Posada de Babel

$$$ | **B&B/INN** | This family-run inn just outside Llanes stands among oak, chestnut, and birch trees on the edge of the Sierra de Cuera. **Pros:** extremely amiable staff; comfy base for hiking; beautiful grounds. **Cons:** slippery stairs to certain rooms; closed in winter; room styles vary. $ *Rooms from: €130* ✉ *La Pereda s/n* ✛ *4 km (2½ miles) southwest of Llanes*

☎ *985/402525* ⊕ *www.laposadadebabel. com* ☉ *Closed Dec.–Easter* ➴ *12 rooms* ❍⃨ *No meals.*

Cangas de Onís

25 km (16 miles) south of Ribadesella, 70 km (43 miles) east of Oviedo.

The first capital of Christian Spain, Cangas de Onís is also the unofficial capital of the Picos de Europa National Park. Partly in the narrow valley carved by the Sella River, it has the feel of a mountain village.

VISITOR INFORMATION

CONTACTS Cangas de Onís ✉ *Av. Covadonga 21* ☎ *985/848043* ⊕ *www.cangasdeonis.es/en.*

Sights

Picos de Europa Visitor Center

INFO CENTER | To help plan your rambles, consult the scale model of the park outside the visitor center; staff inside can advise you on suitable routes. There are various stores on the same street that sell maps and guidebooks, a few in English. ✉ *Av. Covadonga 1* ☎ *985/848005* 🌐 *www.cangasdeonis.com.*

Puente Romano de Congas de Onís sobre el Sella

BRIDGE/TUNNEL | A high, humpback medieval bridge (also known as the Puente Romano, or Roman Bridge, because of its style) spans the Río Sella gorge with a reproduction of Pelayo's Victory Cross, or La Cruz de la Victoria, dangling underneath. ✉ *Cangas de Onís.*

Restaurants

Restaurante Los Arcos

$$$ | **SPANISH** | Situated on one of the town's main squares, this busy tavern serves local cider, fine Spanish wines, and honest regional dishes. The well-prioed lunchtime menu features mouthwatering fare such as *revuelto de morcilla* (scrambled eggs with blood sausage) and *pulpo de pedreu sobre crema fina de patata, oricios y germinados ecologicos* (octopus with creamed potato, sea urchins, and bean sprouts). **Known for:** local cider; lunch menu; scrambled eggs with blood sausage. [$] *Average main: €18* ✉ *Pl. del Ayuntamiento 3* ☎ *985/849277* 🌐 *restaurantlosarcos.com.*

Hotels

Hotel Posada del Valle

$ | **B&B/INN** | British couple Nigel and Joanne Burch converted a rustic, 19th-century, stone-wall farmhouse into an idyllic guesthouse; built near the side of a hill, it faces out over spectacular panoramas of the Picos. **Pros:** surrounded by nature; views of the Picos; wealth of local knowledge at your fingertips. **Cons:** remote and difficult to find; breakfast costs extra; restaurant does not serve lunch. [$] *Rooms from: €88* ✉ *Collía, Arriondas* ☎ *985/841157* 🌐 *www.posadadelvalle.com* 💳 *No credit cards* 🕒 *Closed Nov.–Mar.* 🛏 *12 rooms* 🍴 *No meals.*

★ **Parador de Cangas de Onís**

$$$$ | **HOTEL** | On the banks of the Río Sella just west of Cangas, this friendly parador is made up of an 8th-century Benedictine monastery and a modern wing: the older building has 11 period-style rooms. **Pros:** gorgeous riverside location and mountain views; excellent food; oodles of history. **Cons:** limited menu; chilly corridors; rooms on lower floor can be noisy. [$] *Rooms from: €185* ✉ *Monasterio de San Pedro de Villanueva, Villanueva s/n, Ctra. N625* ✣ *From N634 take right turn for Villanueva* ☎ *985/849402* 🌐 *www.parador.es* 🕒 *Closed Jan.–end Mar.* 🛏 *64 rooms* 🍴 *No meals.*

Activities

The tourist office in Cangas de Onís can help you organize a Picos de Europa trek. The Picos visitor center in Cangas has general information, route maps, and a useful scale model of the range.

HIKING

Astur Sella Aventura

CLIMBING/MOUNTAINEERING | Part of the Hotel Montevedro, Astur Sella Aventura specializes in canoeing and canyon rappelling. ✉ *Ramón Prada Vicente 5* ☎ *985/848370* 🌐 *www.astursellaaventura.com.*

Cangas Aventura Turismo Activo

CAMPING—SPORTS-OUTDOORS | Rafting, canoeing, Jet Skiing, climbing, trekking, horseback riding, paintballing, and snowshoeing packages are all available here. ✉ *Av. Covadonga 17 Bajo* ☎ *985/849261* 🌐 *www.cangasaventura.com.*

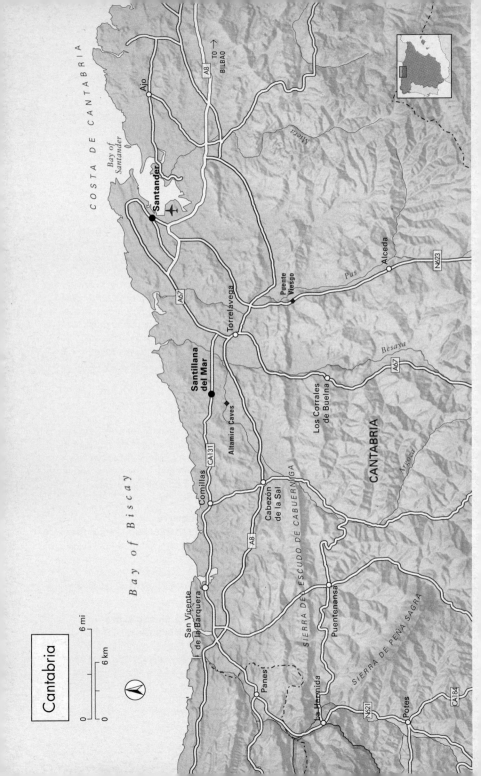

Potes

51 km (31 miles) southwest of San Vicente de la Barquera, 115 km (69 miles) southwest of Santander, 173 km (104 miles) north of Palencia, 81 km (50 miles) southeast of Cangas de Onís.

Known for its fine cheeses, the region of La Liébana is a highland domain also worth exploring for other reasons. Potes, the area's main city, is named for its ancient bridges and surrounded by the stunning 9th-century **monasteries** of Santo Toribio de Liébana, Lebeña, and Piasca. The gorges of the Desfiladero de la Hermida pass are 13 km (8 miles) north, and the rustic town of Mogrovejo is on the way to the vertiginous cable car at Fuente Dé, 10 km (6 miles) west of Potes.

GETTING HERE AND AROUND

Potes is just over two hours from Gijón and Oviedo via the A8, and 1½ hours from Santander via the A8 and N621.

VISITOR INFORMATION

CONTACTS Potes ✉ *Centro de Estudio Lebaniegos, Pl. de la Independencia s/n* ☎ *942/738126.*

Sights

El Mirador del Cable

TOWN | As you approach the parador of Fuente Dé, at the head of the valley northwest of the hamlet of Espinama, you'll see a wall of gray rock rising 6,560 feet straight into the air. Visible at the top is the tiniest of huts: El Mirador del Cable (the cable-car lookout point). Get there via a 2,625-foot funicular (€17 round-trip). At the top, you can hike along the Ávila Mountain pasturelands, rich in wildlife, between the central and eastern massifs of the Picos. There's an official entrance to Picos de Europa National Park here. ✉ *Potes* ☎ *942/736610* 🌐 *www.cantur.com.*

Restaurants

El Bodegón

$$ | **SPANISH** | A simple, friendly, and cozy space awaits behind the ancient stone facade of this restaurant, 200 meters from the main plaza. Part of the house is original, but much has been renovated, providing an attractive combination of traditional mountain design and modern construction. **Known for:** great wine; popular spot; highland comfort food. [$] *Average main: €15* ✉ *C. San Roque 4* ☎ *942/730247* 🕒 *Closed Wed.*

Hotels

Hotel del Oso

$$ | **HOTEL** | **FAMILY** | Offering a great value, this cozy lodge is the perfect base for exploring the surrounding Picos de Europa. **Pros:** great base for hiking; decent restaurant; swimming pool and tennis court. **Cons:** decor is a bit outdated; lower floor rooms can be noisy; some rooms are on the small side. [$] *Rooms from: €92* ✉ *Cosgaya* ☎ *942/733018* 🌐 *www.hoteldeloso.es* 🕒 *Closed Dec. 15–Feb. 15* 🛏 *49 rooms* 🍴 *No meals* 💳 *No credit cards.*

Santander

390 km (242 miles) north of Madrid, 154 km (96 miles) north of Burgos, 116 km (72 miles) west of Bilbao, 194 km (120 miles) northeast of Oviedo.

One of the great ports on the Bay of Biscay, Santander is surrounded by beaches that can often be busy, but it still manages to avoid the package-tour feel of so many Mediterranean resorts. A fire destroyed most of the old town in 1941, so the rebuilt city looks relatively modern. The town gets especially fun and busy in summer, when its summer-university community and music-and-dance festival fill the city with students and performers.

The Altamira Museum's replica of a Paleolithic cave displays paintings of bison.

From the 1st to the 4th century, under the Romans, Santander—then called Portus Victoriae—was a major port. Commercial life accelerated between the 13th and 16th centuries, but the waning of Spain's naval power and a series of plagues during the reign of Felipe II caused Santander's fortunes to plummet in the late 16th century. Its economy revived after 1778, when Seville's monopoly on trade with the Americas was revoked and Santander entered fully into commerce with the New World. In 1910 the Palacio de la Magdalena was built by popular subscription as a gift to Alfonso XIII and his queen, Victoria Eugenia, lending Santander prestige as one of Spain's royal watering holes.

GETTING HERE AND AROUND

Santander itself is easily navigated on foot, but if you're looking to get to El Sardinero beach, take the bus from the central urban transport hub at Jardines de Pereda.

CONTACTS Santander Bus Station ⊠ *C. Navas de Tolosa s/n* ☎ *942/211995.*

Santander Train Station ⊠ *Pl. de las Estaciones s/n* ☎ *912/320320 RENFE* ⊕ *www. renfe.com.*

VISITOR INFORMATION
CONTACTS Santander ⊠ *Jardines de Pereda s/n* ☎ *942/203000* ⊕ *www.turismo. santander.es.*

Sights

Catedral de Santander
RELIGIOUS SITE | The blocky cathedral marks the transition between Romanesque and Gothic. Though largely rebuilt in the neo-Gothic style after serious damage in the town's 1941 fire, the cathedral retained its 12th-century crypt. The chief attraction here is the tomb of Marcelino Menéndez y Pelayo (1856–1912), Santander's most famous literary figure. The cathedral is across Avenida de Calvo Sotelo from the Plaza Porticada. ⊠ *Calle de Somorrostro s/n* ☒ *Free.*

Centro Botín
BUILDING | Inaugurated in 2017, this futuristic-looking museum and cultural

space, designed by architect Renzo Piano, houses contemporary artwork by international artists. Worth a visit for the eye-popping outside and views alone, the building overlooks the harbor and is surrounded by the Jardines de Pereda. ✉ *Jardines de Pereda, Muelle de Albareda s/n* ☎ *942/047147* ⊕ *www.centrobotin.org/en* 🎫 *€8* ⊙ *Closed Mon. (except mid-July–end of Aug.).*

Palacio de la Magdalena

BUILDING | Built on the highest point of the Peninsula de Magdalena and surrounded by 62 acres of manicured gardens and rocky beaches, this elegant palace is the most distinctive building in Santander. Built between 1908 and 1912 as a summer home for King Alfonso XIII and Queen Victoria Eugenia, the building has architectural influences from France and England. Today, the palace is used as a venue for meetings, weddings, and college language classes (summer only). There are also daily guided visits—call in advance to schedule a tour in English. ✉ *Av. Magdalena s/n* ☎ *942/203084* ⊕ *www.palaciomagdalena.com* 🎫 *€3.*

🌊 Beaches

Playa El Sardinero

BEACH—SIGHT | Gently curving round the bay from the Magdalena Peninsula, Santander's longest and most popular beach has a full range of amenities and fine, golden sand. Although this northeast-facing stretch is exposed, moderate waves in summer make it generally fine for bathing, but its location on the Cantabrian coast keeps the water very cold. In winter months it is a favorite of surfers, particularly the part of the beach in front of Hotel Cuiqui. Be sure to arrive at the beach via the sun-dappled Piquío Gardens, where terraces filled with flowers and trees lead the way down to the beach. **Amenities:** food and drink; lifeguards; showers; toilets; water sports. **Best for:** surfing; swimming; walking. ✉ *Santander.*

Puente Viesgo

In 1903, in this 16th-century hamlet in the Pas Valley, four caves were discovered under the 1,150-foot peak of Monte del Castillo, two of which—Cueva del Castillo and Cueva de las Monedas—are open to the public. Bison, deer, bulls, and humanoid stick figures are depicted within the caves; the oldest designs are thought to be 35,000 years old. Most arresting are the paintings of 44 hands (curiously, 35 of them left). The painters are thought to have blown red pigment around their hands through a hollow bone, leaving the negative image. Reservations are essential. ⊕ *cuevas.culturadecantabria.com*

🍴 Restaurants

Bodega del Riojano

$$$$ | SPANISH | The paintings on wine-barrel ends that decorate this classic restaurant have given it the nickname "Museo Redondo" (Round Museum). The building dates back to the 16th century, when it was a wine cellar, which you can see in the heavy wooden beams overhead and the rough and rustic tables. **Known for:** fish of the day; historic setting; specialties from La Rioja. 💲*Average main: €25* ✉ *C. Río de la Pila 5* ☎ *942/216750* ⊕ *www.bodegadelriojano.com* ⊙ *No dinner Sun.*

★ La Casona del Judío

$$$$ | SPANISH | While the à la carte menu at this tasteful, fine-dining establishment is exquisite, and includes a delectable variety of traditional Cantabrian seafood and meat dishes, the real draw are the tasting menus (€52 and €68). This private culinary experience occurs in the romantically lit brick wine cellar below the main restaurant. **Known for:**

tasting menus; interaction with the chef; cannelloni stuffed with morcilla. [$] *Average main: €24* ✉ *Calle de Repuente 20* ☎ *942/342726* 🌐 *www.lacasonadeljudio.com* 💳 *No credit cards.*

Hotels

Abba Santander

$$$ | **HOTEL** | Occupying the building of the historic Hotel México, Abba Santander has gradually been transformed from a family-run inn into a chain hotel with contemporary interiors and modern conveniences. **Pros:** cheerful service; central location; charming architectural details. **Cons:** slippery bathroom floors; busy part of town; additional cost for parking. [$] *Rooms from: €160* ✉ *C. Calderón de la Barca 3* ☎ *942/212450, 942/091516 bookings* 🌐 *www.abbasantanderhotel.com* 🛏 *37 rooms* 🍴 *No meals.*

Hotel Bahía

$$$$ | **HOTEL** | Classical style combined with state-of-the-art technology and contemporary furnishings make this Santander's finest hotel—a grand and comfortable perch overlooking the water. **Pros:** in the center of town; great for watching maritime traffic; friendly service. **Cons:** nearby cathedral bells can be noisy if you're not on the sea side of the hotel; not right on the beach; no gym. [$] *Rooms from: €200* ✉ *Calle Cádiz 22* ☎ *902/570627* 🌐 *www.hotelbahiasantander.com* 🛏 *188 rooms* 🍴 *No meals.*

Las Brisas

$$$ | **B&B/INN** | Jesús García runs his family's century-old mansion as an upscale, cottage-style hotel by the sea. **Pros:** close to the shore; fresh and briny Atlantic air; cozy basement bar and breakfast room. **Cons:** mildly disorganized; some rooms are a bit cramped; a long walk to the city center. [$] *Rooms from: €139* ✉ *C. la Braña 14, El Sardinero* ☎ *942/270111* 🌐 *www.hotellasbrisas.net* 🕒 *Closed Dec. 15–Feb. 15* 🛏 *13 rooms* 🍴 *Free Breakfast.*

Shopping

For most items head to the center: the streets around the ayuntamiento are good for clothing, shoes, and sportswear. At the bustling Mercado de la Esperanza, just behind the ayuntamiento, you can find fish and shellfish that have been freshly plucked from the sea of Cantabria, as well as locally produced cheeses and meat. Open-air fruit and vegetable stalls mark the entrance.

Mantequerías Cántabras

FOOD/CANDY | Fine foods, including the santanderino specialty *dulces pasiegos* (light and sugary cakes), can be sampled and bought here. ✉ *Pl. de Italia s/n* ☎ *942/272899.*

Santillana del Mar

29 km (18 miles) west of Santander.

Santillana del Mar has developed a thriving tourism industry based on the famed cave art discovered 2 km (1 mile) north of town—and the town itself is worth a visit of at least a day. Just as the Altamira Caves have captured the essence of prehistoric life, the streets, plazas, taverns, and manor houses of Santillana del Mar paint a vivid portrait of medieval and Renaissance village life in northern Spain. Its stunning ensemble of 15th- to 17th-century stone houses is one of Spain's greatest architectural collections.

VISITOR INFORMATION

CONTACTS Santillana del Mar ✉ *C. Jesús Otero 20* ☎ *942/818812* 🌐 *www.santillanadelmarturismo.com.*

Did You Know?

Santillana del Mar is sometimes called the Town of Three Lies, because it isn't holy (*santa*), flat (*llana*), or on a sea (*mar*), as implied. The name actually derives from the local martyr, Santa Juliana (Santa Illana), whose remains are kept in the Colegiata.

Sights

Altamira Caves

CAVE | These world-famous caves, 3 km (2 miles) southwest of Santillana del Mar, have been called the Sistine Chapel of prehistoric art for the beauty of their drawings, believed to be some 20,000 years old. First uncovered in 1875, the caves are a testament to early mankind's admiration of beauty and surprising technical skill in representing it, especially in the use of rock forms to accentuate perspective. There's a lottery system for tickets to enter the caves, and only a small number of visitors are allowed in each month—but the reproduction in the **museum** is open to all. ✉ *Museo de Altamira, Marcelino Sanz de Sautuola s/n* ☎ *942/818005* 🌐 *museodealtamira.mcu.es* 🎟 *€3 (free Sat. afternoon and Sun.)* 🕒 *Closed Mon.*

Colegiata de Santa Juliana

BUILDING | Santillana del Mar is built around the Colegiata, Cantabria's finest Romanesque structure. Highlights include the 12th-century cloister, famed for its sculpted capitals, a 16th-century altarpiece, and the tomb of Santa Juliana, who is the town's patron saint and namesake. ✉ *Pl. Abad Francisco Navarro s/n* ☎ *639/830520* 🎟 *€3.*

Museo Diocesano

MUSEUM | Inside the 16th-century Regina Coeli convent is a museum devoted to liturgical art, which includes wooden figures of saints, oil paintings of biblical scenes, altarpieces, and a collection of sacred treasures from the colonial New World. ✉ *C. El Cruce s/n* ☎ *942/840317* 🎟 *€3* 🕒 *Closed Mon.*

Hotels

Casa del Organista

$$ | **B&B/INN** | A typical *casona montañesa* (noble mountain manor) with painstakingly crafted stone and wood details, this intimate hideaway makes a slightly rustic, elegant base for exploring one of Spain's finest Renaissance towns. **Pros:** good base; warm interior design; lovely views of tiled roofs and rolling hills. **Cons:** limited availability and difficult to book in high season; some rooms are very small; no elevator. [$] *Rooms from: €96* ✉ *C. Los Hornos 4* ☎ *942/840352* 🌐 *www.casadelorganista.com* 🕒 *Closed Dec. 21–Jan. 20* 🛏 *14 rooms* 🍴 *No meals.*

★ Parador de Santillana Gil Blas

$$$ | **HOTEL** | Built in the 16th century, this lovely stone palace comes with baronial rooms, with heavy wood beams overhead and splendid antique furnishings. **Pros:** storybook surroundings; elegant decor; attentive service. **Cons:** expensive; a little breezy and chilly in winter; noise carries from the square into the rooms. [$] *Rooms from: €175* ✉ *Pl. Ramón Pelayo 11* ☎ *942/028028* 🌐 *www.parador.es* 🛏 *28 rooms* 🍴 *No meals.*

Chapter 6

THE BASQUE COUNTRY, NAVARRA, AND LA RIOJA

Updated by
Benjamin Kemper

6

⊙ Sights	⑪ Restaurants	🛏 Hotels	🛍 Shopping	🍸 Nightlife
★★★★★	★★★★★	★★★★☆	★★★★☆	★★★☆☆

WELCOME TO THE BASQUE COUNTRY, NAVARRA, AND LA RIOJA

TOP REASONS TO GO

★ **Explore the Basque coast:** From colorful fishing villages to tawny beaches, the craggy Basque coast always delights the eye.

★ **Eat** *pintxos* **(bar snacks) in San Sebastián:** Nothing matches San Sebastián's Parte Vieja, where tavern hoppers graze at counters heaped with eye-catching morsels.

★ **Appreciate Bilbao's art and architecture:** The gleaming titanium Guggenheim and the Museo de Bellas Artes (Fine Arts Museum) shimmer where steel mills and shipyards once stood, while verdant pastures can be seen in the distance.

★ **Party with the world during San Fermín in Pamplona:** The annual festival highlighted by the bull runs draws visitors from around the globe. It'll get your adrenaline pumping whether you're running with a pack of fierce bulls (and people) or watching from the sidelines with a *gin-tónic.*

★ **Drink in La Rioja wine country:** Spain's premier wine region is filled with wine-tasting opportunities, fascinating history, and fine cuisine.

Note: The Basque Country, known as "Euskadi" or "Euskal Herria" in the Basque language, spills over the French border, with two provinces located outside Spain. For ease of reading, we chose not to use qualifiers like "Spanish" when mentioning Spain's autonomous region, as the French Basque Country is not covered in this guide. In addition, although most locales and subjects in this chapter have separate Basque and Castilian (Spanish) spellings, we've given preference to the most prevalent name (e.g., "pintxos" instead of "pinchos" and "San Sebastián" instead of "Donosti").

1 **Bilbao.** Go for the Guggenheim; stay for the pintxos and the quaint *casco viejo* (old town).

2 **Bermeo.** Check out the most important fishing port in the Basque Country.

3 **Mundaka.** Surf with the pros.

4 **Axpe Atxondo.** Live your Basque rural fantasy in a tiny mountain town.

5 **Getaria and Zumaia.** Explore Balenciaga's old stomping grounds and taste the grilled turbot that Anthony Bourdain made famous.

6 **San Sebastián.** Make a pilgrimage to Spain's culinary mecca with more Michelin stars per capita than (almost) any other city on earth.

7 **Vitoria-Gasteiz.** Experience true-blue Basque culture without a tour bus in sight in the region's gritty industrial capital.

8 **Laguardia.** Swirl and sip world-class wine in ultramodern tasting rooms.

9 **Pasaia.** Slow down in a sleepy fishing village just a few minutes' drive from San Sebastián.

10 **Hondarribia.** Stroll among colorful captains' houses before hopping on a ferry to France.

11 **Pamplona.** Run with the bulls (if you dare), or visit in the off-season to steep yourself in Navarran culture.

12 **Puenta la Reina.** A common stop at the junction of the two Camino de Santiago pilgrimage routes from northern Europe.

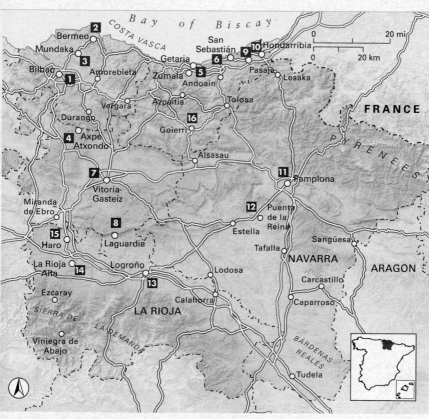

13 Logroño. Make this scrappy, food-focused city your home base for enological adventures in La Rioja.

14 La Rioja Alta. Hop from *bodega* (winery) to bodega in La Rioja's most coveted wine-producing area.

15 Haro. Hole up in La Rioja's most wine-centric town, and post up at Hemingway's favorite *asador*—a restaurant specializing in grilled fish and meats.

EATING AND DRINKING WELL IN THE BASQUE COUNTRY

Basque cuisine, Spain's most prestigious regional gastronomy, may incorporate the refined culinary sensibilities of the French and the no-nonsense country cooking of inland Iberia, but it's no hybrid cuisine.

The distinctive seafood, meat, and vegetable dishes served here are often impossible to find elsewhere in Spain, thanks to hyperlocal ingredients and culinary secrets passed down from generation to generation.

The so-called *nueva cocina vasca* (new Basque cooking) movement began more than 40 years ago as an echo of the nouvelle cuisine of France. Young chefs like Pedro Subijana and Juan Mari Arzak began deconstructing versions of classic Basque dishes like *marmitako* (tuna and potato stew) and *bacalao al pil pil* (salt cod bathed in emulsified garlic sauce) with the aim to redefine and promote Basque cooking globally. Today the region has the world's second-highest concentration of Michelin stars per capita. Although the core of Basque cooking hinges on the art of preparing fish, there is no dearth of lamb, beef, or pork in the Basque diet or on menus.

CIDER

Don't miss a chance to go to a *sagardotegi*, a boisterous cider house where the cider spurts into your glass straight from the barrel to be quaffed in a single gulp. *Txuletas de buey* (juicy rib eyes grilled over coals) and *tortilla de bacalao* (cod omelet) provide ballast for the rustic apple cider. The cider-cod combination is linked to the Basque fishermen and whalers who carried cider, rather than wine, in their galleys.

BABY EELS

Angulas, known as elvers in English, are a Basque delicacy that has become an expensive treat, with prices reaching €1,000 a kilogram. The 3- to 4-inch-long eels look like spaghetti with eyes and are typically served in a small earthenware dish sizzling with olive oil, garlic, and a single slice of chili. A special wooden fork is used to eat them, to avoid any metallic taste and because the wood grips the slippery eels better than metal. Don't be misled by the "gulas" sold in lower-end tapas bars and groceries across Spain. They look just like angulas, but they're made from processed whitefish.

BACALAO

Cod, a Basque favorite since the Stone Age, comes in various guises. Bacalao al pil pil is a classic Bilbao specialty, simmered—rather than fried—with garlic and olive oil in its own juices. The "pil pil" refers to the sound of the emulsion of cod and olive oil bubbling up from the bottom of the pan. Served with a red chili pepper, this is a beloved Basque delicacy.

BESUGO A LA DONOSTIARRA

Besugo (sea bream) cooked San Sebastián style is baked in the oven, covered with flakes of garlic that look like scales, and sprinkled with vinegar and parsley before serving.

OX

Oxen in the Basque Country have traditionally been work animals, fed and maintained with great reverence and care. When slaughtered at the age of 12 or 13, their flesh is tender and marbled with streaks of fat rich with grassy aromas. Most of today's ox steaks and chops (*txuletas de buey,* or "beef chops") aren't cut from work oxen, but a hulking beefsteak, cooked to juicy perfection over coals, is still as beguiling.

TUNA AND POTATO STEW

Marmitako, the Basques' answer to bouillabaisse, is a stick-to-your-ribs potato, yellowfin tuna, and red pepper stew. Beware: it usually has a strong fishy taste. One bite, and you'll understand why the dish, named after the French for cooking pot (*marmite*), has long been the preferred restorative for weather-beaten seafarers.

WINE

Basque Txakoli, a simple, zippy white (and, increasingly, rosé) made from tart indigenous grapes, is refreshing with seafood and pintxos. Those who prefer a red should spring for a wine from Rioja Alavesa, the Basque part of Rioja wine country north of the Ebro.

Northern Spain is a misty land of green hills, low russet roof lines, and colorful fishing villages; it's also home to the formerly industrial city of Bilbao, reborn as a center of art and architecture. The semiautonomous Basque Country—with its steady drizzle (onomatopoetically called the *siri-miri*), verdant landscape, and rugged coastline—is a distinct national and cultural entity.

Navarra is considered Basque in the Pyrenees—indeed, Euskera is spoken in much of the region's north and Navarran in the south, along the Río Ebro. La Rioja, tucked between the Sierra de la Demanda (a mountain range that separates La Rioja from the central Castilian steppe) and the Ebro, is Spain's premier wine country.

Called the País Vasco in Castilian Spanish and Euskadi in the linguistically mysterious, non-Indo-European Basque language, Euskera, the Basque region is essentially a country within a country, or a nation within a state (the semantics are much debated). Though a significant portion of Basques still favor independence from Spain, the separatist terrorist organization ETA (Euskadi Ta Askatasuna, meaning "Basque Homeland and Liberty"), which used to cause some travelers pause, officially disbanded on May 2, 2018. There have been no significant politically motivated acts of violence in the region in more than a decade. Basque culture, with its pre-Roman roots, is unlike that of any other region in Spain. In local festivals, you can still watch as locals play such rural sports as chopping mammoth tree trunks and lifting boulders. The Basques' competitive streak carries over into poetry and gastronomy; *bertsolaris* (amateur poets) improvise duels of sharp-witted verse, and gastronomic societies compete in cooking contests to see who can make the best *sopa de ajo* (garlic soup) or marmitako.

MAJOR REGIONS

Bilbao and Inland Basque Country. Starring Frank Gehry's titanium brainchild, the Museo Guggenheim Bilbao, **Bilbao** has established itself as one of Spain's 21st-century magnets. Medieval Vitoria is the capital of Álava and the whole Basque Country and is relatively undiscovered by tourists; same goes for Goierri and Axpe Atxondo, wooded oases situated in the provinces of Gipuzkoa and Vizcaya, respectively.

San Sebastián and the Basque Coast. With Bilbao and the tiny harbor of Bermeo in the rearview, trace the coastal BI3438 east from the fishing village of Lekeitio toward San Sebastián, and you'll find colorful seaside towns, jaw-dropping views of the Atlantic, and quaint beach resorts, making this snaking highway one of the most scenic drives in all of Spain. After passing the sleepy port of Getaria and a handful of well-to-do beach resorts like Zumaia, you'll arrive in **San Sebastián,** Bilbao's aristocratic cousin, a city that invites you to slow down with its elegant boardwalks and leisurely pintxo crawls. East of the city are **Pasaia** (Spanish: Pasajes), from which the Marquis de Lafayette set off to help the rebel forces in the American Revolution and where Victor Hugo spent a winter writing, and Hondarribia, a brightly painted, flower-festooned port town just shy of the French border. Note to sufers: for the best waves (and surf schools), head to Mundaka, a 45-minute drive north of Bilbao.

Navarra and Pamplona. Bordering the French Pyrenees and populated largely by Basques, Navarra grows progressively less Basque toward its southern and eastern edges. **Pamplona,** the ancient Navarran capital, draws crowds with its annual celebration of San Fermín, where the main event is the running of the bulls. Olite, south of Pamplona, has a storybook castle. The towns of Puente la Reina and Estella are visually indelible stops on the Camino de Santiago.

A rugged compendium of highlands, plains, and vineyards nourished by the Río Ebro, **La Rioja** (named for the Río Oja) has historically produced Spain's finest wines. Most inhabitants live along the Ebro, in the cities of **Logroño** and **Haro,** though the mountains and upper river valleys are arguably the most scenic areas. A mix of Atlantic and Mediterranean climates and cultures with Basque overtones, La Rioja comprises La Rioja Alta (Upper Rioja), the mountainous western end (where most of the region's great wines come from); La Rioja Alavesa, situated north of the Ebro and taking in Álava and Laguardia (with its highly architectural wineries); and La Rioja Baja (Lower Rioja), the parched eastern extremity with a more Mediterranean climate and less prestigious wines. Logroño, the main population center, is a good jumping-off point for all three viticultural areas.

Planning
When to Go

Relatively clear skies and warm temperatures last from mid-April to mid-October, making the warm-weather months the best time of year to visit. Some shops and restaurants close in August.

Pamplona in July is bedlam, though for hard-core party animals it's heaven.

The Basque Country is rainy in the winter, but the bracing Atlantic weather can be invigorating if you're in the right mindset. Foodies will be rewarded for traveling in the off-season as January through May is prime sagardotegi season, when the local producers fling open their doors and serve multicourse, all-you-can-drink meals. Indeed, Basque cuisine's heartiest, richest dishes taste their best when it's cold and damp outside.

The September film festival in San Sebastián coincides with the spectacular whaleboat regattas, while the beaches are still ideal and mostly uncrowded.

When looking for a place to stay, remember that the north is an expensive, well-to-do part of Spain, which is reflected in room rates—though some steals can be found in the off-season (and on Airbnb). San Sebastián is particularly pricey, and Pamplona rates triple during San Fermín in July. Be sure to book far ahead for summer travel.

Planning Your Time

A road trip through the Basque Country, Navarra, and La Rioja would require at least a week, but you can get a good sense of Bilbao and San Sebastián, the region's most essential cities, in two days each. The Baztán Valley, Pamplona, Laguardia, and La Rioja's capital, Logroño, are other top stops.

If you have a spare day or two, visit Mundaka and the coast of Vizcaya west of Bilbao; Getaria, Pasaia, and Hondarribia near San Sebastián; and the wineries of Haro in La Rioja.

La Rioja's Sierra de la Demanda also has some of the finest landscapes in Spain, not to mention culinary pilgrimages to "gastronomical hotel" Echaurren in Ezcaray or Venta de Goyo in Viniegra de Abajo.

Getting Here and Around

AIR TRAVEL
Bilbao's airport serves much of this area, and there are smaller, notoriously expensive airports at Hondarribia (serving San Sebastián), Logroño, and Pamplona, which are generally only used by domestic carriers in high season.

AIRPORTS Aeropuerto de Bilbao ✉ *48180 Loiu, Bilbao* ⊕ *www.aena.es.*

BICYCLE TRAVEL
Bicycle travel in the Basque Country and across the north of Spain is hilly and often wet, but for the intrepid cyclist, it's a scenic way to get from A to B, even if the roads have notoriously narrow shoulders.

BICYCLE RENTALS

BOAT AND FERRY TRAVEL
Brittany Ferries has routes from Portsmouth (United Kingdom) to Bilbao three times a week. The intriguing if impractical trip takes between 27 and 34 hours and costs approximately $85 each way.

BUS TRAVEL
Frequent coach bus service connects the major cities to Madrid, Zaragoza, and Barcelona (with a layover or transfer to Spain's other destinations). The trip

between Barcelona and Bilbao takes seven to eight hours. Reserve online at ⊕ *www.alsa.es.*

Bus service between cities and smaller towns is surprisingly comprehensive—and cheap. Consult Google Maps or visit a local tourist office for route information.

CAR TRAVEL
Even the remotest points are an easy one-day drive from Madrid, and northern Spain is superbly covered by freeways.

The drive from Madrid to Bilbao is 397 km (247 miles), about five hours; follow the A1 past Burgos to Miranda del Ebro, where you pick up the AP68. Car rentals are available in the major cities: Bilbao, Pamplona, San Sebastián, Hondarribia, and Vitoria. A note about signage: the Basque word for "calle" is *kalea.* We have standardized our addresses using "calle" for ease of Google Mapping, but you will see "kalea" on road signs in most Basque locales.

TAXI TRAVEL
In cities, taxis can usually be hailed on the street, and drivers are generally amenable to longer trips (say, from San Sebastián to Astigarraga's cider houses).

TRAIN TRAVEL
For now, standard-speed RENFE trains connect Madrid to Bilbao, San Sebastián, and Logroño, though the much-anticipated AVE (expected to be completed in 2023) will soon make the trip much quicker. Once you've arrived, a car is the most convenient way to get around, but the regional company FEVE runs a delightful (if perpetually late) narrow-gauge train that winds through stunning landscapes. From San Sebastián, lines west to Bilbao (the Euskotren) and east to Hendaye, France, depart from Estación de Amara; most long-distance trains use RENFE's Estación del Norte. *See the Travel Smart chapter for more information about train travel.*

Rideshare Travel

If you don't have access to a car, the fastest and cheapest way to get to the Basque Country, Navarra, and La Rioja is via the Blablacar rideshare app, which boasts more worldwide users than Uber. Simply type your origin and destination into the app, select the itinerary that best suits your schedule, and confirm your booking via credit card. You can then text with the driver to arrange pickup and drop-off locations. Prices remain low because it is a rideshare service as opposed to a taxi-like service, and drivers aren't allowed to make a profit (the fee you pay helps offset the cost of gas and tolls). Download the app in your mobile provider's app store or browse trips on ⊕ www.blablacar.com.

Restaurants

Foodies may never want to leave the Basque Country, where the avant-garde and home cooking merge seamlessly. Everywhere you look in the region's cities and towns, there are mom-and-pop taverns, pintxo bars, and asadores. But this area of Spain is also known for its Michelin-starred destination restaurants, venues sequestered in off-the-beaten-path villages that have become dining meccas, like Asador Etxebarri (Atxondo), Martín Berasategui (Lasarte), and Mugaritz (Errenteria).

Hotels

Ever since the Guggenheim put Bilbao on the map as a design destination, the city's hotel fleet has expanded and reflected (in the case of the Gran Hotel Domine, literally) the glitter and panache of Gehry's museum. Boutique hotels, chic designer properties, and trusted-brand behemoths have made older hotels look small and quaint by comparison. *Hotel reviews have been shortened. For full information, visit Fodors.com.*

What It Costs in Euros

	$	$$	$$$	$$$$
RESTAURANTS				
	under €12	€12–€17	€18–€22	over €22
HOTELS				
	under €90	€90–€125	€126–€180	over €180

Bilbao

34 km (21 miles) southeast of Castro-Urdiales, 116 km (72 miles) east of Santander, 397 km (247 miles) north of Madrid.

Time in Bilbao ("Bilbo" in Euskera) may be recorded as BG or AG (Before Guggenheim or After Guggenheim). Seldom has a single monument of art and architecture so radically changed a city. Frank Gehry's stunning museum, Norman Foster's sleek subway system, the Santiago Calatrava glass footbridge and airport, the leafy César Pelli Abandoibarra park and commercial complex next to the Guggenheim, and the Philippe Starck Azkuna Zentroa cultural center have contributed to an unprecedented cultural revolution in what was once the industry capital of the Basque Country.

Bilbao's new attractions get more press, but the city's old treasures still quietly line the banks of the rust-color Nervión. The **casco viejo** (old quarter)—also known as Siete Calles (Seven Streets)—is a charming jumble of shops, bars, and restaurants on the river's right bank, near the Puente del Arenal. This elegant proto-Bilbao nucleus was carefully restored after devastating floods in 1983. Throughout the casco viejo are ancient mansions emblazoned with family coats of arms, wooden doors, and fine ironwork balconies. The most interesting square is the

64-arch Plaza Nueva, where an outdoor market is pitched every Sunday morning.

On the left bank, the wide, late-19th-century boulevards of the **Ensanche** neighborhood, such as Gran Vía (the main shopping artery) and Alameda de Mazarredo, are the city's more formal face. Bilbao's cultural institutions include, along with the Guggenheim, a major museum of fine arts (the Museo de Bellas Artes) and an opera society (Asociación Bilbaína de Amigos de la Ópera, or ABAO) whose program includes 47 performances attended by more than 90,000 spectators. In addition, epicureans have long ranked Bilbao's culinary offerings among the best in Spain. Attention, *fútbol* fans: don't miss a chance to ride the trolley line, the Euskotren, for a trip along the river from Atxuri Station to Basurto's San Mamés soccer stadium, reverently dubbed "La Catedral del Fútbol" (The Cathedral of Football).

GETTING HERE AND AROUND

Euskotren's Tranvía Bilbao, running up and down the Ría de Bilbao (aka Nervión estuary) past the Guggenheim to the Mercado de la Ribera, is an attraction in its own right: silent, swift, and panoramic as it glides up and down its grassy runway. The Euskotren that leaves from Atxuri Station north of the Mercado de la Ribera runs along a spectacular route through Gernika and the Urdaibai Biosphere Preserve to Mundaka and Bermeo, probably the best way short of a boat to see this lovely wetlands preserve.

Bilbobus provides bus service from 6:15 am to 10:55 pm. Plaza Circular and Plaza Moyúa are the principal hubs for all lines. Once the metro and normal bus routes stop service, take a night bus, known as a Gautxori ("night bird"). Six lines run every 30 minutes between Plaza Circular and Plaza Moyúa and the city limits on Friday from 11:30 pm to 2 am and on Saturday overnight until 7 am.

Metro Bilbao is linear, running down the Nervión estuary from Basauri, above,

or east of, the casco viejo, all the way to the mouth of the Nervión at Getxo, before continuing to the beach town of Plentzia. The Moyúa station is the most central stop and lies in the middle of Bilbao's Ensanche, or modern part. The second subway line runs down the left bank of the Nervión to Santurtzi. The fare is €1.60–€1.90 for a one-way ticket, €3–€3.50 for a return ticket, and just €0.91–€1.19 with the Barik travel card.

The Funicular de Artxanda connects Bilbao to Artxanda Mountain. The fare is €4 round-trip.

BUS AND SUBWAY INFORMATION
Bilbobus ☎ 94/445–3471 ⊕ www.bilbobus.com. **Metro Bilbao** ☎ 94/425–4025 ⊕ www.metrobilbao.eus.

STATIONS Bilbao-Abando Railway Station
✉ Edificio Terminus, Pl. Circular 2, El Ensanche ☎ 94/479–5760 ⊕ www.adif. es. **Euskotren** ✉ Casco Viejo ☎ 90/254–3210 ⊕ www.euskotren.es. **Termibus Bilbao** ✉ Gurtubay 1, San Mamés ☎ 94/439–5077 ⊕ www.termibus.es.

FUNICULAR Funicular de Artxanda ✉ Pl. de Funicular, Matiko ☎ 94/445–4966 ⊕ www.bilbao.net/funicularartxanda Ⓜ Casco Viejo.

VISITOR INFORMATION
CONTACTS Bilbao Tourism Office ✉ Pl. Circular, 1st fl., El Ensanche ☎ 94/479–5760 ⊕ www.bilbaoturismo.net Ⓜ Moyúa.

TOURS
Bilbao Paso a Paso
GUIDED TOURS | Bilbao Paso a Paso organizes walking tours, guided visits to the Guggenheim, hot-air-balloon rides, gastronomical tours around the city, and excursions to nearby sites. ✉ Calle Egaña 17, 5th fl., Suite 4, Casco Viejo ☎ 94/415–3892 ⊕ www.bilbaopasoapaso. com ☞ From €175 Ⓜ Casco Viejo.

Bilbao Turismo
GUIDED TOURS | Weekend guided tours, in English and Spanish, are conducted by the tourist office (reservations required).

The casco viejo tour starts at 10 am at the ground floor of the main tourist office on the Plaza Circular. The Ensanche and Abandoibarra tour begins at noon from the tourist office to the left of the Guggenheim entrance. Both tours last 90 minutes. ⊠ *Pl. Circular 1, El Ensanche* ☎ *94/479–5760* ⊕ *www.bilbaoturismo. net* ⊠ *€5* Ⓜ *Abando.*

Bilboats

BOATING | One- and two-hour boat tours take you downstream from Plaza Pío Baroja the city center, passing some of Bilbao's iconic buildings and bridges. Customized day trips can also be arranged. ⊠ *Pl. Pío Baroja* ☎ *94/642–4157* ⊕ *www. bilboats.com* ⊠ *From €13* Ⓜ *Moyúa.*

 # Sights

Azkuna Zentroa

ARTS VENUE | In the early 20th century this was a municipal wine-storage facility used by Bilbao's Rioja wine barons. Now, the city-block-size, Philippe Starck–designed civic center is filled with shops, cafés, restaurants, movie theaters, swimming pools, fitness centers, and nightlife opportunities at the very heart of the city. Conceived as a hub for entertainment, culture, wellness, and civic coexistence, it added another star to Bilbao's cosmos of architectural and cultural offerings when it opened. The complex regularly hosts film festivals and art exhibitions, and it's a cozy place to take refuge on a rainy afternoon. ⊠ *Pl. Arriquibar 4, El Ensanche* ☎ *94/401–4014* ⊕ *www.azkunazentroa.com/az/ingl/home* Ⓜ *Moyúa.*

Basílica de Nuestra Señora de Begoña

RELIGIOUS SITE | Bilbao's most cherished religious sanctuary, dedicated to the patron saint of Vizcaya, can be reached by the 313 stairs from Plaza de Unamuno or by the gigantic elevator (the Ascensor de Begoña) looming over Calle Esperanza 6 behind the San Nicolás church. The church's Gothic nave was begun in 1519 on the site of an early hermitage, where the Virgin Mary was alleged to have appeared long before. Finished in 1620, the basilica was completed with the economic support of the shipbuilders and merchants of Bilbao, many of whose businesses are commemorated on the inner walls of the church. The high ground the basilica occupies was strategically important during the Carlist Wars of 1836 and 1873, and as a result La Begoña suffered significant damage that was not restored until the beginning of the 20th century. It's comparable in importance to Barcelona's Virgen de Montserrat. ⊠ *Calle Virgen de Begoña 38, Begoñalde* ☎ *94/412–7091* ⊠ *Free* Ⓜ *Casco Viejo.*

Catedral de Santiago (*St. James's Cathedral*)

RELIGIOUS SITE | Bilbao's earliest church was a pilgrimage stop on the coastal route to Santiago de Compostela. Work on the structure began in 1379, but fire delayed completion until the early 16th century. The florid Gothic style with Isabelline elements features a nave in the form of a Greek cross, with ribbed vaulting resting on cylindrical columns. The notable outdoor arcade, or *pórtico*, was used for public meetings of the early town's governing bodies. ⊠ *Pl. de Santiago 1, Casco Viejo* ☎ *94/415–3627* ⊕ *www.catedralbilbao.com* ⊠ *€5* Ⓜ *Casco Viejo.*

Euskal Museoa Bilbao Museo Vasco (*Basque Museum of Bilbao*)

MUSEUM | This be-all-end-all museum on Basque ethnography and Bilbao's cultural history occupies a 16th-century convent. Highlights include El Mikeldi, a pre-Christian, Iron Age stone animal representation that may be 4,000 years old; the room dedicated to Basque shepherds and the pastoral way of life; and the exhibit *Mar de los Vascos* (*Sea of the Basques*) about whaling, fishing, and maritime activities. Placards are in Spanish and Basque only. ⊠ *Pl. Unamuno 4, Casco Viejo* ☎ *94/415–5423* ⊕ *www.*

euskal-museoa.eus/es ⓦ *€3 (free Thurs.)* ◷ *Closed Tues.* Ⓜ *Casco Viejo.*

Funicular de Artxanda

VIEWPOINT | For an easy and quick excursion, take a five-minute spin on the Artxanda Funicular, the railway that joins downtown Bilbao with the summit of Artxanda Mountain. The panorama from the hillsides of Artxanda is the most comprehensive view of Bilbao, and the summit also includes a park, hotel, sports complex, and several restaurants. The asadores, in particular, are excellent. ⓧ *Pl. de Funicular, Matiko* ☎ *94/445–4966* ⓦ *www.bilbao.net/funicularartxanda* ⓦ *€4 round-trip* Ⓜ *Casco Viejo.*

Iglesia de San Nicolás

RELIGIOUS SITE | Honoring the patron saint of mariners, San Nicolás de Bari, the city's early waterfront church was built over an earlier hermitage and consecrated in 1756. With a striking Baroque facade over the Arenal, originally a sandy beach, the church weathered significant damage at the hands of French and Carlist troops in the 19th century. Sculptures by Juan Pascual de Mena adorn the interior. Look for the oval plaque to the left of the door marking the high-water mark of the flood of 1983. ⓧ *Pl. de San Nicolás 1, Casco Viejo* ☎ *94/416–3424* ⓦ *Free* Ⓜ *Casco Viejo.*

★ Mercado de la Ribera

MARKET | This renovated triple-decker ocean liner, with its prow facing down the estuary toward the open sea, is one of the best markets of its kind in Europe—and one of the biggest, with more than 400 retail stands covering 37,950 square feet that run the gamut from fish markets to pintxo bars and wine shops. Like the architects of the Guggenheim and the Palacio de Euskalduna nearly 75 years later, the architect here was playful with this epicurean mecca in the river. From the stained-glass entryway over Calle de la Ribera to the tiny catwalks over the river and the bustling pintxo stalls on the ground floor,

the market is an inviting—if increasingly overtouristed—place. ⓧ *Calle de la Ribera 22, Casco Viejo* ☎ *94/602–3791* ⓦ *mercadodelaribera.biz* ◷ *Closed Sun.* Ⓜ *Casco Viejo.*

★ Museo de Bellas Artes (*Museum of Fine Arts*)

MUSEUM | Considered one of the top five museums in a country that has a staggering number of museums and great paintings, the Museo de Bellas Artes is like a mini Prado, with representatives from every Spanish school and movement from the 12th through 20th centuries. The museum's fine collection of Flemish, French, Italian, and Spanish paintings includes works by El Greco, Francisco de Goya y Lucientes, Diego Velázquez, José Ribera, Paul Gauguin, and Antoni Tàpies. One large and excellent section traces developments in 20th-century Spanish and Basque art alongside works by better-known European contemporaries, such as Fernand Léger and Francis Bacon. Look especially for Zuloaga's famous portrait of La Condesa Mathieu de Moailles and Joaquín Sorolla's portrait of Basque philosopher Miguel de Unamuno. ⓧ *Parque de Doña Casilda de Iturrizar, Pl. Museo 2, El Ensanche* ☎ *94/439–6060* ⓦ *www.museobilbao.com* ⓦ *€10 (free 6–8 pm)* ◷ *Closed Tues.* Ⓜ *Moyúa.*

★ Museo Guggenheim Bilbao

BUILDING | With its eruption of light in the ruins of Bilbao's scruffy shipyards and steelworks, the Guggenheim has dramatically reanimated this onetime industrial city. At once suggestive of a silver-scaled fish and a mechanical heart, Frank Gehry's sculpture in titanium, limestone, and glass is the perfect habitat for the 250 contemporary and postmodern artworks it contains. Artists whose names are synonymous with the art of the 20th century (Kandinsky, Picasso, Miró, Pollock, Calder, and Malevich) and European artists of the 1950s and 1960s (Eduardo Chillida, Antoni Tàpies, Jose Maria Iglesias, Francesco Clemente, and Anselm Kiefer) are joined by contemporary

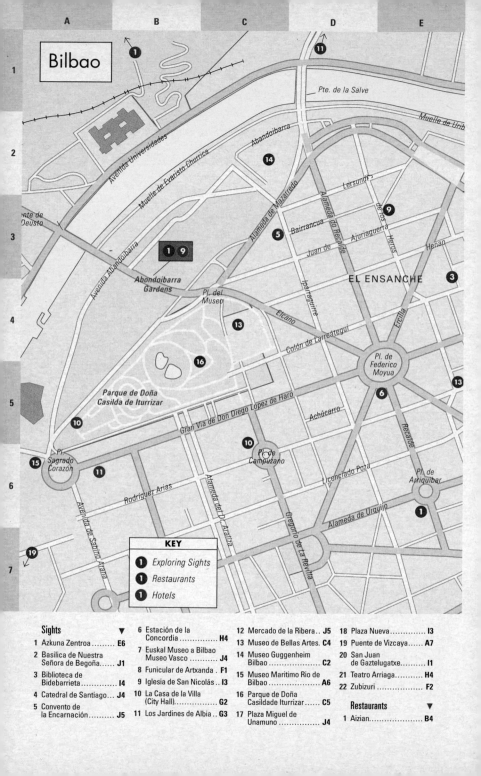

Bilbao

KEY

1 *Exploring Sights*

1 *Restaurants*

1 *Hotels*

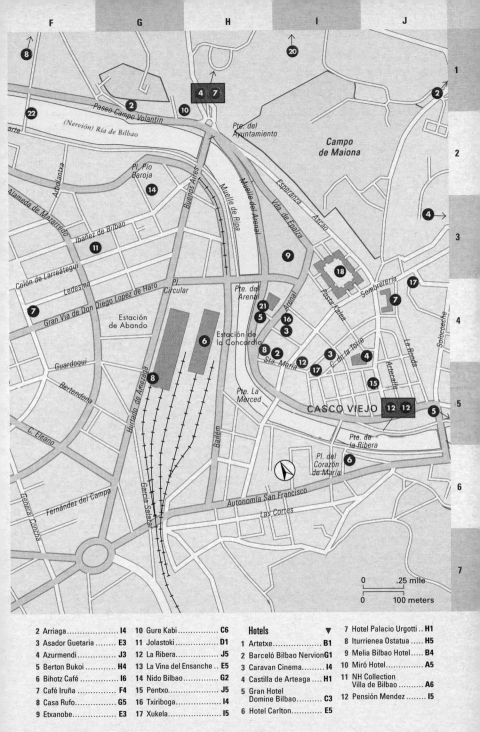

F   G   H   I   J

1

2

3

4

5

6

7

Paseo Campo Volantin

(Nervión) Ría de Bilbao

Pl. Pío Baroja

Campo de Maiona

Pte. del Ayuntamiento

Alameda de Mazarredo

Autolantra

Ibañez de Bilbao

Colón de Larreátegui

Ledesma

Gran Via de Don Diego Lopez de Haro

Estación de Abando

Guardoqui

Bertendona

C. Elcano

General Concha

Fernández del Campo

Hurtado de Amezaga

García Salazar

Bailém

Buenos Aires

Muelle del Arenal

Muelle de Ripa

Vda. de Epaiza

Esperanza

Ascao

Pl. Circular

Pte. del Arenal

Estación de la Concordia

Pte. La Merced

Sta. María

Arenal

posta Kalea

Sombrerería

C. de la Torre

Artecalle

La Ronda

Sotocoeche

Artecalle

CASCO VIEJO

Pte. de la Ribera

Pl. del Corazón de María

Autonomía San Francisco

Las Cortes

0   .25 mile

0   100 meters

figures (Bruce Nauman, Juan Muñoz, Julian Schnabel, Miquel Barceló, and Jean-Michel Basquiat). The ground floor is dedicated to large-format and installation work, some of which—like Richard Serra's *Serpent*—was created specifically for the space. ■TIP➜ **Buy tickets in advance online and from Servicaixa ATMs or, in the Basque Country, the BBK bank machines.** ⊠ *Abandoibarra Etorbidea 2, El Ensanche* ☎ *94/435–9080* ⊕ *www. guggenheim-bilbao.eus* ⊠ *€13* ⊘ *Closed Mon. Sept.–June* Ⓜ *Moyúa.*

Parque de Doña Casilda de Iturrizar

CITY PARK | Bilbao's main park, stretching east toward the river from the Museo de Bellas Artes, is a lush collection of exotic trees, ducks and geese, fountains, falling water, and great expanses of lawns usually dotted with lovers. It's a sanctuary from the hard-edged Ensanche, Bilbao's modern, post-1876 expansion. Doña Casilda de Iturrizar was a well-to-do 19th-century Bilbao matron who married a powerful banker and used his wealth to support various cultural and beneficent institutions in the city, including this grassy refuge. ⊠ *El Ensanche* Ⓜ *San Mamés.*

Plaza Miguel de Unamuno (*Plaza Unamuno*)

PLAZA | Named for Bilbao's all-time-greatest intellectual, figure of fame and fable throughout Spain and beyond, this bright and open space at the upper edge of the casco viejo honors Miguel de Unamuno (1864–1936)—a philosopher, novelist, professor, and wit, as well as a man of character and temperament. Unamuno wrote some of Spain's most seminal works, including *Del sentimiento trágico de la vida en los hombres y los pueblos* (*The Tragic Sense of Life in Men and Nations*); his *Niebla* (*Mist*) has been generally accepted as the first existentialist novel, published in 1914 when Jean-Paul Sartre was but nine years old. ⊠ *Casco Viejo* Ⓜ *Casco Viejo.*

Plaza Nueva (*Plaza Barria*)

PLAZA | This 64-arch neoclassical plaza, built in 1851, is known for its Sunday-morning flea market, December 21 Santo Tomás festivities, and permanent tapas and restaurant offerings. Note the size of the houses' balconies (the bigger the balcony, the richer the original proprietor) and the tiny windows near the top of the facades, where servants' quarters would've been. The building behind the coat of arms at the head of the square was once a government office but is now the **Academia de la Lengua Vasca** (Academy of the Basque Language). The coat of arms shows the tree of Guernica (or Gernika in Basque), symbolic of Basque autonomy, and two wolves, which represent Don Diego López de Haro (López derives from *lupus,* meaning wolf). The bars and shops around the arcades include two **Victor Montes** establishments, one for pintxos at Plaza Nueva 8 and the other for sit-down dining at No. 2. **Café Bar Bilbao** (No. 6), aka Casa Pedro, has Belle Époque interiors accented by photos of early Bilbao, while **Argoitia** (No. 15), across the square, has a nice angle on the midday sun. ⊠ *Casco Viejo* Ⓜ *Casco Viejo.*

★ Puente de Vizcaya (*Hanging Bridge*)

BRIDGE/TUNNEL | One of Bilbao's most extraordinary sights since it was built in 1893, this transporter bridge suspended from cables ferries cars and passengers across the Nervión, uniting two distinct worlds: the exclusive, bourgeois Arenas and Portugalete, a staid, working-class town. Portugalete is a 15-minute walk from Santurce, where the quayside Mandanga Hogar del Pescador serves simple fish specialties. Besugo is the traditional choice, but the grilled sardines are equally sublime at a fraction of the price. ⊠ *Barria 3, Las Arenas* ⊹ *To reach bridge, take subway to Areeta, or drive across Puente de Deusto, turn left on Av. Lehendakari Aguirre, and follow signs for Las Arenas; it's a 10- or 15-min drive from downtown* ☎ *94/480–1012*

⊕ *www.puente-colgante.com* ✉ *From €1*
Ⓜ *Areeta.*

San Juan de Gaztelugatxe

RELIGIOUS SITE | A recent *Game of Thrones* filming location, this solitary stone hermitage clings to a rocky promontory over the Bay of Biscay. A narrow, 231-step passageway connects the 10th-century chapel (perched on what would otherwise be an island) to the mainland, forming one of the region's most dramatic—and photogenic—landscapes. Bilbaínos visit the hermitage on holidays for good luck. ■**TIP➜ A walk around San Juan de Gaztelugatxe's chapel bell tower is said to cure nightmares and insomnia—and to make wishes come true.** ⊠ *San Juan de Gaztelugatxe ✛ 37 km (23 miles) northeast of Bilbao, along the Bay of Biscay, between the towns of Bakio and Bermeo* ⊕ *www.euskoguide.com/places-basque-country/spain/san-juan-de-gaztelugatxe.*

Teatro Arriaga

ARTS VENUE | This 1,500-seat theater was once as exciting a source of Bilbao pride as the Guggenheim is today. Built between 1886 and 1890, when Bilbao's population was a mere 35,000, the Teatro Arriaga represented a gigantic per-capita cultural investment. The original "Nuevo Teatro" (New Theater) de Bilbao was a lavish Belle Époque, neo-baroque jewel modeled after the Paris Opéra, by architect Joaquín Rucoba (1844–1909); it was renamed in 1902 for the bilbaíno musician considered "the Spanish Mozart," Juan Crisóstomo de Arriaga (1806–26). After a 1914 fire, the new version of the theater opened in 1919. Now largely upstaged by the sprawling, modern Palacio de Euskalduna, the Arriaga still hosts its fair share of opera, theater, concerts, and dance events September–June. ⊠ *Pl. Arriaga 1, Casco Viejo* ☎ *94/479–2036* ⊕ *www.teatroarriaga.com* ⊗ *Closed Sun. in July* Ⓜ *Casco Viejo.*

Bilbao Blue

The Guggenheim office building near Jeff Koons's *Puppy* is startlingly, deeply blue. While working on the Guggenheim, Frank Gehry fell in love with this "Bilbao blue," so called for the vivid blue sky seen on rare days when the Atlantic drizzle—the Basque siri-miri—permits. Curiously, as a result of either the Guggenheim's reflected light, less smog, or climate change, Bilbao's blue skies have become more frequent but less intense, leaving the Guggenheim offices and the Perro Chico restaurant, Gehry's favorite, among the few surviving splashes of the city's emblematic color.

Zubizuri

BRIDGE/TUNNEL | Santiago Calatrava's seagull-shaped bridge (the name means "white bridge" in Euskera) connects Campo Volantín on the right bank with El Ensanche on the left and is located just a few minutes from the Guggenheim. Other Calatrava creations in the area include the airport west of Bilbao at Loiu and the bridge at Ondarroa. ⊠ *El Ensanche* Ⓜ *Moyúa.*

🍴 Restaurants

Aizian

$$$$ | SPANISH | Chef José Miguel Olazabalaga's Aizian is anything but a "hotel restaurant," even if it's situated inside the Meliá Bilbao. Sure, his dishes err on the safe side—you won't find tweezed microgreens and dry-ice displays here—but they're dependably delicious: think sautéed wild mushrooms topped with foie gras and a runny egg or seared venison loin with beets and smoked chestnut puree. **Known for:** old-school Basque with a twist; dreamy torrija (Spanish "French" toast); good value for fine dining. $ *Average main: €40* ✉ *Meliá Bilbao, Calle Lehendakari Leizaola 29, El Ensanche* ☎ *94/428–0039* ⊕ *www. restaurante-aizian.com* ⊙ *Closed Sun.* Ⓜ *San Mamés.*

Arriaga

$$$ | BASQUE | The sagardotegi experience is a must in the Basque Country, but if you can't swing a trip to one of the huge cider houses in the countryside, Arriaga is a fine urban stand-in. Expect unlimited *sidra al txotx* (cider drawn straight from the barrel), sausage stewed in apple cider, codfish omelets, txuleta de buey, and Idiazabal cheese with quince preserves. **Known for:** unlimited cider from the kupela (enormous barrel); chargrilled rib eyes; convivial atmosphere. $ *Average main: €22* ✉ *Calle Santa Maria 13, Casco Viejo* ☎ *94/416–5670* ⊕ *www. asadorarriaga.com* Ⓜ *Casco Viejo.*

Asador Guetaria

$$$$ | BASQUE | With a wood-paneled dining room decorated with antiques, this family operation is a longtime local favorite for top-quality fish and meats cooked over coals. The kitchen, open to view, cooks *lubina* (sea bass), besugo, *dorada* (gilthead bream), txuletas de buey, and *chuletas de cordero* (lamb chops) to perfection in a classic asador setting. **Known for:** masterful grilled dishes; familial atmosphere; homey, old-timey dining room. $ *Average main: €50* ✉ *Colón de Larreátegui 12, El Ensanche* ☎ *94/424–3923, 94/423–2527* ⊕ *www. guetaria.com* Ⓜ *Moyúa.*

Azurmendi

$$$$ | BASQUE | This award-winning, highly ranked restaurant, a 10-minute drive from town, is constantly lauded for its envelope-pushing cuisine and industry-leading sustainability practices. The experience begins the moment you enter into its spacious indoor garden, with a chef greeting you with a cocktail before escorting you to the kitchen to be introduced to the "Azurmendi concept." Next is a trip to the sunny greenhouse to nibble on gourmet appetizers made with fresh garden produce, followed by a "picnic" in the lobby with dishes like truffled eggs "cooked inside out." The culinary climax takes place in the dining room with dishes like smoked fish brioche or roasted lobster out of the shell, sluiced with coffee butter. **Known for:** three-Michelin-star dining; most innovative restaurant experience in Bilbao; elegant, minimalist dining room. $ *Average main: €220* ✉ *Legina Auzoa s/n* ☎ *94/455–8866* ⊕ *www.azurmendi.restaurant* ⊙ *Closed Mon.*

Berton Bukoi

$$ | BASQUE | Dinner is served until midnight in this sleek yet casual pintxo spot in the casco viejo. The industrial design—think wood tables with a green-tint polyethylene finish and exposed ventilation pipes—belies a comfort-food-heavy menu with star dishes like grilled octopus brochettes and juicy grilled steaks. **Known for:** top-quality steaks; terrific value; pintxos that punch above their weight. $ *Average main: €15* ✉ *Calle Jardines 8, Casco Viejo* ☎ *94/416–7035* ⊕ *www.berton.eus* Ⓜ *Casco Viejo.*

★ Bihotz Café

$ | CAFÉ | When your feet need a rest, unwind at this third-wave coffeehouse that uses a sleek La Marzocco machine and is furnished with cushy armchairs and floor lamps. There are also small-production vermouths and local craft beers to try alongside soups, sandwiches, and other snacks. **Known for:** best cafés con leche in town; excellent craft beer selection; homey, inviting ambience. $ *Average main: €8* ✉ *Calle Arechaga 6, Casco Viejo* ☎ *94/471–9674* ⊙ *Closed Mon.* Ⓜ *Casco Viejo.*

★ Café Iruña

$$ | CAFÉ | This essential Bilbao haunt (est. 1903) on El Ensanche's most popular garden and square is a favorite for its interior design, boisterous ambience, and tried-and-true classics like Basque steak frites or bacalao al pil pil. The neo-Mudejar

dining room overlooking the square is the place to be—if they try to stuff you in the back dining room, resist or come back another time. **Known for:** no-nonsense Basque comfort food; always packed with locals; intricate neo-Mudejar dining room. $ *Average main: €15* ✉ *Los Jardines de Albia , Calle Berástegui 4, El Ensanche* ☎ *94/423–7021* ⊕ *www. cafeirunabilbao.net* Ⓜ *Moyúa.*

★ Casa Rufo

$$$ | BASQUE | Charming and cozy, this centenarian Bilbao institution is essentially a series of nooks and crannies tucked into a fine food, wine, olive oil, cheese, and ham emporium. Leave it to the affable owners to recommend a house specialty such as the oversize txuleton de buey, which pairs wonderfully with the house Rioja *crianza* (two years in oak, one in bottle) and any number of other bottles from the 1,000-strong wine list. **Known for:** deep wine list with hard-to-find selections; delectable txuleton de buey; homey dining room. $ *Average main: €20* ✉ *Calle Hurtado de Amézaga 5, El Ensanche* ☎ *94/443–2172* ⊕ *www. casarufo.com* ⊘ *Closed Sun.* Ⓜ *Abando.*

Etxanobe

$$$$ | BASQUE | This legendary nueva cocina vasca restaurant relocated to a larger space in 2018 to accommodate two distinct concepts, La Despensa del Etxanobe and Atelier Etxanobe. La Despensa is sexy and informal with dim lighting, neon signage, and look-at-me plating, while the white-tablecloth Atelier features refined seafood-centric cuisine. **Known for:** two restaurants under one roof—one casual and the other refined; impeccable designer decor; pristine seafood. $ *Average main: €70* ✉ *Calle de Juan de Ajuriaguerra 8, El Ensanche* ☎ *94/442–1071* ⊕ *www.atelieretxanobe. com* ⊘ *Closed Tues.* Ⓜ *Uribitarte.*

Gure Kabi

$$$ | SPANISH | FAMILY | This family-friendly restaurant off the tourist track serves a wide range of unfussy, lovingly prepared dishes ranging from creamy squid *croquetas* (croquettes) to griddled European lobster. The best value is the €14 weekday *menú del día* (prix fixe). **Known for:** Basque home cooking; locals-only vibe; killer prix-fixe lunch. $ *Average main: €22* ✉ *Calle Particular de Estraunza 4–6, El Ensanche* ☎ *94/600–4843* ⊕ *www.gurekabi.com* ⊘ *Closed Sun.* Ⓜ *Indautxu.*

Jolastoki

$$$$ | BASQUE | FAMILY | If you find yourself in Getxo, the beach town north of Bilbao where the Puente de Vizcaya is located, treat yourself to a meal at this graceful mansion serving mouthwatering dishes like rice with squid and salsa verde and oxtail in Rioja wine sauce. Set menus, ranging in price from €15 to €75 per person, are a good value whether you're looking to save or splurge. **Known for:** location near the Puente de Vizcaya; locally sourced ingredients; variety of set menus. $ *Average main: €40* ✉ *Av. Los Chopos 21, Neguri* ☎ *94/491–2031* ⊕ *www.restaurantejolastoki.com* ⊘ *Closed Mon. No dinner Sun. and Tues.* Ⓜ *Gobela, Neguri.*

La Ribera

$$$ | BASQUE | FAMILY | Make a beeline to this gastro bar on the ground floor of the eponymous Mercado to satisfy your Basque food cravings after ogling all the shimmering fresh fish, plump *jamónes ibéricos* (Iberian hams), and sweet-smelling fruit. The €14.50 menú del día is a terrific deal, and the highbrow pintxos are consistently tasty. **Known for:** hip, young vibe; good prix-fixe lunch; wide selection of sweet and savory snacks. $ *Average main: €20* ✉ *Mercado de la Ribera, Calle de la Ribera 20, Casco Viejo* ☎ *94/657–5474* ⊕ *www.lariberabilbao. com* ⊘ *Closed Mon. and Tues.* Ⓜ *Casco Viejo.*

★ La Viña del Ensanche

$$$ | BASQUE | Littered with used napkins and furnished with simple wood tables beneath jamones ibéricos hanging from the rafters, this lively, deceptively simple bar attracts locals and tourists alike for its exceptional pintxos. Don't pass up the deconstructed Galician-style octopus on a bed of mashed potatoes laced with *pimentón* (paprika) or the appetizer of homemade foie gras with three preserves. **Known for:** croquetas made with Joselito jamón ibérico; loud, convivial atmosphere; homemade foie gras. $ *Average main: €20* ✉ *Calle Diputazio 10, El Ensanche* ☎ *94/415–5615* ⊕ *www. lavinadelensanche.com* ⊘ *Closed Sun.* Ⓜ *Moyúa.*

★ Nido Bilbao

$$$ | BASQUE | Even the bread is homemade at this wildly popular Basque restaurant on the Left Bank that's renowned for dishes like goose foie gras with raspberry coulis, dry-aged T-bone steaks, and house-made *morcilla* (blood sausage). A list of small-production and organic wines rounds out the hyperlocal dining experience. **Known for:** homemade everything, from sausages to breads and ice creams; natural wines; market-driven cuisine. $ *Average main: €22* ✉ *Calle Barroeta Aldamar 3, El Ensanche* ☎ *94/436–0643* ⊕ *www.nidobilbao.com* ⊘ *Closed Sun.* Ⓜ *Abando.*

★ Pentxo

$$ | BASQUE | FAMILY | Consistently delicious, shockingly affordable, and unapologetically old-school, Pentxo is the sort of restaurant bilbaínos like to keep to themselves. Whether you pop in for a pintxo at the bar (the flash-fried *antxoas rellenas*, or stuffed anchovies, are a must) or come for a €15 prix-fixe lunch (opt for whatever seafood main is listed), you'll leave wishing you could be a regular. **Known for:** local crowd; outstanding pintxos and coffees; unbeatable lunch deal. $ *Average main: €15* ✉ *Calle Belostikale 20, Casco Viejo* ☎ *94/416–9472* ⊕ *www.restaurantepentxo.com* ⊘ *Closed Sun.* Ⓜ *Casco Viejo.*

Txiriboga

$ | TAPAS | Locals flock to this hole-in-the-wall for what might be the city's best croquetas—choose from jamón, chicken, bacalao, or wild mushroom. The *rabas* (fried calamari) also stand out for their nongreasy, ultracrisp exterior. **Known for:** burst-in-your-mouth croquetas; quintessential Basque taberna; terrific calamari. $ *Average main: €9* ✉ *Calle Santa Maria 13, Casco Viejo* ☎ *94/415–7874* ⊘ *Closed Mon.* Ⓜ *Casco Viejo.*

Xukela

$$ | TAPAS | The main draw at this tavern is the pintxos—imaginative, internationally inflected bites ranging from smoked Cantabrian anchovies to mushroom–foie gras toasts. The small place feels like a professor's study, with books and magazines scattered about, and there's a sign on the wall that says, "This is an Atheist establishment." **Known for:** booksy interiors; nueva cocina tapas at taberna prices; varied wine list. $ *Average main: €14* ✉ *Calle de El Perro 2, Casco Viejo* ☎ *94/415–9772* Ⓜ *Casco Viejo.*

Hotels

Artetxe

$ | B&B/INN | FAMILY | With rooms overlooking Bilbao from the heights of Artxanda, this Basque farmhouse with wood trimmings and eager young owners offers excellent value. **Pros:** a peaceful, grassy perch from which to enjoy Bilbao and the Basque countryside; great service; plenty of space for children to play. **Cons:** far from the center, the museums, and the action; BYOB; no evening restaurant service. $ *Rooms from: €65* ✉ *Calle de Berriz 112* ✛ *Off Ctra. Enékuri–Artxanda, Km 7* ☎ *94/474–7780* ⊕ *www.hotelartetxe. com* ⇆ *12 rooms* ⏻ *Free Breakfast.*

★ Barceló Bilbao Nervión

$$$ | HOTEL | Sandwiched between the casco viejo and the industrial area surrounding the Guggenheim, this corporate hotel soars seven stories over the Nervión, and its best rooms boast semicircular windows that make you feel like you're hovering over it. **Pros:** supremely comfortable; great location;

Basque Culture

The Basques are a mystery: nobody knows where they came from or when they arrived in this windswept corner of the Iberian Peninsula. Though the first written records of the Basques are from Roman times, recent studies indicate that this "tribe" of proto-Europeans has inhabited the area for at least 7,000 years. A combination of impenetrable geography and a fierce warrior class kept the Basques somewhat isolated from the rest of the continent for hundreds, if not thousands, of years—enough time to establish and preserve their distinctive mythology, sports, food, and—perhaps most significantly—language, which remains alive and well today.

Basque Language

Although the Basque people speak French north of the border and Spanish south of the border, many (approximately one-quarter of the population on the Spanish side) consider **Euskera** their first language. The mother tongue is so vital to the Basque identity that the cultural signifier "Basque" in Euskera is "Euskalduna," literally "Speaker of Basque." As Europe's only non-Indo-European language, Euskera is one of the great enigmas of linguistic scholarship. To the non-speaker, Euskera sounds like rough, consonant-heavy Spanish, though its highly complex grammar has no relation to the Romance languages.

Basque Cuisine

Traditional Basque cuisine combines the fresh fish of the Atlantic and upland vegetables, beef, and lamb with a love of sauces that is rare south of the Pyrenees. Today the nueva cocina vasca movement has painted Basque food as highly innovative and slightly precious, even if most everyday Basques still eat as they always have. With the sudden trendiness of pintxos (the Basque equivalent of tapas), Basque cuisine is now a part of the culinary zeitgeist in cities from New York to Tokyo.

Basque Sports

A Basque village without a *frontón* (pelota court) is as unimaginable as an American town without a baseball diamond. Pelota, or **jai alai** in Euskera, is the fastest-moving ball sport, according to Guinness World Records, with ball speeds reaching 150 mph. The game is played on a three-walled court 175 feet long and 56 feet wide with 40-foot side walls, and the object is to angle the ball along or off of the side wall so that it cannot be returned. Betting is popular.

Herrikirolak (rural sports) are based on farming and seafaring. Stone lifters (*harrijasotzaileak* in Euskera) heft weights up to 700 pounds. *Aizkolari* (axe men) chop wood in various contests, and the *gizon proba* (man trial) pits three-man teams moving weighted sleds. Then there are the *estropadak*, whaleboat rowers who compete in spectacular regattas (culminating in the September competition off La Concha beach in San Sebastián).

When it comes to **soccer**, Basque goaltenders have developed special fame in Spain, where Bilbao's Athletic Club and San Sebastián's Real Sociedad have won national championships with budgets far inferior to those of Real Madrid or FC Barcelona.

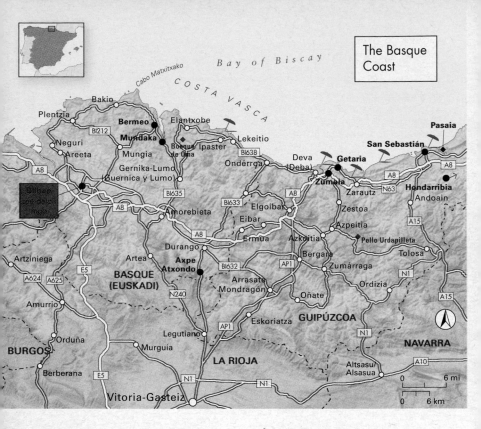

Bay of Biscay

COSTA VASCA

Cabo Matxitxako

Bakio

Plentzia

Neguri
Areeta

Bermeo
Mundaka

Mungia

Gernika-Lumo
(Guernica y Lumo)

Elantxobe

Bosque
de Oma

Ipaster

Lekeitio

Ondárroa

Deva
(Deba)

Getaria

Pasaia

San Sebastián

Zumaia

Zarautz

Hondarribia

Andoain

Amorebieta

Elgoibar

Eibar

Zestoa

Azpeitia

Bilbao
(see detail
map)

Durango

Ermua

Azkoitia

Azkoitia

Pello Urdapilleta

Tolosa

Artziniega

Artea

Axpe
Atxondo

BASQUE
(EUSKADI)

Arrasate
Mondragón

Bergara

Zumárraga

Ordizia

Amurrio

Legutiano

Eskoriatza

Oñate

GUIPÚZCOA

NAVARRA

Orduña

Murguía

BURGOS

Berberana

LA RIOJA

Altsasu/
Alsasua

Vitoria-Gasteiz

0   6 mi

0   6 km

stylish modern decor. **Cons:** no river views from interior rooms; not terribly homey; lacks local flavor. $ *Rooms from: €155* ✉ *Paseo Campo de Volantín 11, Casco Viejo* ☎ *94/445–4700* ⊕ *www. barcelo.com* ↩ *350 rooms* ⦿ *No meals* Ⓜ *Uribitarte.*

★ Caravan Cinema

$$ | **B&B/INN** | This cozy, cinema-themed pension with in-room Nespresso machines and huge TVs is an absolute steal for Bilbao at €100 a night. **Pros:** excellent value; convenient to main sights; cheerful staff. **Cons:** some rooms overlook a dirty little courtyard; inadequate soundproofing; contact proprietor to schedule check-in time. $ *Rooms from: €100* ✉ *Calle Correo 11, Casco Viejo* ☎ *68/886–0907* ⊕ *www.caravan-cinema.com* ↩ *11 rooms* ⦿ *No meals* Ⓜ *Arriaga.*

★ Castillo de Arteaga

$$$$ | **HOTEL** | Built in the mid-19th century for Empress Eugenia de Montijo, wife of Napoléon III, this neo-Gothic limestone castle with rooms in the watchtowers and defensive walls is one of the most extraordinary lodging options in or around Bilbao (and Relais & Châteaux agrees). **Pros:** market-driven restaurant worth a trip in itself; views over the wetlands; palatial digs. **Cons:** isolated from the village and 30 minutes from Bilbao; spotty Wi-Fi in some rooms; restaurant is pricey and there aren't many cheap alternatives in the area. $ *Rooms from: €200* ✉ *Calle Gaztelubide 7, Gautegiz de Arteaga* ⊕ *40 km (25 miles) northwest of Bilbao* ☎ *94/627–0440* ⊕ *www.castillodearteaga.com* ⊙ *Closed late Dec.–early Jan.* ↩ *13 rooms* ⦿ *Free Breakfast.*

Gran Hotel Domine Bilbao

$$$ | HOTEL | This Silken-chain art hotel across from the Guggenheim showcases the conceptual wit of Javier Mariscal, creator of Barcelona's 1992 Olympic mascot Cobi, and the structural know-how of Bilbao architect Iñaki Aurrekoetxea. **Pros:** emblematic of Bilbao's architectural renaissance; breakfasts on the rooftop terrace; spacious, updated rooms. **Cons:** hard on the wallet; a little full of its own glamour; soundproofing could be better. ⓢ *Rooms from: €175* ⊠ *Alameda de Mazarredo 61, El Ensanche* ☎ *94/425–3300, 94/425–3301* ⊕ *www.granhotel-dominebilbao.com* ⌁ *145 rooms* ⑩ *No meals* Ⓜ *Moyúa.*

Hotel Carlton

$$$$ | HOTEL | This grande dame, equidistant from the casco viejo and the Abandoibarra neighborhood, exudes old-world grace and charm along with a sense of history—which it has aplenty: Orson Welles, Ava Gardner, Ernest Hemingway, and Lauren Bacall are a just a few luminaries who posted up here. **Pros:** historic, old-world surroundings; spacious rooms; luxury gym and business center. **Cons:** surrounded by concrete and urban frenzy; "modern" design touches come across as tacky; occasionally grumpy personnel. ⓢ *Rooms from: €200* ⊠ *Pl. Federico Moyúa 2, El Ensanche* ☎ *94/416–2200* ⊕ *www.hotelcarlton.es* ⌁ *142 rooms* ⑩ *Free Breakfast* Ⓜ *Moyúa.*

Hotel Palacio Urgoiti

$$$ | HOTEL | FAMILY | This majestic hotel, occupying a reconstructed 17th-century country palace out toward the airport, is a peaceful country retreat with a 9-hole pitch-and-putt in the hotel gardens and other activities nearby. **Pros:** handy train service into Bilbao; convenient to the airport; elegant environment with easy access to outdoor activities. **Cons:** 15-minute drive to Bilbao; teeth-rattling flights overhead; freezing indoor pool. ⓢ *Rooms from: €135* ⊠ *Calle Arritugane s/n, Mungia* ✈ *13 km (8 miles) west of Bilbao, 2 km (1 mile) from airport* ☎ *94/674–6868* ⊕ *www.palaciourgoiti.com* ⌁ *43 rooms* ⑩ *Free Breakfast.*

★ Iturrienea Ostatua

$$$ | B&B/INN | This quirky, cozy hotel occupies a traditional Basque town house overlooking Bilbao's casco viejo. **Pros:** budget-friendly; attentive personnel; rustic-chic interiors. **Cons:** exterior-facing rooms can be noisy; no on-site parking and the closest lot is expensive; slow Wi-Fi. ⓢ *Rooms from: €130* ⊠ *Calle Santa María 14, Casco Viejo* ☎ *94/416–1500* ⊕ *www.iturrieneaostatua.com* ⌁ *19 rooms* ⑩ *No meals* Ⓜ *Casco Viejo.*

Meliá Bilbao Hotel

$$$ | HOTEL | Designed by architect Ricardo Legorreta and inspired by the work of Basque sculptor Eduardo Chillida (1920–2002), this high-rise hotel was built over what was once the nerve center of Bilbao's shipbuilding industry; fittingly, it recalls a futuristic ocean liner. **Pros:** some rooms face the Guggenheim; high levels of comfort; top-notch dining options. **Cons:** a high-rise colossus; maintenance issues; inconsistent service. ⓢ *Rooms from: €180* ⊠ *Calle Lehendakari Leizaola 29, El Ensanche* ☎ *94/428–0000* ⊕ *www.melia.com* ⌁ *213 rooms* ⑩ *No meals* Ⓜ *San Mamés.*

★ Miró Hotel

$$$ | HOTEL | Between the Guggenheim and Bilbao's excellent Museo de Bellas Artes, this boutique hotel refurbished by Barcelona fashion designer Toni Miró competes with the reflecting facade of Javier Mariscal's Domine Bilbao just up the street. **Pros:** tasteful, ultramodern decor; free coffee, tea, and popcorn in the lobby; views of the Guggenheim. **Cons:** snooty staff; dull bagged breakfast included in some rates; uncozy. ⓢ *Rooms from: €180* ⊠ *Alameda de Mazarredo 77, El Ensanche* ☎ *94/661–1880* ⊕ *www.mirohotelbilbao.com* ⌁ *50 rooms* ⑩ *No meals* Ⓜ *Moyúa.*

NH Collection Villa de Bilbao
$$$ | **HOTEL** | Although a bit "big-city brisk" (very bilbaíno, not unlike New York City), this four-star hotel is a great value for money and offers choice extras—morning newspapers at your door, exceptional breakfasts, well-appointed rooms, and professional service. **Pros:** spacious rooms; has the latest technology and creature comforts; scenic walk to the Bellas Artes and Guggenheim museums. **Cons:** disorganized reception staff; a bit cold and corporate; poor bathroom maintenance. [$] *Rooms from: €150* ✉ *Gran Vía 87, El Ensanche* ☎ *94/441–6000* 🌐 *www.nh-hoteles.com* 🛏 *139 rooms* 🍴 *No meals* [M] *San Mamés.*

Pensión Méndez
$ | **B&B/INN** | This 12-room *pensión* (guesthouse) with shared baths may be the best value in the city center with its small but well-maintained accommodations, some of which (Nos. 1 and 2) overlook the facade of the Palacio Yohn. **Pros:** excellent value and location in the middle of the casco viejo; prices don't fluctuate in high season; family-run business. **Cons:** no a/c; rooms with best views are noisy at night; proprietors don't speak English. [$] *Rooms from: €35* ✉ *Calle Santa María 13, 1st and 4th fls., Casco Viejo* ☎ *94/416–0364* 🌐 *www.pensionmendez.com* 💳 *No credit cards* 🛏 *24 rooms* 🍴 *No meals* [M] *Casco Viejo.*

Activities

SOCCER

Soccer is religion in Bilbao, even if the Athletic Bilbao soccer team hasn't won a league title in around 30 years. The Lions are often in the top half of the league standings and take special pleasure in tormenting powerhouses Madrid and Barcelona. The local rivalry with San Sebastián's Real Sociedad is as bitter as baseball's Yankees–Red Sox feud.

San Mamés Stadium
SOCCER | Athletic Bilbao got a new home in 2013 with the opening of this €213 million stadium on the Nervión that seats over 53,000. Its retractable roof keeps spectators dry, rain or shine. ✉ *Rafael Moreno Pitxitxi s/n, San Mamés* ☎ *94/441–3954* 🌐 *www.bilbaostadium.com* [M] *San Mamés.*

Shopping

The main stores for clothing are found around Plaza Moyúa in El Ensanche along streets such as Iparraguirre and Rodríguez Arias. The casco viejo has dozens of smaller shops, many of them in handsomely restored early houses with gorgeous wooden beams and ancient stones, specializing in an endless variety of products from crafts to antiques. Wool items, gourmet products, and wood carvings from around the Basque Country can be found throughout Bilbao. Basque *txapelas* (berets, or Basque *boinas*) are famous worldwide and make fine gifts.

For international fashion brands, the ubiquitous department store El Corte Inglés is an easy, if unexciting, one-stop shop.

Some shops close on Sunday.

★ La Bendita
FOOD/CANDY | This pocket-size gourmet shop tucked beside the cathedral sells the finest sweets, wines, and *conservas* (preserves) the region has to offer. Slender green Txakoli bottles and vintage-label Cantabrian anchovies make wonderful souvenirs. ✉ *Calle Bidebarrieta 16, Casco Viejo* ☎ *94/652–3623* 🌐 *www.labenditabilbao.com* [M] *Arriaga.*

Malmö
ART GALLERIES | Opened in 2015, this Scandinavian-inflected "concept store" carries art zines, coffee-table books, and designer accessories. Shop wildly patterned Swell thermoses, Cova Orgaz cardboard figurines, and Spanish-made Labobratori notebooks. ✉ *Calle Dorre 7, Casco Viejo* ☎ *94/646–7014* 🌐 *www.malmogallery.com* [M] *Arriaga.*

Mundaka

37 km (23 miles) northeast of Bilbao.

Tiny Mundaka, famous among surfers all over the world for its left-breaking roller at the mouth of the Ría de Gernika, has much to offer nonsurfers as well: the town's elegant summer homes and stately houses bearing family coats of arms compete for pride of place with the hermitage on the Santa Catalina peninsula and the parish church's Renaissance doorway.

VISITOR INFORMATION

CONTACTS Mundaka ⊠ *Calle Josepa Deuna s/n* ☎ *94/617–7201* ⊕ *www.mundakaturismo.com.*

Sights

Bosque de Oma (*Painted Forest*)
FOREST | Outside of town, about 5 km (3 miles) from Gernika, lies the Urdaibai Natural Reserve. Stop here for a stroll through the Bosque de Oma, featuring rows of trees vividly painted by Basque artist Agustín Ibarrola. It's a striking and successful marriage of art and nature. The nearby **Cuevas de Santimamiñe** have important prehistoric cave paintings that can be accessed virtually at a visitor center. ⊠ *Barrio Basondo, Kortezubi* ☎ *94/465–1657* ⊕ *www.bosquedeoma. com* ⊠ *Free.*

Beaches

Mundaka Beach
BEACH—SIGHT | This beach is said to have the longest surf break in Europe and among the best in the world, making it a magnet for surfers. In summer and fall this beach is off-limits to families who just want to splash around. Inland from the beach is the Urdaibai Natural Preserve, a UNESCO-designated biosphere. **Amenities:** lifeguards; water sports. **Best for:** surfing. ⊠ *Calle Matadero.*

 Restaurants

Baserri Maitea
$$$$ | BASQUE | In the village of Forua, about 11 km (7 miles) south of Mundaka and 1 km (½ mile) northwest of Gernika, this restaurant is in a stunning 18th-century caserío. Strings of red peppers and garlic hang from wooden beams in the cathedral-like interior, and the kitchen is famous for its hearty yet refined fish and meat dishes prepared over a wood-fired grill. **Known for:** spectacular ambience in a Basque farmhouse; bacalao dishes; personable waitstaff. $ *Average main: €25* ⊠ *Calle Atxondoa s/n* ☎ *94/625–3408* ⊕ *www.baserrimaitea.com* ۩ *No dinner Sun.–Thurs.*

Restaurante Portuondo
$$$$ | BASQUE | Sweeping beach views, aromas of fresh fish cooking over hot coals, a comfortable country dining room—these are just a few of the reasons Portuondo, a 15-minute walk outside town, is a stalwart Mundaka restaurant. If you're in the mood for something informal, post up at the downstairs pintxo bar. **Known for:** beautiful setting; meats and fish grilled to perfection; buzzy tapas area. $ *Average main: €30* ⊠ *Portuondo Auzoa 1* ✛ *Ctra. Gernika–Bermeo BI2235, Km 47* ☎ *94/687–6050* ⊕ *www.restauranteportuondo.com* ۩ *Closed Mon.*

Hotels

Atalaya
$$ | HOTEL | Tastefully converted from a private house, this 1911 landmark has become a favorite for quick overnight rail getaways from Bilbao, and scenery along the 37-km (23-mile) train ride is spectacular. **Pros:** intimate retreat from Bilbao's sprawl and bustle; well-maintained sauna; free parking. **Cons:** tight quarters in some rooms; limited menu in the restaurant; can be lonely in the off-season. $ *Rooms from: €115* ⊠ *Calle Itxaropen 1* ☎ *94/687–6899* ⊕ *www.atalayahotel.es* ↪ *13 rooms* ۩ *No meals.*

Axpe Atxondo

47 km (29 miles) east of Bilbao, 6 km (4 miles) south of Mundaka.

The village of Axpe, in the valley of Atxondo, sits in the shadow of 4,777-foot Monte Anboto—one of the highest peaks in the Basque Country outside the Pyrenees. According to local lore, the Basque nature goddess Mari lives in a cave close to the summit. Anboto, with its spectral gray rock face, is a sharp contrast to the soft green meadows running up to the very foot of the mountain. In his *Mitología vasca* (*Basque Mythology*), ethnologist José María de Barandiarán describes the goddess as "a beautiful woman, well constructed in all ways except for one foot, which was like that of a goat."

GETTING HERE AND AROUND
To reach Axpe from Bilbao, drive east on the A8/E70 freeway toward San Sebastián. Get off at the Durango exit, 40 km (24 miles) from Bilbao, and take the BI632 toward Elorrio. At Apatamonasterio turn right on to the BI3313 and continue to Axpe.

 Restaurants

★ **Etxebarri**
$$$$ | **BASQUE** | Of all the three-Michelin-star outposts in the Basque Country, Victor Arguinzoniz's Etxebarri may be the most exclusive, since it only opens for lunch (except for Saturday) and reservations are limited. Here, grilling is elevated to an art form, with various types of woods, coals, and tools carefully selected for the preparation of each dish. **Known for:** No. 10 spot on "World's 50 Best" restaurants list; temple of open-hearth cuisine; surprisingly unpretentious, laid-back atmosphere. $ *Average main: €60* ✉ *Pl. San Juan 1* ☎ *94/658–3042* ⊕ *www.asadoretxebarri. com* ⊙ *No dinner Sun.–Fri. Closed Mon. Closed Aug.*

 Hotels

★ **Mendi Goikoa**
$ | **HOTEL** | This handsome collection of hillside farmhouses is among the province of Vizcaya's most exquisite (and secret) hideaways. **Pros:** gorgeous setting; smart and attentive service; sweet, sweet silence. **Cons:** need a car to get here; not open year-round; rooms on the smaller side. $ *Rooms from: €80* ✉ *Barrio San Juan 33* ☎ *94/682–0833* ⊙ *Closed Nov.–Easter* ⇄ *11 rooms* ⦿ *Free Breakfast.*

Getaria and Zumaia

80 km (50 miles) east of Bilbao, 22 km (14 miles) west of San Sebastián.

Getaria (Guetaria in Castilian) is known as *la cocina de Gipuzkoa* (the kitchen of the Gipuzkoa province) for its many restaurants and taverns. It was also the birthplace of Juan Sebastián Elcano (1487–1526), the first circumnavigator of the globe and Spain's most emblematic naval hero. Elcano took over and completed Magellan's voyage after Magellan was killed in the Philippines in 1521. The town's galleon-like church has sloping wooden floors resembling a ship's deck. Zarautz, the next town over, has a wide beach and many taverns and cafés.

Zumaia is a snug little port and summer resort with the estuary of the Urola River flowing—back and forth, according to the tide—through town. Zumaia and Getaria are connected along the coast road and by several good footpaths.

VISITOR INFORMATION
CONTACTS Getaria Tourist Office ✉ *Parque Aldamar 2, Getaria* ☎ *94/314–0957* ⊕ *www.getariaturismo.eus.* **Zumaia Tourist Office** ✉ *Pl. de Kantauri 13, Zumaia* ☎ *94/314–3396* ⊕ *www.zumaia.eus.*

Embattled Gernika

On Monday, April 26, 1937—market day—Gernika, 33 km (20 miles) east of Bilbao, was attacked by German and Italian air brigades at the behest of the Nationalist forces in what would be history's second terror bombing against a civilian population. (The first, much less famous, was against neighboring Durango, about a month earlier.) Gernika, a rural town, had been one of the symbols of Basque identity since the 14th century: as early as the Middle Ages, Spanish sovereigns had sworn under the ancient oak tree of Gernika to respect Basque *fueros* (local courts with the sort of autonomy that was anathema to Generalísimo Francisco Franco's Madrid-centered "National Movement," which promoted Spanish unity over local identity). The planes of the Nazi Luftwaffe were sent with the blessings of Franco to experiment with saturation bombing of civilian targets and to decimate the traditional seat of Basque autonomy.

When the raid ended, between 153 and 1,654 civilians (the exact number of casualties is unclear) lay dead or dying in the ruins, and today Gernika remains a symbol of the atrocities of war, largely thanks to Picasso's famous canvas *Guernica*. The city was destroyed—although the oak tree miraculously emerged unscathed—and has been rebuilt as a modern, architecturally uninteresting town. Not until the 60th anniversary of the event did Germany officially apologize for the bombing.

When Spain's Second Republic commissioned Picasso to create a work for the Paris 1937 International Exposition, little did he imagine that his grim canvas protesting the bombing of a Basque village would become one of the most famous paintings in history.

Picasso's painting had its own struggle. The Spanish Pavilion in the International Exposition nearly substituted a more upbeat work, using *Guernica* as a backdrop. In 1939, Picasso ceded *Guernica* to New York's Museum of Modern Art, stipulating that the painting should return only to a democratic Spain. Over the next 30 years, as Picasso's fame grew, so did *Guernica*'s—as a work of art and a symbol of Spain's captivity.

When Franco died in 1975, two years after Picasso, negotiations with Picasso's heirs for the painting's return to Spain were already under way. Now on display at Madrid's Centro de Arte Reina Sofía, *Guernica* is home for good.

◉ Sights

Cristóbal Balenciaga Museoa

HOUSE | The haute-couture maestro Cristóbal Balenciaga (1895–1972) was born in Getaria, and the impressive museum created in his honor is a must-see, regardless of your fashion sensibilities. The collection and interactive exhibits are distributed between two buildings, the mansion where Balenciaga was born and a starkly geometric monolith inaugurated in 2011. Feast your eyes on couture specimens from the foundation's 1,200-item collection, from suits to gowns and accessories that represent his life's work. "Balenciaga is a couturier in the truest sense of the word," said Coco Chanel of her rival. "The others are simply fashion designers." ✉ *Aldamar Parkea 6, Getaria* ☎ *94/300–8840* ⊕ *www.*

cristobalbalenciagamuseoa.com ✉ *€10*
🕐 *Closed Mon. in Sept.–June.*

Urdapilleta

FARM/RANCH | For a look at a working Basque farmhouse, or caserío, where the Urdapilleta family farms pigs, sheep, cattle, goats, chickens, and ducks, take a detour up to the village of Bidegoian, on the Azpeitia–Tolosa road. Pello Urdapilleta (which means "pile of pigs" in Euskera) sells artisanal cheeses and Basque heritage-breed pork sausages. ✉ *Elola Azpikoa Baserria, Bidegoian ✛ 35 km (22 miles) from Getaria and Zumbia via N634 and Gl631* ☎ *60/570–1204* ⊕ *www. urdapilleta.eu.*

 **Restaurants**

★ Agroturismo Segore Etxeberri

$$$ | **BASQUE** | **FAMILY** | Hidden in the lush, hilly countryside southwest of Tolosa— and many miles off the tourist track—is Agroturismo Segore Etxeberri, a restaurant (and five-room bed-and-breakfast) housed in a traditional caserío perched on a hilltop. After snapping a few pics of the jaw-dropping views, tuck into a soul-satisfying Basque feast of roast chicken (raised on the property), stewed game meats, or freshly caught fish. **Known for:** culinary gem in the middle of nowhere; spectacular views; meats and vegetables from the estate. 💲 *Average main: €18* ✉ *Calle Valle Santa Marina s/n, Albiztur* ☎ *94/358–0976* ⊕ *www.segore. com* 🕐 *Closed Tues. No dinner Mon., Wed., and Thurs.*

Bedua

$$$$ | **BASQUE** | This rustic (if slightly overpriced) asador in business for four generations draws the crowds for its excellent tortilla de bacalao, txuleta de buey, and fish of all kinds, especially the classic besugo cooked *a la donostiarra* (roasted and covered with a sauce of garlic and vinegar). Txakoli from nearby Getaria is the beverage of choice. **Known for:** pristine seafood and home-grown vegetables; top-quality txuleton;

farmhouse-chic ambience. 💲 *Average main: €30* ✉ *Cestona, Barrio Bedua, Cestona ✛ Up Urola, 3 km (2 miles) from Zumaia* ☎ *94/386–0551* ⊕ *www.bedua. es.*

★ Elkano

$$$$ | **SEAFOOD** | Ever since Anthony Bourdain waxed poetic about award-winning Elkano's grilled turbot on *Parts Unknown,* the dish has become something of a holy grail among in-the-know foodies. Order the famous flat fish (at its fatty prime in May and June), and you'll receive what Bourdain called an "anatomy lesson" as the maître d' extols the virtues of each separate cut, culminating with the gelatinous fins—which you're encouraged to suck between your fingers, caveman style. **Known for:** grilled turbot; reputation as an Anthony Bourdain favorite; rare, quirky wines. 💲 *Average main: €45* ✉ *Calle Herrerieta 2, Getaria* ☎ *94/314–0024* ⊕ *www.restauranteelkano.com* 🕐 *Closed Tues.*

 Hotels

Landarte

$ | **B&B/INN** | **FAMILY** | Kick back in this restored 16th-century country manor house 1 km (½ mile) from Zumaia and an hour's walk from Getaria. **Pros:** warm, family-friendly atmosphere; traditional cuisine on request; unusual wall art. **Cons:** some top-floor rooms under the low eaves could be tricky for taller guests; €9 breakfast; can't go far without a car. 💲 *Rooms from: €88* ✉ *Ctra. Artadi Anzoa 1, Zumaia* ☎ *94/386–5358* ⊕ *www.landarte.net* 🕐 *Closed mid-Dec.–Feb.* ⇆ *6 rooms* 🍴 *No meals.*

★ Saiaz Getaria

$$ | **HOTEL** | For panoramic views over the Bay of Biscay, this 15th-century house on Getaria's uppermost street is a perfect choice. **Pros:** historic property; waves lull you to sleep; discounts at nearby spa and gym. **Cons:** soundproofing could be better; spotty Wi-Fi; only two (first-come, first-served) parking spaces. 💲 *Rooms*

from: €109 ⊠ *Roke Deuna 25, Getaria*
☎ *94/314–0143* ⊕ *www.saiazgetaria.com*
⊘ *Closed Dec. 20–Jan. 6* ⤳ *17 rooms*
⊖ *No meals.*

🛍 Shopping

Getaria, Zumaia, and the surrounding villages are great places to pick up locally canned anchovies, tuna, and sardines as well as bottles of Txakoli and *sagardoa,* Basque cider.

Salanort

FOOD/CANDY | This highly regarded conservas company might be most famous for its anchovies, which are always plump and expertly packed, but you can also stock up on local wines and liqueurs here such as *patxaran,* a digestif made with sloe berries. ⊠ *Nagusia 22, Getaria* ☎ *94/314–0036* ⊕ *www.salanort.com.*

San Sebastián

100 km (62 miles) northeast of Bilbao.

San Sebastián (Donostia in Euskera) is a sophisticated city arched around one of the finest urban beaches in the world, **La Kontxa** (The Shell), so named for its shoreline curved like a scallop shell. Ondarreta and Zurriola beaches, also inside the city limits, flank it on either side. The promontories of Monte Urgull and Monte Igueldo serve as bookends for La Kontxa, while Zurriola has Monte Ulía rising over its far end. The best way to take in San Sebastián is on foot: promenades and pathways twist up the hills that surround the city and afford postcard-perfect views. The first records of San Sebastián date to the 11th century. A backwater for centuries, the city had the good fortune in 1845 to attract Queen Isabella II, who was seeking relief from a skin ailment in the icy Atlantic waters. Isabella was followed by much of the aristocracy of the time, and San Sebastián became—and remains—a favored summer retreat for Madrid's well-to-do.

The city is bisected by the **Urumea River,** which is crossed by three ornate bridges inspired by late-19th-century French architecture. At the mouth of the Urumea, the incoming surf smashes the rocks with such force that white foam erupts, and the sound is wild and Wagnerian. The city is laid out with wide streets on a grid pattern, thanks mainly to the dozen times it has been all but destroyed by fire. The last conflagration came after the French were expelled in 1813; English and Portuguese forces occupied the city, abused the population, and torched the place. Today, San Sebastián is a seaside resort on par with Nice and Monte Carlo. It becomes one of Spain's most expensive cities in the summer, when vacationers from France (and, increasingly, America and Great Britain) descend in droves.

Neighborhoods include the scenic, touristy *parte vieja* (old quarter), tucked under Monte Urgull north of the mouth of the Urumea River; hip-and-happening Gros (so named for a corpulent Napoleonic general), across the Urumea to the north; commercial Centro, the urban nucleus around the cathedral; residential Amara, farther east toward the Anoeta sports complex; glitzy La Kontxa, hugging the eponymous beach; and stately El Antiguo, at the western end of La Kontxa. Igueldo is the high promontory over the city at the southwestern side of the bay. Alto de Miracruz is the high ground to the northeast toward France; Errenteria is inland east of Pasaia; Oiartzun is a village farther north; Astigarraga is in apple-cider country to the east of Anoeta.

GETTING HERE AND AROUND

San Sebastián is a very walkable city, though local buses (€1.75) are also convenient. Buses for Pasajes (Pasaia), Errenteria, Astigarraga, and Oiartzun depart from Calle Okendo, one block west of the Urumea River behind the Hotel Maria Cristina. Bus A-1 goes to Astigarraga; A-2 is the bus to Pasajes.

The Euskotren's Metro Donostialdea, the city train, is popularly known as El Topo (The Mole) for the amount of time it spends underground. It originates at the Amara Viejo station in Paseo Easo and tunnels its way to Hendaye, France, every 30 minutes (€2.65; 45 minutes). Euskotren also serves Bilbao by way of Lasarte-Oria, but buses and Blablacar rideshares will get you there in about half the time. Euskotren recently opened new stations that connect the neighboring towns of Lasarte-Oria (€1.75; 12 minutes), Pasaia (€1.65; 12 minutes), and Irun (€2.65; 30 minutes) to San Sebastián.

The station for the funicular up to Monte Igueldo (☎ *94/321–3525* ⊕ *www. monteigueldo.es*; €3.75) is just behind Ondarreta beach at the western end of La Kontxa.

BUS CONTACTS Estación de Autobuses ⊠ *Paseo de Federico García Lorca 1* ☎ *94/347–5150* ⊕ *www.estaciondonostia.com.*

CAR RENTAL Europcar ⊠ *Aeropuerto de San Sebastián, Calle Gabarrari 22, Hondarribia* ☎ *94/366–8530* ⊕ *www.europcar. com.*

TRAIN CONTACTS Estación de Amara (*Estación de Easo*) ⊠ *Pl. Easo 9* ☎ *90/254–3210* ⊕ *www.renfe.com.* **Estación de San Sebastián–Donostia** (*Estación del Norte*) ⊠ *Paseo de Francia 22* ☎ *90/224–3402* ⊕ *www.renfe.com.*

VISITOR INFORMATION
CONTACTS San Sebastián–Donostia Tourist Office ⊠ *Blvd. 8* ☎ *94/348–1166* ⊕ *www. sansebastianturismo.com.*

◉ Sights

Every corner of Spain champions its culinary identity, but San Sebastián's refined fare is in a league of its own. Many of the city's restaurants and pintxos spots are in the **parte vieja,** on the east end of the bay beyond the elegant *casa consistorial* (city

hall) and formal **Alderdi Eder** gardens. The building that now houses city hall opened as a casino in 1887; after gambling was outlawed early in the 20th century, the town council moved here from the Plaza de la Constitución, the parte vieja's main square.

Aquarium Donostia-San Sebastián
ZOO | **FAMILY** | For a stroll through and under some 6,000 marine animals—ranging from tiger sharks to sea turtles, with one participative pool where kids are encouraged to touch and try to pick up fish—the aquarium is a great rainy-day activity. The illustrated history of Basque whaling and boatbuilding is also fascinating. ⊠ *Pl. Carlos Blasco de Imaz 1, Parte Vieja* ☎ *94/344–0099* ⊕ *www. aquariumss.com* ☑ *€13.*

Catedral del Buen Pastor (*Cathedral of the Good Shepherd*)
RELIGIOUS SITE | You can see the facade of this 19th-century cathedral from the river, across town. With the tallest church spire in the province, the Catedral del Buen Pastor was constructed in the neo-Gothic style. It's worth a glimpse inside at beautiful stained-glass windows. ⊠ *Pl. del Buen Pastor, Calle Urdaneta 12, Centro* ☎ *94/346–4516* ☑ *Free* ⊘ *Closed weekends.*

Chillida Leku Museum
MUSEUM | In the Jáuregui section of Hernani, 10 minutes south of San Sebastián (close to both Martín Berasategui's restaurant in nearby Lasarte *and* the cider houses of the Astigarraga neighborhood, like Sidrería Petritegi), the Eduardo Chillida Sculpture Garden and Museum, in a 16th-century farmhouse, got a face-lift to finally reopen in April 2019. It is a treat for anyone interested in contemporary art. Visits are by appointment only via the website. ⊠ *Caserío Zabalaga, Barrio Jáuregui 66, Lasarte* ☎ *94/333–6006* ⊕ *www.museochillidaleku.com* ☑ *From €6* ⊘ *Closed Tues. (except July and Aug.) and Dec. 25–Jan. 1.*

San Sebastián's famed, curving beach, La Kontxa

Iglesia de Santa María del Coro

RELIGIOUS SITE | Just in from the harbor, in the shadow of Monte Urgull, is this baroque church with a stunning carved facade of an arrow-riddled St. Sebastian flanked by two towers. The interior is strikingly restful considering the bustling area. Note the sculptures *The Harmony of Sound,* by Maximilian Peizmann, to the right of the entrance, and *By the Cross to the Light,* by Eduardo Chillida, in the baptistery. ⊠ *Calle Mayor 12, Parte Vieja* ☎ *94/342–3124* 💶 *€3.*

Kursaal

ARTS VENUE | Designed by the world-renowned Spanish architect Rafael Moneo and located at the mouth of the Urumea River, the Kursaal is San Sebastián's postmodern concert hall, film society, and convention center. The gleaming cubes of glass that make up this bright complex were conceived as a perpetuation of the site's natural geography, an attempt to underline the harmony between the natural and the artificial and to create a visual stepping-stone between the heights of Monte Urgull and Monte Ulía. It has two auditoriums, a gargantuan banquet hall, meeting rooms, exhibition space, a set of terraces overlooking the estuary, and a nueva cocina restaurant called Ni Neu. For guided tours of the building, make arrangements in advance. ⊠ *Av. de Zurriola 1, Gros* ☎ *94/300–3000* ⊕ *www. kursaal.eus.*

★ Monte Igueldo

MOUNTAIN—SIGHT | On the western side of the bay, this promontory is a must-visit. You can walk or drive up or take the funicular (€3.75 round-trip), with departures every 15 minutes. From the top, you get a bird's-eye view of San Sebastián's gardens, beaches, parks, wide tree-lined boulevards, and Belle Époque buildings. ⊠ *Igueldo* ☎ *94/321– 3525 for funicular* ⊕ *www.monteigueldo. es* 🕑 *Closed most of Jan. and Wed. Nov.–Feb.*

Tabakalera

ARTS VENUE | Occupying a century-old tobacco factory, this vibrant cultural center, inaugurated in 2015, epitomizes the creative, forward-thinking verve of

San Sebastián. Check the website to see what performances, exhibitions, and screenings are planned ahead of your visit, and drop by to steep yourself in the city's here and now. ✉ *Pl. Andre Zigarrogileak 1, Amara* ☎ *94/311–8855* 🌐 *www.tabakalera.eu.*

Beaches

★ La Kontxa

BEACH—SIGHT | **FAMILY** | San Sebastián's shell-shaped main beach is one of the most famous urban beaches in the world. Night and day, rain or shine, it's filled with locals and tourists alike, strolling and taking in the city's skyline and the uninhabited Isla de Santa Clara just offshore. Several hotels line its curved expanse including the grande dame **Hotel de Londres y de Inglaterra.** The beach has clean, pale sand and few rocks or seaweed, but only a bit of shade, near the promenade wall. Lounge chairs are available for rent. La Kontxa is safe night and day and is especially popular with families. **Amenities:** lifeguards; showers; toilets. **Best for:** sunrise; sunset; walking. ✉ *Calle de la Concha Ibilbidea, La Concha.*

Zurriola

BEACH—SIGHT | Just across the Urumea River from La Kontxa lies this sprawling, less touristy beach. Exposed to the open Atlantic, the beach boasts waves that are big enough to surf—and sometimes too dangerous for kids. **Amenities:** lifeguards; water sports. **Best for:** surfing. ✉ *Zurriola Ibilbidea, Gros.*

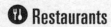

Restaurants

A Fuego Negro

$$$ | **TAPAS** | Sample experimental pintxos here like Kobe beef sliders (the house specialty), béchamel-stuffed mussels, and Basque-style "pastrami" made from indigenous pigs. The dim lighting, industrial decor, and rock posters attract a young, hip crowd. **Known for:** "MakCobe" beef slider; innovative pintxos; cool crowd. [$] *Average main: €20* ✉ *Calle 31 de Agosto 31, Parte Vieja* ☎ *65/013–5373* 🌐 *www.afuegonegro.com* 🕓 *Closed Mon.*

★ Arzak

$$$$ | **BASQUE** | One of the world's great culinary meccas, award-winning Arzak embodies the prestige, novelty, and science-driven creativity of the Basque culinary zeitgeist. The restaurant and its high-tech food lab—both helmed by founder Juan Mari Arzak's daughter Elena these days—are situated in the family's 19th-century home on the outskirts of San Sebastián, and though the space might not be much to look at, the ever-changing dishes are downright thrilling for their trompe l'oeil presentations, unexpected flavor combinations, and rare ingredients. **Known for:** thrilling culinary experience; old-school hospitality; often listed on World's Best Restaurants lists. [$] *Average main: €237* ✉ *Av. Alcalde Jose Elosegui 273, Alto de Miracruz* ☎ *94/327–8465, 94/328–5593* 🌐 *www.arzak.es* 🕓 *Closed Sun. and Mon., June 15–July 2, and 3 wks in early Nov.*

Bergara

$$$ | **TAPAS** | Winner of many a miniature cuisine award (don't miss the prawn-filled *txalupa* tartlet), this Gros neighborhood standby offers a stylish take on traditional tapas and pintxos. It also serves entrée-sized meals. **Known for:** variety of newfangled and traditional pintxos; heavenly foie gras; trendy atmosphere. [$] *Average main: €20* ✉ *Calle General Arteche 8, Gros* ☎ *94/327–5026* 🌐 *www.pinchosbergara.es.*

Bodegón Alejandro

$$$$ | **BASQUE** | Hiding in the basement of a timber building in the heart of the parte vieja, this restaurant—where Martín Berasategui cut his teeth—toes the line between traditional and contemporary Basque cuisine. Its dishes include hake in citrus sauce, filet mignon with soufflé potatoes, and, for dessert, cheese ice cream. **Known for:** affordable and delectable tasting menus; top-quality beef; seasonal vegetable delicacies like de lágrima peas and white asparagus. [$] *Average main: €24* ✉ *Calle de Fermín Calbetón 4, Parte Vieja* ☎ *94/342–7158* 🌐 *www.bodegonalejandro.com.*

★ Casa Urola

$$$$ | BASQUE | FAMILY | Don't be put off by the slightly outdated decor of this parte vieja stalwart—the kitchen at Casa Urola is easily one of the city's most skilled. Savor appetizers made with hard-to-find regional vegetables like cardoon, borage, and *de lágrima* peas before moving onto entrées like seared squab presented with a pâté of its own liver and roasted hake loin with white wine and clams. **Known for:** flawless Basque cuisine; repuation as restaurant industry favorite; signature torrija. [$] *Average main: €28* ✉ *Calle de Fermín Calbetón 20, Parte Vieja* ☎ *94/344–1371* 🌐 *www.casaurolajatetxea.es* ⏲ *Closed Tues.*

★ Ganbara

$$ | TAPAS | This busy bar and restaurant near Plaza de la Constitución is now run by the third generation of the same family. Specialty morsels range from shrimp and asparagus to acorn-fed Iberian ham on croissants and anchovies, sea urchins, and—the house specialty—wild mushrooms topped with an egg yolk. **Known for:** to-die-for wild mushrooms; traditional Basque pintxos; lively and loud atmosphere. [$] *Average main: €14* ✉ *Calle San Jerónimo 21, Parte Vieja* ☎ *94/342–2575* 🌐 *www.ganbarajatetxea.com* ⏲ *Closed Mon. No dinner Sun.*

Goiz Argi

$ | TAPAS | The specialty of this tiny bar—and the reason locals flock here on weekends—is the garlicky seared-shrimp brochette. **Known for:** juicy shrimp skewers; good value; cheerful bartenders. [$] *Average main: €8* ✉ *Calle de Fermín Calbetón 4, Parte Vieja* ☎ *94/342–5204.*

Gorriti

$ | TAPAS | Next to the open-air Brecha Market, this traditional little pintxos bar is a well-priced neighborhood standby filled with good cheer and delicious tapas. **Known for:** fabulous tortilla de bacalao; casual local crowd; simple, well-prepared Basque bites. [$] *Average main: €11* ✉ *Calle San Juan 3, Parte Vieja* ☎ *94/342–8353* 🌐 *www.bargorriti.com* ⏲ *Closed Sun.*

Kokotxa Restaurante

$$$$ | INTERNATIONAL | This simply decorated award-winning restaurant in the heart of the parte vieja hinges on chef Daniel López's clean, innovative cuisine, which plays on traditional Basque and Spanish flavors and often adds an Asian twist. Opt for a market-driven *degustación* or López's classic tasting menu, including signature dishes like whole langoustine with beet rice and sweetbreads with Jerusalem artichokes and truffles. **Known for:** Michelin-starred dining in the city center; Asian-inflected Basque cuisine; surprisingly casual atmosphere. [$] *Average main: €85* ✉ *Calle del Campanario 11, Parte Vieja* ☎ *94/342–1904* 🌐 *www.restaurantekokotxa.com* ⏲ *Closed Mon. No dinner Sun.*

La Cepa

$$$$ | TAPAS | This boisterous tavern established in 1948 has ceilings lined with dangling jamónes, walls covered with old photos of San Sebastián, and a dining room packed with locals and tourists in equal measure. Everything from the Iberian ham to the little olive-pepper-and-anchovy combos called *penaltis* will whet your appetite, but those who opt for a full meal should order the dry-aged txuleton. **Known for:** hand-cut Iberian ham; melt-in-your-mouth steak; amicable staff. [$] *Average main: €25* ✉ *Calle 31 de Agosto 7, Parte Vieja* ☎ *94/342–6394* 🌐 *www.barlacepa.com* ⏲ *Closed Tues. and last 2 wks in Nov.*

★ La Cuchara de San Telmo

$$ | **TAPAS** | You may have to throw an elbow or two to get into this teeming bar, but it's worth braving the sardine-can digs for outstanding pintxos like mushroom-and-Idiazabal risotto and seared foie gras with Basque cider compote. **Known for:** internationally inflected pintxos; constant crowds; fabulous foie gras. [$] *Average main: €12* ✉ *Calle 31 de Agosto 28, Parte Vieja* ☎ *94/343–5446.*

★ La Viña

$$ | **TAPAS** | **FAMILY** | This centrally located, no-frills bar is almost always crowded, drawing busloads of tour groups as well as locals, who come to try the viral "burnt" cheesecake. This silky, creamy dessert pairs perfectly with a cup of coffee, while, on the savory side, the sumptuous pintxos—red peppers stuffed with bacalao, croquetas, or veal meatballs—go well with a glass of Rioja. **Known for:** cheesecake with a cult following; old-timey ambience; wide variety of classic pintxos. [$] *Average main: €15* ✉ *Calle 31 de Agosto 3, Parte Vieja* ☎ *94/342–7495* 🌐 *www.lavinarestaurante.com* 🕒 *Closed Mon.*

★ Martín Berasategui

$$$$ | **CONTEMPORARY** | Basque chef Martín Berasategui has more Michelin stars than any other chef in Spain, and at his flagship in the dewy village of Lasarte-Oria, it's easy to see why. Dishes are Basque at heart but prepared with exacting, French-inflected technique that comes through in dishes like artfully composed salads, elegant caviar preparations, and eel-and-foie-gras mille-feuilles—a Berasategui signature. **Known for:** once-in-a-lifetime dining experience; idyllic, white-tablecloth outdoor terrace; artful mix of classic and avant-garde. [$] *Average main: €88* ✉ *Calle Loidi 4, Lasarte* ✥ *8 km (5 miles) south of San Sebastián* ☎ *94/336–6471, 94/336–1599* 🌐 *www.martinberasategui.com* 🕒 *Closed Mon. and Tues. and mid-Dec.–mid-Jan. No dinner Sun.*

Mugaritz

$$$$ | **SPANISH** | This bucolic farmhouse in the hills above Errenteria, 8 km (5 miles) northeast of San Sebastián, is a veritable laboratory of modern cooking techniques helmed by (arguably) the most experimental chef in Spain today, Andoni Aduriz. The obligatory three-hour, 20-course experience—which might be too abstract for some—includes dishes like "a sip of flowers and warm water" and "memories of a rabbit" complemented by zany wild-card wines. **Known for:** being a bit "out there"; abstract dishes; long, immersive dining experience. [$] *Average main: €210* ✉ *Otzazulueta Baserria, Aldura Aldea 20, Errenteria* ☎ *94/352–2455, 94/351–8343* 🌐 *www.mugaritz.com* 🕒 *Closed Mon. and mid-Dec.–mid-Apr. No lunch Tues. No dinner Sun.*

Ni Neu

$$$ | **CONTEMPORARY** | Chef Mikel Gallo's Ni Neu ("Me, Myself" in Euskera), defined by its experimental comfort-food cuisine, occupies a bright corner of Rafael Moneo's dazzling Kursaal complex at the mouth of the Urumea. The jammy eggs with potatoes and codfish broth and roast monkfish with mustard seeds and tapenade are two of the most popular dishes, though lighter tapas fare is also available in the bar area. **Known for:** €38 tasting menu (a steal); riverside dining; traditional Basque fare with a modern twist. [$] *Average main: €20* ✉ *Av. Zurriola 1, Gros* ☎ *94/300–3162* 🌐 *www.restaurantenineu.com* 🕒 *Closed Mon. No dinner Tues., Wed., and Sun.*

Ormazabal

$$ | **TAPAS** | You'd be hard-pressed to find a homier pintxo bar in San Sebastián. Ormazabal has been luring a mostly local crowd for decades with its juicy tortillas de bacalao and burst-in-your-mouth croquetas. **Known for:** chummy waitstaff; hole-in-the-wall local vibe; old-school dishes like spinach croquetas. [$] *Average main: €15* ✉ *Calle 31 de Agosto 22, Parte Vieja* ☎ *68/663–3025.*

Restaurante Astelena 1997

$$$$ | BASQUE | Chef Ander González has transformed the narrow stone rooms of a defunct banana warehouse into one of the finest spots for modern Basque dining—at a great price. The €33 weekday menú del día and €55 weekend *menú de degustación* (tasting menu) hinge on what's in season, though dishes like seared txuleton and hake in white wine sauce with clams never come off the menu for a reason. **Known for:** unpretentious yet elegant Basque cuisine; fantastic seafood dishes; surprisingly good value for this part of town. $ *Average main: €24* ⊠ *Euskal Herria 3, Parte Vieja* ☎ *94/342–5867* ⊕ *www.restauranteastelena.com* ⊗ *Closed Mon. No dinner Sun. and Wed.*

San Marcial

$$ | TAPAS | Nearly a secret, this quintessential Basque spot has big wooden tables and a monumental bar filled with *cazuelitas* (small earthenware dishes) and tapas of all kinds. It is in the center of town but tucked away downstairs. **Known for:** oversize ham-and-cheese croquettes called gavillas; unfussy Basque pintxos and sandwiches; "hidden" location in the old town off the tourist track. $ *Average main: €13* ⊠ *Calle San Marcial 50, Centro* ☎ *94/343–1720* ⊗ *Closed Tues.*

★ Zelaia

$$$$ | BASQUE | This traditional sagardotegi, located 7 km (4 miles) south of San Sebastián, is where the region's top chefs—Juan Mari Arzak, Martín Berasategui, and Pedro Subijana, to name a few—ring in every cider season with a resounding *¡txotx!* ("cheers" in Basque). Removed from the tourist track and open from mid-January to late April, Zelaia invites guests into its barrel-lined warehouses to chow down on a set menu of bacalao-centric dishes, thick-cut steaks, and—for dessert—local sheep's-milk cheese with quince preserves and walnuts. **Known for:** being an authentic cider house; food that's an echelon above other sagardotegis; unlimited cider

drinking. $ *Average main: €30* ⊠ *B0 Martindegi 29* ☎ *94/355–5851* ⊕ *www.zelaia. es* ⊗ *Closed late Apr.–mid-Jan. and Sun.*

Zuberoa

$$$$ | BASQUE | This is the kind of restaurant where the chef greets every table and meals start with an amuse-bouche of foie gras—in other words, it's an old-world slice of heaven. Market-driven meals (think roasted wild game, Basque de lágrima peas, and strawberry gazpacho) unfold to the backdrop of a 15th-century farmhouse that empties out onto an ivy-lined patio in the summer. **Known for:** Michelin-starred old-world Basque cuisine; wonderfully hospitable chef; dining room in a 15th-century caserío. $ *Average main: €40* ⊠ *Araneder Bidea, Barrio Iturriotz* ☎ *94/349–1228* ⊕ *www.zuberoa.com* ⊗ *Closed Wed., and Sun. June–Oct. No dinner Sun., and Tues. Nov.–May.*

 ## Hotels

Arrizul Congress Hotel

$$$$ | HOTEL | This clean-cut urban hotel, located steps from the river and Zurriola Beach, opened in early 2017 and is a dependable option for families and business travelers alike. **Pros:** feels fresh and modern; triples are available; within walking distance of all the main sights. **Cons:** bad soundproofing means noisy mornings; architectural foibles make some rooms awkward; occasionally unprofessional front-desk staff. $ *Rooms from: €239* ⊠ *Calle Ronda 3, Gros* ☎ *94/332–7026* ⊕ *www.hotelarrizulcongress.com* ⤢ *46 rooms* ¶◎¶ *No meals.*

Astoria7 Hotel

$$$ | HOTEL | Set in the renovated Astoria Cinema, this movie-themed hotel has a spacious lobby adorned with autographed photos of the many movie stars who have attended the famous San Sebastián Film Festival over the years. **Pros:** spacious rooms; fun and campy cinematographic decor; varied, good-quality breakfast. **Cons:** 20-minute

walk (or short bus ride) to beach and the parte vieja; not for noncinephiles; in ugly high-rise building. Ⓢ *Rooms from: €155* ✉ *Calle de la Sagrada Família 1, Centro* ☎ *94/344–5000* ⊕ *www.astoria7hotel. com/en* 🖘 *102 rooms* 🍽 *No meals.*

★ Hotel de Londres y de Inglaterra

$$$$ | HOTEL | On the main beachfront promenade overlooking La Kontxa, this stately hotel has a regal, old-world feel and Belle Époque aesthetic that starts in the elegant marble lobby, with its shimmering chandeliers, and continues throughout the hotel. **Pros:** hotel with best views in town; cozy and comfortable rooms; professional service. **Cons:** street side can be noisy on weekends; unremarkable and unkempt breakfast area; noticeable wear and tear. Ⓢ *Rooms from: €330* ✉ *Zubieta 2, La Concha* ☎ *94/344–0770* ⊕ *www.hlondres.com* 🖘 *148 rooms* 🍽 *No meals.*

Hotel María Cristina

$$$$ | HOTEL | The graceful beauty of the Belle Époque is embodied here, in San Sebastián's most luxurious hotel on the west bank of the Urumea, which has played hosts to countless movie stars and dignitaries since opening in 1912. **Pros:** elaborate breakfasts; old-world elegance with new-world amenities; grand historic building. **Cons:** staff can be a bit starchy; some aspects of recent renovations lack taste; drinks at the bar are expensive. Ⓢ *Rooms from: €580* ✉ *Paseo República Argentina 4, Centro* ☎ *94/343–7600* ⊕ *www.hotel-mariacristi-na.com* 🖘 *136 rooms* 🍽 *No meals.*

★ One Shot Tabakalera House

$$$ | HOTEL | Locals call this four-star newcomer a "hotel within a museum" because of its location inside the Tabakalera cultural center, a hotbed of art and innovation inaugurated in 2015. **Pros:** avant-garde design; located within the city's cultural center; close to the RENFE train station. **Cons:** 10-minute walk into town; no room service; no coffeemakers in most rooms. Ⓢ *Rooms from: €180*

✉ *Paseo Duque de Mandas 52, Amara* ☎ *94/393–0028* ⊕ *www.hoteloneshot-tabakalerahouse.com* 🖘 *33 rooms* 🍽 *No meals.*

Pensión Nuevas Artes

$$ | B&B/INN | This tidy 10-room hotel four blocks east of San Sebastián's cathedral stands out for its rock-bottom prices. **Pros:** terrific value; cozy atmosphere; steps from the Buen Pastor Cathedral and top sights. **Cons:** no check-in between 2 and 5 pm; bad soundproofing; no a/c. Ⓢ *Rooms from: €110* ✉ *Urbieta 64, Centro* ☎ *94/347–4905* ⊕ *www. pension-nuevasartes.com* 🖘 *10 rooms* 🍽 *No meals.*

Villa Soro

$$$$ | HOTEL | The open lobby of this mansion-cum-hotel has vaulted ceilings and curved Victorian stairs that lead to a sunny, stained-glassed sitting area and unique guest rooms. **Pros:** 16 Spanish wines by the glass at the bar; free on-site parking; historic mansion. **Cons:** 10-minute taxi or bus ride from the center of town; basement rooms are dark and depressing; service can be snooty. Ⓢ *Rooms from: €310* ✉ *Av. de Ategor-rieta 61, Gros* ☎ *94/329–7970* ⊕ *www. villasoro.es* 🖘 *25 rooms* 🍽 *No meals.*

🍸 Nightlife

BARS AND PUBS

Gu

BARS/PUBS | The renovated Gu, with its floor-to-ceiling windows overlooking La Kontxa, is a glitzy indoor-outdoor cocktail bar and nightclub housed in a futuristic building resembling a moored cruise ship. ✉ *Ijentea 9, Centro* ☎ *84/398–0775* ⊕ *www.gusansebastian.com.*

MUSIC CLUBS

Akerbeltz

MUSIC CLUBS | This feel-good dive bar is a perfect late-night refuge for music and drinks. ✉ *Calle Mari 19, Parte Vieja* ☎ *94/346–0934, 94/345–1452.*

★ ¡BE! Club

MUSIC CLUBS | Formerly known as Bebop, this San Sebastián classic—which eschews the usual Top 40 in favor of Latin, jazz, and unconventional dance tunes—got a major face-lift in 2018 and is all the better for it. ☒ *Paseo de Salamanca 3, Parte Vieja* ☎ *94/347–8505* ⊕ *www. beclubss.com.*

Performing Arts

Kursaal

ARTS CENTERS | Home of the Orquesta Sinfónica (Symphony Orchestra) de Euskadi, this venue is also a favorite for ballet, opera, theater, and jazz. ☒ *Av. de la Zurriola 1, Gros* ☎ *94/300–3000* ⊕ *www. kursaal.eus.*

Teatro Victoria Eugenia

ARTS CENTERS | In a stunning 19th-century building, this elegant venue offers varied programs of theater, dance, and more. ☒ *Paseo de la República Argentina 2, Centro* ☎ *94/348–1160* ⊕ *www.victoriae-ugenia.eus.*

⬤ Shopping

San Sebastián is a busy shopping town. Wander Calle San Martín and the surrounding pedestrian-only streets to see what's in the windows. Some stores are closed on Sunday.

Alboka Artesanía

CRAFTS | This is the best city-center shop for Basque-made artisanry such as patterned tablecloths and linens, jai alai balls, ceramics, and traditional dress. ☒ *Pl. Constitución 8, Parte Vieja* ☎ *94/342–6300* ⊕ *www.albokaartesania. com.*

Casa Ponsol

CLOTHING | This is the best place to buy boinas. The Leclerq family has been hatting (and clothing) the local male population for four generations, since 1838. ☒ *Calle Narrica 4, at Calle Sarriegui*

3, Parte Vieja ☎ *94/342–0876* ⊕ *www. casaponsol.com.*

Kado

HOUSEHOLD ITEMS/FURNITURE | Pop into this Nordic-inspired boutique for furniture, kitchenware, and splashy artwork. ☒ *Calle Alfonso VIII 3, Centro* ☎ *94/305–0393* ⊕ *www.kadodecoracion.com.*

Mimo

FOOD/CANDY | This posh gourmet food and wine shop also hosts Basque cooking classes and the city's best food tours. ☒ *Calle Okendo 1, Centro* ☎ *94/342–1143* ⊕ *www.mimofood.com.*

Vitoria-Gasteiz

62 km (39 miles) south of Bilbao, 100 km (62 miles) west of Pamplona.

The capital of the Basque Country, and the region's second-largest city after Bilbao, Vitoria-Gasteiz might be Euskadi's least "Basque" city, at least to the naked eye, since it's neither a seafaring port nor a mountain enclave. It sprawls, instead, over the steppe-like *meseta de Álava* (Álava plain) and functions as a modern industrial center with plentiful cultural events, fine restaurants, and museums. The city also boasts a strikingly well-preserved *casco medieval* (medieval quarter). Founded by Sancho el Sabio (the Wise) in 1181, the urban center was built largely of granite, so Vitoria's oldest streets and squares seem especially weathered and ancient.

GETTING AROUND

Take the A1 and the PA34 from Pamplona, which takes one hour by car; buses also run regularly between the two cities. From Bilbao, you should take the AP68 and N622, which takes just 44 minutes. Vitoria is a spread-out city, but the area you'll spend your time in is small, only about 1 square km (½ mile), and easily walked.

BUS STATION Estación de Autobuses de Vitoria–Gasteiz ⊠ *Pl. de Euskaltzaindia s/n, Vitoria* ☎ *94/516–1666* ⊕ *www.vitoria-gasteiz.org.*

VISITOR INFORMATION

CONTACTS Vitoria–Gasteiz ⊠ *Pl. España 1* ☎ *94/516–1598* ⊕ *www.vitoria-gasteiz.org.*

Sights

★ Artium

MUSEUM | Officially named the Centro-Museo Vasco de Arte Contemporáneo, this former bus station was reopened as a museum in 2002 by former king Juan Carlos, who called it "the third leg of the Basque art triangle, along with the Bilbao Guggenheim and San Sebastián's Chillida Leku." The museum's permanent collection—including 20th- and 21st-century paintings and sculptures by Jorge Oteiza, Chillida, Agustín Ibarrola, and Nestor Basterretxea, among many others—makes it one of Spain's finest treasuries of contemporary art. ⊠ *Calle Francia 24, Vitoria* ☎ *94/520–9020* ⊕ *www.artium.org* 🖾 *€5 (by donation Wed. and weekends following exhibition openings)* ⊘ *Closed Mon.*

Bibat

MUSEUM | FAMILY | The 1525 Palacio de Bendaña and adjoining bronze-plated building are home to one of Vitoria's main attractions, the Bibat, which combines the Museo Fournier de Naipes (Playing-Card Museum) with the Museo de Arqueología. The *palacio* houses the playing-card collection of Don Heraclio Fournier, who, in 1868, founded a playing-card factory, started amassing cards, and eventually found himself with 15,000 sets, the largest and finest such collection in the world. There are hand-painted cards, including finely painted sets from Japan and round cards from India. The oldest sets date to the 12th century. The Museo de la Arqueología, in the newest building, has paleolithic dolmens, Roman art and artifacts, medieval objects, and

the famous Stele del Jinete (Stele of the Horseback Rider), an early Basque tombstone. ⊠ *Calle Cuchillería 54, Vitoria* ☎ *94/520–3707* 🖾 *€3* ⊘ *Closed Mon.*

★ Catedral de Santa María

RELIGIOUS SITE | Dating back to the 14th century, the cathedral is currently being restored but is still open to visitors—in fact, that's part of the fun. Tour guides hand out protective hard hats and show you around the restoration site. It's a unique opportunity to study the building's architecture from the foundation up. A prominent and active supporter of the project is British novelist Ken Follett, whose novel *World Without End* is about the construction of the cathedral. A statue of the author has been placed on one side of the cathedral. ⊠ *Pl. Santa Maria, Vitoria* ☎ *94/525–5135* ⊕ *www.catedralvitoria.com* 🖾 *From €9.*

Museo de Bellas Artes (*Museum of Fine Arts*)

MUSEUM | Paintings by Ribera, Picasso, and the Basque painter Zuloaga adorn the walls of this gorgeous baroque building. ⊠ *Paseo Fray Francisco 8, Vitoria* ☎ *94/518–1918* ⊕ *www.araba.eus/web/museobellasartes* 🖾 *Free* ⊘ *Closed Mon.*

Parque de la Florida

CITY PARK | This park, with bridges, gazebos, and man-made hills, offers a nice respite from the hustle and bustle of the city. At Christmastime, it morphs into one enormous nativity scene that kids go nuts over. ⊠ *Calle Florida* ✛ *South of Pl. de la Virgen Blanca.*

Plaza de España

PLAZA | Across Virgen Blanca, past the monument and the handsome Victoria café, this is an arcaded neoclassical square with the austere elegance typical of formal 19th-century squares all over Spain.

Plaza de la Virgen Blanca

PLAZA | In the southwest corner of old Vitoria, this plaza is ringed by noble houses with covered arches and white-trim glass galleries. The monument in the center commemorates the Duke of Wellington's victory over Napoléon's army here in 1813.

San Miguel Arcángel
RELIGIOUS SITE | A jasper niche in the lateral facade of this Gothic church contains the Virgen Blanca (White Virgin), Vitoria's patron saint. ✉ *Pl. Virgen Blanca s/n* ☎ *94/516–1598.*

★ Street Art
PUBLIC ART | In a city as noble and staid as Vitoria, you don't expect to find world-class street art, but that's precisely what's been drawing more and more tourists and artsy types to the parallel streets of Anorbin and Carnicerías in the old town. Feast your eyes on multistory, thought-provoking murals depicting family scenes, landscapes, and political issues. ✉ *Cantón Anorbin, Vitoria.*

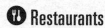

🍴 Restaurants

★ El Portalón
$$$$ | **SPANISH** | With dark, creaky wood floors and staircases, bare brick walls, and ancient beams, pillars, and coats of arms, this 15th-century inn turns out classical Castilian and Basque specialties that reflect Vitoria's geography and social history. Try the *cochinillo lechal asado* (grilled suckling pig) or any of the *rape* (monkfish) preparations. **Known for:** 15th-century dining room; Basque comfort food; deep wine list. [$] *Average main: €23* ✉ *Calle Correría 147, Vitoria* ☎ *94/514–2755* 🌐 *www.restauranteelportalon.com* 🕒 *No dinner Sun.*

★ La Bodeguilla Lanciego
$$$ | **BASQUE** | This inviting white-tablecloth taberna established in 1959 serves soul-satisfying cuisine in a cabin-like dining room decorated with taupe curtains, blond-wood chairs, and original artwork. Steak frites are the go-to here with roast turbot coming in a close second. **Known for:** subtle, tasteful decor; excellent txuletas; peppy staff. [$] *Average main: €19* ✉ *Calle Olagibel 60, Vitoria* ☎ *94/525–0073* 🌐 *www.labodeguillalanciego.com* 🕒 *Closed Sun.*

Toloño
$$ | **TAPAS** | This deceptively simple-looking bar resembles an American diner with shiny white plastic chairs and a sleek wood bar top. But behind this unassuming exterior hides one of Vitoria's culinary jewels, which has won a plethora of awards for its knockout pintxos including *txangurro gratinado* (crab gratin) and ravioli *de conejo* (with rabbit). **Known for:** worth-the-wait creative pintxos; hidden-gem bar; pristine seafood dishes. [$] *Average main: €15* ✉ *Cuesta San Francisco 3, Vitoria* ☎ *94/523–3336* 🌐 *www.tolonobar.com.*

Zaldiarán
$$$$ | **CONTEMPORARY** | There's some tacky plating—think sorbet served in martini glasses— but worthwhile are the contemporary interpretations of classics, such as tempura-battered artichokes and razor clams with yuzu vinaigrette. The tasting menu (€68) changes seasonally. **Known for:** heavenly steak tartare; good-value tasting menus; impress-your-date ambience. [$] *Average main: €25* ✉ *Av. Gasteiz 21, Vitoria* ☎ *94/513–4822* 🌐 *www.restaurantezaldiaran.com* 🕒 *Closed Tues. No dinner Wed. and Sun.*

🛏 Hotels

Etxegana Hotel and Spa
$$$ | **HOTEL** | **FAMILY** | On top of a mountain in the heart of Basque country's "little Switzerland," 20 minutes north of Vitoria-Gasteiz and 40 minutes south of Bilbao, this relaxing retreat features breathtaking views of the surrounding mountains and an excellent restaurant and spa. **Pros:** stunning views; surrounded by nature; family-run and welcoming. **Cons:** half-hour drive to town; it's used as a wedding venue; Wi-Fi could be better in some rooms. [$] *Rooms from: €145* ✉ *Ipiñaburu 38, Zeanuri* ☎ *94/633–8448*

⊕ *www.etxegana.com* ⇄ *18 rooms* ¶⊙¶ *Free Breakfast.*

★ La Casa de los Arquillos

$$ | **B&B/INN** | Brightly lit, with clean Scandinavian design, this well-priced, adorable B&B has the best location in town, just steps from the central Plaza de España de Vitoria. **Pros:** unbeatable location; good breakfast; very cozy. **Cons:** rooms are up two flights of stairs; no convenient parking; no 24-hour reception. $ *Rooms from: €120* ✉ *Paseo los Arquillos 1, Vitoria* ☎ *94/515–1259* ⊕ *www.lacasadelosarquillos.com* ⇄ *8 rooms* ¶⊙¶ *Free Breakfast.*

Parador de Argómaniz

$$$ | **HOTEL** | This 17th-century palace has panoramic views over the Álava plains and retains a powerful sense of mystery and romance, with long stone hallways punctuated by imposing antiques. **Pros:** contemporary rooms and comforts; gorgeous details and surroundings; excellent restaurant. **Cons:** isolated—about a 15-minute drive from Vitoria; no patio furniture on guest-room balconies; noisy radiators might wake you up. $ *Rooms from: €150* ✉ *Calle del Parador 14, (N1, Km 363), Argómaniz* ✛ *East of Vitoria off N104 toward Pamplona* ☎ *94/529–3200* ⊕ *www.parador.es* ⇄ *53 rooms* ¶⊙¶ *No meals.*

Laguardia

45 km (28 miles) south of Vitoria.

Founded in AD 908 to stand guard—as its name suggests—over Navarra's southwestern flank, Laguardia is situated on a promontory overlooking the Río Ebro and the vineyards of La Rioja Alavesa wine country. The peaceful medieval town is an ideal outpost for vineyard-hopping travelers.

VISITOR INFORMATION

CONTACTS Laguardia Tourist Office ✉ *Casa Garcetas, Calle Mayor 52* ☎ *94/560–0845* ⊕ *www.laguardia-alava.com.*

Sights

Starting from the 15th-century Puerta de Carnicerías, or Puerta Nueva, the central portal off the parking area on the east side of town, the first landmark is the 16th-century **ayuntamiento,** with its imperial shield of Carlos V. Farther into the square is the current town hall, built in the 19th century. A right turn down Calle Santa Engracia takes you past impressive facades—the floor inside the portal at No. 25 is a lovely stone mosaic, and a walk behind the triple-emblazoned 17th-century facade of No. 19 reveals a stagecoach, floor mosaics, wood beams, and an inner porch. The Puerta de Santa Engracia, with an image of the saint in an overhead niche, opens out to the right, and on the left, at the entrance to Calle Víctor Tapia, No. 17 bears a coat of arms with the Latin phrase "Laus Tibi" (Praise Be to Thee).

Bodega el Fabulista

WINERY/DISTILLERY | This family-run bodega is famed for its down-to-earth, approachable tours, which take place in the 16th-century caves below Laguardia and are followed by a tasting of two wines for €7. ✉ *Pl. San Juan* ☎ *94/562–1192* ⊕ *www.bodegaelfabulista.com* ✉ *€7* ⊙ *Closed Sun.*

Casa de la Primicia

BUILDING | Laguardia's oldest civil structure, the 15th-century Casa de la Primicia is where tithes of fresh fruit were collected in medieval times. Visit the restored underground bodega, where tours include wine tastings. ✉ *Calle Páganos 78* ☎ *94/562–1266, 94/560–0296* ⊕ *www.bodegascasaprimicia.com* ✉ *€10.*

Eguren Ugarte

WINERY/DISTILLERY | The family behind this majestic winery has been in the business for five generations. Surrounded by vineyards on all sides, the tour showcases traditional wine making at its best and is followed by a tasting of three to five exceptional wines and a pintxo for €5–€12. ✉ *Ctra. A124, Km 61, Páganos* ☎ *94/560–0766* 🌐 *www.egurenugarte.com/en* 🎫 *From €5.*

Galería Juanjo San Pedro
MUSEUM | This gallery is filled with colorful paintings of landscapes and rural life by local artist Juanjo San Pedro. ✉ *Calle Mayor 11* ☎ *65/892–8580* 🌐 *www.juanjosanpedro.es* 🎫 *Free.*

★ Herederos de Marqués de Riscal
BUILDING | The village of Elciego, 6 km (4 miles) southeast of Laguardia, is the site of the historic Marqués de Riscal winery. Tours of the vineyards—among the most legendary in La Rioja—as well as the cellars are conducted in various languages, including English. Reservations are required. The estate also includes the stunning Frank Gehry–designed **Hotel Marqués de Riscal,** crafted out of waves of metal reminiscent of his Guggenheim Bilbao. ✉ *Calle Torrea 1, Elciego* ☎ *94/560–6000* 🌐 *www.marquesderiscal.com* 🎫 *€16.*

★ Santa María de los Reyes
BUILDING | Laguardia's architectural crown jewel is this church's Gothic polychrome portal—the only of its kind in Spain. Protected by a posterior Renaissance facade, the door centers on a lovely, lifelike effigy of La Virgen de los Reyes (Virgin of the Kings), sculpted in the 14th century and painted in the 17th by Ribera. Guided tours can be arranged at the tourist office. ✉ *Calle Mayor 52* ☎ *94/560–0845* 🎫 *Tours €3.*

🛏 Hotels

Hospedería de los Parajes
$$$ | **HOTEL** | While many hotels welcome guests with refreshments at check in, in this quirky hotel, guests check in with a glass of wine in the 16th-century wine cave, which has been converted into a *vinoteca* (wine bar) with traditional wooden tables. **Pros:** charming wine cellar; centrally located; cozy, grandmotherly digs. **Cons:** poor natural light; Wi-Fi spotty in some rooms; expensive and remote parking. [$] *Rooms from: €180* ✉ *Calle Mayor 46–48* ☎ *94/562–1130* 🌐 *www.hospederiadelosparajes.com* 🛏 *18 rooms* 🍴 *Free Breakfast.*

Hotel Collado
$$$$ | **HOTEL** | Guests are treated like royalty in this castle-like 18th-century manor house. **Pros:** old-world European feel; close to the heart of town; website features every room (so ask for the one you want). **Cons:** spotty Wi-Fi in some rooms; underwhelming breakfast; maintenance could be improved. [$] *Rooms from: €192* ✉ *Paseo El Collado 1* ☎ *94/562–1200* 🌐 *www.hotelcollado.com* 🛏 *10 rooms* 🍴 *No meals.*

★ Hotel Marqués de Riscal
$$$$ | **HOTEL** | Frank Gehry's post-Guggenheim hotel concept looks as if a colony from outer space has taken up residence (or crashed) in the middle of one of La Rioja's oldest vineyards. **Pros:** dazzling architecture; five-star environment; superb dining. **Cons:** wildly expensive; interiors are drab in comparison to the exterior; service isn't always five-star. [$] *Rooms from: €410* ✉ *Calle Torrea 1, Elciego* ✥ *6 km (4 miles) southwest of Laguardia* ☎ *94/518–0880* 🌐 *www.hotel-marquesderiscal.com* 🛏 *43 rooms* 🍴 *Free Breakfast.*

Hotel Viura
$$$ | **HOTEL** | The sharp angles and bright colors of this architecturally avant-garde luxury hotel cut a striking contrast to the traditional *pueblo* (village) surrounding it, and the location—12 km (7 miles) west of Laguardia in the sleepy village of Villabuena de Álava—makes it a good base for exploring La Rioja Alavesa and neighboring Rioja Alta. **Pros:** quirky, Instagrammable architecture; rooftop gym and bar; king-size beds. **Cons:** not much to do or see in the village; no spa; soundproofing could be improved. [$] *Rooms from: €165* ✉ *Calle Mayor s/n, Villabuena de Álava*

☎ *94/560–9000* 🌐 *www.hotelviura.com* 🛏 *33 rooms* 🍴 *No meals.*

★ Posada Mayor de Migueloa
$$ | **HOTEL** | With its stone floors and rough-hewn ceiling beams, this 17th-century palace transports you back in time, but it features modern comforts. **Pros:** rustic-chic rooms; off-season specials; restaurant that's a destination in itself. **Cons:** in a pedestrianized area a long way from your car; rooms on the front side exposed to boisterous racket on weekends; no Wi-Fi in some rooms. [$] *Rooms from: €110* ✉ *Calle Mayor de Migueloa 20* ☎ *94/560–0187* 🌐 *www.mayordemigueloa.com* 🕒 *Closed Jan. 8–Feb. 8* 🛏 *8 rooms* 🍴 *Breakfast.*

Pasaia

7 km (4 miles) east of San Sebastián.

Three towns make up the commercial port of Pasaia (Rentería in Spanish): **Pasai Antxo** (Pasajes Ancho), an industrial port; **Pasai de San Pedro** (Pasajes de San Pedro), a large fishing harbor; and historic **Pasai Donibane** (Pasajes de San Juan), a colorful cluster of 16th- and 17th-century buildings. The most scenic way in is via Pasai de San Pedro, on the San Sebastián side of the strait: catch a five-minute launch across the mouth of the harbor (€0.70 one-way, €1.40 round-trip).

In 1777, at the age of 20, General Lafayette set out from Pasai Donibane to aid the American Revolution. Victor Hugo spent the summer of 1843 here writing his *Voyage aux Pyrénées*. The **Victor Hugo House** is the home of the tourist office; the exhibit *Victor Hugo, Traveling Down the Memory* features drawings and documents that belonged to the writer. **Albaola Factory,** a center of maritime culture, is directed by Xabier Agote, who taught boatbuilding in Rockland, Maine.

GETTING HERE AND AROUND

Pasai Donibane can be reached via Pasai de San Pedro from San Sebastián by cab or bus. Or, if you prefer to go on foot, follow the red-and-white-blazed GR trail that begins at the east end of Zurriola Beach—you're in for a spectacular three-hour hike along the rocky coast. By car, take N1 toward France and, after passing Juan Mari Arzak's eponymous restaurant, at Alto de Miracruz, look for a marked left turn into Pasai de San Pedro.

TOURS

Mater Museoa (*Mater Ship Museum*)
BOAT TOURS | **FAMILY** | A former Basque fishing boat now offers a variety of tours of the port and visits to a rowing club and to the Victor Hugo House in Pasai Donibane, as well as a treasure hunt for young and old alike. You can join a one-hour trip or rent the ship out for the whole day (for groups of 10 or more); book ahead, online or by phone. ✉ *Muelle Pesquero, Pasai Donibane* ☎ *61/981–4225* 🌐 *www.matermuseoa.com* 🎟 *From €5.*

VISITOR INFORMATION

CONTACTS Pasaia Tourist Office ✉ *Victor Hugo House, Donibane 63, Pasai Donibane* ☎ *94/334–1556* 🌐 *www.oarsoaldeaturismoa.eus.*

🍴 Restaurants

★ Casa Cámara
$$$$ | **SEAFOOD** | Four generations ago, Pablo Cámara turned this 19th-century fishing wharf on the Pasaia narrows into a first-class seafood restaurant with lovely views over the shipping lane. A steaming *sopa de pescado* (fish soup) on a wet Atlantic day is a memorable event, or try *cangrejo del mar* (spider crab with vegetable sauce) or the superb *merluza con salsa verde* (hake in green sauce). **Known for:** pier-side dining; pristine shellfish; quaint, old-timey ambience. [$] *Average main: €46* ✉ *Calle San Juan 79, Pasai Donibane* ☎ *94/352–3699* 🌐 *www.casacamara.com* 🕒 *Closed Mon., and Wed. Nov.–Easter wk. No dinner Sun.*

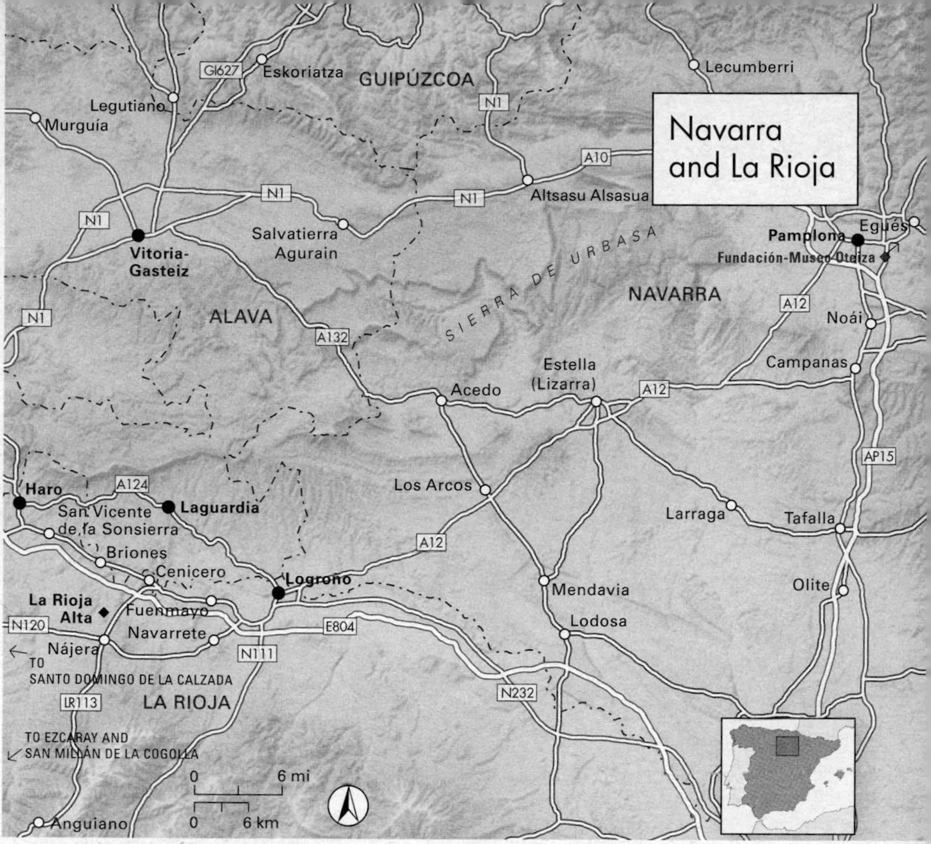
Navarra and La Rioja
GI627
Eskoriatza
GUIPÚZCOA
Lecumberri
Legutiano
Murguía
N1
A10
Altsasu Alsasua
Salvatierra Agurain
Vitoria-Gasteiz
SIERRA DE URBASA
Pamplona
Egüés
Fundación-Museo Oteiza
NAVARRA
ALAVA
A132
A12
Noái
Campanas
Estella (Lizarra)
Acedo
AP15
Los Arcos
Haro
A124
San Vicente de la Sonsierra
Laguardia
Larraga
Tafalla
Briones
Cenicero
Logroño
Mendavia
Olite
La Rioja Alta
Fuenmayor
N120
Navarrete
E804
Lodosa
Nájera
N111
TO SANTO DOMINGO DE LA CALZADA
LR113
LA RIOJA
N232
TO EZCARAY AND SAN MILLÁN DE LA COGOLLA
0
6 mi
0
6 km
Anguiano

Hondarribia

20 km (13 miles) east of Pasaia.

Hondarribia (Fuenterrabía in Spanish) is the last fishing port before the French border and a wonderful day trip from San Sebastián. Lined with fishermen's homes and small fishing boats, the harbor is a scenic if slightly touristy spot. If you have a taste for history, follow signs up the hill to the medieval bastion and onetime castle of Carlos V, now a parador, and keep your eye out for coats of arms emblazoned on the corners of old buildings (as opposed to above entryways)—an Hondarribia peculiarity.

VISITOR INFORMATION

CONTACTS Hondarribia Tourist Office ✉ *Pl. de Armas 9* ☎ *94/364–3677* 🌐 *www.hondarribia.eus.*

Restaurants

Alameda

$$$$ | **BASQUE** | The three Txapartegi brothers—Mikel, Kepa, and Gorka—are the star chefs behind this restaurant, which opened in 1997 after the brothers' apprenticeship with, among others, Martín Berasategui. The elegantly restored house (and its sunny terrace) in upper Hondarribia is a delight, as are the seasonally rotated combinations of carefully chosen ingredients, from fish and duck to vegetables. **Known for:** Michelin-starred dining; freshest seafood and meats; scenic seaside environs. [$] *Average main: €36* ✉ *Calle Minasoroeta 1* ☎ *94/364–2789* 🌐 *www.restaurantealameda.net* 🕒 *No dinner Sun., and Mon. and Tues. late Dec.–early Feb.*

★ Hermandad de Pescadores

$$$ | **SEAFOOD** | One of the Basque country's most historic and typical fishermen's guilds, this central restaurant exudes tradition. At simple wooden tables and a handsome mahogany bar, local volunteers serve simple, hearty fare—think sopa de pescado, *mejillones* (mussels), and *almejas a la marinera* (clams in a thick, garlicky sauce)—at better-than-reasonable prices. **Known for:** dayboat fish; affordable top-quality seafood—a rarity in the region; homey, unfussy dining room. $ *Average main: €20* ✉ *Calle Zuloaga 12* ☎ *94/364–2738* ◷ *Closed Mon., Christmas–Jan., 1 wk in May, and 1 wk in Oct. No dinner Sun.*

Hotels

Casa Artzu

$ | **B&B/INN** | **FAMILY** | Better hosts than this warm, friendly clan are hard to find, and their 13th-century family house and renovated barn offer modern accommodations overlooking the Bidasoa estuary and the Atlantic. **Pros:** good value; family-friendly; free parking. **Cons:** credit cards not accepted; breakfast €3 extra; need a car to get to the beach. $ *Rooms from: €52* ✉ *Barrio Montaña* ☎ *94/364–0530* ⊕ *www.casa-artzu.com* ➡ *No credit cards* ⇩ *6 rooms* ❑ *No meals.*

★ Parador de Hondarribia

$$$$ | **HOTEL** | **FAMILY** | You can live like a medieval lord in this 10th-century bastion, home in the 16th century to Spain's founding emperor, Carlos V—hence its alternative name: Parador El Emperador. **Pros:** great sea views; cozy old-fashioned rooms; terrific breakfasts. **Cons:** no restaurant; no a/c (but ceiling fans); expensive parking. $ *Rooms from: €283* ✉ *Pl. de Armas 14* ☎ *94/364–5500* ⊕ *www.parador.es* ⇩ *36 rooms* ❑ *No meals.*

Pamplona

79 km (47 miles) southeast of San Sebastián.

Pamplona (Iruña in Euskera) is known worldwide for its running of the bulls, made famous by Ernest Hemingway in his 1926 novel *The Sun Also Rises*. The occasion is the festival of San Fermín, July 6–14, when Pamplona's population triples (along with its hotel rates), so reserve rooms months in advance. Every morning at 8 sharp a rocket is shot off, and the bulls kept overnight in the corrals at the edge of town are run through a series of closed-off streets leading to the bullring, a nearly 2,800-foot dash. Running among them are Spaniards and foreigners feeling audacious (or foolhardy) enough to risk getting gored. The degree of peril in the thrilling *encierro* (running, literally "enclosing") is difficult to gauge. Serious injuries occur nearly every day during the festival; deaths are rare but always a possibility. After the bulls' frantic gallop through town, every one of them is killed in the bullring, a fact that draws ire from many anti-bullfighting Spaniards and animal rights groups. Running is free, but tickets to *corridas* (bullfights) can be hard to snag.

Founded by the Roman emperor Pompey as Pompaelo, or Pampeiopolis, Pamplona was successively taken by the Franks, the Goths, and the Moors. In 750, the Pamplonians put themselves under the protection of Charlemagne and managed to expel the Arabs temporarily. But the foreign commander took advantage of this trust to destroy the city walls; when he was driven out once more by the Moors, the Navarrese took their revenge, ambushing and slaughtering the retreating Frankish army as it fled over the Pyrenees through the mountain pass of Roncesvalles in 778. This is the episode depicted in the 11th-century *Song of Roland*, the earliest surviving major work of French literature, although its anonymous French poet cast the aggressors as Moors. For centuries after that, Pamplona remained three argumentative towns until they were forcibly incorporated into one city by Carlos III (the Noble, 1387–1425) of Navarra.

GETTING HERE AND AROUND
BUS STATION Estación de Autobuses de Pamplona ⊠ *Av. de Yanguas y Miranda 2* 🕿 *90/202–3651* ⊕ *www.estaciondeautobusesdepamplona.com.*

CAR RENTALS Europcar ⊠ *Blanca de Navarra Hotel, Av. Pio XII 43* 🕿 *94/817–2523* ⊕ *www.europcar.com* ⊠ *Aeropuerto de Pamplona (Noain), Ctra. Bellaterra s/n* 🕿 *94/831–2798* ⊕ *www.europcar.com.*

TRAIN INFORMATION Estación de Pamplona ⊠ *Pl. de la Estación 1* 🕿 *90/232–0320, 90/243–2343* ⊕ *www.renfe.com.*

VISITOR INFORMATION
CONTACTS Pamplona Tourist Office ⊠ *Calle San Saturnino 2* 🕿 *94/842–0700* ⊕ *www.turismodepamplona.es.*

 # Sights

Archivo Real y General de Navarra
BUILDING | This Rafael Moneo–designed monolith of glass and stone, ingeniously contained within a Romanesque palace, is Pamplona's architectural treasure. Containing papers and parchments going back to the 9th century, the archive holds more than 75,000 linear feet of documents and has room for more than 55,500 feet more. The library and reading rooms are lined with cherrywood and topped with a gilded ceiling. ⊠ *Calle Dos de Mayo s/n* 🕿 *84/842–4667, 84/842–4623* ⊕ *www.cfnavarra.es/agn* 🖃 *Free* ⊙ *Closed weekends.*

Catedral de Pamplona
RELIGIOUS SITE | This is one of the most important religious buildings in northern Spain, thanks to the fragile grace and gabled Gothic arches of its cloister. Inside are the tombs of Carlos III and his wife, marked by an alabaster sculpture. The **Museo Catedralicio Diocesano** (Diocesan Museum) houses religious art from the Middle Ages and the Renaissance. Call in advance for guided tours in English. ⊠ *Calle Curia s/n* 🕿 *94/821–2594* ⊕ *www.catedraldepamplona.com* 🖃 *€5* ⊙ *Museum closed Sun.*

Fundación-Museo Oteiza
MUSEUM | East of Pamplona on the road toward France, this museum dedicated to the father of modern Basque art is a must-visit. Jorge Oteiza (1908–2003), in his seminal treatise, *Quosque tandem,* called for Basque artists to find an aesthetic of their own instead of attempting to become part of the Spanish canon. Rejecting ornamentation in favor of essential form and a noninvasive use of space, Oteiza created a school of artists of which the sculptor Eduardo Chillida (1924–2002) was the most famous. The building itself, Oteiza's home for more than two decades, is a large cube of earth-color concrete designed by Oteiza's longtime friend, Pamplona architect Francisco Javier Sáenz de Oiza. The sculptor's living quarters, his studio and laboratory, and the workshop used for teaching divide the museum into three sections. ⊠ *Calle de la Cuesta 7* ✛ *From town, take Ctra. N150 east for 8 km (5 miles) to Alzuza* 🕿 *94/833–2074* ⊕ *www.museooteiza.org* 🖃 *€4 (free Fri.)* ⊙ *Closed Mon.*

Museo de Navarra
MUSEUM | In a 16th-century building once used as a hospital for pilgrims on their way to Santiago de Compostela, this museum has a collection of regional archaeological artifacts and historical costumes. ⊠ *Cuesta de Santo Domingo 47* 🕿 *84/842–6493* 🖃 *€2 (free Sat. afternoon and Sun.)* ⊙ *Closed Mon.*

Museo Universidad de Navarra
MUSEUM | Designed by local celebrity architect Rafael Moneo, this contemporary art museum opened in 2014 on the University of Navarra campus. It has an exceptional photograph collection

dating to the birth of photography as an art form, and the permanent art collection features classic works by Rothko, Picasso, Kandinsky, and Tàpies. ✉ *Campus Universitario, Calle Universidad* ☎ *94/842–5700* 🌐 *www.museo.unav.edu* 🎫 *€5.*

Plaza del Castillo

NEIGHBORHOOD | One of Pamplona's greatest charms is the warren of narrow streets near the Plaza del Castillo (especially Calle San Nicolás) filled with restaurants, taverns, and bars. ✉ *Pamplona.*

🍴 Restaurants

Café Iruña

$$ | CAFÉ | Pamplona's gentry has been flocking to this ornate, French-style café since 1888, but in 1926 Ernest Hemingway made it part of world literary lore in *The Sun Also Rises*. You can still have a drink with a bronze version of the author in his favorite perch at the far end of the bar, or enjoy views of the plaza from a table on the terrace. **Known for:** long waits; chocolate con churros; grand, ornate dining area. [$] *Average main: €14* ✉ *Pl. del Castillo 44* ☎ *94/822–2064* 🌐 *www.cafeiruna.com.*

Errejota

$$$$ | SPANISH | Previously called Josetxo, this warm, family-run restaurant in a stately mansion with a classically elegant interior is one of Pamplona's foremost addresses for refined cuisine. There's something for everyone on the diverse, internationally inflected menu, whose highlights include baby artichokes with langoustine tails and monkfish with black-olive vinaigrette and soy-anchovy mayonnaise. **Known for:** modern Navarrese cuisine; old-world white-tablecloth dining room; standout artichokes. [$] *Average main: €26* ✉ *Pl. Príncipe de Viana 1* ☎ *94/822–2097* 🌐 *www.errejota.es* 🕒 *Closed Sun. (except during San Fermín), Easter wk, and Aug.*

Europa Restaurante

$$$$ | SPANISH | Pamplona's finest restaurant, in the hotel of the same name, the Europa offers refined, Michelin-starred Navarran cooking with reasonably priced à la carte dining as well as excellent tasting menus available for €46, €63, and €79. The small and light first-floor dining room offers the perfect backdrop to dishes like slow-cooked lamb and pork or the best bacalao al pil pil you may try on your trip. **Known for:** seasonal vegetable dishes; nicest restaurant in town; affordable tasting menus. [$] *Average main: €27* ✉ *Calle Espoz y Mina 11* ☎ *94/822–1800* 🌐 *www.hreuropa.com* 🕒 *Closed Sun.*

★ Gaucho

$ | TAPAS | This legendary tavern, which remains surprisingly calm even during San Fermín, serves some of the best tapas in Pamplona. Opt for classics like garlicky mushroom brochettes and jamón-filled croquetas, or spring for more modern creations such as seared goose liver on toast or almond-encrusted morcilla. **Known for:** delectable foie gras; delicious tapas for all budgets; old-timey atmosphere. [$] *Average main: €9* ✉ *Calle Espoz y Mina 7* ☎ *94/822–5073.*

🛏 Hotels

★ Gran Hotel La Perla

$$$$ | HOTEL | The oldest hotel in Pamplona (and the spot where Ernest Hemingway first conceived of his first novel, *The Sun Also Rises*) underwent several years of refurbishing before it reinvented itself as a high-end lodging option. **Pros:** staff are well versed in history of the property; even entry-level rooms are spacious; good soundproofing. **Cons:** round-the-clock mayhem during San Fermín; prices triple during San Fermín; no pool, gym, or spa. [$] *Rooms from: €183* ✉ *Pl. del Castillo 1* ☎ *94/822–3000* 🌐 *www.granhotellaperla.com* 🛏 *44 rooms* 🍽 *Free Breakfast.*

Hotel Maisonnave

$$ | HOTEL | FAMILY | This modern four-star hotel has a nearly perfect location, tucked away on a relatively quiet pedestrian street, just steps from all the action on Plaza del Castillo and Calle Estafeta. **Pros:** friendly, multilingual staff; great location; lively bar and restaurant. **Cons:** modern interior design lacks local character; more three- than four-star; corporate feel. $ *Rooms from: €91* ✉ *Calle Nueva 20* ☎ *94/822–2600* ⊕ *www.hotelmaisonnave.es* 💬 *138 rooms* ⦿ *No meals.*

Hotel Sercotel Europa

$ | HOTEL | More famous for its world-class Michelin-starred restaurant on the ground floor, this modestly priced hotel is one of Pamplona's best-kept secrets, just a block and half from the bullring and within shouting distance of party central, Plaza del Castillo. **Pros:** central location; good value; special restaurant offers for hotel guests. **Cons:** noisy during the fiesta unless you score an interior room; rooms on the small side; prices can double during San Fermín. $ *Rooms from: €78* ✉ *Calle Espoz y Mina 11* ☎ *94/822–1800* ⊕ *www.hoteleuropapamplona.com* 💬 *25 rooms* ⦿ *Free Breakfast.*

Palacio Guendulain

$$$ | HOTEL | This 18th-century palace in the center of town has been restored to its original grandeur with wooden ceilings, Victorian furniture, and a grand staircase. **Pros:** opportunity to stay in a historical monument; central location; outstanding service. **Cons:** provides little refuge from the mayhem during San Fermín; noise from the street is a problem on weekends; extra charge for parking. $ *Rooms from: €129* ✉ *Calle Zapatería 53* ☎ *94/822–5522* ⊕ *www.palacioguendulain.com* 💬 *25 rooms* ⦿ *Free Breakfast.*

Nightlife

The city has a thumping student life year-round, especially along the length of Calle San Nicolás, whose daytime bars

transform into unpretentious *discotecas* by night. Artsier, more alternative venues line Calle Navarrería, while slightly starchier nightlife spots geared toward the 40-plus crowd can be found around the Plaza de Toros.

Canalla

DANCE CLUBS | Dress up, or you might flunk the bouncer's inspection at this loungy nightclub, filled until dawn with young singles and couples. Cover charge depends on visiting DJs and events, and Fridays are popular student nights. ✉ *Av. Bayona 2* ☎ *67/921–9871* ⊕ *www.canalla.es.*

Ozone

DANCE CLUBS | This techno-music haven is the most popular dance club in town. Cover charge depends on visiting DJs and events; check the website for lineups and prices. ✉ *Calle Monasterio de Velate 5* ☎ *94/826–1593* ⊕ *www.ozonepamplona.com.*

Performing Arts

Edificio Baluarte

MUSIC | The Congress Center and Auditorium, built in 2003 by local architectural star Patxi Mangado, is a sleek assemblage of black Zimbabwean granite. It contains a concert hall of exquisite acoustical perfection utilizing beechwood from upper Navarra's famed Irati *haya* (beech) forest. Performances and concerts, from opera to ballet, are held in this modern venue, built on the remains of one of the five bastions of Pamplona's 16th-century Ciudadela. ✉ *Pl. del Baluarte* ☎ *94/806–6066* ⊕ *www.baluarte.com.*

★ Zentral

CONCERTS | A self-proclaimed gastro club, with food and live music offerings, this clubby venue hosts events ranging from Lindy Hop dance parties to lectures on food science. It morphs into a DJ-driven *discoteca* most nights after 1 am. ✉ *Mercado de Santo Domingo, Calle de Santo*

Running with the Bulls

In *The Sun Also Rises*, Hemingway describes the Pamplona encierro in anything but romantic terms. Jake Barnes hears the rocket, steps out onto his balcony, and watches the crowd run by: men in white with red sashes and neckerchiefs. "One man fell, rolled to the gutter, and lay quiet." It's a textbook move—an experienced runner who falls remains motionless (bulls respond to movement)—and first-rate observation and reporting. In the next chapter, a man is gored and dies. The waiter at Café Iruña mutters, "You hear? Muerto. Dead. He's dead. With a horn through him. All for morning fun." Despite this risk—and humanitarian concerns—generations of Americans and other internationals have turned this barnyard bull-management maneuver into one of the Western world's most famous rites of passage.

The Running Course

At daybreak, six fighting bulls are guided through the streets by 8–10 *cabestros*, or steers (also known as *mansos*, meaning "tame ones"), to the holding pens at the bullring, from which they will emerge later to fight. The course covers 2,706 feet. The Cuesta de Santo Domingo down to the corrals is the most dangerous part of the run, high in terror and short in distance. The walls are sheer, and the bulls pass quickly. The fear here is of a bull hooking along the wall of the Military Hospital on his way up the hill, forcing runners out in front of the speeding pack in a classic hammer-and-anvil movement. Mercaderes is next, cutting left for about 300 feet by the town hall, then right up Calle Estafeta. The outside of each turn and the centrifugal force of 22,000 pounds of bulls and steers are to be avoided here. Calle Estafeta is the bread and butter of the run, the longest (about 1,200 feet), straightest, and least complicated part of the course.

The Classic Run

The classic run, a perfect blend of form and function, is to stay ahead of the horns for as long as possible, fading to the side when overtaken. The long gallop up Calle Estafeta is the place to try it. The trickiest part is splitting your vision so that with one eye you keep track of the bulls behind you and with the other you avoid falling over runners ahead of you.

At the end of Estafeta the course descends left through the *callejón*, or narrow tunnel, into the bullring. The bulls move more slowly here, allowing runners to stay close and even to touch them as they glide down into the tunnel. The only uncertainty is whether there will be a pileup in the tunnel. The most dramatic photographs of the encierro have been taken here, as the pack slams through what occasionally turns into a solid wall of people. If all goes well, the bulls will have arrived in the ring in less than three minutes.

Legal Issues

It is illegal to attempt to attract a bull, thus removing him from the pack and creating a deadly danger. It's also illegal to participate while intoxicated or while taking photos. Sexual assault among the onlookers and partygoers has become an increasing problem. Every year more women report being attacked or inappropriately touched in the crowds.

Domingo s/n, 1st fl. ☎ *94/822–0764*
⊕ *www.zentralpamplona.com.*

Shopping

Botas are the leather wineskins from which Basques typically drink at bull-fights or during fiestas, and the most famous, historic maker, ZZZ, is from Pamplona. The art lies in drinking a stream of wine from a bota held at arm's length without spilling a drop. Some shops are closed on Sunday and during the off-season.

ACCESSORIES
★ Fragment Store
JEWELRY/ACCESSORIES | This well-curated boutique run by young designers is the city's top spot to buy handmade jewelry and accessories, kitchenware, couture garments, and eye-catching stationery. ⊠ *Calle Nueva 4–6* ☎ *84/841–0430* ⊕ *www.fragmentstore.com.*

Olentzero
GIFTS/SOUVENIRS | You can buy botas in most Navarrese towns, but Pamplona's Olentzero gift shop sells the best brand, The Three Zs, written "ZZZ." ⊠ *Calle de la Estafeta 42* ☎ *94/882–0245* ⊕ *www. olentzeroa.com.*

CLOTHING
Caminoteca Pamplona
SPORTING GOODS | Owned by a former pilgrim, this small store stocks everything and anything a hiker embarking on the Camino de Santiago could need, from backpacks, boots, hiking socks, and walking sticks to smaller but equally nec-essary items like blister ointment, rain ponchos, and sporks. ⊠ *Calle de Curia 15* ☎ *94/821–0316* ⊕ *www.caminoteca.com.*

Kukuxumusu
CLOTHING | This chain is famous for color-ful pop-art T-shirt prints with San Fermín and Basque themes. There's another out-post at Mercaderes 19. ⊠ *Calle Sanguesa 19* ☎ *90/278–7092* ⊕ *www.kukuxumusu. com.*

Javier

This gorgeous Navarran hamlet 54 km (33½ miles) southeast of Pamplona, perched atop a lush riverbed and gorge, is the birth-place of the 16th-century Roman Catholic missionary Francis Xavier, cofounder of the Jesuit order. There's a fine **castle,** cathedral, and monastery, two comfortable hotels, three restaurants, and an impres-sive visitor center with rotating exhibits. The town has seen a surge in pilgrim visits since the election of Pope Francis (a Jesuit) in March 2013, but whatever your religious persuasion, it's a beautiful stop on your travels in the Pamplona area. ⊕ *www.javier.es*

FOOD
Gurgur Estafeta
FOOD/CANDY | Come here to buy delicacies from across Navarra, including wines, sweets, cured meats, and cheeses, as well as a variety of bull-themed T-shirts and paraphernalia. ⊠ *Calle Estafeta 21* ☎ *94/820–7992* ⊕ *www.gurgurestafeta. com.*

Manterola
FOOD/CANDY | Here you can buy some toffee called La Cafetera, a local *café con leche* sweet. The shop also sells Navarran wine and other delicacies. ⊠ *Calle Tudela 5* ☎ *94/822–3174* ⊕ *www.manterola.es.*

Torrens Alimentación
FOOD/CANDY | Navarran favorites such as *piquillo* peppers and *chistorra* sausages are sold here. ⊠ *Calle San Miguel 12* ☎ *94/822–4286* ⊕ *www.torrensaliment-acion.com.*

Logroño

85 km (53 miles) southwest of Pamplona.

A scrappy industrial city of 153,000, Logroño has a lovely old quarter bordered by the Ebro and medieval walls, with **Breton de los Herreros** and **Muro Francisco de la Mata** being its principal streets. Wine-loving travelers who prefer the bustle of a city to the quietude of the country should hole up here and take day trips to the outlying vineyards.

Near Logroño, the Roman bridge and the *mirador* (lookout) at **Viguera** are the main sights in the lower Iregua Valley. According to legend, Santiago (St. James) helped the Christians defeat the Moors at the **Castillo de Clavijo,** another panoramic spot. The **Leza (Cañon) del Río Leza** is La Rioja's most dramatic canyon.

GETTING HERE AND AROUND

BUS STATION Estación de Autobuses de Logroño ⊠ *Av. España 1* ☎ *94/123–5983* ⊕ *www.logroño.es.*

TRAIN STATION Estación de Logroño ⊠ *Av. de Colón 83* ☎ *90/243–2343* ⊕ *www. adif.es.*

VISITOR INFORMATION

CONTACTS Oficina de Turismo de Logroño ⊠ *Calle Portales 50* ☎ *94/127–7000* ⊕ *www.logroño.es.*

Sights

Bodegas Baigorri

BUILDING | This sleek, modern winery is an architectural wonder of glass and steel with floor-to-ceiling windows that overlook the vineyards and a state-of-the-art multilevel wine cellar. The two-hour morning tour ends around 2 pm—the perfect time to book lunch at the upstairs restaurant. The tasting menu pairs the three-course menu with four signature wines for €50 and is highly recommended. ⊠ *Ctra. Vitoria–Logroño, Km 53* ☎ *94/560–9420* ⊕ *www.bodegasbaigorri. com* ⊗ *Closed Sun. and Mon.*

Olite

An unforgettable glimpse into the Kingdom of Navarra of the Middle Ages is the reward for journeying to this town, 41 km (25 miles) south of Pamplona. The 11th-century church of San Pedro is revered for its finely worked Romanesque cloisters and portal, but it's the town's castle—restored by Carlos III in the French style and brimming with ramparts, crenellated battlements, and watchtowers—that most captures the imagination. You can walk the ramparts, and should you get tired or hungry, part of the castle has been converted into a parador, making a fine place to catch a bite or a few z's. ⊕ *www.olite.es*

Concatedral de Santa María de la Redonda

RELIGIOUS SITE | Noted for its twin baroque towers, the present-day cathedral was rebuilt in the 16th century in a Gothic style atop ruins of a 12th-century Romanesque church. ⊠ *Calle Portales 14* ☎ *94/125–7611* ⊕ *www.laredonda.org* ☞ *Free.*

Puente de Piedra (*Stone Bridge*)

BRIDGE/TUNNEL | Many of Logroño's monuments, such as this elegant bridge, were built as part of the Camino de Santiago pilgrimage route. ⊠ *Av. de Navarra 1.*

San Bartolomé

RELIGIOUS SITE | The oldest still-standing church in Logroño, San Bartolomé was built between the 13th and 14th centuries in a French Gothic style. Highlights include the 11th-century Mudejar tower and an elaborate 14th-century Gothic doorway. Some carvings on the stone facade depict scenes from the Bible. This is also a landmark on the Camino de Santiago pilgrimage path. ⊠ *Pl. San Bartolomé 2* ☎ *94/125–2254* ☞ *Free.*

Santa María del Palacio

RELIGIOUS SITE | This 11th-century church is known as La Aguja (The Needle) for its pyramid-shaped 135-foot Romanesque-Gothic tower. ⊠ *Calle del Marqués de San Nicolás 30* ⬚ *Free.*

Santiago el Real (*Royal St. James's Church*)

RELIGIOUS SITE | Reconstructed in the 16th century, this church is noted for its equestrian statue of the saint (also known as Santiago Matamoros, or St. James the Moorslayer) presiding over the main door. ⊠ *Calle Barriocepo 6* ☎ *94/120–9501* ⊕ *www.santiagoelreal. org* ⬚ *Free.*

 Restaurants

For tapas, you'll find bars with signature specialties on the connecting streets **Calle del Laurel** and **Travesía de Laurel,** the latter also known as El Sendero de los Elefantes (Path of the Elephants)—an allusion to *trompas* (trunks), Spanish for a snootful. Try Bar Soriano for *champis* (*champiñones,* or mushrooms), Blanco y Negro for *matrimonio* (a green-pepper-and-anchovy sandwich), and La Travesía for *tortilla de patatas.* (Spanish omelet) If you're ordering wine, a young *cosecha* or *clarete* (a rustic local rosé) comes in squat *chato* glasses, a crianza brings out the crystal, and a *reserva* or *gran reserva* (selected grapes aged over three years in oak and bottle) elicits goblets for proper swirling, nosing, and tasting.

Cachetero Comidas

$$$$ | **SPANISH** | A Calle del Laurel standby, this refined taberna with wood-paneled walls serves Riojan specialties like *cochinillo asado* (roast suckling pig) and pimentón-laced potatoes *a la riojana* (potatoes and chorizo stew) as well as risottos and excellent seafood dishes. **Known for:** personable waitstaff; refined Riojan cuisine; butter-soft cochinillo asado. ⓢ *Average main: €25* ⊠ *Calle del Laurel 3* ☎ *94/122–8463* ⊕ *www.*

cachetero.com ⊘ *Closed Tues., and 1st 2 wks in Aug. No dinner Sun.*

★ La Taberna de Baco

$$ | **SPANISH** | This bright, modern bar is a great spot to try seasonal, market-fresh tapas like heirloom tomato salad with chilies and raw onion or cheesy mushroom "carpaccio," but locals flock here for one dish in particular: *oreja a la plancha,* or griddled pig's ear, swimming in punchy *brava* (spicy) sauce. Shatteringly crisp and unapologetically rich, it's one of the best versions you'll have in Spain. **Known for:** offal even the squeamish can learn to love; wide selection of small-production wines; amiable bartenders. ⓢ *Average main: €12* ⊠ *Calle de San Agustín 10* ☎ *94/121–3544* ⊕ *www.latabernade-baco.com.*

★ Tondeluna

$$ | **SPANISH** | A gastro bar that strives to bring haute cuisine to the masses, Tondeluna has six communal tables (with 10 seats each), and all have views into the kitchen, where cooks plate up dishes both novel and familiar like glazed beef cheeks with apple puree and Getaria-style hake with *panadera* (thinly sliced and sauteed) potatoes. **Known for:** good balance of experimental and classic dishes; lively dining room; €20 menú del día. ⓢ *Average main: €16* ⊠ *Calle Muro de la Mata 9* ☎ *94/123–6425* ⊕ *www. tondeluna.com* ⊘ *No dinner Sun.*

Hotels

Marqués de Vallejo

$$ | **HOTEL** | Close to—but not overwhelmed by—the food- and wine-tasting frenzy of nearby Calle del Laurel, this boutique hotel within view of the cathedral is within walking distance of all the major sights. **Pros:** central location; clean, homey rooms; pleasant public areas. **Cons:** street-side rooms can be noisy in summer, when windows are open; furniture looks like it was bought from an early-2000 IKEA catalog; underwhelming breakfast spread. ⓢ *Rooms from: €91*

✉ *Calle Marqués de Vallejo 8* ☎ *94/124–8333* 🌐 *www.hotelmarquesdevallejo.com* 🛏 *50 rooms* 🍴 *No meals.*

NH Herencia Rioja

$$ | **HOTEL** | This modern four-star hotel near the old quarter has contemporary, comfortable rooms, first-rate facilities, a well-trained staff, and a businesslike buzz about it. **Pros:** clean, corporate comfort; two steps from Calle del Laurel's tapas bonanza; excellent breakfast. **Cons:** undistinguished modern building; cheerless interiors; tight, white-knuckle parking. [$] *Rooms from: €95* ✉ *Calle Marqués de Murrieta 14* ☎ *94/121–0222* 🌐 *www.nh-hoteles.com* 🛏 *83 rooms* 🍴 *No meals.*

La Rioja Alta

The Upper Rioja, the most prized subregion of La Rioja's wine country, extends from the Río Ebro to the Sierra de la Demanda. La Rioja Alta has the most fertile soil, the best vineyards and agriculture, the most impressive castles and monasteries, a ski resort at Ezcaray, and the historic economic advantage of being on the Camino de Santiago.

The rivers forming the seven main valleys of the Ebro basin originate in the Sierra de la Demanda, Sierra de Cameros, and Sierra de Alcarama. **Ezcaray** is La Rioja's skiing capital in the **valley of the Río Oja,** just below Valdezcaray in the Sierra de la Demanda. The upper **Najerilla Valley** is La Rioja's mountain sanctuary, an excellent hunting and fishing preserve. The Najerilla River, a rich chalk stream, is one of Spain's best trout rivers. Look for the Puente de Hiedra (Ivy Bridge), its heavy curtain of ivy falling to the surface of the Najerilla. The **Monasterio de Valvanera,** off the C113 near Anguiano, is the sanctuary of La Rioja's patron saint, the Virgen de Valvanera, a 12th-century Romanesque wood carving of the Virgin and Child. **Anguiano** is renowned for its Danza de los Zancos (Dance of the Stilts), held on July 22, when dancers on wooden stilts plummet through the steep streets of the town into the arms of the crowd at the bottom. At the valley's highest point are the Mansilla reservoir and the Romanesque Ermita de San Cristóbal (Hermitage of St. Christopher).

The upper **Iregua Valley,** off N111, has the prehistoric Gruta de la Paz caves at Ortigosa. The artisans of **Villoslada del Cameros** make the region's famous patchwork quilts, called *almazuelas.* Climb to **Pico Cebollera** for a superb view of the valley. Work back toward the Ebro along the Río Leza, through Laguna de Cameros and San Román de Cameros (known for its basket weavers), to complete a tour of the Sierra del Cameros. The upper **Cidacos Valley** leads to the **Parque Jurásico** (Jurassic Park) at Enciso, famous for its dinosaur tracks. The main village in the upper **Alhama Valley** is **Cervera del Rio Alhama,** a center for handmade *alpargatas* (espadrilles).

Sights

Ezcaray

TOWN | Enter the Sierra de la Demanda by heading south from Santo Domingo de la Calzada on LR111. Your first stop is the town of Ezcaray, with its aristocratic houses emblazoned with family crests, of which the **Palacio del Conde de Torremúzquiz** (Palace of the Count of Torremúzquiz) is the most distinguished. Good excursions from here are the Valdezcaray ski station; the source of the Río Oja at Llano de la Casa; La Rioja's highest point, the 7,494-foot Pico de San Lorenzo; and the Romanesque church of Tres Fuentes, at Valgañón. The hamlet is famous for its wild mushroom–gathering residents—and the resulting tapas, too. ✉ *Ezcaray* 🌐 *www.ezcaray.org.*

Nájera

RELIGIOUS SITE | This town was the capital of Navarra and La Rioja until 1076, when the latter became part of Castile and the residence of the Castilian royal family.

The fertile soil and fields of the Ebro River valley make some of Spain's most colorful landscapes.

The monastery of **Santa María la Real** (⊕ *www.santamarialareal.net*), the "pantheon of kings," is distinguished by its 16th-century Claustro de los Caballeros (Cavaliers' Cloister), a flamboyant Gothic structure with 24 lacy, plateresque Renaissance arches overlooking a grassy patio. The sculpted 12th-century tomb of Doña Blanca de Navarra is the monastery's best-known sarcophagus, while the 67 Gothic choir stalls dating from 1495 are among Spain's best. ✉ *Nájera* ☎ *94/136–1083 tourist office* ⊕ *www.najera.es.*

Navarrete

TOWN | This town 14 km (9 miles) west of Logroño via the A12, has noble houses and the 16th-century **Santa María de la Asunción** church. The village is also famous for ceramics; shop at any of the artisan shops in the town center. ⊕ *www.navarrete.es/turismo.*

★ San Millán de la Cogolla

RELIGIOUS SITE | This town, southeast of Santo Domingo de la Calzada, has two jaw-dropping monasteries on the UNESCO World Heritage sites list. There's **Monasterio de Yuso** (⊕ *www.monasteriodeyuso.org*) , where a 10th-century manuscript on St. Augustine's *Glosas Emilianenses* contains handwritten notes in what is considered the earliest example of the Spanish language, the vernacular Latin dialect known as Roman Paladino. And then there's the Visigothic **Monasterio de Suso** (⊕ *www.monasteriodesanmillan.com/suso*), where Gonzalo de Berceo, recognized as the first Castilian poet, wrote and recited his 13th-century verse in the Castilian tongue, now the language of more than 300 million people around the world. ✉ *San Millán de la Cogolla.*

Santo Domingo de la Calzada

TOWN | A key stop on the Camino de Santiago, this town is named after an 11th-century saint who built roads and bridges for pilgrims and founded the hospital that is now the town's parador. The **cathedral** (✉ *Pl. del Santo 4* ☎ *94/134–0033*) is a Romanesque-Gothic pile containing the saint's tomb, choir murals, and a walnut altarpiece carved by Damià

Forment in 1541. The live hen and rooster in a plateresque stone chicken coop commemorate a legendary local miracle in which a pair of roasted fowl came back to life to protest the innocence of a pilgrim hanged for theft. Be sure to stroll through the town's beautifully preserved medieval quarter. ⊠ *Nájera* ⊹ *On N120 20 km (12 miles) west of Nájera* ⊕ *www. santodomingodelacalzada.org.*

 Restaurants

La Herradura

$$ | SPANISH | FAMILY | Rub shoulders with small-town riojanos as you tuck into a bowl of *caparrones,* a local stew made with Riojan red beans, sausage, and fatback. The house wine is an acceptable and inexpensive Uruñuela *cosechero* (young wine of the year) from the Najerilla Valley. **Known for:** caparrones; traditional Rioja; staff with big personalities. $ *Average main: €15* ⊠ *Ctra. de Lerma (N14), Km 42, Anguiano* ☎ *94/137–7151.*

Hotels

★ Echaurren

$$$ | HOTEL | Rioja's renowned "gastro hotel," Echaurren is a veritable foodie paradise with two envelope-pushing restaurants and Relais & Châteaux–certified digs. **Pros:** Rioja's gastronomical mecca; comfortable beds; highly personal service. **Cons:** loud church bells; entry-level rooms are cramped; no bathtubs in most rooms. $ *Rooms from: €180* ⊠ *Calle Padre José García 19, Ezcaray* ☎ *94/135–4047* ⊕ *www.echaurren.com* ⇆ *25 rooms* ⊙ *Free Breakfast.*

Hospedería Abadía de Valvanera

$ | HOTEL | FAMILY | Housed in a monastery atop a 9th-century hermitage, this rural hotel run by a Benedictine community is an ideal base for hiking. **Pros:** cool for the summer; simplicity and silence; rooms of varying sizes for families. **Cons:** spartan accommodations; limited dining choices; decidedly unhip. $ *Rooms from:*

€65 ⊠ *Monasterio de Valvanera, Ctra. LR435, Ezcaray* ☎ *94/137–7044* ⊕ *www. monasteriodevalvanera.es/hospederia* ⇆ *28 rooms* ⊙*No meals.*

Hostería San Millan

$$$ | HOTEL | This magnificent inn occupies a wing of the historic Monasterio de Yuso. **Pros:** historic site; graceful building; good breakfasts. **Cons:** somewhat isolated; monastic interiors; popular among the tour-bus set. $ *Rooms from: €198* ⊠ *Monasterio de Yuso, San Millán de la Cogolla* ☎ *94/137–3277* ⊕ *www. hosteriasanmillan.com* ⇆ *25 rooms* ⊙*No meals.*

Venta de Goyo

$ | B&B/INN | A favorite with anglers and hunters, this cheery spot across from the confluence of the Urbión and Najerilla Rivers has wood-trimmed bedrooms with red-checker bedspreads and an excellent restaurant specializing in venison, wild boar, partridge, woodcock, and game of all kinds. **Pros:** excellent game and mountain cooking; charming rustic bar; unforgettable homemade jams. **Cons:** next to the road; hot in the summer; a bit isolated. $ *Rooms from: €48* ⊠ *Puente Río Neila 2, (Ctra. LR113, Km 24.6), Viniegra de Abajo* ☎ *94/137–8007* ⇆ *22 rooms* ⊙ *All-inclusive.*

Haro

49 km (30 miles) west of Logroño.

Haro is the wine capital of La Rioja. Its casco viejo (old quarter) and best taverns are concentrated along the loop known as La Herradura (The Horseshoe), with the Santo Tomás church at the apex of its curve and Calle San Martín and Calle Santo Tomás leading down to the upper left-hand (northeast) corner of Plaza de la Paz. Up the left side of the horseshoe, Bar La Esquina is the first of many tapas bars. Bar Los Caños, behind a stone archway at San Martín 5, is built into the vaults and arches of the former church of San Martín and serves excellent local crianzas and reservas and a memorable pintxo of quail egg, anchovy, hot pepper, and olive.

VISITOR INFORMATION
CONTACTS Haro Tourist Office ⊠ *Pl. de la Paz 1* ☎ *94/130–3580* ⊕ *www.haroturismo.org.*

Sights

Bodegas (*Wineries*)
WINERY/DISTILLERY | Haro's century-old bodegas have been headquartered in the Barrio de la Estación (Train Station District) since the railroad opened in 1863 and are a fantastic place to go winery-hopping, since they're within walking distance of one another. Guided tours and tastings, some in English, can be arranged at the facilities themselves or through the tourist office. ⊠ *Barrio de la Estación.*

★ Bodegas López de Heredia Viña Tondonia
WINERY/DISTILLERY | Call or email the historic López de Heredia Viña Tondonia winery—known for its vintage-release wines—to reserve a spot on one of the tours, or drop into the Zaha Hadid–designed tasting room for an informal glass or two. ⊠ *Av. Vizcaya 3* ☎ *94/131–0244* ⊕ *www.lopezdeheredia.com* ⊠ *From €10.*

Bodegas Muga
WINERY/DISTILLERY | This sprawling, prestigious bodega offers visits, tours, and tastings as well as a wine bar and restaurant. ⊠ *Barrio de la Estación* ☎ *94/130–6060* ⊕ *www.bodegasmuga.com* ⊠ *€15* ۞ *Closed Sun.*

Santo Tomás
RELIGIOUS SITE | The architectural highlight of Haro, this single-nave Renaissance and late-Gothic church was completed in 1564. It has an intricately sculpted plateresque portal on the south side and a gilded baroque organ facade towering over the choir loft. ⊠ *Calle*

Santo Tomás 5 ☎ *94/131–1690* ⊕ *www.haroturismo.org/en/heritage/churches/church-of-saint-thomas.*

 Restaurants

★ Terete
$$$$ | **SPANISH** | A perennial local favorite, this rustic spot has been roasting lamb in wood ovens since 1877 and serves a hearty *menestra de verduras* (vegetables stewed with bits of ham) that is justly revered as a mandatory sidekick. With rough hand-hewn wooden tables distributed around dark stone and wood-beam dining rooms, the medieval stagecoach-inn environment matches the traditional roasts. **Known for:** 19th-century wood-burning oven; succulent roast lamb and suckling pig; stock of some of La Rioja's best reservas and crianzas. $ *Average main: €30* ⊠ *Calle Lucrecia Arana 17* ☎ *94/131–0023* ⊕ *www.terete.es* ۞ *Closed Mon., 1st 2 wks in July, and last 2 wks in Nov. No dinner Sun.*

Hotels

Hotel Los Agustinos
$$ | **HOTEL** | Across the street from the tourist office, Haro's best hotel is built into a 14th-century monastery with a cloister (now a beautiful covered patio) that's considered one of the finest in La Rioja. **Pros:** gorgeous public rooms; convivial hotel bar; close to town center but in a quiet corner. **Cons:** fusty room interiors; €17-per-day breakfast; €17-per-day parking. $ *Rooms from: €97* ⊠ *Calle San Agustín 2* ☎ *94/131–1308* ⊕ *www.hotellosagustinos.com* ⤴ *62 rooms* ۞ *No meals.*

Chapter 7

THE PYRENEES

7

Updated by
Elizabeth Prosser

👁 **Sights**
★★★☆☆

🍴 **Restaurants**
★★★☆☆

🛏 **Hotels**
★★★☆☆

🛍 **Shopping**
★★☆☆☆

🍸 **Nightlife**
★☆☆☆☆

WELCOME TO THE PYRENEES

TOP REASONS TO GO

★ **Appreciate the Romanesque:** Stop at Taüll and see the exquisite Romanesque churches and mural paintings of the Noguera de Tor Valley.

★ **Explore Spain's Grand Canyon:** The Parque Nacional de Ordesa y Monte Perdido has stunning scenery, along with marmots and mountain goats.

★ **Hike the highlands:** Explore the verdant Basque highlands of the Baztán Valley and follow the Bidasoa River down to colorful Hondarribia and the Bay of Biscay.

★ **Venture off the highway:** Discover the enchanting medieval town of Alquézar, where the impressive citadel, dating back to the 9th century, keeps watch over the Parque Natural Sierra y Cañones de Guara and its prehistoric cave paintings.

★ **Ride the cogwheel train at Ribes de Freser, near Ripoll:** Ascend the gorge to the sanctuary and ski station at Vall de Núria, then hike to the remote highland valley and refuge of Coma de Vaca.

1 Camprodón. A stylish little mountain hub.

2 Beget. Considered Catalonia's cutest town.

3 Sant Joan de les Abadesses. Known for the important 12th-century Romanesque church of Sant Joan.

4 Ripoll. Home to the 9th-century Benedictine Monastery of Santa Maria.

5 Ribes de Freser and Vall de Núria. The starting point of the famous cogwheel train.

6 Puigcerdà. A base for skiers and hikers from both sides of the border.

7 Llívia. A small Spanish enclave completely surrounded by France.

8 La Seu d'Urgell. An ancient town facing the snowy rock wall of the Sierra del Cadí.

9 Sort. The area's epicenter for skiing and fishing.

10 Parc Nacional d'Aigüestortes i Estany de Sant Maurici. A dramatic and unspoiled national park.

11 Taüll. An attractive base for exploring the area.

12 Vielha. A small Pyrenean city close to the French border.

13 Arties. This lively mountain town offers access to hiking, nature, and Romanesque art.

14 Salardú. A convenient base with steep streets and a fortified bell tower.

15 Zaragoza. Home to the famous La Pilarica.

16 Huesca. This Aragonese town is known for its hilly medieval old quarter.

7

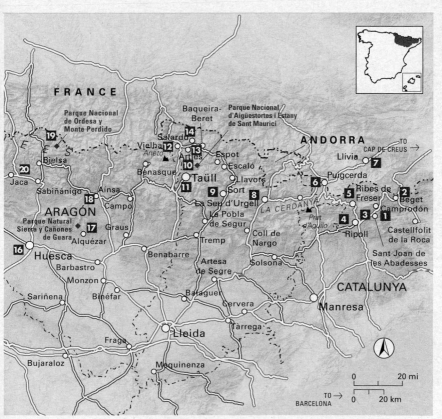

17 Alquézar. One of Aragón's most attractive old towns.

18 Aínsa. A walled medieval town with cobbled streets and pretty views.

19 Parque Nacional de Ordesa y Monte Perdido. A stunning national park with well-marked trails.

20 Jaca. Known for its 11th-century cathedral and fortress and lively eateries.

21 Monasterio de San Juan de la Peña. Popular with seekers of the Holy Grail.

22 Hecho and Ansó Valleys. Pretty mountain villages in spectacular greenery.

23 Roncal Valley. Known for its sheep's-milk cheese and rolling farmlands.

24 Roncesvalles (Orreaga). The first stop for pilgrims on the Camino de Santiago.

25 Burguete (Auritz). Made famous in Hemingway's *The Sun Also Rises*.

26 Baztán Valley. A scenic halfway point between the central Pyrenees and the Atlantic.

EATING AND DRINKING WELL IN THE PYRENEES

Pyrenean cuisine is hearty mountain fare characterized by thick soups, stews, roasts, and local game. Ingredients are prepared with slightly different techniques and recipes in each valley, village, and kitchen.

The three main culinary schools across the Pyrenees match the three main cultural identities of the area—from east to west, they are Catalan, Aragonese, and Basque. Within these three principal groups there are further subdivisions corresponding to the valleys or regions of La Garrotxa, La Cerdanya, Ribagorça, Vall d'Aran, Benasque, Alto Aragón, Roncal, and Baztán. Game is common throughout. Trout, mountain goat, deer, boar, partridge, rabbit, duck, and quail are roasted over coals or cooked in aromatic stews called *civets* in Catalonia and *estofadas* in Aragón and the Basque Pyrenees. Fish and meat are often seared on slabs of slate (*a la llosa* in Catalan, *a la piedra* in Castilian Spanish). Sheep, goat, and cow cheeses vary from valley to valley, along with types of sausages and charcuterie.

WILD MUSHROOMS

Valued for their aromatic contribution to the taste process, wild mushrooms come into season in the autumn. They go well with meat or egg dishes. Favorites include *rovellons* (*Lactarius deliciosus*, or saffron milk cap), sautéed with parsley, olive oil, and garlic, and *camagrocs* (*Cantharellus lutescens*, a type of chanterelle) scrambled with eggs.

HIGHLAND SOUPS

As with all mountain soups, *sopa pirenaica* combines restorative animal protein with vegetables and the high-altitude need for liquids. The Spanish version of the French *garbure*, the classic mountain soup from the north side of the Pyrenees, mixes legumes, vegetables, potatoes, pork, chicken, and sometimes lamb or wild boar into a tasty and energizing meal that will help hikers recover energy and be ready to go again the next morning. *Olha aranesa* (Aranese soup) is another Pyrenean power soup, with vegetables, legumes, pork, chicken, and beef in a long-cooked and slowly simmered unctuous stew. Similar to the ubiquitous Catalan *escudella,* another Pyrenean favorite, the olha aranesa combines chickpeas and pasta with a variety of meats and vegetables and is served, like the *cocido madrileño,* in various stages: soup, legumes, vegetables, and meats.

PYRENEAN STEWS

Wild boar stew is known by different names in the various languages of the Pyrenees—*civet de porc senglar* in Catalan, *estofado de jabalí* in Spanish. A dark and gamy treat in cold weather, wild boar is prepared in many different ways between Catalonia, Aragón, and the Basque Country, but most recipes include onions, carrots, mushrooms, bay leaf, oranges, leeks, peppers, dry

sherry, brown sugar, and sweet paprika. *Civet d'isard* (mountain-goat stew), known as *estofado de ixarso* in the Pyrenees of Aragón, is another favorite, prepared in much the same way but with a more delicate taste.

TRINXAT

The Catalan verb *trinxar* means to chop or shred, and *trinxat* is winter cabbage, previously softened by frost, chopped fine, and mixed with mashed potato and fatback or bacon. A quintessential high-altitude comfort food, trinxat plays the acidity of the cabbage against the saltiness of the pork, with the potato as the unifying element.

DUCK WITH TURNIPS

The traditional dish *tiró amb naps* goes back, as do nearly all European recipes that make use of turnips, to pre-Columbian times, before the potato's arrival from the New World. The frequent use of duck (*pato* in Spanish, *anec* in Catalan, *tiró* in La Cerdanya) in the half-French, half-Spanish, all-Catalan Cerdanya Valley two hours north of Barcelona is a taste acquired from French Catalunya, just over the Pyrenees.

7

The Pyrenees EATING AND DRINKING WELL IN THE PYRENEES

Separating the Iberian Peninsula from the rest of the European continent, the snowcapped Pyrenees have always been a special realm, a source of legend and superstition. To explore the Pyrenees fully—the flora and fauna, the local cuisine, the remote glacial lakes and streams, the Romanesque art in a thousand hermitages—could take a lifetime.

Each of the three autonomous Pyrenean mountain regions that sits between the Mediterranean and the Atlantic is drained by one or more rivers, forming some three dozen valleys, which were all but completely isolated until around the 10th century. Local languages still abound, with Castilian Spanish and Euskera (Basque) in upper Navarra; Aragonese (and its local varieties) in Aragón; and Catalan at the eastern end of the chain from Ribagorça to the Mediterranean.

Throughout history, the Pyrenees were a strategic barrier and stronghold to be reckoned with. The Romans never completely subdued Los Vascones (as Greek historian Strabo [63–21 BC] called the Basques) in the western Pyrenean highlands. Charlemagne lost Roland and his rear guard at Roncesvalles in 778, and his Frankish heirs lost all of Catalonia in 988. Napoléon Bonaparte never completed his conquest of the peninsula, largely because of communications and supply problems posed by the Pyrenees, and Adolf Hitler, whether for geographical or political reasons, decided not to use post–Civil War Spain to launch his

African campaign in 1941. A D-Day option to make a landing on the beaches of northern Spain was scrapped because the Pyrenees looked too easily defendable (you can still see the south-facing German bunkers on the southern flanks of the western Pyrenean foothills). Meanwhile, the mountainous barrier provided a path to freedom for downed pilots, Jewish refugees, and POWs fleeing the Nazis, just as it later meant freedom for political refugees running north from the Franco regime.

MAJOR REGIONS

Eastern Catalan Pyrenees. Catalonia's easternmost Pyrenean valley, the Vall de Camprodón, is still hard enough to reach that, despite pockets of Barcelona summer colonies, it has retained much of its farm culture and mountain wildness. It has several exquisite towns and churches and, above all, mountains like the Sierra de Catllar. Start from Cap de Creus in the Empordà to get the full experience of the Pyrenean cordillera's rise from the sea; then move west through **Beget**, **Camprodón**, the Ter Valley, **Sant Joan de les Abadesses**, and **Ripoll**

before heading north through **Ribes de Freser and Vall de Nuria**. Vallter 2000, La Molina, and Núria are ski resorts at either end of the Pyrenean heights on the north side of the valley.

La Cerdanya. Said to be in the shape of the handprint of God, this high pasture-land is bordered north and south by snow-covered peaks. La Cerdanya starts in France, at Col de la Perche (near Mont Louis) and ends in the Spanish prov-ince of Lleida, at Martinet. Being split between two countries, and subdivided into two more provinces on each side, gives the valley an identity all its own. **Puigcerdà** is the largest town and is a lively base for skiers and hikers, while the Spanish enclave of **Llívia** is easily reached across the border. **Bellver de Cerdanya** showcases examples of tradi-tional Pyrenean architecture, surrounded by refreshing mountain views, while the ancient town of **La Seu d'Urgell** houses the 11th-century chapel of Sant Miquel and the 14th-century convent of Sant Domenec—now a converted parador. Residents on both sides of the border speak Catalan, a Romance language derived from early Provençal French, and regard the valley's political border with undisguised hilarity. Unlike any other val-ley in the upper Pyrenees, this one runs east–west and thus has a record annual number of sunlight hours.

Western Catalan Pyrenees. "The farther from Barcelona, the wilder" is the rule of thumb, and this is true of the rugged countryside and fauna in the western part of Catalonia. Sort, the capital of the Pallars Sobirà (Upper Pallars Valley) is the area's epicenter for skiing, fishing, and white-water kayaking, while three of the greatest destinations in the Pyrenees are in this region: the harmonious, Atlan-tic-influenced Vall d'Aran with its capital, **Vielha**; the Noguera de Tor Valley (aka Vall de Boí), with its matching set of gemlike Romanesque churches in **Taüll**; and **Parc Nacional d'Aigüestortes i Estany de Sant**

Maurici, which has a network of pristine lakes and streams, bordered by Espot (one of the park's main entryways). The main geographical units in this section are the valley of the Noguera Pallaresa River, the Vall d'Aran headwaters of the Atlantic-bound Garonne, and the Noguera Ribagorçana River Valley, Catalonia's western limit.

Aragón and Central Pyrenees. The highest, wildest, and most spectacular range of the Pyrenees is the middle section, farthest from sea level. From Benasque on Aragón's eastern side to **Jaca** at the western edge are the great heights and most dramatic landscapes of Alto Aragón (Upper Aragón), including the Maladeta (11,165 feet), Posets (11,070 feet), and Monte Perdido (11,004 feet) peaks, the three highest points in the Pyre-nean chain. The often-bypassed cities of **Zaragoza** and **Huesca** and are both useful Pyrenean gateways and historic destinations in themselves. Both cities retain an authentic provincial character that is refreshing in today's cosmopoli-tan Spain. Drive east out of Huesca into the Sierra de Guara, a region declared a World Heritage Site by UNESCO in 1998. At its core lies the historic village of **Alquézar**, overlooking the River Vero, where hiking and other outdoor activities abound. Further north, stop at **Aínsa** for its 11th-century citadel and castle. **The Parque Nacional de Ordesa y Monte Perdido** was declared a world heritage site by UNESCO in 1997 and boasts some of the region's best hiking. Deep in Alto Aragón, the city of **Jaca** has a fine 11th-century cathedral and fortress, and a lively per-sonality all its own. The **Hecho and Ansó Valleys** are the westernmost valleys in Aragón and rank among the wildest and most unspoiled reaches of the Pyrenees. With only cross-country (Nordic) skiing available, this is a region less frequented by tourists.

The Navarran and Basque Pyrenees. Begin-ning in the Roncal Valley, the language you hear may be Euskera, the pre-Indo-European tongue of the Basques. The highlands of Navarra, from Roncesvalles and Burguete down through the Baztán Valley to Hondarribia, are a magical realm of rolling hillsides, folklore, and emerald pastures.

Planning

When to Go

If you're a hiker, stick to the summer (June–September, especially July), when the weather is better and there's less chance of a serious snowfall—not to mention blizzards or lightning storms at high altitudes.

October, with comfortable daytime temperatures and chillier evenings, is ideal for enjoying the still-green Pyrenean meadows and valleys and hillside hunts for wild mushrooms. November brings colorful leaves, the last mushrooms, and the first frosts.

For skiing, come December–March. The green springtime thaw, mid-March–mid-April, is spectacular for skiing on the snowcaps and trout fishing or golfing on the verdant valley floors.

August is the only crowded month, when all of Europe is on summer vacation and the cooler highland air is at its best.

Planning Your Time

You could hike all the way from the Atlantic to the Mediterranean in 43 days, but not many have that kind of vacation time. A week is ideal for a single area—La Cerdanya and the Eastern Catalan Pyrenees, easily accessed from Barcelona; the Western Catalan Pyrenees and Vall d'Aran in the Lleida province of Catalonia; Jaca and the central Pyrenees, north of Zaragoza; or the Basque Pyrenees north of Pamplona.

A day's drive up through Figueres (in Catalonia) and Olot will bring you to the town of **Camprodón.** The picturesque villages dotted around this area—in particular **Beget, Sant Joan de les Abadesses,** and **Ripoll**—are all worthy stops, especially for the famous monastery of Santa Maria de Ripoll with its 13th-century Romanesque portal. La Cerdanya's sunny wide plains are popular for walkers and mountain bikers year-round and skiing in La Molina and Masella in winter. **Puigcerdà, Llívia,** and **Bellver de Cerdanya** are must-visits, too.

To the west, the historic town of **La Seu d'Urgell** is an important stop on the way to the **Parc Nacional d'Aigüestortes i Estany de Sant Maurici,** the **Vall d'Aran,** and the winter-sports center Baqueira-Beret. Stop at **Taüll** and the **Noguera de Tor Valley** for Romanesque churches.

The central Aragonese Pyrenees reveal the most dramatic scenery and Aneto, the highest peak in the Pyrenees. The **Parque Nacional de Ordesa y Monte Perdido** is Spain's most majestic canyon—reminiscent of North America's Grand Canyon. **Alquézar** and **Ainsa** are upper Aragón's best-preserved medieval towns, while **Zaragoza, Huesca,** and **Jaca** are the most important cities.

Farther west, the lower Navarran Pyrenees give way to rolling pasturelands. **Roncesvalles** is the first stop off for pilgrims on the life-affirming **Camino de Santiago,** and the peaceful **Baztán Valley** guards a land of ancient traditions.

Getting Here and Around

AIR TRAVEL

Barcelona's international airport, El Prat de Llobregat (⇨ *Barcelona*), is the largest gateway to the Catalan Pyrenees. Farther west, the Pyrenees can be reached by international flights going through Madrid

Barajas airport, or Toulouse Blagnac and Biarritz Airport in France. Smaller airports at Zaragoza, Pamplona, and San Sebastián's Hondarribia (Fuenterrabía) are useful for domestic flights.

BUS TRAVEL

Bus travel in the Pyrenees is the only way to cross from east to west (or vice versa), other than hiking or driving, but requires some zigzagging up and down valleys. In most cases, four buses daily connect the main pre-Pyrenean cities (Barcelona, Zaragoza, Huesca, and Pamplona) and the main highland distributors (Puigcerdà, La Seu d'Urgell, Vielha, Benasque, and Jaca). The time lost waiting for buses makes this option a last resort.

BUS LINES ALSA ⊠ *Estación de Auto-buses, Carrer Yanguas y Miranda s/n, Pamplona* ☎ *902/422242* ⊕ *www.alsa.es.*

Avanza
⊠ *Estación Central de Delicias, Av. Navarra, Zaragoza* ☎ *912/722832* ⊕ *www. avanzabus.com.*

CAR TRAVEL

The easiest way (and in many cases, the *only* way) to tour the Pyrenees is by car—and it comes with the best scenery. The Eje Pirenaico (Pyrenean Axis, or N260) is a carefully engineered, safe cross-Pyrenean route that connects Cap de Creus, the Iberian Peninsula's eastern-most point on the Mediterranean Costa Brava (east of Girona and Cadaqués), with Cabo de Higuer, the lighthouse west of Hondarribia at the edge of the Atlantic Bay of Biscay.

The Collada de Toses (Tosses Pass) to Puigcerdà is the most difficult route into the Cerdanya Valley, but it's toll-free, has spectacular scenery, and you get to include Camprodón, Olot, and Ripoll in your itinerary. Safer and faster but more expensive (tolls total more than €22 from Barcelona to Bellver de Cerdanya) is the E9 through the Tuñel del Cadí. Once you're there, most of the Cerdanya

Valley's two-lane roads are wide and well paved. As you go west, roads can be more difficult to navigate, winding dramatically through mountain passes.

TRAIN TRAVEL

There are three small train stations deep in the Pyrenees: Ribes de Freser in the eastern Catalan Pyrenees; Puigcerdà, in the Cerdanya Valley; and La Pobla de Segur, in the Noguera Pallaresa Valley. The larger gateways are Zaragoza, Huesca, and Lleida. From Madrid, connect through Barcelona for the eastern Pyrenees, Zaragoza and Huesca for the central Pyrenees, and Pamplona or San Sebastián for the Navarran and Basque Pyrenees. For information on timetables and routes, consult ⊕ *www.renfe.com.*

Restaurants

In the Alta Pyrenees, the cozy stone-wall inns, with their hearty cuisine and comfortable interiors, are a welcome sight after a day's hiking or sightseeing. Often family run and relaxed, they rarely have any kind of dress code, and often, a nourishing meal is brought to a close with a complimentary *chupito* (shot) of local liqueur, finishing the night off with a satisfying thump. Back down in the main cities, restaurants take inspiration from these traditional methods but offer a more contemporary style and setting.

Hotels

Most hotels in the Pyrenees are informal and outdoorsy, with a large fireplace in one of the public rooms. They are usually built of wood, glass, and stone, with steep slate roofs that blend in with the surrounding mountains. Most hotel establishments are family operations passed down from generation to generation. *Hotel reviews have been shortened. For full information, visit Fodors.com.*

What It Costs in Euros			
$	$$	$$$	$$$$
RESTAURANTS			
under €12	€12–€17	€18–€22	over €22
HOTELS			
under €90	€90– €125	€126– €180	over €180

Tours

Trekking, horseback riding, adventure sports such as canyoning and ballooning, and more contemplative outings like bird-watching and botanical tours are just a few of the specialties available at the main Pyrenean resorts.

Well populated with trout, the Pyrenees' cold streams provide excellent angling from mid-March to the end of August. Notable places to cast a line are the Segre, Aragón, Gállego, Noguera Pallaresa, Arga, Esera, and Esca Rivers. Pyrenean ponds and lakes also tend to be rich in trout.

Pyrenean Experience

GUIDED TOURS | British expat Georgina Howard specializes in showcasing Basque-Navarran culture, walking, and gastronomy. The walking tours include accommodations and meals. ⊠ Iaulin Borda, Ameztia, Ituren ☎ 650/713759 ⊕ www.pyreneanexperience.com ☒ From €1000.

Camprodón

127 km (79 miles) northwest of Barcelona, 80 km (50 miles) west of Girona.

Camprodón, the capital of its *comarca* (county), lies at the junction of the Ter and Ritort Rivers—both excellent trout streams. The rivers flow by, through, and under much of the town, giving it a highland waterfront character (as well as

a long history of flooding). Its best-known symbol is the elegant 12th-century stone bridge that broadly spans the Ter River in the center of town. The town owes much of its opulence to the summer residents from Barcelona who built mansions along **Passeig Maristany,** the leafy promenade at its northern edge.

GETTING HERE AND AROUND

The C38 runs into the center of town from both north (France) and south (Barcelona, Vic, or Ripoll) directions. If coming from France, the southbound D115 changes into the C38 once over the Spanish border. From either direction, the C38 heads straight toward the center of town. The best way to explore is on foot, as the streets are narrow and can be complicated to navigate by car.

VISITOR INFORMATION

CONTACTS Camprodón ⊠ Carrer Sant Roc 22 ☎ 972/740010 ⊕ www.valldecamprodon.org.

Festivals

Festival de Música de Isaac Albéniz

MUSIC | Camprodón's most famous son is composer Isaac Albéniz (1860–1909), who spent more than 20 years in exile in France, where he became friends with musical luminaries such as Pablo Casals, Claude Debussy, and Gabriel Fauré. His celebrated classical guitar piece *Asturias* is one of Spain's best-known works. In July, during the Isaac Albéniz Music Festival, a series of concerts by renowned artists and young talent from the European classical music scene is held in the monastery of Sant Pere. For an up-to-date concert schedule, contact the tourist office. ⊠ Sant Pere de Camprodón, Carrer Monestir 2 ⊕ www.albeniz.cat.

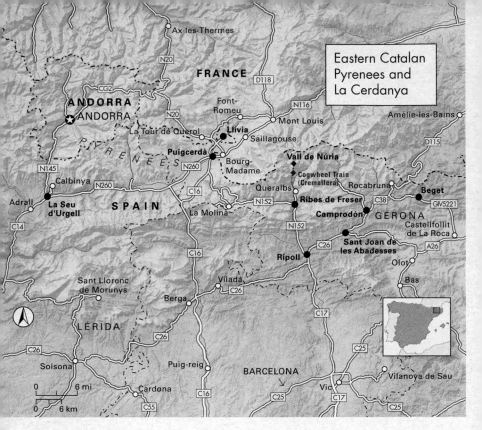

Eastern Catalan Pyrenees and La Cerdanya

0   6 mi
0   6 km

🛏 Hotels

★ Fonda Rigà

$$ | B&B/INN | FAMILY | A highland inn with comfortable modern rooms and spectacular views to the sea, this mountain perch is an excellent base for hiking, horseback riding, and viewing Pyrenean flora and fauna. **Pros:** the views and the peace and quiet; well-maintained rooms and facilities; fabulous dining experience. **Cons:** a serious 5-km (3-mile) drive above the valley floor; remote from Camprodón; bookings only by email or phone. $ *Rooms from: €110* ⊠ *Ctra. de Tregurà de Dalt, Km 4.8* ✛ *At end of Tregurà route, 10 km (6 miles) up Ter Valley from Camprodón* ☎ *972/136000* ⊕ *es.fondariga.com* ⊘ *Closed Nov. 1–15 and 2 wks in late June/early July (dates can vary)* ⇨ *16 rooms* ⊌ *Free Breakfast.*

Hotel Camprodon

$$ | HOTEL | A perfect base for getting a sense of this stylish little mountain hub, this elegant Moderniste building has rooms over the bustling Plaça Dr. Robert on one side and over the river on the other. **Pros:** central location; charming Art Nouveau style and preserved features throughout; wonderful views over the river. **Cons:** no parking; rooms on the square can be noisy in summer; five-night minimum stay in summer. $ *Rooms from: €92* ⊠ *Pl. Dr. Robert 3* ☎ *972/740013* ⊕ *www.hotelcamprodon. com* ⇨ *50 rooms* ⊌ *No meals.*

Hotel Maristany

$$$ | HOTEL | An elegant chalet on Camprodón's grandest promenade, this small but lovely hotel offers a chance to live like the 19th- and 20th-century Barcelona aristocracy who spent summers at this mountain retreat. **Pros:** outside of town center and quiet at night; excellent restaurant; private parking. **Cons:** rooms and baths are somewhat cramped; some noise from the road can carry into the rooms; outside the town's historic core. [$] *Rooms from: €132* ✉ *Av. Maristany 20* ☎ *972/130078* 🌐 *www.hotelmaristany.com* 🕒 *Closed Dec. 11–Easter* 🛏 *10 rooms* 🍴 *Free Breakfast.*

Shopping

Cal Xec

FOOD/CANDY | This legendary sausage and cheese store also sells the much-prized, vanilla-flavored Birbas cookies. It's at the end of the Camprodón Bridge. ✉ *Carrer Isaac Albéniz 1* ☎ *972/740084* 🌐 *www.calxec.com.*

Mercat Setmanal

CRAFTS | Held every Sunday 9–2, this market sells all manner of artisanal food, crafts, clothing, antiques, and bric-a-brac. ✉ *Pl. Dr. Robert.*

Beget

17 km (10 miles) east of Camprodón.

The village of Beget, considered Catalonia's *més bufó* (cutest), was completely cut off from motorized vehicles until the mid-1960s, when a *pista forestal* (jeep track) was laid down. In 1980, Beget was finally fully connected to the rest of the world by an asphalt roadway, which can be hazardous when mist descends, as it often does. The GIV5223 road to Castellfollit de la Roca, 12 km (7 miles) away, is a spectacular drive through former volcanic peaks of the Alta Garrotxa. Beget's 30 houses are eccentric stone structures with heavy wooden doors and a golden color peculiar to the Vall de Camprodón. Archaic stone bridges span the stream where protected trout swim in clear mountain water.

GETTING HERE AND AROUND

Drive northeast out of Camprodón on Carrer Molló (C38) for 2 km (1 mile) before turning right onto the Carretera Camprodón–Beget (GIV5223) for 14 km (9 miles) to Beget. Cars are not allowed to enter the village but there is parking just outside. When leaving, head toward Oix, which leads to Castellfollit de la Roca and the N260, to avoid having to retrace your steps back up the mountain.

Sights

Sant Cristòfol

RELIGIOUS SITE | The 12th-century Romanesque church of Sant Cristòfol (St. Christopher) has a diminutive bell tower and a rare 6-foot Majestat—a polychrome wood carving of the risen and reigning Christ in head-to-foot robes, dating to the 12th century. The church is usually closed, but ask in the bar-restaurant behind the church, or in El Forn de Beget, and someone will direct you to the keeper of the key. A €1 charge is collected for church upkeep. ✉ *Pl. Major s/n* 🎟 *€1.*

Restaurants

Can Po

$ | **CATALAN** | This ancient, ivy-covered, Pyrenean stone-and-mortar farmhouse perched over a deep gully in nearby Rocabruna is famed for carefully prepared local dishes like *vedella amb crema de ceps* (veal in wild mushroom sauce) and the Catalan classic *oca amb peres* (goose stewed with pears). Try the *civet de porc senglar* (stewed wild boar) in winter, or any of the many varieties of wild mushrooms that find their way into the kitchen at this rustic mountain retreat. **Known for:** hearty mountain cuisine; cozy setting; rich and delicious stews. [$] *Average main: €11* ✉ *Ctra. de Beget s/n, Rocabruna* ☎ *972/741045* 💳 *No credit cards* 🕒 *Closed Mon.–Thurs. (except public holidays). Call ahead to check in low season.*

Hotels

El Forn de Beget

$$ | **B&B/INN** | Tucked above the Trull River in the upper part of the village, this little stone hotel and restaurant has panoramic views over Alta Garrotxa. **Pros:** a true hideaway in the Pyrenees; wonderful river views from the dining room; classic mountain food. **Cons:** rooms are small and close together; remote location; need a car to get here. $ *Rooms from: €100* ✉ *Carrer Josep Duñach "En Feliça" 9* ☎ *972/741230* ⊕ *www.elforndebeget. com* ⤳ *4 rooms* ❏ *Free Breakfast.*

Sant Joan de les Abadesses

14 km (9 miles) southwest of Camprodón.

The site of an important church, Sant Joan de les Abadesses is named for the 9th-century abbess Emma and her successors. Emma was the daughter of Guifré el Pilós (Wilfred the Hairy), the hero of the Christian Reconquest of Ripoll and the founder of Catalonia. The town's arcaded Plaça Major offers a glimpse of its medieval past, as does the broad, elegant 12th-century bridge over the Ter.

GETTING HERE AND AROUND

Exit southwest of Camprodón on Carrer Molló (C38) for 9 km (6 miles), passing through Sant Pau de Segúries. At the traffic circle, take the first exit onto the N260 for 4 km (2½ miles) to Sant Joan de les Abadesses. If you're coming from Ripoll, take the northbound N260 for 10 km (6 miles). Once here, it's an easy stroll.

VISITOR INFORMATION

CONTACTS Sant Joan de les Abadesses Tourist Office ✉ *Pl. de la Abadía 9* ☎ *972/720599* ⊕ *www.santjoandelesabadesses.cat.*

Sights

Monastery of Sant Joan de les Abadesses

RELIGIOUS SITE | In the 12th-century Romanesque church of Sant Joan, the altarpiece—a 13th-century polychrome wood sculpture of the Descent from the Cross—is one of the most expressive and human of that epoch. ✉ *Pl. de la Abadía s/n* ☎ *972/722353* ⊕ *www.monestirsantjoanabadesses.cat* 🎫 *€3.*

Ripoll

10 km (6 miles) southwest of Sant Joan de les Abadesses, 105 km (65 miles) north of Barcelona.

One of Catalonia's first Christian strongholds of the Reconquest and a center of religious erudition during the Middle Ages, Ripoll is known as the *bressol* (cradle) of Catalonia's liberation from Moorish domination and the spiritual home of Guifré el Pilós (Wilfred the Hairy), the count of Barcelona who is widely considered to have founded the Catalan nation in the late 9th century. A dark, mysterious country town built around a 9th-century **Benedictine monastery,** Ripoll was a focal point of culture throughout French Catalonia and the Pyrenees, from the monastery's 879 founding until the mid-1800s, when Barcelona began to eclipse it.

GETTING HERE AND AROUND

The C17 northbound from Vic heads into the center of Ripoll. From Camprodón and Sant Joan de les Abadesses, head southwest on the C38, which turns into the N260 to the town center. There are direct trains from Barcelona (⊕ *www. renfe.com*), but bus connections must be made through Girona. It's a 10-minute walk from the station to the center, and the small town is easy to explore on foot.

VISITOR INFORMATION

CONTACTS Ripoll ✉ *Pl. de l'Abat Oliva s/n* ☎ *972/702351* ⊕ *visit.ripoll.cat/es.*

◉ Sights

Monastery of Santa Maria de Ripoll

RELIGIOUS SITE | Decorated with a pageant of biblical figures, the 12th-century doorway to the church is one of Catalonia's great works of Romanesque art, crafted as a triumphal arch by stonemasons and sculptors of the Roussillon school, which was centered on French Catalonia and the Pyrenees. You can pick up a guide to the figures surrounding the portal in the nearby Centro de Interpretación del Monasterio, in Plaça de l'Abat Oliva. The center has an interactive exhibition that explains the historical, cultural, and religious relevance of this cradle of Catalonia. It also provides information about guided tours. ⊠ *Pl. Monasterio s/n* ☎ *972/704203* ⌨ *€6.*

Ribes de Freser and Vall de Núria

14 km (9 miles) north of Ripoll.

The small town of Ribes de Freser is the starting point of the famous *cremallera* (cogwheel) train, which connects passengers with Núria, a small mountaintop ski resort and pilgrimage site, via a spectacular ascent through the Gorges of Núria.

GETTING HERE AND AROUND

The N260 north of Ripoll heads straight to Ribes de Freser. Continue farther north on the GIV5217 to reach Queralbs by car. Both Queralbs and Ribes de Freser are easily explored on foot.

VISITOR INFORMATION

CONTACTS **Vall de Ribes Tourist Office**
⊠ *Ctra. de Bruguera 2, Ribes de Freser* ☎ *972/727728* ⊕ *www.vallderibes.cat.*

◉ Sights

Camí dels Enginyers

TRAIL | From the ski area of Núria, at an altitude of 6,562 feet, the dramatic, occasionally heart-stopping "engineers' path" is best done in the summer months. The three-hour trek, aided at one point by a cable handrail, leads to the remote highland valley of Coma de Vaca, where a cozy refuge and hearty replenishment await. Phone ahead to make sure there's space and check weather conditions. In the morning you can descend along the riverside Gorges de Freser trail, another three-hour walk, to Queralbs, where there are connecting trains to Ribes de Freser. ⊠ *Refugi de Coma de Vaca, Termino Municipal de Queralbs dentro del Espacio protegido Ter Freser, Queralbs* ☎ *649/229012* ⊕ *www.comadevaca.cat/index.php/en* ◔ *Closed Sept.–May.*

★ Cogwheel Train (Cremallera)

TRANSPORTATION SITE (AIRPORT/BUS/FERRY/TRAIN) | FAMILY | The 45-minute train ride from the town of Ribes de Freser up to Núria provides one of Catalonia's most unusual excursions—in few other places in Spain does a train make such a precipitous ascent. The cremallera was completed in 1931 to connect Ribes with the Santuari de la Mare de Déu de Núria (Mother of God of Núria) and with mountain hiking and skiing. ⊠ *Estación de Ribes-Enllaç, Ribes de Freser* ☎ *972/732020* ⊕ *www.valldenuria.cat/es/invierno/cremallera/presentacion* ⌨ *€26 round-trip* ◔ *Closed weekdays in Nov.*

Queralbs

TOWN | The three-hour walk down the mountain from Vall de Núria to the sleepy village of Queralbs follows the course of the cogwheel train on a rather precipitous but fairly easy route, as long as it's not done during the snow season. The path overlooks gorges and waterfalls, overshadowed by sheer peaks, before exiting into the surprisingly charming and tiny village of Queralbs, where houses made of stone and wood cling to the side of the mountain. There is a well-preserved **Romanesque church,** notable for its six-arch portico, marble columns, single nave, and pointed vault. ✉ *Queralbs.*

Santuari de la Mare de Déu de Núria

RELIGIOUS SITE | The legend of this Marian religious retreat is based on the story of Sant Gil of Nîmes, who did penance in the Núria Valley during the 7th century. The saint left behind a wooden statue of the Virgin Mary, a bell he used to summon shepherds to prayer, and a cooking pot; 300 years later, a pilgrim found these treasures in this sanctuary. The bell and the pot came to have special importance to barren women, who, according to local beliefs, were blessed with as many children as they wished after placing their heads in the pot and ringing the bell. ✉ *Vall de Núria* ✣ *26 km (16 miles) north of Ripoll* 🎫 *Free.*

🛏 Hotels

Hostal Les Roquetes

$ | **B&B/INN** | A short walk from the cogwheel train station and the center of the village, this *hostal* has cheerful rooms and some spectacular views. **Pros:** fantastic views; friendly service; good base for walks in the area. **Cons:** limited food options outside of weekends; only accessible by local road or cogwheel train, and those times are limited; simple lodging. [$] *Rooms from: €76* ✉ *Ctra. de Ribes 5, Queralbs* ☎ *972/727369* 🌐 *www.hostalroquetes.com* 🕒 *Closed Nov.* 🔑 *8 rooms* 🍴 *No meals.*

Hotel Vall de Núria

$$$ | **HOTEL** | A mountain refuge and hotel run by the government of Catalonia, this family-oriented base camp with double, triple, and quadruple rooms offers basic lodging and dining at 6,500 feet above sea level within an imposing gray complex. **Pros:** perfect location in the heart of the Pyrenees; pristine mountain air; simplicity. **Cons:** hotel feels institutional, with quasi-monastic austerity; minimum two-night stay in high season; high rates for basic lodging. [$] *Rooms from: €140* ✉ *Estación de Montaña Vall de Núria, Queralbs* ☎ *972/732020* 🌐 *www.valldenuria.cat/en* 💳 *No credit cards* 🕒 *Closed Nov.* 🔑 *65 rooms, 12 apartments* 🍴 *Some meals.*

Puigcerdà

65 km (40 miles) northwest of Ripoll, 170 km (106 miles) northwest of Barcelona.

Puigcerdà is the largest town in the valley; in Catalan, *puig* means "hill," and *cerdà* derives from "Cerdanya." From the promontory upon which it stands, the views down across the meadows of the valley floor and up into the craggy peaks of the surrounding Pyrenees are dramatic. The 12th-century **Romanesque bell tower**—all that remains of the town church of Santa Maria, destroyed in 1936 at the outset of the Spanish Civil War—and the sunny sidewalk cafés facing it are among Puigcerdà's prettiest spots, as is the Gothic church of **Sant Domènec.** Serving primarily as a base for skiers and hikers from both sides of the border, Puigcerdà has lively restaurants and a bustling shopping promenade. On Sunday, markets sell clothes, cheeses, fruits, vegetables, and wild mushrooms to shoppers.

GETTING HERE AND AROUND

From Ripoll take the northwest-bound N260 for 63 km (39 miles) toward Ribes de Freser. Several trains a day (they are less frequent on weekends) run from Barcelona Sants to Puigcerdà (🌐 *www.renfe.com*). Buses go from Barcelona Estación del Nord (🌐 *www.barcelonanord.com*). Once you reach the center, there is ample parking, and the easiest way to get around town is on foot.

VISITOR INFORMATION

CONTACTS Puigcerdà Tourist Office ✉ *Bell tower, Pl. Santa Maria s/n* ☎ *972/880542* 🌐 *www.puigcerda.cat.*

Sights

Le Petit Train Jaune

TRANSPORTATION SITE (AIRPORT/BUS/FERRY/TRAIN) | FAMILY | The "little yellow train" has a service that runs from Bourg-Madame and La Tour de Querol, both easy hikes over the border into France from Puigcerdà (Bourg-Madame is the closest). The border at La Tour, a pretty hour-long hike from Puigcerdà, is marked by a stone painted with the Spanish and French flags. The train can also be picked up in Villefranche. The *carrilet* (narrow-gauge railway) is the last in the Pyrenees and is used for tours as well as transportation; it winds slowly through La Cerdanya to the medieval walled town of Villefranche de Conflent. The 63-km (39-mile) tour can take most of the day, especially if you stop to browse in Mont Louis or Villefranche. The last section, between La Cabanasse and Villefranche, is the most picturesque. In low season the trains are infrequent and subject to change. ✉ *Oficina de Turisme de la Cerdanya, Ctra. Cruïlla N152 N260 s/n* ☎ *972/140665* 🌐 *www.cerdanya.org* 🎫 *€12.*

Plaça Cabrinetty

PLAZA | Along with its porticoes and covered walks, this square is protected from the wind and ringed by two- and three-story houses of various pastel colors, some with decorative sgraffito designs and all with balconies. ✉ *Puigcerdà.*

Santa Maria Bell Tower

BUILDING | The 12th-century Santa Maria church in the center of town was largely destroyed in 1936 during the Spanish Civil War. The only part to have stood the test of time is the bell tower, which is open to visitors. At the top, a 360-degree view of La Cerdanya's towns, bucolic farmlands, and snowy peaks awaits. ✉ *Pl. Santa Maria s/n* ☎ *972/880542* 🎫 *€2.*

Restaurants

Tap de Suró

$$$ | CATALAN | Named for the classic bottle stopper (*tap*) made of cork oak bark (*suró*), this wine store, delicatessen, restaurant, and tapas emporium is the perfect place for sunsets, with views down the length of the Cerdanya Valley accompanied by cheeses, duck and goose liver, and other delicacies. Tucked into the western edge of the town ramparts, it has a varied menu and a frequently changing selection of wines—new and old—from all over Spain and southern France. **Known for:** wine and cava; beautiful views; Iberian ham. [$] *Average main: €20* ✉ *Carrer Querol 21* ☎ *678/655928* 💳 *No credit cards* 🕒 *Closed Mon.*

Hotels

Hotel del Lago

$$ | HOTEL | A comfortable old favorite near Puigcerdà's emblematic lake, this spa hotel has a graceful series of buildings around a central garden. **Pros:** picturesque location on the iconic lake; friendly treatment and service; short walk to the center. **Cons:** rooms can be hot on summer days; pricey for its services; no restaurant (only breakfast). [$] *Rooms from: €115* ✉ *Av. Dr. Piguillem 7* ☎ *972/881000* 🌐 *www.hotellago.com* 🛏 *24 rooms* 🍴 *No meals.*

Shopping

Puigcerdà is one big shopping mall—one that's long been a center for contraband clothes, cigarettes, and other items smuggled across the French border.

Carrer Major

SHOPPING NEIGHBORHOODS | This is an uninterrupted row of stores selling books, jewelry, fashion, sports equipment, and lots more. ✉ *Puigcerdà.*

Pastisseria Confiteria Cosp

FOOD/CANDY | For the best *margaritas* in town (no, not those—these are crunchy-edged madeleines made with almonds) head for the oldest commercial establishment in Catalonia, founded in 1806. ⊠ *Carrer Major 20* ☎ *972/880103.*

Sunday Market

OUTDOOR/FLEA/GREEN MARKETS | On Sunday morning (9–2), head for this weekly market, which, like those in most Cerdanya towns, is a great place to look for local crafts and specialties such as herbs, goat cheese, wild mushrooms, honey, and baskets. ⊠ *Paseo 10 de Abril.*

Llívia

6 km (4 miles) northeast of Puigcerdà.

A Spanish enclave in French territory, Llívia was marooned by the 1659 Peace of the Pyrenees treaty, which ceded 33 villages to France. Incorporated as a *vila* (town) by royal decree of Carlos V—who spent a night here in 1528 and was impressed by the town's beauty and hospitality—Llívia managed to remain Spanish. In the middle of town, look for the mosaic commemorating Lampègia, *princesa de la paul i de l'amor* (princess of peace and of love), erected in memory of the red-haired daughter of the Duke of Aquitania and lover of Munuza, a Moorish warlord who governed La Cerdanya in the 8th century during the Arab domination.

GETTING HERE AND AROUND

From Puigcerdà you could walk to Llívia, as it is only 6 km (4 miles) northbound through the border of France, but there is a bus, which departs from the Puigcerdà train station. By car, follow the Camí Vell de Llívia onto the N154, which goes directly to Llívia.

VISITOR INFORMATION

CONTACTS Llívia Tourist Office ⊠ *Carrer dels Forns 10* ☎ *972/896313.*

Tip

The tourist office on the outskirts of Puigcerdà (*Oficina de Turisme del Consell Comarcal de la Cerdanya,* corner of Ctra. N260 and N152 ☎ 972/880542) has up-to-date information on the best hiking trails in La Cerdanya. If you're planning a long-distance hiking trip, local bus connections will get you to your starting point and retrieve you from the finish line.

◉ Sights

Mare de Déu dels Àngels

ARTS VENUE | At the upper edge of town, this fortified church has wonderful acoustics; check to see if any classical music events are on—especially in August, when it hosts an annual classical music festival. Information about the festival's concerts is released in June. ⊠ *Carrer dels Forns 13* ☜ *Free.*

Museu de la Farmacia

BUILDING | Across from the Mare de Déu dels Àngels church, this ancient pharmacy, housed within the Museo Municipal, was founded in 1415 and has been certified as the oldest in Europe. ⊠ *Carrer dels Forns 10* ☎ *972/896313* ☜ *€4* ☾ *Closed Mon.*

🍴 Restaurants

Can Ventura

$$$ | **SPANISH** | Inside a flower-festooned 17th-century town house made of ancient stones is one of La Cerdanya's best places for both fine cuisine and good value. Beef a la llosa and duck with orange and spices are house specialties, and the wide selection of *entretenimientos* (hors d'oeuvres or tapas) is the perfect way to begin. **Known for:** beef seared on hot slate; cozy mountain lodge setting; additional bar area for drinks and tapas. $ *Average main: €20* ✉ *Pl. Major 1* ☎ *972/896178* ⊕ *www.canventura.com* ⊘ *Closed Mon. and Tues.*

★ La Formatgeria de Llívia

$$$$ | SPANISH | Set on Llívia's eastern edge, this restaurant is inside a former cheese factory, and the proprietors continue the tradition by producing fresh homemade cheese on the premises while you watch. In the restaurant, fine local cuisine and fondues come with panoramic views looking south toward Puigmal and across the valley. **Known for:** fondues and raclettes; homemade cheese; open fire in winter. $ *Average main: €25* ✉ *Pl. de Ro s/n, Gorguja* ☎ *972/146279* ⊕ *www.laformatgeria.com* ⊘ *Closed Tues. and Wed. (except during Aug. and public holidays).*

La Seu d'Urgell

20 km (12 miles) south of Andorra la Vella (in Andorra), 45 km (28 miles) west of Puigcerdà, 200 km (120 miles) northwest of Barcelona.

La Seu d'Urgell is an ancient town facing the snowy rock wall of the Sierra del Cadí. As the seat (*seu*) of the regional archbishopric since the 6th century, it has a rich legacy of art and architecture. The Pyrenean feel of the streets, with their dark balconies and porticoes, overhanging galleries, and colonnaded porches—particularly **Carrer dels Canonges**—makes Seu mysterious and memorable. Look for the medieval **grain measures** at the corner of Carrer Major and Carrer Capdevila. The tiny food shops on the arcaded Carrer Major are good places to assemble lunch for a hike.

GETTING HERE AND AROUND

Take the N260 southwest from Puigcerdà via Bellver de Cerdanya. From the direction of Lleida, head north on the C13 for 63 km (39 miles), then take the C26 after Balaguer, before joining the C14 for 32 km (20 miles) and then the N260 into the center. There are buses daily from Barcelona. The town is compact and can be explored on foot.

CONTACTS ALSA ✉ *Estación de Autobuses, Calle Bisbe de Bell-Loch 1* ☎ *902/422242* ⊕ *www.alsa.es.*

VISITOR INFORMATION
CONTACTS La Seu d'Urgell Tourist Office ✉ *Calle Mayor 8* ☎ *973/351511* ⊕ *www.turismeseu.com.*

Sights

★ Catedral de Santa Maria

MUSEUM | This 12th-century cathedral is the finest in the Pyrenees, and the sunlight casting the rich reds and blues of Santa Maria's southeastern rose window into the deep gloom of the transept is a moving sight. The 13th-century cloister is famous for the individually carved, often whimsical capitals on its 50 columns, crafted by the same Roussillon school of masons who carved the doorway on the church of Santa Maria in Ripoll. Don't miss the haunting, 11th-century chapel of **Sant Miquel** or the **Diocesan Museum,** which has a collection of striking medieval murals from various Pyrenean churches and a colorfully illuminated 10th-century Mozarabic manuscript of the monk Beatus de Liébana's commentary on the apocalypse. ✉ *Pl. del Deganat* ☎ *973/353242* ⊕ *www.museudiocesaurgell.org* 🎫 *€3, includes museum* ⊘ *Closed Sun.*

Hotels

★ Cal Serni

$ | B&B/INN | Ten minutes north of La Seu d'Urgell in the Pyrenean village of Calbinyà, this enchanting 15th-century farmhouse and inn exudes rustic charm and provides inexpensive local gastronomy against a backdrop of panoramic views. **Pros:** mountain authenticity just minutes from La Seu; good value; incredible

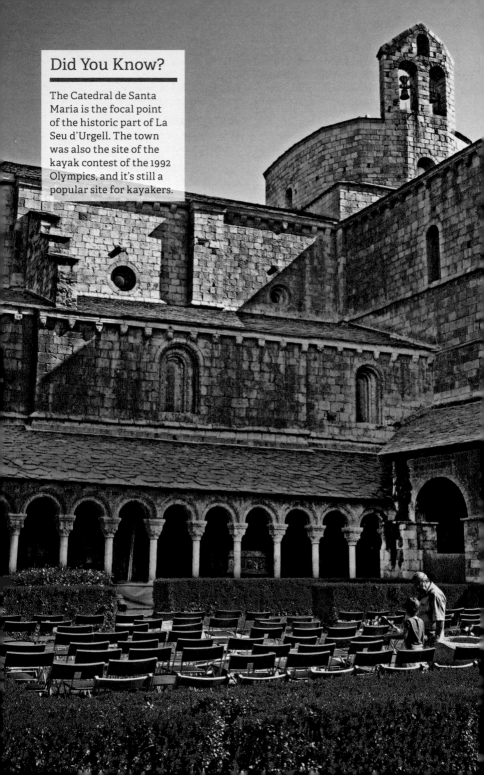

Did You Know?

The Catedral de Santa Maria is the focal point of the historic part of La Seu d'Urgell. The town was also the site of the kayak contest of the 1992 Olympics, and it's still a popular site for kayakers.

views. **Cons:** small guest rooms; tight public spaces; simple lodgings. [$] *Rooms from: €60* ✉ *Ctra. de Calbinyà s/n, Valls de Valira, Calbinyà* ☎ *973/352809* 🌐 *www.calserni.com* 🛏 *6 rooms* 🍴 *No meals.*

Parador de la Seu d'Urgell

$$$ | HOTEL | These comfortable quarters right in the center of town are built into the 14th-century convent of Sant Domènec. **Pros:** next to the Santa Maria cathedral; handy for wandering through the town; historic building. **Cons:** some rooms are small; mediocre restaurant; no parking. [$] *Rooms from: €160* ✉ *Calle Sant Domènec 6* ☎ *973/352000* 🌐 *www.parador.es* 🛏 *79 rooms* 🍴 *No meals.*

Relais & Châteaux El Castell de Ciutat

$$$$ | HOTEL | Just outside town, the setting of this wood-and-slate structure beneath La Seu's castle makes it one of the finest places to stay in the Pyrenees—rooms on the second floor have balconies overlooking the river and surrounding valley, those on the third have slanted ceilings and dormer windows, and suites include a salon. **Pros:** best restaurant for many miles; magnificent Pyrenean panoramas; on-site spa. **Cons:** standard upper-floor rooms feel slightly cramped; next to a busy highway; misses out on the feel of the town. [$] *Rooms from: €200* ✉ *Ctra. de Lleida (N260), Km 229* ☎ *973/350000* 🌐 *www.hotelelcastell.com* 🛏 *33 rooms, 5 suites* 🍴 *Free Breakfast.*

Sort

59 km (37 miles) west of La Seu d'Urgell, 136 km (84 miles) north of Lleida, 259 km (161 miles) northwest of Barcelona.

The capital of the Pallars Sobirà (Upper Pallars Valley) is the area's epicenter for skiing, fishing, and white-water kayaking. The word *sort* is Catalan for "luck," and its local lottery shop, La Bruixa d'Or (The Gold Witch), became a tourist attraction by living up to the town's name and selling more than an average number of winning tickets. Don't be fooled by the town you see from the main road: one block back, Sort is honeycombed with tiny streets and protected corners built to stave off harsh winter weather.

GETTING HERE AND AROUND

Heading westward from La Seu d'Urgell, take the N260 toward Lleida, head west again at Adrall, staying on the N260, and drive 53 km (33 miles) over the Cantó Pass to Sort.

VISITOR INFORMATION

CONTACTS Pallars Sobirà Tourist Office ✉ *Camí de la Cabanera 1* ☎ *973/621002* 🌐 *turisme.pallarssobira.cat.*

🍴 Restaurants

★ Fogony

$$$$ | SPANISH | Come here for seasonal and contemporary creations from an acclaimed chef and supporter of the slow-food movement, with a prix-fixe menu that may include dishes such as *pollo a la cocotte con trufa* (organic bluefoot chicken with truffle) and *solomillo de ternera de los Pirineos con ligero escabeche de verduras y setas* (fillet of Pyrenean veal with marinated vegetables and mushrooms). This restaurant is one of the best of its kind in the Pyrenees and, if you hit Sort at lunchtime, it makes an excellent reason to stop. **Known for:** part of the "slow food" movement; family run; Michelin star. [$] *Average main: €38* ✉ *Av. Generalitat 45* ☎ *973/621225* 🌐 *www.fogony.com* 🕒 *Closed Mon. and Tues. and 2 wks in Jan. No dinner Sun.*

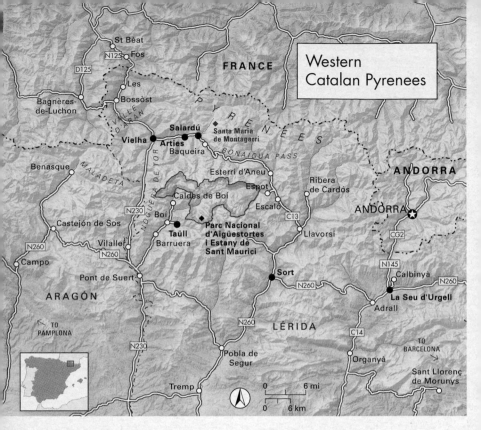

Parc Nacional d'Aigüestortes i Estany de Sant Maurici

33 km (20 miles) north of Sort, 168 km (104 miles) north of Lleida, 292 km (181 miles) northwest of Barcelona.

Catalonia's only national park is a dramatic and unspoiled landscape shaped over 2 million years of glacial activity. Hikers can reach the park from the Noguera Pallaresa and Ribagorçana valleys, from the villages of Espot to the east, and from Taüll and Boí to the west. There are several visitor centers, with maps and information on hiking routes and accommodation, in the villages that border the park, such as Espot and Boí.

GETTING HERE AND AROUND

The C13 north up the Noguera Pallaresa Valley covers 34 km (21 miles) from Sort to Espot. One of the main entrances to the park is 4 km (2 miles) west of Espot, where there is also a parking lot. No cars are allowed inside the park (except official taxis/transport).

VISITOR INFORMATION

CONTACTS Casa del Parc Nacional de Boí (Park Information Center - Boí) ✉ *Ca de Simamet, Carrer de les Graieres, 2, Boí* ☎ *973/696189* ⊕ *www.vallboi.cat/en/visitors-centre-park-house.* **Casa del Parc Nacional d'Espot (Park Information Center)** ✉ *Carrer de Sant Maurici, 5, Espot* ☎ *973/624036.*

◉ Sights

★ Parc Nacional d'Aigüestortes i Estany de Sant Maurici

NATIONAL/STATE PARK | The breathtaking scenery of this national park is formed by jagged peaks, steep rock walls, and an abundance of high mountain terrain, all of which lie in the shadow of the twin peaks of Els Encantats. More than 300 glacial lakes and lagoons trickle through forests and meadows of wildflowers to the meandering Noguera River watercourses: the Pallaresa to the east and the Ribagorçana to the west. The land range sweeps from soft lower meadows below 5,000 feet to the highest crags at nearly double that height. The twin Encantats measure more than 9,000 feet, and the surrounding peaks of Beciberri, Peguera, Montarto, and Amitges hover between 8,700 feet and a little less than 10,000 feet. The park offers an abundance of walking trails. The most popular is a one-day scenic traverse across the park from east to west, starting at the village of Espot and finishing in Boí. ■TIP➔ **Although driving inside the park is not permitted, it is possible to organize taxis to help you on your way from Boí or Espot, and, in summer, buses also provide transportation in and around the park.** ✉ *Espot* ⊕ *www.aiguestortes.info* 🎫 *Free.*

🛏 Hotels

There are no hotels in the park, but the nine refugios have staff who provide basic dormitory-style accommodations, as well as dinner and breakfast for hikers June–October and during shorter periods at Christmas and Easter. When these are not open or staffed, shelter is still available in parts of the park, and fireplaces can be used for cooking, but hikers must supply the food and the utensils. Bookings can be made on the website (⊕ *www.lacentralderefugis.com*). If you plan on only day hikes, there are several hotels and restaurants in the villages of Taüll and Boí, on the western side of the park, or Espot to the east.

Taüll

58 km (35 miles) south of Vielha.

Taüll is a town of narrow streets and tight mountain design—wooden balconies and steep, slate roofs—that makes an attractive base for exploring the Parc Nacional d'Aigüestortes. The high-sided valley also has one of the greatest concentrations of Romanesque architecture in Europe, and the famous Taüll churches of **Sant Climent** and **Santa María** are among the best examples of Romanesque architecture in the Pyrenees. Other important churches near Taüll include Sant Feliu, at Barruera; Sant Joan Baptista, at Boí; Santa Maria, at Cardet; Santa Maria, at Col; Santa Eulàlia, at Erill la Vall; La Nativitat de la Mare de Deu and Sant Quirze, at Durro.

GETTING HERE AND AROUND

Take the N230 northbound from Lleida for 138 km (86 miles), passing through El Pont de Suert. At Erill la Vall, go east for 4 km (2½ miles) toward Boí and Taüll. Taüll is small enough to walk around unless you are headed to the ski resort, in which case a car is needed. Four-wheel-drive taxis into the Parc Nacional d'Aigüestortes can be organized from Espot (☎ *973/624036 for tourist office*).

VISITOR INFORMATION

CONTACTS Centre del Romànic de la Vall de Boí ✉ *Carrer del Batalló 5, Erill la Vall* ☎ *973/696715* ⊕ *www.centreromanic. com.* **Taüll Tourist Office** ✉ *Passeig de St. Feliu 43, Barruera* ☎ *973/694000* ⊕ *www. vallboi.com.*

◉ Sights

★ Sant Climent

RELIGIOUS SITE | At the edge of town, this exquisite three-nave Romanesque church was built in 1123. The six-story belfry has perfect proportions, with Pyrenean stone that changes hues with the light, and a sense of intimacy and balance. In 1922 Barcelona's Museu Nacional d'Art de Catalunya removed the murals for safekeeping, including the famous *Pantocrator,* the work of the "Master of Taüll." The murals presently in the church are reproductions. ✉ *Ctra. de Taüll s/n* 🌐 *www.centreromanic.com* 🎫 *€5.*

🍴 Restaurants

L'Era

$$ | **ECLECTIC** | **FAMILY** | The owners of this rustic restaurant raise their farm animals in ecologically friendly fashion and the menu focuses on the highest quality cuts of organic beef and veal, including grilled steaks and hamburgers, accompanied by sides that include fresh salads. There's also locally cured meat and cheese platters, and the chocolate *coulant* (molten cake) should not be missed. **Known for:** organic cuts of beef; hamburgers and steak; bar and terrace. [$] *Average main: €17* ✉ *Carrer Major 7, Barruera* ☎ *973/694192* 🌐 *www.restaurantlera.com.*

Vielha

79 km (49 miles) northwest of Sort, 297 km (185 miles) northwest of Barcelona, 160 km (99 miles) north of Lleida.

Vielha (Viella in Spanish), capital of the Vall d'Aran, is a lively crossroads vitally involved in the Aranese movement to defend and reconstruct the valley's architectural, institutional, and linguistic heritage. At first glance, the town looks like a typical ski-resort base, but the compact and bustling old quarter has a Romanesque church and narrow streets filled with a good selection of restaurants, shops, and a couple of late-night bars. Hiking and climbing are popular around Vielha; guides are available year-round and can be arranged through the tourist office.

GETTING HERE AND AROUND

From the direction of Taüll, head south on the L500 for 15 km (9 miles) toward El Pont de Suerte. At Campament de Tor turn right onto the Carretera Lleida–Vielha (N230) northbound to Vielha. Vielha's town center is fairly compact and everything can be reached on foot, but you'll need a car to get to Salardú, Arties, and the ski station of Baqueira-Beret.

VISITOR INFORMATION

CONTACTS Vielha Tourist Office ✉ *Carrer Sarriulera 10* ☎ *973/640110* 🌐 *www.visitvaldaran.com.*

👁 Sights

Sant Miquel

RELIGIOUS SITE | Vielha's octagonal, 14th-century bell tower on the Romanesque parish church of Sant Miquel is one of the town's trademarks, as is its 15th-century Gothic altar. The partly damaged 12th-century wood carving *Cristo de Mig Aran,* displayed under glass, evokes a sense of mortality and humanity with a power unusual in medieval sculpture. ✉ *Pl. de la Iglesia.*

🍴 Restaurants

El Molí

$$$ | **SPANISH** | A picturesque riverside location, knotty pine walls, wood beams, and a rustic menu that highlights regional specialties make this a lovely spot for a meal. The restaurant includes a ground-floor dining room with large windows that frame a broad sweep of the river and a second, smaller dining room tucked away in the attic. **Known for:** chuleton de vaca vieja del Pirineo (aged beef, cooked over hot coals); river views; calçots (Catalan green onions). [$] *Average main: €20* ✉ *Carrèr Sarriulèra 26* ☎ *973/641718* 🌐 *www.hotelelmoli.es/en* 🕒 *No dinner Tues. Closed Wed. and Dec. 18–Jan. 18.*

Hiking in the Pyrenees

Walking the Pyrenees, with one foot in France and the other in Spain, is an exhilarating experience.

In fall and winter, the Alberes Mountains between Cap de Creus, the Iberian Peninsula's easternmost point, and the border with France at Le Perthus are a grassy runway between the Côte Vermeille's curving beaches to the north and the green patchwork of the Empordá to the south. The well-marked GR (Gran Recorrido) 11 is a favorite two-day spring or autumn hike, with an overnight stay at the Refugi de la Tanyareda, just below and east of Puig Neulós, the highest point in the Alberes.

The eight-hour walk from Coll de Núria to Ulldeter over the Sierra Catllar, above Setcases, is another grassy corridor in good weather April–October. The luminous Cerdanya Valley is a hiker's paradise year-round, while the summertime round-Andorra hike is a memorably scenic 360-degree tour of the tiny country.

The Parc Nacional d'Aigüestortes i Estany de Sant Maurici is superb for trekking from spring through fall. The ascent of the highest peak in the Pyrenees, the 11,168-foot Aneto peak above Benasque, is a long day's round-trip best approached in summer and only by fit and experienced hikers. Much of the hike is over the Maladeta Glacier, from the base camp at the Refugio de La Renclusa.

In the Parque Nacional de Ordesa y Monte Perdido you can take day trips up to the Cola de Caballo waterfall and back around the southern rim of the canyon or, for true mountain goats, longer hikes via the Refugio de Góriz to La Brèche de Roland and Gavarnie or to Monte Perdido, the parador at La Pineta, and the village of Bielsa. Another prized walk involves bed and dinner in the base-camp town of Torla or a night up at the Refugio de Góriz at the head of the valley.

The section of the Camino de Santiago walk from Saint-Jean-Pied-de-Port to Roncesvalles is a marvelous 8- to 10-hour trek any time of year, though check weather reports carefully October–June.

Local *excursionista* (outing) clubs can help you get started; local tourist offices may also have brochures and rudimentary trail maps. Note that the higher reaches are safely navigable only in summer.

Some useful contacts for hiking are **Cercle d'Aventura** (☎ 972/881017 ⊕ www.cercleaventura.com), **Giroguies** (☎ 636/490830 ⊕ www.giroguies.com), and **Guies de Meranges** (☎ 616/855535 ⊕ www.guiesmeranges.com).

Era Mola (*Restaurante Gustavo y María José*)
$$$ | SPANISH | This rustic former stable with whitewashed walls serves Aranese dishes with a modern, often French twist. Duck, either stewed with apples or served with *carreretes* (wild mushrooms from the valley), and roast lamb are favorites, as is foie gras *de pato con pistachos con caramelo de Pedro Ximenez* (duck foie gras with pistachios and Pedro Ximenez syrup). **Known for:** excellent service; specialty of pigs' trotters stuffed with mushrooms and truffle sauce; traditional cuisine from Vall d'Aran. $ *Average main: €20* ⊠ *Carrer Marrec*

Did You Know?

The ski resort of Baqueira-Beret is part of the Naut Aran (literally "upper valley") municipality of Spain's Vall d'Aran. It is the closest thing to an alpine-ski experience that Spain has to offer and a major draw for skiers, including the king of Spain.

14 ☎ 973/642419 ⏲ Closed May, June, and Oct. No lunch weekdays Dec.–Apr. (except during Christmas and Easter wks).

Hotels

Hotel El Ciervo

$$$ | **B&B/INN** | In Vielha's old quarter, and next to one of the town's attractive pedestrian-only streets, this family-run inn resembles an idyllic winter cottage, and the personal service includes breakfast, available for a small additional charge, which former guests have touted as the best in Spain. **Pros:** quirky and inviting; excellent breakfast; pleasant furnishings. **Cons:** rooms are a little cramped; the feminine, chintz style may not appeal to everyone; breakfast costs extra. [$] *Rooms from: €130 ✉ Pl. de San Orencio 3 ☎ 973/640165 🌐 www.hotelelciervo.net ⏲ Closed Apr.–mid-June and last 2 wks Oct. and Nov. 🛏 20 rooms 🍴 No meals.*

Parador de Vielha

$$$$ | **HOTEL** | The shining star at this modern granite parador is a semicircular salon with huge windows and spectacular views over the Maladeta peaks of the Vall d'Aran. **Pros:** terrific observation post; comfortable and relaxed; on-site spa and swimming pool. **Cons:** overmodern and somewhat lacking in character; beside a busy road; 2 km (1 mile) from Vielha old town. [$] *Rooms from: €190 ✉ Ctra. del Túnel s/n ☎ 973/640100 🌐 www.parador.es ⏲ Closed mid-Oct.–mid-Nov. (dates vary; check ahead) 🛏 118 rooms 🍴 No meals.*

Nightlife

DeVins

BARS/PUBS | This popular wine bar has a prime location overlooking the river and gets busy in the early evening serving tapas, cheese boards, and wine. Later in the evening it becomes a bar dedicated mainly to gin and tonics, but other spirits and a decent wine list are also available. *✉ Carrèr Major 23 ☎ 647/511146.*

Saxo Blu

BARS/PUBS | This is the most popular late-night bar for all ages in downtown Vielha. *✉ Carrer Marrec 6.*

Activities

Skiing, white-water rafting, hiking, climbing, horseback riding, and fly-fishing are just some of the sports available throughout the Vall d'Aran.

SKIING

Baqueira-Beret Estación de Esquí (*Baqueira-Beret Ski Station*)

SKIING/SNOWBOARDING | This ski center offers Catalonia's most varied and reliable skiing. Its 87 km (54 miles) of *pistas* (slopes), spread over 53 runs, range from the gentle Beret slopes to the vertical chutes of Baqueira. The Bonaigua area is a mixture of steep and gently undulating trails, with some of the longest, most varied runs in the Pyrenees. A dozen restaurants and four children's areas are scattered about the facilities, and the thermal baths at Tredós are 4 km (2½ miles) away. *✉ Calle Baqueira Beret ☎ 973/639025 🌐 www.baqueira.es.*

Arties

7 km (4 miles) east of Vielha, 3½ km (2 miles) west of Salardú.

The village of Arties makes a good stop; here you'll find a lively village of Romanesque, Gothic, and Renaissance styles, straddling a clear river that's presided over by the Montarto Peak.

GETTING HERE AND AROUND

The C28 east out of Vielha heads straight to Arties in 7 km (4 miles). The village is small and best explored on foot. Cross over the bridge over the river to hit the main square.

Santa Maria de Montgarri 👁

Partly in ruins, this 11th-century chapel was once an important way station on the route into the Vall d'Aran from France. The beveled, hexagonal bell tower and the rounded stones, which look as if they came from a brook bottom, give the structure a stippled appearance that's a bit like a Pyrenean trout. The Romería de Nuestra Señora de Montgarri (Feast of Our Lady of Montgarri), on July 2, is a country fair with feasting, games, music, and dance. The sanctuary can be reached by following the C142 road until Beret and then walking 6 km (4 miles) along a dirt track that can also be accessed by off-road vehicles. It is difficult to get there during the winter snow season. Partly in ruins, this 11th-century chapel was once an important way station on the route into the Vall d'Aran from France. The beveled, hexagonal Include in print text.

🍴 Restaurants

Tauèrnes Urtau
$$ | **TAPAS** | The area's most happening tapas chain is friendly, fun, and always busy. Customers can help themselves at the bar to an assortment of 40 mouth-watering *pinchos* (creative toppings on bread, held together with a toothpick, such as mini hamburger, king prawn with mushrooms, or ravioli with foie gras), or go for the tapas menu and table service. **Known for:** Basque-style "help yourself at the bar" pinchos; cider and local products; rollicking atmosphere. [$] *Average main: €16* ✉ *Pl. Urtau 12, Arties* ☎ *973/640926* 🌐 *www.urtau.com* 🕒 *Closed 2 wks in Oct. or Nov.*

🛏 Hotels

Casa Irene
$$$ | **B&B/INN** | A rustic haven, Casa Irene's style and spacious, elegant rooms make it a desirable place to stay. **Pros:** small and personalized; aesthetically impeccable; free shuttle service to the slopes. **Cons:** street-side rooms can be noisy on summer nights; restaurant closed Monday; often booked up. [$] *Rooms from: €180* ✉ *Carrer Major 22, 6 km (4 miles) east of Vielha, Arties* ☎ *973/644364* 🌐 *www.hotelcasairene.com* 🕒 *Closed May, June, Oct., and Nov.* ✍ *Reservations essential* 🛏 *22 rooms* 🍽 *Free Breakfast.*

Parador de Arties
$$$ | **HOTEL** | Built around the Casa de Don Gaspar de Portolà, once home to the founder of the colony of California, this modern parador with friendly staff has views of the Pyrenees and is handy for exploring the Romanesque sights in nearby villages. **Pros:** marvelous panoramas; quiet and personal for a parador; mountain-lodge style. **Cons:** neither at the foot of the slopes nor in the thick of the Vielha après-ski vibe; requires driving; feels old-fashioned. [$] *Rooms from: €160* ✉ *Calle San Juan 1, Arties* ☎ *973/640801* 🌐 *www.parador.es* 🕒 *Closed 40 days after Easter wk (dates can vary)* 🛏 *54 rooms, 3 suites* 🍽 *No meals.*

Salardú

9 km (6 miles) east of Vielha.

Salardú is a pivotal point in the Vall d'Aran, convenient to Baqueira-Beret, the Montarto peak, the lakes and Circ de Colomers, Parc Nacional d'Aigüestortes, and the villages of Tredós, Unha, and Montgarri. The town itself, with a little more than 700 inhabitants, is known for its steep streets and its octagonal fortified bell tower.

GETTING HERE AND AROUND

The C28 east out of Vielha goes straight to Salardú and Tredós in 9 km (6 miles) and on to Baqueira-Beret in 13 km (8 miles).

🍴 Restaurants

Casa Rufus

$$$ | SPANISH | Fresh pine on the walls and the floor, red-and-white-check curtains, and snowy-white tablecloths cozily furnish this restaurant in the tiny, gray-stone village of Gessa, between Vielha and Salardú. Try the *conejo relleno de ternera y cerdo* (rabbit stuffed with veal and pork). **Known for:** said to be one of the best restaurants in the area; wide selection of local meat dishes; good stop off on way to or from the Baqueira ski slopes. $ *Average main: €18* ✉ *Carrer Sant Jaume 8, Gessa* ☎ *973/645246* 🕑 *Closed May and June, weekdays in Oct. and Nov., and Sun. Oct.–Apr.*

Taberna Eth Bot

$$$$ | SPANISH | You can feast where the farm animals once grazed in this converted 16th-century stable, where the fixed-price menu features local Aranese dishes such as olha aranesa (a hearty stew from the Aran Valley), *patatas rellenas* (potato stewed with a choice of meat or vegetables), or *estofado de jabalí y arroz* (wild boar stew served with rice). A bottle of wine, water, and bread—and a shot of local liqueur at the end—are thrown in for good measure. **Known for:** atmospheric building; local Aranese cuisine; three-course meal with drinks included in fixed menu. $ *Average main: €35* ✉ *Pl. Mayor 1* ☎ *973/644212.*

🛏 Hotels

Val de Ruda

$$$$ | HOTEL | For rustic surroundings—light on luxury but long on comfort—only a two-minute walk from the ski lift, this modern-traditional construction of glass, wood, and stone is a good choice. **Pros:** pleasant and outdoorsy; warm and welcoming after a day in the mountains; friendly family service. **Cons:** some of the upstairs rooms are cozy but tiny; only open during ski season; not cheap. $ *Rooms from: €255* ✉ *Ctra. Baqueira-Beret Cota 1500* ☎ *973/645258* ⊕ *www.hotelvalderudabaqueira.com* 🕑 *Closed after Easter wk–end Nov.* 🛏 *35 rooms* 🍴 *Free Breakfast.*

Zaragoza

138 km (86 miles) west of Lleida, 307 km (191 miles) northwest of Barcelona, 164 km (102 miles) southeast of Pamplona, 322 km (200 miles) northeast of Madrid.

Despite its hefty size (population 680,000), this sprawling provincial capital midway between Barcelona, Madrid, Bilbao, and Valencia is a detour from the tourist track, yet still accessible via the AVE, Spain's high-speed railroad, with both Madrid and Barcelona only 90 minutes away. The first decade of this century were major boom years here, and it's been rated one of Spain's most desirable places to live because of its good air quality, low cost of living, and low population density.

Straddling Spain's greatest river, the Ebro, Zaragoza was originally named Caesaraugusta, for the Roman emperor Augustus, and established as a thriving river port by 25 BC. Its legacy contains everything from Roman ruins and Jewish baths to Moorish, Romanesque, Gothic-Mudejar, Renaissance, baroque, neoclassical, and Art Nouveau architecture. Parts of the **Roman walls** are visible near the city's landmark **Basílica de Nuestra Señora del Pilar.** Nearby, the medieval **Puente de Piedra** (Stone Bridge) spans the Ebro. Checking out the **Lonja** (Stock Exchange), **La Seo cathedral,** the Moorish **Aljafería**

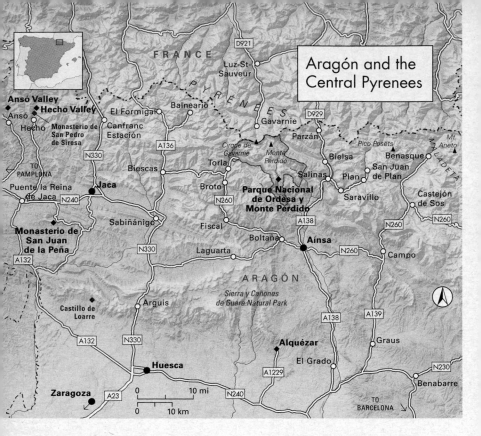

Aragón and the Central Pyrenees

(Fortified Palace and Jewel Treasury), the **Mercado de Lanuza** (Produce Market), and the many **Mudejar churches** in the old town is a good way to navigate Zaragoza's jumble of backstreets.

Worthwhile excursions from Zaragoza include the birthplace of Francisco José de Goya y Lucientes in **Fuendetodos,** 44 km (27 miles) to the southeast, and the **Monasterio de Piedra,** an hour's drive southwest of Zaragoza. Founded in 1195 by Alfonso II of Aragón, this lush oasis of caves, waterfalls, and suspended walkways surrounds a Cistercian monastery that dates back to the 12th century and a 16th-century Renaissance section that is now a private hotel (⊕ www.monasteriopiedra.com).

GETTING HERE AND AROUND

There are several trains per day between Zaragoza and Barcelona, Lleida, and Huesca (⊕ www.renfe.com). The bus company Alosa (⊕ www.alosa.es) runs buses between Zaragoza, Huesca, and Jaca. By car, travel west from Barcelona on the E90 motorway. All of Zaragoza's main sights are accessible on foot, as the center is compact and much of it is traffic-free.

BUS STATION Estación Central de Autobuses ⊠ Calle Miguel Roca i Junyent 7 ☎ 976/700599 ⊕ www.estacion-zaragoza. es.

VISITOR INFORMATION

CONTACTS Zaragoza Tourist Office ⊠ Pl. de Nuestra Señora del Pilar ☎ 902/142008 ⊕ www.zaragozaturismo.es.

◉ Sights

Alma Mater Museum

MUSEUM | Portraits of archbishops (one by Goya), Flemish tapestries, Renaissance and medieval paintings, and the remains of the Romanesque door of Zaragoza's church of Santiago form parts of this museum's collection. ✉ Pl. de la Seo 5 ☎ 976/399488 ⊕ www.almamatermuseum.com ✉ €3 ⊘ Closed Mon.

★ Basílica de Nuestra Señora del Pilar

(Basilica of Our Lady of the Pillar)
RELIGIOUS SITE | Hulking on the banks of the Ebro, the basilica, often known simply as La Pilarica or El Pilar, is Zaragoza's symbol and pride. An immense baroque structure with no fewer than 11 tile cupolas, La Pilarica is the home of the Virgen del Pilar, the patron saint not only of peninsular Spain but of the entire Hispanic world. The fiestas honoring this most Spanish of saints, held the week of October 12, are events of extraordinary pride and Spanish fervor, with processions, street concerts, bullfights, and traditional jota dancing. Among the basilica's treasures are two frescoes by Goya—one of them, El Coreto de la Vírgen, painted when he was young and the other, the famous Regina Martirum, after his studies in Italy. The bombs displayed to the right of the altar of La Pilarica chapel fell through the roof of the church in 1936 and miraculously failed to explode. Behind La Pilarica's altar is the tiny opening where the devout line up to kiss the rough marble pillar where La Pilarica is believed to have been discovered. ✉ Pl. del Pilar s/n ✉ Basilica free, tower €3, museum €2 ⊘ Museum closed Sun. Tower closed Mon. in winter.

EMOZ (Escuela Museo Origami Zaragoza)

MUSEUM | Within Zaragoza's Centro de Historias, EMOZ houses one of the finest collections of origami in the world. These eye-popping exhibitions change themes seasonally, while also revealing the surprising story of Zaragoza's historical connection with the art of paper folding. ✉ Centro de Historias, Pl. de San Agustín 2 ☎ 876/034569 ⊕ www.emoz.es ✉ €3 ⊘ Closed Mon.

IAACC Pablo Serrano

MUSEUM | A collection of works by the famous 20th-century sculptor Pablo Serrano (1908–85) and his wife, Juana Francés, are on display in this museum. ✉ Paseo María Agustín 20 ☎ 976/280659 ⊕ www.iaacc.es ✉ Free ⊘ Closed Mon.

Iglesia de San Pablo

RELIGIOUS SITE | After the basilica and La Seo, this church, with examples of Mudejar architecture in its brickwork, is considered by zaragozanos to be the "third cathedral." ✉ Carrer San Pablo 42 ☎ 976/446296 ⊘ Closed Sun.

La Seo (Catedral de San Salvador)

MUSEUM | Zaragoza's cathedral, at the eastern end of the Plaza del Pilar, is the city's bishopric, or diocesan seo (seat). An amalgam of architectural styles, ranging from the Mudejar brick-and-tile exterior and the Gothic altarpiece to exuberant churrigueresque doorways, La Seo nonetheless has an 18th-century baroque facade that seems to echo those of La Pilarica. The **Museo de Tapices** within contains medieval tapestries. The nearby medieval **Casa y Arco del Deán** form one of the city's favorite corners. ✉ Pl. de la Seo ✉ €4, includes museum.

Museo de Zaragoza

MUSEUM | This museum contains a rich treasury of works by Zaragoza's emblematic painter, Goya, including his portraits of Fernando VII and his best graphic works: Desastres de la Guerra, Caprichos, and La Tauromaquia. ✉ Pl. de los Sitios 6 ☎ 976/222181 ⊕ www.museodezaragoza.es ✉ Free ⊘ Closed Mon.

Museo del Foro

ARCHAEOLOGICAL SITE | Remains of the Roman forum and the Roman sewage system can be seen here. Two more Roman sites, the **thermal baths** at Calle de San Juan y San Pedro and the **river**

port at Plaza San Bruno, are also open to the public. You can organize in advance to see the presentation videos in English through the Museo del Teatro Romano (☎ *976/726075*), and English-language audio guides are also available. ✉ *Pl. de la Seo 2* ☎ *976/721221* 🎟 *€3* ⏲ *Closed Mon.*

Museo del Teatro Romano

ARCHAEOLOGICAL SITE | In addition to the restored Roman amphitheater here, you can also see objects recovered during the excavation process, including theatrical masks, platters, and even Roman hairpins. ✉ *Calle San Jorge 12* ☎ *976/726075* 🎟 *€4* ⏲ *Closed Mon.*

Museo Goya

MUSEUM | A fine collection of Goya's works, particularly engravings, are on view here. ✉ *Carrer Espoz y Mina 23* ☎ *976/397387* 🌐 *museogoya.ibercaja.es* 🎟 *€6.*

Museo Pablo Gargallo

MUSEUM | This is one of Zaragoza's most treasured and admired gems, both for the palace in which it is housed and for its collection—Gargallo, born near Zaragoza in 1881, was one of Spain's greatest modern sculptors. ✉ *Pl. de San Felipe 3* ☎ *976/724922* 🎟 *€4* ⏲ *Closed Mon.*

Palacio de La Aljafería

CASTLE/PALACE | This is one of Spain's three greatest Moorish palaces. If Córdoba's Mezquita shows the energy of the 10th-century Caliphate and Granada's Alhambra is the crowning 14th-century glory of Al-Andalus (the 789-year Moorish empire on the Iberian Peninsula), then the late-11th-century Aljafería can be seen as the intermediate step. Originally a fortress and royal residence, and later a seat of the Spanish Inquisition, the Aljafería is now the home of the Cortes (Parliament) de Aragón. The 9th-century Torre del Trovador (Tower of the Troubadour) appears in Giuseppe Verdi's opera *Il Trovatore.* ✉ *Diputados s/n* ☎ *976/289528* 🌐 *www.cortesaragon.es* 🎟 *€5* ⏲ *Closed Thurs. and Fri. if parliament is in session.*

🍴 Restaurants

★ El Tubo

$$ | **SPANISH** | Zaragoza's famous El Tubo area, around the intersection of Calle Estébanes and Calle Libertad, offers the chance to eat your way through a diverse array of bite-size sharing plates that are meant to be enjoyed standing up or leaning against a barstool. Limit yourself to one tapa per bar so you can sample as much as possible. **El Champi** (Calle Libertad 16) may not be much to look at, but this tiny establishment serves wonderful mushrooms grilled with garlic and olive oil, stacked on bread to soak up the garlic-infused oil. **Known for:** variety of tapas bars; lively atmosphere; narrow, pedestrianized streets. [$] *Average main: €15* ✉ *Calle Estébanes.*

Los Victorinos

$$ | **TAPAS** | Named after a much-feared and respected breed of fighting bull, this rustic tavern, located behind La Seo, is heavily adorned with bullfight-related paraphernalia. It offers an elaborate and inventive selection of pinchos and original tapas of all kinds. *Jamón ibérico de bellota* (acorn-fed Iberian ham), Spain's best-known luxury food, is always a natural choice, though quail eggs or the classic *gilda*—olives, green peppers, and anchovies on a toothpick—are also on the bar and hard to resist. **Known for:** Iberian ham; gilda (olives, green peppers, and anchovies); lively atmosphere. [$] *Average main: €15* ✉ *Calle José de la Hera 6* ☎ *976/394213* 💳 *No credit cards* ⏲ *Closed 2 wks in May. No lunch weekdays. No dinner Sun. Closed Mon.*

Palomeque

$$$ | **TAPAS** | For upscale tapas, larger portions, and a sit-down restaurant atmosphere, Palomeque is a great choice. Using fresh market produce, dishes are

Overlooking the Río Ebro and Zaragoza's Basílica de Nuestra Señora del Pilar

based on traditional recipes and finished off with a clean modern look. **Known for:** duck foie gras shavings on bread; selection of mixed tapas; hidden gem. [$] *Average main: €20* ✉ *Calle Agustín Palomeque 11* ☎ *976/214082* 🌐 *www.restaurantepalomeque.es* 💳 *No credit cards* 🕓 *Closed Sun.*

Tragantua

$$$ | SPANISH | This rollicking spot serves surprisingly great food, including *solomillicos con salsa de trufa* (little beef fillets with truffle sauce), *albóndigas de solomillicos* (meatballs of beef fillet), and a mouthwatering array of seafood. The beer is fresh and cold, and the house wines, usually from Upper Aragón's own Somontano D.O., are of top value and quality. **Known for:** excellent house wines; seafood dishes; nice lunch location. [$] *Average main: €21* ✉ *Pl. Santa Marta s/n* ☎ *976/299174* 🌐 *www.grupoloscabezudos.es* 🕓 *Closed last 2 wks in June and 2nd wk in Jan.*

🛏 Hotels

Catalonia El Pilar

$$ | HOTEL | Overlooking the lovely Plaza Justicia and the baroque Santa Isabel church, this early-20th-century Art Nouveau building is a tourist sight in its own right, featuring an original Moderniste wooden elevator and a facade with wrought-iron decorations. **Pros:** quiet location on one of the city's prettiest squares; five-minute walk from the Basílica de Nuestra Señora del Pilar; spotless and efficient. **Cons:** rooms are immaculate but somewhat characterless; some rooms are on the small side; no on-site parking. [$] *Rooms from: €120* ✉ *Calle Manifestación 16* ☎ *976/205858* 🌐 *www.cataloniahotels.com* 🛏 *66 rooms* 🍴 *Free Breakfast.*

Hotel Sauce

$$ | HOTEL | When it comes to value for money Hotel Sauce couldn't be better, plus it's located right in the center of Zaragoza, a stone's throw from El Pilar and a short walk from El Tubo. **Pros:**

central location; modern facilities and café on-site; excellent value. **Cons:** reception service can be erratic; small rooms; not many rooms. $ *Rooms from: €96* ⊠ *Espoz y Mina 33* ☎ *976/205050* ⊕ *www.hotelsauce.com* ↷ *40 rooms* ⦁⦁⦁ *No meals.*

Palafox

$$$ | **HOTEL** | One of Zaragoza's top hotels, Palafox combines contemporary design with traditional urban service and elegance. **Pros:** top comfort and service; private parking for guests; good restaurant. **Cons:** modern and somewhat antiseptic; rooms not as impressive as the public spaces; tired decor. $ *Rooms from: €150* ⊠ *Calle Marqués Casa Jiménez s/n* ☎ *976/237700* ⊕ *www.palafoxhoteles. com* ↷ *179 rooms* ⦁⦁⦁ *Free Breakfast.*

Huesca

68 km (42 miles) northeast of Zaragoza, 123 km (76 miles) northwest of Lleida.

Once a Roman colony, Huesca would later become the capital of Aragón, until the royal court moved to Zaragoza in 1118. The town's university was founded in 1354 and now specializes in Aragonese studies.

GETTING HERE AND AROUND

From Zaragoza there are several trains a day (⊕ *www.renfe.com*). Alosa (⊕ *www. alosa.es*) runs buses between Huesca and Zaragoza, Lleida, and Jaca. By car from Zaragoza, head northwest toward Huesca on the A23. The center is quite small and it's easier to go on foot to the sights, because the traffic and one-way system can be tricky.

CONTACTS Bus Station ⊠ *Calle José Gil Cávez 10.*

VISITOR INFORMATION

CONTACTS Huesca Tourist Office ⊠ *Pl. Luis López Allué s/n* ☎ *974/292170* ⊕ *www. huescaturismo.com.*

Castillo de Loarre

This massively walled 11th-century monastery, 36 km (22 miles) west of Huesca off Route A132 on A1206, is nearly indistinguishable from the rock outcroppings that surround it. Inside the walls are a church, a tower, a dungeon, and even a medieval toilet with views of the almond and olive groves in the Ebro basin. ⊕ *www.castillodeloarre.es*

◉ Sights

Cathedral

MUSEUM | An intricately carved gallery tops the eroded facade of Huesca's 13th-century Gothic cathedral. Damián Forment, a protégé of the 15th-century Italian master sculptor Donatello, created the alabaster altarpiece, which has scenes from the Crucifixion. ⊠ *Pl. de la Catedral s/n* ☎ *974/231099* ⊠ *€4* ⊙ *Museum closed Sun.*

Museo de Huesca

MUSEUM | This museum occupies parts of the former royal palace of the kings of Aragón and holds paintings by Aragonese primitives, including *La Virgen del Rosario* by Miguel Jiménez, and several works by the 16th-century Maestro de Sigena. The eight chambers of the gallery, set around an octagonal patio, include the **Sala de la Campana** (Hall of the Bell), where, in the 12th century, the beheadings of errant nobles took place. ⊠ *Pl. de la Universidad* ☎ *974/220586* ⊕ *www.museodehuesca. es* ⊠ *Free* ⊙ *Closed Mon.*

San Pedro el Viejo

RELIGIOUS SITE | This church has an 11th-century cloister. Ramiro II and his father, Alfonso I, the only Aragonese kings not entombed at San Juan de la Peña, rest in a side chapel. ⊠ *Pl. de San Pedro s/n* ⊕ *www.sanpedroelviejo.com* ⊠ *€3.*

Mountain trekking in the Huesca province

 Restaurants

Las Torres

$$$$ | SPANISH | Creating a taste of pure upper Aragón, Huesca's top restaurant makes inventive use of first-rate local ingredients like wild mushrooms, wild boar, venison, and lamb. The glass-walled kitchen is as original as the cooking that emerges from it, and the wine list is strong in Somontanos, Huesca's own D.O. **Known for:** showcasing traditional Aragonese dishes with a modern twist; tasting menu with thoughtful presentation; excellent value. $ *Average main: €25* ⊠ *Calle María Auxiliadora 3* ☎ *974/228213* ⊕ *www.lastorres-restaurante.com* ⏱ *No dinner Sun. or Mon. Closed 2 wks over Easter and last 2 wks of Aug.*

Hotels

Hotel Abba Huesca

$$ | HOTEL | This modern hotel in Huesca has comfortable rooms and a buzzing contemporary bar where guests and locals mingle. **Pros:** excellent value; upscale feel; on-site bar and restaurant. **Cons:** slightly outside the center of town; area surrounding the hotel is quiet; functional business hotel decor. $ *Rooms from: €90* ⊠ *Calle de Tarbes 14* ☎ *974/292900* ⊕ *www.abbahuescahotel. com* ⇥ *84 rooms* �🍽 *No meals.*

🛍 Shopping

Ultramarinos La Confianza

FOOD/CANDY | Founded in 1871, La Confianza has been declared the oldest grocery store in Spain. It's in the porticoed Plaza Mayor in the old town and worth popping into to see the tiled floors and hand-painted ceiling, and to browse the shelves stacked high with local products, from dried goods to specialty chocolates and salted cod. ⊠ *Pl. Mayor (Pl. López Allué)* ☎ *974/222632* ⊕ *www.ultramarinoslaconfianza.com.*

Alquézar

51 km (32 miles) northeast of Huesca, 123 km (76 miles) northeast of Zaragoza.

As though carved from the rock itself, Alquézar overlooks the Parque Natural Sierra y Cañones de Guara and is one of Aragón's most attractive old towns. A labyrinth of cobbled, winding streets and low archways coil around the town's central square, and many of the buildings' facades bear coat-of-arms motifs dating back to the 16th century. The uniquely shaped town square, formed with no cohesive plan or architectural style, has a porched area that was built to provide shelter from the sun and rain.

GETTING HERE AND AROUND

From Huesca, travel eastward on the A22 or N240 for 29 km (18 miles) before joining the A1229 toward Alquézar. Cars cannot enter the old quarter, so the only way to see the town is on foot.

VISITOR INFORMATION

CONTACTS Alquézar Tourist Office ✉ *Calle Arrabal 14* ☎ *974/318940* 🌐 *www.alquezar.es.*

👁 Sights

Colegiata de Santa María

RELIGIOUS SITE | Keeping watch over the Sierra de Guara, the Colegiata, originally a 9th-century Moorish citadel, was conquered by the Christians in 1067. An interesting mix of Gothic, Mudejar, and Renaissance details are found in the shaded cloister, and there are biblical murals that date back to the Romanesque era. The church, built in the 16th century, contains an almost life-size Romanesque figure of Christ, but restoration has taken away some of the building's charm—its interior brickwork is now only a painted representation. ✉ *Diseminado Afueras, off Calle la Iglesia* 🎫 *Free.*

San Lorenzo 👁

For an unspoiled Pamplona-like fiesta in another pre-Pyrenean capital, with bullfights, *encierros* (running of the bulls through the streets), and all-night revelry, try Huesca's San Lorenzo celebration (August 9–15). Spain's top bullfighters are the main attraction, along with concerts, street dances, and liberal tastings of the excellent Somontano wines of upper Huesca. *Albahaca* (basil) is the official symbol of Huesca, hence the ubiquitous green sashes and bandanas.

River Vero Cultural Park

NATIONAL/STATE PARK | Declared a UNESCO World Heritage Site in 1998, this park within the Sierra de Guara contains more than 60 limestone caves with prehistoric cave paintings. Some date back to around 22,000 BC, although the majority are between 12,000 BC and 4000 BC. Information and guided tours are available through the interpretation center in Colungo. Hours vary, so call ahead. ✉ *Calle Las Braules 2, Colunga* ✣ *9½ km (6 miles) east of Alquézar* ☎ *974/318185, 974/306006* 🌐 *www.turismosomontano.es* 🎫 *Free.*

🍴 Restaurants

Casa Pardina

$$$$ | **SPANISH** | Elegant, romantic dining at a reasonable price is the draw here, with a choice of two fixed-price menus. Locally sourced ingredients come together to create a traditional Aragonese menu, adapted for contemporary tastes, and the wine is from the nearby Somontano region. **Known for:** terrace with views of the church and Sierra de Guara; no à la carte; locally sourced ingredients and local olive oil. [$] *Average main: €29* ✉ *Calle Medio s/n* ☎ *974/318425* 🌐 *www.*

casapardina.com 🕓 *Closed Tues. No lunch weekdays Oct.–Easter.*

Hotels

Hotel Santa María de Alquézar
$$ | B&B/INN | Just outside the old town walls, this hotel has the best views around—overlooking the Río Vero canyon and the Colegiata de Santa María. **Pros:** breathtaking views; bright rooms; relaxed ambience. **Cons:** noise from the street can be heard in some rooms; outside the walls of the old town; in high season parking is hard to find. [$] *Rooms from: €99* ✉ *Calle Arrabal s/n* ☎ *974/318436* 🌐 *www.hotel-santamaria.com* 🕓 *Closed Jan.–mid-Feb. Call ahead for other seasonal closures* 🛏 *21 rooms* 🍴 *Free Breakfast.*

Activities

The Sierra de Guara is one of Europe's best places for canyoning (descending mountain gorges, usually in or near streams and other water sources).

Avalancha
ADVENTURE TOURS | There are several agencies in Alquézar that specialize in guided private or group trips for all levels and ages. Avalancha is one of the best for canyoning and other adventure activities and provides equipment, including wet suits and helmets. ✉ *Calle Arrabal s/n* ☎ *974/318299* 🌐 *www.avalancha.org.*

Aínsa

66 km (41 miles) southwest of Benasque, 113 km (70 miles) northeast of Huesca, 214 km (133 miles) northeast of Zaragoza.

Wander through the uninspiring outskirts of Aínsa's new town until the road turns sharply upward toward one of Aragón's most impressive walled medieval towns, where houses are jammed together along narrow cobbled streets, offering sweeping views of the surrounding mountains and Parque Nacional de Odesa.

GETTING HERE AND AROUND

Head north out of Huesca on the E7 and then the N260 for a total of 98 km (61 miles), then take the A2205 for 15 km (9 miles). Aínsa can only be explored on foot once you're through the old city walls.

VISITOR INFORMATION

CONTACTS Aínsa Tourist Office ✉ *Av. Ordesa 5* ☎ *974/500767* 🌐 *www.villadeainsa.com.*

Sights

Citadel
CASTLE/PALACE | The citadel and castle, originally built by the Muslims in the 11th century, was conquered by the Christians and reconstructed in the 16th century. ✉ *Old Quarter.*

Santa María
RELIGIOUS SITE | This 12th-century Romanesque church, with its quadruple-vaulted door and 13th-century cloister, is in the corner of the attractive, porticoed Plaza Mayor. ✉ *Calle Santa Cruz* 🎫 *Free.*

Hotels

Hotel Los Siete Reyes
$$ | B&B/INN | One of two boutique hotels in Aínsa's Plaza Mayor, Los Siete Reyes occupies a handsome restored historic house with good-size and artistically decorated bedrooms overlooking the square. **Pros:** charming and atmospheric; central location; good views of the mountain or village. **Cons:** noise from the square; interior design makes rooms dark; patchy Wi-Fi in rooms. [$] *Rooms from: €120* ✉ *Pl. Mayor s/n* ☎ *974/500681* 🌐 *www.lossietereyes.com* 🛏 *6 rooms* 🍴 *No meals.*

Parque Nacional de Ordesa y Monte Perdido

79 km (49 miles) west of Bielsa, 45 km (30 miles) west of Aínsa, 92 km (57 miles) north of Huesca.

This great but often overlooked park was founded by royal decree in 1918 to protect the natural integrity of the central Pyrenees. It has expanded from 4,940 to 56,810 acres as provincial and national authorities have added the Monte Perdido massif, the head of the Pineta Valley, and the Escuain and Añisclo Canyons.

VISITOR INFORMATION

CONTACTS Centro Visitantes de Torla ✉ *Av. Ordesa s/n, Torla* ☎ *974/486472* ⊕ *www.ordesa.net.*

Sights

★ Ordesa and Monte Perdido National Park

NATIONAL/STATE PARK | The entrance to this natural wonder is under the vertical walls of Monte Mondarruego, the source of the Ara River and its tributary, the Arazas, which forms the famous Ordesa Valley. Defined by the Ara and Arazas Rivers, the Ordesa Valley is endowed with lakes, waterfalls, high mountain meadows, and forests of pine, fir, larch, beech, and poplar. Protected wildlife includes trout, boar, chamois, and the *sarrio*, or isard, mountain goat (*Rupicapra pyrenaica*).

Well-marked mountain trails lead to waterfalls, caves, and spectacular observation points. The standard tour, a full day's hike (eight hours), runs from the parking area in the Pradera de Ordesa, 8 km (5 miles) northeast of Torla, up the Arazas River, past the Gradas de Soaso (Soaso Risers, a natural stairway of waterfalls) to the Cola de Caballo (Horse's Tail), a lovely fan of falling water at the head of the Cirque de Cotatuero, a sort of natural amphitheater. There is one refuge, Refugio Gorez, north of the Cola de Caballo. A return walk on the south side of the valley, past the Cabaña de los Cazadores (Hunters' Hut), offers a breathtaking view followed by a two-hour descent back to the parking area. ✉ *Torla* ☎ *974/486472* ⊕ *www.ordesa.net* 🎫 *Free.*

 Restaurants

El Rebeco

$$ | **SPANISH** | In this graceful, rustic building in the upper part of town, the dining rooms are lined with historic photographs of Torla during the 19th and 20th centuries, and in late fall, civets of deer, boar, and mountain goat are the order of the day. In summer, lighter fare and hearty mountain soups restore hikers between treks. **Known for:** traditional Pyrenean architecture; inviting terrace; slow service so adjust accordingly. 💲 *Average main: €14* ✉ *Calle Fatás 55, Torla* ☎ *974/486068* 🕐 *Closed Nov.–Easter.*

Hotels

Villa de Torla

$ | **B&B/INN** | This classic mountain refuge, with sundecks, terraces, and a private dining room, has rooms of various shapes and sizes. **Pros:** in the middle of a postcard-perfect Pyrenean village; helpful staff; restaurant on-site. **Cons:** rooms on the street side can be noisy on weekends and summer nights; not all rooms have a private bathroom; some rooms on the small side. 💲 *Rooms from: €80* ✉ *Pl. Aragón 1, Torla* ☎ *974/486156* ⊕ *www.hotelvilladetorla.com* 🛏 *38 rooms* 🍽 *No meals.*

Jaca

24 km (15 miles) southwest of Biescas, 164 km (102 miles) north of Zaragoza.

Jaca, the most important municipal center in Alto Aragón, is anything but sleepy. Bursting with ambition and

blessed with the natural resources, jacetanos are determined to make their city the site of a Winter Olympics someday. Founded in 1035 as the kingdom of Jacetania, Jaca was an important stronghold during the Christian Reconquest of the Iberian Peninsula and proudly claims never to have bowed to the Moorish invaders. Indeed, on the first Friday of May the town still commemorates the decisive battle in which the appearance of a battalion of women, their hair and jewelry flashing in the sun, intimidated the Moorish cavalry into beating a headlong retreat. Avoid the industrial-looking outskirts and head straight to the atmospheric *casco antiguo* (old town) where there's a splendid 11th-century cathedral and fortress, and where bustling eateries abound.

GETTING HERE AND AROUND

Alosa (⊕ *www.alosa.es*) runs daily buses between Jaca and Zaragoza. There is also a train between Jaca and Huesca or Zaragoza (⊕ *www.renfe.com*). By car, take the E7/N330 northbound from Huesca via Sabiñánigo for 73 km (45 miles). Town sights are easily accessible on foot.

VISITOR INFORMATION

CONTACTS Jaca Tourist Office ⊠ *Pl. San Pedro 11–13* ☎ *974/360098* ⊕ *www.jaca. es.*

 Sights

Canfranc

TOUR—SIGHT | In July and August a guided train tour departs from the Jaca RENFE station, heading to the valley and Canfranc's magnificent Belle Époque train station, now abandoned. Surely the largest and most ornate building in the Pyrenees, the station has a bewitching history and was used as a location in the 1965 film *Doctor Zhivago*. Ask at the tourist office for schedules—it's a good idea to book ahead of time. In addition, a nontourist train runs year-round between Jaca and Canfranc. ⊠ *Canfranc Estación*

En Route: Broto

Broto is a typical Aragonese mountain town with an excellent 16th-century Gothic church. Nearby villages, such as **Oto,** have stately manor houses with classic local features: baronial entryways, conical chimneys, and wooden galleries. **Torla** is Parque Nacional de Ordesa y Monte Perdido's main entry point, with regular buses that go up to the park entrance during summer, and is a popular base camp for hikers.

⊕ *www.elcanfranero.com, www.renfe. com* ☒ *€35.*

Catedral de San Pedro

MUSEUM | An important stop on the pilgrimage to Santiago de Compostela, Jaca's 11th-century Romanesque Catedral de San Pedro has lovely carved capitals and was the first French-Romanesque cathedral in Spain, paving the way for later Spanish Romanesque architecture. Inside the cathedral and near the cloisters, the **Museo Diocesano** is filled with an excellent collection of Romanesque and Gothic frescoes and artifacts. ⊠ *Pl. de San Pedro 1* ☒ *Cathedral free, museum €6.*

Ciudadela

BUILDING | The massive pentagonal Ciudadela is an impressive example of 17th-century military architecture. It has a display of more than 35,000 military miniatures, arranged to represent different periods of history. Check the website to confirm hours. ⊠ *Av. del Primer Viernes de Mayo s/n* ☎ *974/357157* ⊕ *www. ciudadeladejaca.es* ☒ *From €6.*

🍴 Restaurants

La Fragua

$$$ | **SPANISH** | Tucked behind a huge wooden door just off Calle Major hides a cozy stonewalled *asador* (grill house). The fired-up barbecue can be viewed from the dining room, setting the scene nicely for locally sourced meat and fish to be cooked over coals. [$] *Average main: €22* ✉ *Calle Gil Bergés 4* ☎ *974/360618* 🕓 *Closed Tues. No dinner Mon.* 💳 *No credit cards.*

La Tasca de Ana

$$$ | **TAPAS** | For a taste of Spanish tapas in the Pyrenees, this cozy and fun tavern is one of Jaca's finest. With only a handful of tables and standing room by the bar, it's not the setting for a quiet romantic dinner, but it is recommended for anyone spending an evening in Jaca. **Known for:** quick bite; rodolfito langoustine tapa; lively atmosphere. [$] *Average main: €20* ✉ *Calle Ramiro I 3* ☎ *974/363621* 🌐 *www.latascadeana.com* 🕓 *No lunch weekdays. Closed Mon. Closed 2 wks in May and 2 wks in Sept.*

🛏 Hotels

Gran Hotel

$ | **HOTEL** | This rambling hotel—Jaca's traditional official clubhouse—has seen better days, but its central location makes it a practical base. **Pros:** quiet location just west of the town center; professional and polished service; easy walking distance to the sights. **Cons:** modern and functional construction with no special charm or Pyrenean features; neo–motel room style; no frills. [$] *Rooms from: €80* ✉ *Paseo de la Constitución 1* ☎ *974/360900* 🌐 *www.granhoteljaca.com* 🛏 *165 rooms* 🍽 *Free Breakfast.*

★ Hotel Barosse

$$$ | **B&B/INN** | In a small village on the outskirts of Jaca, this intimate, adults-only bed-and-breakfast is worth sacrificing the central-city location to gain sweeping mountain views and helpful, personalized service. **Pros:** peaceful rural setting; boutique-style accommodations; friendly service. **Cons:** a car is necessary; not in the center of Jaca; adults only. [$] *Rooms from: €138* ✉ *Calle de Estirás 4* ☎ *974/360582, 638/845992* 🌐 *www.barosse.com* 🕓 *Closed Nov.* 🛏 *5 rooms* 🍽 *Free Breakfast.*

🍸 Nightlife

Jaca's music bars are concentrated in the casco antiguo, on Calle Ramiro I and along Calle Gil Bergés and Calle Bellido. In the porticoed Plaza de la Catedral, there are a number of bars with terraces, in the shade of the cathedral, to be enjoyed day or evening.

Bar Casa Fau

BARS/PUBS | This busy bar serves coffee and soft drinks, a good selection of wine by the glass, and beer on tap—all of which can be accompanied by tapas and light snacks, and front-row views of the cathedral. ✉ *Pl. de la Catedral 3* ☎ *974/361594.*

Monasterio de San Juan de la Peña

23 km (14 miles) southwest of Jaca, 185 km (115 miles) north of Zaragoza, 90 km (56 miles) east of Pamplona.

South of the Aragonese valleys of Hecho and Ansó is the Monastery of San Juan de la Peña, a site connected to the legend of the Holy Grail and one of the centers of Christian resistance during the 700-year Moorish occupation of Spain.

GETTING HERE AND AROUND

From Jaca, drive 11 km (7 miles) west on the N240 toward Pamplona to a left turn clearly signposted for San Juan de la Peña. From there it's another 11 km (7 miles) on the A1603 to the monastery.

The Monasterio de San Juan de la Peña near Jaca

⊙ Sights

★ Monasterio de San Juan de la Peña

RELIGIOUS SITE | The origins of this arresting religious sanctuary can be traced to the 9th century, when a hermit monk named Juan settled here on the *peña* (cliff). A monastery was founded on the spot in 920, and in 1071 Sancho Ramirez, son of King Ramiro I, made use of the structure, which was built into the mountain's rock wall, to found this Benedictine monastery. The **cloister,** tucked under the cliff, dates to the 12th century and contains intricately carved capitals depicting biblical scenes. The church of the New Monastery contains the **Kingdom of Aragon Interpretation Centre,** where audio guides in English are available. ⊠ *Jaca* ⊹ *Off N240 on A1603* ☎ *974/355119* ⊕ *www. monasteriosanjuan.com* ⊠ *From €7.*

Hecho and Ansó Valleys

The Hecho Valley is 49 km (30 miles) northwest of Jaca. The Ansó Valley is 25 km (15 miles) west of Hecho, 118 km (73 miles) east of Pamplona.

The Ansó Valley is Aragón's western limit. Rich in fauna (mountain goats, wild boar, and even a bear or two), it follows the Veral River up to Zuriza. Towering over the head of the valley is Navarra's highest point, the 7,989-foot **Mesa de los Tres Reyes** (Plateau of the Three Kings), named not for the Magi but for the kings of Aragón, Navarra, and Castile, whose 11th-century kingdoms bordered one another here, allowing them to meet without leaving their respective realms. The **Selva de Oza** (Oza Forest), at the head of the Hecho Valley, is above the **Boca del Infierno** (Mouth of Hell), a tight draw that road and river barely squeeze through.

It's worth stopping at the pretty villages of **Ansó** and **Hecho,** where a preserved collection of stone houses are tightly bunched together along narrow cobbled streets overlooking the valley. In Ansó on the last Sunday in August, residents dress in traditional medieval costumes and perform ancestral dances of great grace and dignity.

GETTING HERE AND AROUND

You can reach the Hecho Valley from Jaca by heading west on the N240 and then north on the A176.

VISITOR INFORMATION

CONTACTS Hecho Tourist Office ⊠ *Ctra. de Oza 38, Hecho* ☎ *974/375505* ⊕ *www. valledehecho.es.*

Sights

Monasterio de San Pedro de Siresa

RELIGIOUS SITE | The area's most important monument, the 9th-century retreat Monasterio de San Pedro de Siresa, presides over the village of Siresa, just 2 km (1 mile) north of Hecho. Although now only the 11th-century church remains, it is a marvelous example of Romanesque architecture. Cheso, a medieval Aragonese dialect descended from the Latin spoken by the Siresa monks, is thought to be the closest to Latin of all Romance languages and dialects. It has been kept alive in the Hecho Valley, especially in the works of the poet Veremundo Méndez Coarasa. ⊠ *Calle San Pedro, Siresa* ⊠ *€2.*

Hotels

Casa Blasquico

$ | B&B/INN | This cozy inn is a typical mountain chalet with flowered balconies and a plethora of memorabilia inside. **Pros:** two cute dormered rooms; fine mountain cuisine; friendly service. **Cons:** rooms lack space; public rooms cluttered; no elevator. $ *Rooms from: €60* ⊠ *Pl. la Fuente 1, Hecho* ☎ *974/375007, 657/892128* ⊕ *www.casablasquico. es* ⊗ *Closed weekdays Nov.–Mar.* 🛏 *6 rooms* 🍽 *No meals.*

En Route

From Ansó, head west to Roncal on the narrow and winding but panoramic 17-km (11-mile) road through the Sierra de San Miguel. To enjoy this route fully, count on taking a good 45 minutes to reach the Esca River and the Roncal Valley.

Roncal Valley

17 km (11 miles) west of Ansó Valley, 72 km (45 miles) west of Jaca, 86 km (53 miles) northeast of Pamplona.

The Roncal Valley, the eastern edge of the Basque Pyrenees, is notable for the sheep's-milk cheese of the same name and as the birthplace of Julián Gayarre (1844–90), the leading tenor of his time. The 34-km (21-mile) drive through the towns of **Burgui** and **Roncal** to **Isaba** winds through green hillsides past *caseríos*, classical Basque farmhouses covered by long, sloping roofs that were designed to house animals on the ground floor and the family up above to take advantage of the body heat of the livestock. Burgui's red-tile roofs backed by rolling pastures contrast with the vertical rock and steep slate roofs of the Aragonese and Catalan Pyrenees; Isaba's wide-arch bridge across the Esca is a graceful reminder of Roman aesthetics and engineering.

GETTING HERE AND AROUND

To get to the valley from Jaca, take the N240 west along the Aragón River; a right turn north on the A137 follows the Esca River from the head of the Yesa Reservoir up the Roncal Valley.

VISITOR INFORMATION

CONTACTS Roncal Tourist Office ⊠ *Barrio Iriartea s/n, Roncal* ☎ *948/475256* ⊕ *www.vallederoncal.es.*

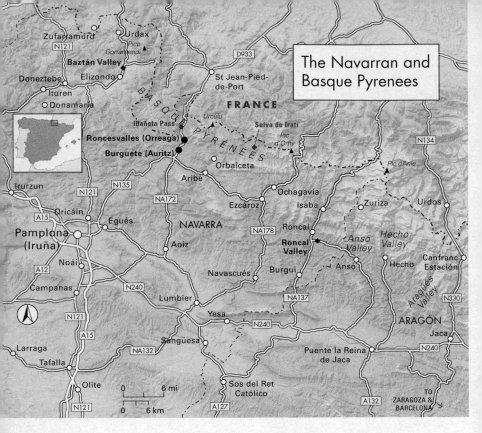

Sights

El Tributo de las Tres Vacas (*The Tribute of the Three Cows*)

FESTIVAL | Try to be in the Roncal Valley for this event, which has been celebrated every July 13 since 1375. The mayors of the valley's villages, dressed in traditional gowns, gather near the summit of San Martín to receive the symbolic payment of three cows from their French counterparts, in memory of the settlement of ancient border disputes. Feasting and celebrating follow. ⊠ *Roncal*.

Ochagavía

TOWN | The road west (NA140) to Ochagavía through the Portillo de Lazar (Lazar Pass) has views of the Anie and Orhi peaks, which tower over the French border. The village itself, with original cobblestone streets and riverside promenade,

makes for a pleasant spot to stretch the legs. ⊠ *Roncal*.

Selva de Irati (*Irati Forest*)

FOREST | A 15-km (9-mile) detour north through the town of Orbaiceta up to the headwaters of the Irati River, at the Irabia Reservoir, gets you a good look at the Selva de Irati, one of Europe's major beech forests and the source of much of the lumber for the Spanish Armada. ⊠ *Roncal*.

Roncesvalles (Orreaga)

64 km (40 miles) northwest of Isaba in the Roncal Valley, 48 km (30 miles) north of Pamplona.

Roncesvalles (often listed as Orreaga, its name in Euskera) is a small village and the site of the Battle of Roncesvalles (or

Battle of Roncevaux Pass), when Charlemagne's army, under the command of Roland, was attacked and overcome by Basque soldiers in AD 778. This battle became the inspiration for one of France's most revered literary poems, *Le Chanson de Roland* (*The Song of Roland*), written in the 11th century.

The village's strategic position, 23 km (14 miles) from the original starting line of Saint-Jean-Pied-de-Port in France, has made it the first stop-off point for pilgrims on the Camino de Santiago since the 10th century. Its Gothic Colegiata (built in the style of the Notre-Dame Cathedral in Paris), hospital, and 12th-century chapel have provided shelter since then. This part of the Camino offers some of the best scenery, and many modern-day pilgrims start in Roncesvalles.

GETTING HERE AND AROUND

The N135 northbound out of Pamplona goes straight to Roncesvalles.

VISITOR INFORMATION

CONTACTS Orreaga-Roncesvalles Tourist Office ✉ *Antiguo Molino, Calle de Nuestra Señora de Roncesvalles, Orreaga* ☎ *948/760301*.

Sights

Colegiata

RELIGIOUS SITE | Built on the orders of King Sancho VII el Fuerte (the Strong), the Collegiate Church houses the king's tomb, which measures more than 7 feet long. ✉ *Calle de Nuestra Señora de Roncesvalles, Orreaga* 🌐 *www.roncesvalles.es*.

Ibañeta Pass

SCENIC DRIVE | This 3,468-foot pass, above Roncesvalles, is a gorgeous route into France. A menhir (monolith) marks the traditional site of the legendary battle in *The Song of Roland*, during which Roland fell after calling for help on his ivory battle horn. The well-marked eight-hour walk to or from Saint-Jean-Pied-de-Port (which does *not* follow the road) is the first and one of the most beautiful and dramatic sections of the Santiago pilgrimage. ✉ *Orreaga*.

Hotels

Casa de Beneficiados

$$ | **HOTEL** | Whether you're embarking on the pilgrimage or not, this hotel, in a restored 18th-century building adjoining the Colegiata, provides warm, atmospheric low-lit, stone-walled common areas and modern, comfortable rooms. **Pros:** historic building; friendly service; oozes pilgrim trail ambience. **Cons:** apartments lack the charm of the common areas; simple food; take caution arriving by car in bad weather. [$] *Rooms from: €90* ✉ *Calle Nuestra Señora de Roncesvalles s/n, Orreaga* ☎ *948/760105* 🌐 *www.hotelroncesvalles.com* 🕒 *Closed mid-Nov.–mid-Mar.* 🛏 *16 rooms* 🍴 *No meals.*

Burguete (Auritz)

2 km (1 mile) south of Roncesvalles.

Burguete (Auritz, in Euskera) lies between two mountain streams forming the headwaters of the Urobi River and is surrounded by meadows and forests. The town was immortalized in Ernest Hemingway's *The Sun Also Rises*, with its evocative description of trout fishing in an ice-cold stream above a Navarran village. Hemingway himself spent time here doing just that, and he stayed at the Hostal Burguete.

GETTING HERE AND AROUND

The N135 northbound out of Pamplona goes to Burguete in 44 km (27 miles). From Roncesvalles, it's just 2 km (1 mile) south on the N135.

Hotels

Hotel Loizu
$$ | **B&B/INN** | An inn for pilgrims since the 18th century, the Loizu is now a country-style hotel that makes an excellent base for exploring the Selva de Irati. **Pros:** family-run; friendly service; comfortable, good-size rooms. **Cons:** bathrooms, although adequate, are small and fairly cramped; basic breakfast; can hear noise from other rooms. [$] *Rooms from: €90* ✉ *Calle San Nicolás 13, Auritz* ☎ *948/760008* 🌐 *www.loizu.com* 🕓 *Closed mid-Dec.–Mar.* 🛏 *27 rooms* 🍴 *No meals.*

Baztán Valley

62 km (38 miles) northwest of Roncesvalles, 80 km (50 miles) north of Pamplona.

Tucked neatly above the headwaters of the Bidasoa River, beneath the peak of the 3,545-foot Gorramendi Mountain that looms over the border with France, is the Baztán Valley. These rounded green hills are a scenic halfway stop-off point between the central Pyrenees and the Atlantic. Here the roads of this enchanted Navarran valley meander through picture-perfect villages of geranium-covered, whitewashed, stone-and-mortar houses with red-tile roofs grouped around a central *frontón* (handball court).

This once-isolated pocket of the Basque-Navarran Pyrenees is peppered with smugglers' trails and is the site of the Camino de Baztanas, the oldest stretch of the Camino de Santiago. You can follow the ancient footsteps of pilgrims starting from the historic village of **Urdax.** Nearby, close to the village of **Zugarramurdi,** you can visit a collection of limestone caves, otherwise knowns as Las Cuevas de las Brujas (Witches' Caves), which bore witness to so-called witches' covens and their pagan rituals before their eventual and brutal persecution in the 1600s. In the valley's main town, **Elizondo,** stately homes and ancestral mansions, built by nobles returning with their fortunes from the Americas, straddle the banks of the Baztán River.

Try to be in the village of Ituren in late September for its Carnival, the Day of the Joaldunak, which has been recognized as one of the oldest celebrations in Europe. Here you can see striking costumes hung with clanging cowbells as participants parade from farm to farm and house to house paying homage to their ancestors; some anthropologists argue that the rituals go back to pagan times. Check the exact dates of the event with the tourist office, as each year's schedule depends on the phases of the moon.

VISITOR INFORMATION

CONTACTS Baztán Valley Tourist Office (*Centro de Turismo Rural de Bértiz*) ✉ *Calle Braulio Iriarte 38, Elizondo* ☎ *948/581517.*

Restaurants

★ Donamaria'ko Benta
$$$$ | **BASQUE** | **FAMILY** | This family-run restaurant and small hotel is notable for its high quality and refined level of service. Created from a former 19th-century residence and stables, the restaurant is cozy in winter, with its crackling fire, and a treat in summer, when you can be seated in the peaceful garden filled with willow trees overlooking the river. **Known for:** pretty outdoor seating in summer; traditional recipes; busy in summer. [$] *Average main: €30* ✉ *Barrio de las Ventas 4, Donamaria* ☎ *948/450708* 🌐 *www.donamariako.com* 🕓 *Closed Mon., and Dec. 10–Jan. 5. No dinner Sun.*

Chapter 8

BARCELONA

8

Updated by
Elizabeth Prosser and
Steve Tallantyre

◉ Sights   🍴 Restaurants   🛏 Hotels   🛍 Shopping   🍸 Nightlife

★★★★★   ★★★★★   ★★★★★   ★★★★★   ★★★★★

WELCOME TO BARCELONA

TOP REASONS TO GO

★ **Explore La Boqueria:** Barcelona's produce market may be the most exciting cornucopia in the world.

★ **Visit Santa Maria del Mar:** The early Mediterranean Gothic elegance, rhythmic columns, and unbroken spaces make this church peerless.

★ **See La Sagrada Família:** Gaudí's unfinished masterpiece is the city's most iconic treasure.

★ **Experience El Palau de la Música Catalana:** This Art Nouveau tour de force is alive with music.

★ **Shop for fashion and design:** How could a city famous for its architecture not offer an abundance of innovative clothing, furniture, and design shops as well?

★ **Watch castellers and sardanas:** Human castles and Catalonia's national dance are two fun ways to appreciate Catalan culture.

1 **La Rambla.** Tourists mix with buskers, street performers, and locals on this stroll.

2 **Barri Gòtic.** Medieval Gothic Quarter.

3 **El Raval.** Home to the stunning Antic Hospital de la Santa Creu; just steps away is Sant Pau del Camp, Barcelona's earliest church.

4 **Sant Pere and La Ribera.** Narrow cobblestone streets are filled with interesting shops and restaurants and the Picasso Museum.

5 **La Ciutedella and Barceloneta.** This waterfront neighborhood has some of the city's best seafood restaurants.

6 **The Eixample.** Home to the Sagrada Família church, Casa Batlló, Casa Milà, and Casa Calvet.

7 **Gràcia.** This former outlying village begins at Gaudí's playful Park Güell and continues past his first commissioned house, Casa Vicens.

8 **Upper Barcelona.** Sarrià is endowed with a gratifying number of gourmet shops and fine restaurants.

9 **Montjuïc and Poble Sec.** A sprawling complex of parks and gardens, sports facilities, open-air theater spaces, and museums.

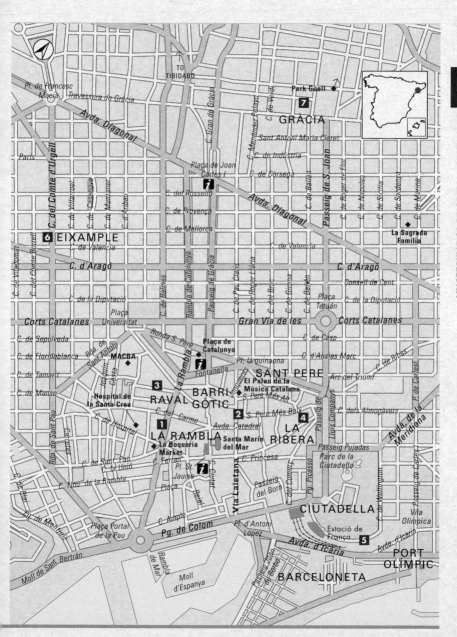

Pl. de Francesc Macià
Travessera de Gràcia
Avda. Diagonal
Paris
Pl. de Francesc Macià
C. del Comte d'Urgell
C. de Vilarroel
C. de Casanova
C. de Muntaner
C. d'Aribau

Park Güell
GRÀCIA
C. Gran de Gràcia
C. Menéndez Pelayo
C. de Verdi
Sant Antoni Maria Claret
C. de Indústria
C. de Còrsega

Plaça de Joan Carles I
C. del Rosselló
C. de Provença
C. de Mallorca

Avda. Diagonal
Passeig de S. Joan
C. de Bailèn
C. de Roger de Flor
C. de Nàpols
C. de Sicília
C. de Sardenya
C. de Marina

La Sagrada Família

EIXAMPLE
C. de València
C. d'Aragó
C. de la Diputació
C. del Comte Borrell
C. del Comte d'Urgell
C. de Viladomat

C. de València
C. d'Aragó
Consell de Cent
Plaça Tetuán
C. de la Diputació
C. de Balmes
Rambla de Catalunya
Passeig de Gràcia
C. de Pau Claris
C. de Roger de Llúria
C. del Bruc
C. de Girona
C. de Bailèn

Corts Catalanes
Plaça Universitat
Gran Via de les
Corts Catalanes
C. de Sepúlveda
C. de Floridablanca
C. de Tamarit
C. de Manso

Ronda S. Pere
Plaça de Catalunya
C. de Casp
C. d'Ausias Marc
C. de Ribes
P. de Carles I
Arc del Triomf
C. dels Almogàvers
Avda. de la Meridiana

Rda. de Sant Antoni
MACBA
La Rambla
Fontanella
SANT PERE
El Palau de la Música Catalana
C. Sant Pere Més Alt
S. Pere Més Baix
Passeig de Lluís Companys

Hospital de la Santa Creu
RAVAL
BARRI GÒTIC
C. del Carme
Avda. Catedral
LA RIBERA
C. de Hospital
C. de Sant Pau
C. la Unió
LA RAMBLA
La Boqueria Market
C. Ferran
Santa Maria del Mar
C. Princesa
Passeig del Born
C. del Comerç
Pg. Picasso

Parc de la Ciutadella
Passeig Pujadas
CIUTADELLA
Vila Olímpica
Estació de França
PORT OLÍMPIC

Pl. St. Jaume
Plaça
Reial
C. Ciutat
C. Nou de la Rambla
C. Ample
Rda. de Sant Pau
Carreras
C. del Blai
Pg. de Montjuïc

Plaça Portal de la Pau
Pg. de Colom
Pl. d'Antoni López
Moll de Sant Bertrán
Moll d'Espanya
Rambla de Mar
Via Laietana
Passeig Joan de Borbó
BARCELONETA
Avda. d'Icària
Passeig de Carles I
C. de Wellington

TO TIBIDABO

EATING AND DRINKING WELL IN BARCELONA

Barcelona cuisine draws from Catalonia's rustic country cooking and uses ingredients from the Mediterranean, the Pyrenees, and inland farmlands. Cosmopolitan influences and experimental contemporary innovation have combined to make Barcelona, historically linked to France and Italy, an important food destination.

The Mediterranean diet of seafood, vegetables, olive oil, and red wine comes naturally to Barcelona. Fish of all kinds, shrimp, shellfish, and rice dishes combining them are common, as are salads of seafood and Mediterranean vegetables. Vegetable and legume combinations are standard. Seafood and upland combinations, the classic *mar i muntanya* (surf and turf) recipes, join rabbit and prawns or cuttlefish and meatballs, while salty and sweet tastes—a Moorish legacy—are found in recipes such as duck with pears or goose with figs.

CAVA

Order "Champagne" in Barcelona and you'll get anything from French bubbly to dirty looks. Ask, instead, for *cava*, sparkling wine from the Penedès region just southwest of the city. The first cava was produced in 1872 after the phylloxera plague wiped out most of Europe's vineyards. Cava (from the "cave" or wine cellar where it ferments) has a drier, earthier taste than Champagne, and slightly larger bubbles.

SALADS

Esqueixada is a cold salad consisting of strips of raw, shredded, salt-cured cod marinated in oil and vinegar with onions, tomatoes, olives, and red and green bell peppers. Chunks of dried tuna can also be included, as well as chickpeas, roast onions, and potatoes, too. *Escalibada* is another classic Catalan salad of red and green bell peppers and eggplant that have been roasted over coals, cut into strips, and served with onions, garlic, and olive oil.

LEGUMES

Botifarra amb mongetes (sausage with white beans) is the classic Catalan sausage made of pork and seasoned with salt and pepper, grilled and served with stewed white beans and *allioli* (an olive oil and garlic emulsion); botifarra can also be made with truffles, apples, eggs, wild mushrooms, and even chocolate. *Mongetes de Sant Pau amb calamarsets* (tiny white beans from Santa Pau with baby squid) is a favorite mar i muntanya.

VEGETABLES

Espinaques a la catalana (spinach with pine nuts, raisins, and garlic) owes a debt to the Moorish sweet-salt counterpoint and to the rich vegetable-growing littoral along the Mediterranean coast north and south of Barcelona. Bits of bacon, fatback, or *jamón ibérico* may be added; some recipes use fine almond

flakes as well. *Albergínies* (eggplant or aubergine) are a favorite throughout Catalonia, whether roasted, stuffed, or stewed, while *carxofes* (artichokes) fried to a crisp or stewed with rabbit is another staple.

FISH

Llobarro a la sal (sea bass cooked in salt) is baked in a shell of rock salt that hardens and requires a tap from a hammer or heavy knife to break and serve. The salt shell keeps the juices inside the fish and the flesh flakes off in firm chunks, while the skin of the fish prevents excessive saltiness from permeating the meat. *Suquet* is favorite fish stew, with scorpion fish, monkfish, sea bass, or any combination thereof, stewed with potatoes, onions, and tomatoes.

DESSERTS

Crema catalana (Catalan cream) is the most popular dessert in Catalonia, a version of the French crème brûlée, custard dusted with cinnamon and confectioner's sugar and burned with a blowtorch (traditionally, a branding iron was used) before serving. The less sweet and palate-cleansing *mel i mató* (honey and fresh cheese) runs a close second in popularity.

The infinite variety and throb of street life, the nooks and crannies of the medieval Barri Gòtic, the ceramic tile and stained glass of Moderniste facades, the art and music, the food (ah, the food!)—one way or another, Barcelona will find a way to get your full attention.

The Catalonian capital greeted the new millennium with a cultural and industrial rebirth comparable only to the late-19th-century Renaixença (Renaissance) that filled the city with its flamboyant Moderniste (Art Nouveau) buildings. An exuberant sense of style—from hip new fashions to cutting-edge interior design, to the extravagant visions of star-status postmodern architects—gives Barcelona a vibe like no other place in the world. Barcelona is Spain's most visited city, and it's no wonder: it's a 2,000-year-old master of the art of perpetual novelty.

Barcelona's present boom began on October 17, 1987, when Juan Antonio Samaranch, president of the International Olympic Committee, announced that his native city had been chosen to host the 1992 Olympics. This single masterstroke allowed Spain's so-called second city to throw off the shadow of Madrid and its 40-year "internal exile" under Franco, and resume its rightful place as one of Europe's most dynamic destinations. The Catalan administration lavished millions in subsidies from the Spanish government for the Olympics, then used the Games as a platform to broadcast the news about Catalonia's cultural and national identity from one end of the planet to the other. More Mediterranean than Spanish, historically closer and more akin to Marseille or Milan than to Madrid, Barcelona has always been ambitious, decidedly modern (even in the 2nd century), and quick to accept the latest innovations. (The city's electric light system, public gas system, and telephone exchange were among the first in the world.) Its democratic form of government is rooted in the so-called Usatges Laws instituted by Ramon Berenguer I in the 11th century, which amounted to a constitution. This code of privileges represented one of the earliest known examples of democratic rule; Barcelona's Consell de Cent (Council of 100), constituted in 1274, was Europe's first parliament and one of the cradles of Western democracy. The center of an important seafaring commercial empire with colonies spread around the Mediterranean as far away as Athens, when Madrid was still a Moorish outpost on the arid Castilian steppe—it was Barcelona that absorbed new ideas and styles first. It borrowed navigation techniques from the Moors. It embraced the ideals of the French Revolution. It nurtured artists like Picasso and Miró, who blossomed in the city's air of freedom and individualism. Barcelona, in short, has always been ahead of the curve.

Planning

Planning Your Time

The best way to get around Barcelona is on foot; the occasional resort to subway, taxi, or tram will help you make the most of your visit. The comfortable FGC (Ferrocarril de la Generalitat de Catalunya) trains that run up the center of the city from Plaça de Catalunya to Sarrià put you within 20- to 30-minute walks of nearly everything. The metro and the FGC close just short of midnight Monday–Thursday and Sunday, and at 2 am on Friday; on Saturday, the metro runs all night. The main attractions you need a taxi or the metro to reach are Montjuïc (Miró Foundation, MNAC, Mies van der Rohe Pavilion, CaixaFòrum, and Poble Espanyol), most easily accessed from Plaça Espanya; Park Güell above Plaça Lesseps; and the Auditori at Plaça de les Glòries. You can reach Gaudí's Sagrada Família by two metro lines (Nos. 2 and 5), but you may prefer the walk from the FGC's Provença stop, as it's an enjoyable half-hour jaunt that passes by three major Moderniste buildings: Palau Baró de Quadras, Casa Terrades (Casa de les Punxes), and Casa Macaia.

Sarrià and Pedralbes are easily explored on foot. The Torre Bellesguard and the Col.legi de les Teresianes are uphill treks; you might want to take a cab. It's a pleasant stroll from Sarrià down through the Jardins de la Vil.la Cecilia and Vil.la Amèlia to the Cátedra Gaudí (the pavilions of the Finca Güell, with Gaudí's amazing wrought-iron dragon gate); from there, you can get to the Futbol Club Barcelona through the Jardins del Palau Reial de Pedralbes and the university campus, or catch a two-minute taxi.

All of the Ciutat Vella (Barri Gòtic, Born-Ribera, La Rambla, El Raval, and Barceloneta) is best explored on foot. If you stay in Barceloneta for dinner (usually not more than €12), have the restaurant call you a taxi to get back to your hotel.

The city bus system is also a viable option—you get a better look at the city as you go—but the metro is faster and more comfortable. The tramway offers a quiet ride from Plaça Francesc Macià out Diagonal to the Futbol Club Barcelona, or from behind the Parc de la Ciutadella out to Glòries and the Fòrum at the east end of Diagonal.

When to Go

For optimal weather and marginally fewer tourists, the best times to visit Barcelona and the rest of Catalonia are April–June and mid-September–mid-December. Catalans and Basques vacation in August, causing epic traffic jams at both ends of the month.

Discounts and Deals

The very worthwhile **Barcelona Card** (⊕ *www.barcelona-card.com*) comes in two-, three-, four-, and five-day versions (€20, €35, €45, and €60). You get unlimited travel on public transport, free admission at numerous museums, and discounts on restaurants, leisure sights, and stores. You can get the card in Turisme de Barcelona offices in Plaça de Catalunya and Plaça Sant Jaume and at the Casa Batlló, the Aquarium, and the Poble Espanyol, among other sites; buy in advance online for a 5% discount.

Getting Here and Around

AIR TRAVEL
Most flights arriving in Spain from the United States and Canada pass through Madrid's Barajas (MAD), but the major gateway to Catalonia and other nearby regions is Spain's second-largest airport, Barcelona's spectacular glass, steel, and marble Prat del Llobregat (BCN). The

T1 terminal, which opened in 2009, is a sleek, ultramodern facility that uses solar panels for sustainable energy and offers a spa, a fitness center, restaurants and cafés, and VIP lounges. This airport is served by numerous international carriers, but Catalonia also has two other airports that handle passenger traffic, including charter flights. One is just south of Girona, 90 km (56 miles) north of Barcelona and convenient to the resort towns of the Costa Brava. Bus and train connections from Girona to Barcelona work well and cheaply, provided you have the time. The other Catalonia airport is at Reus, 110 km (68 miles) south of Barcelona, a gateway to Tarragona and the beaches of the Costa Daurada. Flights to and from the major cities in Europe and Spain also fly into and out of Bilbao's Loiu (BIL) airport. For information about airports in Spain, consult ⊕ www.aena.es.

AIRPORT INFORMATION Aeroport de Girona–Costa Brava (*GRO*) ⊠ *17185 Vilobi de Onyar, Girona* ☎ *902/404704 general info on Spanish airports* ⊕ *www.girona-airport.cat.* **Aeropuerto de Madrid (Adolfo Suárez Madrid-Barajas)** (*MAD*) ⊠ *Av. de la Hispanidad s/n, Madrid* ☎ *902/404704 general info on Spanish airports* ⊕ *www.aeropuertomadrid-barajas.com/eng.* **Aeropuerto de Reus** (*REU*) ⊠ *Autovía Tarragona–Reus, Reus* ☎ *902/404704 general info on Spanish airports* ⊕ *www.aena.es/en/reus-airport/reus.html.* **Aeropuerto Internacional de Bilbao** (*BIL*) ⊠ *Loiu 48180, Bilbao* ☎ *902/404704 general info on Spanish airports* ⊕ *www.aeropuertodebilbao.net/en.* **Barcelona El Prat de Llobregat** (*BCN*) ⊠ *C–32B s/n* ☎ *902/404704 general info on Spanish airports* ⊕ *www.aena.es/en/barcelona-airport/index.html.*

GROUND TRANSPORTATION

Check first to see if your hotel in Barcelona provides airport-shuttle service. If not, visitors typically get into town by train, bus, taxi, or rental car.

Cab fare from the airport into town is €30–€35, depending on traffic, the part of town you're heading to, and the amount of baggage you have (there's a €3.10 surcharge for airport pickups/drop-offs, and a €1 surcharge for each suitcase that goes in the trunk). If you're driving your own car, follow signs to the Centre Ciutat, from which you can enter the city along Gran Vía. For the port area, follow signs for the Ronda Litoral. The journey to the center of town can take 25–45 minutes, depending on traffic.

The Aerobus leaves Terminal 1 at the airport for Plaça de Catalunya every 10 minutes 5:35–7:20 am and 10:25 pm–1:05 am, and every 5 minutes 7:30 am–10:20 pm. From Plaça de Catalunya the bus leaves for the airport every 5 or 10 minutes between 5 am and 12:10 am. The fare is €5.90 one-way and €10.20 round-trip. Aerobuses for Terminals 1 and 2 pick up and drop off passengers at the same stops en route, so if you're outward bound make sure that you board the right one. The A1 Aerobus for Terminal 1 is two-tone light and dark blue; the A2 Aerobus for Terminal 2 is dark blue and yellow.

The train's only drawback is that it's a 10- to 15-minute walk from your gate through Terminal 2 over the bridge. From Terminal 1 a shuttle bus drops you at the train. Trains leave the airport every 30 minutes between 5:42 am and 11:38 pm, stopping at Estació de Sants, for transfer to the Arc de Triomf, then at Passeig de Gràcia and finally at El Clot–Aragó. Trains going to the airport begin at 5:21 am from El Clot, stopping at Passeig de Gràcia at 5:27 am, and Sants at 5:32 am. The trip takes about half an hour, and the fare is €4.10. But the best bargain is the T10 subway card; it gives you free connections within Barcelona plus nine more rides, all for €10.20. Add an extra hour if you take the train to or from the airport.

CITY BUS, SUBWAY, AND TRAM TRAVEL

In Barcelona the underground metro, or subway, is the fastest, cheapest, and easiest way to get around. Metro lines run Monday–Thursday and Sunday 5 am–midnight, Friday to 2 am, Saturday and holiday evenings all night. The FGC trains run 5 am to just after midnight on weekdays and to 1:52 am on weekends and the eves of holidays. Sunday trains run on weekday schedules. Single-fare tickets cost €2.20 (€4.60 to the airport); 10-ride passes cost €10.20

Transfers from a metro line to the FGC (or vice versa) are free within an hour and 15 minutes. Note that in many stations, you need to validate your ticket at both ends of your journey. Maps showing bus and metro routes are available free from the tourist information office in Plaça de Catalunya.

CONTACTS Transports Metropolitans de Barcelona (*TMB*) ☏ *93/214–8000, 93/298–7000* ⊕ *www.tmb.cat/en/home.*

TAXI TRAVEL

In Barcelona taxis are black and yellow and show a green rooftop sign on the front right corner when available for hire. The meter currently starts at €2.10 and rises in increments of €1.07 every kilometer. These rates apply 6 am–10 pm weekdays. At hours outside of these, the rates rise 20%. There are official supplements of €1 per bag for luggage.

Trips to or from a train station entail a supplemental charge of €2.10; a cab to or from the airport, or the Barcelona Cruise Terminal, adds a supplemental charge of €4.20, as do trips to or from a football match. The minimum price for taxi service to or from the Barcelona airport is €20 for terminals T1, T2, and T3, and €39 from T4. There are cabstands (*parades,* in Catalan) all over town, and you can also hail cabs on the street, though if you are too close to an official stand they may not stop. You can call for a cab by phone 24 hours a day. Drivers do not expect a tip, but rounding up the fare is standard.

CONTACTS Barna Taxi ☏ *93/322222* ⊕ *barnataxi.com.* **Radio Taxi 033** ☏ *93/303–3033 to call a cab* ⊕ *radio-taxi033.com.* **Taxi Class Rent** ☏ *93/307–0707* ⊕ *www.taxiclassrent.com/en.*

TRAIN TRAVEL

Spain's intercity services (along with some of Barcelona's local train routes) are the province of the government-run railroad system—RENFE (Red Nacional de Ferrocarriles Españoles). The high-speed AVE train now connects Barcelona and Madrid (via Lleida and Zaragoza) in less than three hours. (Spain has more high-speed tracks in service than any other country in Europe.) The fast TALGO and ALTARIA trains are efficient, though local trains remain slow and tedious. The Catalan government's FGC (Ferrocarril de la Generalitat de Catalunya) also provide train service, notably to Barcelona's commuter suburbs of Sant Cugat, Terrassa, and Sabadell.

Information on the local/commuter lines (*rodalies* in Catalan, *cercanias* in Castilian) can be found at ⊕ *www.renfe.es/cerca-nias.* Rodalies go, for example, to Sitges from Barcelona, whereas you would take a regular RENFE train to, say, Tarragona. It's important to know whether you are traveling on RENFE or on rodalies (the latter distinguished by a stylized C), so you don't end up in the wrong line.

First-class train service in Spain, with the exception of the *coche-cama* (Pullman) overnight service, barely differs from second class or *turista.* The TALGO or the AVE trains, however, are much faster than second-class carriers like the slow-poke Estrella overnight from Barcelona to Madrid, both with limited legroom and general comforts. The AVE is the exception: these sleek, comfortable bullet trains travel between Barcelona and

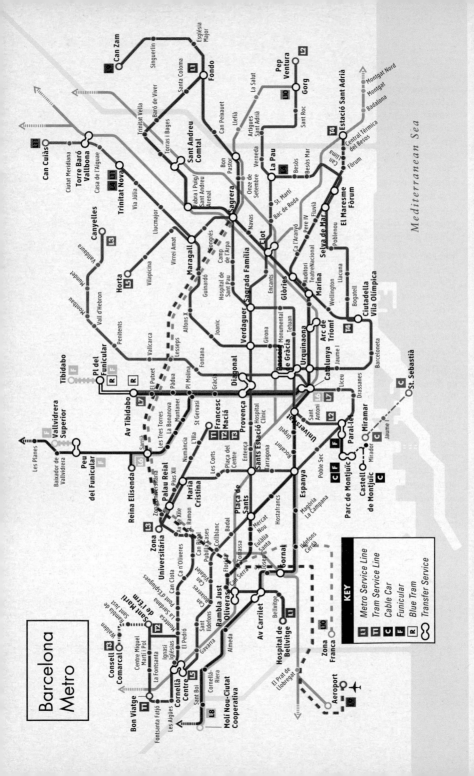

Barcelona Metro

KEY

- Metro Service Line
- Tram Service Line
- Cable Car
- Funicular
- Blue Tram
- Transfer Service

Madrid or between Madrid and Seville. Some 30 AVE trains a day connect Barcelona and Madrid, with departures from 5:50 am to 9:15 pm. Trips take from 2 hours 30 minutes to 3 hours 10 minutes.

STATIONS Estació de França ⊠ *Av. Marquès de l'Argentera 1, Born-Ribera* ☎ *912/320320 RENFE station info* ⊕ *www.renfe.com* Ⓜ *L4 Barceloneta.*
Estació de Passeig de Gràcia ⊠ *Passeig de Gràcia/Carrer Aragó, Eixample* ☎ *912/432343 station info, 912/320320 RENFE general info* ⊕ *www.renfe.com* Ⓜ *L2/L3/L4 Passeig de Gràcia.* **Estació de Sants** ⊠ *Pl. dels Països Catalans s/n, Les Corts* ☎ *912/432343 station info, 902/320320 RENFE general info* ⊕ *www. renfe.com* Ⓜ *L3/L5 Sants Estació.* **Ferrocarrils de la Generalitat de Catalunya (FGC)** ⊠ *Carrer Vergos 44, Sarrià* ☎ *93/366–3000* ⊕ *www.fgc.cat/eng/index.asp* Ⓜ *Sarrià (FGC).* **RENFE** ☎ *912/320320* ⊕ *www.renfe.com.*

INFORMATION AND PASSES Eurail ⊕ *www.eurail.com.* **Rail Europe** ☎ *800/622–8600* ⊕ *www.raileurope.com* ☎ *800/622–8600* ⊕ *www.raileurope.ca.*

Tours

ART TOURS

The Ruta del Modernisme (Moderniste Route), a self-guided tour, provides an excellent guidebook (available in English) that interprets 116 Moderniste sites from the Sagrada Família and the Palau de la Música Catalana to Art Nouveau building facades, lampposts, and paving stones. The €12 Guide, sold at the Pavellons Güell and the Institut Municipal del Paisatge Urbà (*Av. Drassanes 6*), comes with a book of vouchers good for discounts up to 50% on admission to most of the Moderniste buildings and sites in the Guide in Barcelona and 13 other towns and cities in Catalonia, as well as free guided tours in English at Pavellons Güell (daily 10:15 and 12:15)

and the Hospital de Sant Pau (daily at 10, 11, noon, and 1).

The Palau de la Música Catalana offers guided tours in English every hour on the hour from 10 to 3:30. Sagrada Família guided tours cost extra. Casa Milà offers one guided tour daily (6 pm weekdays, 11 am weekends). Architect Dominique Blinder of Urbancultours specializes in explorations of the Barcelona Jewish Quarter but can also provide tours of the Sagrada Família or virtually any architectural aspect of Barcelona.

Centre del Modernisme, Pavellons Güell
SPECIAL-INTEREST | ⊠ *Av. de Pedralbes 7, Pedralbes* ☎ *93/317–7652* ⊕ *www.rutadelmodernisme.com* ☑ *€5* Ⓜ *L3 Palau Real, Maria Cristina.*

Recinte Modernista de Sant Pau
SPECIAL-INTEREST | ⊠ *Carrer Sant Antoni Maria Claret 167, Eixample* ☎ *93/553–7801* ⊕ *www.santpaubarcelona.org/en* ☑ *From €14* Ⓜ *L5 Sant Pau/Dos de Maig.*

CULINARY TOURS

Aula Gastronómica (Cooking Classroom) has different culinary tours, including tours of the Boqueria and Santa Catarina markets with breakfast, cooking classes, and tastings, of €12 per person and up. The locals you'll meet on the tours may struggle a bit in English, but between the guides and the help of fellow travelers, everyone manages. Jane Gregg, founder of Epicurean Ways, offers gourmet and wine tours of Barcelona and Catalonia. Teresa Parker of Spanish Journeys organizes cooking classes, seasonal specials, custom cultural or culinary tours, corporate cooking retreats, or off-the-beaten-path travel.

CONTACTS Aula Gastronómica ⊠ *Carrer Sagristans 5, Entresuelo, Barri Gòtic* ☎ *93/301–1944* ⊕ *www.aulagastronomica.com/cooking-classes* Ⓜ *L4 Jaume I.* **Epicurean Ways** ☎ *434/738–2293 in U.S., 93/802–2688 in Spain* ⊕ *www.epicureanways.com.* **Spanish Journeys** ☎ *508/349–9769* ⊕ *www.spanishjourneys.com.*

BOAT TOURS

Golondrina harbor boats make short trips from the Portal de la Pau, near the Columbus monument. The fare is €7.70 for a 40-minute "Barcelona Port" tour of the harbor and €15.20 for the "Barcelona Sea" 90-minute ride out past the beaches and up the coast to the Fòrum at the eastern end of Diagonal. Departures are spring and summer (Easter week–September), daily 11:15 am–5:15 pm for the Port tour, 12:30 pm and 3:30 pm for the Sea tour; fall and winter, weekends and holidays only, 11 am–5 pm. It's closed mid-December–early January.

CONTACTS **Las Golondrinas** ⊠ *Pl. Portal de la Pau s/n, Moll de les Drassanes, La Rambla* ☎ *93/442–3106* ⊕ *lasgolondrinas. com/en* Ⓜ *L3 Drassanes.*

BUS TOURS

The Bus Turístic (9 or 9:30 am to 7 or 8 pm every 5–25 minutes, depending on the season), sponsored by the tourist office, runs on three circuits with stops at all the important sights. The blue route covers upper Barcelona; the red route tours lower Barcelona; and the green route runs from the Port Olímpic along Barcelona's beaches to the Fòrum at the eastern end of Diagonal (April through September only). A one-day ticket can be bought online (with a 10% discount) for €27 (a two-day ticket is €36). An additional €11.25 ticket (for sale on the same website) covers the fare for the Tramvía Blau, funicular, and Montjuïc cable car across the port.

The product and prices are all but identical, though the Bus Turístic is the official tourist office tour, offering discount vouchers and superior service. In the event of long lines or delays on the Bus Turístic, Hop On Hop Off Tours is a good alternative.

CONTACTS **Barcelona Hop On Hop Off Tours** ⊠ *Eixample* ☎ *871/180–005* ⊕ *www.hop-on-hop-off-bus.com/barcelona-bus-tours.* **Bus Turístic** ⊠ *Pl. de Catalunya 3,*

Eixample ☎ *93/285–3832* ⊕ *www. barcelonabusturistic.cat* Ⓜ *Catalunya.* **Julià Travel** ⊠ *Carrer Balmes 5, Eixample* ☎ *93/402–6900* ⊕ *www.juliatravel.com/ destinations/barcelona* Ⓜ *Catalunya, L1/ L2 Universitat.*

PRIVATE GUIDES

Guides from the organizations listed below are generally competent, though the quality of language skills and general showmanship may vary. For customized tours, including access to some of Barcelona's leading chefs, architects, art historians, and artists, Heritage Tours will set it all up from New York.

Barcelona Guide Bureau

GUIDED TOURS | Daily walking tours of the major sites in Barcelona are available, as well as tours to Montserrat and the Dalí Museum in Girona. Some tours offer fast-track entrance to museums and popular venues like the Sagrada Família. ⊠ *Via Laietana 54, 2–2, Born-Ribera* ☎ *93/268–2422, 667/419140 on weekends* ⊕ *www. barcelonaguidebureau.com* ✉ *From €34* Ⓜ *Urquinaona.*

Heritage Tours

SPECIAL-INTEREST | Private custom-designed tours from this company include hotels, private guides, transportation, and cuisine. ⊠ *121 W. 27th St., Suite 1201, New York* ☎ *800/378–4555 toll-free in U.S., 212/206–8400 in U.S.* ⊕ *www. heritagetours.com* ✉ *Prices vary.*

WALKING TOURS

Turisme de Barcelona offers weekend walking tours of the Barri Gòtic, the Waterfront, Picasso's Barcelona, Modernisme, a shopping circuit, and Gourmet Barcelona in English (at 10:30 am). Prices range from €15 to €21, with 10% discounts for purchases online. For private tours, Julià Travel and Pullmantur *(Bus Tours)* both lead walks around Barcelona. Tours leave from their offices, but you may be able to arrange a pickup at your hotel. Prices per person are €35 for half a day and €90 for a full day, including lunch.

For the best English-language walking tour of the medieval Jewish Quarter, Dominique Tomasov Blinder, of Urbancultours *(Art Tours)* is an architect with 13 years experience in Jewish heritage. Her tour of Jewish Barcelona is a unique combination of history, current affairs, and personal experience; learn more at ⊕ *www.urbancultours.com.*

CONTACTS Urbancultours ⊕ *www.urbancultours.com.*

Visitor Information

Turisme de Barcelona

GUIDED TOURS | In addition to being a useful resource for information, tickets, and bookings, Turisme de Barcelona offers daily walking tours of the Barri Gòtic, Picasso's Barcelona, Modernisme, and Gourmet Barcelona, among others; departure times for tours in English depend on which of the tours you choose. Book online for a 10% discount. The Picasso tour, which includes the entry fee for the Museu Picasso, is a great bargain. Tours depart from the Plaça de Catalunya tourist office. ⊠ *Pl. de Catalunya 17, soterrani, Eixample* ☎ *93/285–3834* ⊕ *bcnshop.barcelonaturisme.com/shopv3/* ⊠ *From €14* Ⓜ *Pl. de Catalunya.*

La Rambla

The promenade in the heart of premodern Barcelona was originally a watercourse, dry for most of the year, that separated the walled Ciutat Vella from the outlying Raval. In the 14th century, the city walls were extended and the arroyo was filled in, so it gradually became a thoroughfare where peddlers, farmers, and tradesmen hawked their wares. (The watercourse is still there, under the pavement. From time to time a torrential rain will fill it, and the water rises up through the drains.) The poet-playwright Federico

García Lorca called this the only street in the world he wished would never end—and in a sense, it doesn't.

Barcelona's most famous boulevard boasts a generous pedestrian strip down the middle and it is a tourist magnet. Much as you may want to avoid the crowds and the tacky, touristy shops and eateries that now cater to the crush of visitors, a stroll here is essential to your Barcelona experience. From the rendezvous point at the head of La Rambla at Café Zurich to La Boqueria produce market, the Liceu opera house, or La Rambla's lower reaches, there are crowds but also gems along this spinal column of Barcelona street life.

Sights

Casa Bruno Cuadros

BUILDING | Like something out of an amusement park, this former umbrella shop was whimsically designed (assembled is more like it) by Josep Vilaseca in 1885. A Chinese dragon with a parasol, Egyptian balconies and galleries, and a Peking lantern all reflect the Eastern style that was very much in vogue at the time of the Universal Exposition of 1888. Now housing a branch office of the Banco Bilbao Vizcaya Artentaria, this prankster of a building is much in keeping with Art Nouveau's eclectic playfulness, though it has never been taken very seriously as an expression of Modernisme and is generally omitted from most studies of Art Nouveau architecture. ⊠ *La Rambla 82, La Rambla* Ⓜ *L3 Liceu.*

★ Gran Teatre del Liceu

ARTS VENUE | Barcelona's opera house has long been considered one of the most beautiful in Europe, a rival to La Scala in Milan. First built in 1848, this cherished cultural landmark was torched in 1861, later bombed by anarchists in 1893, and once again gutted by an accidental fire in early 1994. During that most recent fire, Barcelona's soprano Montserrat

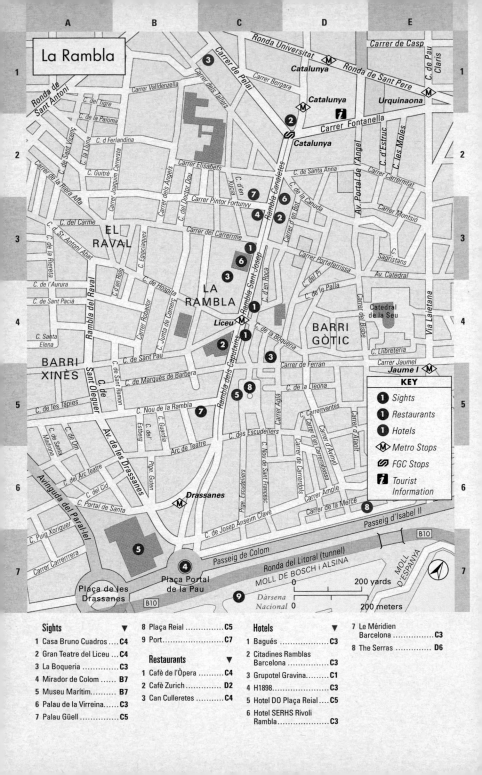

La Rambla

Sights ▼
1 Casa Bruno Cuadros **C4**
2 Gran Teatre del Liceu ... **C4**
3 La Boqueria **C3**
4 Mirador de Colom **B7**
5 Museu Marítim.......... **B7**
6 Palau de la Virreina...... **C3**
7 Palau Güell **C5**

Restaurants ▼
1 Cafè de l'Òpera **C4**
2 Cafè Zurich **D2**
3 Can Culleretes **C4**

Hotels ▼
1 Bagués **C3**
2 Citadines Ramblas
   Barcelona **C3**
3 Grupotel Gravina......... **C1**
4 H1898 .... **C3**
5 Hotel DO Plaça Reial **C5**
6 Hotel SERHS Rivoli
   Rambla.................... **C3**
7 Le Méridien
   Barcelona **C3**
8 The Serras **D6**

Plaça Reial **C5**
Port...................... **C7**

KEY
1 Sights
1 Restaurants
1 Hotels
Ⓜ Metro Stops
𝌆 FGC Stops
𝒊 Tourist Information

Caballé stood on La Rambla in tears as her beloved venue was consumed. Five years later, a restored Liceu, equipped for modern productions, opened anew. Even if you don't see an opera, you can take a tour of the building; some of the Liceu's most spectacular halls and rooms, including the glittering foyer known as the Saló dels Miralls (Room of Mirrors), were untouched by the fire of 1994, as were those of Spain's oldest social club, El Círculo del Liceu—established in 1847 and restored to its pristine original condition after the fire. ⊠ *La Rambla 51–59, La Rambla* ☎ *93/485–9914 express and guided tour information and reservations, 93/485–9931 premium visit reservations* ⊕ *www.liceubarcelona.cat* 🖃 *Variety of tours from €16* Ⓜ *L4 Liceu.*

★ La Boqueria

MARKET | Barcelona's most spectacular food market, also known as the Mercat de Sant Josep, is an explosion of life and color with small tapas bar-restaurants. A solid polychrome wall of fruits, herbs, vegetables, nuts, candied fruits, cheeses, hams, fish, and poultry greets you as you turn in from La Rambla. Under a Moderniste hangar of wrought-iron girders and stained glass, the market occupies a neoclassical square built in 1840. Highlights include the sunny greengrocer's market outside, along with Pinotxo (Pinocchio), just inside to the right, which serves some of the best food in Barcelona. The Kiosko Universal and Quim de la Boqueria both offer delicious alternatives. Don't miss the *fruits del bosc* (fruits of the forest) stand at the back of La Boqueria, with its display of wild mushrooms, herbs, nuts, and berries. To avoid crowds, go before 8 am or after 5 pm. ⊠ *La Rambla 91, La Rambla* ☎ *93/318– 2017 information desk, Tues.–Thurs. 8–3, Fri. and Sat. 8–5, 93/318–2584* ⊕ *www. boqueria.info* ⊙ *Closed Sun.* Ⓜ *Liceu.*

Mirador de Colom (*Columbus Monument*)

MEMORIAL | This Barcelona landmark to Christopher Columbus sits grandly at the foot of La Rambla along the wide harbor-front promenade of Passeig de Colom, not far from the very shipyards (Drassanes Reials) that constructed two of the ships of his tiny but immortal fleet. Standing atop the 150-foot-high iron column—the base of which is aswirl with gesticulating angels—Columbus seems to be looking out at "that far-distant shore" he discovered; in fact he's pointing, with his 18-inch-long finger, in the general direction of Sicily. For a bird's-eye view of La Rambla and the port, take the elevator to the small viewing platform (*mirador*) at the top of the column. The entrance is on the harbor side. ⊠ *Pl. Portal de la Pau s/n, Port Olímpic* ☎ *93/285– 3832* 🖃 *€6* Ⓜ *L3 Drassanes.*

★ Museu Marítim

BUILDING | **FAMILY** | The superb Maritime Museum is housed in the 13th-century Drassanes Reials (Royal Shipyards), at the foot of La Rambla adjacent to the harbor front. This vast covered complex launched the ships of Catalonia's powerful Mediterranean fleet directly from its yards into the port. Today these are the world's largest and best-preserved medieval shipyards. On the Avinguda del Paral·lel side of Drassanes is a completely intact section of the 14th- to 15th-century walls—Barcelona's third and final ramparts—that encircled El Raval along the Paral·lel and the Rondas de Sant Pau, Sant Antoni, and Universitat. Though the shipyards seem more like a cathedral than a naval construction site, the Maritime Museum is filled with vessels, including a spectacular collection of ship models. Headphones and infrared pointers provide a first-rate self-guided tour. The cafeteria-restaurant Norai, open daily 9 am to 8 pm, is Barcelona's hands-down winner for dining in a setting of medieval elegance, and has a charming terrace. ⊠ *Av. de les Drassanes s/n, La Rambla* ☎ *93/342–9920* ⊕ *www.mmb.cat* 🖃 *€10 (includes admission to Santa Eulàlia clipper); free Sun. after 3* ⊙ *Closed Mon.* Ⓜ *L3 Drassanes.*

Visit La Boqueria market early (it opens at 8 am) to avoid the crowds as you discover all this colorful institution has to offer.

Palau de la Virreina (*La Virreina Centre de la Imatge*)

CASTLE/PALACE | The baroque Virreina Palace, built by a viceroy to Peru in the late 18th century, is now a major center for themed exhibitions of contemporary art, film, and photography. The **Tiquet Rambles** office on the ground floor, run by the city government's Institut del Cultura (ICUB), open daily 10–8:30, is the place to go for information and last-minute tickets to concerts, theater and dance performances, gallery shows, and museums. The portal to the palace, and the pediments carved with elaborate floral designs, are a must-see. ⊠ *Rambla de les Flors 99, La Rambla* ☎ *93/316–1000* ⊕ *lavirreina.bcn.cat* 🎟 *Free; €3 charge for some exhibits* 🕙 *Closed Mon.* Ⓜ *Liceu.*

★ Palau Güell

BUILDING | Gaudí built this mansion in 1886–89 for textile baron Count Eusebi de Güell Bacigalupi, his most important patron. The dark facade is a dramatic foil for the brilliance of the inside, where spear-shape Art Nouveau columns frame the windows, rising to support a series of detailed and elaborately carved wood ceilings. The basement stables are famous for the "fungiform" (mushroom-like) columns carrying the weight of the whole building. Don't miss the figures of the faithful hounds, with the rings in their mouths for hitching horses, or the wooden bricks laid down in lieu of cobblestones in the entryway upstairs. The dining room is dominated by an Art Nouveau fireplace in the shape of a deeply curving horseshoe arch and walls with floral and animal motifs. Gaudí is most himself on the roof, where his playful, polychrome ceramic chimneys seem like preludes to later works like the Park Güell and La Pedrera. ⊠ *Nou de la Rambla 3–5, La Rambla* ☎ *93/472–5771, 93/472–5775* ⊕ *www.palauguell.cat/en* 🎟 *€12; free 1st Sun. of month, 5–8 pm* 🕙 *Closed Mon.* ☞ *Guided tours (1 hr) in English Fri. at 10:30 am and Sat. at 2:30 pm at no additional cost* Ⓜ *L3 Drassanes, Liceu.*

Neighborhood Rambles

Carrer dels Escudellers

Named for the terrissaires (earthenware potters) who worked here making escudellas (bowls or stew pots), this colorful loop is an interesting subtrip off La Rambla. Go left at Plaça del Teatre and you'll pass the landmark Grill Room at No. 8, an Art Nouveau saloon with graceful wooden decor and an ornate oak bar; next is La Fonda Escudellers, another lovely, glass- and stone-encased dining emporium. At Nos. 23–25 is Barcelona's most comprehensive ceramics display, Art Escudellers. Farther down, on the right, is Los Caracoles, once among the most traditional of Barcelona's restaurants and now for tourists with deep pockets. Another 100 yards down Carrer Escudellers is Plaça George Orwell, named for the author of Homage to Catalonia, a space created to bring light and air into this formerly iffy neighborhood.

Take a right on on the narrow Carrer de la Carabassa—a street best known in days past for its houses of ill fame, and one of the few remaining streets in the city still entirely paved with cobblestones. It is arched over with two graceful bridges that once connected the houses with their adjacent gardens. At the end of the street, looming atop her own basilica, is Nostra Senyora de la Mercè (Our Lady of Mercy), one of the Barcelona waterfront's most impressive sights. From the Mercè, a walk out Carrer Ample (to the right) leads back to the bottom of La Rambla. The colmado (grocery store) on the corner as you make the turn, La Lionesa (Carrer Ample 21), is one of Barcelona's best-preserved 19th-century shops. At No. 7 is the Calçats Artesans Solé shoe store, known for nearly a century for its handmade footwear.

Carrer Petritxol

Just steps from La Rambla and lined with art galleries, xocolaterías (chocolate shops), and stationers, this narrow passageway dates back to the 15th century, when it was used as a shortcut through the backyard of a local property owner. Working up Petritxol from Plaça del Pi, stop to admire the late-17th-century sgraffito design on the facade over the Ganiveteria Roca knife store, the place for cutlery in Barcelona. Next on the right at Petritxol 2 is the 200-year-old Dulcinea, with a portrait of the great Catalan playwright Àngel Guimerà (1847–1924) over the fireplace; drop in for the house specialty, the suizo ("Swiss" hot chocolate and whipped cream). Note the plaque to Àngel Guimerà over No. 4 and the Art Box gallery at Nos. 1–3 across the street. At No. 5 is Sala Parès, founded in 1840, the dean of Barcelona's art galleries, where major figures like Isidre Nonell, Santiago Russinyol, and Picasso have shown their work. Xocoa at No. 9 is another popular chocolate shop. Look carefully at the "curtains" carved into the wooden door at No. 11; the store is Granja la Pallaresa, yet another enclave of chocolate and ensaimada (a light-looking but deadly sweet Mallorcan pastry, with confectioner's sugar dusted on top).

Plaça Reial

PLAZA | Nobel Prize–winning novelist Gabriel García Márquez, architect and urban planner Oriol Bohigas, and Pasqual Maragall, former president of the Catalonian Generalitat, are among the many famous people said to have acquired apartments overlooking this elegant square, a chiaroscuro masterpiece in which neoclassical symmetry clashes with big-city street funk. Plaça Reial is bordered by stately ocher facades with balconies overlooking the wrought-iron **Fountain of the Three Graces,** and an array of lampposts designed by Gaudí in 1879. Cafés and restaurants—several of them excellent—line the square. Plaça Reial is most colorful on Sunday morning, when collectors gather to trade stamps and coins; after dark it's a center of downtown nightlife for the jazz-minded, the young, and the adventurous (it's best to be streetwise touring this area in the late hours). Bar Glaciar, on the uphill corner toward La Rambla, is a booming beer station for young international travelers. Tarantos has top flamenco performances, and Jamboree offers world-class jazz. ✉ *La Rambla* Ⓜ *L3 Liceu.*

Port

MARINA | Beyond the Columbus monument—behind the ornate Duana (now the Barcelona Port Authority headquarters)—is **La Rambla de Mar,** a boardwalk with a drawbridge designed to allow boats into and out of the inner harbor. La Rambla de Mar extends out to the **Moll d'Espanya,** with its Maremagnum shopping center (open on Sunday, unusual for Barcelona) and the excellent **Aquarium.** Next to the Duana you can board a Golondrina boat for a tour of the port and the waterfront or, from the Moll de Barcelona on the right, take a cable car to Montjuïc or Barceloneta. Trasmediterránea and Baleària passenger ferries leave for Italy and the Balearic Islands from the Moll de Barcelona; at the end of the quay is Barcelona's World Trade Center and the Eurostars Grand Marina Hotel. ✉ *Port Olímpic* Ⓜ *Drassanes.*

 **Restaurants**

Cafè de l'Òpera

$ | CAFÉ | Directly across from the Liceu opera house, this high-ceiling Art Nouveau café has welcomed operagoers and performers for more than 100 years. It's a central point on the Rambla tourist traffic pattern, so locals are increasingly hard to find, but the café has hung onto its atmosphere of faded glory nonetheless. **Known for:** Art Nouveau decor; good for a drink; late-night hours. Ⓢ *Average main: €12* ✉ *La Rambla 74, La Rambla* ☎ *93/317–7585* ⊕ *www.cafeoperabcn. com* Ⓜ *Liceu.*

Cafè Zurich

$ | CAFÉ | This traditional café at the top of La Rambla and directly astride the main metro and transport hub remains the city's prime meeting point. Forget the food and enjoy a beer or coffee at a table on the terrace, perhaps the best spot in the city to observe street life. **Known for:** people-watching far better than the food; sunny terrace; watch for pickpockets. Ⓢ *Average main: €10* ✉ *Pl. de Catalunya 1, La Rambla* ☎ *93/317–9153* Ⓜ *Catalunya.*

Can Culleretes

$ | CATALAN | Just off La Rambla in the Barri Gòtic, this family-run restaurant founded in 1786 displays tradition in both decor and culinary offerings. Generations of the Manubens and Agut families have kept this unpretentious spot—Barcelona's oldest restaurant, listed in the *Guinness World Records*—popular for more than two centuries. **Known for:** Barcelona's oldest restaurant; traditional Catalan cuisine; large portions. Ⓢ *Average main: €10* ✉ *Quintana 5, La Rambla* ☎ *93/317–3022* ⊕ *www.culleretes.com* ⊘ *Closed Mon., and 4 wks in July and 2 wks in Aug. No dinner Sun.* Ⓜ *Liceu5.*

A shipshape collection of nautical wonders is on display at the Museu Marítim.

Hotels

Bagués

$$$$ | HOTEL | The luxury of the Eixample has worked is way down to La Rambla, as this boutique gem (formerly the shop and atelier of the well-known Art Nouveau jeweler of the same name) bears ample witness. **Pros:** steps from the opera house; view of the cathedral and port from the rooftop terrace; free entrance to the Egyptian Museum of Barcelona. **Cons:** rooms a bit small for the price. $ *Rooms from: €291* ✉ *La Rambla 105, La Rambla* ☎ *93/343–5000* ⊕ *www. hotelbagues.com* ⤴ *28 rooms, 3 suites* ⍥ *No meals* Ⓜ *Pl. Catalunya, L3 Liceu.*

Citadines Ramblas Barcelona

$$$$ | HOTEL | FAMILY | Located in two buildings at the upper end of La Rambla, Citadines is an excellent choice for families, groups of friends, or long-term visitors; the accommodations consist of apartments with sitting rooms and one-room studios with kitchenettes and small dining areas. **Pros:** central location; spacious rooms; pet-friendly. **Cons:** basic amenities; no pool; rooms only cleaned during six-night stays (and only once). $ *Rooms from: €280* ✉ *La Rambla 122, La Rambla* ☎ *93/270–1111* ⊕ *www.cita-dines.com* ⤴ *115 studios, 16 apartments* ⍥ *No meals* Ⓜ *Catalunya.*

Grupotel Gravina

$ | HOTEL | On a side street near the Plaça de Catalunya and just five minutes from the MACBA and the Raval, this modern hotel offers comfort and prime location at a very affordable price. **Pros:** great location; room with private terrace for extra €30; friendly, competent staff. **Cons:** rooms are a bit small; generic furniture. $ *Rooms from: €120* ✉ *Gravina 12, La Rambla* ☎ *93/301–6868* ⊕ *www.grupo-telgravina.com* ⤴ *84 rooms* ⍥ *No meals* Ⓜ *Catalunya, L1/L2 Universitat.*

★ H1898

$$$$ | HOTEL | Overlooking La Rambla, this imposing mansion (once the headquarters of the Compañiá General de Tabacos de Filipinas) couldn't be better located—especially for opera fans, with the Liceu

just around the corner. **Pros:** impeccable service; ideal location for exploring the Barri Gòtic; historic spaces plus modern amenities like a spa and roof deck. **Cons:** subway rumble discernible in lower rooms on the Rambla side; no pets; some street noise from the Rambla in lower rooms. Ⓢ *Rooms from: €238* ✉ *La Rambla 109, La Rambla* ☎ *93/552–9552* ⊕ *www.hotel1898.com* ⤴ *169 rooms* ❙⊙❙ *No meals* Ⓜ *Catalunya, Liceu.*

Hotel DO Plaça Reial

$$$$ | HOTEL | Just at the entrance to the neoclassical Plaça Reial, this charming addition to Barcelona's growing collection of boutique hotels—with its three restaurants, La Terraza (under the arcades on the square), El Terrat, and La Cuina (downstairs under graceful brick vaulting)—is a find for foodies and lovers of tasteful design. **Pros:** walking distance from old city center; helpful multilingual staff; 24-hour room service. **Cons:** neighborhood can be rowdy at night; no pets; street noise discernible in lower rooms. Ⓢ *Rooms from: €340* ✉ *Pl. Reial 1, La Rambla* ☎ *93/481–3666* ⊕ *www. hoteldoreial.com* ⤴ *18 rooms* ❙⊙❙ *Free Breakfast* Ⓜ *L3 Liceu.*

Hotel SERHS Rivoli Rambla

$$$ | HOTEL | Behind this traditional upper-Rambla facade lies a surprisingly whimsical interior with marble floors and artwork by well-known Barcelona artist Perico Pastor in the lobby. **Pros:** ideal location; Room 601 is the best in the house; good views from the rooftop terrace. **Cons:** service inconsistent; no pool or spa; two-night minimum stay for online bookings. Ⓢ *Rooms from: €205* ✉ *La Rambla 128, La Rambla* ☎ *93/481–7676* ⊕ *www. hotelserhsrivolirambla.com* ⤴ *126 rooms* ❙⊙❙ *No meals* Ⓜ *Catalunya, L3 Liceu.*

★ Le Méridien Barcelona

$$$$ | HOTEL | There's no dearth of hotels along La Rambla in the heart of the city, but few rival the upscale Le Méridien, popular with businesspeople and visiting celebrities alike for its suites overlooking the promenade and cozy amenities. **Pros:** central location; soaker tubs in deluxe rooms; Mediterranean suites have large private terraces. **Cons:** no pool; rooms small for the price; €60-per-day surcharge for pets. Ⓢ *Rooms from: €249* ✉ *La Rambla 111, La Rambla* ☎ *93/318–6200* ⊕ *www.lemeridien.com/barcelona* ⤴ *231 rooms* ❙⊙❙ *No meals* Ⓜ *Catalunya L3 Liceu.*

The Serras

$$$$ | HOTEL | Picasso had his first studio here (on the sixth floor) when the building was all walk-up flats; today, designer Eva Martinez has found ingenious, tasteful ways to make the best of the space and its limits: a small lobby with a comfortable sofa suite leads back to the long, narrow El Informal, the hotel's excellent restaurant presided over by award-winning young chef Marc Gascons; a mezzanine hosts the 24-hour lounge bar and a small gym. **Pros:** romantic "El Sueño" rooftop terrace with DJ on weekends; fun in-room amenities like yoga mats; excellent restaurant El Formal. **Cons:** no sauna or spa; hard on the budget. Ⓢ *Rooms from: €350* ✉ *Passeig Colom 9, La Rambla* ☎ *93/169–1868* ⊕ *www.hoteltheserrasbarcelona.com* ⤴ *28 rooms* ❙⊙❙ *Free Breakfast* Ⓜ *L4 Barceloneta.*

Nightlife

The liveliest pedestrian promenade in the city bustles with a dizzying array of tourist-baiting shops, eateries, and arched paths to Plaça Reial's euphoric nightlife scene. Casual and unpretentious, the scene erupts nightly with a parade of rambunctious crowds of expats, curious interlopers, and assorted celebrations.

BARS

Boadas

BARS/PUBS | Barcelona's oldest cocktail bar opened its doors in 1933 and quickly gained a reputation as the only place to enjoy a genuine mojito. The faithful—who still include a few of the city's luminaries—have been flocking ever since, despite the bar's decidedly lackluster decor. The space has the look and feel of an old-fashioned private club and is still the spot to watch old-school barmen in dapper duds mixing drinks the way tradition dictates. ✉ *Tallers 1, La Rambla* ☏ *93/318–9592* ⊕ *boadascocktails.com* Ⓜ *Catalunya.*

Jamboree-Jazz and Dance-Club

MUSIC CLUBS | This legendary nightspot has hosted some of the world's most influential jazz musicians since its opening in 1960. Decades later, the club continues to offer two nightly shows and remains a notable haven for new generations of jazz and blues aficionados. After the last performance, the spot transforms into a late-night dance club playing soul, hip-hop, and R&B. ✉ *Pl. Reial 17, La Rambla* ☏ *93/319–1789* ⊕ *www.masimas.com/en/jamboree* Ⓜ *Liceu.*

Barri Gòtic

A labyrinth of medieval buildings, squares, and narrow cobblestone streets, the Barri Gòtic comprises the area around the Catedral de la Seu, built over Roman ruins you can still visit and filled with the Gothic structures that marked the zenith of Barcelona's power in the 15th century. On certain corners you feel as if you're making a genuine excursion back in time.

The Barri Gòtic rests squarely atop the first Roman settlement. Sometimes referred to as the *rovell d'ou* (the yolk of the egg), this high ground the Romans called Mons Taber coincides almost exactly with the early 1st- to 4th-century fortified town of Barcino. Sights to see here include the Plaça del Rei, the remains of Roman Barcino underground beneath the Museum of the History of the City, the Plaça Sant Jaume and the area around the onetime Roman Forum,

the medieval Jewish Quarter, and the ancient Plaça Sant Just.

Sights

Ajuntament de Barcelona

BUILDING | The 15th-century city hall on Plaça Sant Jaume faces the Palau de la Generalitat, with its mid-18th-century neoclassical facade, across the square once occupied by the Roman Forum. The Ajuntament is a rich repository of sculpture and painting by the great Catalan masters, from Marès to Gargallo to Clarà, from Subirachs to Miró and Llimona. Inside is the famous Saló de Cent, from which the Consell de Cent, Europe's oldest democratic parliament, governed Barcelona between 1373 and 1714. The Saló de les Croniques (Hall of Chronicles) is decorated with Josep Maria Sert's immense black-and-burnished-gold murals (1928) depicting the early-14th-century Catalan campaign in Byzantium and Greece under the command of Roger de Flor. The city hall is open to visitors on Sunday mornings 10–1:30, with guided visits in English at 10; on local holidays; and for occasional concerts or events in the Saló de Cent. ✉ *Pl. Sant Jaume 1, Barri Gòtic* ☏ *93/402–7000* ⊕ *ajuntament.barcelona.cat/en* 🆓 *Free* Ⓜ *L4 Jaume I, L3 Liceu.*

Baixada de Santa Eulàlia

RELIGIOUS SITE | Down Carrer Sant Sever from the side door of the cathedral cloister, past Carrer Sant Domènec del Call and the Església de Sant Sever, is a tiny shrine, in an alcove overhead, dedicated to the 4th-century martyr Santa Eulàlia, patron saint of the city. Down this hill, or *baixada* (descent), Eulàlia was rolled in a barrel filled with—as the Jacint Verdaguer verse in ceramic tile on the wall reads—*glavis i ganivets de dos talls* (swords and double-edged knives), the final of the 13 tortures to which she was subjected before her crucifixion at Plaça del Pedró. ✉ *Carrer Sant Sever s/n, Barri Gòtic* Ⓜ *Liceu, Jaume I.*

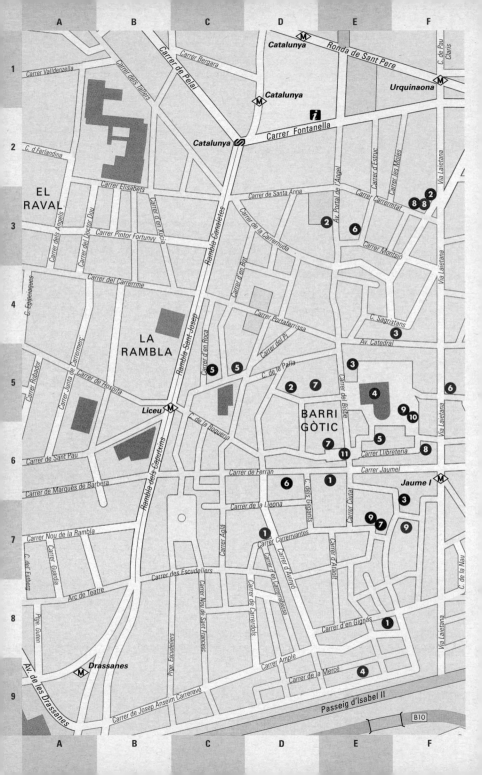

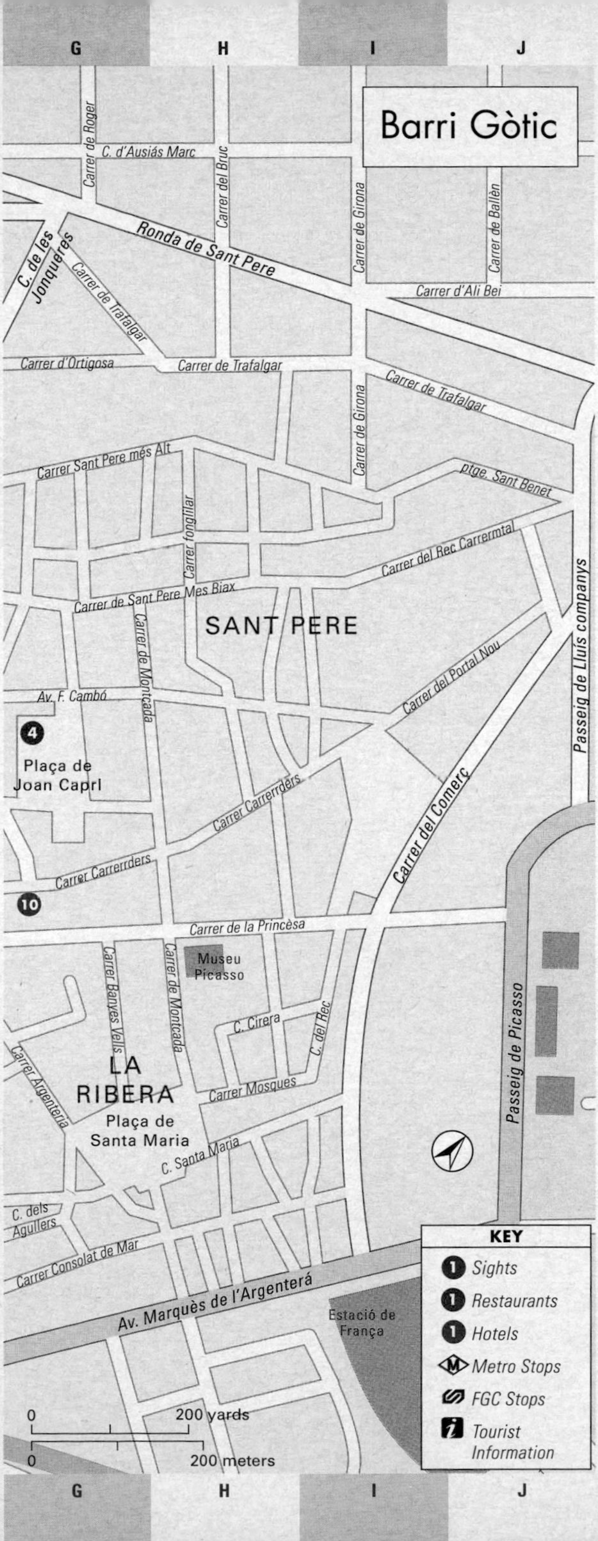

Barri Gòtic

SANT PERE

Plaça de Joan Caprl

LA RIBERA

Plaça de Santa Maria

Museu Picasso

Estació de França

KEY

- ● Sights
- ● Restaurants
- ● Hotels
- Ⓜ Metro Stops
- Ⓕ FGC Stops
- 🛈 Tourist Information

0 — 200 yards
0 — 200 meters

El Call: The Jewish Quarter

Barcelona's Jewish Quarter, El Call (a name derived from the Hebrew word *qahal,* or "meeting place"), is just to the Rambla side of the Palau de la Generalitat. Carrer del Call, Carrer de Sant Domènec del Call, Carrer Marlet, and Arc de Sant Ramón del Call mark the heart of the medieval ghetto. Confined by law to this area at the end of the 7th century (one reason the streets in Calls or Aljamas were so narrow was that their inhabitants could only build into the streets for more space), Barcelona's Jews were the private bankers to Catalonia's sovereign counts (only Jews could legally lend money). The Jewish community also produced many leading physicians, translators, and scholars in medieval Barcelona, largely because the Jewish faith rested on extensive Talmudic and textual study, thus promoting a high degree of literacy. The reproduction of a plaque bearing Hebrew text on the corner of Carrer Marlet and Arc de Sant Ramón del Call was the only physical reminder of the Jewish presence here until the medieval synagogue reopened as a historical site in 2003.

The **Sinagoga Major de Barcelona** (✉ *Carrer Marlet 2, Barri Gòtic* ⊕ *www. calldebarcelona.org* 🔖 *€3* ⊘ *Weekdays 11–5:30, weekends 11–3*), the restored original synagogue at the corner of Marlet and Sant Domènec del Call, is virtually all that survives of the Jewish presence in medieval Barcelona. Tours are given in English, Hebrew, and Spanish, and a booklet in English (€3) explains the history of the community.

The story of Barcelona's Jewish community came to a bloody end in August 1391, when during a time of famine and pestilence a nationwide outbreak of anti-Semitic violence reached Barcelona, with catastrophic results: nearly the entire Jewish population was murdered or forced to convert to Christianity.

Casa de l'Ardiaca (*Archdeacon's House*)
BUILDING | The interior of this 15th-century building, home of the Municipal Archives (upstairs), has superb views of the remains of the 4th-century Roman watchtowers and walls. Look at the Montjuïc sandstone carefully, and you will see blocks taken from other buildings carved and beveled into decorative shapes, proof of the haste of the Romans to fortify the site as the Visigoths approached from the north, when the Pax Romana collapsed. In the center of the lovely courtyard here, across from the Santa Llúcia chapel, is a fountain; on the day of Corpus Christi in June the fountain impressively supports *l'ou com balla,* or "the dancing egg," a Barcelona tradition in which eggs are set to bobbing atop jets of water in various places around the city. ✉ *Carrer de Santa Llúcia 1, Barri Gòtic* ☎ *93/256–2255* Ⓜ *L3 Liceu, L4 Jaume I.*

★ **Catedral de la Seu**
BUILDING | Barcelona's cathedral is a repository of centuries of the city's history and legend—although as a work of architecture visitors might find it a bit of a disappointment. Don't miss the beautifully carved choir stalls of the Knights of the Golden Fleece; the intricately and elaborately sculpted organ loft over the door out to Plaça Sant Iu; the series of 60-odd wood sculptures of evangelical figures along the exterior lateral walls of the choir; and, in the crypt, the tomb of Santa Eulàlia. The leafy, palm tree–shaded **cloister** surrounds a tropical garden,

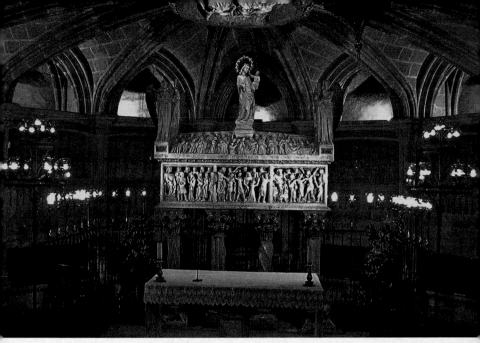

The ornate Gothic interior of the Catedral de la Seu is always enclosed in shadows, even at high noon.

and a pool populated by 13 snow-white geese, one for each of the tortures inflicted upon St. Eulàlia in an effort to break her faith. In front of the cathedral is the grand square of **Plaça de la Seu,** where on Saturday from 6 pm to 8 pm, Sunday morning, and occasional evenings, barcelonins gather to dance the *sardana,* the circular folk dance. ⊠ *Pl. de la Seu s/n, Barri Gòtic* ☎ *93/342–8262* ⊕ *www.catedralbcn.org* ✉ *Free weekdays 8–12:45 and 5:45–7:30, Sat. 8–12:45 and 5:15–8, Sun. 8–1:30 and 5:15–8; €7 donation weekdays 1–5:30, Sat. 1–5, Sun. 2–5; choir €3; rooftop €3* Ⓜ *L4 Jaume I.*

Columnes del Temple d'August (*Columns of the Temple of Augustus*)
ARCHAEOLOGICAL SITE | The highest point in Roman Barcelona is marked with a circular millstone at the entrance to the Centre Excursionista de Catalunya, a club dedicated to exploring the mountains and highlands of Catalonia on foot and on skis. Inside the entryway on the right are some of the best-preserved 1st- and 2nd-century Corinthian Roman columns

in Europe. Massive, fluted, and crowned with the typical Corinthian acanthus leaves in two distinct rows under eight fluted sheaths, these columns remain only because Barcelona's early Christians elected, atypically, not to build their cathedral over the site of the previous temple. The Temple of Augustus, dedicated to the Roman emperor, occupied the northwest corner of the Roman Forum, which coincided approximately with today's Plaça Sant Jaume. ⊠ *Centre Excursionista de Catalunya, Carrer Paradís 10, Barri Gòtic* ☎ *93/315–2311 Centre Excursionista* Ⓜ *L4 Jaume I.*

Els Quatre Gats–Casa Martí
ARTS VENUE | Built by Josep Puig i Cadafalch for the Martí family, this Art Nouveau house, a three-minute walk from the cathedral, was the fountainhead of bohemianism in Barcelona. It was here in 1897 that four friends, notable dandies all—Ramon Casas, Pere Romeu, Santiago Russinyol, and Miguel Utrillo—started a café called the Quatre Gats (Four Cats), meaning to make it *the* place for artists

and art lovers to gather. (One of their wisest decisions was to mount a show, in February 1900, for an up-and-coming young painter named Pablo Picasso.) The exterior was decorated with figures by sculptor Eusebi Arnau (1864–1934). Inside, Els Quatre Gats hasn't changed one iota: pride of place goes to the Casas self-portrait, smoking his pipe, comically teamed up on a tandem bicycle with Romeu. Drop in for a café au lait and you just might end up seated in Picasso's chair. ⊠ *Carrer Montsió 3 bis, Barri Gòtic* ☎ *93/302–4140* ⊕ *www.4gats.com* Ⓜ *Pl. Catalunya, L4 Jaume I, L4 Urquinaona.*

Generalitat de Catalunya

GOVERNMENT BUILDING | Opposite city hall, the Palau de la Generalitat is the seat of the autonomous Catalan government. Seen through the front windows of this ornate 15th-century palace, the gilded ceiling of the Saló de Sant Jordi (St. George's Hall), named for Catalonia's dragon-slaying patron saint, gives an idea of the lavish decor within. Carrer del Bisbe, running along the right side of the building from the square to the cathedral, offers a favorite photo op: the ornate gargoyle-bedecked Gothic bridge overhead, connecting the Generalitat to the building across the street. The Generalitat opens to the public on the second and fourth weekends of the month, with free one-hour guided tours in English (request in advance), through the Generalitat website. There are carillon concerts here on Sunday at noon, another opportunity to see inside. ⊠ *Pl. de Sant Jaume 4, Barri Gòtic* ☎ *93/402–4600* ⊕ *www.gencat.cat* Ⓜ *L4 Jaume I, L3 Liceu.*

★ Museu d'Història de Barcelona

(*Museum of the History of Barcelona [MUHBA]*)

ARCHAEOLOGICAL SITE | This fascinating museum just off Plaça del Rei traces Barcelona's evolution from its first Iberian settlement through its Roman and Visigothic ages and beyond. The Romans took the city during the Punic Wars, and you can tour underground remains of their Colonia Favencia Iulia Augusta Paterna Barcino (Favored Colony of the Father Julius Augustus Barcino) via metal walkways. Some 43,000 square feet of archaeological artifacts, from the walls of houses, to mosaics and fluted columns, workshops (for pressing olive oil and salted fish paste), and street systems, can be found in large part beneath the plaça. See how the Visgoths and their descendants built the early medieval walls on top of these ruins, recycling chunks of Roman stone and concrete, bits of columns, and even headstones. In the ground-floor gallery is a striking collection of marble busts and funerary urns discovered in the course of the excavations. ⊠ *Palau Padellàs, Pl. del Rei s/n, Barri Gòtic* ☎ *93/256–2100* ⊕ *ajuntament.barcelona.cat/museuhistoria/en/* 🎫 *From €7 (free with Barcelona Card, 1st Sun. of month, and all other Sun. after 3)* ⊗ *Closed Mon.* Ⓜ *L4 Jaume I, L3 Liceu.*

Palau del Lloctinent (*Lieutenant's Palace*)

CASTLE/PALACE | The three facades of the Palau face Carrer dels Comtes de Barcelona on the cathedral side, the Baixada de Santa Clara, and Plaça del Rei. Typical of late Gothic–early Renaissance Catalan design, it was constructed by Antoni Carbonell between 1549 and 1557, and remains one of the Gothic Quarter's most graceful buildings. The heavy stone arches over the entry, the central patio, and the intricately coffered wooden roof over the stairs are all good examples of noble 16th-century architecture. The door on the stairway is a 1975 Josep Maria Subirachs work portraying scenes from the life of Sant Jordi and the history of Catalonia. The Palau del Lloctinent was inhabited by the king's official emissary or viceroy to Barcelona during the 16th and 17th centuries; it now houses the historical materials of the Archivo de la Corona de Aragón (Archive of the Crown of Aragon), and offers an excellent exhibit on the life and times of Jaume

I, one of early Catalonia's most important figures. The patio also occasionally hosts early-music concerts, and during the Corpus Christi celebration is one of the main venues for the ou com balla, when an egg "dances" on the fountain amid an elaborate floral display. ⊠ *Carrer dels Comtes de Barcelona 2, Barri Gòtic* ☎ *93/485–4285 archives office* ⊕ *www. mecd.gob.es* Ⓜ *L4 Jaume I.*

★ Plaça del Rei

ARCHAEOLOGICAL SITE | This little square is as compact a nexus of history as anything the Barri Gòtic has to offer. Long held to be the scene of Columbus's triumphal return from his first voyage to the New World—the precise spot where Ferdinand and Isabella received him is purportedly on the stairs fanning out from the corner of the square—the **Palau Reial Major** (admission included in the €7 entrance fee for the Museu d'Història de Barcelona; closed Monday) was the official royal residence in Barcelona. The main room is the **Saló del Tinell,** a magnificent banquet hall built in 1362. To the left is the **Palau del Lloctinent** (Lieutenant's Palace); towering overhead in the corner is the dark 15th-century **Torre Mirador del Rei Martí** (King Martin's Watchtower). ⊠ *Pl. del Rei s/n, Barri Gòtic* Ⓜ *L3 Liceu, L4 Jaume I.*

Plaça Sant Jaume

GOVERNMENT BUILDING | Facing each other across this oldest epicenter of Barcelona (and often on politically opposite sides as well) are the seat of Catalonia's regional government, the Generalitat de Catalunya, in the **Palau de La Generalitat,** and the City Hall, the Ajuntament de Barcelona, in the **Casa de la Ciutat.** This square was the site of the Roman forum 2,000 years ago, though subsequent construction filled the space with buildings. The square was cleared in the 1840s, but the two imposing government buildings are actually much older: the Ajuntament dates back to the 14th century, and the

Generalitat was built between the 15th and mid-17th century. ⊠ *Barri Gòtic* ⊙ *Closed weekdays* ☞ *Tours of Ajuntament (in Catalan, Spanish, and English) weekends 10–2; tours of Generalitat on 2nd and 4th weekends of month 10:30–1, by reservation only (bring your passport)* Ⓜ *Jaume I.*

🍴 Restaurants

Agut

$$ | CATALAN | Wainscoting and 1950s canvases are the background for the mostly Catalan crowd in this homey restaurant in the lower reaches of the Barri Gòtic. Agut was founded in 1924, and its popularity has never waned—after all, hearty Catalan fare at a fantastic value is always in demand. **Known for:** must-try civet of wild boar; local wines; local favorite. Ⓢ *Average main: €17* ⊠ *Gignàs 16, Barri Gòtic* ☎ *93/315–1709* ⊙ *Closed Mon., and 3 wks in Aug. No dinner Sun.* Ⓜ *Jaume I.*

Caelis

$$$$ | CATALAN | Situated in the Hotel Ohla Barcelona, near the Palau de la Música Catalana, Caelis keeps its starred, fine-dining style and adds the pizzazz of open-kitchen show cooking. The two tasting menus (€92 and €135) change regularly and you can pick a course from them as an à la carte alternative. **Known for:** refined fine dining; open kitchen; Michelin-starred. Ⓢ *Average main: €42* ⊠ *Via Laietana 49, Barri Gòtic* ☎ *93/510–1205* ⊕ *www.caelis.com* ⊙ *Closed Sun. and Mon. No lunch Tues.* Ⓜ *Urquinaona.*

Cafè de l'Acadèmia

$$ | CATALAN | With wicker chairs, stone walls, and classical music, this place is sophisticated-rustic in style. Contemporary Mediterranean cuisine specialties such as *timbal d'escalibada amb formatge de cabra* (roast vegetable salad with goat cheese) make it more than just a café. **Known for:** lively terrace; great set lunch; private wine cellar for larger

groups. $ *Average main: €16* ✉ *Lledó
1, Barri Gòtic* ☎ *93/319–8253* ☉ *Closed
weekends, and 3 wks in Aug.* Ⓜ *Jaume I.*

Cuines Santa Caterina

$ | **ECLECTIC** | A lovingly restored market
designed by the late Enric Miralles and
completed by his widow Benedetta
Tagliabue provides a spectacular setting
for one of the city's most original dining
operations. Under the undulating wood-
en superstructure of the market, the
breakfast and tapas bar offers a variety of
international culinary specialties. **Known
for:** open all day; vegetarian options;
Mediterranean fare. $ *Average main: €14*
✉ *Av. Francesc Cambó 16, Born-Ribera*
☎ *93/268–9918* ⊕ *www.grupotragaluz.
com* Ⓜ *Urquinaona, Jaume I.*

Irati Taverna Basca

$$ | **BASQUE** | There's only one drawback
to this lively Basque bar between Plaça
del Pi and La Rambla: it's narrow at the
street end, and harder to squeeze into
than the Barcelona metro at rush hour.
Skip the tapas on the bar and opt for the
plates brought out piping-hot from the
kitchen. **Known for:** quick bites; Basque
specialties; txakoli sparkling wine. $ *Av-
erage main: €21* ✉ *Cardenal Casañas
17, Barri Gòtic* ☎ *93/302–3084* ⊕ *www.
iratitavernabasca.com* Ⓜ *Liceu.*

La Cerería

$ | **VEGETARIAN** | At the corner of Baixada
de Sant Miquel and Passatge de Crèdit,
this humble terrace and musical instru-
ment store/café has charm to spare. The
tables in the Passatge itself are shady
and breezy in summer, and the vegetar-
ian and vegan cuisine is organic and cre-
ative. **Known for:** creative vegetarian and
vegan cuisine; tasty escalivada; next to
birthplace of Catalan painter Joan Miró.
$ *Average main: €10* ✉ *Baixada de Sant
Miquel 3–5, Barri Gòtic* ☎ *93/301–8510*
☉ *Closed Mon.* Ⓜ *Liceu.*

La Palma

$ | **CAFÉ** | Behind the Plaça Sant Jaume's
ajuntament (city hall), toward the post
office, sits this cozy and ancient café.
An old favorite of 20th-century artists
ranging from Salvador Dalí to Pablo Picas-
so, it has marble tables, wine barrels,
sausages hanging from the ceiling, and
newspapers to pore over. **Known for:** local
wines; historic setting; authentic tapas.
$ *Average main: €12* ✉ *Palma Sant Just
7, Barri Gòtic* ☎ *93/315–0656* ⊕ *www.
bodegalapalma.com* ▭ *No credit cards*
☉ *Closed Sun.* Ⓜ *Jaume I.*

La Plassohla

$ | **TAPAS** | A trendy international crowd
packs this place, sampling tapas such
as free-range eggs cooked at low
temperature with mushrooms, and
charcoal-grilled fresh mussels with
tomato sauce. The stylish, high-ceilinged
space keeps noise levels under control,
and huge windows allow both natural
light and views of passing street life.
Known for: sophisticated atmosphere;
open late; cheap fixed lunch. $ *Average
main: €15* ✉ *Via Laietana 49, Barri Gòtic*
☎ *93/504–5100* ⊕ *www.ohlabarcelona.
com* Ⓜ *Urquinaona.*

Pla

$$ | **CATALAN** | Filled with couples night
after night, this combination music,
drinking, and dining place is candlelit and
sleekly designed in glass over ancient
stone, brick, and wood. The cuisine is
light and contemporary, featuring inventive salads and fresh seafood, as well
as options for vegetarians and vegans.
Known for: romantic ambience; extensive
wine list; vegetarian options. $ *Aver-
age main: €18* ✉ *Bellafila 5, Barri Gòtic*
☎ *93/412–6552* ⊕ *www.restaurantpla.cat*
☉ *No lunch weekdays* Ⓜ *Jaume I.*

8

Barcelona BARRI GÒTIC

Barcelona's Sweet Tooth

For a long time, desserts were the Achilles heel of the Barcelona culinary scene. Diners groaning in anticipation after devouring their lovingly prepared starters and entrées often experienced disappointment when the final course arrived at the table—straight from the local supermarket's deep freeze. Occasionally, the waiter delivered a good, homemade *crema catalana* (crème brûlée), but the odds of a truly memorable ending to one's meal weren't favorable. To find Barcelona's sweet spot, you needed to skip the *postres* and head to the local *pastiseria*.

These neighborhood bakeries have always supplied Catalans with a cornucopia of seasonal treats. Some of the most beloved delectables include *xuixos* (pastries stuffed with, yes, crema catalana) and *pastissets de cabell d'àngel* (half-moon pastries). *Coques* are flatbreads, usually enjoyed around Easter, Christmas, or on saints' days. They're often topped with pine nuts and candied fruit, or even some delicious sweet-and-savory combinations, such as pork crackling and

sugar. *Panellets* are another local favorite, worth seeking out in autumn: balls of baked marzipan and pine nuts served with a sweet wine.

More acclaimed establishments have raised the bar for Barcelona desserts, and local chefs are applying the lessons learned in prestigious local cooking schools. One of them, the dazzlingly innovative school-restaurant Espai Sucre (Sugar Space), specializes in all things sweet.

For the best treats in town, try the chocolate. Oriol Balaguer sells pure black gold at his two shops, which look more like exquisite jewelry stores than food retailers. Often rated among the world's top chocolatiers, he competes with Enric Rovira for the crown of Catalonia's best. Another contender for top haute confectioner is Cacao Sampaka, founded by Quim Capdevilla. Travelers with children should consider a trip to the Museu de la Xocolata (Chocolate Museum) in El Born, where they can enjoy some finger-licking fun in the workshops, and shop for delicious sweets in the museum shop.

🛏 Hotels

★ Arai 4* Aparthotel Barcelona (*Arai-Palau Dels Quatre Rius Monument*)
$$$$ | **HOTEL** | **FAMILY** | You couldn't ask for a better location from which to explore Barcelona's Barri Gòtic—or for a bivouac more elegant—than one of the aparthotel suites in this stunning restoration. **Pros:** warm and attentive service; historic character retained in former palace; welcome set with a bottle of wine. **Cons:** somewhat seedy area; on busy street; rooms on the top floor lack historic

charm. $ *Rooms from: €370* ✉ *Avinyó 30, Barri Gòtic* ☎ *93/320–3950* ⊕ *www. hotelarai.com* ⇱ *31 rooms* ❍ *No meals* Ⓜ *L3 Liceu.*

Catalunya Portal d'Angel
$$$ | **HOTEL** | Converted in 1998 from a historic stately home dating back to 1825, the Catalunya Portal d'Angel beckons with its neoclassic facade and original grand marble staircase. **Pros:** pet-friendly; includes walking tours of the Old City and the Eixample; pleasant breakfast pavilion in the garden. **Cons:** small rooms;

faces busy pedestrian mall; lighting needs improvement. $ *Rooms from: €200* ✉ *Av. Portal d'Angel 17, Barri Gòtic* ☎ *93/318–4141* ⊕ *www.hoteles-catalonia.com* ▭ *No credit cards* ⤳ *82 rooms, 1 suite* ⦿ *No meals* Ⓜ *Pl. Catalunya.*

Colón

$$$$ | HOTEL | Around since 1951, the quiet and conservative Colón feels like it's been around forever, and is reasonably priced for the location: near the Catedral de la Seu, which is spectacular when illuminated at night. **Pros:** central location; some rooms have balconies overlooking square; rooftop terrace with heated Jacuzzi. **Cons:** can feel a bit stodgy; narrow bathrooms. $ *Rooms from: €240* ✉ *Av. Catedral 7, Barri Gòtic* ☎ *93/301–1404* ⊕ *www.hotelcolon.es* ⤳ *141 rooms* ⦿ *No meals* Ⓜ *L4 Jaume I.*

★ Duquesa de Cardona

$$ | HOTEL | A refurbished 17th-century town house, built when the Passeig de Colom in front was lined with the summer homes of the nobility, this hotel on the waterfront is a five-minute walk from everything in the Barri Gòtic and Barceloneta, and no more than a 30-minute walk to the Eixample. **Pros:** 24-hour room service; menu of fragrances to order for your room; glass of cava on check-in. **Cons:** rooms on the small side; no spa; no parking. $ *Rooms from: €147* ✉ *Passeig de Colom 12, Barri Gòtic* ☎ *93/268–9090* ⊕ *www.hduquesadecardona.com* ⤳ *51 rooms* ⦿ *No meals* Ⓜ *L4 Barceloneta, L3 Drassanes.*

★ el Jardí

$ | HOTEL | FAMILY | Facing charming Plaça del Pi and Plaça Sant Josep Oriol, in a pair of conjoined buildings that date to 1860, this family-friendly little budget hotel couldn't be better situated for exploring La Rambla and the Barri Gòtic. **Pros:** central location; friendly English-speaking staff; some rooms have balconies overlooking the square. **Cons:** no room service; no pool, gym,

or spa; no place for suitcases in small rooms. $ *Rooms from: €100* ✉ *Pl. Sant Josep Oriol 1, Barri Gòtic* ☎ *93/301–5900* ⊕ *www.eljardi-barcelona.com* ⤳ *40 rooms* ⦿ *No meals* Ⓜ *L3 Liceu, L4 Jaume I, Catalunya.*

Grand Hotel Central

$$$$ | HOTEL | FAMILY | At the edge of the Gothic Quarter, very near the Barcelona cathedral, this fashionable midtown hotel is popular with business and pleasure travelers alike, with contemporary decor and upscale amenities. **Pros:** excellent location between the Gothic Quarter and the Born; infinity pool with city views; Mediterranean City Bar and Restaurant on-site. **Cons:** no pets; busy thoroughfare outside; pricey breakfast. $ *Rooms from: €300* ✉ *Via Laietana 30, Barri Gòtic* ☎ *93/295–7900* ⊕ *www.grandhotelcentral.com* ⤳ *147 rooms* ⦿ *No meals* Ⓜ *L4 Jaume I.*

★ Hotel Neri

$$$$ | HOTEL | Just steps from the cathedral, in the heart of the city's old Jewish Quarter, this elegant, upscale, boutique hotel, part of the prestigious Relais & Chateaux hotel group, marries ancient and avant-garde designs. **Pros:** central location (close to Barri Gòtic); barbecue and occasional live music on the rooftop terrace; 24-hour room service. **Cons:** noisy on summer nights and school days; pets allowed only in deluxe rooms with terraces (pricey surcharge); lighting over beds could improve. $ *Rooms from: €350* ✉ *Carrer Sant Sever 5, Barri Gòtic* ☎ *93/304–0655* ⊕ *www.hotelneri.com/en* ⤳ *22 rooms* ⦿ *No meals* Ⓜ *L3 Liceu, L4 Jaume I.*

Hotel Ohla

$$$$ | HOTEL | One of Barcelona's top design hotels (also with incredible food), the Ohla has a neoclassical exterior (not counting the playful eyeballs stuck to the facade) that belies its avant-garde interior, full of witty, design-conscious touches. **Pros:** rooftop terrace and pool;

remarkable restaurant Caelis on-site; high-end wines at Vistro 49. **Cons:** adjacent to noisy Via Laietana; uncomfortable furniture in lobby. $ *Rooms from: €280* ⊠ *Via Laietana 49, Barri Gòtic* 📞 *93/341–5050* ⊕ *www.ohlabarcelona. com* ⇄ *74 rooms* ⊙ *Free Breakfast* Ⓜ *L4 Urquinaona.*

Mercer Hotel Barcelona

$$$$ | **HOTEL** | On a narrow side street near Plaça Sant Jaume, this romantic boutique hotel, a medieval town house, is among the latest examples of Barcelona's signature genius for the redesign and rebirth of historical properties. **Pros:** minutes from the Old City; comfortable rooftop terrace with a plunge pool and (in season) a bar-café; breakfast in glassed-in patio. **Cons:** very pricey; no gym or spa; expensive breakfast. $ *Rooms from: €480* ⊠ *Carrer dels Lledó 5, Barri Gòtic* 📞 *93/310–7480* ⊕ *www.mercerhoteles. com* ⇄ *28 rooms* ⊙ *No meals* Ⓜ *L4 Jaume I.*

Mercer House Bòria Bcn

$$$ | **HOTEL** | **FAMILY** | Blink and you miss it: on a small side street between the Santa Caterina market and the Picasso Museum, this boutique hotel (just six rooms and five suites) announces itself with no more than a name etched in the glass on its discreet front door. **Pros:** walking distance to great attractions; pleasant rooftop terrace and solarium; en suite kitchens in suites and lofts. **Cons:** no restaurant or bar; no room service; no pool. $ *Rooms from: €179* ⊠ *Carrer de la Bòria 24–26, Barri Gòtic* 📞 *93/295–5893* ⊕ *www.boriabcn.com* ⇄ *6 double rooms, 5 suites* ⊙ *No meals* Ⓜ *L4 Jaume I.*

Nightlife

Medieval Barri Gòtic is a wanderer's paradise filled with ancient winding streets, majestic squares, and myriad period-perfect wine bars and dimly lighted pubs found in the hidden corners of labyrinthine alleyways. The adjoining La Rambla, the liveliest pedestrian promenade in the city, bustles with a dizzying array of tourist-baiting shops, eateries, and arched paths to Plaça Reial's euphoric nightlife scene. Casual and unpretentious, the scene erupts nightly with a parade of rambunctious crowds of expats, curious interlopers, and assorted celebrations.

BARS

El Paraigua

BARS/PUBS | This eatery's stunning Moderniste facade—intricately carved wood, an exquisite vintage register, and other delicate reminders of its former incarnation as a turn-of-the-20th-century umbrella shop—is usually enough to lure newcomers inside for a closer look. But for fiesta-loving night owls, the real attraction is downstairs in the arched, exposed-brick cocktail club, a former convent basement offering first-rate cocktails and weekend jazz concerts in a note-perfect setting. ⊠ *Carrer del Pas de l´Ensenyança 2, Barri Gòtic* 📞 *93/317–1479* ⊕ *www.elparaigua.com* Ⓜ *Jaume I.*

Harlem Jazz Club

MUSIC CLUBS | Located on a rare tree-lined street in the Barri Gòtic, this club attracts patrons of all ages and musical tastes. Listen to live Cuban salsa, swing, and reggae while enjoying killer cocktails in a relaxed and friendly atmosphere. Most concerts start at 10 pm and finish around 1 am, and many people linger until closing time. ⊠ *Comtessa de Sobradiel 8, Barri Gòtic* 📞 *93/310–0755* ⊕ *www. harlemjazzclub.es* Ⓜ *Jaume I, Liceu.*

La Vinateria del Call

WINE BARS—NIGHTLIFE | Located in the heart of Barcelona's former Jewish Quarter, this rustic charmer serves a wide variety of hearty national wines paired with regional cheeses, meats, and tapas. Popular with wine-loving romantics for its antique carved-wood furnishings and candlelit setting, the venue also attracts visitors and regulars looking for a respite from the area's chaotic pace. ⊠ *Sant Domènec del Call 9, Barri Gòtic*

☎ 93/302–6092 ⊕ www.lavinateriadelcall. com Ⓜ Liceu, Jaume I.

Milk

BARS/PUBS | Resembling a prim parlor lounge with touches of kitsch, this cozy bar bistro with plush sofas, gilded mirrors, handmade knickknacks, and tastefully worn tapestry wallpaper has been a favorite hangout for young expats for more than a decade. Try the Michelada, a dramatic alternative Bloody Mary reserved for the strongest constitutions: Corona beer mixed with hot sauce, Worcestershire, and tomato juice. ✉ Gignas 21, Barri Gòtic ☎ 93/268–0922 ⊕ www.milkbarcelona.com Ⓜ Jaume I.

★ Ocaña

BARS/PUBS | Located in a trio of ancient mansions on buzzy Plaça Reial's southern flank, this venue is dedicated to Jose Peréz Ocaña, a cross-dressing artist and proud bohemian, and a dominating figure of Barcelona's decadent post-Franco explosion of alternative culture. With an adjoining Mexican restaurant, as well as a sizable café bar, club, and cocktail lounge, Ocaña also has the fiercest drag queen hostesses on the square. ✉ Pl. Reial 13–15, Barri Gòtic ☎ 93/676–4814 ⊕ www.ocana.cat Ⓜ Drassanes.

Sidecar Factory Club

BARS/PUBS | A mainstay of the decadent nightlife centered on Plaça Reial, this long-running music club has never fallen out of fashion—in fact, it attracts new fans just as the old ones bow out. With a firm focus showcasing up-and-coming indie talent, the venue offers a way to discover new favorites in moody neon red surroundings. ✉ Pl. Reial 7, Barri Gòtic ☎ 93/317–7666 ⊕ www.sidecarfactory-club.com Ⓜ Drassanes.

🎭 Performing Arts

FLAMENCO

Barcelona's flamenco scene is surprisingly vibrant for a culture so far removed from Andalusia. Los Tarantos, in Plaça

Catalan Flamenco

Barcelona has a burgeoning and erudite flamenco scene, even if the dance is imported from Andalusia. For the best flamenco in Barcelona, consult listings and concierges and don't be put off if the venue seems touristy—these venues often book the best artists. Barcelona-born *cantaors* include Mayte Martín and Miguel Poveda. Keep an eye on the billboards for such names as Estrella Morente (daughter of the late, great Enrique Morente) and Chano Domínguez (who often appears at the Barcelona Jazz Festival).

Reial, is a must for its authentic flamenco performances.

Los Tarantos

DANCE | This small basement boîte spotlights some of Andalusia's best flamenco in 30-minute shows of dance, percussion, and song. These shows are a good intro to the art and feel much less touristy than most standard flamenco fare. Shows are daily at 7:30, 8:30, and 9:30 pm, with an additional 10:30 pm show June–September. ✉ Pl. Reial 17, Barri Gòtic ☎ 93/304–1210 ⊕ www.masimas. com/en/tarantos Ⓜ Liceu.

🛍 Shopping

The Barri Gòtic was built on trade and cottage industries, and there are plenty of nimble fingers producing artisan goods in the old-world shops along its stone streets. Start at the cathedral and work your way outward.

ART GALLERIES
Sala Parès
ART GALLERIES | The dean of Barcelona's art galleries, this place is the oldest art gallery in Barcelona. It opened in 1840 as an art-supplies shop; as a gallery, it dates to 1877 and has shown every Barcelona artist of note since then. Picasso and Miró exhibited their work here, as did Casas and Rossinyol before them. Nowadays, Catalan artists like Perico Pastor and Carlos Morago get pride of place. ⊠ *Petritxol 5, Barri Gòtic* ☎ *93/318–7020* ⊕ *salapares.com* Ⓜ *Liceu, Catalunya.*

CERAMICS AND GLASSWARE
★ Art Escudellers
CERAMICS/GLASSWARE | Ceramic pieces from all over Spain are on display at this large store across the street from the restaurant Los Caracoles; more than 140 different artisans are represented, with maps showing what part of Spain the work is from. Wine, cheese, and ham tastings are held downstairs, and you can even throw a pot yourself in the workshop. There are four other branches of Art Escudellers in the old city, including one on the Carrer Avinyó. ⊠ *Escudellers 23–25, Barri Gòtic* ☎ *93/412–6801* ⊕ *www.artescudellers.com* Ⓜ *Liceu, Drassanes.*

CLOTHING
Sombrereria Obach
CLOTHING | This *sombrerería* (hat shop) is as much part of the Barri Gòtic's landscape as any of its medieval churches. Occupying a busy corner in El Call—the old Jewish district—curved glass windows displays the sort of hats, caps, and berets that have been dressing heads in Barcelona since 1924. Styles are classic and timeless, from traditional Basque berets to Stetsons and panamas. ⊠ *Call 2, Barri Gòtic* ☎ *93/318–4094* ⊕ *www.sombrereriaobach.com* Ⓜ *Jaume I, Liceu.*

FOOD
Caelum
FOOD/CANDY | At the corner of Carrer de la Palla and Banys Nous, this café and shop sells wines and foodstuffs such as honey, biscuits, chocolates, and preserves made in convents and monasteries all over Spain. You can pop in to pick up an exquisitely packaged pot of jam, or linger longer in the tearoom, part of which is housed in an old medieval bathhouse in the candlelit basement. ⊠ *De la Palla 8, Barri Gòtic* ☎ *93/302–6993* ⊕ *www.caelumbarcelona.com* Ⓜ *Liceu, Jaume I.*

Formatgeria La Seu
FOOD/CANDY | Scotswoman Katherine McLaughlin has put together the Gothic Quarter's most delightful cheese-tasting sanctuary on the site of an ancient buttery. (A 19th-century butter churn is visible in the back room.) A dozen artisanal cow, goat, and sheep cheeses from all over Spain, and olive oils, can be tasted and taken home. La Seu is named for a combination of La Seu Cathedral, as the "seat" of cheeses, and for cheese-rich La Seu d'Urgell in the Pyrenees. Katherine's wrapping paper, imaginatively chosen sheets of newspaper, give a final flourish to purchases. ⊠ *Dagueria 16, Barri Gòtic* ☎ *93/412–6548* ⊕ *www.formatgerialaseu.com* Ⓜ *Jaume I.*

La Casa del Bacalao
FOOD/CANDY | This cult store decorated with cod-fishing memorabilia specializes in salt cod and books of codfish recipes. Slabs of salt and dried cod, used in a wide range of Catalan recipes (such as esqueixada, in which shredded strips of raw salt cod are served in a marinade of oil and vinegar) can be vacuum-packed for portability. ⊠ *Comtal 8 , just off Porta de l'Àngel, Barri Gòtic* ☎ *93/301–6539* Ⓜ *Catalunya.*

GIFTS AND SOUVENIRS
Artesania Catalunya – CCAM

GIFTS/SOUVENIRS | In 2010 the Catalan government created the registered trademark Empremtes de Catalunya to represent Catalan artisans and to make sure that visitors get the real deal when buying what they believe to be genuine products. The official shop now sells jewelry re-created from eras dating back to pre-Roman times, Gaudí-inspired sculptures, traditional Cava mugs, and some bravely avant-garde objects from young artisans—all officially sanctioned as fit to represent the city. ⊠ *Banys Nous 11, Barri Gòtic* ☎ *93/653–7214* ⊕ *www. bcncrafts.com/en/* Ⓜ *Jaume I, Liceu.*

Cereria Subirà

GIFTS/SOUVENIRS | Known as the city's oldest shop, having remained open since 1761 (though it was not always a candle store), this "waxery" (*cereria*) offers candles in all sizes and shapes, ranging from wild mushrooms to the Montserrat massif, home of the Benedictine abbey dear to the heart of every barcelonin. ⊠ *Baixada Llibreteria 7, Barri Gòtic* ☎ *93/315–2606* ⊕ *www.cereriasubira.cat/ en/* Ⓜ *Jaume I.*

MARKETS
Mercat Gòtic

OUTDOOR/FLEA/GREEN MARKETS | A browser's bonanza, this interesting if somewhat pricey Thursday market for antique clothing, jewelry, and art objects occupies the plaza in front of the cathedral. ⊠ *Av. Plaça de la Catedral, Barri Gòtic* ⊕ *www.mercatgoticbcn.com* Ⓜ *Jaume I, Urquinaona.*

Plaça del Pi

OUTDOOR/FLEA/GREEN MARKETS | This little square fills with the interesting tastes and aromas of a natural-produce market (honeys, cheeses) throughout the month, while neighboring Plaça Sant Josep Oriol holds a painter's market every Sunday. ⊠ *Pl. del Pi, Barri Gòtic* Ⓜ *Catalunya, Liceu.*

SHOES
★ La Manual Alpargatera

SHOES/LUGGAGE/LEATHER GOODS | If you appreciate old-school craftsmanship in footwear and reasonable prices, visit this boutique just off Carrer Ferran. Handmade rope-sole sandals and espadrilles are the specialty, and this shop has sold them to everyone—including the pope. The flat, beribboned espadrilles model used for dancing the sardana is available, as are fashionable wedge heels with peep toes and comfy slippers. The cost of a pair of espadrilles here might put you back about $50, which is far less than the same quality shoes in the United States. ⊠ *Avinyó 7, Barri Gòtic* ☎ *93/301–0172* ⊕ *www.lamanualalpargatera.es* Ⓜ *Liceu, Jaume I.*

El Raval

El Raval (from *arrabal,* meaning "suburb" or "slum") is the area to the west of La Rambla, on the right as you walk toward the port. Originally a rough quarter outside the second set of city walls that ran down the left side of La Rambla, El Raval was once notorious for its Barri Xinès (or Barrio Chino) red-light district, the lurid attractions of which are known to have fascinated a young Pablo Picasso.

El Raval, though still rough-and-tumble, has been gentrified and much improved since 1980, largely as a result of the construction of the Museu d'Art Contemporani de Barcelona (MACBA) and other cultural institutions nearby, such as the Centre de Cultura Contemporània (CCCB), Filmoteca, and the Convent dels Àngels. La Rambla del Raval has been opened up between Carrer de l'Hospital and Drassanes, bringing light and air into the streets of the Raval for the first time in a thousand years. The medieval Hospital de la Santa Creu, Plaça del Pedró, the Mercat de Sant Antoni, and Sant Pau del Camp are highlights of this funky, rough-edged part of Barcelona.

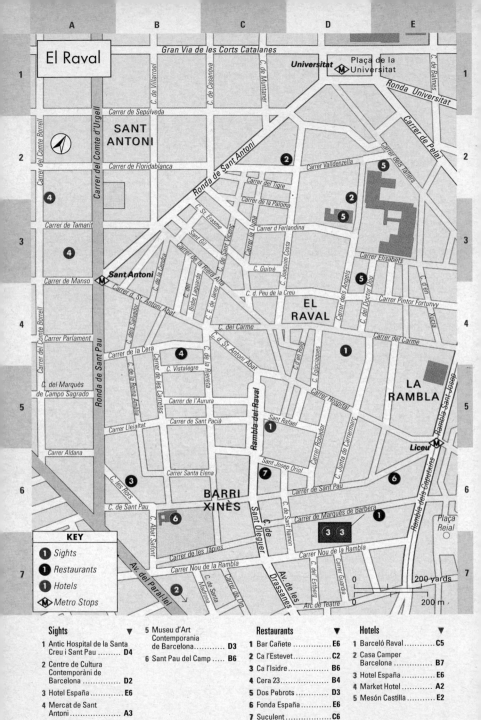

El Raval

Sights ▼

1 Antic Hospital de la Santa Creu i Sant Pau D4

2 Centre de Cultura Contemporàni de Barcelona D2

3 Hotel España E6

4 Mercat de Sant Antoni A3

5 Museu d'Art Contemporania de Barcelona............ D3

6 Sant Pau del Camp B6

Restaurants ▼

1 Bar Cañete E6

2 Ca l'Estevet............... C2

3 Ca l'Isidre B6

4 Cera 23.................... B4

5 Dos Pebrots............... D3

6 Fonda España E6

7 Suculent C6

Hotels ▼

1 Barceló Raval C5

2 Casa Camper Barcelona B7

3 Hotel España E6

4 Market Hotel A2

5 Mesón Castilla E2

KEY

1 Sights

1 Restaurants

1 Hotels

M Metro Stops

Sights

★ Antic Hospital de la Santa Creu i Sant Pau

BUILDING | Founded in the 10th century as one of Europe's earliest medical complexes, the mostly 15th- and 16th-century complex contains some of Barcelona's most impressive Gothic architecture. From the grand entrance, the first building on the left is the 18th-century **Reial Acadèmia de Cirurgia i Medicina** (Royal Academy of Surgery and Medicine); the surgical amphitheater is kept just as it was in the days when students learned by observing dissections. Through a gate to the left of the Casa de Convalescència is the garden-courtyard of the hospital complex, the **Jardins de Rubió i Lluc,** centered on a baroque cross and lined with orange trees. On the right is the **Biblioteca Nacional de Catalunya,** Catalonia's national library. The library is spectacular: two parallel halls—once the core of the hospital—230 feet long, with towering Gothic arches and vaulted ceilings, designed in the 15th century by the architect of the church of Santa Maria del Pi, Guillem Abiell. This was the hospital where Antoni Gaudí was taken, unrecognized and assumed to be a pauper, after he was struck by a trolley on June 7, 1926. ⊠ *Carrer Hospital 56 (or Carrer del Carme 45), El Raval* ☎ *93/317–1686 Reial Acadèmia de Medecina, 93/270–2300 Biblioteca de Catalunya* ⊕ *www.bnc. cat* ☒ *From €8* ☉ *Royal Academy of Medicine: closed Sun.–Tues., Thurs., and Fri; Biblioteca de Catalunya and Capella: closed Sun.* Ⓜ *L3 Liceu.*

Centre de Cultura Contemporànea de Barcelona (*CCCB*)

ARTS VENUE | Just next door to the MACBA, this multidisciplinary gallery, lecture hall, and concert and exhibition space offers a year-round program of cultural events and projects. The center also has a remarkable film archive of historic shorts and documentaries, free to the public. Housed in the restored and renovated Casa de la Caritat, a former medieval convent and hospital, the CCCB, like the Palau de la Música Catalana, is one of the city's shining examples of contemporary flare added to traditional architecture and design. A smoked-glass wall on the right side of the patio, designed by architects Albert Villaplana and Helio Piñon, reflects out over the rooftops of El Raval to Montjuïc and the Mediterranean beyond. ⊠ *Carrer Montalegre 5, El Raval* ☎ *93/306–4100* ⊕ *www.cccb.org* ☒ *Exhibitions €6; Sun. 3–8, free. Admission to CCCB Film Archive is free* ☉ *Closed Mon.* Ⓜ *L1/L2 Universitat, Catalunya.*

Hotel España

BUILDING | Just off La Rambla behind the Liceu opera house on Carrer Sant Pau is the Hotel España, remodeled in 1904 by Lluís Domènech i Montaner, architect of the Moderniste flagship Palau de la Música Catalana. Completely refurbished in 2010, the interior is notable for its Art Nouveau decor. The sculpted marble Eusebi Arnau fireplace in the bar, the Ramon Casas undersea murals in the salon (mermaids singing each to each), and the lushly ornate dining room are the hotel's best artistic features. The España is so proud of its place in the cultural history of the city—and justly so—it opens to the public for 40-minute guided tours, usually twice a week. Check their website for times. (Note that tours are usually in Spanish or Catalan, but English can be requested.) ⊠ *Carrer Sant Pau 9–11, El Raval* ☎ *93/550–0000* ⊕ *www. hotelespanya.com* ☒ *Tour €5* Ⓜ *L3 Liceu.*

Mercat de Sant Antoni

MARKET | A mammoth hangar at the junction of Ronda de Sant Antoni and Comte d'Urgell, designed in 1882 by Antoni Rovira i Trias, the Mercat de Sant Antoni is considered the city's finest example of wrought-iron architecture. The Greek-cross-shaped market covers an entire block on the edge of the Eixample, and some of the best Moderniste stall facades in Barcelona distinguish this exceptional space. Fully functioning as of 2017 after years of painstaking restoration to incorporate medieval archaeological remains underneath, the market is a foodie paradise of fruit, vegetables, fish, cheeses, and more. On Sunday morning, visit Sant Antoni, and wander the outdoor stalls of the weekly flea market full of stamps and coins, comic books and trading cards, VHS, CDs, vinyl, and vintage clothing. ⊠ *Carrer Comte d'Urgell s/n, El Raval* ☎ *93/426–3521* ⊕ *www. mercatdesantantoni.com* ⊘ *Closed Sun.* Ⓜ *L2 Sant Antoni.*

★ Museu d'Art Contemporani de Barcelona
(*Barcelona Museum of Contemporary Art, MACBA*)

MUSEUM | FAMILY | Designed by American architect Richard Meier in 1992, this gleaming explosion of light and geometry in El Raval houses a permanent collection of contemporary art, and regularly mounts special thematic exhibitions of works on loan. Meier gives a nod to Gaudí (with the Pedrera-like wave on one end of the main facade), but his minimalist building otherwise looks unfinished. That said, the MACBA is unarguably an important addition to the cultural capital of this once-shabby neighborhood. The MACBA's 20th-century art collection (Calder, Rauschenberg, Oteiza, Chillida, Tàpies) is excellent, as is the guided tour in English (at 4 pm on Mondays): a useful introduction to the philosophical foundations of contemporary art as well as the pieces themselves. The museum also offers wonderful workshops and activities for kids. ⊠ *Pl. dels Àngels 1, El Raval* ☎ *93/412–0810* ⊕ *www.macba.cat* ⊠ *€10 (valid for 1 month)* ⊘ *Closed Tues.* Ⓜ *L1/L2 Universitat, L1/L3 Catalunya.*

★ Sant Pau del Camp
BUILDING | Barcelona's oldest church was originally outside the city walls (*del camp* means "in the fields") and was a Roman cemetery as far back as the 2nd century, according to archaeological evidence.

What you see now was built in 1127 and is the earliest Romanesque structure in Barcelona. Elements of the church—the classical marble capitals atop the columns in the main entry—are thought to be from the 6th and 7th centuries. The hulking, mastodonic shape of the church is a reminder of the church's defensive posture in the face of intermittent Roman persecution and later, Moorish invasions and sackings. Check for musical performances here, as the church is an acoustical gem. The tiny cloister is Sant Pau del Camp's best feature, and one of Barcelona's semisecret treasures. ⊠ *Carrer de Sant Pau 101, El Raval* ☎ *93/441–0001* ⊠ *Free when Masses are celebrated; guided tour Sun. at 12:45, €3* ⊘ *Cloister closed Sun. during Mass; no tours Sun. in mid-Aug.* Ⓜ *L3 Paral.lel.*

 Restaurants

Bar Cañete
$$$ | TAPAS | A superb tapas and *platillos* (small plates) emporium, this spot is just around the corner from the Liceu opera house. The long bar overlooking the burners and part of the kitchen leads down to the 20-seat communal tasting table at the end of the room. **Known for:** Spanish ham specialists; superb tapas; secreto ibérico. Ⓢ *Average main: €24* ⊠ *Unió 17, El Raval* ☎ *93/270–3458* ⊕ *www.barcanete.com/en* ⊘ *Closed Sun.* Ⓜ *Liceu.*

Ca l'Estevet
$$ | CATALAN | This restaurant has been serving up old-school Catalan cuisine to local and loyal customers since 1940 (and under a different name for 50 years before that), and the practice has been made perfect. Tuck into the likes of grilled botifarra sausages or roasted kid. **Known for:** Catalan specialties; large portions of escudella i carn d'olla (meat stew); historic location. Ⓢ *Average main: €16* ⊠ *Valldonzella 46, El Raval* ☎ *93/301– 2939* ⊕ *www.restaurantestevet.com* ⊘ *No dinner Sun.* Ⓜ *Universitat.*

One of the earliest medical complexes in Europe is the Antic Hospital de la Santa Creu i Sant Pau.

★ Ca l'Isidre

$$$$ | **CATALAN** | A throwback to an age before foams and food science took over the gastronomic world, this restaurant has elevated simplicity to the level of the spectacular since the early 1970s. Isidre and Montserrat share their encyclopedic knowledge of local cuisine with guests, while their daughter Núria cooks traditional Catalan dishes. **Known for:** once frequented by Miró and Dalí; locally sourced produce; art collection. $ *Average main: €36* ⊠ *Flors 12, El Raval* ☎ *93/441–1139* ⊕ *www.calisidre.com* ⊙ *Closed Sun., and 1st 2 wks of Aug.* Ⓜ *Paral.lel.*

Cera 23

$$ | **SPANISH** | Top pick among a crop of modern restaurants putting the razzle back into the run-down Raval, Cera 23 offers a winning combination of great service and robust cooking in a fun, friendly setting; stand at the bar and enjoy a blackberry mojito while you wait for your table. The open kitchen is in the dining area, so guests can watch the cooks create contemporary presentations of traditional Spanish dishes. **Known for:** volcano black rice; open kitchen viewable to diners; exceptional service. $ *Average main: €16* ⊠ *Cera 23, El Raval* ☎ *93/442–0808* ⊕ *www.cera23.com* ⊙ *No lunch weekdays* Ⓜ *Sant Antoni.*

★ Dos Pebrots

$$ | **MEDITERRANEAN** | Albert Raurich of Dos Palillos has transformed his favorite neighborhood haunt into a retro cutting-edge tapas bar that explores the history of Mediterranean cuisine. Everything from the Roman condiment *garum* to 10th-century Xarab fruit salad gets reinvented in a contemporary context. **Known for:** historical-themed tapas; unique dishes like pigs' nipples; restored original exterior. $ *Average main: €20* ⊠ *Doctor Dou 19, El Raval* ☎ *93/853–9598* ⊕ *www.dospebrots.com* ⊙ *Closed Mon. and Tues. No lunch Wed. and Thurs. Closed 2 wks at Christmas.* Ⓜ *Catalunya.*

Fonda España

$$ | **CATALAN** | The sumptuous glory of this restored late-19th-century Art Nouveau dining room now has food to match, courtesy of superstar chef Martín Berasategui. Go for broke with the "gastronomic voyage" tasting menu or feast à la carte on updated period dishes such as "the mermaids"—a smooth cod pil pil (a Basque sauce)—and pigeon with a liver paté heart. **Known for:** Art Nouveau decor; satisfying traditional dishes; excellent set lunches. [$] *Average main: €22* ✉ *Sant Pau 9, El Raval* ☎ *93/550–0000* 🌐 *www.hotelespanya.com* 🕒 *No dinner Sun. No lunch in Aug.* [M] *Liceu.*

★ Suculent

$$ | **CATALAN** | This is a strong contender for the crown of Barcelona's best bistro, as chef Antonio Romero continues to turn out Catalan tapas and dishes that have roots in rustic classics but reach high modern standards of execution. The name is a twist on the Catalan *sucar lent* (to dip slowly), and excellent bread is duly provided to soak up the sauces. **Known for:** obligatory set menus, except at the bar; must-try steak tartare on marrow bone; big, bold flavors. [$] *Average main: €18* ✉ *Rambla del Raval 45, El Raval* ☎ *93/443–6579* 🌐 *www.suculent.com* 🕒 *Closed Mon. and Tues.* [M] *Liceu.*

🛏 Hotels

Barceló Raval

$$$ | **HOTEL** | With an edgy contemporary design, reasonable rates, and location in one of Barcelona's most colorful neighborhoods, Barceló Raval is a welcome addition to the city's hotel scene. **Pros:** 10 minutes from La Rambla; 360-degree vistas from rooftop terrace; DJ during Sunday brunch. **Cons:** Rambla del Raval a bit dicey at night; mood lighting not to everyone's taste; pool on terrace is very small. [$] *Rooms from: €200* ✉ *Rambla del Raval 17–21, El Raval* ☎ *93/320–1490* 🌐 *www.barcelo.com/en-us/hotels/spain/barcelona/barcelo-raval* 🔑 *186 rooms* 🍴 *No meals* [M] *L3 Liceu.*

★ Casa Camper Barcelona

$$$ | **HOTEL** | **FAMILY** | A marriage between the Camper footwear empire and the (now defunct) Vinçon design store produced this 21st-century hotel halfway between La Rambla and the MACBA (Museum of Contemporary Art), with a focus on sustainability (think solar panels and water recycling) and a unique "one big family" feel. **Pros:** great buffet breakfast with dishes cooked to order; just steps from MACBA and the Boqueria; complimentary 24-hour snack bar. **Cons:** expensive for what you get; extra per person charge for children over three years old; no in-room minibar. [$] *Rooms from: €220* ✉ *Carrer Elisabets 11, El Raval* ☎ *93/342–6280* 🌐 *www.casacamper.com* 🔑 *40 rooms* 🍴 *Free Breakfast* [M] *Catalunya, L3 Liceu.*

★ Hotel España

$$$$ | **HOTEL** | This beautifully renovated Art Nouveau gem is the second oldest (after the nearby Sant Agustí) and among the best of Barcelona's smaller hotels. **Pros:** near Liceu opera house and La Rambla; alabaster fireplace in the bar lounge; lavish breakfast buffet. **Cons:** lower rooms facing Carrer Sant Pau get some street noise; bed lighting could be improved; no views. [$] *Rooms from: €250* ✉ *Carrer Sant Pau 9–11, El Raval* ☎ *93/550–0000* 🌐 *www.hotelespanya.com* 🔑 *83 rooms* 🍴 *No meals* [M] *L4 Liceu.*

Market Hotel

$ | **HOTEL** | Wallet-friendly and design conscious, this boutique hotel named for the Mercat de Sant Antoni (a block away) is one of Barcelona's best bargains and walking distance from all of El Raval and the Gothic Quarter sites and attractions. **Pros:** excellent-value Catalan cuisine at on-site restaurant; friendly staff; great showers. **Cons:** standard rooms on lower floors are a little cramped; soundproofing needs upgrade; some rooms have no views. [$] *Rooms from: €100* ✉ *Carrer del Comte Borrell 68, El Raval*

☎ *93/325–1205* 🌐 *www.hotelmarketbarcelona.com* 🛏 *68 rooms* 🍴 *No meals* [M] *L2 Sant Antoni, L1 Urgell.*

★ Mesón Castilla
$$ | **HOTEL** | **FAMILY** | A few steps down Carrer Tallers from the top of La Rambla, on a short side street, there's almost nothing Barcelona about the Mesón Castilla, which feels like a well-appointed country hotel or a parador in Castile or La Mancha: classically Spanish, with mosaic tile floors and sconces, painted coffered ceilings and coats of arms, rooms with antique carved headboards and painted wooden armoires. **Pros:** close to medieval Barcelona and the Eixample; spotlessly kept; lush patio for dining in warm weather. **Cons:** no terrace, pool, or spa; no laundry or room service; bathrooms a bit cramped. [$] *Rooms from: €130* ✉ *Carrer Valldonzella 5, El Raval* ☎ *93/318–2182* 🌐 *www.atiramhotels.com* 🛏 *57 rooms* 🍴 *No meals* [M] *Catalunya, L1/L2 Universitat.*

🍸 Nightlife

El Raval has slowly evolved from a forgotten, seedy no-man's-land into one of the choicest districts to enjoy provocative modern art and a pulsating, boho-glam party scene. Though not to everyone's taste, hippie students, tattooed misfits, artists, and more recently trend-seeking nomads routinely bar crawl up and down a stretch of nightlife-friendly streets (Joaquin Costa is one) featuring a wide assortment of divey dens, music bars, pubs, and funky *coctelerias.*

BARS

Ambar
BARS/PUBS | Right off the tree-lined Rambla del Raval, the clientele at this popular watering hole is as colorful as the snazzy, red-quilted bar and moody green-blue lighting: expat students and pierced young artists rub shoulders with visiting rabble-rousers warming up for a wild night out. With its basic menu of classic cocktails and long drinks, the main attraction is arguably the space itself, strewn with a calculated mix of modern and retro. ✉ *Sant Pau 77, El Raval* ☎ *93/441–3725.*

Casa Almirall
BARS/PUBS | The twisted wooden fronds framing the bar's mirror, an 1888 vintage bar-top iron statue of a muse, and Art Nouveau touches such as curvy door handles make this one of the most authentic bars in Barcelona. It's also the second oldest, dating to 1860. (The oldest is the Marsella, another Raval favorite.) It's a good spot for evening drinks after hitting the nearby MACBA (Museu d'Art Contemporani de Barcelona) or for a prelunch *vermut* (vermouth) on weekends. ✉ *Joaquín Costa 33, El Raval* ☎ *93/318–9917* 🌐 *www.casaalmirall.com/en* [M] *Universitat.*

La Confitería
BARS/PUBS | Located in a former pastry shop, this vintage bar has retained so much of the 19th-century Moderniste facade and interior touches (onetime cake display cases are now filled with period memorabilia) that visitors undoubtedly experience the sensation of time standing still. Divided into two equally inviting spaces and open unconventionally late for a bar (3 am), the front is usually packed with regulars, while the granite-and-metal tables in the back are popular with couples. ✉ *Sant Pau 128, El Raval* ☎ *93/140–5435* 🌐 *www.confiteria.cat* [M] *Paral.lel.*

Manchester
BARS/PUBS | There's no doubt about what the name of this laid-back Raval hangout pays tribute to: that of the early '80s Manchester scene, with the Joy Division and Happy Mondays and the Stone Roses. The sheer number of people (both locals and foreigners) crowding around the wood tables and dancing in the spaces in between suggest that a tribute is welcome. ✉ *Valldonzella 40, El Raval* ☎ *627/733–081* [M] *Catalunya.*

Marsella

BARS/PUBS | Inaugurated in 1820, this historic venue, a favored haunt for artistic notables such as Gaudí, Picasso, and Hemingway, has remained remarkably unchanged since its celebrated heyday. The chipped paint on the walls and ceiling, cracked marble tables, and elaborate spiderwebs on chandeliers and bottles all add to the charm, but the main reason patrons linger is one special shot: Marsella is one of few establishments serving homemade absinthe (*absenta* in Spanish), a potent aniseed-flavored spirit meant to be savored and rumored to enhance productivity. ⊠ *Sant Pau 65, El Raval* ☎ *93/442–7263* Ⓜ *Liceu*.

33/45

BARS/PUBS | From the street, this indie-cool hipster haven seems too brightly lighted for gritty-glam Raval. But its mismatched sofas with oversize pillows and eclectic selection of flavored gins, tequila blends, and imported beer attracts a steady flow of lounge lizards. ⊠ *Joaquin Costa 4, El Raval* ☎ *93/187–4138* Ⓜ *Sant Antoni.*

Ultramarinos

BARS/PUBS | Gintonic (in Spanish it's all one word), the cocktail of choice for many a hip barcelonin, is the undisputed star of this retro-fabulous neighborhood bar. Old-school aficionados favor the saucy collection of signature Hendricks blends, but for those with more curious palates, more than 175 international gins are flavored, perfumed, and/or mixed into no less than 25 killer concoctions. ⊠ *Sant Pau 126, El Raval* ☎ *653/582424* Ⓜ *Paral.lel.*

MUSIC CLUBS: JAZZ AND BLUES
Jazz Sí Club

MUSIC CLUBS | Run by the Barcelona contemporary music school next door, this workshop and (during the day) café is a forum for musicians, teachers, and fans to listen to and debate their art. There is jazz on Monday; pop, blues, and rock jam sessions on Tuesday; jazz Wednesday; Cuban salsa on Thursday; flamenco on Friday; and rock and pop on weekends. The small cover charge (€6–€10, depending on which night you visit) includes a drink; Wednesday has no cover charge. Gigs start between 6:30 and 8:45 pm. ⊠ *Requesens 2, El Raval* ☎ *93/329–0020* ⊕ *tallerdemusics.com/en/jazzsi-club* Ⓜ *Sant Antoni.*

 Performing Arts

THEATER
Teatre Apolo

DANCE | This historic player in Barcelona's theater life stages musicals, comedies, and dramas. ⊠ *Av. del Paral.lel 59, El Raval* ☎ *93/441–9944* ⊕ *www.teatreapolo.com* Ⓜ *Paral.lel.*

 Shopping

Shopping in the Raval reflects the district's multicultural and bohemian vibe. Around MACBA (Barcelona Museum of Contemporary Art) you'll find dozens of designer-run start-ups selling fashion, crafts, and housewares, while the edgier southernmost section has an abundance of curious establishments chock-full of ethnic foods (along Calles Hospital and Carme) and vintage clothing (on Calle Riera Baixa).

BOOKS
La Central del Raval

BOOKS/STATIONERY | This luscious bookstore in the former chapel of the Casa de la Misericòrdia sells books amid stunning architecture and holds regular cultural events. ⊠ *C/Elisabets 6, El Raval* ☎ *933/189979* ⊕ *www.lacentral.com* Ⓜ *Catalunya.*

MARKETS
Flea Market BCN

OUTDOOR/FLEA/GREEN MARKETS | Barcelona's current rage for retro and vintage reaches its pinnacle once a month on a little square behind the medieval shipyards.

Flea Market BCN sees hipsters and hippies, dads and dealers empty out their wardrobes and garages so that you can walk away with art-deco wall clocks or a 1970s hand mixer. Flea Market BCN is held on the second Sunday of every month, while the smaller Fleedonia takes places on the Plaça Salvador Seguí on the first Sunday of every month. ⊠ *Pl. Blanquerna* ⊕ *www.fleamarketbcn.com* Ⓜ *Drassanes.*

Mercat de Sant Antoni

FOOD/CANDY | Just outside the Raval at the end of Ronda Sant Antoni, this steel hangar colossus is an old-fashioned food and secondhand clothing and books (many in English) market. Sunday morning is the most popular time to browse through the used-book and video game market. ⊠ *Comte d'Urgell 1, El Raval* ⊕ *www.mercatdesantantoni.com* Ⓜ *Sant Antoni.*

Sant Pere and La Ribera

Sant Pere, Barcelona's old textile neighborhood, is centered on the church of Sant Pere. A half mile closer to the port, the Barri de la Ribera and the former market of El Born, now known as the Born-Ribera district, were at the center of Catalonia's great maritime and economic expansion of the 13th and 14th centuries. Surrounding the basilica of Santa Maria del Mar, the Born-Ribera area includes Carrer Montcada, lined with 14th- to 18th-century Renaissance palaces; Passeig del Born, where medieval jousts were held; Carrer Flassaders and the area around the early mint; the antiques shop- and restaurant-rich Carrer Banys Vells; Plaça de les Olles; and Pla del Palau, where La Llotja, Barcelona's early maritime exchange, housed the fine-arts school where Picasso, Gaudí, and Domènech i Montaner all studied, as did many more of Barcelona's most important artists and architects.

Long a depressed neighborhood, La Ribera began to experience a revival in the 1980s; now replete with intimate bars, cafés, and trendy boutiques, it continues to enjoy the blessings of gentrification. An open excavation in the center of El Born, the onetime market restored as a multipurpose cultural center, offers a fascinating view of pre-1714 Barcelona, dismantled by the victorious troops of Felipe V at the end of the War of the Spanish Succession. The Passeig del Born, La Rambla of medieval Barcelona, is once again a pleasant leafy promenade.

◉ Sights

Capella d'en Marcús (*Marcús Chapel*)
RELIGIOUS SITE | This Romanesque hermitage looks as if it had been left behind by some remote order of hermit-monks who meant to take it on a picnic in the Pyrenees. The tiny chapel, possibly—along with Sant Llàtzer—Barcelona's smallest religious structure, and certainly one of its oldest, was originally built in the 12th century on the main Roman road into Barcelona, the one that would become Cardo Maximo just a few hundred yards away as it passed through the walls at Portal de l'Àngel. Bernat Marcús, a wealthy merchant concerned with public welfare and social issues, built a hospital here for poor travelers; the hospital chapel that bears his name was dedicated to the Mare de Déu de la Guia (Our Lady of the Guide). As a result of its affiliation, combined with its location on the edge of town, the chapel eventually became the headquarters of the Confraria del Correus a Cavall (Brotherhood of the Pony Express), also known as the *troters* (trotters), that made Barcelona the key link in overland mail between the Iberian Peninsula and France. ⊠ *Carrer Carders 2 (Placeta d'en Marcús), Born-Ribera* ☏ *93/310–2390* Ⓜ *Jaume I.*

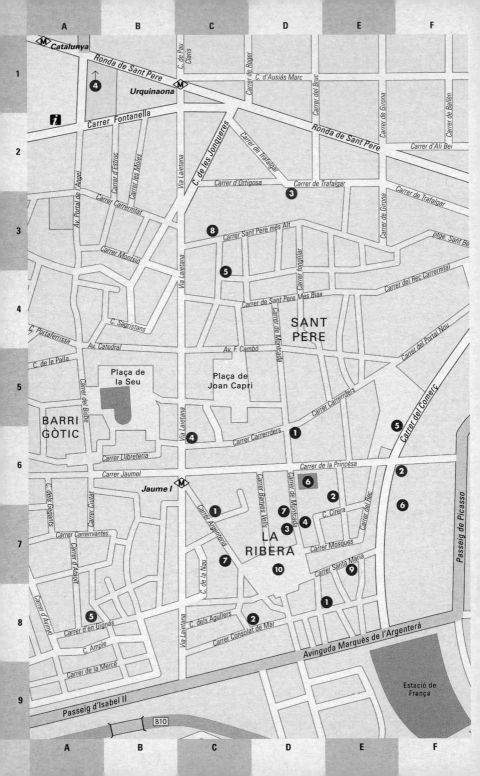

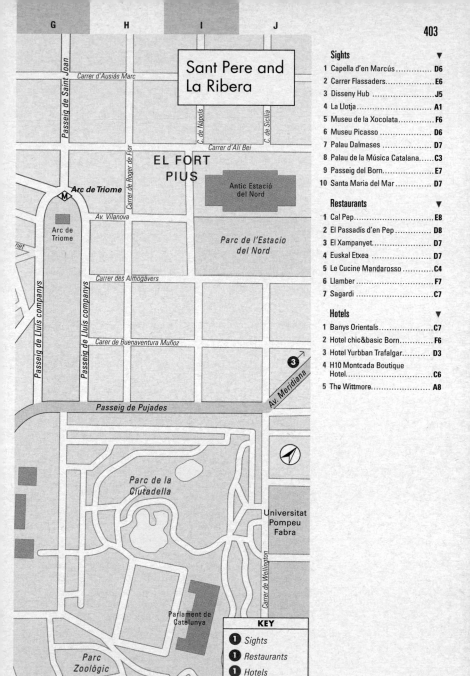

Sant Pere and La Ribera

EL FORT PIUS

Arc de Triome

Arc de Triome

Antic Estació del Nord

Parc de l'Estacio del Nord

Passeig de Saint Joan

Carrer d'Ausiàs Marc

C. de Nàpols

C. de Sicília

Carrer d'Alí Bei

Av. Vilanova

Carrer de Roger de Flor

Carrer des Almogàvers

Carrer de Buenaventura Muñoz

Passeig de Lluís companys

Passeig de Lluís companys

Carrer de Lluís companys

Passeig de Pujades

Av. Meridiana

Parc de la Ciutadella

Universitat Pompeu Fabra

Carrer de Wellington

Parlament de Catelunya

Parc Zoològic

Pg. Circumval lació

Sights ▼

1	Capella d'en Marcús	D6
2	Carrer Flassaders	E6
3	Disseny Hub	J5
4	La Llotja	A1
5	Museu de la Xocolata	F6
6	Museu Picasso	D6
7	Palau Dalmases	D7
8	Palau de la Música Catalana	C3
9	Passeig del Born	E7
10	Santa Maria del Mar	D7

Restaurants ▼

1	Cal Pep	E8
2	El Passadís d'en Pep	D8
3	El Xampanyet	D7
4	Euskal Etxea	D7
5	Le Cucine Mandarosso	C4
6	Llamber	F7
7	Sagardi	C7

Hotels ▼

1	Banys Orientals	C7
2	Hotel chic&basic Born	F6
3	Hotel Yurbban Trafalgar	D3
4	H10 Montcada Boutique Hotel	C6
5	The Wittmore	A8

KEY

- ❶ Sights
- ❶ Restaurants
- ❶ Hotels
- Ⓜ Metro Stops
- 🛈 Tourist Information

0   200 yards
0   200 meters

Carrer Flassaders

COMMERCIAL CENTER | Named for the weavers and blanket makers whom this street belonged to in medieval times, Carrer Flassaders begins on Carrer Montcada opposite La Xampanyet, one of La Ribera's most popular bars for tapas and cava. Duck into the short, dark Carrer Arc de Sant Vicenç; at the end you'll find yourself face to face with **La Seca,** the Royal Mint, where money was manufactured until the mid-19th century. Turn left on Carrer de la Seca to Carrer de la Cirera; overhead to the left is the image of **Santa Maria de Cervelló** , one of the patron saints of the Catalan fleet. Turn right on Carrer de la Cirera past the Otman shop and tearoom, and arrive at the corner of **Carrer dels Flassaders.** Walk left past several shops to the upbeat food court **Mercat Princesa** at No. 21 and the gourmet **Montiel** restaurant at No. 19. Wander through Flassaders' boutiques. Look up to your right at the corner of the gated Carrer de les Mosques, famous as Barcelona's narrowest street. The mustachioed countenance peering down at you was once a medieval advertisement for a brothel. **Hofmann,** at No. 44, is the excellent pastry shop of famous Barcelona chef Mey Hofmann; don't pass up the mascarpone croissants. ✉ *Carrer Flassaders, Born-Ribera* Ⓜ *Jaume I.*

★ Disseny Hub

MUSEUM | This center of activity represents the efforts of Barcelona's urban planners to put all the city's designer eggs in one basket and to plant an eye-catching architectural anchor in the long-delayed renewal project on Plaça de les Glòries. The new building is home to no less than four museum collections: the **Museu de Arts Tèxtil i Indumentària** (Textiles and Clothing Museum) of fashion, embroidery, jewelry, and accessories from ancient times to modern haute couture; the **Museu de Ceràmica** (Ceramics Museum), tracing the evolution of ceramic arts from 13th-century Moorish influences to the present, with a number of pieces by Miró and Picasso; the **Museu de les Arts Decoratives** (Museum of Decorative Arts), devoted mainly to the historical high arts of furniture and furnishings; and the **Gabinet de les Arts Gràfiques** (Graphic Arts Collection) of posters, packaging, typographic styles, and printed papers. ✉ *Edific DHUB, Pl. de les Glòries Catalans 37–8, Sant Martí* ☎ *93/256–6800* ⊕ *www.museudeldisseny.cat* 🎫 *€6, valid for 2 days; free Sun. 3–8 and all day 1st Sun. every month; 30% discount with Bus Turistic tickets* ⊘ *Closed Mon.* Ⓜ *L1 Glòries.*

La Llotja (*Maritime Exchange*)

BUILDING | Barcelona's maritime trade center, the Casa Llotja de Mar, was designed to be the city's finest example of civil architecture, built in the Catalan Gothic style between 1380 and 1392. At the end of the 18th century the facades were (tragically) covered in the neo-classical uniformity of the time, but the interior, the great Saló Gòtic (Gothic Hall), remained unaltered, and was a grand venue for balls throughout the 19th century. The hall, with its graceful arches and columns and floors of light Carrara and dark Genovese marble, has now been brilliantly restored. The building, which is not typically open to the general public, now houses the Barcelona Chamber of Commerce. The **Reial Acadèmia Catalana de Belles Arts de Sant Jordi** (Royal Catalan Academy of Fine Arts of St. George) still has its seat in the Llotja, and its museum is one of Barcelona's semisecret collections of art, from medieval paintings by unknown artists to modern works by members of the Academy itself. ■**TIP**➔ **To slip into the Saló Gòti, walk down the stairs from the museum to the second floor, then take the marble staircase down and turn right.** ✉ *Casa Llotja, Passeig d'Isabel II 1, Born-Ribera* ☎ *93/319–2432 Reial Acadèmia, 670/466260 guided visits to museum* ⊕ *www.racba.org* 🎫 *Free* ⊘ *Museum closed weekends* Ⓜ *L4 Barceloneta.*

Museu de la Xocolata

MUSEUM | FAMILY | The elaborate, painstakingly detailed chocolate sculptures, which have included everything from La Sagrada Família to Don Quixote's windmills, delight both youthful and adult visitors to this museum, set in an imposing 18th-century former monastery and developed by the Barcelona Provincial Confectionery Guild. Other exhibits here touch on Barcelona's centuries-old love affair with chocolate, the introduction of chocolate to Europe by Spanish explorers from the Mayan and Aztec cultures in the New World, and both vintage and current machinery and tools used to create this sweet delicacy. The beautiful shop and café offers rich hot and cold chocolate drinks, boxes and bars of artisanal chocolate, and house-made cakes and pastries. Classes on making and tasting chocolate are offered, too. ⊠ Carrer del Comerç 36, Born-Ribera ☎ 93/268–7878 ⊕ www. museuxocolata.cat ⊠ €6 Ⓜ L4 Jaume 1, L1 Arc de Triomf.

★ Museu Picasso (Picasso Museum)

MUSEUM | The Picasso Museum is housed in five adjoining palaces on Carrer Montcada, a street known for Barcelona's most elegant medieval palaces. Picasso spent his key formative years in Barcelona (1895–1904), and this collection, while it does not include a significant number of the artist's best paintings, is particularly strong on his early work. Displays include childhood sketches, works from Picasso's Rose and Blue periods, and the many famous 1950s Cubist variations on Velázquez's Las Meninas (in Rooms 22–26). The lower-floor sketches, oils, and schoolboy caricatures and drawings from Picasso's early years in A Coruña are perhaps the most fascinating part, showing the facility the artist seemed to possess almost from the cradle. On the second floor are works from his Blue Period in Paris, a time of loneliness, cold, and hunger for the artist. ■TIP→ Admission is free the first Sunday of the month and every Thursday 6–9:30 pm. Arrive early to avoid the long lines and crowds. ⊠ Carrer Montcada 15–19, Born-Ribera ☎ 93/256–3000, 93/256–3022 guided tour and group reservations ⊕ www.museupicasso.bcn.cat ⊠ €12; free Thurs. 6–9:30 pm, and 1st Sun. of month ⊙ Closed Mon. ☞ Guided tours of permanent collection (in English) Wed. at 3 and Sun. at 11 (except Aug.); free with admission Ⓜ L4 Jaume I, L1 Arc de Triomf.

Palau Dalmases

ARTS VENUE | If you can get through the massive wooden gates that open onto Carrer Montcada (at the moment, the only opportunity is when the first-floor café-theater Espai Barroc is open) you'll find yourself in Barcelona's best 17th-century Renaissance courtyard, built into a former 15th-century Gothic palace. Note the door knockers up at horseback level; then take a careful look at the frieze of "The Rape of Europa" running up the stone railing of the elegant stairway at the end of the patio. It's a festive abduction: Neptune's chariot, cherubs, naiads, dancers, tritons, and musicians accompany Zeus, in the form of a bull, as he carries poor Europa up the stairs and off to Crete. The stone carvings in the courtyard, the 15th-century Gothic chapel, with its reliefs of angelic musicians, and the vaulting in the reception hall and salon, are all that remain of the original 15th-century palace. ⊠ Carrer Montcada 20, Born-Ribera ☎ 93/310–0673 Espai Barroc ⊕ palaudalmases.com ⊠ Shows €25 (includes 1 drink) Ⓜ L4 Jaume I.

★ Palau de la Música Catalana

ARTS VENUE | One of the world's most extraordinary music halls, with facades that are a riot of color and form, the Music Palace is a landmark of Carrer Amadeus Vives, set just across Via Laietana, a 10-minute walk from Plaça de Catalunya. The Palau is a flamboyant tour de force designed in 1908 by Lluís Domènech i Montaner. Originally conceived by the Orfeó Català musical society as a vindication of the importance of music at a popular level—as opposed to the Liceu opera house's identification with the Catalan aristocracy—the Palau was for many decades an opposing crosstown force with the Liceu. The exterior is remarkable in itself. The Miquel Blay sculptural group is Catalonia's popular music come to life, with everyone included from St. George the dragonslayer to women and children, fishermen, and every strain and strata of popular life and music. The Palau's over-the-top decor overwhelms the senses even before the first note of music is heard. ✉ *Carrer Palau de la Música 4–6, Born-Ribera* ☎ *93/295–7200, 902/442882 box office* 🌐 *www.palaumusica.cat/en* 🎟 *Tour €20* [M] *L1/L4 Urquinaona.*

★ Passeig del Born

ARCHAEOLOGICAL SITE | Once the site of medieval jousts and autos-da-fé of the Inquisition, the passeig, at the end of Carrer Montcada behind the church of Santa Maria del Mar, was early Barcelona's most important square. Late-night cocktail bars and miniature restaurants with tiny spiral stairways now line the narrow, elongated plaza. Walk down to the Born—a great iron hangar, once a produce market designed by Josep Fontseré, in the Plaça Comercial, across the street from the end of the promenade. The initial stages of the construction of a public library in the Born uncovered the remains of the lost city of 1714, complete with blackened fireplaces, taverns, wells, and the canal that brought water into the city. The streets of the 14th- to 18th-century Born-Ribera lie open in the sunken central square of the old market; around it, on the ground level, are a number of new multifunctional exhibition and performance spaces; these give the city one of its newest and liveliest cultural subcenters. ✉ *Passeig del Born, Born-Ribera* ☎ *93/256–6851 El Born Centre de Cultura i Memòria* 🌐 *elbornculturaimemoria.barcelona.cat* 🎟 *Free to upper galleries, €6 to the archaeological site* 🕒 *Closed Mon.* [M] *L4 Jaume I/Barceloneta.*

★ Santa Maria del Mar

BUILDING | The most beautiful example of early Catalan Gothic architecture, Santa Maria del Mar is extraordinary for its unbroken lines and elegance, and the lightness of the interior is especially surprising considering the blocky exterior. The site was home to a Christian cult from the late 3rd century. Built by mere stonemasons who chose, fitted, and carved each stone hauled down from a Montjuïc quarry, the church is breathtakingly and nearly hypnotically symmetrical. The medieval numerological symbol for the Virgin Mary, the number eight (or multiples thereof) runs through every element of the basilica: the 16 octagonal pillars are 2 meters in diameter and spread out into rib vaulting arches at a height of 16 meters; the painted keystones at the apex of the arches are 32 meters from the floor; and the central nave is twice as wide as the lateral naves (8 meters each). Although anticlerical anarchists burned the basilica in 1936, it was restored after the end of the Spanish Civil War by Bauhaus-trained architects. ✉ *Pl. de Santa Maria 1, Born-Ribera* ☎ *93/310–2390* 🌐 *www.santamariadelmarbarcelona.org* 🎟 *Tour from €10* [M] *L4 Jaume I.*

🍴 Restaurants

Cal Pep

$$ | TAPAS | A two-minute walk east of Santa Maria del Mar, Cal Pep has been in a permanent feeding frenzy for more than 30 years, intensified even further by the hordes of tourists who now flock here. Pep serves a selection of tapas, cooked and served hot over the counter. **Known for:** excellent fish fry; delicious potato omelet; lively counter scene. [$] *Average main: €22* ✉ *Pl. de les Olles 8, Born-Ribera* ☎ *93/310–7961* 🌐 *www.calpep.com* 🕒 *Closed Sun., and 3 wks in Aug. No lunch Mon.* [M] *Jaume I, Barceloneta.*

El Passadís d'en Pep

$$$ | **SEAFOOD** | Hidden away at the end of a narrow unmarked passageway off the Pla del Palau, near the Santa Maria del Mar church, this restaurant is a favorite with well-heeled and well-fed gourmands who tuck in their napkins before devouring some of the city's best traditional seafood dishes. Sit down and waiters will begin serving delicious starters of whatever's freshest that day in the market in rapid-fire succession. **Known for:** fresh seafood; starters served in rapid-fire succession; no menu, but you can prebook a set menu online. [$] *Average main: €28* ✉ *Pl. del Palau 2, Born-Ribera* ☎ *93/310–1021* 🌐 *www.passadis.com* 🕓 *Closed Sun., and 3 wks in Aug.* [M] *Jaume I.*

El Xampanyet

$ | **TAPAS** | Just down the street from the Museu Picasso, dangling *botas* (leather wineskins) announce one of Barcelona's liveliest and most visually appealing taverns, with marble-top tables and walls decorated with colorful ceramic tiles. It's usually packed to the rafters with a rollicking mob of local and out-of-town celebrants. **Known for:** perfect Iberian ham; mouthwatering pa amb tomàquet; real cava. [$] *Average main: €12* ✉ *Montcada 22, Born-Ribera* ☎ *93/319–7003* 💳 *No credit cards* 🕓 *Closed Mon., and 2 wks in Aug. No dinner Sun.* [M] *Jaume I.*

Euskal Etxea

$$$ | **BASQUE** | An elbow-shaped, pine-paneled space, this bar-restaurant (one of the Sagardi group of Basque restaurants) is one of the better grazing destinations in the Born, with a colorful array of tapas and canapés on the bar, ranging from the olive-pepper-anchovy on a toothpick to chunks of tortilla. Other good bets include the *pimientos de piquillo* (red piquillo peppers) stuffed with codfish paste. **Known for:** Basque pintxos; art gallery on-site; excellent Euskal Txerria confit. [$] *Average main: €23* ✉ *Placeta de Montcada 1–3, Born-Ribera* ☎ *93/310–2185* 🌐 *www.gruposagardi.com* [M] *Jaume I.*

Le Cucine Mandarosso

$ | **ITALIAN** | This no-frills, big-flavor southern-Italian restaurant near the Via Laietana is a favorite with locals. Like Naples itself, it's cheap, charming, and over-full, with generous portions of lasagne, carbonara, and so on, featuring authentic ingredients from the in-store deli. **Known for:** reservations not accepted; long wait times; great homemade pastas. [$] *Average main: €12* ✉ *Verdaguer i Callís 4, Born-Ribera* ☎ *93/269–0780* 🌐 *www.lecucinemandarosso.com* 🕓 *Closed Mon.* [M] *Urquinaona.*

Llamber

$$ | **TAPAS** | It may look like one of the stylish, tourist-trap tapas restaurants that have sprung up recently, but Llamber's culinary pedigree sets it apart from the competition; chef Francisco Heras earned his chops in Spain's top restaurants. This dapper, friendly space attracts a mixed crowd with its excellent wine list and well-crafted tapas based on classic Catalan and Asturian recipes. **Known for:** well-crafted tapas; pig's trotters with rice; good late-night option. [$] *Average main: €17* ✉ *Fusina 5, Born-Ribera* ☎ *93/319–6250* 🌐 *www.llamber.com* [M] *Jaume 1.*

Sagardi

$$$ | **BASQUE** | An attractive wood-and-stone cider-house replica, Sagardi piles the counter with a dazzling variety of cold tapas; even better, though, are the hot offerings straight from the kitchen. The restaurant in back serves Basque delicacies like veal sweetbreads with artichokes and *txuletas de buey* (beef steaks) grilled over coals. **Known for:** multiple locations, all equally good; veal sweetbreads; charcoal grill. [$] *Average main: €23* ✉ *Argenteria 62, Born-Ribera* ☎ *93/319–9993* 🌐 *www.gruposagardi.com* [M] *Jaume I.*

Hotels

Banys Orientals

$$ | **HOTEL** | Despite its name, the "Oriental Baths" has no spa, but it does have chic high-contrast design, with dark stained wood and crisp white bedding, and is reasonably priced for the location. **Pros:** Rituals toiletries; tasteful design; steps from the port, Picasso Museum, and the Born area. **Cons:** rooms are on the small side; no room service; no terrace. [$] *Rooms from: €150* ✉ *Argenteria 37, Born-Ribera* ☎ *93/268–8460* 🌐 *www.hotelbanysorientals.com* 🛏 *43 rooms* 🍴 *No meals* [M] *L4 Jaume I.*

Hotel chic&basic Born

$ | **HOTEL** | The lobby of this hip little boutique hotel in the Born with its leather sofa and banquettes might remind you of a Starbucks, but the rooms tell a different story: the concept for chic&basic was whimsical, edgy accommodations at affordable prices, and designer Xavier Claramunt rose to the occasion. **Pros:** near upbeat Born-Ribera scene; bicycle rentals for guests; remote lets you change color of lights in room. **Cons:** no room service or minibars; no children under 12; clothing storage limited, on open racks. [$] *Rooms from: €120* ✉ *Carrer Princesa 50, Born-Ribera* ☎ *93/295–4652* 🌐 *www.chicandbasic.com* 🛏 *31 rooms* 🍴 *No meals* [M] *L4 Jaume I.*

H10 Montcada Boutique Hotel

$$$ | **HOTEL** | A short walk from the attractions of the Gothic Quarter and the Born-Ribera district, the Montcada is one of the 50 properties in the sleek H10 chain and a good choice for comfort and convenience. **Pros:** astounding rooftop deck with Jacuzzi; great location; pleasant breakfast room. **Cons:** wardrobes a tight fit by the bed; bed lighting could improve; no pets. [$] *Rooms from: €209* ✉ *Via Laietana 24, Born-Ribera* ☎ *93/268–8570* 🌐 *www.h10hotels.com* 🛏 *80 rooms* 🍴 *No meals* [M] *Jaume I.*

★ Hotel Yurbban Trafalgar

$$ | **HOTEL** | Guests and locals alike rave about the rooftop terrace at the Yurbban Trafalgar, and with good reason: the panoramic view is hands down one of the best in the city at this hip yet sophisticated hotel. **Pros:** free cheese and wine tasting nightly (8–9 pm); bicycles free for guests; minutes from Palau de la Música. **Cons:** small rooms; room service ends at 11 pm; small shower stalls. [$] *Rooms from: €160* ✉ *Carrer Trafalgar 30, Born-Ribera* ☎ *93/268–0727* 🌐 *yurbban.com/en* 🛏 *56 rooms* 🍴 *No meals* [M] *L1/L3 Urquinaona.*

★ The Wittmore

$$$$ | **HOTEL** | Opened in 2016, the Wittmore is the adults-only romantic hideaway par excellence, tucked away in a tiny cul-de-sac in the maze of streets just north of the marina, a short walk to the Plaça Colón. **Pros:** rooms include robes and slippers; cocktail bar with fireplace; plunge pool and bar on rooftop terrace. **Cons:** no spa or gym; budget-busting rates. [$] *Rooms from: €350* ✉ *Riudares 7, Born-Ribera* ☎ *93/550–0885* 🌐 *www.thewittmore.com* 🛏 *21 rooms* 🍴 *No meals* [M] *L3 Drassanes.*

Nightlife

La Ribera, considered one of Barcelona's most posh areas during medieval times, is still home to some of the city's loveliest ancient architecture. It exudes a tranquil yet distinctive vibe, the very same atmosphere found in the select number of bars, galleries, and eateries sprinkled between patches of greenery and arched stone passageways. El Born, the most voguish part of this district, provides a more eclectic collection of bars and lounge spots specializing in everything from craft beer to organic wines.

BARS
Ale&Hop

BARS/PUBS | Ale&Hop leads the pack in the latest craft-beer-bar invasion to hit the city. A slick microbrewery with exposed brick walls, monochrome wallpaper, and indie beats, Ale&Hop serves artisanal brews on tap or directly from the bottle. A slew of eco-wines and vegetarian snacks provide a health-conscious change of pace. ✉ *Basses de Sant Pere 10, Sant Pere* ☎ *93/126–9094* Ⓜ *Arc de Triomf.*

Bar Brutal

WINE BARS—NIGHTLIFE | Whimsically fashionable with its red tabletops, arched ceiling, and lacquered bar counter, Bar Brutal (and its adjoining bodega Can Cisa) is revered for its dedication to sustainability. The bar's entire stock of wines (300 and counting) is organically produced and much of it served straight from the barrel, without a lick of artificial additives to spoil the natural flavors. ✉ *Barra de Ferro 1, Born-Ribera* ☎ *93/295–4797* ⊕ *www.cancisa.cat* Ⓜ *Jaume I.*

La Vinya del Senyor

WINE BARS—NIGHTLIFE | Ambitiously named "The Lord's Vineyard," this romantic wine bar directly across from the entrance to the Santa Maria del Mar is etched into the ground floor of an ancient building. There's an extensive wine list and bite-size edibles, and ardent aficionados order by the bottle and favor tables found up a rickety ladder on the pint-size mezzanine or on the terrace. ✉ *Pl. de Santa Maria 5, Born-Ribera* ☎ *93/310–3379* Ⓜ *Jaume I.*

Paspartu

BARS/PUBS | Dark and inviting with just a smidgen of whimsy (check out the pop art posters and wooden crate stools), Paspartu boasts 25 gin flavors and the unspoken invitation to settle in and try each one—what else could comfy pillows, nonintrusive music, and bite-size nibbles mean? ✉ *Basses de Sant Pere 12* ☎ *699/546252* Ⓜ *Arc de Triomf.*

★ Rubí Bar

BARS/PUBS | The whimsical apothecary-like spirits cabinet, exposed-stone wall, and dramatic red lighting will be the first things to catch your eye at this cozy hidden gem, tucked away in the mazelike backstreets of El Born. However, it's the friendly service, relaxed atmosphere, and inventive selection of cocktails—most notably a choice of home-brewed flavored gins tantalizingly displayed on the bar shelves in hand-labeled bottles—that brings patrons back time and again. Add to the mix an eclectic playlist of funk, soul, rock, and pop classics, tasty snacks, and inexpensive mojitos that attract locals, expats, and the curious, ages 25–50 and beyond. ✉ *Banys Vells 6, Born-Ribera* ☎ *671/441888* Ⓜ *Jaume I.*

THEATER
La Puntual (*Putxinel·lis de Barcelona*)

THEATER | FAMILY | As one of the city's pioneering puppet (in Catalan, *putxinel·li*) theaters, this beloved venue features entertaining marionette, puppet, and shadow puppet performances. Private events for schools or birthday parties can be organized in Spanish, Catalan, and English. Weekend matinee performances are major kid magnets and tend to sell out fast, so arrive early or reserve a ticket in advance online. ✉ *Allada Vermell 15, Born-Ribera* ☎ *639/305353* ⊕ *www.lapuntual.info* Ⓜ *Jaume I.*

🛍 Shopping

The Ribera and Born neighborhoods, the old waterfront district around the Santa Maria del Mar basilica, seem to breed boutiques and shops of all kinds continuously. Interior design and clothing shops are the main draw. Check along Carrer Argenteria and Plaça de Santa Maria before zipping up Carrer Banys Vells. Two streets north of Carrer Montcada, go to Carrer Rec for designer haute couture clothing, jewelry, and knickknacks of all kinds. Carrer Vidrieria is lined with shops all the way over to Plaça de les Olles, where hometown clothing designer Custo Barcelona owns the corner across from the wildly popular tapas bar Cal Pep. Around Santa Maria del Mar basilica, the aromatic Casa Gispert on Carrer Sombrerers is not to be missed, nor is Baraka, the Moroccan goods expert on Carrer Canvis Vells. Vila Viniteca up Carrer Agullers near Via Laietana is always an interesting Bacchic browse.

CERAMICS AND GLASSWARE
Baraka

CERAMICS/GLASSWARE | Barcelona's prime purveyor of Moroccan goods, ceramics chief among them, Baraka is the city's general cultural commissar for matters relating to Spain's neighbor to the south. The prehaggled goods here are generally cheaper (and the quality better) than you could bring back from Morocco. Other African countries are represented, such as spectacular busts covered in tiny beads from Camaroon. ⊠ *Canvis Vells 2, Born-Ribera* ☎ *93/268–4220* ⊕ *www.barakaweb.com* Ⓜ *Jaume I.*

Helena Rohner

JEWELRY/ACCESSORIES | In a small shop on a backstreet in the Born, Helena Rohner is worth seeking out for its clean lines and minimal fuss—it's reminiscent of Georg Jensen, whom she worked for in the past. Simple silver ring, earring, and pendant settings hold semiprecious stones and enamel disks in on-trend colors, conceived for accessorizing this season's wardrobe. ⊠ *L' Espasseria 13, Born-Ribera* ☎ *93/319–8879* ⊕ *www.helenarohner.com* Ⓜ *Jaume I.*

CLOTHING
Anna Povo

CLOTHING | This stylish boutique near Plaça de les Olles displays an elegant and innovative selection of relaxed knits, coats, and dresses. In general, Anna Povo's designs are sleek and minimalist and colors follow this aesthetic, with cool tones in gray and beige. ⊠ *Vidrieria 11, Born-Ribera* ☎ *93/319–3561* ⊕ *www.annapovo.com* Ⓜ *Jaume I.*

Custo Barcelona

CLOTHING | Ever since Custo Dalmau and his brother David returned from a round-the-world motorcycle tour with visions of California surfing styles dancing in their heads, Custo Barcelona has been a runaway success with its clingy cotton tops in bright and cheery hues. Now with three branches in Barcelona (including an outlet shop at Plaça del Pi 2, in the Barri Gòtic) and many more across the globe, Custo is scoring even more acclaim by expanding into coats, dresses, and kids' wear. ⊠ *Pl. de les Olles 7, Born-Ribera* ☎ *93/268–7893* ⊕ *www.custo.com* Ⓜ *Jaume I.*

El Ganso

CLOTHING | Who would have thought that two Madrid-born brothers could out-Brit the Brits? One of Spain's more recent fashion success stories, El Ganso makes very appealing preppy-inspired men's, women's, and children's wear—striped blazers, pleated skirts, and tailored suits made for upper-class frolics. The label's Born shop only stocks male clothing, while its store on Rambla Catalunya (Rambla Catalunya 116) caters to men and women. ⊠ *Vidrieria 7, Born-Ribera* ☎ *932/689257* ⊕ *www.elganso.com* Ⓜ *Jaume I.*

FOOD
★ Casa Gispert

FOOD/CANDY | On the inland side of Santa Maria del Mar, this shop is one of the most aromatic and picturesque in Barcelona, bursting with teas, coffees, spices, saffron, chocolates, and nuts. The star element in this olfactory and pictur-esque feast is an almond-roasting stove in the back of the store—purportedly the oldest in Europe, dating from 1851 like the store itself. Don't miss the acid engravings on the office windows or the ancient wooden back door before picking up a bag of freshly roasted nuts to take with you. ⊠ *Sombrerers 23, Born-Ribera* ☎ *93/319–7535* ⊕ *www.casagispert.com* Ⓜ *Jaume I.*

Demasié

FOOD/CANDY | The shop's motto, "galetes Exageradament Bones" (biscuits that are exaggeratedly good) may seem like a bit of hype, but these rich colorful cookies are exceptionally tasty. They are best enjoyed with a cup of coffee at the bar inside, or you can have them wrapped up in a pretty duck-egg-blue box to take home with you. There is a Demasié café at Roger de Llúria 8 in the Eixample. ⊠ *Princesa 28, Born-Ribera* ☎ *93/269–1180* ⊕ *www.demasie.es* Ⓜ *Jaume I.*

La Botifarreria de Santa Maria

FOOD/CANDY | This busy emporium next to the church of Santa Maria del Mar stocks excellent cheeses, hams, pâtés, and homemade *sobrassadas* (pork pâté with paprika). Botifarra is the main item here, with a wide range of varieties, including egg sausage for meatless Lent and sausage stuffed with spinach, asparagus, cider, cinnamon, and Cabrales cheese. ⊠ *Santa Maria 4, Born-Ribera* ☎ *93/319–9123* ⊕ *www.labotifarreria.com* Ⓜ *Jaume I.*

★ Vila Viniteca

WINE/SPIRITS | Near Santa Maria del Mar, this is perhaps the best wine treasury in Barcelona, with a truly massive catalogue, tastings, courses, and a panoply of events, including a hugely popular street party to welcome in new-harvest wines (usually late October or early November). Under the same ownership, the tiny grocery store next door offers exquisite artisanal cheeses ranging from French goat cheese to Extremadura's famous Torta del Casar. There are a few tables inside, and, for a corkage fee, you can enjoy a bottle of wine together with a tasting platter. ⊠ *Agullers 7, Born-Ribera* ☎ *93/777–7017* ⊕ *www.vilaviniteca.es* Ⓜ *Jaume I.*

GIFTS AND SOUVENIRS
★ Natura

GIFTS/SOUVENIRS | A gracefully decorated store in the Spanish Natura chain, this crafts specialist stocks a good selection of global trifles, including pieces from India and North Africa. Incense, clothing, tapestries, candles, shoes, gadgets, and surprises of all kinds appear in this cross-cultural craft shop. ⊠ *Argenteria 78, Born-Ribera* ☎ *93/268–2525* ⊕ *www. naturaselection.com* Ⓜ *Jaume I.*

La Ciutedella and Barceloneta

Barceloneta and La Ciutadella fit together historically. In the early 18th century, some 1,000 houses in the Barrio de la Ribera, then the waterfront neighborhood around Plaça del Born, were ordered torn down, to create fields of fire for the cannon of La Ciutadella, the newly built fortress that kept watch over the rebellious Catalans. Barceloneta, then a marshy wetland, was filled in and developed almost four decades later, in 1753, to house the families who had lost homes in La Ribera.

Open water in Roman times, and gradually silted in only after the 15th-century construction of the port, it became Barcelona's fishermen's and stevedores' quarter. Eventually it became a sort of a safety valve, a little fishing village next door where locals could go to escape the formalities and constraints of city life, for a Sunday seafood lunch on the beach and a stroll through what felt like a freer world. With its tiny original apartment blocks, and its history of seafarers and gypsies, Barceloneta even now maintains its spontaneous, carefree flavor.

◉ Sights

Arc del Triomf

MEMORIAL | This exposed-redbrick arch was built by Josep Vilaseca as the grand entrance for the 1888 Universal Exhibition. Similar in size and sense to the traditional triumphal arches of ancient Rome, this one refers to no specific

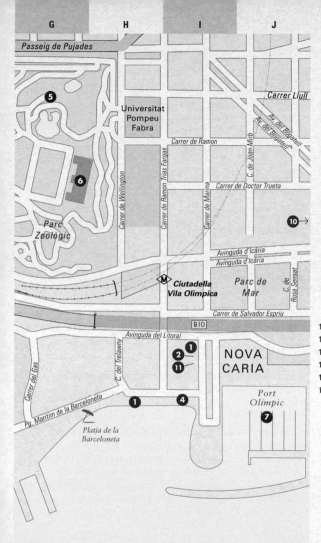

Passeig de Pujades

Carrer Llull

Universitat Pompeu Fabra

Carrer de Ramon

Av. del Bogatell

Av. del Bogatell

C. de Joan Miró

Carrer de Ramon Trias Fargas

Carrer de Wellington

Carrer de Marina

Carrer de Doctor Trueta

Parc Zoològic

Avinguda d'Icària

Avinguda d'Icària

Parc de Mar

C. de Rosa Sensat

Ciutadella Vila Olímpica

Carrer de Salvador Espriu

B10

Avinguda del Litoral

NOVA CARIA

C. del Trelawny

Carrer del Gas

Pg. Marítim de la Barceloneta

Port Olímpic

Platja de la Barceloneta

Sights ▼

1 Arc de Triomf F1
2 El Transbordador Aeri del Port ... B7
3 Estació de França E3
4 Museu d'Història
de Catalunya D4
5 Parc de la Ciutadella G1
6 Parlament de Catalunya G2
7 Port Olímpic J5
8 Port Vell D4
9 Sant Miquel del Port E5

Restaurants ▼

1 Agua H5
2 Arola I5
3 Barceloneta C6
4 Bestial I5
5 Blue Spot A8
6 Can Majó E6
7 Can Solé D5
8 1881 Per Sagardi D4
9 El Vaso de Oro E4
10 Els Pescadors J3
11 Enoteca I5
12 La Cova Fumada D5
13 La Mar Salada D6
14 Mana 75º A9
15 Pez Vela A9

Hotels ▼

1 Hotel Arts Barcelona I5
2 Hotel 54 Barceloneta D6
3 Soho House Barcelona B3
4 W Barcelona A9

KEY

1 Sights
1 Restaurants
1 Hotels
Ⓜ Metro Stops

Formerly an obsolete harbor, Port Vell is a modern yacht-basin and lively entertainment center.

military triumph anyone can recall. In fact, Catalonia's last military triumph of note may have been Jaume I el Conqueridor's 1229 conquest of the Moors in Mallorca—as suggested by the bats (always part of Jaume I's coat of arms) on either side of the arch itself. The Josep Reynés sculptures adorning the structure represent Barcelona hosting visitors to the exhibition on the western side (front), while the Josep Llimona sculptures on the eastern side depict the prizes being given to its outstanding contributors. ✉ *Passeig de Sant Joan, La Ciutadella* Ⓜ *L1 Arc de Triomf.*

El Transbordador Aeri del Port (*port cable car*)

TRANSPORTATION SITE (AIRPORT/BUS/FERRY/ TRAIN) | This hair-raising cable-car ride over the Barcelona harbor from Barceloneta to Montjuïc (with a midway stop in the port) is an adrenaline rush with a view. The rush comes from being packed in with 18 other people (standing-room only) in a tiny gondola swaying a hundred feet or so above the Mediterranean. The cable car leaves from the tower at the end of Passeig Joan de Borbó and connects the Torre de San Sebastián on the Moll de Barceloneta, the tower of Jaume I in the port boat terminal, and the Torre de Miramar on Montjuïc. ■**TIP➜ The Torre de Altamar restaurant in the tower at the Barceloneta end serves excellent food and wine.** ✉ *Passeig Joan de Borbó 88, Barceloneta* ☎ *93/441–4820* ⊕ *www. telefericodebarcelona.com* 🎫 *From €11* Ⓜ *L4 Barceloneta.*

Estació de França

TRANSPORTATION SITE (AIRPORT/BUS/FERRY/ TRAIN) | Barcelona's main railroad station until about 1980, and still in use, the elegant Estació de França is outside the west gate of the Ciutadella. Rebuilt in 1929 for the International Exhibition and restored in 1992 for the Olympics, this mid-19th-century building sits on Estació de Sants, the city's main intercity and international terminus. The marble and bronze, the Moderniste decorative details, and the delicate tracery of its wrought-iron roof girders make this one of the most beautiful buildings of its kind. Stop in for a sense of the bygone romance of European travel. ⊠ *Av. Marquès de l'Argentera s/n, La Ciutadella* ☎ *902/320230 RENFE office, 902/240505 ticket sales and reservations* Ⓜ *L4 Barceloneta.*

Museu d'Història de Catalunya

MUSEUM | Established in what used to be a port warehouse, this state-of-the-art interactive museum makes you part of Catalonian history, from prehistoric times to the contemporary democratic era. After centuries of "official" Catalan history dictated from Madrid (from 1714 until the mid-19th century Renaixença, and from 1939 to 1975), this offers an opportunity to revisit Catalonia's autobiography. Explanations of the exhibits appear in Catalan, Castilian, and English. Guided tours are available Sunday at noon and 1 pm. The rooftop restaurant has excellent views over the harbor and is open to the public (whether or not you visit the museum itself) during museum hours. ⊠ *Pl. de Pau Vila 3, Barceloneta* ☎ *93/225–4700* ⊕ *www.en.mhcat.net* ☜ *€5* ⊘ *Closed Mon.* Ⓜ *L4 Barceloneta.*

Parc de la Ciutadella (*Citadel Park*)

CITY PARK | FAMILY | Once a fortress designed to consolidate Madrid's military occupation of Barcelona, the Ciutadella is now the city's main downtown park. The clearing dates from shortly after the War of the Spanish Succession in the early 18th century, when Felipe V demolished some 1,000 houses in what was then the Barri de la Ribera to build a fortress and barracks for his soldiers and a *glacis* (open space) between rebellious Barcelona and his artillery positions. The fortress walls were pulled down in 1868 and replaced by gardens laid out by Josep Fontseré. In 1888 the park was the site of the Universal Exposition that put Barcelona on the map as a truly European city. ⊠ *Passeig de Picasso 21, La Ciutadella* Ⓜ *L4 Barceloneta, Ciutadella– Vila Olímpica, L1 Arc de Triomf.*

Parlament de Catalunya

BUILDING | Once the arsenal for the Ciutadella—as evidenced by the thickness of the building's walls—this is the only surviving remnant of Felipe V's fortress. For a time it housed the city's museum of modern art, before it was repurposed to house the unicameral Catalan Parliament. Under Franco, the Generalitat—the regional government—was suppressed, and the Hall of Deputies was shut fast for 37 years. Call or go online (⊕ *eed-ucativa@parlament.cat*) to book and schedule a free 45-minute guided tour of the building; the website makes it a bit complicated to register for a booking, but the grand "Salon Rose" is worth a visit in itself. ⊠ *Pl. de Joan Fiveller, Parc de la Ciutadella s/n, La Ciutadella* ☎ *93/304– 6500, 93/304–6645 guided visits* ⊕ *www. parlament.cat/document/cataleg/48179. pdf* ☜ *Free* Ⓜ *L4 Ciutadella/Vila Olímpica.*

Port Olímpic

BEACH—SIGHT | Filled with yachts, restaurants, tapas bars, and mega-restaurants serving reasonably decent fare continuously from 1 pm to 1 am, the Olympic Port is 2 km (1 mile) up the beach from Barceloneta, marked by the mammoth shimmering goldfish sculpture in its net of girders by starchitect Frank Gehry. In the shadow of Barcelona's first real skyscraper, the Hotel Arts, the Olympic Port draws thousands of young people of all nationalities on Friday and Saturday nights, especially in summer, to the beach at Nova Icària, generating a buzz redolent of spring break in Cancún. ⊠ *Port Olímpic, Port Olímpic* Ⓜ *L4 Ciuta-della/Vila Olímpica.*

Port Vell (*Old Port*)

MARINA | From Pla del Palau, cross to the edge of the port, where the Moll d'Espanya, the Moll de la Fusta, and the Moll de Barceloneta meet. (*Moll* means docks.) Just beyond the colorful Roy Lichtenstein sculpture in front of the post office, the modern Port Vell complex—an IMAX theater, aquarium, and Maremagnum shopping mall—stretches seaward to the right on the Moll d'Espanya. The Palau de Mar, with rows of somewhat pricey, tourist-oriented quayside terrace restaurants (try La Gavina, the Merendero de la Mari, or El Magatzem), stretches down along the Moll de Barceloneta to the left. Key points in the Maremagnum complex are the grassy hillside (popular on April 23, Sant Jordi's Day) and the *Ictineo II*, a replica of the world's first submarine created by Narcis Monturiol (1819–85), launched in the Barcelona port in 1862. ✉ *Port Vell, Barceloneta* Ⓜ *L4 Barceloneta.*

Sant Miquel del Port

RELIGIOUS SITE | Have a close look at this baroque church with its modern (1992), pseudo-bodybuilder version of the winged archangel Michael himself, complete with sword and chain, in the alcove on the facade. (The figure is a replica; the original was destroyed in 1936.) One of the first buildings to be completed in Barceloneta, Sant Miquel del Port was begun in 1753 and finished by 1755 under the direction of architect Damià Ribes. Due to strict orders to keep Barceloneta low enough to fire La Ciutadella's cannon over, Sant Miquel del Port had no bell tower and only a small cupola until Elies Rogent added a new one in 1853. Interesting to note are the metopes: palm-sized gilt bas-relief sculptures around the interior cornice and repeated outside at the top of the facade. These 74 Latin-inscribed allegories each allude to different attributes of St. Michael. For example, the image of a boat and the Latin inscription "iam in tuto" (finally safe), alludes to the saint's protection against the perils of the sea. ✉ *Carrer de Sant Miquel 39, Barceloneta* ☎ *93/221–6550* Ⓜ *L4 Barceloneta.*

 Beaches

Platja de la Barceloneta

BEACHES | Just to the left at the end of Passeig Joan de Borbó, this is the easiest Barcelona beach to get to, hence the most crowded and the most fun for people-watching—though itinerant beach vendors can be a nuisance. Along with swimming, there are windsurfing and kitesurfing rentals to be found just up behind the beach at the edge of La Barceloneta. Rebecca Horn's sculpture L'Estel Ferit, a rusting stack of cubes, expresses nostalgia for the beach-shack restaurants that lined the beach here until 1992. Surfers trying to catch a wave wait just off the breakwater in front of the excellent beachfront Agua restaurant. **Amenities:** food and drink; lifeguards; showers; toilets; water sports. **Best for:** partiers; surfing; swimming; walking; windsurfing. ✉ *Passeig Marítim de la Barceloneta s/n, Barceloneta* Ⓜ *Ciutadella/Vila Olímpica.*

Platja de la Mar Bella

BEACHES | Closest to the Poblenou metro stop near the eastern end of the beaches, this is a thriving gay enclave and the unofficial nudist beach of Barcelona (although clothed bathers are welcome, too). The water-sports center Base Nàutica de la Mar Bella rents equipment for sailing, surfing, and windsurfing. Outfitted with showers, safe drinking fountains, and a children's play area, La Mar Bella also has lifeguards who warn against swimming near the breakwater. The excellent Els Pescadors restaurant is just inland on Plaça Prim. **Amenities:** food and drink; lifeguards; showers; toilets; water sports. **Best for:** partiers; nudists; swimming; windsurfing. ✉ *Passeig Marítim del Bogatell, Poblenou* Ⓜ *Poblenou.*

Platja de la Nova Icària

BEACHES | One of Barcelona's most popular beaches, this strand is just east of Port Olímpic, with a full range of entertainment and refreshment venues close at hand. (Xiringuito Escribà is one of the most popular restaurants overlooking neighboring Bogatell beach.) The wide beach is directly across from the neighborhood built as the residential Olympic

Village for Barcelona's 1992 Olympic Games, an interesting housing project that has now become a popular residential neighborhood. Vendors prowl the sand, offering everything from sunglasses to cold drinks to massages. **Amenities:** food and drink; lifeguards; showers; toilets; water sports. **Best for:** partiers; swimming; walking; windsurfing. ✉ *Passeig Marítim del Port Olímpic s/n, Port Olímpic* [M] *Ciutadella/Vila Olímpic.*

Platja de Sant Sebastià

BEACHES | Barceloneta's most southwestern platjas (to the right at the end of Passeig Joan de Borbó), Sant Sebastià is the oldest and most historic of the city beaches; it was here that 19th-century barcelonins cavorted in bloomers and bathing costumes. Neglected (and a bit disreputable) during the Franco years, it's had a rebirth of popularity since the pre-Olympic redesign of the city's waterfront. Between the beach and the Torre Sant Sebastia cable car terminus is the Club Natació Atlètic de Barcelona; the Hotel W Barcelona is at the far south end. **Amenities:** food and drink; lifeguards; showers; toilets. **Best for:** partiers; swimming. ✉ *Passeig Maritim de la Barceloneta s/n, Barceloneta* [M] *L4, Barceloneta.*

🍴 Restaurants

Barceloneta and the Port Olímpic (Olympic Port) have little in common beyond their seaside location. Port Olímpic offers a somewhat massive-scaled and modern environment with a crazed disco strip, while Barceloneta has retained its traditional character as a blue-collar neighborhood, even if few fishermen live here now. Traditional family restaurants and tourist traps can look similar from the street; a telltale sign of unreliable establishments is the presence of hard-selling waiters outside, aggressively courting passing customers.

East of the Eixample and extending to the sea just beyond Port Olímpic, Poblenou's formerly rough-around-the-edges neighborhood with a historical heart has lately seen an influx of edgy art studios, design shops, and even a few hip restaurants—many of these spaces are installed in converted warehouses and industrial concerns.

Agua

$$ | **MEDITERRANEAN** | Hit Agua's terrace on warm summer nights and sunny winter days, or just catch rays inside the immense windows. Either way you'll have a prime spot for beachside people-watching. **Known for:** fresh seafood; must reserve in advance; popular tourist spot. [$] *Average main: €19* ✉ *Passeig Marítim de la Barceloneta 30, Port Olímpic* ☎ *93/225–1272* 🌐 *www.grupotragaluz.com* [M] *Ciutadella–Vila Olímpica.*

Arola

$$$ | **TAPAS** | Top-class tapas on a terrace are surprisingly hard to find, which is why sophisticated snack-seekers head for the eponymous restaurant of Michelin-starred chef Sergi Arola in the Hotel Arts. DJs provide a chilled-out evening atmosphere where diners can sip cocktails and enjoy views of Frank Gehry's Mediterranean-facing *Fish* statue. **Known for:** signature patatas bravas; novel presentation of dishes; superior quality. [$] *Average main: €28* ✉ *Marina 19–21, Port Olímpic* ✢ *Entrance is via lift near street-level entrance to Hotel Arts* ☎ *93/483–8090* 🌐 *www.hotelarts-barcelona.com* ⏲ *Closed Tues. and Wed.* [M] *Ciutadella/Vila Olimpica.*

Barceloneta

$$$ | **SEAFOOD** | This restaurant in an enormous riverboat-like building at the end of the yacht marina in Barceloneta is definitely geared up for high-volume business. The food—paellas and grilled fish dishes are the specialties—is delicious, the service impeccable, and the hundreds of fellow diners make the place feel like a cheerful New Year's Eve celebration. **Known for:** lively waterside spot; excellent salads, rice, and fish dishes;

free valet parking. ⓢ *Average main: €25* ✉ *Escar 22, Barceloneta* ☎ *93/221–2111* ⊕ *www.restaurantbarceloneta.com* Ⓜ *Barceloneta.*

Bestial

$$ | MEDITERRANEAN | Sea views from a multilevel terrace are Bestial's most obvious attraction, but its luxury location beneath Frank Gehry's *Fish* statue is in no way diminished by the food. On the menu, spicy clams and seasonal soups lead up to a star dish of roasted wild fish on a bed of waxy potatoes. **Known for:** beachfront terrace; fresh seafood; pre-club crowd. ⓢ *Average main: €20* ✉ *Ramon Trias Fargas 2–4, Port Olímpic* ☎ *93/224–0407* ⊕ *www.grupotragaluz. com* ⊘ *No dinner Sun.–Wed.* Ⓜ *Ciutadel-la-Vila Olimpica.*

★ Blue Spot

$$ | MEDITERRANEAN | An architect-designed dining room with jaw-dropping views (up and down the coast, in this case) is all too often a predictor of humdrum cooking, at least in Barcelona. Blue Spot—on the eighth floor of a building at the southernmost tip of Barceloneta's beach—breaks this mold with some assured and original Mediterranean-inspired dishes. **Known for:** stunning views; charcoal-grilled food; fashionable crowd. ⓢ *Average main: €21* ✉ *Edifici Ocean, Passeig Joan de Borbó 101, Barceloneta* ☎ *93/144–7866* ⊕ *www.encompaniadelo-bos.com* Ⓜ *Barceloneta.*

Can Majó

$$$ | SEAFOOD | FAMILY | One of Barcelona's best-known seafood restaurants sits by the beach in Barceloneta and specializes in such house favorites as *caldero de bogavante* (a cross between paella and lobster bouillabaisse) and *suquet* (fish stewed in its own juices), but the full range of typical Spanish rice and seafood dishes are also available. Can Majó doesn't consistently reach the standards that once made it famous, but the cooking is still a notch above most of the

touristy haunts nearby. **Known for:** terrace overlooking the Mediterranean; Spanish rice and fish dishes; excellent paella. ⓢ *Average main: €25* ✉ *Almirall Aixada 23, Barceloneta* ☎ *93/221–5455* ⊕ *www. canmajo.es* ⊘ *Closed Mon. No dinner Sun.* Ⓜ *Barceloneta.*

★ Can Solé

$$$ | SEAFOOD | With no sea views or touts outside to draw in diners, Can Solé has to rely on its reputation as one of Barceloneta's best options for seafood for more than 100 years. Faded photos of half-forgotten local celebrities line its walls, but there's nothing out-of-date about the food. **Known for:** open kitchen; fresh fish daily; traditional Spanish rice dishes. ⓢ *Average main: €27* ✉ *Sant Carles 4, Barceloneta* ☎ *93/221–5012* ⊕ *restaurantcansole.com* ⊘ *Closed Mon. and 2 wks in Aug. No dinner Sun.* Ⓜ *Barceloneta.*

1881 Per Sagardi

$$ | BASQUE | Views of yachts sailing out into the glittering Mediterranean sea and the aroma of a wood-fired grill that turns out classic Basque cuisine are a compelling combination here. The Sagardi group's most stylish establishment is perched atop a handsomely renovated former warehouse, which now houses the Catalan History Museum. **Known for:** pleasant terrace; all-day kitchen; sea views. ⓢ *Average main: €22* ✉ *Pl. de Pau Vila 3, Barceloneta* ☎ *93/221–0050* ⊕ *www.gruposagardi. com* Ⓜ *Barceloneta.*

★ El Vaso de Oro

$ | TAPAS | A favorite with gourmands, this often overcrowded little counter serves some of the best beer and tapas in town. The house-brewed artisanal draft beer—named after the Fort family who own and run the bar—is drawn and served with loving care by veteran epauletted waiters who have it down to a fine art. **Known for:** old-school service; stand-up dining; beef fillet is a favorite. ⓢ *Average main: €15*

✉ *Balboa 6, Barceloneta* ☎ *93/319–3098* 🌐 *www.vasodeoro.com* ⏲ *Closed 1st 3 wks of Sept.* [M] *Barceloneta.*

Els Pescadors

$$$ | **SEAFOOD** | **FAMILY** | Northeast of the Port Olímpic, in the newly fashionable Poblenou neighborhood, this handsome late-19th-century dining room has a lovely terrace on a little square shaded by immense ombú trees. Kids can play safely in the traffic-free square while their parents feast on well-prepared seafood specialties such as paella, fresh fish, *fideuà* (a paella-like noodle dish), and the succulent suquet. **Known for:** village-square atmosphere; standard-setting rice and fish dishes; pretty terrace. [$] *Average main: €27* ✉ *Pl. de Prim 1, Port Olímpic* ☎ *93/225–2018* 🌐 *www.elspescadors.com* [M] *Poblenou* ✥ *H6.*

Enoteca

$$$$ | **CATALAN** | Located in the Hotel Arts, Enoteca is the Barcelona outlet for the talents of five?Michelin star chef Paco P?rez, two of which he has earned here. His creative and technically accomplished cooking uses peerless Mediterranean and Pyrenean products, transforming them into astonishing dishes that are both surprising and satisfying. **Known for:** superstar chef; extensive wine list; two Michelin stars. [$] *Average main: €40* ✉ *Hotel Arts, Marina 19, Port Olímpic* ☎ *93/483–8108* 🌐 *enotecapacoperez.com/en* ⏲ *Closed Sun., Mon., 2 wks in Mar., and 2 wks at Christmas. No dinner Tues.–Fri.* [M] *Ciutadella–Vila Olímpica.*

★ La Cova Fumada

$ | **TAPAS** | There's no glitz, no glamour, and not even a sign on the wall, but the battered wooden doors of this old, family-owned tavern hide a tapas bar to be treasured. Loyal customers queue for the market-fresh seafood, served hot from the furiously busy kitchen. **Known for:** impromptu live music; the original "bomba" fried potato croquette; erratic opening times. [$] *Average main: €10* ✉ *Baluard 56, Barceloneta* ☎ *93/221–4061* ⏲ *Closed Sun. No dinner Mon.–Wed. and Sat.* [M] *Barceloneta.*

La Barceloneta, Land of Paella

Paella is Valencian, not Catalan, but Sunday paella in La Barceloneta is a classic Barcelona family outing. *Paella marinera* is a seafood rice boiled in fish stock and seasoned with clams, mussels, prawns, and jumbo shrimp, while the more traditional paella valenciana omits seafood but includes chicken, rice, and snails. *Arròs negre* (black rice) is rice cooked in squid ink, and *arròs caldòs* is a soupier dish that often includes lobster. *Fideuá* is made with vermicelli noodles mixed with the standard ingredients. Paella is for a minimum of two diners—it's usually enough for three.

★ La Mar Salada

$$ | **SEAFOOD** | This restaurant stands out on a street of seafood specialists by offering creative twists on classic dishes at rock-bottom prices. Traditional favorites such as paella, black rice, and fideuà (a paella-like pasta dish) are reinvigorated, and freshness is assured as ingredients come directly from the lonja fish quay across the street, a lively auction where Barcelona's small fishing fleet sells its wares. **Known for:** fresh in-season ingredients; excellent-value seafood; creative desserts. [$] *Average main: €19* ✉ *Passeig Joan de Borbó 58, Barceloneta* ☎ *93/221–2127* 🌐 *www.lamarsalada.cat* ⏲ *Closed Tues.* [M] *Barceloneta.*

Mana 75º

$$ | **MEDITERRANEAN** | **FAMILY** | Catalan fashion firm Desigual, whose offices sit above Mana 75º, has added fabrics and flair to the restaurant's beautifully airy interior, which evokes a sophisticated

sea shack. Service is friendly and the high-tech open kitchen fires out precisely perfect rice dishes such as paella, but portion sizes are on the ungenerous side. **Known for:** superb paellas and rice dishes; open kitchen; free parking. $ *Average main: €19* ⊠ *Passeig de Joan de Borbó 101, Barceloneta* ☎ *93/832–6415* ⊕ *www.mana75.es* ⊘ *Closed Mon. No dinner Sun. and Tues.–Thurs.* Ⓜ *Barceloneta.*

Pez Vela

$$ | SPANISH | FAMILY | The quality of beachside dining in Barcelona has surged in recent years, and this pseudo- *chiringuito* (beach bar) beneath the towering W Hotel is as good a place as any to combine paella with a perfect view of the sea. Rice dishes are better than at many better-known seafood specialists. **Known for:** Galician-style octopus; zingy lemon pie; beachside location and views. $ *Average main: €19* ⊠ *Passeig del Mare Nostrum 19–21, Barceloneta* ☎ *93/221–6317* ⊕ *www.grupotragaluz.com* Ⓜ *Barceloneta.*

🛏 Hotels

★ Hotel Arts Barcelona

$$$$ | HOTEL | This luxurious Ritz-Carlton-owned, 44-story skyscraper overlooks Barcelona from the Port Olímpic, providing stunning views of the Mediterranean, the city, the Sagrada Família, and the mountains beyond. **Pros:** excellent tapas restaurant on-site; fine art throughout hotel; free cava served on club floors daily. **Cons:** a 20-minute hike or more from central Barcelona; very pricey. $ *Rooms from: €355* ⊠ *Carrer de la Marina 19–21, Port Olímpic* ☎ *93/221–1000* ⊕ *www.hotelartsbarcelona.com* ⇌ *483 rooms* ⓘⓞⓘ *No meals* Ⓜ *L4 Ciutadella–Vila Olímpica.*

Hotel 54 Barceloneta

$$ | HOTEL | Just a few minutes' walk from the beach, this 2007 addition to the Barcelona hotel scene has much to offer in location, comfort, and economy. **Pros:**

rooftop terrace with great views of the marina and the Old Port; competent multilingual staff; pleasant rustic breakfast room. **Cons:** noisy around the clock on Passeig Joan de Borbó; bathrooms lack space and privacy. $ *Rooms from: €150* ⊠ *Passeig Joan de Borbó 54, Barceloneta* ☎ *93/225–0054* ⊕ *www.hotel54barceloneta.es* ⇌ *28 rooms* ⓘⓞⓘ *No meals* Ⓜ *L4 Barceloneta.*

Soho House Barcelona

$$$$ | HOTEL | Not a hotel in the usual sense, Soho House is one of a group of private members' clubs for people professionally involved in one way or another in the arts; the concept originated in London in 1995 and now involves facilities worldwide. **Pros:** vibrant atmosphere; "Sunday Feast" brunch in the glassed-in atrium restaurant; well located for exploring the port, Barceloneta, and the Born-Ribera quarter. **Cons:** hard on the budget; some lounge areas and facilities are members-only; feels a bit exclusive. $ *Rooms from: €340* ⊠ *Plaça del Duc de Medinaceli 4, Port Olímpic* ☎ *93/220–4600* ⊕ *www.sohohouse.com* ⇌ *57 rooms* ⓘⓞⓘ *No meals* Ⓜ *L4 Barceloneta, L3 Drassanes.*

★ W Barcelona

$$$$ | HOTEL | This towering sail-shaped monolith dominates the skyline on the Barcelona waterfront; architect Ricardo Bofill's W, now part of the Marriott International chain, is a stunner inside and out, from the six-story atrium lobby with black ceramic tile floors, suspended basket chairs, and glitter walls, to the adjacent bar-lounge with direct access to the "WET" lounge deck, chill-out divans, and pool. **Pros:** unrivaled views; excellent restaurants on-site; transfer service to/from airport and cruise dock. **Cons:** extra amenities can get pricey; far from public transportation (20-minute hike); loud music in public areas. $ *Rooms from: €280* ⊠ *Pl. de la Rosa dels Vents 1, Moll de Llevant, Barceloneta* ☎ *93/295–2800*

⊕ *www.w-barcelona.com* ↵ *473 rooms* ⫠○⫠ *No meals* Ⓜ *L4 Barceloneta.*

Nightlife

The stretch of seaside between Port Vell and Port Olímpic is bursting with Barceloneta's trendy chiringuitos (beach shacks), laid-back bars, and terraced seafood restaurants. In sharp contrast, Port Olímpic's posh nightclub scene caters to the city's fashionable glitterati, aged 21 and over.

Once the city's central industrial hub, Poblenou's contrasting faces—a quaint tree-lined rambla surrounded by vast warehouse spaces and ultramodern edifices—are the main reason for its recent metamorphosis into Barcelona's hippest enclave. Once-abandoned spaces have been renovated into chic artists' lofts and work spaces while vintage shops and nondescript restos are now enjoying new lives as retro-fab bars and lounges oozing with charm.

BARS
★ Balius Bar
BARS/PUBS | Named after the historic hardware store that once stood here, Balius Bar has retro-chic decor, a snazzy playlist (don't miss the live jazz sessions on Sunday), and a puckish "no standing" policy that attract hepcats aged 30 and above looking to kick back with a good cocktail and a side of nostalgia. Afternoons are reserved for vermouth and all the fixings or a chilled cava cocktail paired with fresh, often eco-conscious, bites. In the evenings, creative cocktails are the main draw. ⊠ *Pujades 196, Poblenou* ☎ *93/315–8650* ⊕ *baliusbar. com* Ⓜ *Poblenou.*

★ Eclipse Bar
BARS/PUBS | The sensational shoreline views from the 26th floor of the seaside W Hotel are undoubtedly a major part of Eclipse's attraction. Add to the mix an ultraslick interior design, an impressive

roster of international DJs spinning themed parties every day of the week, and deluxe cocktails decadently paired with sushi, and it's little wonder that this is a favorite spot for glitterati to be seen and heard. ⊠ *Pl. de la Rosa dels Vents 1, Barceloneta* ☎ *93/295–2800* ⊕ *www. eclipse-barcelona.com* Ⓜ *Drassanes.*

La Cervecita Nuestra de Cada Día
BARS/PUBS | For craft beer lovers, this modern high-ceilinged bar and shop is must. Filled to the brim with more than 300 international craft brands plus several local artisanal beers on tap, the venue solidifies its devotion to everything cerveza with organized tastings, pairings, and courses. Claim your spot early as regulars routinely dominate the seating at the long bar or the cozy corner tables up front. ⊠ *Llull 184, Poblenou* ☎ *93/486–9271* Ⓜ *Llacuna.*

Madame George
BARS/PUBS | Everything about this stylish bar is a happy contradiction: the chandeliered space has large gilded mirrors and polished chocolate brown stools that curiously complement the rickety antiques and quirky touches (check out the bathtub sofa in the back room). Cocktails run the full gamut from classic to creative (the piscopolitan, a perfect marriage of Peruvian pisco and the classic cosmo cocktail, is a triumph.) ⊠ *Pujades 179, Poblenou* ☎ *93/500–5151* ⊕ *www. madamegeorgebar.com* Ⓜ *Poble Nou.*

Més de Vi
BARS/PUBS | The brainchild of two Catalan sommeliers, Més de Vi is a chic wine bar with a purpose: to educate visitors on the art of Spanish wines, with a particular focus on regional vintages. Depending on mood and company, there are plenty of seating options: a tasting table for serious aficionados, romantic tête-à-tête tables for a memorable night out, and a bar area for socializing. ⊠ *Marià Aguiló 123, Poblenou* ☎ *93/007–9151* ⊕ *www. mesdvi.cat* Ⓜ *Poble Nou.*

The Eixample

The Eixample (ay-shompla) is an open-air Moderniste museum. Designed as a grid, in the best Cartesian tradition, the Eixample is oddly difficult to find your way around in; the builders seldom numbered the buildings and declined to alphabetize the streets, and even Barcelona residents can get lost in it. The easiest orientation to grasp is the basic division between the well-to-do Dreta, to the right of Rambla Catalunya looking inland, and the more working-class Ezquerra to the left. Eixample locations are also either *mar* (on the ocean side of the street) or *muntanya* (facing the mountains).

Sights

Casa Amatller

BUILDING | The neo-Gothic Casa Amatller was built by Josep Puig i Cadafalch in 1900, when the architect was 33 years old. Puig i Cadafalch's architectural historicism sought to recover Catalonia's proud past, in combination with eclectic elements from Flemish and Dutch architectural motifs. Note the Eusebi Arnau sculptures—especially his St. George and the Dragon, and the figures of a drummer with his dancing bear. The first-floor apartment, where the Amatller family lived, is a museum, with the original furniture and decor (guided tours are offered in English daily at 11 am). ✉ *Passeig de Gràcia 41, Eixample* ☎ *93/461–7460 tour info and ticket sales* ⊕ *amatller.org/en/* ✄ *Tours from €19* Ⓜ *L2/L3/L5 Passeig de Gràcia, FGC Provença.*

Casa Batlló

BUILDING | **FAMILY** | Gaudí at his most spectacular, the Casa Batlló is actually a makeover: it was originally built in 1877 by one of Gaudí's teachers, Emili Sala Cortés, and acquired by the Batlló family in 1900. Batlló wanted to tear down the undistinguished Sala building and start over, but Gaudí persuaded him to remodel the facade and the interior, and the result is astonishing. The facade— with its rainbow of colored glass and *trencadís* (polychromatic tile fragments) and the toothy masks of the wrought-iron balconies projecting outward toward the street—is an irresistible photo op. Nationalist symbolism is at work here: the scaly roof line represents the Dragon of Evil impaled on St. George's cross, and the skulls and bones on the balconies are the dragon's victims, allusions to medieval Catalonia's code of chivalry and religious piety. On summer evenings, you can listen to a concert (starts at 8 pm) and enjoy a drink on the terrace, as part of the "Magic Night" program. ✉ *Passeig de Gràcia 43, Eixample* ☎ *93/216–0306* ⊕ *www.casabatllo.es* ✄ *From €25* Ⓜ *L2/ L3/L4 Passeig de Gràcia, FGC Provença.*

Casa Calvet

HOUSE | This exquisite but more conventional town house (for Gaudí, anyway) was the architect's first commission in the Eixample (the second was the dragon-like Casa Batlló, and the third, and last—he was never asked to do another—was the stone quarry–esque Casa Milà). Peaked with baroque scroll gables over the unadorned (no ceramics, no color, no sculpted ripples) Montjuïc sandstone facade, Casa Calvet compensates for its structural conservatism with its Art Nouveau details, from the door handles to the benches, chairs, vestibule, and spectacular glass-and-wood elevator. The only part of the building accessible to visitors is the ground-floor **Casa Calvet** restaurant, originally the suite of offices for Calvet's textile company, with its exuberant Moderniste decor. ✉ *Carrer Casp 48, Eixample* ⊕ *www.casacalvet.es (restaurant)* Ⓜ *L1/L4 Urquinaona.*

Casa de les Punxes (*House of the Spikes*)

BUILDING | Also known as Casa Terrades for the family that owned the house and commissioned Puig i Cadafalch to build it, this extraordinary cluster of six conical towers ending in impossibly sharp needles is another of Puig i Cadafalch's inspirations, this one rooted in the Gothic architecture of northern European countries. One of the few freestanding Eixample buildings, visible from 360 degrees, this ersatz Bavarian or Danish castle in downtown Barcelona is composed entirely of private apartments, some of them built into the conical towers themselves on three circular levels, connected by spiral stairways. The ground floor, first level, terrace, and towers are now open to the public; check the website for the schedule of guided tours in English. ✉ *Av. Diagonal 416–420, Eixample* ☎ *93/018–5242* ⊕ *casadelespunxes.com* 🚇 *From €13* Ⓜ *L4/L5 Verdaguer, L3/L5 Diagonal.*

Casa Golferichs (*Golferichs Civic Center*)
ARTS VENUE | Gaudí disciple Joan Rubió i Bellver built this extraordinary house, known as El Xalet (The Chalet), for the Golferichs family when he was not yet 30. The rambling wooden eaves and gables of the exterior enclose a cozy and comfortable dark-wood-lined interior with a pronounced verticality. The top floor, with its rich wood beams and cerulean walls, is often used for intimate concerts; the ground floor exhibits paintings and photographs. The building serves now as the quarters of the Golferichs Centre Civic, which offers local residents a range of conferences and discussions, exhibitions and adult education courses, and organizes various thematic walking tours of the city. ✉ *Gran Via 491, Eixample* ☎ *93/323–7790* ⊕ *www.golferichs.org* 🕙 *Closed Sun.* Ⓜ *L1 Rocafort, Urgell.*

★ **Casa Milà**
BUILDING | Usually referred to as *La Pedrera* (The Stone Quarry), with a wavy, curving stone facade that undulates around the corner of the block, this building, unveiled in 1910, is one of Gaudí's most celebrated yet initially reviled designs. Seemingly defying the laws of gravity, the exterior has no straight lines, and is adorned with winding balconies covered with wrought-iron foliage sculpted by Josep Maria Jujol. Gaudí's rooftop chimney park, alternately interpreted as veiled Saharan women or helmeted warriors, is as spectacular as anything in Barcelona, especially in late afternoon when the sunlight slants over the city into the Mediterranean. Inside, the handsome **Espai Gaudí** (Gaudí Space) in the attic has excellent critical displays of Gaudí's works from all over Spain. The Pis de la Pedrera apartment is an interesting look into the life of a family that lived in La Pedrera in the early 20th century. Entrance lines can be long; book ahead for tours. ✉ *Passeig de Gràcia 92, Eixample* ☎ *93/214–2576* ⊕ *www.lapedrera.com/en/home* 🚇 *From €22* Ⓜ *L2/L3/L5 Diagonal, FGC Provença.*

Casa Montaner i Simó–Fundació Tàpies
BUILDING | Built in 1880, this former publishing house, and the city's first building to incorporate iron supports, has been handsomely converted to hold the work of preeminent contemporary Catalan painter Antoni Tàpies, and a collection of works by many important modern artists that he acquired over his lifetime. Tàpies, who died in 2012, was an abstract painter, but was also influenced by surrealism, which accounts for the *Núvol i Cadira* (*Cloud and Chair*) sculpture atop the structure. The modern airy split-level gallery also has a bookstore that's strong on Tàpies, Asian art, and Barcelona art and architecture. ✉ *Carrer Aragó 255, Eixample* ☎ *93/487–0315* ⊕ *www.fundaciotapies.org* 🚇 *€7* 🕙 *Closed Mon.* Ⓜ *L2/L3/L4 Passeig de Gràcia.*

Museu del Modernisme de Barcelona (*Museum of Catalan Modernism: MMBCN*)
MUSEUM | Unjustly bypassed in favor of rival displays in the Casa Milà, Casa Batlló, and the DHUB Design Museum in Plaça de les Glòries, this museum houses a small but rich collection of Moderniste furnishings, paintings and posters, sculpture (including works by Josep Limona), and decorative arts. Don't

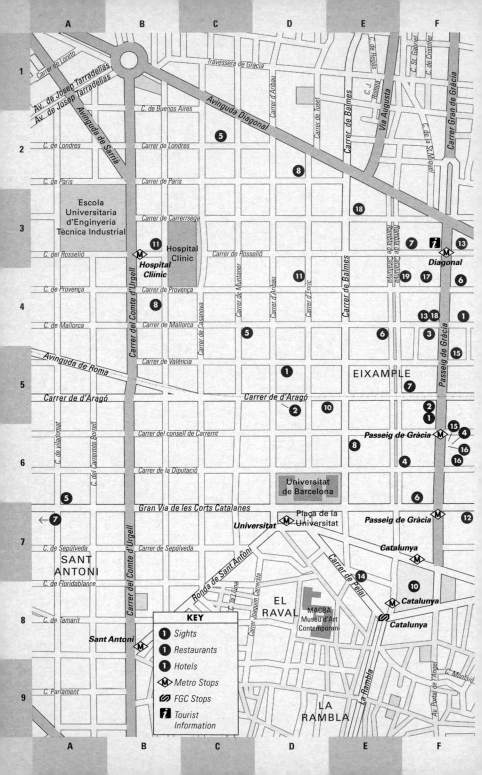

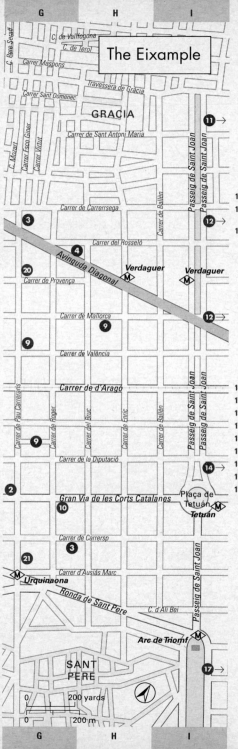

The Eixample

miss the section devoted to Gaudí-designed furniture. ✉ *Carrer Balmes 48, Eixample* ☎ *93/272–2896* ⊕ *www. mmbcn.cat* 🖾 *€10* ⊙ *Closed Mon.* Ⓜ *L1/ L2 Universitat.*

Passatge Permanyer

NEIGHBORHOOD | Cutting through the middle of the block bordered by Pau Claris, Roger de Llúria, Consell de Cent, and Diputació, this charming, leafy mid-Eixample sanctuary is one of 46 passatges (alleys or passageways) that cut through the blocks of this gridlike area. Once an aristocratic enclave and hideaway for pianist Carles Vidiella and poet, musician, and illustrator Apel·les Mestre, Passatge Permanyer is, along with the nearby Passatge Méndez Vigo, the best of these through-the-looking-glass downtown Barcelona alleyways. ✉ *Passatge Permanyer, Eixample* Ⓜ *L2/L3/L4 Passeig de Gràcia.*

Plaça de Catalunya

PLAZA | Barcelona's main bus-and-metro hub is the frontier between the Old City and the post-1860 Eixample. Fountains and statuary, along with pigeons and backpackers in roughly equal numbers, make the Plaça de Catalunya an open space to scurry across on your way to somewhere quieter, shadier, and gentler on the senses. Across the street on the west side is **Café Zurich,** the classic Barcelona rendezvous point at the top of La Rambla, by the steps down to the metro. The block behind the Zurich, known as El Triangle, houses a collection of megastores, chief among them FNAC (for electronics, books, and music) and Massimo Dutti (for designer garb). ✉ *Pl. de Catalunya, Eixample* Ⓜ *Pl. Catalunya.*

★ Recinte Modernista de Sant Pau

BUILDING | Set in what was one of the most beautiful public projects in the world—the Hospital de Sant Pau—the Recinte Modernista (Modernist Complex) is sadly, no longer a hospital, but it is a UNESCO World Heritage site that's extraordinary in its setting, style, and the idea that inspired it. Architect Lluis Domènech i Montaner believed that trees, flowers, and fresh air were likely to help people recover from what ailed them more than anything doctors could do in emotionally sterile surroundings. The hospital wards were set among gardens, their brick facades topped with polychrome ceramic tile roofs in extravagant shapes and details. Domènech also believed in the therapeutic properties of form and color, and decorated the hospital with Pau Gargallo sculptures and colorful mosaics, replete with motifs of hope and healing and healthy growth. Tours are offered in English daily at 10:30 am. ✉ *Carrer Sant Antoni Maria Claret 167, Eixample* ☎ *93/553–7801* ⊕ *www. santpaubarcelona.org/en* 🖾 *From €14; free 1st Sun. of month* Ⓜ *L5 Sant Pau/ Dos de Maig.*

★ Temple Expiatori de la Sagrada Família

BUILDING | Barcelona's most emblematic architectural icon, Antoni Gaudí's Sagrada Família, is still under construction some 135 years after it was begun. This striking and surreal creation was conceived as a gigantic representation of the entire history of Christianity. Begun in 1882 under architect Francesc Villar and passed on in 1891 to Gaudí (until his death in 1926), the church is now in the final stage of construction. No building in Barcelona and few in the world are more deserving of the investment of a few hours to the better part of a day. The apse of the basilica, consecrated by Pope Benedict XVI in 2010, has space for 15,000 people and a choir loft for 1,500. The towers still to be completed over the apse include those dedicated to the four evangelists—Matthew, Mark, Luke, and John—the Virgin Mary, and the highest of all, dedicated to Christ the Savior. By 2022, the 170th anniversary of the birth of Gaudí, the great central tower and dome, resting on four immense columns of Iranian porphyry, considered the hardest of all stones, will soar to a height of 564 feet, making the Sagrada Família Barcelona's tallest building. By 2026, the 100th anniversary of Gaudí's death, after 144 years of construction, the Sagrada Família may be complete enough to be called finished. Take an elevator up the bell towers for spectacular views. The museum displays Gaudí's scale models and photographs showing the progress of construction. The architect is buried to the left of the altar in the crypt. ■**TIP→ Lines to enter the church can stretch around the block. Buy your tickets online, with a reserved time of entry, and jump the queue.** ✉ *Pl. de la Sagrada Família, Carrer Mallorca 401, Eixample* ☎ *93/207–3031, 93/208–0414 visitor info* 🌐 *www.sagradafamilia.cat* 🎫 *From €15* [M] *L2/L5 Sagrada Família.*

🍴 Restaurants

The sprawling blocks of the Eixample contain Barcelona's finest selection of restaurants, from upscale and elegant traditional cuisine in Moderniste houses to high-concept fare in sleek minimalist-experimental spaces.

The Alchemix

$$ | **ASIAN** | Traditionalists tempted to run screaming from The Alchemix's blend of creative cocktails and Asian-influenced, avant-garde gastonomy should think again. Against the odds, this strange brew is a transformative triumph. **Known for:** original cocktails; imaginative cuisine; expert bar staff. [$] *Average main: €18* ✉ *València 212, Eixample* ☎ *93/833–7678* 🌐 *www.thealchemix.com* ⏲ *Closed Sun. and Wed. No lunch Mon., Tues., and Fri.* [M] *Universitat.*

Angle

$$$$ | **CATALAN** | ABaC may hog the spotlight, but chef Jordi Cruz's second restaurant, the relatively humble Angle, is an oft-overlooked star in its own right. Eschewing the gonzo creativity of the mothership, it instead focuses on a greatest hits menu of Cruz's dishes that have proven their appeal over the years. **Known for:** value fixed lunch; Bloody Mary appetizer; celebrity chef. [$] *Average main: €85* ✉ *Aragó 214, Eixample* ☎ *93/216–7777* 🌐 *www.anglebarcelona.com* [M] *Universitat.*

Bar Mut

$$$ | **CATALAN** | Just above Diagonal, this elegant retro space serves first-rate products ranging from wild sea bass to the best Ibérico hams. Crowded, noisy, chaotic, delicious—it's everything a great tapas bar or restaurant should be. **Known for:** upmarket tapas; great wine list; snacks at nearby spin-off Entrepanes Diaz. [$] *Average main: €28* ✉ *Pau Claris 192, Eixample* ☎ *93/217–4338* 🌐 *www.barmut.com* [M] *Diagonal.*

Blanc

$$$ | **CATALAN** | Overseen by feted chef Carme Ruscalleda, Blanc's menu couples traditional Catalan cuisine with her love of Asian cuisine, resulting in combinations such as suckling pig and cardamom or Galician tenderloin with sweet potato and daikon. The dining room is in a bright, white atrium at the heart of the Mandarin Oriental and feels lively at almost any time of day, right from when the first bleary hotel guests crawl in for the (excellent) breakfast. **Known for:** Catalan fused with Asian touches; superb Sunday brunch; airy atrium setting. [$] *Average main: €23* ✉ *Passeig de Gràcia 38–40, Eixample* ✥ *Entrance via Hotel Mandarin Oriental* ☎ *93/151–8783* 🌐 *www.mandarinoriental.com/barcelona/fine-dining/bars/blanc* [M] *Passeig de Gràcia.*

Blau BCN

$ | **CATALAN** | Despite its name, there's nothing about Marc Roca's restaurant that will give you the blues; its stylish interior featuring black-and-white photos sets an elegant stage for jazzed-up versions of rustic Catalan dishes that attract discerning local diners. Slow-cooked beef cheeks, a salad of tomatoes picked the same day, and wild-mushroom-studded cannelloni all impress, but the menu is ruled by a mighty alpha-cheesecake that

Continued on page 435

TEMPLE EXPIATORI DE LA
SAGRADA FAMÍLIA

Antoni Gaudí's striking and surreal masterpiece was conceived as nothing short of a Bible in stone, an arresting representation of the history of Christianity. Today this Roman Catholic church is Barcelona's most emblematic architectural icon. Looming over Barcelona like a mid-city massif of grottoes and peaks, the Sagrada Família strains skyward in piles of stalagmites. Construction is ongoing and continues to stretch toward the heavens.

CONSTRUCTION, PAST AND PRESENT

"My client is not in a hurry," was Gaudí's reply to anyone curious about his project's timetable . . . good thing, too, because the Sagrada Família was begun in 1882 under architect Francesc Villar, passed on in 1891 to Gaudí, and is still thought to be more than a decade from completion. Gaudí added Art Nouveau touches to the crypt and in 1893 started the Nativity facade. Conceived as a symbolic construct encompassing the complete story and scope of the Christian faith, the church was intended by Gaudí to impress the viewer with the full sweep and force of the Gospel. At the time of his death in 1926 only one tower of the Nativity facade had been completed.

By 2026, the 100th anniversary of Gaudí's death, after 144 years of construction in the tradition of the great medieval and Renaissance cathedrals of Europe, the Sagrada Família may well be complete enough to call finished. Architect Jordi Bonet continues in the footsteps of his father, architect Lluís Bonet, to make Gaudí's vision complete as he has since the 1980s.

(left) Sagrada Família interior. (top) Shepherds gather to witness the birth of Christ in the Nativity facade.

DETAILS TO DISCOVER: THE EXTERIOR

GAUDÍ IN THE PASSION FACADE

Subirachs pays double homage to the great Moderniste master in the Passion facade: Gaudí himself appears over the left side of the main entry making notes or drawings, the evangelist in stone, while the Roman soldiers are modeled on Gaudí's helmeted, Star Wars–like warriors from the roof of La Pedrera.

Gaudí in the Passion facade

TOWER TOPS

Break out the binoculars and have a close look at the pinnacles and peaks of the Sagrada Família's towers. Sculpted by Japanese artist Etsuro Sotoo, these clusters of grapes and different kinds of fruit are symbols of fertility, of rebirth, and of the Resurrection of Christ.

Sotoo's ornamental fruit

SUBIRACHS IN THE PASSION FACADE

At Christ's feet in the entombment sculpture is a blocky figure with a furrowed brow, thought to be a portrayal of the agnostic's anguished search for certainty. This figure is generally taken as a self-portrait of Subirachs, characterized by the sculptor's giant hand and an "S" on his massive right arm.

DONKEY ON THE NATIVITY FACADE

On the left side of the Nativity facade over the Portal of Hope is a *burro*, a small donkey, known to have been modeled from a donkey that Gaudí saw near the work site. The *ruc català* (Catalan donkey) is a beloved and iconic symbol of Catalonia, often displayed on Catalonian bumpers as a response to the Spanish fighting bull.

The donkey in the Nativity facade

THE ROSE TREE DOOR

The richly sculpted Rose Tree Door, between the Nativity facade and the cloisters, portrays Our Lady of the Rose Tree with the infant Jesus in her arms, St. Dominic and St. Catherine of Siena in prayer, with three angels dancing overhead. The sculptural group on the wall known as "The Death of the Just" portrays the Virgin and child comforting a moribund old man, the Spanish prayer "Jesús, José, y María, asistidme en mi última agonía" (Jesus, Joseph, and María, help me in my final agony). The accompanying inscriptions in English, "Pray for us sinners now and at the hour of our death, Amen" are the final words of the Ave María prayer.

The heavily embelished Rose door

COLUMN FROM THE PORTAL OF CHARITY

The column, dead center in the Portal of Charity, is covered with the genealogy of Christ going back through the House of David to Abraham. At the bottom of the column is the snake of evil, complete with the apple of temptation in his mouth, closed in behind an iron grate, symbolic of Christianity's mission of neutralizing the sin of selfishness.

The column in the Portal of Charity

FACELESS ST. VERONICA

Because her story is considered legendary, not historical fact, St. Veronica appears faceless in the Passion facade. Also shown is the veil she gave Christ to wipe his face with on the way to Calvary that was said to be miraculously imprinted with his likeness. The veil is torn in two overhead and covers a mosaic that Subirachs allegedly disliked and elected to conceal.

St. Veronica with the veil

STAINED-GLASS WINDOWS

The stained-glass windows of the Sagrada Família are work of Joan Vila-Grau. The windows in the west central part of the nave represent the light of Jesus and a bubbling fountain in a bright chromatic patchwork of shades of blue with green and yellow reflections. The main window on the Passion facade represents the Resurrection. Gaudí left express instructions that the windows of the central nave have no color, so as not to alter the colors of the tiles and trencadis (mosaics of broken tile) in green and gold representing palm leaves. These windows will be clear or translucent, as a symbol of purity and to admit as much light as possible.

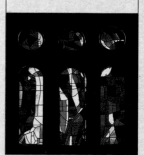

Stained-glass windows

TORTOISES AND TURTLES

Nature lover Gaudí used as many elements of the natural world as he could in his stone Bible. The sea tortoise beneath the column on the Mediterranean side of the Portal of Hope and the land turtle supporting the inland Portal of Faith symbolize the slow and steady stability of the cosmos and of the church.

SAINT THOMAS IN THE BELL TOWER

Above the Passion facade, St. Thomas demanding proof of Christ's resurrection (thus the expression "doubting Thomas") and perched on the bell tower is pointing to the palm of his hand asking to inspect Christ's wounds.

CHRIST RESURRECTED ABOVE PASSION FACADE

High above the Passion facade, a gilded Christ sits resurrected, perched between two towers.

Christ resurrected

MAKING THE MOST OF YOUR TRIP

The Nativity facade

WHEN TO VISIT

To avoid crowds, come first thing in the morning. Or, plan to visit during mid-morning and mid to late-afternoon when golden light streams through the stained glass windows.

WHAT TO WEAR AND BRING

Visitors are encouraged not to wear shors and to cover bare shoulders. It's a good idea to bring binoculars to absorb details all the way up.

TIMING

If you're just walking around the exterior, an hour or two is plenty of time. If you'd like to go inside to the crypt, visit the museum, visit the towers, and walk down the spiraling stairway, you'll need three to four hours.

BONUS FEATURES

The **museum** displays Gaudí's scale models and shows photographs of the construction. The **crypt** holds Gaudí's remains. The excellent gift shop has a wide selection of Gaudi-related articles including, sculptures, jewelry, miniature churches, and beautiful books.

PLAN AHEAD

Advance reservations (available up to two months in advance) are essential to avoid disappointment. Also, book a private tour for context and more time: it's worth it here, especially in peak season."

VISITOR INFORMATION

✉ Pl. de la Sagrada Família, Eixample
☎ 93/207–3031 ⊕ www.sagradafamilia.org
🎫 €17, with towers, €32, with audio guides €25
🕐 Oct.–Mar., daily 9–6; Apr.–Sept., daily 9–8
Ⓜ Sagrada Família.

WHICH TOWER?

We do not recommend visiting the towers while construction is ongoing but if you must, choose the Nativity Façade. These are the oldest of the Sagrada Família's towers and the only ones that Gaudí worked on. Also, there's a small bridge which affords better views and a close-up of parts of the façade.

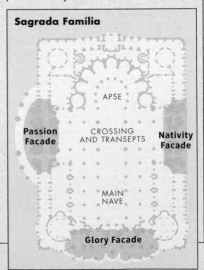

Sagrada Família

APSE

Passion Facade

CROSSING AND TRANSEPTS

Nativity Facade

MAIN NAVE

Glory Facade

combines an iron fist of Roquefort in a velvet Brie glove. **Known for:** delightful wild-mushroom-studded cannelloni; tasty slow-cooked beef cheeks; killer cheese-cake. $ *Average main: €15* ✉ *Londres 89, Eixample* ☎ *93/419–3032* ⊕ *blaubcn.com* ⊙ *Closed Sun.* Ⓜ *Hospital Clínic.*

Cervecería Catalana
$$ | **TAPAS** | **FAMILY** | A bright and booming tapas bar with a few tables outside, this spot is always packed for a reason: good food at reasonable prices. Try the small *solomillos* (filets mignons), mini-morsels that will take the edge off your carnivorous appetite without undue damage to your wallet, or the jumbo shrimp brochettes. **Known for:** affordable tapas; perfect jumbo shrimp brochettes; lively atmosphere. $ *Average main: €16* ✉ *Mallorca 236, Eixample* ☎ *93/216–0368* Ⓜ *Diagonal, Provença (FGC).*

★ Cinc Sentits
$$$$ | **CATALAN** | Obsessively local, scrupulously sourced, and masterfully cooked, the dishes of Catalan-Canadian chef Jordi Artal put the spotlight on the region's finest ingredients in an intimate, sophisticated setting. It's hard to believe that this garlanded restaurant is Jordi's first, but there's no arguing with the evidence of your *cinc sentits* (five senses). **Known for:** excellent chef; cutting-edge techniques; tasting menu only. $ *Average main: €99* ✉ *Entença 60, Eixample* ☎ *93/323–9490* ⊕ *cincsentits.com* ⊙ *Closed Sun. and Mon.* Ⓜ *Provença.*

★ Disfrutar
$$$$ | **ECLECTIC** | Three former head chefs from the now-closed "World's Best Restaurant" elBulli have combined their considerable talents to create this roller-coaster ride of culinary fun. Sun streams into the gorgeous interior through skylights, spotlighting tasting menus of dazzling inventiveness and good taste. **Known for:** otherworldly desserts; tasting menus only; excellent beetroot meringues. $ *Average main: €150*

✉ *Villarroel 163, Eixample* ☎ *93/348–6896* ⊕ *www.disfrutarbarcelona.com* ⊙ *Closed weekends and 2 wks in Mar.* Ⓜ *Hospital Clínic.*

Embat
$$ | **CATALAN** | An *embat* is a puff of wind in Catalan, and this little bistro is a breath of fresh air in the sometimes stuffy Eixample. The highly affordable market cuisine is always impeccably fresh and freshly conceived, from flavorful brunches to a bargain lunch selection and a more elaborate evening menu. **Known for:** modern, unfussy fare; stylish minimalist interior; delicious cod. $ *Average main: €16* ✉ *Mallorca 304, Eixample* ☎ *93/458–0855* ⊕ *embatrestaurant.com/* ⊙ *Closed Sun. No dinner Mon.–Wed.* Ⓜ *Verdaguer.*

★ La Pastisseria
$ | **BAKERY** | This stylish *pastisseria* looks more like a designer jewelry store than a bakery. Rows of world-class cakes and pastries gleam temptingly in glass cases, ready to be taken away or enjoyed in-store with coffee or a glass of cava. **Known for:** award-winning cakes; handmade delicacies; high-quality ingredients. $ *Average main: €9* ✉ *Aragó 228, Eixample* ☎ *93/451–8401* ⊕ *www.lapastisseriabarcelona.com* ⊙ *Closed Sun. evening* Ⓜ *Passeig de Gràcia.*

La Taverna Del Clínic
$$ | **SPANISH** | The Simoes brothers have earned a solid reputation with discerning and deep-pocketed locals for serving creative and contemporary tapas. Their bar spills out onto a sunny street-side terrace where customers can enjoy truffle cannelloni and an award-winning variation on patatas bravas, paired with selections from the excellent wine list. **Known for:** contemporary tapas; award-winning patatas bravas; superb cheese selection. $ *Average main: €20* ✉ *Rosselló 155, Eixample* ☎ *93/410–4221* ⊕ *www.latavernadelclinic.com* ⊙ *Closed Sun.* Ⓜ *Hospital Clinic.*

La Yaya Amelia

$$ | **CATALAN** | Just two blocks uphill from Gaudí's Sagrada Família church, this kitchen serves lovingly prepared and clued-in dishes ranging from warm goat-cheese salad to foie (duck or goose liver) to *chuletón de buey a la sal* (beef cooked in salt). Decidedly old-school, the interior is largely unchanged since the restaurant opened in 1976. **Known for:** old-fashioned charm; great value; medley of Basque and Catalan cuisine. [$] *Average main: €16* ✉ *Sardenya 364, Eixample* ☎ *678–355162* [M] *Sagrada Família.*

★ Lasarte

$$$$ | **BASQUE** | Martin Berasategui, one of San Sebastián's corps of master chefs, placed his Barcelona kitchen in the capable hands of Paolo Casagrande in 2006, and it has been a culinary triumph ever since. It's now widely considered Barcelona's best restaurant. **Known for:** inventive cuisine at one of the best restaurants in Barcelona; magnificent tasting menu; heavenly grilled pigeon. [$] *Average main: €59* ✉ *Mallorca 259, Eixample* ☎ *93/445–3242* 🌐 *www.restaurantlasarte.com* 🕒 *Closed Sun., Mon., 2 wks in Jan., 1 wk at Easter, and 3 wks in Aug./Sept.* [M] *Diagonal, Passeig de Gràcia, Provença (FGC).*

★ Manairó

$$$ | **CATALAN** | A *manairó* is a mysterious Pyrenean elf, and Jordi Herrera may be the culinary version; his ingenious meat-cooking methods—such as filet mignon *al faquir* (heated from within on red-hot spikes) or blowtorched on a homemade centrifuge—may seem eccentric but produce diabolically good results. Melt-in-your-mouth meat dishes form the centerpiece of Manairó's menus, but they are ably supported by a bonanza of bold and confident creations that aren't frightened of big flavors. **Known for:** innovative contemporary cuisine; delicious meat dishes; sculptures and artworks by the chef. [$] *Average main: €26* ✉ *Diputació 424, Eixample* ☎ *93/231–0057* 🌐 *www.jordiherrera.es/manairo* 🕒 *Closed Sun. and 1st wk of Jan.* [M] *Monumental.*

★ Moments

$$$$ | **CATALAN** | Inside the ultrasleek Hotel Mandarin Oriental Barcelona, this restaurant continues the glamour with mod white chairs and glinting goldleaf on the ceiling. The food by Raül Balam and his mother—the legendary Carme Ruscalleda—lives up to its stellar pedigree, with original preparations that draw on deep wells of Catalan culinary traditions. **Known for:** chef's table; elaborate tasting menus; outstanding wine list. [$] *Average main: €56* ✉ *Passeig de Gràcia 38–40, Eixample* ☎ *93/151–8781* 🌐 *www.mandarinoriental.com* 🕒 *Closed Sun., Mon., and 2 wks in Jan.* [M] *Passeig de Gràcia.*

Tapas 24

$$$ | **TAPAS** | The tapas emporium of celebrity chef Carles Abellán shows us how much he admires traditional Catalan and Spanish bar food, from patatas bravas to *croquetes de pollastre rostit* (roast chicken croquettes). The counter and terrace are constantly crowded, but the slightly pricey food is worth elbowing your way through the crowd for. **Known for:** traditional tapas with a twist; all-day kitchen; bikini Carles Abellán (ham-and-cheese toastie with truffle oil). [$] *Average main: €24* ✉ *Diputació 269, Eixample* ☎ *93/488–0977* 🌐 *www.carlesabellan.com/mis-restaurantes/tapas-24* [M] *Passeig de Gràcia.*

Tragaluz

$$$ | **MEDITERRANEAN** | *Tragaluz* means "skylight" (the sliding roof opens to the stars in good weather), and this is an excellent choice if you're still on a design high. The Mediterranean cuisine is traditional yet light and will please most palates, and it's a popular lunch spot. **Known for:** open-air dining; coffee or post-dinner drink upstairs; entrance is through Japanese tavern. [$] *Average main: €25* ✉ *Passatge de la Concepció 5, Eixample*

☏ 93/487–0621 ⊕ grupotragaluz.com Ⓜ Diagonal.

Xerta

$$$$ | CATALAN | The restaurant of the new Ohla Eixample hotel won a Michelin star in its first year. Much of Xerta's menu is the expected swanky fine-dining fare, but it stands out for its unique produce from the deltas and rivers of the Terres de l'Ebre region, such as sweet miniature *canyuts* (razor clams). **Known for:** produce from Terres de l'Ebre region; outstanding seafood and rice dishes; sweet miniature canyuts (razor clams). Ⓢ *Average main: €30* ✉ *Còrsega 289, Eixample* ☏ *93/737–9080* ⊕ *www.xertarestaurant.com* ◷ *Closed Sun. and Mon.* Ⓜ *Provença.*

Hotels

★ Alma Hotel Barcelona

$$$$ | HOTEL | Only the facade is left to recall the Moderniste origins of the building; the inside spaces were completely redesigned in 2011, and the Alma emerged as Barcelona's sleekest mid-Eixample hotel. **Pros:** British afternoon tea served daily (open to the public); gorgeous garden with sushi bar; complementary minibar. **Cons:** budget-stretching room rates; pricey buffet breakfast. Ⓢ *Rooms from: €300* ✉ *Carrer Mallorca 271, Eixample* ☏ *93/216–4490* ⊕ *www. almahotels.com* ⤳ *72 rooms* ⑩ *No meals* Ⓜ *L3/L5 Diagonal, L4 Girona, FGC Provença.*

★ Almanac Barcelona

$$$$ | HOTEL | FAMILY | Occupying a prime position on Barcelona's Gran Via de les Corts Catalanes, a stone's throw from Gaudí's modernist buildings on Passeig de Gràcia, this is a boutique-style hotel wrapped up in supreme luxury. **Pros:** superb location one block from Passeig de Gràcia; unbeatable rooftop views; top-quality service. **Cons:** hard on the wallet; additional charge for the spa; no pets. Ⓢ *Rooms from: €350* ✉ *Gran Via de les Corts Catalanes 619-621, Eixample*

☏ 93/018–7000 ⊕ www.almanachotels. com ⤳ 91 rooms ⑩ No meals Ⓜ L2/L3/ L4 Passeig de Gràcia.

Condes de Barcelona

$$$ | HOTEL | One of Barcelona's most popular hotels, the Condes de Barcelona is perfectly placed for exploring the sights (and shops) of the city's most fashionable quarter, and—for the privileged location—offers exceptional value. **Pros:** elegant building with subdued contemporary furnishings; prime spot in the middle of the Eixample; excellent value. **Cons:** no spa; no pets; rooftop plunge pool is small. Ⓢ *Rooms from: €190* ✉ *Passeig de Gràcia 73, Eixample* ☏ *93/467–4780* ⊕ *www.condesdebarcelona.com* ⤳ *126 rooms* ⑩ *No meals* Ⓜ *L3/L5 Diagonal, Provença (FGC).*

★ Continental Palacete

$$ | HOTEL | FAMILY | This former palatial family home, or *palacete*, provides a splendid drawing room, a location nearly dead-center for Barcelona's main attractions, views over leafy Rambla de Catalunya, and a 24-hour free buffet. **Pros:** ornate design; attentive staff; ideal location. **Cons:** room decor is relentlessly pink and overdraped; bathrooms are a bit cramped; some street noise. Ⓢ *Rooms from: €153* ✉ *Rambla de Catalunya 30, at Diputació, Eixample* ☏ *93/445–7657* ⊕ *www.hotelcontinental.com* ⤳ *22 rooms* ⑩ *Free Breakfast* Ⓜ *L2/L3/L4 Passeig de Gràcia, Plaça Catalunya.*

The Corner Hotel

$$$ | HOTEL | This hip addition to the city's boutique hotel scene, positioned (yep, you guessed it) on a corner, has been fashioned from a handsome, turn-of-the-century building in Barcelona's stylish Eixample district, within a few blocks walking distance of Gaudí's key sights on Passeig de Gràcia. **Pros:** walking distance to Passeig de Gràcia; rooms include complimentary bottle of water plus coffee and tea; popular Sunday brunch. **Cons:** far from the old town; interior-facing rooms lack natural light; extra charge for

parking. Ⓢ *Rooms from: €190* ✉ *Mallorca, 178, Eixample* ☎ *93/554-2400* ⊕ *www.thecornerhotel-barcelona.com* ✈ *72 rooms* |◯| *No meals* Ⓜ *FGC Provença; L5 Hospital Clinic.*

El Avenida Palace

$$$$ | HOTEL | A minute's walk from Plaça Catalunya and the Passeig de Gràcia, this 1952 hotel earns top marks for location—and for nostalgia. **Pros:** prime location; excellent soundproofing; "Beatles suite" (the band stayed here in 1965). **Cons:** not for fans of minimalism or cutting-edge design; service can be snooty; low ceilings on guest room floors. Ⓢ *Rooms from: €250* ✉ *Gran Via 605-607, Eixample* ☎ *93/301-9600* ⊕ *www.avenidapalace.com* ✈ *151 rooms* |◯| *No meals* Ⓜ *L2/L3/L4 Passeig de Gràcia, Pl. Catalunya.*

Gallery Hotel

$$ | HOTEL | In the upper part of the Eixample below the Diagonal, this contemporary hotel offers impeccable service and a superb central location for exploring, with the city's prime art-gallery district just a few blocks away on Consell de Cent. **Pros:** two large rooftop terraces with year-round pools; DJ or live music on summer weekends; recently renovated. **Cons:** small closet space; rooftop deck does not offer great views. Ⓢ *Rooms from: €165* ✉ *Roselló 249, Eixample* ☎ *93/415-9911* ⊕ *www.galleryhotel.com* ✈ *105 rooms* |◯| *No meals* Ⓜ *L3/L5 Diagonal, Provença (FGC).*

Hotel Astoria

$$ | HOTEL | Three blocks west of Rambla Catalunya, near the upper middle of the Eixample, this renovated classic property, part of the cutting-edge Derby Hotels Collection group of brilliant artistic restorations, is a trove for the budget-minded. **Pros:** prime location; excellent value for price; free entrance to the Egyptian Museum of Barcelona. **Cons:** gym has only three machines; rooms on lower floors on the street side can be noisy; rooftop terrace pool is small. Ⓢ *Rooms from: €140* ✉ *Carrer Paris 203, Eixample* ☎ *93/209-8311* ⊕ *www.hotelastoria-barcelona.com* ✈ *117 rooms* |◯| *No meals* Ⓜ *Provença (FGC), L3/L5 Diagonal.*

★ Hotel Claris Grand Luxe Barcelona

$$$$ | HOTEL | Acclaimed as one of Barcelona's best hotels, the Claris is an icon of design, tradition, and connoisseurship. **Pros:** first-rate restaurant La Terraza; Mayan Secret Spa with temazcal and pure chocolate skin treatment; rooms in a variety of styles. **Cons:** basic ("Superior") rooms small for the price; rooftop terrace noise at night can reach down into sixth-floor rooms; capacity bookings can sometimes overwhelm the staff. Ⓢ *Rooms from: €270* ✉ *Carrer Pau Claris 150, Eixample* ☎ *93/487-6262* ⊕ *www.hotelclaris.com* ✈ *124 rooms* |◯| *No meals* Ⓜ *L2/L3/L4 Passeig de Gràcia.*

★ Hotel El Palace Barcelona

$$$$ | HOTEL | Founded in 1919 by Caesar Ritz, the original Ritz (the grande dame of Barcelona hotels) was renamed in 2005 but kept its lavish Old European style intact, from the liveried doorman in top hat and tails to the lobby's ormolu clocks and massive crystal chandelier. **Pros:** equidistant from Barri Gòtic and central Eixample; L'Éclair features live jazz and more; Mayan-style sauna in the award-winning spa. **Cons:** €30-per-night surcharge for small pets; equally pricey; formal atmosphere. Ⓢ *Rooms from: €360* ✉ *Gran Vía de les Corts Catalanes 668, Eixample* ☎ *93/510-1130* ⊕ *www.hotelpalacebarcelona.com* ✈ *120 rooms* |◯| *No meals* Ⓜ *L2/L3/L4 Passeig de Gràcia.*

★ Hotel Granados 83

$$$ | HOTEL | Designed in the style of a New York City loft and seated on a tree-shaded street in the heart of the Eixample, this hotel blends exposed brick, steel, and glass with Greek and Italian marble and Indonesian tamarind wood to achieve downtown cool. **Pros:** luxurious duplexes with private terraces and semi-private pools; wide variety of good casual restaurants nearby; free entrance to the

8 Barcelona THE EIXAMPLE

Egyian Museum of Barcelona. **Cons:** rooftop terrace pool quite small; standard rooms need more storage space; Wi-Fi can be patchy. $ *Rooms from: €195* ✉ *Carrer Enric Granados 83, Eixample* ☎ *93/492–9670* ⊕ *www.hotelgranados83.com* ⇄ *84 rooms* |◎| *No meals* Ⓜ *Provença (FGC).*

★ Hotel Granvía

$$ | HOTEL | A 19th-century palatial home (built for the owner of the Bank of Barcelona), the Granvía opened as a hotel in 1935, and reopened in 2013 after a lengthy renovation, with its original features still intact: an art deco cupola in the entrance, coffered ceilings, pillared arches, and a marble grand staircase. **Pros:** historical setting; pleasant terrace; British-style high tea served in the salon daily 5–7 pm. **Cons:** no pool, gym, or spa; most standard rooms have twin beds yoked together rather than doubles; bathrooms a bit cramped; few amenities. $ *Rooms from: €170* ✉ *Gran Vía de les Corts Catalanes 642, Eixample* ☎ *93/318–1900* ⊕ *www.hotelgranvia.com* ⇄ *58 rooms* |◎| *Free Breakfast* Ⓜ *L2/L3/ L4 Passeig de Gràcia.*

★ Hotel Omm

$$$$ | HOTEL | FAMILY | The lobby of this postmodern architectural stunner tells you what to expect throughout: perfect comfort, cutting-edge design, and meticulous attention to every detail. **Pros:** perfect location for the upper Eixample; fireplace in lounge; superb spa. **Cons:** small plunge pools; restaurant is pricey and a little precious; parking is expensive. $ *Rooms from: €275* ✉ *Roselló 265, Eixample* ☎ *93/445–4000* ⊕ *www. hotelomm.com* ⇄ *91 rooms* |◎| *No meals* Ⓜ *L3/L5 Diagonal, Provença (FGC).*

Hotel Regina

$$$ | HOTEL | FAMILY | What it lacks in bells and whistles, this family-friendly little hotel makes up for in its unparalleled location—on a side street just steps from Plaça Catalunya—and its relaxed contemporary feel. **Pros:** just steps from Plaça Catalunya; charming breakfast room has excellent buffet; live sessions in the piano bar Tuesdays at 9 pm. **Cons:** no pool or gym (but privileges at nearby fitness center); bathrooms in some superior rooms are really small; no pets. $ *Rooms from: €180* ✉ *Calle Bergara 4, Eixample* ☎ *93/301–3232* ⊕ *www.reginahotel.com/en* ⇄ *99 rooms* |◎| *No meals* Ⓜ *Catalunya.*

★ Majestic Hotel & Spa

$$$$ | HOTEL | With an unbeatable location on Barcelona's most stylish boulevard, steps from Gaudí's La Pedrera and near the area's swankiest shops, a leafy rooftop terrace with killer views of the city's landmarks including the Sagrada Familia, this hotel is a near-perfect place to stay. **Pros:** excellent restaurant and spa; beloved city landmark with interesting history; art (including Miró prints) from owner's private collection. **Cons:** some standard rooms a bit small for the price; pricey (but award-winning) buffet breakfast. $ *Rooms from: €325* ✉ *Passeig de Gràcia 68, Eixample* ☎ *93/488–1717* ⊕ *www. hotelmajestic.es* ⇄ *275 rooms* |◎| *No meals* Ⓜ *L2/L3/L4 Passeig de Gràcia, Provença (FGC)* ⚓ *D2.*

Mandarin Oriental Barcelona

$$$$ | HOTEL | FAMILY | A carpeted ramp leading from the elegant Passeig de Gràcia (flanked by Tiffany and Brioni boutiques) lends this hotel the air of a privileged—and pricey—inner sanctum. **Pros:** outstanding Moments restaurant; babysitters and parties for the kids, on request; Mimosa interior garden great for drinks. **Cons:** rooms relatively small for a five-star accommodation; Wi-Fi free in rooms only if booked online; lighting a bit dim. $ *Rooms from: €575* ✉ *Passeig de Gràcia 38–40, Eixample* ☎ *93/151–8888* ⊕ *www.mandarinoriental.com/barcelona* ⇄ *120 rooms* |◎| *No meals* Ⓜ *L2/L3/ L4 Passeig de Gràcia, L3/L5 Diagonal, Provença (FGC).*

Meliá Barcelona Sky

$$ | **HOTEL** | At a bit of a remove from the major tourist attractions, east along Diagonal from Plaça de les Glòries, the Meliá hotel group's Barcelona Sky gets much of its business from professional and trade conference organizers, but wins high marks as well from recreational visitors for its luxurious appointments and lively design. **Pros:** handy to Sagrada Família, beach, and Poble Nou nightlife scene; great views from rooftop deck; 24-hour free drinks and snacks on terrace. **Cons:** inconvenient to Eixample and Gothic Quarter; high-rise glass-and-concrete slab architecture; "open concept" bedroom/bathroom layout lacks privacy. [$] *Rooms from: €160* ✉ *Carrer Pere IV 272–286, Eixample* ☎ *902/144440* 🌐 *www.melia.com* 🛏 *258 rooms* 🍴 *No meals* [M] *L4 Poble Nou.*

★ **Monument Hotel**

$$$$ | **HOTEL** | Originally the home of Enric Battló, a brother of the textile magnate who commissioned Gaudí to redesign the Moderniste masterpiece Casa Battló, and a minute's walk away on the Passeig de Gràcia, the historic 1898 building that houses the Monument went through several incarnations before architect Oscar Tusquets and his project team transformed it into the elegant upmarket hotel it is today. **Pros:** helpful, professional multilingual staff; ideal mid-Eixample location; underfloor heating in the bathrooms. **Cons:** hard on the budget; most "junior suites" are in effect large doubles with seating areas; pricey American breakfast. [$] *Rooms from: €300* ✉ *Passeig de Gràcia 73, Eixample* ☎ *93/548–2000* 🌐 *www.monument-hotel.com* 🛏 *158 rooms* 🍴 *No meals* [M] *L3/L5 Diagonal, Provença (FGC).*

★ **Murmuri Barcelona**

$$$ | **HOTEL** | **FAMILY** | British designer Kelly Hoppen took this 19th-century town house on La Rambla de Catalunya and transformed it into a chic, intimate urban retreat, with room decor in velvety brown, beige, and black, with big mirrors, dramatic bed lighting, and arresting photography. **Pros:** private terraces in Privilege doubles; strategic Eixample location; exclusive rooftop terrace open year-round. **Cons:** no pool, gym, or spa (though guest privileges at the nearby affiliated Majestic hotel); no pets, except in the apartments; Design doubles a bit small. [$] *Rooms from: €185* ✉ *Rambla de Catalunya 104, Eixample* ☎ *93/550–0600* 🌐 *www.murmuri.com* 🛏 *61 rooms* 🍴 *No meals* [M] *L3/L5 Diagonal, Provença (FGC).*

The One Hotel

$$$$ | **HOTEL** | **FAMILY** | This highly rated H10 hotel chain property with smart, elegant interiors (courtesy of Barcelona-based design studio, Jaime Beriestain) occupies a prime position one block from Gaudí's Casa Milà. **Pros:** prime position for Gaudí sights and shopping; wonderful city views from the rooftop; generously sized rooms. **Cons:** no private on-site parking (additional cost); charge for pets; restaurant in the lobby feels a little generic. [$] *Rooms from: €300* ✉ *C/ Provença 277, Eixample* ☎ *93/214–2070* 🌐 *www.h10hotels.com* 🛏 *88 rooms* 🍴 *No meals* [M] *L5/L3 Diagonal.*

the5rooms

$$ | **B&B/INN** | **FAMILY** | This charming little boutique B&B in the heart of the city has been expanded into a complex of nine spacious guest rooms and three suites, with two full residential apartments next door. **Pros:** a sense of home away from home; comfortable contemporary design; honesty bar in the common area. **Cons:** no bar or restaurant; Pau Claris a busy and noisy artery; no reception after 9 pm. [$] *Rooms from: €155* ✉ *Carrer Pau Claris 72, Eixample* ☎ *93/342–7880* 🌐 *www.the5rooms.com* 🛏 *12 rooms, 2 apartments* 🍴 *Breakfast* [M] *L1/L4 Urquinaona, L2/L3/L4 Passeig de Gràcia.*

Nightlife

Home to a magnificent array of Modernist architectural wonders, including Gaudí masterpieces Casa Milà, Casa Batlló, and La Sagrada Família, Barcelona's modish L'Eixample district is at once the largest and most diverse nightlife destination in town.

BARS

★ Banker's Bar

BARS/PUBS | With allusions to its past life as a bank (like the safety deposit boxes on the wall), the swank cocktail bar of the 5* Mandarin Oriental Hotel lounge is perfect for an opulent night out. DJs play relaxing jazz, swing, and blues tunes on weekends. Wednesday night is reserved for live musical performances. Oversize brown leather chairs and taupe-color detailing surround the black lacquer bar manned by barmaids dressed in matching Asian-inspired qipaos serving fare from a biannually changing "East meets West" menu that includes classic cocktail favorites alongside signature creations paired with light, bicontinental bites. ✉ Hotel Mandarin Oriental, Passeig de Gràcia 38–40, Eixample ☎ 93/151–8782 ⊕ www.mandarinoriental.es/barcelona Ⓜ Passeig de Gràcia.

★ Dry Martini

BARS/PUBS | An homage to the traditional English martini bar of decades past, this stately spot is paradise for cocktail aficionados seeking the most expertly mixed drinks in town (martinis even have their own prep section). From the wood-paneled fixtures of the mirrored bar featuring a vintage brass register, to the knowledgeable barmen dressed in impeccable white coats and ties, to the wall of vintage spirit bottles overlooking plush and regal turquoise and red leather seating, each detail aims to transport the loyal clientele back to an era of inspired excellence. ✉ Aribau 162, Eixample ☎ 93/217–5072 ⊕ www.drymartiniorg.com Ⓜ Provença.

La Vinoteca Torres

WINE BARS—NIGHTLIFE | In a space ideally located on Barcelona's exclusive shopping avenue, Passeig de Gràcia, the acclaimed Torres wine dynasty offers an ample selection of their international wines and spirits to accompany delectable Mediterranean fish or meat dishes such as the signature oxtail in Sangre de Toro red wine sauce. The dark, ultramodern space is adorned with walls of stacked wine bottles, and strategic lighting illuminates the natural wood tables. ✉ Passeig de Gràcia 78, Eixample ☎ 93/272–6625 ⊕ www.lavinotecatorres.com Ⓜ Passeig de Gràcia, Diagonal.

Les Gens que J'aime

BARS/PUBS | Bohemia meets the Moulin Rouge at this intimate, below-street-level bordello-inspired pub with turn-of-the-20th-century memorabilia, including fringed lampshades, faded period portraits, stacked blue light chandelier, and comfy wicker sofas cushioned with lush red velvet. First opened in 1967, this jazz-playing dark and dusty spot offers attentive yet laid-back service, allowing guests to linger for a cocktail (whiskey sours are popular), a telling tarot card reading, or a romantic tête-à-tête by Tiffany lamplight. ✉ València 286, bajos, Eixample ☎ 93/215–6879 ⊕ www.lesgensquejaime.com Ⓜ Passeig de Gràcia.

Milano

BARS/PUBS | For more than a decade, this "secret" basement bar, located in an area otherwise dominated by student pubs and tourist traps, has had a rotating lineup of international acts including blues, soul, jazz, flamenco, swing, and pop. In a space resembling a 1940s cabaret, you'll find paneled oak, a brass bar, spotlit photo prints of previous acts, and red banquette-style seating alongside matching armchairs and tables. Milano is open from noon for tapas lunch with cocktails (classic and creative), and shows run nightly at 9 pm and 11 pm. ✉ Ronda Universitat 35, Eixample

☎ 93/112–7150 ⊕ www.camparimilano. com/en Ⓜ Catalunya, Universitat.

★ Monvínic

WINE BARS—NIGHTLIFE | Conceptualized to celebrate wine culture at its finest, this spectacular space, aptly called "Wineworld" in Catalan, features a ritzy wine bar complete with tablet wine lists, a cavernous culinary space, a reference library, a vertical garden, and the pièce de résistance: a vast cellar housing a mind-blowing 3,500 vintages from around the world. Small plates of regional jamón and inventive riffs on classical Catalan cuisine complement the vino. Wine tastings, both traditional and creative, are held regularly for groups or individuals looking to become oenophiles. ✉ Diputació 249, Eixample ☎ 93/272–6187 ⊕ www.monvinic.com Ⓜ Passeig de Gràcia.

Morro Fi

BARS/PUBS | Tiny and unpretentious yet decidedly on trend, this untraditional vermuteria is reintroducing classic vermouth to the masses. Opened by a trio of vermouth aficionados, Morro Fi (loosely translates as "refined palate") was originally a foodie blog that morphed into a bar determined to educate visitors about enjoying vermouth (they even produce their own brand) with select tapas. The result? Locals and the odd expat routinely spilling out into the streets, drink in hand while indie music blares. ✉ Consell de Cent 171, Eixample ⊕ www.morrofi.cat Ⓜ Urgell.

Senyor Vermut

BARS/PUBS | This snazzy, high-ceilinged vermuteria has guests lining up to sample a generous selection of more than 40 vermuts served with traditional tapas. From bitter to earthy or aged in a barrel, this classic aperitif is clearly the star attraction despite other offerings including wine, beer, juices, and hot beverages. ✉ Carrer de Provença 85, Eixample ☎ 93/532–8865 Ⓜ Entença.

★ Solange Cocktails and Luxury Spirits

BARS/PUBS | The latest venture from the Pernia brothers—the trio whose Tandem Cocktail Bar (Aribau 86) pioneered Barcelona's emerging cocktail scene back in the '80s—is a sleek, golden-hued, luxurious lounge space aptly named after Solange Dimitrios, 007's original Bond girl. The homage continues with signature cocktails that reference Bond films, characters, and even a "secret mission" concoction for the more daring. ✉ Carrer Aribau 143, Eixample ☎ 93/164–3625 Ⓜ Hospital Clínic, Diagonal.

🎭 Performing Arts

ART GALLERIES

Fundació Antoni Tàpies

ARTS CENTERS | This foundation created in 1984 by Catalonia's then-most important living artist continues to promote the work of important Catalan artists and writers, particularly that of the late Antoni Tàpies, whose passion for art and literature still echos in the halls of this enchanting Modernist building by esteemed architect Domènech i Montaner. It hosts thought-provoking temporary exhibitions, a comprehensive lecture series, and film screenings, and houses an excellent library specializing in contemporary art. ✉ Aragó 255, Eixample ☎ 93/487–0315 ⊕ www.fundaciotapies. org Ⓜ Passeig de Gràcia.

FLAMENCO

Palacio del Flamenco

DANCE | This Eixample music hall showcases some of the city's best flamenco. Prices start at €45 for a drink and a show, up to €110. (Save money by purchasing tickets online in advance.) Late shows are slightly cheaper. ✉ Balmes 139, Eixample ☎ 93/218–7237 ⊕ www. palaciodelflamenco.com Ⓜ Provença, Diagonal.

THEATER
Teatre Nacional de Catalunya
THEATER | Near Glòries, the area with the highest concentration of development in recent years at the eastern end of the Diagonal, this grandiose glass-enclosed classical temple was designed by Ricardo Bofill, architect of Barcelona's airport. Programs cover everything from Shakespeare to avant-garde theater. Most productions, as the name suggests, are in Catalan but beautiful to witness all the same. ✉ *Pl. de les Arts 1, Eixample* ☎ *93/306–5700* ⊕ *www.tnc.cat* Ⓜ *Glòries, Monumental.*

Teatre Tívoli
DANCE | One of the city's most beloved traditional theater and dance venues, the Tívoli has staged timeless classics and has hosted everyone from the Ballet Nacional de Cuba to flamenco and teeny-bopper treats. ✉ *Casp 8, Eixample* ☎ *93/215–9570* ⊕ *www.grupbalana.com* Ⓜ *Catalunya.*

Gràcia

Lying above the Diagonal from Carrer de Còrsega all the way up to Park Güell, Gràcia is bound by Via Augusta and Carrer Balmes to the west and Carrer de l'Escorial and Passeig de Sant Joan to the east. Today the area is filled with hip little bars and trendy restaurants, movie theaters, outdoor cafés, gourmet shops and designer boutiques, and the studios of struggling artists: this is where Barcelona's young cohort want to live, and come to party. Mercé Rodoreda's novel *La Plaça del Diamant* (translated by the late David Rosenthal as *The Time of the Doves*) begins and ends in Gràcia during the August Festa Major, a festival that fills the streets with the rank-and-file residents of this always lively, intimate little pocket of general resistance to Organized Life.

Sights

Casa-Museu Gaudí
HOUSE | Up the steps of **Park Güell** and to the right is the whimsical Alice-in-Wonderland-esque house where Gaudí lived with his niece from 1906 to his death in 1926. Now a small museum, exhibits include Gaudí-designed furniture and decorations, drawings, and portraits and busts of the architect. Stop by if you are in the area, but the museum is not worth traveling far for. ✉ *Park Güell, Carretera del Carmel 23A, Gràcia* ☎ *93/219–3811* ⊕ *www.casamuseugaudi.org* ✉ *€6* Ⓜ *L3 Lesseps, Vallcarca.*

★ Casa Vicens
HOUSE | Antoni Gaudí's first important commission as a young architect began in 1883 and finished in 1889. For this house Gaudí still used his traditional architect's tools, particularly the T square. The historical eclecticism (that is, borrowing freely from past architectural styles around the world) of the early Art Nouveau movement is evident in the Orientalist themes and Mudejar (Moorish-inspired) motifs lavished throughout the design. The client, Don Manuel Vicens Montaner, owned a brick and tile factory—which explains the lavish use of the green and yellow ceramic tiles, in checkerboard and floral patterns, that animate the facade. (Casa Vicens was in fact the first polychromatic facade to appear in Barcelona.) The chemaro palm leaves decorating the gate and surrounding fence are thought to be the work of Gaudí's assistant Francesc Berenguer; the comic iron lizards and bats oozing off the facade are Gaudí's playful version of the Gothic gargoyle. ✉ *Carrer de les Carolines 24–26, Gràcia* ⊕ *www.casavicens. org* Ⓜ *L3 Fontana, Lesseps.*

Gran de Gràcia
NEIGHBORHOOD | This highly trafficked central artery up through Gràcia is lined with buildings of great artistic and architectural interest, beginning with the hotel

Can Fuster. Built between 1908 and 1911 by Palau de la Música Catalana architect Lluís Domènech i Montaner in collaboration with his son Pere Domènech i Roure, the building shows a clear move away from the chromatically effusive heights of Art Nouveau. More powerful, and somehow less superficial, than much of that style of architecture, it uses the winged supports under the balconies and the floral base under the corner tower as important structural elements instead of as pure ornamentation, as Domènech i Montaner the elder might have. As you move up Gran de Gràcia, probable Francesc Berenguer buildings can be identified at No. 15; No. 23, with its scrolled cornice; and Nos. 35, 49, 51, 61, and 77. ⊠ *Gran de Gràcia, Gràcia* Ⓜ *L3 Fontana, Lesseps; FGC Gràcia.*

Mercat de la Llibertat

MARKET | This uptown version of the Rambla's Boqueria market is one of Gràcia's coziest spaces, a food market big enough to roam in and small enough to make you feel at home. Built by Francesc Berenguer between 1888 and 1893, the Llibertat market reflects, in its name alone, the revolutionary and democratic sentiment strong in Gràcia's traditionally blue-collar residents. Look for Berenguer's decorative swans swimming along the roof line and the snails surrounding Gràcia's coat of arms. ⊠ *Pl. Llibertat 27, Gràcia* ☎ *93/217–0995* ⊕ *www.bcn.es/ mercatsmunicipals* ⊘ *Closed Sun.* Ⓜ *FGC Gràcia.*

★ Park Güell

CITY PARK | FAMILY | Alternately shady, green, floral, or sunny, this park is one of Gaudí's, and Barcelona's, most visited venues. Named for and commissioned by Gaudí's main patron, Count Eusebi Güell, it was originally intended as a gated residential community based on the English Garden City model, with a covered marketplace. The pillars of the market support the main public square above it, where impromptu dances and plays were performed. Gaudí highlights include the gingerbread gatehouses; the **Casa-Museu Gaudí**, where the architect lived; the Room of a Hundred Columns; and the fabulous serpentine polychrome bench that snakes along the main square by Gaudí assistant Josep Maria. Visitors must pay an entrance fee to the "monumental area," where the main attractions are located; the rest of the park remains free to enter. Tickets should be booked online up to three months in advance. ⊠ *Carrer d'Olot s/n, Gràcia* ☎ *93/409– 1831* ⊕ *www.parkguell.cat/en* 🎫 *From €9* Ⓜ *L3 Lesseps, Vallcarca.*

Plaça de la Vila de Gràcia

PLAZA | Originally named (until 2009) for the memorable Gràcia mayor Francesc Rius i Taulet, this is the town's most emblematic and historic square, marked by the handsome clock tower in its center. The tower, built in 1862, is just over 110 feet tall. It has water fountains around its base, royal Bourbon crests over the fountains, and an iron balustrade atop the octagonal brick shaft stretching up to the clock and belfry. The symbol of Gràcia, the clock tower was bombarded by federal troops when Gràcia attempted to secede from the Spanish state during the 1870s. ⊠ *Pl. de la Vila de Gràcia, Gràcia* Ⓜ *L3 Fontana, Gràcia (FGC).*

Plaça de la Virreina

PLAZA | The much-damaged and oft-restored church of Sant Joan de Gràcia in this square stands where the Palau de la Virreina once stood, the mansion of the same *virreina* (wife, or in this case, widow of a viceroy) whose 18th-century palace, the Pallau de la Virreina, stands on the Rambla. (The Palau is now a prominent municipal museum and art gallery.) The story of La Virreina, a young noblewoman widowed at an early age by the death of the elderly viceroy of Peru, is symbolized in the bronze sculpture in the center of the square: it portrays Ruth of the Old Testament, represented carrying the sheaves of wheat she was

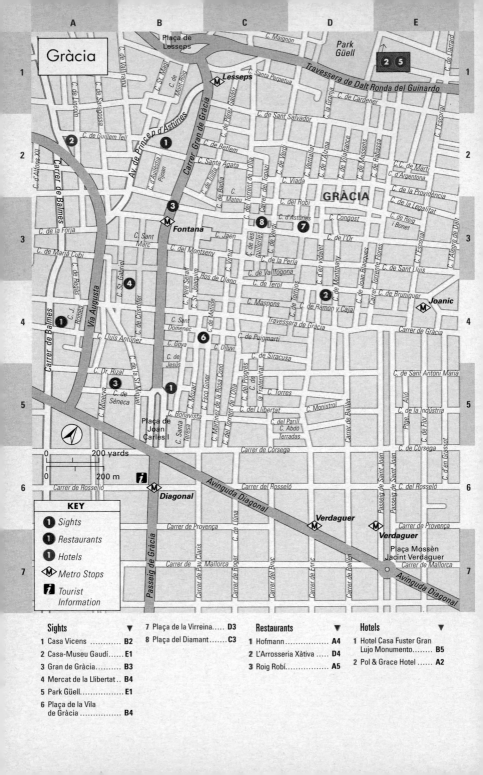

Gràcia

Sights ▼
1 Casa Vicens **B2**
2 Casa-Museu Gaudí **E1**
3 Gran de Gràcia **B3**
4 Mercat de la Llibertat .. **B4**
5 Park Güell **E1**
6 Plaça de la Vila
  de Gràcia **B4**
7 Plaça de la Virreina **D3**
8 Plaça del Diamant **C3**

Restaurants ▼
1 Hofmann **A4**
2 L'Arrosseria Xàtiva **D4**
3 Roig Robí **A5**

Hotels ▼
1 Hotel Casa Fuster Gran
  Lujo Monumento **B5**
2 Pol & Grace Hotel **A2**

KEY
🔴 Sights
🔴 Restaurants
🔴 Hotels
Ⓜ Metro Stops
ℹ Tourist
   Information

gathering when she learned of the death of her husband, Boaz. Ruth is the Old Testament paradigm of wifely fidelity to her husband's clan, a parallel to La Virreina—who spent her life doing good deeds with her husband's fortune. ✉ *Pl. de la Virreina, Gràcia* Ⓜ *L3 Fontana.*

Plaça del Diamant

PLAZA | This little square is of enormous sentimental importance in Barcelona as the site of the opening and closing scenes of 20th-century Catalan writer Mercé Rodoreda's famous 1962 novel *La Plaça del Diamant*. Translated by the late American poet David Rosenthal as *The Time of the Doves*, it is the most widely translated and published Catalan novel of all time: a tender yet brutal story of a young woman devoured by the Spanish Civil War and, in a larger sense, by life itself. The bronze birds represent the pigeons that Colometa spent her life obsessively breeding; the male figure on the left pierced by bolts of steel is Quimet, her first love and husband, whom she met at a dance in this square and later lost in the war. ✉ *Pl. del Diamant* Ⓜ *L3 Fontana.*

🍽 Restaurants

This lively and intimate neighborhood is home to many of Barcelona's artists, musicians, and actors. The bohemian atmosphere is reflected in an eclectic collection of restaurants encompassing everything from street food and affordable ethnic cuisine to thoroughly sophisticated dining.

Hofmann

$$$$ | MEDITERRANEAN | The late Mey Hofmann, German-born and Catalonia-trained, was revered for decades for her creative Mediterranean and international cuisine based on carefully selected raw materials prepared with unrelenting quality. Her team carries on her legacy at her locale, a graceful designer space with a glassed-in kitchen as center stage.

Known for: sardine tartare; foie gras in puff pastry; prawn risotto. Ⓢ *Average main: €35* ✉ *La Granada del Penedès 14–16, Gràcia* ☎ *93/218–7165* ⊕ *www. hofmann-bcn.com* ⏳ *Closed Sun. and Aug. No lunch Sat.* Ⓜ *Gràcia, Diagonal.*

L'Arrosseria Xàtiva

$$ | SPANISH | This rustic dining room in Gràcia, a spin-off from the original in Les Corts, evokes the rice paddies and lowlands of Valencia. Low lighting imparts a warm glow over exposed brick walls, wood-beam ceilings, and bentwood chairs, and it's a great spot to savor some of Barcelona's finest paellas and rice dishes. **Known for:** traditional paella; lovingly prepared food; all-day kitchen on weekends. Ⓢ *Average main: €20* ✉ *Torrent d'en Vidalet 26, Gràcia* ☎ *93/284–8502* ⊕ *www.grupxativa.com* Ⓜ *Joanic.*

Roig Robí

$$$ | CATALAN | Rattan chairs and a garden terrace characterize this polished dining spot in the bottom corner of Gràcia just above the Diagonal (near Vía Augusta). Rustic and relaxed, Roig Robí (ruby red in Catalan, as in the color of certain wines) maintains a high level of culinary excellence, serving traditional Catalan market cuisine with original touches directed by chef Mercé Navarro. **Known for:** top-notch guinea-fowl canelón; seasonal specials; helmed by excellent chef. Ⓢ *Average main: €26* ✉ *Sèneca 20, Gràcia* ☎ *93/218–9222* ⊕ *www.roigrobi. com* ⏳ *Closed Sun., and 2 wks in Aug. No lunch Sat.* Ⓜ *Diagonal, Gràcia (FGC).*

🛏 Hotels

★ Hotel Casa Fuster Gran Lujo Monumento

$$$$ | HOTEL | This hotel offers one of two chances (the other is the Hotel España) to stay in an Art Nouveau building designed by Lluís Domènech i Montaner, architect of the sumptuous Palau de la Música Catalana. **Pros:** well situated for exploring both Gràcia and the Eixample;

ample rooms with luxury-level amenities; all the Moderniste details you could want. **Cons:** rooms facing Passeig de Gràcia could use better soundproofing; no pets; service can be a bit stiff. Ⓢ *Rooms from: €290* ✉ *Passeig de Gràcia 132, Gràcia* ☎ *93/255–3000* ⊕ *www.hotelcasafuster. com* ⇄ *105 rooms* ᵀᴼᴵ *No meals* Ⓜ *L3/L5 Diagonal.*

Pol & Grace Hotel

$$ | **HOTEL** | Renovated and reopened in 2015 under new ownership—the hip young enthusiastic pair renamed the hotel after themselves—the Pol & Grace is strategically located for exploring Gràcia, a short walk to Gaudí's Casa Vicens, and well connected by FGC train to the head of the Rambla. **Pros:** fun and laid-back atmosphere; children under 10 stay free; book exchange and DVD collection in the lobby. **Cons:** no restaurant on-site; building of no particular architectural interest; no gym or pool. Ⓢ *Rooms from: €130* ✉ *Guillem Tell 49, Gràcia* ☎ *93/415–4000* ⊕ *www.polgracehotel.es* ⇄ *64 rooms* ᵀᴼᴵ *No meals* Ⓜ *Sant Gervasi, Pl. Molina (FGC).*

Upper Barcelona: Sarrià and Pedralbes

Sarrià was originally a country village, overlooking Barcelona from the foothills of the Collserola. Eventually absorbed by the westward-expanding city, the village, 15 minutes by FGC commuter train from Plaça de Catalunya, has become a unique neighborhood made up of old-timers, who speak only Catalan; writers, artists, and other creatives; gourmet shops and upscale restaurants; and expats, who prize the neighborhood for its proximity to the international schools.

Cross Avinguda Foix from Sarrià and you're in Pedralbes—the wealthiest residential neighborhood in the city. (Fútbol superstar Leo Messi has his multimillion-euro home here, and the exclusive Real Club de Tenis de Barcelona is close by.) The centerpiece of this district is the 14th-century Monestir (Monastery) de Pedralbes. The Futbol Club at Barcelona's Camp Nou stadium and the museum are another 20 minutes' walk, down below the Diagonal.

 Sights

Col·legi de les Teresianes

COLLEGE | Built in 1889 for the Reverend Mothers of St. Theresa, when Gaudí was still occasionally using straight lines, the upper floors of this former operating school are reminiscent of those in Berenguer's apartment at Carrer de l'Or 44, with its steep peaks and verticality. Hired to take over for another architect, Gaudí found his freedom of movement somewhat limited in this project. The dominant theme here is the architect's use of steep, narrow catenary arches and Mudejar exposed-brick pillars. The most striking effects are on the second floor, where two rows of a dozen catenary arches run the width of the building, each of them unique; as Gaudí explained, no two things in nature are identical. The brick columns are crowned with T-shaped brick capitals (for St. Theresa). ✉ *Ganduxer 85, Sant Gervasi* ☎ *93/212–3354* ⊕ *ganduxer.escolateresiana.com* Ⓜ *La Bonanova, Les Tres Torres (FGC).*

★ Monestir de Pedralbes

MUSEUM | This marvel of a monastery, named for its original white stones (*pedres albes*), is really a convent, founded in 1326 for the Franciscan order of Poor Clares by Reina (Queen) Elisenda. The three-story Gothic cloister, one of the finest in Europe, surrounds a lush garden. The day cells, where the nuns spend their mornings praying, sewing, and studying, circle the arcaded courtyard. The queen's own cell, the Capella de Sant Miquel, just to the right of the

A quiet space for reflection: the courtyard of the Monestir de Pedralbes

entrance, has murals painted in 1346 by Catalan master Ferrer Bassa. Look for the letters spelling out *Joan no m'oblides* ("John, do not forget me") scratched between the figures of St. Francis and St. Clare (with book and quill), written by a brokenhearted novice. The nuns' upstairs dormitory contains the convent's treasures: paintings, liturgical objects, and seven centuries of artistic and cultural patrimony. ✉ *Baixada del Monestir 9, Pedralbes* ☎ *93/256–3434* ⊕ *monestirpedralbes.bcn.cat/en* ⊠ *€5; free Sun. after 3 pm, and 1st Sun. of every month* ⊙ *Closed Mon.* Ⓜ *Reina Elisenda (FGC).*

Museu Verdaguer–Vil·la Joana

HOUSE | Catalonian poet Jacint Verdaguer died in this house in 1902. The story of Verdaguer's reinvention of Catalan nationalism in the late 19th century, and his ultimate death in disgrace, defrocked and impoverished, is a fascinating saga. Considered the national poet of Catalonia and the most revered and beloved voice of the Catalan "Renaixença" of the 19th century, Verdaguer—universally known as Mossèn Cinto (Mossèn is Catalan for priest; Cinto is from Jacinto)—finally succumbed to tuberculosis and a general collapse triggered by economic, existential, and doctrinal religious troubles. Priest, poet, mystic, student, hiker, and lover of the Pyrenees, he was seen as a virtual saint, and wrote works of great religious and patriotic fervor such as *Idilis* and *Cants mistichs,* as well his famous long masterpiece, *Canigó* (1886). In *La Atlàntida* (1877), eventually to become a Manuel de Falla opera-oratorio, he wrote about prehistoric myths of the Iberian Peninsula and the Pyrenees. Verdaguer's death provoked massive mourning. ✉ *Vil. la Joana, Ctra. de l'Església 104, Vallvidrera* ☎ *93/256–2122* ⊕ *www.museuhistoria.bcn.cat/es/muhba-villa-joana* ⊠ *Free* Ⓜ *Baixador de Vallvidrera (FGC).*

Palau Reial de Pedralbes (*Royal Palace of Pedralbes*)

CASTLE/PALACE | Built in the 1920s as the palatial estate of Count Eusebi Güell—one of Gaudí's most important patrons—this mansion was transformed

Upper Barcelona: Sarrià and Pedralbes

into a royal palace by architect Eusebi Bona i Puig and completed in 1929. King Alfonso XIII, grandfather of Spanish king Juan Carlos I, visited the palace in the mid-1920s before its completion. In 1931, during the Second Spanish Republic, the palace became the property of the municipal government, and it was converted to a decorative arts museum in 1932. (The museum is now part of the Disseny Hub complex in Plaça de les Glòries Catalanes.) In 1936 the rambling, elegant country-manor-house palace was used as the official residence of Manuel Azaña, last president of the Spanish Republic. The gardens and grounds are open to the public; the buildings are not. ⊠ *Av. Diagonal 686, Pedralbes* Ⓜ *L3 Palau Reial.*

Pavellons de la Finca Güell–Càtedra Gaudí
BUILDING | Work on the Finca began in 1883 as an extension of Count Eusebi Güell's family estate. Gaudí, the count's architect of choice, was commissioned to do the gardens and the two entrance pavilions (1884–87); the rest of the project was never finished. The fierce wrought-iron dragon gate is Gaudí's reference to the Garden of the Hesperides, as described by national poet Jacint Verdaguer's epic poem *L'Atlàntida* (1877)—the *Iliad* of Catalonia's historic-mythic origins. The property is open for guided tours in English on weekends at 10:15 and 12:15. Admission is limited to 25 visitors: call ahead, or book on the Ruta del Modernisme website. The Ruta is a walking tour covering 120 masterworks of the Moderniste period, including those by Gaudí, Domènech i Montaner, and Puig i Cadafalch. ⊠ *Av. Pedralbes 7, Pedralbes* ☎ *93/256–2504 guided tours* ⊕ *www.rutadelmodernisme.com* ☜ *Tours €5* Ⓜ *L3 Palau Reial.*

Sarrià
LOCAL INTEREST | The village of Sarrià was originally a cluster of farms and country houses overlooking Barcelona from the hills. Once dismissively described as nothing but "winds, brooks, and convents," this quiet enclave is now a prime residential neighborhood at the upper edge of the city. Start an exploration at the square—the locus, at various times, of antique and bric-a-brac markets, book fairs, artisanal food and wine fairs, sardana dances (Sunday morning), concerts, and Christmas pageants. The 10th-century Romanesque **Church of Sant Vicenç** dominates the main square, Plaça de Sarrià; the bell tower, illuminated on weekend nights, is truly impressive. Across Passeig de la Reina Elisenda from the church (50 yards to the left) is the 100-year-old Moderniste **Mercat de Sarrià.** Allow a few hours to wander the surrounding streets and to stop at Sarrià's famous **Foix** pastry shops. ⊠ *Sarrià* Ⓜ *Sarrià (FGC Line L6).*

Tibidabo
AMUSEMENT PARK/WATER PARK | FAMILY | One of Barcelona's two promontories, this hill bears a distinctive name, generally translated as "To Thee I Will Give." It refers to the Catalan legend that this was the spot from which Satan tempted Christ with all the riches of the earth below (namely, Barcelona). On a clear day, the views from this 1,789-foot peak are legendary. Tibidabo's skyline is marked by a neo-Gothic church, the work of Enric Sagnier in 1902, and—off to one side, near the village of Vallvidrera—the 854-foot communications tower, the **Torre de Collserola,** designed by Sir Norman Foster. If you're with kids, take the San Francisco–style Tramvía Blau (Blue Trolley) from Plaça Kennedy to the overlook at the top, and transfer to the funicular to the 100-year-old **amusement park** at the summit. ⊠ *Pl. Tibidabo 3–4, Tibidabo* ☎ *93/211–7942 amusement park* ⊕ *www.tibidabo.cat* ☜ *Amusement park €29* Ⓜ *FGC L7 Tibidabo, then Tramvía Blau.*

★ Torre Bellesguard

HOUSE | For an extraordinary Gaudí experience, climb up above Plaça de la Bonanova to this private residence built between 1900 and 1909 over the ruins of the summer palace of the last of the sovereign count-kings of the Catalan-Aragonese realm, Martí I l'Humà (Martin I the Humane), whose reign ended in 1410. In homage to this medieval history, Gaudí endowed the house with a tower, gargoyles, and crenellated battlements; the rest—the catenary arches, the trencadís in the facade, the stained-glass windows—are pure Art Nouveau. Look for the red and gold Catalan senyera (banner) on the tower, topped by the four-armed Greek cross Gaudí often used. The visit includes access to the roof, which Gaudí designed to resemble a dragon, along with the gardens, patio, and stables. ■ **TIP➤ Reservations required for the highly recommended guided tour (reserva@bellesguardgaudi.com).** ✉ *Calle Bellesguard 16–20, Sant Gervasi* ☎ *93/250–4093* ⊕ *www.bellesguardgaudi.com* ✆ *From €9* ⊗ *Closed Mon.* Ⓜ *Av. Tibidabo (FGC).*

🍴 Restaurants

Take an excursion to the upper reaches of town for an excellent selection of bars, cafés, and restaurants, along with cool summer evening breezes and a sense of well-heeled village life.

ABaC

$$$$ | **CATALAN** | Jordi Cruz is a culinary phenomenon in Spain. The only choice here is between the two tasting menus, and you can trust this chef to give you the best he has; the hypercreative sampling varies wildly from season to season, but no expense or effort is ever spared. **Known for:** celebrity chef; creative in-season dishes; elegant setting in elegant boutique hotel. Ⓢ *Average main: €180* ✉ *Av. del Tibidabo 1–7, Tibidabo* ☎ *93/319–6600* ⊕ *www.abacbarcelona. com* Ⓜ *Tibidabo.*

Acontraluz

$$ | **CATALAN** | A stylish covered terrace in the leafy upper-Barcelona neighborhood of Tres Torres, Acontraluz has a strenuously varied market-based menu ranging from game in season, such as *rable de liebre* (stewed hare) with chutney, to the more northern *pochas con almejas* (beans with clams). All dishes are prepared with care and talent, and the lunch menu is a relative bargain. **Known for:** stylish dining room with a retractable roof; bargain lunch menu; excellent stewed hare. Ⓢ *Average main: €20* ✉ *Milanesat 19, Tres Torres* ☎ *93/203–0658* ⊕ *acontraluz.com* ⊗ *No dinner Sun. Closed 2 wks in Aug.* Ⓜ *Les Tres Torres.*

Bar Tomás

$ | **TAPAS** | Famous for its *patatas bravas amb allioli* (potatoes with fiery hot sauce and allioli, an emulsion of crushed garlic and olive oil), accompanied by freezing mugs of San Miguel beer, this old-fashioned Sarrià classic is worth seeking out as a contrast to the bland designer tapas bars that are ubiquitous in Barcelona. You'll have to elbow your way to a tiny table and shout to be heard over the hubbub, but you'll get an authentic taste of local bar life. **Known for:** excellent patatas bravas; traditional tavern atmosphere; San Miguel beer in frozen mugs. Ⓢ *Average main: €8* ✉ *Major de Sarrià 49, Sarrià* ☎ *93/203–1077* ⊕ *www.eltomasdesarria. com* ✉ *No credit cards* ⊗ *Closed Wed. and Sun. Closed Aug.* Ⓜ *Sarrià.*

★ Coure

$$$ | **MEDITERRANEAN** | *Cuina d'autor* is Catalan for creative or original cooking, and that is exactly what you get in this smart subterranean space on the intimate and restaurant-centric Passatge Marimón, just above the Diagonal thoroughfare. The upstairs bar gets busy with a post-work crowd of food-loving locals, but downstairs is a cool, minimalist restaurant. **Known for:** interesting wine list; great local fish; seasonal mushrooms. Ⓢ *Average main: €24* ✉ *Passatge*

Marimón 20, Sant Gervasi ☎ 93/200–7532 🕓 Closed Sun. and Mon. Closed 3 wks in Aug. [M] Diagonal.

Dole Café

$ | **CAFÉ** | Little more than a slender slot on the corner of Capità Arenas and Manuel de Falla, this famous upper Barcelona café is absolutely vital to the Sarrià and Capità Arenas neighborhoods. Sandwiches and pastries here are uncannily well made and tasty. **Known for:** top-notch sandwiches and pastries; popeye sandwich is a favorite; often packed. [$] *Average main: €10 ✉ Manuel de Falla 16–18, Sarrià ☎ 93/204–1120 🕓 Closed Sun. No dinner Mon.–Sat. [M] Metro: Maria Cristina, FGC: Sarrià.*

★ El Asador de Aranda

$$$ | **SPANISH** | **FAMILY** | It's a hike to get to this immense palace a few minutes' walk above the Avenida Tibidabo train station—but it's worth it. The kitchen, featuring a vast, wood-fired clay oven, specializes in Castilian cooking, with *cordero lechal* (roast suckling lamb), *morcilla* (black sausage), and pimientos de piquillo as star players. **Known for:** beautiful Art Nouveau setting; excellent roasted lamb; spectacular city views from terrace. [$] *Average main: €25 ✉ Av. del Tibidabo 31, Tibidabo ☎ 93/417–0115 🌐 www.asadordearanda.net [M] Tibidabo (FGC).*

Fishhh!

$$ | **SEAFOOD** | Housed inside the L'Illa Diagonal shopping mall, you can combine retail therapy with a seafood feast at Fishhh!, a first-rate oyster bar and fish restaurant. Owner Lluís de Buen is long a major seafood supplier of Barcelona's top restaurants (check out his seafood-central command post off the back left corner of the Boqueria market) and his staff have put together a lively and popular dining space that exudes Boqueria market–style excitement in the midst of a busy shopping venue. **Known for:** oysters and Champagne; seafood specialties; king crab served table-side. [$] *Average main: €15 ✉ Av. Diagonal 557, Sant Gervasi, Les Corts ☎ 93/444–1139 🌐 fishhh.net 🕓 Closed Sun. [M] Les Corts.*

Gouthier

$$ | **SEAFOOD** | This Paris-style oyster bar spills out onto a pretty square in the former village of Sarrià. Pristine oysters of all kinds are shucked and served fresh alongside rye bread and creamy pats of French butter. **Known for:** supplies oysters to leading restaurants; quiet location; pleasant terrace. [$] *Average main: €18 ✉ Mañé i Flaquer 8, Sarrià ✣ Located on Pl. Vicenç de Sarrià ☎ 93/205–9969 🌐 www.gouthier.es 🕓 Closed Sun. and Mon. [M] Sarrià.*

★ Hisop

$$$ | **CATALAN** | The minimalist interior design of Oriol Ivern's small restaurant is undistinguished, but his cooking is stellar. This is budget-conscious fine dining that avoids exotic ingredients but lifts local dishes to exciting new heights. **Known for:** great-value cuisine; Michelin star; delicious cod with morel sauce. [$] *Average main: €25 ✉ Passatge de Marimón 9, Sant Gervasi ☎ 93/241–3233 🌐 www.hisop.com 🕓 Closed Sun., and 1st wk of Jan. No lunch Sat. [M] Diagonal.*

★ Tram-Tram

$$$ | **CATALAN** | At the end of the old tram line above the village of Sarrià, this restaurant offers one of Barcelona's finest culinary stops, with Isidre Soler and his wife, Reyes, at the helm. Perfectly sized portions and an airy white space within this traditional Sarrià house add to the experience. **Known for:** menú de degustació (tasting menu); pleasant interior garden patio; refined Catalan cuisine. [$] *Average main: €24 ✉ Major de Sarrià 121, Sarrià ☎ 93/204–8518 🌐 tram-tram.com 🕓 Closed Mon., and 2 wks in Aug. No dinner Sun. and Tues. [M] Sarrià.*

★ Via Veneto

$$$$ | **CATALAN** | Open since 1967, this family-owned temple of fine Catalan dining offers a contemporary menu punctuated by old-school classics. Service from

the veteran waiters is impeccable, and diners can safely place themselves in the hands of the expert sommelier to guide them through a daunting 10,000-bottle-strong wine list. **Known for:** favorite of Salvador Dalí and now sports stars; incredible roast duck; smoking room for postprandial cigars. $ *Average main: €37* ✉ *Ganduxer 10, Sant Gervasi* ☎ *93/200–7244* ⊕ *www.viavenetobarcelona.com* ⊙ *Closed Sun. and Aug. No lunch Sat.* Ⓜ *La Bonanova (FGC), Maria Cristina.*

Hotels

ABaC Hotel

$$$$ | HOTEL | This classy boutique hotel with a Michelin-starred restaurant is located in the environs of Gràcia, at the base of Avenida Tibidabo, and provides a complete respite from the bustle of the city—and the busy thoroughfare on which it is placed. **Pros:** oasis-style rooms, completely soundproofed; the best restaurant in town; walk through the kitchen whenever you choose. **Cons:** far from the old town and beaches; only 15 rooms, so it's easily booked up; layout of hotel can be disorientating. $ *Rooms from: €310* ✉ *Av. Tibidabo 1, Sant Gervasi* ☎ *93/319–6600* ⊕ *www.abacbarcelona. com/en* ⥁ *15 rooms* ‖◯‖ *No meals* Ⓜ *FGC L7 Avinida Tibidabo.*

★ Primero Primera

$$$$ | HOTEL | FAMILY | The Perez family converted their apartment building on a leafy side street in the quiet, upscale, residential neighborhood of Tres Torres and opened it as an exquisitely designed, homey boutique hotel in 2011. **Pros:** retro-modern ambience; 24-hour free snack bar; electric bicycle rentals for guests. **Cons:** bit of a distance from downtown; very small pool; service can be uneven. $ *Rooms from: €230* ✉ *Doctor Carulla 25–29, Sant Gervasi* ☎ *93/417–5600* ⊕ *www.primeroprimera.com* ⥁ *30 rooms* ‖◯‖ *Free Breakfast* Ⓜ *Tres Torres (FGC).*

Sansi Pedralbes

$$ | HOTEL | A contemporary polished-marble-and-black-glass box, with Japanese overtones, a stone's throw from the gardens of the Monestir de Pedralbes, this hotel may be a bit removed from the action downtown, but there's a stop on the Bus Turistic just across the street, and the views up into the Collserola Hills above Barcelona are splendid. **Pros:** small and intimate; close to Carretera de les Aigües, Barcelona's best running track; quiet area near the Güell Pavilions. **Cons:** the nearest subway stations are 15–20 minutes away on foot; no pets; pricey breakfast. $ *Rooms from: €150* ✉ *Av. Pearson 1–3, Pedralbes* ☎ *93/206–3880* ⊕ *www.sansihotels.com* ⥁ *60 rooms* ‖◯‖ *No meals* Ⓜ *Reina Elisenda (FGC), L3 Maria Cristina.*

Activities

SOCCER
Futbol Club Barcelona

SOCCER | Founded in 1899, FC Barcelona won its third European Championship in 2009, the Liga championship, and its 27th Copa del Rey (King's Cup)—Spain's first-ever *triplete*—and did it again in 2015. Even more impressive was its razzle-dazzle style of soccer, rarely seen in the age of cynical defensive lockdowns and muscular British-style play. Barça, as the club is known, is Real Madrid's nemesis (and vice versa) and a sociological and historical phenomenon of deep significance in Catalonia. Ticket windows at Access 14 to the Camp Nou stadium are open Monday–Thursday 9–5, Friday 9–2:30, and Saturday 9–1:30 (if there's a match at home). You can also buy tickets online through the FC Barcelona website, or from Ticketmaster (*www.ticketmaster. es*) or Entradas (*www.entradas.es*). Tours of the stadium and museum can also be organized through the FC Barcelona website. ✉ *Camp Nou, Aristides Maillol 12, Les Corts* ☎ *902/189900* ⊕ *www. fcbarcelona.com* Ⓜ *Collblanc, Palau Reial.*

Montjuïc and Poble Sec

A bit remote from the hustle and bustle of Barcelona street life, Montjuïc more than justifies a day or two of exploring. The Miró Foundation, the Museu Nacional d'Art de Catalunya, the minimalist Mies van der Rohe Pavilion, the lush Jardins de Mossèn Cinto Verdaguer, and the gallery and auditorium of the CaixaForum (the former Casaramona textile factory) are all among Barcelona's must-see sights.

Other Montjuïc attractions include the fortress, the Olympic stadium, the Palau Sant Jordi, and the Poble Espanyol. There are buses within Montjuïc that visitors can take from sight to sight.

◉ Sights

★ CaixaForum (Casaramona)
ARTS VENUE | FAMILY | This 1911 neo-Mudejar Art Nouveau masterpiece, originally built to house a factory by Josep Puig I Cadafalch (architect of Casa de les Punxes, Casa Amatller, Casa Martí, and Casa Quadras) is a center for art exhibits, concerts, lectures, and cultural events, and well worth keeping an eye on in newspaper and magazine leisure listings for special exhibitions. The CaixaForum also regularly lays on a whole range of films, concerts, and hands-on learning activities for kids. The original brickwork is spectacular; the restoration is a brilliant example of the fusion of ultramodern design techniques with traditional (even Art Nouveau) architecture. ⊠ Av. Francesc Ferrer i Guàrdia 6–8, Montjuïc ☎ 93/476–8600 ⊕ www.obrasocial. lacaixa.es ⊡ €4 Ⓜ L1/L3 Pl. d'Espanya.

Castell de Montjuïc
CASTLE/PALACE | Built in 1640 by rebels against Felipe IV, the castle has had a dark history as a symbol of Barcelona's military domination by foreign powers, usually the Spanish army. The fortress was stormed several times, most

famously in 1705 by Lord Peterborough for Archduke Carlos of Austria. In 1808, during the Peninsular War, it was seized by the French under General Dufresne. Later, during an 1842 civil disturbance, Barcelona was bombed from its heights by a Spanish artillery battery. After the 1936–39 civil war, the castle was used as a dungeon for political prisoners. Lluís Companys, president of the Generalitat de Catalunya during the civil war, was executed by firing squad here on October 14, 1940. In 2007 the fortress was formally ceded back to Barcelona. A popular weekend park and picnic area, the moat contains attractive gardens, with one side given over to an archery range, and the various terraces have panoramic views over the city and out to sea. ⊠ Ctra. de Montjuïc 66, Montjuïc ☎ 93/256–4440, 93/302–3553 for Sala Montjuic ⊕ www.bcn.cat/castelldemontjuic ⊡ €5 (free Sun. from 3 pm); Sala Montjuic tickets €7 Ⓜ L2/L3 Paral.lel and Funicular.

Estadi Olímpic Lluís Companys (Olympic Stadium)
MUSEUM | Open for visitors, the Olympic Stadium was originally built for the International Exhibition of 1929, with the idea that Barcelona would then host the 1936 Olympics (ultimately staged in Hitler's Berlin). After failing twice to win the nomination, the city celebrated the attainment of its long-cherished goal by renovating the semi-derelict stadium—preserving the original facade and shell—in time for 1992, providing seating for 70,000. The nearby **Museu Olímpic i de l'Esport**, a museum about the Olympic movement in Barcelona, shows audiovisual replays from the 1992 Olympics, and provides interactive simulations for visitors to experience the training and competition of Olympic athletes. An information center traces the history of the modern Olympics from Athens in 1896 to the present. ⊠ Av. de l'Estadi s/n, Montjuïc ☎ 93/426–2089 Estadi

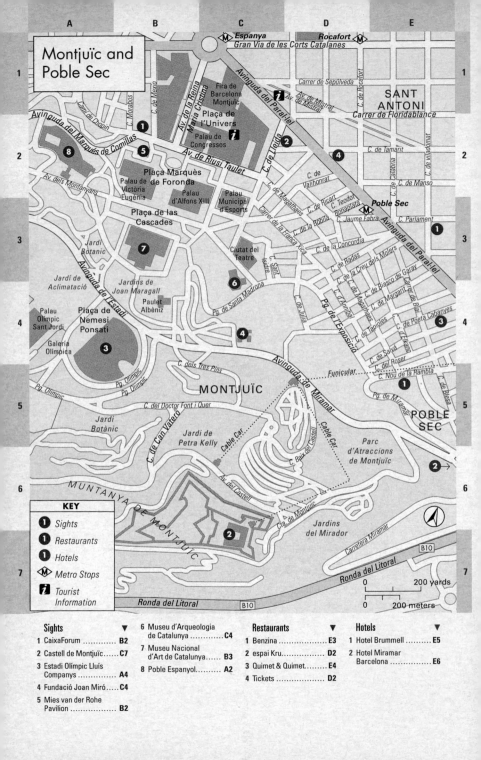

Montjuïc and Poble Sec

	A	B	C	D	E	

M Espanya
Gran Via de les Corts Catalanes
Rocafort **M**

Avinguda del Paral·lel

Carrer de Sepúlveda

SANT
ANTONI

Av. de Mistral

Carrer de Floridablance

Camí de Chopin

C. de Morabos

C. de Mexio

C. de la Reina
Maria Cristina

Fira de
Barcelona
Montjuïc

7

Plaça de
l'Univers

Palau de
Congressos

7

C. de Lleida

C. de Rocafort

C. de Calabria

C. de Viladomat

Avinguda del Marquès de Comillas

8

5

1

Av. dels Montanyans

Av. de Riusi Taulet

C. de Tamarit

C. de Manso

Plaça Marquès
de Foronda

Palau
Victòria
Eugènia
d'Alfons XIII

Palau
Municipal
d'Esports

C. de Magalhães

C. de Vallhonrat

C. de Ricart

C. Teodot
Bonaplata

Poble Sec **M**

C. de Jaume Fabra

C. Parlament

1

Plaça de
Nemesi
Ponsati

Palau de
Foronda

Palau

Plaça de las
Cascades

Jardí
Botànic

7

Ciutat del
Teatre

Carrer de la Fança Xica

C. de la Bòbila

C. de la Concordia

C. de Rades

C. de la Creu dels Molers

Avinguda del Paral·lel

C. de Magalhães

C. de Blasco de Garay

C. de Margarit

Carrer de Blai

3

Jardí de
Aclimatació

Avinguda de l'Estadi

Jardins de
Joan Maragall

Paulet
Albèniz

6

Pg. de Santa Madrona

C. Sant
Isidra

C. de Julia

C. d'Amàlia

Pg. de l'Exposició

C. de Tapioles

C. de Poeta Cabanyes

3

C. d'Elkano

Palau
Olímpic
Sant Jordi

Plaça de
Nemesi
Ponsati

3

Galería
Olímpica

C. dels Tres Pins

4

C. de Salvà

C. del Roser

C. Nou de la Rambla

1

C. de Blasa

Pg. Olímpic

Pg. Olímpic

Pg. Olímpic

C. del Doctor Font i Quer

MONTJUÏC

Avinguda de Miramar

Funicular

Pg. de Miramar

**POBLE
SEC**

Jardí
Botànic

Jardí de
Petra Kelly

Cable Car

Cable Car

Parc
d'Atraccions
de Montjuïc

2

MUNTANYA DE MONTJUÏC

Av. del Castell

Ctra. de Montjuïc

2

Jardins
del Mirador

Carretera Miramar

B10

Ronda del Litoral

Ronda del Litoral   B10

0   200 yards
0   200 meters

KEY

1 Sights
1 Restaurants
1 Hotels
M Metro Stops
7 Tourist Information

Sights ▼
1 CaixaForum B2
2 Castell de Montjuïc...... C7
3 Estadi Olímpic Lluís Companys A4
4 Fundació Joan Miró..... C4
5 Mies van der Rohe Pavilion B2

6 Museu d'Arqueologia de Catalunya C4
7 Museu Nacional d'Art de Catalunya...... B3
8 Poble Espanyol.......... A2

Restaurants ▼
1 Benzina E3
2 espai Kru................. D2
3 Quimet & Quimet........ E4
4 Tickets D2

Hotels ▼
1 Hotel Brummell E5
2 Hotel Miramar Barcelona E6

Olímpic, 93/292–5379 Museu Olímpica ⊕ www.fundaciobarcelonaolimpica.es ⊠ Free 𝕆 Museum closed Mon. Ⓜ L1/L3 Espanya.

★ Fundació Joan Miró

MUSEUM | The Miró Foundation, a gift from the artist Joan Miró to his native city, is one of Barcelona's most exciting showcases of modern and contemporary art. The airy white building, with panoramic views north over Barcelona, was designed by the artist's close friend and collaborator Josep Lluís Sert and opened in 1975; an extension was added by Sert's pupil Jaume Freixa in 1988. Miró's playful and colorful style, filled with Mediterranean light and humor, seems a perfect match for its surroundings, and the exhibits and retrospectives that open here tend to be progressive and provocative—look for Alexander Calder's fountain of moving mercury. Miró himself rests in the cemetery on Montjuïc's southern slopes. ⊠ Av. Miramar 71–75, Parc de Montjuïc, Montjuïc ☎ 93/443–9470 ⊕ www.fmirobcn.org ⊠ €12 𝕆 Closed Mon. Ⓜ L1/L3 Pl. Espanya; L3 Paral.lel, then Funicular de Montjuïc.

Mies van der Rohe Pavilion

BUILDING | One of the masterpieces of the Bauhaus School, the legendary Pavelló Mies van der Rohe—the German contribution to the 1929 International Exhibition, reassembled between 1983 and 1986—remains a stunning "less is more" study in interlocking planes of white marble, green onyx, and glass. In effect, it is Barcelona's aesthetic antonym (in company with Richard Meier's Museu d'Art Contemporani and Rafael Moneo's Auditori) to the flamboyant Art Nouveau—the city's signature Modernisme—of Gaudí and his contemporaries. Note the mirror play of the black carpet inside the pavilion with the reflecting pool outside, or the iconic Barcelona chair designed by Ludwig Mies van der Rohe (1886–1969); reproductions have graced modern interiors around the world for decades. ⊠ Av. Francesc Ferrer i Guàrdia 7, Montjuïc ☎ 93/423–4016, 93/215–1011 ⊕ miesbcn.com ⊠ €5 Ⓜ L1/L3 Pl. Espanya.

Museu d'Arqueologia de Catalunya

MUSEUM | Just downhill to the right of the Palau Nacional, the Museum of Archaeology holds important finds from the Greek ruins at Empúries, on the Costa Brava. These are shown alongside fascinating objects from, and explanations of, megalithic Spain. ⊠ Passeig Santa Madrona 39–41, Montjuïc ☎ 93/423–2149 ⊕ www.mac.cat/eng ⊠ €5; last Tues. of month; free Oct.–June 𝕆 Closed Mon. Ⓜ L1/L3 Pl. Espanya.

★ Museu Nacional d'Art de Catalunya (Catalonian National Museum of Art, MNAC)

MUSEUM | Housed in the imposingly domed, towered, frescoed, and columned **Palau Nacional,** built in 1929 as the centerpiece of the International Exposition, this superb museum was renovated in 1995 by Gae Aulenti, architect of the Musée d'Orsay in Paris. In 2004 the museum's three holdings (Romanesque, Gothic, and the Cambó Collection—an eclectic trove, including a Goya, donated by Francesc Cambó) were joined by the 19th- and 20th-century collection of Catalan impressionist and Moderniste painters. Also now on display is the Thyssen-Bornemisza collection of early masters, with works by Zurbarán, Rubens, Tintoretto, Velázquez, and others. Pride of place goes to the Romanesque exhibition, the world's finest collection of Romanesque frescoes, altarpieces, and wood carvings, most of them rescued from chapels in the Pyrenees during the 1920s. The central hall of the museum, with its enormous pillared and frescoed cupola, is stunning. ⊠ Palau Nacional, Parc de Montjuïc s/n, Montjuïc ☎ 93/622–0360 ⊕ www.museunacional.cat ⊠ From €12 (valid for day of purchase and 1 other day in same month); free Sat. after 3 pm and 1st Sun. of month 𝕆 Closed Mon. Ⓜ L1/L3 Pl. Espanya.

★ **Poble Espanyol** (*Spanish Village*)
BUILDING | **FAMILY** | Created for the 1929
International Exhibition, the Spanish
Village is a sort of open-air architectural
museum, with faithful replicas to scale
of building styles, from an Aragonese
Gothic-Mudejar bell tower to the tower
walls of Ávila, drawn from all over Spain;
the ground-floor spaces are devoted to
boutiques, cafés and restaurants, workshops, and studios. The liveliest time to
come is at night, and a reservation at
one of the half dozen restaurants gets
you in for free, as does the purchase of a
ticket for either of the two discos or the
Tablao del Carmen flamenco club. ⊠ *Av.
Francesc Ferrer i Guàrdia 13, Montjuïc*
☎ *93/508–6300* ⊕ *www.poble-espanyol.
com* ⊠ *€14 (€13 online); after 8 pm €7
(€6 online)* Ⓜ *L1/L3 Pl. Espanya.*

 Restaurants

Benzina
$$ | **ITALIAN** | Named in homage to the
gas station that once sat here, Benzina
blends industrial elements with splashes
of color, supremely comfortable chairs,
and excellent music (on vinyl, naturally)
to create a hip but cozy Italian restau-
rant that would not look out of place
in New York. The food is center stage,
however; the freshly made pasta—com-
bined with classic sauces or the chef's
whims—is among the best in the city.
Known for: chic decor; fresh house-made
pastas; new twists on traditional dishes.
Ⓢ *Average main: €17* ⊠ *Passatge Pere
Calders 6, Born-Ribera* ☎ *93/659–5583*
⊕ *www.benzina.es* ⊗ *No lunch weekdays*
Ⓜ *Poble Sec.*

★ **espai Kru**
$$$ | **ECLECTIC** | What happens when one
of Barcelona's most venerable seafood
restaurants joins the creative cooking
revolution? The answers can be found at
espai Kru, upstairs from the eye-water-
ingly expensive Rías de Galicia, where
the finest ingredients from the deep are
given a more modestly priced makeover

in contemporary surroundings. **Known
for:** fresh seafood; oyster bar; light-as-air
lobster sandwiches. Ⓢ *Average main:
€26* ⊠ *Lleida 7, Poble Sec* ☎ *93/424–8152*
⊕ *www.espaikru.com* ⊗ *Closed Mon.
No dinner Tues.–Sat. No lunch Sun.* Ⓜ *Pl.
Espanya/Poble Sec.*

Quimet & Quimet
$ | **TAPAS** | A foodie haunt, this tiny tapas
place is hugely popular with locals and
in-the-know visitors alike; if you show
up too late, you might not be able to get
in—come before 1:30 pm or 7:30 pm,
however, and you might snag a stand-
up table. Fourth-generation chef-owner
Quim and his family improvise ingenious
canapés. **Known for:** local wines; family-run; intimate space (long wait times).
Ⓢ *Average main: €15* ⊠ *Poeta Cabanyes
25, Poble Sec* ☎ *93/442–3142* ⊗ *Closed
Sun. and Aug. No dinner Sat.* Ⓜ *Paral.lel.*

Tickets
$$$ | **TAPAS** | Ferran and Albert Adrià of
former "World's Best Restaurant" elBulli
fame are the ringleaders behind this
circus-themed big top of creative tapas.
Tickets offers tapas twists you've never
dreamed of, like strawberry-bearing trees
(complete with pruning scissors) with
pistachio acorns, and a round-the-world
ride of oysters. **Known for:** off-the-wall
creativity; online reservations only;
enthusiastic and knowledgeable wait-
staff. Ⓢ *Average main: €25* ⊠ *Av. Paral.lel
164, Poble Sec* ⊕ *www.ticketsbar.es/en*
⊗ *Closed Sun. and Mon., 2 wks in Aug.,
and 1 wk at Christmas. No lunch Tues.–
Fri.* Ⓜ *Poble Sec.*

 Hotels

Hotel Brummell
$$$ | **HOTEL** | Opened in 2015, the Brum-
mell is among the more recent of the
stylish new ventures now starting to
give the once-scruffy neighborhood of
Poble Sec a different buzz. **Pros:** young,
friendly international staff; smart TVs;
excellent brunch. **Cons:** no room service;

Find replicas of buildings from all over Spain and see craftspeople at work in the Spanish village, at the foot of Montjuïc.

storage is limited; vending machines in lieu of in-room minibars. [$] *Rooms from: €180* ✉ *Nou de la Rambla 174, Poble Sec* ☎ *93/125–8622* 🌐 *www.hotelbrummell.com* 🛏 *20 rooms* 🍴 *No meals* [M] *L3 Paral.lel.*

★ Hotel Miramar Barcelona

$$$ | **HOTEL** | **FAMILY** | Only the facade remains of this imposing "palace," built in 1929 for Barcelona's second Universal Expositionas and later acquired by a TV network as its studio headquarters, then abandoned from 1983 until 2006, when it was gutted and transformed by architect Oscar Tusquets into an elegant, romantic hillside resort. **Pros:** complimentary glass of cava on check-in; easy access to beach and Barceloneta by cable car; parking free if booked online (otherwise €12 outside, €18 inside). **Cons:** no shuttle service; pricey breakfast. [$] *Rooms from: €220* ✉ *Pl. Carlos Ibáñez 3, Montjuïc* ☎ *93/281–1600* 🌐 *www.hotelmiramar-barcelona.com* 🛏 *66 doubles, 8 suites* 🍴 *No meals* [M] *L3 Drassanes.*

Nightlife

Sant Antoni's after-dark offerings may seem quiet in comparison to other iconic neighbors, but bars and bodegas here exude a genuine and welcoming quality only found in tourist-free zones. Poble Sec, on the other hand, is a stone's throw away from the huge L'Eixample district and offers an eclectic collection of fashionable cafés, bars, and eateries.

BARS

Bodega 1900

BARS/PUBS | Celebrated chef Albert Adrià (Tickets, at Avenida del Paral.lel 164, is just across the street) pays homage to time-honored traditional *vermuterias* by combining his creative culinary wizardry with conventional products, resulting in elevated versions of turn-of-the-20th-century dishes and drinks. Sleekly decorated in white and aged wood, this contemporary eatery resembles a dreamy but traditional vermouth bar with steep prices. ✉ *Tamarit 91, Poble Sec* ☎ *93/325–2659* 🌐 *www.bodega1900.com* [M] *Poble Sec.*

Celler Cal Marino

BARS/PUBS | Rustic and charming with an arched, brick-walled center, barrel tables, and rows of multicolor *sifón* fizzy-water bottles, this homey venue serves wine by the glass or liter (for takeaway) from the wine cellar, artisanal beers, and vermouth paired with homemade tapas. Tuesday through Friday the special is three drinks matched with three tapas, while Sunday is often dedicated to live jazz concerts and vermouth aperitifs. ⊠ *Margarit 54, Poble Sec* ☎ *93/329–4592* ⊕ *www.calmarino.com* Ⓜ *Poble Sec, Paral.lel.*

El Rouge

BARS/PUBS | El Rouge has a bohemian vibe, complete with a selection of mismatched, threadbare furniture, posters of impressionist paintings tacked to the wall, and the low light created by red pashmina shawls draped over lampshades. Here you'll find an excellent mixologist and tasteful lounge music playing in the background. ⊠ *Poeta Cabanyes 21, Poble Sec* ☎ *634/127581* ◷ *Closed Wed. and Sun.* Ⓜ *Paral.lel.*

★ Jonny Aldana

BARS/PUBS | This cheery technicolor bar-resto, featuring a tiled facade and open-window bar with stools inside and out, is bursting with 1950s iconography. Wines are sold by the glass, beer is served from the tap, but it's the superb vermouths and cocktails combined with veggie and vegan tapas that reel in patrons. ⊠ *Aldana 9, Poble Sec* ☎ *93/174– 2083* Ⓜ *Paral.lel.*

★ Xixbar

BARS/PUBS | The interior of this Alice in Wonderland–like venue of checkered half walls, a marble bar, and contempo objets d'art rarely seen on ceilings is the first clue that you've landed somewhere special. Beyond that, with 50-plus flavors of gins and infusions on offer and a lounge-friendly 3 am curfew on weekends, Xix turns conventional cocktail drinkers into card-carrying gin lovers. ⊠ *Carrer de Rocafort 19, Poble Sec* ☎ *93/423–4314* ⊕ *www.xixbar.com* Ⓜ *Poble Sec.*

⊕ Performing Arts

FLAMENCO
El Tablao de Carmen

DANCE | Large tour groups come to this venerable flamenco dinner-theater venue in the Poble Espanyol named after, and dedicated to, the legendary dancer Carmen Amaya. Die-hard flamenco aficionados might dismiss the ensembles that perform here as a tad touristy, but the dancers, singers, and guitarists are pros. Visitors can enjoy one of the two nightly performances over a drink or over their choice of a full-course, prix-fixe meal. Reservations are recommended. Dinner shows are held daily at 6 pm and 8:30 pm. ⊠ *Poble Espanyol, Av. Francesc Ferrer i Guàrdia 13, Montjuïc* ☎ *93/325–6895* ⊕ *www.tablaodecarmen.com* Ⓜ *Espanya.*

Chapter 9

CATALONIA, VALENCIA, AND THE COSTA BLANCA

Updated by
Elizabeth Prosser

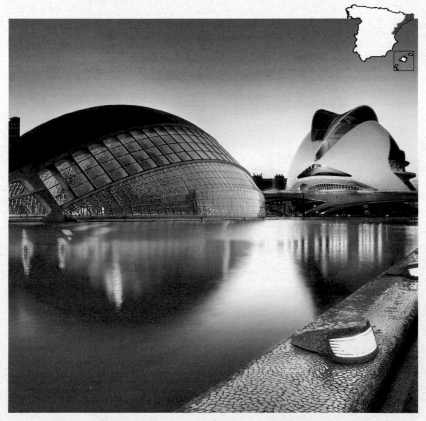

👁 Sights	🍴 Restaurants	🛏 Hotels	🛍 Shopping	🍸 Nightlife
★★★★☆	★★★★☆	★★★☆☆	★★★☆☆	★★★☆☆

WELCOME TO CATALONIA, VALENCIA, AND THE COSTA BLANCA

TOP REASONS TO GO

★ **Girona:** Explore a city where monuments of Christian, Jewish, and Islamic cultures have coexisted for centuries and are just steps apart.

★ **Valencia reborn:** The city has seen a transformation of the Turia River into a treasure trove of museums, concert halls, parks, and architectural wonders.

★ **Great restaurants:** Foodies argue that the fountainhead of creative gastronomy has moved from France to Spain—and in particular to the great restaurants of the Empordà and Costa Brava.

★ **Dalí's home and museum:** "Surreal" doesn't begin to describe the Teatre-Museu Dalí in Figueres or the wild coast of the artist's home at Cap de Creus.

★ **Las Fallas festival:** Valencia's Las Fallas in mid-March, a week of fireworks and solemn processions with a finale of spectacular bonfires, is one of the best festivals in Europe.

Year-round, Catalonia is the most visited of Spain's autonomous communities. The Pyrenees, which separate it from France, provide some of the country's best skiing, and the rugged Costa Brava in the north and the Costa Daurada to the south are havens for sunseekers. Excellent rail, air, and highway connections link Catalonia to the beach resorts of Valencia, its neighbor to the south.

1 Girona

2 Figueres

3 Besalú

4 Olot

5 Tossa de Mar

6 Sant Feliu de Guixols

7 S'Agaró

8 Calella de Palafrugell and Around

9 Begur and Around

10 Cadaqués and Around

11 Montserrat

12 Sitges

13 Santes Creus

14 Santa Maria de Poblet

15 Valencia

16 Albufera Nature Park

17 Dénia

18 Calpe

19 Altea

20 Alicante

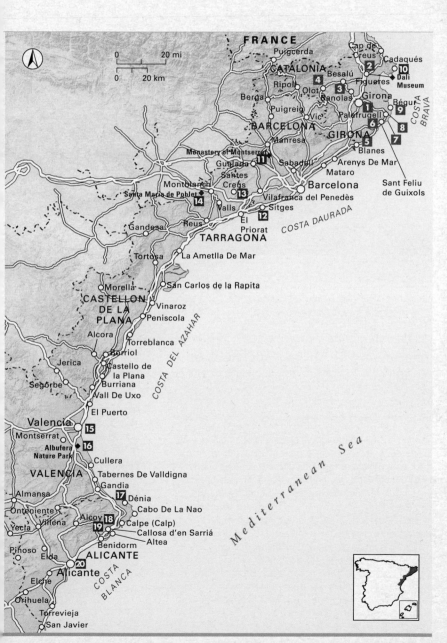

0   20 mi

0   20 km

FRANCE

Puigcerda

Cap de
Creus

2

Cadaqués

CATALONIA

10

Dalí
Museum

Ripoll

Besalú

4

Figueres

Olot

Berga

3

Girona

Banolas

Bégura

Puigreig

1

9

Vic

Palafrugell

COSTA
BRAVA

BARCELONA

GIRONA

6

Manresa

5

8

Monastery of Montserrat

11

Sabadell

7

Gualada

Blanes

Santes
Creus

Arenys De Mar

Montblanch

Barcelona

Mataro

Santa Maria de Poblet

13

14

Vilafranca del Penedès

Sant Feliu
de Guixols

Valls

Sitges

12

Reus

El
Priorat

COSTA DAURADA

Gandesa

TARRAGONA

Tortosa

La Ametlla De Mar

Morella

San Carlos de la Rapita

**CASTELLON
DE LA
PLANA**

Vinaroz

Peniscola

Alcora

COSTA DEL AZAHAR

Torreblanca

Jerica

Borriol

Castello de
la Plana

Segorbe

Burriana

Vall De Uxo

El Puerto

Valencia

Montserrat

15

Albufera
Nature Park

16

VALENCIA

Cullera

Almansa

Tabernes De Valldigna

Ontoniente

Gandia

Yecla

Villena

Alcoy

17

Dénia

18

Cabo De La Nao

Piñoso

Calpe (Calp)

19

Callosa d'en Sarriá

Elda

Benidorm

Altea

ALICANTE

20

COSTA
BLANCA

Alicante

Elche

Mediterranean Sea

Orihuela

Torrevieja

San Javier

EATING AND DRINKING WELL IN CATALONIA

Cuisine in both Catalonia and Valencia includes classic Mediterranean dishes, and Catalans feel right at home with paella valenciana (Valencian paella). Fish preparations are similar along the coast, though inland favorites vary from place to place.

The grassy inland meadows of Catalonia's northern Alt Empordà region put quality beef on local tables; from the Costa Brava comes fine seafood, such as anchovies from L'Escala and *gambas* (prawns) from Palamós, both deservedly famous. *Romesco*—a blend of almonds, peppers, garlic, and olive oil—is used as a vegetable, fish, and seafood sauce in Tarragona, especially during the *calçotadas* (spring onion feasts) in February. *Allioli*, garlicky mayonnaise, is another popular topping. The Ebro Delta is renowned for fresh fish, oysters, and eels, as well as *rossejat* (fried rice in a fish broth). Valencia and the Mediterranean coast are the homeland of paella valenciana. *Arròs a banda* is a variant in which the fish and rice are cooked separately.

CALÇOTS

The *calçot* is a sweet spring onion developed by a 19th-century farmer who discovered how to extend the edible portion by packing soil around the base. It is grilled on a barbecue, then peeled and dipped into romesco sauce. In January, the town of Valls holds a *calçotada* where upward of 30,000 people gather for meals of onions, sausage, lamb chops, and red wine.

RICE

Paella valenciana is one of Spain's most famous gastronomic contributions. A simple country dish dating to the early 18th century, "paella" refers to the wide frying pan with short, sturdy handles that's used to cook the rice. Anything fresh from the fields that day, along with rice and olive oil, traditionally went into the pan, but paella valenciana has particular ingredients: short-grain rice, chicken, rabbit, *garrofó* (a local legume), tomatoes, green beans, sweet peppers, olive oil, and saffron. *Paella marinera* (seafood paella) is a different story: rice, cuttlefish, squid, mussels, shrimp, prawns, lobster, clams, garlic, olive oil, sweet paprika, and saffron, all stewed in fish broth. Other paella variations include *paella negra*, a black rice dish made with squid ink; *arròs a banda* made with peeled seafood; and *fideuà*, paella made with noodles.

SEAFOOD STEWS

Sèpia amb pèsols is a vegetable and seafood *mar i muntanya* ("surf and turf") beloved on the Costa Brava: cuttlefish and peas are stewed with potatoes, garlic, onions, tomatoes, and a splash of wine. The *picadillo*—the finishing touches of flavors and textures—includes parsley, black pepper, fried bread, pine nuts, olive oil, and salt. *Es niu* ("the nest") of game fowl, cod, tripe, cuttlefish, pork, and

rabbit is another Costa Brava favorite. Stewed for a good five hours, this is a much-celebrated wintertime classic. You'll also find *suquet de peix*, the Catalan fish stew, at restaurants along the Costa Brava.

FRUITS AND VEGETABLES

Valencia and the eastern Levante region have long been famous as Spain's *huerta*, or garden. The alluvial soil of the littoral produces an abundance of everything from tomatoes to asparagus, peppers, chard, spinach, onions, artichokes, cucumbers, and the whole range of Mediterranean bounty. Catalonia's Maresme and Empordà regions are also fruit and vegetable bowls, making this coastline a true cornucopia of fresh produce.

WINES

The Penedès wine region west of Barcelona has been joined by new wine Denominations of Origin from all over Catalonia. Alt Camp, Tarragona, Priorat, Montsant, Costers del Segre, Pla de Bages, Alella, and Empordà all produce excellent reds and whites to join Catalonia's sparkling cava on local wine lists. The rich, full-bodied reds of Montsant and Priorat, especially, are among the best in Spain.

The long curve of the Mediterranean from the French border to Cabo Cervera below Alicante encompasses the two autonomous communities of Catalonia and Valencia, with the country's second- and third-largest cities (Barcelona and Valencia, respectively). Rivals in many respects, the two communities share a language, history, and culture that set them apart from the rest of Spain.

Girona is the gateway to Northern Catalonia's attractions—the Pyrenees, the volcanic region of La Garrotxa, and the beaches of rugged Costa Brava. Northern Catalonia is memorable for the soft, green hills of the Empordà farm country and the Alberes mountain range at the eastern end of the Pyrenees. Across the landscape are *masías* (farmhouses) with staggered-stone roofs and square towers that make them look like fortresses. Even the tiniest village has its church, arcaded square, and *rambla,* where villagers take their evening *paseo* (stroll).

Salvador Dalí's deep connection to the Costa Brava is enshrined in the Teatre-Museu Dalí in Figueres: he's buried in the crypt beneath it. His wife Gala is buried in his former home, a castle in Púbol. His summer home in Port Lligat Bay, north of Cadaqués, is now a museum of his life and work.

The province of Valencia was incorporated into the Kingdom of Aragón, Catalonia's medieval Mediterranean empire, when it was conquered by Jaume I in the 13th century. Along with Catalonia, Valencia became part of the united Spanish state in the 15th century, but defenders of its separate cultural and linguistic identity still resent the centuries of Catalan domination. The Catalan language prevails in Tarragona, a city and province of Catalonia, but Valenciano—a dialect of Catalan—is spoken and used on street signs in the Valencian provinces.

The coastal farmland and beaches that attracted the ancients now call to modern-day tourists, though in parts, a number of "mass-tourism" resorts have marred the shore. Inland, however, local culture survives intact. The rugged and beautiful territory is dotted with small fortified towns, several of which bear the name of Spain's 11th-century national hero, El Cid, commemorating the battles he fought here against the Moors some 900 years ago.

MAJOR REGIONS

For many, **Northern Catalonia** is one of the top reasons reason to visit Spain. The historic center of **Girona**, its principal city, is a labyrinth of climbing cobblestone streets and staircases, with remarkable

Gothic and Romanesque buildings at every turn. El Call, the Jewish Quarter, is one of the best-preserved areas of its kind in Europe, and the Gothic cathedral is an architectural masterpiece. Streets in the modern part of the city are lined with smart shops and boutiques, and the overall quality of life in Girona is considered among the best in Spain. Nearby towns **Besalú** and **Figueres** are vastly different. Figueres is an unremarkable town made exceptional by the Dalí Museum. Besalú is a picture-perfect Romanesque village on a bluff overlooking the Riu Fluvià, with one of the most prestigious restaurants in Catalonia. Lesser known are the medieval towns in and around the volcanic (now extinct) area of La Garrotxa: Vic, Rupit, and Olot boast the best produce in the region.

The Costa Brava (Wild Coast) is a nearly unbroken series of sheer rock cliffs dropping down to clear blue-green waters, punctuated by innumerable coves and tiny beaches on narrow inlets, called *calas*. It basically begins at Blanes and continues north along 135 km (84 miles) of coastline to the French border at Portbou. Although the area does have spots of real-estate excess, the rocky terrain of many pockets (**Tossa de Mar, Begur,** and **Cadaqués**) has discouraged overbuilding. On a good day here, the luminous blue of the sea contrasts with red-brown headlands and cliffs, and the distant lights of fishing boats reflect on wine-color waters at dusk. Small stands of umbrella pine veil the footpaths to many of the secluded coves and little patches of white sand—often, the only access is by boat.

The **Southern Catalonia** area is home to **Montserrat,** home to the shrine of La Moreneta (the Black Virgin of Montserrat), the lively coastal town of **Sitges,** the Cistercian monasteries of **Santes Creus** and **Santa Maria de Poblet,** and the region's principal town of Tarragona. Farther south lies **Valencia,** Spain's

third-largest city and the capital of its region and province, equidistant from Barcelona and Madrid. For a day trip there's the **Albufera,** a scenic coastal wetland teeming with native wildlife, especially migratory birds.

The Costa Blanca (White Coast) begins at **Dénia,** south of Valencia, and stretches down roughly to Torrevieja, below Alicante. It's best known for its magical vacation combo of sand, sea, and sun, with popular beaches and more secluded coves and stretches of sand. **Alicante** itself has two long beaches, a charming old quarter, and mild weather most of the year.

Planning

When to Go

Come for the beaches in the hot summer months, but expect crowds and serious heat—in some places up to 40°C (104°F). The Mediterranean coast is more comfortable in May and September.

February and March are the peak months for skiing in the Pyrenees. Winter travel in the region has other advantages: Valencia still has plenty of sunshine, and if you're visiting villages and wineries in the countryside, you might have the place all to yourself. Note that many restaurants and hotels outside the major towns may close on weekdays or longer in winter, so call ahead. Many museums and sites close early in winter (6 pm).

The Costa Brava and Costa Blanca beach areas get hot and crowded in summer, and accommodations are at a premium. In contrast, spring is mild and an excellent time to tour the region, particularly the rural areas, where blossoms infuse the air with pleasant fragrances and wildflowers dazzle the landscape.

Planning Your Time

Not far from Barcelona, the beautiful towns of Vic, Girona, and Cadaqués are easily reachable from the city by bus or train in a couple of hours. Figueres is a must if you want to see the Teatre-Museu Dalí. Girona makes an excellent base from which to explore La Garrotxa—for that, you'll need to rent a car.

Valencia is three hours by express train from Barcelona. Historic Valencia and the Santiago Calatrava–designed City of Arts and Sciences complex can be covered in two days, but stay longer and indulge in the city's food and explore the nightlife in the Barrio del Carmen.

Getting Here and Around

AIR TRAVEL

El Prat de Llobregat in Barcelona is the main international airport for the Costa Brava; Girona is the closest airport to the region, with bus connections directly into the city and to Barcelona. Valencia has an international airport with direct flights to London, Paris, Brussels, Lisbon, Zurich, and Milan as well as regional flights from Barcelona, Madrid, Málaga, and other cities in Spain. There is a regional airport in Alicante serving the Valencian region and Murcia.

BOAT AND FERRY TRAVEL

Many short-cruise lines along the coast offer the chance to view the Costa Brava from the sea. Visit the port areas in the main towns and you'll quickly spot several tourist cruise lines. Plan to spend around €15–€27, depending on the length of the cruise. Many longer cruises include a stop en route for a swim. The glass-keel Nautilus boats for observation of the Medes Islands underwater park cost around €20 and run daily April–October and weekends November–March.

The shortest ferry connections to the Balearic Islands originate in Dénia. Balearia sails from there to Ibiza, Formentera, and Mallorca.

BOAT AND FERRY INFORMATION
Balearia ☎ 902/160180, 865/608423 from abroad ⊕ www.balearia.com. **Nautilus** ⊠ Passeig Marítim 23, L'Estartit ☎ 972/751489 ⊕ www.english.nautilus. es.

BUS TRAVEL

Private companies run buses down the coast and from Madrid to Valencia, and to Alicante. ALSA is the main bus line in this region; check local tourist offices for schedules. Sarfa operates buses from Barcelona to Blanes, Lloret, Sant Feliu de Guixols, Platja d'Aro, Palamos, Begur, Roses, L'Escala, and Cadaqués.

CONTACTS ALSA ☎ 902/422242 ⊕ www. alsa.es. **Moventis Sarfa** ⊠ Estació del Nord, Alí Bei 80, Barcelona ☎ 902/302025 ⊕ compras.moventis.es/en-GB Ⓜ Arc de Triomf. **Sagalés** ⊠ Estació del Nord, Alí Bei 80, Barcelona ☎ 902/130014 tickets ⊕ www.sagales.com Ⓜ Arc de Triomf. **Sagalés AirportLine** ☎ 902/130014 ⊕ www.sagalesairportline.com.

CAR TRAVEL

A car is necessary for explorations inland and convenient for reaching locations on the coast, where drives are smooth and scenic. Catalonia and Valencia have excellent roads; the only drawbacks are the high cost of fuel and the high tolls on the autopistas (highways, usually designated by the letters "AP"). The national roads (starting with the letter N) can get clogged, however, so you're often better off on toll roads if your time is limited.

TRAIN TRAVEL

Most of the Costa Brava is not served directly by railroad. A local line runs up the coast from Barcelona to Blanes, then turns inland and connects at Maçanet-Massanes with the main line up to France. Direct trains stop only at major connections, such as Girona, Flaçà, and Figueres. To visit one of the smaller towns in between, you can take a fast direct train from Barcelona to Girona, for instance, then get off and wait for a local to come by.

Express intercity trains reach Valencia from all over Spain, arriving at the new Joaquin Sorolla station; from there, a shuttle bus takes you to the Estación del Norte, the terminus in the center of town, for local connections. From Barcelona there are 15 trains a day, including the fast train TALGO, which takes 3½ hours. There are 22 daily trains to Valencia from Madrid; the high-speed train takes about 1 hour 40 minutes.

For the Costa Blanca, the rail hub is Alicante.

CONTACTS RENFE ☎ 912/320320 ⊕ www. renfe.com.

Farmhouse Stays in Catalonia

Dotted throughout Catalonia are farm-houses (casas rurales in Spanish, and cases de pagès or masíes in Catalan), where you can spend a weekend or longer. Accommodations vary from small rustic homes to spacious luxurious farm-houses with fireplaces and pools. Stay in a guest room at a bed-and-breakfast, or rent an entire house and do your own cooking. Most tourist offices, including the main Catalonia Tourist Office, have information and listings. Several organi-zations in Spain have detailed listings and descriptions of Catalonia's farmhouses.

CONTACTS Agroturisme.org ☎ 932/680900 ⊕ www.agroturisme.cat. **Cases Rurals** ☎ 660/576834 ⊕ www.casesrurals.com.

Restaurants

Catalonia's eateries are deservedly famous. Girona's El Celler de Can Roca was voted Best Restaurant in the World multiple times in recent years in the annual critics' poll conducted by British magazine Restaurant, and a host of other first-rate establishments continue to offer inspiring fine dining in Catalonia, which began in the hinterlands at the legendary Hotel Empordà. Yet you needn't go to an internationally acclaimed restaurant to dine well. Superstar chef Ferran Adrià of the former foodie paradise elBulli dines regularly at dives in Roses, where straight-up fresh fish is the attraction. Northern Catalonia's Empordà region is known for seafood and rich assortment of inland and upland products. Beef from Girona's verdant pastureland is prized throughout Catalonia, while wild mush-rooms from the Pyrenees and game from the Alberes range offer seasonal depth to menus across the region. From a simple beachside paella or llobarro (sea bass) at a chiringuito (beach shack) with tables on the sand, to the splendor of a meal at El Celler de Can Roca, playing culinary hopscotch through Catalonia is a good way to get to know the region.

Hotels

Lodgings on the Costa Brava range from the finest hotels to spartan pensions. The better accommodations have splendid views of the seascape. If you plan to visit during the high season (July and August), be sure to book reservations well in advance at almost any hotel in the area; the Costa Brava remains one of the most popular summer resort areas in Spain. Many Costa Brava hotels close down in the winter season (November–March).

Hotel reviews have been shortened. For full information, visit Fodors.com.

What It Costs in Euros			
$	$$	$$$	$$$$
RESTAURANTS			
under €12	€12–€17	€18–€22	over €22
HOTELS			
under €90	€90–€125	€126–€180	over €180

Girona

97 km (60 miles) northeast of Barcelona.

At the confluence of four rivers, Northern Catalonia's Girona (population: 97,000) keeps intact the magic of its historic past; with its brooding hilltop castle, soaring Gothic cathedral, and dreamy riverside setting, it resembles a vision from the Middle Ages. Today, as a university center, Girona combines past and vibrant present: art galleries, chic cafés, and trendy boutiques have set up shop in many of the restored buildings of the old quarter, known as the Força Vella (Old Fortress), which is on the east side of the Riu Onyar. Built on the side of the mountain, it presents a tightly packed labyrinth of medieval buildings and monuments on narrow cobblestone streets with connecting stairways. You can still see vestiges of the Iberian and Roman walls in the cathedral square and in the patio of the old university. In the central quarter is El Call, one of Europe's best-preserved medieval (12th- to 15th-century) Jewish communities and an important center of Kabbalistic studies.

The main street of the Força Vella is Carrer de la Força, which follows the old Via Augusta, the Roman road that connected Rome with its provinces.

GETTING HERE AND AROUND

There are more than 20 daily trains from Barcelona to Girona (continuing on to the French border). Regional trains can take between one and two hours, and can be picked up from a number of stations in Barcelona, while the high-speed AVE train service is a convenient option, running from Barcelona Sants station to Girona in under 40 minutes (it's advisable to prebook the AVE). The train station is about a 20-minute walk from the old quarter; alternatively, taxis can be picked up in front of the train station on arrival. There are frequent Sagales buses to Girona Airport; they take an average of 75 minutes and cost €16 one-way, €25 round-trip. The Sagales 602 and 603 buses run from Barcelona's El Prat de Llobregat airport and Estació del Nord, in the city center of Barcelona, to Girona city bus station. Getting around the city is easiest on foot or by taxi; several bridges connect the historic old quarter with the more modern town across the river.

CONTACTS Sagalés ☎ *902/130014* ⊕ *www.sagales.com.*

DISCOUNTS AND DEALS

The GironaMuseus discounts admission to all the city's museums. ■**TIP**→ **Some are free on the first Sunday of every month.** Check the tourist office or at the Punt de Benvinguda welcome center, which can also arrange guided tours.

TOURS
Bike Breaks

BICYCLE TOURS | In recent times, Girona has developed a passion for all things bike related. Bike Breaks provides bike rentals and tours so that you can get to know the city and its surroundings on two wheels. ⊠ *Carrer Nou 14 E* ☎ *972/205465* ⊕ *www.gironacyclecentre. com* ✉ *Tours from €25.*

Northern Catalonia
and the Costa Brava

VISITOR INFORMATION Girona Office of Tourism ✉ *Rambla de la Llibertat 1* ☎ *972/010001* ⊕ *www.girona.cat/turisme.* **Punt de Benvinguda** ✉ *Berenguer Carnicer 3* ☎ *972/211678, 972/011669* ⊕ *www. gironawalks.com.*

⊙ Sights

Banys Arabs (*Arab Baths*)

HOT SPRINGS | A misnomer, the Banys Arabs were actually built by Morisco craftsmen (workers of Moorish descent) in the late 12th century, long after Girona's Islamic occupation (714–797) had ended. Following the old Roman model that had disappeared in the West, the custom of bathing publicly may have been brought back from the Holy Land with the Crusaders. These baths are sectioned off into three rooms in descending order: a *frigidarium*, or cold bath, a square room with a central octagonal pool and a skylight with cupola held up by two stories of eight fine columns; a *tepidarium*, or warm bath; and a *caldarium*, or steam room, beneath which is a chamber where a fire was kept burning. Here the inhabitants of old Girona came to relax, exchange gossip, or do business. It is known from another public bathhouse in Tortosa, Tarragona, that the various social classes came to bathe by sex and religion on fixed days of the week: Christian men on one day, Christian women on another, Jewish men on still another, Jewish women (and prostitutes) on a fourth, Muslims on others: ✉ *Carrer Ferran el Catòlic s/n* ☎ *972/190969* ⊕ *www.banysarabs.org* 🎟 *€2.*

There's more to Girona's cathedral than the 90 steps to get to it; inside there's much to see, including the Treasury.

Basilica of Sant Feliu

RELIGIOUS SITE | One of Girona's most beloved churches and its first cathedral until the 10th century, Sant Feliu was repeatedly rebuilt and altered over four centuries and stands today as an amalgam of Romanesque columns, a Gothic nave, and a baroque facade. The vast bulk of this structure is landmarked by one of Girona's most distinctive belfries, topped by eight pinnacles. The basilica was founded over the tomb of St. Felix of Africa, a martyr under the Roman emperor Diocletian. ⊠ *Pujada de Sant Feliu 29* ☎ *972/201407* ⌁ *From €7.*

★ Cathedral

BUILDING | At the heart of the Força Vella, the cathedral looms above 90 steps and is famous for its nave—at 75 feet, the widest in the world and the epitome of the spatial ideal of Catalan Gothic architects. Since Charlemagne founded the original church in the 8th century, it has been through many fires and renovations. Take in the rococo-era facade, "eloquent as organ music" and impressive flight of 17th-century stairs, which rises from its own *plaça*. Inside, three smaller naves were compressed into one gigantic hall by the famed architect Guillermo Bofill in 1416. The change was typical of Catalan Gothic "hall" churches, and it was done to facilitate preaching to crowds. Note the famous silver canopy, or *baldaquí* (baldachin). The oldest part of the cathedral is the 11th-century Romanesque **Torre de Carlemany** (Charlemagne Tower) ⊠ *Pl. de la Catedral s/n* ☎ *972/427189* ⊕ *www.catedraldegirona.cat* ⌁ *From €7.*

★ El Call

HISTORIC SITE | Girona is especially noted for its 13th-century Jewish Quarter, El Call, which branches off Carrer de la Força, south of the Plaça Catedral. The quarter is a network of lanes that crisscross above one another, and houses built atop each other in disorderly fashion along narrow stone medieval streets. With boutique shopping, artsy cafés, and lots of atmospheric eateries and bars, there is plenty to explore. ⊠ *Girona.*

Monestir de Sant Pere de Galligants

MUSEUM | The church of St. Peter, across the Galligants River, was finished in 1131, and is notable for its octagonal Romanesque belfry and the finely detailed capitals atop the columns in the cloister. It now houses the **Museu Arqueològic** (Museum of Archaeology), which documents the region's history since Paleolithic times and includes some artifacts from Roman times. ⊠ *Carrer Santa Llúcia 8* ☏ *972/202632* ⊕ *www.macgirona.cat* 🎫 *€5* ⊘ *Closed Mon.*

Museu d'Art

MUSEUM | The Episcopal Palace near the cathedral contains the wide-ranging collections of Girona's main art museum. On display is everything from superb Romanesque *majestats* (carved wood figures of Christ) to reliquaries from Sant Pere de Rodes, illuminated 12th-century manuscripts, and works of the 20th-century Olot school of landscape painting. ⊠ *Pujada de la Catedral 12* ☏ *972/203834* ⊕ *www.museuart.com* 🎫 *€5* ⊘ *Closed Mon.*

Museum of Jewish History

MUSEUM | Housed in a former synagogue and dedicated to the preservation of Girona's Jewish heritage, this center organizes conferences, exhibitions, and seminars and contains 21 stone tablets, one of the finest collections in the world of medieval Jewish funerary slabs. These came from the old Jewish cemetery of Montjuïc, revealed when the railroad between Barcelona and France was laid out in the 19th century. Its exact location, about 1½ km (1 mile) north of Girona on the road to La Bisbal and known as La Tribana, is being excavated. The center also holds the **Institut d'Estudis Nahmànides,** with an extensive library of Judaica. ⊠ *Carrer de la Força 8* ☏ *972/216761* ⊕ *www.girona.cat/call/eng/museu.php* 🎫 *€4.*

Passeig Arqueològic

ARCHAEOLOGICAL SITE | The landscaped gardens of this stepped archaeological walk are below the restored walls of the Força Vella (which you can walk, in parts) and enjoy superlative views of the city from belvederes and watchtowers. From there, climb through the Jardins de la Francesa to the highest ramparts for a view of the cathedral's 11th-century Torre de Carlemany. ⊠ *Girona.*

🍴 Restaurants

Cal Ros

$$$ | CATALAN | Tucked under the arcades just behind the north end of Plaça de la Llibertat, this restaurant combines ancient stone arches with crisp, contemporary furnishings and cheerful lighting. The menu changes regularly, featuring organically raised local produce in season, and fresh fish in updated versions of traditional Catalan cuisine. **Known for:** rice dishes; tucked under the arches of the old quarter; updated traditional cuisine. 🟈 *Average main: €22* ⊠ *Carrer Cort Reial 9* ☏ *972/219176* ⊘ *Closed Mon. and Tues. No dinner Sun.*

★ El Celler de Can Roca

$$$$ | CONTEMPORARY | Anointed twice (in 2013 and 2015) by an international panel of food critics and chefs as the best restaurant in the world, El Celler de Can Roca is a life-changing culinary experience. The Roca brothers—Joan, Josep, and Jordi—showcase their masterful creations in two tasting menus, at €180 and €205. **Known for:** extensive wine selection; one of the best restaurants in the world; reservations required many months or even a year ahead. 🟈 *Average main: €180* ⊠ *Can Sunyer 48* ☏ *972/222157* ⊕ *cellercanroca.com* ⊘ *Closed Sun. and Mon., Easter wk, 1 wk in Aug., and Dec. 23–Jan. 16. No lunch Tues.*

With its picturesque rivers, Girona is often called the Spanish Venice.

La Fabrica

$ | **CAFÉ** | Christian, a professional cyclist, and his wife, Amber, opened this inviting space, serving brunch and superb coffee, in an old carpentry factory (La Fabrica means "the factory" in Spanish). There are raw concrete floors, exposed brick walls, high ceilings, and an abundance of bike memorabilia. **Known for:** bike-friendly stop; excellent coffee; setting in converted factory. [$] *Average main: €9* ✉ *Carrer de la Llebre 3* ☎ *972/296622* 🌐 *www.lafabricagirona.com* 🕒 *No dinner.*

Rocambolesc

$ | **CAFÉ** | **FAMILY** | Couldn't get a table at El Celler de Can Roca? Keep trying, but in the meantime there's Rocambolesc, the latest of the Roca family culinary undertakings. **Known for:** ice cream and sorbet; popsicles; fun toppings. [$] *Average main: €5* ✉ *Carrer Santa Clara 50* ☎ *972/416667* 🌐 *www.rocambolesc.com* 💳 *No credit cards.*

Hotels

★ Alemanys 5

$$$$ | **RENTAL** | **FAMILY** | Award-winning architect Anna Noguera and partner Juan-Manuel Ribera transformed a 16th-century house steps from the cathedral into two extraordinary apartments: one for up to five people, the other for six. **Pros:** perfect for families or small groups; ideal location; superb architectural design. **Cons:** difficult to navigate the small streets by car (hotel provides instructions); minimum stay required; needs booking in advance. [$] *Rooms from: €300* ✉ *Carrer Alemanys 5* ☎ *649/885136* 🌐 *www.alemanys5.com* 🛏 *2 apartments* 🍴 *No meals.*

Bellmirall

$ | **B&B/INN** | This pretty little *hostal* (guesthouse) in the old city, on the edge of El Call, makes up in value and location what it lacks in amenities and services; when there's no staff on call, you come and go with your own key. **Pros:** steps from the important sites; charming sitting room; good value. **Cons:** bedrooms are small; some rooms have shared bathrooms; no elevator. $ *Rooms from: €88* ✉ *Carrer de Bellmirall 3* ☎ *972/204009* ⊕ *www.bellmirall.eu* ⊗ *Closed Jan.* ⤳ *7 rooms* ⦿ *Free Breakfast.*

Hotel Peninsular
$$ | HOTEL | In a handsomely restored early-20th-century building across the Riu Onyar, with views into Girona's historic Força Vella, this modest but useful hotel occupies a strategic spot at the end of the Pont de Pedra (Stone Bridge), a Girona landmark in the center of the shopping district. **Pros:** good location at the hub of Girona life; near the stop for the bus from Girona airport; friendly staff. **Cons:** smallish rooms; basic decor; no frills. $ *Rooms from: €90* ✉ *Carrer Nou 3, Av. Sant Francesc 6* ☎ *972/203800* ⊕ *www.hotelpeninsulargirona.com* ⤳ *48 rooms* ⦿ *No meals.*

 ## Shopping

FOOD, CANDY, AND WINE
Gluki
FOOD/CANDY | This chocolatier and confectioner has been in business since 1870. ✉ *Carrer Nou 9* ☎ *972/201989* ⊕ *www.gluki.cat.*

La Simfonia
WINE/SPIRITS | At this relaxed wine shop and bar, you can be guided through a stellar range of regional wines (and cheeses)—and sample before you buy. ✉ *Pl. de l'Oli 6* ☎ *972/411253* ⊕ *www.lasimfonia.com.*

JEWELRY
Baobab
JEWELRY/ACCESSORIES | A lot of designer Anna Casal's original jewelry seems at first sight to be rough-hewn; it takes a second careful look to realize how sophisticated it really is. This shop doubles as her studio. ✉ *Carrer de les Hortes 18* ☎ *972/410227.*

Figueres

37 km (23 miles) north of Girona.

Figueres is the capital of the *comarca* (county) of the Alt Empordà, the bustling county seat of this predominantly agricultural region. Local people come from the surrounding area to shop at its many stores and stock up on farm equipment and supplies. Thursday is market day, and farmers gather at the top of La Rambla to do business and gossip, taking refreshments at cafés and discreetly pulling out and pocketing large rolls of bills, the result of their morning transactions. What brings the tourists to Figueres in droves, however, has little to do with agriculture and everything to do with Salvador Dalí's jaw-droppingly surreal "theater-museum"—one of the most visited museums in Spain.

GETTING HERE AND AROUND
Figueres is one of the stops on the regular train service from Barcelona to the French border. Local buses are also frequent, especially from nearby Cadaqués, with more than eight scheduled daily. If you're driving, take the AP7 north from Girona. The town is small enough to explore on foot.

VISITOR INFORMATION
CONTACTS Figueres ✉ *Pl. de l'Escorxador 2* ☎ *972/503155* ⊕ *en.visitfigueres.cat.*

 ## Sights

Castell de Sant Ferran
CASTLE/PALACE | Just a minute's drive northwest of Figueres is this imposing 18th-century fortified castle, one of the largest in Europe—only when you start exploring can you appreciate how immense it is. The parade grounds extend for acres, and the arcaded stables can hold more than 500 horses; the perimeter is roughly 4 km (2½ miles around). This castle was the site of the

Figueres's Famous Son

With a painterly technique that rivaled that of Jan van Eyck, a flair for publicity so aggressive it would have put P. T. Barnum to shame, and a penchant for the shocking (he loved telling people Barcelona's historic Barri Gòtic should be knocked down), artist Salvador Dalí, whose most lasting image may be the melting watches in his iconic 1931 painting *The Persistence of Memory*, enters art history as one of the foremost proponents of surrealism, the movement launched in the 1920s by André Breton. The artist, who was born in Figueres and died there in 1989, decided to create a museum-monument to himself during the last two decades of his life. Dalí often frequented the Cafeteria Astòria at the top of La Rambla (still the center of social life in Figueres), signing autographs for tourists or just being Dalí: he once walked down the street with a French omelet in his breast pocket instead of a handkerchief.

last official meeting of the Republican parliament (on February 1, 1939) before it surrendered to Franco's forces. Ironically, it was here that Lieutenant Colonel Antonio Tejero was imprisoned after his failed 1981 coup d'état in Madrid. ■TIP➔ **Call ahead and arrange for the two-hour Catedral de l'Aiguas guided tour in English (€15), which includes a trip through the castle's subterranean water system by Zodiac pontoon boat.** ✉ *Pujada del Castell s/n* ☎ *972/506094* ⊕ *www.castillosanfernando.org/en/* 🎫 *€4* ⊘ *Closed Mon. (except public holidays).*

Museu del Joguet de Catalunya

MUSEUM | FAMILY | Hundreds of antique dolls and toys are on display here—including collections owned by, among others, Salvador Dalí, Federico García Lorca, and Joan Miró. The museum also hosts Catalonia's only *caganer* exhibit. These playful little figures answering nature's call have long had a special spot in the Catalan *pessebre* (Nativity scene). Farmers are the most traditional figures, squatting discreetly behind the animals, but these days you'll find Barça soccer players and politicians, too. ✉ *Carrer de Sant Pere 1* ☎ *972/504585* ⊕ *www.mjc.*

cat 🎫 *€7* ⊘ *Closed Mon. Oct.–May and late Jan.–mid-Feb.*

★ Teatre-Museu Dalí

BUILDING | "Museum" was not a big enough word for Dalí, so he christened his monument a theater. In fact, the building was once the Força Vella theater, reduced to a ruin in the Spanish Civil War. Now topped with a glass geodesic dome and studded with Dalí's iconic egg shapes, the multilevel museum pays homage to his fertile imagination and artistic creativity. It includes gardens, ramps, and a spectacular drop cloth Dalí painted for Les Ballets de Monte Carlo. Don't look for his greatest paintings here, although there are some memorable images, including *Gala at the Mediterranean*, which takes the body of Gala (Dalí's wife) and morphs it into the image of Abraham Lincoln once you look through coin-operated viewfinders. The sideshow theme continues with other coin-operated pieces, including *Taxi Plujós* (*Rainy Taxi*), in which water gushes over the snail-covered occupants sitting in a Cadillac once owned by Al Capone, or *Sala de Mae West,* a trompe-l'oeil vision in which a pink sofa, two fireplaces, and two paintings morph into the

The Dalí Museum in Figueres is itself a work of art. Note the eggs on the exterior: they're a common image in the artist's work.

face of the onetime Hollywood sex symbol. Fittingly, another "exhibit" on view is Dalí's own crypt. ✉ *Pl. Gala-Salvador Dalí 5* ☎ *972/677500* 🌐 *www.salvador-dali.org* 🎟 *€15* 🕒 *Closed Mon. Oct.–May (except public holidays).*

🍴 Restaurants

★ Hotel Empordà

$$$$ | **CATALAN** | Just 1½ km (1 mile) north of town, this restaurant run by Jaume Subirós—housed within a rather nondescript, 42-room hotel—has been hailed as the birthplace of modern Catalan cuisine and has become a beacon for gourmands. The menu changes seasonally and may contain dishes such as *cordero lechal al romero, cebollitas, pera, y boniato* (suckling lamb with rosemary, onion, pear, and sweet potato) or *espárragos de Riumors, al perfume de trufa blanca y pecorino* (asparagus from Riumors, with white truffle parfum and pecorino). **Known for:** historic culinary destination; birthplace of modern Catalan cuisine; impeccable service. [$] *Average main: €30* ✉ *Av. Salvador Dalí i Domènech 170* ☎ *972/500562* 🌐 *www.hotelemporda.com.*

🛏 Hotels

Hotel Duràn

$$ | **HOTEL** | Dalí had his own private dining room in this former stagecoach relay station, though the guest rooms, refurbished in bland pale-wood tones and standard contemporary furnishings, offset the hotel's historic 19th-century exterior. **Pros:** good central location; dining room has pictures of Dalí; family-friendly. **Cons:** rooms lack character; parking inconvenient and an extra charge; no pets. [$] *Rooms from: €90* ✉ *Carrer Lasauca 5* ☎ *972/501250* 🌐 *www.hotelduran.com* 🛏 *65 rooms* 🍴 *No meals.*

Dali's Castle

Castell Gala Dalí - Púbol The third point of the Dalí triangle is the medieval castle of Púbol, where the artist's wife and perennial model, Gala, is buried in the crypt. During the 1970s this was Gala's residence, though Dalí also lived here in the early 1980s. It contains paintings and drawings, Gala's haute-couture dresses, and other objects chosen by the couple. It's also a chance to wander through another Daliesque landscape, with lush gardens, fountains decorated with masks of Richard Wagner (the couple's favorite composer), and distinctive elephants with giraffe's legs and claw feet. Púbol, a small village roughly between Girona and Figueres, is near the C66. If you are traveling by train, get off at the Flaçà station on RENFE's Barcelona–Portbou line; walk or take a taxi 4 km (2½ miles) to Púbol. The Sarfa bus company also has a stop in Flaçà and on the C66 road, some 2 km (1¼ miles) from Púbol. ⊠ *Pl. Gala-Dalí s/n, Púbol* ☎ *972/488655* ⊕ *www.salvador-dali.org* ⌑ *€8* ⏱ *Closed early Jan.– mid-Mar. and Mon. mid-Mar.–mid-June and mid-Sept.–early-Jan. (except public holidays).*

Besalú

34 km (21 miles) northwest of Girona, 25 km (15 miles) west of Figueres.

Besalú, the capital of a feudal county until power was transferred to Barcelona at the beginning of the 12th century, remains one of the best-preserved medieval towns in Catalonia. Among its main sights are the 12th-century Romanesque fortified bridge over the Riu Fluvià; two churches—Sant Vicenç (set on an attractive, café-lined plaza) and Sant Pere; and the ruins of the convent of Santa Maria on the hill above town.

GETTING HERE AND AROUND

With a population of less than 2,500, the village is easily small enough to stroll through—restaurants and sights are within walking distance of each other. There is bus service to Besalú from Figueres and the surrounding Costa Brava resorts.

VISITOR INFORMATION

CONTACTS Besalú Tourist Office ⊠ *Carrer del Pont 1* ☎ *972/591240* ⊕ *www.besalu. cat.*

◉ Sights

Església de Sant Pere

RELIGIOUS SITE | This 12th-century Romanesque church is part of a 10th-century monastery, still in an excellent state of preservation. ⊠ *Pl. de Sant Pere s/n.*

Església de Sant Vicenç

BUILDING | Founded in 977, this pre-Romanesque gem contains the relics of St. Vincent as well as the tomb of its benefactor, Pere de Rovira. La Capella de la Veracreu (Chapel of the True Cross) displays a reproduction of an alleged fragment of the True Cross brought from Rome by Bernat Tallafer in 977 and stolen in 1899. ⊠ *Pl. Sant Vicenç s/n.*

Jewish ritual baths

ARCHAEOLOGICAL SITE | The remains of this 13th-century *mikvah*, or Jewish ritual bath, were discovered in the 1960s; it's one of the few surviving in Spain. A stone stairway leads down into the chamber where the water was drawn from the river, but little else indicates the role that the baths played in the medieval Jewish community. Access is by guided tour only (organized through the tourist office).

Besalú contains astonishingly well-preserved medieval buildings.

✉ *Calle de Pont Vell 1* ☎ *972/591240 tourist office* 🎫 *€3* 🕒 *Admission by guided tour only.*

Pont Fortificat

BRIDGE/TUNNEL | The town's most emblematic feature is this Romanesque 11th-century fortified bridge with crenellated battlements spanning the Riu Fluvià. ✉ *Carrer del Pont.*

🍴 Restaurants

★ Els Fogons de Can Llaudes

$$$$ | **CATALAN** | A faithfully restored 10th-century Romanesque chapel holds proprietor Jaume Soler's outstanding restaurant—one of Catalonia's best. A typical dish could be *confitat de bou i raïm glacejat amb el seu suc* (beef confit au jus with glacé grapes), but the menu changes weekly. **Known for:** rotating fixed-price menu only; excellent decor; Romanesque chapel. [$] *Average main: €80* ✉ *Pl. de Prat de Sant Pere 6* ☎ *972/590858* 🕒 *Closed Tues., and last 2 wks of Nov.*

Olot

21 km (13 miles) west of Besalú, 55 km (34 miles) northwest of Girona.

Capital of the comarca (administrative region) of La Garrotxa, Olot is famous for its 19th-century school of landscape painters and has several excellent Art Nouveau buildings, including the Casa Solà-Morales, which has a facade by Lluís Domènech i Montaner, architect of Barcelona's Palau de la Música Catalana. The Sant Esteve church at the southeastern end of Passeig d'en Blay is famous for its El Greco painting *Christ Carrying the Cross* (1605).

The villages of Vall d'En Bas lie south of Olot, off the C153. A freeway cuts across this countryside to Vic, but you'll miss a lot by taking it. The twisting old road leads you through rich farmland past farmhouses with dark wooden balconies bedecked with bright flowers. Turn off for Sant Privat d'En Bas and Els Hostalets d'En Bas. Farther on, the picturesque medieval village of **Rupit** has excellent restaurants serving the famous *patata de Rupit*, potato stuffed with duck and beef, while the rugged Collsacabra mountains offer some of Catalonia's most pristine landscapes.

Restaurants

Ca l'Enric

$$$$ | CATALAN | Chefs Jordi and Isabel Juncà have become legends in the town of La Vall de Bianya, just north of Olot, with exquisite cuisine that's firmly rooted in local products. Dishes star game of all sorts, truffles, and wild mushrooms, and are served in a historic stone-walled 19th-century inn. **Known for:** local ingredients; rotating menu; fixed-price menus. Ⓢ *Average main: €85* ✉ *Ctra. de Camprodon s/n, La Vall de Bianya* ✛ *Nacional 260, Km 91* ☎ *972/290015* ⊕ *www.restaurantcalenric.cat* ⊘ *Closed Mon., Dec. 27–Jan. 17, and 1st 2 wks of July (can vary). No dinner Sun.–Wed.*

Les Cols

$$$$ | CATALAN | Chef Fina Puigdevall has made this sprawling 18th-century *masia* (Catalan farmhouse) a triumph. In the restaurant, the cuisine on the prix-fixe menu (no à la carte option) is seasonal and based on locally grown products, from wild mushrooms to the extraordinarily flavorful legumes and vegetables produced by the rich, volcanic soil of La Garrotxa. **Known for:** local ingredients; seasonal fixed-price menu; incredible decor. Ⓢ *Average main: €60* ✉ *Mas les Cols, Ctra. de la Canya s/n* ☎ *972/269209* ⊕ *www.lescols.com* ⊘ *Closed Mon., and 1st 3 wks of Jan. No dinner Sun. and Tues.*

Tossa de Mar

80 km (50 miles) northeast of Barcelona, 41 km (25 miles) south of Girona.

Christened "Blue Paradise" by painter Marc Chagall, who summered here for four decades, Tossa's pristine beaches are among Catalonia's best. Set around a blue buckle of a bay, Tossa de Mar is a symphony in two parts: the Vila Vella (Old Town) and the Vila Nova (New Town), the latter a lovely district open to the sea and threaded by 18th-century lanes. The Vila Vella is a knotted warren of steep cobblestone streets with many restored buildings. It sits on the Cap de Tossa promontory that juts out into the sea.

The beaches and town act as a magnet for many vacationers in July and August. Out of season, it's far more sedate, but the mild temperatures make it an ideal stop for coastal strolls.

GETTING HERE AND AROUND

By car, the fastest way to Costa Brava's Tossa de Mar from Barcelona is to drive up the inland AP7 tollway toward Girona, then take Sortida 10 (Exit 10). The old national route, N11, can also get you there, but is slow, heavily traveled, and more dangerous, especially in summer. The main bus station (as well as the local tourist office inside the station) is on Plaça de les Nacions Sense Estat.

⊙ Sights

Museu Municipal

MUSEUM | In a lovingly restored 14th-century house, this museum is said to be Catalonia's first dedicated to modern art. It is home to one of the only three Chagall paintings in Spain, *Celestial Violinist*. ✉ *Pl. Pintor Roig i Soler 1* ☎ *972/340709* 🎫 *€3* ⊘ *Closed Mon.*

Did You Know?

In the 1950s, Tossa de Mar was famous for the arrival of Ava Gardner to film "The Flying Dutchman" with James Mason. In 1998 a bronze statue was erected within the castle walls to honor her.

Vila Vella and Castillo de Tossa de Mar

CASTLE/PALACE | Listed as a national artistic-historic monument in 1931, Tossa de Mar's **Vila Vella** (Old Town) is the only remaining example of a fortified medieval town in Catalonia. Set high above the town on a promontory, the Old Town is presided over by the ramparts and towers of the 13th-century **Castillo de Tossa de Mar,** and is situated on a steep yet worthy climb up from the main town, accessed from the western side of Platja Gran Tossa de Mar (Playa Grande). The cliff-top views, particularly at sunset, are remarkable, and the labyrinth of narrow, cobblestone lanes lined with ancient houses (some dating back to the 14th century) is a delight to explore at a leisurely pace. **■TIP→ At Bar del Far del Tossa (Carrer del Far 14), near the lighthouse, you can enjoy the best views in town. Reviving post-climb drinks, snacks, and light meals are available.** ✉ *Passeig de Vila Vella 1.*

Beaches

Mar Menuda (*Little Sea*)

BEACH—SIGHT | Just north of the town center, this gentle 460-foot sandy crescent is a pleasant Blue Flag beach that's popular with local families. The sand is coarse, but the sparkling, calm, shallow waters make it ideal for children. Fishing boats bob peacefully in the water nearby after completing their morning's work. At the top of the beach there is a second cove called La Banyera de Ses Dones (the women's bathtub), which provides ideal conditions for diving, though if the sea is not calm, it is dangerous for swimmers. By day there is little natural shade, so bring adequate sunblock and an umbrella if you plan a long beach session. It gets extremely busy in high season. **Amenities:** none. **Best for:** snorkeling; sunset; swimming. ✉ *Av. Mar Menuda.*

Platja Gran (*Big Beach*)

BEACH—SIGHT | Sweeping past the Vila Vella, this well-maintained, soft-sand beach runs along the front of town to meet the base of the Cap de Tossa. One of the most photographed coastlines in this area of Spain, it is also, at the height of summer, one of the busiest. Conditions are normally fine for swimming (any warnings are announced via loudspeaker). A rising number of motorboats is impacting on the water quality, but for now it retains its Blue Flag status. Running behind the beach, there is no shortage of cafés and kiosks selling ice cream and snacks. There is no natural shade, but you can rent deck chairs and umbrellas. **Amenities:** food and drink; lifeguards; showers; toilets; water sports. **Best for:** snorkeling; sunset; swimming. ✉ *Av. de sa Palma.*

🍴 Restaurants

La Cuina de Can Simon

$$$$ | CATALAN | Elegantly rustic, this restaurant right beside Tossa de Mar's medieval walls serves a combination of classical Catalan cuisine with up-to-date, innovative touches. The menu changes with the season; two tasting menus (€68 and €135) provide more than enough to sample, and you can also order à la carte. **Known for:** top-notch service; seasonal menu; welcoming tapa and cava upon entrance. [$] *Average main: €30* ✉ *Carrer del Portal 24* ☎ *972/341269* 🌐 *www.restaurantcansimon.com* 🕒 *Closed Mon. and Tues.*

🛏 Hotels

Hotel Capri

$$ | HOTEL | FAMILY | Located on the beach, this hotel is in hailing distance of the old quarter in the medieval fortress; rooms are simple, and those with sea views have private terraces. **Pros:** family-friendly option; perfect location; good value. **Cons:** rooms are small; minimal amenities; no private parking. $ *Rooms from: €106* ⊠ *Passeig del Mar 17* ☎ *972/340358* ⊕ *www.hotelcapritossa.com* ⊘ *Closed Nov.–Feb.* ⨼ *22 rooms* ⊙⊢ *Free Breakfast.*

★ Hotel Diana

$$$$ | HOTEL | Built in 1906 by architect Antoni de Falguera i Sivilla, disciple of Antoni Gaudí, this Moderniste gem sits on the square in the heart of the Vila Vella, steps from the beach. **Pros:** attentive service; ideal location, with sea views; Moderniste touches. **Cons:** minimal amenities; room rates unpredictable; some rooms are small. $ *Rooms from: €250* ⊠ *Pl. de Espanya 6* ☎ *972/341886* ⊕ *www.hotelesdante.com* ⊘ *Closed Nov.–Mar.* ⨼ *21 rooms* ⊙⊢ *Free Breakfast.*

Hotel Sant March

$$ | HOTEL | FAMILY | This family hotel in the center of town is two minutes from the beach, with guest rooms that open onto a pleasant interior garden that serve as an oasis of tranquillity in a sometimes hectic town. **Pros:** warm personal touch; good value; central location. **Cons:** no elevator; rooms a bit small; few exterior views. $ *Rooms from: €110* ⊠ *Av. Pelegrí 2* ☎ *972/340078* ⊕ *www.hotelsantmarch.com* ⊘ *Closed Oct. 15–Mar.* ⨼ *29 rooms* ⊙⊢ *Free Breakfast.*

Sant Feliu de Guixols

23 km (14 miles) northeast of Tossa de Mar.

The little fishing port of Sant Feliu de Guixols is set on a small bay; Moderniste mansions line the seafront promenade, recalling a time when the cork industry made this one of the wealthier towns on the coast. In front of them, a long crescent beach of fine white sand leads around to the fishing harbor at its north end. Behind the promenade, a well-preserved old quarter of narrow streets and squares leads to a 10th-century gateway with horseshoe arches (all that remains of a pre-Romanesque monastery); also here is a church that combines Romanesque, Gothic, and baroque styles. Nearby, the iron-structured indoor market, which dates back to the 1930s, sells the freshest and finest local produce, with colorful stalls often overflowing onto the Plaça del Mercat in front.

GETTING HERE AND AROUND

To get here, take the C65 from Tossa de Mar—though adventurous souls might prefer the harrowing hairpin curves of the G1682 coastal corniche.

Sights

Museu d'Història de Sant Feliu de Guíxols

MUSEUM | The Romanesque Benedictine monastery houses this museum, which contains interesting exhibits about the town's cork and fishing trades, and displays local archaeological finds. ⊠ *Pl. del Monestir s/n* ☎ *972/821575* ⊕ *www.museu.guixols.cat* ⊠ *€2.*

 Restaurants

Can Segura

$$ | CATALAN | Half a block in from the beach at Sant Feliu de Guixols, this restaurant serves home-cooked seafood and upland specialties. The dining room is always full, with customers waiting their turn in the street, but the staff is good at finding spots at the jovially long communal tables. **Known for:** first-rate seafood specialties; communal dining; excellent rice dishes. $ *Average main: €13* ⊠ *Carrer de Sant Pere 11* ☎ *972/321009.*

El Dorado Mar

$$$ | SEAFOOD | FAMILY | Around the southern end of the beach at Sant Feliu de Guixols, perched over the entrance to the harbor, this family seafood restaurant offers superb sea views as well as fine fare at unbeatable prices. Whether straight seafood such as *lubina* (sea

bass) or *dorada* (gilt-head bream) or *revuelto de setas* (eggs scrambled with wild mushrooms), everything served here is fresh and flavorful. **Known for:** affordable cuisine; knockout egg scramble; fresh seafood. $ *Average main: €18* ⌧ *Passeig President Irla 15* ☎ *972/321818* ⊕ *www. grupeldorado.com* ⊙ *No dinner Tues. Closed Wed.*

Hotels

Hostal del Sol

$$ | **HOTEL** | **FAMILY** | Once the summer home of a wealthy family, this Moderniste hotel has a grand stone stairway and medieval-style tower, as well as a garden and a lawn where you can relax by the pool. **Pros:** family-friendly option; good value; good breakfast. **Cons:** bathrooms a bit claustrophobic; far from the beach; on a busy road. $ *Rooms from: €120* ⌧ *Ctra. a Palamós 194* ☎ *972/320193* ⊕ *www. hostaldelsol.cat/en* ⊙ *Closed mid-Oct.–Easter* ⮐ *41 rooms* ⦿ *Free Breakfast.*

S'Agaró

3 km (2 miles) north of Sant Feliu.

S'Agaró is an elegant gated community on a rocky point at the north end of the cove. The 30-minute walk along the **sea wall** from Hostal de La Gavina to Sa Conca Beach is a delight, and the one-hour hike from Sant Pol Beach over to Sant Feliu de Guixols offers views of the Costa Brava at its best.

🍴 Restaurants

Villa Mas

$$$$ | **CATALAN** | This Moderniste villa on the coast road from Sant Feliu to S'Agaró, with a lovely turn-of-the-20th-century zinc bar, serves up typical Catalan and seasonal Mediterranean dishes like *arròs a la cassola* (deep-dish rice) with shrimp brought fresh off the boats in Palamos,

just up the coast. The terrace is a popular and shady spot just across the road from the beach. **Known for:** dining on terrace; across from beach; fresh seafood catches. $ *Average main: €28* ⌧ *Passeig de Sant Pol 95, Sant Feliu de Guixols* ☎ *972/822526* ⊕ *www.restaurantvilla-mas.com* ⊙ *Closed Mon.; no dinner Sun. or Tues.–Thurs.*

Hotels

★ L'Hostal de la Gavina

$$$$ | **HOTEL** | Opened in 1932 by farmer-turned-entrepreneur Josep Ensesa, the original hotel grew from a cluster of country villas into a sprawling complex of buildings of extraordinary splendor that have attracted celebrity guests from Orson Welles and Ava Gardner to Sean Connery. **Pros:** in a gated community; impeccable service and amenities; sea views, including from pool and terrace. **Cons:** hard on the budget; walls are thin; expensive restaurant. $ *Rooms from: €490* ⌧ *Pl. Roserar s/n, S'Agar¿* ☎ *972/321100* ⊕ *www.lagavina.com* ⊙ *Closed Nov.–Easter* ⮐ *74 rooms* ⦿ *Free Breakfast.*

Calella de Palafrugell and Around

25 km (15½ miles) north of S'Agaró.

Up the coast from S'Agaró, the C31 brings you to Palafrugell and Begur; to the east are some of the prettiest, least developed inlets of the Costa Brava. One road leads to **Llafranc**, a small port with waterfront hotels and restaurants, and forks right to the fishing village of **Calella de Palafrugell**, known for its July habaneras festival. (The *habanera* is a form of Cuban dance music brought to Europe by Catalan sailors in the late 19th century; it still enjoys a nostalgic cachet here.) Just south is the panoramic promontory of **Cap Roig,** with views of the barren Formigues Isles.

North along the coast lie **Tamariu, Aiguablava, Fornell, Platja Fonda,** and (around the point at Cap de Begur) **Sa Tuna** and **Aiguafreda.** There's not much to do in any of these hideaways, but you can luxuriate in wonderful views, some of the Costa Brava's best beaches and coves, and the soothing quiet. Tamariu, a largely unspoiled former fishing village backed by simple whitewashed houses and a small strip of seafood restaurants that hug the shoreline, is reached by descending a vertiginous road set between mountains and pine forests. Farther north, toward Begur, the small, sheltered Aiguablava beach sets the stage for memorable sunsets. Its restaurant, Toc Al Mar, is a firm favorite with barcelonins (Barcelona residents) on weekend coastal jaunts and offers picture-perfect views.

🍴 Restaurants

★ Pa i Raïm

$$$ | **CATALAN** | "Bread and Grapes" in Catalan, Pa i Raïm is an excellent restaurant set in writer Josep Pla's ancestral family home in Palafrugell. It has one rustic dining room as well as another in a glassed-in winter garden, plus a leafy terrace, which is the place to be in summer. **Known for:** traditional country cuisine; contemporary fare; standout prawns tempura. *[$] Average main: €20 ✉ Torres i Jonama 56, Palafrugell ☎ 972/447278 🌐 www.pairaim.com 🕓 Closed Mon. No dinner Sun.–Thurs.*

🛏 Hotels

El Far Hotel-Restaurant

$$$$ | **B&B/INN** | **FAMILY** | Rooms in this 17th-century hermitage attached to a 15th-century watchtower have original vaulted ceilings, hardwood floors, and interiors accented with floral prints; the larger doubles and the suite can accommodate extra beds for children. **Pros:** friendly service; graceful architecture; spectacular views of bay. **Cons:** a bit of a distance from the beach; pricey for the value; need car. *[$] Rooms from: €235 ✉ Muntanya de Sant Sebastia, Carrer Uruguai s/n, Llafranc ☎ 972/301639 🌐 www.elfar.net 🕓 Closed Jan.–early Feb. 🛏 9 rooms 🍽 Free Breakfast.*

Begur and Around

11 km (7 miles) north of Calella de Palafrugell.

From Begur, go east through the calas or take the inland route past the rose-color stone houses and ramparts of the restored medieval town of **Pals.** Nearby **Peratallada** is another medieval fortified town with an 11th-century castle, tower, and palace. The name is derived from *pedra tallada,* meaning "carved stone," and behind the town's well-preserved walls is a maze of narrow streets and ivy-covered houses built from stone that was carved from the moat, which still encircles the town. In the center, the arcaded Plaça de les Voltes is alive with restaurants, shops, and cafés. North of Pals there are signs for **Ullastret,** an Iberian village dating to the 5th century BC. **L'Estartit** is the jumping-off point for the spectacular natural park surrounding the Medes Islands, famous for its protected marine life and consequently for diving and underwater photography.

👁 Sights

Empúries

ARCHAEOLOGICAL SITE | The Greco-Roman ruins here are Catalonia's most important archaeological site, and this port is one of the most monumental ancient engineering feats on the Iberian Peninsula. As the Greeks' original point of arrival in Spain, Empúries was also where the Olympic

Flame entered Spain for Barcelona's 1992 Olympic Games. ✉ *Puig i Cadafalch s/n* ☎ *972/770208* ⊕ *www.macempuries.cat* 🍽 *€6* ⊙ *Closed Mon. mid-Nov.–mid-Feb.*

Medes Islands (*Underwater Natural Park*) **NATURE PRESERVE** | The marine reserve around the Medes Islands, an archipelago of several small islands, is just off the coastline of L'Estartit, and is touted as one of the best places in Spain to scuba dive. Thanks to its protected status, the marine life—eels, octopus, starfish, and grouper—is tame, and you can expect high visibility unless the weather is bad. If diving doesn't appeal, you can take one of the glass-bottomed boats that frequent the islands from the mainland and view from above. ✉ *L'Estartit.*

Restaurants

Restaurant Ibèric
$$$ | **CATALAN** | This excellent pocket of authentic Costa Brava cuisine serves everything from snails to wild boar in season. The terrace is ideal for leisurely dining. **Known for:** eclectic cuisine; high-quality seasonal fare; traditional setting. 🖫 *Average main: €20* ✉ *Carrer Valls 11, Ullastret* ☎ *972/757108* ⊕ *www. restaurantiberic.com* ⊙ *Closed Mon. No dinner Tues.–Thurs. and Sun.*

Hotels

El Convent Hotel and Restaurant
$$$$ | **HOTEL** | Built in 1730, this elegant former convent is a 10-minute walk to the beach at the Cala Sa Riera—the quietest and prettiest inlet north of Begur. **Pros:** outstanding architecture; quiet and private; terrace for dining. **Cons:** minimum three-night stay in summer; rooms are not soundproofed; need car. 🖫 *Rooms from: €240* ✉ *Ctra. de la Platja del Racó 2, Begur* ☎ *972/623091* ⊕ *www.hotel-conventbegur.com* 🛏 *25 rooms* 🍽 *Free Breakfast.*

★ Hotel Aigua Blava
$$$$ | **HOTEL** | **FAMILY** | What began as a small hostal in the 1920s is now a sprawling luxury hotel, run by the fourth generation of the same family. **Pros:** impeccable service; gardens and pleasant patios at every turn; private playground. **Cons:** no elevator; no beach in the inlet; expensive restaurant. 🖫 *Rooms from: €330* ✉ *Platja de Fornells s/n, Begur* ☎ *972/622058* ⊕ *www.aiguablava. com* ⊙ *Closed Nov.–Mar.* 🛏 *85 rooms* 🍽 *Free Breakfast.*

Cadaqués and Around

70 km (43 miles) north of Begur.

Spain's easternmost town, Cadaqués, still has the whitewashed charm that transformed this fishing village into an international artists' haunt in the early 20th century. Salvador Dalí's house, now a museum, is at Port Lligat, a 15-minute walk north of town.

Sights

★ Cap de Creus
NATURE SITE | North of Cadaqués, Spain's easternmost point is a fundamental pilgrimage, if only for the symbolic geographical rush. The hike out to the lighthouse—through rosemary, thyme, and the salt air of the Mediterranean—is unforgettable. The Pyrenees officially end (or rise) here. New Year's Day finds mobs of revelers awaiting the first emergence of the "new" sun from the Mediterranean. Gaze down at heart-pounding views of the craggy coast and crashing waves with a warm mug of coffee in hand or fine fare on the table at **Bar Restaurant Cap de Creus,** which sits on a rocky crag above the Cap de Creus. On a summer evening, you may be lucky and stumble upon some live music on the terrace. ✉ *Carrer de Cadaqués al Cap de Creus.*

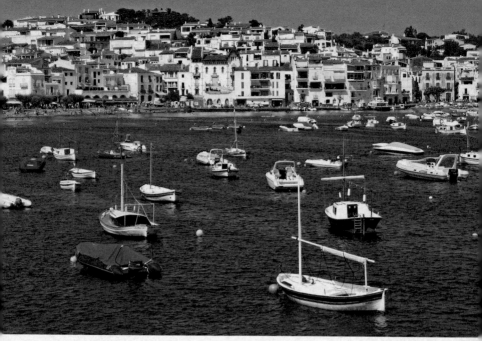

The popular harbor of Cadaqués

Casa Salvador Dalí - Portlligat

HOUSE | This was Dalí's summerhouse and a site long associated with the artist's notorious frolics with everyone from poets Federico García Lorca and Paul Eluard to filmmaker Luis Buñuel. Filled with bits of the surrealist's daily life, it's an important point in the "Dalí triangle," completed by the castle at Púbol and the Teatre-Museu Dalí in Figueres. You can get here by a 3-km (2-mile) walk north along the beach from Cadaqués. Only small groups of visitors are admitted at any given time, and reservations in advance are required. ⊠ *Portlligat s/n, Cadaqués* ☎ *972/251015* ⊕ *www.salvador-dali.org* ✆ *€12; advance reservation required* ☉ *Closed Mon. mid-Feb.–mid-Mar. and Nov. and Dec. Closed Jan. 7–mid-Feb.*

★ Sant Pere de Rodes

RELIGIOUS SITE | The monastery of Sant Pere de Rodes, 7 km (4½ miles) by car (plus a 20-minute walk) above the pretty fishing village of El Port de la Selva, is a spectacular site. Built in the 10th and 11th centuries by Benedictine monks— and sacked and plundered repeatedly since—this restored Romanesque monolith commands a breathtaking panorama of the Pyrenees, the Empordà plain, the sweeping curve of the Bay of Roses, and Cap de Creus. (Topping off the grand trek across the Pyrenees, Cap de Creus is a spectacular six-hour walk from here on the well-marked GR11 trail.) ■**TIP**➔ **In July and August, the monastery is the setting for the annual Festival Sant Pere (www.festivalsantpere.com), drawing top-tier classical musicians from all over the world.** Find event listings online (in Catalan); phone for reservations or to book a postconcert dinner in the monastery's refectory-style restaurant: ☎ *972/194233, 610/310073.* ⊠ *Camí del Monestir s/n, El Porte de la Selva* ☎ *972/387559* ⊕ *www. festivalsantpere.com* ✆ *€6* ☉ *Closed Mon.*

🍴 Restaurants

★ Casa Anita

$$$$ | **SEAFOOD** | Simple, fresh, and generous dishes are the draw at this informal little eatery, an institution in Cadaqués. It sits on the street that leads to Port Lligat and Dalí's house. **Known for:** no menu; regional wines; famous clientele. [$] *Average main: €25* ✉ *Carrer Miquel Rosset 16, Cadaqués* ☎ *972/258471* 🕒 *Closed Mon., and mid-Oct.–1st wk in Dec.*

Compartir

$$$$ | **CATALAN** | The concept may be similar, but Compartir ("to share") is no tapas restaurant. This award-winning restaurant bases its menu on a small-plate sharing approach that has been taken to another level by the culinary team of Mateu Casañas, Oriol Castro, and Eduard Xatruch (all former elBulli chefs), who transform traditional recipes into an outstanding gourmet experience. **Known for:** sharing plates; creative gastronomy; beautiful courtyard setting. [$] *Average main: €24* ✉ *Riera Sant Vicenç s/n, Cadaqués* ☎ *972/258482* 🌐 *www.compartircadaques.com* 🕒 *Closed Mon., and Jan.–early Feb.*

🛏 Hotels

Hotel Playa Sol

$$$$ | **HOTEL** | **FAMILY** | In business for more than 50 years, this hotel on the cove of Es Pianc, just a five-minute walk from the village center, is a good option for families, due to its connecting rooms, swimming pool, and bike rental. **Pros:** attentive, friendly service; family-friendly; great views. **Cons:** decor could be more colorful; rooms with balcony and sea views are harder to book; small rooms. [$] *Rooms from: €250* ✉ *Riba Es Pianc 3, Cadaqués* ☎ *972/258100* 🌐 *www.playasol.com* 🕒 *Closed Nov.–mid-Mar.* 🛏 *48 rooms* 🍴 *No meals.*

Llané Petit

$$$ | **HOTEL** | This intimate, typically Mediterranean bay-side hotel caters to people who want to make the most of their stay in the village and don't want to spend too much time in their hotel. **Pros:** semiprivate beach next to hotel; free Wi-Fi; good breakfast. **Cons:** small rooms; somewhat lightweight beds and furnishings; some soundproofing issues. [$] *Rooms from: €142* ✉ *Pl. Llane Petit s/n, Cadaqués* ☎ *972/251020* 🌐 *www.llanepetit.com* 🕒 *Closed Nov.–Mar.* 🛏 *37 rooms* 🍴 *Free Breakfast.*

Montserrat

50 km (31 miles) west of Barcelona.

A popular side trip from Barcelona is a visit to the dramatic, sawtooth peaks of Montserrat, where the shrine of La Moreneta (the Black Virgin of Montserrat) sits. Montserrat is as memorable for its strange topography as it is for its religious treasures. The views over the mountains that stretch all the way to the Mediterranean and, on a clear day, to the Pyrenees, are breathtaking. The rugged, boulder-strewn terrain makes for exhilarating walks and hikes.

GETTING HERE AND AROUND

By car from Barcelona, follow the A2/A7 autopista on the upper ring road (Ronda de Dalt), or from the western end of the Diagonal as far as Salida 25 to Martorell. Bypass this industrial center and follow signs to Montserrat. You can also take the FGC train from the Plaça d'Espanya metro station (hourly 7:36 am–5:41 pm, connecting with either the cable car at Aeri Montserrat or with the rack railway (Cremallera) at Monistrol Montserrat. Both the cable car and rack railway take 15 minutes and depart every 20 minutes and 15 minutes, respectively. Once you arrive at the monastery, several funiculars can take you farther up the mountain.

A Musical Side Trip

Museu Pau Casals The family house of renowned cellist Pau (Pablo) Casals (1876–1973) is on the beach at Sant Salvador, just east of the town of El Vendrell. Casals, who left Spain in self-imposed exile after Franco seized power in 1939, left a museum of his possessions here, including several of his cellos, original music manuscripts, paintings, and sculptures. Other exhibits describe the Casals campaign for world peace ("Pau," in Catalan, means both Paul and peace), his speech at the United Nations in 1971 (at the age of 95), and his haunting interpretation of *El Cant dels Ocells* (*The Song of the Birds*), his homage to his native Catalonia. Across the street, the Auditori Pau Casals holds frequent concerts and, in July and August, a classical music festival. The museum is about 32 km (20 miles) south of Sitges, en route to Tarragona. ✉ *Av. Palfuriana 67, Sant Salvador, Tarragona* ☎ *977/684276* ⊕ *www.paucasals. org* 🎫 *€8* 🕐 *Closed Mon.*

👁 Sights

★ La Moreneta

RELIGIOUS SITE | The shrine of La Moreneta, one of Catalonia's patron saints, resides in a Benedictine monastery high in the Serra de Montserrat, surrounded by—and dwarfed by the grandeur of—sheer, jagged peaks. The crests above the monastic complex bristle with chapels and hermitages. The shrine and its setting have given rise to countless legends about what happened here: St. Peter left a statue of the Virgin Mary carved by St. Luke, Parsifal found the Holy Grail, and Wagner (who wrote the opera *Parsifal*) sought musical inspiration. The shrine is world famous and one of Catalonia's spiritual sanctuaries, and not just for the monks who reside here—honeymooning couples flock here by the thousands seeking La Moreneta's blessing on their marriages, and twice a year, on April 27 and September 8, the diminutive statue of Montserrat's Black Virgin becomes the object of one of Spain's greatest pilgrimages. Only the basilica and museum are regularly open to the public.

■**TIP→** The famous Escolania de Montserrat boys' choir sings the Salve and Virulai from the liturgy weekdays at 1 pm and Sunday at noon. ✉ *Montserrat* ☎ *No phone* ⊕ *www.montserratvisita.com* 🎫 *€16 sanctuary, audio guide, museum, and audiovisual presentation.*

Sitges

43 km (27 miles) southwest of Barcelona.

Sitges is the prettiest and most popular resort in Barcelona's immediate environs, with an excellent beach and a whitewashed and flowery old quarter. It's also one of Europe's premier gay resorts. From April through September, the fine white sand of the Sitges beach is elbow-to-elbow with sun worshippers. On the eastern end of the strand is an alabaster statue of the 16th-century painter El Greco, usually associated with Toledo, where he spent most of his professional career. The artist Santiago Rusiñol is responsible for this surprise; he was such a Greco fan that he not only installed two of his

Whitewashed buildings dominate the landscape in Sitges.

paintings in his Museu del Cau Ferrat but also had this sculpture planted on the beach.

Sitges and the two nearby Cistercian monasteries to the west of it, Santes Creus and Santa Maria de Poblet, are a trio of attractions that can be seen in a day.

GETTING HERE AND AROUND
By car from Barcelona, head southwest along Gran Vía or Passeig Colom to the freeway that passes the airport on its way to Castelldefels. From here, the freeway and tunnels will get you to Sitges in 20–30 minutes. En route, the small village of Garraf is a worthwhile pit stop, with narrow lanes flanked by whitewashed houses that cling to a promontory looking out to sea. It has a small beach backed by colorful beach huts, providing a quieter refuge from the crowds in Sitges (although it too gets busy in high season).

Just over 30 minutes by train (€3.80 each way), there's regular service from all three Barcelona stations. Buses, roughly the same price, run at least hourly from Plaza Espanya and take about 45 minutes, depending how many stops they make. If you're driving head south on the C32.

Sights

Bodegas Torres
WINERY/DISTILLERY | This family vineyard-winery provides tours and tastings of some excellent Penedès wines. There are also pairings on offer—wine with cheese or wine and Ibérico ham. ⊠ Finca "El Maset", Ctra. BP2121 (direction Sant Martí Sarroca), Vilafranca del Penedès ⟳ From Sitges, make straight for the AP–2 autopista by way of Vilafranca del Penedès ☎ 938/177400 ⊕ www.torres.es 🖾 From €12; includes tour and wine tasting.

Museu del Cau Ferrat
MUSEUM | This is the most interesting museum in Sitges, established by the bohemian artist and cofounder of the Quatre Gats café in Barcelona, Santiago Rusiñol (1861–1931), and containing some of his own paintings together with two by El Greco. Connoisseurs of wrought iron will love the beautiful collection of *cruces terminales,* crosses that once marked town boundaries. Next door is the **Museu Maricel de Mar,** with more artistic treasures. ✉ *Carrer Fonollar 6, Sitges* ☎ *938/940364* 🌐 *www.museusdesitges.com* 🎫 *€10, includes Museu Maricel de Mar* 🕒 *Closed Mon.*

Passeig Maritim
BEACH—SIGHT | A focal point of Sitges life, this long esplanade is an iconic pedestrianized promenade that sweeps past the bay of Sitges. It's backed by upmarket villas, mountain vistas, and ocean views. ✉ *Sitges.*

🍴 Restaurants

Vivero
$$$ | **SEAFOOD** | Perched on a rocky point above the bay at Playa San Sebastián, Vivero specializes in paellas and seafood; try the *mariscada,* a meal-in-itself ensemble of lobster, mussels, and prawns. Weather permitting, the best seats in the house are on the terraces, with wonderful views of the water. **Known for:** outdoor dining; excellent mariscada; wonderful water views. $ *Average main: €22* ✉ *Passeig Balmins s/n, Playa San Sebastián, Sitges* ☎ *938/942149* 🌐 *www.elviverositges.com.*

Santes Creus

95 km (59 miles) west of Barcelona.

Sitges, with its beach and its summer festivals of dance and music, film and fireworks, is anything but solemn. Head inland, however, some 45 minutes' drive west, and you discover how much the art and architecture—the very tone of Catalan culture—owes to its medieval religious heritage. Monolithic Romanesque architecture and beautiful cloisters characterize the Cistercian monasteries at Santes Creus and Poblet.

GETTING HERE AND AROUND

It takes about 45 minutes to drive to Santes Creus from Sitges. Take the C32 west, then get onto the C51 and TP2002, or drive inland toward Vilafranca del Penedès and the AP-7 freeway, followed by the AP-2 (Lleida).

Regular trains leave Sants and Passeig de Gràcia stations for Sitges, Garraf, and Vilafranca del Penedès; the ride takes a half hour to an hour. To get to Santes Creus or Poblet from Sitges, take a Lleida-bound train to L'Espluga de Francolí, 4 km (2½ miles) from Poblet; there's one direct train in the morning at 7:37 and four more during the day with transfers at Sant Vicenç de Calders. From L'Espluga, take a cab to the monastery.

👁 Sights

Montblanc
TOWN | The ancient gates are too narrow for cars, and a walk through its tiny streets reveals Gothic churches with stained-glass windows, a 16th-century hospital, and medieval mansions. ✉ *Off AP-2, Salida 9 (Exit 9).*

Santes Creus
RELIGIOUS SITE | Founded in 1157, Santes Creus is the first of the monasteries you'll come upon as the A2 branches

west toward Lleida; take Exit 11 off the highway. Three austere aisles and an unusual 14th-century apse combine with the restored cloisters and the courtyard of the royal palace. ⊠ *Pl. Jaume el Just s/n, Santes Creus* ☏ *977/638329* 🎫 *€6* 🕐 *Closed Mon.*

Santa Maria de Poblet

8 km (5 miles) west of Santes Creus.

This splendid Cistercian monastery, located at the foot of the Prades Mountains, is one of the great masterpieces of Spanish monastic architecture. Declared a UNESCO World Heritage site, the cloister is a stunning combination of lightness and size, and on sunny days the shadows on the yellow sandstone are extraordinary.

GETTING HERE AND AROUND
The Barcelona–Lleida train can drop you at L'Espluga de Francolí, from where it's a 4-km (2½-mile) walk to the monastery. Buses from Tarragona or Lleida will get you a little closer, with a 2¾-km (1½-mile) walk. The drive from Sitges takes about an hour, via the C32 and AP-2 (Exit 9 when coming from Sitges).

◉ Sights

★ Monasterio de Santa María de Poblet
BUILDING | Founded in 1150 by Ramón Berenguer IV in gratitude for the Christian Reconquest, the monastery first housed a dozen Cistercians from Narbonne. Later, the Crown of Aragón used Santa Maria de Poblet for religious retreats and burials. The building was damaged in an 1836 anticlerical revolt, and monks of the reformed Cistercian Order have managed the difficult task of restoration since 1940. Today, a community of monks and novices still pray before the splendid retable over the tombs of Aragonese rulers, restored to

Celebrated Onions

Valls This town, famous for its early spring *calçotada* (onion feast) held on the last Sunday of January, is 10 km (6 miles) from Santes Creus and 15 km (9 miles) from Poblet. Even if you miss the big day, calçots are served November through April at rustic farmhouses such as **Cal Ganxo** in nearby Masmolets (*Carrer de la Font F 14* ☏ *977/605960*).

their former glory by sculptor Frederic Marès; they also sleep in the cold, barren dormitory and eat frugal meals in the stark refectory. ⊠ *Off AP-2 (Exit 9 from Barcelona, Exit 8 from Lleida), Pl. Corona de Aragón 11* ☏ *977/870089* ⊕ *www. poblet.cat* 🎫 *€9.*

Valencia

351 km (218 miles) southwest of Barcelona, 357 km (222 miles) southeast of Madrid.

Valencia, Spain's third-largest municipality, is a proud city with a thriving nightlife and restaurant scene, quality museums, and spectacular contemporary architecture, juxtaposed with a thoroughly charming historic quarter, making it a popular destination year in and year out. During the civil war, it was the last seat of the Republican Loyalist government (1935–36), holding out against Franco's National forces until the country fell to 40 years of dictatorship. Today it represents the essence of contemporary Spain— daring design and architecture along with experimental cuisine—but remains deeply conservative and proud of its traditions. Although it faces the Mediterranean, Valencia's history and geography

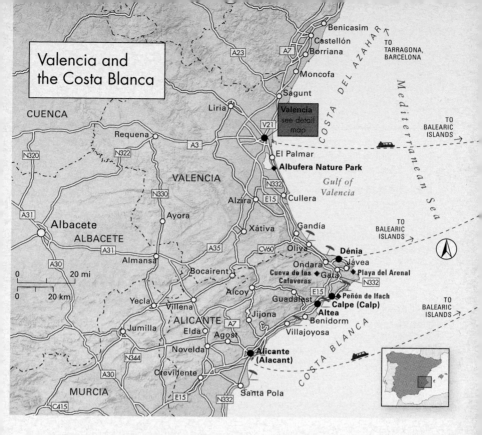

Valencia and
the Costa Blanca

have been defined most significantly by the Turia River and the fertile huerta that surrounds it.

GETTING HERE AND AROUND

By car, Valencia is about 3½ hours from Madrid via the A3 motorway, and about the same from Barcelona on the AP-7 toll road. Valencia is well connected by bus and train, with regular service to and from cities throughout the country, including nine daily AVE high-speed express trains from Madrid, making the trip in 1 hour 40 minutes, and six Euromed express trains daily from Barcelona, taking about 3½ hours. Valencia's bus station is across the river from the old town; take Bus No. 8 from the Plaza del Ayuntamiento. Frequent buses make the four-hour trip from Madrid and the five-hour trip from Barcelona. Dozens of

airlines, large and small, serve Valencia airport, connecting the city with dozens of cities throughout Spain and the rest of Europe.

Once you're here, the city has an efficient network of bus, tram, and metro service. For timetables and more information, stop by the local tourist office. The double-decker Valencia Bus Turístic runs daily 9:30–7:45 (until 9:15 in summer) and departs every 20–30 minutes from the Plaza de la Reina. It travels through the city, stopping at most of the main sights: 24- and 48-hour tickets (€17 and €19, respectively) let you get on and off at eight main boarding points, including the Institut Valencià d'Art Modern, the Museo de Bellas Artes, and the Ciutat de les Arts i les Ciències. The same company also offers a two-hour guided trip (€17) to Albufera Nature Park, including an excursion by boat through the wetlands, departing from the Plaza de la Reina. In summer (and sometimes during the rest of the year) Valencia's tourist office organizes tours of Albufera. You see the port area before continuing south to the lagoon itself, where you can visit a traditional *barraca* (thatch-roof farmhouse).

BUS CONTACT Valencia Bus Station ⊠ *Carrer de Menendez Pidal 11* ☎ *963/466266.*

FESTIVALS

Gran Fira de València (Great Valencia Fair)

ARTS FESTIVALS | Valencia's monthlong festival, in July, celebrates theater, film, dance, and music. ⊠ *Valencia* ⊕ *www.granfiravalencia.com.*

★ Las Fallas

FESTIVALS | If you want nonstop nightlife at its frenzied best, come during the climactic days of Las Fallas, March 15–19 (the festival begins March 1), when revelers throng the streets to see the gargantuan *ninots,* effigies made of wood, paper, and plaster depicting satirical scenes and famous people. Last call at many bars and clubs isn't until the wee hours, if at all. On the last night, all the effigies but one (the winner is spared) are burned to the ground during La Crema, and it seems as though the entire city is ablaze. ⊠ *Valencia* ⊕ *www.visitvalencia.com/en/whats-on-offer-valencia/festivities/the-fallas.*

TOURS

Valencia Bus Turístic

BUS TOURS | Valencia's tourist bus allows you to hop on and hop off as you please, while audio commentary introduces the city's history and highlights. ⊠ *Pl. de la Reina s/n* ☎ *699/982514* ⊕ *www.valenciabusturistic.com* 🎫 *From €17.*

VISITOR INFORMATION

CONTACTS Valencia Tourist Office ⊠ *Pl. del Ayuntamiento 1* ☎ *963/524908* ⊕ *www.visitvalencia.com/en.*

 # Sights

★ Catedral de Valencia

BUILDING | Valencia's 13th- to 15th-century cathedral is the heart of the city. The building has three portals—Romanesque, Gothic, and rococo. Inside, Renaissance and baroque marble were removed to restore the original Gothic style, as is now the trend in Spanish churches. The Capilla del Santo Cáliz (Chapel of the Holy Chalice) displays a purple agate vessel purported to be the Holy Grail (Christ's cup at the Last Supper) and thought to have been brought to Spain in the 4th century. Behind the altar is the left arm of **St. Vincent,** martyred in Valencia in 304. Stars of the cathedral **museum** are Goya's two famous paintings of St. Francis de Borja, Duke of Gandia. Left of the entrance is the octagonal tower **El Miguelete,** which you can climb (207 steps) to the top: the roofs of the old town create a kaleidoscope of orange and brown terra-cotta, with the sea in the background. ⊠ *Pl. de l'Almoina, s/n, Ciutat Vella* ☎ *963/918127* ⊕ *www.catedraldevalencia.es* 🎫 *€7, includes audio guide* 🕐 *Closed Sun. Nov.–Mar.*

★ Ciutat de les Arts i les Ciències

ARTS VENUE | FAMILY | Designed mainly by native son Santiago Calatrava, this sprawling futuristic complex is the home of Valencia's **Museu de les Ciències Príncipe Felipe** (Prince Philip Science Museum), **L'Hemisfèric** (Hemispheric Planetarium), **L'Oceanogràfic** (Oceanographic Park), and **Palau de les Arts** (Palace of the Arts, an opera house and cultural center). With resplendent buildings resembling combs and crustaceans, the Ciutat is a favorite of architecture buffs and curious kids. The Science Museum has soaring platforms filled with lasers, holograms, simulators, hands-on experiments, and a swell "zero gravity" exhibition on space exploration. The eye-shape planetarium projects 3-D virtual voyages on its huge IMAX screen. At l'Oceanogràfic (the work of architect Felix Candela), the largest marine park in Europe, you can take a submarine ride through a coastal marine habitat. Other attractions include an amphitheater, an indoor theater, and a chamber-music hall. ⊠ *Av. del Profesor López Piñero 7* ☎ *961/974686* ⊕ *www. cac.es* ✉ *Museu de les Ciències from €8, L'Oceanogràfic from €30, L'Hemisfèric from €8. Combined ticket €39.*

★ **Lonja de la Seda** (*Silk Exchange*)
BUILDING | On the Plaza del Mercado, this 15th-century building is a product of Valencia's golden age, when the city's prosperity as one of the capitals of the Corona de Aragón made it a leading European commercial and artistic center. The Lonja was constructed as an expression of this splendor and is widely regarded as one of Spain's finest civil Gothic buildings. Its facade is decorated with ghoulish gargoyles, complemented inside by high vaulting and slender helicoidal (twisted) columns. Opposite the Lonja stands the **Iglesia de los Santos Juanes** (Church of the St. Johns), gutted during the 1936–39 Spanish Civil War, and, next door, the Moderniste **Mercado Central** (Central Market, ⇨ *see Shopping*), with its wrought-iron girders and stained-glass windows. ⊠ *Lonja 2, Ciutat Vella* ☎ *962/084153* ✉ *€2.*

★ **Mercado Central (Central Market)**
FOOD/CANDY | This bustling food market (at nearly 88,000 square feet, one of the largest in Europe) is open from 7 am to 3 pm, Monday through Saturday. Locals and visitors alike line up at the 1,247 colorful stalls to shop for fruit, vegetables, meat, fish, and confectionery. Hop on a stool at The Central Bar, located in the heart of the throng, and taste award-winning chef Ricard Camarena's casual yet no less tasty take on tapas and *bocadillos* (sandwiches), while enjoying front-row-seat viewing of the action. ⊠ *Pl. Ciudad de Brujas s/n* ☎ *963/829100* ⊕ *www.mercadocentralvalencia.es* ☾ *Closed Sun.*

★ **Museo de Bellas Artes** (*Museum of Fine Arts*)
MUSEUM | Valencia was a thriving center of artistic activity in the 15th century—one reason that the city's Museum of Fine Arts, with its lovely palm-shaded cloister, is among the best in Spain. To get here, cross the old riverbed by the Puente de la Trinidad (Trinity Bridge) to the north bank; the museum is at the edge of the **Jardines del Real** (Royal Gardens; open daily 8–dusk), with its fountains, rose gardens, tree-lined avenues, and small zoo. The permanent collection of the museum includes many of the finest paintings by Jacomart and Juan Reixach, members of the group known as the Valencian Primitives, as well as work by Hieronymus Bosch—or El Bosco, as they call him here. The ground floor has a number of brooding, 17th-century Tenebrist masterpieces by Francisco Ribalta and his pupil José Ribera, a Diego Velázquez self-portrait, and a room devoted to Goya. ⊠ *Calle San Pío V 9, Trinitat* ☎ *963/870300* ⊕ *www. museobellasartesvalencia.gva.es* ✉ *Free* ☾ *Closed Mon.*

Palacio del Marqués de Dos Aguas (*Ceramics Museum*)
CASTLE/PALACE | Since 1954, this palace has housed the **Museo Nacional de Cerámica,** with a magnificent collection of local and artisanal ceramics. Look for the Valencian kitchen on the second floor. The building itself, near Plaza Patriarca, has gone through many changes over the years and now has elements of several architectural styles, including a fascinating baroque alabaster facade. Embellished with carvings of fruits and vegetables, the facade was designed in 1740 by Ignacio Vergara. It centers on the two voluptuous male figures representing the Dos Aguas (Two Waters), a reference to Valencia's two main rivers and the origin of the noble title of the Marqués de Dos Aguas. The museum's collection centers around traditional Valencian ceramics, textiles, furniture, and clothing as well as

Valencia

KEY

- ● Sights
- ● Restaurants
- ● Hotels

Sights ▼

1 Casa Museo José Benlliure **C3**

2 Ciutat de les Arts i les Ciències **E7**

3 Lonja de la Seda **B3**

4 Mercado Central (Central Market) **B4**

5 Museo de Belles Artes **D1**

6 Palacio del Marqués de Dos Aguas **C4**

7 Plaza del Ayuntamiento **C5**

8 Real Colegio del Corpus Christi **D4**

9 San Nicolás **B2**

Restaurants ▼

1 La Casa Montaña **E6**

2 La Pepica **E6**

3 La Riuà **D3**

4 La Sucursal **A1**

Hotels ▼

1 Ad Hoc Monumental ... **D2**

2 Antigua Morellana **C3**

3 Caro Hotel **D2**

4 Palau de la Mar **E6**

5 Westin Valencia **E6**

a section on antique pottery from Greek, Iberian, and Roman times through to the 20th century. ⊠ *Rinconada Federico García Sanchiz 6* ☎ *963/516392* ✉ *Palace and museum €3; free Sat. 4–8 and Sun.* ⊘ *Closed Mon.*

Plaza del Ayuntamiento

BUILDING | With the massive baroque facades of the Ayuntamiento (City Hall) and the Correos (central Post Office) facing each other across the park, this plaza is the hub of city life. The Ayuntamiento itself houses the municipal tourist office and a museum of paleontology. ■TIP→ **Pop in just for a moment to marvel at the Post Office, with its magnificent stained-glass cupola and ring of classical columns. They don't build 'em like that any more.** ⊠ *Plaza del Ayuntamiento, Casco Antiguo* ☎ *963/525478* ⊕ *www.visitvalencia.com* ⊘ *Ayuntamiento closed weekends. Post Office closed Sun.*

Real Colegio del Corpus Christi (*Iglesia del Patriarca*)

MUSEUM | This seminary, with its church, cloister, and library, is the crown jewel of Valencia's Renaissance architecture. Founded by San Juan de Ribera in the 16th century, it has a lovely Renaissance patio and an ornate church, and its museum—Museum of the Patriarch—holds artworks by Juan de Juanes, Francisco Ribalta, and El Greco. ⊠ *Calle de la Nave 1, Casco Antiguo* ☎ *963/514176* ⊕ *www.seminariocorpuschristi.org* ✉ *€3* ⊘ *Closed Sun.*

San Nicolás

RELIGIOUS SITE | A small plaza contains Valencia's oldest church (dating to the 13th century), once the parish of the Borgia Pope Calixtus III. The first portal you come to, with a tacked-on, rococo bas-relief of the Virgin Mary with cherubs, hints at what's inside: every inch of the originally Gothic church is covered with exuberant ornamentation. ⊠ *Calle Caballeros 35, Casco Antiguo* ☎ *963/913317* ⊕ *www.sannicolasvalencia.com* ✉ *€5* ⊘ *Closed Mon.*

Beaches

Playa las Arenas

BEACH—SIGHT | This wide (nearly 450 feet) and popular grand municipal beach stretches north from the port and the America's Cup marina more than a kilometer (½ mile), before it gives way to the even busier and livelier Platja de Malvarossa. The Paseo Marítimo promenade runs the length of the beach and is lined with restaurants and small hotels, including the **Neptuno** and the upscale **Las Arenas Balneario** resort. There's no shade anywhere, but the fine golden sand is kept pristine and the water is calm and shallow. **Amenities:** food and drink; lifeguards; showers; toilets; water sports. **Best for:** sunset; swimming; walking; windsurfing. ⊠ *Valencia* ⊕ *www.playadelasarenas.com/en.*

Restaurants

La Casa Montaña

$$$ | TAPAS | The walls are lined with rotund wine barrels at this welcoming bodega with a Moderniste facade, tucked down a side street in the city's old fishermen's quarter. Established in 1836, the restaurant serves a large and varied selection of tapas, from melt-in-your-mouth jamón to rustic stews and grilled seafood, all well accompanied by a superlative, regularly updated selection of wines. **Known for:** good tapas and shared plates; loads of character; quality wine list. $ *Average main: €21* ⊠ *Carrer de Josep Benlliure 69* ☎ *963/672314* ⊕ *www.emilianobodega.com* ⊘ *No dinner Sun.*

La Pepica

$$$ | SPANISH | Locals regard this bustling, informal restaurant, on the promenade at El Cabanyal beach, as the best in town for seafood paella. Founded in 1898, the walls of the establishment are covered with signed pictures of appreciative visitors, from Ernest Hemingway to King Juan Carlos and the royal family. **Known**

Valencia's L'Oceanogràfic (Ciutat de les Arts i les Ciències) has amazing exhibits, as well as an underwater restaurant.

for: locally revered seafood paella; fruit tarts; historic locale. [$] *Average main: €20* ✉ *Av. Neptuno 6* ☎ *963/710366* 🌐 *www.lapepica.com* 🕒 *Closed last 2 wks in Nov. and last 2 wks in Jan. No dinner Sun.–Thurs.*

La Riuà

$$ | **SPANISH** | A favorite of Valencia's well connected and well-to-do since 1982, this family-run restaurant a few steps from the Plaza de la Reina specializes in seafood dishes like *anguilas* (eels) prepared with *all i pebre* (garlic and pepper), *parrillada de pescado* (selection of freshly grilled fish), and traditional paellas. Lunch begins at 2 and not a moment before. **Known for:** specialty eel dish; award-winning dining; longtime family-run establishment. [$] *Average main: €16* ✉ *Calle del Mar 27, bajo* ☎ *963/914571* 🌐 *www.lariua.com* 🕒 *Closed Sun. No dinner Mon.*

La Sucursal

$$$$ | **MEDITERRANEAN** | This thoroughly modern but comfortable restaurant in the Institut Valencià d'Art Modern is likely to put a serious dent in your budget, but it's unlikely you'll sample better venison carpaccio anywhere else, or partake of any finer an *arroz caldoso de bogavante* (soupy rice with lobster). The dinner menu is prix-fixe (€70). [$] *Average main: €60* ✉ *Carrer Guillem de Castro 118, El Carmen* ☎ *963/746665* 🌐 *www.restaurantelasucursal.com.*

🛏 Hotels

Ad Hoc Monumental

$$ | **HOTEL** | This nicely designed 19th-century town house sits on a quiet street at the edge of the old city, a minute's walk from the Plaza Almoina and the cathedral in one direction, and steps from the Turia gardens in the other. **Pros:** close to sights but quiet; courteous, helpful staff; great value. **Cons:** parking can be a nightmare; not especially family-oriented; small rooms. [$] *Rooms from: €90* ✉ *Carrer Boix 4, Ciutat Vella* ☎ *963/919140* 🌐 *www.adhochoteles.com* 🛏 *28 rooms* 🍴 *No meals.*

★ Antigua Morellana

$ | **B&B/INN** | Run by four convivial sisters, this 18th-century town house provides the ultimate no-frills accommodation in the heart of the old city. **Pros:** friendly service; excellent location; complimentary tea in the lounge. **Cons:** no parking; simple amenities; small rooms. [$] *Rooms from: €70* ✉ *Carrer d'En Bou 2, Ciutat Vella* ☎ *963/915773* 🌐 *www.hostalam.com* 🛏 *18 rooms* 🍴 *No meals.*

★ Caro Hotel

$$$$ | **HOTEL** | A triumph of design, opened in 2012, this elegant modern hotel is seamlessly wedded to an important historical property: a 14th-century Gothic palace, built on the 12th-century Arabic wall and over the Roman Circus, fragments of which are on show. **Pros:** good location, a few minutes' walk from the cathedral; spot-on, attentive service; oasis of quiet. **Cons:** the two top-floor rooms have low, slanted ceilings; valet parking is rather pricey; decidedly not family-friendly. [$] *Rooms from: €200* ✉ *Carrer Almirante 14* ☎ *963/059000* 🌐 *www.carohotel.com* 🛏 *26 rooms* 🍴 *No meals.*

Palau de la Mar

$$$$ | **HOTEL** | In a restored 19th-century palace, this boutique hotel looks out at the Porta de La Mar, which marked the entry to the old walled quarter of Valencia. **Pros:** big bathrooms with double sinks; great location near the sights and shops; courtyard and garden. **Cons:** top-floor rooms have low, slanted ceilings; rooms overlooking road can be noisy; small gym. [$] *Rooms from: €240* ✉ *Av. Navarro Reverter 14, Ciutat Vella* ☎ *963/162884* 🌐 *www.hospes.com/en/palau-mar* 🛏 *66 rooms* 🍴 *Free Breakfast.*

Westin Valencia

$$$$ | **HOTEL** | Built in 1917 as a cotton mill, with successive recyclings as a fire station and a stable for the mounted National Police Corps, this classic property was transformed in 2006 into a luxury hotel. **Pros:** attentive, professional, multilingual staff; location steps from the metro that connects directly to the airport; pet-friendly. **Cons:** rates rise to astronomical during special events; some rooms could use refreshing; patchy Wi-Fi. [$] *Rooms from: €200* ✉ *Av. Amadeo de Saboya 16, Pl. del Reial* ☎ *963/625900* 🌐 *www.westinvalencia.com* 🛏 *135 rooms* 🍴 *No meals.*

🍸 Nightlife

Valencianos have perfected the art of doing without sleep. Nightlife in the old town centers on Barrio del Carmen, a lively web of streets that unfolds north of Plaza del Mercado. Popular bars and pubs dot Calle Caballeros, starting at Plaza de la Virgen; the Plaza del Tossal also has some popular cafés, as does Calle Alta, off Plaza San Jaime.

Some of the funkier, newer places are in and around Plaza del Carmen. Across the river, look for appealing hangouts along Avenida Blasco Ibáñez and on Plaza de Cánovas del Castillo. Out by the sea, Paseo Neptuno and Calle de Eugenia Viñes are lined with clubs and bars, lively in summer. The monthly English-language nightlife and culture magazine *24/7 Valencia* (🌐 *www.247valencia.com*) is free at tourist offices and various bars and clubs; leisure guides in Spanish include *Hello Valencia* (🌐 *www.hello-valencia.es*) and *La Guía Go* (🌐 *www.laguiago.com*).

BARS AND CAFÉS

Café de las Horas

BARS/PUBS | This surreal bordello-style bar is an institution for Valencia's signature cocktail, Agua de Valencia (a syrupy blend of cava or Champagne, orange juice, vodka, and gin). The bar's warm atmosphere and convivial vibe are perfect for whiling away the hours at the start (or end) of the night. ✉ *Calle del Conde de Almodóvar 1* ☎ *963/917336* 🌐 *www.cafedelashoras.com.*

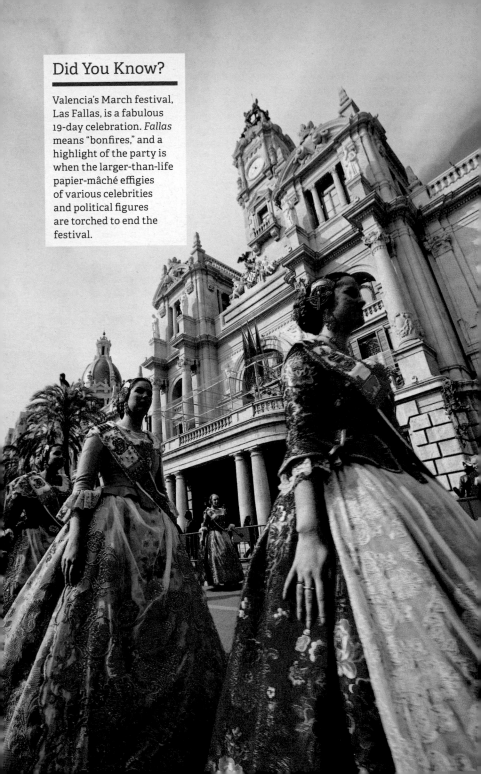

Did You Know?

Valencia's March festival, Las Fallas, is a fabulous 19-day celebration. *Fallas* means "bonfires," and a highlight of the party is when the larger-than-life papier-mâché effigies of various celebrities and political figures are torched to end the festival.

Café del Duende

CAFES—NIGHTLIFE | For a taste of *el ambiente andaluz* (Andalusian atmosphere), stop by this flamenco club in the heart of the Barrio del Carmen. It's open Thursday–Saturday from 10 pm (performances start at 10:30 pm on Thursday and at 11 pm on Friday and Saturday). On Sunday performances start at 8 pm. Get there early to secure a seat. ⊠ *Carrer Túria 62, El Carmen* ☎ *630/455289* ⊕ *www.cafedelduende.com.*

Tyris On Tap

BARS/PUBS | Valencia's first craft-beer brewery, Cerveza Tyris, has an animated bar opposite the Mercado Central. Visitors can sample a smorgasbord of locally brewed beers on tap and fill up on tapas, chili dogs, and burgers to a background of well-selected music. ⊠ *Carrer de la Taula de Canvis 6, El Carmen* ☎ *961/132873* ⊕ *www.cervezatyris.com.*

MUSIC CLUBS

Jimmy Glass Jazz Bar

MUSIC CLUBS | Aficionados of modern jazz gather at this bar (check website for details as opening hours vary according to performances booked), which books an impressive range of local and international combos and soloists. ⊠ *Carrer Baja 28, El Carmen* ⊕ *www.jimmyglassjazz.net.*

Radio City

MUSIC CLUBS | The airy, perennially popular, bar–club–performance space at Radio City offers eclectic nightly shows featuring music from flamenco to Afro-jazz fusion. ⊠ *Carrer Santa Teresa 19, El Carmen* ☎ *963/914151* ⊕ *www.radiocity-valencia.com.*

Performing Arts

MUSIC

Palau de la Música

CONCERTS | On one of the nicest stretches of the Turia riverbed is this huge glass vault, Valencia's main concert venue. Home of the Orquesta de Valencia, the main hall also hosts touring performers from around the world, including chamber and youth orchestras, opera, and an excellent concert series featuring early, baroque, and classical music. It's worth popping in to see the building even without concert tickets, and there is also an **art gallery,** which hosts free changing exhibitions by renowned modern artists. ⊠ *Passeig de l'Albereda 30* ☎ *963/375020* ⊕ *www.palauvalencia.com.*

Palau de les Arts Reina Sofía

CONCERTS | This visually arresting performing arts venue and concert hall, designed by Santiago Calatrava, hosts a rich calendar of opera and classical music throughout the year. ⊠ *Av. del Professor López Piñero (Historiador de la Medicina) 1* ☎ *902/202383 information and tickets* ⊕ *www.lesarts.com.*

🛍 Shopping

Nela

CRAFTS | Browse here, in the heart of the old city, for *abanicos* (traditional silk folding fans), hand-embroidered *mantillas* (shawls), and parasols. ⊠ *Calle San Vicente Mártir 2, Ciutat Vella* ☎ *963/923023.*

Plaza Redonda

GIFTS/SOUVENIRS | A few steps from the cathedral, off the upper end of Calle San Vicente Mártir, the restored Plaza Redonda ("Round Square") is lined with stalls selling all sorts of souvenirs and traditional crafts. ⊠ *Pl. Redonda, El Carmen.*

Albufera Nature Park

11 km (7 miles) south of Valencia.

South of Valencia, Albufera Nature Park is one of Spain's most spectacular wetland areas. Home to the largest freshwater lagoon on the peninsula, this protected area and bird-watcher's paradise is bursting with unusual flora and fauna, such as rare species of wading birds. Encircled by a tranquil backdrop of rice fields, it's no surprise that the villages that dot this picturesque place have some of the best options in the region for trying classic Valencian paella or *arròs a banda* (rice cooked in fish stock).

GETTING HERE AND AROUND

From Valencia, buses depart for the park from the corner of Sueca and Gran Vía de Germanías every hour, and every half hour in summer, 7 am–9 pm daily.

Sights

★ Albufera Nature Park

NATURE PRESERVE | This beautiful freshwater lagoon was named by Moorish poets—*albufera* means "the sun's mirror." The park is a nesting site for more than 250 bird species, including herons, terns, egrets, ducks, and gulls. Bird-watching companies offer boat rides all along the Albufera. For maps, guides, and tour arrangements, start your visit at the park's information center, the Centre d'Interpretació Raco de l'Olla in El Palmar. ✉ *Ctra. de El Palmar s/n, El Palmar* ☎ *963/868050* 🌐 *www.albufera.com* 🎫 *Free.*

El Palmar

TOWN | This is the major village in the area, with streets lined with restaurants specializing in various types of paella. The most traditional kind is made with rabbit or game birds, though seafood is also popular in this region because it's so fresh. ✉ *El Palmar.*

Restaurants

Maribel Arroceria

$$ | SPANISH | So tasty is the paella here that even valencianos regularly travel out of the city to Maribel Arroceria, off the main drag in El Palmar. While you sit surrounded by the rice fields of Albufera Nature Park, during the week you can devour a fixed-price lunchtime *menu del dia* (€20) of four starters to share, a paella, and dessert, served in the contemporary, air-conditioned dining room or outside at pavement tables overlooking the canal. **Known for:** highly prized paellas; reasonable prix-fixe lunch menus, plus à la carte options; authentic setting in area considered the birthplace of paella. [$] *Average main: €17* ✉ *Carrer de Francisco Monleón 5, El Palmar* ☎ *961/620060* 🌐 *www.arroceriamaribel.com* 🕒 *Closed Wed. No dinner.*

Dénia

The stretch of coastline known as the Costa Blanca (White Coast) begins at Dénia, south of Valencia. Dénia is the port of departure on the Costa Blanca for the ferries to Ibiza, Formentera, and Mallorca—but if you're on your way to or from the islands, stay a night in the lovely little town in the shadow of a dramatic cliff-top fortress. Or, spend a few hours wandering in the Baix la Mar, the old fishermen's quarter with its brightly painted houses, and exploring the historic town center. The town has become something of a culinary hot spot and is home to award-winning restaurants, which for its compact size is something of an achievement.

GETTING HERE AND AROUND

Dénia is linked to other Costa Blanca destinations via Line 1of the Alicante–Benidorm narrow-gauge TRAM train. There's also regular bus service from major towns and cities, including Madrid (7¼–9 hours) and Valencia (1¾–2½ hours). Local buses can get you around all of the Costa Blanca communities.

The Playa del Arenal, a tiny bay cut into the larger one, is worth a visit in summer. You can reach it via the coastal road (CV736) between Dénia and Jávea.

VISITOR INFORMATION
CONTACTS Visitor Information Dénia
✉ *Pl. Oculista Buigues 9* ☎ *966/422367* ⊕ *www.denia.net.*

Sights

Castillo de Dénia
ARCHAEOLOGICAL SITE | The most interesting architectural attraction here is the castle overlooking the town, and the **Palau del Governador** (Governor's Palace) inside. On the site of an 11th-century Moorish fortress, the Renaissance-era palace was built in the 17th century and was later demolished. A major restoration project is under way. The fortress has an interesting archaeological **museum** as well as the remains of a Renaissance bastion and a Moorish portal with a lovely horseshoe arch. ✉ *Av. del Cid–Calle San Francisco s/n* ☎ *966/422367* 🎫 *€3 (includes entrance to archaeological museum).*

Cueva de las Calaveras (*Cave of the Skulls*)
CAVE | **FAMILY** | About 15 km (9 miles) inland from Dénia, this 400-yard-long cave was named for the 12 Moorish skulls found here when it was discovered in 1768. The cave of stalactites and stalagmites has a dome rising to more than 60 feet and leads to an underground lake. ✉ *Ctra. Benidoleig–Pedreguera, Km 1.5, Benidoleig* ☎ *966/404235* ⊕ *www.cuevadelascalaveras.com* 🎫 *€4.*

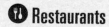 Restaurants

El Raset
$$$ | **SEAFOOD** | Across the harbor, this Valencian favorite has been serving traditional cuisine with a modern twist for more than 30 years. From a terrace with views of the water you can choose from an array of excellent seafood dishes, including house specialties such as *arroz en caldero* (rice with monkfish, lobster, or prawns) and *gambas rojas* (local red prawns). À la carte dining can be expensive, while set menus are easier on your wallet. **Known for:** excellent seafood dishes; reasonably priced set menus; tasty paella. 💲 *Average main: €20* ✉ *Calle Bellavista 7* ☎ *965/785040* ⊕ *www.grupoelraset.com.*

La Seu
$$$ | **SPANISH** | Under co-owners Fede and Diana Cervera and chef Xicu Ramón, this distinguished restaurant in the center of town continues to reinvent and deconstruct traditional Valencian cuisine. The setting is an architectural tour de force: a 16th-century town house transformed into a sunlit modern space with an open kitchen and a three-story-high wall sculpted to resemble a billowing white curtain. **Known for:** creative tapas; unbeatable midweek menu prices; inventive take on Valencian cuisine. 💲 *Average main: €20* ✉ *Calle Loreto 59* ☎ *966/424478* ⊕ *www.laseu.es* 🕙 *Closed early Jan.–early Feb. Closed Mon.*

🛏 Hotels

★ Art Boutique Hotel Chamarel
$$ | **B&B/INN** | Ask the staff and they'll tell you that *chamarel* means a "mixture of colors," and this hotel brimming with charm, built as a grand family home in 1840, is certainly an eccentric blend of styles, cultures, periods, and personalities. **Pros:** friendly, helpful staff; individual attention; pet-friendly. **Cons:** no pool; not on the beach; rooms over the street are noisy. 💲 *Rooms from: €110* ✉ *Calle Cavallers 3* ☎ *966/435007* ⊕ *www.hotelchamarel.com* 🛏 *15 rooms* 🍴 *Free Breakfast.*

Dénia's massive fort overlooks the harbor and provides a dramatic element to the skyline, with the Montgü mountains in the background.

★ Hostal Loreto

$ | **HOTEL** | Travelers on tight budgets will appreciate this basic yet impeccable lodging, on a central pedestrian street in the historic quarter just steps from the Town Hall. **Pros:** great central location in former nunnery; good value; broad, comfy roof terrace. **Cons:** no elevator; no amenities; rooms can be dark. [$] *Rooms from: €82* ✉ *Calle Loreto 12* ☎ *966/435419* 🌐 *www.hostalloreto.com* 🛏 *43 rooms* 🍴 *Free Breakfast.*

★ Hotel El Raset

$$$ | **B&B/INN** | Just across the esplanade from the port, where the Balearia ferries depart for Mallorca and Ibiza, this upscale boutique hotel has amenities that few lodgings in Dénia offer. **Pros:** staff is friendly, attentive, and multilingual; good location; good restaurant from same owners down the street. **Cons:** no pool; dim overhead lighting in rooms; pricey private parking. [$] *Rooms from: €160* ✉ *Calle Bellavista 1, Port* ☎ *965/786564* 🌐 *www.hotelelraset.com* 🛏 *20 rooms* 🍴 *Free Breakfast.*

★ La Posada del Mar

$$$$ | **HOTEL** | A few steps across from the harbor, this hotel in the 13th-century customs house has inviting rooms with seafront views; there's a subtle nautical theme, most evident in the sailor's-knot ironwork along the staircase. **Pros:** serene environment; close to center of town; lovely sea views. **Cons:** pricey parking; no pool; rooms overlooking the main road can be noisy. [$] *Rooms from: €198* ✉ *Puerto de Denia, Pl. de les Drassanes 2, Port* ☎ *966/432966* 🌐 *www.laposadadelmar.com* 🛏 *31 rooms* 🍴 *Free Breakfast.*

Calpe (Calp)

35 km (22 miles) south of Dénia.

Calpe has an ancient history, as it was chosen by the Phoenicians, Greeks, Romans, and Moors as a strategic point from which to plant their Iberian settlements. The real-estate developers were the latest to descend upon it: much

of Calpe today is overbuilt with high-rise resorts and *urbanizaciónes*. But the old town is a delightful maze of narrow streets and small squares, archways and cul-de-sacs, with houses painted in Mediterranean blue, red, ocher, and sandstone; wherever there's a broad expanse of building wall, you'll likely discover a mural. Calpe is a delightful place to wander.

GETTING HERE AND AROUND

The narrow-gauge TRAM railway from Dénia to Alicante also serves Calpe, as do local buses.

VISITOR INFORMATION

CONTACTS Visitor Information Calpe ✉ *Av. Ejércitos Españoles 44, Calp* ☎ *965/836920* 🌐 *www.calpe.es.*

Sights

Fish Market

MARKET | The fishing industry is still very important in Calpe, and every evening the fishing boats return to port with their catch. The subsequent auction at the fish market can be watched from the walkway of La Lonja de Calpe. ✉ *Port, Calp* 🕑 *Closed weekends.*

Mundo Marino

TOUR—SIGHT | Choose from a wide range of sailing trips, including cruises up and down the coast. Glass-bottom boats make it easy to observe the abundant marine life. ✉ *Puerto Pesquero, Calp* ☎ *966/423066* 🌐 *www.mundomarino.es* 🎫 *From €15.*

Peñón d'Ifach Natural Park

NATURE SITE | The landscape of Calpe is dominated by this huge calcareous rock more than 1,100 yards long, 1,090 feet high, and joined to the mainland by a narrow isthmus. The area is rich in flora and fauna, with more than 300 species of plants and 80 species of land and marine birds. A visit to the top is not for the fainthearted; wear shoes with traction for the hike, which includes a trip through a tunnel to the summit. The views are spectacular, reaching to the island of Ibiza on a clear day. Check with the local visitor information center about guided tours for groups. ✉ *Calp.*

Restaurants

Patio de la Fuente

$$$ | **MEDITERRANEAN** | In an intimate little space with wicker chairs and pale mauve walls, this restaurant in the old town serves a bargain Mediterranean three-course prix-fixe dinner, wine included; you can also order à la carte. In summer, dine on the comfortable patio out back. **Known for:** outdoor dining; good-value three-course dinner; divine Scotch egg. [$] *Average main: €18* ✉ *Carrer Dos de Mayo 16, Calp* ☎ *965/831695* 🌐 *www.patiodelafuente.com* 🕑 *Closed Sun. and Mon. No lunch.*

Hotels

Pensión el Hidalgo

$ | **B&B/INN** | This family-run pension near the beach has small but cozy rooms with a friendly, easygoing feel, and several have private balconies overlooking the Mediterranean. **Pros:** beachfront location; reasonable prices; breakfast terrace with sea views. **Cons:** basic design; you must book far ahead in summer; weak Wi-Fi connection in some rooms. [$] *Rooms from: €70* ✉ *Av. Rosa de los Vientos 19, Calp* ☎ *965/839862* 🌐 *www.pensionelhidalgo.com* 🔑 *9 rooms* 🍴 *No meals.*

Altea

11 km (7 miles) southwest of Calpe.

Perched on a hill overlooking a bustling beachfront, Altea (unlike some of its neighboring towns) has retained much of its original charm, with an atmospheric old quarter laced with narrow cobblestone streets and stairways, and gleaming white houses. At the center

is the striking church of Nuestra Señora del Consuelo, with its blue ceramic-tile dome, and the Plaza de la Iglesia in front.

GETTING HERE AND AROUND

Also on the Dénia–Alicante narrow-gauge TRAM train route, Altea is served by local buses, with connections to major towns and cities. The old quarter is mainly pedestrianized.

VISITOR INFORMATION

CONTACTS Visitor Information Altea ✉ *Calle Sant Pere 14* ☎ *965/844114* 🌐 *www.visitaltea.es.*

🍴 Restaurants

La Costera

$$$ | **FRENCH** | This popular restaurant focuses on fine French fare, with such specialties as house-made foie gras (simply called foie), roasted lubina (sea bass), and beef entrecôte. There's also a variety of game in season, including venison and partridge. **Known for:** bucolic outdoor terrace; in-season game; French specialties. [$] *Average main: €20* ✉ *Costera Mestre de Música 8* ☎ *965/840230* 🌐 *www.lacosteradealtea.es* ⏲ *Closed Mon. No lunch Tues.–Thurs. No dinner Sun.*

Oustau de Altea

$$ | **EUROPEAN** | In one of the prettiest corners of Altea's old town, this eatery was formerly a cloister and a school. Today the dining room and terrace combine contemporary design gracefully juxtaposed with a rustic setting, and the restaurant is known for serving polished international cuisine with French flair. **Known for:** cuisine with French style; dishes named after classic films; contemporary artwork. [$] *Average main: €15* ✉ *Calle Mayor 5, Casco Antiguo* ☎ *965/842078* 🌐 *www.oustau.com* ⏲ *Closed Mon. and Feb. No lunch.*

🛏 Hotels

Hostal Fornet

$ | **HOTEL** | The pièce de résistance at this simple, pleasant hotel, at the highest point of Altea's historic center, is the roof terrace with its stunning view; from here, you look out over the church's distinctive blue-tiled cupola and the surrounding tangle of streets, with a Mediterranean backdrop. **Pros:** lovely views; top value; multilingual owners. **Cons:** no pool or beach; small rooms; door is locked when reception is not staffed, and you have to call to be let in. [$] *Rooms from: €49* ✉ *Calle Beniardá 1, Casco Antiguo* ☎ *965/843005* 🌐 *www.hostalfornetaltea.com* 🔑 *23 rooms* 🍽 *No meals.*

Alicante (Alacant)

82 km (51 miles) northeast of Murcia, 183 km (114 miles) south of Valencia, 52 km (32 miles) south of Altea.

The Greeks called it Akra Leuka (White Summit) and the Romans named it Lucentum (City of Light). A crossroads for inland and coastal routes since ancient times, Alicante has always been known for its luminous skies. The city is dominated by the 16th-century grande dame castle, **Castillo de Santa Bárbara,** a top attraction. The best approach is via the elevator cut deep into the mountainside. Also memorable is Alicante's grand **Esplanada,** lined with date palms. Directly under the castle is the city beach, the Playa del Postiguet, but the city's pride is the long, curved Playa de San Juan, which runs north from the Cap de l'Horta to El Campello.

GETTING HERE AND AROUND

Alicante has two train stations: the main Estación de Madrid and the local Estación de la Marina, from which the local FGV line runs along the Costa Blanca from Alicante to Dénia. The Estación de la Marina is at the far end of Playa

Alicante's Esplanada de España, lined with date palms, is the perfect place for a stroll. The municipal brass band offers concerts on the bandstand of the Esplanada on Sunday evenings in July and August.

Postiguet and can be reached by Buses C1 and C2 from downtown.

The slower narrow-gauge TRAM train goes from the city center on the beach to El Campello. From the same open-air station in Alicante, the Line 1 train departs to Benidorm, with connections on to Altea, Calpe, and Dénia.

VISITOR INFORMATION

CONTACTS Tourist Information Alicante
✉ *Rambla Méndez Núñez 41, Alicante*
☎ *965/200000* ⊕ *www.alicanteturismo. com.* **TRAM** ✉ *Alicante-Luceros, Alicante*
☎ *900/720472* ⊕ *www.tramalicante.es.*

Sights

Ayuntamiento

BUILDING | Constructed between 1696 and 1780, the town hall is a beautiful example of baroque civic architecture. Inside, a gold sculpture by Salvador Dalí of San Juan Bautista holding the famous cross and shell rises to the second floor in the stairwell. Ask gate officials for permission to explore the ornate halls

and rococo chapel on the first floor. Look for the plaque on the first step of the staircase that indicates the exact sea level, used to define the rest of Spain's altitudes "above sea level." ✉ *Pl. de Ayuntamiento, Alicante* ☎ *965/149100* ⊙ *Closed weekends.*

Basílica de Santa María

BUILDING | Constructed in a Gothic style over the city's main mosque between the 14th and 16th century, this is Alicante's oldest house of worship. The main door is flanked by beautiful baroque stone-work by Juan Bautista Borja, and the interior highlights are the golden rococo high altar, a Gothic image in stone of St. Mary, and a sculpture of Sts. Juanes by Rodrigo de Osona. ✉ *Pl. de Santa María s/n, Alicante* ☎ *965/200000 tourist office (for information)* ⊙ *Closing times can vary due to religious services.*

★ Castillo de Santa Bárbara (*St. Barbara's Castle*)

ARCHAEOLOGICAL SITE | One of the largest existing medieval fortresses in Europe, Castillo de Santa Bárbara sits atop

545-foot-tall Monte Benacantil. From this strategic position you can gaze out over the city, the sea, and the whole Alicante plain for many miles. Remains from civilizations dating from the Bronze Age onward have been found here; the oldest parts of the castle, at the highest level, are from the 9th through 13th century. The castle is most easily reached by taking the elevator from Avenida Juan Bautista Lafora. The castle also houses the Museo de la Ciudad de Alicante (MUSA), which uses audiovisual presentations and archaeological finds to tell the story of Alicante, its people, and the city's enduring relationship with the sea. ✉ *Monte Benacantil s/n, Alicante* ☎ *965/152969* 🌐 *www.castillodesantabarbara.com* 🎫 *Castle and museum free, elevator €3.*

Concatedral of San Nicolás de Bari

BUILDING | Built between 1616 and 1662 on the site of a former mosque, this church (called a *con*catedral because it shares the seat of the bishopric with the Concatedral de Orihuela) has an austere facade designed by Agustín Bernardino, a disciple of the great Spanish architect Juan de Herrera. Inside, it's dominated by a dome nearly 150 feet high, a pretty cloister, and a lavish baroque side chapel, the Santísima Sacramento, with an elaborate sculptured stone dome of its own. Its name comes from the day that Alicante was reconquered (December 6, 1248) from the Moors, the feast day of St. Nicolás. ✉ *Pl. Abad Penalva 2, Alicante* ☎ *965/212662* 🎫 *Free* 🕓 *Closed Sun. except services.*

Museo Arqueológico Provincial

MUSEUM | Inside the old hospital of San Juan de Dios, the MARQ has a collection of artifacts from the Alicante region dating from the Paleolithic era to modern times, with a particular emphasis on Iberian art. ✉ *Pl. Dr. Gómez Ulla s/n, Alicante* ☎ *965/149000* 🌐 *www.marqalicante.com* 🎫 *€3* 🕓 *Closed Mon.*

Museu de Fogueres

MUSEUM | Bonfire festivities are popular in this part of Spain, and the ninots, or effigies, can be elaborate and funny, including satirized political figures and celebrities. Every year the best effigies are saved from the flames and placed in this museum, which also has an audiovisual presentation of the festivities, scale models, photos, and costumes. ✉ *Rambla de Méndez Nuñez 29, Alicante* ☎ *965/146828* 🎫 *Free* 🕓 *Closed Mon. Closed Sun. and Mon. in Aug.*

🍴 Restaurants

El Portal

$$$ | **SPANISH** | Blending tradition with novelty is not always an easy task, but it is what draws people back to El Portal in droves. Chef Sergio Sierra runs a slick operation, from the restaurant's extravagant decor (think modern interpretation of Roaring '20s) to a menu that is committed to offering the best flavors of the region—from the freshest seafood to premium cuts of meat to seasonal produce. **Known for:** montadito de solomillo de vacuno con trufa (steak sandwich with truffle oil); unique decor and DJ soundtrack; cocktails, wine, and dinner all in one place. [$] *Average main: €22* ✉ *C. Bilbao 2, Alicante* ☎ *965/144 444* 🌐 *www.elportaltaberna.es.*

★ La Taberna del Gourmet

$$$ | **TAPAS** | This wine bar and restaurant in the heart of the *casco antiguo* (old town) earns high marks from locals and international visitors alike. A bar with stools and counters offers a selection of fresh seafood tapas—oysters, mussels, razor clams—to complement a well-chosen list of wines from La Rioja, Ribera del Duero, and Priorat, and the two dining rooms are furnished with thick butcher-block tables and dark brown leather chairs. **Known for:** excellent wine list; fresh seafood tapas; reservations essential. [$] *Average main: €20* ✉ *Calle*

San Fernando 10, Alicante ☎ *965/204233* 🌐 *www.latabernadelgourmet.com.*

Nou Manolín

$$$ | **SPANISH** | An Alicante institution, this inviting exposed-brick and wood-lined restaurant is generally packed with locals, here for the excellent-value tapas and daily menu. It's a superb place to tuck into fish freshly caught that afternoon, a tribute to the city's enduring relationship with the sea. **Known for:** market-fresh produce; authentic local vibe; a favorite of culinary superstar Ferran Adrià. [$] *Average main: €22* ✉ *Calle Villegas 3, Alicante* ☎ *965/616425* 🌐 *www.grupo-gastronou.com.*

Hotels

Hostal Les Monges Palace

$ | **HOTEL** | In a restored 1912 building, this family-run hostal in Alicante's central casco antiguo features lovingly preserved exposed stone walls, ceramic tile floors, and rooms furnished with eccentric artwork and quirky charm. **Pros:** personalized service; ideal location with rooftop terrace; lots of character. **Cons:** the newer, modern part is not as atmospheric; must book well in advance; bathrooms in standard rooms are small. [$] *Rooms from: €75* ✉ *Calle San Agustín 4, Alicante* ☎ *965/215046* 🌐 *www.lesmonges.es* 🛏 *24 rooms* 🍴 *Free Breakfast.*

Nightlife

El Barrio, the old quarter west of Rambla de Méndez Núñez, is the prime nightlife area of Alicante, with music bars and discos every couple of steps. In summer, or after 3 am, the liveliest places are along the water, on Ruta del Puerto and Ruta de la Madera.

El Coscorrón

BARS/PUBS | It's an Alicante tradition to start an evening out here, with El Coscorrón's generous mojitos. ✉ *Calle Tarifa 5, Alicante* ☎ *965/212727.*

Shopping

Mercado Central

FOOD/CANDY | Bulging with fish, vegetables, and other local items, this is the place to stop by and discover Alicante's fresh produce, traded from this Moderniste-inspired building since 1921. ✉ *Av. Alfonso el Sabio 10, Alicante.*

Chapter 10

IBIZA AND THE BALEARIC ISLANDS

Updated by
Elizabeth Prosser

⊙ Sights	🍴 Restaurants	🛏 Hotels	🛍 Shopping	🍸 Nightlife
★★★☆☆	★★★★☆	★★★★☆	★★★☆☆	★★★☆☆

WELCOME TO
IBIZA AND THE BALEARIC ISLANDS

TOP REASONS TO GO

★ **Pamper yourself:** Luxurious boutique hotels on restored and redesigned rural estates are *the* hip places to stay in the Balearics. Many have their own holistic spas: restore and redesign yourself at one of them.

★ **Enjoy seafood delicacies:** Seafood specialties come straight from the boat to portside restaurants all over the islands.

★ **Party hard:** Ibiza's summer club scene is the biggest, wildest, and glitziest in the world.

★ **Take in the gorgeous views:** The *miradores* (viewpoints) of Mallorca's Tramuntana, along the road from Valldemossa to Sóller, highlight the most spectacular seacoast in the Mediterranean.

★ **Discover Palma:** Capital of the Balearics, Palma is one of the great unsung cities of the Mediterranean—a showcase of medieval and modern architecture, a venue for art and music, a mecca for sailors, and a killer place to shop for shoes.

The Balearic Islands lie 80–305 km (50–190 miles) off the Spanish mainland, roughly between Valencia and Barcelona. In the center, Mallorca, with its rolling eastern plains and mountainous northwest, is the largest of the group. Menorca, its closest neighbor, is virtually flat; but like Ibiza and tiny Formentera to the west, it has a rugged coastline of small inlets and sandy beaches.

1 Ibiza. Sleepy from November to May, the island is Party Central in midsummer for retro hippies and nonstop clubbers. Dalt Vila, the medieval quarter of Eivissa, the capital, on the hill overlooking the town, is a UNESCO World Heritage Site.

2 Formentera. Day-trippers from Ibiza chill out on this (comparatively) quiet little island with long stretches of protected beach.

3 Mallorca. Palma, the island's capital, is a trove of art and architectural gems. The Tramuntana, in the northwest, is a region of forested peaks and steep sea cliffs that few landscapes in the world can match.

4 Menorca. Mahón, the capital city, commands the largest and deepest harbor in the Mediterranean. Many of the houses above the port date to the 18th-century occupation by the British Navy.

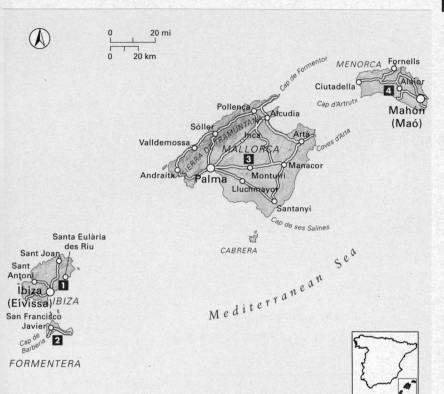

0   20 mi

0   20 km

Cap de Formentor

MENORCA Fornells

Ciutadella   Alaior

Cap d'Artrutx   **4**

Mahón
(Maó)

Pollença   Alcudia

Sóller   Inca   Artà

Valldemossa   *SIERRA DE TRAMUNTANA*   Coves d'Arta

MALLORCA

3

Andraitx   Manacor

Palma   Monturi

Lluchmayor

Santanyi

Cap de ses Salines

CABRERA

Santa Eulària
des Riu

Sant Joan

Sant
Antoni

Ibiza   **1**
(Eivissa)   *IBIZA*

San Francisco
Javier   **2**

Cap de
Barberia

FORMENTERA

Mediterranean Sea

EATING AND DRINKING WELL IN THE BALEARIC ISLANDS

Mediterranean islands should guarantee great seafood—and the Balearics deliver, with superb products from the crystalline waters surrounding the archipelago. Inland farms supply free-range beef, lamb, goat, and cheese.

Ibiza's fishermen head out into the tiny inlets for sea bass and bream, which are served in beach shacks celebrated for *bullit de peix* (fish casserole), *guisat* (fish and shellfish stew), and *burrida de ratjada* (ray with almonds). Beyond the great seafood, there are traditional farm dishes that include *sofrit pagès* (lamb or chicken with potatoes and red peppers), *botifarron* (blood sausage), and *rostit* (oven-roasted pork). Mallorcans love their *sopas de peix* (fish soup) and their *panades de peix* (fish-filled pastries), while Menorca's harbor restaurants are famous for *llagosta* (spiny lobster), grilled or served as part of a *caldereta*—a soupy stew. Interestingly, mayonnaise is widely believed to have been invented by the French in Mahón, Menorca, after they took the port from the British in 1756.

BALEARIC ALMONDS

Almonds are omnipresent in the Balearics, used in sweets as well as seafood recipes. Typically used in the *picada*—the ground nuts, spices, and herbs on the surface of a dish—almonds are essential to the Balearic economy. After a 19th-century phylloxera plague decimated Balearic vineyards, almond trees replaced vines and the almond crop became a staple.

VEGETABLES

The *tumbet mallorquin* is a classic Balearic dish made of layers of fried zucchini, bell peppers, potatoes, and eggplant with tomato sauce between each layer. It's served piping hot in individual earthenware casseroles.

SEAFOOD

There are several seafood dishes to look out for in the Balearics. Burrida de ratjada is boiled ray baked between layers of potato with almonds. The picada covering the ray during the baking includes almonds, garlic, egg, a slice of fried bread, parsley, salt, pepper, and olive oil. *Caldereta de llagosta* (spiny lobster soup) is a quintessential Menorcan staple sometimes said to be authentic only if the Menorcan spiny lobster is used. *Guisat de marisc* (shellfish stew) is an Ibiza stew of fish and shellfish cooked with a base of onions, potatoes, peppers, and olive oil. Nearly any seafood from the waters around Ibiza may well end up in this staple.

PORK

Rostit is baked in the oven with liver, eggs, bread, apples, and plums. *Sobrasada* (finely ground pork seasoned with sweet red paprika and stuffed in a sausage skin) is one of Mallorca's two most iconic food products (the other is the *ensaimada,* a sweet spiral pastry made with *saim,* or lard). Sobrasada originated in Italy but

became popular in Mallorca during the 16th century.

MENORCAN CHEESE

Mahón cheese is a Balearic trademark, and Menorca has a Denominación de Origen (D.O.), one of the 12 officially designated cheese-producing regions in Spain. The *curado* (fully cured) cheese is the tastiest.

WINE

With just 2,500 acres of vineyards (down from 75,000 in 1891), Mallorca's two D.O. wine regions—Binissalem, near Palma, and Pla i Llevant on the eastern side of the island—will likely remain under the radar to the rest of the world. While you're here, though, treat yourself to a Torre des Canonge white, a fresh, full, fruity wine, or a red Ribas de Cabrera from the oldest vineyard on the island, Hereus de Ribas in Binissalem, founded in 1711. Viticulture on Menorca went virtually extinct with the reversion of the island to Spain after its 18th-century British occupation, but since the last half of the 20th century, a handful of ambitious, serious winemakers—mainly in the area of Sant Lluís—have emerged to put the local product back on the map.

BEST BEACHES OF THE BALEARICS

When it comes to oceanfront property, the Balearic Islands have vast and varied resources: everything from long sweeps of beach on sheltered bays to tiny crescents of sand in rocky inlets and coves called calas—some so isolated you can reach them only by boat.

Not a few of the Balearic beaches, like their counterparts on the mainland coasts, have become destinations for communities of holiday chalets and retirement homes, usually called *urbanizaciónes,* their waterfronts lined with the inevitable shopping centers and pizza joints—skip these and head to the simpler and smaller beaches in or adjoining the Balearics' admirable number of nature reserves. Granted you'll find few or no services, and be warned that smaller beaches mean crowds in July and August, but these are the Balearics' best destinations for sun and sand. The local authorities protect these areas more rigorously, as a rule, than they do those on the mainland, and the beaches are gems.

BEACH AMENITIES

Be prepared: services at many of the smaller Balearic beaches are minimal or nonexistent. If you want a deck chair or something to eat or drink, bring it with you or make sure to ask around to see if your chosen secluded inlet has at least a *chiringuito*: a waterfront shack where the food is likely to feature what the fisherman pulled in that morning.

SES SALINES, IBIZA

Easy to reach from Eivissa, Ibiza's capital, this is one of the most popular beaches on the island, but the setting—in a protected natural park area—has been spared overdevelopment. The beach is relatively narrow, but the fine golden sand stretches more than a kilometer along the curve of Ibiza's southernmost bay. Two other great choices, on the east coast, are Cala Mastella, a tiny cove tucked away in a pine woods where a kiosk on the wharf serves the fresh catch of the day, and Cala Llenya, a family-friendly beach in a protected bay with shallow water.

BENIRRÁS, IBIZA

Benirrás is a small cove tucked away on Ibiza's northern coast backed by pine-clad hills. Known for its sunsets and laid-back vibe, it's popular with artists and hippies. Every Sunday at sunset, drummers gather to form ritualistic drum circles, one of the island's most popular events. On other days, it's a peaceful stretch of soft sand with calm water to spend a few hours.

PLATJES DE SES ILLETES, FORMENTERA

The closest beach to the port at La Sabina, where the ferries come in from Ibiza, Ses Illetes is Formentera's preeminent party scene: some 3 km (2 miles) of fine white sand with beach bars and

snack shacks, and Jet Skis and windsurfing gear for rent.

ES TRENC, MALLORCA

One of the few long beaches on the island that's been spared resort development, this pristine 3-km (2-mile) stretch of soft, white sand southeast of Palma, near Colònia Sant Jordi, is a favorite with nude bathers—who stay mainly at the west end—and day-trippers who arrive by boat. The water is crystal-clear blue and shallow for some distance out. The 10-km (6-mile) walk along the beach from Colònia Sant Jordi to the Cap Salines lighthouse is one of Mallorca's treasures.

CALA MACARELLA/CALA MACARETTA, MENORCA

This pair of beautiful, secluded coves edged with pines is about a 20-minute walk through the woods from the more developed beach at Santa Galdana, on Menorca's south coast. Macarella is the larger and busier of the two; Macaretta, a few minutes farther west along the path, is popular with nude bathers and boating parties. Cala Pregonda, on the north coast, is a lovely crescent cove with pine and tamarisk trees behind and dramatic rock formations at both ends.

Could anything go wrong in a destination that gets, on average, 300 days of sunshine a year? True, the water is only warm enough for a dip May–October, but the climate does seem to give the residents of the Balearics a sunny disposition year-round. They are a remarkably hospitable people, not merely because tourism accounts for such a large chunk of their economy, but because history and geography have combined to put them in the crossroads of so much Mediterranean trade and traffic.

The Balearic Islands were outposts, successively, of the Phoenician, Carthaginian, and Roman empires before the Moors invaded in 902 and took possession for some 300 years. In 1235, Jaume I of Aragón ousted the Moors, and the islands became part of the independent kingdom of Mallorca until 1343, when they returned to the Crown of Aragón under Pedro IV. With the marriage of Isabella of Castile to Ferdinand of Aragón in 1469, the Balearics were joined to a united Spain. Great Britain occupied Menorca in 1704, during the War of the Spanish Succession, to secure the superb natural harbor of Mahón as a naval base, but returned it to Spain in 1802 under the Treaty of Amiens.

During the Spanish Civil War, Menorca remained loyal to Spain's democratically elected Republican government, while Mallorca and Ibiza sided with Francisco Franco's insurgents. Mallorca then became a base for Italian air strikes against the Republican holdouts in Barcelona. This topic is still broached delicately on the islands; they remain fiercely independent of one another in many ways. Even Mahón and Ciutadella, at opposite ends of Menorca—all of 44 km (27 miles) apart—remain estranged over differences dating to that war.

The tourist boom, which began during Franco's regime (1939–75), turned great stretches of Mallorca's and Ibiza's coastlines into strips of high-rise hotels, fast-food restaurants, and discos.

Planning

When to Go

July and August are peak season in the Balearics; it's hot, and even the most secluded beaches are crowded. Weatherwise, May and October are ideal, with June and September just behind. Winter is quiet; it's too cold for the beach but fine for hiking, golfing, and exploring— though on Menorca the winter winds are notoriously fierce. The clubbing season on Ibiza begins in June.

Note: between November and March or April many hotels and restaurants are closed for their own vacations or seasonal repairs.

Planning Your Time

Most European visitors to the Balearics pick one island and stick with it, but you could easily see all three. Start in Mallorca with **Palma**. Begin early at the cathedral and explore the Llotja, the Almudaina palace, and the Plaça Major. The churches of Santa Eulàlia and Sant Francesc and the Arab Baths are a must. Staying overnight in Palma means you can sample the nightlife and have time to visit the museums.

Take the old train to **Sóller** and rent a car for a trip over the Sierra de Tramuntana to **Deià, Son Marroig,** and **Valldemossa.** The roads are twisty, so give yourself a full day. Spend the night in Sóller, and you can drive from there in less than an hour via **Lluc** and **Pollentia** to the Roman and Moorish ruins at **Alcúdia.**

By fast ferry it's just over three hours from Port d'Alcúdia to **Ciutadella,** on Menorca; the port, the **cathedral,** and the narrow streets of the old city can be explored in half a day. Make your way across the island to **Mahón,** and devote an afternoon to the highlights there.

From Mahón, you can take a 30-minute interisland flight to **Eivissa.** On Ibiza, plan a full day for the UNESCO World Heritage Site **Dalt Vila** and the shops of **Sa Penya,** and the better part of another for **Santa Gertrudis** and the north coast. If you've come to Ibiza to party, of course, time has no meaning.

Getting Here and Around

AIR TRAVEL

The easiest way to reach Mallorca, Menorca, and Ibiza is to fly. Each of the three islands is served by an international airport, all of them within 15–20 minutes by car or bus from their respective capital cities. There are daily domestic connections to each from Barcelona (about 50 minutes), Madrid, and Valencia: no-frills and charter operators fly to Eivissa, Palma, and Mahón from many European cities, especially during the summer. There are also flights between the islands. Book early in high season.

BIKE TRAVEL

The Balearic Islands—especially Ibiza and Formentera—are ideal for exploration by bicycle. Ibiza is relatively flat and easy to negotiate, though side roads can be in poor repair. Formentera is level, too, with bicycle lanes on all connecting roads. Parts of Mallorca are quite mountainous, with challenging climbs through spectacular scenery; along some country roads, there are designated bike lanes. Bicycles are easy to rent, and tourist offices have details of recommended routes. Menorca is relatively flat, with lots of roads that wander through pastureland and olive groves to small coves and inlets.

BOAT AND FERRY TRAVEL

From Barcelona: The Acciona Trasmediterránea and Balearia car ferries serve Ibiza, Mallorca, and Menorca from Barcelona. The most romantic way to get to the Balearic Islands is by overnight ferry from Barcelona to Palma, sailing (depending on the line and the season) between 11 and 11:30 pm; you can watch the lights of Barcelona sinking into the horizon for hours—and when you arrive in Palma, around 7 am, see the spires of the cathedral bathed in the morning sun. Overnight ferries have lounges and private cabins. Round-trip fares vary with the line, the season, and points of departure and destination but from Barcelona are from around €110 for lounge seats or €270 per person for a double cabin (tax included).

Faster ferries operated by Balearia, with passenger lounges only, speed from Barcelona to Eivissa (Ibiza), to Palma and Alcúdia (Mallorca), and to Mahón (Menorca). Depending on the destination, the trip takes between three and six hours.

From Valencia: Acciona Trasmediterránea ferries leave Valencia late at night for Ibiza, arriving early in the morning. Balearia fast ferries (no vehicles) leave Valencia for Sant Antoni on Ibiza in the late afternoon, making the crossing in about 2½ hours. Acciona Trasmediterránea and Balearia have services from Valencia to Mallorca, and Trasmediterránea also runs a service to Mahón (Menorca). Departure days and times vary with the season, with service more frequent in summer.

From Dénia: Balearia runs a daily three-hour fast ferry service for passengers and cars between Dénia and Ibiza, another between Dénia and Formentera, and a similar eight-hour service between Dénia and Palma on weekends.

Interisland: Daily fast ferries connect Ibiza and Palma; one-way fares run €66–€81, depending on the type of accommodations. The Pitiusa and Trasmapi lines offer frequent fast ferry and hydrofoil service between Ibiza and Formentera (€27 one-way, €40–€44 round-trip). Daily ferries connect Alcúdia (Mallorca) and Ciutadella (Menorca) in three to four hours, depending on the weather; a hydrofoil makes the journey in about an hour.

BOAT AND FERRY CONTACTS Acciona Trasmediterránea ☎ *902/454645* ⊕ *www. trasmediterranea.es/en.* **Balearia** ☎ *902/160180* ⊕ *www.balearia.com.* **Mediterranea Pitiusa** ☎ *609/741067 reservations, 971/314461 for Eivissa ticket office* ⊕ *www.mediterraneapitiusa. com.* **Trasmapi** ☎ *971/314433 information, 971/310711 for Eivissa ticket office* ⊕ *www.trasmapi.com.*

BUS TRAVEL

There is bus service on all the islands, though it's not extensive, especially on Formentera. ⇨ *Check each island's Getting Here and Around section for details.*

CAR TRAVEL

Ibiza is best explored by car or motor scooter: many of the beaches lie at the end of rough, unpaved roads. Tiny Formentera can almost be covered on foot, but renting a car or a scooter at La Sabina is a time saver. A car is essential if you want to beach-hop on Mallorca or Menorca and explore beyond the main cities and resorts.

TAXI TRAVEL

On Ibiza, taxis are available at the airport and in Eivissa, Figueretas, Santa Eulàlia, and Sant Antoni. On Formentera, there are taxis in La Sabina and Es Pujols. Legal taxis on Ibiza and Formentera are metered, but it's a good idea to get a rough estimate of the fare from the driver before you climb aboard. Taxis in Palma are metered. For trips beyond the city, charges are posted at the taxi stands. On Menorca, you can pick up a taxi at the airport or in Mahón or Ciutadella.

TRAIN TRAVEL

The public Ferrocarriles de Mallorca railroad track connects Palma and Inca, with stops at about half a dozen villages en route.

A journey on the privately owned Palma–Sóller railroad is a must: completed in 1912, it still uses the carriages from that era. The train trundles across the plain to Bunyola, then winds through tremendous mountain scenery to emerge high above Sóller. An ancient tram connects the Sóller terminus to Port de Sóller, leaving every hour on the hour 8–7; the Palma terminal is near the corner of the Plaça d'Espanya, on Calle Eusebio Estada next to the Inca train station.

Restaurants

On the Balearic Islands many restaurants tend to have short business seasons. This is less true of Mallorca, but on Menorca, Ibiza, and especially on Formentera, it might be May (or later) before the shutters are removed from that great seafood shack you've heard so much about. Really fine dining experiences are in short supply on the islands, although this tide is changing; in the popular beach resorts, the promenades can seem overrun with paella and pizza joints. Away from the water, however, there are exceptional meals to be had—and the seafood couldn't be any fresher.

Hotels

Many hotels on the islands include a continental or full buffet breakfast in the room rate.

IBIZA

Ibiza's high-rise resort hotels and holiday apartments are mainly in Sant Antoni, Talamanca, Ses Figueretes, and Playa d'en Bossa. Overbuilt Sant Antoni has little but its beach to recommend it. Playa d'en Bossa, close to Eivissa, is prettier but lies under a flight path. To get off the beaten track and into the island's largely pristine interior, look for *agroturismo* lodgings in Els Amunts (the Uplands) and in villages such as Santa Gertrudis or Sant Miquel de Balanzat.

FORMENTERA

If July and August are the only months you can visit, reserve well in advance. Accommodations on Formentera, the best of them on the south Platja de Mitjorn coast, tend to be small private properties converted to studio apartment complexes, rather than megahotels.

MALLORCA

Mallorca's large-scale resorts—more than 1,500 of them—are concentrated mainly on the southern coast and primarily serve the package-tour industry. Perhaps the best accommodations on the island are the number of grand old country estates and town houses that have been converted into boutique hotels, ranging from simple and relatively inexpensive agroturismos to stunning outposts of luxury.

MENORCA

Aside from a few hotels and hostals in Mahón and Ciutadella, almost all of Menorca's tourist lodgings are in beach resorts. As on the other islands, many of these are fully reserved by travel operators in the high season and often require a week's minimum stay, so it's generally most economical to book a package that combines airfare and accommodations. Or inquire at the tourist office about boutique and country hotels, especially in and around Sant Lluís.

Hotel reviews have been shortened. For full information, visit Fodors.com.

WHAT IT COSTS in Euros			
$	$$	$$$	$$$$
RESTAURANTS			
under €12	€12–€17	€18–€22	over €22
HOTELS			
under €90	€90–€125	€126–€180	over €180

Tours

Ibiza resorts run trips to neighboring beaches and to smaller islands. Trips from Ibiza to Formentera include an escorted bus tour. In Sant Antoni, there are a number of tour organizers to choose from.

Most Mallorca hotels and resorts offer guided tours. Typical itineraries are the Caves of Artà or Drac, on the east coast, including the nearby Auto Safari Park and an artificial-pearl factory in Manacor; the Chopin museum in the old monastery at Valldemossa, returning through the writers' and artists' village of Deià; the port of Sóller and the Arab gardens at Alfàbia; the Thursday market and leather factories in Inca; Port de Pollença; Cap de Formentor; and the northern beaches.

Excursions a Cabrera

BOAT TOURS | Several options are available for visits to Cabrera, from a three-hour sunset tour, including sparkling wine and dessert, to a daylong tour, with time to explore independently. One option for this is to take a self-guided tour of the island's underwater ecosystem—using a mask and snorkel with their own sound system; the recording explains the main points of interest as you swim. Boats generally depart from Colònia Sant Jordi, 47 km (29 miles) southeast of Palma. You can buy tickets on the dock at Carrer Babriel Roca or online. ✉ *Colònia de Sant Jordi* ☎ *971/649034* ⊕ *www.excursionscabrera.es* ✈ *From €35.*

Yellow Catamarans

BOAT TOURS | On Menorca, sightseeing trips on glass-bottom catamarans leave Mahón's harbor from the quayside near the Xoriguer gin factory. Departure times vary; check with the tourist information office on the Moll de Ponent, at the foot of the winding stairs from the old city to the harbor. ✉ *Moll de Llevant 12, Mahón* ☎ *971/352307, 639/676351 for reservations* ⊕ *www.yellowcatamarans.com* ✈ *€13.*

Ibiza

Tranquil countryside, secluded coves, and intimate luxury lodging to the north; sandy beaches and party venues by the score to the south; a capital crowned with a historic UNESCO World Heritage Site, and laid-back (and English-speaking) hospitality islandwide—Ibiza is a vacation destination not to be missed. Settled by the Carthaginians in the 5th century BC, Ibiza has seen successive waves of invasion and occupation, the latest of which began in the 1960s, when it became a tourist destination. With a full-time population of barely 140,000, it now gets some 2 million visitors a year. It's blessed with beaches—56 of them, by one count—and also has the world's largest nightclub. About a quarter of the people who live on Ibiza year-round are expats.

October through April, the pace of life here is decidedly slow, and many of the island's hotels and restaurants are closed. In the 1960s and early 1970s, Ibiza was discovered by sun-seeking hippies and eventually emerged as an icon of counterculture chic. Ibizans were—and still are—friendly and tolerant of their eccentric visitors. In the late 1980s and 1990s, club culture took over. Young ravers flocked here from all over the world to dance all night and pack the sands of built-up beach resorts like Sant Antoni. That party-hearty Ibiza is still alive and well, but a new wave of luxury rural hotels, offering oases of peace and privacy, with spas and high-end restaurants, marks the most recent transformation of the island into a venue for more upscale tourism. In fact, it is entirely feasible to spend time on Ibiza and not see any evidence of the clubbing and nightlife scene it is so famous for.

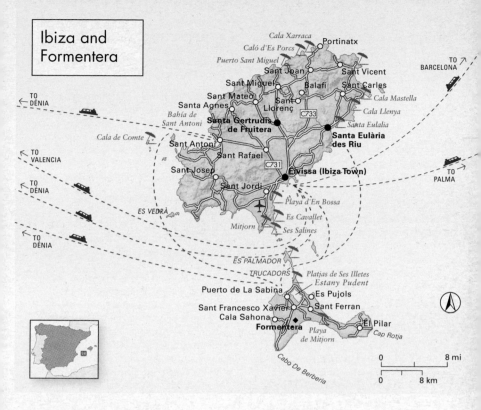

Ibiza and Formentera

GETTING HERE AND AROUND

Ibiza is a 55-minute flight or a nine-hour ferry ride from Barcelona.

Ibizabus serves the island. Buses run to Sant Antoni every 15–30 minutes 7:30 am–midnight (until 10:30 pm November–May) from the bus station on Avenida d'Isidor Macabich in Eivissa, and to Santa Eulàlia every half hour 6:50 am–11:30 pm Monday–Saturday (until 10:30 November–April), with late buses on Saturday in the summer party season at midnight, 1, and 2 am; Sunday service is hourly 7:30 am–11:30 pm (until 10:30 pm November–April). Buses to other parts of the island are less frequent, as is the cross-island bus between Sant Antoni and Santa Eulàlia.

On Ibiza, a six-lane divided highway connects the capital with the airport and Sant Antoni. Traffic circles and one-way streets make it a bit confusing to get in and out of Eivissa, but out in the countryside driving is easy and in most cases is the only way of getting to some of the island's smaller coves and beaches.

BUS CONTACT Ibizabus ☎ *971/340382, 600/482972 for Discobus* ⊕ *www.ibizabus.com.*

TAXI CONTACTS Cooperativa Limitada de Taxis de Sant Antoni ✉ *Carrer del Progrés, Sant Antoni* ☎ *971/343764.* **Radio-Taxi** ☎ *971/398483* ⊕ *www.taxi-eivissa.com.*

Eivissa (Ibiza Town)

Hedonistic and historic, Eivissa (Ibiza, in Castilian) is a city jam-packed with cafés, nightspots, and trendy shops;

looming over it are the massive stone walls of **Dalt Vila**—the medieval city declared a UNESCO World Heritage Site in 1999—and its Gothic cathedral. Squeezed between the north walls of the old city and the harbor is **Sa Penya,** a long labyrinth of stone-paved streets with some of the city's best offbeat shopping, snacking, and exploring.

TOURS
Dalt Vila Tours
SPECIAL-INTEREST | FAMILY | On nearly every Saturday evening, a 75-minute dramatized tour of Dalt Vila departs from the Portal de Ses Taules, at the foot of the walls. Three performers in period costume enact a legendary 15th-century love story as they move through the medieval scenes. Reservations are essential. The tour is in Spanish, though English speakers can be accommodated for groups of 10 or more. ⊠ *Portal de Ses Taules, Dalt Vila* ☎ *971/399232* ☎ *From €10.*

VISITOR INFORMATION
CONTACTS **Ibiza Tourist Office** ⊠ *La Cúria, Pl. de la Catedral s/n, Dalt Vila* ☎ *971/399232.*

 Sights

Bastió de Sant Bernat (*Bastion of St. Bernard*)
ARCHAEOLOGICAL SITE | From here, behind the cathedral, a promenade with sea views runs west to the bastions of Sant Jordi and Sant Jaume, past the **Castell**—a fortress formerly used as an army barracks. In 2007 work began to transform it into a luxury parador, but archaeological discoveries under the work site have delayed the reconstruction indefinitely. The promenade ends at the steps to the **Portal Nou** (New Gate). ⊠ *Eivissa.*

Cathedral
MUSEUM | Built on a site used for temples and other religious buildings since the time of the Phoenicians, Ibiza's cathedral has a Gothic tower and a baroque nave, and a small museum of religious art and artifacts. It was built in the 13th and 14th centuries and renovated in the 18th century. ⊠ *Pl. de la Catedral s/n, Dalt Vila* ☎ *971/312773* ☎ *Museum €1.*

Centre d'Interpretació Madina Yabisa
MUSEUM | A few steps from the cathedral, this small center has a fascinating collection of audiovisual materials and exhibits on the period when the Moors ruled the island. ⊠ *Carreró de la Soledat, 2, Dalt Vila* ☎ *971/392390* ☎ *€2* ⊘ *Closed Mon.*

Museu d'Art Contemporani
MUSEUM | Just inside the old city portal arch, this museum houses a collection of paintings, sculpture, and photography from 1959 to the present. The scope of the collection is international, but the emphasis is on artists who were born or lived in Ibiza during their careers. There isn't much explanatory material in English, however. There is also an underground archaeological site in the basement, some of which dates back as far as the 6th century BC. ⊠ *Ronda Narcís Puget s/n, Dalt Vila* ☎ *971/302723* ⊕ *www.mace.eivissa.es* ☎ *Free* ⊘ *Closed Mon.*

Sant Domingo
RELIGIOUS SITE | The roof of this 16th-century church is an irregular arrangement of tile domes. The nearby *ajuntament* (town hall) is housed in the church's former monastery. ⊠ *Carrer General Balanzat 6, Dalt Vila* ⊘ *Closed Mon.*

 Beaches

Es Cavellet Beach
BEACH—SIGHT | This wild stretch of white sand hugged by turquoise waves is popular with nudist sunbathers and can be reached on foot from Ses Salines beach (20-minute walk) or by car it's a 10-km (6-mile) drive from Eivissa, through the salt flats. Parts are backed by sand dunes, and on a clear day it serves up views of Eivissa and Formentera. El Chiringuito bar and restaurant, one of Ibiza's favorite waterfront beach bars, is

known for its relaxed vibe, good food and cocktails, and its lively season-opening and season-closing parties. **Amenities:** food and drink; parking (fee); showers. **Best for:** nudists; swimming. ✉ *Sant Josep de sa Talaia.*

Ses Salines

BEACH—SIGHT | Very much a place to see and be seen, the beach at Ses Salines is a mile-long narrow crescent of golden sand about 10 minutes' drive from Eivissa, in a wildlife conservation area. Trendy restaurants and bars, like the Jockey Club and Malibu, bring drinks to you on the sand and have DJs for the season, keeping the beat in the air all day long. The beach has different areas: glitterati in one zone, naturists in another, gay couples in another. There are no nearby shops, but the commercial vacuum is filled by vendors of bags, sunglasses, fruit drinks, and so on, who can be irritating. The sea is shallow, with a gradual drop-off, but on a windy day breakers are good enough to surf. **Amenities:** food and drink; lifeguards; parking (fee); showers; toilets; water sports. **Best for:** nudists; partiers; swimming; windsurfing. ✉ *Eivissa* ✥ *10 km (6 miles) west on E20 ring road from Eivissa toward airport, then south on PM802 local road to beach.*

🍴 Restaurants

Restaurante Jardín La Brasa

$$$$ | **MEDITERRANEAN** | A perennial favorite, La Brasa is tucked down a side street close to the walls of the Dalt Vila. Here you can dine on traditional Ibizan cuisine, such as barbecued entrecôte steak, lamb chops, or grilled squid, within a tree-filled courtyard lit by fairy lights and candles—a haven from the bustling surroundings. **Known for:** grilled meat; courtyard setting; reservations needed in high season. [$] *Average main: €25* ✉ *Carrer de Pere Sala 3, Eivissa* ☎ *971/301202* 🌐 *www.labrasaibiza.com.*

★ Sa Brisa Gastro Bar

$$$ | **CONTEMPORARY** | Time was, you could search in vain for innovative cuisine in Eivissa, but that changed with the opening of this stylish place. Enjoy a menu of tapas, salads, seafood, and meat dishes with imaginative Latin touches including delicious homemade *croquetas* (croquettes), shrimp quesadillas with guacamole, and Iberian pork. **Known for:** innovative dishes; stylish, modern interior; great location on the main promenade. [$] *Average main: €18* ✉ *Passeig Vara de Rey 15, Ibiza Nueva* ☎ *971/090649* 🌐 *www.sabrisagastrobar.com.*

🛏 Hotels

Boutique Hostal Salinas

$$$$ | **B&B/INN** | After several changes of ownership, this little bed-and-breakfast finally found its groove, and the location is ideal for beach addicts. **Pros:** minutes' walk to the beach; family-friendly; excellent buffet breakfast. **Cons:** small armoires; pricey in high season, with a five-day minimum stay May 20–October; rooms need soundproofing. [$] *Rooms from: €242* ✉ *Ctra. Sa Canal, Km 6, Ses Salinas, Sant Josep de sa Talaia* ☎ *971/308899, 647/912906* 🌐 *www.boutiquehostalsalinas.com* 🕒 *Closed late Oct.–Apr. (dates can vary)* 🔑 *11 rooms* 🍽 *Free Breakfast.*

Hostal Parque

$$$ | **HOTEL** | This is the top contender for a budget-friendly billet in the heart of town, and its location at the foot of Dalt Vila couldn't be better. **Pros:** good value; strategic location; views over the square. **Cons:** not much closet space; square in front of the hotel is noisy until the wee hours in high season; erratic service. [$] *Rooms from: €160* ✉ *Pl. del Parque 4, Dalt Vila* ☎ *971/301358* 🌐 *www.hostalparque.com* 🔑 *30 rooms* 🍽 *No meals.*

An evening stroll among the shops in Eivissa

La Ventana

$$$$ | **B&B/INN** | Inside the medieval walls, this intimate hillside hotel has fine views of the old town and the harbor from some of the rooms. **Pros:** historic setting; good value; roof terrace. **Cons:** rooms are small; lots of stairs to climb, especially if you want a room with a view; surroundings can be noisy until late. $ *Rooms from: €215* ⊠ *Sa Carrossa 13, Eivissa* ☎ *971/390857* ⊕ *www.laventanaibiza. com* ⇗ *12 rooms, 2 suites* ⏺ *No meals.*

Nightlife

Ibiza's discos are famous throughout Europe. Keep your eyes open during the day for free invitations handed out on the street—these can save you expensive entry fees. Between June and September, an all-night "Discobus" service (☎ *600/482972* ⊕ *www.discobus.es*) runs between Eivissa, Sant Antoni, Santa Eulàlia/Es Canar, Playa d'En Bossa, and the major party venues. The cost is €3 for one ride, €12 for a five-trip ticket.

BARS AND GATHERING PLACES
Calle Santa Creu

GATHERING PLACES | **FAMILY** | Hidden behind the walls of the Dalt Vila, this narrow lane is lined with bustling eateries. It's at its most atmospheric in the evening, when you can enjoy a candlelit dinner on the cobblestones as the world slowly saunters past. ⊠ *Dalt Vila.*

Carrer de la Mare de Déu (*Calle de la Virgen*)

GATHERING PLACES | Gay nightlife converges on this street in Sa Penya. ⊠ *Eivissa.*

Sunset Ashram

BARS/PUBS | There are many places to take in a spectacular sunset in Ibiza, but this one ranks as one of the White Isle's top spots. Set above a beautiful stretch of unspoiled coastline, boho Sunset Ashram mixes beach casual with ambient music, tasty cocktails, and unobstructed panoramic views of the golden hour. Dinner is also served here (reservations essential). ⊠ *Cala Conta s/n, San Agustin des Vedra* ☎ *661/347222* ⊕ *www.sunsetashram.com/en.*

DANCE CLUBS
Amnesia
DANCE CLUBS | This popular club in San Rafael opened in 1980 and it's still going strong, with several ample dance floors that throb to house and funk. Like most of the clubs on the island, it opens for the season at the end of May, with a gala bash. ☒ *Ctra. Eivissa–Sant Antoni, Km 5, San Rafael* ☎ *971/198041* ⊕ *www. amnesia.es.*

Keeper
DANCE CLUBS | Clubbers start the evening here, where there's no cover and the action starts at 11 pm. The indoor space at Keeper can get a bit cramped, but out on the terrace freedom reigns. ☒ *Marina Botafoch, Paseo Juan Carlos I s/n, Ibiza Nueva* ☎ *971/310509.*

Pacha
DANCE CLUBS | A young, international crowd gathers after 2 am at the flagship venue of this club empire, where each of the five rooms offers a different style, including techno, house music, R&B, and hip-hop. ☒ *Av. 8 de Agosto s/n, Eivissa* ☎ *971/318564* ⊕ *www.pacha.com.*

Privilege
DANCE CLUBS | Billing itself as the largest club in the world, the long-running center of Ibiza's nightlife has a giant dance floor, a swimming pool, and more than a dozen bars. ☒ *Urbanización San Rafael s/n, San Rafael* ☎ *971/198160.*

 Activities

BICYCLING
Extra Rent
BICYCLING | You can rent cars, Vespas, and scooters here. ☒ *Av. Santa Eulária des Riu 25–27, Eivissa* ☎ *971/191717, 900/506013 for info and booking* ⊕ *www. extrarent.com.*

BOATING
Coral Yachting
BOATING | You can charter all sorts of power craft, sailboats (small and large), and catamarans here, by the day or by the week, with or without a skipper. ☒ *Marina Botafoc, Local 323–324, Eivissa* ☎ *971/313926* ⊕ *www.coralyachting. com.*

IbizAzul Charters
BOATING | A variety of motorized craft and sailboats are available for rent here, and 40-foot live-aboard "Goleta" yachts are available for weekend or weeklong charters. ☒ *Ctra. Ibiza–Portinatx, Km 16.5, Sant Joan* ☎ *971/325264* ⊕ *www. ibizazul.com.*

HORSEBACK RIDING
Can Mayans
HORSEBACK RIDING | Hire horses here for rides along the coast and inland. Can Mayans has a riding school and a gentle touch with beginners. It's closed on Monday. ☒ *Ctra. Santa Gertrudis–Sant Lorenç, Km 3, San Lorenzo de Balafia* ☎ *690/922144* ⊕ *www.can-mayans.com.*

SCUBA DIVING
Active Dive
BOATING | Instruction and guided dives, as well as kayaking, parasailing, and boat rentals are available here. ☒ *Surf Lounge Ibiza, Calle des Molí 10, Sant Antoni* ☎ *679/333782* ⊕ *www.active-dive.com.*

Arenal Diving
SCUBA DIVING | Book lessons and dives here, from beginner level to advanced, with PADI-trained instructors and guides. ☒ *Av. Doctor Fleming 16, Sant Antoni* ☎ *617/280055* ⊕ *www.arenaldiving.com/ en.*

Sea Horse Scuba Diving Centre
SCUBA DIVING | A short distance from Sant Antoni, this aquatic center offers basic scuba training as well as excursions to spectacular nearby dive sites, especially the Cala d'Hort Marine Nature Reserve and the Pillars of Hercules underwater caves. ☒ *Edificio Yais 5, Calle Vizcaya 8, Playa Port des Torrent, Sant Josep de sa Talaia* ☎ *629/349499, 678/717211* ⊕ *www.seahorsedivingibiza.com.*

TENNIS

Ibiza Club de Campo

TENNIS | With six clay courts, seven paddle tennis courts, a 25-meter pool, and a gym, this is the best-equipped club on the island. Nonmembers can play tennis here for €8 per hour per person. ✉ *Ctra. Ibiza–Sant Josep, Km 2.5, Sant Josep de sa Talaia* ☎ *971/300088* 🌐 *www.ibizaclubdecampo.es.*

Shopping

Although the Sa Penya area of Eivissa still has a few designer boutiques, much of the area is now given over to the so-called hippie market, with stalls selling clothing and crafts of all sorts May–October. Browse Avenida Bartolomeu Rosselló and the main square of Dalt Vila for casual clothes and accessories.

Divina

CLOTHING | With no shortage of shops in Eivissa selling clothing in the classic white Ibiza style, Divina stands out for its range of clothes for kids and its modest selection of real Panama hats. ✉ *Pl. de la Vila 17, Dalt Vila* ☎ *971/300815.*

Enotecum

WINE/SPIRITS | This store has a good range of wines, including labels produced in the Balearics, and spirits. ✉ *Av. d'Isidoro Macabich 36, Eivissa* ☎ *971/399167.*

Santa Eulària des Riu

15 km (9 miles) northeast of Eivissa.

At the edge of this town on the island's eastern coast, to the right below the road, a Roman bridge crosses what some claim is the only permanent river in the Balearics (hence *des Riu,* or "of the river"). The town itself follows the curve of a long sandy beach, a few blocks deep with restaurants, shops, and vacation apartments. From here it's a 10-minute drive to Sant Carles and the open-air hippie market, Las Dalias, held there every Saturday morning. The popular Las Dalias night market offers shopping with live music, food, and drinks and runs from June to September, every Monday and Tuesday (and on Sunday in August).

GETTING HERE AND AROUND

By car, take the C733 from Eivissa. From May to October, buses run from Eivissa every half hour Monday–Saturday and every hour on Sunday. Service is less frequent the rest of the year.

VISITOR INFORMATION

CONTACTS Santa Eularia des Riu ✉ *Carrer Mariano Riquer Wallis 4* ☎ *971/330728* 🌐 *www.visitsantaeulalia.com.*

Restaurants

Mezzanotte

$$ | **ITALIAN** | This charming little portside Italian restaurant has just 12 tables inside, softly lit with candles and track lighting. The kitchen prides itself on hard-to-find fresh ingredients flown in from Italy. **Known for:** fresh Italian cuisine; sidewalk seating in summer; dried and salted mullet roe from Sardinia. [$] *Average main: €15* ✉ *Paseo de s'Alamera 18* ☎ *971/319498* 🕒 *Closed Jan. and Feb.*

Oleoteca Ses Escoles

$$ | **MEDITERRANEAN** | Chef-owner Miguel Llabres honed his craft at starred restaurants in Mallorca and opened here in 2014, to local acclaim. He keeps the menu short and focuses on garden-fresh seasonal vegetables and free-range local meats. **Known for:** free-range local meats; gourmet shop; Ibizan potato salad. [$] *Average main: €17* ✉ *Ctra. Ibiza-Portinatx, Km 9.8, Sant Joan de Labritja* ☎ *871/870229* 🌐 *www.canmiquelguasch.com* 🕒 *Closed Jan., and Mon. Oct.–Apr.*

Hotels

Can Curreu

$$$$ | **B&B/INN** | The traditional architecture here, reminiscent of a Greek island village, features a cluster of low buildings with thick whitewashed walls, the edges and corners gently rounded off—and each room has one of these buildings to itself, with a private patio artfully separated from its neighbors. **Pros:** friendly, efficient staff; horseback riding stables; luxurious spa. **Cons:** pricey; bit of a drive to the nearest beaches; patchy Wi-Fi. [$] *Rooms from: €295* ✉ *Ctra. de Sant Carles, Km 12* ☎ *971/335280* 🌐 *www.cancurreu.com* 🛏 *18 rooms* 🍴 *Free Breakfast.*

★ Can Gall

$$$$ | **B&B/INN** | Santi Marí Ferrer remade his family's *finca* (farmhouse), with its massive stone walls and native *savina* wood beams, into one of the island's friendliest and most comfortable country inns. **Pros:** family friendly; oasis of quiet; poolside pergola for events and yoga sessions. **Cons:** 15-minute drive to beaches; some private terraces a bit small; often booked out for weddings. [$] *Rooms from: €220* ✉ *Ctra. Sant Joan, Km 17.2, San Lorenzo de Balafia* ☎ *971/337031, 670/876054* 🌐 *www.agrocangall.com* ⏲ *Closed Nov.–Mar.* 🛏 *2 rooms, 9 suites* 🍴 *Free Breakfast.*

Hostal Yebisah

$$ | **HOTEL** | The longtime residents and civic boosters Toni and Tanya Molio, who are credited with the idea of dredging sand from the bay to create the beach at Santa Eulària, run this simple lodging on the little promenade in the heart of town. **Pros:** friendly service; ideal location; good value. **Cons:** bathrooms a bit cramped; minimal amenities; best rates only for minimum booking of four nights. [$] *Rooms from: €110* ✉ *Paseo S'Alamera 13* ☎ *971/330160* 🌐 *www.hostalyebisah.com* ⏲ *Closed Nov.–Apr.* 🛏 *26 rooms* 🍴 *No meals.*

Activities

BICYCLING

Kandani

BICYCLING | Bicycle rentals start at €15 for one day or €10 per day for weeklong rentals, and accessories are also available, as are guided cycling tours. ✉ *Carrer César Puget Riquer 27* ☎ *971/339264* 🌐 *www.kandani.es.*

DIVING

Punta Dive Ibiza

SCUBA DIVING | With three separate locations, this is one of the best-equipped and best-staffed diving centers on the island, for beginners and experienced PADI-qualified divers alike. ✉ *Playa Cala Martina s/n* ☎ *971/336726* 🌐 *www.puntadive.com.*

Subfari

SCUBA DIVING | This is one of the best places to come for diving off the north coast of the island. ✉ *Puerto de Portinatx s/n, Sant Joan de Labritja* ✣ *22 km (14 miles) north via C733* ☎ *971/337558, 677/466040* 🌐 *www.subfari.net.*

GOLF

Club de Golf Ibiza

GOLF | Ibiza's only golf club combines the 9 holes at the Club Roca Llisa resort complex (Course II) with the newer and more challenging 18-hole Course I nearby. Fairway maintenance on Course II leaves a bit to be desired. ✉ *Ctra. Jesús–Cala Llonga s/n* ☎ *971/196052* 🌐 *www.golfibiza.com* 🎫 *Course I, €98; Course II, €65* ⛳ *Course I: 18 holes, 6561 yards, par 72; Course II: 9 holes, 6265 yards (2 rounds), par 71.*

Santa Gertrudis de Fruitera

15 km (9 miles) north of Eivissa.

Blink and you miss it: that's true of most of the small towns in the island's interior and especially so of Santa Gertrudis. It's not much more than a bend in the road, but it's worth a look. The brick-paved town square is closed to vehicle traffic—perfect for the sidewalk cafés and boutique stores. From here, you are only a few minutes' drive from some of the island's flat-out best resort hotels and spas and the most beautiful secluded northern coves and beaches: **S'Illa des Bosc, Benirrás** (where they have drum circles to salute the setting sun), **S'Illot des Renclí, Portinatx,** and **Caló d'En Serra.** Artists and expats like it here: they've given the town an appeal that now makes for listings of half a million dollars or more for a modest two-bedroom house.

GETTING HERE AND AROUND
By car, take the C733 from Eivissa. From May to October, buses run from Eivissa every 90 minutes on weekdays, less frequently on weekends and the rest of the year.

 ## Restaurants

Can Caus
$$ | SPANISH | Ibiza might pride itself on its seafood, but there comes a time for meat and potatoes. When that time comes, take the 20-minute drive to the outskirts of Santa Gertrudis to this family-style roadside restaurant where you can feast on skewers of barbecued sobrasada, goat chops, and lamb kebabs. **Known for:** grilled meats; local vibe; Ibizan home cooking. Ⓢ *Average main: €16* ✉ *Ctra. Sant Miquel, Km 3.5, Santa Gertrudis* ☎ *971/197516* ⊕ *www.cancaus. com* ⊘ *Closed Mon. and in low season (varies).*

La Paloma
$$ | MEDITERRANEAN | Channeling that Ibiza-boho vibe, La Paloma feels like a refuge for artists and hippies, nestled amid the shady overhang of orange and lemon trees. The eclectic and concise menu uses freshly prepared seasonal produce, often featuring crunchy salads, Middle Eastern and North African–inspired dishes, fish, and homemade pasta (the chef is Italian and many of the

ingredients come directly from there). Ⓢ *Average main: €16* ✉ *Calle Can Pou 4, San Lorenzo de Balafia* ⊹ *7 km (4½ miles) from Santa Gertrudis de Fruitera* ☎ *971/325543* ⊕ *www.palomaibiza.com* ⊘ *Closed Nov. and Mon. Oct.–May.*

 ## Hotels

★ Cas Gasí
$$$$ | B&B/INN | A countryside setting on a hillside overlooking a valley makes this lovely late-19th-century manor house a quiet escape in a lively destination, with photo-ready views of Ibiza's only mountain (1,567-foot Sa Talaiassa). **Pros:** great views; attentive personal service; peace and quiet; free yoga classes in the morning. **Cons:** minimum stay required in July and August; not geared to families; very expensive. Ⓢ *Rooms from: €675* ✉ *Cami Vell a Sant Mateu s/n, Santa Gertrudis* ☎ *971/197700* ⊕ *www.casgasi.com* ⛵ *9 rooms, 1 suite* ⎷⊙⎸ *Free Breakfast.*

 ## Shopping

te Cuero
SHOES/LUGGAGE/LEATHER GOODS | This store specializes in hand-tooled leather bags and belts with great designer buckles, boots, and sandals. ✉ *Pl. de la Iglesia 6, Santa Gertrudis* ☎ *971/197100* ⊘ *Closed Sun. and Dec.–Mar.*

Formentera

Environmental protection laws shield much of Formentera, making it a calm respite from neighboring Ibiza's dance-until-you-drop madness. Though it does get crowded in the summer, the island's long white-sand beaches are among the finest in the Mediterranean; inland, you can explore quiet country roads by bicycle in relative solitude.

From the port at La Savina, it's only 3 km (2 miles) to Formentera's capital, **Sant**

Francesc Xavier, a few yards off the main road. There's an active hippie market in the small plaza in front of the church. At the main road, turn right toward Sant Ferran, 2 km (1 mile) away. Beyond Sant Ferran the road continues for 7 km (4 miles) along a narrow isthmus, staying slightly closer to the rougher northern side, where the waves and rocks keep yachts—and thus much of the tourist trade—away.

The plateau on the island's east side ends at the lighthouse **Faro de la Mola.** Nearby is a **monument to Jules Verne,** who set part of his 1877 novel *Hector Servadac* (published in English as *Off on a Comet*) in Formentera. The rocks around the lighthouse are carpeted with purple thyme and sea holly in spring and fall.

Back on the main road, turn right at Sant Ferran toward Es Pujols. The few hotels here are the closest Formentera comes to beach resorts, even if the beach is not the best. Beyond Es Pujols the road skirts **Estany Pudent,** one of two lagoons that almost enclose La Savina. Salt was once extracted from Pudent, hence its name, which means "stinking pond," although the pond now smells fine. At the northern tip of Pudent, a road to the right leads to a footpath that runs the length of **Trucadors,** a narrow sand spit. The long, windswept beaches here are excellent.

GETTING HERE AND AROUND
Formentera is a one-hour ferry ride from Ibiza or 25 minutes on the jet ferry. Balearia operates ferry services to Formentera from Ibiza and Dénia, the nearest landfall on the Spanish mainland.

On Ibiza, you can also take ferries from Santa Eulària and Sant Antoni to La Savina (1 hour, €23) as well as numerous ferries to the coves and calas on the east and west coasts of the island. Day-trippers can travel to Formentera for a few hours in the sun before heading back to Ibiza to plug into the nightlife.

A very limited bus service connects Formentera's villages, shrinking to one bus each way between San Francisco and Pilar on Saturday and disappearing altogether on Sunday and holidays.

FERRY CONTACTS Balearia ⊕ *www. balearia.com.*

TAXI CONTACTS Parada de Taxis La Savina ☎ *971/322002.*

VISITOR INFORMATION
CONTACTS Formentera Tourist Office ⊠ *Estación Maritima s/n, La Savina* ☎ *971/322057.*

 Beaches

★ **Platjas de Ses Illetes**
BEACH—SIGHT | The closest beach to the port at La Savina is an exquisitely beautiful string of dunes stretching to the tip of the Trucador Peninsula at Es Pau. Collectively called Ses Illetes, they form part of a national park and are consistently voted by travel site contributors as among the five best beaches in the world. Ibiza clubbers like to take the fast ferry over from Eivissa after a long night and chill out here, tapping the sun for the energy to party again; this sort of photosynthesis is especially popular with young Italian tourists. The water is fairly shallow and the meadows of seagrass in it shelter colorful varieties of small fish; the fairly constant breezes are good for windsurfing. Nude and topless sunbathing raises no eyebrows anywhere along the dunes. Be warned: there's no shade here at all, and rented umbrellas fetch premium prices. **Amenities:** food and drink; lifeguards; showers; toilets; water sports. **Best for:** nudists; snorkeling; swimming; windsurfing. ⊠ *La Savina* ⊹ *4 km (2½ miles) north of La Savina.*

Hotels

Can Aisha

$$$$ | **B&B/INN** | With only five apartments, this converted stone farmhouse can feel like a family compound, especially when everyone is gathered on the sundeck or around the communal barbecue. **Pros:** all apartments have private terraces; shops and restaurants nearby; kitchenettes with basic equipment. **Cons:** no kids and no pets; short season; often booked out. [$] *Rooms from: €350* ✉ *Venda de Sa Punta 3205, Es Pujols* ☎ *616/654982* 🌐 *www.canaisha.com* 🕒 *Closed roughly Oct.–May* 🛏 *5 apartments* 🍴 *Free Breakfast.*

Shopping

El Pilar is the chief crafts village here. Stores and workshops sell handmade items, including ceramics, jewelry, and leather goods. El Pilar's crafts market draws shoppers on Sunday and Wednesday from May to mid-October. May through mid-October, crafts are sold in the morning at the San Françesc Xavier market and in the evening in Es Pujols.

Activities

DIVING

Vell Marí

SCUBA DIVING | You can take diving courses Monday–Saturday here. ✉ *Puerto de la Savina, Marina de Formentera, Local 14–16, La Savina* ☎ *971/322105.*

Mallorca

Saddle-shape Mallorca is more than five times the size of Menorca or Ibiza. The Sierra de Tramuntana, a dramatic mountain range soaring to nearly 5,000 feet, runs the length of its northwest coast, and a ridge of hills borders the southeast shores; between the two lies a flat plain that in early spring becomes a sea of almond blossoms, the so-called snow of Mallorca. The island draws more than 10 million visitors a year, many of them bound for summer vacation packages in the coastal resorts. The beaches are beautiful, but save time for the charms of the northwest and the interior: caves, bird sanctuaries, monasteries and medieval towns, local museums, outdoor cafés, and village markets.

GETTING HERE AND AROUND

From Barcelona, Palma de Mallorca is a 50-minute flight, an 8-hour overnight ferry, or a 4½-hour catamaran journey.

If you're traveling by car, Mallorca's main roads are well surfaced, and a four-lane, 25-km (15-mile) motorway penetrates deep into the island between Palma and Inca. The Vía Cintura, an efficient beltway, rings Palma. For destinations in the north and west, follow the "Andratx" and "Oeste" signs on the beltway; for the south and east, follow the "Este" signs. Driving in the mountains that parallel the northwest coast and descend to a corniche (cliff-side road) is a different matter; you'll be slowed not only by the narrow winding roads but also by tremendous views, tourist traffic, and groups of cyclists.

VISITOR INFORMATION

CONTACTS Oficina de Turismo de Mallorca ✉ *Aeropuerto de Mallorca, Son Sant Joan s/n, Palma* ☎ *971/789556* 🌐 *www.infomallorca.net.*

Palma de Mallorca

If you look north of the cathedral (La Seu, or the seat of the bishopric, to Mallorcans) on a map of the city of Palma, you can see around the Plaça Santa Eulàlia a jumble of tiny streets that made up the earliest settlement. Farther out, a ring of wide boulevards traces the fortifications built by the Moors to defend the larger city that emerged by the 12th century. The zigzags mark the bastions that jutted

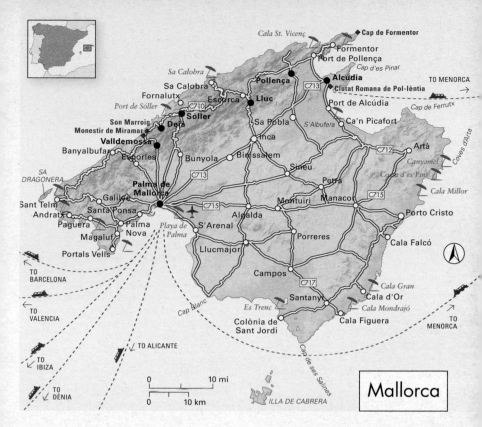

Map labels:
Cala St. Vicenç · Cap de Formentor · Formentor · Port de Pollença · Cap d'es Pinar · TO MENORCA · Sa Calobra · Pollença · Alcúdia · Ciutat Romana de Pol·lèntia · Sa Calobra · Fornalutx · Escorca · Lluc · Port de Sóller · Port de Alcúdia · Cap de Ferrutx · Son Marroig · Sóller · Sa Pobla · Can Picafort · Monestir de Miramar · Deià · S'Albufera · Valldemossa · Inca · Coves d'Arta · Banyalbufar · Esporles · Bunyola · Binissalem · Artà · C712 · Sineu · Canyamel · SA DRAGONERA · Palma de Mallorca · Cala d'es Pins · Petra · Cala Millor · Sant Telm · Galilea · Montuïri · Manacor · C715 · Andratx · Santa Ponsa · C715 · Algaida · Porto Cristo · Paguera · Palma Nova · S'Arenal · Cala Falcó · Magaluf · Playa de Palma · Porreres · Portals Vells · Llucmajor · TO BARCELONA · Campos · Cala Gran · TO VALENCIA · Cap Blanc · Es Trenc · Santanyí · Cala d'Or · Cala Mondrajó · TO MENORCA · Colònia de Sant Jordi · Cala Figuera · TO ALICANTE · TO IBIZA · Cap de ses Salines · TO DÉNIA · 0 10 mi · 0 10 km · ILLA DE CABRERA · **Mallorca**

out at regular intervals. By the end of the 19th century, most of the walls had been demolished; the only place where you can still see the massive defenses is at Ses Voltes, along the seafront west of the cathedral.

A *torrent* (streambed) used to run through the middle of the old city, dry for most of the year but often a raging flood in the rainy season. In the 17th century it was diverted to the east, along the moat that ran outside the city walls. Two of Palma's main arteries, La Rambla and the Passeig des Born, now follow the stream's natural course. The traditional evening paseo takes place on the bustling Born.

If you come to Palma by car, park in the garage beneath the Parc de la Mar (the ramp is just off the highway from the airport, as you reach the cathedral) and stroll along the park. Beside it run the huge bastions guarding the Palau Reial de l'Almudaina; the cathedral, golden and massive, rises beyond. Where you exit the garage, there's a **ceramic mural** by the late Catalan artist and Mallorca resident Joan Miró, facing the cathedral across the pool that runs the length of the park.

If you begin early enough, a walk along the ramparts at Ses Voltes from the mirador beside the cathedral is spectacular. The first rays of the sun turn the upper pinnacles of La Seu bright gold and then begin to work their way down the sandstone walls. From the Parc de la Mar, follow Avinguda Antoni Maura past the steps to the palace. Just below the Plaça de la Reina, where the **Passeig des Born** begins, turn left on Carrer de la Boteria into the Plaça de la Llotja. (If the

Llotja itself is open, don't miss a chance to visit—it's the Mediterranean's finest Gothic-style civic building.) From there stroll through the Plaça Drassana to the **Museu d'Es Baluard,** at the end of Carrer Sant Pere. Retrace your steps to Avinguda Antoni Maura. Walk up the Passeig des Born to Plaça Joan Carles I, then right on Avenida de La Unió.

GETTING HERE AND AROUND

Palma's Empresa Municipal de Transports (EMT) runs 65 bus lines and a tourist train in and around the Mallorcan capital. Most buses leave from the Intermodal station, next to the Inca railroad terminus on the Plaça d'Espanya; city buses leave from the ground floor, while intercity buses leave from the underground level. The tourist office on the Plaça d'Espanya has schedules. Bus No. 1 connects the airport with the city center and the port; No. 2 circumnavigates the historic city center; Nos. 3 and 20 connect the city center with the Porto Pi commercial center; No. 46 goes to the Fundació Pilar i Joan Miró, and No. 21 connects S'Arenal with the airport. The fare for a single local ride is €1.50; to the airport it's €3.

You can hire a horse-drawn carriage with driver at the bottom of the Born, and also on Avinguda Antonio Maura, in the nearby cathedral square, and on the Plaça d'Espanya, at the side farthest from the train station. A tour of the city costs €30 for a half hour, €50 for an hour. ■TIP→ **Haggle firmly, and the driver might come down a bit off the posted fare.**

Boats from Palma to neighboring beach resorts leave from the jetty opposite the Auditorium, on the Passeig Marítim. The tourist office has a schedule.

BUS INFORMATION Empresa Municipal de Transports ⊠ *Calle Josep Anselm Clavé 5* ☎ *971/214444* ⊕ *www.emtpalma.es.*

BUS STATION Estació Intermodal ⊠ *Pl. d'Espanya s/n* ☎ *971/177777* ⊕ *www. tib.org.*

TAXI INFORMATION Radio-Taxi Ciutat ⊠ *Francesc Sancho 7* ☎ *971/201212* ⊕ *www.radiotaxiciutat.com.*

VISITOR INFORMATION

CONTACTS Oficine d'Informació Turística ⊠ *Pl. de la Reina 2* ☎ *971/173990* ⊕ *www.infomallorca.net.*

TOURS

City Sightseeing

SELF-GUIDED | The open-top City Sightseeing bus leaves from behind the Palau de la Aludaina every 20–25 minutes starting at 9:30 am and makes 16 stops throughout the town, including Plaça de la Reina, the Passeig Marítim, and the Castell de Bellver. Tickets are valid for 24 or 48 hours, and you can get on and off as many times as you wish. All Palma tourist offices have details. ⊠ *Av. Antoni Maura 24* ⊕ *www.city-ss.es/en/destination/palma* ☎ *From €18.*

Sights

Ajuntament (*Town Hall*)

BUILDING | Along Carrer Colom is the 17th-century ajuntament. Stop in to see the collection of *gigantes,* the huge painted and costumed mannequins paraded through the streets during festivals, which are on display in the lobby. The olive tree on the right side of the square is one of Mallorca's so-called *olivos milenarios*—purported to be more than 1,000 years old. The adjacent building is the Palau del Consell, the headquarters of the island's government, a late-19th-century building on the site of a medieval prison. The *palau* (palace) has its own collection of gigantes and an impressive stained-glass window over the ornate stone staircase; visits inside can be arranged by appointment (*visites@conselldemallorca.net*). ⊠ *Pl. Cort 1, Centro* ☎ *971/225900* ⊕ *www. palmademallorca.es.*

Cathedral of Palma de Mallorca

Banys Arabs (*Arab Baths*)

ARCHAEOLOGICAL SITE | One of Palma's oldest monuments, the 10th-century public bathhouse has a wonderful walled garden of palms and lemon trees. In its day, it was not merely a place to bathe but a social institution where you could soak, relax, and gossip with your neighbors. ✉ *Carrer Can Serra 7, Centro* ☎ *637/046534* 🖾 *€3.*

Bodegas José Ferrer

WINERY/DISTILLERY | One of the largest of Mallorca's wineries, Bodegas José Ferrer can be visited for tastings. Ferrer wines consistently do well at international competitions in France and Germany; Pedra de Binissalem, their ecological red, is a subtle blend of Cabernet Sauvignon and the local varietal Manto Negro—well worth a try. ✉ *Carrer del Conquistador 103, Binissalem* ☎ *971/100100* ⊕ *www. vinosferrer.com* 🖾 *From €11* ⊙ *Closed Sun. Nov.–Feb.*

Caixa Forum (*Grand Hotel*)

BUILDING | Built between 1901 and 1903 by Luis Domènech i Montaner, originator of Barcelona's Palau de la Música Catalana, this former hotel has an alabaster facade sculpted like a wedding cake, with floral motifs, angelic heads, and coats of arms. The original interiors are gone, however. The building is owned and used by the Fundació La Caixa, a cultural and social organization funded by the region's largest bank. Don't miss the permanent exhibit of paintings by the Mallorcan impressionist Hermenegildo Anglada Camarasa. ✉ *Pl. Weyler 3, Centro* ☎ *971/178500, 971/178512* ⊕ *obrasocial.lacaixa.es/nuestroscentros/ caixaforumpalma_es.html* 🖾 *€4* ⊙ *Closed Dec. 25–Jan. 6.*

Can Corbella

BUILDING | On the corner of Carrer de Jaume II is this gem of Palma's early Moderniste architecture, designed in the 1890s by Nicolás Lliteras. ✉ *Pl. Cort, Centro.*

Can Forteza Rei

BUILDING | Designed by Luis Forteza Rei in 1909, this Art Nouveau delight has twisted wrought-iron railings and surfaces inlaid with bits of polychrome tile which are signature touches of Antoni Gaudí and his contemporaries. A wonderful carved stone face in a painful grimace, flanked by dragons, ironically frames the stained-glass windows of a third-floor dental clinic. There's a chocolate shop on the ground floor. ⊠ *Pl. Marqués Palmer 1, Centro.*

Castell de Bellver (*Bellver Castle*)

CASTLE/PALACE | Overlooking the city and the bay from a hillside, the castle was built at the beginning of the 14th century in Gothic style but with a circular design—the only one of its kind in Spain. It houses an archaeological museum of the history of Mallorca and a small collection of classical sculpture. The Bus Turístic 50 and the EMT municipal buses Nos. 3, 20, and 46 all stop a 20-minute walk from the entrance. On Thursday evenings in July, from 9:30, there are classical music concerts in the courtyard, performed by the Ciutat de Palma Symphony Orchestra. ⊠ *Carrer de Camilo José Cela s/n* ☎ *971/735065, 971/225900 concerts box office* ⊕ *castelldebellver. palmademallorca.es* ☒ *€4 (free Sun.)* ⊘ *Closed Mon.*

★ Catedral de Majorca (*La Seu*)

RELIGIOUS SITE | Palma's cathedral is an architectural wonder that took almost 400 years to build. Begun in 1230, the wide expanse of the nave is supported by 14 70-foot-tall columns that fan out at the top like palm trees. The nave is dominated by an immense rose window, 40 feet in diameter, dating to 1370. Over the main altar (consecrated in 1346) is the surrealistic *baldoquí* (baldachin) by Antoni Gaudí, completed in 1912. This enormous canopy, with lamps suspended from it like elements of a mobile, rises to a Crucifixion scene at the top. To the right, in the Chapel of the Santísimo, is an equally remarkable 2007 work by the sculptor Miquel Barceló: a painted ceramic tableau covering the walls like a skin. ■TIP➜ **From April through October you can take a guided tour of the bell tower and the cathedral's terraces overlooking panoramic views of the city. Reservations must be made in advance on the website.** ⊠ *Pl. Almoina s/n, Centro* ☎ *971/723130, 902/022445* ⊕ *www.catedraldemallorca. org* ☒ *€8.*

★ Museu d'Es Baluard (*Museum of Modern and Contemporary Art of Palma*)

MUSEUM | West of the city center, this museum rises on a long-neglected archaeological site, parts of which date back to the 12th century. The building itself is an outstanding convergence of old and new: the exhibition space uses the surviving 16th-century perimeter walls of the fortified city, including a stone courtyard facing the sea and a promenade along the ramparts. There are three floors of galleries, and the collection includes work by Miró, Picasso, and Antoni Tàpies, among other major artists. The courtyard café–terrace Es Baluard (no dinner Sunday–Wednesday October–mid-June) affords a fine view of the marina. To get here, take the narrow Carrer de Sant Pere through the old fishermen's quarter, from Plaça de la Drassana. ⊠ *Pl. Porta de Santa Catalina 10* ☎ *971/908200* ⊕ *www. esbaluard.org/en* ☒ *€6* ⊘ *Closed Mon.*

Museu Fundació Pilar y Joan Miró (*Pilar and Joan Miró Foundation Museum*)

MUSEUM | The permanent collection here includes a great many drawings and studies by the Catalan artist, who spent his last years on Mallorca, but it exhibits far fewer finished paintings and sculptures than the Fundació Miró in Barcelona. While the exhibits are fairly limited, the setting and views of Palma alone are worth taking the detour. ⊠ *Carrer Saridakis 29* ☎ *971/701420* ⊕ *www. miromallorca.com* ☒ *€8 (free Sat. after 3)* ⊘ *Closed Mon.*

Illa de Cabrera

Off the south coast of Mallorca, this verdant isle is one of the last unspoiled places in the Mediterranean—the largest of the 19 islands that make up the Cabrera Archipelago. To protect its dramatic landscape, varied wildlife, and lush vegetation, it was declared a national park in 1991. Throughout its history, Cabrera has had its share of visitors, from the Romans to the Arabs. Today, the only intact historical remains are those of a 14th-century castle overlooking the harbor. Tours are operated daily by the **Marcabrera** company. Boats depart from Colònia Sant Jordi, 47 km (29 miles) southeast of Palma. Full-day trips, starting at 10 and returning at 3, with a stop to swim or snorkel in the mysterious Cueva Azul (Blue Cave), start from €450; two-hour excursions by speedboat, leaving three times a day, between 1 and 5, are €49. ⊕ www.marcabrera.com

Museu Fundación Juan March
MUSEUM | A few steps from the north archway of the Plaça Major is the Museu Fundación Juan March. This fine little museum was established to display what had been a private collection of modern Spanish art. The building itself was a sumptuous private home built in the 18th century. The second and third floors were redesigned to accommodate a series of small galleries, with one or two works at most—by Pablo Picasso, Joan Miró, Juan Gris, Salvador Dalí, Antoni Tàpies, and Miquel Barceló, among others—on each wall. ⊠ *Sant Miquel 11, Centro* ☎ *971/713515* ⊕ *www.march.es/arte/palma* 🎟 *Free* ⊙ *Closed Sun.*

Palau Reial de l'Almudaina (*Royal Palace of La Almudaina*)
CASTLE/PALACE | Opposite Palma's cathedral, this palace was originally an Arab citadel, then became the residence of the ruling house during the Middle Ages. It's now a military headquarters and the king's official residence when he is in Mallorca. Guided tours generally depart hourly during open hours. If you want to explore on your own, audio guides are available. ■ TIP➜ **Try to catch the changing of the Honor Guard ceremony, which takes place in front of the palace at noon on the last Saturday of the month (except July and August).** ⊠ *Carrer Palau Reial s/n, Centro* ☎ *971/214134* ⊕ *www.patrimonionacional.es/real-sitio/palacio-real-de-la-almudaina* 🎟 *€7* ⊙ *Closed Mon.*

Passeig des Born
PROMENADE | While it's known as one of the best streets in Palma to hit the shops, this tree-lined promenade is also a favored place to *pasear* (stroll), lined with palatial-style stone residences (most of which have now been converted into hotels and shops) and busy café-terraces. Bar Bosch, straddling Passeig des Born and Plaza Rei Joan Carles I, has been a key gathering point for locals since 1936. ⊠ *Palma.*

Plaça Major
PLAZA | A crafts market fills this elegant neoclassical space 10–2 on Friday and Saturday (Monday–Saturday in July and August). Until 1823, this was the local headquarters of the Inquisition. A flight of steps on the east side of the Plaça Major leads down to **Las Ramblas,** a pleasant promenade lined with flower stalls. ⊠ *Centro.*

Sa Llotja (*Exchange*)
BUILDING | On the seafront west of the Plaça de la Reina, the 16th-century Llotja connects via an interior courtyard to the **Consolat de Mar** (Maritime Consulate). With its decorative turrets, pointed

battlements, fluted pillars, and Gothic stained-glass windows—part fortress, part church—it attests to the wealth Mallorca achieved in its heyday as a Mediterranean trading power. The interior (the Merchants' Chamber) often hosts free art exhibitions. ⊠ Pl. Llotja 5 ✉ Free ⊘ Closed Mon.

Sant Francesc

RELIGIOUS SITE | The 13th-century monastery church of Sant Francesc was established by Jaume II when his eldest son took monastic orders and gave up rights to the throne. Fra Junípero Serra, the missionary who founded San Francisco, California, was later educated here; his statue stands to the left of the main entrance. The basilica houses the tomb of eminent 13th-century scholar Ramón Llull. The cloisters (enter via the side door, on the right) are especially beautiful and peaceful. The €5 entrance fee includes entrance to five other churches. ⊠ Pl. Sant Francesc 7, Centro ☎ 971/712695 ✉ €5 ⊘ Closed Sun.

Santa Eulàlia

RELIGIOUS SITE | Carrer de la Cadena leads to this imposing Gothic church, where, in 1435, 200 Jews were forced to convert to Christianity after their rabbis were threatened with being burned at the stake. ⊠ Pl. Santa Eulalia 2, Centro ☎ 971/714625 ✉ Free.

Teatre Principal

ARTS VENUE | Take time to appreciate the neoclassical symmetry of this theater, Palma's chief venue for classical music. The opera season here usually runs mid-March–June. ⊠ Carrer de la Riera 2, Centro ☎ 971/219700 information, 971/219696 tickets ⊕ www.teatreprincipal.com ✉ Performances vary.

🏖 Beaches

Es Trenc

BEACH—SIGHT | FAMILY | Even though it's nearly an hour's drive from Palma, this pristine 2-km (1-mile) stretch of fine

Cuevas del Drach

Mallorca's "Dragon Caves" comprise four large caves that reach a depth of 80 feet below the surface, one of the largest underground lakes in the world, and a dazzling array of stalagmites and stalactites that form identifiable shapes such as the Virgin of the Cave, the Buddha, and the Valley of Montserrat. The hour-long tour includes a visit to the caves, a boat trip (optional) across Lake Martel, and a short classical music concert performed on the lake by musicians in an illuminated boat. ⊕ www.cuevasdeldrach.com/en

white sand on Mallorca's southern coast, much longer than it is wide, is one of the most popular beaches on the island—arrive late on a Saturday or Sunday in summer, and you'll be hard-pressed to find a space to stretch out. At times the water can be a bit choppy, and there are occasional patches of seaweed—but otherwise the clear, clean water slopes off gently from the shore for some 30 feet, making it ideal for families with younger kids. Es Trenc is in a protected natural area free of hotels and other developments, which makes for good bird-watching. Naturists lay their claim to part of the beach's eastern end. **Amenities:** food and drink; lifeguards; parking (fee); toilets. **Best for:** nudists; partiers; swimming; walking. ⊠ MA6040, Colònia de Sant Jordi ⊕ 10 km (6 miles) south of Campos, 6½ km (4 miles) east of Colònia Sant Jordi.

🍴 Restaurants

Café La Lonja (Sa Llotja)

$ | TAPAS | A great spot for hot chocolate or a unique tea or coffee, this classic establishment in the old fishermen's neighborhood has a young vibe that goes well with the style of the place. Both the sunny terrace in front of the Llotja and the bar inside are excellent places for drinks and sandwiches. **Known for:** quick pit stop; terrace with views of the Llotja; coffee and snacks. $ Average main: €9 ✉ Carrer Sa Lonja del Mar 2 ☎ 971/722799.

Ca'n Joan de S'aigo

$ | CAFÉ | This café, on a side street behind the church of Sant Francesc, is one of Palma's venerable institutions, in business since 1700. Drop in for coffee or hot chocolate with an *ensaimada crema*—a spiral-shape Mallorcan pastry with a rich cream-cheese filling. $ Average main: €8 ✉ Carrer de Ca'n Sanç 10, Centro ☎ 971/710759.

Forn de Sant Joan

$$$$ | MEDITERRANEAN | This former bakery turned restaurant (*forn* means "bakery" or "oven" in Mallorquin) dates back to the 19th century and features exposed brick walls, colorful floor tiles, modern art on the walls, and picture-perfect Mediterranean-style tapas. There's a cocktail bar on the ground floor that overlooks the street, and one of the three distinct dining areas is the area where bread dough was once prepared. **Known for:** former 19th-century bakery; elevated tapas and Mediterranean dishes; cocktail bar. $ Average main: €25 ✉ Carrer de Sant Joan 4 ☎ 971/728422 ⊕ www.forndesantjoan.com.

La Bóveda

$$ | TAPAS | This popular restaurant serves huge, tasty portions of tapas and inexpensive platters such as chicken or ham croquetas, grilled cod, garlic shrimp, and *revueltos de ajos con morcilla* (scrambled eggs with garlic and black sausage).

Within hailing distance of the Llotja, the tables in the back are always at a premium (they're cooler on summer days), but there's additional seating at the counter or on stools around upended wine barrels. **Known for:** down-to-earth portions of traditional tapas; ham croquettes; local vibe. $ Average main: €14 ✉ Carrer de la Botería 3 ☎ 971/714863 ⏱ Closed Sun.

★ Marc Fosh

$$$$ | CONTEMPORARY | While Palma suffers no dearth of rough-and-ready eateries, Marc Fosh has little or no competition in the fine-dining category. The renowned chef Marc Fosh offers several tasting menus, which are executed superbly, with the best local seasonal produce transformed into remarkable dishes with surprising twists. **Known for:** award-winning cuisine; tasting menus based on local produce; good-value weekday lunch menu. $ Average main: €89 ✉ Carrer de la Missió 7A ☎ 971/720114 ⊕ www.simplyfosh.com/en.

🛏 Hotels

★ Cap Rocat

$$$$ | HOTEL | What was once a 19th-century military fortress on the southern flank of the Bay of Palma has been converted into one of Mallorca's—and arguably Europe's—most distinctive hotels. **Pros:** stunning backdrop; superb cuisine; impeccable service. **Cons:** isolated from the bustle—and nightlife; lacks a sandy beach; sky-high prices. $ Rooms from: €500 ✉ Ctra. de Enderrocat s/n, Cala Blava ☎ 971/747878 ⊕ www.caprocat.com ⏱ Closed Nov.–mid-Mar. ⟿ 30 rooms ⧓ Free Breakfast.

Dalt Murada

$$$ | B&B/INN | In an ideal location in the old part of Palma, a minute's walk to the cathedral, this town house, dating back to the 15th century, was the Sancho Moragues home until 2001, when the family opened it as a hotel. **Pros:** rooftop terrace with views; modern touches in historic

home; steps from the cathedral. **Cons:** thin walls; no parking; erratic service. $ *Rooms from: €160* ⊠ *Carrer Almudaina 6A, Centro* ☎ *971/425300* ⊕ *www.dalt-murada.com* ⊙ *Closed Nov.–Apr.* ⇗ *23 rooms* ⊚ *No meals.*

Hostal Apuntadores

$$ | **HOTEL** | A favorite among budget travelers, this lodging in the heart of the old town, within strolling distance of the bustling Passeig des Born, has a rooftop terrace with what is arguably the city's best view—overlooking the cathedral and the sea. **Pros:** good value; rooms have a/c and heat; some rooms have balconies. **Cons:** can be noisy; the cheapest rooms share bathrooms; basic decor. $ *Rooms from: €119* ⊠ *Carrer Apuntadores 8, Centro* ☎ *971/713491* ⊕ *www.apuntado-reshostal.com* ⇗ *28 rooms* ⊚ *No meals.*

Hotel Almudaina

$$$ | **HOTEL** | Business travelers from the mainland favor this comfortable, central hotel, and it's an excellent choice for vacationers as well. **Pros:** steps from Palma's upscale shopping; courteous, efficient service; rooftop terrace and bar. **Cons:** public spaces are small; limited parking; rooms directly below the Sky Bar can be noisy. $ *Rooms from: €150* ⊠ *Av. Jaume III 9, Centro* ☎ *971/727340* ⊕ *www.hotelalmudaina.com* ⇗ *70 rooms* ⊚ *Free Breakfast.*

★ Hotel Born

$$$ | **HOTEL** | Romanesque arches and a giant palm tree spectacularly cover the central courtyard and reception area of this shabby-chic hotel, which occupies the former mansion of a noble Mallorcan family. **Pros:** convenient for sightseeing; romantic courtyard floodlit at night; good value. **Cons:** small rooms on the street side; poor soundproofing; mediocre breakfast. $ *Rooms from: €158* ⊠ *Carrer Sant Jaume 3* ☎ *971/712942* ⊕ *www. hotelborn.com* ⇗ *30 rooms* ⊚ *Free Breakfast.*

Palau Sa Font

$$$$ | **B&B/INN** | Warm Mediterranean tones and crisp, clean lines give this boutique hotel in the center of the shopping district an atmosphere very different from anything else in the city. **Pros:** buffet breakfast until 11; helpful English-speaking staff; 16th-century former Episcopal palace. **Cons:** pool is small; good soundproofing, but area can be noisy in summer; rooms a bit small for the price. $ *Rooms from: €189* ⊠ *Carrer Apuntadores 38* ☎ *971/712277* ⊕ *www.palausa-font.com* ⊙ *Closed early-Jan.–mid-Feb.* ⇗ *19 rooms* ⊚ *Free Breakfast.*

⊙ Nightlife

Mallorca's nightlife is never hard to find. Many of the hot spots are concentrated 6 km (4 miles) west of Palma at **Punta Portals,** in Portals Nous, where the royal yacht is moored when former king Juan Carlos I comes to Mallorca in early August for the Copa del Rey international regatta. Another major area is **Avinguda Gabriel Roca.** This section of the Passeig Marítim holds many taverns, pubs, and clubs. The network of streets in the old town, around Carrer Apuntadores, is also prime barhopping territory.

BARS AND CAFÉS

★ Bar Abaco

BARS/PUBS | The over-the-top baroque exuberance of this bar sets it far apart from its setting in an otherwise unfunky, old neighborhood. There are urns and baskets of fresh flowers and fruit tumbling out on to the floor, stone pillars and vaulted ceilings, tall candles, and ambient opera music. Be warned: Abaco's signature cocktails are pricey. It's open 8 pm–1 am Monday–Thursday, and until 3 am on Friday and Saturday. ⊠ *Carrer de Sant Joan 1* ☎ *971/714939* ⊕ *www.bar-abaco.es.*

Carrer Apuntadores

BARS/PUBS | On the west side of Passeig des Born in the old town, this street is lined with casual bars and cafés that appeal to night owls in their twenties and thirties. On the weekend, you can often come across impromptu live rock and pop acts performed on small stages. ⊠ *Palma.*

Plaça de la Llotja
BARS/PUBS | This square, along with the surrounding streets, is the place to go for *copas* (drinking, tapas sampling, and general carousing). ⊠ *Palma.*

Wineing
TAPAS BARS | Tucked down Calle Apuntadores, Wineing offers a unique way to try wines from across the island and beyond. Sample wines via a card-operated system that dispenses small tastings (or larger glasses, if you feel inclined). There is also a menu of tapas, cheese platters, and grilled meats to share. ⊠ *Calle Apuntadores 24* ☎ *971/214011* ⊕ *www.wineing.es.*

DANCE CLUBS
Tito's
DANCE CLUBS | Outdoor elevators transport you from the street to the dance floor at the sleek and futuristic Tito's. ⊠ *Passeig Marítim, Av. Gabriel Roca 31* ☎ *971/730017* ⊕ *www.titosmallorca.com.*

MUSIC CLUBS
Jazz Voyeur Club
MUSIC CLUBS | Some of Palma's best jazz combos—and the occasional rock group—play this small, smoky club in the old port-side neighborhood. There's music every night, and it keeps going until 3 am on Friday and Saturday. ⊠ *Carrera Apuntadores 5* ☎ *971/720780* ⊕ *www.jazzvoyeurclub.com.*

 Activities

BALLOONING
Majorca Balloons
BALLOONING | For spectacular views of the island, float up in a hot-air balloon, which lifts off daily April–October, weather permitting, at sunrise and sunset. Call for a reservation: the office is open 10–1

and 5–8. Feeling romantic? The company offers moonlight flights for two, for a mere €600. ⊠ *C. Farallo 4, Manacor* ☎ *971/596969* ⊕ *www.mallorcaballoons. com* ☒ *1-hr flights €165 per person.*

BICYCLING
With long, flat stretches and heart-pounding climbs, Mallorca's 675 km (420 miles) of rural roads adapted for cycling make the sport the most popular on the island; many European professional teams train here. Tourist-board offices have excellent leaflets on bike routes with maps, details about the terrain, sights, and distances. The companies below can rent you bikes for exploring Palma and environs.

Embat Ciclos
BICYCLING | Some 10 km (6 miles) from the city center, on the beach in Platja de Palma, Embat has both standard touring and electric bikes for rent and will happily assist with organizing tours of the island. ⊠ *Bartolomé Riutort 27, Can Pastilla* ☎ *971/492358* ⊕ *www.embatciclos.com.*

Palma on Bike
BICYCLING | This bike-rental shop, just below the Plaça de la Reina in Palma, is open daily 9:30–3 and 4–8. You can also organize a tour from here. ⊠ *Av. Antoni Maura 10, Centro* ☎ *971/718062* ⊕ *www. palmaonbike.com.*

BIRD-WATCHING
Mallorca has two notable nature reserves.

Sa Dragonera
BIRD WATCHING | This island and its large colony of sea falcons are accessible by boat from Sant Elm, at the western tip of Mallorca. The boats, run by the operator Cruceros Margarita, leave from in front of El Pescador restaurant at the port of Sant Elm daily every 30 minutes. ⊠ *Sant Elm* ☎ *629/606614, 639/617545 for Cruceros Margarita* ⊕ *www.crucerosmargarita.com* ☒ *Boat €13.*

Mallorca is a popular place for cyclists, and many European professionals train here.

S'Albufera de Mallorca

BIRD WATCHING | This is the largest wetlands zone in Mallorca. ✉ *Ctra. Port d'Alcúdia–Ca'n Picafort, Alcúdia* ☎ *971/892250* ⊕ *www.mallorcaweb.net/salbufera* ☞ *Stop at Centre de Recepció (Reception Center) sa Roca for permission to enter park.*

GOLF

Mallorca has more than 20 18-hole golf courses, among them PGA championship venues of fiendish difficulty. The Federación Balear de Golf (Balearic Golf Federation) can provide more information.

Canyamel Golf

GOLF | This club, some 64 km (40 miles) from Palma, at the far eastern tip of the island, has wonderful views of the sea. Fans of the club say the 475-yard 13th hole (par 5) is a heartbreaker. ✉ *Av. d'Es Cap Vermell s/n, Capdepera* ☎ *971/841313* ⊕ *www.canyamelgolf.com* ⛳ *€83–€105 for 18 holes, depending on the season* 🏌 *18 holes, 6562 yards, par 73.*

★ Golf Alcanada

GOLF | This 18-hole course, designed by Robert Trent Jones Jr., is widely regarded as the best club on the island, with spectacular views of the bay and lighthouse. ✉ *Ctra. del Faro s/n, Alcúdia* ☎ *971/549560* ⊕ *www.golf-alcanada.com/en* ⛳ *€105–€165 for 18 holes, €62–€83 for 9 holes (depending on season)* 🏌 *18 holes, 7107 yards, par 72.*

HIKING

Mallorca is excellent for hiking. In the Sierra de Tramuntana, you can easily arrange to trek one way and take a boat, bus, or train back. Ask the tourist office for the free booklet *20 Hiking Excursions on the Island of Mallorca,* with detailed maps and itineraries.

Grup Excursionista de Majorca (*Mallorcan Hiking Association*)

HIKING/WALKING | This association can provide hiking information. ✉ *Carrer dels Horts 1* ☎ *971/718823* ⊕ *www.gemweb.org.*

SAILING
Cruesa Majorca Yacht Charter

SAILING | A wide range of yachts, cruisers, and catamarans are available for rent here, by the day or the week. ✉ *Av. Antonio Maura 18, entlo 2 izq* ☎ *971/282821* ⊕ *www.cruesa.com/en.*

Federación Balear de Vela (*Balearic Sailing Federation*)

SAILING | For information on sailing, contact the federation. ✉ *Edificio Palma Arena, Av. Uruguay s/n* ☎ *971/402412* ⊕ *www.federacionbalearvela.org.*

SCUBA DIVING
Big Blue

SCUBA DIVING | This dive center, next to the Hotel Hawaii on the beach boardwalk in Palmanova, offers PADI-certified courses for beginners (€269), including two dives with full equipment: tanks, wet suits, regulators, masks, and fins. ✉ *Carrer Martin Ros Garcia 6, Palmanova* ☎ *971/681686* ⊕ *www.bigbluediving.net.*

TENNIS

Tennis is very popular here—the more so for world champion Rafael Nadal being a Mallorcan. There are courts at many hotels and private clubs, and tennis schools as well. The Federació de Tennis de les Illes Balears (Balearics Tennis Federation) can provide information about playing in the area.

Federació de Tennis de les Illes Balears (*Balearic Tennis Federation*)

TENNIS | ✉ *Edificio Palma Arena, Calle Uruguay s/n* ☎ *971/720956* ⊕ *www.ftib.es/es/welcome.*

🛍 Shopping

Mallorca's specialties are shoes and leather clothing, utensils carved from olive wood, porcelain and handblown glass, and artificial pearls. Look for designer fashions on the **Passeig des Born** and for antiques on **Costa de la Pols,** a narrow little street near the Plaça Riera. The **Plaça Major** has a modest crafts market Friday and Saturday 10–2 (in summer the market is also open on weekdays). During summer, there's a crafts market on the seafront at Sa Llotja. Palma has a range of food markets, including Mercat Oliva, where you can browse stalls piled high with local produce, meat, and fish. At the recently opened San Juan Gastronomic Market (⊕ *www.mercadosanjuanpalma.es*) sample street-style food, cocktails, and wine in an impressive Moderniste building, constructed in the 1900s.

Many of Palma's best shoe shops are on Avenida Rei Jaime III, between the Plaça Joan Carles I and the Passeig Mallorca.

FOOD
Colmado Santo Domingo

FOOD/CANDY | This is a wonderful little shop for the artisanal food specialties of Mallorca: sobresada of black pork, sausages of all sorts, cheeses, jams, and honeys and preserves. ✉ *Carrer Santo Domingo 1, Centro* ☎ *971/714887* ⊕ *www.colmadosantodomingo.com.*

GLASS AND CERAMICS
Gordiola

CERAMICS/GLASSWARE | Glassmakers since 1719, Gordiola has a factory showroom in Algaida, on the Palma–Manacor road, where you can watch the glass being blown and even try your hand at making a piece. ✉ *Ctra. Palma–Manacor, Km 19, Algaida* ☎ *971/665046* ⊕ *www.gordiola.com.*

SHOES AND LEATHER GOODS
Alpargatería La Concepción

SHOES/LUGGAGE/LEATHER GOODS | Mallorca's most popular footwear is the simple, comfortable slip-on espadrille (usually with a leather front over the first half of the foot and a strap across the back of the ankle). Look for a pair here. ✉ *Carrer de la Concepción 17* ☎ *971/710709* ⊕ *www.zapateriamallorca.com.*

Lottusse

SHOES/LUGGAGE/LEATHER GOODS | Shop here for high-end shoes, leather coats, and accessories. ⊠ *Av. Jaume III 2* ☎ *971/710203* ⊕ *www.lottusse.com.*

Mercat de Sineu

OUTDOOR/FLEA/GREEN MARKETS | The island's biggest market takes place every Wednesday, 8 am to 1 pm, in the town of Sineu, 34 km (21 miles) east of Palma. The market, among the island's oldest, dates back to the 14th century, when livestock was auctioned—a practice that continues to this day. Come early if you want to see the auction, which takes place in and around the main square. Local crafts and produce, plants and flowers, clothing and leather goods are traded throughout the village along the labyrinth of narrow streets, which can get very busy. In the 14th century, King Jaime II chose Sineu as the new capital of Mallorca, connecting Palma with Sineu via a long, straight road that can still be traced today. The remains of the ancient palace and former residence of King Jaime II, as well as other important monuments, can be visited across the town. ⊠ *Pl. Es Fossar.*

Valldemossa

18 km (11 miles) north of Palma.

The jumping-off point for a drive up the spectacular coast of the Tramuntana, this pretty little town, north of Palma, is famous for the vast complex of the Reial Cartuja monastery. Surrounded by natural beauty and stunning views, it was also here where Chopin spent the winter of 1838 with George Sand. As most tourists tend to bus in during the day for a few hours and leave, it is worth spending an evening in Valldemossa to soak up the true atmosphere of this beautiful village. At sundown, the quiet streets and *plaças* are a delight to wander through, flanked by sandy stone houses with green shutters and overflowing plant pots. A classical music festival paying tribute to Chopin (among other composers) is held every August, with most performances taking place in the Reial Cartuja monastery.

GETTING HERE AND AROUND
Valldemossa is a 20-minute drive from Palma on the MA1130. Regular bus service from the Plaça d'Espanya in Palma gets you to Valldemossa in about a half hour.

VISITOR INFORMATION
CONTACTS Valldemossa Tourist Office
⊠ *Av. de Palma 7* ☎ *971/612019.*

 Sights

★ **Cartoixa de Valldemossa** (*Royal Carthusian Monastery*)
MUSEUM | The monastery was founded in 1339, but after the monks were expelled in 1835, it acquired a new lease on life by offering apartments to travelers. The most famous lodgers were Frédéric Chopin and his lover, the Baroness Amandine Dupin, the French novelist better known by her pseudonym, George Sand. The two spent three difficult months here in the cold, damp winter of 1838–39.

In the **church,** note the frescoes above the nave—the monk who painted them was Goya's brother-in-law. The **pharmacy,** made by the monks in 1723, is almost completely preserved. A long corridor leads to the apartments, furnished in period style, occupied by Chopin and Sand (the piano is original). Nearby, another set of apartments houses the local **museum,** with mementos of Archduke Luis Salvador and a collection of old printing blocks. From here you return to the ornately furnished **King Sancho's palace,** a group of rooms originally built by King Jaume II for his son. The tourist office, in Valldemossa's main plaza, sells a ticket good for all of the monastery's attractions. ⊠ *Pl. de la Cartuja s/n* ☎ *971/612986* ⊕ *www.cartujadevalldemossa.com* ⊠ *€10* ⊗ *Closed Sun.*

🛏 Hotels

⭐ Gran Hotel Son Net

$$$$ | **HOTEL** | About equidistant from Palma and Valldemossa, this restored estate house—parts of which date back to 1672—is one of Mallorca's most luxurious hotels. **Pros:** attentive staff; family-friendly; convenient to Palma. **Cons:** a bit far from the beaches; all this luxury comes at a high price; need car. Ⓢ *Rooms from: €500* ✉ *Carrer Castillo de Son Net s/n, Puigpunyent* ☎ *971/147000* ⊕ *www.sonnet.es* ⤳ *26 rooms* ⦿ *Free Breakfast.*

⭐ Mirabó de Valldemossa

$$$$ | **B&B/INN** | At the far end of a winding dirt road in the hills overlooking the Reial Cartuja, across the valley of Valldemossa, this luxurious little agroturismo is a romantic hideaway that's hard to reach and even harder to tear yourself away from. **Pros:** friendly personal service; peace and quiet; incredible views. **Cons:** no restaurants nearby; no gym or spa; those low stone doorways can be a headache. Ⓢ *Rooms from: €290* ✉ *Ctra. Valldemossa, Km 16* ☎ *661/285215* ⤳ *9 rooms* ⦿ *Free Breakfast.*

Deià

9 km (5½ miles) southwest of Sóller.

Deià is perhaps best known as the adopted home of the English poet and writer Robert Graves, who lived here off and on from 1929 until his death in 1985. His grave can be found in the small cemetery at the top of the village. Deià is still a favorite haunt of writers and artists, including Graves's son Tomás, author of *Pa amb Oli* (*Bread and Olive Oil*), a guide to Mallorcan cooking, and British painter David Templeton. Ava Gardner lived here for a time; so, briefly, did Picasso. The setting is unbeatable—all around Deià rise the steep cliffs of the Sierra de Tramuntana. There's live jazz on summer evenings, and on warm afternoons literati gather at the beach bar in the rocky cove at Cala de Deià, 2 km (1 mile) downhill from the village. Walk up the narrow street to the village church; the small **cemetery** behind it affords views of mountains terraced with olive trees and of the coves below. It's a fitting spot for Graves's final resting place, in a quiet corner.

About 4 km (2½ miles) west of Deià is **Son Marroig,** a former estate of Austrian archduke Luis Salvador (1847–1915), which is now preserved as a museum, with a lovely garden and stunning coastal views. If you're driving, the best way to reach Son Marroig is the twisty MA10.

GETTING HERE AND AROUND

The Palma–Port de Sóller bus (€4.35) passes through Deià six times daily in each direction Monday–Saturday, five times on Sunday. Taxis to Deià from Palma cost €45 by day, €50 at night; from the airport the fares are €50/€55, and from Sóller €22/€24. Intrepid hikers can walk from Deià through the mountains to Sóller, on a trail of moderate difficulty, in about 2½ hours.

👁 Sights

Ca N'Alluny (*La Casa de Robert Graves*)

HOUSE | The Fundació Robert Graves opened this museum dedicated to Deià's most famous resident in the house he built in 1932. The seaside house is something of a shrine: Graves's furniture and books, personal effects, and the press he used to print many of his works are all preserved. ✉ *Ctra. Deià-Sóller s/n* ☎ *971/636185* ⊕ *www.lacasaderobert-graves.com* 🎟 *€7* 🕑 *Closed Sun.*

Monestir de Miramar

RELIGIOUS SITE | On the road south from Deià to Valldemossa, this monastery was founded in 1276 by Ramón Llull, who established a school of Asian languages here. It was bought in 1872 by the Archduke Luis Salvador and restored as a mirador. Explore the garden and the tiny cloister, then walk below through the olive groves to a spectacular lookout. ✉ *Diseminado Miramar 1, Ctra. Deià–Valldemossa (MA10), Km 67* ☎ *971/616073* 🎟 *€4* 🕒 *Closed Sun.*

Son Marroig

HOUSE | This estate belonged to Austrian archduke Luis Salvador, who arrived here as a young man and fell in love with the place. He acquired huge tracts of land along the northwestern coast, building miradores at the most spectacular points but otherwise leaving the pristine beauty intact. Below the mirador, you can see **Sa Foradada,** a rock peninsula pierced by a huge archway, where the archduke moored his yacht. Now a museum, the estate house contains the archduke's collections of Mediterranean pottery and ceramics, Mallorcan furniture, and paintings. The garden is especially fine. From April through early October, the Deià International Festival holds classical concerts here. ✉ *Ctra. Deià–Valldemossa (MA10), Km 65* ☎ *971/639158* 🌐 *www.sonmarroig.com* 🎟 *€4* 🕒 *Closed Sun.*

Beaches

Cala Deia

BEACH—SIGHT | Encircled by high pine-topped cliffs, this rocky cove connects to various coastal walking paths as well as a narrow road that twists its way down from the village. Year-round, clear turquoise water makes it great for snorkeling and swims. The popular Ca's Patro March restaurant, hewn into the rocks, overhangs the sea and stirring views; it's often booked out days in advance. There is also a simple beach bar. Best for: swimming, snorkelling. ✉ *Cala Deia.*

Hotels

★ Belmond La Residencia

$$$$ | **HOTEL** | **FAMILY** | Two 16th- and 17th-century manor houses, on a hill facing the village of Deià, have been artfully combined to make this exceptional hotel, superbly furnished with Mallorcan antiques, modern canvases, and canopied four-poster beds. **Pros:** some rooms have private plunge pools; private shuttle to the sea; tennis coach, pro shop, and clinic. **Cons:** expensive; narrow stairs to the Tower Suite. [$] *Rooms from: €730* ✉ *Son Canals s/n* ☎ *971/639011* 🌐 *www.belmond.com/la-residencia-mallorca* 🛏 *67 rooms, 1 villa* 🍴 *Free Breakfast.*

★ Hotel Es Molí

$$$$ | **HOTEL** | A converted 17th-century manor house in the hills above the valley of Deià, this peaceful hotel is known for its traditional sense of luxury. **Pros:** attentive service; heated pool with spacious terrace; chamber music concerts twice a week during the summer. **Cons:** steep climb to annex rooms; short season; three-night minimum for some stays in high season. [$] *Rooms from: €365* ✉ *Ctra. Valldemossa–Deià s/n* ☎ *971/639000* 🌐 *www.esmoli.com* 🕒 *Closed Nov.–Mar.* 🛏 *87 rooms* 🍴 *Free Breakfast.*

s'Hotel D'es Puig

$$$ | **B&B/INN** | **FAMILY** | This family-run "hotel on the hill" has a back terrace with a lemon-tree garden and a wonderful view of the mountains. **Pros:** peaceful setting; two pools (one heated); private parking for guests. **Cons:** public spaces can feel a bit cramped; no pets; books out quickly. [$] *Rooms from: €170* ✉ *Carrer d'es Puig 4* ☎ *971/639409, 637/820805* 🌐 *www.hoteldespuig.com* 🕒 *Closed Dec. and Jan.* 🛏 *14 rooms* 🍴 *Free Breakfast.*

Sóller

13 km (8 miles) north of Jardins d'Alfàbia, 30 km (19 miles) north of Palma.

All but the briefest visits to Mallorca should include at least an overnight stay in Sóller, one of the most beautiful towns on the island, with palatial homes built in the 19th and early 20th centuries by the landowners and merchants who thrived on the export of the region's oranges, lemons, and almonds. Many of the buildings here, like the **Church of Sant Bartomeu** and the **Bank of Sóller,** on the Plaça Constitució, and the nearby **Can Prunera,** are gems of the Moderniste style, designed by contemporaries of Antoni Gaudí. The tourist information office in the **town hall,** next to Sant Bartomeu, has a walking-tour map of the important sites.

GETTING HERE AND AROUND

You can travel in retro style from Palma to Sóller on one of the six daily trains (four daily in February, March, November, and December; €25 round-trip) operated by Ferrocarril de Sóller, which depart from Plaça d'Espanya. With a string of wooden rail cars with leather-covered seats dating to 1912, the train trundles along for about an hour, making six stops along the 27-km (17-mile) route; the scenery gets lovely—especially at Bunyola and the Mirador Pujol—as you approach the peaks of the Tramuntana. From the train station in Sóller, a charming old trolley car, called the Tranvía de Sóller, threads its way down through town to the Port de Sóller. The fare is €7 each way. You can also buy a combination round-trip ticket for the train and the trolley for €32. The mountain road between Palma and Sóller is spectacular—lemon and olive trees on stone-walled terraces, farmhouses perched on the edges of forested cliffs—but demanding. ■TIP➔ If **you're driving to Sóller, take the tunnel at Alfabía instead. Save your strength for even better mountain roads ahead.**

TRAIN AND TROLLEY CONTACT Ferrocarril de Sóller ⊠ *Pl. d'Espanya 6, Palma* ☎ *971/752051 in Palma, 971/752028 in Palma, 971/630130 in Sóller* ⊕ *www.trendesoller.com.*

VISITOR INFORMATION CONTACTS Sóller Tourist Office ⊠ *Pl. Espanya 15* ☎ *971/638008.*

◉ Sights

Can Prunera

HOUSE | A minute's walk or so from the Plaça de la Constitució, along Sóller's main shopping arcade, brings you to this charming museum, where Moderniste style comes to life. In the lovingly restored family rooms on the first floor of this imposing town house you can see how Sóller's well-to-do embraced the art deco style: the ornate furniture and furnishings, the stained glass and ceramic tile, and the carved and painted ceilings all helped announce their status In turn-of-the-century Mallorcan society. Upstairs, Can Prunera also houses a small collection of paintings by early modern masters, among them Man Ray, Santiago Rusiñol, Paul Klee, and Joan Miró; the garden is an open-air museum in its own right, with sculptures by José Siguiri, Josep Sirvent, and other Mallorcan artists. ⊠ *Carrer de la Lluna 86–90* ☎ *971/638973* ⊕ *www.canprunera.com* ☎ *€5* ⊗ *Closed Mon. Nov.–Feb.*

Station Building Galleries

MUSEUM | Maintained by the Fundació Tren de l'Art, these galleries have two small but remarkable collections—one of engravings by Miró, the other of ceramics by Picasso. ⊠ *Soller Railway Station, Pl. Espanya 6* ☎ *Free.*

 Restaurants

Sa Cova

$$ | **CATALAN** | On Sóller's busy central square, this friendly and informal restaurant specializes in traditional local cooking, with a nod to touristic expectations. Skip the inevitable paella, and opt instead for the *sopas mallorquines*, thick vegetable soups served over thin slices of bread, or the Mallorcan pork loin, stuffed with nuts and raisins. **Known for:** sopas mallorquines; outdoor seating; great people-watching. $ *Average main: €16* ⊠ *Pl. Constitució 7* ☎ *971/633222.*

Hotels

Ca'n Abril

$$ | B&B/INN | About a minute's walk from the main square, this family-friendly boutique hotel is an oasis of quiet in summer, when Sóller gets most of its tourist traffic. **Pros:** friendly service; honesty bar; excellent value. **Cons:** no elevator; no pets; parking off-site (€10 per day). $ *Rooms from: €125* ⊠ *Carrer Pastor 26* ☎ *971/633579, 672/360507* ⊕ *www. hotel-can-abril-soller.com* ⊙ *Closed Nov.– mid-Mar.* ⟿ *10 rooms* ⓞⓘ *Free Breakfast.*

Ca'n Isabel

$$ | B&B/INN | Just across the tram tracks from the train station, this former home still feels much like a family hideaway. **Pros:** convenient location; good value; pretty gardens. **Cons:** rooms on the small side; no elevator; no private parking. $ *Rooms from: €132* ⊠ *Carrer Isabel II 13* ☎ *971/638097* ⊕ *www.canisabel.com* ⊙ *Closed Nov.–Feb.* ⟿ *6 rooms* ⓞⓘ *Free Breakfast.*

Gran Hotel Sóller

$$$$ | HOTEL | A former private estate with an imposing Moderniste facade, this is the biggest hotel in town. **Pros:** friendly and efficient service in at least five languages; short walk from town center; convenient to trams. **Cons:** pricey for what you get; small pools; functional decor. $ *Rooms from: €240* ⊠ *Carrer Romaguera 18* ☎ *971/638686* ⊕ *www. granhotelsoller.com* ⟿ *40 rooms* ⓞⓘ *Free Breakfast.*

Fornalutx

This pretty little mountain village nestled amid lemon and orange groves, 4 km (2½ miles) north of Sóller, is a worthy scenic detour. Much of its appeal emanates from the narrow pedestrianized streets, blond-stone houses speckled with bougainvillea and topped with red-tiled roofs, and the views over the Sóller valley.

La Vila Hotel and Restaurant

$$$ | B&B/INN | Owner Toni Oliver obviously put a lot of work into this lovingly restored town house on Sóller's central square. **Pros:** friendly service; good location; lovely Art Nouveau features. **Cons:** rooms on the square can be noisy; no elevator; no pets. $ *Rooms from: €152* ⊠ *Pl. de la Constitució 14* ☎ *971/634641* ⊕ *www.lavilahotel.com* ⟿ *8 rooms* ⓞⓘ *Free Breakfast.*

Activities

Ten minutes or so from the center of Sóller on the trolley, the beachfront at Port de Sóller offers all sorts of water-based fun.

Nautic Sóller

WATER SPORTS | On the northwest coast at Port de Sóller, this place has sea kayaks and motorboats available for rent May–October. ⊠ *Calle de la Marina 4, Port de Sóller* ☎ *609/354132* ⊕ *www.nauticsoller. com.*

Alcúdia

54 km (34 miles) northeast of Palma.

Nothing if not strategic, Alcúdia is the ideal base for exploring Mallorca's north coast, with the 13-km-long (8-mile-long) beach from Port d'Alcúdia to C'an Picafort

Mallorca's Sierra de Tramuntana provides excellent views for hikers.

and the adjacent Playa de Muro, the bird-watchers' paradise in the S'Albufera wetlands, and the spectacular drive along the corniche to Cap de Formentor. The charming little walled town itself is a capsule version of Mallorcan history: the first city here was a Roman settlement, in 123 BC. The Moors reestablished a town here, and after the Reconquest it became a feudal possession of the Knights Templar; the first ring of city walls dates to the early 14th century. Begin your visit at the **Church of Sant Jaume** and walk through the maze of narrow streets inside to the **Porta de Xara,** with its twin crenellated towers.

GETTING HERE AND AROUND

Porta de Alcúdia, where the ferry arrives from Ciutadella, is a 3-km (2-mile) taxi ride from the center of Alcúdia. There is also direct bus service from Palma.

VISITOR INFORMATION

CONTACTS Alcúdia Tourist Office ⊠ *Passeig de Pere Ventayol s/n* ☎ *971/549022* ⊕ *www.alcudiamallorca.com.*

👁 Sights

Ciutat Romana de Pol·lèntia

ARCHAEOLOGICAL SITE | Archaeological remains of the ancient city of Pollentia, which dates to about 70 BC, include La Portella residential area, the Forum, and the 1st-century-AD Roman theater. The Museu Monogràfic de Pollentia has a small collection of statuary and artifacts from the nearby excavations of the Roman capital of the island. ⊠ *Av. dels Prínceps d'Espanya s/n* ☎ *971/547004, 971/897102* ⊕ *www.pollentia.net* 🎫 *€4, includes museum and archaeological site* 🕙 *Closed 1 pm on weekends.*

Pollença

8 km (5 miles) from Alcúdia, 50 km (31 miles) from Palma.

This is a pretty little town, with a history that goes back at least as far as the Roman occupation of the island; the only trace of that period is the stone **Roman Bridge** at the edge of town. In the 13th

century, Pollença and much of the land around it was owned by the Knights Templar, who built the imposing church of **Nuestra Senyora de Los Ángeles** on the west side of the present-day Plaça Major. The church looks east to the 1,082-foot peak of the Puig de Maria, with the 15th-century sanctuary at the top. The **Calvari** of Pollença is a flight of 365 stone steps to a tiny chapel and a panoramic view as far as Cap de Formentor. There's a colorful weekly market at the foot of the steps on Sunday mornings.

GETTING HERE AND AROUND

Pollença is a fairly easy drive from Palma on the MA013. A few buses each day connect Pollença with Palma and Alcúdia.

VISITOR INFORMATION

CONTACTS Pollença Tourist Office ✉ *Guillen Cifre de Colonya s/n* ☎ *971/535077.*

Festival de Pollença

MUSIC | An acclaimed international music event, this festival is held each July and August. Since its inception, in 1961, it has attracted such performers as Mstislav Rostropovich, Jessye Norman, the St. Petersburg Philharmonic, the Camerata Köln, and the Alban Berg Quartet. Concerts are held in the cloister of the Convent of Sant Domingo. ✉ *Pollença* ☎ *971/534011* 🌐 *www.festivalpollenca.com.*

Sights

Cap de Formentor

SCENIC DRIVE | The winding road north from Port de Pollença to the tip of the island is spectacular. Stop at the Mirador de la Cruete, where the rocks form deep, narrow inlets of multishaded blue. A stone tower called the Talaia d'Albercuix marks the highest point on the peninsula. Continue on, around hairpin bends—and past superb coastal views—to reach Cala Formentor beach. The drive is certainly not for the fainthearted, but the beach at the end is one of Mallorca's best, with fine white sand and calm turquoise water, backed by a forest of pine trees that offer shade. ✉ *Formentor.*

Hotels

Hotel Juma

$$ | **B&B/INN** | This little hotel, which opened in 1907, is on Pollença's main square, making it a good choice for a weekend stay because of the Sunday market that takes place there. **Pros:** great location; tasty breakfast in the bar; good value. **Cons:** parking can be a problem; rooms overlooking square can be noisy; basic decor and amenities. [$] *Rooms from: €125* ✉ *Pl. Major 9* ☎ *971/535002* 🌐 *www.pollensahotels.com* 🕓 *Closed mid-Nov.–mid-Mar.* 🛏 *7 rooms* 🍴 *Free Breakfast.*

★ Hotel Son Sant Jordi

$$$$ | **B&B/INN** | A favorite way station for groups of cyclists touring the island, the Son Sant Jordi is a small, family-friendly gem of a boutique hotel, formerly the convent of the adjacent Church of Sant Jordi. **Pros:** pleasant patio garden; lots of character and charm; great location. **Cons:** a tad pricey; three-night minimum stay June–September; no parking on-site. [$] *Rooms from: €180* ✉ *Carrer Sant Jordi 29* ☎ *971/530389* 🌐 *www.hotelsonsantjordi.com/en* 🛏 *12 rooms* 🍴 *Free Breakfast.*

★ Son Brull Hotel and Spa

$$$$ | **RESORT** | "Oasis" is what springs to mind when driving up through family vineyards to this brilliantly restored medieval monastery, reborn as a deluxe resort hotel. **Pros:** charm and sophistication; strategic location for exploring Pollença, Alcúdia, and the S'Albufereta wildlife reserve; free daily yoga and Pilates sessions. **Cons:** pricey; minimum booking for some arrivals in high season; no sea view might disappoint some. [$] *Rooms from: €700* ✉ *Ctra. Palma–Pollença, Km 50* ☎ *971/535353* 🌐 *www.sonbrull.com* 🕓 *Closed Dec. and Jan.* 🛏 *13 rooms, 10 suites* 🍴 *Free Breakfast.*

Lluc

20 km (12 miles) southwest of Pollença.

The Santuari de Lluc, which holds the Black Virgin and is a major pilgrimage site, is widely considered Mallorca's spiritual heart.

GETTING HERE AND AROUND
The Santuari is about midway between Sóller and Pollença on the hairpin route over the mountains (MA10). Two buses daily connect these towns, stopping in Lluc. Taxi fare from either town is about €35.

Sights

Santuari de Lluc

MUSEUM | La Moreneta, also known as La Virgen Negra de Lluc (the Black Virgin of Lluc), is a votary statue of the Virgin Mary that's held in a 17th-century **church,** the center of this sanctuary complex. The **museum** has an eclectic collection of pre-historic and Roman artifacts, ceramics, paintings, textiles, folk costumes, votive offerings, Nativity scenes, and work by local artists. Between September and June, a children's choir sings psalms in the chapel at morning and evening services, Monday–Saturday, and at 11 am for Sunday Mass. The Christmas Eve performance of the "Cant de la Sibila" ("Song of the Sybil"), based on a medieval prophecy of the end of the world, is an annual choral highlight. ⊠ *Pl. dels Peregrins 1* ☎ *971/871525* ⊕ *www.lluc. net/en* 🎫 *€5.*

Menorca

Menorca, the northernmost of the Balearics, is a knobby, cliff-bound plateau with some 193 km (120 miles) of coastline and a central hill called El Toro, from the 1,100-foot summit of which you can see the whole island. Prehistoric monuments—*taulas* (huge stone T-shapes), *talayots* (spiral stone cones), and *navetes* (stone structures shaped like overturned boats)—left by the first Neolithic settlers are all over the island.

Tourism came late to Menorca, which aligned with the Republic in the Spanish Civil War; Franco punished the island by discouraging the investment in infrastructure that fueled the Balearic boom on Mallorca and Ibiza. Menorca has avoided many of the problems of overdevelopment: there are still very few high-rise hotels, and the herringbone road system, with a single central highway, means that each resort is small and separate. There's less to see and do on Menorca, and more unspoiled countryside than on the other Balearics. The island, home to some 220 species of birds and more than 1,000 species of plants, was designated a Biosphere Reserve in 1993. Menorca is where Spaniards and Catalans tend to take their families on vacation.

GETTING HERE AND AROUND
To get to Menorca from Barcelona take the overnight ferry, or a 40-minute flight. It's around a one-hour ferry ride from Palma.

Several buses a day run the length of Menorca between Mahón and Ciutadella, stopping en route at Alaior, Mercadal, and Ferreries. The bus line Autos Fornells serves the northeast; Transportes Menorca connects Mahón with Ciutadella and with the major beaches and calas around the island. From smaller towns there are daily buses to Mahón and connections to Ciutadella. In summer, regular buses shuttle beachgoers from the west end of Ciutadella's Plaça Explanada to the resorts to the south and west; from Mahón, excursions to Menorca's most remote beaches leave daily from the jetty next to the Nuevo Muelle Comercial.

If you want to beach-hop in Menorca, it's best to have your own transportation, but most of the island's historic sights are in Mahón or Ciutadella, and once you're

Menorca

in town everything is within walking distance. You can see the island's archaeological remains in a day's drive, so you may want to rent a car for just that part of your visit.

BUS CONTACTS Autocares Torres
☎ 902/075066 ⊕ www.bus.e-torres.net/en. **Autos Fornells** ☎ 971/154390 ⊕ www.autosfornells.com. **Transportes Menorca** ☎ 971/360475 ⊕ www.tmsa.es.

Mahón (Maó)

Established as the island's capital in 1722, when the British began their nearly 80-year occupation, Mahón still bears the stamp of its former rulers. The streets nearest the port are lined with four-story Georgian town houses; the Mahónese drink gin and admire Chippendale furniture; English is widely spoken. The city is

quiet for much of the year, but between June and September the waterfront pubs and restaurants swell with foreigners.

GETTING HERE AND AROUND
There's ferry service here from Mallorca, but it's much less frequent than to Ciutadella. Within Mahón, Autocares Torres has three bus routes around the city and to the airport.

BUS STATION Estació Autobuses ✉ Carrer Moll de Llevant 1, Mahón ☎ 971/360475.

TAXI CONTACT Radio-Taxi ☎ 971/367111, 971/482222 ⊕ www.taxismenorca.com.

VISITOR INFORMATION
CONTACTS Aeropuerto de Menorca Tourist Office ✉ Arrivals terminal, Mahón ☎ 971/356944 ⊕ www.menorca.es. **Mahón Tourist Office (Port)** ✉ Moll de Llevant 2, Mahón ☎ 971/355952 ⊕ www.menorca.es.

Sights

Carrer Isabel II

HISTORIC SITE | This street is lined with many Georgian homes. To get here, walk up Carrer Alfons III and turn right at the ajuntament. ⊠ *Mahón.*

Mercat Des Claustre

MARKET | This church has a fine painted and gilded altarpiece. Adjoining the church are the cloisters, now a **market,** with stalls selling fresh produce and a variety of local cheeses and sausages. The central courtyard is a venue for a number of cultural events throughout the year. ⊠ *Pl. del Carme, Mahón* ☎ *638/920259.*

Santa María

RELIGIOUS SITE | Dating to the 13th century, this church was rebuilt in the 18th century, during the British occupation, and then restored again after being sacked during the Spanish Civil War. The church's pride is its 3,006-pipe baroque organ, imported from Austria in 1810. Organ concerts are given here at 7:30 on Saturday evening, and at 11 am and 7 pm on Sunday. The altar, and the half-domed chapels on either side, have exceptional frescoes. ⊠ *Pl. de la Constitució s/n, Mahón.*

Teatre Principal

ARTS VENUE | Opera companies from Italy en route to Spain made the Teatre Principal in Mahón their first port of call; if the maoneses gave a production a poor reception, it was cut from the repertoire. Built in 1824, it has five tiers of boxes, red plush seats, and gilded woodwork: La Scala in miniature. Lovingly restored, it still hosts a brief opera season. If you're visiting in the first week of December or June, buy tickets well in advance. ⊠ *Carrer Costa Deià 40, Mahón* ☎ *971/355603* ⊕ *www.teatremao.com.*

Torralba

ARCHAEOLOGICAL SITE | Puzzle over Menorca's prehistoric past at this megalithic site with a number of stone constructions, including a massive taula. Behind it, from the top of a stone wall, you can see, in a nearby field, the monolith **Fus de Sa Geganta** (the Giantess's Spindle). ⊠ *Mahón* ⊹ *From Mahón, drive west and turn south at Alaior on road to Cala en Porter; it's 2 km (1 mile) ahead at bend in road, marked by an information kiosk on left.*

Torre d'en Gaumés

ARCHAEOLOGICAL SITE | This is a complex set of Talaiotic stone constructions—fortifications, monuments, deep pits of ruined dwellings, huge vertical slabs, and taulas. ⊠ *Alaior* ⊹ *Head south toward Son Bou on west side of Alaior and, after about 1 km (½ mile), the 1st fork left leads to ruins.*

Beaches

Cala Galdana

BEACH—SIGHT | **FAMILY** | A smallish horseshoe curve of fine white sand, framed by almost vertical pine-covered cliffs, is where Menorca's only river, the Agendar, reaches the sea through a long limestone gorge. The surrounding area is under environmental protection—the handful of resort hotels and chalets above the beach (usually booked solid June–September by package-tour operators) were grandfathered in. Cala Galdana is family friendly in the extreme, with calm, shallow waters, and a nearby water park–playground for the kids. A favorite with Menorcans and visitors alike, it gets really crowded in high season, but a 20-minute walk through the pine forest leads to the otherwise inaccessible little coves of Macarella and Macaretta, remote beaches popular with naturists and boating parties. **Amenities:** food and drink; lifeguards; showers; water sports. **Best for:** swimming; walking. ⊠ *35 km (21 miles) from Mahón, Ferreries* ⊹ *Take ME1 to Ferreries, then head south from there on local ME22.*

🍴 Restaurants

El Jàgaro

$$$$ | **SEAFOOD** | This simple waterfront restaurant, at the east end of the harbor promenade, is a local favorite. The lunchtime crowd comes for the platter of lightly fried mixed fish with potatoes; knowledgeable clients home in on local specialties like *cap-roig* (scorpionfish) with garlic and wine sauce, or paella *bogavante* (with clawed lobster). **Known for:** spiny lobster stew (caldereta); harbor-front setting; local flavor. [$] *Average main: €27* ✉ *Moll de Llevant 334, Mahón* ☎ *971/362390* 🕒 *Closed Mon. No dinner Sun. Nov.–Mar.*

★ Es Molí de Foc

$$$$ | **SPANISH** | Originally a flour mill, this is the oldest building in the village of Sant Climent, and the food is exceptional. Taste seasonal dishes, which can include prawn carpaccio with cured Mahón cheese and artichoke oil, black paella with monkfish and squid, and *carrilleras de ternera* (beef cheeks) with potato. **Known for:** historic building; brewery on-site; rustic local food with style. [$] *Average main: €24* ✉ *Carrer Sant Llorenç 65, Sant Climent* ✥ *4 km (2½ miles) southwest of town* ☎ *971/153222* 🌐 *www.esmolidefoc.es* 🕒 *Closed Mon. Oct.–June. No lunch Mon. in July and Aug., and Tues.–Sun. Oct.–June.*

🛏 Hotels

Hotel Port Mahón

$$$$ | **HOTEL** | This standby may not win many prizes for imaginative design, but it's a solid choice, with rooms with hardwood floors, generic but comfortable furniture, and plenty of closet space. **Pros:** decent value; good buffet breakfast; some rooms have private terraces with impressive views. **Cons:** pool and garden front on the Passeig Marítim; no a/c; uninspired design. [$] *Rooms from: €200* ✉ *Av. Port de Maó s/n, Mahón* ☎ *971/362600* 🌐 *www.sethotels.com/en/port-mahon-hotel-en.html* 🛏 *82 rooms* 🍽 *Free Breakfast.*

★ Hotel Rural y Restaurante Biniarroca

$$$$ | **B&B/INN** | Antique embroidered bed linens, shelves with knickknacks, and comfy chairs—this is an English vision of a peaceful and secluded rural retreat, and its glory is the garden of irises, lavender, and flowering trees. **Pros:** excellent food on-site; some suites have private terraces; peaceful surroundings. **Cons:** bit of a drive to the beach; some low ceilings; adults only. [$] *Rooms from: €220* ✉ *Cami Vell 57, Sant Lluís* ☎ *971/150059* 🌐 *www.biniarroca.com* 🕒 *Closed Nov.–Easter* 🛏 *18 rooms* 🍽 *Free Breakfast.*

★ Jardi de Ses Bruixes Boutique Hotel

$$$$ | **B&B/INN** | Built in 1811 by a Spanish ship captain, this *casa señorial* (town house) in the heart of Mahón was lovingly restored by architect and co-owner Fernando Pons and opened in 2014 as a boutique hotel. **Pros:** amiable, eager-to-please staff; strategic location; at-home atmosphere. **Cons:** difficult to reach by car, though there is free public parking a few minutes' walk away; bathtubs in the bedrooms sacrifice privacy to design; thin walls. [$] *Rooms from: €250* ✉ *Calle de San Fernando 26, Mahón* ☎ *971/363166* 🌐 *www.hotelsesbruixes.com* 🛏 *16 rooms* 🍽 *Free Breakfast.*

Sant Joan de Binissaida

$$$$ | **B&B/INN** | An avenue lined with chinaberry and fig trees leads to this lovely restored farmhouse with environmental credentials, including some solar power and organic produce from the farm. **Pros:** vistas clear to the port of Mahón; huge pool; excellent restaurant. **Cons:** bit of a drive to the nearest beach; rooms in the annex lack privacy; short season, with three-night minimum stay in summer. [$] *Rooms from: €340* ✉ *Camí de Binissaida 108, Es Castell* ☎ *971/355598* 🌐 *www.binissaida.com* 🕒 *Closed Nov.–Apr.* 🛏 *12 rooms* 🍽 *Free Breakfast.*

Nightlife

Akelarre Jazz and Dance Club

MUSIC CLUBS | This stylish bar near the port has a café-terrace downstairs and live jazz and blues on Thursday and Friday night. It's open year-round 10:30 am–4 am and serves tapas and snacks to share in the evening. ✉ *Moll de Ponent 41–43, Mahón* ☎ *971/368520.*

Casino Sant Climent

MUSIC CLUBS | From May to September, catch live jazz on Tuesday evening at the Casino bar and restaurant. Book ahead for tables on the terrace. ✉ *Sant Jaume 4, Sant Climent* ✛ *4 km (2½ miles) southwest of Mahón* ☎ *971/153418* ⊕ *www. casinosantcliment.com.*

Cova d'en Xoroi

DANCE CLUBS | The hottest spot in Menorca is *the* place to catch the sun going down, drink in hand, a 20-minute drive from Mahón in the beach resort of Cala en Porter. This dance-until-dawn club is in a series of caves in a cliff high above the sea, which, according to local legend, was once the refuge of a castaway Moorish pirate. In addition to the nighttime DJs, there are afternoon–evening chill-out events with live music. ✉ *Carrer de Sa Cova s/n, Cala en Porter* ☎ *971/377236* ⊕ *www.covadenxoroi. com.*

Es Cau

MUSIC CLUBS | Dug like a cave into the bluff of the little cove of Cala Corb, this is where locals gather (Thursday–Saturday 10 pm–3 am) to sing and play guitar: *habañeras,* love songs, songs of exile and return—everyone knows the songs and they all join in. It's hard to find, but anybody in Es Castell can point the way. ✉ *Cala Corb s/n, Es Castell.*

Activities

BICYCLING
Asociación Cicloturista de Menorca

BICYCLING | Ask here about organized bike tours of the island. ✉ *Moll de Llevant 173, Mahón* ☎ *971/364816, 610/464816* ⊕ *www.menorcacicloturista.com/en.*

Bike Menorca

BICYCLING | Rent a road bike or mountain bike by the day (from €15) from this full-service outfitter. ✉ *Av. Francesc Femenías 44, Mahón* ☎ *971/353798* ⊕ *www.bikemenorca.com.*

DIVING

The clear Mediterranean waters here are ideal for diving. Equipment and lessons are available at Cala En Bosc, Son Parc, Fornells, Ciutadella, and Cala Tirant, among others.

Blue Islands Diving

DIVING/SNORKELING | ✉ *Passatge Riu 7, Serpentona, Cala Galdana* ⊕ *www.blueislandsdiving.com.*

GOLF
Golf Son Parc

GOLF | Menorca's sole golf course, designed by Dave Thomas, is 9 km (6 miles) east of Mercadal, about a 20-minute drive from Mahón. Rocky bunkers, and the occasional stray peacock on the fairways, make this an interesting and challenging course. The club, open year-round, also has two composition tennis courts and a restaurant ✉ *Urbanització Son Parc s/n, Mercadal* ☎ *971/188875* ⊕ *www.golfsonparc.com/en* 🔖 *€35–€50 for 9 holes, €49–€77 for 18 holes, depending on season* 🏌 *18 holes, 5653 yards, par 69.*

WALKING

In the south, each cove is approached by a *barranca* (ravine or gully), often from several miles inland. The head of **Barranca Algendar** is down a small, unmarked road immediately on the right of the Ferreries–Cala Galdana road; the barranca ends at the local beach resort, and from there you have a lovely walk north along the sea to an unspoiled half moon of sand at **Cala Macarella.** Extend your walk north, if time allows, through the forest along the riding trail to **Cala Turqueta,** where you'll find some of the island's most impressive grottoes.

📥 Shopping

Menorca is known for shoes and leather goods, as well as cheese, gin, and wine. Wine was an important part of the Menorcan economy as long ago as the 18th century: the British, who knew a good place to grow grapes when they saw one, planted the island thick with vines. Viticulture was abandoned when Menorca returned to the embrace of Spain, and it has reemerged only in the past few years.

Boba's

SHOES/LUGGAGE/LEATHER GOODS | Duck into the little alley between Carrer Nou and Carrer de l'Angel, and discover the atelier where Llorenç Pons makes his *espardenyes d'autor* (traditional rope-sole sandals) in original and surprising designs. ⊠ *Pont de l'Angel 4, Mahón* ☎ *647/587456.*

★ Bodegas Binifadet

WINE/SPIRITS | This is the most promising of the handful of the local wineries, with robust young reds and whites on store shelves all over Menorca. The owners have expanded their product line into sparkling Chardonnay (sold only on the premises), olive oil, jams and conserves, and wine-based soaps and cosmetics. It's well worth a visit, not merely for tastings and guided tours (the website has details), but—weather permitting—for a meal on the terrace (Easter–October, noon–4; mid-May–September, noon–midnight). The kitchen puts an international touch on traditional Menorcan recipes and products; the local red prawns in sea salt (€23) are great. In midsummer, reservations are a must. You can also simply drop by for a glass of wine on the terrace; the surroundings are picturesque and peaceful. ⊠ *Ctra. Sant Lluís–Es Castell, Km 0.5, Sant Lluís* ☎ *971/150715* ⊕ *www.binifadet.com.*

Pons Quintana

SHOES/LUGGAGE/LEATHER GOODS | This showroom has a full-length window overlooking the factory where its very chic women's shoes are made. ⊠ *Carrer Sant Antoni 120, Alaior* ✛ *13 km (8 miles) northeast of Mahón* ☎ *971/371050* ⊕ *www.ponsquintana.com/en.*

Xoriguer

WINE/SPIRITS | One gastronomic legacy of the British occupation was gin. Visit this distillery on Mahón's quayside near the ferry terminal, where you can sample various types of gin, and buy some to take home. ⊠ *Moll de Ponent 91, Mahón* ☎ *971/362197* ⊕ *www.xoriguer.es.*

Ciutadella

44 km (27 miles) west of Mahón.

Ciutadella was Menorca's capital before the British settled in Mahón, and its history is richer. Settled successively by the Phoenicians, Greeks, Carthaginians, and Romans, Ciutadella fell to the Moors in 903 and became a part of the Caliphate of Córdoba until 1287, when Alfonso III of Aragón reconquered it. He gave estates in Ciutadella to nobles who aided him in the battle, and to this day the old historic center of town has a distinctly aristocratic tone. In 1558 a Turkish armada laid siege to Ciutadella, burning the city and enslaving its inhabitants. It was later rebuilt but never quite regained its former stature.

As you arrive via the ME1, the main artery across the island from Mahón, turn left at the second traffic circle and follow the ring road to the Passeig Marítim; at the end, near the **Castell de Sant Nicolau** is a **monument to David Glasgow Farragut,** the first admiral of the U.S. Navy, whose

Ciutadella's harbor, just below the main square and lined with restaurants, is perfect for a summer evening stroll.

father emigrated from Ciutadella to the United States. From here, take Passeig de Sant Nicolau to the **Plaëa de s'Esplanada** and park near the Plaça d'es Born. Navigate your way from the cathedral through the narrow, medina-like streets of the old town to the 19th century wrought iron Mercat de Peix speckled in green and white tiles—and a hive of activity. Bar Ulisses does a roaring trade day and night, while providing the perfect people-watching perch.

GETTING HERE AND AROUND

Autocares Torres has a single bus line running between Ciutadella and the beaches and calas near the city.

BUS CONTACT Autocares Torres
☎ *902/075066* ⊕ *www.bus.e-torres.net/en.*

BUS STATION Estación de Autobuses de Ciutadella ✉ *Pl. dels Pins.*

TAXI CONTACT Radio Taxi Menorca
☎ *971/482222* ⊕ *www.taximenorca.es.*

VISITOR INFORMATION
CONTACTS Ciutadella Tourist Office
✉ *Edifici Ajuntament, Pl. d'es Born s/n*
☎ *971/484155* ⊕ *www.menorca.es.*

Sights

Cathedral

RELIGIOUS SITE | Carrer Major leads to this Gothic edifice, which has some beautifully carved choir stalls. The side chapel has round Moorish arches, remnants of the mosque that once stood on this site; the bell tower is a converted minaret. ✉ *Pl. de la Catedral* ☎ *971/380739* 🏷 *€6.*

Convento de Sant Agustí (*El Socorro*)

ARTS VENUE | Carrer del Seminari is lined on the west side with some of the city's most impressive historic buildings. Among them is this 17th-century convent, which hosts Ciutadella's summer festival of classical music (contact *admin@jjmmciutadella.com* for details) in its lovely cloister, and the Diocesan Museum collection of paintings, archaeological finds, and liturgical objects. The room housing the historical library and archives is especially impressive. ✉ *Carrer del Seminari at Carrer Obispo Vila* ☎ *971/481297* 🎫 *€6 (includes cathedral).*

Mirador d'es Port

VIEWPOINT | From a passage on the left side of Ciutadella's columned and crenellated ajuntament on the west side of the Born, steps lead up to this lookout. From here you can survey the harbor. ✉ *Pl. d'Es Born.*

Museu Municipal

MUSEUM | The museum houses artifacts of Menorca's prehistoric, Roman, and medieval past, including records of land grants made by Alfons III to the local nobility after defeating the Moors. It occupies an ancient defense tower, the Bastió de Sa Font (Bastion of the Fountain), at the east end of the harbor. ✉ *Pl. de Sa Font s/n* ☎ *971/380297* 🌐 *www.ciutadella.org/museu* 🎫 *€3 (free Wed.).*

Palau Salort

HOUSE | This is the only noble house in Ciutadella that's open to the public, albeit at limited times, and you can view five rooms of the palace and the interior garden. The coats of arms on the ceiling are those of the families Salort (*sal* and *ort,* a salt pit and a garden) and Martorell (a marten). ✉ *Carrer Major des Born* 🎫 *€3.*

Port

NEIGHBORHOOD | Ciutadella's port is accessible from steps that lead down from Carrer Sant Sebastià. The waterfront here is lined with seafood restaurants, some of which burrow into caverns far under the Born. ✉ *Ciutadella.*

Beaches

Cala Macarella and Cala Macaralleta

BEACH—SIGHT | What just might be the two most beautiful of Menorca's small beaches are reachable three ways: by boat, by car from the Mahón–Ciutadella highway (ME1), or, if you're feeling robust and ambitious, on foot from the little resort town of Cala Galdana. Cala Macarella is a little crescent of white sand lapped by breathtakingly turquoise and blue waters that are calm and shallow, and sheltered by rocks on both sides. Remote as it is, it's popular with locals as well as vacationers. A 10-minute walk along the cliffs brings you to the even smaller and more tranquil Cala Macaralleta, where there are no amenities and fewer sunseekers. **Amenities:** food and drink; lifeguards; parking (no fee); toilets. **Best for:** swimming; walking. ✉ *Urbanització Serpentona.*

🍴 Restaurants

Cafe Balear

$$$ | **SEAFOOD** | Seafood doesn't get much fresher than here, as the owners' boat docks nearby every day except Sunday. The relaxed atmosphere welcomes either a quick bite or a full dining experience. **Known for:** lobster caldereta; port-side location; fresh-off-the-boat catches. [$] *Average main: €21* ✉ *Pl. de San Juan 15* ☎ *971/380005* 🕒 *Closed Nov. and Mon.*

S'Amarador

$$$ | **SEAFOOD** | At the foot of the steps that lead down to the port, this restaurant has a café-terrace out front that's perfect for people-watching, drinks, and tapas. Fresh seafood in any form is a sure bet here: try the John Dory, baked, grilled, or fried with garlic—or splurge on the caldereta (€65). **Known for:** bustling terrace; flavorsome lobster stew; good-value fixed-price lunch menu. [$] *Average main: €20* ✉ *Pere Capllonch 42* ☎ *971/383524, 619/421518* 🌐 *www.samarador.com.*

Smoix

$$$ | **MEDITERRANEAN** | Creative, contemporary Menorcan cuisine is the draw here, in an industrial-style setting with a small leafy courtyard and low-key cosmopolitan vibe. Start things off with a local gin, and choose from two tasting menus (€34.50 or €44.50) or from a small list of à la carte dishes that change according to the season. **Known for:** crayfish ravioli; brochette with chicken, prawns, shiitake mushrooms and lime; local gin. $ *Average main: €21* ✉ *Av. Jaume Conqueridor 38* ☎ *971/489198* ⊕ *www.smoix.com.*

 Hotels

Hotel Rural Sant Ignasi

$$$ | **B&B/INN** | **FAMILY** | About 10 minutes by car from the central square, and set in a centuries-old oak forest, this comfortable manor house dates to 1777 and is a favorite with young Spanish families. **Pros:** good value; friendly staff; tennis and paddle tennis courts. **Cons:** kids in the pool all day; short season; three-night minimum stay in summer. $ *Rooms from: €180* ✉ *Ronda Norte s/n* ✛ *Take Ronda Norte to 2nd traffic circle at Polígono Industrial; just past traffic circle turn left on Son Juaneda and follow signs* ☎ *971/385575* ⊕ *www.santignasi.com* ☾ *Closed mid-Oct.–Apr.* ⛺ *25 rooms* ⦿ *Free Breakfast.*

★ Hotel Tres Sants

$$$$ | **B&B/INN** | This chic boutique hotel is in the heart of Ciutadella, on a narrow cobblestone street behind the cathedral, and has killer views from the rooftop terrace, extending over the old city and (in good weather) across the ocean as far as Mallorca. **Pros:** suites for families; ideal location for exploring the city; on-site spa access 24 hours. **Cons:** no parking; no elevator; communal breakfasts don't suit everyone. $ *Rooms from: €290* ✉ *Carrer Sant Cristofol 2* ☎ *626/053536* ⊕ *www. grupelcarme.com/en/tres-sants* ⛺ *8 rooms* ⦿ *Free Breakfast.*

 Activities

HORSEBACK RIDING

Horseback riding, breeding, and dressage have been traditions on the island for hundreds of years, and the magnificent black Menorcan horses play an important role, not only as work animals and for sport, but also in shows and colorful local festivals. There are 17 riding clubs on the island, a number of which offer excursions on the rural lanes of the unspoiled countryside. The Camí de Cavalls is a riding route in 20 stages that completely circumnavigates the island. Cavalls Son Angel in Ciutadella, Centre Equestre Equimar in Es Castell, and Menorca a Cavall in Ferreries organize excursions for adults and children. Son Martorellet, on the road to the beach at Cala Galdana, is a ranch where you can visit the stables and watch dressage training exhibitions every Wednesday and Thursday afternoon at 3:30; there's an equestrian show in traditional costume every Saturday at 4:30, February–November.

Cavalls Son Àngel

HORSEBACK RIDING | **FAMILY** | This equestrian center specializes in excursions along the Cami de Cavalls, the horseback route that circumnavigates the island, with rides that range from one to two hours for beginners (€22–€40) to three- or five-day trips (September–June only) with lunches en route. Riders on the longer excursions need to arrange their own overnight accommodations. ✉ *Camí d'Algaiarens s/n* ☎ *609/833902, 649/488098* ⊕ *www.cavallssonangel.com.*

Menorca a Cavall

HORSEBACK RIDING | **FAMILY** | Hour-and-a-half-long excursions, along portions of the Camí de Cavalls, are €30 in autumn and winter, €40 in spring and summer. Longer rides run €60–€100, depending on the season. Single- and two-day routes along the south coast of Menorca can also be organized autumn through spring. ✉ *Finca Es Calafat, Ctra. Ferreries–Cala Galdana (ME22), Km 4.3, Ferreries* ☎ *971/374637, 685/990545* ⊕ *www.menorcaacavall.com.*

Son Martorellet

HORSEBACK RIDING | **FAMILY** | The equestrian performances at the Son Martorellet stables, featuring demonstrations of dressage with the famed

Menorcan horses, are offered Wednesday and Thursday afternoons. ✉ *Ctra. Ferreries–Cala Galdana, Km 1.7, Ferreries* ☎ *971/373406, 639/156851* ⊕ *www. sonmartorellet.com.*

🛍 Shopping

The *polígono industrial* (industrial complex) on the right as you enter Ciutadella has a number of shoe factories, each with a shop. Prices may be the same as in stores, but the selection is wider. In Plaça d'es Born, a market is held on Friday and Saturday.

For the best shopping, try the Ses Voltes area, the Es Rodol zone near Plaça Artrutx, and along the Camí de Maó between Plaça Palmeras and Plaça d'es Born.

Hort Sant Patrici
FOOD/CANDY | This is a good place to buy the tangy, Parmesan-like Mahón cheese. There's a shop, beautiful grounds with a small vineyard, a sculpture garden and botanical garden, and a display of traditional cheese-making techniques and tools. On Monday, Tuesday, Thursday, and Saturday from 9 to 11 am you can watch the cheese being made. Guided tours (by reservation; €8) are available on Tuesday, Thursday, and Saturday at 10 am. Hort Sant Patrici has its own vineyards and olive trees, and nestled among them is a B&B, the **Ca Na Xini** (*www.canaxini.com/ en/rural-boutique-hotel-menorca*), with eight rooms done in dazzling minimalist white. ✉ *Camí Sant Patrici s/n, Ferreries* ✛ *18 km (11 miles) east of Ciutadella; exit ME1 at 2nd traffic circle after Ferreries onto Camí Sant Patrici* ☎ *971/373702* ⊕ *www.santpatrici.com* ⊘ *Closed Sun. in summer, weekends in winter.*

Maria Juanico
JEWELRY/ACCESSORIES | Interesting plated and anodized silver jewelry and accessories are created by Maria at a workshop in the back of her store. ✉ *Carrer Seminari 38* ☎ *971/480879* ⊕ *www. mariajuanico.com/en/tienda.*

Nadia Rabosio
JEWELRY/ACCESSORIES | This inventive designer has created an original selection of jewelry and hand-painted silks. ✉ *Carrer Santissim 4* ☎ *971/384080.*

El Toro

24 km (15 miles) northwest of Mahón.

The peak of El Toro is Menorca's highest point, at all of 1,555 feet. From the monastery on top you can see the whole island and across the sea to Mallorca.

GETTING HERE AND AROUND
Follow signs in Es Mercadal, the crossroads at the island's center.

🍴 Restaurants

Es Molí d'es Recó
$$$ | **CATALAN** | A great place to stop for a lunch of typical local cuisine, this restaurant is in an old windmill at the west end of Es Mercadal, on the ME1 about halfway between Mahón and Ciutadella and about 4 km (2½ miles) from El Toro. It has fortress-grade, whitewashed stone walls and low vaulted ceilings, and a constant air of cheerful bustle. **Known for:** Menorcan specialties; pretty terrace; sopa menorquina. ⓢ *Average main: €21* ✉ *Carrer Major 53, Mercadal* ☎ *971/375392.*

Fornells

35 km (22 miles) northwest of Mahón.

A little village (full-time population: 500) of whitewashed houses with red-tile roofs, Fornells comes alive in the summer high season, when Spanish and Catalan families arrive in droves to open their holiday chalets at the edge of town and in the nearby beach resorts. The bay—Menorca's second largest and deepest—is good for windsurfing, sailing, and scuba diving. The first fortifications built here to defend the Bay of Fornells from pirates date to 1625.

GETTING HERE AND AROUND
Buses leave the Estació Autobusos on Calle José Anselmo Clavé in Mahón for the 50-minute, 40-km (25-mile) trip to Fornells at 10:30, 12:30, 3, 5, and 7. By car, it's an easy half-hour drive north on the PM710.

 Activities

SAILING
Several miles long and a mile wide but with a narrow entrance to the sea and virtually no waves, the Bay of Fornells gives the beginner a feeling of security and the expert plenty of excitement.

Wind Fornells
SAILING | Here, on the beach just off Carrer del Rosari, you can rent windsurfing boards and dinghies and take lessons, individually or in groups. It's open May–October. ⊠ *Ctra. Es Mercadal–Fornells s/n, Mercadal* ☎ *664/335801* ⊕ *www. windfornells.com.*

Cova des Coloms

35 km (22 miles) northwest of Mahón.

There are caverns and grottoes all over the Balearics, some of them justly famous because of their size, spectacular formations, and subterranean pools. This one is well worth a visit.

GETTING HERE AND AROUND
Take the road from Ferreries to Es Migjorn Gran, park by the cemetery, and follow the signs on the footpath, about 30 minutes' walk toward the beach at Binigaus. Signs direct you to the gully, where you descend to the cave.

 Sights

Cova des Coloms (*Cave of Pigeons*)
CAVE | This massive cave is the most spectacular on Menorca, with eerie rock formations rising up to a 77-foot-high ceiling. When planning your visit, bear in mind that it's a 30-minute walk each way from the nearest parking. ⊠ *Ciutadella* ✛ *On eastern side of ravine from Es Migjorn Gran to beach.*

Chapter 11

ANDALUSIA

Updated by
Joanna Styles

👁 Sights	🍴 Restaurants	🛏 Hotels	🛍 Shopping	🍸 Nightlife
★★★★☆	★★★★★	★★★★☆	★★★☆☆	★★★☆☆

WELCOME TO ANDALUSIA

TOP REASONS TO GO

★ **Appreciate exquisite architecture:** Granada's Alhambra and Córdoba's Mezquita are two of Spain's—if not the world's—most impressive sites.

★ **Dance the flamenco:** "Olé" deep into the night at a heel-clicking flamenco performance in Jerez de la Frontera, the "cradle of flamenco."

★ **Admire priceless paintings:** Bask in the golden age of Spanish art at Seville's Museo de Bellas Artes.

★ **Explore ancient glory:** Cádiz, believed to be the oldest port in Europe, is resplendent with its sumptuous architecture and a magnificent cathedral.

★ **Visit the white villages:** Enjoy the simple beauty of a bygone age by exploring the gleaming *pueblos blancos.*

1 Seville. Food, architecture, and flamenco abound in this vibrant little city.

2 Carmona. Only 30 minutes from Seville, this charming town is a great base for exploring the region.

3 Italica. Known for the ruins of its Roman city.

4 Ronda. Famous for its dramatic escarpments, views, and gorge.

5 Around Ronda. Caves, mountain villages, and gorges.

6 Grazalema and the Sierra de Grazalema. One of Spain's most ecologically outstanding areas.

7 Doñana National Park. A World Heritage-listed park with incredible wildlife and nature.

8 La Rábida. Columbus planned his voyage from this pretty, peaceful village.

9 Aracena. A region known for its cured Iberian hams.

10 Jerez de la Frontera. The capital of horse culture and sherry.

11 Arcos de la Frontera. A classic Andalusian pueblo blanco.

12 Cádiz. So old that Julius Caesar once held public office here.

13 Córdoba. Home to the stunning Mezquita—a must visit.

14 Montilla. Vineyards, olive groves, and centuries of history.

15 Baena. A charming old town and good base for exploring the Sierras.

16 Zuheros. One of Andalusia's most beautiful white villages.

17 Priego de Córdoba. An olive farming town famous for its mansions and Baroque churches.

18 Jaén. Rich in history, with an impressive hilltop castle-parador.

19 Baeza. One of the best-preserved old towns in Spain.

20 Ubeda. Slightly larger than Baeza, this town is known for its architecture, artisan crafts, and olive groves.

21 Cazorla. Surrounded by fields of olive trees, with mountains as a backdrop.

22 Granada. Beautiful city home to the Alhambra and the tomb of the Catholic Monarchs.

23 Side Trips from Granada. Find some of Andalusia's prettiest, most ancient villages, including Fuente Vaqueros and the Alpujarras.

EATING AND DRINKING WELL IN ANDALUSIA

Andalusian cuisine, as diverse as the geography of seacoast, farmland, and mountains, is held together by its Moorish aromas. Cumin seed and other Arabian spices, along with salty-sweet combinations, are ubiquitous.

The eight Andalusian provinces cover a wide geographical and culinary spectrum. Superb seafood is center stage in Cádiz, Puerto de Santa María, and Sanlúcar de Barrameda. *Jamón ibérico de bellota* (Iberian acorn-fed ham) and other Iberian pork products rule from the Sierra de Aracena in Huelva to the Pedroches Mountains north of Córdoba. In Seville look for products from the Guadalquivir estuary, the Sierra, and the rich Campiña farmland all prepared with great creativity. In Córdoba try *salmorejo cordobés* (a thick gazpacho), *rabo de toro* (oxtail stew), or representatives of the salty-sweet legacy from Córdoba's Moorish heritage such as *cordero con miel* (lamb with honey). Spicy *crema de almendras* (almond soup) is a Granada favorite along with *habas con jamón* (broad beans with ham) from the Alpujarran village of Trevélez.

SHERRY

Dry sherry from Jerez de la Frontera (fino) and from Sanlúcar de Barrameda (manzanilla), share honors as favorite tapas accompaniments. Manzanilla, the more popular choice, is fresher and more delicate, with a slight marine tang. Both are the preferred drinks at Andalusian *ferias* (fairs), particularly in Seville in April and Jerez de la Frontera in May.

COLD VEGETABLE SOUPS

Spain's most popular contribution to world gastronomy after paella may well be gazpacho, a simple peasant soup served cold and filled with scraps and garden ingredients. Tomatoes, cucumber, garlic, oil, bread, and chopped peppers are the ingredients, and side plates of chopped onion, peppers, garlic, tomatoes, and croutons accompany, to be added to taste. Salmorejo cordobés, a thicker cold vegetable soup with the same ingredients but a different consistency, is used to accompany tapas.

MOORISH FLAVORS

Andalusia's 781-year sojourn at the heart of Al-Andalus, the Moorish empire on the Iberian Peninsula, left as many tastes and aromas as mosques and fortresses. Cumin-laced *boquerones en adobo* (marinated anchovies) or the salty-sweet cordero con miel are two examples, along with coriander-spiked *espinacas con garbanzos* (spinach with garbanzo beans) and *perdiz con dátiles y almendras* (partridge stewed with dates and almonds). Desserts especially reflect the Moorish legacy in morsels such as *pestiños,* cylinders or twists of fried dough in anise-honey syrup.

FRIED FISH

Andalusia is famous for its fried fish, from *pescaito frito* (fried whitebait) to *calamares fritos* (fried squid rings). Andalusians are masters of deep-frying techniques using very hot olive and vegetable oils that produce peerlessly crisp, dry *frituras* (fried seafood); much of Andalusia's finest tapas repertory is known for being served up piping hot and crunchy. Look for *tortillita de camarones,* a delicate lacework of tiny fried shrimp.

STEWS

Guisos are combinations of vegetables, with or without meat, cooked slowly over low heat. Rabo de toro is a favorite throughout Andalusia, though Córdoba claims the origin of this dark and delicious stew made from the tail of a fighting bull. The segments of tail are cleaned, browned, and set aside before leeks, onions, carrots, garlic, and bay leaves are stewed in the same pan. Cloves, salt, pepper, a liter of wine, and a half liter of beef broth are added to the stew with the meat, and they're all simmered for two to three hours until the meat is falling off the bone and thoroughly tenderized. *Alboronía,* also known as *pisto andaluz,* is a traditional stew of eggplant, bell peppers, and zucchini.

FLAMENCO

Rule one about flamenco: You don't see it. You feel it. The pain and yearning on the dancers' faces and the eerie voices are real. If the dancers manage to summon the *duende* and allow this soulful state of emotion to take over, then they have done their jobs well.

FLAMENCO 101

Origins: The music is largely Arabic in its beginnings, but you'll detect echoes of Greek dirges and Jewish chants, with healthy doses of Flemish and traditional Castilian thrown in. Hindu sways, Roman mimes, and other movement informs the dance, but we may never know the specific origins of flamenco. The dance, along with the nomadic Gypsies, spread throughout Andalusia and within a few centuries had developed into many variations and styles, some of them named after the city where they were born (such as malaguenas and *sevillanas*) and others taking on the names after people, emotions, or bands. In all, there are more than 50 different styles (or *palos*) of flamenco, four of which are the stylistic pillars others branch off from—differing mainly in rhythm and mood: *toná, soleá,* fandango, and seguidilla.

Clapping and castanets: The sum of its parts are awe-inspiring, but if you boil it down, flamenco is a combination of music, singing, and dance. Staccato hand-clapping almost sneaks in as a fourth part—the sounds made from all the participants' palms, or *palmas,* is part of the duende— but this element remains more of a connector that all in the performance take part in when their hands are free.

Hand-clapping was likely flamenco's original key instrument before the guitar, *cajón* (wooden box used for percussion), and other instruments arrived on the scene. Perhaps the simplest way to augment the clapping is to add a uniquely designed six-string guitar, in which case you've got yourself a *tablao,* or people seated around a singer and clapping. Dance undoubtedly augments the experience, but isn't necessary for a tablao. These exist all throughout Andalusia and are usually private affairs with people who love flamenco. One needn't be a Gypsy in order to take part in it. But it doesn't hurt. Castanets (or *palillos*) were absorbed by the Phoenician culture and adopted by the Spanish, now part of their own folklore. They accompany other traditional folk dances in Spain and are used pervasively throughout flamenco (though not always present in some forms of dance).

Flamenco now: Flamenco's enormous international resurgence has been building for the past few decades. Much of this revival can be attributed to pioneers like legendary singer Camarón de la Isla, guitarist Paco de Lucía, or even outsiders like Miles Davis fusing flamenco with other genres like jazz and rock. Today the most popular flamenco fusion artists include Rosalía and Fuel Fandango.

FLAMENCO HEAD TO TOE

Wrists rotate while hands move, articulating each finger individually, curling in and out. The trick is to have it appear like an effortless flourish. Facial expression is considered another tool for the dancer, and it's never plastered on but projected from some deeper place. For women, the hair is usually pulled back in touring flamenco performances in order to give the back row a chance to see more clearly the passionate expressions. In smaller settings like tablaos, hair is usually let down and is supposed to better reveal the beauty of the female form overall. The dancer carries the body in an upright and proud manner: the chest is out, shoulders back. Despite this position, the body should never carry tension—it needs to remain pliable and fluid. With professional dancers, the feet can move so quickly, they blur like hummingbird wings in action. When they move slowly, you can watch the different ways a foot can strike the floor. A *planta* is when the whole foot strikes the floor, as opposed to when the ball of the foot or the heel (*taco*) hits. Each one must be a "clean" strike or the sound will be off.

Gypsies, flamenco, horses, bulls—Andalusia is the Spain of story and song, simultaneously the least and most surprising part of the country: least surprising because it lives up to the hype and stereotype that long confused all of Spain with the Andalusian version, and most surprising because it is, at the same time, so much more.

To begin with, five of the eight Andalusian provinces are maritime, with colorful fishing fleets and a wealth of seafood usually associated with the north. Second, there are snowcapped mountains and ski resorts in Andalusia, the kind of high sierra resources normally associated with the Alps, or even the Pyrenees, yet the Sierra Nevada—with Granada at the foothills—is within sight of North Africa. Third, there are wildlife-filled wetlands and highland pine and oak forests rich with game and trout streams, not to mention free-range Iberian pigs. And last, there are cities like Seville that somehow manage to combine all of this with the creativity and cosmopolitanism of London or Barcelona.

Andalusia—for 781 years (711–1492) a Moorish empire and named for al-Andalus (Arabic for "Land of the West")—is where the authentic history and character of the Iberian Peninsula and Spanish culture are most palpably, visibly, audibly, and aromatically apparent.

An exploration of Andalusia must begin with the cities of Seville, Córdoba, and Granada as the fundamental triangle of interest and identity. All the romantic images of Andalusia, and Spain in general, spring vividly to life in Seville: Spain's fourth-largest city is a cliché of matadors, flamenco, tapas bars, Gypsies, geraniums, and strolling guitarists, but there's so much more than these urban treasures. A more thorough Andalusian experience includes such unforgettable natural settings as Huelva's Sierra de Aracena and Doñana wetlands, Jaén's Parque Natural de Cazorla, Cádiz's pueblos blancos, and Granada's Alpujarras mountains.

MAJOR REGIONS

Seville and Around Seville. Long Spain's chief riverine port, the captivating city of Seville sits astride the Guadalquivir River, which launched Christopher Columbus to the New World and Ferdinand Magellan around the globe. South of the capital is fertile farmland; in the north are highland villages. Worthy daytrips and side trips from Seville include **Carmona**, **Italica**, **Ronda**, and **Grazalema**.

Huelva. Famed as oak-forested grazing grounds for the treasured *cerdo ibérico* (Iberian pig), the province's **Doñana National Park** is another of Spain's greatest national treasures. **La Rabida** is worth a visit for its Christopher-Columbus associations and **Aracena** is a fresh and leafy mountain getaway on the border of Portugal.

Cádiz Province and Jerez de la Frontera. Almost completely surrounded by water, the city of **Cádiz** is Western Europe's oldest continually inhabited city, a dazzling bastion at the edge of the Atlantic. **Jerez de la Frontera** is known for its sherry, flamenco, and equestrian culture. Other notable villages worth visiting are **Arcos de la Frontera** and **El Puerto de Santa María.**

Cordoba and Side Trips from Cordoba. **Córdoba,** a center of world science and philosophy in the 9th and 10th centuries, is a living monument to its past glory. Its prized building is the Mezquita (mosque). In the countryside, acorns and olives thrive and must-visit villages include **Montilla, Baena, Zuheros,** and **Priego de Córdoba.**

Jaén Province. Andalusia's northeastern-most province is a striking contrast of olive groves, pristine wilderness, and Renaissance towns with elegant palaces and churches like **Baeza** and **Ubeda.** **Cazorla,** at the east end of the province has a remote, mountain setting and endless miles of olive groves.

Granada. Christian and Moorish cultures are dramatically counterposed in Granada, especially in the graceful enclaves of **La Alhambra** and **Realejo.** To the west of the Darro are the neighborhoods of **Sacromonte** and **Albayzin.** The **Centro** or city center is the main shopping area.

Planning

When to Go

The best months to go to Andalusia are October and November and April and May. It's blisteringly hot in the summer; if that's your only chance to come, plan

time in the Pedroches of northern Córdoba province, Granada's Sierra Nevada and Alpujarras highlands, or the Sierra de Cazorla in Jaén to beat the heat. Autumn catches the cities going about their business, the temperatures are moderate, and you will rarely see a line form.

December through March tends to be cool, uncrowded, and quiet, but come spring, it's fiesta time, with Seville's Semana Santa (Holy Week, between Palm Sunday and Easter) the most moving and multitudinous. April showcases whitewashed Andalusia at its floral best, every patio and facade covered with flowers from bougainvillea to honeysuckle.

Planning Your Time

A week in Andalusia should include visits to Córdoba, Seville, and Granada to see, respectively, the Mezquita, the cathedral and its Giralda minaret, and the Alhambra. Two days in each city nearly fills the week, though the extra day would be best spent in Seville, Andalusia's most vibrant concentration of art, architecture, culture, and excitement.

Indeed, a week or more in Seville alone would be ideal, especially during the Semana Santa celebration, when the city becomes a giant street party. With more time on your hands, Cádiz, Jerez de la Frontera, and Sanlúcar de Barrameda form a three- or four-day jaunt through flamenco, sherry, Andalusian equestrian culture, and tapas emporiums.

A three-day trip through the Sierra de Aracena will introduce you to a lovely Atlantic upland, filled with Mediterranean black pigs deliciously fattened on acorns, while the Alpujarras, the mountain range east of Granada, is famed for its pueblos blancos. In this region you can find anywhere from three days to a week of hiking and trekking opportunities in some of the highest and wildest reaches in Spain. For nature enthusiasts, the highland

Cazorla National Park and the wetland Doñana National Park are Andalusia's highest and lowest outdoor treasures.

Getting Here and Around

AIR TRAVEL

Andalusia's regional airports can be reached via Spanish domestic flights or from major European hubs. Málaga Airport (*see Costa del Sol and Costa de Almería*) is one of Spain's major hubs and a good access point for exploring this part of Andalusia.

The region's second-largest airport, after Málaga, is in Seville. The smaller Aeropuerto de Jerez is 7 km (4 miles) northeast of Jerez on the road to Seville. Buses run from the airport to Jerez and Cádiz. Flying into Granada's airport from Madrid or Barcelona is also a good option if you want to start your trip in Andalusia. It's easy to get into Granada from the airport.

BUS TRAVEL

The best way to get around Andalusia, if you're not driving, is by bus. Buses serve most small towns and villages and are faster and more frequent than trains. ALSA is the major bus company; tickets can be booked online, but be aware that non-Spanish credit cards occasionally cause problems with the system. Payment via PayPal is usually problem-free.

BUS CONTACTS ALSA ☎ *902/422242* ⊕ *www.alsa.es.*

CAR TRAVEL

If you're planning to explore beyond Seville, Granada, and Córdoba, a car makes travel convenient.

The main road from Madrid is the A4 through Córdoba to Seville, a four-lane *autovía* (highway). From Granada or Málaga, head for Antequera, then take the A92 autovía by way of Osuna to Seville. Road trips from Seville to the Costa del Sol (by way of Ronda) are slow but scenic. Driving in western Andalusia is easy—the terrain is mostly flat land or slightly hilly, and the roads are straight and in good condition. From Seville to Jerez and Cádiz, the A4 highway gets you to Cádiz in under an hour. The only way to access Doñana National Park by road is to take the A49 Seville–Huelva highway, exit for Almonte/Bollullos Par del Condado, then follow the signs for El Rocío and Matalascañas. The A49 west of Seville will also lead you to the freeway to Portugal and the Algarve. There are some beautiful scenic drives here, about which the respective tourist offices can advise you. The A369, heading southwest from Ronda to Gaucín, passes through stunning whitewashed villages.

With the exception of parts of the Alpujarras, most roads in this region are smooth, and touring by car is one of the most enjoyable ways to see the countryside. Local tourist offices can advise about scenic drives. One good route heads northwest from Seville on the A66 passing through stunning scenery; turn northeast on the A461 to Santa Olalla de Cala to the village of Zufre, dramatically set at the edge of a gorge. Backtrack and continue on to Aracena. Return via the Minas de Riotinto (signposted from Aracena), which will bring you back to the A66 heading east to Seville.

RENTAL CONTACT Autopro ☎ *952/176545* ⊕ *www.autopro.es.*

FERRY TRAVEL

From Cádiz, Trasmediterránea operates ferry services to the Canary Islands with stops at Las Palmas de Gran Canaria (39 hours) and connecting ferries on to Fuerteventura, Lanzarote, La Palma, and Santa Cruz de Tenerife. There are no direct ferries from Seville.

CONTACT Acciona Trasmediterránea ✉ *Estación Marítima, Cádiz* ☎ *902/454645* ⊕ *www.trasmediterranea.es.*

TAXI TRAVEL

Taxis are plentiful throughout Andalusia and may be hailed on the street or from specified taxi stands. Fares are reasonable, and meters are strictly used; the minimum fare is about €4. You are not required to tip taxi drivers, although rounding off the amount is appreciated. Uber and Cabify services, available via mobile app, operate in some parts of Andalusia; Uber is in Córdoba, Granada, and Seville, while Cabify is in Seville.

In Seville or Granada, expect to pay around €20–€25 for cab fare from the airport to the city center.

TRAIN TRAVEL

From Madrid, the best approach to Andalusia is via the high-speed AVE. In just 2½ hours, the spectacular ride winds through olive groves and rolling fields of Castile to Córdoba and on to Seville.

Seville, Córdoba, Jerez, and Cádiz all lie on the main rail line from Madrid to southern Spain. Trains leave Madrid for Seville (via Córdoba), and two of the non-AVE trains continue to Jerez and Cádiz. Travel time from Seville to Cádiz is 1½ hours. Trains also depart regularly for Barcelona (4 daily, 5½ hours), and Huelva (3 daily, 1½ hours). From Granada, Málaga, Ronda, and Algeciras, trains go to Seville via Bobadilla.

Restaurants

Eating out is an intrinsic part of the Andalusian lifestyle. Whether it's sharing some tapas with friends over a prelunch drink or a three-course à la carte meal, many Andalusians eat out at some point during the day. Unsurprisingly, there are literally thousands of bars and restaurants throughout the region catering to all budgets and tastes.

At lunchtime, check out the *menús del día* (daily menus) offered by many restaurants, usually three courses and excellent value (expect to pay €8–€15,

depending on the type of restaurant and location). Roadside restaurants, known as *ventas*, usually provide good food in generous portions and at reasonable prices. Be aware that many restaurants add a service charge (*cubierto*), which can be as much as €3 per person, and some restaurant prices don't include value-added tax (*impuesto sobre el valor añadido/I.V.A.*) at 10%. Note also that restaurants with tasting menus (*menús de degustación*) usually require everyone at the table to have the menu.

Andalusians tend to eat later than their fellow Spaniards: lunch is 2–4 pm, and dinner starts at 9 pm (10 pm in the summer). In cities, many restaurants are closed Sunday night, and fish restaurants tend to close on Monday; in inland towns and cities, some restaurants close for all of August.

Hotels

Seville has grand old hotels, such as the Alfonso XIII, and a number of former palaces converted into sumptuous hostelries.

The Parador de Granada, next to the Alhambra, is a magnificent way to enjoy Granada. Hotels on the Alhambra hill, especially the parador, must be reserved far in advance. Lodging establishments in Granada's city center, around the Puerta Real and Acera del Darro, can be unbelievably noisy, so if you're staying there, ask for a room toward the back. Though Granada has plenty of hotels, it can be difficult to find lodging during peak tourist season (Easter through late October).

In Córdoba, several pleasant hotels occupy houses in the old quarter, close to the mosque. Other than during Holy Week and the Festival de los Patios in May, it's easy to find a room in Córdoba, even without a reservation.

Rental accommodations bookable on portals such as Airbnb are popular in large towns and cities, although quality varies so double-check reviews before you book.

Not all hotel prices include value-added tax (I.V.A.) and the 10% surcharge may be added to your final bill. Check when you book. *Hotel reviews have been shortened. For full information, visit Fodors. com.*

Tours

Alúa
ADVENTURE TOURS | For help with planning and getting the equipment for hiking, rock climbing, mountain biking, caving, and other active sports throughout Andalusia, this is a good place to start. ✉ *Calle Concejal Francisco Ruiz Librero, Bormujos* ☎ *955/110776* ⊕ *www.alua.es* ✉ *From €15.*

★ annie b's Spanish Kitchen
SPECIAL-INTEREST | Based in Vejer de la Frontera (Cádiz), Scottish-born Annie B offers food and wine experiences, including sherry tours, tuna *almadraba* (an age-old way of trapping) trips, and cooking classes. ✉ *Calle Viñas, 11, Vejer de la Frontera* ☎ *620/560649* ⊕ *www. anniebspain.com* ✉ *From €75.*

Cabalgar Rutas Alternativas
EXCURSIONS | This is an established Alpujarras equestrian agency that organizes horseback riding in the Sierra Nevada. ✉ *C. Ermita, Bubión* ☎ *958/763135* ⊕ *www.ridingandalucia.com* ✉ *Rides from €25, tours from €795.*

Faro del Sur
ADVENTURE TOURS | Activities such as trekking, cycling, sailing, and kayaking in western Andalusia are available, and tours include kayaking along the Guadalquivir River and sailing along the Huelva coastline. ✉ *Puerto Deportivo L-1, Isla Cristina* ☎ *959/344490* ⊕ *www. farodelsur.com* ✉ *From €400.*

Glovento Sur
AIR EXCURSIONS | Up to five people at a time are taken in balloon trips above Granada, Ronda, and Seville. ✉ *Placeta Nevot 4, #1A, Granada* ☎ *958/290316* ⊕ *www.gloventosur.com* ✉ *From €200.*

Guías de Cazorla
ADVENTURE TOURS | Guided hikes, horseback riding, canyoning, and four-wheel-drive tours in the Sierra de Cazorla are offered. ✉ *Calle Pósteles 18, Cazorla* ☎ *953/720112* ⊕ *guiasdecazorla.es* ✉ *From €30.*

Nevadensis
GUIDED TOURS | Based in the Alpujarras, Nevadensis leads guided hiking, climbing, and skiing tours of the Sierra Nevada. Note that prices are per group. ✉ *Pl. de la Libertad, Pampaneira* ☎ *958/763127* ⊕ *www.nevadensis.com* ✉ *From €150.*

Sierra eXtreme
ADVENTURE TOURS | Choose from a wide range of adventure sports such as walking, climbing, caving, and canyoning in the Andalusian mountains with this company. ☎ *637/727365* ⊕ *www. sierraextreme.net* ✉ *From €25.*

Sierra Trails
EXCURSIONS | Trail rides in the Alpujarras, lasting up to a week, can be organized through this company. The price includes airport transfers, overnight stays, and most meals. ✉ *Ctra. de la Sierra, Bubión* ☎ *608/453802* ⊕ *www.spain-horse-riding.com* ✉ *Rides from €95, tours from €675.*

Seville

550 km (340 miles) southwest of Madrid.

Seville's whitewashed houses bright with bougainvillea, ocher-color palaces, and baroque facades have long enchanted both sevillanos and travelers. It's a city for the senses—the fragrance of orange blossom (orange trees line many streets) suffuses the air in spring, the sound of flamenco echoes through the alleyways in Triana and Santa Cruz, and views of the great Guadalquivir River accompany you at every turn. This is also a fine city in its architecture and people—stroll down the swankier pedestrian shopping streets and you can't fail to notice just how good-looking everyone is. Aside from being blessed with even features and flashing dark eyes, Sevillanos exude a cool sophistication that seems more Catalan than Andalusian.

The layout of the historic center of Seville makes exploring easy. The central zone—**Centro**—around the cathedral, Calle Sierpes, and Plaza Nueva, is splendid and monumental, but it's not where you'll find Seville's greatest charm. **El Arenal,** home of the Maestranza bullring, the Teatro de la Maestranza concert hall, and a concentration of picturesque taverns, still buzzes the way it must have when stevedores loaded and unloaded ships from the New World. Just southeast of Centro, the medieval Jewish quarter, **Barrio de Santa Cruz,** is home to the *Real Alcázar* (fortress) and a lovely, whitewashed tangle of alleys. The **Barrio de la Macarena** to the northeast is rich in sights and authentic Seville atmosphere. The fifth and final neighborhood to explore, on the far side of the Río Guadalquivir, is in many ways the best of all—**Triana,** the traditional habitat for sailors, bullfighters, and flamenco artists, as well as the main workshop for Seville's renowned ceramicists.

GETTING HERE AND AROUND
AIR TRAVEL
Seville's airport is about 7 km (4½ miles) east of the city. There's a bus from the airport to the center of town every half hour daily (5:20 am–1:15 am; €4 one-way, €6 return). Taxi fare from the airport to the city center is around €22 during the day and €25 at night and on Sunday. A number of private companies operate private airport-shuttle services.

BIKE TRAVEL
As an almost completely flat city, Seville is perfect for bike travel, and there are several bike rental companies within the city, including Bici4City and Oh my bikes!

CONTACTS Bici4City ⊠ *Calle Peral 6, Centro* ☎ *954/229883* ⊕ *bici4city.com.* **Oh my bikes!** ⊠ *Av. Menéndez y Pelayo 11, Barrio de Santa Cruz* ☎ *954/536017* ⊕ *www.ohmybikes.com.*

BUS TRAVEL
Seville has two intercity bus stations: Estación Plaza de Armas, the main one, with buses serving Córdoba, Granada, Huelva, and Málaga in Andalusia, plus Madrid and Portugal and other international destinations; and the smaller Estación del Prado de San Sebastián, serving Cádiz and nearby towns and villages.

Certain routes operate limited night service from midnight to 2 am Monday through Thursday, with services until 5 am Friday through Sunday. Single rides cost €1.40, but if you're going to be busing a lot, it's more economical to buy a rechargeable multitravel pass, which works out to €0.69 per ride. Special Tarjetas Turísticas (tourist passes) valid for one or three days of unlimited bus travel cost (respectively) €5 and €10. Tickets are sold at newsstands and at the main bus station, Prado de San Sebastián.

CONTACTS Estación del Prado de San Sebastián ⊠ *Calle Vázquez Sagastizábal, El Arenal* ☎ *955/479290.* **Estación Plaza de Armas** ⊠ *Puente Cristo de la Expiración, Centro* ☎ *955/038665* ⊕ *www.autobus-esplazadearmas.es.*

CAR TRAVEL
Getting in and out of Seville by car isn't difficult, thanks to the SE30 ring road, but getting around in the city by car is problematic. We advise leaving your car at your hotel or in a lot while you're here.

TAXI TRAVEL
CONTACTS Radio Taxi Sevilla
☎ 954/580000.

TRAIN TRAVEL
Train connections include the high-speed AVE service from Madrid, with a journey time of less than 2½ hours.

CONTACTS Estación Santa Justa ⊠ *Av. Kansas City, El Arenal* ☎ *912/320320.*

TOURS
Azahar Sevilla Tapas Tours
SPECIAL-INTEREST | Local food and wine expert Shawn Hennessey leads guided tours around Seville's best tapas bars (traditional and gourmet). Choose from several different tours, lunch or evening. ⊕ *azahar-sevilla.com/sevilletapas/tapas-tours* ➔ *From €70.*

History and Tapas Tour
GUIDED TOURS | Glean local, historical, and culinary knowledge on a variety of tours around sights and tapas bars. ⊕ *www.sevilleconcierge.com* ➔ *From €60.*

Sevilla Bike Tour
BICYCLE TOURS | Guided tours, leaving from the Makinline Shop on Calle Arjona at 10:30 am, take in the major sights of the city and offer interesting stories and insider information along the way. You'll cover about 10 km (6 miles) in three hours. Reservations are required on weekends and recommended on weekdays. ⊠ *Calle Arjona 8, Centro* ☎ *954/562625* ⊕ *www.sevillabiketour.com* ➔ *From €25.*

Sevilla Walking Tours
WALKING TOURS | A choice of three walking tours are conducted in English: the City Walking Tour, leaving Plaza Nueva from the statue of San Fernando; the Alcázar Tour, leaving Plaza del Triunfo from the central statue; and the Cathedral Tour, also leaving from the Plaza del Triunfo central statue. ⊠ *Seville* ☎ *902/158226, 616/501100* ⊕ *sevillawalkingtours.com* ➔ *From €12.*

Where's Columbus?

Christopher Columbus knew both triumph and disgrace, yet he found no repose—he died, bitterly disillusioned, in Valladolid in 1506. No one knows for certain where he's buried; he was reportedly laid to rest for the first time in the Dominican Republic and then moved over the years to other locations. A portion of his remains can be found in Seville's cathedral.

Your First Flamenco Experience
SPECIAL-INTEREST | Local dancer Eva Izquierdo from Triana teaches you how to clap in time, stand, and take your first dance steps, in authentic costume. ⊠ *Seville* ☎ *626/007868* ⊕ *www.ishowusevilla.com* ➔ *From €35.*

VISITOR INFORMATION
CONTACTS City of Seville ⊠ *Paseo Marqués de Contador s/n, Barrio de Santa Cruz* ✛ *On waterfront, by Torre de Oro* ☎ *955/471232* ⊕ *www.visitasevilla.es.*

Centro

The Centro area is the heart of Seville's commercial life. It has bustling shopping streets, several of which are pedestrianized, and leafy squares lined with bars and cafés. The residential streets contain some of the best examples of colonial architecture; noteworthy features include fine facades and roof gables topped with local ceramics. Centro is also home to several of the city's most beautiful churches.

Seville's cathedral is the largest and tallest cathedral in Spain, the largest Gothic building in the world, and the third-largest church in the world, after St. Peter's in Rome and St. Paul's in London.

 Sights

Calle Sierpes

NEIGHBORHOOD | This is Seville's classy main shopping street. Near the southern end, at No. 85, a plaque marks the spot where the Cárcel Real (Royal Prison) once stood. Miguel de Cervantes began writing *Don Quixote* in one of its cells. ✉ *Centro.*

★ Catedral de Sevilla

RELIGIOUS SITE | Seville's cathedral can be described only in superlatives: it's the largest and highest cathedral in Spain, the largest Gothic building in the world, and the world's third-largest church, after St. Peter's in Rome and St. Paul's in London. After Ferdinand III captured Seville from the Moors in 1248, the great mosque begun by Yusuf II in 1171 was used as a Christian cathedral. In 1401 Seville pulled down the old mosque, leaving only its minaret and outer courtyard, and built a new cathedral in just over a century. The magnificent *retablo* (altarpiece) in the Capilla Mayor (Main Chapel) is the largest in Christendom. The Capilla Real (Royal Chapel) is concealed behind a curtain, but duck in if you're quick, quiet, and properly dressed (no shorts or sleeveless tops). Don't forget the Patio de los Naranjos (Courtyard of Orange Trees), where the fountain in the center was used for ablutions before people entered the original mosque. ✉ *Pl. Virgen de los Reyes, Centro* ☎ *954/214971* ⊕ *www.catedraldesevilla.es* 🎫 *€9 (free Mon. 4:30–6 pm if you book via the website).*

Metropol Parasol

ARCHAEOLOGICAL SITE | This huge square, at the west end of Calle Cuna, is home to the world's largest wooden structure, 492 feet long by 230 feet wide. The design represents giant trees, reminiscent of Gaudí, and walkways run through the "tree tops" affording great views of the city, especially at sunset. At ground level, there are interesting archaeological remains (mostly Roman) and a large indoor food market. ✉ *Pl. de la Encarnación, Centro* 🎫 *€3.*

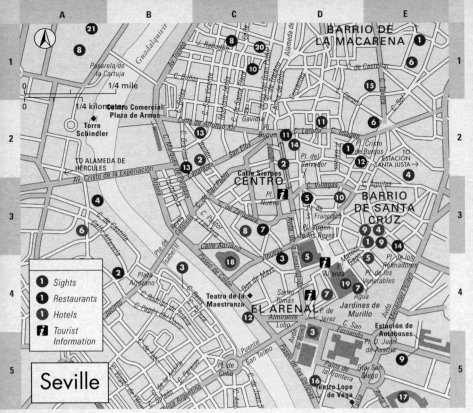

Sights ▼

1 Basílica de la
Macarena **E1**

2 Calle Sierpes **C2**

3 Capilla de los
Marineros **B4**

4 Casa de Pilatos **E2**

5 Catedral de
Sevilla **D4**

6 Convento de
Santa Paula **E1**

7 Hospital de los
Venerables **D4**

8 Isla de
La Cartuja **A1**

9 Jewish Quarter **E3**

10 Museo del Baile
Flamenco **D3**

11 Metropol Parasol **D2**

12 Monasterio de
Santa María
de las Cuevas **C4**

13 Museo de
Bellas Artes **C2**

14 Palacio de la
Condesa de Lebrija **D2**

15 Palacio de las Dueñas .. **E1**

16 Parque de
María Luisa **D5**

17 Plaza de España **E5**

18 Plaza de Toros
Real Maestranza **C4**

19 Real Alcázar **D4**

20 San Lorenzo y Jesús
del Gran Poder **C1**

21 Torre del Oro **A1**

Restaurants ▼

1 Bache San Pedro **D2**

2 Bar Las Golondrinas **B4**

3 Casa Morales **C4**

4 De la O **A3**

5 El Pintón **D3**

6 El Rinconcillo **E2**

7 Enrique Becerra **C3**

8 Espacio Eslava **C1**

9 Ispal **E5**

10 La Azotea **C1**

11 La Campana **D2**

12 Palo Cartao **E2**

13 Vermutería
Yo Soy Tu Padre **B2**

14 Vinería San Telmo **E3**

Hotels ▼

1 Casa del Poeta **E3**

2 Gran MeliáColón **C2**

3 Hotel Alfonso XIII **D4**

4 Hotel Amadeus
la Música **E3**

5 Hotel Casa 1800 .... **E4**

6 Hotel Monte Triana **A3**

7 Legado Alcazar **D4**

8 Mercer **C3**

9 Pensión Córdoba **E3**

★ Palacio de la Condesa de Lebrija

CASTLE/PALACE | This lovely palace has three ornate patios, including a spectacular courtyard graced by a Roman mosaic taken from the ruins in Itálica, surrounded by Moorish arches and fine *azulejos* (painted tiles). The side rooms house a collection of archaeological items. The second floor contains the family apartments and visits are by guided tour only. **■TIP➔ It's well worth paying the extra for the second-floor tour, which gives an interesting insight into the collections and the family.** ✉ *Calle Cuna 8, Centro* ☎ *954/227802* 🎟 *From €6 (free Mon. 6–7 pm).*

Palacio de las Dueñas

HOUSE | The 15th-century home and official residence of the late 18th Duchess of Alba in Seville is an oasis of peace and quiet in the bustling city. Set around an ornate patio with Mudejar arches and a central fountain, the house includes antiques and paintings, as well as memorabilia relating to the duchess herself. Revered in the city and one of Spain's most important noblewomen and society figures, Cayetana de Alba loved bullfighting, flamenco, and ceramics. The visit (first floor only) also includes the stables, gardens (said to have inspired some of the poet Antonio Machado's most famous early verses), and a Gothic chapel. ✉ *Calle Dueñas 5, Centro* ☎ *954/214828* 🎟 *€10 (free Mon. beginning at 4).*

🍴 Restaurants

Casa Morales

$ | **TAPAS** | Down a side street off the Avenida de la Constitución, this historic bar (formerly a wine store) takes you back to 19th-century Seville, and it is still run by the same family that established it in 1850. Locals pack the place at lunchtime, when popular dishes include *menudo con garbanzos* (tripe with chickpeas) and *albóndigas de choco* (cuttlefish croquettes). **Known for:** local atmosphere; wine list; tripe with chickpeas. [$] *Average main: €8* ✉ *Calle García de Vinuesa 11, Centro* ☎ *954/221242* 🕓 *Closed Sun.*

El Pintón

$$ | **FUSION** | With a privileged spot a block north from the cathedral, this central restaurant offers two dining spaces: on the traditional inside patio, where wood, mirrors, and tasteful lighting create an intimate but airy space, or outside on the pleasant terrace. The cuisine combines Andalusian dishes with a modern touch, with menu items such as bloody gazpacho, *huevo en tempura con parmentier trufado* (egg in batter with truffled potato puree), red tuna tartare, and *solomillo ibérico relleno de setas* (Iberian pork steak filled with mushrooms). **Known for:** attractive interior; value quick bites; Mediterranean dishes. [$] *Average main: €12* ✉ *Calle Francos 42, Centro* ☎ *955/075153* 🌐 *elpinton.com.*

★ Espacio Eslava

$$ | **TAPAS** | The crowds gathered outside this local favorite off the Alameda de Hercules may be off-putting at first, but the creative, inexpensive tapas (from €3) are well worth the wait—and so is the house specialty, the Basque dessert *sokoa.* Try delicacies like the *solomillo de pato con pan de queso y salsa de peras al vino* (duck fillet with cheesy bread and pears in wine sauce). **Known for:** tapas; sokoa, a Basque dessert; vegetable strudel. [$] *Average main: €12* ✉ *Calle Eslava 3, Centro* ☎ *954/906568* 🕓 *Closed Mon. No dinner Sun.*

La Azotea

$$ | **SPANISH** | With a young vibe and a vast and inventive menu (which changes seasonally), this tiny restaurant offers a welcome change from Seville's typical fried fare. The owners' haute-cuisine ambitions are reflected in excellent service and lovingly prepared food—but not in the prices. **Known for:** creative tapas; seasonal menu; local vibe. [$] *Average main: €15* ✉ *Calle Jesus del Gran Poder*

31, Centro ☎ *955/116748* 💳 *No credit cards* 🕒 *Closed Sun. and Mon.*

★ La Campana

FOOD/CANDY | Under the gilt-edged ceiling at Seville's most celebrated pastry outlet (founded in 1885), you can enjoy the flan-like *tocino de cielo,* or "heavenly bacon." For breakfast, enjoy a traditional feed of toasted bread with tomato and a strong coffee, served at a standing bar. Prices are reasonable despite its popularity. ✉ *Calle Sierpes 1, Centro* ☎ *954/223570* 🌐 *confiterialacampana.com.*

Hotels

★ Mercer

$$$$ | **HOTEL** | Housed in a 19th-century mansion, Mercer is one of the city's top boutique hotels, featuring a lofty patio with a fountain, a stunning marble staircase, and a striking geometric chandelier atop a glass gallery. **Pros:** luxury lodging; spacious rooms; rooftop terrace with plunge pool. **Cons:** pricey; a little too prim; patio rooms have no views. [$] *Rooms from: €450* ✉ *Calle Castelar 26, Centro* ☎ *954/223004* 🌐 *www.mercersevilla.com* 🛏 *10 rooms* 🍴 *Free Breakfast.*

Nightlife

Naima Café Jazz

MUSIC CLUBS | This tiny bar off Alameda de Hércules features jazz, blues, or jam sessions every night. It's open from 8 pm till late. ✉ *Calle Trajano 47, Centro* ☎ *954/382485* [M] *Sevilla–Santa Justa.*

Shopping

Ángela y Adela Taller de Diseño

CLOTHING | Come to this shop for privately fitted and custom-made flamenco dresses. ✉ *Calle Luchana 6, Centro* ☎ *954/227186.*

Buffana

JEWELRY/ACCESSORIES | This shop carries handmade hats and caps for all occasions, especially weddings. ✉ *Calle Don Alonso el Sabio 8, Centro* ☎ *954/537824* 🌐 *patriciabuffuna.com.*

Lola Azahares

CLOTHING | For flamenco wear, this is one of Seville's most highly regarded stores. ✉ *Calle Cuna 31, Centro* ☎ *954/222912.*

Plaza del Duque

CRAFTS | A few blocks north of Plaza Nueva, Plaza del Duque has a crafts market Thursday through Saturday. ✉ *Centro.*

Barrio de Santa Cruz

The most romantic neighborhood in the city, Santa Cruz offers the visitor quintessential Seville: whitewashed houses with colorful geraniums and bourgainvillea cascading down their facades, winding alleyways, and intimate squares scented with orange blossoms in the spring, all lit by old-style lamps at night. This neighborhood is also the busiest and most touristic part of Seville—so stray from the main thoroughfares and lose yourself in the side streets to discover a place where time seems to have stopped and all you hear is birdsong.

Sights

★ Casa de Pilatos

HOUSE | With its fine patio and superb azulejo decorations, this palace is a beautiful blend of Spanish Mudejar and Renaissance architecture and is considered a prototype of an Andalusian mansion. It was built in the first half of the 16th century by the dukes of Tarifa, ancestors of the present owner, the Duke of Medinaceli. It's known as Pilate's House because Don Fadrique, first marquis of Tarifa, allegedly modeled it on Pontius Pilate's house in Jerusalem, where he had gone on a pilgrimage in 1518. The upstairs apartments, which you can see on a guided tour, have frescoes, paintings, and antique furniture. Admission includes an audio guide in English.

Seville's grand alcázar is a UNESCO World Heritage Site and an absolute must-see.

✉ *Pl. de Pilatos 1, Barrio de Santa Cruz* ☎ *954/225298* ✈ *From €10.*

Hospital de los Venerables

HOSPITAL—SIGHT | Once a retirement home for priests, this baroque building has a splendid azulejo patio with an interesting sunken fountain (designed to cope with low water pressure) and an upstairs gallery, but the highlight is the chapel, featuring frescoes by Valdés Leal and sculptures by Pedro Roldán. The building now houses a cultural foundation that organizes on-site art exhibitions. ✉ *Pl. de los Venerables 8, Barrio de Santa Cruz* ☎ *954/562696* ✈ *€8, includes audio guide (free 1st Thurs. of month)* 🕑 *Closed Mon.–Wed.*

★ Jewish Quarter

NEIGHBORHOOD | The twisting alleyways and traditional whitewashed houses add to the tourist charm of this *barrio*. On some streets, bars alternate with antiques and souvenir shops, but most of the quarter is quiet and residential. On the Plaza Alianza, pause to enjoy the antiques shops and outdoor cafés. In the Plaza de Doña Elvira, with its fountain and azulejo benches, young sevillanos gather to play guitars. Just around the corner from the hospital, at Callejón del Agua and Jope de Rueda, Gioacchino Rossini's Figaro serenaded Rosina on her Plaza Alfaro balcony. Adjoining the Plaza Alfaro, in the Plaza Santa Cruz, flowers and orange trees surround a 17th-century filigree iron cross, which marks the site of the erstwhile church of Santa Cruz, destroyed by Napoléon's general Jean-de-Dieu Soult. ✉ *Barrio de Santa Cruz.*

Museo del Baile Flamenco

MUSEUM | This private museum in the heart of Santa Cruz (follow the signs) was opened in 2007 by the legendary flamenco dancer Cristina Hoyos and includes audiovisual and multimedia displays explaining the history, culture, and soul of Spanish flamenco. There are also regular classes and shows. ✉ *Calle Manuel Rojas Marcos 3, Barrio de Santa Cruz* ☎ *954/340311* ⊕ *www.museoflamenco. com* ✈ *€10.*

★ Real Alcázar
CASTLE/PALACE | The Plaza del Triunfo forms the entrance to the Mudejar palace built by Pedro I (1350–69) on the site of Seville's former Moorish alcázar. Though the alcázar was designed and built by Moorish workers brought in from Granada, it was commissioned and paid for by a Christian king more than 100 years after the Reconquest of Seville. Highlights include the oldest parts of the building, the 14th-century Sala de Justicia (Hall of Justice) and, next to it, the intimate Patio del Yeso (Courtyard of Plaster); Pedro's Mudejar palace, arranged around the beautiful Patio de las Doncellas (Court of the Damsels); the Salón de Embajadores (Hall of the Ambassadors), the most sumptuous hall in the palace; the Renaissance Palacio de Carlos V (Palace of Carlos V), endowed with a rich collection of Flemish tapestries; and the Estancias Reales (Royal Chambers), with rare clocks, antique furniture, paintings, and tapestries. ✉ *Pl. del Triunfo, Santa Cruz* ☎ *954/502324* 🌐 *www.alcazarsevilla.org* 🎫 *€12 (free 1 hr Mon.: 6–7 pm Apr.–Sept. and 4–5 pm Oct.–Mar.).*

🍴 Restaurants

Ispal
$$$$ | **SPANISH** | At this fine-dining venue near the Prado de San Sebastián bus station, chef Antonio Rodríguez Bort (the winner of several prestigious national tapas awards) has created one of the city's most exciting and innovative menus, using ingredients only from the province of Seville. The two tapas tasting menus (€49 and €69) include dishes such as *papas con choco, churros y castaña* (potatoes, cuttlefish, churros, and chestnuts) and *estofado de habas baby con bacalao* (baby broad bean stew with cod). **Known for:** exceptional tapas; regional wine list; suckling pig. [$] *Average main: €49* ✉ *Pl. de San Sebastián 1, Barrio de Santa Cruz* ☎ *954/547127* 🌐 *restauranteispal.com* 🕒 *Closed Mon. No dinner Sun.*

Vermutería Yo Soy Tu Padre
$ | **SPANISH** | Vermouth tasting comes into its own at this tiny venue, home to five home brews created using a secret recipe with a sherry base (manzanilla or fino) and herbs. Take the barman Esteban's advice on which to try and pair it with cold plates such as *trifásico de ahumados* (three types of smoked fish) and nearly two dozen types of cheese. **Known for:** homemade vermouth; authentic atmosphere; pairing tapas. [$] *Average main: €6* ✉ *Calle Gravina 70, Centro* ☎ *619/470784.*

★ Vineria San Telmo
$$ | **SPANISH** | Offering dining in a dimly lit dining room or on the street-level terrace, this popular Argentinean-owned restaurant near the touristy alcázar has a menu full of surprises. All dishes—which come as tapas, half portions, or full portions (ideal for sharing)—are superb and sophisticated, especially the eggplant stew with tomato, goat cheese, and smoked salmon; the Iberian pork with potato; and the oxtail in phyllo pastry. *It can get very crowded and noisy at times, thus it's not always the ideal place for a romantic meal for two.* **Known for:** creative tapas; extensive choice of Spanish vinos; Iberian pork with potato. [$] *Average main: €14* ✉ *Paseo Catalina de Ribera 4, Santa Cruz* ☎ *954/410600.*

🛏 Hotels

Casa del Poeta
$$$$ | **HOTEL** | Up a narrow alleyway, behind an ordinary facade, a 17th-century palace that was the haunt of Seville's poets at the end of the 19th century is now an oasis of calm. **Pros:** peaceful, central location; authentic palatial atmosphere; rooftop with a view. **Cons:** difficult to reach by car (call shortly before arrival for staff to meet you); could be too traditional for some; service can be a little

slow. $ Rooms from: €200 ⊠ Calle Don Carlos Alonso Chaparro 3, Santa Cruz ☎ 954/213868 ⊕ www.casadelpoeta.es ⇆ 17 rooms |☉| No meals.

★ Hotel Amadeus La Música de Sevilla
$$$ | HOTEL | With regular classical concerts, a music room off the central patio, and instruments for guests to use, including pianos in some of the sound-proofed rooms, this 18th-century manor house is ideal for touring professional musicians and music fans in general. **Pros:** small but charming rooms; roof terrace; friendly service. **Cons:** no direct car access; ground-floor rooms can be dark; layout slightly confusing. $ Rooms from: €150 ⊠ Calle Farnesio 6, Santa Cruz ☎ 954/501443 ⊕ www.hotelamadeussevilla.com ⇆ 43 rooms |☉| No meals.

★ Hotel Casa 1800
$$$$ | B&B/INN | This classy boutique hotel, in a refurbished 19th-century mansion, is a refuge in bustling Santa Cruz. **Pros:** top-notch amenities; great service; central location. **Cons:** rooms facing the patio can be noisy; no restaurant; on noisy side street. $ Rooms from: €280 ⊠ Calle Rodrigo Caro 6, Santa Cruz ☎ 954/561800 ⊕ www.hotelcasa1800sevilla.com ⇆ 33 rooms |☉| No meals.

Legado Alcázar
$$$ | HOTEL | Nestled next to the alcázar—the monument and hotel share walls—this 17th-century noble house offers a tasteful boutique experience in a very quiet corner. **Pros:** very quiet but central location; historic features; views of the alcázar. **Cons:** no restaurant on-site; room size varies; could be too traditional for some. $ Rooms from: €174 ⊠ Calle Mariana de Pineda 18, Barrio de Santa Cruz ☎ 954/091818 ⊕ www.legadoalcazarhotel.com ⇆ 18 rooms |☉| No meals.

Pensión Córdoba
$ | HOTEL | Just a few blocks from the cathedral, nestled in the heart of Santa Cruz, this small, family-run inn is an excellent value. **Pros:** quiet, central

location; friendly staff; rooms have a/c. **Cons:** no entry after 3 am; no breakfast; no elevator to second floor. $ Rooms from: €70 ⊠ Calle Farnesio 12, Santa Cruz ☎ 954/227498 ⊕ www.pensioncordoba.com ⇆ 11 rooms |☉| No meals.

▶ Nightlife

EME Catedral Hotel
CAFES—NIGHTLIFE | This rooftop terrace has some of the best views of the cathedral in town. Sip your cocktail to the sound of resident DJs most nights. The terrace is open daily beginning at 2 pm. ⊠ Calle Alemanes 27, Barrio de Santa Cruz ☎ 954/560000 ⊕ www.emecatedralhotel.com Ⓜ Puerta de Jerez.

🎭 Performing Arts

FLAMENCO
★ La Casa del Flamenco
THEMED ENTERTAINMENT | Catch an authentic professional performance in the heart of Santa Cruz on the atmospheric patio of a 15th-century house where the excellent acoustics mean there's no need for microphones or amplifiers. Shows start daily at 7 pm and 8:30 pm. ⊠ Calle Ximénez de Enciso 28, Barrio de Santa Cruz ☎ 954/500595 ⊕ www.lacasadelflamencosevilla.com 🎟 €18.

Los Gallos
DANCE | This intimate club in the heart of Santa Cruz attracts mainly tourists. Flamenco performances are entertaining and reasonably authentic. ⊠ Pl. Santa Cruz 11, Santa Cruz ☎ 954/216981 ⊕ www.tablaolosgallos.com 🎟 €35, includes one drink.

🛍 Shopping

Pleita
CERAMICS/GLASSWARE | This shop sells ceramics in the traditional Seville blue and white, plus handmade esparto grass accessories and bags. ⊠ Calle Aguilas 14, Barrio de Santa Cruz ☎ 955/091141.

The half moon of Plaza de España

El Arenal and Parque María Luisa

Parque María Luisa is part shady, midcity forestland and part monumental esplanade. El Arenal, named for its sandy riverbank soil, was originally a neighborhood of shipbuilders, stevedores, and warehouses. The heart of El Arenal lies between the Puente de San Telmo, just upstream from the Torre de Oro, and the Puente de Isabel II (Puente de Triana). El Arenal extends as far north as Avenida Alfonso XII to include the Museo de Bellas Artes. Between the park and El Arenal is the university.

Sights

★ Museo de Bellas Artes (*Museum of Fine Arts*)

MUSEUM | This museum—one of Spain's finest for Spanish art—is in the former convent of La Merced Calzada, most of which dates from the 17th century. The collection includes works by Murillo (the city celebrated the 400th anniversary of his birth in 2018) and the 17th-century Seville school, as well as by Zurbarán, Diego Velázquez, Alonso Cano, Valdés Leal, and El Greco. You will also see outstanding examples of Sevillian Gothic art and baroque religious sculptures in wood (a quintessentially Andalusian art form). In the rooms dedicated to Sevillian art of the 19th and 20th centuries, look for Gonzalo Bilbao's *Las Cigarreras*, a group portrait of Seville's famous cigar makers. An arts-and-crafts market is held outside the museum on Sunday. ⊠ *Pl. del Museo 9, El Arenal* ☎ *954/542931* ⊕ *www.museosdeandalucia.es* ☑ *€2* ⊘ *Closed Mon.*

★ Parque de María Luisa

CITY PARK | Formerly the garden of the Palacio de San Telmo, this park blends formal design and wild vegetation. In the burst of development that gripped Seville in the 1920s, it was redesigned for the 1929 World's Fair, and the impressive villas you see now are the fair's remaining pavilions, many of them consulates or schools; the old casino holds the Teatro Lope de Vega, which puts on mainly musicals. Note the Anna Huntington **statue of El Cid** (Rodrigo Díaz de Vivar, 1043–99), who fought both for and against the Muslim rulers during the Reconquest. The statue was presented to Seville by the Massachusetts-born sculptor for the 1929 World's Fair. ⊠ *Main entrance, Glorieta San Diego, Parque Maria Luisa.*

Plaza de España

PLAZA | FAMILY | This grandiose half-moon of buildings on the eastern edge of the Parque de María Luisa was Spain's centerpiece pavilion at the 1929 World's Fair. The brightly colored azulejo pictures represent the provinces of Spain, while the four bridges symbolize the medieval kingdoms of the Iberian Peninsula. In fine weather you can rent small boats to row along the arc-shape canal. To escape the crowds and enjoy views of the square from above, pop upstairs. ⊠ *Parque Maria Luisa.*

Plaza de Toros Real Maestranza (*Royal Maestranza Bullring*)

PLAZA | Sevillanos have spent many a thrilling evening in this bullring, one of the oldest and loveliest *plazas de toros* in Spain, built between 1760 and 1763. The 20-minute tour (in English) takes in the empty arena, a museum with elaborate costumes and prints, and the chapel where matadors pray before the fight. Bullfights take place in the evening Thursday–Sunday from April through July and in September. Tickets can be booked online or by phone; book well in advance to be sure of a seat. ⊠ *Paseo de Colón 12, El Arenal* ☎ *954/210315 for visits, 954/560759 for bullfights* ⊕ *www. realmaestranza.es for tours, www.plaza-detorosdelamaestranza.com for tickets* ☞ *Tours €8 (free Mon. 3–7).*

Torre del Oro (*Tower of Gold*)

LIGHTHOUSE | Built by the Moors in 1220 to complete the city's ramparts, this 12-sided tower on the banks of the

Guadalquivir served to close off the harbor when a chain was stretched across the river from its base to a tower on the opposite bank. In 1248, Admiral Ramón de Bonifaz broke through the barrier, and Ferdinand III captured Seville. The tower houses a small naval museum. ⊠ *Paseo Alcalde Marqués de Contadero s/n, El Arenal* ☎ *954/222419* ☞ *€3 (free Mon.).*

🍴 Restaurants

★ Enrique Becerra

$$$ | SPANISH | Excellent tapas (try the lamb kebab with dates and couscous), a lively bar, and an extensive wine list await at this restaurant run by the fifth generation of a family of celebrated restaurateurs. The menu focuses on traditional, home-cooked Andalusian dishes, such as cod in a green sauce, pork fillet in whiskey, and *cola de toro guisado con salsa de vino tinto* (stewed oxtail in red wine sauce). **Known for:** traditional Andalusian dishes; fried eggplant stuffed with prawns; stewed oxtail. $ *Average main: €20* ⊠ *Calle Gamazo 2, El Arenal* ☎ *954/213049* ⊕ *enriquebecerra.com.*

🛏 Hotels

Gran Meliá Colón

$$$$ | HOTEL | Originally opened for 1929's Ibero-American Exposition, this classic hotel retains many original features, including a marble staircase leading up to a central lobby crowned by a magnificent stained-glass dome and crystal chandelier. **Pros:** good central location; excellent restaurant; some great views. **Cons:** some rooms overlook air shaft; on a busy and noisy street; pricey. $ *Rooms from: €360* ⊠ *Calle Canalejas 1, El Arenal* ☎ *954/505599* ⊕ *www.melia.com* ⇨ *189 rooms* ⑪ *No meals.*

★ Hotel Alfonso XIII

$$$$ | HOTEL | Inaugurated by King Alfonso XIII in 1929 when he visited the World's Fair, this grand hotel next to the university is a splendid, historic, Mudejar-style

palace, built around a central patio and surrounded by ornate brick arches. **Pros:** both stately and hip; impeccable service; historic surroundings. **Cons:** a tourist colony; expensive; too sophisticated for some. $ *Rooms from: €375* ⊠ *Calle San Fernando 2, El Arenal* ☎ *954/917000* ⊕ *www.hotel-alfonsoxiii-seville.com* ⊰ *148 rooms* ❄ *Free Breakfast.*

Performing Arts

Teatro de la Maestranza

OPERA | Long prominent in the opera world, Seville is proud of its opera house. Tickets go quickly, so book well in advance (online is best). ⊠ *Paseo de Colón 22, El Arenal* ☎ *954/223344 for info, 954/226573 for tickets* ⊕ *www. teatrodelamaestranza.es.*

Teatro Lope de Vega

ARTS CENTERS | Classical music, ballet, and musicals are performed here. Tickets are best booked online. ⊠ *Av. María Luisa s/n, Parque Maria Luisa* ☎ *954/472828 for info, 600/950746 for tickets* ⊕ *www. teatrolopedevega.org.*

🛍 Shopping

Artesanía Textil

TEXTILES/SEWING | You can find blankets, shawls, and embroidered tablecloths woven by local artisans at this textile shop. ⊠ *Calle García de Vinuesa 33, El Arenal* ☎ *954/215088.*

El Postigo

CRAFTS | This permanent arts-and-crafts market opposite El Corte Inglés is open every day except Sunday. ⊠ *Pl. de la Concordia, El Arenal.*

Barrio de la Macarena

This immense neighborhood covers the entire northern half of historic Seville and deserves to be walked many times. Most of the best churches, convents, markets, and squares are concentrated around the

center in an area delimited by the Arab ramparts to the north, the Alameda de Hercules to the west, the Santa Catalina church to the south, and the Convento de Santa Paula to the east. The area between the Alameda de Hercules and the Guadalquivir is known to locals as the Barrio de San Lorenzo, a section that's ideal for an evening of tapas grazing.

◉ Sights

Basílica de la Macarena

RELIGIOUS SITE | This church holds Seville's most revered image, the Virgin of Hope— better known as La Macarena. Bedecked with candles and carnations, her cheeks streaming with glass tears, the Macarena steals the show at the procession on Holy Thursday, the highlight of Seville's Semana Santa pageant. The patron of Gypsies and the protector of the matador, her charms are so great that young sevillano bullfighter Joselito spent half his personal fortune buying her emeralds. When he was killed in the ring in 1920, La Macarena was dressed in widow's weeds for a month. The adjacent museum tells the history of Semana Santa traditions through processional and liturgical artifacts amassed by the Brotherhood of La Macarena over four centuries. ⊠ *Calle Bécquer 1, La Macarena* ☎ *954/901800* 🎟 *Basilica free, museum €5.*

★ Convento de Santa Paula

RELIGIOUS SITE | This 15th-century Gothic convent has a fine facade and portico, with ceramic decoration by Nicolaso Pisano. The chapel has some beautiful azulejos and sculptures by Martínez Montañés. It also contains a small museum and a shop selling delicious cakes and jams made by the nuns. ⊠ *Calle Santa Paula 11, La Macarena* ☎ *954/536330* 🎟 *€4* ⊗ *Closed Mon.*

San Lorenzo y Jesús del Gran Poder

RELIGIOUS SITE | This 17th-century church has many fine works by such artists as Martínez Montañés and Francisco

Pacheco, but its outstanding piece is Juan de Mesa y Velasco's *Jesús del Gran Poder* (*Christ Omnipotent*). ✉ *Pl. San Lorenzo 13, La Macarena* ☎ *954/915672* 🎟 *Free.*

🍴 Restaurants

Bache San Pedro

$$ | **SPANISH** | Barack Obama's chosen spot for tapas when he visited the city in April 2019 has outside seating on a small terrace with views of the square or spots inside, where traditional Seville tiles blend perfectly into the sleek industrial vibe. Bringing the taste of Cádiz to Seville, dishes here come as tapas or sharing plates (€3.50–€15) and include *croquetas de puchero* (stew croquettes), a taco of *chicharrones* (pork crackling) with Payoyo goat's cheese, and possibly the spiciest *patatas bravas* (fried potatoes) in town. **Known for:** innovative cuisine; friendly service; delicious desserts. [$] *Average main: €13* ✉ *Pl. Cristo de Burgos 23* ☎ *954/502934* 🌐 *www.bachesevilla.com* 🕒 *Closed Mon.*

El Rinconcillo

$$ | **SPANISH** | Founded in 1670, this lovely spot serves a classic selection of dishes, such as the *pavía de bacalao* (fried breaded cod), a superb *salmorejo* (a purée consisting of tomato and bread), and espinacas con garbanzos all in generous portions. The views of the Iglesia de Santa Catalina out the front window upstairs are unbeatable, and your bill is chalked up on the wooden counters as you go (tapas are attractively priced from €2). **Known for:** tapas; crowds of locals; views of Iglesia de Santa Catalina. [$] *Average main: €12* ✉ *Calle Gerona 40, La Macarena* ☎ *954/223183* 🌐 *www.elrinconcillo.es.*

Palo Cortao

$ | **SPANISH** | Down an uninspiring side street but with a very quiet terrace with views of San Pedro Church, this bar with stool seating around high tables offers tranquil dining and, most notably, one of the best sherry menus in town. Known as an *abacería* (grocer's store), it serves more than 30 finos, amontillados, and olorosos, plus homemade vermouth on the drinks menu, and each pairs perfectly with a food choice. **Known for:** excellent sherry; pairing menu; ajoblanco (cold garlic soup). [$] *Average main: €5* ✉ *Calle Merceds de Velilla 4, La Macarena* ☎ *649/446120* 🌐 *www.palo-cortao.com* 🕒 *Closed Sun.*

Fiesta Time!

Seville's color and vivacity are most intense during Semana Santa, when lacerated Christs and bejeweled, weeping Mary statues are paraded through town on floats borne by often-barefoot penitents. Two weeks later, sevillanos throw Feria de Abril, featuring midday horse parades with men in broad-brim hats and Andalusian riding gear astride prancing steeds, and women in ruffled dresses riding sidesaddle behind them. Bullfights, fireworks, and all-night singing and dancing complete the spectacle.

Triana

Triana used to be Seville's Gypsy quarter. Today, it has a tranquil, neighborly feel by day and a distinctly flamenco feel at night. Cross over to Triana via the **Puente de Isabel II,** an iron bridge built in 1852 and the first to connect the city's two sections. Start your walk in the **Plaza del Altozano,** the center of the Triana district and traditionally the meeting point for travelers from the south crossing the river to Seville. Admire the facade of the Murillo pharmacy here before walking up **Calle Jacinto.** Look out for the fine **Casa de los Mensaque** (now the district's administrative office and usually open on weekday mornings), home to some of Triana's finest potters and housing some stunning examples of Seville ceramics. To reach attractions in La Cartuja, take Bus C1.

Sights

Capilla de los Marineros

RELIGIOUS SITE | This seamen's chapel is one of Triana's most important monuments and home to the Brotherhood of Triana, whose Semana Santa processions are among the most revered in the city. There's also a small museum dedicated to the Brotherhood. ✉ *Calle Pureza 2, Triana* ☎ *954/332645* 🎟 *Free, museum €4.*

Isla de La Cartuja

ISLAND | Named after its 14th-century Carthusian monastery, this island in the Guadalquivir River across from northern Seville was the site of the decennial Universal Exposition (Expo) in 1992. The island has the Teatro Central, used for concerts and plays; Parque del Alamillo, Seville's largest and least-known park; and the Estadio Olímpico, a 60,000-seat covered stadium. The best way to get to La Cartuja is by walking across one or both (one each way) of the superb Santiago Calatrava bridges spanning the river. The Puente de la Barqueta crosses to La Cartuja, and downstream the Puente del Alamillo connects the island with Seville. Buses C1 and C2 also serve La Cartuja. ✉ *Triana.*

Monasterio de Santa María de las Cuevas

(*Monasterio de La Cartuja*)

MUSEUM | The 14th-century monastery was regularly visited by Christopher Columbus, who was also buried here for a few years. Part of the building houses the **Centro Andaluz de Arte Contemporáneo,** which has an absorbing collection of contemporary art. ✉ *Isla de la Cartuja, Av. Américo Vespucio, Triana* ☎ *955/037070* 🎟 *€2* 🕒 *Closed Mon.*

Restaurants

Bar Las Golondrinas

$$ | **SPANISH** | Run by the same family for more than 50 years and lavishly decorated in the colorful tiles that pay tribute to the neighborhood's potters, Las Golondrinas is a fixture of Triana life. The staff never change, and neither does the menu—the recipes for the *punta de solomillo* (sliced sirloin), *chipirones* (fried baby squid), and *caballito de jamón* (ham on bread) have been honed to perfection, and they're served as tapas, or *raciones*, (€2) that keep everyone happy. **Known for:** vibrant atmosphere; traditional tapas; good value. [$] *Average main: €12* ✉ *Calle Antillano Campos 26, Triana* ☎ *954/332616.*

De la O

$$ | **SPANISH** | Tucked away on the riverfront in Triana next to Puente Cristo de la Expiración, this modern venue advocates local produce in traditional Andalusian recipes along with a long wine list of Andalusian wines. The long, narrow interior has striking wood-paneled walls with a verdant vertical garden in the middle, while outside dining takes in panoramic views of the river on the intimate terrace. **Known for:** quality local produce; homemade sausages; dishes presented artistically. [$] *Average main: €12* ✉ *Paseo de Nuestra Señora de la O 29, Triana* ☎ *954/339000* 🌐 *www.delaorestaurante.com* 🕒 *Closed Mon. No dinner Sun.*

Hotels

Hotel Monte Triana

$$ | **HOTEL** | Comfortable, squeaky-clean facilities and excellent value for the cost are two key reasons for choosing this hotel to the north of the heart of Triana. **Pros:** good value; private car park; friendly and helpful staff. **Cons:** 20-minute walk into city center; decor too basic for some; no on-site restaurant. [$] *Rooms from: €110* ✉ *Calle Clara de Jesús Montero 24, Triana* ☎ *954/343111* 🌐 *www.hotelesmonte.com* 🛏 *114 rooms* 🍴 *No meals.*

🎭 Performing Arts

FLAMENCO
Lola de los Reyes

DANCE | This venue in Triana presents reasonably authentic shows and hosts "flamenco afternoons" on Friday and Saturday—check the website for details. Entrance is free, but there's a one-drink minimum. ⊠ *Calle Pureza 107, Triana* ☎ *667/631163* ⊕ *www.loladelosreyes.es* Ⓜ *Blas Infante/Parque de los Principes.*

Teatro Central

ARTS CENTERS | This modern venue on the Isla de la Cartuja stages theater, dance (including flamenco), and classical and contemporary music. Tickets can be bought at El Corte Inglés stores or via ⊕ *www.elcorteingles.es.* ⊠ *Calle José de Gálvez 6, Triana* ☎ *955/542155 for information* ⊕ *www.teatrocentral.es.*

🛍 Shopping

Potters' District
CERAMICS/GLASSWARE | Look for traditional azulejo tiles and other ceramics in the Triana potters' district, on Calle Alfarería and Calle Antillano Campos. ⊠ *Triana.*

Carmona

32 km (20 miles) east of Seville off A4.

Wander the ancient, narrow streets here and you'll feel as if you've been transported back in time. Claiming to be one of the oldest inhabited places in Spain (both Phoenicians and Carthaginians had settlements here), Carmona, on a steep, fortified hill, became an important town under the Romans and the Moors. There are many Mudejar and Renaissance churches and convents (several are open weekend mornings only), medieval gateways, and simple whitewashed houses of clear Moorish influence, punctuated here and there by a baroque palace. Local fiestas are held in mid-September.

GETTING HERE AND AROUND
There's excellent bus service between Seville and Carmona—the journey takes under 40 minutes, making it an easy day trip. Within Carmona itself, it's easy to get around on foot.

VISITOR INFORMATION
CONTACTS **Carmona** ⊠ *Alcázar de la Puerta de Sevilla* ☎ *954/190955* ⊕ *www.turismo.carmona.org.*

👁 Sights

Alcázar del Rey Don Pedro (*King Pedro's Fortress*)

CASTLE/PALACE | This Moorish structure was built on Roman foundations and converted by King Pedro the Cruel into a Mudejar palace. Pedro's summer residence was destroyed by a 1504 earthquake, and all that remains are ruins that can be viewed but not visited. However, the parador within the complex has a breathtaking view, and the café and restaurant are lovely spots to have a refreshment or meal. ⊠ *Calle Los Alcázares s/n.*

Museo de la Ciudad

MUSEUM | FAMILY | This interesting museum behind Santa María has exhibits on Carmona's history with particular emphasis on Roman finds. There's plenty for children, and the interactive exhibits are labeled in English and Spanish. ⊠ *Calle San Ildefonso 1* ☎ *954/140128* ⊕ *www.museociudad.carmona.org* ⊡ *€3 (free Tues.).*

Roman Necropolis

MEMORIAL | At the western edge of town 900 tombs were placed in underground chambers between the 4th and 2nd centuries BC. The necropolis walls, decorated with leaf and bird motifs, have niches for burial urns and tombs such as the **Elephant Vault** and the **Servilia Tomb,** a complete Roman villa with colonnaded arches and vaulted side galleries. ⊠ *Calle Enmedio* ☎ *600/143632* ⊡ *€2* ⊙ *Closed Mon.*

11

Andalusia CARMONA

Santa María

RELIGIOUS SITE | This Gothic church was built between 1424 and 1518 on the site of Carmona's former Great Mosque and retains its beautiful Moorish courtyard, studded with orange trees. ⊠ *Calle Martín* ⬚ *€3* ⊘ *Closed Mon.*

 Hotels

Parador Alcázar del Rey Don Pedro (*Parador de Carmona*)

$$$$ | HOTEL | This parador has superb views from its hilltop position among the ruins of Pedro the Cruel's summer palace. **Pros:** unbeatable views over the fields; great sense of history; restaurant serves local specialties. **Cons:** 30 minutes away from Seville. $ *Rooms from: €225* ⊠ *Calle del Alcázar* ☎ *954/141010* ⊕ *www.parador.es* ⤴ *63 rooms* ❍| *No meals.*

Itálica

12 km (7 miles) north of Seville, 1 km (½ mile) beyond Santiponce.

Neighboring the small town of Santiponce, Itálica is Spain's oldest Roman site and one of its greatest, and it is well worth a visit when you're in Seville. If you're here during July, try to get tickets for the International Dance Festival held in the ruins (⊕ *www.festivalitalica.es*).

GETTING HERE AND AROUND

The M170A bus route runs frequently (daily 8 am–3:30 pm) between the Plaza de Armas bus station in Seville and Itálica. Journey time is 20 minutes. If you have a rental car, you could include a visit to the ruins on your way to Huelva. Allow at least two hours for your visit.

 Sights

★ **Itálica**

ARCHAEOLOGICAL SITE | One of Roman Iberia's most important cities in the 2nd century, with a population of more than 10,000, Itálica today is a monument of Roman ruins. Founded by Scipio Africanus in 205 BC as a home for veteran soldiers, Itálica gave the Roman world two great emperors: Trajan (AD 52–117) and Hadrian (AD 76–138). You can find traces of city streets, cisterns, and the floor plans of several villas, some with mosaic floors, though all the best mosaics and statues have been removed to Seville's Museum of Archaeology. Itálica was abandoned and plundered as a quarry by the Visigoths, who preferred Seville. It fell into decay around AD 700. The remains include the huge, elliptical **amphitheater,** which held 40,000 spectators, a **Roman theater,** and **Roman baths.** Part of the last season of *Game of Thrones* was filmed here in 2018. The small visitor center offers information on daily life in the city. ⊠ *Av. Extremadura 2, Santiponce* ☎ *600/141767* ⊕ *www.juntadeandalucia. es/cultura/museos* ⬚ *€2* ⊘ *Closed Mon.*

Around Ronda: Caves, Romans, and Pueblos Blancos

This area of spectacular gorges, remote mountain villages, and ancient caves is fascinating to explore and a dramatic contrast to the clamor and crowds of the nearby Costa del Sol.

GETTING HERE AND AROUND

Public transportation is very poor in these parts. Your best bet is to visit by car—the area is a short drive from Ronda.

Andalusia's classic pueblos blancos look like Picasso paintings come to life.

Sights

★ Acinipo

ARCHAEOLOGICAL SITE | Old Ronda, 20 km (12 miles) north of Ronda, is the site of this old Roman settlement, a thriving town in the 1st century AD that was abandoned for reasons that still baffle historians. Today it's a windswept hillside with piles of stones, the foundations of a few Roman houses, and what remains of a theater. Views across the Ronda plains and to the surrounding mountains are spectacular. The site's opening hours vary depending on staff availability and excavations—check with the Ronda tourist office by phone before visiting. ⊠ *Ronda* ✛ *Take A376 toward Algodonales; turnoff for ruins is 9 km (5 miles) from Ronda on MA449* ☎ *951/041452* 🖾 *Free.*

Cueva de la Pileta *(Pileta Cave)*

CAVE | At this site 20 km (12 miles) west of Ronda, a Spanish guide (who speaks some English) will hand you a paraffin lamp and lead you on a roughly 60-minute walk that reveals prehistoric wall paintings of bison, deer, and horses outlined in black, red, and ocher. One highlight is the Cámara del Pescado (Chamber of the Fish), whose drawing of a huge fish is thought to be 15,000 years old. Tours take place on the hour and last around an hour. ⊠ *Benaoján* ✛ *Drive west from Ronda on A374 and take left exit for village of Benaoján from where caves are well signposted* ☎ *687/133338* 🖾 *€10.*

Olvera

TOWN | Here, 13 km (8 miles) north of Setenil, two imposing silhouettes dominate the crest of the hill: the 11th-century castle Vallehermoso, a legacy of the Moors, and the neoclassical church of La Encarnación, reconstructed in the 19th century on the foundations of the old mosque.

Setenil de las Bodegas

TOWN | This small city, in a cleft in the rock cut by the Río Guadalporcín, is 8 km (5 miles) north of Acinipo. The streets resemble long, narrow caves, and on many houses the roof is formed by a projecting ledge of heavy rock.

Zahara de la Sierra

TOWN | A solitary watchtower dominates a crag above this village, its outline visible for miles around. The tower is all that remains of a Moorish castle where King Alfonso X once fought the emir of Morocco; the building remained a Moorish stronghold until it fell to the Christians in 1470. Along the streets you can see door knockers fashioned like the hand of Fatima: the fingers represent the five laws of the Koran and are meant to ward off evil. ✥ *From Olvera, drive 21 km (13 miles) southwest to the village of Algodonales, then south on A376 for 5 km (3 miles).*

Grazalema and the Sierra de Grazalema

28 km (17 miles) northwest of Ronda.

The village of Grazalema is the prettiest of the pueblos blancos. Its cobblestone streets of houses with pink-and-ocher roofs wind up the hillside, red geraniums splash white walls, and black wrought-iron lanterns and grilles cling to the house fronts.

The Sierra de Grazalema Natural Park encompasses a series of mountain ranges known as the Sierra de Grazalema, which straddle the provinces of Málaga and Cádiz. These mountains trap the rain clouds that roll in from the Atlantic, and the area has the distinction of being the wettest place in Spain, with an average annual rainfall of 88 inches. Because of the park's altitude and prevailing humidity, it's one of the last habitats for the rare fir tree *Abies pinsapo*; it's also home to ibex, vultures, and birds of prey. Parts of the park are restricted, accessible only on foot and when accompanied by an official guide.

GETTING HERE AND AROUND

The village of Grazalema itself is quite small and is best reached by private car as there's little public transport.

VISITOR INFORMATION

CONTACTS Grazalema ✉ *Pl. de los Asomaderos 7, Grazalema* ☎ *956/132052.*

Sights

El Bosque

TOWN | An excursion from Grazalema takes you through the heart of this protected reserve, home to a trout stream and information center. Follow the A344 west through dramatic mountain scenery, past Benamahoma. ✉ *Grazalema.*

Ubrique

TOWN | From Grazalema, the A374 takes you to this town on the slopes of the Saltadero Mountains, known for its leather tanning and embossing industry. Look for the **Convento de los Capuchinos** (Capuchin Convent), the church of **San Pedro,** and, 4 km (2½ miles) away, the ruins of the Moorish castle **El Castillo de Fátima.** ✉ *Grazalema.*

Hotels

★ La Mejorana

$ | **B&B/INN** | An ideal base for exploring the area, this is the spot to find rural simplicity and stunning mountain views. **Pros:** in the center of the village; tastefully furnished; home-away-from-home atmosphere. **Cons:** no TV in rooms; rustic feel not for everyone. [$] *Rooms from: €64* ✉ *Calle Santa Clara 6, Grazalema* ☎ *956/132327* 🌐 *www.lamejorana.net* 🔑 *6 rooms* 🍴 *Free Breakfast.*

Doñana National Park

100 km (62 miles) southwest of Seville.

The jewel in Spain's crown when it comes to national parks, and one of Europe's most important wetlands, Doñana is a paradise for wildlife in their natural habitat. Most of the park is heavily protected and closed to visitors, although you can visit with one of the authorized

Andalusia's White Villages

Andalusia's pueblos blancos are usually found nestled on densely wooded hills, clinging to the edges of deep gorges, or perched on hilltops. The picturesque locations of the pueblos blancos usually have more to do with defense than anything else, and many have crumbling fortifications that show their use as defensive structures along the frontier between the Christian and Moorish realms. In a few, the remains of magnificent Moorish castles can be spied. The suffix *de la frontera*, literally meaning "on the frontier," tacked onto a town's name reflects this historical border position.

Vejer de la Frontera

This dazzling white town is perched high on a hill, perfectly positioned to protect its citizens from the threat of marauding pirates. Today it is one of the most charming pueblos blancos on the Cádiz coast, known for its meandering cobbled lanes, narrow arches, and large number of atmospheric bars and restaurants. Vejer is popular with an artsy crowd that has brought art galleries, boutique hotels, crafts shops, and sophisticated restaurants.

Frigiliana

This impossibly pretty whitewashed village is 7 km (4½ miles) north of the well-known resort of Nerja. Despite the encroachment of modern apartment buildings, the old center has remained relatively unchanged. Pots of crimson geraniums decorate the narrow streets, while the bars proudly serve the local sweet wine. Frigiliana is a good place for seeking out ceramics made by the town's craftspeople. Hikers can enjoy the 3-km (2-mile) hike from the old town to El Fuerte, the hilltop site of a 1569 skirmish between the Moors and the Christians (⇨ *see Chapter 12*).

Gaucín

The countryside surrounding Ronda is stunning, especially in the spring when the ground is carpeted with wildflowers, including exquisite purple orchids. Not surprisingly, the Serranía de Ronda (as this area is known) is famous for its superb walking. Gaucín is a lovely village crowned by a ruined Moorish castle. It is popular with artists who open their studios to the public each year in late spring (visit ⊕ *artgaucin.com* for dates). The town also has several excellent restaurants and sophisticated boutique hotels.

Pitres and La Taha

Granada's Alpujarras mountains are home to some of Andalusia's most unspoiled white villages. Two of the best known are Bubión and Capileira, while the Pitres and La Taha villages of Mecina, Mecinilla, Fondales, Ferreirola, and Atalbéitar are lovely hamlets separated by rough tracks that wind through orchards and woodland, set in a valley that attracts few visitors.

Grazalema

About a half hour from Ronda, Grazalema is the prettiest—and the whitest—of the white towns. It's a small town, worth some time wandering, and well situated for a visit to the mountains of the Sierra de Grazalema Natural Park.

tour companies who organize visits by jeep, foot, or horseback.

GETTING HERE AND AROUND

To explore Doñana and its surroundings you need your own transportation, particularly to get to the different visitor centers, all some distance apart.

VISITOR INFORMATION

In addition to the centers listed here, there is a visitor center for the park at Sanlúcar de Barrameda called La Fábrica de Hielo.

CONTACTS El Acebuche ☎ *959/439629.* **La Rocina Visitor Center** ☎ *959/439569.* **Palacio de Acebrón** ✉ *Ctra. de la Rocina* ☎ *959/506162.*

Sights

★ Doñana National Park

NATIONAL/STATE PARK | FAMILY | One of Europe's most important swaths of unspoiled wilderness, these wetlands spread out along the west side of the Guadalquivir estuary. The site was named for Doña Ana, wife of a 16th-century duke, who, prone to bouts of depression, one day crossed the river and wandered into the wetlands, never to be seen alive again. The 188,000-acre park sits on the migratory route from Africa to Europe and is the winter home and breeding ground for as many as 150 rare species of birds. Habitats range from beaches and shifting sand dunes to marshes, dense brushwood, and sandy hillsides of pine and cork oak. Two of Europe's most endangered species, the imperial eagle and the lynx, make their homes here, and kestrels, kites, buzzards, egrets, storks, and spoonbills breed among the cork oaks. ✉ *Huelva* 🌐 *www.andalucia.org/en/natural-spaces/national-parks/donana.*

Beaches

Playa de Mazagón

BEACH—SIGHT | The 5-km (3-mile) stretch of fine golden sand running from Mazagón to the frontier of the Doñana National Park forms one of the last unspoiled beaches in Andalusia. Dunes flank most of the beach, along with attractive sandstone cliffs; the Parador de Mazagón perches here. At the western end, the beach is popular with locals and visitors, beach bars are plentiful, and towel space at a premium in August. Walk in an easterly direction, however, and the beach becomes a much quieter affair. Bathing is generally safe, but watch for rip currents when it's windy. **Amenities:** food and drink (June 15–September 15); lifeguards; showers; toilets; water sports. **Best for:** sunset; swimming; walking. ✉ *Mazagón.*

Hotels

Toruño

$ | HOTEL | Despite its location behind the famous Rocío shrine, the theme at this simple, friendly hotel is nature. **Pros:** views over the wetlands; bird-watching opportunities; restaurant serving reasonably priced traditional food. **Cons:** not great for extended stays; basic accommodation; busy during pilgrimage week. [$] *Rooms from: €80* ✉ *Pl. del Acebuchal 22, El Rocío* ☎ *959/442323* 🌐 *www.toruno.es* 🛏 *30 rooms* 🍴 *Free Breakfast.*

La Rábida

8 km (5 miles) northwest of Mazagón.

La Rábida's monastery is worth a stop if you're a history buff. It's nicknamed "the birthplace of America" because in 1485 Columbus came from Portugal with his son Diego to stay in the Mudejar-style Franciscan monastery, where he discussed his theories with friars Antonio

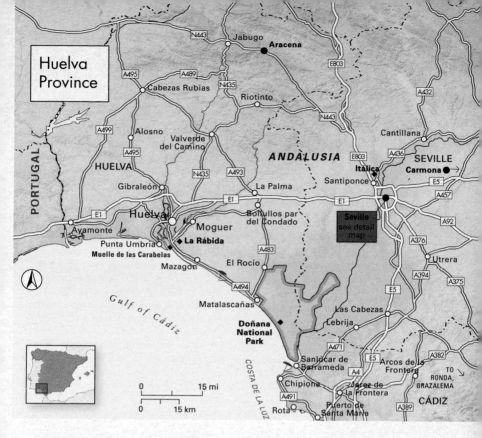

de Marchena and Juan Pérez. They interceded on his behalf with Queen Isabella, who had originally rejected his planned expedition.

◉ Sights

Muelle de las Carabelas (*Caravel's Wharf*)
LIGHTHOUSE | Set two kilometers (1 mile) from La Rábida's monastery, on the seashore, is a reproduction of a 15th-century port. The star exhibits here are the full-size models of Columbus's flotilla, the *Niña, Pinta,* and *Santa María,* built using the same techniques as in Columbus's day. You can go aboard each and learn more about the discovery of the New World in the adjoining museum. ⊠ *Paraje de la Rábida* ☎ *959/530597* ▦ *€4* ⊙ *Closed Mon.*

Santa María de La Rábida
RELIGIOUS SITE | The Mudejar-style Franciscan monastery of this church has a much-venerated 14th-century statue of the **Virgen de los Milagros** (Virgin of Miracles). There are relics from the discovery of America displayed in the museum and the **frescoes** in the gatehouse were painted by Daniel Vázquez Díaz in 1930. ⊠ *C. del Monasterio, Ctra. de Huelva* ☎ *959/350411* ▦ *€4* ⊙ *Closed Mon.*

Aracena

105 km (65 miles) northeast of Huelva, 100 km (62 miles) northwest of Seville.

Stretching north of the provinces of Huelva and Seville is the 460,000-acre Sierra de Aracena nature park, an expanse of hills cloaked in cork and holm oak.

This region is known for its cured Iberian hams, which come from the prized free-ranging Iberian pigs that gorge on acorns in the autumn months before slaughter; the hams are buried in salt and then hung in cellars to dry-cure for at least two years. The best Iberian hams have traditionally come from the village of **Jabugo.**

GETTING HERE AND AROUND

Because this area is remote and with little reliable public transportation, it's best to get around by car.

VISITOR INFORMATION

CONTACTS Aracena ⊠ *Calle Pozo de la Nieve, at cave entrance* ☎ *663/937877.*

Sights

Gruta de las Maravillas (*Cave of Marvels*)
CAVE | FAMILY | In the town of Aracena, the capital of the region, the main attraction is this spectacular cave. Its 12 caverns contain long corridors, stalactites and stalagmites arranged in wonderful patterns, and stunning underground lagoons. Only 1,000 people may visit per day, so go early if visiting in high season. ⊠ *Calle Pozo de la Nieve* ☎ *663/937876* 💳 *€10.*

🍴 Restaurants

Montecruz
$$ | SPANISH | The downstairs bar here serves simple tapas, but it's the upstairs restaurant that makes it worth a visit. The rustic dining room is decorated with wall paintings and hunting trophies, and the kitchen serves regional produce and dishes—try the *gurumelos salteados con jamón y gambas* (a type of mushroom stir-fried with ham and shrimp), *lomo de jabalí* (boar tenderloin), or the outstanding ham; chestnut stew is the standout for dessert. **Known for:** tapas; lomo de jabalí; gurumelos salteados con jamón y gambas (mushroom stir-fried with ham and shrimp). $ *Average main: €14* ⊠ *Pl. de San Pedro* ☎ *959/126013.*

Cádiz

32 km (20 miles) southwest of Jerez, 149 km (93 miles) southwest of Seville.

With the Atlantic Ocean on three sides, Cádiz is a bustling town that's been shaped by a variety of cultures and has the varied architecture to prove it. Founded as Gadir by Phoenician traders in 1100 BC, Cádiz claims to be the oldest continuously inhabited city in the Western world. Hannibal lived in Cádiz for a time, Julius Caesar first held public office here, and Columbus set out from here on his second voyage, after which the city became the home base of the Spanish fleet. In the 18th century, when the Guadalquivir silted up, Cádiz monopolized New World trade and became the wealthiest port in Western Europe. Most of its buildings—including the cathedral, built in part with wealth generated by gold and silver from the New World—date from this period. The old city is African in appearance and immensely intriguing—a cluster of narrow streets opening onto charming small squares. The golden cupola of the cathedral looms above low white houses, and the whole place has a slightly dilapidated air. Spaniards flock here in February to revel in the carnival celebrations, and ever more cruise ships visit the harbor, but in general it's not too touristy.

GETTING HERE AND AROUND

Every day, around 15 local trains connect Cádiz with Seville, Puerto de Santa María, and Jerez. The city has two bus stations. The main one, run by Comes, serves most destinations in Andalusia and farther afield; the other, run by Socibus, serves Córdoba and Madrid. There are buses to and from Sanlúcar de Barrameda (14 on weekdays), Arcos de la Frontera (9 daily), and the Costa del Sol (via Seville, 4 daily). Cádiz is easy to get to and navigate by car. Once there, the old city is easily explored by foot.

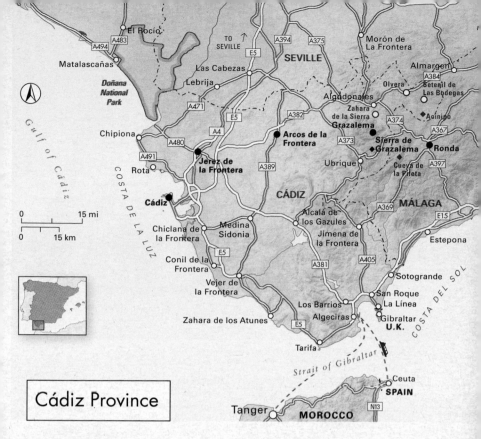

BUS STATION Cádiz–Estación de Autobuses Comes ✉ *Pl. de Sevilla* ☎ *956/807059.* **Cádiz-Estación de Autobuses Socibus** ✉ *Av. Astilleros s/n* ☎ *956/257415.*

TAXI CONTACT Radiotaxi ☎ *956/212121.*

TRAIN STATION Cádiz ✉ *Pl. de Sevilla s/n* ☎ *912/320320.*

VISITOR INFORMATION
CONTACTS Local Tourist Office ✉ *Paseo de Canalejas* ☎ *956/241001* ⊕ *www.turis-mo.cadiz.es.* **Regional Tourist Office** ✉ *Av. Ramón de Carranza s/n* ☎ *956/203191* ⊕ *www.cadizturismo.com.*

👁 Sights

Begin your explorations in the Plaza de Mina, a large, leafy square with palm trees and plenty of benches. Look out for the ornamental facade on the Colegio de Arquitectos (College of Architects), on the west side of the square.

Cádiz Cathedral

RELIGIOUS SITE | Five blocks southeast of the Torre Tavira are the gold dome and baroque facade of Cádiz's cathedral, which offers history as well as views from atop the Clock Tower (*Torre del Reloj*)—making the climb to the top worth it. The building's structure was begun in 1722, when the city was at the height of its power. The Cádiz-born composer Manuel de Falla, who died in 1946 at the age of 70, is buried in the **crypt.** The **museum,** on Calle Acero, displays gold, silver, and jewels from the New World, as well as Enrique de Arfe's processional cross, which is carried in the annual Corpus Christi parades. The cathedral is known as the New Cathedral because it supplanted the original

Cádiz's majestic cathedral, as seen from the Plaza de la Catedral

13th-century structure next door, which was destroyed by the British in 1592, rebuilt, and rechristened the church of **Santa Cruz** when the New Cathedral came along. ✉ *Pl. Catedral* ☎ *956/286154* 📠 *€6, includes crypt, museum, tower, and church of Santa Cruz.*

Gran Teatro Manuel de Falla

ARTS VENUE | Four blocks west of Santa Inés is the Plaza Manuel de Falla, overlooked by this amazing neo-Mudejar redbrick building. The classic interior is impressive as well—try to attend a performance. ✉ *Pl. Manuel de Falla* ☎ *956/220828.*

Museo de Cádiz (*Provincial Museum*)

MUSEUM | On the east side of the Plaza de Mina is Cádiz's provincial museum. Notable pieces include works by Murillo and Alonso Cano as well as the *Four Evangelists* and a set of saints by Zurbarán. The archaeological section contains two extraordinary marble Phoenician sarcophagi from the time of this ancient city's birth. ✉ *Pl. de Mina* ☎ *856/105023* 📠 *€2* 🕙 *Closed Mon.*

Museo de las Cortes

MUSEUM | Next door to the Oratorio de San Felipe Neri, this small but pleasant museum has a 19th-century mural depicting the establishment of the Constitution of 1812. Its real showpiece, however, is a 1779 ivory-and-mahogany model of Cádiz, with all of the city's streets and buildings in minute detail, looking much as they do now. ✉ *Calle Santa Inés 9* ☎ *956/221788* 📠 *Free* 🕙 *Closed Mon.*

Oratorio de la Santa Cueva

RELIGIOUS SITE | A few blocks east of the Plaza de Mina, next door to the Iglesia del Rosario, this oval 18th-century chapel has three frescoes by Goya. On Good Friday, the *Sermon of the Seven Words* is read and Haydn's *Seven Last Words* played. ✉ *Calle Rosario 10* ☎ *956/222262* 📠 *€4 (free Sun.)* 🕙 *Closed Mon.*

Oratorio de San Felipe Neri

RELIGIOUS SITE | A walk up Calle San José from the Plaza de Mina will bring you to this church, where Spain's first liberal constitution (known affectionately as La Pepa) was declared in 1812. It was here, too, that the Cortes (Parliament) of Cádiz met when the rest of Spain was subjected to the rule of Napoléon's brother, Joseph Bonaparte (more popularly known as Pepe Botella, for his love of the bottle). On the main altar is an *Immaculate Conception* by Murillo, the great sevillano artist who in 1682 fell to his death from a scaffold while working on his *Mystic Marriage of St. Catherine* in Cádiz's Chapel of Santa Catalina. ✉ *Calle Santa Inés 38* ☎ *662/642233* 🎟 *€4 (free Sun.)* 🕓 *Closed Mon.*

Roman Theater

ARCHAEOLOGICAL SITE | Next door to the church of Santa Cruz are the remains of a 1st-century-BC Roman theater, one of the oldest and largest in Spain. The stage remains unexcavated (it lies under nearby houses), but you can visit the entrance and large seating area as well as the visitor center. ✉ *Campo del Sur s/n, Barrio del Pópulo* 🎟 *Free* 🕓 *Closed 1st Mon. of month.*

★ Torre Tavira

BUILDING | **FAMILY** | At 150 feet, this watchtower is the highest point in the old city. More than a hundred such structures were used by Cádiz ship owners to spot their arriving fleets. A camera obscura gives a good overview of the city and its monuments; the last show is a half hour before closing time. ✉ *Calle Marqués del Real Tesoro 10* ☎ *956/212910* 🌐 *www.torretavira.com/en* 🎟 *€6.*

🍴 Restaurants

★ Casa Manteca

$ | **SPANISH** | Cádiz's most quintessentially Andalusian tavern is in the neighborhood of La Viña, named for the vineyard that once grew here. *Chacina* (Iberian ham or sausage) and *chicharrones de Cádiz* (cold pork) served on waxed paper and washed down with manzanilla (sherry from Sanlúcar de Barrameda) are standard fare at the low wooden counter that has served bullfighters and flamenco singers, as well as dignitaries from around the world, since 1953. The walls are covered with colorful posters and other memorabilia from the annual carnival, flamenco shows, and ferias. **Known for:** atmospheric interior; delicious cold cuts; manzanilla. [$] *Average main: €9* ✉ *Corralón de los Carros 66* ☎ *956/213603* 🕓 *No dinner Sun. and Mon.*

Código de Barra

$$$ | **SPANISH** | Local produce comes under the Dutch microscope at one of the most up-and-coming dining venues in Cádiz, under the direction of chef Léon Griffioen and earmarked by the *New York Times.* With only a few tables, and in minimalist surroundings, the restaurant, decked in black and gray, offers a tasting menu (€35 for 7 dishes, €47.50 for 10; pairing options available) that comes with several surprises including an "olive" and long, thin tortillitas de camarones —it is one explosion of flavor after another. **Known for:** creative take on traditional local cuisine; an excellent-value tasting menu; good and long wine list (ask the staff for pairing suggestions). [$] *Average main: €19* ✉ *Pl. Candelaria 12* ☎ *635/533303* 🕓 *Closed Mon. No dinner Sun.*

Columbus Sets Sail

On August 2, 1492, the *Niña*, the *Pinta*, and the *Santa María* set sail from the town of Palos de la Frontera. At the door of the church of **San Jorge** (1473), the royal letter ordering the levy of the ships' crew and equipment was read aloud, and the voyagers took their water supplies from the fountain known as La Fontanilla at the town's entrance.

Riders fill the streets during Jerez's Feria del Caballo (Horse Fair) in early May.

El Faro

$$$ | SPANISH | This famous fishing-quarter restaurant near Playa de la Caleta is deservedly known as one of the best in the province. From the outside, it's one of many whitewashed houses with ocher details and shiny black lanterns; inside it's warm and inviting, with half-tile walls, glass lanterns, oil paintings, and photos of old Cádiz. **Known for:** fresh fish; rice dishes; tapas. $ *Average main: €22* ✉ *Calle San Felix 15* ☎ *956/211068* ⊕ *www.elfarodecadiz.com.*

La Candela

$ | SPANISH | A block north of Plaza Candelaria and on one of Cádiz's narrow pedestrian streets, La Candela is a good place to try local fare with a modern twist. The salmorejo comes baked with pork loin tartare, the red tuna comes in a variety of ways, and several dishes have Asian touches, served tempura style or with wasabi sauce. **Known for:** tapas; homemade cheesecake; Spanish-Asian fusion food. $ *Average main: €10* ✉ *Calle Feduchy 1* ☎ *956/221822.*

Hotels

Hotel Argantonio

$$$ | HOTEL | This small, family-run hotel in the historic center of town combines traditional style and modern amenities. **Pros:** friendly and helpful staff; great location; good-size bathrooms. **Cons:** rooms in the original building on the small side; street-facing rooms can be noisy; not easy to find. $ *Rooms from: €130* ✉ *Calle Argantonio 3* ☎ *956/211640* ⊕ *www.hotelargantonio.com* ⇄ *17 rooms* ❍| *No meals.*

Hotel Patagonia Sur

$$$ | HOTEL | With a handy central location just two blocks from the cathedral, this modern hotel offers functional and inexpensive lodging, especially during low season. **Pros:** central location; good value; top-floor rooms have a private terrace. **Cons:** small rooms; street noise can be intrusive; five-night minimum stay in summer. $ *Rooms from: €145* ✉ *Calle Cobos 11* ☎ *856/174647* ⊕ *www.hotelpatagoniasur.es* ⇄ *16 rooms* ❍| *No meals.*

Parador de Cádiz
$$$$ | **HOTEL** | With a privileged position overlooking the bay, this parador has spacious public areas and large modern rooms, most with balconies facing the sea. **Pros:** great views of the bay; pool; bright and cheerful. **Cons:** expensive parking; very quiet in the off season; lacks historic appeal of other paradores. *[$] Rooms from: €280 ✉ Av. Duque de Nájera 9 ☎ 956/226905 🌐 www.parador.es/en/paradores/parador-de-cadiz 🛏 124 rooms 🍴 No meals.*

Arcos de la Frontera

31 km (19 miles) east of Jerez.

Its narrow and steep cobblestone streets, whitewashed houses, and finely crafted wrought-iron window grilles make Arcos the quintessential Andalusian pueblo blanco. Make your way to the main square, the **Plaza de España,** the highest point in the village; one side of the square is open, and a balcony at the edge of the cliff offers views of the Guadalete Valley. On the opposite end is the church of **Santa María de la Asunción,** a fascinating blend of architectural styles—Romanesque, Gothic, and Mudejar—with a plateresque doorway, a Renaissance retablo, and a 17th-century baroque choir. The *ayuntamiento* (town hall) stands at the foot of the old castle walls on the northern side of the square; across is the Casa del Corregidor, onetime residence of the governor and now a parador. Arcos is the westernmost of the 19 pueblos blancos dotted around the Sierra de Cádiz.

GETTING HERE AND AROUND

Arcos is best reached by private car, but there are frequent bus services here from Cádiz, Jerez, and Seville on weekdays. Weekend services are less frequent.

Notable Residents

Christopher Columbus and author Washington Irving once lived in the small fishing village of El Puerto de Santa María.

VISITOR INFORMATION

CONTACTS Arcos de la Frontera ✉ *Cuesta de Belén 5* ☎ *956/702264* 🌐 *www.turismoarcos.com.*

Restaurants

Restaurante Aljibe
$$ | **FUSION** | Local cooking meets Moroccan cuisine on one of the best fusion menus in the province at this venue with small dining spaces and an Arabian theme. White prawns, *ensalada de higos y payoyo* (fig and goat's cheese salad) and *bacalao confitado con calabacín* (cod with zucchini) sit perfectly next to *pastela* (game pie) and couscous dishes. **Known for:** Andalusian-Moroccan fusion; good service with a smile; Moroccan sweetmeats for dessert. *[$] Average main: €14 ✉ Cuesta del Belén 10 ☎ 622/836527 🕒 Closed Tues.*

Restaurante Tamizia
$$ | **SPANISH** | The old town has only one real formal restaurant—within the parador hotel—and it boasts perhaps the best views ever from a table, because wherever you choose to sit (bar, terrace, or restaurant), you'll dine looking over miles of green countryside beyond. Parador fare is justly famed in Spain, and the food on offer here is no exception. **Known for:** views from your dinner table; dishes using local produce; rabo de toro. *[$] Average main: €16 ✉ Parador Casa del Corregidor , Pl. del Cabildo s/n ☎ 956/700500.*

Hotels

★ El Convento

$ | B&B/INN | Perched atop the cliff behind the town parador, this tiny hotel in a former 17th-century convent shares the amazing view of another hotel in town, its swish neighbor (La Casa Grande). **Pros:** picturesque location; intimacy; value. **Cons:** small spaces; lots of stairs; no restaurant. $ Rooms from: €85 ⊠ Calle Maldonado 2 ☎ 956/702333 ⊕ www.hotelelconvento.es ⊙ Closed Jan. and Feb. ⇄ 13 rooms ☂ No meals.

★ La Casa Grande

$$ | B&B/INN | Built in 1729, this extraordinary 18th-century mansion encircles a central patio with lush vegetation and is perched on the edge of the 400-foot cliff to which Arcos de la Frontera clings. **Pros:** attentive owner; impeccable aesthetics; amazing views. **Cons:** inconvenient parking; long climb to the top floor; interior is a little dark. $ Rooms from: €120 ⊠ Calle Maldonado 10 ☎ 956/703930 ⊕ www.lacasagrande.net ⇄ 7 rooms ☂ No meals.

Parador Casa del Corregidor

$$$ | HOTEL | Expect a spectacular view from the terrace, as this parador clings to the cliffside, overlooking the rolling valley of the Río Guadalete. **Pros:** gorgeous views from certain rooms; elegant interiors; good restaurant. **Cons:** public areas a little tired; expensive bar and cafeteria; not all rooms have views. $ Rooms from: €150 ⊠ Pl. del Cabildo s/n ☎ 956/700500 ⊕ www.parador.es ⇄ 24 rooms ☂ No meals.

Jerez de la Frontera

97 km (60 miles) south of Seville.

Jerez, world headquarters for sherry, is surrounded by vineyards of chalky soil, producing palomino and Pedro Ximénez grapes that have funded a host of churches and noble mansions. Names such as González Byass, Domecq,

Harvey, and Sandeman are inextricably linked with Jerez. The word "sherry," first used in Great Britain in 1608, is an English corruption of the town's old Moorish name, Xeres. Both sherry and thoroughbred horses (the city was European Capital of Horses in 2018) are the domain of Jerez's Anglo-Spanish aristocracy, whose Catholic ancestors came here from England centuries ago. At any given time, more than half a million barrels of sherry are maturing in Jerez's vast aboveground cellars.

GETTING HERE AND AROUND

Jerez is a short way from Seville with frequent daily trains (journey time is around an hour) and buses (1 hour 15 minutes), fewer on weekends. If you're traveling to the city by car, park in one of the city-center lots or at your hotel as street parking is difficult. Jerez Airport is small and served by a number of flights to destinations in northern Europe and within Spain.

AIRPORT Jerez de la Frontera Airport ⊠ Ctra. N-IV, Km 628.5 ☎ 902/404704 ⊕ www.aena.es.

BUS STATION Jerez de la Frontera ⊠ Pl. de la Estación ☎ 956/149990.

TAXI CONTACT Tele Taxi ☎ 956/344860, 956/350537.

TRAIN STATION Jerez de la Frontera ⊠ Pl. de la Estación s/n, off Calle Diego Fernández Herrera ☎ 912/320320.

VISITOR INFORMATION

CONTACTS Jerez de la Frontera ⊠ Edificio Los Arcos, Pl. del Arenal ☎ 956/338874 ⊕ www.turismojerez.com.

 Sights

Alcázar

CASTLE/PALACE | Once the residence of the caliph of Seville, the 12th-century alcázar in Jerez de la Frontera and its small, octagonal **mosque** and **baths** were built for the Moorish governor's private

Winery Tours in Jerez

On a bodega visit, you'll learn about the *solera* method of blending old wine with new, and the importance of the *flor* (yeast that forms on the wine as it ages) in determining the kind of sherry.

Phone ahead for an appointment to make sure you join a group that speaks your language. Admission fees start at €8 (more for extra wine tasting or tapas), and tours, which last 60–90 minutes, go through the aging cellars, with their endless rows of casks. (You won't see the actual fermenting and bottling, which take place in more modern, less romantic plants outside town.) Finally, you'll be invited to sample generous amounts of pale, dry fino, nutty amontillado, rich, deep oloroso, and sweet Pedro Ximénez and, of course, to purchase a few robustly priced bottles in the winery shop.

use. The baths have three sections: the *sala fría* (cold room), the larger *sala templada* (warm room), and the *sala caliente* (hot room) for steam baths. In the midst of it all is the 17th-century **Palacio de Villavicencio,** built on the site of the original Moorish palace. A camera obscura, a lens-and-mirrors device that projects the outdoors onto a large indoor screen, offers a 360-degree view of Jerez. ⊠ *Calle Alameda Vieja* ☎ *956/149955* 🖭 *From €5.*

Álvaro Domecq

WINERY/DISTILLERY | This is Jerez's oldest *bodega* (winery), founded in 1730. Aside from sherry, Domecq makes the world's best-selling brandy, Fundador. Harveys Bristol Cream is also part of the Domecq group. Visits must be booked in advance by phone or email. ⊠ *Calle San Ildefonso 3* ☎ *956/339634* ⊕ *www.alvarodomecq. com* 🖭 *From €13.*

★ Bodegas Tradición

WINERY/DISTILLERY | Tucked away on the north side of the old quarter and founded in 1998, this is one of the youngest bodegas, but it has the oldest sherry. The five types sit in the casks for at least 20 years and most are older. Visits (book in advance by phone or email) include a tour of the winery, a lesson in how to pair each sherry type, and a tour of the unique Spanish art collection that includes works by El Greco, Zurburán, Goya, and Velázquez. ⊠ *Pl. de los Cordobeses 3* ☎ *956/168628* ⊕ *www.bodegas-tradicion.es* 🖭 *€30* ⊙ *Closed Sun.*

Catedral de Jerez

RELIGIOUS SITE | Across from the alcázar and around the corner from the González Byass winery, the cathedral has an octagonal cupola and a separate bell tower, as well as Zurbarán's canvas *La Virgen Niña Meditando* (*The Virgin as a Young Girl*). ⊠ *Pl. de la Encarnación* ☎ *956/169059* 🖭 *From €6* ⊙ *Closed Sun.*

González Byass

WINERY/DISTILLERY | Home of the famous Tío Pepe, this is one of the most commercial bodegas. The tour, which is in English, is well organized and includes La Concha, an open-air aging cellar designed by Gustave Eiffel. ⊠ *Calle Manuel María González* ☎ *956/357016* ⊕ *www.gonzalezbyass.com* 🖭 *€16.*

Museo Arqueológico

MUSEUM | Diving into the maze of streets that form the scruffy San Mateo neighborhood east of the town center, you come to one of Andalusia's best archaeological museums. The collection is strongest on the pre-Roman period, and the star item, found near Jerez, is a Greek helmet dating to the 7th century BC. ⊠ *Pl. del Mercado s/n* ☎ *956/149560*

Just about the whole city turns out for Jerez's Feria del Caballo, and traditional Andalusian costumes are a common sight.

🎟 *From €5 (free 1st Sun. of month)*
🕐 *Closed Mon.*

★ Plaza de la Asunción

PLAZA | Here on one of Jerez's most intimate squares you can find the Mudejar church of **San Dionisio,** patron saint of the city, (open 10–noon Monday–Thursday) and the ornate *cabildo municipal* (city hall), with a lovely plateresque facade dating to 1575. ⊠ *Jerez de la Frontera* 🎟 *Church free* 🕐 *Church closed for touring Fri.–Sun.*

★ Real Escuela Andaluza del Arte Ecuestre
(*Royal Andalusian School of Equestrian Art*)

SPORTS VENUE | FAMILY | This prestigious school operates on the grounds of the Recreo de las Cadenas, a 19th-century palace. The school was masterminded by Álvaro Domecq in the 1970s, and every Tuesday and Thursday (Thursday only in January and February) as well as each Friday in August and September, the Cartujana horses—a cross between the native Andalusian workhorse and the Arabian—and skilled riders in 18th-century riding costume demonstrate intricate dressage techniques and jumping in the spectacular show *Cómo Bailan los Caballos Andaluces* (roughly, *The Dancing Horses of Andalusia*). ■TIP➜ **Reservations are essential.** The price of admission depends on how close to the arena you sit; the first two rows are the priciest. At certain other times you can visit the museum, stables, and tack room and watch the horses being schooled. ⊠ *Av. Duque de Abrantes* 🕾 *956/318008 for information* ⊕ *www.realescuela.org* 🎟 *From €21.*

San Miguel

RELIGIOUS SITE | One block from the Plaza del Arenal, near the alcázar, stands the church of San Miguel. Built over the 15th and 16th centuries, its interior illustrates the evolution of Gothic architecture, with various styles mixed into the design. ⊠ *Pl. de San Miguel* 🕾 *956/343347* 🎟 *€2* 🕐 *Closed weekends.*

Sandeman

WINERY/DISTILLERY | The Sandeman brand of sherry is known for its dashing man-in-a-cape logo. Tours of the sherry bodegas in Jerez give you some insight into his history and let you visit the cellars. Some visitors purchase tapas to have with their sherry tastings. There is also a museum and shop on-site. ⊠ *Calle Pizarro 10* ☎ *675/647177* ⊕ *www.sandeman.com/visit-us/jerez/sherry-bodegas* ◪ *From €8.*

Yeguada de la Cartuja

FARM/RANCH | This farm just outside Jerez de la Frontera specializes in Carthusian horses. In the 15th century, a Carthusian monastery on this site started the breed for which Jerez and the rest of Spain are now famous. Visits include a full tour of the stables and training areas and a show. Book ahead. ⊠ *Finca Fuente El Suero, Ctra. Medina–El Portal, Km 6.5* ☎ *956/162809* ⊕ *www.yeguadacartuja.com* ◪ *From €16.*

Zoobotánico

ZOO | FAMILY | Just west of the town center, the Jerez zoo is set in lush botanical gardens where you can usually spy up to 33 storks' nests. Primarily a place for the rehabilitation of injured or endangered animals native to the region, the zoo also houses white tigers, elephants, a giant red panda, and the endangered Iberian lynx (the only place where you can see the lynx in captivity). ⊠ *Calle Madreselva* ☎ *956/149785* ⊕ *www.zoobotanicojerez.com* ◪ *€10* ◷ *Closed Mon. mid-Sept.–mid-June.*

🍴 Restaurants

★ Albores

$$ | SPANISH | Opposite the city hall, this busy restaurant with swift service has pleasant outdoor seating under orange trees and a modern interior with low lighting, and serves innovative, modern dishes with a traditional base. The menu is extensive and changes often, although must-try staples include *barriga de atún con salsa de soja y mermelada de tomate* (tuna belly with soy sauce and tomato jam) and *lomo de ciervo* (venison steak). **Known for:** tuna cooked any which

way; generous portions (sharing is encouraged; half portions are also available); desserts like crème brûlée with white chocolate and a house apple pie. Ⓢ *Average main: €16* ⊠ *Calle Consistorio 12* ☎ *956/320266* ⊕ *www.restaurantealbores.com.*

Bar Juanito

$ | SPANISH | Traditional bars don't come more authentic than Bar Juanito, which has been serving local dishes for more than 70 years and pairs everything, of course, with sherry. You can eat standing at the bar or seated in the pleasant patio restaurant, where there's often live music on Saturday. **Known for:** tapas (52 on the menu); artichoke dishes in season (early spring); pork-based stew. Ⓢ *Average main: €10* ⊠ *Calle Pescadería Vieja 8–10* ☎ *956/342986.*

★ La Carboná

$$$ | SPANISH | In a former bodega, this eatery has a rustic atmosphere with arches, wooden beams, and a fireplace for winter nights, and in summer you can often enjoy live music and sometimes flamenco dancing while you dine. The chef has worked at several top restaurants, and his menu includes traditional grilled meats as well as innovative twists on classic dishes, such as foie gras terrine with pear and cardamom, and *mero con curry de palo cortado* (grouper fish with sherry curry). **Known for:** multiple-course sherry tasting menu; bodega setting; innovative dishes. Ⓢ *Average main: €22* ⊠ *Calle San Francisco de Paula 2* ☎ *956/347475* ◷ *Closed Tues.*

Mesón del Asador

$ | SPANISH | Just off the Plaza del Arenal, this rustic meat restaurant is always packed with young locals who crowd around the bar for cheap and generous tapas (from €3). Oxtail stew, fried chorizo, black pudding, and pig's-cheek stew come in huge portions, resulting in an incredibly inexpensive meal. **Known for:** grilled meats; generous portions; inexpensive tapas. Ⓢ *Average main: €11*

✉ *Calle Remedios 2–4* ☎ *952/322658* 💳 *No credit cards.*

Venta Esteban

$$ | **SPANISH** | **FAMILY** | This restaurant is slightly off the beaten track, but well worth seeking out for traditional Jerez cuisine in a pleasant setting. Choose tapas in the bar or à la carte in the spacious and airy dining rooms. **Known for:** seafood; traditional stews; homemade custard. [$] *Average main: €16* ✉ *Colonia de Caulina C.11–03* ✥ *Just off Seville highway exit* ☎ *956/316067* 🌐 *www.restauranteventaesteban.es.*

Hotels

★ Casa Palacio Maria Luisa

$$$$ | **HOTEL** | Once home to Jerez's gentlemen's club (known as the Casino) and something of a symbol of the city's sherry heyday, this restored 19th-century mansion is arguably the most comfortable luxurious hotel in town and the only five-star grand-luxe one. **Pros:** beautifully designed, uber-comfortable rooms; excellent service; lovely outside terrace. **Cons:** might be too grandiose for some. [$] *Rooms from: €280* ✉ *Calle Tornería 22* ☎ *956/926263* 🌐 *casapalaciomarialuisa.com* 🛏 *21 rooms* 🍴 *No meals.*

Hotel Doña Blanca

$ | **HOTEL** | Slightly off the main tourist route but still within easy walking distance to attractions, this traditional town-house hotel offers spacious accommodations with some of the best prices in the city. **Pros:** private terrace in some rooms; great value; generously sized rooms. **Cons:** cold breakfast choices only; not right in the city center; might be too basic for some. [$] *Rooms from: €60* ✉ *Calle Bodegas 11* ☎ *956/348761* 🌐 *www.hoteldonablanca.com* 🛏 *30 rooms* 🍴 *No meals.*

Hotel Villa Jerez

$$$ | **B&B/INN** | Tastefully furnished, this hacienda-style hotel offers luxury on the outskirts of town. **Pros:** elegant gardens; Italian restaurant on site; saltwater swimming pool. **Cons:** outside of town center; some areas need updating; breakfast is average. [$] *Rooms from: €140* ✉ *Av. de la Cruz Roja 7* ☎ *956/153100* 🌐 *www.hace.es/hotelvillajerez* 🛏 *15 rooms* 🍴 *No meals.*

Hotel YIT Casa Grande

$$ | **HOTEL** | This cozy hotel, right in the city center with all the main attractions on its doorstep, comes complete with its original 1920s Art Nouveau design and period antiques. **Pros:** central location; personalized service; roof terrace. **Cons:** no pool; decor might not appeal to everyone; some rooms have street noise. [$] *Rooms from: €100* ✉ *Pl. de las Angustias 3* ☎ *956/345070* 🌐 *www.hotelcasagrandejerez.com* 🛏 *15 rooms* 🍴 *No meals.*

La Fonda Barranco

$ | **HOTEL** | A block away from the cathedral and behind the police station, this typical Jerez town house has been restored to its full bourgeois glory, preserving original tiled floors, beamed ceilings, and a light central patio. **Pros:** personalized attention; central location; good value. **Cons:** some rooms are dark; no elevator; basic breakfast. [$] *Rooms from: €65* ✉ *Calle Barranco 12* ☎ *956/332141* 🌐 *www.lafondabarranco.com* 🛏 *8 rooms, 2 apartments* 🍴 *Free Breakfast.*

Activities

Circuito Permanente de Velocidad

AUTO RACING | Formula One Grand Prix races—including the Spanish motorcycle Grand Prix on the first weekend in May—are held at Jerez's racetrack. ✉ *Ctra. Arcos, Km 10* ☎ *956/151100* 🌐 *www.circuitodejerez.com.*

Shopping

Calle Corredera and **Calle Bodegas** are the places to go if you want to browse for wicker and ceramics.

Córdoba

166 km (103 miles) northwest of Granada, 407 km (250 miles) southwest of Madrid, 239 km (143 miles) northeast of Cádiz, 143 km (86 miles) northeast of Seville.

Strategically located on the north bank of the Guadalquivir River, Córdoba was the Roman and Moorish capital of Spain, and its old quarter, clustered around its famous Mezquita, remains one of the country's grandest and yet most intimate examples of its Moorish heritage. Once a medieval city famed for the peaceful and prosperous coexistence of its three religious cultures—Islamic, Jewish, and Christian—Córdoba is also a perfect analogue for the cultural history of the Iberian Peninsula.

Córdoba today, with its modest population of a little more than 330,000, offers a cultural depth and intensity—a direct legacy from the great emirs, caliphs, philosophers, physicians, poets, and engineers of the days of the caliphate—that far outstrips the city's current commercial and political power. Its artistic and historical treasures begin with the Mezquita-Catedral (mosque-cathedral), as it is generally called, and continue through the winding, whitewashed streets of the Judería (the medieval Jewish quarter); the jasmine-, geranium-, and orange-blossom-filled patios; the Renaissance palaces; and the two dozen churches, convents, and hermitages, built by Moorish artisans directly over former mosques.

GETTING HERE AND AROUND
BIKE TRAVEL
Never designed to support cars, Córdoba's medieval layout is ideal for bicycles, and there's a good network of designated bicycle tracks.

Rent a Bike Córdoba
Bicycle (electric or manual) rental is available here at reasonable rates (from €5 for 3 hours). The company also offers bike tours around the city and to Medinat Al-Zahra. ✉ *Calle Góngora 11* ☎ *679/685175* ⊕ *rentabikecordoba.com.*

BUS TRAVEL
Córdoba is easily reached by bus from Granada, Málaga, and Seville. The city has an extensive public bus network with frequent service. Buses usually start running at 6:30 or 7 am and stop around midnight. You can buy 10-trip passes at newsstands and the bus office in Plaza de Colón. A single-trip fare is €1.30.

Córdoba has organized open-top bus tours of the city that can be booked via the tourist office.

CONTACTS Córdoba ✉ *Glorieta de las Tres Culturas* ☎ *957/404040* ⊕ *www.estacion-autobusescordoba.es.*

CAR TRAVEL
The city's one-way system can be something of a nightmare to navigate, and it's best to park in one of the signposted lots outside the old quarter.

TAXI TRAVEL
CONTACTS Radio Taxi ☎ *957/764444.*

TRAIN TRAVEL
The city's modern train station is the hub for a comprehensive network of regional trains, with regular high-speed train service to Seville, Málaga, Madrid, and Barcelona. Trains for Granada change at Bobadilla.

CONTACTS Train Station ✉ *Glorieta de las Tres Culturas* ☎ *912/320320.*

VISITOR INFORMATION
CONTACTS Tourist Office ✉ *Pl. de las Tendillas 5, Centro* ☎ *902/201774* ⊕ *www.turismodecordoba.org.*

⊙ Sights

Córdoba is an easily navigable city, with twisting alleyways that hold surprises around every corner. The main city subdivisions used in this book are the **Judería** (which includes the Mezquita); **Sector Sur,**

Córdoba's History

The Romans invaded Córdoba in 206 BC, later making it the capital of Rome's section of Spain. Nearly 800 years later, the Visigoth king Leovigildus took control, but the tribe was soon supplanted by the Moors, whose emirs and caliphs held court here from the 8th to the early 11th century. At that point Córdoba was one of the greatest centers of art, culture, and learning in the Western world; one of its libraries had a staggering 400,000 volumes. Moors, Christians, and Jews lived together in harmony within Córdoba's walls. In that era, it was considered second in importance only to Constantinople; but in 1009, Prince Muhammad II and Omeyan led a rebellion that broke up the caliphate, leading to power flowing to separate Moorish kingdoms.

Córdoba remained in Moorish hands until it was conquered by King Ferdinand in 1236 and repopulated from the north of Spain. Later, the Catholic Monarchs used the city as a base from which to plan the conquest of Granada. In Columbus's time, the Guadalquivir was navigable as far upstream as Córdoba, and great galleons sailed its waters. Today, the river's muddy water and marshy banks evoke little of Córdoba's glorious past, but an old Arab waterfall and the city's bridge—of Roman origin, though much restored by the Arabs and successive generations, most recently in 2012—recall a far grander era.

around the **Torre de la Calahorra** across the river; the area around the **Plaza de la Corredera,** a historic gathering place for everything from horse races to bullfights; and the **Centro Comercial,** from the area around Plaza de las Tendillas to the Iglesia de Santa Marina and the Torre de la Malmuerta. Incidentally, the last neighborhood is much more than a succession of shops and stores. The town's real life, the everyday hustle and bustle, takes place here, and the general atmosphere is very different from that of the tourist center around the Mezquita, with its plethora of souvenir shops. Some of the city's finest Mudejar churches and best taverns, as well as the Palacio de los Marqueses de Viana, are in this pivotal part of town well back from the Guadalquivir waterfront.

Some of the most characteristic and rewarding places to explore in Córdoba are the parish churches and the taverns that inevitably accompany them, where you can taste fino de Moriles, a dry, sherry-like wine from the Montilla-Moriles

D.O., and *tentempiés* (tapas—literally, "keep you on your feet"). The *iglesias fernandinas* (churches named for their construction after Fernando III's conquest of Córdoba) are nearly always built over mosques with stunning horseshoe-arch doorways and Mudejar towers, and taverns tended to spring up around these populous hubs of city life. Examples are the Taberna de San Miguel (aka Casa el Pisto) next to the church of the same name, and the Bar Santa Marina (aka Casa Obispo) next to the Santa Marina Church.

■**TIP→ Córdoba's officials frequently change the hours of the city's sights; before visiting an attraction, confirm hours with the tourist office or the sight itself.**

Alcázar de los Reyes Cristianos (*Fortress of the Christian Monarchs*)
CASTLE/PALACE | Built by Alfonso XI in 1328, the alcázar in Córdoba is a Mudejar-style palace with splendid gardens. (The original Moorish alcázar stood beside the Mezquita, on the site

of the present Bishop's Palace.) This is where, in the 15th century, the Catholic monarchs held court and launched their conquest of Granada. Boabdil was imprisoned here in 1483, and for nearly 300 years this alcázar served as the Inquisition's base. The most important sights here are the Hall of the Mosaics and a Roman stone sarcophagus from the 2nd or 3rd century. ⊠ Pl. Campo Santo de los Mártires, Judería ✛ Next to Guadalquivir River ☎ 957/201716 ⊕ alcazardelosreyescristianos.cordoba.es ⊠ €5 ⊘ Closed Mon.

★ Calleja de las Flores
NEIGHBORHOOD | A few yards off the northeastern corner of the Mezquita, this tiny street has the priettiest patios, many with ceramics, foliage, and iron grilles. The patios are key to Córdoba's architecture, at least in the old quarter, where life is lived behind sturdy white walls—a legacy of the Moors, who honored both the sanctity of the home and the need to shut out the fierce summer sun. Between the first and second week of May—right after the early-May **Cruces de Mayo** (Crosses of May) competition, when neighborhoods compete at setting up elaborate crosses decorated with flowers and plants—Córdoba throws a **Patio Festival,** during which private patios are filled with flowers, opened to the public, and judged in a municipal competition. Córdoba's tourist office publishes an itinerary of the best patios in town (downloadable from patios.cordoba.es/en)—note that most are open only in the late afternoon on weekdays but all day on weekends. ⊠ Judería.

★ Madinat Al-Zahra (Medina Azahara)
ARCHAEOLOGICAL SITE | Built in the foothills of the Sierra Morena by Abd ar-Rahman III for his favorite concubine, al-Zahra (the Flower), this once-splendid summer pleasure palace was begun in 936. Historians say it took 10,000 men, 2,600 mules, and 400 camels 25 years to erect this fantasy of 4,300 columns in dazzling pink, green, and white marble and jasper brought from Carthage. A palace, a mosque, luxurious baths, fragrant gardens, fish ponds, an aviary, and a zoo stood on three terraces here, until, in 1013, it was sacked and destroyed by Berber mercenaries. In 1944 the Royal Apartments were rediscovered, and the throne room carefully reconstructed. The outline of the mosque has also been excavated. The only covered part is the Salon de Abd ar-Rahman III (currently being restored); the rest is a sprawl of foundations and arches that hint at the original splendor. First visit the nearby museum and then continue with a walk among the ruins. ⊠ Ctra. de Palma del Río, Km 5.5 ✛ 8 km (5 miles) west of Córdoba on C431 ☎ 957/104933 ⊕ www.museosdeandalucia.es ⊠ €2 ⊘ Closed Mon.

★ Mezquita (Mosque)
RELIGIOUS SITE | Built between the 8th and 10th centuries, Córdoba's mosque is one of the earliest and most transportingly beautiful examples of Spanish Islamic architecture. Inside, some 850 columns rise before you in a forest of jasper, marble, granite, and onyx. The Mezquita has served as a cathedral since 1236, but it was founded as a mosque in 785 by Abd ar-Rahman I. The beautiful **mihrab** (prayer niche) is the Mezquita's greatest jewel. In front of the mihrab is the **maksoureh**, a kind of anteroom for the caliph and his court; its mosaics and plasterwork make it a masterpiece of Islamic art. In the 13th century, Christians had the **Capilla de Villaviciosa** built by Moorish craftsmen, its Mudejar architecture blending with the lines of the mosque. Not so the heavy, incongruous baroque structure of the cathedral, sanctioned in the heart of the mosque by Carlos V in the 1520s. ⊠ Calle de Torrijos, Judería ☎ 957/470512 ⊕ mezquita-catedraldecordoba.es ⊠ Mezquita €10 (free Mon.–Sat. 8:30–9:30 am), Torre del Alminar €2.

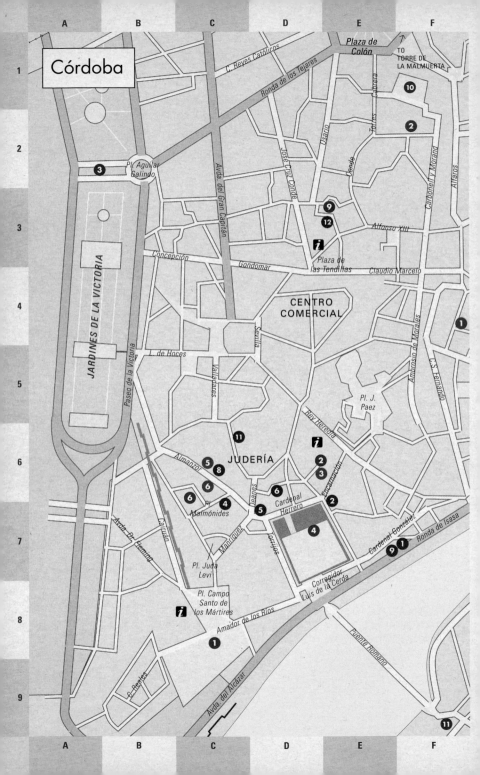

KEY

- **1** Sights
- **1** Restaurants
- **1** Hotels
- **i** Tourist Information

Sights ▼

1 Alcázar de los Reyes Cristianos **C8**
2 Calleja de las Flores **E6**
3 Madinat Al-Zahra **A2**
4 Mezquita **D7**
5 Museo de Bellas Artes. **G6**
6 Museo Taurino **C6**
7 Palacio de Viana **G1**
8 Plaza de los Dolores **G1**
9 Plaza de San Miguel **E3**
10 Plaza de Santa Marina **F1**
11 Torre Calahorra **F9**

Restaurants ▼

1 Amaltea **F7**
2 Bar Santos **E6**
3 Bodegas Campos **H6**
4 Casa Mazal **C7**
5 Casa Pepe de la Judería **D7**
6 El Caballo Rojo **D6**
7 El Choco **I4**
8 El Churrasco **C6**
9 La Regadera **E7**
10 La Tinaja **G6**
11 Salón de Té **C6**
12 Taberna de San Miguel **E3**
13 Taberna Sociedad de Plateros **G6**

Hotels ▼

1 Casa de los Azulejos **F4**
2 Hospes Palacio del Bailío **F2**
3 Hotel Balcón de Córdoba **E6**
4 Hotel Maestre **G6**
5 La Llave de la Judería ... **C6**
6 NH Collection Amistad Córdoba **C6**
7 Viento 10 .... **I5**

Córdoba's stunning Mezquita charts the evolution of Western and Islamic architecture over a 1,300-year period.

★ Museo de Bellas Artes

MUSEUM | Hard to miss because of its deep-pink facade, Córdoba's Museum of Fine Arts, in a courtyard just off the Plaza del Potro, belongs to a former Hospital de la Caridad (Charity Hospital). It was founded by Ferdinand and Isabella, who twice received Columbus here. The collection, which includes paintings by Murillo, Valdés Leal, Zurbarán, Goya, and Joaquín Sorolla y Bastida, concentrates on local artists. Highlights are altarpieces from the 14th and 15th centuries and the large collection of prints and drawings, including some by Fortuny, Goya, and Sorolla. ✉ *Pl. del Potro 1, San Francisco* ☎ *957/103659* ✈ *€2* ⌚ *Closed Mon.*

Museo Taurino (*Museum of Bullfighting*)

MUSEUM | Two adjoining mansions on the Plaza Maimónides (or Plaza de las Bulas) house this museum, and it's worth a visit, as much for the chance to see a restored mansion as for the posters, Art Nouveau paintings, bull's heads, suits of lights (bullfighting outfits), and memorabilia of famous Córdoban bullfighters, including the most famous of all, Manolete. To the surprise of the nation, Manolete, who was considered immortal, was killed by a bull in the ring at Linares in 1947. ✉ *Pl. de Maimónides 1, Judería* ☎ *957/201056* ✈ *€4* ⌚ *Closed Mon.*

Palacio de Viana

CASTLE/PALACE | This 17th-century palace is one of Córdoba's most splendid aristocratic homes. Also known as the **Museo de los Patios,** it contains 12 interior patios, each one different; the patios and gardens are planted with cypresses, orange trees, and myrtles. Inside the building are a carriage museum, a library, embossed leather wall hangings, filigree silver, and grand galleries and staircases. As you enter, note that the corner column of the first patio has been removed to allow the entrance of horse-drawn carriages. ✉ *Pl. Don Gomé 2, Centro* ☎ *957/496741* ✈ *From €5* ⌚ *Closed Mon.*

Plaza de los Dolores
PLAZA | The 17th-century Convento de Capuchinos surrounds this small square north of Plaza San Miguel. The square is where you feel most deeply the city's languid pace. In its center, a statue of **Cristo de los Faroles** (Christ of the Lanterns) stands amid eight lanterns hanging from twisted wrought-iron brackets. ✉ *Centro.*

Plaza de San Miguel
NEIGHBORHOOD | The square and café terraces around it, and its excellent tavern, Taberna San Miguel–Casa El Pisto, form one of the city's finest combinations of art, history, and gastronomy. The San Miguel church has an interesting facade with Romanesque doors built around Mudejar horseshoe arches, and a Mudejar dome inside. ✉ *Centro.*

Plaza Santa Marina
PLAZA | At the edge of the **Barrio de los Toreros,** a quarter where many of Córdoba's famous bullfighters were born and raised, stands a statue of the famous bullfighter Manolete (1917–47) opposite the lovely fernandina church of Santa Marina de Aguas Santas (St. Marina of Holy Waters). Not far from here, on the Plaza de la Lagunilla, is a bust of Manolete. ✉ *Centro.*

Torre Calahorra
BUILDING | The tower on the far side of the Puente Romano (Roman Bridge), which was restored in 2008, was built in 1369 to guard the entrance to Córdoba. It now houses the **Museo Vivo de Al-Andalus** ("al-Andalus" is Arabic for "Land of the West"), with films and audiovisual guides (in English) on Córdoba's history. Climb the narrow staircase to the top of the tower for the view of the Roman bridge and city on the other side of the Guadalquivir. ✉ *Av. de la Confederación s/n, Sector Sur* ☎ *957/293929* 🌐 *www.torrecalahorra.es* 🎫 *€5, includes audio guide.*

🍴 Restaurants

Amaltea
$$ | INTERNATIONAL | Satisfying vegetarians, vegans, and their meat-eating friends, this organic restaurant includes some meat and fish on the menu. There's a healthy mix of Mexican, Asian, Spanish, and Italian-influenced dishes, including pasta with artichokes, chicken curry with mango and apricots, and couscous. **Known for:** vegetarian food; inviting interior with relaxed vibe; pasta with artichokes. [$] *Average main: €15* ✉ *Ronda de Isasa 10, Centro* ☎ *957/491968* ⏲ *No dinner Sun. No lunch Aug.*

Bar Santos
$ | TAPAS | This very small, quintessentially Spanish bar, with no seats and numerous photos of matadors and flamenco dancers, seems out of place surrounded by the tourist shops and overshadowed by the Mezquita, but its appearance—and its prices—are part of its charm. Tapas (from €2.50) such as *albóndigas en salsa de almendras* (meatballs in almond sauce) and *bocadillos* (sandwiches that are literally "little mouthfuls") are excellent in quality and value, while the *tortilla de patata* (potato omelet) is renowned and celebrated both for its taste and its heroic thickness. **Known for:** tortilla de patata; inexpensive tapas; being busy. [$] *Average main: €6* ✉ *Calle Magistral González Francés 3, Judería* ☎ *957/488975.*

★ Bodegas Campos
$$$ | SPANISH | A block east of the Plaza del Potro, this traditional old bodega with high-quality service is the epitome of all that's great about Andalusian cuisine. The dining rooms are in barrel-heavy rustic rooms and leafy traditional patios (take a look at some of the signed barrels—you may recognize a name or two, such as the former U.K. prime minister Tony Blair). **Known for:** bodega setting; regional dishes; excellent tapas bar. [$] *Average main: €22* ✉ *Calle Los Lineros 32, San*

Pedro ☎ *957/497500* 🌐 *www.bodegas-campos.com.*

Casa Mazal

$$$ | **ECLECTIC** | In the heart of the Judería, this pretty little restaurant serves a modern interpretation of Sephardic cuisine, with organic dishes that are more exotic than the usual Andalusian fare. The many vegetarian options include gazpacho with orange, ginger, and tea, and the *confitura de cordero con espárragos trigueros* (caramelized lamb with baby asparagus) and *atún rojo empedrado en sésamo* (red tuna steak in sesame seeds) are delicious. **Known for:** traditional Sephardic cuisine; romantic ambience; vegetarian dishes. [$] *Average main: €18* ✉ *Calle Tomás Conde 3, Judería* ☎ *957/941888.*

Casa Pepe de la Judería

$$$ | **SPANISH** | Geared toward a tourist clientele, this place is always packed, noisy, and fun, and there is live Spanish guitar music on the roof terrace most summer nights. Antiques and some wonderful old oil paintings fill this three-floor labyrinth of rooms just around the corner from the mosque, near the Judería. **Known for:** traditional Andalusian food; croquetas de jamón; live music on the roof terrace in summer. [$] *Average main: €20* ✉ *Calle Romero 1, off Deanes, Judería* ☎ *957/200744.*

El Caballo Rojo

$$$ | **SPANISH** | Though now under new ownership, this has been one of the most famous traditional restaurants in Andalusia, frequented by royalty and society folk. The interior resembles a cool, leafy Andalusian patio, and the dining room is furnished with stained glass and dark wood; the upstairs terrace overlooks the Mezquita. **Known for:** fine traditional dining; rabo de toro; modern specialties like clams in sweet sherry-like wine. [$] *Average main: €22* ✉ *Calle Cardenal Herrero 28, Judería* ☎ *957/475375* 🌐 *www.elcaballorojo.com.*

★ El Choco

$$$$ | **SPANISH** | The city's most exciting restaurant, which has renewed its Michelin star annually since 2012, El Choco has renowned chef Kisko Garcia at the helm whipping up innovative dishes based on his 10 Commandments to preserve good cooking. One of them is that taste always comes first, and that plays out well during a meal at this minimalist restaurant with charcoal-color walls, glossy parquet floors, and dishes offering new sensations and amazing presentations. **Known for:** creative Andalusian cooking; good value Michelin-star tasting menu; innovative presentation. [$] *Average main: €95* ✉ *Compositor Serrano Lucena 14, Centro* ☎ *957/264863* 🌐 *www.restaurantechoco.es* 🕓 *Closed Mon. and Aug. No dinner Sun. or Tues.*

El Churrasco

$$$ | **SPANISH** | The name suggests grilled meat, but this restaurant in the heart of the Judería serves much more than that. In the colorful bar try tapas (from €3.50) such as the *berenjenas crujientes con salmorejo* (crispy fried eggplant slices with thick gazpacho), while in the restaurant, opt for the supremely fresh grilled fish or the steak, which is the best in town, particularly the namesake *churrasco ibérico* (grilled pork, served here in a spicy tomato-based sauce). **Known for:** grilled meat; tapas; alfresco dining. [$] *Average main: €20* ✉ *Calle Romero 16, Judería* ☎ *957/290819* 🕓 *Closed Aug.*

La Regadera

$$ | **SPANISH** | It feels as if you could be outside at this bright venue on the river whose fresh interior comes with miniature wall gardens and lots of watering cans (*regaderas*)—there's even a fresh herb garden in the middle. Local produce takes center stage on the menu, where you'll find a mix of traditional and modern dishes including house specials such as slow-cooked lamb, carpaccio *ibérico*, and violet ice cream with strawberries. **Known for:** good wine list; garden-like interior;

tuna tartare. $ *Average main: €14* ✉ *Ronda de Isasa 10, Judería* ☎ *957/101400* ⊕ *www.regadera.es* ◷ *Closed Mon.*

La Tinaja

$$ | SPANISH | On the river to the east of the city, this bodega-bar has kept its original 18th-century-house layout, which means that you can eat in different rooms as well as outside on the pleasant terrace. The food is traditional, with an emphasis on local produce and Córdoba staples such as *mazamorra con atún rojo ahumado* (traditional almond soup with smoked tuna) and *alcachofas confitadas con castaña asada* (artichokes with roast chestnuts) as well as oxtail and salmorejo. **Known for:** grilled meat; riverside terrace; homemade foie gras. $ *Average main: €14* ✉ *Paseo de la Ribera 12, Centro* ☎ *957/047998* ⊕ *latinajadecordoba. com.*

Salón de Té

BARS/PUBS | A few blocks from the Mezquita, this place is a beautiful spot for tea, with a courtyard, side rooms filled with cushions, and a shop selling Moroccan clothing. It's open daily 10 am–10 pm. ✉ *Calle del Buen Pastor 13, Judería* ☎ *957/487984.*

Taberna de San Miguel

$$ | TAPAS | Just a few minutes' walk from the Plaza de las Tendillas and opposite the lovely San Miguel Church, this popular tapas spot—also known as the Casa el Pisto (Ratatouille House)—was established in 1880. You can choose to squeeze in at the bar and dine on tapas (€2.50) or spread out a little more on the patio decked with ceramics and bullfighting memorabilia, where half and full portions are served. **Known for:** tapas, including pisto; historic ambience; patio with bullfighting memorabilia. $ *Average main: €12* ✉ *Pl. San Miguel 1, Centro* ☎ *957/470166* ⊕ *www.casaelpisto.com* ◷ *Closed Sun. and Aug.*

Taberna Sociedad de Plateros

$ | TAPAS | On a narrow side street just steps away from the Plaza del Potro, this delightful spot dates to the 17th century. One of the city's most historic inns, it has a large patio that adjoins a traditional marble bar where locals meet. **Known for:** tapas; home-style cooking; local haunt. $ *Average main: €8* ✉ *Calle San Francisco 6, Plaza de la Corredera* ☎ *957/470042* ◷ *Closed Mon. Sept.–June, and Sun. in July and Aug.*

🛏 Hotels

Casa de los Azulejos

$$ | B&B/INN | This 17th-century house still has original details like the majestic vaulted ceilings and, with the use of stunning azulejos—hence the name—it mixes Andalusian and Latin American influences. **Pros:** interesting architecture; generous breakfast buffet; tropical central patio. **Cons:** hyperbusy interior design; limited privacy; plunge pool is only open in summer. $ *Rooms from: €90* ✉ *Calle Fernando Colón 5, Centro* ☎ *957/470000* ⊕ *www.casadelosazulejos.com* ⇲ *9 rooms* ⵏ⊙⵿ *Free Breakfast.*

★ Hospes Palacio del Bailío

$$$$ | HOTEL | One of the city's top lodging options, this tastefully renovated 17th-century mansion is built over the ruins of a Roman house (visible beneath glass floors) in the historic center of town. **Pros:** dazzling interiors; impeccable comforts; central location. **Cons:** not easy to access by car; pricey; parking is limited. $ *Rooms from: €250* ✉ *Calle Ramírez de las Casas Deza 10–12, Plaza de la Corredera* ☎ *957/498993* ⊕ *www. hospes.com/palacio-bailio* ⇲ *53 rooms* ⵏ⊙⵿ *No meals.*

★ Hotel Balcón de Córdoba

$$$$ | HOTEL | Located in a tastefully restored 17th-century convent, this boutique hotel has spacious, quiet rooms, and the Mezquita is almost within arm's reach from the rooftop terrace. **Pros:**

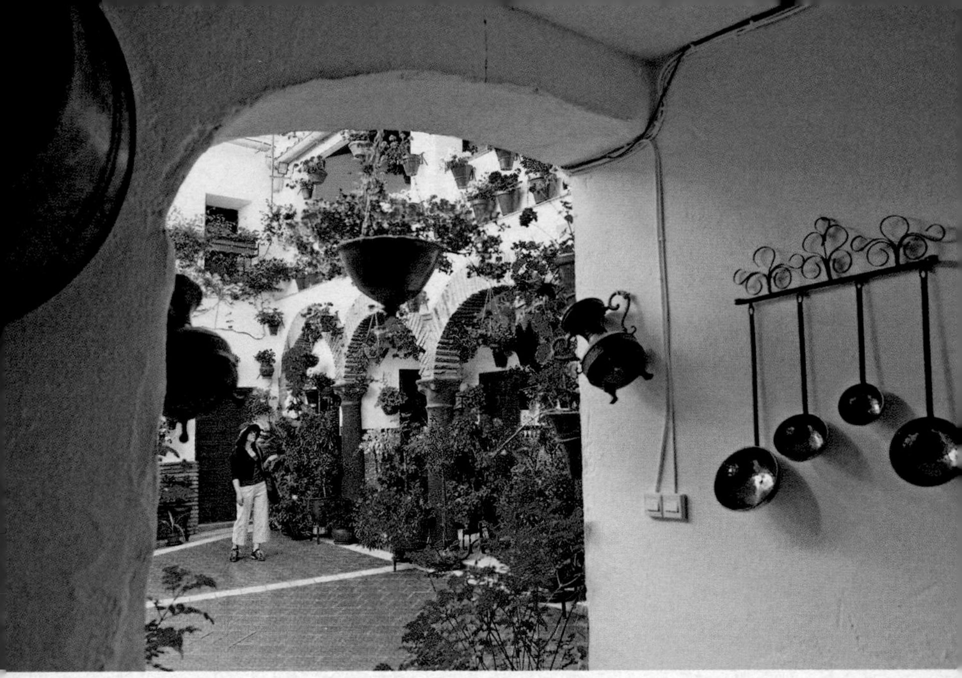

A typical Córdoba patio, filled with flowers

central location; historic building; rooftop views of the Mezquita. **Cons:** difficult to access by car; very quiet; small breakfast area. [$] *Rooms from: €230* ✉ *Calle Encarnación 8, Judería* ☎ *957/498478* 🌐 *balcondecordoba.com* 🛏 *10 rooms* 🍴 *Free Breakfast.*

Hotel Maestre

$ | **HOTEL** | Around the corner from the Plaza del Potro, this is an affordable hotel in which Castilian-style furniture, gleaming marble, and high-quality oil paintings add elegance to excellent value. **Pros:** good location; great value; helpful reception staff. **Cons:** no elevator and lots of steps; ancient plumbing; could be too basic for some. [$] *Rooms from: €60* ✉ *Calle Romero Barros 4–6, San Pedro* ☎ *957/472410* 🌐 *www.hotelmaestre.com* 🛏 *26 rooms* 🍴 *No meals.*

★ La Llave de la Judería

$$$ | **B&B/INN** | This small hotel, occupying a collection of houses just a stone's throw from the Mezquita, combines enchanting antique furnishings with modern amenities, but its greatest asset is its exceptionally helpful staff. **Pros:** beautiful interiors; rooms are equipped with computers; close to the Mezquita. **Cons:** rooms facing street can be noisy; direct car access is difficult; dark reception area. [$] *Rooms from: €160* ✉ *Calle Romero 38, Judería* ☎ *957/294808* 🌐 *www.lallavedelajuderia.es* 🛏 *9 rooms* 🍴 *Free Breakfast.*

NH Collection Amistad Córdoba

$$$ | **HOTEL** | Two 18th-century mansions overlooking Plaza de Maimónides in the heart of the Judería have been melded into a modern business hotel with a cobblestone Mudejar courtyard, carved-wood ceilings, and a plush lounge. **Pros:** pleasant and efficient service; large rooms; central location. **Cons:** parking is difficult; main access via steep steps with no ramp; a little impersonal. [$] *Rooms from: €140* ✉ *Pl. de Maimónides 3, Judería* ☎ *957/420335* 🌐 *www.nh-hoteles.es* 🛏 *108 rooms* 🍴 *No meals.*

Viento 10

$$ | **HOTEL** | Tucked away to the east of the old quarter, but within just 10

minutes' walk of the Mezquita is a quiet, romantic haven, once part of the 17th-century Sacred Martyrs Hospital. **Pros:** quiet location; pillow menu; Jacuzzi and sauna. **Cons:** some walking distance to the main monuments; a little plain; not easy to find. [$] *Rooms from: €120* ✉ *Calle Ronquillo Briceño 10, San Pedro* ☎ *957/764960* 🌐 *www.hotelviento10.es* 🕓 *Closed Jan.* 🛏 *8 rooms* 🍴 *No meals.*

Nightlife

For nightlife, Córdoba locals hang out mostly in the areas of Ciudad Jardín (the old university area), Plaza de las Tendillas, and the Avenida Gran Capitán.

Bodega Guzman
BARS/PUBS | For some traditional tipple, check out this atmospheric bodega near the old synagogue. Its sherries are served straight from the barrel in a room that doubles as a bullfighting museum. ✉ *Calle de los Judios 6, Judería.*

Café Málaga
MUSIC CLUBS | A block from Plaza de las Tendillas, this is a laid-back hangout for jazz and blues aficionados. There's live music most days and occasional flamenco nights. ✉ *Calle Málaga 3, Centro* ☎ *957/474107.*

Performing Arts

FLAMENCO

Tablao El Cardenal
DANCE CLUBS | Córdoba's most famous flamenco club offers performances by established artists on a pleasant open-air patio. Admission is €23 (including a drink) and the 90-minute shows take place Monday through Thursday at 8:15 pm and on Friday and Saturday at 9. ✉ *Calle Buen Pastor 2, Judería* ☎ *619/217922.*

Shopping

Córdoba's main shopping district is around Avenida Gran Capitán, Ronda de los Tejares, and the streets leading away from Plaza Tendillas.

Meryan
SHOES/LUGGAGE/LEATHER GOODS | This is one of Córdoba's best workshops for embossed leather. ✉ *Calleja de las Flores 2* ☎ *957/475902* 🌐 *www.meryancor.com.*

Montilla

46 km (28 miles) south of Córdoba toward Málaga.

In the countryside around Montilla, hills are ablaze with sunflowers in early summer near the vineyards of the Montilla-Moriles D.O. Every fall, 47,000 acres' worth of Pedro Ximénez grapes are crushed here to produce the region's rich Montilla wines, which are similar to sherry. Montilla-Moriles has also developed a young white wine similar to Portugal's Vinho Verde.

GETTING HERE AND AROUND

Regular buses connect Montilla with Córdoba and Granada, but to make the most of your time, visit Montilla en route by car to either city. Montilla's small size makes it an easy pedestrian destination. Allow half a day to visit.

VISITOR INFORMATION

CONTACTS Montilla ✉ *Calle Castillo s/n* ☎ *957/652354* 🌐 *www.montillaturismo.es.*

Sights

Bodegas Alvear
WINERY/DISTILLERY | Founded in 1729, this bodega in the center of town is Andalusia's oldest. Besides being informative, the fun tour and wine tasting give you the chance to buy a bottle or two of Alvear's tasty version of the sweet Pedro

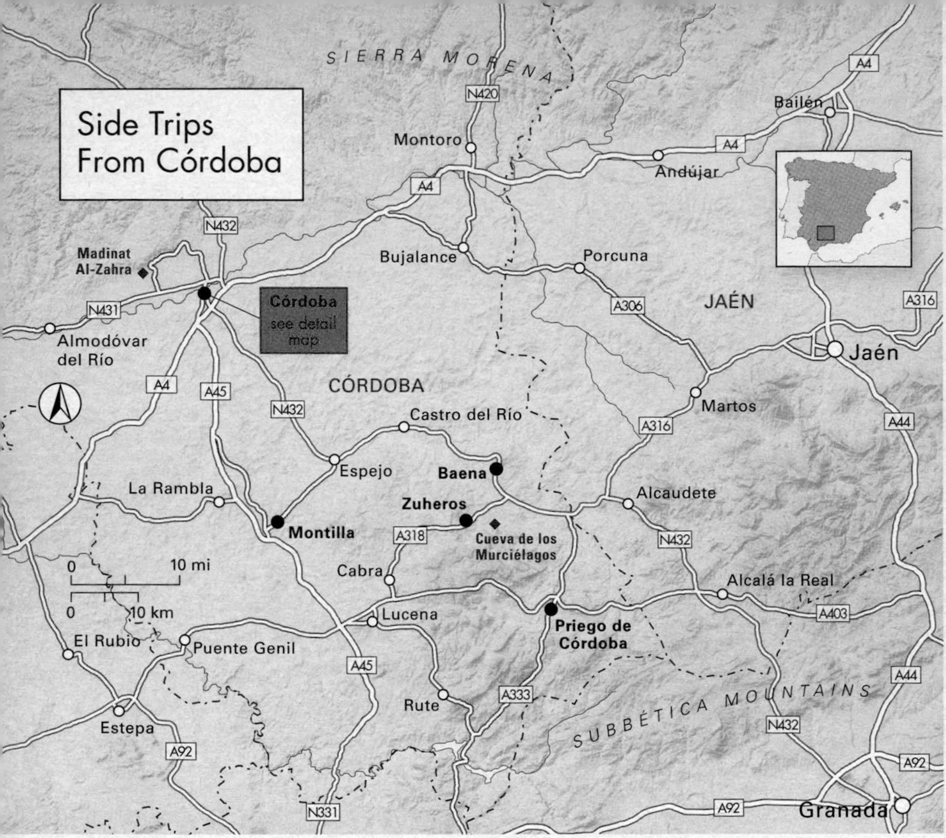

Ximénez aged wine. **■TIP→ Phone ahead to book a tour in English.** ✉ *Calle María Auxiliadora 1* ☎ *957/652939* 🌐 *www.alvear.es* 🎫 *From €9.*

🍴 Restaurants

Taberna Bolero

$ | **SPANISH** | Local fare comes into its own at this venue in the town center decorated with barrels and Moorish stars in keeping with Córdoba's traditions and history. Dine on excellent fried fish or the slightly more elaborate *bacalao en salsa de naranja* (cod in orange sauce) or go for the provincial staple, oxtail. **Known for:** good traditional dishes; local wines; fried fish. [$] *Average main: €10* ✉ *Calle Fuente Álamo 9* ☎ *679/398002* 🕒 *Closed Mon. No dinner Sun.*

🛍 Shopping

On the outskirts of town, coopers' shops produce barrels of various sizes, some small enough to serve as creative souvenirs.

Tonelería J. L. Rodríguez

WINE/SPIRITS | On Montilla's main road, it is worth stopping here not just to buy barrels and local wines, but also to pop in the back and see the barrels being made. ✉ *Ctra. Córdoba–Málaga (N331), Km 43.3* ☎ *957/650563* 🌐 *www.toneleriajlrodriguez.com.*

Baena

66 km (43 miles) southeast of Córdoba, 42 km (26 miles) east of Montilla.

Outside the boundaries of Subbética and surrounded by chalk fields producing top-quality olives, Baena is an old town of narrow streets, whitewashed houses, ancient mansions, and churches clustered beneath Moorish battlements.

Sights

Museo del Olivar y el Aceite

MUSEUM | This museum is housed in the old olive mill owned and operated by Don José Alcalá Santaella until 1959. The machinery on display dates to the middle of the 19th century, when the mill was capable of processing up to three tons of olives a day. The museum aims to demonstrate the way of life of workers in this important industry. You can taste and buy olive oil at the shop. ✉ *Calle Cañada 7* ☎ *957/671757* 🌐 *www.museoaceite.com* 🎟 *€2* 🕒 *Closed Mon.*

Zuheros

80 km (50 miles) southeast of Córdoba.

At the northern edge of the Subbética mountain range and at an altitude of 2,040 feet, Zuheros is one of the most attractive villages in the province of Córdoba. From the road up, it's hidden behind a dominating rock face topped by the dramatic ruins of a castle built by the Moors over a Roman castle. There's an expansive view back over the valley from here. Next to the castle is the Iglesia de Santa María, built over a mosque. The base of the minaret is the foundation for the bell tower.

GETTING HERE AND AROUND

Several daily buses connect Zuheros with Seville and Córdoba, although the schedule isn't ideal for sightseeing. Driving is the best option for exploring the surrounding area, including the Cueva de los Murciélagos (Cave of the Bats). Zuheros is compact and easy to get around, although there's a steep climb from the car park to the village.

Sights

Cueva de los Murciélagos (*Cave of the Bats*)

CAVE | Some 4 km (2½ miles) above Zuheros along a winding road, the Cueva de los Murciélagos runs for about 2 km (1 mile), although only about half of that expanse is open to the public. The cave is thought to have been inhabited as far back as tens of thousands of years ago, but what you can see today (by guided tour only) are the wall paintings that archeologists date to the Neolithic Age (6000–3000 BC) and Chalcolithic Age (3000–2000 BC). The cave also is interesting geologically. Visits must be booked in advance by phone or email (*turismo@zuheros.es*). *A museum in town (Museo Histórico-Arqueológico Municipal) displays some of the items found in area caves.* ✉ *CV247* ✣ *Off Calle Santo* ☎ *957/694545 Tues.–Fri. 10–1:30* 🎟 *€8* 🕒 *Closed Mon.*

Hotels

Zuhayra

$ | **B&B/INN** | Fresh from a refurbishment in 2017, this small hotel on a narrow street has comfortable rooms painted a sunny yellow with views over the village rooftops to the valley below. **Pros:** cozy public spaces; stunning vistas; best dining in the village. **Cons:** plain decor; thin walls; a few rooms have no view. [$] *Rooms from: €65* ✉ *Calle Mirador 10* ☎ *957/694693* 🌐 *www.zercahoteles.com* 🛏 *18 rooms* 🍴 *Free Breakfast.*

Priego de Córdoba

103 km (64 miles) southeast of Córdoba, 25 km (15 miles) southeast of Zuheros.

The jewel of Córdoba's countryside is Priego de Córdoba, a town of 23,500 inhabitants at the foot of Monte Tinosa. Wander down Calle del Río, opposite the town hall, to see 18th-century mansions, once the homes of silk merchants. At the end of the street is the Fuente del Rey (King's Fountain), with some 130 water jets, built in 1803. Don't miss the lavish baroque churches of La Asunción and La Aurora or the Barrio de la Villa, an old Moorish quarter with a maze of narrow streets of white-walled buildings.

GETTING HERE AND AROUND

Priego has reasonable bus service from Córdoba (2½ hours) and Granada (1½ hours), although your best bet is to visit by car en route to either of these cities. Once there, it's perfect for pedestrian exploration.

VISITOR INFORMATION

CONTACTS Priego de Córdoba ✉ *Pl. de la Constitución 3* ☎ *957/700625* ⊕ *www. turismodepriego.com.*

 Restaurants

La Pianola (*Casa Pepe*)
$ | SPANISH | Expect cheap, cheerful, and lively dining at this small venue, a couple of blocks south of the castle and usually packed with locals. On the menu are usual Córdoba staples including oxtail, but the specialty here is *bacalao frito* (fried cod). **Known for:** value dining; good tapas; delicious French toast for dessert. $ *Average main: €9* ✉ *Calle Obispo Caballero 6* ☎ *957/700409* ⊘ *Closed Mon.*

Hotels

Hotel-Museo Patria Chica
$$ | HOTEL | This charming hotel opened in 2017, housed in a fully restored 19th-century mansion, and is complete with a pretty interior patio and peaceful private garden. **Pros:** central location; period furnishings; pool and restaurant on-site. **Cons:** quiet; slightly out of the town center; some rooms face the street. $ *Rooms from: €100* ✉ *Carrera de las Monjas 47* ☎ *957/058385* ⊕ *www. hotelpatriachica.com* ➴ *15 rooms* ⦿ *Free Breakfast.*

La Posada Real
$ | B&B/INN | In the heart of Priego's Barrio de la Villa, this restored basic town house has two sections, each with geranium-decked balconies and typical Andalusian touches. **Pros:** friendly owner; traditional town house; center of town. **Cons:** rooms on the small side; car access difficult; two-night minimum stay. $ *Rooms from: €60* ✉ *Calle Real 14* ☎ *957/541910* ➴ *7 rooms* ⦿ *No meals.*

Jaén

107 km (64 miles) southeast of Córdoba, 93 km (58 miles) north of Granada.

Nestled in the foothills of the Sierra de Jabalcuz, Jaén is surrounded by towering peaks and olive-clad hills. The modern part of town holds little interest for travelers these days, but the old town is an atmospheric jumble of narrow cobblestone streets hugging the mountainside. Jaén's grand parador, in the city's hilltop castle, is a great reason to stop here.

The Arabs called this land Geen (Route of the Caravans) because it formed a crossroad between Castile and Andalusia. Captured from the Moors by Ferdinand III in 1246, Jaén became a frontier province, the site of many a skirmish and battle over the following 200 years between the Moors of Granada and Christians from the north and west.

Olive groves near Priego de Córdoba

GETTING HERE AND AROUND

You can reach Jaén by bus from Granada, Madrid, and Málaga (*ALSA* ☎ *902/422242* ⊕ *www.alsa.es*) and also by train from Granada and Málaga. Jaén is compact and all sights are easy to visit on foot, with the exception of the castle, 3 km (2 miles) from the center and a steep climb—if you can't face the ascent, take a taxi.

VISITOR INFORMATION

CONTACTS Jaén ⊠ *Calle Maestra 8* ☎ *953/190455* ⊕ *www.turjaen.org*.

 Sights

★ Baños Árabes

ARCHAEOLOGICAL SITE | Explore the narrow alleys of old Jaén as you walk from the cathedral to the Baños Árabes (Arab Baths), which once belonged to Ali, a Moorish king of Jaén, and probably date to the 11th century. In 1592, a viceroy of Peru named Fernando de Torres y Portugal built himself a mansion, the **Palacio de Villardompardo,** right over the baths,

so it took years of painstaking excavation to restore them to their original form. The palace contains a fascinating, albeit small, museum of folk crafts and a larger museum devoted to native art. ⊠ *Palacio de Villardompardo, Pl. Luisa de Marillac* ☎ *953/248068* 🖼 *Free* ⊙ *Closed Mon.*

Basílica Menor de San Ildefonso (*Smaller Basilica of Saint Ildefonso*)

RELIGIOUS SITE | Set on the square and in the district of the same name, this large church is one of Jaén's treasures. Built mainly in the Gothic style with baroque details, the magnificent gilded altar is the highlight. ⊠ *Pl. de San Ildefonso* ☎ *953/190346* 🖼 *Free.*

★ Castillo de Santa Catalina

CASTLE/PALACE | This castle, perched on a rocky crag 400 yards above the center of town, is Jaén's star monument. It may have originated as a tower built by Hannibal, but whatever its origins, the site was fortified continuously over the centuries. The Nasrid king Alhamar, builder of Granada's Alhambra, constructed an alcázar here, but Ferdinand III

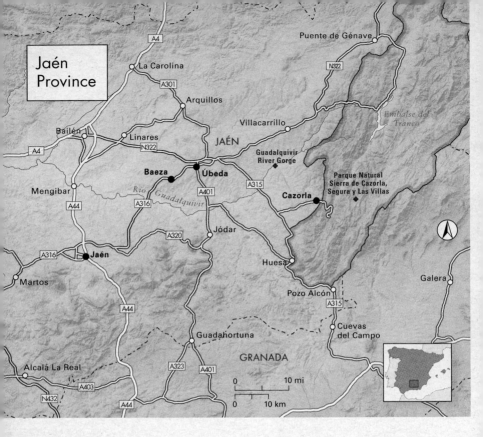

captured it from him in 1246 on the feast day of Santa Catalina (St. Catherine). Catalina consequently became Jaén's patron saint, so when the Christians built a castle and chapel here, they dedicated both to her. Guided tours are available twice daily. ⊠ *Ctra. del Castillo de Santa Catalina* ☎ *953/120733* ➡ *€4 (free last 3 hrs Wed.).*

Jaén Cathedral

RELIGIOUS SITE | Looming above the modest buildings around it, the cathedral was begun in 1492 on the site of a former mosque and took almost 300 years to build. Its chief architect was Andrés de Vandelvira (1509–75)—many more of his buildings can be seen in Úbeda and Baeza. The ornate facade was sculpted by Pedro Roldán, and the figures on top of the columns include San Fernando (Ferdinand III) and the four evangelists.

The cathedral's most treasured relic is the **Santo Rostro** (Holy Face), the cloth with which, according to tradition, St. Veronica cleansed Christ's face on the way to Calvary, leaving his image imprinted on the fabric. The *rostro* (face) is displayed every Friday 10:30–noon and 5–6. In the underground **museum,** look for the paintings *San Lorenzo,* by Martínez Montañés; the *Immaculate Conception,* by Alonso Cano; and a Calvary scene by Jácobo Florentino. ⊠ *Pl. Santa María s/n* ☎ *953/241448* ➡ *€5.*

Museo de Jaén

MUSEUM | This museum is divided into two sections within the rooms of a 1547 mansion: archaeological finds and fine art. The Bronze Age and Roman era are particularly well represented; highlights here include the Dama de los Robles statue and the first-century marble room.

The patio showcases the facade of the erstwhile Church of San Miguel. The fine-arts section has a room full of Goya lithographs. ✉ *Paseo de la Estación 29* ☎ *953/101366* 🎫 *€2* 🕒 *Closed Mon.*

Museo Íbero

MUSEUM | The long-awaited Iberian Museum opened in late 2017 to much acclaim in a striking modern building on the site of the old prison that once housed Franco's political prisoners. It has one of the best collections of Iberian (pre-Roman, from the 6th to 1st century BC) artifacts in Spain including 20 life-size Iberian sculptures discovered by chance near the village of Porcuna in 1975. The wolf's head is particularly striking. Exhibitions portray the Iberian lifestyle and culture and showcase some of the 3,500 pieces in the immense collection. ✉ *Paseo de la Estación 41* ☎ *953/001692* 🎫 *€2* 🕒 *Closed Mon.*

🍴 Restaurants

Bagá

$$$$ | **SPANISH** | Just around the corner from the Basílica Menor de San Ildefonso, Jaén's only Michelin-starred restaurant to date opened in fall 2018 with chef Pedro Sánchez pushing the standard for local food very high. The three tables plus barstools have a direct view of the kitchen, so you can watch the tasting menu being prepared. **Known for:** fine dining with the slogan "Sentir Jaén" ("Feel Jaén"); innovative, seasonal dishes; local produce. [$] *Average main: €65* ✉ *Calle Reja de la Capilla 3* ☎ *953/047450* 🌐 *www.bagagastronomico.com* 🕒 *Closed Sun. and Mon. No lunch Tues.*

Restaurante Casa Antonio

$$$ | **SPANISH** | Exquisite Andalusian food with a contemporary twist is served at this somber yet elegant restaurant with three small dining rooms, all with cherrywood-paneled walls and dramatic contemporary artwork. Try the *arroz con conejo y caracoles* (rice with rabbit and snails) or *mero blanco con cliflor crujiente* (white grouper fish with crispy cauliflower). **Known for:** fresh local produce; suckling pig; local extra-virgin olive oil. [$] *Average main: €18* ✉ *Calle Fermín Palma 3* ☎ *953/270262* 🌐 *www.casantonio.es* 🕒 *Closed Mon. and Aug. No dinner Sun.*

🛏 Hotels

★ Parador de Jaén

$$$ | **HOTEL** | Built amid the mountaintop towers of the Castillo de Santa Catalina, this 13th-century castle reopens in March 2020 and is one of the showpieces of the parador chain and reason enough to visit Jaén. **Pros:** architectural grandeur; panoramic views; historic and atmospheric building. **Cons:** outside Jaén; long walk down to sights (and steep climb up again); could be too grandiose for some. [$] *Rooms from: €150* ✉ *Calle Castillo de Santa Catalina* ☎ *953/230000* 🌐 *www.parador.es* 🛏 *45 rooms* 🍽 *No meals.*

Baeza

48 km (30 miles) northeast of Jaén on N321.

The historic town of Baeza, nestled between hills and olive groves, is one of the best-preserved old towns in Spain. Founded by the Romans, it later housed the Visigoths and became the capital of a Moorish taifa, one of some two dozen mini-kingdoms formed after the Ummayad Caliphate was subdivided in 1031. Ferdinand III captured Baeza in 1227, and for the next 200 years it stood on the frontier of the Moorish kingdom of Granada. In the 16th and 17th centuries, local nobles gave the city a wealth of Renaissance palaces.

GETTING HERE AND AROUND

Frequent buses (16 per day on weekdays, 12 per day on weekends; *ALSA* ☎ *902/422242* 🌐 *www.alsa.es*) connect

The Fortress of Alcalá la Real

About 75 km (46½ miles) south of Jaén on N432 and A316, lies Alcalá la Real. Dominating the town as well as the area for miles around is the hilltop fortress, the Fortaleza de la Mota. Installed by the Moors in 727, it sits imperiously at an elevation of 3,389 feet. Spectacular views of the peaks of the Sierra Nevada are visible on the southern horizon.

This ancient city, known to the Iberians and Romans, grew to prominence under the Moors who ruled here for more than 600 years. It was they who gave it the first part of its name, Alcalá, which originated from a word meaning "fortified settlement." During the 12th century the city changed hands frequently as the Moors fought to maintain control of the area. Finally, in 1341, Alfonso XI conquered the town for good, adding *real* (royal) to its name. It remained of strategic importance until the Catholic Monarchs took Granada in 1492—indeed, it was from here that they rode out to accept the keys of the city and the surrender. Hundreds of years later, French forces left the town in ruins after their retreat in the early 19th century.

The town of Alcalá la Real itself was gradually rebuilt, but the hilltop fortress (Fortaleza de la Mota), consisting of the *alcazaba* (citadel) and the abbey church that Alfonso XI built, was more or less ignored. Up until the late 1990s, exposed skeletons were visible in some open tombs on the floor of the church. Today visitors can wander around the ruins and visit the small archaeological museum.

Getting here and around: Alcalá la Real can be reached by bus from Córdoba, Granada, and Jaén, but the easiest way to reach it is by car. Once there, the town is easily explored on foot. The fortress is about a 15-minute walk from the city center.

Baeza with Jaén and Úbeda, although a private car is the best option given the remoteness of the town and that you may want to explore nearby Úbeda on the same day. Baeza is small and flat, and with its sights clustered around the very center it's very easy to explore on foot.

TOURS
Semer Guided Tours
GUIDED TOURS | Two-hour guided tours around Baeza (in English, minimum two people, Tuesday—Sunday) recount the history, culture, and traditions of the town. Tours of Úbeda are also available, with a discount for combined tours of both towns. ✉ Calle Rastro de la Carniceria 3 ☎ 953/757916 ⊕ www.semerturismo.com ☞ From €11.

VISITOR INFORMATION
CONTACTS Baeza ✉ Pl. del Pópulo ☎ 953/779982.

 ## Sights

Ayuntamiento (*Town Hall*)
GOVERNMENT BUILDING | Baeza's town hall was designed by cathedral master Andrés de Vandelvira. The facade is ornately decorated with a mix of religious and pagan imagery. Look between the balconies for the coats of arms of Felipe II, the city of Baeza, and the magistrate Juan de Borja. Ask at the tourist office about visits to the *salón de plenos,* a meeting hall with painted, carved woodwork. ✉ Pl. Cardenal s/n.

Baeza Cathedral
RELIGIOUS SITE | Originally begun by Ferdinand III on the site of a former mosque, the cathedral was largely rebuilt by Andrés de Vandelvira, architect of Jaén's cathedral, between 1570 and 1593, though the west front has architectural influences from an earlier period. A fine 14th-century rose window crowns the 13th-century Puerta de la Luna (Moon Door). Don't miss the baroque silver monstrance (a vessel in which the consecrated Host is exposed for the adoration of the faithful), which is carried in Baeza's Corpus Christi processions—the piece is kept in a concealed niche behind a painting, but you can see it in all its splendor by putting a coin in a slot to reveal the hiding place. Next to the monstrance is the entrance to the clock tower, where a small donation and a narrow spiral staircase take you to one of the best views of Baeza. The remains of the original mosque are in the cathedral's Gothic cloisters. ✉ *Pl. de Santa María* ☎ *953/744157* 🎟 *€4.*

Casa del Pópulo
HOUSE | Located in the central paseo—where the Plaza del Pópulo (or Plaza de los Leones) and Plaza de la Constitución (or Plaza del Mercado Viejo) merge to form a cobblestone square—this graceful town house was built around 1530. The first Mass of the Reconquest was supposedly celebrated on its curved balcony; it now houses Baeza's tourist office. ✉ *Pl. del Pópulo.*

Convento de San Francisco
RELIGIOUS SITE | This 16th-century convent is one of Vandelvira's religious architectural masterpieces. The building was spoiled by the French army and partially destroyed by a light earthquake in the early 1800s, but you can see its restored remains. ✉ *Calle de San Francisco.*

Museo de Baeza
MUSEUM | Tucked away behind the tourist office, the Baeza Museum is in itself a museum piece. Housed in a 15th-century noble palace, the facade and interiors are home to an interesting display of Baeza's history, from Roman remains to more recent religious paintings. ✉ *Calle Casas Nuevas* ☎ *953/741582* 🎟 *€2* 🕒 *Closed Mon.*

🍴 Restaurants

Palacio de Gallego
$$$ | **SPANISH** | With a special location next to the cathedral, this is one of the best restaurants in town, known most of all for its barbecue dishes. Red tuna steak stars on the *asados* (roasted dishes) menu, but you can also try meat, including game, as well as *almejas* (clams). **Known for:** barbecue; red tuna steak; outdoor terrace. [$] *Average main: €20* ✉ *Calle Santa Catalina* ☎ *667/760184* 🕒 *Closed Tues. No dinner Wed.*

🛏 Hotels

Hotel Puerta de la Luna
$$ | **HOTEL** | This beautifully restored 17th-century palace, one of Baeza's finest accommodation options, is centered on two patios—one with a pond and views of the cathedral tower, the other with a small pool. **Pros:** stunning architecture; central location; good food on-site. **Cons:** difficult to find; basic breakfast; a bit too quiet. [$] *Rooms from: €100* ✉ *Calle Canónigo Melgares Raya 7* ☎ *953/747019* 🌐 *www.hotelpuertadelaluna.com* 🛏 *44 rooms* 🍽 *No meals.*

Úbeda

9 km (5½ miles) northeast of Baeza on N321.

Úbeda's *casco antiguo* (old town) is one of the most outstanding enclaves of 16th-century architecture in Spain. It's a stunning surprise in the heart of Jaén's olive groves, set in the shadow of the wild Sierra de Cazorla mountain range. For crafts enthusiasts, this is Andalusia's capital for many kinds of artisan goods. Follow signs to the Zona Monumental, where there are countless Renaissance palaces and stately mansions, though most are closed to the public.

GETTING HERE AND AROUND

Frequent buses (16 weekdays, 12 weekends; *ALSA* ☎ *902/422242* ⊕ *www. alsa.es*) connect Úbeda with Jaén and Baeza, although a private car is the best option given the remoteness of the town and that you may want to explore nearby Baeza in the same day. Úbeda's sights are all within easy reach of the center so exploring on foot is easy.

TOURS
Semer Guided Tours

Two-hour guided tours around Úbeda (in English, minimum two people, Tuesday through Sunday) recount the history, culture, and traditions of the town. Tours of Baeza are also available, with a discount on combined tours of both towns. ⊠ *Calle Juan Montilla 3* ☎ *953/757916* ⊕ *www.semerturismo.com* ⯈ *From €11.*

VISITOR INFORMATION

CONTACTS Úbeda ⊠ *Pl. de Andalucía 5* ☎ *953/779204* ⊕ *www.turismodeubeda. com.*

 Sights

Ayuntamiento Antiguo (*Old Town Hall*)
BUILDING | Begun in the early 16th century but restored as a beautiful arcaded baroque palace in 1680, the former town hall is now a conservatory of music. From the hall's upper balcony, the town council watched celebrations and autos-da-fé ("acts of faith"—executions of heretics sentenced by the Inquisition) in the square below. You can't enter the town hall, but on the north side you can visit the 13th-century church of San Pablo, with an Isabelline south portal. ⊠ *Pl. Primero de Mayo* ✛ *Off Calle María de Molina* ☎ *953/750637* ⯈ *Church free* ☾ *Closed Mon.*

Hospital de Santiago
HOSPITAL—SIGHT | Sometimes jokingly called the Escorial of Andalusia (in allusion to Felipe II's monolithic palace and monastery outside Madrid), this is a huge, angular building in the modern section of town and yet another one of Vandelvira's masterpieces in Úbeda. The plain facade is adorned with ceramic medallions, and over the main entrance is a carving of Santiago Matamoros (St. James the Moorslayer) in his traditional horseback pose. Inside are an arcaded patio and a grand staircase. Now a cultural center, it holds some of the events at the International Spring Dance and Music Festival (⊕ festivaldeubeda.com). ⊠ *Av. Cristo Rey* ☎ *953/750842* ⯈ *Free* ☾ *Closed Sun. in July, and weekends in Aug.*

Sacra Capilla de El Salvador
RELIGIOUS SITE | The Plaza Vázquez de Molina, in the heart of the casco antiguo, is the site of this building, which is photographed so often that it's become the city's unofficial symbol. It was built by Vandelvira, but he based his design on some 1536 plans by Diego de Siloé, architect of Granada's cathedral. Considered one of the masterpieces of Spanish Renaissance religious art, the chapel was sacked in the frenzy of church burnings at the outbreak of the civil war, but it retains its ornate western facade and altarpiece, which has a rare Berruguete sculpture. ⊠ *Pl. Vázquez de Molina* ☎ *609/279905* ⯈ *€5 (free Mon.–Sat. 9:30–10, Sun. 6–7).*

★ Sinagoga del Agua
RELIGIOUS SITE | This 13th-century synagogue counts among Úbeda's most amazing discoveries. Entirely underground and known as the Water Synagogue for the wells and natural spring under the mikvah, it comprises seven areas open to visitors, including the main area of worship, mikvah, women's gallery, and rabbi's quarters. During summer solstice the sun's rays illuminate the

stairway, providing the only natural light in the synagogue. ✉ *Calle Roque Rosas* ☎ *953/758150* 🌐 *www.sinagogadelagua.com* 🎟 *€5.*

🍴 Restaurants

Asador de Santiago

$$$ | **SPANISH** | At this adventurous restaurant just off the main street, the chef prepares both Spanish classics, like white shrimp from Huelva or suckling pig from Segovia, and innovative dishes like *ensalada de queso de cabra en hojaldre con membrillo* (salad with goat's cheese pastry and quince) and *lomo de ciervo en escabeche* (venison steak in pickled sauce). The candle-filled interior is more traditional than the bar and has terra-cotta tiles, dark wood furnishings, and crisp white linens. **Known for:** fine dining; Spanish classics; tasting menu. [$] *Average main: €20* ✉ *Av. Cristo Rey 4* ☎ *953/750463* 🌐 *asadordesantiago.com* 🕒 *No dinner Sun.*

Cantina La Estación

$$$ | **SPANISH** | Meals at one of Úbeda's top restaurants are served in a train-carriage interior decorated with railway memorabilia, while tapas reign at an outside terrace and at the bar. Highly rated by locals who flock here on weekends, this distinctive eatery serves creative dishes like *humus con berenjenas, pimientos rojos y anchoas* (eggplant hummus with red peppers and anchovies), *b ombón de foie envuelto en oro y queso de cabra* (gold-glazed foie with goat's cheese), and *bacalao confitado* (caramelized cod). **Known for:** extensive and reasonably priced wine menu; value tasting menu; fun interior. [$] *Average main: €18* ✉ *Cuesta de la Rodadera 1* ☎ *687/777230* 🕒 *Closed Wed. No dinner Tues.*

Taberna Misa de 12

$$$ | **SPANISH** | This small bar has the best position on the leafy square, one block from the Plaza del Ayuntamiento, and the pleasant outside terrace is the best place to enjoy the tapas. Despite the tiny kitchen, the menu stretches long and includes homemade croquettes and roasted peppers, red tuna tartare, and Iberian pork cuts. **Known for:** tapas; wine list; outdoor dining. [$] *Average main: €18* ✉ *Pl. Primero de Mayo 7* ☎ *622/480049* 🌐 *www.misade12.com* 🕒 *Closed Mon. and Tues.*

🛏 Hotels

Hotel El Postigo

$ | **HOTEL** | Tucked away in the center of town, this is a modern surprise among Úbeda's historical buildings and an oasis of peace and quiet. **Pros:** central location; tasty breakfast; patio with a pool. **Cons:** difficult to access by car; lacks character; mediocre breakfast. [$] *Rooms from: €80* ✉ *Calle Postigo 5* ☎ *953/795550* 🌐 *www.hotelelpostigo.com* 🔑 *26 rooms* 🍽 *Free Breakfast.*

★ Palacio de la Rambla

$$$ | **B&B/INN** | In old Úbeda, this stunning 16th-century mansion has been in the same family since it was built—it still hosts the Marquesa de la Rambla when she's in town—and eight of the rooms are available for overnighters. **Pros:** central location; elegant style; all rooms have access to the garden. **Cons:** little parking; grandiosity not for everyone; some areas a little tired. [$] *Rooms from: €132* ✉ *Pl. del Marqués 1* ☎ *953/750196* 🌐 *www.palaciodelarambla.com* 🕒 *Closed July and Aug.* 🔑 *8 rooms* 🍽 *Free Breakfast.*

★ Parador de Úbeda

$$$ | **HOTEL** | Designed by Andrés de Vandelvira, this splendid parador is in a 16th-century ducal palace in a prime location on the Plaza Vázquez de Molina, next to the Capilla del Salvador. **Pros:** elegant surroundings; perfect location; excellent restaurant. **Cons:** parking is difficult; church bells in the morning; could be too formal for some. [$] *Rooms from: €170* ✉ *Pl. Vázquez de Molina s/n* ☎ *953/750345* 🌐 *www.parador.es* 🔑 *36 rooms* 🍽 *No meals.*

🛍 Shopping

Little Úbeda is the crafts capital of Andalusia, with workshops devoted to carpentry, basket weaving, stone carving, wrought iron, stained glass, and, above all, the city's distinctive green-glaze pottery. Calle Valencia is the traditional potters' row, running from the bottom of town to Úbeda's general crafts center, northwest of the casco antiguo (follow signs to Calle Valencia or Barrio de Alfareros).

Úbeda's most famous potter was Paco Tito, whose craft is carried on at three different workshops run by two of his sons, Pablo and Juan, and a son-in-law, Melchor, each of whom claims to be the sole true heir to his father's art.

Alfarería Góngora

CERAMICS/GLASSWARE | All kinds of ceramics are sold here. ⊠ *Calle Cuesta de la Merced 32* ☎ *953/754605.*

Alfarería Tito

CERAMICS/GLASSWARE | The extrovert Juan Tito can often be found at the potter's wheel in his rambling shop, which is packed with ceramics of every size and shape. You can also shop online. ⊠ *Pl. del Ayuntamiento 12* ☎ *953/751302* ⊕ *www. alfareriatito.com.*

Melchor Tito

CERAMICS/GLASSWARE | You can see classic green-glazed items—the focus of Melchor Tito's work—being made in his workshops in Calle Valencia and Calle Fuenteseca 17, which are both also shops. ⊠ *Calle Valencia 44* ☎ *953/753692.*

Pablo Tito

CERAMICS/GLASSWARE | Clay sculptures of characters from *Don Quixote,* fired by Pablo Tito in an old Moorish-style kiln, are the specialty of this studio and shop. There is also a museum (Monday through Saturday 8–2 and 4–8, Sunday 10–2) on the premises. ⊠ *Calle Valencia 22* ☎ *953/751496.*

Cazorla

48 km (35 miles) southeast of Úbeda.

Unspoiled and remote, the village of Cazorla is at the east end of Jaén province. The pine-clad slopes and towering peaks of the Cazorla and Segura sierras rise above the village, and below it stretch endless miles of olive groves. In spring, purple jacaranda trees blossom in the plazas.

GETTING HERE AND AROUND

The remoteness and size of the Parque Natural Cazorla plus the lack of frequent public transportation make this somewhere that is good to explore by car.

For a change of scenery, after exploring the Parque Natural, leave by an alternative route—drive along the spectacular gorge carved by the Guadalquivir River, a rushing torrent beloved by kayaking enthusiasts. At the Tranco Dam, follow signs to Villanueva del Arzobispo, where the N322 takes you back to Úbeda, Baeza, and Jaén.

VISITOR INFORMATION

CONTACTS **Cazorla Tourist Office** ⊠ *Paseo Santo Cristo 19* ☎ *953/710102* ⊕ *www. cazorla.es.*

👁 Sights

★ **Parque Natural Sierra de Cazorla, Segura y Las Villas** (*Cazorla, Segura, and Las Villas Nature Park*)
NATURE PRESERVE | FAMILY | For a break from man-made sights, drink in the scenery or watch for wildlife in this park, a carefully protected patch of mountain wilderness 80 km (50 miles) long and 30 km (19 miles) wide. Deer, wild boars, and mountain goats roam its slopes, and hawks, eagles, and vultures soar over the 6,000-foot peaks. Early spring is the ideal time to visit; try to avoid the summer and late-spring months, when the park teems with tourists and locals. It's often difficult, though by no means

The picturesque town of Cazorla

impossible, to find accommodations in fall, especially on weekends during hunting season (September through February). Between June and October, the park maintains seven well-equipped campgrounds. For information on hiking, camping, canoeing, horseback riding, or guided excursions, contact the **Agencia de Medio Ambiente** (*Calle Martínez Falero 11, Cazorla* ☎ *953/711534*), or the park visitor center. ✉ *Cazorla* 🌐 *www.sierrasdecazorlaseguraylasvillas.es/en*.

Centro de Interpretación Torre del Vinagre
INFO CENTER | A short film shown in the interpretive center introduces the park's main sights. Displays explain the plants and geology, and there's a small hunting museum. Staff can advise on camping, fishing, and hiking trails. ✉ *Ctra. del Tranco (A319), Km 48, Torre del Vinagre* ☎ *953/713017* 🌐 *www.sierrasdecazorlaseguraylasvillas.es*.

🍴 Restaurants

Leandro
$$ | SPANISH | One of the best places to eat in the village, this atmospheric restaurant decorated in traditional local style serves up mountain game such as venison, goat, and wild boar, cooked on the barbecue or on hot stones. Other house specialties include homemade burgers, local trout, and partridge pâté. **Known for:** barbecue game meat; cheese mille-feuille pastry; good value. [$] *Average main: €16* ✉ *Calle Hoz 3* ☎ *953/720632* 🌐 *www.mesonleandro.com*.

🛏 Hotels

Casa Rural Plaza de Santa Maria
$ | B&B/INN | In the heart of the village with lovely views of the castle, this restored 17th-century mansion offers some of the best value lodging in the area. **Pros:** quiet, central location; stunning castle views; large terraces with loungers. **Cons:** a little basic; inconsistent decor; difficult car access. [$] *Rooms*

from: €60 ✉ Callejón de la Plaza de Santa María ☎ 953/722087 🌐 www.plazade-santamaria.com 🛏 9 rooms 🍴 Free Breakfast.

Parador de Cazorla

$$$ | **HOTEL** | You'll find this modern parador isolated in a valley at the edge of the nature reserve, 26 km (16 miles) north of Cazorla, in a quiet place that's popular with hunters and anglers. **Pros:** lovely views from the pool; restaurant serves excellent mountain game; bucolic setting. **Cons:** not all rooms have views; access is difficult; uninspiring exterior. [$] *Rooms from: €130 ✉ Sierra de Cazorla s/n ☎ 953/727075 🌐 www.parador.es ⏲ Closed Jan. 🛏 34 rooms 🍴 No meals.*

Granada

430 km (265 miles) south of Madrid, 261 km (162 miles) east of Seville, 160 km (100 miles) southeast of Córdoba.

The Alhambra and the tomb of the Catholic Monarchs are the pride of Granada. The city rises majestically from a plain onto three hills, dwarfed—on a clear day—by the Sierra Nevada. Atop one of these hills perches the reddish-gold Alhambra palace, whose stunning view takes in the sprawling medieval Moorish quarter, the caves of the Sacromonte, and, in the distance, the fertile *vega* (plain), rich in orchards, tobacco fields, and poplar groves. In 2013, Granada celebrated its 1,000th anniversary as a kingdom.

Split by internal squabbles, Granada's Moorish Nasrid dynasty gave Ferdinand of Aragón his opportunity in 1491. Spurred by Isabella's religious fanaticism, he laid siege to the city for seven months, and on January 2, 1492, Boabdil, the "Rey Chico" (Boy King), was forced to surrender the keys of the city. As Boabdil fled the Alhambra via the Puerta de los Siete Suelos (Gate of the Seven Floors), he asked that the gate be sealed forever.

Granada's main shopping streets, centering on the Puerta Real, are the Gran Vía de Colón, Reyes Católicos, Zacatín, and Recogidas. Most antiques shops are on Cuesta de Elvira and Alcaicería—off Reyes Católicos. Cuesta de Gomérez, on the way up to the Alhambra, also has several handicrafts shops and guitar workshops. A Moorish aesthetic pervades Granada's ceramics, marquetry (especially the *taraceas,* wooden boxes with inlaid tiles on their lids), woven textiles, and silver-, brass-, and copper-ware.

GETTING HERE AND AROUND

AIR TRAVEL

Five daily flights connect Granada with Madrid and four connect it with Barcelona.

CONTACTS Aeropuerto de Granada (*Aeropuerto Federico García Lorca*) *☎ 902/404704.*

BUS TRAVEL

Granada's main bus station is at Carretera de Jaén, 3 km (2 miles) northwest of the center of town beyond the end of Avenida de Madrid. Most buses operate from here, except for buses to nearby destinations such as Fuentevaqueros, Viznar, and some buses to Sierra Nevada, which leave from the city center's Plaza del Triunfo near the RENFE station. Luggage lockers (*la consigna*) are available at the main bus and train stations, and you can also leave your luggage at City Locker (Placeta de las Descalzas 3) and Lock & Be Free (Calle Salamanca 13).

Autocares Bonal operates buses between Granada and the Sierra Nevada. **ALSA** buses run to and from Las Alpujarras (3 times daily), Córdoba (17 times daily), Seville (9 times daily), Málaga (20 times daily), and Jaén, Baeza, Úbeda, Cazorla, Almería, Almuñécar, and Nerja (several times daily).

In Granada, **airport** buses (€3) run between the center of town and the airport, leaving roughly every hour 7 am–8:45 pm from the Palacio de Congresos and making a few other stops along the way to the airport. Times are listed at the bus stop.

Granada has an extensive public bus network within the city. You can buy 5-, 10-, and 20-trip discount passes on the buses and at newsstands. The single-trip fare is €1.50. Granada Cards include bus trips plus guaranteed tickets for the Alhambra and other main monuments (without having to wait in lines). The card costs from €36.50, saving at least a third on regular prices. You can purchase the cards at the municipal tourist office, but it's best to buy them online via (⊕ www.granadatur.com/granada-card) in advance of your visit; you can download them on your cell phone, or print at home or the tourist office.

CONTACTS Granada Bus Station ⊠ Ctra. Jaén ☎ 902 /422242.

TAXI TRAVEL
CONTACTS Taxi Genil ☎ 958/132323. **Tele Radio Taxi** ☎ 958/280654.

TRAIN TRAVEL
There are regular trains from Seville and Almería, but service from Málaga and Córdoba is less convenient, necessitating a change at Bobadilla. A new AVE high-speed fast track entered operation in mid-2019; it reduced journey times considerably (50 minutes to Málaga and 90 minutes to Seville). There are a couple of daily trains from Madrid, Valencia, and Barcelona.

CONTACTS Train Station ⊠ Av. de los Andaluces ☎ 912/320320.

TOURS
Cycling Country
BICYCLE TOURS | For information about cycling tours around Granada (Andalusia and Spain), 1–10 days long, contact this company, run by husband-and-wife team Geoff Norris and Maggi Jones in a town about 55 km (33 miles) away. ⊠ Calle Salmerones 18, Alhama de Granada ☎ 958/360655 ⊕ www.cyclingcountry.com ✉ From €30.

Granada Tapas Tours
GUIDED TOURS | Long-time British resident Gayle Mackie offers a range of tapas tours lasting up to three hours. ⊠ Granada ☎ 619/444984 ⊕ www.granadatapastours.com ✉ From €40, including 6 tapas.

VISITOR INFORMATION
CONTACTS Municipal Tourist Office ⊠ Pl. del Carmen 9, Centro ☎ 958/248280 ⊕ www.granadatur.com. **Provincial Tourist Office** ⊠ Calle Cárcel Baja 3, Centro ☎ 958/247128 ⊕ www.turgranada.es.

La Alhambra

◉ Sights

★ Alhambra
CASTLE/PALACE | With more than 2.7 million visitors a year, the Alhambra is Spain's most popular attraction. This sprawling palace-fortress was the last bastion of the 800-year Moorish presence on the Iberian Peninsula. Composed of royal residential quarters, court chambers, baths, and gardens, surrounded by defense towers and massive walls, the Alhambra is an architectural gem. The courtyards, patios, and halls offer an ethereal maze of Moorish arches, columns, and domes containing intricate stucco carvings and patterned ceramic tiling. The heart of the Alhambra, the **Palacios Nazaríes** contain delicate apartments, lazy fountains, and tranquil pools, and are divided into three sections: the *mexuar*, where business, government, and palace administration were headquartered; the *serrallo*, state rooms where the sultans held court; and the harem. ■**TIP→ Booking tickets in advance is essential to avoid disappointment**. ⊠ Cuesta de Gomérez,

Granada

Sights

1 Abadía de Sacromonte ... F1
2 Alhambra ... E2
3 Capilla Real ... B2
4 Carmen de los Mártire ... F3
5 Casa de los Pisa ... C2
6 Casa de los Tiros ... C3
7 Casa-Museo de Manuel de Falla ... F3
8 Casas del Chapiz ... F1
9 Cathedral ... B2
10 Centro José Guerrero ... B3
11 Corral del Carbón ... C3
12 El Bañuelo ... D1
13 El Cuarto Real ... C3
14 Fundación Rodríguez-Acosta/Instituto Gómez Moreno ... D3
15 Museo Cuevas del Sacromonte ... E1
16 Palacio de los Córdova ... F1
17 Palacio Madraza ... B2
18 Paseo Padre Manjón ... E1

Restaurants

1 Alacena de las Monjas ... C3
2 Bar Los Diamantes ... C2
3 Bodegas Castañeda ... C2
4 Café Botánico ... A2
5 Cunini ... B3
6 Damasqueros ... D3
7 El Trillo ... C1
8 La Bodega de Antonio ... A3
9 La Brujidera ... C2
10 Oliver ... B3
11 Paprika ... B1
12 Pilar del Toro ... C2
13 Ruta del Azafrán ... E1
14 Tinta Fina ... B3

Hotels

1 Carmen de la Acubilla del Caracol ... D3
2 Casa Morisca ... E1
3 Hospes Palacio de los Patos ... F2
4 Hostal Rodri ... A2
5 Hotel Alhambra Palace ... E3
6 Hotel Casa 1800 ... D2
7 Hotel Palacio Santa Inés ... D2
8 Hotel Párraga Siete ... A3
9 Palacio de los Navas ... B3
10 Parador de Granada ... F2

KEY

- Sights
- Restaurants
- Hotels
- Tourist Information

0 1/8 mi
0 200 meters

Jardines del Generalife

TO SACROMONTE

ALBAYZIN

CENTRO

REALEJO

Campo del Príncipe

Mirador de San Nicolás

Cuesta de la Alhacaba

Basílica de San Juan de Dios

PLAZA DE TOROS

Alhambra ☎ 858/953616 tickets, 958/027971 information ⊕ www.tickets. alhambra-patronato.es ⓢ From €14, Museo de la Alhambra and Palacio de Carlos V free ⓥ Museo de Bellas Artes and Museo de la Alhambra closed Mon.

Carmen de los Mártires

HOUSE | Up the hill from the Hotel Alhambra Palace, this turn-of-the-20th-century *carmen* (private villa) and its gardens— the only area open to tourists—are like a Generalife in miniature. ⊠ Paseo de los Mártires, Alhambra ☎ 958/849103 ⓢ Free.

Casa-Museo de Manuel de Falla

HOUSE | The composer Manuel de Falla (1876–1946) lived and worked for many years in this rustic house tucked into a charming hillside lane with lovely views of the Alpujarras. In 1986 Granada paid homage to him by naming its new concert hall (down the street from the Carmen de los Mártires) the Auditorio Manuel de Falla—from this institution, fittingly, you have a view of his little white house. Note the bust in the small garden: it's placed where the composer once sat to enjoy the sweeping vista. ⊠ Calle Antequeruela Alta 11, Alhambra ☎ 958/222189 ⊕ museomanueldefalla. com ⓢ €3 ⓥ Closed Mon.

Hotels

★ Carmen de la Alcubilla del Caracol

$$$ | B&B/INN | In a traditional granadino villa on the slopes of the Alhambra, this privately run lodging is one of Granada's most stylish hotels. **Pros:** great views; bright, airy rooms; walking distance to the Alhambra. **Cons:** tough climb in hot weather. ⓢ Rooms from: €150 ⊠ Calle Aire Alta 12, Alhambra ☎ 958/215551 ⊕ www.alcubilladelcaracol.com ⓥ Closed mid-July–Aug. ⤳ 7 rooms ⓣⓞⓣ No meals.

Hotel Alhambra Palace

$$$$ | HOTEL | Built by a local duke in 1910, this neo-Moorish hotel is on leafy grounds at the back of the Alhambra hill, and has a very *Arabian Nights* interior (think orange-and-brown overtones, multicolor tiles, and Moorish-style arches and pillars). **Pros:** bird's-eye views; location near the Alhambra; large, warmly decorated rooms. **Cons:** steep climb up from Granada; often packed with business people (it doubles as a convention center); might be too grandiose for some. ⓢ Rooms from: €250 ⊠ Pl. Arquitecto García de Paredes 1, Alhambra ☎ 958/221468 ⊕ www.h-alhambrapalace. es ⤳ 126 rooms ⓣⓞⓣ No meals.

★ Parador de Granada

$$$$ | HOTEL | This is Spain's most expensive and most popular parador, right within the walls of the Alhambra. **Pros:** good location; lovely interiors; garden restaurant. **Cons:** no views in some rooms; removed from city life; very expensive. ⓢ Rooms from: €410 ⊠ Calle Real de la Alhambra, Alhambra ☎ 958/221440 ⊕ www.parador.es/en/paradores/parador-de-granada ⤳ 40 rooms ⓣⓞⓣ No meals.

Realejo

Sights

Casa de los Tiros

MUSEUM | This 16th-century palace, adorned with the coat of arms of the Grana Venegas family who owned it, was named House of the Shots for the musket barrels that protrude from its facade. The stairs to the upper-floor displays are flanked by portraits of miserable-looking Spanish royals, from Ferdinand and Isabella to Felipe IV. The highlight is the carved wooden ceiling in the Cuadra Dorada (Hall of Gold), adorned with gilded lettering and portraits of royals and knights. Old lithographs, engravings, and photographs show life in Granada in the 19th and early 20th centuries. ⊠ Calle Pavaneras 19, Realejo-San Matías ☎ 600/143175 ⊕ www.juntadeandalucia.es/cultura/museos/MCTGR ⓢ €2 ⓥ Closed Mon.

El Cuarto Real

BUILDING | Just a block away from Casa de los Tiros is the newly restored El Cuarto Real, a 13th-century Nasrid palace which has decorations almost identical to the Alhambra. Only the fortified tower remains standing with its exquisite *qubba* (reception room) with stunning walls and ceiling motifs. The adjoining modern extension houses temporary art exhibitions, and the formal gardens make a peaceful place to rest. ✉ *Pl. de los Campos 6, Realejo-San Matías* ☎ *958/849111* 🎫 *Free.*

Fundación Rodríguez-Acosta/Instituto Gómez-Moreno

MUSEUM | This nonprofit organization was founded at the behest of the painter José Marí Rodríguez-Acosta. Inside a typical carmen, it houses works of art, archaeological finds, and a library (currently closed to visitors) collected by the Granada-born scholar Manuel Gómez-Moreno Martínez. Other exhibits include valuable and unique objects from Asian cultures and the prehistoric and classical eras. ✉ *Callejón Niños del Rollo 8, Realejo-San Matías* ☎ *958/227497* 🌐 *www.fundacionrodriguezacosta.com* 🎫 *€5.*

🍴 Restaurants

Alacena de las Monjas

$$$ | **SPANISH** | Just as popular with locals as visitors, this restaurant in the heart of the Realejo district sits on the first floor and basement of a 14th-century convent—you can see the original clay vats that supplied the water downstairs. You can also dine outside in the lovely, quiet square. **Known for:** historic setting; red tuna; steak. [$] *Average main: €20* ✉ *Pl. del Padre Suarez 5, Realejo-San Matías* ☎ *958/229519* 🌐 *www.alacenadelasmonjas.com* ⏲ *Closed Tues. No dinner Mon.*

★ Damasqueros

$$$$ | **SPANISH** | The modern, wood-paneled dining room and warm lighting form the perfect setting for the creative Andalusian cuisine cooked here by local chef Lola Marín, who learned her trade with some of Spain's top chefs, such as Martín Berasategui. The tasting menu changes weekly and always includes in-season produce in its five courses (cold and hot starters, fish, meat, and dessert). **Known for:** fresh local produce; wine pairing; service. [$] *Average main: €39* ✉ *Calle Damasqueros 3, Realejo-San Matías* ☎ *958/210550* 🌐 *www.damasqueros.com* ⏲ *Closed Mon. No dinner Sun.*

Sacromonte

The third of Granada's three hills, the Sacromonte rises behind the Albayzín. The hill is covered with prickly pear cacti and riddled with caverns. The Sacromonte has long been notorious as a domain of Granada's Gypsies and thus a den of thieves and scam artists, but its reputation is largely undeserved. The quarter is more like a quiet Andalusian *pueblo* (village) than a rough neighborhood. Many of the quarter's colorful *cuevas* (caves) have been restored as middle-class homes, and some of the old spirit lives on in a handful of *zambras* (flamenco performances in caves, which are garishly decorated with brass plates and cooking utensils). These shows differ from formal flamenco shows in that the performers mingle with you, usually dragging one or two onlookers onto the floor for an improvised dance lesson. Ask your hotel to book you a spot on a cueva tour, which usually includes a walk through the neighboring Albayzín and a drink at a tapas bar in addition to the zambra.

Continued on page 642

ALHAMBRA: PALACE-FORTRESS

 Floating mirage-like on its promontory overlooking Granada, the mighty and mysterious Alhambra shimmers vermilion in the clear mountain air, with the white peaks of the Sierra Nevada rising behind it. This sprawling palace-fortress, named from the Arabic for "red citadel" (*al-Qal'ah al-Hamra*), was the last bastion of the 800-year Moorish presence on the Iberian Peninsula. Composed of royal residential quarters, court chambers, baths, and gardens, surrounded by defense towers and massive walls, the Alhambra is an architectual gem where Moorish kings worked and played—and murdered their enemies.

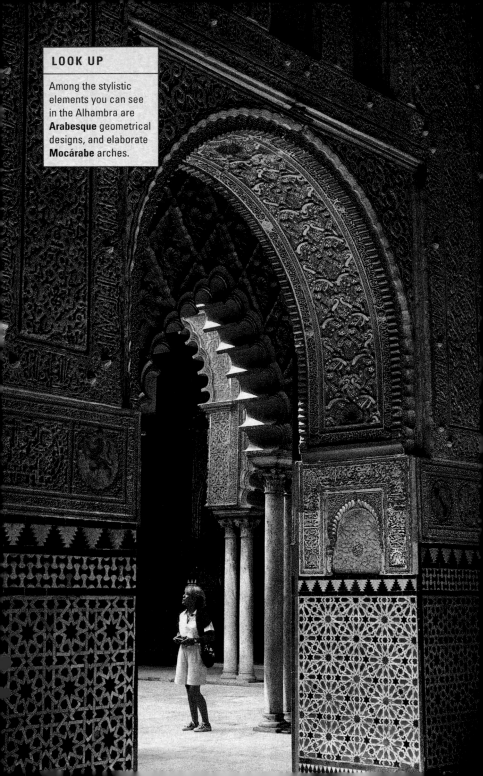

LOOK UP

Among the stylistic elements you can see in the Alhambra are **Arabesque** geometrical designs, and elaborate **Mocárabe** arches.

Built of perishable materials, the Alhambra was meant to be forever replenished and replaced by succeeding generations. The Patio de los Leones' (above) has recently been restored to its original appearance.

INSIDE THE FORTRESS

More than 3 million annual visitors come to the Alhambra today, making it Spain's top attraction. Vistors revel in the palace's architectural wonders, most of which had to be restored after the alterations made after the Christian reconquest of southern Spain in 1492 and the damage from an 1821 earthquake. Incidentally, Napoléon's troops commandeered the site in 1812 with intent to level it but their attempts were foiled.

The courtyards, patios, and halls offer an ethereal maze of Moorish arches, columns, and domes containing intricate stucco carvings and patterned ceramic tiling. The intimate arcades, fountains, and light-reflecting pools throughout are identified in the ornamental inscriptions as physical renderings of paradise taken from the Koran and Islamic poetry. The contemporary visitor to this dreamlike space feels the fleeting embrace of a culture that brought its light to a world emerging from medieval darkness.

ARCHITECTURAL TERMS

Arabesque: An ornament or decorative style that employs flower, foliage, or fruit, and sometimes geometrical, animal, and figural outlines to produce an intricate pattern of interlaced lines.

Mocárabe: A decorative element of carved wood or plaster based on juxtaposed and hanging prisms resembling stalactites. Sometimes called

muquarna (honeycomb vaulting), the impression is similar to a beehive and the "honey" has been described as light.

Mozárabe: Sometimes confused with Mocárabe, the term Mozárabe refers to Christians living in Moorish Spain. Thus, Christian artistic styles or recourses in Moorish architecture (such as the paintings in the Sala de los

Reyes) are also identified as *mozárabe*, or, in English, mozarabic.

Mudéjar: This word refers to Moors living in Christian Spain. Moorish artistic elements in Christian architecture, such as horseshoe arches in a church, also are referred to as Mudéjar.

ALHAMBRA'S ARCHITECTURAL HIGHLIGHTS

The **columns** used in the construction of the Alhambra are unique, with extraordinarily slender cylindrical shafts, concave base moldings, and carved rings decorating the upper extremities. The capitals have simple cylindrical bases under prism-shaped heads decorated in a variety of vegetal motifs. Nearly all of these columns support false arches constructed purely for decorative purposes. The 124 columns surrounding the Patio de los Leones (Court of the Lions) are the best examples.

Court of the Lions

Cursive epigraphy is used to quote the Koran and Arabic poems. Considered the finest example of this are the Ibn-Zamrak verses that decorate the walls of the Sala de las Dos Hermanas.

Cursive epigraphy

Glazed ceramic tiles covered with geometrical patterns in primary colors cover the walls of the Alhambra with a profusion of styles and shapes. Red, blue, and yellow are the colors of magic in Sufi tradition, while green is the life-giving color of Islam.

Ceramic tiles

The **horseshoe arch**, widening before rounding off with lower ends extending around the circle until they begin to converge, was the quintessential Moorish architectural innovation, used not only for aesthetic and decorative purposes but because it allowed greater height than the classical, semicircular arch inherited from the Greeks and Romans. The horseshoe arch also had a mystical significance in recalling the shape of the *mihrab*, the prayer niche in the *qibla* wall of a mosque indicating the direction of prayer and suggesting a door to Mecca or to paradise. Horseshoe arches and arcades are found throughout the Alhambra.

Gate of Justice

The Koran describes paradise as "gardens underneath which rivers flow," and **water** is used as a practical and ornamental architectural element throughout the Alhambra. Whether used musically, as in the canals in the Patio de los Leones or visually, as in the reflecting pool of the Patio de los Arrayanes, water is used to enhance light, enlarge spaces, or provide musical background for a desert culture in love with the beauty and oasis-like properties of hydraulics in all its forms.

Alhambra fountains

The Alcazaba was built chiefly by Nasrid kings in the 1300s.

LAY OF THE LAND

The complex has three main parts: the Alcazaba, the Palacio Nazaríes (Nasrid Royal Palace), and the Generalife. Across from the main entrance is the original fortress, the **Alcazaba**. Here, the watchtower's great bell was once used to announce the opening and closing of the irrigation system on Granada's great plain.

A wisteria-covered walkway leads to the heart of the Alhambra, the **Palacios Nazaríes**. Here, delicate apartments, lazy fountains, and tranquil pools contrast vividly with the hulking fortifications outside. It is divided into three sections: the *mexuar*, where business, government, and palace administration were headquartered; the *serrallo*, a series of state rooms where the sultans held court and entertained their ambassadors; and the *harem*, which in its time was entered only by the sultan, his family, and their most trusted servants, most of them eunuchs. Nearby is the Renaissance **Palacio de Carlos V** (Palace of Charles V), featuring a perfectly square exterior but a circular interior courtyard. Designed by Pedro Machuca, a pupil of Michelangelo, it is where the sultan's private apartments once stood. Part of the building houses the free **Museo de la Alhambra**, devoted to Islamic art. Upstairs is the more modest **Museo de Bellas Artes**.

Over on Cerro del Sol (Hill of the Sun) is **Generalife**, the ancient summer palace of the Nasrid kings.

TIMELINE

1238 First Nasrid king, Ibn el-Ahmar, begins Alhambra.

1391 Nasrid Palaces is completed.

1492 Boabdil surrenders Granada to Ferdinand and Isabella, parents of King Henry VIII's first wife, Catherine of Aragon.

1524 Carlos V begins Renaissance Palace.

1812 Napoléonic troops arrive with plans to destroy Alhambra.

1814 The Duke of Wellington sojourns here to escape the pressures of the Peninsular War.

1829 Washington Irving lives on the premises and writes Tales of the *Alhambra*, reviving interest in the crumbling palace.

1862 Granada municipality begins Alhambra restoration that continues to this day.

ALHAMBRA'S PASSAGES OF TIME

From Columbus's commissioning to a bloody murder, historic events as well as everyday affairs happened between these walls.

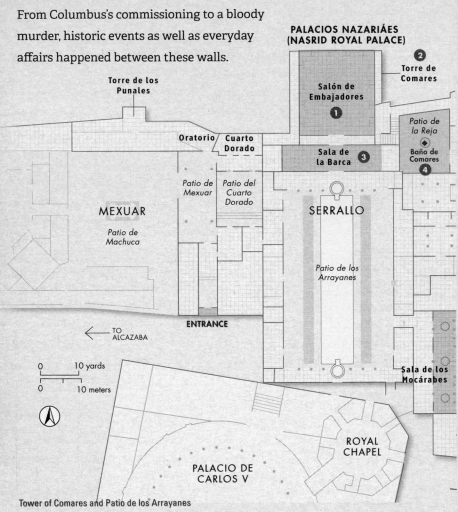

PALACIOS NAZARIÉES (NASRID ROYAL PALACE)

Torre de los Punales

Torre de Comares ❷

Salón de Embajadores ❶

Patio de la Reja

Oratorio / Cuarto Dorado

Sala de la Barca ❸

Baño de Comares ❹

Patio de Mexuar

Patio del Cuarto Dorado

MEXUAR

SERRALLO

Patio de Machuca

Patio de los Arrayanes

ENTRANCE

← TO ALCAZABA

0   10 yards
0   10 meters

Sala de los Mocárabes

ROYAL CHAPEL

PALACIO DE CARLOS V

Tower of Comares and Patio de los Arrayanes

❶ In **El Salón de Embajadores**, Boabdil drew up his terms of surrender, and Christopher Columbus secured royal support for his historic voyage in 1492. The carved wooden ceiling is a portrayal of the seven Islamic heavens, with six rows of stars topped by a seventh-heaven cupulino or micro-cupola.

❷ **Torre de Comares**, a lookout in the corner of this hall is where Carlos V uttered his famous line, "Ill-fated the man who lost all this."

❸ Mistakenly named from the Arabic word *baraka* (divine blessing), **Sala de la Barca** has a carved wooden ceiling often described as an inverted boat.

Sala de los Reyes

7 Shhh, don't tell a secret here. In the **Sala de los Ajimeces**, a whisper in one corner can be clearly heard from the opposite corner.

8 In the **Sala de las Dos Hermanas**, twin slabs of marble embedded in the floor are the "sisters," though Washington Irving preferred the story of a pair of captive Moorish beauties.

9 In the **Patio de Los Leones** (Court of the Lions), a dozen crudely crafted lions (restored to their former glory in 2012) support the fountain at the center of this elegant courtyard, representing the signs of the zodiac sending water to the four corners.

10 In the **Sala de los Abencerrajes**, Muley Hacen (father of Boabdil) murdered the male members of the Abencerraje family in revenge for their chief's seduction of his daughter Zoraya. The rusty stains in the fountain are said to be bloodstains left by the pile of Abencerraje heads.

The star-shaped cupola, reflected in the pool, is considered the Alhambra's most beautiful example of stalactite or honeycomb vaulting. The octagonal dome over the room is best viewed at sunset when the 16 small windows atop the dome admit sharp, low sunlight that refracts kaleidoscopically through the beehive-like prisms.

11 In the **Sala de los Reyes**, the ceiling painting depicts the first 10 Nasrid rulers. It was painted by a Christian artist since Islamic artists were not allowed to usurp divine power by creating human or animal figures.

The overhead painting of the knight rescuing his lady from a savage man portrays chivalry, a concept introduced to Europe by Arabic poets.

12 The terraces of **Generalife** grant incomparable views of the city.

Generalife gardens

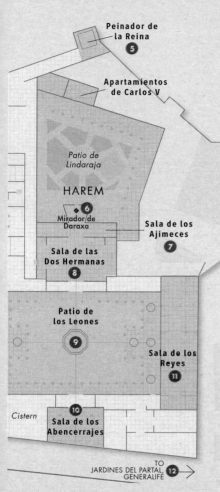

4 The **Baño de Comares** is where the sultan's favorites luxuriated in brightly tiled pools beneath star-shape pinpoints of light from the ceiling above.

5 **El Peinador de la Reina**, a nine-foot-square room atop a small tower was the Sultana's boudoir. The perforated marble slab was used to infiltrate perfumes while the queen performed her toilette. Washington Irving wrote his *Tales of the Alhambra* in this romantic tree-house-like perch.

6 Sultana Zoraya often found refuge in this charming little balcony (**Mirador de Daraxa**) overlooking the Lindaraja garden.

👁 Sights

Abadía de Sacromonte

CAVE | The caverns on Sacromonte are thought to have sheltered early Christians; 15th-century treasure hunters found bones inside and assumed they belonged to San Cecilio, the city's patron saint. Thus, the hill was sanctified—*sacro monte* (holy mountain)—and an abbey built on its summit, the Abadía de Sacromonte. Tours in English are at 2 and 5:30. ✉ *C. del Sacromonte, Sacromonte* ☎ *958/221445* ⊕ *sacromonteabbey.com* 🎟 *€4.*

Museo Cuevas del Sacromonte

MUSEUM | The ethnographical museum here shows how people lived in this area, and elsewhere in this interesting complex looks at Granada's flora and fauna. During the summer months, there are live flamenco concerts. ⚠ **It's a steep walk to reach the center, even if you take Bus No. C2 (from Plaza Nueva) to shorten the distance.** ✉ *Barranco de los Negros, Sacromonte* ☎ *958/215120* ⊕ *www.sacromontegranada.com* 🎟 *€5.*

Albayzín

Covering a hill of its own, across the Darro ravine from the Alhambra, this ancient Moorish neighborhood is a mix of dilapidated white houses and immaculate carmenes. It was founded in 1228 by Moors who had fled Baeza after Ferdinand III captured the city. Full of cobblestone alleyways and secret corners, the Albayzín guards its old Moorish roots jealously, though its 30 mosques were converted to baroque churches long ago. A stretch of the Moors' original city wall runs beside the ridge called the **Cuesta de la Alhacaba.** If you're walking—the best way to explore—you can enter the Albayzín from either the Cuesta de Elvira or the Plaza Nueva. Alternatively, on foot or by taxi (parking is impossible), begin in the Plaza Santa Ana and follow the

Bicycling in Granada

At the foot of the Iberian Peninsula's tallest mountain—the 11,427-foot Mulhacén peak—Granada offers challenging mountain-biking opportunities, and spinning through the hairpin turns of the Alpujarras east of Granada is both scenic and hair-raising. For organized cycling tours, contact **Cycling Country** *(Tours).*

Carrera del Darro, Paseo Padre Manjón, and Cuesta del Chapíz. One of the highest points in the quarter, the plaza in front of the church of San Nicolás (*€2; open mornings only*)—the **Mirador de San Nicolás**—has one of the finest views in all of Granada: on the hill opposite, the turrets and towers of the Alhambra form a dramatic silhouette against the snowy peaks of the Sierra Nevada. The sight is most magical at dawn, dusk, and on nights when the Alhambra is floodlighted. Take note of the mosque just next to the church—views of the Alhambra from the mosque gardens are just as good as those from the Mirador de San Nicolás and a lot less crowded. Interestingly, given the area's Moorish history, the two sloping, narrow streets of Calderería Nueva and Calderería Vieja that meet at the top by the Iglesia San Gregorio have developed into something of a North African bazaar, full of shops and vendors selling clothes, bags, crafts, and trinkets. The numerous little teahouses and restaurants here have a decidedly Moroccan flavor.

Many of the streets are cobbled so wear sturdy footwear with thick soles.

👁 Sights

Casa de los Pisa

MUSEUM | Originally built in 1494 for the Pisa family, the claim to fame of this house is its relationship to San Juan de Dios, who came to Granada in 1538 and founded a charity hospital to take care of the poor. Befriended by the Pisa family, he was taken into their home when he fell ill in February 1550. A month later, he died there, at the age of 55. Since that time, devotees of the saint have traveled from around the world to this house with a stone Gothic facade, now run by the Hospital Order of St. John. Inside are numerous pieces of jewelry, furniture, priceless religious works of art, and an extensive collection of paintings and sculptures depicting St. John. ⊠ *Calle Convalecencia 1, Albaicín* 🕿 *958/222144* 🎫 *€3* 🕙 *Closed Sun.*

El Bañuelo (*Little Bath House*)

HOT SPRINGS | These 11th-century Arab steam baths might be a little dark and dank now, but try to imagine them some 900 years ago, filled with Moorish beauties. Back then, the dull brick walls were backed by bright ceramic tiles, tapestries, and rugs. Light comes in through star-shape vents in the ceiling, à la a bathhouse in the Alhambra. ⊠ *Carrera del Darro 31, Albaicín* 🕿 *958/229738* 🎫 *€5.*

Palacio de los Córdova

CASTLE/PALACE | At the end of the Paseo Padre Manjón, this 17th-century noble house today holds Granada's municipal archives and is used for municipal functions and art exhibits. You're free to wander about the large garden, the only area open to visitors. ⊠ *Cuesta del Chapiz 4, Albaicín* 🕿 *958/180021* 🎫 *Free.*

Paseo Padre Manjón

Along the Río Darro, this paseo is also known as the Paseo de los Tristes (Promenade of the Sad Ones) because funeral processions once passed this way. The cafés and bars here are a good place for a coffee break. The park, dappled with wisteria-covered pergolas, fountains, and stone walkways, has a stunning view of the Alhambra's northern side. ⊠ *Albaicín.*

🍴 Restaurants

★ El Trillo

$$$ | **SPANISH** | Tucked away in the warren of alleyways in a restored Albayzín villa, this lovely small restaurant offers perhaps the best food in the area. There's a formal dining room, outside garden with pear and quince trees, plus a roof terrace with Alhambra views. **Known for:** fine dining; views of the Alhambra; rice with wild boar. $ *Average main: €18* ⊠ *Callejón del Aljibe del Trillo 3, Albaicín* 🕿 *958/225182* ⊕ *www.restaurante-eltrillo.com.*

Paprika

$$ | **VEGETARIAN** | Inside a pretty brick building and with an informal terrace sprawling over the wide steps of the Cuesta de Abarqueros, Paprika offer unpretentious vegan food. Most ingredients and wines are organic, and dishes include salads, stir-fries, and curries, such as Thai curry with tofu, coconut, and green curry sauce. **Known for:** choice of vegan food; value plate of the day; organic ingredients. $ *Average main: €12* ⊠ *Cuesta de Abarqueros 3, Albaicín* 🕿 *958/804785* ⊕ *www.paprika-granada.com.*

Pilar del Toro

$$ | **SPANISH** | This bar and restaurant, just off Plaza Nueva, is in a 17th-century palace with a stunning patio (complete with original marble columns) and peaceful garden. The menu emphasizes meat dishes such as *chuletas de cordero* (lamb chops) and the house specialty, braised rabo de toro and fried artichokes or eggplant. **Known for:** atmospheric patio; oxtail; elegant upstairs restaurant. $ *Average main: €15* ⊠ *Calle Hospital de Santa Ana 12, Albaicín* 🕿 *958/225470* ⊕ *pilardeltoro.es.*

Ruta del Azafrán
$$ | **SPANISH** | A charming surprise nestled at the foot of the Albayzín by the Darro—this sleek contemporary space in the shadow of the Alhambra offers a selection of specialties. The menu is interesting and diverse and includes dishes like chicken pastela, tuna *tataki* (a method of pounding fish in Japanese cuisine) with pineapple, and several different risottos. **Known for:** wide choice of dishes; views of the Alhambra, especially at night; tasting menus. [$] *Average main: €16* ✉ *Paseo de los Tristes 1, Albaicín* ☎ *958/226882* 🌐 *rutadelazafran.com.*

Hotels

★ Casa Morisca
$$$ | **B&B/INN** | The architect who owns this 15th-century building transformed it into a hotel so distinctive that he received Spain's National Restoration Award for his preservation of original architectural elements, including barrel-vaulted brickwork, wooden ceilings, and the original pool. **Pros:** historic location; award-winning design; easy parking. **Cons:** stuffy interior rooms; no full restaurant on-site; slightly out of the town center. [$] *Rooms from: €150* ✉ *Cuesta de la Victoria 9, Albaicín* ☎ *958/221100* 🌐 *www.hotelcasamorisca.com* 🛏 *14 rooms* 🍴 *Free Breakfast.*

Hotel Casa 1800
$$$$ | **HOTEL** | A stone's throw from the Paseo de los Tristes, this restored 17th-century mansion has a fine, tiered patio. **Pros:** historic building; deluxe suite has balcony with views of the Alhambra; walking distance to most sights. **Cons:** on a street that doesn't permit cars; rooms are small (but comfortable); no bar. [$] *Rooms from: €250* ✉ *Calle Benalua 11, Albaicín* ☎ *958/210700* 🌐 *www.hotelcasa1800granada.com* 🛏 *25 rooms* 🍴 *No meals.*

Hotel Palacio Santa Inés
$$$ | **HOTEL** | It's not often you get to stay in a 16th-century palace—and this one has a stunning location in the heart of the Albayzín. **Pros:** perfect location for exploring the Albayzín; quirky interiors; some rooms have Alhambra views. **Cons:** can't get there by car; some rooms rather dark; breakfast is average. [$] *Rooms from: €150* ✉ *Cuesta de Santa Inés 9, Albaicín* ☎ *958/222362* 🌐 *www.palaciosantaines.es* 🛏 *35 rooms* 🍴 *No meals.*

Performing Arts

FLAMENCO

Cueva de la Rocío
DANCE | This is a good spot for authentic flamenco shows, staged nightly at 9, 10, and 11. ✉ *C. del Sacromonte 70, Albaicín* ☎ *958/227129* 🌐 *cuevalarocio.es.*

El Tabanco
MUSIC CLUBS | In the heart of the Albayzín, this small venue is an art gallery by day and live music venue (mostly flamenco and jazz) by night. Book in advance to be sure of a seat. ✉ *Cuesta de San Gregorio 24, Albaicín* ☎ *662/137046* 🌐 *www.eltabanco.com.*

El Templo del Flamenco
DANCE | Slightly off the beaten track (take a taxi to get here) and less touristy because of it, this venue has shows at 8 and 10 daily. ✉ *Calle Parnaleros Alto 41, Albaicín* ☎ *622/500052* 🌐 *templodelflamenco.com.*

Eshavira Club
MUSIC CLUBS | At this dimly lighted club you can hear sultry jazz. There's also flamenco at 11 pm on Thursday and Friday. Admission fee includes a drink. ✉ *Calle Postigo de la Cuna 2, Albaicín* ☎ *958/290829.*

Jardines de Zoraya
DANCE | This show doesn't take place in a cave, but the music and dance are some of the most authentic available. Daily flamenco shows are at 8 and 10:30

pm, and at 3 pm on weekends. ⊠ *Calle Panaderos 32, Albaicín* ☎ *958/206266* ⊕ *www.jardinesdezoraya.com.*

Peña La Platería

DANCE | This private club in the Albayzín is devoted to flamenco. Performances are usually on Thursday and Saturday evenings—check the club's Facebook page for details (⊕ *www.facebook.com/plateriaflamenco*). ⊠ *Calle Plazoleta de Toqueros 7, Albaicín* ☎ *958/210650.*

Centro

Sights

Capilla Real (*Royal Chapel*)

RELIGIOUS SITE | Catholic Monarchs Isabella of Castile and Ferdinand of Aragón are buried at this shrine. When Isabella died in 1504, her body was first laid to rest in the Convent of San Francisco. The architect Enrique Egas began work on the Royal Chapel in 1506 and completed it 15 years later, creating a masterpiece of the ornate Gothic style now known in Spain as Isabelline. In 1521 Isabella's body was transferred to the Royal Chapel crypt, joined by that of her husband, Ferdinand, and later her daughter, Juana la Loca (Joanna the Mad), son-in-law, Felipe el Hermoso (Philip the Handsome), and Prince Felipe of Asturias. The **crypt** containing the coffins is simple, but it's topped by elaborate marble tombs showing Ferdinand and Isabella lying side by side. The **altarpiece** comprises 34 carved panels depicting religious and historical scenes. The **sacristy** holds Ferdinand's sword, Isabella's crown and scepter, and a fine collection of Flemish paintings once owned by Isabella. ⊠ *Calle Oficios, Centro* ☎ *958/227848* ⊕ *www.capillareal-granada.com* ⊠ *€5.*

Cathedral

RELIGIOUS SITE | Carlos V commissioned the cathedral in 1521 because he considered the Capilla Real "too small for so much glory" and wanted to house his illustrious late grandparents someplace more worthy. Carlos undoubtedly had great intentions, as the cathedral was created by some of the finest architects of its time: Enrique Egas, Diego de Siloé, Alonso Cano, and sculptor Juan de Mena. Alas, his ambitions came to little, for the cathedral is a grand and gloomy monument, not completed until 1714 and never used as the crypt for his grandparents (or parents). Enter through a small door at the back, off the Gran Vía. Old hymnals are displayed throughout, and there's a museum, which includes a 14th-century gold-and-silver monstrance given to the city by Queen Isabella. ⊠ *Gran Vía, Centro* ☎ *958/222959* ⊠ *€5 (including audio guide).*

Centro José Guerrero

MUSEUM | Just across a lane from the cathedral and Capilla Real, this building houses colorful modern paintings by José Guerrero. Born in Granada in 1914, Guerrero traveled throughout Europe and lived In New York in the 1950s before returning to Spain. The center also runs excellent temporary contemporary art shows. ⊠ *Calle Oficios 8, Centro* ☎ *958/225185* ⊕ *www.centroguerrero.org* ⊠ *Free* ⊙ *Closed Mon.*

Corral del Carbón (*Coal House*)

HOUSE | This building was used to store coal in the 19th century, but its history is much longer. Dating to the 14th century, it was used by Moorish merchants as a lodging house, and then by Christians as a theater. It's one of the oldest Moorish buildings in the city and the only Arab structure of its kind in Spain. ⊠ *Calle Mariana Pineda, Centro* ⊠ *Free.*

Palacio Madraza

CASTLE/PALACE | This building conceals the Islamic seminary built in 1349 by Yusuf I. The intriguing baroque facade is elaborate; inside, across from the entrance, an octagonal room is crowned by a Moorish dome. It hosts occasional free art and cultural exhibitions. ⊠ *Calle Zacatín, Centro* ☎ *958/241299* ⊠ *€2.*

🍴 Restaurants

Bar Los Diamantes

$$ | **TAPAS** | This cheap and cheerful bar is a big favorite with locals and draws crowds whatever the time of year. Specialties include fried fish and seafood—try the *surtido de pescado* (assortment of fried fish) to sample the best—as well as *mollejas fritas* (fried lambs' brains). **Known for:** fried fish; no seating; busy atmosphere. [$] *Average main: €12* ✉ *Calle Navas 28, Centro* ☎ *958/222572* 🌐 *www.barlosdiamantes.com* 💳 *No credit cards.*

Bodegas Castañeda

$$$ | **SPANISH** | A block from the cathedral across Gran Vía, this is a delightfully typical Granada bodega with low ceilings and dark wood furniture. In addition to the wines, specialties here are plates of cheese, pâté, and *embutidos* (cold meats). **Known for:** tapas; atmospheric bar; Spanish tortilla with creamy aioli. [$] *Average main: €18* ✉ *Calle Almireceros 1–3, Centro* ☎ *958/215464.*

★ Café Botánico

$$ | **TAPAS** | Southeast of Granada's cathedral, this is a modern hot spot, a world apart from Granada's usual traditional tapas bar. Here you'll find a bright-orange-and-beige interior and an eclectic crowd of students, families, and businesspeople. **Known for:** international menu; good-value lunch deal; homemade desserts. [$] *Average main: €14* ✉ *Calle Málaga 3, Centro* ☎ *958/271598.*

Cunini

$$$$ | **SPANISH** | Around the corner from the cathedral, this is one of Granada's longest-established fish restaurants. Catch-of-the-day fish and shellfish, fresh from the boats at Motril, are displayed in the window at the front of the tapas bar, adjacent to the cozy wood-paneled dining room. **Known for:** fresh seafood; the only place in town serving angulas (glass eels); outdoor dining. [$] *Average main: €22* ✉ *Pl. Pescadería 14, Centro* ☎ *958/250777* 🕑 *Closed Mon. No dinner Sun.*

La Bodega de Antonio

$$ | **SPANISH** | Just off Calle Puentezuelas, this authentic patio complete with original pillars provides a cozy vibe. Specials include the house cod (with prawns and clams) and Galician-style octopus, best enjoyed with a *cerdito* (a "little pig" ceramic jug of sweet white wine, so named for its snout pourer). **Known for:** generous portions; tapas; Galician-style octopus. [$] *Average main: €12* ✉ *Calle Jardines 4, Centro* ☎ *958/252275* 🕑 *Closed Wed. and Aug.*

★ La Brujidera

$$ | **TAPAS** | Also known simply as Casa de Vinos (Wine House), this place, up a pedestrian street just behind Plaza Nueva, is a must for Spanish wine lovers. The cozy interior is reminiscent of a ship's cabin, with wood paneling lining the walls, along with bottles of more than 150 Spanish wines. **Known for:** long wine list; meat and cheese boards; vermouth and sherries on tap. [$] *Average main: €12* ✉ *Monjas del Carmen 2, Centro* ☎ *958/222595* 🕑 *Closed 1 wk in Feb.*

Oliver

$$ | **SPANISH** | The interior may look a bit bare, but whatever this fish restaurant lacks in warmth it makes up for with the food. Less pricey than its neighbor Cunini, it serves simple but high-quality dishes like grilled mullet, dorado baked in salt, prawns with garlic, and monkfish in saffron sauce. **Known for:** tapas bar; fresh fish; migas (fried bread crumbs). [$] *Average main: €17* ✉ *Pl. Pescadería 12, Centro* ☎ *958/262200* 🌐 *restauranteoliver.com* 🕑 *Closed Sun.*

Tinta Fina

$$$ | **SPANISH** | Underneath the arches just off Puerta Real, this modern bar and restaurant has a reputation for being one of Granada's most chic venues. This trendy spot is especially known for fresh seafood, including oysters and red

shrimp, tuna tartare, and grilled octopus. **Known for:** seafood; cocktail and G&T menus; chic atmosphere. $ *Average main: €20* ✉ *Calle Angel Ganivet 5, Centro* ☎ *958/100041* ⊕ *www.tintafin-arestaurante.com.*

Hotels

Hospes Palacio de los Patos
$$$$ | HOTEL | This beautifully restored palace is unmissable, sitting proudly on its own in the middle of one of Granada's busiest shopping streets. **Pros:** central location; historic setting; great spa and restaurant. **Cons:** expensive parking; some street noise; basement rooms are dark. $ *Rooms from: €300* ✉ *Calle Solarillo de Gracia 1, Centro* ☎ *958/535790* ⊕ *www.hospes.es* ⤳ *42 rooms* ⊚ *No meals.*

★ Hostal Rodri
$ | HOTEL | This very comfortable and quiet hostel lies conveniently off Plaza de la Trinidad near the cathedral and is a good option for cheaper lodging in a city with so many upscale accommodations. **Pros:** central location; clean, comfortable rooms; value. **Cons:** some rooms on small side; no direct car access; could be too basic for some. $ *Rooms from: €55* ✉ *Calle Laurel de las Tablas 9, Centro* ☎ *958/288043* ⊕ *www.hostalrodri.com* ⤳ *10 rooms* ⊚ *No meals.*

Hotel Párraga Siete
$$ | HOTEL | This family-run hotel in the heart of the old quarter within easy walking distance of sights and restaurants offers excellent value and amenities superior to its official two-star rating. **Pros:** central, quiet location; good on-site restaurant; easy nearby parking. **Cons:** difficult to access by car; interiors might be too sparse for some; no historic character. $ *Rooms from: €100* ✉ *Calle Párraga 7, Centro* ☎ *958/264227* ⊕ *www.hotelparragasiete.com* ⤳ *20 rooms* ⊚ *No meals.*

Palacio de los Navas
$$$ | B&B/INN | In the center of the city, this palace was built by aristocrat Francisco Navas in the 16th century and it later became the Casa de Moneda (the Mint); its original architectural features blend well with modern ones. **Pros:** great location; peaceful oasis during the day; rooms are set around a beautiful interior patio. **Cons:** can be noisy at night; breakfast uninspiring. $ *Rooms from: €150* ✉ *Calle Navas 1, Centro* ☎ *958/215760* ⊕ *www.hotelpalaciodelosnavas.com* ⤳ *19 rooms* ⊚ *Free Breakfast.*

Nightlife

Bohemia Jazz Café
MUSIC CLUBS | This atmospheric jazz bar has piano performances and occasional live bands. ✉ *Pl. de los Lobos 11, Centro.*

Shopping

Artesanías González
CRAFTS | Not far from La Alhambra, this is one of the best and longest-established places to buy taracea on handmade chessboards, boxes, side tables, and coasters. ✉ *Cuesta de Gomérez 12, Centro* ☎ *858/122382* ⊗ *Closed Sun.*

Espartería San José
CRAFTS | For wicker baskets and esparto-grass mats and rugs, head to this shop off the Plaza Pescadería. ✉ *Calle Jáudenes 3, Centro* ☎ *958/267415.*

Outskirts of Granada

Sights

Casa-Museo Federico García Lorca
MUSEUM | Granada's most famous native son, the poet Federico García Lorca, gets his due here, in the middle of a park devoted to him on the southern fringe of the city. Lorca's onetime summer home, **La Huerta de San Vicente,** is now a museum (guided tours only)—run

by his niece Laura García Lorca—with such artifacts as his beloved piano and changing exhibits on specific aspects of his life. ✉ *Parque García Lorca, Virgen Blanca, Arabial* ☎ *958/258466* ⊕ *www. huertadesanvicente.com* ✉ *€3 (free Wed.)* ⊘ *Closed Mon.*

Monasterio de la Cartuja

RELIGIOUS SITE | This Carthusian monastery in northern Granada (2 km [1 mile] from the center of town and reached by Bus No. N7) was begun in 1506 and moved to its present site in 1516, though construction continued for the next 300 years. The exterior is sober and monolithic, but inside are twisted, multicolor marble columns; a profusion of gold, silver, tortoiseshell, and ivory; intricate stucco; and the extravagant sacristy—it's easy to see why it has been called the Christian answer to the Alhambra. Among its wonders are the trompe l'oeil spikes, shadows and all, in the Sanchez Cotan cross over the *Last Supper* painting at the west end of the refectory. If you're lucky, you may see small birds attempting to land on these faux perches. ✉ *C. de Alfacar, Cartuja* ☎ *958/161932* ✉ *€5.*

Parque de las Ciencias (*Science Park*)

MUSEUM | **FAMILY** | Across from Granada's convention center and easily reached on Bus No. C4, this museum (one of the most visited in Andalusia) has a planetarium and interactive demonstrations of scientific experiments. The 165-foot observation tower has views to the south and west. ✉ *Av. del Mediterráneo s/n, Zaidín* ☎ *958/131900* ⊕ *www.parqueciencias.com* ✉ *From €3* ⊘ *Closed Mon.*

🍴 Restaurants

Restaurante Arriaga

$$$$ | **BASQUE** | Run by Basque chef Álvaro Arriaga, this restaurant sits on the top floor of the Museo de la Memoria de Andalucía just outside the city (it's well worth the taxi drive) and enjoys panoramic views of Granada with the Sierra

Nevada behind. Choose from two tasting menus (€55 for six dishes and €70 for nine dishes), both with one surprise after another. À la carte specialties include Basque cod in garlic sauce, slow-cooked beef, and hake cheeks in traditional green sauce. **Known for:** tasting menus; culinary surprises (the menu starts with dessert!); panoramic views of Granada. Ⓢ *Average main: €28* ✉ *Av. de las Ciencias 2, Armilla* ☎ *958/132619* ⊕ *www. restaurantearriaga.com* ⊘ *Closed Mon. and Tues.*

Side Trips from Granada

The fabled province of Granada spans the Sierra Nevada, with the beautifully rugged Alpujarras and the highest peaks on mainland Spain—Mulhacén at 11,407 feet and Veleta at 11,125 feet. This is where you can find some of the prettiest, most ancient villages, and it's one of the foremost destinations for Andalusia's increasingly popular rural tourism. Granada's vega, covered with orchards, tobacco plantations, and poplar groves, stretches for miles around.

Twelve kilometers (8 miles) south of Granada on A44, the road reaches a spot known as the **Suspiro del Moro** (Moor's Sigh). Pause here a moment and look back at the city, just as Granada's departing "Boy King" Boabdil did 500 years ago. As he wept over the city he'd surrendered to the Catholic Monarchs, his scornful mother pronounced her now legendary rebuke: "You weep like a woman for the city you could not defend as a man."

Fuente Vaqueros

19½ km (12 miles) northwest of Granada.

Museo Casa Natal Federico García Lorca

HOUSE | Born in the village of Fuentevaqueros on June 5, 1898, the poet lived here until age six. His childhood home opened as a museum in 1986, when Spain commemorated the 50th anniversary of his assassination (he was shot without trial by Nationalists at the start of the civil war in August 1936) and celebrated his reinstatement as a national figure after 40 years of nonrecognition during the Francisco Franco regime. The house has been restored with original furnishings, and the former granary, barn, and stables have been converted into exhibition spaces, with temporary art shows and a permanent display of photographs, clippings, and other memorabilia. A two-minute video shows the only existing footage of Lorca. Visits are by guided tour only. ⊠ *C. del Poeta García Lorca 4* ☏ *958/516453* ⊕ *www.patronatogarcialorca.org/casamuseo.php* ✉ *€2* ⊘ *Closed Mon.*

The Sierra Nevada

The drive southeast from Granada to Pradollano along the A395—Europe's highest road, by way of Cenes de la Vega—takes about 45 minutes. It's wise to carry snow chains from mid-November to as late as April or even May. The mountains here make for an easy and worthwhile excursion, especially for those keen on trekking.

◉ Sights

Mulhacén

MOUNTAIN—SIGHT | To the east of Granada, the mighty Mulhacén, the highest peak in mainland Spain, soars to 11,427 feet. Legend has it that it came by its name when Boabdil, the last Moorish king of Granada, deposed his father, Abul Hassan Ali, and had the body buried at the summit of the mountain so that it couldn't be desecrated. For more information on trails to the two summits, check the National Park Service's site (⊕ *www.nevadensis.com*). ⊠ *Sierra Nevada.*

Pico de Veleta

MOUNTAIN—SIGHT | Peninsular Spain's second-highest mountain is 11,125 feet high. The view from its summit across the Alpujarras to the sea at distant Motril is stunning, and on a very clear day you can see the coast of North Africa. When the snow melts (July and August) you can drive or take a minibus from the Albergue Universitario (Universitario mountain refuge) to within around 400 yards of the summit—a trail takes you to the top in around 45 minutes. ■TIP➔ **It's cold up there, so take a warm jacket and scarf, even if Granada is sizzling hot.** ⊠ *Sierra Nevada.*

⚐ Activities

SKIING

Estación de Esquí Sierra Nevada

SKIING/SNOWBOARDING | FAMILY | Europe's southernmost ski resort is one of its best equipped. At the Pradollano and Borreguiles stations, there's good skiing from December through April or May; each has a special snowboarding circuit, floodlighted night slopes, a children's ski school, and après-ski sun and swimming in the Mediterranean less than an hour away. In winter, buses to Pradollano leave Granada's bus station three times a day on weekdays and four times on weekends and holidays. Tickets are €9 round-trip. As for Borreguiles, you can get there only on skis. There's an information center (⊕ *www.sierranevada.es*) at Plaza de Andalucía 4. ⊠ *Sierra Nevada.*

The Alpujarras

Village of Lanjarón: 46 km (29 miles) south of Granada.

A trip to the Alpujarras, on the southern slopes of the Sierra Nevada, takes you to one of Andalusia's highest, most remote, and most scenic areas, home for decades to painters, writers, and a considerable foreign population. The Alpujarras region was originally populated by Moors fleeing the Christian Reconquest (from Seville after its fall in 1248, then from Granada after 1492). It was also the final fiefdom of the unfortunate Boabdil, conceded to him by the Catholic Monarchs after he surrendered Granada. In 1568 rebellious Moors made their last stand against the Christian overlords, a revolt ruthlessly suppressed by Felipe II and followed by the forced conversion of all Moors to Christianity and their resettlement farther inland and up Spain's eastern coast. The villages were then repopulated with Christian soldiers from Galicia, who were granted land in return for their service. To this day, the Galicians' descendants continue the Moorish custom of weaving rugs and blankets in the traditional Alpujarran colors of red, green, black, and white, and they sell their crafts in many of the villages. Be on the lookout for handmade basketry and pottery as well.

Houses here are squat and square; they spill down the southern slopes of the Sierra Nevada, bearing a strong resemblance to the Berber homes in the Rif Mountains, just across the Mediterranean in Morocco. If you're driving, the road as far as Lanjarón and Orgiva is smooth sailing; after that come steep, twisting mountain roads with few gas stations. Beyond sightseeing, the area is a haven for outdoor activities such as hiking and horseback riding. Inquire at the **Information Point** at Plaza de la Libertad, at Pampaneira.

Sights

Lanjarón and Nearby Villages

TOWN | The western entrance to the Alpujarras is some 46 km (29 miles) from Granada at Lanjarón. This spa town is famous for its mineral water, collected from the melting snows of the Sierra Nevada and drunk throughout Spain. **Orgiva,** the next and largest town in the Alpujarras, has a 17th-century castle. Here you can leave the A348 and follow

signs for the villages of the Alpujarras Altas (High Alpujarras), including **Pampaneira, Capileira,** and especially **Trevélez,** which lies on the slopes of the Mulhacén at 4,840 feet above sea level. Reward yourself with a plate of the local jamón serrano. Trevélez has three levels—the Barrio Alto, Barrio Medio, and Barrio Bajo—and the butchers are concentrated in the lowest section (Bajo). The higher levels have narrow cobblestone streets, whitewashed houses, and shops.

Hotels

Hotel Alcadima

$ | HOTEL | FAMILY | One of the best-value hotels in the area, this pleasant if unfancy hotel in the rustic spa town of Lanjarón makes a good base for exploring the lower part of the Alpujarras. **Pros:** swimming pool; excellent restaurant; two-bedroom suites are ideal for families. **Cons:** Lanjarón isn't the prettiest village in the area; could be too plain for some; down an unattractive side street. $ Rooms from: €60 ⊠ Calle Francisco Tarrega 3 ☎ 958/770809 ⊕ www.alcadima.com 🛏 45 rooms ⬦ No meals.

Los Tinaos

$ | RENTAL | Located on the way to Trevélez in the pretty whitewashed village of Bubión that almost clings to the mountainside, these comfortable apartments (for two or four people) come squeaky-clean, with open log fires as well as central heating, and sweeping views across the valley. **Pros:** valley views; a short walk from Pitres; bar serving locally produced wine. **Cons:** steep walk down. $ Rooms from: €60 ⊠ Calle Parras 2, Bubión ☎ 958/763217 ⊕ www.lostinaos.com 🛏 10 rooms ⬦ No meals.

Chapter 12

COSTA DEL SOL AND COSTA DE ALMERÍA

12

Updated by
Joanna Styles

👁 Sights   🍽 Restaurants   🛏 Hotels   🛍 Shopping   🍸 Nightlife

★★★★☆   ★★★★★   ★★★★☆   ★★★★☆   ★★★☆☆

WELCOME TO COSTA DEL SOL AND COSTA DE ALMERÍA

TOP REASONS TO GO

★ **Enjoy the sun and sand:** Relax at any of the beaches; they're all free, though in summer there isn't much towel space.

★ **Soak up the atmosphere:** Spend a day in Málaga, Picasso's birthplace, visiting the museums, exploring the old town, and strolling the Palm Walkway in the port.

★ **Check out Puerto Banús:** Wine, dine, and celebrity-watch at the Costa del Sol's most luxurious and sophisticated port town.

★ **Visit Cabo de Gata:** This protected natural reserve is one of the wildest and most beautiful stretches of coast in Spain.

★ **Shop for souvenirs:** Check out the weekly market in one of the Costa resorts to pick up bargain-price souvenirs, including ceramics.

The towns and resorts along the southeastern Spanish coastline vary considerably according to whether they lie to the east or to the west of Málaga. To the east are the Costa de Almería and the Costa Tropical, less developed stretches of coastline. Towns like Nerja act as a gateway to the dramatic mountainous region of La Axarquía. West from Málaga along the Costa del Sol proper, the strip between Torremolinos and Marbella is the most densely populated. Seamless though it may appear, as one resort merges into the next, each town has a distinctive character, with its own sights, charms, and activities.

1 The Cabo de Gata Nature Reserve

2 Agua Amarga

3 Almería

4 Almuñécar

5 Nerja

6 The Axarquía

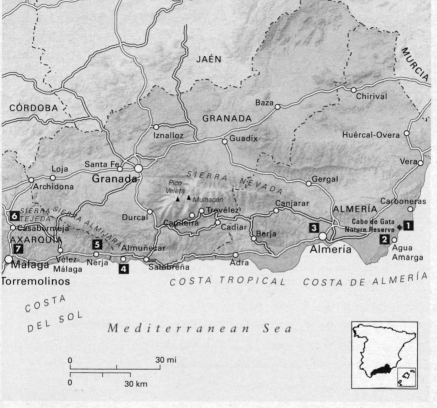

0   30 mi

0   30 km

7 Málaga	**13** Marbella
8 Antequera	**14** Ojén
9 The Guadalhorce Valley	**15** Estepona
10 Torremolinos	**16** Casares
11 Fuengirola	**17** Tarifa
12 Mijas	**18** Gibraltar

EATING AND DRINKING WELL ALONG SPAIN'S SOUTHERN COAST

Spain's southern coast is known for fresh fish and seafood, grilled or quickly fried in olive oil. Sardines roasted on spits are popular along the Málaga coast, while upland towns offer more robust mountain fare, especially in Almería.

Chiringuitos, small shanties along the beaches, are summer-only Costa del Sol restaurants that serve fish fresh off the boats. Málaga is known for seafood restaurants serving *fritura malagueña de pescaíto* (fried fish). In mountain towns, you'll find superb *rabo de toro* (oxtail), goat and sheep cheeses, wild mushrooms, and game dishes. Almería shares Moorish aromas of cumin and cardamom with its Andalusian sisters to the west but also turns the corner toward its northern neighbor, Murcia, where delicacies such as *mojama* (salt-dried tuna) and *hueva de maruca* (ling roe) have been favorites since Phoenician times. Almería's wealth of vegetables and legumes combine with pork and game products for a rougher, more powerful culinary canon of thick stews and soups.

TO DRINK

Málaga has long been famous for the sweet Muscatel wine that Russian empress Catherine the Great loved so much she imported it to Saint Petersburg duty free in 1792. In the 18th century, Muscatel was sold medicinally in pharmacies for its curative powers and is still widely produced and often served as accompaniment to dessert or tapas.

COLD ALMOND AND GARLIC SOUP

Ajoblanco, a summer staple in Andalusia, is a refreshing salty-sweet combination served cold. Exquisitely light and sharp, the almond and garlic soup has a surprisingly creamy and fresh taste. Almonds, garlic, hard white bread, olive oil, water, sherry vinegar, and a topping of muscat grapes are standard ingredients.

FRIED FISH MÁLAGA STYLE

A popular dish along the Costa del Sol and the Costa de Almería, fritura malagueña de pescaíto is basically any sort of very small fish—such as anchovies, cuttlefish, baby squid, whitebait, and red mullet—fried in oil so hot that the fish end up crisp and light as a feather. The fish are lightly dusted in white flour, crisped quickly, and drained briefly before arriving piping hot and bone-dry on your plate. For an additional Moorish aroma, fritura masters add powdered cumin to the flour.

ALMERÍA STEWS

Almería is known for heartier fare than neighboring Málaga. *Puchero de trigo* (wheat and pork stew) is a fortifying winter comfort stew of boiled whole grains of wheat cooked with chickpeas, pork, black sausage, fatback, potatoes, saffron, cumin, and fennel. *Ajo colorao* (also known as *atascaburras*) is another popular stew, which consists

of potatoes, dried peppers, vegetables, and fish that are simmered into a thick red-orange stew *de cuchara* (eaten with a spoon). Laced with cumin and garlic and served with thick country bread, it's a stick-to-your-ribs mariner's soup.

ROASTED SARDINES

Known as *moraga de sardinas,* or *espeto de sardinas,* this method of cooking sardines is popular in the summer along the Pedregalejo and Carihuela beaches east and west of Málaga: the sardines are skewered and extended over logs at an angle so that the fish oils run back down the skewers instead of falling into the coals and causing a conflagration. Fresh fish and cold white wine or beer make this a beautiful and relaxing sunset beach dinner.

A THOUSAND AND ONE EGGS

In Andalusia and especially along the Costa del Sol, *huevos a la flamenca* (eggs flamenco style) is a time-tested dish combining peppers, potatoes, ham, and peas with an egg broken over the top and baked sizzling hot in the oven. Other musts: *Revuelto de setas y gambas* (scrambled eggs with wild mushrooms and shrimp) and the universal Iberian potato omelet, the *tortilla de patatas.*

BEST BEACHES OF THE SOUTHERN COAST

Tourists have been coming to the Costa del Sol since the 1950s, attracted by its magical combination of brochure-blue sea, miles of beaches, and reliably sunny weather.

The beaches here range from the gravel-like shingle in Almuñécar, Nerja, and Málaga to fine, gritty sand from Torremolinos westward. The best (and most crowded) beaches are east of Málaga and those flanking the most popular resorts of Nerja, Torremolinos, Fuengirola, and Marbella. For more secluded beaches, head west of Estepona and past Gibraltar to Tarifa and the Cádiz coast. The beaches change when you hit the Atlantic, becoming appealingly wide with fine golden sand. The winds are usually quite strong here, which means that although you can't read a newspaper while lying out, the conditions for windsurfing and kiteboarding are near perfect.

Beaches are free, and busiest in July, August, and on Sundays May–October when malagueño families arrive for a full day on the beach and lunch at a chiringuito.

OVER THE TOPLESS

In Spain, as in many parts of Europe, it is perfectly acceptable for women to go topless on the beach, although covering up is the norm at beach bars. There are several nude beaches on the Costas; look for the *playa naturista* sign. The most popular are in Maro (near Nerja), Benalnatura (Benalmádena Costa), Cabo Pino (Marbella), and near Tarifa.

LA CARIHUELA, TORREMOLINOS

This former fishing district of Torre-molinos has a wide stretch of beach. The chiringuitos here are some of the best on the Costa, and the promenade, which continues until Benalmádena port, with its striking Asian-inspired architecture and great choice of restaurants and bars, is delightful for strolling.

CARVAJAL, FUENGIROLA

Backed by low-rise buildings and greenery, the beach here is unspoiled and refreshingly low-key. East of Fuengirola center, the Carvajal beach bars have young crowds, with regular live music in summer. It's also an easily accessible beach on the Málaga–Fuengirola train, with a stop within walking distance of the sand.

PLAYA LOS LANCES, TARIFA

This white sandy beach is one of the least spoiled in Andalusia. Near lush vegetation, lagoons, and the occasional campground and boho-chic hotel (*see listing for the Hurricane Hotel*), Tarifa's main beach is famed throughout Europe for its windsurfing and kite-boarding, so expect some real winds: *levante* from the east and *poniente* from the west.

CABO DE GATA, ALMERÍA

Backed by natural parkland, with volcanic rock formations creating dramatic cliffs and secluded bays, Almería's stunning Cabo de Gata coastline includes superb beaches and coves within the protected UNESCO Biosphere Reserve. The fact that most of the beaches here are only accessible via marked footpaths adds to their off-the-beaten-track appeal.

PUERTO BANÚS, MARBELLA

Looking for action? Some great beach scenes flank the world-famous luxurious port. Pedro's Beach is known for its excellent, laid-back Caribbean-style seafood restaurants, good music, and hip, good-looking crowd. Another superb sandy choice are the coves west of the marina, so-called boutique beaches, with club areas and massages available, as well as attractive beaches and tempting shallow waters.

EL SALADILLO, ESTEPONA

Between Marbella and Estepona (take the Cancelada exit off the A7), this relaxed and inviting beach is not as well known as its glitzier neighbors. It's harder to find, so mainly locals in the know frequent it. There are two popular seafood restaurants here, plus a volleyball net, showers, and sun beds and parasols for rent.

With roughly 320 days of sunshine a year, the Costa del Sol well deserves its nickname, "the Sunshine Coast." It's no wonder much of the coast has been built up with resorts and high-rises. Don't despair, though; you can still find some classic Spanish experiences, whether in the old city of Marbella or one of the smaller villages like Casares. And despite the hubbub of high season, visitors can always unwind here, basking or strolling on mile after mile of sandy beach.

Technically, the stretch of Andalusian shore known as the Costa del Sol runs west from the Costa Tropical, near Granada, to the tip of Tarifa, the southernmost point in Europe, just beyond Gibraltar. For most of the Europeans who have flocked here over the past 50 years, though, the Sunshine Coast has been largely restricted to the 70-km (43-mile) sprawl of hotels, vacation villas, golf courses, marinas, and nightclubs between Torremolinos, just west of Málaga, and Estepona, down toward Gibraltar. Since the late 1950s this area has mushroomed from a group of impoverished fishing villages into an overdeveloped seaside playground and retirement haven. The city of Almería and its coastline, the Costa de Almería, is southwest of Granada's Alpujarras region and due east of the Costa Tropical (around 147 km [93 miles] from Almuñécar).

MAJOR REGIONS

South of Spain's Murcia Coast lie the shores of Andalusia, beginning with the **Costa de Almería.** Several of the coastal towns here, including **Agua Amarga,** have a laid-back charm, with miles of sandy beaches and a refreshing lack of high-rise developments. The mineral riches of the surrounding mountains gave rise to Iberia's first true civilization, whose capital can still be glimpsed in the 4,700-year-old ruins of Los Millares, near the village of Santa Fe de Mondújar. The small towns of Níjar and Sorbas maintain an age-old tradition of pottery making and other crafts, and the western coast of **Almería** has tapped unexpected wealth from a parched land, thanks to modern techniques of growing produce in plastic greenhouses. In contrast to the inhospitable landscape of the mountain-fringed Andarax Valley, the area east of Granada's Alpujarras, near Alhama, has a cool climate and gentle landscape, both conducive to making fine wines.

East of Málaga and west of Almería lies the **Costa Tropical.** Housing developments resemble buildings in Andalusian villages rather than the bland high-rises elsewhere, and its tourist onslaught has been mild. A flourishing farming center, the area earns its keep from tropical fruit, including avocados, mangoes, and pawpaws (also known as custard apples). You may find packed beaches and traffic-choked roads at the height of the season, but for most of the year the Costa Tropical is relatively free of other tourists, if not also devoid of expatriates.

The Málaga Province, with the city of **Málaga** and the provincial towns of the upland hills and valleys to the north, creates the kind of contrast that makes travel in Spain so tantalizing. The region's Moorish legacy—tiny streets honeycombing the steamy depths of Málaga, the layout of the farms, and the crops themselves, including olives, grapes, oranges, and lemons—is a unifying visual theme. Ronda and the whitewashed villages of Andalusia behind the Costa del Sol make for one of Spain's most scenic and emblematic driving routes.

To the west of Málaga, along the coast, the sprawling outskirts of **Torremolinos** signal that you're entering the Costa del Sol, with its beaches, high-rise hotels, and serious numbers of tourists. On the far west, you can still discern Estepona's fishing village and Moorish old quarter amid its booming coastal development. Just inland, **Casares** piles whitewashed houses over the bright-blue Mediterranean below.

Planning

When to Go

May, June, and September are the best times to visit this coastal area, when there's plenty of sunshine but fewer tourists than in the hottest season of July and August. Winter can have bright sunny days, but you may feel the chill, and many hotels in the lower price bracket have heat for only a few hours a day; you can also expect several days of rain. Holy Week, the week before Easter Sunday, is a fun time to visit to see the religious processions.

Planning Your Time

Travelers with their own wheels who want a real taste of the area in just a few days could start by exploring the relatively unspoiled villages of the Costa Tropical: wander around quaint Salobreña, then hit the larger coastal resort of Nerja and head inland for a look around pretty Frigiliana.

Move on to Málaga next; it has lots to offer, including several top art museums, excellent restaurants, and some of the best tapas bars in the province. It's also easy to get to stunning, mountaintop Ronda (⇨ *see Chapter 11*), which is also on a bus route.

Hit the coast at Marbella, the Costa del Sol's swankiest resort, and then take a leisurely stroll around Puerto Banús. Next, head west to Gibraltar for a day of shopping and sightseeing before returning to the coast and Torremolinos for a night on the town.

Choose your base carefully, as the various areas here make for very different experiences. Málaga is a vibrant Spanish city, virtually untainted by mass tourism, while Torremolinos is a budget destination catering mostly to the mass market. Fuengirola is quieter, with a large population of middle-aged expatriates; farther west, the Marbella–San Pedro de Alcántara area is more exclusive and expensive.

Getting Here and Around

AIR TRAVEL

Delta Airlines runs direct flights from JFK (New York) to Málaga late May–September and via Charles de Gaulle (Paris) the rest of the year. All other flights from the United States connect in Madrid. British Airways flies several times daily from London (City, Gatwick, and Heathrow) to Málaga, and several budget airlines, such as easyJet, Norwegian Air, and Ryanair also link the two cities. There are direct flights to Málaga from most other major European cities on Iberia or other airlines. Iberia Express/Vueling has five flights daily from Madrid (1 hour 15 minutes), five flights daily from Barcelona (1½ hours), and regular flights from other Spanish cities.

Málaga's Costa del Sol airport is 10 km (6 miles) west of town and is one of Spain's most modern. Trains from the airport into town run every 20 minutes 6:44 am–12:54 am (12 minutes, €1.80) and from the airport to Fuengirola every 20 minutes 5:32 am–11:42 pm (34 minutes, €2.70), stopping at several resorts en route, including Torremolinos and Benalmádena.

From the airport there's also bus service to Málaga every half hour 7 am–midnight and then three buses between midnight and 6 am (€3). At least 10 daily buses (more frequently July–September) run between the airport and Marbella (45 minutes, €6.15–€8.20). Taxi fares from the airport to Málaga, Torremolinos, and other resorts are posted inside the terminal: from the airport to Marbella is about €65, to Torremolinos €20, and to Fuengirola €35. Many of the better hotels and all tour companies will arrange for

pickup at the airport. Uber operates from Málaga Airport to Costa del Sol resorts and Cabify from the airport to Málaga city center. Both services are slightly cheaper than taxis and available via their respective online apps.

AIRPORT CONTACT Aeropuerto Costa del Sol (AGP) (*Aeropuerto de Málaga*) ⊠ *Av. Comandante García Morato s/n, Málaga* ☎ *952/048804* ⊕ *www.aena.es.*

BIKE TRAVEL

The Costa del Sol is famous for its sun and sand, but many people supplement their beach time with mountain-bike forays into the hilly interior, particularly around Ojén, near Marbella, and along the mountain roads around Ronda. One popular route, which affords sweeping vistas, follows the mountain road from Ojén west to Istán. The Costa del Sol's temperate climate is ideal for biking, though it's best not to exert yourself on the trails in July and August, when temperatures soar. There are numerous bike-rental shops in the area, particularly in Marbella, Ronda, and Ojén; many shops also arrange bike excursions. The cost to rent a mountain bike for the day is around €20. Guided bike excursions, which include bikes, support staff, and cars, generally start at about €50 a day.

BIKE RENTAL CONTACT Bike Tours Malaga ⊠ *Calle Vendeja 6, Málaga* ☎ *951/252264* ⊕ *www.biketoursmalaga.com.* **Marbella Rent a Bike** ☎ *952/811062* ⊕ *www.marbellarentabike.com.*

BUS TRAVEL

Until the high-speed AVE train line opens between Antequera and Granada in late 2019, buses are the best way to reach the Costa del Sol from Granada, and, aside from the train service from Málaga to Fuengirola, the best way to get around once you're here. During holidays it's wise to reserve your seat in advance for long-distance travel.

On the Costa del Sol, bus services connect Málaga with Cádiz (2 daily),

Córdoba (4 daily), Granada (20 daily), and Seville (7 daily). In Fuengirola you can catch buses for Mijas, Marbella, Estepona, and Algeciras. The Avanzabus bus company serves most of the Costa del Sol. ALSA serves Granada, Córdoba, Seville, and Nerja. Los Amarillos serves Jerez and Ronda, and Comes runs services to Cádiz. There are also daily buses between Málaga airport and Granada and Seville.

BUS CONTACTS ALSA ☎ *902/422242* ⊕ *www.alsa.es.* **Avanzabus** ☎ *912/722832* ⊕ *www.avanzabus.com.* **Comes** ☎ *956/291168* ⊕ *www.tgcomes.es.* **Los Amarillos** ☎ *902/210317* ⊕ *www. losamarillos.es.*

CAR TRAVEL

A car allows you to explore Andalusia's mountain villages. Mountain driving can be hair-raising but is getting better as highways are improved.

Málaga is 536 km (333 miles) from Madrid, taking the A4 to Córdoba, then the A44 to Granada, the A92 to Antequera, and the A45; 162 km (101 miles) from Córdoba via Antequera; 220 km (137 miles) from Seville; and 131 km (81 miles) from Granada by the shortest route of the A92 to Loja, then the A45 to Málaga.

To take a car into Gibraltar you need, in theory, an insurance certificate and a logbook (a certificate of vehicle ownership). In practice, all you need is your passport as well as a valid driving license. Head for the well-signposted multistory parking garage, as street parking on the Rock is scarce.

NATIONAL CAR-RENTAL AGENCIES Helle Hollis ☎ *952/245544* ⊕ *www.hellehollis. com.*

TAXI TRAVEL

Taxis are plentiful throughout the Costa del Sol and may be hailed on the street or from specified taxi ranks marked "Taxi." Restaurants are usually happy to call a

taxi for you, too. Fares are reasonable, and meters are strictly used. You are not required to tip taxi drivers, though rounding up the amount will be appreciated. Uber operates throughout the Costa del Sol, and Cabify services are available in Málaga city.

TRAIN TRAVEL

Málaga is the main rail terminus in the area, with 13 high-speed trains per day from Madrid (2 hours 30 minutes–3 hours, depending on the train). Málaga is also linked by high-speed train with Barcelona (6 daily, 5 hours 45 minutes–6 hours 35 minutes, depending on the train). Six daily trains also link Seville with Málaga in just under two hours.

High-speed AVE trains from Granada to Málaga began operation in late 2019 and have reduced the journey time to 50 minutes. Málaga's train station is a 15-minute walk from the city center, across the river.

RENFE connects Málaga, Torremolinos, and Fuengirola, stopping at the airport and all resorts along the way. The train leaves Málaga every 20 minutes 5:20 am–11:30 pm, and Fuengirola every 20 minutes 6:10 am–12:20 am. For the city center, get off at the last stop. A daily train connects Málaga and Ronda via the dramatic Chorro gorge (2 hours 30 minutes).

Restaurants

Málaga is best for traditional Spanish cooking, with a wealth of bars and seafood restaurants serving fritura malagueña, the city's famous fried seafood. Torremolinos's Carihuela district is also a good destination for lovers of Spanish seafood. The area's resorts serve every conceivable foreign cuisine, from Thai to the Scandinavian smorgasbord. For delicious cheap eats, try the chiringuitos. Strung out along the beaches, these summer-only restaurants serve seafood fresh off the boats. Because there are so many foreigners here, meals on the coast are served earlier than elsewhere in Andalusia; most restaurants open at 1 or 1:30 for lunch and 7 or 8 for dinner.

Hotels

Most hotels on the developed stretch between Torremolinos and Fuengirola offer large, functional rooms near the sea at competitive rates, but the area's popularity as a budget destination means that most such hotels are booked in high season by package-tour operators. Finding a room at Easter, in July and August, or over holiday weekends can be difficult if you haven't reserved in advance. In July and August many hotels require a stay of at least three days. Málaga is an increasingly attractive base for visitors to this corner of Andalusia and has some good hotels. Marbella, meanwhile, has more than its fair share of grand lodgings, including some of Spain's most expensive rooms. Gibraltar's handful of hotels tends to be more expensive than most comparable lodgings in Spain.

There are also apartments and villas for short- or long-term stays, ranging from traditional Andalusian farmhouses to luxury villas. One excellent source for apartment and villa rentals is **Spain Holiday** (☎ 951/204601 ⊕ www.spain-holiday. com). For Marbella, you can also try **Nordica Rentals** (☎ 952/811552 ⊕ www.nordicarentals.com), and, for high-end rentals, **The Luxury Villa Collection** (⊕ www. theluxuryvillacollection.com). Our local writers vet every hotel to recommend the best overnights in each price category, from budget to expensive. Unless otherwise specified, you can expect a private bath, phone, and TV in your room. *Hotel reviews have been shortened. For full information, visit Fodors.com.*

What It Costs in Euros

	$	$$	$$$	$$$$
RESTAURANTS				
	under €12	€12–€17	€18–€22	over €22
HOTELS				
	under €90	€90–€125	€126–€180	over €180

Golf in the Sun

Nicknamed the "Costa del Golf," the Sun Coast has over 70 golf courses within putting distance of the Mediterranean. Most of the courses are between Rincón de la Victoria (east of Málaga) and Gibraltar. The best time for golfing is October–June; greens fees are lower in high summer. Check out the comprehensive website ⊕ www.golfinspain.com for up-to-date information.

Tours

Several companies run one- and two-day excursions from Costa del Sol resorts. You can book with local travel agents and hotels; excursions leave from Málaga, Torremolinos, Fuengirola, Marbella, and Estepona, with prices varying by departure point. Most tours last half a day, and in most cases you can be picked up at your hotel. Popular tours include Málaga, Gibraltar, the Cuevas de Nerja, Mijas, Tangier, and Ronda. The Costa del Sol's varied landscape is also wonderful for hiking and walking, and several companies offer walking or cycling tours.

TOUR OPERATORS
Birdaytrip
SPECIAL-INTEREST | One-day trips, holidays and scheduled trips to bird-watch on the Costa del Sol. Costs are per group of maximum four people. ⊠ *Málaga* ⊕ *www.birdaytrip.es* ✉ *From €135.*

John Keo Walking Tours

WALKING TOURS | This company provides guided walks and hikes around the eastern Costa del Sol, weekdays only. Reservations are essential. ☎ *647/273502* ⊕ *www.hikingwalkingspain.com* ✉ *From €25.*

Sierra MTB

BICYCLE TOURS | A good range of rural and urban guided cycling tours suit all levels. Weekend and weeklong packages, including accommodations and a different bike ride every day, are available in addition to day trips. ✉ *Málaga* ☎ *616/295251* ⊕ *www.sierracycling.com* ✉ *From €80.*

Viajes Rusadir

EXCURSIONS | This local firm specializes in Costa del Sol excursions and private tours. ☎ *952/463458* ⊕ *www.viajesrusadir.com* ✉ *From €30.*

Visitor Information

The official website for the Costa del Sol is ⊕ *www.visitacostadelsol.com*; it has good information on sightseeing and events, guides to towns and villages, and contact details for the regional and local tourist offices, which are listed under their respective towns and cities. Tourist offices are generally open Monday–Saturday 10–7 (until 8 in summer) and Sunday 10–2.

The Cabo de Gata Nature Reserve

40 km (25 miles) east of Almería, 86 km (53 miles) south of Mojácar.

The southeast corner of Spain is one of the country's last unspoiled wildernesses, and much of the coastline is part of a highly protected nature reserve. San José, the largest village, has a pleasant bay, though these days the village has rather outgrown itself and can be very busy in summer. Those preferring smaller, quieter destinations should look farther north, at places such as Agua Amarga and the often-deserted beaches nearby.

GETTING HERE AND AROUND

You need your own wheels to explore the nature reserve and surrounding villages, including San José. When it's time to hit the beach, Playa de los Genoveses and Playa Monsul, to the south of San José, are some of the best. A rough road follows the coast around the spectacular cape, eventually linking up with the N332 to Almería. Alternatively, follow the signs north for the towns of Níjar (approximately 20 km [12 miles] north) and Sorbas (32 km [20 miles] northeast of Níjar); both towns are famed for their distinctive green-glazed pottery, which you can buy directly from workshops.

◉ Sights

Parque Natural Marítimo y Terrestre Cabo de Gata–Níjar

NATURE PRESERVE | Birds are the main attraction at this nature reserve just south of San José; it's home to several species native to Africa, including the *camachuelo trompetero* (large-beaked bullfinch), which is not found anywhere else outside Africa. Check out the Centro Las Amoladeras visitor center at the park entrance, which has an exhibit and information on the region and organizes guided walks and tours of the area. ✉ *San José* ✛ *Road from Almería to Cabo de Gata, Km 6* ☎ *950/160435* ⊕ *www.juntadeandalucia.es* ⊘ *Closed Mon. and Tues.*

⊕ Beaches

El Playazo

BEACH—SIGHT | *Playazo* literally means "one great beach," and this sandy cove is certainly one of the gems in the Cabo de Gata nature reserve. Just a few minutes' drive from the village of Rodalquilar (once home to Spain's only gold mine), the yellow-sand beach is surrounded by ocher-color volcanic rock; an 18th-century fortress stands at one end. These are sheltered waters, so bathing is safe and warm, and the offshore rocks make for great snorkeling. This beach is deserted during most of the year, and its isolation and lack of amenities mean that even in the summer months you won't come across too many other beachgoers. Although nude bathing isn't officially allowed here, it is tolerated. **Amenities:** none. **Best for:** snorkeling; solitude; sunrise. ✉ *Rodalquilar, San José.*

Playa de los Genoveses
BEACH—SIGHT | Named after the Genovese sailors who landed here in 1127 to aid King Alfonso VII, this beach is one of the area's best known and most beautiful. The long, sandy expanse is backed by pines, eucalyptus trees, and low-rising dunes. The sea is shallow, warm, and crystal clear here—snorkeling is popular around the rocks at either end of the cove. Free parking is available mid-September–mid-June; in July and August, you must park in nearby San José and take a free shuttle bus to the beach. The beach can also be reached via an easy coastal walk from San José, a 7-km (4½-mile) round-trip. The beach has no amenities to speak of, so take plenty of water if it's hot. **Amenities:** parking. **Best for:** snorkeling; solitude; sunset; walking. ✉ *San José.*

🛏 Hotels

Hostal La Isleta
$ | **B&B/INN** | This low-rise, white, blocky building with blue trim is nothing fancy—what you're paying for is the location, within a stone's throw of the beach on a charming bay, with superb, relaxing sea views. **Pros:** waterfront location; excellent seafood restaurant; traditional Spanish hostal. **Cons:** no frills; can be noisy with families in summer; basic breakfast. [$] *Rooms from: €70* ✉ *Calle Isleta del Moro, San José* ☎ *950/389713* 🛏 *10 rooms* 🍴 *No meals.*

Agua Amarga

22 km (14 miles) north of San José, 55 km (34 miles) east of Almería.

Like other coastal hamlets, Agua Amarga started out in the 18th century as a tuna-fishing port. These days, as perhaps the most pleasant village on the Cabo de Gata coast, it attracts lots of visitors, although it remains much less developed than San José. One of the coast's best beaches is just to the north: the dramatically named **Playa de los Muertos** (Beach of the Dead), a long stretch of fine gravel bookended with volcanic outcrops.

GETTING HERE AND AROUND

If you're driving here from Almería, follow signs to the airport, then continue north on the A7; Agua Amarga is signposted just north of the Parque Natural Cabo de Gata. The village itself is small enough to explore easily on foot.

🍴 Restaurants

La Palmera
$$ | **SPANISH** | At the far eastern end of the beach, the terrace at this hotel restaurant sits right on the sand; get a table here rather than inside the less impressive dining room. Fresh fish, locally caught and grilled, is the highlight of the menu, which also includes simple salads and plates of fried fish. **Known for:** locally caught fish; beachfront dining; arroz a banda (rice with fish and aioli). [$] *Average main: €16* ✉ *Calle Aguada 4* ☎ *950/138208* 🌐 *hostalrestaurantelapalmera.net/en* 🕒 *Closed for 6 wks in winter. Call to check.*

Dramatic views of the coastline from the Cabo de Gata natural park

Hotels

Hotel El Tío Kiko

$$$ | **HOTEL** | On a hill to the west of the village, this modern luxury hotel has commanding sea views and is close enough to the main beach to walk (but far enough to enjoy peace and quiet). **Pros:** sea views; rooms have balconies, some with hot tubs; varied breakfast. **Cons:** up a hill; could be too quiet for some; adults-only from mid-June–mid-September. [$] *Rooms from: €180* ✉ *Calle Embarque 12* ☎ *950/138080* 🌐 *www.eltiokiko.com* 🛏 *27 rooms* 🍴 *Free Breakfast.*

Almería

183 km (114 miles) east of Málaga.

Warmed by the sunniest climate in Andalusia, Almería is a youthful Mediterranean city, basking in sweeping views of the sea from its coastal perch and close to several excellent beaches. It's also a capital of the grape industry, thanks to its wonderfully mild climate in spring and fall. Rimmed by tree-lined boulevards and some landscaped squares, the city's core is a maze of narrow, winding alleys formed by flat-roofed, distinctly Mudejar houses. Now surrounded by modern apartment blocks, these dazzlingly white older homes continue to give Almería an Andalusian flavor. Barely touched by tourism, this compact city is well worth a visit—allow an overnight stay to take in the main sights en route to or from Cabo de Gata or Málaga. Almería was Gastronomic Capital of Spain in 2019 so be sure to try the local fare and tapas bars, where you'll be offered a free (and usually elaborate) tapa with your drink.

GETTING HERE AND AROUND

Bus No. 30 (€1.05) runs roughly every 35 minutes 7 am–11 pm from Almería airport to the center of town (Calle del Doctor Gregorio Marañón).

The city center is compact, and most of the main sights are within easy strolling distance of each other.

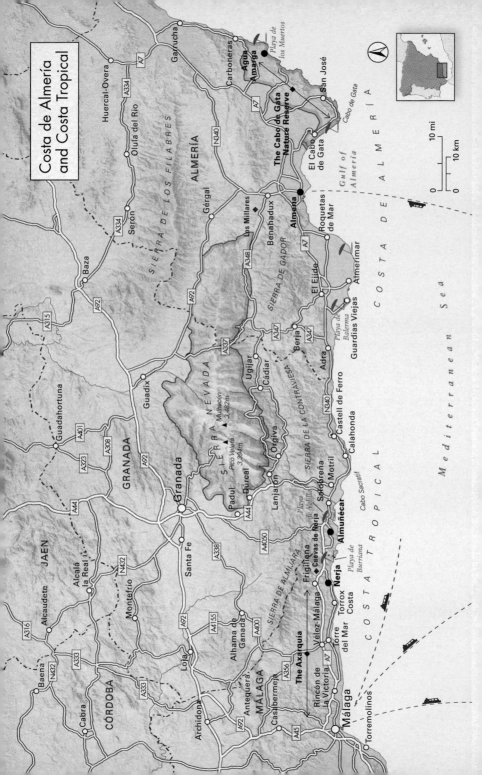

VISITOR INFORMATION

CONTACTS Almería Visitor Information

✉ *Pl. de la Constitución* ☎ *950/210538*
⊕ *www.turismodealmeria.org.*

 Sights

Alcazaba

MILITARY SITE | Dominating the city is this fortress, built by Caliph Abd ar-Rahman I and given a bell tower by Carlos III. From here you have sweeping views of the port and city. Among the ruins of the fortress, which was damaged by earthquakes in 1522 and 1560, are landscaped gardens of rock flowers and cacti. ✉ *Calle Almanzor* ☎ *950/801008* 🗹 *Free* ⊙ *Closed Mon.*

Cathedral

RELIGIOUS SITE | Below the *alcazaba* (citadel) is the local cathedral, with buttressed towers that give it the appearance of a castle. It's in Gothic style, but with some classical touches around the doors. Guided tours are available, and admission includes a visit to the ecclesiastical museum. ✉ *Pl. de la Catedral* ☎ *950/234848* 🗹 *€5.*

Mercado Central de Almería

MARKET | Built in 1892 in a Modernist style, Almería's main market provides a colorful insight into the province's long list of fresh produce. The iron structure, characteristic of late 19th-century buildings, is enclosed by a pretty tiled facade. Don't miss the plaque marking Marie Curie's visit here in 1931. ✉ *Calle Aguilar de Campo s/n* ⊙ *Closed Sun.*

★ Refugios de la Guerra Civil (*Civil War Shelters*)

HISTORIC SITE | Almería, the last bastion of the Republican government during the Spanish Civil War, was hit by 754 bombs launched via air and sea by Nationalist forces. To protect civilians, 4½ km (2¾ miles) of tunnels were built under the city to provide shelter for more than 34,000 people. About 1 km (½ mile)

Los Millares

This important archaeological site is nearly 2½ km (1½ miles) southwest from the village of Santa Fe de Mondújar and 19 km (12 miles) from Almería. This collection of ruins scattered on a windswept hilltop was the birthplace of civilization in Spain nearly 5,000 years ago. Large tombs show that the community had an advanced society, and the formidable defense walls indicate it had something to protect. A series of concentric fortifications shows that the settlement grew, eventually holding some 2,000 people. The town was inhabited from 2700 to 1800 BC and came to dominate the entire region. Guided tours are available: call in advance to book.

can now be visited on a guided tour that covers the food stores, sleeping quarters, and an operating theater for the wounded, with its original medical equipment. ✉ *Pl. Manuel Pérez García s/n* ☎ *950/268696* 🗹 *€3* ⊙ *Closed Mon.*

🍴 Restaurants

La Encina

$$$ | **SPANISH** | This justly popular restaurant is housed in an 1860s building that also incorporates an 11th-century Moorish well. Time may have stood still with the setting, but the cuisine reflects a modern twist on traditional dishes, including seafood mains like *bacalao con cebolla, miel y pasas con cruijiente de espinacas* (cod with onion, honey, and raisins) or *rabo de novillo con almendras* (oxtail stew with almonds). **Known for:** creative tapas; wine list; bacalao. 🅢 *Average main: €18* ✉ *Calle Marín 3* ☎ *950/273429* ⊕ *www.restaurantelaencina.net* ⊙ *Closed Mon.*

Valentín

$$$ | **SPANISH** | This popular, central spot serves fine regional specialties, such as *arroz de marisco* (rice with seafood), *cazuela de rape en salsa de almendras* (monkfish stew with almond sauce), and the delicious *kokotxas de bacalao en salsa de ostras* (cod cheeks in oyster sauce). The surroundings are rustic-yet-elegant Andalusian: whitewashed walls, dark wood, and exposed brick. **Known for:** rice dishes; rustic-chic setting; can be hard to get a table. [$] *Average main: €21* ✉ *Calle Tenor Iribarne 10* ☎ *950/264475* ⏲ *Closed Jan.*

Hotels

Aire Hotel

$$ | **HOTEL** | In the heart of the old quarter, early-19th-century architecture is paired with comfortable and up-to-date amenities in this boutique hotel with strong design features. **Pros:** central location; terrace with great views; underground Arab baths are included in the rate. **Cons:** in-room showers offer no privacy; street noise in some rooms; some rooms have no views. [$] *Rooms from: €110* ✉ *Pl. de la Constitución 4* ☎ *950/282096* 🌐 *www.airehotelalmeria.com* 🛏 *10 rooms* 🍴 *No meals.*

Hotel Catedral

$ | **HOTEL** | In full view of the cathedral, this small hotel combines traditional charm (it has kept many of its original mid-19th-century features, including a stunning arched entryway) with modern elegance. **Pros:** cathedral views; rooftop terrace with plunge pool; good breakfast. **Cons:** reception staff could be friendlier; hotel events can be noisy; cathedral church bells not for everyone. [$] *Rooms from: €75* ✉ *Pl. de la Catedral 8* ☎ *950/278178* 🌐 *www.hotelcatedral.net* 🛏 *20 rooms* 🍴 *No meals.*

Nuevo Torreluz Hotel

$ | **HOTEL** | Value is the overriding attraction at this comfortable and elegant modern hotel, which has slick, bright rooms and the kind of amenities you'd expect to come at a higher price. **Pros:** great central location; large rooms; good value. **Cons:** no pool; breakfast served in hotel next door; rooms in the main building are more expensive. [$] *Rooms from: €70* ✉ *Pl. Flores 10* ☎ *950/234399* 🌐 *www.torreluz.com* 🛏 *98 rooms* 🍴 *No meals.*

Nightlife

In Almería, the action's on **Plaza Flores,** moving down to the beach in summer.

Performing Arts

★ **Peña El Taranto**

DANCE | For more than 55 years, this excellent venue (home to the city's Arab water deposits) has been one of the main centers for flamenco in Andalusia, and foot-stomping live flamenco and concerts are performed every two weeks. Check in advance for exact times and dates. ✉ *Calle Tenor Iribarne 20* ☎ *950/235057* 🌐 *www.eltaranto.com.*

Almuñécar

85 km (53 miles) east of Málaga.

This small-time resort with a shingle beach is popular with Spanish and Northern European vacationers. It's been a fishing village since Phoenician times, 3,000 years ago, when it was called Sexi; later, the Moors built a castle here for the treasures of Granada's kings. The road west from Motril and Salobreña passes through what was the empire of the sugar barons, who brought prosperity to Málaga's province in the 19th century: the cane fields now give way to lychees, limes, mangoes, pawpaws, and olives.

A religious procession in Almuñécar

The village is actually two, separated by the dramatic rocky headland of Punta de la Mona. To the east is Almuñécar proper, and to the west is **La Herradura,** a quiet fishing community. Between the two is the Marina del Este yacht harbor, which, along with La Herradura, is a popular diving center. A renowned jazz festival takes place annually in July, often showcasing big names.

GETTING HERE AND AROUND

The A7 runs north of town. There is an efficient bus service to surrounding towns and cities, including Málaga, Granada, Nerja, and, closer afield, La Herradura. Almuñécar's town center is well laid out for strolling, and the local tourist office has information on bicycle and scooter rental.

VISITOR INFORMATION

CONTACTS Almuñécar ⊠ *Palacete de la Najarra, Av. de Europa* ☎ *958/631125* ⊕ *www.turismoalmunecar.es.*

Sights

Castillo de San Miguel (*St. Michael's Castle*)

CASTLE/PALACE | A Roman fortress once stood here, later enlarged by the Moors, but the castle's present aspect, crowning the city, owes more to 16th-century additions. The building was bombed during the Peninsular War in the 19th century, and what was left was used as a cemetery until the 1990s. You can wander the ramparts and peer into the dungeon; the skeleton at the bottom is a reproduction of human remains discovered on the spot. ⊠ *Calle San Miguel Bajo* ☎ *958/838623* ⊠ *€3, includes admission to Cueva de Siete Palacios* ⊗ *Closed Mon.*

Cueva de Siete Palacios (*Cave of Seven Palaces*)

HISTORIC SITE | Beneath the Castillo de San Miguel is this large, vaulted stone cellar of Roman origin, now Almuñécar's archaeological museum. The collection is small but interesting, with Phoenician,

Roman, and Moorish artifacts. ✉ *Calle San Miguel Bajo* ☎ *958/838623* 🎫 *€3, includes admission to Castillo de San Miguel* ◷ *Closed Mon.*

Restaurants

★ El Arbol Blanco Playa
$$ | INTERNATIONAL | Now located on the seafront (it was once a hike to get to the former hilltop location), this superb restaurant has a light and airy dining room, an outside terrace, and stunning sea views. The dishes, all creatively presented, include traditional options like oven-baked lamb as well as more innovative choices such as skate in Champagne sauce, a perfect pair for the excellent local white wine, Calvente blanco. The desserts are sublime, particularly the cheesecake. 💲 *Average main: €16* ✉ *Paseo Marítimo Reina Sofía* ✛ *Next to Aquatrópic* ☎ *958/634038* ◷ *Closed Wed. and Jan. and Feb.*

🛏 Hotels

Casablanca
$$ | HOTEL | This quaint, family-run hotel comes with a pink-and-white neo-Moorish facade, a choice location next to the beach and near the botanical park, and comfortable rooms that are all different. **Pros:** great location; intimate, family-run atmosphere; all rooms have private balconies or views. **Cons:** rooms vary, and some are small; parking can be difficult; only some rooms have sea views. 💲 *Rooms from: €95* ✉ *Pl. San Cristóbal 4* ☎ *958/635575* ⊕ *www.hotelcasablancaalmunecar.com* ↻ *39 rooms* ⦿ *No meals.*

Nerja

52 km (32 miles) east of Málaga, 22 km (14 miles) west of Almuñécar.

Nerja—the name comes from the Moorish word *narixa*, meaning "abundant springs"—has a large community of

Salobreña

About 13 km (8 miles) east of Almuñécar, this unspoiled village of near-perpendicular streets and old white houses on a steep hill beneath a Moorish fortress is a true Andalusian *pueblo* (village), separated from the beachfront restaurants and bars in the newer part of town. It's great for a quick visit, and the pebbly beach makes a nice walk. You can reach Salobreña by descending through the mountains from Granada or by continuing west from Almería on the A7.

expats, who live mainly outside town in *urbanizaciones* ("village" developments). The old village is on a headland above small beaches and rocky coves, which offer reasonable swimming despite the gray, gritty sand. In July and August, Nerja is packed with tourists, but the rest of the year it's a pleasure to wander the old town's narrow streets.

GETTING HERE AND AROUND
Nerja is a speedy hour's drive east from Málaga on the A7. If you're driving, park in the underground lot just west of the Balcón de Europa (it's signposted) off Calle La Cruz. The town is small enough to explore on foot.

VISITOR INFORMATION
CONTACTS Nerja ✉ *Calle Carmen 1* ☎ *952/521531* ⊕ *turismo.nerja.es.*

Sights

★ Balcón de Europa
PROMENADE | FAMILY | The highlight of Nerja, this tree-lined promenade is on a promontory just off the central square, with magnificent views of the mountains and sea. You can gaze far off into the horizon using the strategically placed telescopes, or use this as a starting point

for a horse-and-carriage clip-clop ride around town. Open-air concerts are held here in July and August. ✉ *Nerja*.

Cuevas de Nerja (*Nerja Caves*)
CAVE | Between Almuñécar and Nerja, these caves are on a road surrounded by giant cliffs and dramatic seascapes. Signs point to the cave entrance above the village of Maro, 4 km (2½ miles) east of Nerja. Its spires and turrets, created by millennia of dripping water, are now floodlit for better views. One suspended pinnacle, 200 feet long, is the world's largest known stalactite. The cave painting of seals discovered here may be the oldest example of art in existence—and the only one known to have been painted by Neanderthals. The awesome subterranean chambers create an evocative setting for concerts and ballets during the Nerja Festival of Music and Dance, held annually during June to July. There is also a bar-restaurant near the entrance with a spacious dining room that has superb views. ■ TIP→ **Afternoon visits are by guided tour only, September–June. They take around 45 minutes so arrive at least an hour before closing time. Private tours in English are available (€15, bookable online) All ticket prices are cheaper online.** ✉ *Maro* ☎ *952/529520* ⊕ *www.cuevadenerja. com* 🎫 *€10*.

Beaches

Las Alberquillas
BEACH—SIGHT | One of the string of coves on the coastline west of Nerja, this beach of gray sand mixed with shingle is backed by pine trees and scrub that perfume the air. Reachable only via a stony track down the cliffs, this protected beach is one of the few on the Costa del Sol to be almost completely untouched by tourism. Its moderate waves mean you need to take care when bathing. The snorkeling around the rocks at either end of the beach is among the best in the area. This spot's seclusion makes the beach a favorite with couples and

Frigiliana

On an inland mountain ridge overlooking the sea, this pretty village has spectacular views and an old quarter of narrow, cobbled streets and dazzling white houses decorated with pots of geraniums. It was the site of one of the last battles between the Christians and the Moors. Frigiliana is a short drive from the highway to the village; if you don't have a car, you can take a bus here from Nerja, which is 8 km (5 miles) away.

nudists—it's reasonably quiet even at the height of summer. Limited parking is available off the N340 highway, but there are no amenities, so take plenty of water. **Amenities:** none. **Best for:** nudists; snorkeling; solitude. ✉ *N340, Km 299*.

🍴 Restaurants

★ Oliva
$$$$ | MEDITERRANEAN | Mediterranean cuisine based on fresh, local produce takes center stage at this restaurant, which has both a minimalist, intimate dining room and a pleasant patio that's heated in winter. Highlights include the sole mille-feuille, baby garlic, and ginger mayo, and *pluma ibérica* (Iberian pork) with *ras el hanout* (Moroccan spice mix) and eggplant puree. **Known for:** the best innovative cuisine in town; wine list; Iberian pork. 💲 *Average main: €25* ✉ *Calle La Pintada 7* ☎ *952/522988* ⊕ *www. restauranteoliva.com*.

🛏 Hotels

★ Hotel Carabeo
$$ | B&B/INN | Down a side street near the center of town but still near the sea, this British-owned boutique hotel combines a great location and views with

comfortable, pleasant rooms. **Pros:** sea views; great location; excellent restaurant. **Cons:** not open out of season; difficult to get a room in high season; rooms are comfortable but compact. $ *Rooms from: €100* ✉ *Calle Hernando de Carabeo 34* ☎ *952/525444* ⊕ *www.hotelcarabeo. com* ⊘ *Closed late Oct.–late Mar.* ⬡ *7 rooms* ⭐ *Free Breakfast.*

🎭 Performing Arts

El Colono
DANCE | Although the flamenco show is undeniably touristy, this club has an authentic *olé* atmosphere with good dancers. The food is reasonable, and local specialties, including paella and seafood soup, are served. Dinner shows (€38), with a three-course meal, begin at 7:30 pm on Wednesday. ✉ *Calle Granada 6* ☎ *678/672350* ⊘ *Closed Jan.–Easter.*

The Axarquía

Vélez-Málaga: 36 km (22 miles) east of Málaga.

The Axarquía region stretches from Nerja to Málaga, and the area's charm lies in its mountainous interior, peppered with pueblos, vineyards, and tiny farms. Its coast consists of narrow, pebbly beaches and drab fishing villages on either side of the high-rise resort town of Torre del Mar.

GETTING HERE AND AROUND
Although bus routes are fairly comprehensive throughout the Axarquía, reaching the smaller villages may involve long delays; renting a car is convenient and lets you get off the beaten track and experience some of the beautiful unspoiled hinterland in this little-known area. The four-lane A7 highway cuts across the region a few miles in from the coast; traffic on the old coastal road (N340) is slower.

VISITOR INFORMATION
CONTACTS Cómpeta ✉ *Av. de la Constitución, Cómpeta* ☎ *952/553685* ⊕ *www.competa.es.*

TOURS
La Rosilla
SPECIAL-INTEREST | Experience local food and culture at a traditional *finca* (traditional estate or ranch) in the heart of the Axarquía. ☎ *659/734401* ⊕ *larosilla-catering.com/cooking-culture* ⬡ *From €65.*

👁 Sights

Ruta del Sol y del Vino and Ruta de la Pasa
SCENIC DRIVE | The Axarquía has a number of tourist trails that take in the best of local scenery, history, and culture. Two of the best are the Ruta del Sol y del Vino (Sunshine and Wine Trail), through Algarrobo, Cómpeta (the main wine center), and Nerja; and the Ruta de la Pasa (Raisin Trail), which goes through Moclinejo, El Borge, and Comares. The trails are especially spectacular during the late-summer grape harvest or in late autumn, when the leaves of the vines turn gold.

Vélez-Málaga
TOWN | The capital of the Axarquía is a pleasant agricultural town of white houses, mango and avocado orchards, and vineyards. It's worth a half-day trip to see the **Thursday market,** Contemporary Art Centre (CAC), the ruins of a **Moorish castle,** and the church of **Santa María la Mayor,** built in the Mudejar style on the site of a mosque that was destroyed when the town fell to the Christians in 1487. The town also has a thriving flamenco scene with regular events (⊕ *www. flamencoabierto.com).* ✉ *Vélez-Málaga.*

🍴 Restaurants

El Convento
$$ | **SPANISH** | Housed in a restored convent, this cozy restaurant offers atmospheric dining inside and a pleasant terrace outside. Excellent tapas and

tostas (toppings on toasted bread) are available at the bar in addition to an extensive menu of local and international dishes in the restaurant. **Known for:** good value dining; tostas; croquettes. [$] *Average main: €12* ✉ *Calle de los Moros 5, Vélez-Málaga* ☎ *951/250100.*

🛏 Hotels

Hotel Palacio Blanco

$$ | **HOTEL** | This light and airy boutique hotel is housed in a charmingly restored 18th-century mansion just a short distance from the castle. **Pros:** spacious rooms; rooftop terrace with pool; central location. **Cons:** no on-site parking; first-floor rooms are a little dark; few facilities. [$] *Rooms from: €95* ✉ *Calle Felix Lomas 4, Vélez-Málaga* ☎ *952/549174* 🌐 *www.palacioblanco.com* 🛏 *9 rooms* 🍴 *Free Breakfast.*

Málaga

175 km (109 miles) southeast of Córdoba.

Málaga is one of southern Spain's most welcoming and happening cities, and it more than justifies a visit. Visitor figures soared after the Museo Picasso opened in 2003 and again after a new cruise-ship terminal opened in 2011, and the city has had a well-earned face-lift, with many of its historic buildings restored or undergoing restoration. The area between the river and the port has been transformed into the Soho art district, and since the arrival of three new art museums in 2015, the city has become one of southern Europe's centers for art. Alongside all this rejuvenation, some great shops and lively bars and restaurants have sprung up all over the center.

True, the approach from the airport certainly isn't that pretty, and you'll be greeted by huge 1970s high-rises that march determinedly toward Torremolinos. But don't give up: in its center and eastern suburbs, this city of about 550,000 people is a pleasant port, with ancient streets and lovely villas amid exotic foliage. Blessed with a subtropical climate, it's covered in lush vegetation and averages some 324 days of sunshine a year.

Central Málaga lies between the Río Guadalmedina and the port, and the city's main attractions are all here. The Centro de Arte Contemporáneo (CAC) sits next to the river; to the east lies the Soho district, hoisted from its former seedy red-light reputation to a vibrant cultural hub with galleries and up-and-coming restaurants. Around La Alameda boulevard (mostly pedestrianized in 2019), with its giant weeping fig trees, is old-town Málaga: elegant squares, pedestrian shopping streets such as Calle Marqués de Larios, and the major monuments, which are often tucked away in labyrinthine alleys.

Eastern Málaga starts with the pleasant suburbs of El Palo and Pedregalejo, once traditional fishing villages. Here you can eat fresh fish in the numerous chiringuitos and stroll Pedregalejo's seafront promenade or the tree-lined streets of El Limonar. A few blocks west is Málaga's bullring, **La Malagueta,** built in 1874, and Muelle Uno (port-front commercial center), whose striking glass cube is home to the Centre Pompidou. It's great for a drink and for soaking up views of the old quarter.

GETTING HERE AND AROUND

If you're staying at one of the coastal resorts between Málaga and Fuengirola, the easiest way to reach Málaga is via the train (every 20 minutes). If you're driving, there are several well-signposted underground parking lots, and it's not that daunting to negotiate by car. Málaga has two metro lines from the west, and both reach central train and bus stations; extension to the center is due in late 2020.

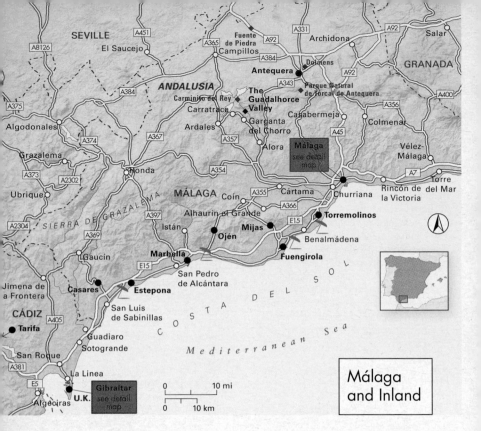

Málaga is mostly flat, so the best way to explore it is on foot or by bike via the good network of designated bike paths. To get an overview of the city in a day, hop on the Málaga Tour City Sightseeing Bus. There is a comprehensive bus network, too, and the tourist office can advise on routes and schedules. Taxis are readily available and Cabify and Uber both operate in Málaga city.

BIKE RENTAL CONTACT Málaga Bike Tours ✉ *Calle Trinidad Grund 5* ☎ *606/978513* ⊕ *www.malagabiketours.eu.*

BUS CONTACT Málaga Bus Station ✉ *Paseo de los Tilos* ☎ *952/350061* ⊕ *www.estabus.emtsam.es.*

CAR RENTAL CONTACTS Europcar ✉ *Málaga Costa del Sol Airport* ☎ *911/505000* ⊕ *www.europcar.es.* **Niza**

Cars ✉ *Málaga Costa del Sol Airport* ☎ *952/236179* ⊕ *www.nizacars.es.*

TAXI COMPANY Unitaxi ☎ *952/320000* ⊕ *www.unitaxi.es.*

TRAIN INFORMATION Málaga Train Station ✉ *Esplanada de la Estación* ☎ *912/320320* ⊕ *www.renfe.com.*

TOURS
Málaga Tour City Sightseeing Bus
BUS TOURS | This open-top, hop-on hop-off tour bus gives you an overview of Málaga's main sites in a day, including the Gibralfaro. Buy tickets online ahead of your trip or when you board the bus. ✉ *Málaga* ⊕ *www.city-sightseeing.com* 🎫 *€18.*

Spain Food Sherpas
GUIDED TOURS | Eat your way around Málaga with the Taste of Tapas Tour or the evening Wine and Tapas Tour with

local guides who know their stuff when it comes to the city's culinary culture. ⊠ *Málaga* ☎ *644/329806* ⊕ *www.spain-foodsherpas.com* ⊠ *From €61.*

VISITOR INFORMATION
CONTACTS Guide to Malaga ⊕ *www. guidetomalaga.com* . **Málaga** ⊠ *Pl. de la Marina, Paseo del Parque* ☎ *951/926620* ⊕ *www.malagaturismo.com.*

👁 Sights

Alcazaba
ARCHAEOLOGICAL SITE | Just beyond the ruins of a Roman theater on Calle Alcazabilla stands Málaga's greatest monument. This fortress was begun in the 8th century, when Málaga was the principal port of the Moorish kingdom, although most of the present structure dates to the 11th century. The inner palace was built between 1057 and 1063, when the Moorish emirs took up residence; Ferdinand and Isabella lived here for a while after conquering the city in 1487. The ruins are dappled with orange trees and bougainvillea and include a small museum; from the highest point you can see over the park and port. ⊠ *Málaga* ⊹ *Entrance on Calle Alcazabilla* 🎫 *From €4 (free Sun. from 2 pm).*

Centre Pompidou Málaga
MUSEUM | The only branch outside France of the Centre Pompidou in Paris opened in March 2015 in the striking glass cube designed by Daniel Buren at Muelle Uno on Málaga port. Housing more than 80 paintings and photographs, the museum showcases 20th- and 21st-century modern art, with works by Kandinsky, Chagall, Scurti, Miró, and Picasso on permanent display. There are also regular temporary exhibitions each year. ⊠ *Pasaje Doctor Carrillo Casaux s/n* ☎ *951/926200* ⊕ *www.centrepompidou-malaga. eu* 🎫 *From €7 (free Sun. from 4 pm)* ⊘ *Closed Tues.*

Centro de Arte Contemporáneo (*Contemporary Arts Center*)
MUSEUM | This museum includes photographic studies and paintings, some of them immense. The 7,900 square feet of bright exhibition space is used to showcase ultramodern artistic trends—the four exhibitions feature changing exhibits from the permanent collection, two temporary shows, and one show dedicated to up-and-coming Spanish artists. The gallery attracts world-class modern artists like Mark Ryden, KAWS, and Ai Weiwei. Outside, don't miss the giant murals behind the museum painted by the street artists Shepard Fairey (aka Obey) and Dean Stockton (aka D*Face). ⊠ *Alemania s/n* ☎ *952/120055* ⊕ *www. cacmalaga.org* 🎫 *Free* ⊘ *Closed Mon.*

Gibralfaro (*Fortress*)
HISTORIC SITE | Surrounded by magnificent vistas and floodlit at night, these fortifications were built for Yusuf I in the 14th century; the Moors called them Jebelfaro, from the Arab word for "mount" and the Greek word for "lighthouse," after a beacon that stood here to guide ships into the harbor and warn of pirates. The lighthouse has been succeeded by a small parador. ⊠ *Gibralfaro Mountain* ⊹ *Drive by way of Calle Victoria, or take Bus No. 35 (10 departures per day, roughly every 45 mins 10–7) from stop in park near Pl. de la Marina* 🎫 *From €4 (free Sun. from 2 pm).*

La Concepción
GARDEN | This botanical garden was created in 1855 by the daughter of the British consul, who married a Spanish shipping magnate—the captains of the Spaniard's fleet had standing orders to bring back seedlings and cuttings from every "exotic" port of call. The wisteria pergola, in bloom in early April, is one of the highlights. The garden is just off the exit road to Granada—too far to walk, but well worth the cab fare or the bus journey (No. 2 from La Alameda, then a 20-minute walk or on the Málaga Tour

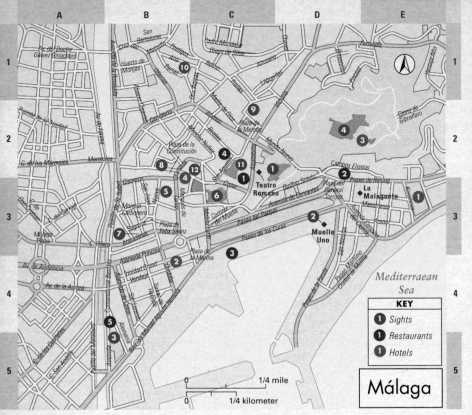

Sights ▼

1 Alcazaba.................**C2**

2 Centre Pompidou
   Málaga...................**D3**

3 Centro de Arte
   Contemporáneo.........**B5**

4 Gibralfaro...............**D2**

5 La Concepción..........**B3**

6 Málaga Cathedral.......**C3**

7 Mercado de
   Atarazanas.............**B3**

8 Museo Carmen Thyssen
   Málaga..................**B2**

9 Museo Casa Natal
   de Picasso..............**C2**

10 Museo del Vidrio y
   Cristal..................**B1**

11 Museo Picasso
   Málaga..................**C2**

12 Pasaje Chinitas.........**B2**

Restaurants ▼

1 Eboka.....................**C3**

2 El Ambigú
   de la Coracha...........**D2**

3 El Palmeral...............**C3**

4 Los Patios de Beatas....**C2**

5 Oleo Restaurante.......**B4**

Hotels ▼

1 Gran Hotel Miramar.....**E3**

2 Hotel Castilla
   Guerrero.................**B4**

3 Parador de Málaga–
   Gibralfaro...............**D2**

4 Room Mate Larios......**B3**

Bus) from the city center. ✉ *Ctra. de las Pedrizas, Km 216* ☎ *951/926180* ⊕ *www.laconcepcion.malaga.eu* 🎟 *€6 (free Sun. all day Oct.–Mar., 3:30–7:30 Apr.–Sept.)* ⊘ *Closed Mon.*

Málaga Cathedral

RELIGIOUS SITE | Built between 1528 and 1782, the cathedral is a triumph, although a generally unappreciated one, having been left unfinished when funds ran out. Because it lacks one of its two towers, the building is nicknamed "La Manquita" (the One-Armed Lady). The enclosed choir (restored in 2019), which miraculously survived the burnings of the civil war, is the work of 17th-century artist Pedro de Mena, who carved the wood wafer-thin in some places to express the fold of a robe or shape of a finger. The choir also has a pair of massive 18th-century pipe organs, one of which is still used for the occasional concert. Adjoining the cathedral is a small museum of religious art and artifacts. A walk around the cathedral on Calle Cister will take you to the magnificent Gothic Puerta del Sagrario. A rooftop walkway (guided tours only) gives you stunning views of the ocher domes and the city. ✉ *Calle Molina Lario* ☎ *640/871711* 🎟 *From €6 (free 9–10 am Mon.–Thurs.).*

Mercado de Atarazanas

HISTORIC SITE | From the Plaza Felix Saenz, at the southern end of Calle Nueva, turn onto Sagasta to reach the Mercado de Atarazanas. The typical 19th-century iron structure incorporates the original **Puerta de Atarazanas,** the exquisitely crafted 14th-century Moorish gate that once connected the city with the port. Don't miss the magnificent stained-glass window depicting highlights of this historic port city as you stroll round the stalls, filled with local produce. The bars at the entrance offer good-value tapas, open at lunchtime only. ✉ *Calle Atarazanas* ⊘ *Closed Sun.*

Museo Carmen Thyssen Málaga

MUSEUM | Like Madrid, Málaga has its own branch of this museum, with more than 200 works from Baroness Thyssen's private collection. Shown in a renovated 16th-century palace, the collection features mainly Spanish paintings from the 19th century but also has work from two great 20th-century artists, Joaquín Sorolla y Bastida and Romero de Torres. The museum also hosts regular exhibitions, talks, and art workshops. ✉ *Calle Compañia 10* ☎ *902/303131* ⊕ *www.carmenthyssenmalaga.org* 🎟 *From €10 (free Sun. from 5 pm)* ⊘ *Closed Mon.*

Museo Casa Natal de Picasso (*Picasso's Birthplace*)

MUSEUM | Málaga's most famous native son, Pablo Picasso, was born here in 1881. The building has been painted and furnished in the style of the era and houses a permanent exhibition of the artist's early sketches and sculptures, as well as memorabilia, including his christening robe and family photos. ✉ *Pl. de la Merced 15* ☎ *951/926060* ⊕ *www.fundacionpicasso.malaga.eu* 🎟 *€3.*

Museo del Vidrio y Cristal (*Museum of Glass and Crystal*)

MUSEUM | More than 3,000 pieces of glass and crystal, lovingly collected by the owner, are displayed throughout this 18th-century mansion, which is a museum piece in its own right. The pieces, whether ancient Egyptian or from Europe's Lalique and Whitefriars, give a unique insight into man's decorative use of glass. Visits are by guided tour only. ✉ *Plazuela Santísimo Cristo de la Sangre 2* ☎ *952/220271* ⊕ *www.museovidrioy-cristalmalaga.com* 🎟 *€6* ⊘ *Closed Mon., and Aug.*

★ Museo Picasso Málaga

MUSEUM | Part of the charm of this art gallery, one of the city's most prestigious museums, is that its small collection is such a family affair. These are the works that Pablo Picasso kept for himself or gave to his family, including the exquisite

Portrait of Lola, the artist's sister, which he painted when he was 13, and the stunning *Three Graces*. The holdings were largely donated by two family members—Christine and Bernard Ruiz-Picasso, the artist's daughter-in-law and her son. The works are displayed in chronological order according to the periods that marked Picasso's 73-year development as an artist. The museum is housed in a former palace where, during restoration work, Roman and Moorish remains were discovered. These are now on display, together with the permanent collection of Picassos and temporary exhibitions. **■TIP➔ Guided tours in English are available; book at least five days ahead.** ✉ *Calle San Agustín* ☎ *952/127600* 🌐 *www.museopicassomalaga.org* 🎟 *€8 (free last 2 hrs on Sun.).*

Pasaje Chinitas

NEIGHBORHOOD | The narrow streets and alleys on each side of Calle Marqués de Larios have charms of their own. The most famous is Pasaje Chinitas, off Plaza de la Constitución and named for the notorious Chinitas cabaret here. Peep into the dark, vaulted *bodegas* (wineries) where old men down glasses of *seco añejo* or Málaga Virgen, local wines made from Málaga's muscatel grapes. Silversmiths and vendors of religious books and statues ply their trades in shops that have changed little since the early 1900s. Backtrack across Larios, and, in the streets leading to Calle Nueva and Calle San Juan, you can see shoeshine boys, lottery-ticket vendors, Gypsy guitarists, and tapas bars serving wine from huge barrels. ✉ *Málaga.*

🍴 Restaurants

Eboka

$$ | **SPANISH** | Tucked behind the Picasso Museum, Eboka has quickly established a reputation as an excellent gastro bar serving Mediterranean dishes made from local produce. Inside, the restaurant is contemporary with low lighting and plant motifs on the walls, and outside there's a pleasant terrace. **Known for:** sharing plates; wine list; outdoor terrace. [$] *Average main: €15* ✉ *Calle Pedro de Toledo 4* ☎ *952/124671* 🌐 *www.ebokarestaurante.com.*

El Ambigú de la Coracha

$$ | **MEDITERRANEAN** | Located beneath the Gibralfaro, this modern restaurant with a lovely terrace offers sweeping views of Málaga below—more than worth the climb to get here—and local cuisine with an international influence. Starters, like king prawn ceviche with local avocado, make ideal sharing plates. **Known for:** views of Málaga; local wines and produce; olive oil tasting. [$] *Average main: €15* ✉ *Calle Campo Eliseos* ☎ *951/900046* 🌐 *elambigudelacoracha.com* 🕓 *Closed Mon.*

El Palmeral

$$$ | **MEDITERRANEAN** | Set among the Palm Walk near the cruise-ship terminal and with first-class views of the harbor, this restaurant has become a firm favorite with locals and visitors. Sit inside the modern glass cube for elegant dining or outside for a more informal meal (or just coffee). **Known for:** harbor views; paella; croquetas. [$] *Average main: €18* ✉ *Muelle 2* ☎ *674/277645* 🌐 *www.palmeralmalaga.com.*

★ Los Patios de Beatas

$$$ | **SPANISH** | Sandwiched between the Museo Picasso and Fundación Picasso is

Something Sweet 🍴

For coffee and cakes, malagueños favor Lepanto, the classy shop at Calle Marqués de Larios 7, where uniform-clad staff serve a variety of pastries, cakes, and other sweets. Just next door at Casa Mira is delicious homemade ice cream.

one of Málaga's largest wine collections (there are more than 500 on the list). The two historic mansions that make up this restaurant include an original patio and 17th-century stone wine vats; you can sit on barstools in the beamed tapas section, where the walls are lined with dozens of wine bottles, or dine on the airy patio, which is covered with stained glass. **Known for:** wine list; innovative tapas; stunning interior. $ *Average main: €20* ✉ *Calle Beatas 43* ☎ *952/210350* ⊕ *www.lospatiosdebeatas.com* ▭ *No credit cards.*

Óleo Restaurante

$$$ | INTERNATIONAL | Attached to the Centro de Arte Contemporáneo, this small restaurant offers a range of Mediterranean dishes and sushi best enjoyed on the riverside terrace. Sharing plates include hummus or Vietnamese rolls with Málaga kid goat; highlights on the main menu are *carrillada ibérica* (stewed Iberian pork) with couscous, tuna steak, and a long list of sushi. **Known for:** sushi; stewed Iberian pork; riverside dining. $ *Average main: €18* ✉ *Calle Alemania* ✛ *Next to CAC* ☎ *952/219062* ⊕ *www.oleorestaurante. es* ⊗ *Closed Mon.*

 Hotels

Gran Hotel Miramar

$$$$ | HOTEL | Málaga's giant "wedding-cake" palace was opened by King Alfonso XIII in 1926 as one of the city's first hotels and fully restored to its former glory in 2017; if you can't splurge on a room, at least treat yourself to a coffee or cocktail here. **Pros:** most luxurious accommodations in town; personal butler service; stunning interior patio. **Cons:** faces a busy road; short walk from city center; pricey. $ *Rooms from: €270* ✉ *Paseo de Reding 22* ☎ *952/603000* ⊕ *www.granhotelmiramarmalaga.com* ⤻ *190 rooms* ⭗ *No meals.*

Hotel Castilla Guerrero

$ | HOTEL | This centrally located and gracious hotel has well-priced rooms that are small but functional, with double glazing to block out any late-night street revelry—those facing the side street or the interior patio are the quietest. **Pros:** great location between the city center and the port; parking; rooms are clean and modern. **Cons:** rooms are small; friendly owners don't speak much English; breakfast is not free in adjoining cafe. $ *Rooms from: €85* ✉ *Calle Córdoba 7* ☎ *952/218635* ⊕ *www.hotelcastillaguerrero.com* ⤻ *51 rooms* ⭗ *No meals.*

★ Parador de Málaga–Gibralfaro

$$$$ | HOTEL | The attractive rooms at this cozy, gray-stone parador are some of the best in Málaga, with spectacular views of the city and the bay, so reserve well in advance. **Pros:** flawless Málaga-and-Mediterranean vistas from balconies; popular restaurant; rooftop pool. **Cons:** some distance uphill from town; tired communal areas; can be very busy. $ *Rooms from: €190* ✉ *Monte de Gibralfaro s/n, Monte* ☎ *952/221902* ⊕ *www.parador.es* ⤻ *38 rooms* ⭗ *No meals.*

Room Mate Larios

$$$$ | HOTEL | On the central Plaza de la Constitución, in the middle of a sophisticated shopping area, this elegantly restored 19th-century building holds luxuriously furnished rooms. **Pros:** stylish; king-size beds; rooftop bar with cathedral views. **Cons:** daytime noise from shopping street; interior rooms are dark; Cathedral bells ring every 15 mins (from 7am to midnight). $ *Rooms from: €190* ✉ *Marqués de Larios 2* ☎ *952/222200* ⊕ *www.room-matehotels.com* ⤻ *45 rooms* ⭗ *No meals.*

🎭 Performing Arts

Málaga's main nightlife districts are Maestranza, between the bullring and the Paseo Marítimo, and the beachfront in the suburb of Pedregalejo. Central

Málaga also has a lively bar scene around the Plaza Uncibay and Plaza de la Merced. Malaga holds a biennial flamenco festival with events throughout the year; the next one is in 2021.

Museo de Flamenco Juan Breva
CULTURAL FESTIVALS | The Juan Breva Flamenco Museum offers flamenco performances featuring local artists on Thursday and Saturday at 8:30 pm. Get there early to admire the museum's extensive collection of flamenco memorabilia. ⊠ *Calle Ramón Franquelo 8* ☎ *687/607526* ⊠ *€15.*

Antequera

64 km (40 miles) north of Málaga, 87 km (54 miles) northeast of Ronda.

The town of Antequera holds a surprising number of magnificent baroque monuments (including some 30 churches)—it provides a unique snapshot of a historic Andalusian town, one a world away from the resorts on the Costa del Sol. It became a stronghold of the Moors after their defeat at Córdoba and Seville in the 13th century. Its fall to the Christians in 1410 paved the way for the Reconquest of Granada; the Moors' retreat left a fortress on the town heights.

Next to the town fortress is the former church of **Santa María la Mayor.** Built of sandstone in the 16th century, it has a ribbed vault and is now used as a concert hall. The church of **San Sebastián** has a brick baroque Mudejar tower topped by a winged figure called the Angelote (Big Angel), the symbol of Antequera. The church of **Nuestra Señora del Carmen** (Our Lady of Carmen) has an extraordinary baroque altarpiece that towers to the ceiling. On Thursday, Friday, and Saturday evening, mid-June–mid-September, many monuments are floodlit and open until late.

GETTING HERE AND AROUND
There are several daily buses from Málaga and Ronda to Antequera. Drivers will arrive via the A367 and A384, and should head for the underground parking lot on Calle Diego Ponce in the center of town, which is well signposted. Antequera is small and compact, and most monuments are within easy walking distance, although the castle is up a fairly steep hill. You need a car to visit the Dolmens.

VISITOR INFORMATION
CONTACTS **Municipal Tourist Office**
⊠ *Calle Encarnación 4* ☎ *952/702505* ⊕ *turismo.antequera.es.*

 Sights

Archidona
TOWN | About 8 km (5 miles) from Antequera's Lovers' Rock, the village of Archidona winds its way up a steep mountain slope beneath the ruins of a Moorish castle. This unspoiled village is worth a detour for its **Plaza Ochavada,** a magnificent 17th-century octagon resplendent with contrasting red and ocher stone. ⊠ *A45, Archidona.*

★ Dolmens
ARCHAEOLOGICAL SITE | These mysterious prehistoric megalithic burial chambers, just outside Antequera, were built some 4,000 years ago out of massive slabs of stone weighing more than 100 tons each. The best-preserved dolmen is La Menga. Declared UNESCO World Heritage sites in 2016, the Dolmens offer an interesting insight into the area's first inhabitants and their burial customs, well explained at the visitor center. Note that gates close 30 minutes before closing time. ⊠ *Antequera ✛ Signposted off Málaga exit rd.* ☎ *952/712206* ⊠ *Free.*

Laguna de Fuente de Piedra
NATURE PRESERVE | Europe's major nesting area for the greater flamingo is a shallow saltwater lagoon. In February and March, these birds arrive from Africa by the thousands to breed, returning to Africa

in August when the water dries up. The visitor center has information on wildlife. Bring binoculars if you have them. On weekends and public holidays in April–June—flamingo hatching time—the visitor center suspends its usual lunchtime closure. Guided tours are available in English (€8 per person; book ahead online). ✉ *Antequera* ✣ *10 km (6 miles) northwest of Antequera, off A92 to Seville* ☎ *952/712554* 🌐 *www.reservatuvisita.es* 🎟 *Free* ⏲ *Closed lunchtime.*

Museo de la Ciudad de Antequera
MUSEUM | The town's pride and joy is *Efebo,* a beautiful bronze statue of a boy that dates back to Roman times. Standing almost 5 feet high, it's on display along with other ancient, medieval, and Renaissance art and artifacts in this impressive museum. ✉ *Pl. Coso Viejo* ☎ *952/708300* 🌐 *turismo.antequera.es* 🎟 *€3 (free Sun.)* ⏲ *Closed Mon.*

★ **Parque Natural del Torcal de Antequera**
(*El Torcal Nature Park*)
NATURE PRESERVE | Well-marked walking trails (stay on them) guide you at this park, where you can walk among eerie pillars of pink limestone sculpted by aeons of wind and rain. Guided hikes (in Spanish only) can be arranged, as well as stargazing in July and August. The visitor center has a small museum. ✉ *Centro de Visitantes* ✣ *10 km (6 miles) south on Ctra. C3310* ☎ *952/243324* 🎟 *Free.*

Peña de los Enamorados
NATURE SITE | The dramatic silhouette of the Peña de los Enamorados (Lovers' Rock) is an Andalusian landmark. Legend has it that a Moorish princess and a Christian shepherd boy eloped here one night and cast themselves to their deaths from the peak the next morning. The rock's outline is often likened to the profile of the cordobés bullfighter Manolete. ✉ *Antequera* ✣ *East on A45.*

🍴 Restaurants

El Mesón Ibérico Dehesa Las Hazuelas
$$ | **SPANISH** | Down the road from the tourist office, this ordinary-looking restaurant serves excellent and abundant Spanish cooking for some of the best prices in the area. Inside, traditional wine barrels share space with modern leather stools, pine furniture, and a flat-screen television, and there's also a pleasant outside terrace. **Known for:** tapas; generous portions; gin list. [$] *Average main: €12* ✉ *Calle Encarnación 9* ☎ *661/563658.*

Restaurante Arte de Cozina
$$ | **SPANISH** | As the name suggests, this cozy restaurant offers art in cooking, and its take on typical local dishes is one of the best in Málaga province. The menu is seasonal with an emphasis on local produce; it might include *porrilla de espinacas con huevo* (spinach stew with egg) and the *choto malagueño* (kid goat in spicy sauce). **Known for:** traditional dishes; kid goat; bienmesabe dessert. [$] *Average main: €14* ✉ *Calle Calzada 25* ☎ *952/840014* 🌐 *artedecozina.com.*

🛏 Hotels

Parador de Antequera
$$$ | **HOTEL** | Within a few minutes' walk of the historic center, this parador provides a welcome oasis of calm for relaxing after sightseeing, and panoramic vistas of the Peña de los Enamorados can be seen from the gardens, restaurant, and some rooms. **Pros:** quiet, romantic setting; views; pool with loungers. **Cons:** slightly out of town; interior design could be too impersonal for some; not all rooms have views. [$] *Rooms from: €150* ✉ *Pl. García del Olmo 2* ☎ *952/840261* 🌐 *www.parador.es* 🛏 *58 rooms* 🍽 *No meals.*

The Guadalhorce Valley

About 34 km (21 miles) from Antequera, 66 km (41 miles) from Málaga.

The awe-inspiring **Garganta del Chorro** (Gorge of the Stream) is a deep limestone chasm where the Río Guadalhorce churns and snakes its way some 600 feet below the road. The railroad track that worms in and out of tunnels in the cleft was, amazingly, the main line heading north from Málaga for Bobadilla junction and, eventually, Madrid until the AVE track was built.

North of the gorge, the Guadalhorce has been dammed to form a series of scenic reservoirs surrounded by piney hills, which constitute the **Parque de Ardales** nature area. Informal, open-air restaurants overlook the lakes and a number of picnic spots. Driving along the southern shore of the lake, you reach Ardales and, turning onto the A357, the old spa town of **Carratraca**. Once a favorite watering hole for both Spanish and foreign aristocracy, it has a Moorish-style *ayuntamiento* (town hall) and an unusual polygonal bullring. Today the 1830 guesthouse has been renovated into the luxury Villa Padierna spa hotel. The splendid Roman-style marble-and-tile bathhouse has benefited from extensive restoration.

GETTING HERE AND AROUND

Coming from Antequera, take the "El Torcal" exit, turning right onto the A343, then from the village of Alora, follow the minor road north. From Málaga go west on the A357 through Cártama, Pizarra, Carratraca, and Ardales. There's also a train (one service daily) from Málaga to El Chorro station, which is handy if you're planning to walk the Caminito del Rey.

Sights

★ Caminito del Rey

TRAIL | Clinging to the cliff side in the valley, the "King's Walk" is a suspended catwalk built for a visit by King Alfonso XIII at the beginning of the 19th century. It reopened in March 2015 after many years and a €9 million restoration and is now one of the province's main tourist attractions—as well as one of the world's dizziest. No more than 400 visitors are admitted daily for the walk, which includes nearly 3 km (2 miles) on the boardwalk itself and nearly 5 km (3 miles) on the access paths. It takes four to five hours to complete, and it's a one-way walk, so you need to make your own way back to the start point at the visitor center at the Ardales end (shuttle buses offer regular service; check when the last bus leaves and time your walk accordingly). A certain level of fitness is required and the walk is not recommended for young children or anyone who suffers from vertigo. ■**TIP**→ **This is one of the Costa del Sol's busiest attractions; book ahead.** ✉ *Valle del Guadalhorce* ⊕ *www.caminitodelrey.info* ✉ *From €10* ⌫ *Closed Mon.*

Torremolinos

11 km (7 miles) west of Málaga, 16 km (10 miles) northeast of Fuengirola, 43 km (27 miles) east of Marbella.

Torremolinos is all about fun in the sun. It may be more subdued than it was in the action-packed 1960s and '70s, but it remains the gay capital of the Costa del Sol. Scantily attired Northern Europeans of all ages still jam the streets in season, shopping for bargains on Calle San Miguel, downing sangria in the bars of La Nogalera, and congregating in the bars and English pubs. By day, the sunseekers flock to El Bajondillo and La Carihuela beaches, where, in high summer, it's hard to find towel space on the sand.

Torremolinos has two sections. The first, Central Torremolinos, is built around the Plaza Costa del Sol, refurbished and fully pedestrianized in 2019; Calle San Miguel, the main shopping street; and the brash Plaza de la Nogalera, which is full of overpriced bars and restaurants. The Pueblo Blanco area, off Calle Casablanca, is more pleasant; and the Cuesta del Tajo, at the far end of Calle San Miguel, winds down a steep slope to El Bajondillo beach. Here, crumbling walls, bougainvillea-clad patios, and old cottages hint at the quiet fishing village of bygone years.

The second, more sedate, section of Torremolinos is La Carihuela. To get here, head west out of town on Avenida Carlota Alessandri and turn left following the signs. This more authentically Spanish area still has a few fishermen's cottages and excellent seafood restaurants. The traffic-free esplanade is pleasant for strolling, especially on a summer evening or Sunday at lunchtime, when it's packed with Spanish families. Just 10 minutes' walk north from the beach is the Parque de la Batería, a very pleasant park with fountains, ornamental gardens, and good views of the sea.

GETTING HERE AND AROUND

Torremolinos is a short train or bus journey from Málaga. The town itself is mostly flat, except for the steep slope to El Bajondillo—if you don't want to walk, take the free elevator.

BUS CONTACT Bus Station ✉ *Calle Hoyo* ☎ *No phone.*

TAXI CONTACT Radio Taxi Torremolinos ☎ *952/380600.*

VISITOR INFORMATION

CONTACTS La Carihuela ✉ *Paseo Marítimo* ✣ *Next to Hotel Tropicana on seafront* ☎ *952/372956* 🌐 *www.turismotorremolinos.es.* **Torremolinos** ✉ *Pl. Comunidades Autónomas* ☎ *951/954379.*

Beaches

La Carihuela

BEACH—SIGHT | FAMILY | This 2-km (1-mile) stretch of sand running from the Torremolinos headland to Puerto Marina in Benalmádena is a perennial favorite with Málaga residents as well as visitors. Several hotels, including the Tropicana, flank a beach promenade that's perfect for a stroll, and there are plenty of beach bars where you can rent a lounger and parasol—and also enjoy some of the best *pescaíto frito* (fried fish) on the coast. The gray sand is cleaned regularly, and the moderate waves make for safe bathing. Towel space (and street parking) is in short supply during the summer months, but outside high season this is a perfect spot for soaking up some winter sunshine. **Amenities:** food and drink; lifeguards (mid-June–mid-September); showers; toilets; water sports. **Best for:** swimming; walking. ✉ *Torremolinos* ✣ *West end of town, between center and Puerto Marina.*

Restaurants

Casa Juan

$$ | SEAFOOD | Thanks to the malagueño families who flock here on weekends for the legendary fresh seafood, this restaurant seats 170 inside and 150 outside in an attractive square, one block back from the seafront. Try for a table overlooking the mermaid fountain. **Known for:** zarzuela de marisco (seafood stew); fried fish; rice dishes. [$] *Average main: €14* ✉ *Pl. San Ginés, La Carihuela* ☎ *952/373512.*

Yate El Cordobes

$$ | SPANISH | Ask the locals which beachfront chiringuito they prefer and El Yate will probably be the answer. Run and owned by an affable cordobés family, the menu holds few surprises, but the seafood is freshly caught, and meat and vegetables are top quality. **Known for:** fresh seafood; grilled dorada (sea

Beach umbrellas at the edge of the surf in Torremolinos

bream); beachside dining. **$** *Average main: €13* ⊠ *Paseo Marítimo Playamar s/n* ☎ *952/384956* ⊘ *Closed Jan.*

 ## Hotels

Hotel Fénix

$$$ | **HOTEL** | One of the handful of adults-only hotels here, Hotel Fénix offers easy access to both the city center via the main entrance and El Bajondillo beach (one block away) via the first floor. **Pros:** handy location; good breakfast; sea views. **Cons:** some rooms have limited view; not on the beachfront; no kids allowed. **$** *Rooms from: €180* ⊠ *Av. de las Mercedes 22* ☎ *952/051994* ⊕ *www. thepalmexperiencehotels.com* ⤴ *126 rooms* ¶⊘¶ *No meals.*

Hotel La Luna Blanca

$$$ | **HOTEL** | A touch of Asia comes to Torremolinos at Spain's only Japanese hotel, tucked away at the western end of the resort and a few minutes' walk from La Carihuela. **Pros:** peaceful; close to La Carihuela; free parking. **Cons:** can be difficult to find; steep walk back from the beach. **$** *Rooms from: €140* ⊠ *Pasaje del Cerrillo 2* ☎ *952/053711* ⊕ *www.hotel-lalunablanca.com* ⤴ *11 rooms* ¶⊘¶ *Free Breakfast.*

Hotel MS Tropicana

$$$ | **HOTEL** | **FAMILY** | On the beach at the far end of La Carihuela, in one of the most pleasant parts of Torremolinos, this low-rise resort hotel has a loyal following for its friendly and homey style and comfortable, bright rooms. **Pros:** great for families; surrounded by bars and restaurants; has its own beach club. **Cons:** can be noisy; a half-hour walk to the center of Torremolinos; minimum four-night stay in July and August. **$** *Rooms from: €140* ⊠ *Trópico 6, La Carihuela* ☎ *952/386600* ⊕ *www.hotelmstropicana.com* ⤴ *84 rooms* ¶⊘¶ *Free Breakfast.*

 ## Nightlife

Most nocturnal action is in the center of Torremolinos, and most of its gay bars are in or around the Plaza de la Nogalera, in the center, just off the Calle San Miguel.

Parthenon

DANCE CLUBS | One of the longest-established gay bars in Torremolinos has live music and drag shows most nights. Check the club's Facebook page for details. ⊠ *La Nogalera 716* ☏ *678/479381.*

🎭 Performing Arts

Taberna Flamenca Pepe López

DANCE | Many of the better hotels stage flamenco shows, but you may also want to check out this venue, which has shows throughout the year (call or check the website to confirm times). ⊠ *Pl. de la Gamba Alegre* ☏ *952/381284* ⊕ *www.tabernaflamencapepelopez.com* 🎟 *€30.*

Fuengirola

16 km (10 miles) west of Torremolinos, 27 km (17 miles) east of Marbella.

Fuengirola is less frenetic than Torremolinos. Many of its waterfront high-rises are vacation apartments that cater to budget-minded sunseekers from Northern Europe and, in summer, a large contingent from Córdoba and other parts of Spain. The town is also a haven for British retirees (with plenty of English and Irish pubs to serve them) and a shopping and business center for the rest of the Costa del Sol. The Tuesday market here is the largest on the coast and a major tourist attraction.

GETTING HERE AND AROUND

Fuengirola is the last stop on the train line from Málaga. There are also regular buses that leave from Málaga's and Marbella's main bus stations.

BIKE RENTAL CONTACT Route Electric Bike ⊠ *Paseo Marítimo Rey de España 10* ☏ *951/405150* ⊕ *www.route-electricbike.com.*

BUS CONTACT Bus Station ⊠ *Av. Alfonso XIII 5* ☏ *No phone.*

TAXI CONTACT Radio Taxi Fuengirola ☏ *952/471000.*

VISITOR INFORMATION
CONTACTS Fuengirola Tourist Office ⊠ *Av. Jesús Santos Rein 6* ☏ *952/467457* ⊕ *turismo.fuengirola.es.*

👁 Sights

Bioparc Fuengirola

ZOO | FAMILY | In this modern zoo, wildlife live in a cageless environment as close as possible to their natural habitats. The Bioparc is involved in almost 50 international breeding programs for species in danger of extinction and also supports conservation projects in Africa and several prominent ecological initiatives. Four different habitats have been created, and chimpanzees, big cats, and crocodiles may be viewed, together with other mammals such as white tigers and pygmy hippos, as well as reptiles and birds. There are also daily shows and exhibitions, and various places to get refreshments. In July and August the zoo stays open until 11 pm to allow visitors to see the nocturnal animals. ⊠ *Av. José Cela 6* ☏ *952/666301* ⊕ *www.bioparc-fuengirola.es* 🎟 *€20.*

Castillo de Sohail

CASTLE/PALACE | On the hill at the far west of town is the impressive Castillo de Sohail, built as a fortress against pirate attacks in the 10th century and named for the Moorish term for Fuengirola. Don't miss the views of the valley, sea, and coast from the battlements. Concerts are held here during the summer months. ⊠ *Calle Tartessos* ✛ *15-min walk west from center* ☏ *952/589349* 🎟 *Free* ⊗ *Closed Mon.*

🏖 Beaches

Carvajal

BEACH—SIGHT | FAMILY | Lined with low-rises and plenty of greenery, this typically urban beach is between Benalmádena and Fuengirola. One of the Costa del

Sol's Blue Flag holders (awarded to the cleanest beaches with the best facilities), the 1¼-km (¾-mile) beach has yellow sand and safe swimming conditions, which make it very popular with families. Beach bars rent lounge chairs and umbrellas, and there's regular live music in the summer. Like most beaches in the area, Playa Carvajal is packed throughout July and August, and most summer weekends, but at any other time this beach is quite quiet. The Benalmádena end has a seafront promenade and street parking, and the Carvajal train station (on the Fuengirola–Málaga line) is just a few yards from the beach. **Amenities:** food and drink; lifeguards (mid-June–mid-September); parking (no fee); showers; toilets; water sports. **Best for:** sunrise; swimming. ✉ *N340, Km 214–216.*

🍴 Restaurants

Bodega Charolais

$$$ | **SPANISH** | Andalusian cuisine fuses perfectly with Basque tradition in this atmospheric restaurant. Fresh local produce features high on the menu. Dine inside or out or try the tapas at the bar. Excellent wine list with over 100 labels. [$] *Average main: €18* ✉ *Calle Larga 14* ☎ *952/475441* 🌐 *www.bodegacharolais.com.*

Restaurante Bodega La Solera

$$ | **SPANISH** | Tucked into the elbow of a narrow street near the main church square, this restaurant serves up superb Spanish dishes, including *albóndigas de ibérico en salsa de almendras* (Iberian pork meatballs in almond sauce) and *bacalao frito sobre pisto de verduras* (fried cod on ratatouille). The three-course daily menu with a half bottle of wine (€16.50) offers a wide range of choices. **Known for:** Iberian pork meatballs; good-value daily menu; wine selection. [$] *Average main: €15* ✉ *Calle Capitán 13* ☎ *952/467708* 🌐 *www.restaurantelasolera.es* 🕓 *Closed Tues.*

★ Vegetalia

$ | **VEGETARIAN** | This attractive, long-established vegetarian restaurant has a large, pleasant dining space decorated with vibrant artwork. It's best known for its excellent, and vast, lunchtime buffet (€8.95), which includes salads and hot dishes like red-lentil croquettes, vegetable paella, and soy "meatballs." Leave room for the house-made desserts, especially the peach-mousse cheesecake. **Known for:** vegetable dishes; lunch buffet; soy meatballs. [$] *Average main: €9* ✉ *Calle Santa Isabel 8* ☎ *952/586031* 🌐 *www.restaurantevegetalia.com* 🕓 *No dinner. Closed July, Aug., and Sun.*

🛏 Hotels

Hostal Italia

$ | **B&B/INN** | Right off the main plaza and near the beach, this deservedly popular family-run hotel has bright and comfortable but small rooms; guests return year after year, particularly during the October *feria* (fair). **Pros:** friendly owners; most rooms have balconies; surrounded by restaurants and bars. **Cons:** some street noise; rooms are small. [$] *Rooms from: €75* ✉ *Calle de la Cruz 1* ☎ *952/474193* 🌐 *www.hostalitalia.com* 🛏 *40 rooms* 🍴 *No meals.*

Hotel Florida Spa

$$$ | **HOTEL** | This glossy spa hotel has a sophisticated edge on its high-rise neighbors, with light and airy rooms and private terraces overlooking the port and surrounding beach. **Pros:** great location; in-house spa; views of mountains and coast. **Cons:** can be an overload of tour groups; very small pool; three-night minimum stay in July and August. [$] *Rooms from: €160* ✉ *Calle Dr. Galvez Ginachero* ☎ *952/922700* 🌐 *www.hotel-florida.es* 🛏 *184 rooms* 🍴 *No meals.*

Horsewomen in Fuengirola's El Real de la Feria

Performing Arts

Salón Varietés Theater

CONCERTS | From October through June, amateur local troupes stage plays and musicals in English here. The venue also hosts occasional touring tribute acts. ✉ *Calle Emancipación 30* ☎ *952/474542* ⊕ *www.salonvarietestheatre.com.*

Mijas

8 km (5 miles) north of Fuengirola, 18 km (11 miles) west of Torremolinos.

Mijas is in the foothills of the sierra just north of the coast. Long ago foreign retirees discovered the pretty, whitewashed town, and though the large, touristy square may look like an extension of the Costa, beyond it are hilly residential streets with timeworn homes. Try to visit late in the afternoon, after the tour buses have left.

Mijas extends down to the coast, and the coastal strip between Fuengirola and

Marbella is officially called **Mijas-Costa.** This area has several hotels, restaurants, and golf courses.

GETTING HERE AND AROUND

Buses leave Fuengirola every half hour for the 25-minute drive through hills peppered with large houses. If you have a car and don't mind a mildly hair-raising drive, take the more dramatic approach from Benalmádena-Pueblo, a winding mountain road with splendid views. You can park in the underground parking garage signposted on the approach to the village.

VISITOR INFORMATION

CONTACTS **Mijas Tourist Office** ✉ *Av. Virgen de la Peña* ☎ *952/589034* ⊕ *turismo. mijas.es.*

Sights

Centro de Arte Contemporáneo

MUSEUM | This modern art center contains more than 400 works from the Remedios Medina Collection, including the second largest collection of Picasso ceramics in the world. A total of 130 works by Picasso are on display alongside paintings, etchings, and other pieces by artists such as Dalí, Braque, and Foujita. ⊠ *Calle Málaga 28* ☎ *952/590442* ⊕ *www.cacmijas.info* ⊠ *€3* ⊘ *Closed Mon.*

Iglesia Parroquial de la Inmaculada Concepción (*Immaculate Conception*)
RELIGIOUS SITE | This delightful village church, up the hill from the bullring, is worth a visit. It's impeccably decorated, especially at Easter, and the terrace and spacious gardens have a splendid panoramic view. ⊠ *Pl. de la Constitución* ⊠ *Free.*

Museo Mijas
MUSEUM | This charming museum occupies the former ayuntamiento. Its themed rooms, including an old-fashioned bakery and bodega, surround a patio, and regular art exhibitions are mounted in the upstairs gallery. ⊠ *Pl. de la Libertad* ☎ *952/590380* ⊠ *€1.*

 Restaurants

Casa 5
$$$ | MEDITERRANEAN | Just a five-minute walk from the contemporary art museum, this welcoming restaurant offers a seasonal menu with nods to Mediterranean and Asian cuisine. Staples include the *pulpo ahumado lima y limó n* (smoked octopus with lemon and lime) and *arroz a la dehesa con pimientos caramelizados y secreto ibérico* (country-style rice with caramelized peppers and Iberian pork belly). **Known for:** Mediterranean-Asian fusion; smoked octopus; alfresco dining. $ *Average main: €20* ⊠ *Calle Málaga 5* ☎ *952/591152* ⊘ *Closed Mon.*

Restaurante El Mirlo Blanco
$$$ | SPANISH | In an old house on the pleasant Plaza de la Constitución, this restaurant is run by a Basque family that's been in the Costa del Sol restaurant business since 1968. The cozy indoor dining room, with log fire for cooler days,

---

Take a Boat

A 30-minute ferry trip runs between Marbella and Puerto Banús (*€8.50 one-way March–November* ⊕ *www.fly-blue.com*), giving you the chance to admire the Marbella mountain backdrop and maybe catch a glimpse of the local dolphins. If you're feeling energetic, walk back the 7 km (4½ miles) along the beachfront promenade stopping at one of the many beach bars for a welcome refreshment or ice cream.

---

is welcoming and intimate, with original and noteworthy artwork interspersed among the arches, hanging plants, and traditional white paintwork. **Known for:** Basque specialties; reputation as a local institution; Grand Marnier soufflé. $ *Average main: €22* ⊠ *Calle Cuesta de la Villa 13* ☎ *952/485700* ⊕ *www.mirlo-blanco.es* ⊘ *Closed Jan.*

Tomillo Limón
$ | INTERNATIONAL | A bright and airy tapas bar offering traditional Spanish staples—croquettes and *patatas bravas* (spicy potatoes)—as well more modern takes on quick bites. Try the Sri Lankan–style chickpeas or the *morcilla bric* (black sausage roll). **Known for:** patatas bravas; delicious desserts; quick bites. $ *Average main: €5* ⊠ *Av. Virgen de la Peña 11* ☎ *951/437298.*

Marbella

27 km (17 miles) west of Fuengirola, 28 km (17 miles) east of Estepona, 50 km (31 miles) southeast of Ronda.

Thanks to its year-round mild climate and a spectacular natural backdrop, Marbella has been a playground for the rich and famous since the 1950s, when wealthy Europeans first put it on the map as a high-end tourist destination. Grand hotels, luxury restaurants, and multimillion-euro mansions line the waterfront. The town is a mixture of a charming *casco antiguo* (old quarter), where visitors can get a taste of the real Andalusia; an ordinary, tree-lined main thoroughfare (Avenida Ricardo Soriano) flanked by high-rises; and a buzzing Paseo Marítimo (Seafront Promenade), which now stretches some 10 km (6 miles) to San Pedro in the west. The best beaches are to the east of the town between El Rosario and the Don Carlos Hotel. Puerto Banús, the place to see and be seen during the summer, is Spain's most luxurious marina, home to some of the most expensive yachts you will see anywhere. A bevy of restaurants, bars, and designer boutiques are nearby.

GETTING HERE AND AROUND

There are regular buses from and to the surrounding resorts and towns, including Fuengirola, Estepona (both every 30 minutes), and Málaga (hourly).

BUS CONTACT Bus Station ⊠ *Av. Trapiche* ☎ *No phone.*

VISITOR INFORMATION

CONTACTS Marbella Tourist Office ⊠ *Pl. de los Naranjos 1* ☎ *952/768707* ⊕ *www. marbellaexclusive.com.*

👁 Sights

Museo del Grabado Español Contemporáneo

MUSEUM | In a restored 16th-century palace in the casco antiguo, this museum shows some of the best in contemporary Spanish prints. Some of Spain's most famous 20th-century artists, including Picasso, Miró, and Tàpies, are on show. Temporary exhibitions are also mounted here. ⊠ *Calle Hospital Bazán* ☎ *952/765741* ⊕ *www.mgec.es* ✆ *€3* ⊗ *Closed Sun. and Mon.*

Plaza de los Naranjos

PLAZA | Marbella's appeal lies in the heart of its casco antiguo, which remains surprisingly intact. Here, a block or two back from the main highway, narrow alleys of whitewashed houses cluster around the central Plaza de los Naranjos (Orange Tree Square), where colorful, albeit pricey, restaurants vie for space under the orange trees. Climb onto what remains of the old fortifications and stroll along the Calle Virgen de los Dolores to the Plaza de Santo Cristo. ⊠ *Marbella.*

Puerto Banús

MARINA | Marbella's wealth glitters most brightly along the Golden Mile, a tiara of star-studded clubs, restaurants, and hotels west of town and stretching from Marbella to Puerto Banús. A mosque and the former residence of Saudi Arabia's late King Fahd reveal the influence of Middle Eastern oil money in this wealthy enclave. About 7 km (4½ miles) west of central Marbella (between Km 175 and Km 174), a sign indicates the turnoff leading down to Puerto Banús. Though now hemmed in by a belt of high-rises, Marbella's plush marina, with 915 berths, is a gem of ostentatious wealth, a Spanish answer to St. Tropez. Huge yachts and countless expensive stores and restaurants make for a glittering parade of beautiful people that continues long into the night. The backdrop is an Andalusian pueblo—built in the 1960s to resemble the fishing villages that once lined this coast. ⊠ *Marbella.*

🏖 Beaches

Marbella East Side Beaches

BEACH—SIGHT | **FAMILY** | Marbella's best beaches are to the east of town, between the Monteros and Don Carlos hotels, and include Costa Bella and El Alicate. The 6-km (4-mile) stretch of yellow sand is lined with residential complexes and sand dunes (some of the last remaining on the Costa del Sol). The sea remains shallow for some distance, so bathing is safe. Beach bars catering to all tastes and budgets dot the sands, as do several exclusive beach clubs (look for Nikki Beach, for instance, where luxury yachts are anchored offshore). Tourists

12

Costa del Sol and Costa de Almería MARBELLA

and locals flock to these beaches in the summer, but take a short walk away from the beach bars and parking lots, and you'll find a less crowded spot for your towel. **Amenities:** food and drink; lifeguards (mid-June–mid-September); parking (fee in summer); showers; toilets; water sports. **Best for:** swimming; walking. ✉ *A7, Km 187–193.*

Playas de Puerto Banús
BEACH—SIGHT | These small sandy coves are packed almost to bursting in the summer, when they're crowded with young, bronzed, perfect bodies: topless sunbathing is almost de rigueur. The sea is shallow along the entire stretch, which is practically wave free and seems warmer than other beaches nearby. In the area are excellent Caribbean-style beach bars with good seafood and fish, as well as lots of options for sundown drinks. This is also home to the famous Ocean and Sala Beach clubs with their oversize sun beds, Champagne, and nightlong parties. **Amenities:** food and drink; lifeguards (mid-June–mid-September); showers; toilets; water sports. **Best for:** partiers; sunset; swimming. ✉ *Puerto Banús.*

🍴 Restaurants

Altamirano
$$ | SEAFOOD | The modest, old-fashioned exterior of this local favorite is a bit deceiving: inside you'll be greeted not with stodgy decor but rather with three spacious dining rooms with Spanish soccer memorabilia, photos of famous patrons, and tanks of fish. Seafood choices run long and include fried or grilled squid, spider crab, lobster, sole, red snapper, and sea bass. **Known for:** seafood; homemade rice pudding; outdoor dining. [$] *Average main: €13* ✉ *Pl. Altamirano* ☎ *952/824932* 🌐 *www.baraltamirano.es.*

★ Cappuccino
$$$ | INTERNATIONAL | Just under the Don Pepe Hotel and right on the promenade, this is the perfect spot for some refreshment before or after you tackle a long stroll along the seafront. Done in navy and white with wicker chairs, this outdoor café-restaurant has a fitting nautical theme, and if the temperature drops, blankets and gas heaters are at the ready. **Known for:** ocean views; brunch; stylish terrace. [$] *Average main: €18* ✉ *Calle de José Meliá* ☎ *952/868790.*

Kava Marbella
$$$$ | INTERNATIONAL | This rising star on the Marbella dining scene might be a new arrival, but it looks set to pick up the baton from Dani García whose Michelin-starred restaurant closed in fall 2019. At just 25, chef Fernando Alcalá won the Best New Chef award at Madrid Fusion in 2019, and his dishes based on seasonal produce certainly rank among the finest in town. **Known for:** innovative cuisine; famous cheesecake; good-value tasting menu. [$] *Average main: €24* ✉ *Av. Antonio Belón 4* ☎ *952/824108* 🌐 *www.kavamarbella.com* 🕒 *Sun. and Mon.*

La Niña del Pisto
$ | SPANISH | Tucked away in the casco antiguo, this small venue with upstairs and downstairs dining offers a taste of Córdoba tapas and Montilla wine in Marbella. There is a good choice of tapas and sharing plates, including homemade croquettes, cold cuts, fried fish (the squid is particularly good), and the house *pisto* (ratatouille) served with a fried egg or pork. **Known for:** tapas; pisto; Montilla wine. [$] *Average main: €10* ✉ *Calle Lázaro 2* ☎ *633/320022* 🕒 *No lunch. Closed Sun. and Mon.*

Messina
$$$$ | MEDITERRANEAN | Between the casco antiguo and the seafront, this innovative restaurant has an unpromising plain exterior, but forge ahead: the interior's chocolate browns and deep reds make for cozy surroundings for a quiet dinner from chef Mauricio Giovanni, who renewed his Michelin star in 2018. The menu has an Italian slant, with more than a sprinkling of Spanish cuisine in its unusual fusion dishes. **Known for:** innovative

dining; good-value tasting menus; cozy atmosphere. [$] *Average main: €28* ✉ *Av. Severo Ochoa 12* ☎ *952/864895* 🌐 *www.restaurantemessina.com* 🕓 *No lunch. Closed Sun.*

Paellas y Más

$$$ | **SPANISH** | Located on the west side of town, about a 10-minute walk from the center, this modern restaurant specializes in rice dishes; there are 14 on the menu, including the signature baked rice with pork and the squid rice with prawns and chickpeas. Sit inside in the elegant dining room or outside on the shady terrace on the plaza. *Fideuá* (similar to paella but made with noodles instead of rice) also features on the menu. **Known for:** rice dishes; fideuá (a noodle version of paella); baked rice with pork. [$] *Average main: €20* ✉ *Calle Hermanos Salom 3* ☎ *952/822511* 🌐 *www.restaurantepaellasymas.com.*

Hotels

Hotel Lima

$$$$ | **HOTEL** | Two blocks from the beach and a short walk from the casco antiguo stands one of Marbella's oldest hotels, which had a total overhaul in 2019 to elevate it to a four-star property. **Pros:** downtown location is good for town and beach; newly refurbished ; open all year. **Cons:** room size varies considerably; street noise in some rooms; lacks character of other properties. [$] *Rooms from: €230* ✉ *Av. Antonio Belón 2* ☎ *952/770500* 🌐 *hotellimamarbella.com* 🛏 *61 rooms* 🍴 *No meals.*

La Morada Mas Hermosa

$$$ | **HOTEL** | On one of Marbella's prettiest plant-filled pedestrian streets (on the right just up Calle Ancha), this small hotel has a warm, homey feel, and the rooms are lovely. **Pros:** real character; quiet street, yet near the action; short walk from the beach. **Cons:** some rooms accessed by steep stairs; no parking; breakfast is a little basic. [$] *Rooms from: €165* ✉ *Calle Montenebros 16A* ☎ *952/924467* 🌐 *www.lamoradamashermosa.com* 🕓 *Closed Jan.–mid-Feb.* 🛏 *7 rooms* 🍴 *Free Breakfast.*

La Villa Marbella

$$ | **HOTEL** | Just a short walk from the Plaza de los Naranjos, these private rooms and apartments, decorated in Asian style with Thai screens, offer a quiet hideaway. **Pros:** central but quiet location; rooftop terrace and pool; good breakfast. **Cons:** multiple buildings; no on-site parking; three-night minimum stay in July and August. [$] *Rooms from: €120* ✉ *Calle Príncipe 10* ☎ *952/766220* 🌐 *www.lavillamarbella.com* 🛏 *12 rooms* 🍴 *No meals.*

★ Marbella Club

$$$$ | **HOTEL** | The grande dame of Marbella hotels offers luxurious rooms, tropical grounds, and sky-high rates; the sense of seclusion is emphasized by its lofty palm trees, dazzling flower beds, and a beachside tropical pool area. **Pros:** luxurious, classic hotel; superb facilities; some bungalow rooms have private pools. **Cons:** a drive from Marbella's restaurants and nightlife; extremely expensive; three-night minimum stay in July and August. [$] *Rooms from: €900* ✉ *Blvd. Principe Alfonso von Hohenlohe at Ctra. de Cádiz, Km 178* ✣ *3 km (2 miles) west of Marbella* ☎ *952/822211* 🌐 *www.marbellaclub.com* 🛏 *130 rooms* 🍴 *No meals.*

★ The Town House

$$$ | **HOTEL** | In a choice location on one of old Marbella's prettiest squares, this former family home is now a luxurious boutique hotel. **Pros:** upbeat design; great central location; rooftop terrace and bar. **Cons:** no parking; street-facing rooms are noisy on weekends; while charming, the attic rooms are not for tall guests. [$] *Rooms from: €150* ✉ *Pl. Tetuan, Calle Alderete 7* ☎ *952/901791* 🌐 *www.townhousemarbella.com* 🛏 *9 rooms* 🍴 *Free Breakfast.*

Nightlife

Much of the nighttime action in Marbella revolves around Puerto Banús—the main marina—in bars like Sinatra's and Joys Bar, but there are cosmopolitan nightspots elsewhere in the town, too, centered on the small marina and the old quarter, along with a sophisticated casino.

Casino Marbella
CASINOS | This chic gambling spot is in the Hotel Andalucía Plaza, just west of Puerto Banús. Shorts and sports shoes are not allowed, and passports are required. It's open daily 8 pm–4 am (9 pm–5 am in August). ✉ *Hotel Andalucía Pl., N340* ☎ *952/814000* 🌐 *www.casinomarbella.com.*

La Sala Banús
DANCE CLUBS | This is one of Marbella's most popular nightspots for "older" clubbers (those out or nearly out of their twenties). Dine in before you dance to the live music. ✉ *Calle Belmonte, near bullring, Puerto Banús* ☎ *952/814145* 🌐 *www.lasalabanus.com.*

Olivia Valére
DANCE CLUBS | Marbella's most famous nightspot, with an impressive celebrity guest list, attracts a sophisticated crowd with its roster of big-name DJs and stylish surroundings that resemble a Moorish palace. To get here, head inland from the town's mosque (it's easy to spot). Doors open at midnight (daily in July and August; Friday and Saturday only, September–June) and close at 7 am. ✉ *Ctra. de Istán, Km 0.8* ☎ *952/828861.*

Ojén

10 km (6 miles) north of Marbella.

For a contrast to the glamour of the coast, drive up to Ojén, in the hills above Marbella. Take note of the beautiful pottery and, if you're here the first week in August, don't miss the **Festival de Flamenco,** which attracts some of Spain's most respected flamenco names, including Juan Peña Fernández (aka El Lebrijano), Miguel Póveda, and Marina Heredia. Four kilometers (2½ miles) from Ojén is the **Refugio del Juanar,** a former hunting lodge in the heart of the Sierra Blanca, at the southern edge of the Serranía de Ronda, a mountainous wilderness. A walking trail takes you a mile from the *refugio* to the *mirador* (lookout), with a sweeping view of the Costa del Sol and the coast of North Africa.

GETTING HERE AND AROUND

Approximately three buses leave from the Marbella main bus station for Ojén on weekdays, two on Saturday and none on Sunday.

Hotels

La Posada del Angel
$$ | B&B/INN | With friendly Dutch owners and rooms with lots of traditional Andalusian features and even a few Moroccan touches, this hotel makes a perfect rural retreat. **Pros:** chance to sample Andalusian village life; heated pool; some rooms have terraces with a view. **Cons:** could be too quiet for some; slightly off the beaten track; minimum two-night stay mid-July–mid-September. [$] *Rooms from: €98* ✉ *Calle Mesones 21* ☎ *952/881808* 🌐 *www.laposadadelangel.net* 🛏 *16 rooms* 🍴 *Free Breakfast.*

Refugio del Juanar
$ | HOTEL | Once an aristocratic hunting lodge (King Alfonso XIII came here), this secluded hotel and restaurant was sold to its staff in 1984 for the symbolic sum of 1 peseta and is a world apart from the glamour of Marbella, just 30 minutes' drive away. **Pros:** access to hiking routes; traditional Andalusian looks; tucked away in a pine forest. **Cons:** can seem very cut off; some areas are a little tired; menu is limited. [$] *Rooms from: €88* ✉ *Sierra*

Blanca s/n ☎ 952/881000 ⊕ www.juanar. com ⬗ 25 rooms ⦿ Free Breakfast.

Estepona

17 km (11 miles) west of San Pedro de Alcántara, 22 km (14 miles) west of Marbella.

Estepona is a pleasant and relatively tranquil seaside resort, despite being surrounded by lots of urban developments. The beach, more than 1 km (½ mile) long, has better-quality sand than the Costa norm, and the promenade is lined with well-kept, aromatic flower gardens. The gleaming white **Puerto Deportivo** is packed with bars and restaurants, serving everything from fresh fish to Chinese food. Back from the main Avenida de España, the old quarter of cobbled narrow streets and squares is surprisingly unspoiled and decorated with flowerpots. Keep your eyes open for the many modern sculptures in the squares and 30-odd giant murals that cover entire facades throughout the town. The tourist office provides a guide to the artists and a mural map.

GETTING HERE AND AROUND
Buses run every half hour 6:30 am–11 pm from Marbella to Estepona and there are around four buses a day from Málaga Airport. The town is compact enough to make most places accessible via foot.

BUS CONTACT Bus Station ⊠ *Av. de España.*

VISITOR INFORMATION
CONTACTS Estepona Tourist Office ⊠ *Pl. de las Flores s/n* ☎ *952/802002* ⊕ *www. estepona.es/turismo.*

Sights

Museo de Arte de la Diputación
MUSEUM | Housed in the historic 18th-century Casa de las Tejerinas palace, this art museum, which opened in 2018

and is known as MAD, showcases contemporary Andalusian and Spanish artists. Focusing on work produced this century, the museum has 50 pieces from artists including Málaga-born Dadi Dreucol and Chema Lumbreras, Santiago Idáñez from Seville, and Judas Arrieta from the Basque Country. Also worthy of note are the central patio and ornate facade. ⊠ *Casa de las Tejerinas, Pl. de las Flores* ☎ *952/069695* ⊕ *www.madantequera.com* ✉ Free ◷ Closed Sun. and Mon.

★ Orchidarium
GARDEN | This lush green space in the middle of Estepona houses Europe's largest orchidarium. More than 1,600 species, from South America and Asia, are exhibited under a futuristic 100-foot glass dome containing a giant cascade. Guided tours are available. ⊠ *Calle Terraza 86* ☎ *951/517074* ⊕ *www.orchidariumestepona.com* ✉ €3 ◷ Closed Mon.

Beaches

El Saladillo
BEACH—SIGHT | Something of a Costa del Sol secret, this quiet 4-km (2½-mile) beach of gray sand has long, empty stretches with plenty of room for towels, even in high summer, making it a great place to relax, walk, or swim. The water's safe for swimming when waves are low, but watch out for the undertow when it's windy. Between San Pedro and Estepona, and flanked by residential developments, El Saladillo has the occasional beach bar. **Amenities:** food and drink; lifeguards (mid-June–mid-September); showers; toilets; water sports. **Best for:** solitude; sunset; walking. ⊠ *A7, Km 166–172.*

 Restaurants

La Casa del Rey
$$$ | SPANISH | Just a block from Plaza de las Flores, a 200-year-old building hides this sleek, modern wine bar, serving

some of the best tapas in town. Choose from a long list of hot and cold *pinchos* (small snacks)—the *rabo de toro en hojaldre* (oxtail in pastry) and *graten de bacalao* (cod gratin) are perennial favorites—tostas, and miniburgers, or from the à la carte menu, where meat dishes star. **Known for:** tapas; wine list; rabo de toro. *$ Average main: €18 ✉ Calle Raphael 7 ☎ 951/965414 🌐 lacasadelreyestepona.com.*

La Escollera

$$ | SPANISH | Located at the heart of Estepona port, this is one of the best places on the western Costa del Sol to try simply cooked fresh fish, delivered daily off the restaurant's own boat. The very busy venue (on weekends it's packed to bursting) has excellent service and a quick turnaround so you never have to wait very long for a table. **Known for:** fresh fish; liveliness on weekends; authentic atmosphere. *$ Average main: €14 ✉ Calle Puerto Pesquero s/n ✣ Near lighthouse at east end of port ☎ 952/806354 ⏲ No dinner Sun. Closed Mon.*

Hotels

Hotel Boutique Casa Veracruz

$$ | HOTEL | Housed in a beautifully restored historic mansion, this family-run hotel offers cozy accommodations off a stunning central patio. **Pros:** steps to Estepona's old quarter and the beach; historic building; complimentary refreshments. **Cons:** interior rooms dark; decor may be a little too flowery for some; reception not manned all day. *$ Rooms from: €115 ✉ Calle Veracruz 22 ☎ 951/466470 🌐 www.hotelboutiquecasaveracruz.com 🛏 10 rooms 🍽 Free Breakfast.*

Kempinski Hotel Bahía

$$$$ | RESORT | Entirely refurbished in 2018, this luxury resort, between the coastal highway and the sea, looks like a cross between a Moroccan casbah and a take on the Hanging Gardens of Babylon, with tropical gardens and a succession of large swimming pools meandering down to the beach. **Pros:** great location; excellent amenities; all rooms have balconies with sea views. **Cons:** so-so beach; some distance from Estepona; expensive. *$ Rooms from: €490 ✉ Playa El Padrón, Ctra. A7, Km 159 ☎ 952/809500 🌐 www.kempinski.com 🛏 144 rooms 🍽 Free Breakfast.*

Casares

20 km (12 miles) northwest of Estepona.

The mountain village of Casares lies high above Estepona in the Sierra Bermeja, with streets of ancient white houses piled one on top of the other, perched on the slopes beneath a ruined but impressive Moorish castle. The heights afford stunning views over orchards, olive groves, and woods to the Mediterranean sparkling in the distance.

GETTING HERE AND AROUND

Buses are few and far between to Casares and the best way to visit the village is by your own means. Be prepared for some steep slopes when you sightsee.

Restaurants

Sarmiento

$$ | SPANISH | FAMILY | Opened in late 2018, this restaurant has quickly gained a loyal following among locals and visitors with its stunning location—the terrace has far-reaching views over the village and to the Strait of Gibraltar (don't miss the eagles soaring the thermals above you)—and delicious food. Local produce takes center stage, and you can try Casares cheese, goat, and lamb as well as locally sourced tropical fruits and fresh fish from the coast. **Known for:** stunning views; Casares cheese, goat, and lamb; meat croquettes. *$ Average main: €18*

Windsurfing at Tarifa

✉ *Ctra. de Casares, Km 12.5, Estepona* ☎ *952/895035* ⊕ *restaurantesarmiento. com* ⊗ *No dinner Sun. and Mon. Closed Tues.*

Tarifa

74 km (46 miles) southwest of San Roque.

Tarifa's strong winds helped keep it off the tourist maps for years, but now it is Europe's biggest center for windsurfing and kiteboarding, and the wide, white-sand beaches stretching north of the town have become a huge attraction. Those winds have proven a source of wealth in more direct ways also, via the electricity created by vast wind farms on the surrounding hills. This town at the southernmost tip of mainland Europe—where the Mediterranean and the Atlantic meet—has continued to prosper. Downtown cafés, which not that long ago were filled with men playing dominoes and drinking *anís* (a Spanish

liquor), now serve croissants with their *café con leche* and make fancy tapas for a cosmopolitan crowd. The lovely hilltop village of Vejer de la Frontera, 51 km (32 miles) west of Tarifa, is an easy side trip, and its coastline offers stunning beaches and the historic Cape Trafalgar, where the English Armada beat Napoléon in an epic naval battle in 1805.

GETTING HERE AND AROUND
Buses connect Tarifa and Vejer de la Frontera with Algeciras, but this is an area best visited by car, especially if you want to explore the coastline. There's no public transportation to Baelo Claudia or NMAC.

VISITOR INFORMATION
CONTACTS Tarifa Tourist Office ✉ *Paseo de la Alameda s/n* ☎ *956/680993* ⊕ *turis-modetarifa.com.*

Sights

★ Baelo Claudia
ARCHAEOLOGICAL SITE | On the Atlantic coast, 24 km (15 miles) north of Tarifa, stand the impressive Roman ruins of

Baelo Claudia, once a thriving production center of garum, a salty, pungent fish paste appreciated in Rome. The visitor center includes a museum. Concerts are regularly held at the restored amphitheater during the summer months. ✉ *Tarifa* ✛ *Take N340 toward Cádiz 16 km (10 miles), then turn left for Bolonia on CA8202* ☎ *956/106797* ✐ *€2* ⊘ *Closed Mon.*

Castle

CASTLE/PALACE | Tarifa's 10th-century castle is famous for the siege of 1292, when the defender Guzmán el Bueno refused to surrender even though the attacking Moors threatened to kill his captive son. In defiance, he flung his own dagger down to them, shouting, "Here, use this," or something to that effect (they did indeed kill his son). The Spanish military turned the castle over to the town in the mid-1990s, and it now has a **museum** about Guzmán and the sacrifice of his son. There are impressive views of the African coast from the battlements and towers. ✉ *Av. Fuerza Armadas* ✐ *€4* ⊘ *Closed Mon. Nov.–Mar.*

★ Fundación NMAC (*Contemporary Art and Nature*)

MUSEUM | The rolling hills and forest between Tarifa and Vejer provide the perfect stage for this unique outdoor art museum. The sculptures and installations are placed along the guided route and in restored army barracks, and include works by international and Spanish artists such as Olafur Eliasson, Marina Abramovic, James Turrell, Pascale Marthine Tayou, and Fernando Sánchez Castillo. Visit first thing to avoid the crowds and get the best of the birdsong. ✉ *Dehesa de Montenmedio, Ctra. N340, Km 42.5, Vejer de la Frontera* ☎ *956/455134* ⊕ *www.fundacionnmac.org* ✐ *€5 (free 1st Sun. of month)* ⊘ *Closed Mon.*

⊛ Beaches

Playa Los Lances

BEACH—SIGHT | This part of the Atlantic coast consists of miles of white and mostly unspoiled beaches, and this, to the north of Tarifa and the town's main beach, is one of the longest. Backed by low-lying scrub and lagoons, the beach is also close to the odd campground, boho-chic hotel, and kitesurfing school. Its windswept sands make for perfect kitesurfing: together with Punta Paloma (just up the coast) it's where you'll see most sails surfing the waves and wind. Amenities are concentrated at the Tarifa end of the beach, where there are a few bars and cafés, usually open mid-June–mid-September, and this is naturally where the crowds congregate in the summer. Otherwise, most of the beach is deserted year-round. Swimming is safe here, except in high winds, when there's a strong undertow. **Amenities:** food and drink (mid-June–mid-September); lifeguards; showers; toilets. **Best for:** solitude; sunset; walking; windsurfing. ✉ *Tarifa.*

🛏 Hotels

★ Hotel V...

$$$ | **HOTEL** | The spacious rooms at this restored 16th-century mansion in the heart of the spectacular village of Vejer de la Frontera overlook the coast and the countryside with white villages speckling the horizon. **Pros:** stunning views; exquisite decor; rooftop terrace. **Cons:** no elevator; no on-site parking; roads around hotel too narrow to drive. $ *Rooms from: €160* ✉ *Calle Rosario 11–13, Vejer de la Frontera* ☎ *956/451757* ⊕ *www. hotelv-vejer.com* ⊠ *11 rooms* ❙⊙❙ *Free Breakfast.*

Hurricane Hotel

$$$ | **HOTEL** | Surrounded by lush subtropical gardens and fronting the beach, the Hurricane is one of the best-loved hip hotels on this stretch of coastline, famous for its Club Mistral wind- and kitesurfing school and its horseback-riding center. **Pros:** fun and sophisticated; excellent restaurant; lovely gardens with beach access. **Cons:** 6 km (3½ miles) from Tarifa proper; rooms are plain; some noise from the highway. $ *Rooms from: €164* ✉ *N340, Km 78* ☎ *956/684919* ⊕ *www.hotelhurricane.com* ⇄ *21 rooms* �

 Free Breakfast.

Gibraltar

20 km (12 miles) east of Algeciras, 77 km (48 miles) southwest of Marbella.

The Rock of today is a bizarre anomaly of Moorish, Spanish, and—especially—British influences. There are double-decker buses, "bobbies" in helmets, and red mailboxes. Millions of pounds have been spent in developing its tourist potential, and a steady flow of expat Brits comes here from Spain to shop at Morrisons supermarket and other stores. This tiny British colony—nicknamed "Gib" or simply "the Rock"—whose impressive silhouette dominates the strait between Spain and Morocco, was one of the two Pillars of Hercules in ancient times, marking the western limits of the known world and commanding the narrow pathway between the Mediterranean Sea and the Atlantic Ocean. The Moors, headed by Tariq ibn Ziyad, seized the peninsula in 711, preliminary to the conquest of Spain. The Spaniards recaptured Tariq's Rock in 1462. The English, heading an Anglo-Dutch fleet in the War of the Spanish Succession, gained control in 1704, and, after several years of local skirmishes, Gibraltar was finally ceded to Great Britain in 1713 by the Treaty of Utrecht. Spain has been trying to get it back ever since. In 1779 a combined French and Spanish force laid siege to the Rock for three years, to no avail. During the Napoleonic Wars, Gibraltar served as Admiral Horatio Nelson's base for the decisive naval Battle of Trafalgar, and during the two world wars, it served the Allies well as a naval

and air base. In 1967 Franco closed the land border with Spain to strengthen his claims over the colony, and it remained closed until 1985.

There are likely few places in the world that you enter by walking or driving across an airport runway, but that's what happens in Gibraltar. First you show your passport; then you make your way out onto the narrow strip of land linking Spain's Línea with Britain's Rock. Unless you have a good reason to take your car—such as loading up on cheap gas or duty-free goodies—you're best off leaving it in a guarded parking area in La Línea, the Spanish border town. Don't bother hanging around here; it's a seedy place. In Gibraltar you can hop on buses and take taxis that expertly maneuver the narrow, congested streets. The Official Rock Tour—conducted either by minibus or, at a greater cost, taxi—takes about 90 minutes and includes all the major sights, allowing you to choose where to come back and linger later.

In 2019, tensions between Gibraltar and Spain continued to be high, particularly with regard to Gibraltar's status with regard to Brexit. As a result, lines for leaving the colony, both via car and on foot, can be long—it can take up to three hours to cross the border into Spain. This situation is unlikely to change, as there's little sign of any progress on any sort of joint Anglo-Spanish sovereignty, which the majority of Gibraltarians fiercely oppose.

When you call Gibraltar from Spain or another country, prefix the seven-digit telephone number with 00–350. Gibraltar's currency is the Gibraltar pound (£), whose exchange rate is the same as the British pound. Euros are accepted everywhere, although you will get a better exchange rate if you use pounds.

The Rock of Gibraltar

GETTING HERE AND AROUND
There are frequent day tours organized from the Costa del Sol resorts, either via your hotel or any reputable travel agency.

VISITOR INFORMATION
CONTACTS Gibraltar ⊠ *Grand Casemates Sq.* ☎ *200/45000* ⊕ *www.visitgibraltar.gi.*

Sights

Apes' Den
NATURE PRESERVE | The famous Barbary Apes are a breed of cinnamon-color, tailless macaques (not apes, despite their name) native to Morocco's Atlas Mountains. Legend holds that as long as they remain in Gibraltar, the British will keep the Rock; Winston Churchill went so far as to issue an order for their preservation when their numbers began to dwindle during World War II. They are publicly fed twice daily, at 8 and 4, at Apes' Den, a rocky area down Old Queens Road near the Wall of Carlos V. Among the macaques' talents are their grabbing of food, purses, cell phones, and cameras,

so be on guard. ⊠ *Old Queens Rd.* ☎ *200 /71633* 💷 *£5 to enter Upper Rock Nature Reserve.*

★ Cable Car
VIEWPOINT | You can reach St. Michael's Cave—or ride all the way to the top of Gibraltar—on a cable car. The car doesn't go high off the ground, but the views of Spain and Africa from the Rock's pinnacle are superb. It leaves from a station at the southern end of Main Street, which is known as the Grand Parade. ⊠ *Grand Parade* 💷 *£16 round-trip.*

Gibraltar Museum
MUSEUM | Often overlooked by visitors heading to the Upper Rock Reserve, this museum houses a beautiful 14th-century Moorish bathhouse and an 1865 model of the Rock; the displays evoke the Great Siege and the Battle of Trafalgar. There's also a reproduction of the "Gibraltar Woman," the Neanderthal skull discovered here in 1848. The museum also serves as an interpretation hub for the prehistoric remains found in the limestone caves of Gorham's Cave Complex, which received

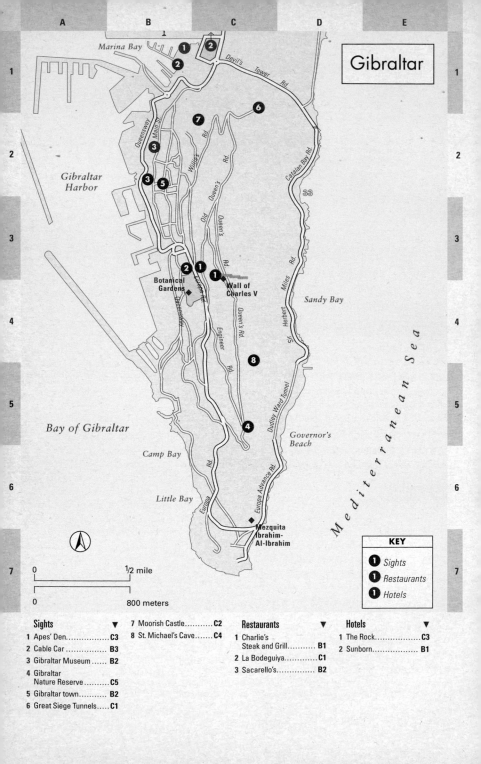

Gibraltar

Sights ▼
1 Apes' Den.............C3
2 Cable Car B3
3 Gibraltar Museum B2
4 Gibraltar
  Nature Reserve C5
5 Gibraltar town...........B2
6 Great Siege Tunnels.....C1
7 Moorish Castle...........C2
8 St. Michael's Cave.......C4

Restaurants ▼
1 Charlie's
  Steak and Grill...........B1
2 La Bodeguiya.............C1
3 Sacarello's...............B2

Hotels ▼
1 The Rock...............C3
2 Sunborn.................B1

KEY
1 *Sights*
1 *Restaurants*
1 *Hotels*

0   ½ mile
0   800 meters

UNESCO heritage status in 2016. ✉ *Bomb House La.* ☎ *200/74289* ⊕ *www.gibmuseum.gi* ✉ *£5* ⊘ *Closed Sun.*

Gibraltar Nature Reserve

NATURE PRESERVE | The reserve, accessible from Jews' Gate, includes St. Michael's Cave, the Apes' Den, the Great Siege Tunnels, the Moorish Castle, and the Military Heritage Center, which chronicles the British regiments that have served on the Rock. The Skywalk, a glass viewing platform opened (appropriately) by Mark Hamill, aka Luke Skywalker, in 2018, offers 360-degree views of the Rock and ocean from 370 yards up. You can access the reserve via the cable car. ⊹ *From Rosia Bay, drive along Queensway and Europa Rd. as far as Casino, above Alameda Gardens. Make a sharp right here, up Engineer Rd. to Jews' Gate, a lookout over docks and Bay of Gibraltar toward Algeciras* ☎ *200/71633* ✉ *£13 for all attractions.*

Gibraltar Town

TOWN | The dignified Regency architecture of Great Britain blends well with the shutters, balconies, and patios of southern Spain in colorful, congested Gibraltar town, where shops, restaurants, and pubs beckon on Main Street. At the Governor's Residence, the ceremonial Changing of the Guard takes place six times a year, and the Ceremony of the Keys takes place twice a year. Make sure you see the Anglican Cathedral of the Holy Trinity; the Catholic Cathedral of St. Mary; and the Crowned Law Courts, where the famous case of the sailing ship *Mary Celeste* was heard in 1872.

Great Siege Tunnels

HISTORIC SITE | Formerly known as the Upper Galleries, these tunnels were carved out during the Great Siege of 1779–82. At the northern end of Old Queen's Road, you can plainly see the openings from which the guns were pointed at the Spanish invaders. They form part of what is arguably the most impressive defense system anywhere in the world. The privately managed World War II tunnels nearby (prebooking essential via email) are also open to the public but are less dramatic. ✉ *Old Queen's Rd.* ✎ *naturereserve@gibraltar.gov.gi* ⊕ *www.visitgibraltar.gi/see-and-do/military-history/the-great-siege-tunnels-50* ✉ *£13 for Nature Reserve, Upper Rock, and attractions including tunnels.*

Moorish Castle

CASTLE/PALACE | The castle was built by the descendants of the Moorish general Tariq ibn Ziyad (670–720), who conquered the Rock in 711. The present Tower of Homage dates to 1333, and its besieged walls bear the scars of stones from medieval catapults (and later, cannonballs). Admiral George Rooke hoisted the British flag from its summit when he captured the Rock in 1704, and it has flown here ever since. The castle may be viewed from the outside only. ✉ *Willis's Rd.*

St. Michael's Cave

CAVE | This is the largest of Gibraltar's 150 caves; a visit here is part of the tour of the Upper Rock Nature Preserve. This series of underground chambers full of stalactites and stalagmites is sometimes used for very atmospheric (albeit damp) concerts and other events. The skull of a Neanderthal woman (now in the British Museum) was found at the nearby Forbes Quarry eight years before the world-famous discovery in Germany's Neander Valley in 1856; nobody paid much attention to it at the time, which is why the prehistoric species is called Neanderthal rather than *Homo calpensis* (literally, "Gibraltar Man," after the Romans' name for the Rock: Calpe).

This is the largest of Gibraltar's 150 caves; a visit here is part of the tour of the Upper Rock Nature Preserve. This series of underground chambers full of stalactites and stalagmites is sometimes used for very atmospheric (albeit damp) concerts and other events. The skull of a Neanderthal woman (now in the British Museum) was found at the nearby Forbes Quarry eight years before the world-famous discovery in Germany's Neander Valley in 1856; nobody paid much attention to it at the time, which is why the prehistoric species is called Neanderthal rather than *Homo calpensis* (literally, "Gibraltar Man," after the Romans' name for the Rock: Calpe). ✉ *Queen's Rd.* 🌐 *gibraltarinfo.gi/top-10-attractions/#st-michaels-cave* 🎫 *Included in Nature Reserve ticket (£13); £25 for tour of Lower Cave.*

Restaurants

Charlie's Steak and Grill

$$ | **STEAKHOUSE** | Don't let the brash neon exterior put you off: inside is one of the best steak houses in the region. Hugely popular among locals for its long list of juicy steaks, this diner-style venue also serves lamb, fried fish, and Indian curries. **Known for:** steak; Indian curries; English desserts. 💲 *Average main: £14* ✉ *Marina Bay, 4/5 Britannia House* ☎ *200/69993* 🌐 *www.charliessteakandgrill.com.*

La Bodeguiya

$ | **SPANISH** | After nearly two decades on the Spanish side of the Rock, the owners of La Bodeguiya decided to open a sister Spanish tapas bar at this location in Gibraltar. Packed to the brim at lunchtime, the restaurant serves tapas of Iberian pork and seafood (shrimp and king prawn are specialties), plus Spanish staples such as croquettes and potato salad. **Known for:** tapas; loyal following; Iberian pork and seafood. 💲 *Average main: £10* ✉ *10 Chatham Courterguard* ☎ *200/64211* ⏲ *Closed Sun. and Mon.*

Sacarello's

$ | **BRITISH** | Right off Main Street, this busy restaurant is as well known for its excellent coffee and cakes as it is for the rest of its food. There's a varied salad and quiche buffet, as well as stuffed baked potatoes and daily specials, which could include beef curry, or baked lamb with honey mustard. **Known for:** coffee and cakes; lunch menu; cozy, old-fashioned English setting. 💲 *Average main: £10* ✉ *57 Irish Town* ☎ *200/70625* 🌐 *www.sacarellosgibraltar.com* ⏲ *Closed Sun. No dinner.*

Hotels

The Rock

$$$ | **HOTEL** | This hotel overlooking the straits first opened in 1932, and although furnishings in the rooms and restaurants are elegant and colorful, they still preserve something of the English colonial style, with bamboo, ceiling fans, and a terrace bar covered with wisteria. **Pros:** old-world atmosphere; magnificent bay views; good breakfast. **Cons:** inconvenient for shopping; up a steep hill; some bathrooms are very small. 💲 *Rooms from: £140* ✉ *3 Europa Rd.* ☎ *200/73000* 🌐 *www.rockhotelgibraltar.com* *84 rooms* 🍽 *No meals.*

Sunborn

$$$$ | **HOTEL** | This giant yacht hotel (it's seven floors high and 155 yards long) has a permanent home in Gibraltar's marina and offers luxury accommodations complete with ocean views, a casino, a spa, and a restaurant on the top deck, plus lots of luxury extras. **Pros:** unusual place to stay; luxury extras; central, waterfront location. **Cons:** some may find it claustrophobic; not all cabins have views; noise from airport and nearby bars. 💲 *Rooms from: £210* ✉ *35 Ocean Village Promenade* ☎ *200/16000* 🌐 *www.sunborngibraltar.com* *189 rooms* 🍽 *No meals.*

Nightlife

Lord Nelson

BARS/PUBS | A restaurant during the day and a lively bar at night, the Lord Nelson has karaoke on Saturday night and jam sessions and live music during the week. Many ales are on tap. ✉ *Grand Casemates Sq.* ☎ *200/50009* 🌐 *www.lordnelson.gi.*

Chapter 13

THE CANARY ISLANDS

Updated by
Benjamin Kemper

⊙ Sights	🍴 Restaurants	🛏 Hotels	⬤ Shopping	🍸 Nightlife
★★★★☆	★★★☆☆	★★★★☆	★★★☆☆	★★★★☆

WELCOME TO THE CANARY ISLANDS

TOP REASONS TO GO

★ **Carnaval:** Judge for yourself if Carnaval festivities in Santa Cruz de Tenerife and Las Palmas rival those of Rio.

★ **El Teide:** Be blown away by the views of Spain's highest peak, visible from most of the island of Tenerife.

★ **Relaxation:** Seek out solitude and tranquillity in and beyond the dunes of Maspalomas, in Gran Canaria.

★ **Volcanoes:** Marvel at the stark beauty of Lanzarote's volcanoes and lava flows.

★ **Wine:** Go vineyard-hopping and taste distinctive award-winning wines made from Canarian grapes.

★ **Beaches:** Relax on the pure white sands that are bathed by pristine turquoise sea on Fuerteventura.

1 Tenerife. Tenerife, with the largest population of the Canaries, also has the most attractions—even if it has suffered terribly at the hands of tasteless developers. Ride a cable car up the slopes of El Teide, swim in a huge artificial lake, wander botanical gardens, or dance at glittering discos. The beaches are small, with mostly black sand. The verdant (read: rainy) north coast has some unspoiled villages, while the southern Playa de las Américas's skyline is filled with modern high-rise hotels.

2 Gran Canaria. The hot spot of the '60s, Gran Canaria no longer draws as many visitors as Tenerife (it does have one of Europe's biggest and brightest gay scenes, though). Maspalomas beach is one of the islands' most arresting, and the magnificent sand dunes behind it are a must-visit nature reserve. The volcanic center is a succession of dramatic peaks and canyons veined with white-knuckle mountain roads that lead to hidden villages. The seaside capital, Las Palmas, is the Canaries' most cosmopolitan city and is always abuzz with locals and tourists. The old town around Vegueta and Triana is quaint and

authentic, and there's a sparkling stretch of beach downtown, with a lantern-lit boardwalk lined with restaurants and bars.

3 Lanzarote. Lanzarote is a desert isle that improbably escaped the ravages of rampant speculation that scarred Tenerife and Gran Canaria. That's largely thanks to renowned

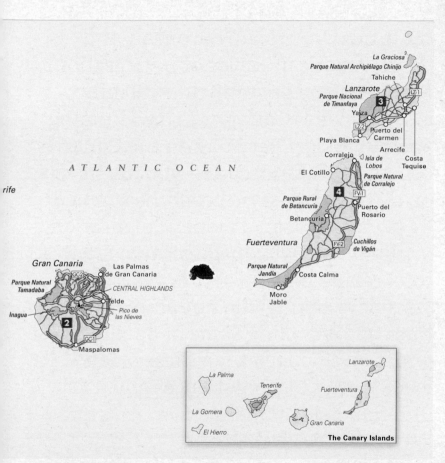

ATLANTIC OCEAN

rife

La Graciosa

Parque Natural Archipiélago Chinijo

Tahiche

Lanzarote

Parque Nacional de Timanfaya

Yaiza

LZ-1

3

LZ-2

Puerto del Carmen

Playa Blanca

Arrecife

Corralejo

Isla de Lobos

Costa Tequise

El Cotillo

Parque Natural de Corralejo

FV-1

4

Puerto del Rosario

Parque Rural de Betancuria

Betancuria

Fuerteventura

FV-2

Cuchillos de Vigán

Parque Natural Jandía

Costa Calma

Moro Jable

Gran Canaria

Las Palmas de Gran Canaria

Parque Natural Tamadaba

GC2

CENTRAL HIGHLANDS

Telde

Pico de las Nieves

Inagua

2

GC1

Maspalomas

La Palma

Tenerife

Lanzarote

Fuerteventura

La Gomera

El Hierro

Gran Canaria

The Canary Islands

architect and activist César Manrique, who pioneered most of the development of responsible tourist attractions on the island. Lanzarote has golden beaches, white villages, caves, and a volcanic national park where heat from an eruption in 1730 is still rising through vents in the earth.

Vegetation is scarce, but the grapes grown by farmers in volcanic ash produce a distinctive Canarian wine.

4 Fuerteventura. Fuerteventura is the least visited of the four largest islands, but construction of new hotels has kept up with the demands of tourists, who come to windsurf and

kitesurf and enjoy the endless white beaches, reminiscent of those in the Caribbean. Luxury hotels dot the coastal resorts, though the barren interior remains largely the domain of goats.

A historic way station between the Old and New Worlds, the Canary Islands have been influenced over the centuries by African, European, and South American waves of immigration. Perhaps that constant cultural influx is what makes Canarians so welcoming and outgoing. Every day on the Canaries brings a new landscape—you might relax on a Caribbean-style beach, be startled by giant lizards in a tropical plantation, or climb a snowcapped volcano. From total relaxation in a luxury resort to strenuous hiking via mountain refuge huts, and sampling some of Spain's finest wines on a bodega tour, these small islands offer big experiences and a very different side of Spain.

A volcanic archipelago 1,280 km (800 miles) southwest of mainland Spain and 112 km (70 miles) off the coast of southern Morocco, the seven Canary Islands lie at about the same latitude as central Florida. La Gomera and El Hierro, as well as parts of La Palma and Gran Canaria, are fertile and overgrown with exotic tropical vegetation, while Lanzarote, Fuerteventura, and stretches of Tenerife are as dry as a bone, with lava caves and desert sand dunes. Even so, Spain's highest peak, Mt. Teide, on Tenerife, is sometimes capped with snow. Geographically, the Canaries are African, but culturally they're European, and spiritually probably Latin American (many islanders have close blood ties to Cuba and Venezuela). The Spanish that's spoken here is, in pronunciation and intonation (but less so in vocabulary), more Latin American than Iberian. Salsa and reggaeton, less popular in mainland Spain, are basically all you'll hear at the wild Carnaval fiestas here.

Before the Spanish arrived, the Canaries were populated by cave-dwelling people called Guanches who were genetically similar to the Berber tribes of northern Africa. In the late 15th century the islands fell one by one to Spanish conquistadores. Columbus resupplied his ships here in 1492 before heading west to the New World and helped establish the archipelago as an important trading center. The Guanches were decimated by slave traders by the end of the 16th century, and to this day, their customs and culture remain largely a mystery. The most significant Guanche remains are the Cenobio de Valerón ruins on Gran Canaria and the mummies on display at the Museo de la Naturaleza y el Hombre in Santa Cruz de Tenerife.

Each of the seven islands is a world unto itself with unique charms, landscapes, and patrimony. Our coverage focuses on the four largest and most-visited islands: Tenerife, Gran Canaria, Lanzarote, and Fuerteventura. The smaller western isles of El Hierro, La Gomera, and La Palma are no less attractive: if you have a few days to spare, visit them from the larger islands via plane or boat.

Planning

WHEN TO GO

The Canaries enjoy warmth in the winter and cool breezes in summer. Regardless of the time of year you visit, expect highs of about 75°F and lows of about 60°F. Winter, especially Christmas and Easter are peak tourism periods for northern Europeans, while Spaniards and Italians tend to come in the summer, particularly August, to escape the sweltering heat. October, when the summer heat and the winds drop, and spring, when a profusion of wildflowers colors the islands, are the most beautiful times to be here. Since the Canaries are a year-round destination, prices tend to be roughly the same no matter when you come, barring the

holiday season. You may have some luck negotiating discounts during the slowest months, May and November.

GETTING HERE AND AROUND
AIR TRAVEL

There are no nonstop flights to the Canary Islands from the United States, though as of 2019, there are mumblings in aviation circles of a possible direct flight between New York City and Tenerife. Americans usually transfer in Madrid or elsewhere in Europe. Iberia, its budget carrier Vueling, and Air Europa have direct flights daily to Tenerife, Gran Canaria, Lanzarote, and Fuerteventura from several cities in mainland Spain (three hours from Madrid). Budget airlines like Ryanair and Easyjet often have unbeatable deals.

Interisland flights are handled by carriers Binter Canarias and Canaryfly using small jets and turboprop planes with great low-altitude views of the islands.

FLIGHT INFORMATION Air Europa ☎ 911/401501 ⊕ www.aireuropa. com. **Binter Canarias** ☎ 902/875787 ⊕ www.bintercanarias.com. **Canaryfly** ☎ 902/808065 ⊕ www.canaryfly.es. **Iberia** ☎ 901/111500 ⊕ www.iberia.com. **Vueling** ☎ 902/808005 ⊕ www.vueling. com.

AIRPORTS Fuerteventura ☎ 913/211000 ⊕ www.aena.es. **Gran Canaria** ☎ 928/579130 ⊕ www.aena.es. **Lanzarote** ☎ 902/404704 ⊕ www.aena.es. **Tenerife North** ☎ 902/404704 ⊕ www.aena.es. **Tenerife South** ☎ 902/404704 ⊕ www. aena.es.

Tenerife has two airports: Tenerife South (TFS), near Playa de las Américas, and Tenerife North (TFN), near the capital city of Santa Cruz. Choose the airport closest to the area of the island that you'll be spending the most time in. The TITSA bus (Route 343, €9.70) connects the airports directly; travel takes about 50 minutes. Driving time from one airport to the other is also about 50 minutes; you can hire a taxi for about €90 or rent a car for around €35.

BOAT AND FERRY TRAVEL

Trasmediterránea runs a slow, comfortable ferry service weekly between Seville and Cádiz and the Canary Islands: Tenerife (Santa Cruz de Tenerife), 49 hours; Gran Canaria (Las Palmas), 40 hours; Lanzarote (Arrecife), 34 hours 30 minutes. The boat has cabins, a tiny pool, restaurants, a recreation room, and a dance club, but it's not a luxury cruise and clearly rather impractical, both money- and time-wise.

Fred Olsen, Naviera Armas, Líneas Romero, and Trasmediterránea operate inexpensive ferries between all seven islands, although if you're traveling to or from El Hierro, La Gomera, or La Palma to the eastern islands, you usually need to get a connecting ferry from Tenerife. Most interisland trips take one to four hours; the few boats departing near midnight are equipped with sleeping cabins. Note that schedules change, particularly in high winds or storms, so it's imperative to call ahead to double-check. Fred Olsen has several ultrasleek trimarans, which accommodate vehicles and are the quickest way to go between islands.

CONTACTS Fred Olsen ☎ 902/100107 *general information* ⊕ *www.fredolsen. es.* **Líneas Romero** ☎ 928/596107 ⊕ *www. lineasromero.com.* **Naviera Armas** ☎ 902/456500 *general information* ⊕ *www.navieraarmas.com.* **Trasmediterránea** ☎ 902/454645 *general information* ⊕ *www.trasmediterranea.es.*

BUS TRAVEL

On the Canaries, buses are known as *guaguas* (pronounced *wa*-was), likely a hispanicization of the English word "wagon." A bus terminal is usually called an *intercambiador* rather than an *estación de autobuses*. Expect to see these terms on signs and brochures.

Bus travel is generally good between the main resorts, airports, and capitals.

In Tenerife, TITSA runs a wide-reaching network of routes connecting the airports with Santa Cruz and the south, and Los Rodeos airport with Santa Cruz and Puerto de la Cruz. Global on Gran Canaria connects the capital and the south with the airport. Buses also transport ferry passengers to and from bus terminals and ports.

Each island has its own bus service geared toward residents. Buses generally leave each village early in the morning for the capital, then depart from the main plaza in early afternoon. Tourist offices have details.

CONTACTS Fuerteventura ☎ 928/855726 ⊕ *www.tiadhe.com.* **Gran Canaria** ☎ 928/939407 ⊕ *www.globalsu.net.* **Lanzarote** ☎ 928/811522 ⊕ *www.intercity-buslanzarote.es.* **Tenerife** ☎ 922/531300 ⊕ *www.titsa.com.*

CAR TRAVEL

Most travelers rent a car for at least part of their stay on the Canaries, as this is by far the best way to explore the countryside. Note that the roads are not always kind to those with vertigo; they often curve over high mountain cliffs with nothing but the sea below. Mountain roads are often narrow, which can be hair-raising if you meet a bus coming the other way. Expect traffic, especially around urban centers.

Car-rental companies abound on every island. Reservations are usually necessary in high season. Cicar and Europcar, with branches in all the airports and major towns on all seven islands, tend to have the best rates.

CONTACTS **Cicar Fuerteventura** ✉ *Aeropuerto de Fuerteventura, Puerto del Rosario* ☎ *928/822900* ⊕ *www.cicar.com.* **Cicar Gran Canaria** ✉ *Aeropuerto de Las Palmas, Gando* ☎ *928/822900* ⊕ *www. cicar.com.* **Cicar Lanzarote** ✉ *Aeropuerto de Lanzarote, Arrecife* ☎ *928/822900* ⊕ *www.cicar.com* ✉ *Tenerife North Airport, La Laguna* ☎ *928/822900* ⊕ *www. cicar.com.* **Cicar Tenerife South** ✉ *Tenerife South Airport, Granadilla de Abona* ☎ *928/822900* ⊕ *www.cicar.com.* **Europcar Fuerteventura** ✉ *Aeropuerto de Fuerteventura* ☎ *902/105055* ⊕ *www.europcar. es.* **Europcar Gran Canaria** ✉ *Aeropuerto de Las Palmas* ☎ *902/105055* ⊕ *www. europcar.es.* **Europcar Lanzarote** ✉ *Aeropuerto de Lanzarote* ☎ *902/105055* ⊕ *www.europcar.es.* **Europcar Tenerife North** ✉ *Tenerife North Airport, La Laguna* ☎ *902/105055* ⊕ *www.europcar. es.* **Europcar Tenerife South** ✉ *Tenerife South Airport, Granadilla de Abona* ☎ *902/105055* ⊕ *www.europcar.es.*

CRUISE TRAVEL

The Canaries are increasingly popular cruise destinations. Las Palmas de Gran Canaria and Santa Cruz de Tenerife are Spain's most visited cruise ports after Barcelona and Palma de Mallorca. The islands are frequent stops on cruises that also visit Madeira, the Azores, and the west coast of Africa.

TAXI TRAVEL

In major towns, taxis can be hailed on the street. Alternately, ask for the nearest taxi stand (*parada de taxi*). Taxis use meters to calculate the fare; passengers may be charged extra fees for luggage

and holiday, weekend, and late-night trips.

TAXI COMPANIES **Lanzarote Taxi** (*Asociación Cooperativa de Taxistas Ajey–Tamia*) ☎ *630/207305* ⊕ *www.lanzarotetaxi.com.* **Radio-Taxi San Marcos Tenerife** ☎ *922/641112, 922/641459, 682/391930 mobile/WhatsApp* ⊕ *www.taxisanmarcos.es.* **Taxis Fuerteventura** ☎ *928/850216* ⊕ *www.taxisfuerteventura.es.* **Taxi Radio Gran Canaria** (*Taragranca Sociedad Cooperativa de Taxistas*) ☎ *928/460000* ⊕ *www.taragranca.org.*

RESTAURANTS

Traditional Canarian cuisine hinges on local seafood, tropical fruits, potatoes, bread, and goat cheese. Meals often begin with *platos de cuchara,* hearty dishes eaten with a spoon, such as *potaje canario* (containing garden vegetables, pork, potatoes, and chickpeas), *rancho canario* (with beef, noodles, and legumes), and *potaje de berros* (watercress soup). *Gofio,* a savory porridge made with corn or wheat flour and enriched with milk or stock, adds ballast to otherwise light meals. The main culinary event is often fresh native fish, the best of which are *vieja, cherne,* and *sama,* all firm-flesh white rockfish. But perhaps the most inescapable Canarian delicacy is *papas arrugadas,* "wrinkled" new potatoes cooked in an abundance of salt water. The best examples use *papas bonitas* ("pretty potatoes"), the moniker for locally grown heirloom varieties.

Other specialties include *cabrito* (roast baby goat) and *conejo* (rabbit), both served in *salmorejo,* a slightly spicy paprika sauce. Finally, no Canarian meal is complete without a dab of *mojo rojo,* a sometimes-spicy sauce made with *pimientas palmeras* (mild red chilies), garlic, and vinegar, plus any number of secret ingredients. No two mojos are alike. Most restaurants serve the sauce virtually by default, and Canarians heap it liberally on dishes as varied as fish and papas arrugadas. The tamer, and fresher, version is *mojo verde,* made with cilantro and/or parsley. Another island specialty is goat cheese, made best in La Palma.

Canarian wines are good and varied. The most popular red grape is listán negro, which makes a fruity, highly drinkable wine with a faint smokiness—probably that volcanic soil talking. Common whites include malvasía and listán blanco, often blended to create floral, fruity expressions. Confusingly, off-dry wines are frequently labled as *afrutados* ("fruity"), so if you like your whites on the dry side, ask for a *vino seco.* Wine production on the Canaries dates back centuries—the Malmsey (fortified sweet) wines from Lanzarote were a favorite with Shakespeare's Falstaff. On the stronger side, the Canaries are also famous for dark rum and liqueurs flavored with everything from coffee to cocoa and hazelnut.

■ **TIP→ Although the tap water in the Canary Islands is technically safe to drink according to the Ministry of Health, most of it comes from desalination plants and is of inferior quality (and taste). Bottled water is the norm in both hotels and restaurants, and hotels generally do not charge restocking fees. To cut down on plastic waste, purchase large-format bottles, and ask your hotel to recycle empties. As of 2019, Fuente Alta is the only bottled water brand in the Canaries that uses recycled materials in its production.**

WHAT IT COSTS In Euros

$	$$	$$$	$$$$
AT DINNER			
Under €12	€12–€17	€18–€22	over €22

HOTELS

There are hundreds of hotels on the Canary Islands, so it's important to choose wisely and not jump at the first seemingly good deal. With a few exceptions, noted in the individual reviews, it's best to stay in newer facilities, ones that weren't built shoddily during the Canaries' tourism boom many decades ago. Many hotels include either a full buffet breakfast or a meal plan of breakfast and lunch or dinner in the price of a room. Hotels with spas and pools generally include the use of these in their rates, but be sure to check the fine print when comparing prices.

Apartment and cabin rentals have become wildly popular in recent years, particularly on Tenerife and Lanzarote. Airbnb is the most common booking resource. These accommodations are usually simply furnished with a kitchenette and small living space, though there are certainly diamond-in-the-rough design properties to be discovered for those willing to pony up the extra euros.

If you organize your trip through a package tour, you'll probably receive a good rate for a hotel room, but rates for independent travelers can vary hugely at such resorts, and you may pay more than necessary. Check for offers on hotel websites and inquire about discounts for long stays or during low season. Always call properties directly before booking via a third party to see if they'll offer you a lower rate. As always, check hotel-rate comparison sites.

Advance booking is almost always a must, since hotels are often booked solid several months out by package travelers.

High season varies depending on the island and locale. In Tenerife and Gran Canaria, high season is from November to April with a second spike in July and August. Lanzarote and Fuerteventura's high seasons are during December and January plus July and August. Airfare to Tenerife and Gran Canaria increases during those islands' respective Carnaval celebrations in late February, so if you're keen to attend, plan on making reservations at least a few months ahead of time.

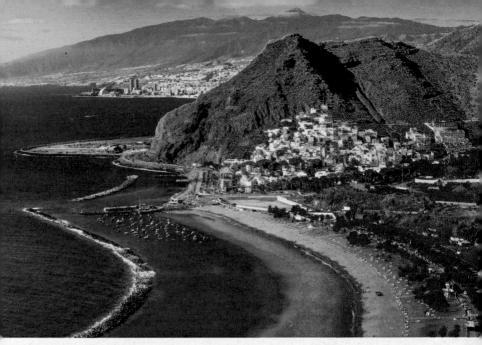

Playa de las Teresitas is one of Tenerife's most popular beaches, thanks to its golden sand, many facilities, and beachfront restaurants.

Note that many four- and five-star hotels have fusty dress codes that require you to change out of beachwear, shorts, and flip-flops at mealtimes.

WHAT IT COSTS In Euros

$	$$	$$$	$$$$
FOR TWO PEOPLE			
under €90	€90–€125	€126–€180	over €180

Tenerife

Tenerife is the largest of the Canary Islands. Its standout feature is the volcanic peak of El Teide (also known as Mount Teide or Monte Teide), which, at 12,198 feet, is Spain's highest mountain. The slopes leading up to Teide are blanketed with pines in the north and with barren lava fields in the south. Tenerife's capital, Santa Cruz de Tenerife, is a giant urban center—forget whitewashed villas and sleepy streets, and imagine the traffic, activity, and crowds of an important shipping port. In the wetter north, mixed among the tourist attractions, are banana plantations and vineyards. In the dry south, the resorts lining the coast have sprung up at the edge of a virtual desert.

VISITOR INFORMATION
Santa Cruz de Tenerife
✉ Pl. de España s/n, Santa Cruz de Tenerife ☎ 922/892903 ⊕ www.webtenerife.com.

VILLA AND APARTMENT RENTAL
Villas and apartments abound in the Canary Islands. The self-catering apartments are competitively priced, and you can often find excellent deals, particularly if you stay for a week or more and do price comparisons on Airbnb and similar sites; the downside is that many apartments are often in drab, cement complexes surrounded by throngs of other vacationing sunseekers, usually from England and Germany. For detailed listings and photos of apartments, villas and hotels throughout the islands, check

Pleasures and Pastimes

Beaches

The sun is what draws most people to the Canaries, and each island has different kinds of beaches for soaking it up. The longest and most pristine—and also the windiest—are the white-sand strands of Fuerteventura. Lanzarote and Gran Canaria offer golden-sand beaches with lounge chairs and parasailing. Tenerife has few natural beaches and makes do with crowded, man-made ones with imported yellow sand plus a few black-sand ones, usually in rock-flanked coves with limited accessibility. The Atlantic Ocean can be rough and chilly in winter, so most high-end hotels provide heated pools to compensate.

Carnaval

There may be no more raucous street party on earth than Carnaval in the Canaries, specifically the rival festivals of Las Palmas de Gran Canaria and Santa Cruz de Tenerife. The two island capitals whip themselves up into 10 days of all-night partying.

Canary *carnavales* are like drunken Halloween nights set to Latin music: of the half-million people swarming the streets in each city, it's hard to spot one person not in costume. Although Las Palmas's Carnaval lasts one month, the serious fun begins with the start of Santa Cruz's, the weekend before Ash Wednesday and running through the final Sunday. It's possible to experience both cities' mayhem, even on the same night, by jet foil; don't miss Las Palmas's Drag Queen gala or Santa Cruz's hilarious mock "sardine burial," which marks the end of the fiesta.

Shopping

The Canary Islands are free ports, which means no value-added tax (VAT) is charged on luxury goods, but you should still expect to pay vacation prices, especially in popular resort areas. The islands are also known for intricately embroidered tablecloths and place mats. If you're looking for the real thing, be prepared to pay for it, and watch out for imitations.

out ⊕ *www.booking.com*, ⊕ *www.homeaway.co.uk*, ⊕ *www.airbnb.com*, and ⊕ *www.spain-holiday.com*.

LOCAL AGENTS Atlantic Horizons
⊠ *Av. Amsterdam 3, Los Cristianos* ☎ *922/790299* ⊕ *www.atlantichorizons.com*. **Tenerife Royal Gardens** ⊠ *Apartamentos Royal Gardens 4, Playa de las Américas* ☎ *922/790211* ⊕ *www.tenerife-holiday-apartments.com*.

Santa Cruz de Tenerife

10 km (6 miles) southeast of Los Rodeos Airport, 75 km (45 miles) northeast of Playa de las Américas.

Although Tenerife's busy capital is smaller, quieter, and less attractive than Las Palmas in Gran Canaria, it has its share of worthwhile attractions and elegant monuments. Until 1833, the island's capital was La Laguna, not Santa Cruz, making the latter "new," at least by Spanish standards; the city's oldest buildings (the fishermen's houses on Calle de la Noria) date to the 18th century. At the busy Plaza de España, modernized in 2006 by Swiss architects Herzog & de Meuron, there are several pedestrian streets leading north and to the area west of the port, where you'll find the city's stunning auditorium and maritime park. Be sure to go for a stroll down the ramblas, long,

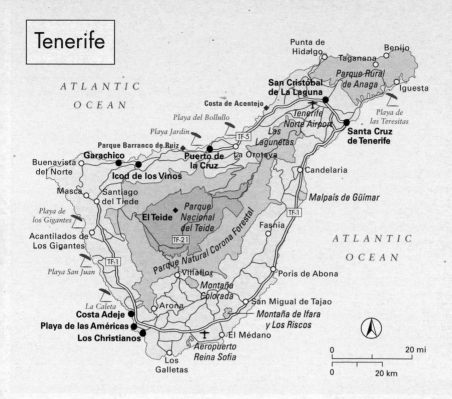

Tenerife

ATLANTIC OCEAN

Punta de Hidalgo
Benijo
Taganana
Parque Rural de Anaga
Iguesta
San Cristóbal de La Laguna
Costa de Acentejo
Playa del Bollullo
Playa de las Teresitas
Tenerife Norte Airport
Playa Jardín
Las Lagunetas
Santa Cruz de Tenerife
Parque Barranco de Ruiz
Garachico
Puerto de la Cruz
La Orotava
Buenavista del Norte
Icod de los Vinos
Candelaria
Masca
Santiago del Tiede
Malpaís de Güímar
Playa de los Gigantes
El Teide
Parque Nacional del Teide
Fasnia
Acantilados de Los Gigantes
TF-21
Parque Natural Corona Forestal
ATLANTIC OCEAN
TF-1
Playa San Juan
Villaflor
Poris de Abona
La Caleta
Montaña Colorada
Costa Adeje
Arona
San Miguel de Tajao
Playa de las Américas
Montaña de Ifara y Los Riscos
Los Christianos
El Médano
Aeropuerto Reina Sofía
Los Galletas

0   20 mi
0   20 km

tree-lined boulevards that fall steeply from the north end of the city to the sea.

Santa Cruz is also an ideal home base for adventures into the Parque Rural de Anaga (Anaga Nature Park), one of Tenerife's most scenic and untouched corners. If you can brave the white-knuckle switchbacks, you'll be rewarded with subtropical forests, volcanic formations, and charming villages.

GETTING HERE AND AROUND

If you're arriving by sea, it can be a long and fairly uninteresting walk from your cruise ship into town, so take a shuttle bus if one's provided (most cruise companies do) to the Estación Marítima cruise station. From here, you can hop on the sightseeing bus or walk to the Plaza de España (about a 10-minute walk), where there's a branch of the tourist office and all main sights are within walking distance. If you're heading south to Los Cristianos or north to Puerto de la Cruz, go to the bus terminal (about a 15-minute walk from Plaza de España), where there are frequent bus connections. La Laguna can be reached by tram: there are stops at the bus station and near the Puente General Serrador.

From Tenerife you can catch a ferry to any of the other six islands. From Santa Cruz, sail to Gran Canaria's two main ports: Agaete in the west (Fred Olsen is the quickest, at about an hour) or Las Palmas in the north. Ferries to La Palma (Santa Cruz de la Palma), La Gomera (San Sebastián), and El Hierro (Puerto de la Estaca) leave from Los Cristianos, in southern Tenerife. La Gomera can also be reached by a ferry from Los Cristianos (55 minutes; 35 minutes by Fred Olsen's trimaran).

Sights

Auditorio de Tenerife Adán Martín

ARTS VENUE | A magnificent avant-garde auditorium designed by Santiago Calatrava dominates the west end of the city. To keep its pearly-white *trencadís* (broken tile mosaics) exterior clear of pooping pigeons, a falconer comes twice a day to scare them off with his raptors. The auditorium has a year-round program of concerts and opera, though you can sometimes catch impromptu music acts rehearsing or performing in the adjacent square overlooking the sea. Guided tours (10, noon, 2, and 4) are given in English and Spanish; book ahead by phone or email. ⊠ *Av. de la Constitución 1* ☎ *922/568625* ⊕ *www.auditoriodetenerife.com* ⤳ *Tours €8* ⊗ *No tours Sun.*

Castillo de San Cristóbal (*St. Christopher's Castle*)

MUSEUM | **FAMILY** | The walls of this castle were uncovered when the car park under the Plaza de España was being built. The site is now a small museum that includes the 18th-century "Tigre Cannon" that reputedly cost Britain's Admiral Nelson his right arm in an attack he led in 1797. Entrance to the museum is via a stairway opposite the lake. ⊠ *Pl. de España* ⤳ *Free* ⊗ *Closed Sun.*

Iglesia de Nuestra Señora de la Concepción (*Church of Our Lady of the Conception*)

RELIGIOUS SITE | A six-story Moorish bell tower tops this church, which was renovated as part of an urban-renewal project that razed blocks of slums in this area. Church opening times vary, but you can generally visit before and after Mass. ⊠ *Pl. de la Iglesia* ☎ *922/242387* ⤳ *Free.*

Mercado de Nuestra Señora de Africa (*La Recova Market*)

MARKET | **FAMILY** | This colorful city market is part bazaar and part food emporium. Stalls outside sell household goods; inside, stands displaying everything from flowers to canaries are arranged around a patio. Downstairs, a stroll through the seafood section will acquaint you with the local fish. A flea market with antiques and secondhand goods is held here on Sunday mornings. Check the website for a monthly schedule of night-time activities. ⊠ *Av. de San Sebastián* ⊕ *www.la-recova.com.*

Museo de la Naturaleza y Arqueología (*Museum of Nature and Archaeology*)

MUSEUM | Primitive ceramics and mummies are this museum's highlights. The ancient Guanches mummified their dead by rubbing the bodies with pine resin and salt and leaving them in the sun to dry for two weeks. ⊠ *Calle Fuente Morales s/n* ☎ *922/535816* ⊕ *www.museosdetenerife.org* ⤳ *€5 (free Fri. and Sat. 4–8)* ⊗ *Closed Mon.*

Museo Municipal de Bellas Artes (*Museum of Fine Arts*)

MUSEUM | This 14-room, two-story gallery is lined with canvases by Breughel, Coecke, and Ribera as well as other famed works created between the 16th and 20th centuries. Many depict local events. The museum is on the Plaza Príncipe de Asturias. ⊠ *Calle José Murphy 12* ☎ *922/274786* ⤳ *Free* ⊗ *Closed Mon.*

Palmetum

GARDEN | **FAMILY** | Up on the hill just behind Parque Marítimo is Europe's largest collection of palms with some 600 species. The 29½-acre site, built over the former city dump and opened in 2014, houses palm trees from all over the world set around waterfalls and lagoons, all with panoramic views of the ocean and city. Guided tours in English are available for €3 extra and last approximately one hour. ⊠ *Av. Constitución 5* ☎ *697/651127* ⊕ *palmetumtenerife.es* ⤳ *€6* ⊗ *Closed Mon.*

Parque Marítimo César Manrique

CITY PARK | **FAMILY** | West of the auditorium, this public maritime park with its three saltwater pools and tropical gardens is a favorite with locals. Designed by the Lanzarote-born architect César Manrique, it combines volcanic rock with palms and local flora. ⊠ *Av. de la Constitución 5* ☎ *922/229368* ⊕ *www. parquemaritimosantacruz.es* 🎫 *€3.*

Plaza de España

PLAZA | The heart of Santa Cruz de Tenerife is the Plaza de España. The cross at the southern end is a memorial to those who died in the Spanish Civil War, which—it bears remembering—was launched from Tenerife by General Franco during his exile here. The controversial monument's architect was Juan de Ávalos, who also designed the Francoist memorial and basilica at Valle de los Caídos. A 2006 refresh of the entire square by Swiss firm Herzog & de Meuron added a shallow oblong pond, new pavilions, and modern lighting The plaza is a vibrant center for Carnaval festivities. Castillo San Cristóbal and the tourist office are both here. ⊠ *Santa Cruz de Tenerife.*

★ Tenerife Espacio de las Artes *(TEA)*

MUSEUM | This museum is the leader in contemporary art on the islands due to its sleek low-rise design and avant-garde exhibitions. Designed by the Swiss architects Herzog & de Meuron, it's next to the Museo de la Naturaleza. Expect 20th- and 21st-century art with a political or sociological bent (a 2019 exhibition explored the complex relationship between tourism and art). TEA's crown jewel is the hall dedicated to tinerfeño surrealist artist Óscar Domínguez. ⊠ *Av. San Sebastián 8* ☎ *922/849057* ⊕ *www. teatenerife.es* 🎫 *€7* 🕑 *Closed Mon.*

Beaches

Playa de las Teresitas

BEACH—SIGHT | FAMILY | Santa Cruz's beach, Las Teresitas, is about 7 km (4½ miles) northeast of the city, near the town of San Andrés. The 1½ km (1 mile) of beach was created using white sand imported from the Sahara in 1973 and adorned with palms. Beachgoers

Parque Rural de Anaga 👁

Thanks to its ornery terrain, Anaga Nature Park has managed to keep the tour-bus crowd (mostly) at bay—their loss. This magical oasis takes in misty laurel forests (aka laurisilva) with numerous endemic species, bizarre rock formations that jut above the trees, and hidden mountain villages like Taganana, founded in 1501. Explore the area by car, stopping to take a dip at Playa de Benijo, where you can catch a hiking trail into the surrounding countryside, and to snap a few postcard-worthy pics at the Pico de Inglés viewpoint.

in the '70s were purportedly bitten by the occasional scorpion that had hitched a ride from Africa (they've since been eradicated). A man-made barrier runs parallel to the sands and ensures rip-tide-free bathing. Busy in the summer and on weekends, this beach is especially popular with local families. The 910 TITSA bus route connects the beach with Santa Cruz. There's a good choice of bars and restaurants, and plenty of lounge chairs for rent. **Amenities:** food and drink; lifeguards; parking (no fee); showers; toilets. **Good for:** sunrise; swimming; walking. ⊠ *San Andrés.*

🍴 Restaurants

El Coto de Antonio

$$ | SPANISH | FAMILY | This down-home Santa Cruz standby got a leg up in 2018 when famed Spanish radio show host Carlos Herrera called it his favorite Santa Cruz restaurant on the air; since then, tables have been in high demand, so call ahead. You'll agree that the buzz is well deserved when you sample chef Carlos's steak tartare, the best in town, or his rustic snail stew enriched with trotters (don't knock it till you try it). **Known for:** homey atmosphere; Canarian comfort food; knockout steak tartare. $ *Average main: €17* ✉ *Calle de General Goded 13* ☎ *922/272105* ⊙ *No dinner Sun.*

El Lateral 27

$$ | SPANISH | FAMILY | Situated on the main shopping street, this restaurant is a convenient place to stop for a meal after sightseeing, especially since the kitchen is open from 11 am to midnight. Try to snag a table on the terrace that overflows onto the leafy pedestrian street (the interior dining room is comparatively drab). **Known for:** wide selection of salads; fresh fish; good value for the city center. $ *Average main: €15* ✉ *Calle Bethencourt Alfonso 27* ☎ *922/287774* ⊙ *Closed Sun.*

La Garriga

$ | SPANISH | FAMILY | Some of the best sandwiches in town are made here, and the *tortilla* (potato omelet) may be the tastiest on the island. You can also buy cold and local cheeses. **Known for:** greasy-spoon sandwiches; terrific tortilla; fine cheeses and charcuterie. $ *Average main: €3* ✉ *Calle Pérez Galdós 24* ☎ *922/285501* ▭ *No credit cards* ⊙ *Closed Sun. No dinner Sat.*

Los Pinchitos

$$ | SEAFOOD | FAMILY | Los Pinchitos is one of those dying-breed restaurants where you can eat your fill of pristine seafood without maxing out your credit card. Settle in for a leisurely no-frills feast of octopus, scallops, squid, and whatever other sea creatures were hauled up onto the pier that morning, and wash it all down with a carafe of (surprisingly solid) house wine. **Known for:** heaping seafood platters; homey atmosphere; mojo-topped limpets. $ *Average main: €14* ✉ *Calle Guillén 14* ☎ *643/176630.*

★ San Sebastián 57

$$$$ | FUSION | To fully grasp the potential of Canarian cuisine, book a table at this white-tablecloth standby that coaxes market ingredients—such as *patudo* (bigeye) tuna, black potatoes, and local heirloom tomatoes—into flawless, modern preparations like *tataki* (lightly seared), *ensaladilla rusa* (salade Olivier), and vinaigrette, respectively. Staff aren't on island time and happily attend to your every need. **Known for:** Canarian fusion cuisine; rave-worthy tasting menus; subdued, minimalist decor. $ *Average main: €24* ✉ *Av. de San Sebastián 57* ☎ *822/104325* ⊙ *Closed Sun.*

Tasca Tagoror

$ | SPANISH | FAMILY | Opposite the Iberostar Grand Mencey, this tiny no-frills bar serves simple Canarian cuisine—think grilled sardines and tomato-avocado salads—in abundant portions at reasonable prices. The dining room has a beamed ceiling, low wooden stools, and barrels for tables—in other words, it's fine for a quick bite but not ideal for lingering. **Known for:** casual local crowd; budget-friendly tapas; solid seafood and Spanish omelet. $ *Average main: €10* ✉ *Calle Dr. José Naveiras 9* ☎ *922/274163* ⊙ *Closed Sun.*

Hotels

Hotel Colón Rambla

$ | HOTEL | FAMILY | This cheery budget hotel is situated in a residential area north of the city center, just off the Rambla Santa Cruz. **Pros:** quiet oasis in the city center; well-maintained pool; large bathrooms. **Cons:** breakfasts don't vary; some rooms get noise from street traffic; could use an update. $ *Rooms from: €70* ✉ *Calle Viera y Clavijo 49* ☎ *922/272550* ⊕ *www.hotelcolonrambla.com* ⤴ *40 rooms* ⊙ *No meals.*

★ Iberostar Grand Mencey

$$$ | HOTEL | The ancient Guanches' name for their kings was "Mencey," and you'll feel like one at this grand, white stucco-and-marble hotel north of the city center. **Pros:** quiet, leafy neighborhood;

well-oiled-machine staff; fairy-tale garden. **Cons:** far from the action; jacked-up fees for parking and spa access; no kid-centric areas or programming. $ *Rooms from: €128* ⊠ *Calle Dr. José Naveiras 38* ☎ *922/609900* ⊕ *www.iberostar.com* ⬎ *286 rooms* ⦿⦿ *No meals.*

ⓨ Nightlife

Santa Cruz nightlife revolves around Calle Antonio D. Alfonso, known locally as Calle de la Noria, west of the Iglesia de la Concepción. Here you'll find plenty of good cocktail bars and pubs. If you're looking for tapas, try Callejón del Combate, west of the Plaza del Príncipe. For upscale disco bars and dance clubs, head for **Avenida Anaga,** facing the port.

★ Bambú Lounge

DANCE CLUBS | Shimmy—and twerk, if you dare—at this Southeast Asian–inflected rooftop *discoteca* that attracts a young local crowd. Sunday nights are reserved for Latin (salsa, bachata, and more) dance parties. ⊠ *Calle Fernando Arozena Quintero 5* ☎ *922/202296* ⊕ *www.bambulounge.es.*

Café Atlántico

CAFES—NIGHTLIFE | Opposite the tourist office, this is one of the city's oldest café-bars (est. 1945), famous as a venue for business and cultural gatherings. The original interior includes Moorish tiling, typical Canary wooden beams, and a very large oil painting of Mt. Teide. Open all day from 10 am until late, this is the place for a relaxed cocktail or *café con leche.* A 2018 row between the management company and original owners has put the café's future in jeopardy, so get there soon, before it closes or loses its old-timey essence. ⊠ *Pl. de España 1* ☎ *922/246909.*

🏃 Activities

GOLF
Real Club de Golf de Tenerife

GOLF | This club, which celebrated its 85th birthday in 2017, has the second-oldest course in Spain and comes with paranomic views. The course, to the north of the city, is only open to nonmembers on weekdays from 8 to 12:30, and reservations are essential. ⊠ *El Peñon, Tacoronte* ☎ *922/636607* ⊕ *www.realclubgolftenerife.com* ⛳ *Green fees from €65* 🏌 *18 holes, 5750 yards, par 71.*

🛍 Shopping

Santa Cruz de Tenerife is a major shopping center, even if it doesn't have quite the variety and number of stores found in Las Palmas. Calle Castillo, the main pedestrian street through the center of town, is lined with souvenir shops, trendy boutiques, and big-brand apparel stores (e.g., Massimo Dutti, Bimba y Lola, Foot Locker). Calle del Pilar has higher-end fashions and the department stores Marks & Spencer and El Corte Inglés (another branch is next to the bus terminal).

Artenerife

CRAFTS | Traditional crafts sold at this kiosk near the tourist office are made by local artisans and guaranteed by the island's government as *productos artesanos.* The selection includes Tenerifan *calado*—exquisitely embroidered linen tablecloths and place mats—and clay pottery made using the same methods as those used by the island's aboriginal settlers. (The aborigines didn't use potter's wheels; rather, they rolled the clay into *churros,* or cylindrical strips, and hand-kneaded these into bowls. Pebbles, branches, and shells were used to buff the results.) ⊠ *Pl. de España* ☎ *922/291523* ⊕ *www.artenerife.com* ⊗ *Closed Sat. afternoon and Sun.*

San Cristóbal de La Laguna

5 km (3 miles) northwest of Santa Cruz.

Known colloquially as "La Laguna," this university town was the first capital of Tenerife. It was planned and built in a Renaissance style in 1500, a design that was later adopted in New World cities like La Habana (modern-day Havana) and Cartagena de Indias (in Colombia), and many original, UNESCO-protected buildings remain. The old town has kept its colonial feel through the centuries with its tree-lined promenades, pastel-colored facades, and elegant palaces. Pick up a map at the tourist office, on Calle Obispo Rey Redondo, and snake your way through the pedestrianized streets to be transported to Spain's Golden Age.

GETTING HERE AND AROUND

Tram

This comfortable tram goes from central Santa Cruz, with stops at the bus station and Fundación, to La Laguna, a trip of 35 minutes. A one-way ticket, which costs €1.35, can be bought at the automated kiosks before you board. ✉ *La Laguna* 🌐 *www.metrotenerife.com.*

VISITOR INFORMATION

La Laguna Tourist Office

Free guided tours in English leave from the tourist office on weekday mornings with no set timetable. Call ahead to confirm a time slot. ✉ *Calle Obispo Rey Redondo 7* ☎ *922/631194* 🌐 *www.turismodelalaguna.com* ☞ *Closed weekends.*

👁 Sights

Museo de Historia y Antropología (*Museum of History and Anthropology of Tenerife*)

MUSEUM | Occupying the splendid 17th-century palace of an Italian merchant, this museum chronicles Tenerife's sociocultural history from the 15th to the 20th century with documents, artifacts, and religious relics. Signage is in Spanish only, but you can download a free English audio guide on your smartphone (ask museum personnel for details). The elegant courtyard blends Italian Renaissance architecture, like white marble columns, with local materials such as hardy Canary Island pine. ✉ *Calle San Agustín 22* ☎ *922/825949* 🌐 *www.museosdetenerife.org* 🎫 *€5 (free Fri. and Sat. 4–8).*

Parroquia Matriz de Nuestra Señora de la Concepción

RELIGIOUS SITE | **FAMILY** | The arcaded bell tower of this 16th-century church is an architectural icon of La Laguna, visible from almost everywhere in the city. Climb to the top for 360-degree views of the city and surrounding countryside. ✉ *Pl. de la Concepción 10* 🎫 *€1.*

🍴 Restaurants

★ Tasca el Obispado

$$ | **SPANISH** | **FAMILY** | Figurines of the Virgin Mary and other religious paraphernalia line the walls of this eclectic tavern with low ceilings and a cozy, countrified feel. Hand-cut *jamón* (ham) and runny-in-the-center tortillas make wonderful appetizers; save room for the *conejo en salmorejo* (roast rabbit in a paprika-garlic sauce) and homemade desserts. **Known for:** cheery service; rustic decor; one of the best tortillas on the island. [$] *Average main: €15* ✉ *Calle Herradores 88* ☎ *922/251450* 🕒 *Closed Sun.*

Zumería Tamarindo

$ | **SPANISH** | **FAMILY** | Students and penny-pinching travelers flock to this no-frills juice bar, as famous for its colorful smoothies (made with local fruit) as it is for its club sandwiches and filling *platos combinados* (combo platters), served with fries and salad. **Known for:** tropical fruit juices and smoothies; full lunches for under €5; collegiate atmosphere. [$] *Average main: €4* ✉ *Calle Consistorio 22* ☎ *922/314353* 🕒 *Closed Sun.*

La Laguna was the first unwalled colonial city and still preserves its original 15th century layout almost intact.

Hotels

Hotel Aguere

$ | **HOTEL** | Get a taste of historic life in La Laguna at this 18th-century palace that became a hotel in 1885. **Pros:** historic building; good value; welcoming staff. **Cons:** small rooms with basic furnishings; antique doors and walls mean poor soundproofing; no elevator and steep stairs. [$] *Rooms from: €80* ✉ *Calle Obispo Rey Redondo 55* ☎ *922/314036* 🌐 *www.hotelaguere.es* 🛏 *23 rooms* 🍴 *Free Breakfast.*

★ **La Laguna Gran Hotel**

$$ | **HOTEL** | This chic four-star hotel housed in an 18th-century palace opened in 2017. **Pros:** rooftop pool, gym, and bar; varied breakfasts with local items; Michelin-starred restaurant on-site. **Cons:** poor soundproofing; still ironing out kinks; inconsistent service. [$] *Rooms from: €97* ✉ *Calle Nava y Grimon 18* ☎ *922/108080* 🌐 *lalagunagranhotel.com* 🛏 *123 rooms* 🍴 *No meals.*

Activities

Centro Hípico La Esperanza

HORSEBACK RIDING | **FAMILY** | This equestrian center, 8 km (5 miles) west of La Laguna, offers trail rides and equitation lessons. Advanced riders shouldn't miss the "Adrenaline" experience that lets you do what most other riding companies won't: gallop at full tilt. ✉ *Camino Guillén s/n, La Esperanza* ☎ *677/479544* 🌐 *centrohipicolaesperanza.com* 🎫 *From €50.*

Puerto de la Cruz

36 km (22 miles) west of Santa Cruz.

This is the oldest resort in the Canaries, and sadly, cheap mass tourism and urban sprawl have all but drained it of local charm and island character. There are a few diamonds in the rough, though, and several sights on the outskirts of town make the area worth a visit. Don't stay at any of the bland, overpriced resorts by the beach, and when exploring, stick to the old sections of town, which have colonial plazas and paseos for evening strolls.

GETTING HERE AND AROUND

An excellent bus service connects Puerto de la Cruz with the airport and Santa Cruz's bus terminal. Buses leave every 30 minutes weekdays and every 45–60 minutes on weekends; the journey takes around 50 minutes. You can also rent a car (from €30 a day) or take a taxi (€42).

The town is very hilly and getting anywhere outside the port involves a steep climb. To visit the Jardín Botánico or Parque Taoro, your best bet is to take a cab or rent a motorcycle or bike.

VISITOR INFORMATION

Más que Motos Tenerife
 Save yourself the trek up and down the hills by renting a motorbike or motorcycle, ideal for exploring Puerto de la Cruz and surroundings. As the name implies, quads and dirt bikes are also available. Motorcycle rentals are from €20 a day including helmet and insurance. ⊠ *Av. Marques Villanueva del Prado 15, Local 8* ☎ *922/371131* ⊕ *www.masquemotostenerife.com.*

Sights

★ Casa del Vino del Tenerife

MUSEUM | FAMILY | Wine and food lovers shouldn't miss this wine museum and tasting room, opened by the Canary Islands' government to promote local vintners. The surprisingly well-appointed museum, which describes local grapes, viticultural methods, and history, has English-language placards; reasonably priced tastings in various formats are held in the abutting bar area, and you can buy your favorite bottle in the shop. The complex also has a tapas bar and a restaurant with creative Canarian fare and a curious little **honey museum** with exhibits and tastings. Casa del Vino lies about halfway between Puerto de la Cruz and Tenerife North Airport, at the El Sauzal exit on the main highway. ⊠ *Calle*

San Simon 49, at Autopista General del Norte, Km 21, Sauzal ☎ *922/572535* ⊕ *www.casadelvinotenerife.com* ☎ *€3* ☉ *Closed Mon.*

Costa Martiánez (*Lago Martiánez*)
AMUSEMENT PARK/WATER PARK | FAMILY | Because Puerto de la Cruz has uninviting black-sand beaches, the town commissioned Lanzarote artist César Manrique in 1965 to build Costa Martiánez, a forerunner of today's water parks. It's an immense, and immensely fun, public pool on the waterfront, with landscaped islands, bridges, and a volcano-like fountain that sprays sky-high. The complex also includes several smaller pools and a restaurant-nightclub. All facilities are cash-only. ⊠ *Av. de Colón s/n* ☎ *922/385955* ⊕ *www.ociocostamartianez.com* ☎ *From €6.*

Jardín Botánico (*Botanical Garden*)
GARDEN | FAMILY | Filled with more than 4,000 varieties of tropical trees and plants, and sonorous birds, the Jardín Botánico was founded in 1788, on the orders of King Carlos III, to propagate warm-climate species brought back to Spain from the Americas. The gardens are closed during stormy weather or when the wind speed exceeds 40 kph (25 mph). ⊠ *Calle Retama 2* ☎ *922/383572* ☎ *€3.*

Loro Parque
AMUSEMENT PARK/WATER PARK | FAMILY | This huge subtropical garden and zoo holds 1,300 parrots, many of which are trained to ride bicycles and perform other tricks. The garden also has the world's largest penguin zoo. The dapper Antarctic birds receive round-the-clock care from marine biologists and other veterinary specialists in a climate-controlled environment. Also here is one of Europe's largest aquariums, with an underwater tunnel, a dolphin and killer-whale (orca) show, and some gorillas. Free trains leave for the park from the Plaza Reyes Católicos. ⊠ *Av. Loro Parque s/n* ☎ *922/373841* ⊕ *www.loroparque.com* ☎ *€35.*

Jardín Beach in Puerto de la Cruz is a famous beach filled with dark-colored volcanic sand, palm trees, and hotels.

Plaza de la Iglesia

PLAZA | Stroll from Lago Martiánez along the coastal walkway to reach the Plaza de la Iglesia, which is beautifully landscaped with flowering plants. Be sure to visit the Nuestra Señora de la Peña Church (open before and after Mass) with its baroque altarpiece and elaborate pulpit. ✉ *Puerto de la Cruz.*

Plaza del Charco

PLAZA | It's a two-minute walk from the Plaza de la Iglesia to this plaza, one of the prettiest and liveliest in town, with plenty of cafés and tapas bars. ✉ *Puerto de la Cruz.*

Tourist Office

GOVERNMENT BUILDING | Occupying a meticulously preseved royal customhouse from the 17th century, the tourist office is outfitted with balconies, an interior patio, and intricate wood carvings. ✉ *Casa de la Aduana, Calle Las Lonjas s/n* ☎ *922/386000* 🌐 *www.webtenerife.com.*

🍴 Restaurants

Bodegas Monje

$$ | **SPANISH** | A five-minute drive from the Casa del Vino, in the township of El Sauzal, you'll find this award-winning winery and restaurant perched on a bluff overlooking the ocean. After a lunch of crackly pulled (local heritage-breed *cochino negro*) pork and roasted potatoes, waddle over to the bodega for a tour and tasting, and if you're looking for a gluggable souvenir, snap up a bottle of the Tintilla, a smoky, complex red aged in French oak barrels that's nearly impossible to find in shops. **Known for:** heritage-breed pulled pork; mojo-making demonstrations (call ahead to book); production of some of the finest wines on the island. [$] *Average main: €14* ✉ *Calle Cruz de Leandro 36, Sauzal* ☎ *922/585027* 🌐 *www.bodegasmonje.com* 🕓 *No dinner.*

★ Casa Pache

$ | **SPANISH** | **FAMILY** | Down a plant-lined alley off the Plaza del Charco, this family-run restaurant is in a typical local house, with a labyrinth of small rooms leading off the main hall; you might find yourself sitting next to a collection of old photos, a pile of hats, or some rustic artifacts. Standouts on the traditional Canarian menu include *puchero canario* (chickpea stew with vegetables, pork, and chicken), *piñas con costillas y papas* (corn on the cob with spareribs and potatoes), and conejo en salmorejo . **Known for:** romantic ambience; Canarian comfort food; staff who treat you like family. *[$] Average main: €10 ✉ Calle La Verdad 6 ☎ 922/372524 💳 No credit cards ⏲ Closed Wed.*

Tropical

$ | **SPANISH** | Those in the know come here for typical Canarian food, especially the local dayboat fish. The best tables are outside on the pedestrian street, a couple of blocks behind the port, but the interior's cheap and cheerful wooden tables and fishing nets have their charm. **Known for:** ocean-fresh seafood; unbeatable set lunch deal; local wines. *[$] Average main: €9 ✉ Calle El Lomo 7 ☎ 922/385312 ⏲ Closed Sat. and July.*

Hotels

★ Hacienda Cuatro Ventanas

$$$ | **RENTAL** | Until recently, if you wanted luxury on Tenerife, you had to settle for one of the big-brand resorts in the south—no longer; Cuatro Ventanas, hidden among rolling banana plantations that tumble into the sea, is the kind of place a celebrity might rent to disappear to for a few weeks. **Pros:** highly Instagrammable infinity pool; a world away from the tourist hubbub; high-design interiors. **Cons:** a bit remote; no full-time staff or daily cleaning service; slow Wi-Fi. *[$] Rooms from: €162 ✉ Calle Playa del Socorro 1–2 ☎ 660/866678 🌐 www.haciendacuatroventanas.com 🛏 4 rooms 🍴 No meals.*

What's in a Name?

You may be surprised to learn that the Canary Islands were named not for the yellow songbirds but for a breed of dog (*canum* in Latin) found here by ancient explorers. The birds were later named after the islands.

Hotel Tigaiga

$$ | **HOTEL** | Take in sweeping views of the city, ocean, La Palma island, and Mt. Teide from the lush tropical gardens at this family-owned hotel above Taoro Park. **Pros:** intimate, noncorporate feel; magnificent views; well-appointed breakfast buffet. **Cons:** slightly dated rooms; 230-stair climb to the hotel from the city; older clientele means it's quiet. *[$] Rooms from: €124 ✉ Parque Taoro 28 ☎ 922/383500 🌐 www.tigaiga.com 🛏 76 rooms 🍴 Free Breakfast.*

Monopol

$ | **HOTEL** | Monopol has had more than a century to perfect its brand of hospitality: built as a private home in 1742, opened as a hotel in 1888, and run by the same family for more than 70 years, this three-star has neatly furnished rooms with wooden balconies set around a verdant courtyard. **Pros:** central location; historic building; serene pool area. **Cons:** communal areas could use refurbishment; dowdy decor; proximity to loud church bells. *[$] Rooms from: €65 ✉ Calle Quintana 15 ☎ 922/384611 🌐 www.monopoltf.com 🛏 92 rooms 🍴 No meals.*

Nightlife

Hotels often have live music or other entertainment at night, mostly geared toward an older (50s and up) crowd.

The side streets of Avenida Colón are packed with bars and underground clubs catering to a wider range of ages and musical tastes. For the pop and DJ beats, head to Blanco Bar and Pub Limbo on Calle Blanco.

Azúcar
DANCE CLUBS | You can dance to Cuban rhythms and live Latin jams at this busy nightclub that opens at 11 nightly. ⊠ *Calle Obispo Pérez 12* 🕾 *682/286705.*

Casino Puerto de la Cruz
CASINOS | Try your luck in games of chance in the beautiful surroundings of Costa Martiánez. You must be over 18 and flash a photo ID to get into this unfancy casino. No beachwear or shorts are allowed. ⊠ *Costa Martiánez, Av. de Colón s/n* 🕾 *922/368842* ⊕ *www.casinos-tenerife.com* 🔁 *€3.*

 Performing Arts

Teatro Timanfaya
MUSIC CLUBS | The town's theater (a five-minute walk south of Plaza del Charco) has a year-round calendar of cultural events including a classical music concert every Sunday at noon (€10). Purchase tickets for events at the tourist office. ⊠ *Calle Las Damas 1* 🕾 *922/376106.*

Icod de los Vinos

26 km (16 miles) west of Puerto de la Cruz.

Attractive plazas rimmed by unspoiled colonial architecture and pine balconies form the heart of Tenerife's most historic wine district. A 1,000-year-old **dragon tree,** the natural symbol of Tenerife, towers 57 feet above the coastal highway, C820. It's arguably the oldest living specimen of this species on earth, and special measures (like installing an electrical fan inside its trunk to prevent mold) have been undertaken to preserve it. The Guanches worshiped these trees as symbols of fertility and knowledge; the sap, which turns red upon contact with air, was used in healing rituals.

GETTING HERE AND AROUND
Buses run every hour between here and Santa Cruz, and there's also reasonably frequent service from Puerto de la Cruz. Otherwise, drive here so you can also explore farther afield.

Garachico

5 km (3 miles) west of Icod de los Vinos.

Garachico is one of the most idyllic and historic towns on the islands, and it's well worth a quick visit. It was the main port of Tenerife until May 5, 1706, when Mt. Teide blew its top, sending twin rivers of lava downhill—one filled Garachico's harbor, and the other wiped out about 90% of the town (hence Garachico's nickname: "Pompeii of the Canaries"). Though most of the buildings are faithful reconstructions from the 18th century, a handful of original structures survived including the **Castillo de San Miguel,** a tiny 16th-century fortress on the waterfront. Save for the odd art exhibition or cultural event, it's closed to the public. The restored **Convento de San Francisco** (open Monday–Saturday), was also unscathed, as was the 18th-century parish church of **Santa Ana** with its elaborate baroque altarpiece.

Sights

Piscinas Naturales El Caletón
HOT SPRINGS | **FAMILY** | Lava flows formed these seaside natural pools, to which stairs, paths, and railings have been added for easy access. There's a pleasant café selling drinks and snacks and a conventional swimming pool that comes in handy when the surf is rough. Far from luxurious or exclusive, the pools are owned by the town and popular with born-and-bred tinerfeños of all ages. ⊠ *Av. Tome Cano 5.*

Hotels

★ Boutique Hotel San Roque

$$$ | HOTEL | Museum-quality art by well-known painters lines the walls of this Bauhaus-inspired design property occupying a colonial palace in the old town. **Pros:** art by renowned artists; paradisiacal pool and spa; 17th-century building with great bones. **Cons:** kids not allowed; gloomy rooms and bathrooms; cold when the weather is uncooperative. [$] *Rooms from: €177* ✉ *Calle Esteban de Ponte 31* ☎ *922/133435* 🌐 *www.hotel-sanroque.com* 🛏 *20 rooms* 🍴 *No meals.*

Shopping

Tabacos Arturo

TOBACCO | Snap up local cigars at this tiny mom-and-pop shop that rolls its own smokes on-site. ✉ *Av. Tome Cano 8* ☎ *689/359158* 🕒 *Closed Sun.*

El Teide

60 km (36 miles) southwest of Puerto de la Cruz, 63 km (39 miles) north of Playa de las Américas.

The dormant volcano of El Teide, Spain's highest peak, looms large on the horizon no matter where you are on the island, and its (often snowcapped) peak is visible from the neighboring islands of Gran Canaria and La Palma on clear days. You need a special permit (approximate processing time: two months; apply at 🌐 *www.reservasparquesnacionales.es*) to reach the highest point, but most hikers and tourists will be content with hitching a ride up most of the way on the cable car.

GETTING HERE AND AROUND

Four roads lead to El Teide from different parts of Tenerife, each getting you to the park in about an hour, but the most beautiful approach is the road from Orotava, which is a mile uphill from Puerto de la Cruz. Orotava has a row of stately mansions on Calle San Francisco, north of the baroque church Nuestra Señora de la Concepción. Roads into the park are occasionally closed due to icy conditions; try to visit early on in your trip so you have an opportunity to return if this is the case.

Sights

★ Parque Nacional del Teide (*Teide National Park*)

NATURE SITE | FAMILY | This park includes the volcano itself and the **Cañadas del Teide,** a violent jumble of volcanic leftovers from El Teide and the neighboring Pico Viejo. The last eruption here was in 1798. Within the park you can find blue-tinged hills (the result of a process called hydrothermal alteration); spiky, knobby rock protrusions; and lava in varied colors and textures. The bizarre, photogenic rock formations known as **Los Roques de García** are especially memorable; a two-hour trail around these rocks—one of 30 well-marked hikes inside the park—is a highlight. Visit in late May or early June to see the crimson, horn-shaped *tajinaste* flowers in bloom, a dramatic sight.

You enter the Parque Nacional del Teide at El Portillo. Exhibits at the visitor center explain the region's natural history; a garden outside labels the flora found within the park. The center also offers trail maps, video presentations, guided hikes, and bus tours. A second park information center is located near Los Roques de García beside the Parador Nacional Cañadas del Teide. ✉ *La Orotava* ☎ *922/922371*.

Cable Car

TRANSPORTATION SITE (AIRPORT/BUS/FERRY/TRAIN) | On its way to the top of El Teide, the cable car soars over sulfur steam vents. You can get a good view of southern Tenerife and Gran Canaria from the top, although you'll be confined to the tiny terrace of a bar. The station also has a basic restaurant. It's strongly

The last eruption of the mountain El Teide was in 1909, on the northwestern flank of the volcano.

recommended to reserve your spot online, though it's important to note that there are no ticket refunds should the cable car be closed due to wind. ✉ *La Orotava* ☎ *922/010440* 🌐 *www.volcano-teide.com* 🎫 *€14.*

Climbing the Teide Crater

NATIONAL/STATE PARK | If you're planning on hiking in the park, plan ahead. Take warm clothing even in summer, suitable footwear, sun protection, snacks, and plenty of drinking water. The trail to the top (No. 10) of the volcano is closed when it's snowy, usually three or four months of the year. The difficult final 656 feet to the volcano crater itself take about 40 minutes to climb, and you need a special (free) pass to do so—apply online (at least two months in advance in high season). If you stay at the refuge and access the crater before 9 am, you don't need a pass. ✉ *Teide National Park, La Orotava* 🌐 *www.reservasparquesnacionales.es.*

Hotels

Parador de Las Cañadas del Teide

$$$ | **HOTEL** | This mountain retreat may be an eyesore, but it occupies a privileged position as the only hotel located within the park. **Pros:** stunning surroundings; good Canarian cuisine; views from most guest rooms. **Cons:** could be a bit remote for some; swarming with tourists; ugly building. $ *Rooms from: €145* ✉ *Cañadas del Teide, La Orotava* ☎ *922/386415* 🌐 *www.parador.es* 🛏 *37 rooms* 🍴 *No meals.*

Activities

Diga Sports

HIKING/WALKING | This company organizes day hikes to the summit of El Teide. The challenging walk takes between five and eight hours, and you need to be in good shape to make it to the top. Gentler walks are also available on the island and on La Gomera. ✉ *Hotel Park Club Europe, Av. Rafael Puig 23, Playa*

de las Américas ☎ *922/793009* ⊕ *www.*
diga-sports.de.

Shopping

Not surprisingly for one of the most
visited places in Spain, the area around El
Teide provides plenty of places for buying
souvenirs. Beware of imitation lace and
embroidery.

Casa de los Balcones

TEXTILES/SEWING | Regional arts and crafts
are available here. ⊠ *La Orotava ⊹ Next
to cable car* ☎ *922/694060* ⊕ *www.
casa-balcones.com.*

Los Cristianos, Playa de las Américas, and Costa Adeje

*74 km (44 miles) southwest of Santa
Cruz, 10 km (6 miles) west of Reina Sofía
Airport.*

The sunniest (and most woefully tacky)
tourist area on Tenerife is the southwestern coastline, where high-rise hotels are
built chockablock above the beaches
without a lick of feng-shui sensibility.
Costa Adeje, to the west of Playa de las
Américas, is the newest addition with
lower-rise apartments and hotels packed
into the hillside. Sun, beaches, and
nightlife—not cultural or nature activities—constitute the attractions here for
millions of northern Europeans desperate
for sunshine in the winter months. Playa
de las Américas, particularly in the area
around Las Verónicas, is a loud and brash
resort, not to everyone's taste. Los Cristianos and Costa Adeje are quieter, more
sedate areas, attracting a more mature
crowd of holidaymakers. However, if
you're looking for peace and quiet, you'll
probably want to give this area a wide
berth.

GETTING HERE AND AROUND

Hourly buses connect the southern part
of the island with the capital, stopping
at Tenerife South Airport on the way. If
you rent a car from Santa Cruz (from €30
a day), expect to get to the southern
resorts in just over an hour. Once there,
a good bus service connects the different
locales, and hotels that are not within
easy walking distance of the beach provide a shuttle service to the seafront.

Sights

Siam Park

AMUSEMENT PARK/WATER PARK | **FAMILY** |
This giant Southeast Asian–themed water
park covers just about all the aquatic
bases, from sleepy, restful pools to the
heart-stopping Tower of Power, which
drops you 90 feet into a "shark-infested"
aquarium. ⊠ *Autopista del Sur, Exit 28 or
29, Santa Cruz de Tenerife* ☎ *822/070000*
⊕ *www.siampark.net* ⊠ *€38.*

Beaches

El Médano

BEACH—SIGHT | Stretching for more than
2 km (1 mile), this is the longest beach
on the island and also one of the most
distinctive—the conical top of Montaña
Roja (Red Mountain) lies at its southern
tip. The golden sands and exemplary
facilities earn it the country's "Blue Flag"
rating, and the gentle waves make for
safe swimming. Strong winds make it
a good beach for those who want to try
their hand at windsurfing. To get here,
drive along the TF1 past the Reina Sofía
Airport and take the TF64 south shortly
afterward. **Amenities:** food and drink;
lifeguards; showers; toilets; water sports.
Best for: sunset; swimming; walking;
windsurfing. ⊠ *Arona.*

Las Vistas

BEACH—SIGHT | Part of the eight beach-
es making up the sands in Playa de
las Américas and Los Cristianos, Las
Vistas has clean yellow sand and perfect

bathing conditions thanks to a series of breakwalls that protect the beaches from high waves. Lounge chairs and parasols are available for rent. After sunbathing on this Blue Flag beach, take a stroll along the seafront promenade, one of the longest of its kind in Europe. **Amenities:** food and drink; lifeguards; showers; toilets; water sports. **Best for:** sunset; swimming; walking. ✉ *Los Cristianos.*

Los Cristianos

BEACH—SIGHT | This was the first beach on the island to receive international tourists en masse, from the '60s on; today its golden sands are flanked by apartment blocks and hotels. The nearby port protects the beach from high winds and waves, so bathing is safe. Lounge chairs and parasols are available for rent. This is a lively beach, with frequent concerts and sporting events, and finding a space for your towel can be a challenge in the summer. **Amenities:** food and drink; lifeguards; showers; toilets; water sports. **Best for:** partiers; sunset; swimming. ✉ *Los Cristianos.*

★ Playa de los Guíos

BEACH—SIGHT | This small, placid cove situated 12 km (7 miles) from Playa de las Américas is dwarfed by Los Gigantes, the towering cliffs nearby. Its natural black sand, striking in appearance, can be hot on the toes, so be sure to strap on some sandals. A nearby marina provides boat trips along the coast to take in the full beauty of the cliffs. **Amenities:** food and drink; lifeguards; showers; toilets; water sports. **Best for:** sunset; swimming. ✉ *Los Gigantes, Santiago del Teide.*

🍴 Restaurants

Bar Baku

$ | **RUSSIAN** | Try wrapping your head around the fact that there's an Azerbaijani restaurant in Tenerife where you can find Georgian specialties served by Russian waiters. Improbably, the food here—hand-threaded lamb kebabs, lemony stuffed grape leaves, plump pelmeni, juicy *khinkali* (Georgian soup dumplings), and other Russian and Caucasian delicacies—is fresh, well-spiced, and wildly affordable. **Known for:** Caucasian cuisine like it's made in the Old Country; grilled kebabs and boiled dumplings; Russian crowd. [$] *Average main: €9* ✉ *Centro Comercial Terra Nova, Av. de España 25, Costa Adeje* ✣ *Follow "Bar Baku" signs from shopping center's main entrance* ☎ *662/028096.*

Masca

Approximately 16 km (10 miles) north of Guía de Isora, tucked deep in the Macizo de Teno mountains, lies Masca, colloquially known as the Macchu Picchu of the Canaries. If you squint, you can see the resemblance—the huddle of houses is perched on a misty ridge beneath a massive, pyramid-shaped rock. Scale down the cobblestone steps into the town center, grab a quick coffee or sandwich, and, if you're feeling adventurous, embark on the three-hour (each way) hike down to the beach.

La Cúpula

$$$$ | **SPANISH** | The best of French cuisine fuses with Canarian and Spanish touches at this sophisticated venue in the Jardines de Nivaria Hotel. Dine inside under chandeliers and in classic French style or outside on the pleasant terrace. **Known for:** roasted meats; sophisticated dining; lovely terrace and great views. [$] *Average main: €25* ✉ *Jardines de Nivaria Hotel, Calle Bruselas, Playa de Fanabé* ☎ *922/7713333* 🌐 *www.restaurantelacupula.com* ⏲ *Closed Sun. No lunch.*

La Vieja

$$$ | **SPANISH** | A few minutes' drive from Costa Adeje lies this oceanfront restaurant overlooking the quaint harbor

of La Caleta. Watch the sun set over La Gomera island while you savor fresh local fish and shellfish and Tenerife wines. **Known for:** ocean views; fresh fish; local wines. $ *Average main: €20* ⊠ *Edificio Las Terrazas 1, La Caleta* ☏ *922/711548* ⊕ *www.restaurantelavieja.com.*

Hotels

Arona Gran Hotel

$$$ | **HOTEL** | Prime views of the marina at Los Cristianos and La Gomera island are what you get from the balconies at this hotel, which is especially popular among retirees. **Pros:** adults-only policy means plenty of peace and quiet; professional, amicable service; good choice for those with mobility difficulties. **Cons:** younger guests may feel out of place; poolside real estate fills up fast; access to spa and infinity pool costs extra. $ *Rooms from: €154* ⊠ *Av. Juan Carlos I 38, Los Cristianos* ☏ *922/750678* ⊕ *www.aronahotel. com* ⊅ *392 rooms* ⊚ *Some meals.*

★ Bahía del Duque

$$$$ | **RESORT** | **FAMILY** | Built to resemble a 19th-century Canarian village—complete with a bell tower, Italianate villas, and leafy courtyards—this sprawling luxury resort takes in eight restaurants, five swimming pools, a 24-hour gym, and two tennis courts. **Pros:** warm, helpful staff; excellent breakfast buffet with made-to-order eggs; bountiful poolside real estate. **Cons:** most pools aren't climatized; leaks in public areas when it rains; overpriced spa treatments. $ *Rooms from: €250* ⊠ *Av. de Bruselas s/n, Adeje* ☏ *922/746932* ⊕ *www.thetaishotels.com* ⊅ *351 rooms* ⊚ *No meals.*

Jardines de Nivaria

$$$$ | **HOTEL** | Step inside from views of Mt. Teide to a world of Tiffany glass, palms, and orchids crowned by the largest privately owned stained-glass window in the world. **Pros:** fantastic spa; tranquil atmosphere; seafront location. **Cons:** some may prefer a more modern

style; evening entertainment sometimes a snooze; dinner always in the same dated restaurant. $ *Rooms from: €215* ⊠ *Calle Bruselas, Playa de Fanabé* ☏ *922/713333* ⊕ *www.hoteljardinesnivaria.com* ⊟ *No credit cards* ⊅ *271 rooms* ⊚ *Free Breakfast.*

The Ritz-Carlton Abama

$$$$ | **RESORT** | **FAMILY** | Rising like a Moorish citadel from the banana fields, the Ritz-Carlton Abama is an architectural stunner with a coral-red exterior, a semiprivate beach, seven pools, and a two-Michelin-star restaurant and award-winning golf course. **Pros:** top-notch gym, spa, and restaurants; gorgeous ocean views; kids club with original activities. **Cons:** small beach with ugly views; the main building and pools can be overrun with families; below-average breakfast. $ *Rooms from: €258* ⊠ *TF47, Km 9, Guía de Isora* ☏ *922/126000* ⊕ *www.ritzcarlton.com* ⊅ *461 rooms* ⊚ *No meals.*

Vincci Selección La Plantación del Sur

$$$$ | **HOTEL** | Centering around an original banana plantation house, this modern hotel retains its colonial essence with spacious communal areas, teak furniture, and potted palms. **Pros:** tranquil ambience; excellent service; views of the mountains and Costa Adeje. **Cons:** some distance from beach; 10- to 15-minute walk to nightlife; some noise from other rooms. $ *Rooms from: €210* ⊠ *Calle Roque Nublo 1, Costa Adeje* ☏ *902/454585* ⊕ *www.vinccihoteles.com* ⊅ *165 rooms* ⊚ *Free Breakfast.*

Activities

DIVING
Dive Center Aquanautic Club Tenerife

DIVING/SNORKELING | This PADI-licensed diving center in the small resort of Playa Paraíso is one of the most well established on the island. ⊠ *Lago Playa Paraíso, Playa Paraíso, Adeje* ☏ *922/741881* ⊕ *www.diving-tenerife.com.*

GOLF

Southern Tenerife has five of the island's eight golf courses, and these five lie within 20 km (12 miles) of each other.

Amarilla Golf Club

GOLF | In San Miguel, not far from Campo Golf, this 18-hole course has greens that front the ocean. ⊠ *Urbanizacion Amarilla Golf, San Miguel* ☎ *922/730319* ⊕ *www. amarillagolf.com* ↟ *18 holes, 6684 yards, par 72.*

Campo Golf del Sur

GOLF | Near Reina Sofía Airport, this course has 27 holes and spectacular greens that are surrounded by cacti and palms. ⊠ *Urbanizacion Golf del Sur, Av. Galván Bello, San Miguel* ☎ *922/738170* ⊕ *www.golfdelsur.es* ↟ *27 holes, 6458 yards, par 72.*

Centro de Golf Los Palos

GOLF | In Arona, near Los Cristianos, Centro de Golf Los Palos has 9 holes (par 27) and is a good practice course. ⊠ *Ctra. Guaza, Las Galletas, Km 7, Los Cristianos* ☎ *922/169080* ⊕ *www.golflospalos.com* ↟ *9 holes, 1040 yards, par 27.*

Golf Abama

GOLF | This exclusive course surrounded by banana plantations boasts more than 22 lakes and 90,000 palms along its 18 holes. It's part of the Ritz-Carlton Abama resort complex. ⊠ *Playa de San Juan, Ctra. Gral TF47, Km 9, Guía de Isora* ☎ *922/126000* ⊕ *www.abamagolf.com* ↟ *18 holes, 6858 yards, par 72.*

Golf Costa Adeje

GOLF | There's a 27-hole course that runs alongside the ocean and has a small number of palm trees dotted throughout, black volcanic sand bunkers, and views of the sea. ⊠ *Fince de los Olivos, Adeje* ☎ *922/710000* ⊕ *www.golfcostaadeje. com* ↟ *27 holes, 6440 yards, par 72.*

Golf Las Américas

GOLF | Adjacent to Playa de las Américas, Golf Las Américas has an 18-hole course with views of the ocean and La Gomera island. ⊠ *Playa de las Américas, Arona* ☎ *922/752005* ⊕ *www.golf-tenerife.com* ↟ *18 holes, 6409 yards, par 72.*

KITESURFING

Azul Kiteboarding

WINDSURFING | Kiteboard, surfboard, and windboard rentals and classes are available at this club on the seafront in Playa del Médano, which happens to be one of the best places on the island for beginners. If you're experienced and enjoy big waves, try Playa El Cabezo. ⊠ *Edificio El Toscón, Paseo Nuestra Señora de Roja 26, El Médano* ☎ *922/178314* ⊕ *www. azulkiteboarding.com.*

Gran Canaria

Gran Canaria has three distinct identities: Its capital, Las Palmas (pop. 379,000), is a thriving business center and important shipping and cruise port; the white-sand beaches of the south coast are tourist magnets; and the rural interior has a forgotten-in-time allure and spectacular landscapes.

Las Palmas, the largest city in the Canary Islands, is overrun by tourists, traffic, exhaust-spewing buses, and hordes of shoppers—in other words, it's a *city,* the likes of which most first-time travelers don't readily associate with the archipelago. (Even so, it consistently ranks as number one in air quality among Spanish metropolises.) But there are plenty of diamonds in the rough including the 7-km (4½-mile) Canteras beach and well-preserved old town.

The south coast, a boxy '60s development along wide avenues, is a family resort, popular with millions of northern Europeans. At the southern tip of the island, the Playa del Inglés (a popular gay-friendly retreat) gives way to the vast empty dunes of Maspalomas. The isle's interior is a steep highland that reaches 6,435 feet at Pozo de las Nieves. Although it's green in winter, Gran

Gran Canaria

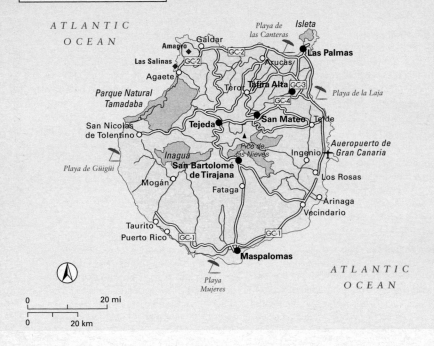

ATLANTIC OCEAN

Playa de las Canteras

Isleta

Gáldar
Amagro
Las Salinas
GC-2
Agaete

Parque Natural Tamadaba

Teror
Tafira Alta GC-3
GC-4

Playa de la Laja

San Nicolás de Tolentino
Tejeda
San Mateo
Telde

Inagua
Pico de las Nieves
Ingenio
Aueropuerto de Gran Canaria

San Bartolomé de Tirajana

Playa de Güigüi

Mogán
Fataga

Los Rosas

Arinaga
Vecindario

Taurito
Puerto Rico
GC-1
GC-1

Maspalomas

ATLANTIC OCEAN

Playa Mujeres

Las Palmas

Arucas

0 ——— 20 mi
0 ——— 20 km

Canaria does not have the luxurious tropical foliage of the archipelago's western islands, and the landscape is often stark the rest of the year.

Las Palmas

35 km (21 miles) north of Gran Canaria Airport, 60 km (36 miles) north of Maspalomas.

Las Palmas is a long, sprawling city, strung out for 10 km (6 miles) along two waterfronts of a peninsula. Though most of the action centers on the peninsula's northern end along the lovely Las Canteras beach, the historical sights are clustered around the city's southern edge. Begin in the old quarter, La Vegueta, at the **Plaza Santa Ana** (don't miss the bronze dog statues), for a tour through attractive colonial architecture.

Then make your way to the neighboring quarter of Triana, a treasure trove of small shops and cafés and restaurants. Both neighborhoods are protected by UNESCO. It's quite a walk from one end of town to the other, so at any point you may want to hop on one of the many canary-yellow buses. Buses 1, 2, and 12 run the length of the city.

VISITOR INFORMATION
Las Palmas Cruise Terminal
✉ *Las Canteras.*

GETTING HERE AND AROUND
It's a short stroll from the cruise terminal into the northern part of Las Palmas. Here you can explore the beach and check out the market and the stores in El Muelle shopping mall and Calle Mesa y López, or take a bus (1, 2, or 12) into the older part of the city.

If you're planning to go north to Agaete or Teror, or south to Maspalomas or Puerto Mogán, good bus services run frequently from the Santa Catalina terminal just outside the port. You can also get an airport bus from here. Alternatively, you can rent a car (from €30 a day) or take a taxi.

For those planning to island-hop, Las Palmas and Agaete have good connections with Santa Cruz de Tenerife. Fred Olsen provides the quickest travel between Santa Cruz de Tenerife and Gran Canaria (Agaete)—the trimaran takes an hour. Free bus service is provided between Agaete and Las Palmas in both directions. You can also ferry to Lanzarote (Arrecife) and Fuerteventura (Puerto del Rosario and Morro Jable). Fred Olsen runs several ferries a week between Las Palmas, Lanzarote (Arrecife), and Fuerteventura (Puerto del Rosario).

Note that Las Palmas and the highway south are always busy with traffic, so allow plenty of time for your journey, particularly on the way back. Even a bus trip from one end of Las Palmas to the other can take up to an hour during rush hour.

TOURS
Several companies offer various sightseeing and themed tours. The hop-on, hop-off, service is also good for just getting around.

City Sightseeing Bus
BUS TOURS | Visiting the main sites of Las Palmas, this hop-on, hop-off, bus has a Monumental City Tour (nine stops) and the Atlantic City Tour, with two additional stops. The buses leave from Parque Santa Catalina and Parque San Telmo. Tickets (cheaper if bought online) include a free walking tour in Vegueta. ⊠ *Las Palmas* ⊕ *www.city-sightseeing.com* ✆ *€18.*

Trip Gran Canaria
SPECIAL-INTEREST | This company's tours in Las Palmas cover Vegueta and Triana. Tours take between two and three hours, and booking ahead is a good idea. ⊠ *Calle Colón 2, Vegueta* ☎ *674/128849*

⊕ *www.tripgrancanaria.com* ✆ *From €8 Vegueta and Triana tours; from €28 for gastronomic tour* ☞ *Vegueta and Triana tours from €6; gastronomic tours farther afield from €42.*

 ## Sights

★ Casa Museo Colón (*Columbus Museum*)
HOUSE | FAMILY | In a palace where Christopher Columbus may have stayed when he stopped to repair the *Pinta*'s rudder, nautical instruments, copies of early navigational maps, and models of Columbus's three ships are on display in addition to interactive exhibits. The palace, which retains many original features, has two rooms holding pre-Columbian artifacts and one floor dedicated to paintings from the 16th to the 19th century. There's a glaring absence of criticism of Columbus's complicated legacy. ⊠ *Calle Colón 1, Vegueta* ☎ *928/312373* ⊕ *www. casadecolon.com* ✆ *€4 (free Sun.).*

Catedral Santa Ana
RELIGIOUS SITE | It took four centuries to complete St. Anne's Cathedral, so the neoclassical Roman columns of the 19th-century exterior contrast sharply with the Gothic ceiling vaulting of the interior. Baroque statues are displayed in the cathedral's **Museo de Arte Sacro** (Museum of Religious Art), arranged around a peaceful cloister. Ask the curator to open the *sala capitular* (chapter house) to see the 16th-century Valencian-tile floor. Be sure to check out the black-bronze dog sculptures outside the cathedral's main entrance—these are four examples of the Gran Canaria hounds that gave the island its name. ⊠ *Calle Espíritu Santo 20, facing Pl. Santa Ana, Vegueta* ☎ *928/314430* ✆ *Cathedral free, museum €2* ⊗ *Closed Sun.*

Centro Atlántico de Arte Moderno (*Atlantic Center for Modern Art*)
MUSEUM | This art gallery has earned a name for curating some of the best

The irregularity of house shapes in the colorful barrios of San Nicolas and San Juan in Las Palmas are an iconic image of the city.

avant-garde shows in Spain, with a year-round calendar of exhibitions. The excellent permanent collection includes Canarian art from the 1930s and 1940s and works by the well-known Lanzarote artist César Manrique. The center also has a fine collection of contemporary African art. ⊠ *Calle los Balcones 11, Vegueta* ☎ *928/311800* ⊕ *www.caam.net* ✉ *Free* ⏲ *Closed Mon.*

Ermita de San Telmo (*Parroquia de San Bernardo*)

RELIGIOUS SITE | Destroyed by Dutch attackers in 1599, this chapel was rebuilt in the 17th century. Inside is a fine baroque altarpiece with rich gold leaf and wooden details. The chapel is generally open only before and after Mass. ⊠ *Pl. de San Telmo, Triana.*

Fundación de Arte y Pensamiento Martín Chirino

CASTLE/PALACE | Housed in the Castillo de la Luz—the Canary Islands' oldest defensive fortress that once protected the port from pirates and other invaders—the Fundación de Arte y Pensamiento Martín Chirino opened in 2015 to celebrate the legacy of the Canaries' most famous modern sculptor. Chirino's swooping, abstract designs are more poignant than ever given his death in 2019. ⊠ *Calle Juan Rejón s/n, Las Canteras* ☎ *928/463162* ⊕ *www.fundacionmartinchirino.org* ✉ *€4* ⏲ *Closed Mon.*

Parque de Santa Catalina

CITY PARK | FAMILY | Ride a guagua to this park, where you can visit the **Museo Néstor,** home to neoclassical and modernist works by brothers Miguel (architect) and Néstor (artist) Martín Fernández. There's also a kids' play area and cultural center with temporary exhibitions. On the way there, stop off at the neighboring Parque Doramas (stops are listed on big yellow signs; Buses 2, 3, and 12 generally cover the entire city), to peek at the elegant Santa Catalina Hotel. Next to the Parque Doramas is the **Pueblo Canario,** a model village with typical Canarian architecture. ⊠ *Calle León y Castillo.*

Poema del Mar Aquarium

ZOO | 2017 saw the opening of this ultramodern fresh- and saltwater aquarium that's organized by altitude: you start your visit gazing at the aquatic life of mountain lakes and rivers and finish in a room dedicated to alien-like deep-sea critters. The coral-filled pool is a highlight. ✉ *Muelle del Sanapú 22* ☎ *928/010350* 🌐 *www.poema-del-mar.com* 🎟 *€25.*

Beaches

Although it can't quite compete with the endless stretches of golden sand to the south of the island, the northern beach here, frequented by locals of all ages, is one of Las Palmas's major attractions.

★ Las Canteras

BEACH—SIGHT | **FAMILY** | One of the best urban beaches in Spain is found at the northwest end of the city. Its yellow sands are flanked by a pleasant promenade that stretches more than 3 km (nearly 2 miles) from the Alfredo Kraus Auditorium, in the south, where surfers congregate, to the Playa del Confital, in the north. The beach is protected by a natural volcanic reef, La Barra, which runs parallel to the shore and makes for safe swimming. Lounge chairs and sunshades can be rented year-round. **Amenities:** food and drink; lifeguards; showers; toilets; water sports. **Best for:** sunset; surfing; swimming; walking. ✉ *Paseo Las Canteras.*

Restaurants

Bikina

$ | **INTERNATIONAL** | **FAMILY** | Skip the middling tourist-packed cafés and sandwich shops on the Las Canteras boardwalk and grab a bite at this sunny, casual storefront instead that serves tropical fare ranging from tacos to Cubano melts to pad Thai. **Known for:** "slow" fast food; craveable tacos and quesadillas; beachside patio. [$] *Average main: €8* ✉ *Paseo las Canteras 63* ☎ *828/065357* 🕒 *Closed Tues.*

Need a Break?

Cafetería Casa Suecia (Swiss Tea House) Escape to the tranquil, air-conditioned quiet of the Casa Suecia Salon de Té on Tomás Miller 70—near Playa de las Canteras—for comfortable booths, foreign newspapers, picture windows, pastries, breakfast plates, sandwiches, and perhaps the only free coffee refills on the islands. ✉ *Calle Tomás Miller 70* ☎ *928/271626* 🕒 *Closed Mon.*

Deliciosa Marta

$$ | **SPANISH** | Tables are hard to come by at this busy restaurant: there's usually a line outside the door. Much of the original design of this typical Triana house has been preserved, with plain stone walls and wooden beams, although the industrial-chic lighting and metal shelves add a modern touch. **Known for:** steak tartare; consistently fantastic food quality; well-heeled local crowd. [$] *Average main: €15* ✉ *Calle Pérez Galdos 23, Triana* ☎ *928/370882* 🕒 *Closed Sun.*

★ El Santo

$$ | **FUSION** | Freshly dug baby potatoes with mojo "snow," tempura octopus with aerated spirulina, Canarian blood sausage soufflé with beer ice cream—these are a few of the palate-bending dishes you'll find on the menu at El Santo, one of Gran Canaria's most exciting fusion spots. Rustic stone walls give the restaurant an intimate, relaxed feel, while the white tablecloths and professional waiters hint that young-gun chef Abraham Ortega means business. **Known for:** experimental Canarian cuisine; subdued yet stylish dining room; foams, reductions, and fine-dining touches. [$] *Average main: €22* ✉ *Calle Escritor Benito Pérez Galdós 23* ☎ *928/283366* 🌐 *www.elsantorestaurante.com* 🕒 *Closed Sun. and Mon.*

Guirlache

$ | **CAFÉ** | **FAMILY** | For a sweet treat, try Guirlache. There are at least 20 ice-cream flavors, and many of the cakes are made with that island staple, condensed milk. **Known for:** delicious cakes, ice creams, and chocolates; quality ingredients; popular with locals. [$] *Average main: €4* ✉ *Calle Triana 68, Triana* ☎ *928/366723* 🌐 *www.guirlachelaspalmas.com.*

La Champiñonería

$ | **SPANISH** | Halfway up a pleasant pedestrian street in Vegueta, this French café-style restaurant with deep red walls lined with wood and old photos of Las Palmas specializes in mushroom dishes. Choose from more than 15 different preparations, or forego the fungi and try the meat dishes and giant scrambled-egg *revueltos*. **Known for:** mushroom everything; large portions for the money; cozy atmosphere. [$] *Average main: €8* ✉ *Calle Mendizábal 30, Vegueta* ☎ *928/334516* 💳 *No credit cards* 🕒 *Closed Mon.*

Neodimio 60

$$$ | **FUSION** | If you manage to snag one of the four tables at this *nueva cocina* (new cuisine) restaurant, you're in for a decadent feast of local seafood, meats, and vegetables prepared with Latin and Asian twists (think chipotle-rubbed octopus, cod ceviche with passion fruit and ginger, and ricotta-stuffed agnolotti with fresh corn sauce). The cocktails, which could be described as "cheffy," don't disappoint either. **Known for:** fine-dining fusion cuisine without the smoke and mirrors; concise market-driven menu; pocket-size digs. [$] *Average main: €21* ✉ *Calle Alfredo L. Jones 28* ☎ *674/746695* 🕒 *Closed Sun. and Mon.*

Te Lo Dije Pérez

$ | **INTERNATIONAL** | Just below the cathedral square is one of the island's best bars for having a beer—there's a huge selection—along with some tapas. The bar feels a bit like a French café, with high ceilings and black and red furnishings. **Known for:** choice of beers; fun ambience; good tapas. [$] *Average main: €8* ✉ *Calle Obispo Codina 6, Vegueta* ☎ *928/249087* 🌐 *www.telodijeperez.com* 💳 *No credit cards* 🕒 *Closed Sun.*

Zoe Food

$ | **VEGETARIAN** | A magnet for vegetarians and vegans, this restaurant has retro decor and a pleasant, shady terrace. Specialties include vegetable woks with tofu, vegan meatballs, and healthy organic breakfasts. **Known for:** €10 menú del día (prix fixe); range of vegan, gluten-free, and vegetarian options; organic produce. [$] *Average main: €8* ✉ *Calle Domingo J. Navarro 35, Triana* ☎ *928/586507* 🕒 *Closed Sun. No dinner.*

🛏 Hotels

Bull Reina Isabel and Spa

$$ | **HOTEL** | **FAMILY** | With a location right on Las Canteras, this is a good midrange option for visiting the city and taking in its beach. **Pros:** rooftop swimming pool; beachfront location; solid breakfasts and dining in general. **Cons:** some areas look a little tired; street-view rooms are dreary; steep competition to get a sunbed by the pool. [$] *Rooms from: €120* ✉ *Calle Alfredo Jones 40, Las Canteras* ☎ *928/260100* 🌐 *www.bullhotels.com* 💳 *No credit cards* 🛏 *225 rooms* 🍴 *Free Breakfast.*

Hotel Verol

$ | **HOTEL** | **FAMILY** | This no-frills budget hotel has an uninspiring facade, but its location, sandwiched between the Las Canteras seafront promenade and the main shopping street, makes a great base for exploring and beachgoing. **Pros:** excellent value; beachside location; kid and pet friendly. **Cons:** basic, with small bathrooms; some street noise; poor-quality bath amenities. [$] *Rooms from: €55* ✉ *Calle Sagasta 25, Las Canteras* ☎ *928/262104* 🌐 *www.hotelverol.com* 🛏 *25 rooms* 🍴 *No meals.*

★ Veintiuno

$$ | **HOTEL** | This boutique adults-only hotel is a social-media darling, thanks to its drool-worthy rooftop pool overlooking the cathedral. **Pros:** serene and stylish decor; rooftop splash pool; local art and quirky library. **Cons:** noisy ground-floor room; cramped breakfast area; no tea- and coffee-making facilities in entry-level rooms. [$] *Rooms from: €100* ✉ *Calle Espíritu Santo 21* ☎ *683/369723* 🌐 *www.hotelveintiuno.com* 🛏 *11 rooms* 🍴 *No meals.*

Nightlife

Lively and sometimes a little rough around the edges, the bars and discos in Las Palmas are clustered between Playa de las Canteras and Parque Santa Catalina. The seafront promenade and **Calle Tomás Miller** are lined with restaurants serving dishes from every corner of the globe. Live music and entertainment are common—check out the online La Brújula guide for a lowdown on cultural events (🌐 *www.labrujulaocioycultura.com*).

Ginger

BARS/PUBS | Sip a colorful tiki drink while watching the tide come in at this Las Canteras hotspot, whose fishbowl *gin-tónics* and zippy mojitos lure a mixed local and international crowd until 2 am. ✉ *Paseo de las Canteras 2* ☎ *696/728992.*

Orquesta Filarmónica de Gran Canaria

CONCERTS | One of Spain's oldest orchestras, the Filarmónica has an ample calendar of concerts between September and July that take place at the emblematic Auditorio Alfonso Kraus at the southwestern end of the Las Canteras seafront promenade. ✉ *Paseo Príncipe de Asturias s/n* ☎ *928/472570* 🌐 *www.ofgrancanaria.com.*

★ TAO Club and Garden

DANCE CLUBS | Open until 5 am on weekends and past 1 am every other night, this swanky tropical nightclub playing a mix of pop and DJ music draws a local crowd of revelers ages 25 and up. The palm-lined outdoor terrace, with music and its own bar, is one of the city's top see-and-be-seen spots in the summer. Be sure to dress to impress (no shorts, sandals, or tanks). ✉ *Paseo Alonso Quesada s/n* ☎ *928/243730* 🌐 *www.taolaspalmas.com.*

Teatro Pérez Galdós

CULTURAL TOURS | A varied program of plays, concerts, and opera is performed throughout the year at this century-old theater at the end of the Vegueta district. Spanish theater buffs shouldn't miss the guided 40-minute tours, which take place Monday through Saturday at 10:15, 11:15, and 12:15 (€5; no reservation required). ✉ *Pl. Stagno 1, Vegueta* ☎ *928/433334, 928/491770 box office* 🌐 *www.auditorio-teatrolaspalmasgc.es.*

Activities

GOLF

El Cortijo Club de Campo

GOLF | Just outside Las Palmas on the freeway to the south, this 18-hole, par-72 course is one of the longest in Spain. Set among magnificent palm groves and six lakes, it has several holes with ocean views. ✉ *Autopista del Sur, Km 6.4, Telde* ☎ *928/711111* 🌐 *www.elcortijo.es* ⛳ *18 holes, 6899 yards, par 72.*

Real Club de Golf de Las Palmas

GOLF | Founded in 1891, the Real Club de Golf de Las Palmas is Spain's oldest course. Redesigned and relocated in 1956, it has 18 holes (par 71), two putting greens, two tennis courts, a restaurant, and a bar. Fifteen minutes outside Las Palmas, the course sits on the rim of the impressive Bandama Crater overlooking the extinct Bandama Volcano. The club also rents horses; it has 48 stables and five riding rings. ✉ *Ctra. de Bandama s/n, Santa Brígida* ☎ *928/351050* 🌐 *www.realclubdegolfdelaspalmas.com* ⛳ *18 holes, 6288 yards, par 71.*

Shopping

Las Palmas easily has the best shopping on the islands. The main commercial areas are located around Calle Mesa y López (south of the port) and Triana in the old quarter. Here you'll find all the major international and Spanish fashion stores, duty-free stores, and shops selling local crafts, hats and clothes, tackle for fishing and catching crabs, surf gear, and lots more.

Artesanía Santa Catalina

CRAFTS | Genuine crafts, souvenirs, and handiwork can be found in this shop two blocks west of Parque Santa Catalina. ⊠ *Calle Ripoche 4, Las Canteras* ☎ *928/229596.*

Fundación Para El Estudio y Desarrollo de la Artesanía Canaria (FEDAC)

CRAFTS | This government-funded shop carries a selection of Gran Canaria crafts and handiwork. ⊠ *Calle Domingo J. Navarro 7, Triana* ☎ *928/369661* ⊕ *www.fedac.org* ⊘ *Closed weekends.*

José Juan Sosa

CRAFTS | Out of his studio in Gáldar, a town west of Las Palmas, this award-winning knife maker sells handmade blades with ornate handles made from ebony, gold, silver, steel, and nickel. Every piece is one of a kind. Visits are by email appointment only: *kneron77@gmail.com.* ⊠ *Lomo San Antón, 90B* ⊕ *www.cuchilloscanarios.blogspot.com.*

TRAStornados

HOUSEHOLD ITEMS/FURNITURE | Part furniture showroom, part fashion boutique, and part home decorating store, this ultracool shopping spot sells designer wares from Spanish and international brands. If you're looking for a fancy gift for someone special—a beautiful handmade vase, perhaps, or a scented candle—you've come to the right place. ⊠ *Calle Pérez Galdós 13* ☎ *928/433053* ⊘ *Closed Sun.*

Visanta

DUTY-FREE | Score deals on duty-free electronic equipment, perfume, and cosmetics at this store behind the Parque Santa Catalina. ⊠ *Calle Ripoche 9* ☎ *928/228818* ⊕ *www.visanta.com* ⊘ *Closed Sun.*

Maspalomas and the Southern Coast

60 km (36 miles) southwest of Las Palmas, 25 km (15 miles) southwest of Gran Canaria Airport.

One of the first places in Spain to welcome international tourists (starting in 1962), Maspalomas remains a beach resort with all the trappings. It's improbably backed by empty sand dunes that resemble the Sahara—despite beachfront overdevelopment in the town—and retains appealing stretches of isolated beach on the outskirts, as well as a bird sanctuary. Much of the area around the dunes is a protected nature reserve.

GETTING HERE AND AROUND

From Las Palmas, a short bus journey (45 minutes, longer at rush hour) runs to the southern resorts. Note that not all return buses go to the bus terminal near the port (Intercambiador de Parque Santa Catalina); some end at Intercambiador de San Telmo in central Las Palmas. You may therefore need to take a bus from here to the port if you're on a cruise (Buses 1 and 12 are the best options). If you rent a car from the port, it's an easy drive to the south coast via the GC1 highway, and there's plenty of parking in and around Maspalomas. Allow extra time for the journey back to the port if you're traveling during rush hour.

Sights

Aqualand Maspalomas

AMUSEMENT PARK/WATER PARK | FAMILY | The largest water park in the Canary

The dunes of Maspalomas were formed by sand from the bottom of the ocean, during the last ice age.

Islands has wave pools, slides, and just about everything else splash related. ⊠ *Ctra. Palmitos Park, Km 3, Maspalomas* ☎ *928/140525* ⊕ *www.aqualand.es* ✉ *€29.*

Palmitos Park

GARDEN | FAMILY | One of the main attractions in this part of the island, inland from Maspalomas, this part botanical garden and part zoo has 1,500 tropical birds, a butterfly sanctuary, an orchid house, 160 species of tropical fish, many crocodiles, and parrot shows. ⊠ *Ctra. Palmitos, Km 6, Maspalomas* ☎ *928/797070* ⊕ *www.palmitospark.es* ✉ *€32.*

Beaches

The below beaches abut one another, and you can walk them in sequence (hindered only by a pair of rocky dividers) along the shore. A boardwalk links Playa de Tarajalillo to the rest of the beaches until the dunes separate the boardwalk from the Maspalomas beach and Playa de la Mujer.

★ Maspalomas

BEACH—SIGHT | The island's most emblematic beach and one of the most beautiful, Maspalomas has golden sand that stretches for 2¾ km (1¾ miles) along the southern tip of Gran Canaria. Behind this beach are the famous Maspalomas dunes as well as palm groves and a saltwater lagoon, which lend an air of isolation and refuge to the beach. Bathing is safe everywhere except at La Punta de Maspalomas, where currents converge. Topless bathing is acceptable, and there's a nudist area at La Cañada de la Penca. This beach is busy year-round. **Amenities:** food and drink; lifeguards; showers; toilets. **Best for:** nudists; sunrise; sunset; walking. ⊠ *Maspalomas.*

Playa de las Burras

BEACH—SIGHT | Sandwiched between Playa del Inglés and Playa de San Agustín, this little sandy beach is protected by a breakwall, making it a favorite with families. Small fishing boats are moored in the bay, and the seafront promenade connects the neighboring resorts. Swimming is safe. There are plenty of lounge chairs and sunshades. **Amenities:** food and drink; lifeguards; showers; toilets. **Best for:** sunrise; swimming. ⊠ *San Agustín*.

Playa de las Mujeres

BEACH—SIGHT | The co-ed "Women's Beach" is around the corner from the Maspalomas lighthouse in Meloneras. A natural beach with gray shingles and small rocks, this quiet enclave currently has no amenities, although the expansion of Meloneras, along with the construction of several high-end hotels, may change that in the future. Swimming is generally safe. **Amenities:** none. **Best for:** solitude; sunset. ⊠ *Meloneras*.

Playa de San Agustín

BEACH—SIGHT | To the east of Maspalomas, this smaller beach consists of brown-black sand and some rocks. The promenade has lush vegetation nearby, making it one of the most picturesque on the island. This is a quieter beach than Maspalomas and Playa del Inglés. Bathing is safe in calm conditions, but watch out for strong currents when the waves get up. Lounge chairs and sunshades line the beach. **Amenities:** food and drink; lifeguards; showers; toilets; water sports. **Best for:** sunrise; walking. ⊠ *San Agustín*.

Playa del Inglés

BEACH—SIGHT | Rivaling Maspalomas for popularity, Playa del Inglés has a lot going for it, including partying at the beach bars, sports, competitions, and concerts. There are nearly 3 km (2 miles) of golden sands, flanked by a pleasant seafront promenade that's great for early-morning and evening strolls. Swimming is generally safe, although windy conditions can create waves—it's a favorite spot with surfers. Lounge chairs and sunshades are available along the beach, and there's also a nudist area, which is signposted. **Amenities:** food and drink; lifeguards; showers; toilets; water sports. **Best for:** nudists; partiers; swimming; windsurfing. ⊠ *Playa del Inglés*.

 Restaurants

El Portalón

$$$ | **BASQUE** | **FAMILY** | In the center of Playa del Inglés, this modern Basque restaurant has made a name for itself for its well-priced classic cuisine. Interiors are a bit passé (a bit like a wedding reception hall), but there are two pleasant terraces outside. **Known for:** fine Basque dining; generous portions; good wine list. $ *Average main: €20* ⊠ *Av. Tirajana 27, Playa del Inglés* ☎ *928/771622* ▭ *No credit cards*.

La Tapita Los Joses

$ | **SPANISH** | Cheap and cheerful sums up this small bar-restaurant at the north end of Maspalomas. It's usually packed with locals, who flock here for good and inexpensive Spanish classics, including *revuelto de papas con jamón serrano* (scrambled eggs with potatoes and Iberian ham) and *bacalao con tomate* (cod in tomato sauce), and tapas. **Known for:** traditional tapas; value set menu; local crowds. $ *Average main: €10* ⊠ *Calle Plácido Domingo 12, Maspalomas* ☎ *928/769680* ▭ *No credit cards* ☾ *Closed Sun. and late Aug.–late Sept.*

Restaurante Etiopico Afrika

$$ | **ETHIOPIAN** | Maspalomas is an unlikely place to find some of the best Ethiopian food in Spain, but make no mistake—Etiopico Afrika is worth going out of your way to visit. Every entrée—from lentil stews and split pea purees to *doro wat* (berbere-spiced braised meat)—comes atop a spongy round of injera, a pliable Ethiopian flatbread made from teff flour. **Known for:** spice-packed Ethiopian dishes; live guitar music in the evenings; vegetarian friendly. $ *Average main: €14* ⊠ *Calle La Palma 9, Maspalomas* ☎ *648/760498* ⊕ *www.restauranteafrika.es* ☾ *Closed Mon.*

Rías Bajas

$$$ | **SPANISH** | Seafood lovers, look no further: This Galician restaurant serves some of the most pristine fish and shellfish on the island, from *rape a la marinera* (monkfish cooked in wine and garlic) and *zarzuela de pescado y marisco* (fish and seafood stew) to various rice dishes such as paella. It's a well-established favorite with islanders—many travel all the way here from Las Palmas just for dinner. **Known for:** fresh seafood; fish and seafood stew; rice dishes. [$] *Average main: €18* ✉ *Edificio Playa del Sol, Av. de Tirajana at the corner of Av. EEUU, Playa del Inglés* ☎ *928/764033.*

Hotels

★ Bohemia Suites and Spa

$$$$ | RESORT | When Swiss architect Pia Smith was tasked with refurbishing the Hotel Apolo, the first hotel on the Playa del Inglés, she reached for the sledgehammer. **Pros:** standout spa and brand-new wellness facilities; most avant-garde cocktail bar in the Canaries; characterful modern decor. **Cons:** garden-view rooms face noisy construction site; poolside waiter service is slow; certain areas undergoing renovation or repair. [$] *Rooms from: €186* ✉ *Av. Estados Unidos 28, Maspalomas* ☎ *928/563400* 🌐 *www.bohemia-grancanaria.com* 🛏 *67 rooms* 🍴 *Free Breakfast.*

Bull Eugenia Victoria and Spa

$$$ | HOTEL | One of the first hotels to pop up in the Playa del Inglés area in 1975, this is a longtime favorite among older northern Europeans in search of sun. **Pros:** Dead Sea pool; rooms overlook the pool and garden area; huge spa and gym. **Cons:** not beachfront; one-night stays not possible; young travelers may feel out of place among older crowd. [$] *Rooms from: €140* ✉ *Av. Gran Canaria 26, Maspalomas* ☎ *928/762500* 🌐 *www.bullhotels.com* 🛏 *400 rooms* 🍴 *Free Breakfast.*

Costa Canaria

$$$$ | HOTEL | One of the few hotels in the south of the island with direct access to the beach, Costa Canaria sits just behind the Blue Flag sands on Playa de San Agustín. **Pros:** unbeatable oceanfront location; beautiful gardens; ultramodern pool facilities. **Cons:** some distance from attractions; young travelers may feel out of place given older clientele; unremarkable food. [$] *Rooms from: €200* ✉ *Calle Las Retamas 1, San Agustín* ☎ *928/760200* 🌐 *www.bullhotels.com* 🛏 *229 rooms, 15 bungalows* 🍴 *All-inclusive.*

Parque Tropical

$$$ | HOTEL | One of the first hotels to be built in Playa del Inglés, Parque Tropical remains a peaceful oasis of tropical palms, colorful blooms, and cascades. **Pros:** made-to-order pancakes at breakfast; meticulously maintained gardens; direct beach access. **Cons:** some rooms are dark because of vegetation; only twin beds available; antiquated no-shorts policy at dinner. [$] *Rooms from: €144* ✉ *Av. Italia 1, Playa del Inglés* ☎ *928/774012* 🌐 *www.hotelparquetropical.com* 💳 *No credit cards* 🛏 *221 rooms* 🍴 *Free Breakfast.*

★ Seaside Palm Beach

$$$$ | HOTEL | Sophisticated and luxurious, this hotel is a stone's throw from the edge of Maspalomas beach. **Pros:** exceptional design and facilities; above-and-beyond service; room cleaning twice a day. **Cons:** expensive in high season; small bathrooms; almost everyone is German and over 60. [$] *Rooms from: €300* ✉ *Av. del Oasis s/n, Maspalomas* ☎ *928/721032* 🌐 *www.hotel-palm-beach.es* 🛏 *328 rooms* 🍴 *Free Breakfast.*

Nightlife

The days may be long, but the nights are even longer in Maspalomas and Playa del Inglés, party central of the Canary Islands. Freshly tanned vacationers pack the pubs at sundown; later, the clubs fill with writhing masses dancing to disco. Gran Canaria is one of Europe's biggest gay destinations, and gay bars and clubs abound near the four-story Yumbo

Centrum shopping center at Playa del Inglés. Las Meloneras is another nightlife center, where Aqua Ocean Club is one of the big attractions.

Eiffel Bar

BARS/PUBS | Slurping down a strawberry Daiquiri at the gay-friendly Eiffel Bar is a rite of passage on the Playa del Inglés nightlife circuit; every cocktail comes with a complimentary bowl of peanuts and marshmallows. ✉ *Yumbo Centrum, Av. Estados Unidos, Planta baja, local 121, Playa del Inglés* ☎ *634/310227.*

Pacha Gran Canaria

DANCE CLUBS | The Canarian outpost of this renowned discotheque megachain doesn't disappoint with its DJ beats and sundown-to-sunup dancing. Expect a mix of locals and foreigners; the club isn't gay per se but is gay-friendly. ✉ *Av. Sargentos Provisionales 10, Maspalomas* ☎ *928/771730* ⊕ *www.pachagrancanaria. com.*

Activities

BICYCLING
Bike 10Mil

BICYCLING | **FAMILY** | The tours offered by this company cater to all ages and fitness levels, or you can rent a bike and go it alone. ✉ *IFA Hotel Continental, Av. de Italia 2, Playa del Inglés* ☎ *663/535038* ⊕ *www.happybiking.info.*

BOAT TOURS
CoolPlaySail

SAILING | **FAMILY** | Hop on a sunset cruise or full-day sailing adventure on this 15.5-meter yacht complete with refreshments, tunes, and paddleboards. ✉ *Puerto Deportivo Pasito Blanco, Maspalomas* ☎ *629/505606* ⊕ *www.coolplaysail.com.*

Multiacuatic

WHALE-WATCHING | Two-hour whale- and dolphin-watching trips leave from Playa de Puerto Rico, about 13 km (8 miles) west of Maspalomas. Avoid rough-sea

Detour

Artenara From the road leading to the Parador Cruz de Tejeda, follow signs west to the village of Artenara (about 13 km [8 miles]) for views of the rocky valley and its chimney-like formations. You can see both Roque Nublo and Roque Ventaiga, sitting like temples on a long ridge in the valley. ✉ *Artenara* ⊕ *www. artenara.es.*

days. ✉ *Muelle Puerto Base, Puerto Rico* ☎ *626/982152* ⊕ *www.dolphinwhales. es* ✉ *€29.*

CAMEL RIDES
Camello Safari

LOCAL SPORTS | **FAMILY** | Join a quick camel trek across the Maspalomas dunes. The rides, which take about 30 minutes, leave every 15 minutes. ✉ *Calle Oceania s/n, Maspalomas* ☎ *928/760781* ⊕ *www. camellosafari.com* ✉ *€12.*

GOLF
Lopesan Meloneras Golf

GOLF | Half of the 18 holes at this par-71 course face the mountains, and the other half face the sea. Several are practically on the beach. ✉ *Autopista GC 500 s/n, Meloneras* ☎ *928/145309* ⊕ *www.gran-canariagolf.com* ✉ *Green fees €72* 🏌 *18 holes, 6350 yards, par 71.*

Maspalomas Golf

GOLF | Surrounded by the famous Maspalomas dunes, this 18-hole, par-73 course has ocean views from many of its long, wide greens. The course was designed by Mackenzie Ross. ✉ *Av. T. O. Neckerman s/n, Maspalomas* ☎ *928/762581* ⊕ *www.maspalomasgolf.net* ✉ *Green fees €70; golf cart €18* 🏌 *18 holes, 6723 yards, par 73.*

HORSEBACK RIDING

El Salobre

HORSEBACK RIDING | Horseback riding trips near Maspalomas are for one (€30) or two (€45) hours, with longer trips available on request. The company can pick you up from your hotel and take you to the stables. ✉ *Calle Islas Malvinas 3, El Salobre* ☎ *616/418363* 🌐 *www.elsalobrehr.es.*

WINDSURFING

Pro Surfing

SURFING | Learn from scratch or improve your windsurfing, kitesurfing, and paddle-boarding skills here; they also have gear to rent. ✉ *CC Eurocenter Loc. 80, Av. de Moya 6, Playa del Inglés* ☎ *928/769719* 🌐 *www.prsurfing.es.*

San Bartolomé de Tirajana

23 km (14 miles) north of Maspalomas, 20 km (12 miles) east of Cruz de San Antonio.

The administrative center of the south coast, San Bartolomé de Tirajana is an attractive town planted with pink geraniums. At its popular Sunday-morning market, held every two weeks in front of the church, you'll find tropical produce and island crafts. To the east, the village of **Santa Lucía** has crafts shops and a small museum devoted to Guanche artifacts.

Tejeda

About 7 km (4½ miles) southwest of Las Palmas.

At the misty mountain village of Tejeda, the road begins to ascend through a pine forest dotted with picnic spots to the **Parador Cruz de Tejeda.** From the parador, continue uphill about 21 km (13 miles) to the **Mirador Pico de las Nieves,** the highest lookout on Gran Canaria. Here, too, is the **Pozo de la Nieve,** a well built by clergymen in 1699 to store snow. Tejeda is locally famous for its fragrant almonds, which bakers incorporate into delectable confections sold in the town center.

Side Trip

Drive up to the Cruz Grande summit on GC520. To the left are several of the island's reservoirs, known as the lakes of Gran Canaria; they're stocked with trout and carp, and you can fish in them with a permit (obtained in advance) from the island environmental agency (*928/301591*). Continue along GC520 in the direction of Tejeda, past rural mountain villages. On the right is the Roque Nublo, an eroded volcanic chimney worshiped by the Guanches that juts 80 meters (262 feet) into the air. Explore the Roque and its surrounding trails, pausing for a picnic in the shade.

Hotels

Parador Cruz de Tejeda

$$ | **HOTEL** | Right in the geographical center of the island, this is the perfect spot to get away from it all and to take in some of Gran Canaria's best views. **Pros:** large rooms; fantastic spa (€25 fee); incredible sunsets from the rooms. **Cons:** limited dining options outside hotel; difficult access up a mountain road; inconsistent service. [$] *Rooms from: €100* ✉ *Calle Cruz de Tejeda, Tejeda* ☎ *928/012500* 🌐 *www.parador.es* 🛏 *43 rooms* 🍴 *No meals.*

San Mateo

15 km (9 miles) northeast of Parador Cruz de Tejeda.

From Tejeda, the road winds down to San Mateo, whose goat cheese is famous across Gran Canaria. You can find it at the weekend market and in shops the island over. Pass **Santa Brigida** and turn right toward the golf club on the rim of the Bandama Crater. Continue to the village of Atalaya, where there are cave houses and pottery workshops carrying on a millennia-old tradition.

Tafira Alta

7 km (4½ miles) west of Las Palmas.

Along the main road leading into Las Palmas from San Mateo is Tafira Alta, an exclusive suburb with a colonial air where many of the city's wealthiest families live.

 Sights

Jardín Botánico Canario "Viero y Clavijo"
GARDEN | In Tafira Alta (just north of Las Palmas) is one of Spain's largest botanical gardens, with plants from all the islands grouped in their natural habitats. ⊠ *Ctra. de Centro, Km 7, Tafira Alta* ☏ *928/219580* ⊕ *www.jardincanario.org.*

Lanzarote

With hardened lava fields, black and red dunes, and treeless mountainsides, Lanzarote's interior is right out of a science-fiction movie (literally—*Clash of the Titans, One Million Years B.C.,* and a number of other blockbusters were filmed here). The entire island is a UNESCO biosphere reserve. There are no springs or lakes, and it rarely rains, so all freshwater comes from desalination plants. Despite its surreal and sometimes intimidating volcanic landscape, Lanzarote—the fourth-largest Canary—has turned itself into an inviting resort through good planning (although not so good around Playa Blanca, where illegal construction is slightly out of hand), an emphasis on outdoor adventure, and

conservation of its natural beauty. No buildings taller than two stories are allowed in most places, and billboards are forbidden, leaving views of the spectacular geology unobstructed.

Lanzarote was named for the Italian explorer Lancelotto Alocello, who arrived in the 14th century, but the name most synonymous with the island today is César Manrique, the internationally acclaimed artist and architect who helped shape modern-day Canarian culture and share it on the world stage. Manrique designed many of the island's tourist attractions and convinced authorities to require that all new buildings be painted white with green or brown trim (white with blue on the coast), to suggest coolness and fertility. He also led the fight against overdevelopment, lying down in front of bulldozers and galvanizing local activists. All over this island, and especially in Arrecife, Lanzarote has a North African feel. Like Moroccans, many locals sip their hot drinks, in this case *café bombón* (coffee with condensed milk), from little glasses rather than mugs.

Vying with Fuerteventura for the title of warmest island, Lanzarote often bakes in the summer. It's also very windy, particularly during July and August, when the trade winds (*vientos alisios*) from the northeast batter the island.

Despite the heat and lack of precipitation, the island produces some surprisingly excellent wine. Vines are buried (sometimes up to several feet deep) in a mantle of black lava shingle known as *picón* that attracts and retains moisture from dew, the only source of water for vines on this arid island. There are two designated wine tours that take in the main vineyards on the west side of the island. Ask at a tourist office for a wine-tour map.

VISITOR INFORMATION
Airport Tourist Office
✉ *Arrecife* ☎ *928/820704* ⊕ *www.turis-molanzarote.com.*

Arrecife Tourist Office
✉ *Parque Municipal, Arrecife* ☎ *928/811762.*

Arrecife

6 km (4 miles) east of the airport.

Although Arrecife houses one-third of Lanzarote's population (146,000), it exudes a leisurely island energy, unlike bustling Santa Cruz or Las Palmas. Real talk: It's not an especially pretty city, and some Canarians will even tell you to skip it altogether, but it does have some of the best shopping and nightlife on the island. It's also a practical place to crash before an early-morning departure or after a late-night landing. The coastline is strung with line after line of rocky reefs (in fact, "reef" is what *arrecife* means in Spanish). While you're here, don't miss its two castles or its inland saltwater lagoon, Charco de San Ginés, where there's a gorgeous fleet of small fishing craft. A stroll around the backstreets near the lagoon gives you an idea of the old Arrecife. The local Playa del Reducto is a good place to squeeze in some beach time if you're spending the day here.

From Arrecife, you can walk or bike to Puerto del Carmen along the 12-km (7½-mile) seafront promenade, which takes in lovely stretches of golden sand and views of the Ajaches mountains in the south. Stop for a bite to eat in Playa Honda, and take the bus back if you're not up for the return trip.

GETTING HERE AND AROUND
Cruise ships dock at Puerto Mármoles, about 3 km (2 miles) east of the capital. A walkway traces the shore from the port into the town, but it's a long and unattractive walk. Consider hopping on a shuttle bus or hailing a taxi outside the terminal.

Once in Arrecife, there are buses to Costa Teguise, Puerto del Carmen, and Playa Blanca run by the ambitiously named Intercity Bus company (⊕ *www.intercitybuslanzarote.es*). If you want to travel farther afield, it's best to rent a car.

Island-hopping is possible by ferry from Arrecife to Fuerteventura and on to Gran Canaria, although the quickest way to get to Fuerteventura is from Playa Blanca. Southern Lanzarote and northern Fuerteventura are linked by two companies, Fred Olsen and Naviera Armas, both of which make six round trips a day from Lanzarote. Interisland planes link Lanzarote quickly and frequently with the other islands.

VISITOR INFORMATION
Tourist Office Center
INFO CENTER | Arrecife isn't the most attractive part of Lanzarote, but the old town is interesting, particularly the area around the Charco de San Ginés (lagoon). The **tourist office**, housed in the original bandstand in the municipal park, has detailed maps and information about local points of interest. ✉ *Parque Municipal* ☎ *928/811762* ⊗ *Closed Sun.*

Tourist Office Cruise Terminal
The tourist office right on the port opens for three hours after cruise-ship arrivals. ✉ *Muelle de los Mármoles s/n* ☎ *928/844690.*

Sights

Castillo San Gabriel
CASTLE/PALACE | This double-wall fortress was once used to keep pirates at bay. You can walk out to the fortress over Puente de las Bolas with lovely views of the port and city and then explore the small (Spanish-only) museum inside. ✉ *Arrecife* 🖼 *€3.*

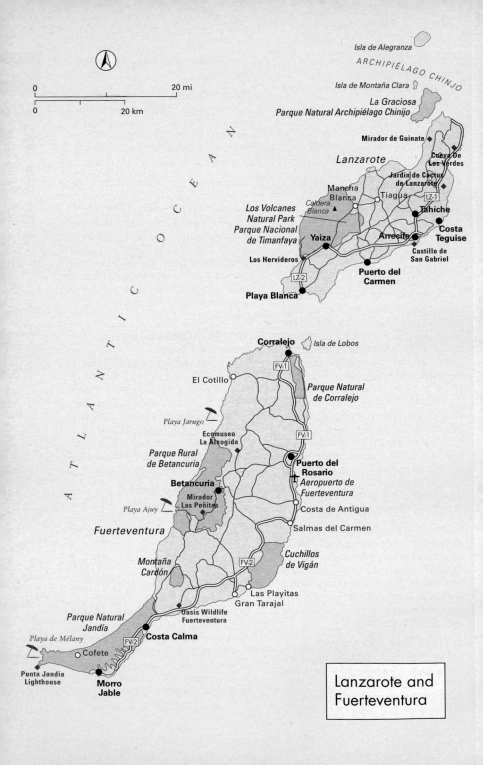

Lanzarote and Fuerteventura

Museo Internacional de Arte Contemporáneo Castillo de San José (*MIAC*)
CASTLE/PALACE | The old waterfront fortress **Castillo San José** was turned into this stunning modern art museum by the architect César Manrique. One of his paintings is on display, along with other works by artists such as Cardenas, Beaudin, Zóbel, and Tàpies. ✉ *Av. de Naos s/n* ☎ *901/200300* 🎟 *€4.*

Beaches

Playa del Reducto
BEACH—SIGHT | It may not be in the same league as some of the beaches in the south, but Playa del Reducto is still an attractive urban beach, ideal for relaxing after you've looked around Arrecife. It's well maintained and protected by natural reefs, so swimming is usually like swimming in a warm lake (though do watch out for rocky outcrops at low tide). The beach, overlooked at the eastern end by the high-rise Arrecife Gran Hotel, is backed by a pleasant promenade that goes all the way to Puerto del Carmen. **Amenities:** food and drink; showers; toilets. **Best for:** sunrise; walking. ✉ *Arrecife.*

Restaurants

Casa Ginory
$ | **SPANISH** | Decorated in a nautical theme, Casa Ginory has indoor and outdoor seating, with tables overlooking the sea or the Charco de San Ginés lagoon. House specials include *matrimonio* (a "marriage" of squid rings and fish) and *almejas* (clams) washed down with local wines. **Known for:** fresh fish; waterfront views; local vibe. [$] *Average main: €9* ✉ *Calle Juan de Quesada 7* ☎ *922/804046* 💳 *No credit cards* 🕒 *Closed Sun.*

Lilium
$$ | **SPANISH** | Creative cooking with Canarian roots is the philosophy behind the dishes at this modern restaurant east of the San Ginés lagoon. Although there are a few tables outdoors, the dining mainly takes place inside, where copper and chocolate tones accompany floral touches. **Known for:** finest dining on the island; innovative cuisine; tasting menu. [$] *Average main: €15* ✉ *Av. Olof Palme s/n* ☎ *928/524978* 🌐 *restaurantelilium.com* 🕒 *Closed Sun.*

Naia
$$ | **SPANISH** | From your patio table overlooking the harbor, feast on attractively plated modern Spanish fare such as heirloom tomato salmorejo , griddled Iberian pork with sautéed vegetables, and slow-poached cod over black rice. The interior dining area is almost as charming with pendant lights and mismatched vintage chairs. **Known for:** artfully plated dishes; pleasant harborside patio; creative Canarian cuisine. [$] *Average main: €13* ✉ *Av. César Manrique 33* ☎ *928/805797* 🌐 *www.restaurantenaia.com* 🕒 *Closed Sun.*

Hotels

Arrecife Gran Hotel
$$ | **HOTEL** | This 17-story glass tower is a bit of an eyesore on an island where low-rises are the norm, but once inside, it's hard to hate the bird's-eye views from the rooms and the inviting, comfy communal areas. **Pros:** great views; spacious rooms; soothing, well-maintained spa. **Cons:** cleanliness not quite five-star; average breakfast; slow, forgetful service staff. [$] *Rooms from: €110* ✉ *Av. Fred Olsen 1* ☎ *928/800000* 🌐 *www.aghotelspa.com* 🛏 *160 rooms* 🍴 *No meals.*

Hotel Lancelot
$ | **HOTEL** | Facing the attractive Playa del Reducto, this is a good budget option for a quick overnight. **Pros:** beachside location; good value; rooftop pool. **Cons:** dull breakfast that stops at 10 am; mattresses can be a little uncomfortable; dingy environs. [$] *Rooms from: €76* ✉ *Av. de la Mancomunidad 9* ☎ *928/805099*

Lanzarote is known for its year-round warm weather, volcanic landscape, and conservation of its natural beauty.

⊕ *www.hotellancelot.com* ⤴ *110 rooms* ⦿ *No meals.*

Nightlife

The Garden
DANCE CLUBS | This 21-plus nightclub plays mostly chart-topping bangers to a stylish local set. Drinks are reasonably priced. No shorts, sandals, or beachwear allowed. ⊠ *Calle Luis Morote 7* ☎ *651/120883.*

The Red Lion
BARS/PUBS | Grab a beer at this quirky locals-only sports bar to watch spirited *fútbol* matches and bet on horse races. An Elvis impersonator frequently provides the musical entertainment. ⊠ *Av. de las Islas Canarias, Local 10* ☎ *651/593485.*

Activities

★ Eco Insider
TOUR—SPORTS | FAMILY | Discover hidden corners of Lanzarote with this company's specialty trips, which include bird-watching, volcano walks, food and wine tours, and visits to the remote islets of La Graciosa and uninhabited La Alegranza. Tours are led by local experts. The company can pick you up by prior arrangement from your hotel or cruise ship; book well in advance. Prices include lunch and transportation. ☎ *650/819069* ⊕ *www. eco-insider.com* ✉ *From €42.*

💼 Shopping

Shopping is low-key in Arrecife. The main shops are on and around the pedestrian-only Calle León y Castilla.

Queso Project
FOOD/CANDY | Some of Lanzarote's top artisan cheeses (and a wide selection of mainland European ones) are sold at this charming city-center shop. ⊠ *Calle José Molina 7* ☎ *636/714348* ⊕ *www.queso-project.com* ⊗ *Closed Sun. and Mon.*

Costa Teguise

7 km (4½ miles) northeast of Arrecife.

A green-and-white complex of apartments and several large hotels, Costa Teguise is a typical '80s resort that some would say is past its heyday, although it still draws thousands of visitors every year. King Juan Carlos used to own a villa here, near the Meliá Salinas hotel. Teguise proper (also known as La Villa de Teguise or, colloquially, "La Villa"), on the other hand, is situated 15 km (9 miles) inland from the coastal enclave and is another experience entirely: it is Lanzarote's historic capital and the oldest settlement in the archipelago, dating to 1402. Many of local visionary artist César Manrique's architectural masterpieces are situated withing easy driving distance of Teguise.

GETTING HERE AND AROUND

Lanzarote Intercity buses connect the resort and Arrecife. On weekdays, a bus leaves every 20 minutes, and every 30 minutes on weekends. The trip takes about 20 minutes.

VISITOR INFORMATION
Costa Teguise Tourist Office
⊠ *Av. Islas Canarias s/n* ☎ *928/592542* ⊕ *www.turismoteguise.com.*

Sights

Castillo de Santa Bárbara (*Museo de la Piratería*)
CASTLE/PALACE | **FAMILY** | For sweeping aerial views of Lanzarote's craggy coast and parched volcanic landscape, climb to the top of this 16th-century fortress that, since 2011, houses the Canaries' Museo de la Piratería (Piracy Museum). The *castillo* warded off pirates for centuries from its perch on the Guanapay volcano. ⊠ *Calle Herrera y Rojas 5, Teguise* ☎ *928/594802, 686/470376* ⊕ *www.museodelapirateria.com.*

★ **César Manrique House Museum**
HOUSE | On a hillock overlooking the sleepy town of Haría you'll find César Manrique's final home, preserved as if in amber. The artist lived in this architecturally stunning estate, which he built for himself, until his untimely death by auto accident in 1992. Plant-filled courtyards lead into Bohemian living areas brimming with sculptures, paintings, and iconic furniture; the bathroom, with a floor-to-ceiling window into a leafy garden, is a highlight, as is the outdoor pool area and art studio, kept precisely how it was left on the day he died. ⊠ *Calle Elvira Sánchez 30, Haria* ☎ *928/843138* ⊕ *www.fcmanrique.org* ⊠ *€10.*

Cueva de los Verdes (*Green Caves*)
CAVE | Guided walks take you through this 1-km (½-mile) section of an underground volcanic tunnel, said to be the longest in the world. It's one of the most stunning natural sights on the island. You'll find the entrance to the north of Costa Teguise, beyond Punta Mujeres. ⊠ *LZ204* ☎ *901/200300* ⊠ *€10.*

★ **Jardín de Cactus** (*Cactus Garden*)
GARDEN | North of Costa Teguise between Guatiza and Mala, this cactus garden with 10,000 specimens of more than 1,500 varieties was César Manrique's last creation for Lanzarote. Look beyond the park and you'll see prickly pear fields: for centuries locals have cultivated these plants for their cochineal, an insect living on the cacti from which scarlet carmine dye is extracted. ⊠ *Ctra. General del Norte s/n, Guatiza* ☎ *901/200300* ⊠ *€6.*

Los Jameos del Agua
NATURE SITE | These water caverns, 15 km (9 miles) north of the Costa Teguise, were created when molten lava streamed through an underground tunnel and hissed into the sea. Look for the tiny albino crabs on the rocks in the underground lake—this species, which is blind, is found nowhere else in the world. There are bars and restaurants around the lake, and the **Casa de los Volcanes** is a

The incredible Jardín de Cactus was designed by César Manrique, the island's most influential artist and architect.

good museum of volcanic science. Night visits are possible on Saturday. ⊠ *Punta de Mujeres* ☎ *901/200300* 🎟 *€10.*

Mirador del Río

BUILDING | Designed by César Manrique, this lookout at the northerly tip of a hair-pin bend in the LZ202 road lets you see the islet of **La Graciosa** from an altitude of 1,550 feet. From the lookout you can also see smaller protected isles—Montaña Clara, Alegranza (the Canary closest to Europe), and Roque del Este. Try to arrive early to beat the crowds. ⊠ *LZ202* 🎟 *€5.*

Órzola

TOWN | The little fishing village of Órzola is 9 km (5½ miles) north of Los Jameos del Agua. Small-boat excursions leave here each day for the neighboring islet of La Graciosa , where there are fewer than 500 residents and plenty of quiet beaches. ⊠ *Órzola.*

Beaches

Playa de Famara

BEACH—SIGHT | Directly opposite Costa Teguise on the north coast of Lanzarote is one of the island's most attractive beaches. Set in a natural cove, its 6 km (4 miles) of sand are flanked by spectacular cliffs. The riptide here makes for excellent surfing and windsurfing, and Playa de Famara is regularly used for world championships for those sports. That said, the strong currents mean swimming can be dangerous. **Amenities:** food and drink; lifeguards; showers; toilets; water sports. **Best for:** sunset; surfing; walking; wind-surfing. ⊠ *Av. el Marinero, Las Palmas.*

Playa de la Garita

BEACH—SIGHT | **FAMILY** | Not far from the Jardín de Cactus, Playa de la Garita is a wide bay of crystalline water favored by surfers in winter and snorkelers in summer. Almost a kilometer (½ mile) of golden sands is safe for swimming, making this a popular spot for families. The beach gets busy in the summer but is reasonably quiet the rest of the year. Lounge chairs and umbrellas are available for rent. **Amenities:** food and drink; lifeguards; showers; toilets; water sports. **Best for:** snorkeling; surfing; swimming. ⊠ *Arrieta.*

Playa de las Cucharas

BEACH—SIGHT | This is the best of Costa Teguise's several small beaches. The sands are protected from high wind and waves by the natural bay formed in the coastline. A pleasant seafront promenade takes you around the beach and into the southern stretches of the resort. Getting a spot for your towel in the summer can be a challenge, especially on weekends. **Amenities:** food and drink; lifeguards; showers; toilets; water sports. **Best for:** sunrise; swimming. ⊠ *Av. Arenas Blancas.*

🍴 Restaurants

El Navarro

$$ | **INTERNATIONAL** | Although it's on a busy access road and inside a drab building, this restaurant is well worth a stop. Grab a table that's outside if possible. **Known for:** curry croquettes; good service; killer cheesecake. $ *Average main: €14* ⊠ *Av. del Mar 13* 🕾 *928/592145* ▭ *No credit cards* 🕓 *Closed Tues. and July.*

Restaurante Las Caletas Casa Tomás

$ | **SPANISH** | Off the tourist track, this no-frills seafood restaurant with stunning sea views is a favorite with locals. The outdoor terrace seems to hover over the sea. **Known for:** ocean views; pleasant terrace; affordable seafood dishes. $ *Average main: €8* ⊠ *Calle Bambilote 2* 🕾 *928/591046* 🕓 *Closed Mon. and Tues.*

🛏 Hotels

H10 Lanzarote Gardens

$$$ | **RESORT** | **FAMILY** | For a good, all-inclusive deal in tropical surroundings, this is one of the best bets in the area for families. **Pros:** good value; excellent service;

entertainment for all ages. **Cons:** can be crowded in high season; no elevators; noisy breakfasts. $ *Rooms from: €160* ⊠ *Av. Islas Canarias 13* 🕾 *900/444666* ⊕ *www.hotelh10lanzarotegardens.com* ⬧ *242 rooms* 🍽 *Free Breakfast.*

Santa Rosa

$ | **RESORT** | Outstanding value in pristine surroundings is the hallmark of the Santa Rosa resort, a collection of one- and two-bedroom apartments centered around a large swimming pool. **Pros:** great value; spotlessly clean; well-appointed gym. **Cons:** longish walk to the beach; single beds only; maintenance could be improved. $ *Rooms from: €87* ⊠ *Av. del Mar 19* 🕾 *928/346038* ⊕ *www.apartamentossantarosa.com* ⬧ *128 rooms* 🍽 *Free Breakfast.*

Activities

BICYCLING
Evolution Bikes

BICYCLING | **FAMILY** | Both novice and expert cyclists are well-served at this shop that rents mountain bikes, road bikes, quadricycles, and more. Child seats and trailers are also available. Should any technical issues arise while riding, a store associate will drive out and fix it. Rates start at €11 per day. ⊠ *Complejo La Galea, Paseo Marítimo 2* 🕾 *672/330251* ⊕ *www.evolution-bikes.com.*

DIVING

One of the island's official diving centers is near Las Cucharas beach.

Aquatis Diving Center

SCUBA DIVING | Diving Lanzarote rents equipment, leads dives, and offers a certification course. Adrenaline junkies shouldn't miss the "Diving With Sharks" outing. ⊠ *Playa de las Cucharas, Local 6* 🕾 *928/590407* ⊕ *www.diving-lanzarote.net.*

Calipso Diving Lanzarote

DIVING/SNORKELING | This well-established dive school has PADI Resort Center status and offers experiences for kids and adults. Hotel pickup can be arranged. ✉ *Centro Comercial Calipso, Av. Islas Canarias, Local 3* ☎ *928/590879* ⊕ *www.calipso-diving.com.*

GOLF
Costa Teguise Golf

GOLF | These 18 holes, which are outside the Costa Teguise development, have unusual sand traps filled with black-lava cinders. ✉ *Av. del Golf s/n* ☎ *928/590512* ⊕ *www.lanzarote-golf.com* ⅄ *18 holes, 7082 yards, par 72.*

SURFING

Some of the best surfing in the world is on Lanzarote's west coast, particularly at Famara beach where regular surfing championships take place. The variety of beaches and winds on the island makes it an excellent location for surfers of all abilities.

★ Surf Canarias

SURFING | Surfers of all experience levels can take classes and rent gear from this company. ✉ *Calle Achique 14, Teguise* ☎ *928/528528* ⊕ *www.surfcanarias.com.*

WINDSURFING
Windsurfing Club Las Cucharas

WINDSURFING | The most thrilling place on the island for windsurfing is at Playa de las Cucharas; this club provides lessons and equipment rental. ✉ *CC Las Maretas 2, Calle de Marajo* ☎ *928/590731* ⊕ *www.lanzarotewindsurf.com.*

🛍 Shopping

For island crafts and produce, go to the open market (one of the largest on the islands) in the village of **Teguise** on Sunday between 9 and 2. Some vendors set up stalls in the plaza; others just lay out a blanket in the street and sell embroidered tablecloths, leather goods, costume jewelry, African masks, and other items.

Aloe Plus Lanzarote

PERFUME/COSMETICS | A wide range of lotions, balms, and serums made from locally grown aloe vera are sold at this shop, which also has a small "museum" detailing the history and uses of the plant. There are other branches in Yaiza, Arrieta, Punta Mujeres, and La Graciosa. ✉ *Pl. de la Constitución 4, Teguise* ☎ *928/594894* ⊕ *www.aloepluslanzarote.com* ⊙ *Closed Sun. afternoon.*

Puerto del Carmen

11 km (7 miles) southwest of Arrecife.

Most beach-bound travelers to Lanzarote wind up in the sandy strands of the Puerto del Carmen area, the island's busiest resort. The small fishing port and historic marina (called El Varadero) are surrounded by numerous cafés and restaurants, with the main commercial center behind them. The charming Puerto Carlero, 6 km (4 miles) west, is the newest addition to the resort and makes a quieter base.

GETTING HERE AND AROUND

Take the bus from Arrecife or the airport. Services run every 20 minutes on weekdays and every 30 on weekends. The trip takes 40 minutes. If you're feeling energetic, you could instead walk or bike on the seafront promenade all the way to Puerto del Carmen from the capital.

VISITOR INFORMATION
Puerto del Carmen Tourist Office

✉ *Av. de las Playas 6* ☎ *928/513351* ⊕ *www.puertodelcarmen.com.*

Beaches

Playa de los Pocillos

BEACH—SIGHT | Slightly north of Puerto del Carmen, this beach is near most of the area's development; hotels and apartments are restricted, however, to the other side of the highway, leaving the 2-km (1-mile) yellow-sand beach surprisingly pristine. Finding a spot to lay your towel can be difficult in summer. Lounge chairs and umbrellas are available. **Amenities:** food and drink; lifeguards; showers; toilets; water sports. **Best for:** sunrise; swimming; walking. ⊠ *Av. de las Playas, Tías.*

Playa Grande
BEACH—SIGHT | Puerto del Carmen's main beach is a busy strip of yellow sand that's as close as you can get to an urban beach on Lanzarote outside Arrecife. Lounge chairs and umbrellas are available for rent. Backing the beach is a seafront promenade with plenty of souvenir shops and restaurants. You can take the promenade all the way to Arrecife. **Amenities:** food and drink; lifeguards; showers; toilets; water sports. **Best for:** swimming. ⊠ *Av. de las Playas.*

Playa Matagorda
BEACH—SIGHT | On this northern extension of Playa de los Pocillos, there are alternating sections of gravel and gray sand. A perpetually windy spot, this busy beach has gentle waves that are perfect for those learning to surf. Lounge chairs and beach umbrellas are available. **Amenities:** food and drink; lifeguards; showers; toilets; water sports. **Best for:** surfing; swimming; walking. ⊠ *Av. de las Playas, Tías.*

🍴 Restaurants

Everest Indian Restaurant
$ | INDIAN | FAMILY | When you can't look at another plate of fish and taters without moaning—*mira*, it happens to the best of us in the Canaries—spring for a palate-jolting curry at Everest, whose heady dishes ranging from vindaloo to korma and *jalfrezi* (curry dish) are probably better than your neighborhood Indian joint's renditions. **Known for:** blistered made-to-order naan; unapologetically spicy curries; cheery service. Ⓢ *Average main: €10* ⊠ *Av. de las Playas 41* ☎ *928/511181.*

La Lonja
$ | TAPAS | Every morning, fishermen haul in their catch steps from this converted fishermen's warehouse whose upstairs dining room has sweeping views of the busy harbor. The Canarian menu includes simply roasted and fried fish and papas arrugadas. **Known for:** heaping seafood and fish platters; harbor and sea views; great value. Ⓢ *Average main: €11* ⊠ *Calle Varadero 22* ☎ *928/511377.*

★ Mardeleva
$$ | SEAFOOD | On a hill overlooking the port, this small family-run restaurant is all about the catch of the day (try the barracuda if available), served either fried or grilled and always accompanied by papas arrugadas. *Arroz caldoso con bogavante* (soupy rice with lobster) is another highlight. Try to score a table on the outdoor terrace, where you can watch the boats ply across the harbor; inside, eclectic family artworks are on display. **Known for:** pleasant marina views; pristine seafood; intimate, family-run atmosphere. Ⓢ *Average main: €12* ⊠ *Calle los Infantes 10* ☎ *928/510686.*

🛏 Hotels

Hotel Costa Calero Talaso and Spa
$$ | HOTEL | Sprawling gardens and serene pools await guests at this modern hotel, just south of Puerto del Carmen in the Puerto Calero marina. **Pros:** quiet location with lovely gardens; free shuttle bus to the beach; spa with Roman baths. **Cons:** slightly off the beaten track; dull entertainment; little food variety. Ⓢ *Rooms from: €124* ⊠ *Urbanización Puerto Calero s/n* ☎ *928/849595* ⊕ *www.hotelcosta-calero.es* ↝ *312 rooms, 12 suites* ¹⁰¹ *Free Breakfast.*

Seaside Los Jameos Playa
$$$ | HOTEL | FAMILY | César Manrique disciples were behind this giant colonial resort, where the tropical gardens, wooden balconies, and cane furniture all evoke old-school Havana. **Pros:** stunning

Did You Know?

The grapes used to make wines in Lanzarote are cultivated in a singular manner. Here, rows of volcanic stone semi-circles replace patchwork green fields. Called Zocos, these have been built for each individual vine and provide much needed protection from the sometimes-fierce winds.

architecture; complimentary glass of cava at check-in; renowned tennis club. **Cons:** communal areas need a refresh; not much variety for vegetarians; kids' activities are sometimes lackluster. $ *Rooms from: €170* ✉ *Calle Marte 2, Playa de los Pocillos* ☎ *928/763308* 🌐 *www.los-jameos-playa.es* 🛏 *526 rooms, 4 suites* 🍴 *Free Breakfast.*

Nightlife

This is the center of Lanzarote's nightlife. The main party strip is Avenida de las Playas. For a more relaxed night out, head to the old town, where most locals spend their time. The crowd is still mostly foreign, but the bars are more intimate and the drinks cheaper.

The Dubliner Live Music Lounge

MUSIC CLUBS | These cover musicians are pros at getting everyone into party mode (and they keep it bumping till 3:30)—so grab a pint of Guinness and jump on the dance floor. Nobody takes themselves too seriously at the Dubliner, and that's precisely its allure. ✉ *Centro Comercial Marítimo, Av. de las Playas* ☎ *636/713861.*

Gran Casino de Lanzarote

CASINOS | Try your luck at the only casino on Lanzarote—it's as laid-back as the island itself. You must be over 18 and must show your passport to get in. ✉ *Av. de las Playas 12* ☎ *928/515000* 🌐 *www.grancasinolanzarote.com.*

Ruta 66

BARS/PUBS | At the American bar Ruta 66, you can sip a frothy mixed drink on a cushioned wicker chair while taking in catchy tunes and ocean views. This is also the town's liveliest spot to catch a sports game and root for your team among fellow fans. ✉ *Av. de las Playas 19.*

Scotch Corner Bar

BARS/PUBS | Guitars hang from the ceiling, and old pictures of Scotland adorn the walls in the Scotch Corner Bar. There's live music nightly usually acoustic and sometimes Scottish. Regulars love the mojitos. ✉ *Calle Tenerife 14.*

Activities

Lanzarote Golf

GOLF | This 18-hole course, which is between Puerto del Carmen and Tías, comes with spectacular ocean views along its wide greens. ✉ *Ctra. del Puerto del Carmen–Tías s/n* ☎ *928/514050* 🌐 *www.lanzarotegolfresort.com* ⛳ *18 holes, 6707 yards, par 72.*

Tahíche

5 km (3 miles) south of Teguise.

Only one thing makes Tahíche a destination rather than a drive-through town between Arrecife and the north of the island: the former estate of César Manrique.

GETTING HERE AND AROUND

By car, head north out of Arrecife on the main avenue, Avenida Campoamor. The Fundación César Manrique is off to the left before you enter the village (follow the signs). From Arrecife, Buses 7 and 9 go this way several times a day; Bus 10 runs weekdays only; all stop at the César Manrique Crossing.

Sights

★ Fundación César Manrique

HOUSE | César Manrique (1919–92) made this high-design bachelor pad called Taro de Tahíche for himself in 1968 upon returning from New York City, where he'd been living and working thanks to a grant from Nelson Rockefeller. The artist managed to turn a barren lava field into an inviting and architecturally stunning abode—the first of its kind in the Canaries—that would play host to international celebrities and become the islands' most emblematic residence. The artist called

Taro home for 20 years and created some of his most celebrated works while residing here; his studio now displays original paintings. The real attraction is the house itself with its cave dwellings outfitted with splashy furniture, crystalline pools tucked between boulders, and palms shooting up through holes between floors. ✉ *Calle Jorge Luis Borges 16* ☎ *928/843138* ⊕ *www.fcmanrique.org* ✆ *€8.*

Yaiza

13 km (8 miles) west of Puerto del Carmen.

Yaiza is a quiet whitewashed village with good restaurants. Largely destroyed by a river of lava in the 1700s, it's best known as the gateway to the volcanic national park. The hamlet of El Golfo, situated within the Yaiza municipality, is a whitewashed coastal town with seafood restaurants and views of the **Charco Verde,** or "Green Lake."

GETTING HERE AND AROUND
Bus service is infrequent, so rent a car to get here. To get to the volcanoes, you have to take a tour bus, as there's no access for private vehicles.

Sights

El Charco Verde (*Charco de los Clicos*)
BODY OF WATER | This bizarre green lagoon, which looks like something out of a sci-fi thriller, is situated at the outer limits of Timanfaya National Park just uphill from El Golfo. It gets its radioactive hue from its sulfuric content and *Ruppia maritima* seagrass. It's forbidden to walk to the lake as it's within the reserve, but there's a viewpoint that's clearly marked at the turn-off to El Golfo where you can snap some excellent photos, especially at sunset. ✉ *Yaiza.*

★ **Parque Nacional de Timanfaya** (*Timanfaya National Park*)
NATIONAL/STATE PARK | FAMILY | Popularly known as "the Fire Mountains," this national park takes up much of southern Lanzarote. As you enter the park from Yaiza, you'll see the staging area for the Canaries' best-known **camel rides**; a bumpy camel trek among the rust-red dunes lasts about 20 minutes. The volcanic landscape inside Timanfaya is a violent jumble of exploded craters, cinder cones, lava formations, and heat fissures. The park is protected, and you can't drive or hike through it yourself (leave your car in the lot beside the volcano-top restaurant, **El Diablo**); the only way to see the central volcanic area is on a 14-km (9-mile) bus circuit called the **Ruta de los Volcanes** , designed to have minimal environmental impact. (Photographers will be bummed that the only pics you can take on tour are through smudged windows.)

A taped English commentary explains how the parish priest of Yaiza took notes during the 1730 eruption that buried two villages. He had plenty of time—the eruption lasted six years, making it the longest known eruption in volcanic history. By the time it was over, more than 75% of Lanzarote was covered in lava. Throughout the park, on signs and road markers, you'll see a little devil with a pitchfork; this *diablito* was designed by Manrique. ■TIP→ **During summer, visit in late afternoon to avoid the crowds.**

✉ *Centro de Visitantes Mancha Blancha, Ctra. de Yaiza a Tinajo, Km 11.5, Tinajo* ☎ *928/118042* ✆ *Ruta de los Volcanes €9.*

🍴 Restaurants

El Diablo
$$ | SPANISH | This must be one of the world's most unusual restaurants. Here, in the heart of Timanfaya National Park, chicken, steaks, and spicy sausages are

The spectacular volcanic landscape of Timanfaya National Park was created over six years of near-continuous volcanic eruptions that took place between 1730 and 1736.

cooked over a volcanic crater using the earth's natural heat. **Known for:** unique location; volcano views; food cooked over crater. $ *Average main: €15* ✉ *Timanfaya National Park, Tinajo* ☎ *928/840057.*

★ La Bodega de Santiago

$$ | SPANISH | Shaded by a splendid ficus that keeps the terraza cool in the midday heat, La Bodega de Santiago is worth going out of your way to visit. The traditional Canarian menu is exquisite, integrating meats and produce from the surrounding farms and complementing dishes with island wines. **Known for:** romantic dining beneath a gorgeous tree; terrific goat and roast meats; locavore cuisine. $ *Average main: €17* ✉ *Calle Montañas del Fuego 27* ☎ *928/836204* ⊕ *www.labodegadesantiago.es* ⊙ *Closed Mon.*

Restaurante Mar Azul

$$ | SEAFOOD | Of all the seafood restaurants in the tiny hamlet of El Golfo, this harborside standby stands out for its ultra-fresh fish and homemade Canarian dishes. Order the *parrillada de marisco,* or grilled seafood platter, for a sampling of local fish (the barracuda is consistently exceptional), calamari, and fried shellfish, all of which soar to new heights when dunked in cilantro-packed mojo verde. **Known for:** bountiful seafood platters; not-your-average mojos; romantic seaside terrace. $ *Average main: €15* ✉ *Av. Marítima 42* ☎ *928/173132.*

Shopping

Ahumadería de Uga

FOOD/CANDY | The hamlet of Uga is the improbable home of what's arguably Spain's finest smoked salmon producer. The Guerrero family won't relinquish its secret recipe, but what we know is that the salmon is imported from Scotland and Norway, cured with salt culled from nearby Janubio beach, and smoked over La Geria grapevines. The smoked fish is so delectable that the tiny shop sells more than 200 pounds of it each day. ✉ *LZ2 3* ☎ *928/830132.*

Playa Blanca

15 km (9 miles) south of Yaiza.

Playa Blanca is Lanzarote's newest resort. Tourists come for the white-sand beaches at **Punta de Papagayo,** which can only be reached by driving on hard-packed dirt. The town beaches are small sandy coves, often packed to bursting in the summer. Apart from the few large hotels that dominate the east side of the beachfront, accommodations are all inside freestanding houses. The town itself is small, stretching along the sea from the lighthouse in the west to the marina (Marina Rubicón) in the east.

Just north of Playa Blanca lies Lanzarote's agricultural belt and wine country: **La Geria.** Here, scraggly vines erupt from pits of lapilli or "picón" soil ringed by volcanic rock. These crude stone walls have been used for centuries to shield the vines from the wind. Farmers in this area often cover the topsoil with a layer of ash to allow easy filtration and retention of dew and water, another age-old viticulture technique.

GETTING HERE AND AROUND

Rent a car to access the beaches and coastline. There's an hourly bus service (Línea 60) between Arrecife and Playa Blanca.

Island hopping to Fuerteventura (just across the strait) is easy from Playa Blanca.

VISITOR INFORMATION
Playa Blanca Tourist Office
⊠ *Calle Don Jaime Quesada El Maestro 3* ☎ *928/518150.*

Sights

★ **Bodegas El Grifo – Museo del Vino**
MUSEUM | Established in 1775, El Grifo is the Canaries' first winery and one of the oldest in Spain. Tour the grounds, which include a serene cactus garden

and wine museum, before ponying up for a tasting. El Grifo's wines are fruity and crowd-pleasing—and slightly less complex than those produced at neighboring Los Bermejos. Guided museum tours, which include a glass of wine, cost €9 and take place Monday–Sunday at 11, 1, and 4:30. ⊠ *Lugar de El Grifo* ☎ *928/524036* ⊕ *www.elgrifo.com* 🎫 *€5 museum entry.*

Los Bermejos
WINERY/DISTILLERY | Visit the winery that the *New York Times's* wine critic, Eric Asimov, deemed the Canaries' "star producer." In the small, modern tasting area, situated on a terrace overlooking the vines, sip one of Spain's top rosés, made from indigenous listán negro grapes, and wonderfully fragrant Malvasía whites. Walk-ins are accepted. ⊠ *Camino a Los Bermejos 7, San Bartolomé de Tirajana* ☎ *928/522463* ☉ *Closed weekends.*

Beaches

The most popular beach is **Playa de Papagayo,** though there are several others that are worth a visit.

Playa de Papagayo
BEACH—SIGHT | The rugged coastline east of Playa Blanca has several stunning beaches, but Playa de Papagayo is considered to be the area's—if not the island's—most picturesque. This small bay with fine white sand is perfect for sunbathing as it's protected from the wind by cliffs at both ends. You have to walk along a dirt path to get here, so take suitable footwear and bottled water. Despite its remoteness, Papagayo is a busy beach, particularly in summer. **Amenities:** none. **Best for:** snorkeling; sunrise; swimming. ⊠ *Playa Blanca.*

Playa Mujeres
BEACH—SIGHT | Squint and you could be in the Caribbean—this long white-sand beach situated within the protected area of Papagayo has turquoise water and generally calm surf. It faces west toward

Fuerteventura and the Isla de Lobos and is popular among nudists. The sandy bay provides safe swimming conditions, and the beach is cleaned regularly. Amenities are limited to a few small bars. On the way to the beach, look out for the ruins of some bunkers from World War II. **Amenities:** food and drink. **Best for:** snorkeling; nudists; sunset; swimming. ✉ *Playa Blanca* 🎫 *€3 per vehicle.*

Hotels

★ Hotel Casa del Embajador
$$$$ | **B&B/INN** | Tucked behind one of Lanzarote's typically green front doors is an oasis of calm where all you'll want to do is curl up in one of the loungers and take in the views of Fuerteventura and the Isla de Lobos. **Pros:** peace and quiet by the sea; good breakfast; fresh fruit in the rooms. **Cons:** no a/c; rooms need a revamp; pricey for what it is. [$] *Rooms from: €270* ✉ *Calle La Tegala 56* ☎ *928/519191* 🌐 *www.hotelcasadelembajador.com* 🛏 *13 rooms* 🍴 *Free Breakfast.*

Iberostar Selection Lanzarote Park
$$$ | **RESORT** | **FAMILY** | Travelers looking for accessible luxury and all-inclusive pampering should look no further than this Iberostar outpost, a chic yet unpretentious oceanfront resort that reopened in 2017 after major renovations. **Pros:** separate family and adults-only areas; spacious rooms; newly renovated public areas. **Cons:** underwhelming food across the board; you can hear the evening entertainment from some rooms; bland interiors convey no sense of place. [$] *Rooms from: €176* ✉ *Av. Archipiélago 7* ☎ *928/517048* 🌐 *www.iberostar.com* 🛏 *388 rooms* 🍴 *No meals.*

Princesa Yaiza Suite Hotel Resort
$$$$ | **HOTEL** | **FAMILY** | It might be big, but this sprawling white hotel still manages to do luxury with a capital *L*. **Pros:** great service; superb spa; fantastic buffet breakfast with eggs cooked to order. **Cons:** long walk to some rooms; overpriced food at pool bar; communal areas need a refresh. [$] *Rooms from: €192* ✉ *Av. de Papagayo s/n* ☎ *928/519300* 🌐 *www.princesayaiza.com* 🛏 *385 rooms* 🍴 *Free Breakfast.*

Activities

Papagayo Bike
BICYCLING | Daily bike rental starts at €12. Guided bike tours are also available. ✉ *Calle La Tegala 13* ☎ *928/349861* 🌐 *www.papagayobike.com.*

Fuerteventura

Some of Fuerteventura's towering sand dunes blew in from the Sahara Desert, 96 km (60 miles) away, and indeed it's not hard to imagine Fuerteventura as a detached piece of Africa. Despite being the second-largest Canary Island by area, Fuerteventura's population only reaches 115,000. Tourism arrived relatively late on the island, compared to Gran Canaria and Lanzarote, and it's still a comparatively minor tourist destination. Visitors come mainly to enjoy the stunning white beaches and to windsurf; there's little else to do. The two main resort areas are at the island's far north and south ends: Corralejo, across from Lanzarote, known for its miles of protected dunes, and the Jandía peninsula with dozens of long beaches, respectively. Fuerteventura didn't fully escape the Spanish construction boom of the early 2000s, but it remains a relatively unspoiled island and has been a UNESCO biosphere reserve since 2009.

Prior to being conquered in the early 15th century by French crusaders, the island was inhabited by a tribal people called the Maxos with roots in in North Africa; at the time of the colonists' arrival, the Maxos were split between two kingdoms, Jandía, in the south, and Maxorata, in the north. A stone wall, remnants of which have survived to the present, divided the two areas. The Catholic Monarchs claimed sovereignty over Fuerteventura in 1476 but were met with dozens of pirate attacks in the following decades, which led them to decree the construction of several fortifications along the coast, some of which are still visible today. The island was largely dismissed by Spaniards as a desert wasteland until famed novelist Miguel de Unamuno chronicled his exile there in the 1920s under Primo de Rivera's reign—contrary to the dictator's wishes, Unamuno found Fuerteventura rather paradisiacal and would come to appreciate its "eternal springtime" temperatures and "naked hills that look like camels' humps."

Like Lanzarote, Fuerteventura is often windy, especially during the summer, when the northeast trade winds blow hard for days at a time. It's also one of the hottest islands in the summer, and its winters are warm and dry.

VISITOR INFORMATION
Airport Tourist Office
✉ *Fuerteventura Airport, Puerto del Rosario* ☎ *928/860604* ⊕ *www.visit-fuerteventura.es.*

Center Tourist Office
This tourist office is on the seafront, opposite the large fountain sculpture. ✉ *Av. Reyes de España s/n, Puerto del Rosario* ☎ *928/530844.*

Puerto del Rosario

Fuerteventura's capital, Puerto del Rosario, has suffered from an image problem for a long time. It used to be called Puerto de Cabra (Goat Port), but the "rebranding" as Rosary Port has not changed the fact that there's little of interest here to the average traveler. If you arrive by boat, your best bet is to rent a car (from €20 a day; Cicar has an office by the cruise

terminal), skip town, and explore the island's natural wonders.

If you find yourself in Puerto del Rosario with an hour or two to spare before your boat leaves, stroll round the Parque Escultórico (Park of Sculptures) in the center of town, where there are more than 50 works on display. The tourist office outside the port can provide a map and guide to the 15 most prominent sculptures.

GETTING HERE AND AROUND
Cruise ships dock at a terminal that's within easy walking distance of the town center. From there you can take a bus to Caleta de Fuste or Corralejo (departures every 30 minutes) or Morro Jable (every hour). If you plan to visit the southern beaches, make sure you rent a vehicle that's suitable for the dirt roads—you may need a 4x4 (inquire at the rental agency).

Ferries leave from Puerto del Rosario for Arrecife in Lanzarote and Las Palmas (via Morro Jable). Southern Lanzarote (Playa Blanca) and northern Fuerteventura (Corralejo) are linked by two companies, Fred Olsen and Naviera Armas. They both make six daily round trips from Lanzarote.

Tiadhe Fuerteventura Bus
✉ *Bus Station, Av. de la Constitución s/n* ☎ *928/855726* ⊕ *www.tiadhe.com.*

 Activities

Natouraladventure
TOUR—SPORTS | Bike rentals and guided tours and hikes around the island are all available from this company, which can tailor excursions to different fitness levels. Horseback riding and boat trips can also be arranged. ✉ *Calle Marisco 7* ☎ *664/849411* ⊕ *www.natouraladventure.com.*

GOLF
Fuerteventura Golf Club
GOLF | This course with ocean views is near Caleta de Fuste, just south of Puerto del Rosario. ⊠ *Ctra. de Jandía, Km 11, Antigua* ☎ *928/160034* ⊕ *www.fuerteventuragolfclub.com* ⅄ *18 holes, 6637 yards, par 70.*

Golf Club Salinas de Antigua
GOLF | Just down the road from Fuerteventura Golf Club, this course is surrounded by sand dunes. ⊠ *Ctra. de Jandía, Km 12, Antigua* ☎ *928/877272* ⊕ *www.salinasgolf.com* ⅄ *18 holes, 6105 yards, par 70.*

Corralejo

38 km (23 miles) north of Puerto del Rosario.

Most people visit this part of Fuerteventura for its magnificent sand dunes. Corralejo, a small port town, has one street of tourist restaurants and some pedestrian plazas with good seafood.

GETTING HERE AND AROUND
A bus service that leaves every 30 minutes connects Corralejo with Puerto del Rosario. Ferries leave from the marina, next to the original fishing port, for Lanzarote and Isla de Lobos, an uninhabited island that sits off the northwest coast.

Sights

Casa de los Coroneles (*The Colonels' House*)
HOUSE | The island's most famous historic building is 19 km (11 miles) south on the inland road. Military governors built the immense house in the 1600s and ruled the island from it until the turn of the 20th century. The interior, which you can see in under 30 minutes, is defined by heavy wooden doors and charming courtyards, though rooms are devoid of furniture. Placards are in Spanish only. ⊠ *Calle los Coroneles 28, La Oliva*

⊕ *www.lacasadeloscoroneles.org* ☎ *€3* ⊘ *Closed Sun. and Mon.*

El Cotillo
TOWN | On Fuerteventura's most northwesterly tip, this fishing village has quaint and colorful houses and a sleepy, lost-in-time feel. Go at sunset, when the surrounding sands take on a red-orange glow, and peek into the 17th-century Castillo de El Tostón (Tostón Tower), which often holds temporary art exhibits. ⊠ *Corralejo.*

Beaches

Playa de Corralejo
BEACH—SIGHT | Also known as Grandes Playas, Playa de Corralejo runs about 3½ km (2 miles) south from the Tres Islas hotel to the Playa de la Barreta. Its white sands are fringed by high sand dunes on one side and the ocean and Isla de Lobos on the other, so views are magnificent. Like many Fuerteventura beaches, it's windy, so waves can be rough. Lounge chairs and umbrellas are available on some parts of the beach, and nude sunbathing is common at the more remote spots. **Amenities:** food and drink; lifeguards; showers; toilets; water sports. **Best for:** nudists; sunrise; walking; windsurfing. ⊠ *Corralejo.*

Playa del Aljibe de la Cueva
BEACH—SIGHT | On the northwest side of the island, this beach has a castle that once repelled pirates. The small stretch of white sand is rather isolated and is popular with locals. The beach is backed by dramatic ocher cliffs, and the sea tends to be rough. **Amenities:** none. **Best for:** solitude; nudists; sunset; windsurfing. ⊠ *Corralejo.*

 Restaurants

La Taberna
$$ | **SPANISH** | Behind the Atlantic Center shopping mall, this well-established favorite is one of the oldest restaurants in town and has been under the same

Spanish management since 1989. As you might expect from the name, its interior resembles a typical Spanish tavern, with wooden furniture and beams and cozy lighting. **Known for:** cheery staff; to-die-for paella; traditional Spanish ambience. $ *Average main: €14* ✉ *Calle Hernán Cortés 3* ☎ *928/535027* ⊘ *Closed Sun. No lunch.*

★ Restaurante El Moral

$$ | SPANISH | In the small town of Villaverde, halfway between Puerto del Rosario and Corralejo, is one of the island's best-kept culinary secrets. At this small restaurant, Canarian dishes are served family style in the center of the table. **Known for:** homemade Canarian tapas; good value; excellent house wines. $ *Average main: €12* ✉ *Ctra. General 94, Villaverde* ☎ *928/868285* ⊘ *Closed Mon.*

Hotels

★ Avanti

$$$ | HOTEL | Fresh, ultramodern (and ultra-Instagrammable) design defines the aesthetic at Avanti, a 15-room adults-only hotel with gleaming blue-and-white rooms and an elegant rooftop bar. **Pros:** destination-worthy restaurant; trendy interiors; exclusive (but not stuffy) feel. **Cons:** first-floor rooms are noisy; small Jacuzzis; rooftop bar open only in high season. $ *Rooms from: €145* ✉ *Calle Delfín 1* ☎ *928/867523* ⊕ *www.avanti-hotelboutique.com* ⊘ *Restaurant closed Wed.* ⇌ *15 rooms* ℃ *Free Breakfast.*

★ Gran Hotel Atlantis Bahía Real

$$$ | RESORT | Straight out of the *Arabian Nights*, this oceanfront resort makes an extremely romantic retreat. **Pros:** excellent service; luxurious retreat; first-class cuisine. **Cons:** no bars or shops in the vicinity; rooms beginning to show wear; overpriced restaurant. $ *Rooms from: €176* ✉ *Av. Grandes Playas s/n* ☎ *928/537153* ⊕ *www.atlantisbahiareal. com* ⇌ *170 rooms, 72 suites* ℃ *Free Breakfast.*

Hotel Riu Palace Tres Islas

$$$ | RESORT | You can step right onto Grandes Playas, one of the best beaches on the island, from this hotel, which resembles a cruise ship with its six stories and curved white facade. **Pros:** two large, well-maintained pools; excellent service; beachfront location. **Cons:** some distance from Corralejo; older clientele may not make it the best fit for families; dull entertainment. $ *Rooms from: €170* ✉ *Av. Grandes Playas* ☎ *928/535700* ⊕ *www.riu.es* ⇌ *372 rooms* ℃ *Free Breakfast.*

Activities

BICYCLING
Easy Riders

BICYCLING | In additional to bike rental, Easy Riders also runs guided tours around the north of the island that cover 20–80 km (12½–50 miles) and can be made to suit most fitness levels. Some include a visit to the Isla de Lobos, off the north coast of the island. ✉ *Suite Atlantis Fuerteventura Resort, Las Dunas s/n, Local 2* ☎ *928/867005* ⊕ *www. easyriders-bikecenter.com.*

BOATING AND OTHER WATER SPORTS

The channel between Corralejo and the tiny Isla de Lobos is rich in undersea life and favored by divers as well as sport fishermen.

Dive Center Corralejo

DIVING/SNORKELING | This company organizes dives every day except Sunday as well as PADI courses. ✉ *Calle Nuestra Señora del Pino 22* ☎ *627/809948* ⊕ *www. divecentercorralejo.com.*

Fuertecharter Boat Trips

BOATING | This company, located in the marina, offers boat and fishing trips. ✉ *Marina, Muelle Deportivo* ☎ *928/344734* ⊕ *www.fuertecharter. com.*

Kailua Surf School Fuerteventura

SURFING | Even if you've never surfed before, let the enthusiastic staff at Kailua show you the ropes. Classes for more advanced surfers are also available in addition to 7- and 14-night surf camps. Rates start at €40 per four-hour group lesson. ✉ *Av. Corralejo Grandes Playas 75* ☎ *630/345560* ⊕ *www.kailuasurf-school.com.*

Betancuria

25 km (15 miles) west of Puerto del Rosario.

Betancuria (pop. 839), set in the fertile center of the island, was once Fuerteventura's capital and has several historical monuments. Its quiet streets display typical Fuerteventura architecture.

GETTING HERE AND AROUND
Betancuria and surroundings are best explored by car (hire from €20 a day in Puerto del Rosario).

Sights

Molino de Antigua (*Antigua Windmill*)
MUSEUM | In Antigua, 8 km (5 miles) east of Betancuria, you can visit a restored, white Don Quixote–style windmill that was once used for grinding *gofio* flour and now displays an exhibition about cheese-making on the island. Next to the windmill are a craft shop and cactus garden. Incidentally, the modern metal windmills throughout the island were imported from the United States and are used for pumping water. ✉ *Antigua* ☎ *928/878041* 💶 *€2* ⏱ *Closed Sun. and Mon.*

Museo de la Iglesia
MUSEUM | The town's Church Museum contains a replica of the banner carried by the Norman conqueror Juan de Bethancourt when he seized Fuerteventura in the 15th century. Most of the artwork was salvaged from the nearby convent, now in ruins. The museum is generally open weekday mornings, but it has no official opening hours, so don't be

surprised to find it closed. ✉ *Betancuria* 💶 *€2.*

Santa María de Betancuria
RELIGIOUS SITE | The weatherworn colonial church of Santa María de Betancuria was built in the early 15th century as the island's main church when Betancuria was the capital. The church was almost completely destroyed by Berbers in 1593 and then rebuilt. Outside Mass times, the church has no official opening hours, though weekday mornings are often a safe bet. ✉ *Pl. Santa María de Betancuria 1* 💶 *€3.*

Costa Calma

7 km (4½ miles) south of Matas Blancas.

As you continue south along the coast from Matas Blancas, the beaches get longer, the sand gets whiter, and the water gets bluer.

GETTING HERE AND AROUND
The bus connecting Puerto del Rosario and Morro Jable stops at Costa Calma. Buses leave roughly every 30 minutes weekdays and every hour on weekends.

Beaches

Playa Costa Calma
BEACH—SIGHT | Like so many of the Fuerteventura beaches, this is yet another stretch of perfect white sands. Playa Costa Calma is actually made up of three beaches, a large one flanked by two smaller ones. You can walk along all three at low tide, but don't be caught by the rising tide: the rocky outcrops between the beaches will prevent your return. Lounge chair and umbrella rental is available near the hotels. Windy conditions draw windsurfers here. **Amenities:** food and drink; lifeguards; showers; toilets; water sports. **Best for:** sunrise; swimming; walking; windsurfing. ✉ *Costa Calma.*

Surrounded by mountains, Betancuria is a charming colonial village with cobbled streets, whitewashed cottages, and friendly villagers.

Playa de Sotavento

BEACH—SIGHT | This famous stretch of pure white sand rivals Corralejo for the title of best Fuerteventura beach. It extends for 6½ glorious km (4 miles)—at low tide you can walk over to neighboring beaches for 9 km (5½ miles). A sandbank that runs parallel to the beach creates a shallow lagoon that's perfect for swimming and for getting down the basics of windsurfing. Nude sunning is favored here, except directly in front of hotels—these areas are also the only place where amenities are available. **Amenities:** food and drink; water sports. **Best for:** nudists; solitude; sunrise; windsurfing. ⊠ *Jandía.*

 Hotels

H10 Tindaya

$$$$ | **HOTEL** | Tuscany meets the Canary Islands at this neoclassical hotel with soaring towers and ocher-colored columns. **Pros:** hotel has its own sheltered beach; squeaky-clean; good service. **Cons:** all dining is buffet style; entertainment can be noisy at times; small beach.

Ⓢ *Rooms from: €200* ⊠ *Punta del Roquito s/n* ☎ *900/444666* ⊕ *www.hotelh10tindaya.com* ⤢ *354 rooms* ⏹ *All-inclusive.*

Risco del Gato Suites The Senses Collection

$$$ | **HOTEL** | A far cry from the big-box resorts that abound on Fuerteventura, this suites-only sanctuary has spectacular ocean views—it's 2 km (1 mile) to the west of Costa Calma resort and perched about 650 feet above the magnificent Playa de Sotavento. **Pros:** tranquil location and setting; intriguing architecture; quality service. **Cons:** slightly out of town; some rooms could use a refresh; evening meals are bland. Ⓢ *Rooms from: €160* ⊠ *Calle Sicasumbre 2* ☎ *902/160630* ⊕ *www.hotelriscodelgato.com* ⤢ *51 suites* ⏹ *No meals.*

🍸 Nightlife

Los Piratas de Costa Calma

BARS/PUBS | Pedro, the bartender at this popular tiki joint, will happily get you buzzed on his flamboyantly garnished concoctions. ⊠ *Calle Punta de los Molinillos s/n* ☎ *663/357689.*

Activities

GOLF
Playitas Golf
GOLF | This challenging course designed by Scottish golf course architect John Chilver Stainer is between Caleta de Fuste and Costa Calma. ⊠ *Guanchinerfe 2, Las Playitas* ☎ *928/860400* ⊕ *www. playitas.net* ⫪ *18 holes, 5276 yards, par 67.*

Morro Jable

At the southernmost tip of the island.

The old fishing port of Morro Jable, at the southern tip of Fuerteventura, has a long stretch of golden sand. Many more miles of virgin coast stretch beyond here—down a dirt road that eventually leads to the lighthouse—and beaches along the entire windward side of the peninsula remain untouched.

GETTING HERE AND AROUND
You can get to Morro Jable by bus from Puerto del Rosario. Buses leave every 30 minutes on weekdays and every hour weekends, but if you want to explore the main attraction in this part of the island (the stunning beaches), a car is a must.

Beaches

Beyond the town of Morro Jable, a dirt road leads to the isolated hamlet of Puerto de la Cruz, where there's a lighthouse. If you follow the dirt path across the narrow strip of land (make sure ahead of time that your rental is up to it), you can enjoy the equally empty beaches here. For scuba diving and snorkeling, head for the rocky outcrops on the windward side of Jandía.

Playa de Barlovento de Jandía
BEACH—SIGHT | Barlovento is yet another spectacular and unspoiled beach in this part of Fuenteventura. The fact that it can only be reached by 4x4s or other heavy-duty vehicles means it receives few visitors; in low season you could have this 6-km (4-mile) stretch practically to yourself. Take plenty of drinking water, and watch out for strong currents, especially when the wind is strong. **Amenities:** none. **Best for:** solitude; nudists; sunset; windsurfing. ⊠ *Morro del Jable.*

Playa de Cofete
BEACH—SIGHT | Along with Barlovento next door, Playa de Cofete is one of Spain's most pristine beaches. This 14-km (9-mile) strip of golden sand faces north, making it the perfect spot for sunbathing, walking, and just getting away from it all. Currents are strong here, particularly when it's gusty. Take plenty of drinking water. **Amenities:** none. **Best for:** solitude; nudists; sunset; walking; windsurfing. ⊠ *Morro del Jable.*

Playa de Morro Jable
BEACH—SIGHT | The long stretch of powdery white sand and safe swimming conditions make Morro Jable's beach one of the island's most emblematic. It gets busy on weekends and during the summer, and finding a space for your towel can be difficult unless you're prepared to walk a ways. Lounge chairs and umbrellas are both available. **Amenities:** food and drink; lifeguards; showers; toilets; water sports. **Best for:** sunset; swimming; walking; windsurfing. ⊠ *Morro del Jable.*

Index

Photo Credits

Notes

Notes

Notes

Fodor's ESSENTIAL SPAIN 2020

Publisher: Stephen Horowitz, *General Manager*

Editorial: Douglas Stallings, *Editorial Director*; Jacinta O'Halloran, Amanda Sadlowski, *Senior Editors*; Kayla Becker, Alexis Kelly, Teddy Minford, Rachael Roth, *Editors*

Design: Tina Malaney, *Director of Design and Production*; Jessica Gonzalez, *Graphic Designer*; Mariana Tabares, *Design & Production Intern*

Production: Jennifer DePrima, *Editorial Production Manager*; Carrie Parker, *Senior Production Editor*; Elyse Rozelle, *Production Editor*; Jackson Pranica, *Editorial Production Assistant*

Maps: Rebecca Baer, *Senior Map Editor*; Mark Stroud (Moon Street Cartography), David Lindroth, *Cartographers*

Photography: Viviane Teles, *Senior Photo Editor*; Namrata Aggarwal, Ashok Kumar, Carl Yu, *Photo Editors*; Rebecca Rimmer, *Photo Intern*

Business & Operations: Chuck Hoover, *Chief Marketing Officer*; Robert Ames, *Group General Manager*; Tara McCrillis, *Director of Publishing Operations*; Victor Bernal, *Business Analyst*

Public Relations and Marketing: Joe Ewaskiw, *Senior Director Communications & Public Relations*; Esther Su, *Senior Marketing Manager*

Fodors.com Jeremy Tarr, *Editorial Director*; Rachael Levitt, *Managing Editor*

Technology: Jon Atkinson, *Director of Technology*; Rudresh Teotia, *Lead Developer*; Jacob Ashpis, *Content Operations Manager*

Writers: Lauren Frayer, Benjamin Kemper, Elizabeth Prosser, Joanna Styles, Steve Tallantyre

Editor: Jacinta O'Halloran

Production Editor: Jennifer DePrima

ISBN 978-1-64097-182-0

ISSN 2471–920X

Library of Congress Control Number 9780804143929

All details in this book are based on information supplied to us at press time. Always confirm information when it matters, especially if you're making a detour to visit a specific place. Fodor's expressly disclaims any liability, loss, or risk, personal or otherwise, that is incurred as a consequence of the use of any of the contents of this book.

SPECIAL SALES
This book is available at special discounts for bulk purchases for sales promotions or premiums. For more information, e-mail SpecialMarkets@fodors.com.

PRINTED IN THE UNITED STATES OF AMERICA

10 9 8 7 6 5 4 3 2 1

About Our Writers

 Benjamin Kemper followed the siren song of Ibérico ham from New York to Madrid, Spain, where he writes about the places that make him hungriest. The Caucasus, Portugal, France, and—por supuesto—Spain are his main beats. Beyond Benjamin's frequent collaborations with Fodor's, his work has appeared in the *Wall Street Journal, Condé Nast Traveler, AFAR, Smithsonian Magazine*, and *Travel + Leisure*, among other publications.

 Originally from the north of England, **Elizabeth Prosser** has lived in Barcelona since 2007. When she is not indulging in her passion for travel, she works as a freelance writer and editor covering a range of topics including travel, lifestyle, property and technology for a range of print and online publications.

 Joanna Styles is a freelance writer based in Malaga, Andalusia, just about the perfect place to live. Since she first spotted orange trees in the sunshine and the snow-capped Sierra Nevada, she's been passionate about Andalusia, its people, places, and culture. Thirty years later she's still discovering hidden corners. Joanna is the author of www.guidetomalaga.com.

 Steve Tallantyre is a British journalist and copywriter. He moved from Italy to Barcelona in the late 1990s. Married to a Catalan native, with two "Catalangles" children, Steve writes about the region's restaurants, and food culture for leading international publications. He also owns a popular blog about Barcelona cuisine ⊕ *www.foodbarcelona. com* and is the founder of a copywriting agency ⊕ *www.BCNcontent.com*.